God With Us

God With Us

An Introduction to Adventist Theology

John C. Peckham

Berrien Springs, Michigan

published in
association with

Andrews University Press
Sutherland House
8360 W. Campus Circle Dr.
Berrien Springs, MI 49104-1700
Telephone: 269-471-6134
Fax: 269-471-6224
Email: aupo@andrews.edu
Website: http://universitypress.andrews.edu

Copyright © 2023 by the Biblical Research Institute

All rights reserved. No part of this book may be used or reproduced in any manner or translated into other languages without written permission from the publisher except in the case of brief quotations embodied in critical articles and reviews.

ISBN 978-1-940980-33-1

Library of Congress Control Number: 2024950673

Printed in China

29 28 27 26 25   2 3 4 5 6

Unless otherwise indicated, Scripture quotations are taken from the (NASB®) New American Standard Bible®, Copyright © 1960, 1971, 1977, 1995, 2020 by The Lockman Foundation. Used by permission. All rights reserved. www.lockman.org

Project Director	Ronald Alan Knott
Project Editor	Deborah L. Everhart
Theological Editor	Frank M. Hasel
Cover Design	Types & Symbols
Image Design	L. S. Baker, Jr.
Editorial Assistance	Daniela Pusic, Abigail Cancel, Alyssa Caruthers

Original cover illustration after Robert Zünd, *Road to Emmaus*, 1877

Produced with the assistance of Livingstone (www.LivingstoneCorp.com). Project staff includes: Ashley Taylor, Taylor Frecker, Monica Allen, Larry Taylor, and Tom Shumaker

DEDICATION

This book is dedicated to my beloved son,
Joel Samuel Peckham.

I pray that you will always remember that God is *with* you
and that you will walk *with* Him all the days of your life
and dwell *with* Him forever.

CONTENTS

Foreword	ix
Preface	xi
Acknowledgments	xvii
Introduction	xix
Competing Theories in Christian Theology	xxiii
Abbreviations	xxv

PART ONE — 1

THE STORY OF GOD WITH US: A PRELUDE

1 The Story of God with Us: Presence Ruptured and Renewed	3
2 The Story of God with Us: Presence Coming and Coming Again	31
3 Is the Story True? Presence with Us in Truth	67

PART TWO — 99

GOD WITH US IN THREE PERSONS

4 Christ: God with Us in the Flesh	101
5 The Holy Spirit: God with Us in the Spirit	139
6 Father, Son, and Holy Spirit: The Trinity of Love	165

PART THREE — 191

GOD FOR US WHO LOVES, PROVIDES, AND REVEALS

7 The Almighty Creator Who Suffers with Us: The Covenantal God of Love	193
8 The Eternal, All-Knowing God Who Dwells with Us: The Ever-Present God of Love	223
9 The God Who Provides All Good Things and Conquers Evil: Divine Providence and Cosmic Conflict	253

10 The Testimony of the King: Divine Revelation and Scripture as Covenant Witness Document	**291**
Excursus The Emmaus Approach: How to Understand Scripture and Do Theology	**331**

PART FOUR — 345
GOD FOR US WHO MAKES US, SAVES US, AND COVENANTS WITH US

11 God Creates Us in God's Image: Human Nature, Identity, and Value	**347**
12 Life and Death: Human Freedom, Sinfulness, and Conditional Immortality	**381**
13 God Saves Us: The Process of Salvation	**415**
14 God Covenants with Us: Understanding Covenant and Law	**453**
15 The Gift of the Sabbath: Temple in Time and Day of Rest, Grace, and Deliverance	**497**

PART FIVE — 529
GOD WITH US AGAIN, FOREVER

16 God Makes a Way to Dwell with Us: The Sanctuary	**531**
17 God with Us in the Church: The Fellowship of the Lamb	**581**
18 The Mission of the Church: The Way of the Lamb vs. The Way of the Dragon	**619**
19 The End of the Beginning: Last Things	**649**

Epilogue: Ask, Seek, Knock	**685**
Appendix: Seventh-day Adventist Fundamental Beliefs	**687**
Endnotes	**701**

FOREWORD

John C. Peckham's *God with Us* provides a comprehensive overview of Seventh-day Adventist theology that touches the heart and stimulates the intellect. Although the subtitle qualifies it as an "introduction," it goes beyond a mere introductory work in that it successfully combines breadth with depth. As the book unfolds, the various doctrinal and theological topics are expounded in their relation to God—the most important person in the universe and the most sublime subject of theological reflection and personal commitment. Topics such as the Trinity, creation, Sabbath, incarnation, sanctuary, and the Second Coming of Jesus are integrated with depth and simplicity within the broad framework of the biblical picture of a personal, omnipotent, and loving God. Therefore, a truthful and beautiful picture of God emerges—not the impassible god of classical philosophy nor the romantic and sugary pop-culture god, but the creator and covenant God revealed in Scripture who loves us so much that He became one of us in Jesus Christ.

Among the many significant contributions of this volume, two deserve special mention. One is the clear explanation of Christ's work of atonement, a much-misunderstood subject often distorted by sociocultural concerns and sensibilities. This volume explains Christ's work on the cross and its reverberation in the heavenly sanctuary, consistent with the multifaceted testimony of Scripture. It is important to remember that a proper understanding of Christ's sacrifice on the cross is not a theoretical matter but has a practical bearing on our relationship with Jesus and our fellow humans. After all, the cross, as the supreme manifestation of God's love for us, compels us not only to give our lives to Jesus but also to love our neighbor as Jesus loved us.

The second significant contribution to be noted is the presentation of the cosmic conflict, which provides a coherent framework to better understand the problem of evil. Admittedly, the age-old question of why bad things happen to good people remains a difficult problem for theology and philosophy. Given the major tragedies that have befallen the world, from wars and natural catastrophes to individual suffering, the so-called problem of evil remains a point of contention to which philosophers and theologians have scrambled to provide answers. But in contrast to many philosophizing and theologizing, this book offers a straightforward approach based on Scripture, which explains evil as having originated in the rebellion of a free creature against God's loving sovereignty. Such an explanation not only gives an insightful glimpse into evil and sin but provides a framework for understanding the plan of redemption, which will culminate in the resolution of the cosmic conflict. Many other aspects of this book deserve mention, but for the sake of space, only the two aforementioned subjects have been noted. I now invite readers to continue their journey through this volume and experience the benefits of such a clear, profound, and accessible exposition of biblical truth.

Finally, it bears noting that this volume has been produced with a main purpose and audience: to serve as a textbook for college students. But I must add that this work can also be very helpful to pastors, laypersons, and anyone interested in a deeper understanding of Scripture. Thus, I hope that in such a time as this, when a variety of competing philosophical and cultural currents threaten to subvert and deconstruct the God of Scripture, this book will provide its readers with a solid understanding of who God is and what He has accomplished on our behalf in Jesus Christ. Ultimately, this book provides a broad and integrated overview of biblical doctrine to help us better understand God, His plan for us, and our place in the universe. It is not a mere compendium of individual doctrinal pieces but an integrated work offering an overarching view of biblical truth.

Elias Brasil de Souza, Director
Biblical Research Institute
April 2023

PREFACE

For as long as I can remember, I've had a lot of questions, especially "why" questions.[1] As a child, more than once I could not sleep at night because so many questions were bouncing around inside my head; particularly questions about God and His love and justice. I remember struggling with the question, "Why would a loving God finally destroy sinners?" I figured the answer would be in one of my dad's books.

So I prayed, and I read and read and read some more. As it got later and later into the night, I kept thinking, "If I just look a little bit longer, surely I'll find the answer." Sometimes I found answers that I took to be satisfactory, yet, I came to learn that even such "answers" led to more questions.

I continue to ask a lot of questions now; this has been *one* of the keys in my experience to coming to know God better and love God more. However, perhaps you have been taught or heard someone teach that we should be careful not to ask too many (theological) questions.

It is common in some circles to downgrade the importance of asking questions and seeking a deeper knowledge of God. "It doesn't matter what we know," some say. Cultural trends in recent times seem to undergird this. As Martin Luther King Jr. once stated: "Rarely do we find men who willingly engage in hard, solid thinking. There is an almost universal quest for easy answers and half-baked solutions. Nothing pains some people more than having to think."[2]

Is it important to seek knowledge about God? Indeed. Yet, we must distinguish between true knowledge and that which is "falsely called 'knowledge'" (1 Tim. 6:20). True knowledge is frequently praised throughout Scripture. For example, "The fear of the Lord is the beginning of knowledge; fools despise wisdom and instruction" (Prov. 1:7; cf. 10:14; 12:1; 14:18; 19:2).

In Hosea 4:6, God emphatically proclaims: "My people are destroyed for lack of knowledge. Since you have rejected knowledge, I also will reject you from being My priest. Since you have forgotten the Law of your God, I also will forget your children." Jesus said that the greatest commandment is to love the Lord our God with all our heart, soul, strength, and mind (Luke 10:27).

And Paul emphasizes a battle of the mind, "We are destroying arguments and all arrogance raised against the knowledge of God, and we are taking every thought captive to the obedience of Christ" (2 Cor. 10:5; cf. Phil. 1:8–11).

Questions and Answers

The knowledge of God that Paul refers to here requires plowing deep into God's revelation, particularly in His Word. Doing this requires a great deal of humility and teachability. If you think you already know enough, you are very unlikely to learn. If you are unwilling to ask questions and seek answers, how will you come to the knowledge of God?

Although many fear asking questions of God, it is striking to see how often God welcomes questions in Scripture. Genesis 18 records a conversation Abraham has with God. The patriarch's question concerns the exceedingly wicked cities of Sodom and Gomorrah: "Will You indeed sweep away the righteous with the wicked? Suppose there are fifty righteous people within the city; will You indeed sweep it away and not spare the place for the sake of the fifty righteous who are in it? Far be it from You to do such a thing, to kill the righteous with the wicked, so that the righteous and the wicked are treated alike. Far be it from You! Shall not the Judge of all the earth deal justly?" (Gen. 18:23–25).

God replies, "'If I find in Sodom fifty righteous within the city, then I will spare the entire place on their account.' And Abraham replied, 'Now behold, I have ventured to speak to the Lord, although I am only dust and ashes'" (Gen. 18:26, 27). Notice that not only does Abraham ask very difficult and pointed questions, but he also does so with great humility and reverence.

Abraham does not stop with his first question. He repeats the same basic question: What if there are only forty-five, only forty, only thirty, only twenty, and finally: "'Oh may the Lord not be angry, and I shall speak only this once: suppose ten are found there?' And He said, 'I will not destroy it on account of the ten'" (Gen. 18:32).

Moses also repeatedly asks God hard questions. To take just one of many examples: when the Israelites murmur against Moses at the increased workload laid upon them by Pharaoh after Moses asks for their release, Moses asks God: "Lord, why have You brought harm to this people? Why did You ever send me? Ever since I came to Pharaoh to speak in Your name, he has done harm to this people, and You have not rescued Your people at all" (Exod. 5:22–23; cf. 32–34; Num. 21).

Did God answer Moses? Indeed, with wondrous miracles and deliverance, culminating with the Exodus itself.

In a similar fashion, Gideon asks God about the severe oppression by the Midianites: "O my lord, if the LORD is with us, why then has all this happened to us? And where are all His miracles which our fathers told us about, saying, 'Did the LORD not bring us up from Egypt?' But now the LORD has abandoned us and handed us over to Midian" (Judg. 6:13). Again, God unmistakably answers Gideon, bringing deliverance to His people.

Psalm 88:14 agonizingly expresses the thoughts of many who are undergoing trials: "LORD, why do You reject my soul? Why do You hide Your face from me?" (cf. Isa. 63:15). Such questions demanding an answer from God for personal agony and suffering are common throughout the Bible.

Consider the case of Job. Or read through the book of Lamentations. The lesson we should learn is that it is acceptable to ask questions of God, even hard questions, if they are humbly asked in the right spirit. However, be prepared to receive God's answer, which may not be what you expect or seek (cf. Hab. 1:5–17). In the New Testament, likewise, imprisoned and deeply discouraged, John the Baptist sends the question to Jesus: "Are You the Coming One, or are we to look for someone else?" (Matt. 11:3). And then Jesus Himself, hanging on the cross, asks the most striking question of all: "MY GOD, MY GOD, WHY HAVE YOU FORSAKEN ME?" (Mark 15:34).

Exceedingly difficult questions indeed. Yet, Jesus encourages us to ask, though always in faith: "Ask, and it will be given to you; seek, and you will find; knock, and it will be opened to you" (Matt. 7:7). Thus, the Bereans were commended as "noble-minded" because "they received the word [of the apostles] with great eagerness, examining the Scriptures daily to see whether these things were so" (Acts 17:11; cf. 1 Thess. 5:21).

Theology Is Relational

Nevertheless, more and more often, we seem to hear sayings like: "I don't want theology, I just want Jesus" (as if you could receive one without the other). "Don't give me religion, give me relationship." Teaching systematic theology, I am often made aware that some have negative opinions of theology. They often think of theology as cold, abstract, and dry.

Theology is nothing of the sort! What is at the center of true theology? God! And what is the character of God? Love. And what is love if not relational? It is a terrible misunderstanding to say, "I love God, but I don't want theology." It is almost like saying to my wife, "I love you, but I don't want to know anything about you. Don't ask me any questions, and I won't ask you any questions." That is not the way a relationship in marriage works. Because I love my wife, I want to know her as intimately as I possibly can.

In an analogous fashion, theology is relational. While there is an abundance of counterfeit theology, genuine theology is coming to know the living God of love Himself! "This is eternal life, that they may know You, the only true God, and Jesus Christ whom You have sent" (John 17:3).

Good Questions

We hear so often: "You ask too many questions." "You just don't have enough faith." Or, "We should not ask questions like that!" Yet, in this age of increasing biblical, theological, and spiritual apathy, when people ask us questions, should we not be excited that they are asking questions instead of turning them away because their questions make us uncomfortable?

Many react negatively to questions because they perceive such questions to be a threat. Yet, I believe that the better we come to know God, the more we come to love Him and the less threatened we are by honest questions. Truth loses nothing by close investigation.

To wrestle with God is acceptable, even as Jacob did (Gen. 32), as long as you refuse to let go of Him. Some people try to wrestle God away from themselves with their questions. God can handle our questions. He is far bigger than our questions. But, we need to remember to hold onto Him while we ask, seek, and knock (see Matt. 7:7)—seeking the truth in His Word.

We are not invited to be skeptics (John 20:24–27) but to ask in faith. At the same time, we should always be "ready to make a defense [*apologia*] to everyone who asks you to give an account for the hope that is in you, but with gentleness and respect" (1 Pet. 3:15). Yet, in doing so, we need not be *defensive*.

How can I know that I am asking the right questions? It is not the content of a question that makes it good or bad but the motivation. Do you ask because you do not want to believe? Is your question itself a thinly veiled attack? Do you intend your question to be a defense mechanism? A question wielded as a weapon is a bad question. On the other hand, good questions are motivated by the sincere quest for answers. Are you asking because you genuinely desire to know while recognizing that the answer may extend beyond your grasp?

Jesus often entertained and even elicited these kinds of good questions from honest seekers, drawing them to ask the right questions that would lead them to the most important answers (e.g., with Nicodemus in John 3 and with the woman at the well in John 4).

In seeking answers, we must remember how little we know—indeed, that we do not even know how much we do not know. At times, we find what we take to be satisfactory answers to our questions, yet each "answer" may lead to more questions. Indeed, each answer may be only a partial answer, one more piece of the grand puzzle that we are still trying to put together, though we no longer may expect to complete the puzzle. Given that only God is all-knowing, there will always be more to learn.

Yet, one thing we must do is to respond regularly to the invitation of James 1:5: "But if any of you lacks wisdom, let him ask of God, who gives to all generously and without reproach, and it will be given to him." Asking theological questions has led me to some of the most profound worship experiences of my life.

My faith in God and love for Him have grown and taken deeper and deeper root, which I hope is manifest in my life. Of course, I still have more questions. But I never want to stop getting to know God better, similar to the way in which I enjoy growing in my relationship with my wife year after year, not seeking an endpoint where I am finished getting to know her. How could we say to God, "I love You, but I don't want to know You more deeply?"

I want to know Him more and still more. How about you?

ACKNOWLEDGMENTS

What a privilege and also a great responsibility it has been to write a book such as this. So many people have encouraged or supported me in one way or another along the way.

First, I owe special thanks to those who taught (and continue to teach) me, beginning with my parents, who first introduced me to the living God of the Bible and themselves served many years ministering to others. I had the privilege to grow up in a ministry-involved family, and that shaped my outlook and thinking from a very early age. Thank you, mom and dad, not only for your love and support for me but also for modeling how to follow God and serve others.

Additionally, I have been blessed to have many great Adventist teachers over the years, particularly the faculty of the Seventh-day Adventist Theological Seminary of Andrews University, where I received my theological training and now have the privilege to serve on the faculty. I could not have even begun to write this work were it not for the outstanding contributions of these and many other faithful Adventist theologians over the years. My own work and thinking has been shaped by countless excellent pastors, teachers, and scholars. I will not attempt to enumerate all of them here, but special thanks are owed to Fernando Canale, Richard Davidson, Roy Gane, and Miroslav Kiš.

Further, I particularly want to thank my current and former colleagues in the Theology and Christian Philosophy Department—Jo Ann Davidson, Denis Fortin, Martin Hanna, Darius Jankiewicz, and Ante Jerončić. It has been a blessing and a privilege to work alongside and learn from you in such a collegial department. Thank you for all of your support and feedback. Jo Ann Davidson, Denis Fortin, and Martin Hanna warrant double thanks as I have not only been privileged to serve as their colleague, but they each were once my teachers, and I learned (and continue to learn) much from each one of them.

I also owe a particular debt of gratitude to Andrews University for granting me a sabbatical during the fall of 2021 to complete the writing of this manuscript. In this regard, I am especially thankful to

Jiří Moskala for approving the sabbatical and to my department chair, Ante Jerončić, for supporting the idea.

I am also deeply grateful for the support of the members of the Biblical Research Institute, who commissioned me to write this book and provided helpful direction and feedback along the way. I am particularly thankful to Ekkhardt Mueller, who initially extended the invitation to me to write this work. I am also deeply thankful to Kwabena Donkor for his support and considerable feedback on the manuscript and to Frank Hasel, who expertly served as an editor of this project and also provided extensive and very helpful feedback and support. I am also thankful to all the members of the Biblical Research Institute Committee who read and provided helpful encouragement and feedback on a number of chapters in this manuscript.

Many thanks are also due to Ronald Knott, Deborah Everhart, Scottie Baker, Daniela Pusic, and the rest of the team at Andrews University Press for their work in bringing this manuscript to publication.

Finally, I wish to thank my beloved wife, Brenda, and our beloved son, Joel. Brenda, I cannot thank you enough—you never cease to amaze me, and I am thankful beyond words for you. Joel, thank you for being my best buddy. I love you very much, and I am grateful that I get to be your dad. I will always fondly remember slowly reading through this book with you as we prepared for your baptism. This book is for you.

INTRODUCTION

This book is an introduction to Christian theology from an Adventist perspective. In this work, I aim to provide an introduction that allows readers to see biblical teachings for themselves, not only to be introduced to Adventist beliefs but to see how they flow from the *story* of Scripture itself. I have thus focused primarily on offering a biblically-based introduction to the main elements of Adventist theology.

Some prominent aspects of Seventh-day Adventist theology may be illuminated by a brief reflection on the name Seventh-day Adventist. In Christian theology, "Advent" (derived from a Latin term meaning "coming") refers specifically to the coming of Jesus. Jesus's first coming was the first Advent, and His Second Coming will be the second Advent. The "Adventist" part of the name "Seventh-day Adventist" thus conveys the expectation and hope of the Second Coming of Christ and the restoration of the intimate personal presence of God with humans.

Adventist theology is thus deeply concerned with God's presence. The label "Adventist" refers specifically to a people eagerly awaiting and preparing for the Second Coming of Christ—the second Advent. Adventist theology, then, is a theology directed toward the hope of the restoration of the special and personal presence of the living God *with us* when God will again "tabernacle" with us (Rev. 21:3).

The "Seventh-day" part of the name highlights the Sabbath, the seventh day of the week set apart by God for worship and restful communion with God—a temple in time and (among many other things) a memorial of creation and deliverance. In this and other regards, Adventist theology is bound up with the hope and expectation of communion with God in space and time. Accordingly, in Adventist theology, there is an emphasis on God's presence in both time and space—an emphasis on God as God *with us*.

This theme of divine presence that is so integral to Adventist theology is itself a central theme of the Bible. Indeed, the matter of God's presence with us is so prominent in Scripture that some would even identify it as *the* main theme of Scripture.[1] The story and teachings of Scripture revolve around the matter of divine presence, with God Himself becoming human in Christ—becoming "God with us"—standing at the pinnacle of the story of redemption. As we will see, God's work of redemption itself is the work of reconciling humans to Himself so that we can be with Him again in the special ways He intended from the beginning, temporarily ruptured by the entrance of evil.

This story of Scripture is largely the story of God making a way to overcome sin and defeat evil so that God can be *with us* in fullness. That is, the story of Scripture is the story of God's desire to be specially and personally present *with us* in a union of love. This personal presence of God with us in love relationship is the best possible good for all creation, which God desires to restore so much that God became human (in Christ)—to be "God with us" (Immanuel) in human flesh.

The story of redemption is interwoven with Scripture's emphasis on God's presence "with us" in space and time, which Scripture highlights in terms of sacred places (e.g., the sanctuary), sacred times (e.g., the Sabbath), and sacred promises (e.g., the covenants) regarding His special presence *with* His people and many other promises. Scripture includes many assurances of a future wherein God's covenant promises are fulfilled (through the second Advent), not least of which is the repeated promise: "I will be with you and be your God."

Christ's works to save the world, from becoming human (in the incarnation) to giving Himself on the cross to Christ's ongoing priestly ministry and His Second Coming and final judgment, are aimed at bringing about the reconciliation necessary for the full restoration of the personal and special presence of God *with* all creation. The story of redemption is, thus, itself the story of the restoration of the fullness of God's special and personal presence *with us* forevermore.

This book begins with an introduction to the story of God with us, consisting of three preliminary chapters—two chapters that provide an overview of the story of Scripture and a third chapter that addresses reasons one might believe this story is true and place confidence in the Bible. This is followed by sixteen chapters that address core doctrines one by one, each set within the story of Scripture as the story of God with us. I have included the preliminary chapters that summarize the story of Scripture in order to orient readers to the grand story of Scripture in which all the doctrines this book covers are situated, which provides the framework for understanding the grand story of redemption as the story of God's desire and action to be present *with us*. This will be particularly helpful for readers who might not already be familiar with the main storylines of Scripture, but I think it will also be a helpful refresher and orienting starting point for readers for whom most of the material in these chapters is not new. Whatever the reader's background, having a basic and fresh grasp of the overarching story of Scripture in mind is crucial to understanding the richness of the theology of Scripture that the rest of this book aims to introduce.

I have tried to make this book as reader-friendly as possible—theology for everyone, as accessible as I could produce in a volume such as this while still conveying the material I have been commissioned to convey. Since this book is an introduction, I have been very selective in what I discuss and do not discuss. Where appropriate, I introduce an Adventist perspective on difficult theological questions *without claiming all Adventists see such things alike*.

Each topic, however, involves more questions and nuances than can be addressed in an introductory work. Each topic warrants at least a monograph all its own. There is much more to say about each of the theological issues briefly introduced and addressed in each chapter but I have selected what to include and what issues to engage (and in what depth) according to the intended audience, which is undergraduate-level college students and interested laypersons. My hope is that this book will be useful not only in college-level classes but also as an accessible primer on Adventist theology for use in local church contexts.

In the attempt to make this volume highly accessible and readable, I have tried to keep theological jargon to a minimum. For those who may wish to pursue more formal theological study, familiarity with some theological terminology is needed and, thus, I introduce some basic terms throughout the text. Moreover, some of the technical material that is needed to cover the bases, so to speak, I have relegated to the endnotes in order to make the reader experience flow more smoothly. Readers may feel free to ignore the endnotes except in cases where they have a question and may look to the endnote to see if it might be addressed there.

Each doctrinal chapter concludes with some questions for reflection and some suggestions for further reading. The recommendations in the further reading sections include works that will be beneficial for readers to understand the theological landscape. Inclusion of a book in the list for further reading does not constitute an endorsement of all the content in the source. I have included materials that convey positions with which I disagree.

In this regard, one of the tradeoffs for an introductory book such as this is that I cannot deal with historical theology or the contemporary landscape of Christian thought in any detail (at least not without making this book far longer). In lieu of such treatment, I have included brief sections throughout the book ("Competing Theories in Christian Theology"), which introduce the landscape of various views in Christian theology, leaving the main body of the text to focus on constructive introductory theology that explains the various doctrines from Scripture in a way that (I hope) the reader can see develop from Scripture for himself or herself.

For those who may wish to use this as a textbook in classes that require more engagement with the history and broader landscape of Christian thought, I would recommend coupling this book with Alister McGrath's *Christian Theology: An Introduction* (Wiley-Blackwell) so that students will also be exposed to the sweep of the history of Christian thought. For a longer treatment of historical theology, one might see Justo L. González's excellent work, *A History of Christian Thought* (Abingdon).[2] For a brief and accessible introduction to the development of Adventist thought specifically, I recommend George R. Knight's book, *A Search for Identity: The Development of Seventh-day Adventist Beliefs* (Review and Herald).[3]

I pray this book will be a blessing to all who read it.

COMPETING THEORIES IN CHRISTIAN THEOLOGY

The Divinity and Humanity of Christ	121
The Relationship between Christ's Divinity and Humanity	127
The Nature of the Holy Spirit	153
The Trinity	172
Relations within the Trinity	182
Issues in Origins	199
Divine Immutability and Passibility	208
Divine Presence	229
Divine Eternity	233
Divine Foreknowledge	237
Divine Providence and Human Free Will	258
The Problem of Evil	265
Divine Revelation	302
Inspiration	309
The Biblical Canon	317
The Image of God	351
The Nature of Sin	385
The State of the Dead and Human Constitution	395
Models of Atonement	425
Justification and Sanctification	439
Covenant Issues	471
The Sabbath	499
Typology	539
The Heavenly Sanctuary	567
The Nature of the Church	586
Sacramentalism	591
Church Governance	599
The Mission of the Church	622
The Second Advent	653
The Millennium	661
Competing Views of "Hell"	666

ABBREVIATIONS

AB	Anchor Bible
ABD	*Anchor Bible Dictionary.* Edited by D. N. Freedman. 6 vols. New York: Doubleday, 1992.
ANF	Ante-Nicene Fathers
BDAG	Danker, F. W., W. Bauer, W. F. Arndt, and F. W. Gingrich. *Greek-English Lexicon of the New Testament and Other Early Christian Literature,* 3rd ed. Chicago: University of Chicago Press, 2000.
BDB	Brown, F., S. R. Driver, and C. A. Briggs. *A Hebrew and English Lexicon of the Old Testament.* Oxford: Oxford University Press, 1907.
BSac	*Bibliotheca sacra*
CEV	Scripture quotations marked (CEV) are from the Contemporary English Version Copyright © 1991, 1992, 1995 by American Bible Society. Used by Permission.
CSB	Scripture quotations marked (CSB) are from the Christian Standard Bible. Copyright © 2017 by Holman Bible Publishers. Used by permission. Christian Standard Bible®, and CSB® are federally registered trademarks of Holman Bible Publishers, all rights reserved.
ESV	Scripture quotations marked (ESV) are from the ESV® Bible (The Holy Bible, English Standard Version®). ESV® Text Edition: 2016. Copyright © 2001 by Crossway, a publishing ministry of Good News Publishers. The ESV® text has been reproduced in cooperation with and by permission of Good News Publishers. Unauthorized reproduction of this publication is prohibited. All rights reserved
HALOT	*Hebrew and Aramaic Lexicon of the Old Testament* by Ludwig Koehler, Walter Baumgartner, and J. J. Stamm, translated and edited under the supervision of M. E. J. Richardson, 5 vols. Leiden/New York: Brill, 1994–2000

HCSB	Scripture quotations marked HCSB are taken from the Holman Christian Standard Bible®, Copyright ©1999, 2000, 2002, 2003, 2009 Holman Bible Publishers. Holman Christian Standard Bible®, Holman CSB®, and HCSB® are federally registered trademarks of Holman Bible Publishers.
JETS	*Journal of the Evangelical Theological Society*
JSOT	*Journal for the Study of the Old Testament*
KJV	King James Version
LCL	Loeb Classical Library
LXX	Septuagint
NIB	*The New Interpreter's Bible*
NIDNTT	*New International Dictionary of New Testament Theology.* Edited by C. Brown. 4 vols. Grand Rapids, MI: Zondervan, 1975–1985
NIDOTTE	*New International Dictionary of Old Testament Theology and Exegesis.* Edited by W. A. VanGemeren. 5 vols. Grand Rapids, MI: Zondervan, 1997
NIV	Scripture quotations marked (NIV) are taken from the Holy Bible, New International Version®, NIV®. Copyright © 1973, 1978, 1984, 2011 by Biblica, Inc.™ Used by permission of Zondervan. All rights reserved worldwide. www.zondervan.com The "NIV" and "New International Version" are trademarks registered in the United States Patent and Trademark Office by Biblica, Inc.™
NKJV	Scripture quotations marked NKJV are taken from the New King James Version®. Copyright © 1982 by Thomas Nelson. Used by permission. All rights reserved.
NPNF1	*Nicene and Post-Nicene Fathers*, Series 1
NPNF2	*Nicene and Post-Nicene Fathers*, Series 2
NRSVue	Scripture quotations marked NRSVue are taken from the New Revised Standard Version Updated Edition. Copyright © 2021 National Council of Churches of Christ in the United States of America. Used by permission. All rights reserved worldwide.
par.	Paragraph

TDOT	*Theological Dictionary of the Old Testament.* Edited by G. J. Botterweck and H. Ringgren. Translated by J. T. Willis, G. W. Bromiley, and D. E. Green. 17 vols. Grand Rapids: Eerdmans, 1974–2021
TLOT	*Theological Lexicon of the Old Testament.* Edited by E. Jenni, with assistance from C. Westermann. Translated by M. E. Biddle. 3 vols. Peabody, MA: Hendrickson, 1997
WCF	Westminster Confession of Faith

PART ONE

THE STORY OF GOD WITH US: A PRELUDE

1

THE STORY OF GOD WITH US: PRESENCE RUPTURED AND RENEWED

The earth shook.[1] Rocks split. The temple veil was torn in two. All this and more occurred when Jesus of Nazareth died on the cross just outside Jerusalem's walls roughly two thousand years ago. In that moment, even Roman soldiers concluded of Jesus, "Truly this was the Son of God!"[2]

Indeed, He was. And He is. And He is to come.

The story of Jesus stands at the center of the story of God *with us*, which is the greatest story ever told, or that ever could be told. The greatest love story, the greatest adventure, with the greatest tragedy, and *eventually* the greatest triumph—the victory of love and justice. It is an epic like no other, a cosmic drama, the story of stories in which every person's story has a part, including *your* story, which matters more to God than you can imagine.

God, the Creator of all, loves *you* and wants to be *with you*. The story of Scripture is the story of God's love and desire to be *with us*, the story of the relentless mission of God to be *with us*, God's quest for covenant love relationship with us—love freely given, freely received, and freely reflected to others.

> **God, the Creator of all, loves you and wants to be with you.**

The story of love itself is the story of the one true God—the story of God *with us*. It is the story of the God of Abraham, Isaac, and Jacob; the God revealed supremely in Jesus, the Christ (Messiah); the story of the God who *is* love.

Presence with Us Established

In the beginning, there was nothing but God.

But, God was not lonely because, from the beginning, before all creation, God enjoyed love relationship within God's own nature.[3] Indeed, as was progressively revealed and unfolded to humans throughout the story of redemption, there is only one God, yet God *is* three persons—the Father, the Son, and the Holy Spirit.[4]

The Father loves the Son and the Spirit, the Son loves the Father and the Spirit, and the Spirit loves the Father and the Son. Before any creatures existed, the Father, Son, and Spirit were united in love—as they always have been and always will be. God is love.

God did not *need* to create. God needs nothing.[5] Yet, God *freely* created the world.[6] In so doing, God committed Himself to love relationship with creatures, to a *covenant* of love with creation—to be God *with us.*

Everything else exists only because God, who alone exists of Himself, created the universe and sustains all things even now.[7] God is love.[8]

In the beginning, God—Father, Son, and Spirit—created the world.

God created and formed this planet and filled it with creatures. God lovingly created fish, birds, cattle, wild animals, and indeed all creatures.[9] And God deeply cares for animals and all of creation.[10]

Accordingly, in creation, God instituted both the moral and natural order—the moral law of unselfish love and the physical laws of nature, which, left unbroken and uncorrupted, would yield the endless and uninterrupted flourishing of all creation.[11]

On the sixth day of creation week, God "formed the man of dust from the ground, and breathed into his nostrils the breath of life; and the man became a living person."[12] Later that day, God created woman from the side of the man, and they were joined together as husband and wife, becoming "one flesh."[13]

God thus created humans—male and female—in His own image; to love God and one another, and to *lovingly* rule and care for this planet as stewards of God's good creation. Thus, God said, "Let us make humans in our image, according to our likeness; and let them have dominion over the fish of the sea and over the birds of the air and over the cattle and over all the wild animals of the earth and over every creeping thing that creeps upon the earth."[14]

God saw everything that He had made, and it was *very* good.[15] It was flawless. And, though God needs no rest, God rested on the seventh day and blessed and sanctified it.[16]

Thereafter, God was present in a special way *with* His creation (i.e., *specially* present, see chapter 8).[17] In Eden, a garden paradise, the first humans lived in perfect bliss, enjoying perfect love relationship with God and one another.

Imagine, if you can, life in the paradise of Eden. Whatever you might imagine, the reality of life *with* God in the paradise of Eden was unimaginably greater.

But tragedy followed. God's special presence with creation was disrupted by evil. The order in creation that God established for the flourishing of all creation was corrupted and subjected to futility instead.[18] Humans lost their home in the paradise of Eden and forfeited the rulership over this world that God had given them, giving it over to a diabolical ruler who hates love itself and has reigned with cruelty ever since.

Presence with Us Ruptured

"You certainly will not die," the serpent told Eve in the garden, directly contradicting what God had told Eve.[19]

Eve had a choice to make. Someone had lied to her. Was it the serpent or God?

God gave Adam and Eve permission to eat from *every* tree in the garden *except one*—the tree of the knowledge of good and evil. If they ate from that tree, God warned, they would surely die.[20]

The serpent said otherwise, deceptively twisting God's words. He drew Eve into conversation by misleadingly asking whether God *really* said humans shall not eat from any tree of the garden—nearly the opposite of God's instruction.

After Eve corrected him, the serpent directly contradicted God's warning, alleging that God was lying to keep humans from becoming like Him, for God knew that if they ate the forbidden fruit they would "become like God, knowing good and evil."[21]

Eve decided "the tree was good for food" and ate the forbidden fruit.[22] Adam ate also. These were the first human sins, which changed everything.

Sin plunged humanity and the entire planet into the misery of unrelenting decay, disease, and death, against which all creation groans for deliverance.[23]

By eating the fruit, Adam and Eve became like God *only* in the sense of gaining knowledge of evil and its awful results, from which God was protecting them. In countless other ways, however, they became much more unlike God, who is only and always good and loving and never does evil.[24]

The serpent tempted Eve not only to disbelieve God and doubt His perfectly good and loving intentions for her, but also to make herself like God in the sense of becoming a *ruler* and *lawgiver* unto herself (thus seeking to take on a kind of *autonomy* that belongs to God alone).

Eve was already free, having been granted moral freedom—freedom to choose between good and evil—by God Himself, as seen in God's command not to eat from that one tree.[25] But, only God is autonomous in the ways the serpent tempted Eve to try to become.

God alone is essentially good in and of Himself—the very source and ground of moral goodness and love.[26] God's moral law of unselfish love, then, is not arbitrary, as if something intrinsically evil (for example, rape) could be declared good or vice versa. Rather, the very law of unselfish love itself flows from God's unchanging essential nature of love such that God's law of love is unchangeable.[27]

> **God alone is essentially good in and of Himself—the very source and ground of moral goodness and love.**

Because God is perfectly and entirely good and loving, evil *cannot* remain where God dwells (in the *fullness* of God's presence).[28]

By eating the forbidden fruit, Adam and Eve actually lost *some* of their freedom, effectively banishing the special intimate presence of God they previously enjoyed and plunging themselves (and others) into the oppressive and enslaving rule of the serpent whom Scripture later identifies as the devil, the singularly cruel father of all slavery, oppression, and suffering who "deceives the whole world."[29] Indeed, by their choice to join the serpent in his rebellion against God's rule, Adam and Eve gave rulership of this world over to the serpent—the dragon ruler who wars against God with his army of fallen angels and works behind and through evil and oppressive empires throughout history.[30] Elsewhere, Jesus Himself identifies the devil as "the father of lies" and "the ruler of this world."[31] Indeed, Jesus "appeared for this purpose, to destroy the works of the devil," doing so through the ultimate demonstration of God's goodness and love at the cross, defeating the devil's lies.[32]

In Eden, the devil effectively claimed God was a liar who did not want what was best for Eve.[33] From this story onward, throughout Scripture, the devil stands as the enemy of God and His creation, seeking to overthrow God's government, operating by deception and lies to slander God's character and breed distrust of God, which effectively breaks love relationship.

The Eden story itself thus indicates that evil had already erupted elsewhere in the universe. Not only was there a tree of the knowledge of good and evil in Eden, but the serpent's lies and slander against God demonstrate the serpent was already evil. Earlier in Genesis, God declared that everything He had made "was very good."[34] Thus, we can be sure that the enemy manifested in the serpent was an evil intruder from elsewhere, already waging war against God and His rule of love.[35]

The devil's war against God began in heaven. The being who became the devil through rebellion was created by God without flaw and was even a covering cherub beside God's throne in the heavenly temple. But, he corrupted himself and sought to elevate himself to rule in God's place. Toward this end, he tried to convince the angels in heaven that God is not really perfectly good and loving, slandering God's character and God's law.[36]

Neither Satan nor any other mere creature could oppose God at the level of sheer power. This cosmic war, then, is not a conflict of sheer power but a conflict of another kind—a cosmic conflict over slanderous allegations against God's character lodged by the devil in the courtroom of heaven and beyond.[37]

While the devil cannot defeat God's kingdom by force, his strategy is to bring God's kingdom down by undermining confidence in God's goodness and love so that creatures distrust God, resulting in the breaking of love relationship (which hinges on trust), disrupting the perfect harmony of love and justice that otherwise flows unabated from God's moral government of unselfish love.

On earth, the horrible fruits of evil, the yield of the enemy's rule, struck home immediately. Adam and Eve had enjoyed perfect love relationship with God and one another, but their rebellion against God's law of love—their sin—resulted in brokenness in their relationship with God and one another and their relationship to nature. They had regularly enjoyed God's special presence with them, but after they sinned, when "they heard the sound of the Lord God walking in the garden in the cool of the day," they "hid themselves from the presence of the Lord God among the trees of the garden" because they were afraid.[38] Then, when God asked them what they'd done, Adam blamed Eve and indirectly blamed God, saying, "The woman whom You gave to be with me, she gave me some of the fruit of the tree, and I ate."[39] In turn, Eve blamed the serpent.

Adam and Eve's sin brought curses upon creation that corrupted nature, including human nature, introducing suffering and death. Sin brought excruciating pain in childbirth, a curse against the ground such that great toil was required to bring forth food, the emergence of thorns and thistles, and other causes of pain, and death.[40]

Yet, even in the midst of this Fall, God bestowed amazing grace.[41] Despite their rebellion, God continued to give Adam and Eve life. And, God promised He would put enmity between the serpent and the woman, and that the woman's Seed (one of her descendants) would be struck by the serpent but ultimately deliver a fatal blow to defeat the serpent.[42] This glimpse of the conflict between the serpent and the woman's Seed is mirrored in the conflict between the dragon (the devil) and the child born to the woman depicted in Revelation 12 (Christ). Indeed, from Genesis to Revelation, the story of Scripture reveals glimpses of this ongoing cosmic conflict behind the scenes of earth's history.

The promise was that deliverance would come through a descendant of Eve. But Eve did not give birth to the promised deliverer. She gave birth to a son named Cain. But, the joy of his birth gave way to tragedy because Cain later murdered his brother, Abel.[43]

And things only got worse. Humanity spiraled ever downward into greater and greater evil, the inevitable result of departure from God's law of unselfish love. Evil increased so much over the generations that it came to threaten the existence of humanity itself.

By the time of Noah, "the wickedness of mankind was great on the earth" and "every intent of the thoughts of their hearts was only evil continually."[44] If things continued this way, all would be lost. Humanity would utterly destroy itself. God was deeply pained and grieved.[45]

The whole earth was "filled with violence" and "all flesh had corrupted its ways upon the earth."[46] Evil pervaded the world such that all aspects of human life were saturated with evil and the immense degradation, violence, and suffering that inevitably results from evil.

Think of the deepest evil you can. Now, imagine it spread all over the world such that it occupies the thoughts and designs of all humans at all times. Had God not intervened, humans would have inflicted more and still more horrors upon one another, eventually destroying themselves entirely.

Yet, before humans entirely destroyed themselves, God stepped in with judgment in the form of the flood while also delivering the human race in the ark. Like all of God's judgments, this judgment came as a last resort, only after much warning and provision such that anyone could be saved if only they would heed God's warnings. Judgment came only after God's provision was rejected and there was no remedy.

Specifically, a man named "Noah found favor in the eyes of the LORD," for he "was a righteous man" and "walked with God."[47] Through Noah, God made provision to save all who were willing to be saved, calling and instructing Noah to build a large boat—an ark, which would save humans and all kinds of animals from the flood.[48]

Through Noah, God gave humanity a new start and a new hope—the promised deliverer (Christ) would eventually come through Noah's line. After the flood, God made a covenant (a special kind of solemn agreement) with Noah, including promises that extended to all peoples and to animals also.[49] Here and elsewhere in the story of Scripture, God consistently makes and keeps covenants, always keeping His promises.

Although God graciously spared a remnant in the ark, before long their descendants mounted massive rebellion against God, rejecting God's covenant with Noah and threatening to return the world to the pre-flood critical mass of evil.

At Babel, they decided to build a tower up to the heavens to make a name for themselves and avoid being scattered, a rejection of God's covenant instructions and promises, amounting to the rejection of God's rulership. God is love and does not force Himself on anyone, so He gave them over to their decisions.

To disperse them from uniting in great evil, God confused their language, so they were scattered over all the earth.[50] But, having rejected God's rulership, the people gave themselves over to the rulership of the enemy, serving celestial beings whom they thought were "gods" but were actually Satan's horde of demons masquerading as gods.[51]

The peoples of the earth thus rejected covenant relationship with God, which (absent special divine action) would leave God without a covenant people. What, then, of the promised Seed of the woman? Was there no hope for deliverance from the serpent? Through whom would the promised Son—the Messiah—come?

Presence with Us Renewed

He was called to leave nearly everything he knew—his home, his family, and the "gods" he'd been taught to worship. "Go," God told Abram, "To the land which I will show you; And I will make you into a great nation, and I will bless you" and "you shall be a blessing" for "in you all the families of the earth will be blessed."[52]

Although the peoples of the earth had rejected God's covenants at Babel and given themselves over to the rulership of demons masquerading as "gods," the one true Creator God made a way to reclaim the world from the enemy's oppressive rule. At every turn, *God countered evil with love.*

> **At every turn, God countered evil with love.**

Out of the scattered peoples of Babel, God called Abram, from whom He created a new nation to be His allotted people—His own treasured possession, through whom He would bless "all the families of the earth" and ultimately rescue the world. Thereby, God created a people where there was no people, the elect nation of Israel, claiming them as His allotted portion through the lineage of whom (in the Messiah) He would redeem the world from enemy rule.[53]

God could not immediately reclaim the entire world as His covenant people (as He wished) because God's moral government operates only by the principles of love.[54] Genuine love cannot be coerced but must be freely given and freely received.[55] This means God's love can be rejected and with it covenant relationship with God, which is based on love.

Through their decisions, humans gave the rebel, Satan, temporary and limited rulership over this world.[56] By their sin, Adam and Eve effectively joined the enemy's rebellion, temporarily giving the rulership of this world, which God had given to Adam and Eve, over to the enemy.[57] And, by their rebellion at Babel, the people rejected God's covenant promises and rulership and gave themselves over to the worship and rule of false gods (demons in disguise).[58]

While God continued to work for the good of all nations, the people's rejection of God's covenant promises and rule created a situation in which (absent special divine action) God would have no covenant people through whom to manifest His character and carry out the plan of redemption.

To rectify this, God created a people by calling Abram out of the Mesopotamian culture of idolatry, electing him, and making a covenant with him that would bring blessing to all peoples.[59] Through this one man, God made a new nation, the elect nation of Israel, and did so in order to bless *all* nations, taking Israel as His allotted portion, through whom He would reclaim the entire world from enemy rule.[60]

The nation of Israel was not elected only for her own sake, then, but for the sake of the entire world. Through the covenant people of Israel, the promised Son—the Messiah—would come to defeat the serpent and save the world, restoring God's special presence *with us.*

Covenant People Established:
The Abrahamic Covenant and Beyond

God promised He would make Abram "the father of a multitude of nations," including God's special covenant people. God thus changed Abram's name to Abraham, which means "father of many."[61]

But, despite trying, Abraham and his wife Sarai had no children.

What, then, of God's promises? How could the promised Son come?

Sarai and Abraham devised a plan that led to much strife and tragedy. Abraham took Sarai's Egyptian maidservant Hagar as a wife and had a child with her, named Ishmael.[62]

But Ishmael was not the promised son.

And, as one might expect, contention and jealousy ensued in the family, causing Hagar and Ishmael to be sent away many years later.[63]

Soon after Ishmael was born, Sarai harshly mistreated Hagar. So, Hagar ran away. But God did not leave Hagar alone. The angel of the Lord came to Hagar in the midst of her hardship and assured her of God's concern for her, promising to "greatly multiply" her "descendants so that they will be too many to count."[64] Many years later, the angel of the Lord again visited Hagar, and God promised her, "I will make a great nation of" Ishmael.[65] "God was with" Ishmael, who fathered many nations that settled throughout Arabia.

Though Ishmael was not the promised son of the covenant, God cared for Hagar and Ishmael, as He does for all peoples. While God worked through His covenant people in a special way for the blessing of all nations, God was also always working in various ways in the lives of all other peoples.

When Abraham and Sarai were greatly advanced in years, long past childbearing age, God changed Sarai's name to Sarah and promised Abraham, "your wife Sarah will bear you a son" and "I will establish My covenant with him as an everlasting covenant for his descendants after him."[66]

This seemed utterly impossible. So much so that both Abraham and Sarah laughed at God's promise.[67]

Yet, at the very time God foretold, the promised son was born to Sarah.[68] Not without a sense of humor, God Himself named this miracle child "Isaac," which means "he laughs."[69]

From a merely human perspective, the birth of Isaac by Sarah would have been laughable indeed. Not only were Abraham and Sarah far too old, but before Isaac was born, Sarah was twice taken from Abraham by powerful rulers who desired to make Sarah their wife—first by the Pharaoh of Egypt and years later by Abimelech, King of Gerar. In both cases, God intervened, and Sarah was returned to Abraham unharmed.[70]

Further, after his birth, the promised son's life seemed to be in jeopardy when God commanded Abraham to sacrifice his beloved son Isaac on Mount Moriah. God never intended that Abraham actually sacrifice Isaac. The angel of the Lord stopped Abraham from doing so.[71] But, the story foreshadowed Christ, the beloved Son of God, sacrificing Himself for us.

In the story of Abraham and beyond, at nearly every turn, the very existence of the promised son of the covenant seemed to be in jeopardy.[72]

God works in mysterious ways indeed. Throughout the story of Scripture, the path to the fulfillment of God's promises is often a circuitous one. God works around countless impediments, challenges, and oppositions to His covenant promises, stemming from human failures and rebellions as well as the enemy's relentless attacks behind the scenes.

Isaac himself was to have a son to carry on the promised covenant line that would become the nation of Israel. But Isaac's wife, Rebekah, was also barren until Isaac prayed. God answered Isaac's prayer, and Rebekah gave birth to twins—Esau and Jacob.[73]

Esau was born first, but he was not the promised covenantal son. God told Rebekah that both sons would be the father of nations, but "the older will serve the younger."[74]

Jacob and Rebekah deviously took it into their own hands to gain the blessing typically bestowed on the firstborn son as his birthright, bringing much strife and hardship.

One day when Esau was hungry, Jacob sold him some lentil stew in exchange for Esau's birthright.[75] Later, Rebekah helped Jacob pretend to be Esau so that his father Isaac, nearly blind by then, would bestow the firstborn birthright blessing on Jacob. This ill-conceived deception was successful but led to Jacob going into exile to avoid Esau's wrath.[76]

Nevertheless, God was with Jacob. He gave Jacob a dream in which "a ladder was set up on the earth with its top reaching to heaven; and behold, the angels of God were ascending and descending on it."[77] And, God promised Jacob, "Your descendants will also be like the dust of the earth," and "in your descendants shall all the families of the earth be blessed. Behold, I am with you," and "I will not leave you until I have done what I have promised you."[78]

Yet, the covenant line of Israel was threatened again in the very next generation. Jacob's favorite son Joseph was sold into slavery by his own brothers due to jealousy, an act of treachery that eventually led to the nation of Israel being enslaved in Egypt for centuries.[79]

Along the way, God worked through Joseph to deliver many peoples from famine, but the events brought the people of Israel to live in Egypt, where a later Pharaoh would enslave them, and generations of Israelites would cry out for deliverance and liberation.[80]

Covenant People Liberated: The Exodus and the Mosaic Covenant

Israel was enslaved in Egypt for centuries. Generations of Israelites did not know what it was like to live free. But, another chosen *son*, Moses, arose to bring deliverance.

Like many chosen sons before and after, Moses's very existence was in jeopardy from the start. At the time Moses was born, concerned about the growing population of Israel, the Pharaoh of Egypt commanded that male newborn Hebrews be put to death. But the brave midwives Shiphrah and Puah "feared God" and "let the boys live."[81] So Pharaoh commanded that every male newborn Israelite be cast into the Nile river to die.[82]

Moses was born under a death sentence.

But Moses lived.

His mother, Jochebed, hid Moses for months. When that would no longer work, she hid Moses in a basket covered with tar and pitch set among the reeds by the bank of the Nile river, stationing his sister Miriam to keep watch.

Then, Pharaoh's daughter found the infant when she went to bathe in the Nile. She took pity on him and took him as her own.[83]

Seeing this, Miriam asked Pharaoh's daughter, "Shall I go and call a woman for you who is nursing from the Hebrew women, so that she may nurse the child for you?"[84] Pharaoh's daughter agreed, and Moses was raised by his mother and brought back to Pharaoh's daughter when he was older.[85]

Though educated in Pharaoh's household, Moses did not forget his Hebrew brothers and sisters. One day, upon seeing an Egyptian beating a Hebrew, Moses killed the Egyptian in a fit of rage and then fled from Egypt to exile in Midian, remaining there as a shepherd for forty years.[86]

Moses was powerless to rescue his people from slavery. But, in the wilderness, he encountered the One who could.

While shepherding by Mount Sinai, Moses saw a bush burning with fire, yet not consumed.

Amazing.

From the midst of the burning bush, the "angel of the Lord" appeared, and God told Moses, "remove your sandals from your feet, for the place on which you are standing is holy ground."[87]

God told Moses He heard the cries of the people and would deliver them from slavery and bring them to the promised land—the land God promised to Abraham's descendants.[88]

But where had God been all those years they were enslaved? How could God's covenant people be enslaved for so long?

In this and other regards, the story of Scripture makes it perfectly clear that being part of God's people does not thereby spare one from hardship or suffering. Sometimes God's chosen people suffer even more than others under the enemy's harsh attacks.

We'll see much more about why evil seems to prosper later in this book (see chapter 9). For now, it is crucial to recognize that even in the midst of hardship, God was *with* His people.

Centuries before, God foretold to Abraham that his offspring would be enslaved and oppressed for hundreds of years. But, God promised, "I will bring judgment on the nation that they serve, and afterward they shall come out with great possessions. As for yourself, you shall go to your ancestors in peace; you shall be buried in a good old age. And they shall come back here in the fourth generation, for the iniquity of the Amorites [people who lived in the promised land of Canaan] is not yet complete."[89]

God fulfilled His promises.

God sent Moses and his brother Aaron to deliver God's message to Pharaoh, "Israel is My son, My firstborn," so "Let My son go so that he may serve Me."[90]

When Pharaoh refused, just as God foretold, Pharaoh was shown God's power by miracles (such as turning a wooden staff into a serpent) and warned that judgments in the form of plagues would come if he did not let God's people go.

Yet, Pharaoh stubbornly refused to let Israel go.

So, God brought a series of ten plagues, with a warning calling Pharaoh to let Israel go preceding each one. Pharaoh refused each time until finally, after the tenth plague, Pharaoh finally agreed to let them go.[91]

God Himself led Israel out "in a pillar of cloud by day" and "in a pillar of fire by night to give them light."[92]

Pharaoh and his officials soon changed their minds, however, and sent an army after Israel.[93]

Before long, Israel seemed trapped. The Red Sea was in front of them, and the army of Egypt was quickly closing in from behind.

But then, the angel of the LORD moved behind them along with the pillar of cloud, dividing the camp of Egypt from that of Israel through the night. Then, God "swept the sea back by a strong east wind all night, and turned the sea into dry land" so Israel could cross through safely on dry land, with the waters "*like* a wall" on their right and left.[94]

Afterward, the Egyptian army pursued Israel into the midst of the sea on dry land. But God brought confusion on them and caused their chariot wheels to swerve and finally caused the waters to return and cover the Egyptian army.

Thus, God liberated Israel from slavery in what is known as the Exodus.[95]

In the Exodus, each of the ten plagues targeted particular "gods" of Egypt, the "gods" thought to be responsible for (or associated with) different elements afflicted by the plagues (e.g., the sun god Ra was triumphed over in the plague of darkness). Through the plagues, then, God not only delivered Israel from the Egyptian empire but also judged and triumphed "against all the gods of Egypt," the demonic rulers behind human rulers (see chart on pages 18–19).[96]

This served not only to liberate Israel from slavery in Egypt so they would know the true God by experience, it also served as a revelation of the one true Creator God for the Egyptians and surrounding peoples even decades later—providing an opportunity to know the true God and turn to Him and join themselves to Him.

Notably, some Egyptians (and others) joined Israel and left with them in the Exodus.[97] And, decades later, the Canaanite Rahab of Jericho chose to follow God and become part of Israel, reporting that she and her people had "heard how the LORD dried up the water of the Red Sea before you when you came out of Egypt" and other mighty acts of God, showing that "the LORD your God, He is God in heaven above and on earth below."[98]

This same Rahab was an ancestor of Jesus Himself.[99]

While the people of Israel were formed from the specially chosen descendants of Abraham, Isaac, and Jacob, the issue was not ethnicity but covenant fidelity. Many of the physical descendants of Israel were both Hebrew and Egyptian by birth. For example, Joseph's wife Asenath was Egyptian, the mother of the tribes of Ephraim and Manasseh.[100] And, those who were not physical descendants could become part of Israel if they were willing to enter into special covenant relationship with God, according to the instructions God gave Moses.[101]

After graciously rescuing and liberating Israel, God expanded on the covenant promises He made to Abraham, giving special covenant instructions with laws and promised blessings to Israel in what is known as the Mosaic (or Sinaitic) covenant.[102] Here and elsewhere, God's gracious actions precede and establish relationship, followed by covenant laws and promises. Among other things, God promised His covenant people, "I will make My dwelling among you, and My soul will not reject you. I will also walk among you and be your God, and you shall be My people."[103]

After the Exodus, Israel visited Mount Sinai, where God previously spoke to Moses from the burning bush. There, the glory of God appeared to the people of Israel, and God Himself inscribed the Ten Commandments on two tablets of stone.[104] These commandments were part of the moral law Christ later summed up in the two greatest commandments, love the LORD God with all your heart, soul, strength, and mind, and love your neighbor as yourself.[105]

The Mosaic covenant also included laws to keep order in society (civil laws) as they were learning to live as free people, and laws regarding services and festivals (ceremonial laws) that would teach them of God and the ways He would ultimately save the world.[106]

Further, while others (such as Aaron and Miriam) manifested the gift of prophecy at times, God set up Moses as a special prophet with special covenantal authority.[107]

Within the instructions of the Mosaic covenant, God commanded that the people "construct a sanctuary for Me, so that I may dwell among them."[108] God could dwell in the midst of sinful people only if He made a way to cover and eventually cleanse their sins, to shield them from the full glory of His utterly pure and holy special presence, in which evil cannot remain.

The sanctuary was a wilderness tabernacle in which priests ministered, conducting various rituals that were symbols (or types) that

EGYPTIAN PLAGUES

PLAGUE	PASSAGE	EXPLANATION	EGYPTIAN "GODS" AFFECTED
Blood	Exodus 7:14–25	The Egyptians believed that the gods were the source of the Nile, sent gifts by the Nile, and governed life in the Nile. This plague was therefore an attack on the gods and the very thing that made life possible in Egypt.	Hapi, Khnum, Sobek, Taweret, among others
Frogs	Exodus 8:1–15	A relentless and continuous advance of frogs out of the river where everything had just died would have made all aspects of life difficult. The Egyptians believed that Hekhet, a frog-headed goddess, granted the breath of life to all living creatures, making this a direct attack on her ability to regulate life.	Hekhet
Lice	Exodus 8:16–19	The Egyptians believed that the god Geb was the earth and the foundation of life. Therefore, when this plague came, they would have been horrified that their god was turned into lice. This plague was not deadly but was a third attack on the Egyptian concepts of the fundamentals of life (water, breath, and land).	Geb
Flies	Exodus 8:20–32	This was the first of three plagues that attacked health and wellness. Biting flies were used as symbols of valor in battle. The Egyptian army was likened to hornets or biting flies as an illustration of the blessing and aid of the gods. When the flies were turned against Egypt, their gods proved powerless to intercede or to heal wounds.	Khepri, Ra, Thoth, Bity, among others
Pestilence	Exodus 9:1–7	This plague targeted beasts of burden, commerce, transportation, and war that were also the animals used to symbolize many gods. The death of these animals was thus an attack on the gods thought to provide Egyptian productivity and strength. Major food sources and production would have also been greatly hindered.	Sekhmet, Khnum, Hathor, Ptah, among others

PLAGUE	PASSAGE	EXPLANATION	EGYPTIAN "GODS" AFFECTED
Boils	Exodus 9:8–12	The Egyptian priests were specifically spoken of as not being able to stand before Moses due to the boils. Since the priests were integral to the Egyptian cult, the religious system was attacked. Unhealed wounds also put the focus on gods associated with wellness.	Thoth, Isis, and Selket, among others
Hail	Exodus 9:13–35	The first of three plagues that destroyed Egyptian infrastructure by devastating orchards, crops, and shelters and damaging boats, carts, and anything left out in the elements. The Egyptian gods of earth, sky, agriculture, and weather all proved powerless to stop the plague.	Geb, Nut, Isis, Seth, Sekhmet, among others
Locusts	Exodus 10:1–20	Locusts were known and feared. A swarm empowered by the God of Israel proved that the Egyptian gods associated with agriculture were powerless. Egypt exported tons of food each year, making this an attack not just on agriculture but on commerce.	Geb, Nut, Shu, Isis, Seth, Sekhmet, Nepri, among others
Darkness	Exodus 10:21–29	The Egyptians believed that the sun traveled through the underworld each night. When it reemerged each morning, it signaled that there was balance in the universe. The sun going dark was therefore a direct challenge to the ability of the gods to rule, and the Egyptians would have seen this as a signal that the forces of chaos had won and the end of the world was upon them.	Ra, Aten, Thoth, Seth, among others
Death	Exodus 11:1—12:32	The firstborn was the future leader of each family, making this an attack on the future. The god Horus was believed to be embodied by the living Pharaoh. The crown-prince (the firstborn) would be the next Horus. Thus, the death of the first-born prince was a direct attack on Horus (i.e., Pharaoh) himself by taking away his choice of successor.	Horus

prefigured (among many other things) how God makes a way to forgive sins while remaining perfectly just so that He can dwell *with* His people.

The sanctuary rituals included daily sacrifices that represented the future, once-for-all sacrifice of Jesus on the cross as "the Lamb of God who takes away the sin of the world!"[109] And, once a year, the sanctuary was ritually cleansed on the Day of Atonement, which prefigured the second phase of Christ's atoning work—Christ's work as our high priest in the sanctuary in heaven of which earthly sanctuaries were miniature models (types).[110] Only through Christ's atoning works (prefigured in the sanctuary system) can humans ultimately be *with* God again in the full, special sense God intended from the beginning.[111]

Yet, while God was giving Moses instructions on Mount Sinai integral to God dwelling *with* them, the people committed an egregious act of rebellion. They demanded that Aaron make them a golden calf to worship as if *it* delivered them from Egypt.[112]

Only a short time after God had miraculously delivered them from slavery in Egypt, they decided to make and worship a golden calf idol. Akin to a wife cheating on her husband (or vice versa), this was a horrible betrayal of their covenant relationship with God, which was even more sacred than the exclusive union of husband and wife. They trampled on this sacred union, deeply paining God, who loved them more than any other has ever loved anyone.

They did not only worship an idol; they "got up to engage in lewd behavior," a reference to ritual sexual acts and other depraved acts.[113] They thus turned their backs on God, choosing instead the ways of the cruel and evil "gods" that God had delivered them from. The nations had given themselves over to demonic rule at Babel. And now, mere weeks after the Exodus, it seemed that God's allotted covenant people would also give themselves over. The sanctuary was not yet built—and it seemed like it might never be.

When Moses came down from the mountain, he was furious at what he saw. He threw down the tablets containing the Ten Commandments, shattering them. By the people's evil acts, the covenant itself was shattered like the shards of the stone tablets Moses threw down.[114]

It seemed like all was lost. And were it not for God's abundant grace and compassion, all would have been lost.

God had every right to abandon them then and there. Without His special protection and provision, they would have surely perished in the wilderness.

But God did not leave them nor forsake them.

Instead, God made a way to continue to remain *with* them, even in their midst, and He promised Moses: "My presence shall go with you, and I will give you rest."[115] By continuing to go *with* them, God demonstrated the surpassingly gracious, compassionate, and long-suffering nature of His character of love.

Requesting assurance that God would indeed renew covenant relationship with Israel and go *with* them, even in their midst, Moses asked God: "Please, show me Your glory!"[116]

"I Myself will make all My goodness pass before you," God responded, "and will proclaim the name of the LORD before you; and I will be gracious to whom I will be gracious, and will show compassion to whom I will show compassion."[117] Then, God made His special presence pass by Moses, protecting Moses by putting him in the cleft of the rock and covering Moses while He passed by.[118] Amazing.

Before, at the burning bush, God identified Himself as "I AM WHO I AM."[119] In the aftermath of the golden calf rebellion, God added to this self-description. Not only is He the one who is—the only one who exists of Himself and is the ground of everything else that exists, but He is also "The LORD, the LORD, a God merciful and gracious, slow to anger, and abounding in steadfast love and faithfulness, keeping steadfast love for the thousandth generation, forgiving iniquity and transgression and sin, yet by no means clearing the guilty."[120]

As we will see, love and justice go together; they are inseparable. Though God's compassion and grace exceed all reasonable expectations, with God there is no injustice. But God makes a way to forgive the sins of His people, taking the consequences of sin on Himself so we can be saved (much more on this later).

> Love and justice go together; they are inseparable.

Even after the golden calf rebellion, those willing to repent were restored, and the covenant was renewed.[121] The sanctuary was built. God established a special priesthood to minister in the sanctuary on behalf of the people, and "the glory of the LORD filled the tabernacle" and continued to go *with* them and lead them in the wilderness.[122]

Sadly, the golden calf rebellion was not the only time the people broke the covenant. Over and over again, they pained God and grieved the holy one of Israel.[123] Even as God miraculously gave them food and drink—including food from heaven (called manna)—they muttered and grumbled and complained, refused to believe, and rebelled many times over, repeatedly breaking God's heart, who nevertheless bore exceedingly long with them with amazing longsuffering and unmatched faithfulness.[124]

When they were on the cusp of entering the promised land, they refused to go in because they were afraid. Though God had miraculously delivered them from the far mightier nation of Egypt, they were afraid of the Canaanites.

Twelve men were sent to spy out the promised land of Canaan, one from each tribe of Israel. After forty days, they returned and reported that it was a plentiful land, but "the people who live in the land are strong, and the cities are fortified and very large."[125] Most of the spies claimed, "We are not able to go up against the people, because they are too strong for us."[126]

Two of them, however, said otherwise. Joshua and Caleb urged that the people should not rebel against God's instructions but go into the land as God instructed, trusting God's promises. But, the people did not listen to these two, and "all the congregation said to stone them with stones." But then, "the glory of the Lord appeared in the tent of meeting to all the sons of Israel."[127]

Here, again, the people should have been cut off. But God once again pardoned them.[128] However, due to their repeated rebellions, the first generation would not see the promised land (except for Joshua and Caleb, no men of the first generation entered the promised land).[129]

Instead of crossing into the promised land, they wandered in a circle in the wilderness for forty years (corresponding to the forty days they had spied out the land).[130] Afterward, a new generation of Israel crossed over into the promised land.

Even Moses himself did not cross over into the promised land because of his own failures.[131] Here and elsewhere, it is worth noting that the biblical story does not sugarcoat the lives of the people—even great heroes were deeply flawed, and their flaws are not covered up. The people of Israel and humanity as a whole needed a hero, but such a hero could not come from the line of *merely* human leaders.

Covenant Judges and Kings: The Davidic Covenant and Fallen Kings

Moses was gone. Joshua was appointed to succeed Moses and led the Israelites into the promised land of Canaan.[132]

But the people continued to rebel. After Joshua's death, things only got worse, much worse, in a cycle of rebellion.[133] Another generation arose that forgot what God did in the Exodus and beyond, and they committed great evils, serving the false gods of the nations, forsaking God despite what He'd done for them.

By repeated rebellion, the people rejected God and His special protection, leaving themselves open to invasion and oppression by surrounding nations, which attacked and plundered them just as God had warned.

Yet even though they forsook and betrayed Him, God *still* did not leave them alone. God raised up judges who delivered them from their oppressors. But, as time passed, they repeatedly fell away again, further betraying their special relationship with the one true God in favor of serving the gods of the nations, leaving themselves open to more attacks by surrounding nations.

Over and over again, God "was moved to pity by their groaning because of those who tormented and oppressed them."[134] And, over and over again, God raised up judges to deliver the people. But, soon after, "they would turn back and act more corruptly" than the last generation, following the "gods" of the nations and sinking deeper and deeper into the evil ways of those "gods."[135]

Deborah was one of the mighty judges God raised up to deliver Israel along the way.[136] Both a prophet and a judge, she instructed (and went with) a commander named Barak to lead Israel to defeat Jabin (the king of Canaan who'd oppressed the people for twenty years), bringing peace in the land for forty years.[137]

Later, God raised up Gideon and delivered His people in mighty ways, giving a company of only three hundred men victory over a large army.

So successful was Israel under Gideon that they tried to make him king. But he refused. God alone was to be the King of Israel.[138]

For centuries after the Exodus, there was no human king in Israel. Judges functioned as leaders, akin to governors, who were to function as stewards of God—the one true King of Israel. Yet, over and over, the covenant people rejected God's rule.

Although the judges God raised up temporarily rallied the people to faithfulness, the people descended into greater wickedness over time. Not only did they worship the gods of the nations, some also set up their own invented god with their own invented priesthood.[139] Not only were they oppressed by surrounding nations, but many of them likewise became oppressors and did violence against one another. They committed horrible acts. The downward spiral of rebellion continued generation after generation for centuries, with people indulging in great violence and descending into chaos, with atrocities among the people of Israel that turn the stomach; including rape and brutal war.[140]

As much as ever before, they needed a hero to restore justice and rule with righteousness and love. But, they'd rejected God's rule: "there was no king in Israel; everyone did what was right in his own eyes."[141]

Then, God did a new thing again.

Nearly four hundred years had passed since the Exodus. God had appeared to be silent for decades. The priests in Israel were deeply corrupt, especially the sons of the high priest, who used the temple rituals to enrich themselves and even "slept with the women who served at the doorway of the tent of meeting."[142]

Surrounding nations like the Philistines were a continual threat—so much so that at one point, the Philistines even stole the ark of the covenant and held it for months. Thus, it was said, "The glory has departed from Israel, because the ark of God has been taken."[143] Yet, God showed His power over the false "gods" of the Philistines, and they fearfully sent the ark back to Israel.[144]

Nevertheless, there was not much reason for hope in Israel. The people needed to hear from God, who alone could deliver them. But, "word from the Lord was rare in those days; visions were infrequent."[145] Then, God raised up a great prophet and judge.

In the midst of such problems in Israel, a woman named Hannah was distraught. She desperately wanted a child, but she had none. One day, while praying and weeping bitterly near the temple in the city of Shiloh, she vowed that if God would give her a son, she would give him to serve God all his life.[146]

Soon after, Hannah did have a son and named him Samuel because God heard her prayers.[147] After raising Samuel for some years, she took him to the temple and dedicated him to God, where he remained to serve with Eli, the high priest.[148]

One night, Samuel heard God calling him by name, and he delivered God's message to Eli.[149] Afterward, Samuel continued to grow, "the LORD was with him, and He let none of his words fail" and "all Israel . . . knew that Samuel was confirmed as a prophet of the LORD. And the LORD appeared again at Shiloh, because the LORD revealed Himself to Samuel at Shiloh by the word of the LORD."[150]

Samuel was a great prophet and judge in Israel and led the people to repent from serving the "gods" of the nations. They turned to serving God, and God gave them deliverance from their oppressors, the Philistines.[151]

When Samuel grew old, he appointed his sons as judges. But Samuel's sons did not faithfully serve God. Like Eli's sons before, they were wicked; they "turned aside after dishonest gain, and they took bribes and perverted justice."[152]

Israel's enemies rose up once again and attacked and oppressed Israel. And the people cried out, demanding to have a human king like the other nations, defying God's repeated warnings against having a human king at that time.[153] Then, like long before through Moses, God warned that human kings would become power-hungry agents of injustice and oppression among them.[154] But, the people did not listen.

Samuel felt like his leadership was thus rejected. But God assured Samuel, "they have not rejected you, but they have rejected Me from being King over them."[155]

God assured Samuel, "they have not rejected you, but they have rejected Me from being King over them."

Reluctantly, God gave them a king according to their demands; a man named Saul.[156] Despite their previous rebellions, God "would now have established" Saul's "kingdom over Israel forever." But, by repeated disobedience, Saul eventually forfeited his kingdom.[157]

To replace Saul, God chose a shepherd boy named David, "a man after His own heart."[158] David himself was the great-grandson of Ruth, a non-Israelite woman from the nation of Moab.[159] After her Israelite husband died, in a great display of love and fidelity, Ruth had moved to Israel with her mother-in-law, Naomi. There, Ruth eventually married Boaz, himself a son of the Canaanite woman Rahab of Jericho.[160] These women from other nations were not only ancestors of David, but also of Jesus of Nazareth.[161]

Roughly one thousand years before Christ, God made a covenant with David, promising, "I will establish the throne of [David's] kingdom forever. I will be a father to him and he will be a son to Me."[162] And, as David explained to his son Solomon, God promised: "If your sons are careful about their way, to walk before Me in truth with all their heart and all their soul, you shall not be deprived of a man to occupy the throne of Israel."[163] Later, God told Solomon that if he would be faithful, God would establish His kingdom "over Israel forever." However, if Solomon or his children "turn away from following" God and keeping His commandments, serving other "gods" instead, then God would "cut Israel off from the land which" He gave them.[164]

Solomon inherited a glorious kingdom. Rulers from all over the world came to marvel at the blessings God bestowed on Israel.[165] Early on, Solomon asked wisdom of God. And God gave him wisdom like no other.[166] Solomon built the glorious temple in Jerusalem, of unmatched beauty and splendor, a wonder of the world. And, the special presence of God dwelt there—"the glory of the LORD filled the house of the LORD."[167]

God's special presence would have remained with His people, in their midst, by way of the temple. But over and over and over again, the people rebelled. Tragically, over time Solomon himself descended into unfaithfulness. He took many wives, went after and served other "gods," and the people followed in his wake, plunging Israel back into the cycle of rebellion with the demonic "gods" of the nations.[168]

When Solomon's reign ended, Israel was divided into two kingdoms—the northern kingdom of Israel and the southern kingdom of Judah, which were often in conflict with one another thereafter. Solomon's once glorious kingdom was followed by a line of mostly rebellious kings in Israel and Judah.[169]

At one point, during the reign of a particularly wicked king and queen named Ahab and Jezebel, the people of Israel had descended so far into worshiping false gods (and the evils that accompanied such worship) that the prophet Elijah stood alone in a showdown on Mount Carmel against 450 prophets of the false god Baal and 400 prophets of the false goddess Asherah (Baal's consort). There, God triumphed over the false gods by bringing fire from heaven, showing Himself to be the one true God.[170]

Here and elsewhere, much of Israel's history among the nations manifests the two paths of human history: loyalty to the "gods" of the nations or loyalty to the one true God of Israel—the Creator of all. God's amazing display at Mount Carmel should have turned the people of Israel around, but Ahab and Jezebel led the people into yet more rebellion.

God repeatedly sent prophets to call His covenant people to return. Yet, God's loving calls were spurned, deeply grieving God.[171]

God also worked to draw the other nations to Him, calling them away from evil. For example, God sent Jonah to the Assyrian city of Nineveh to warn them of judgment to come. In response, the entire city deeply repented, sparing them from judgment.[172]

Israel was supposed to serve as a light to the nations, continually attracting others to recognize and serve the one true God. Instead, over time, the covenant people were attracted to be like the other nations and served their gods—"They even sacrificed their sons and their daughters to the demons" to "the idols of Canaan."[173]

Covenant People in Exile

"My people did not listen to My voice, and Israel did not obey Me. So I gave them over to the stubbornness of their heart, to walk by their own plans. Oh that My people would listen to Me, that Israel would walk in My ways! I would quickly subdue their enemies and turn My hand against their adversaries."[174]

These words of God expressed His grief. God wanted so much to deliver His people, to heal and restore them, but they were not willing.[175] "I called, but no one answered; I spoke, but they did not listen. Instead, they did evil in My sight and chose that in which I did not delight."[176]

This deeply pained God.[177] God sent them prophets who decried the two great sins: failure to love God (idolatry) and failure to love one another (social injustice). Through the prophets, God cried out to His people as a loving husband cries out to his unfaithful wife, or as a loving mother calls after her wayward children to return.

God implored them: "Stop doing evil, learn to do good; seek justice, rebuke the oppressor, obtain justice for the orphan, plead for the widow's case."[178] Yet, the people repeatedly practiced cruel injustice against one another and betrayed God in favor of the "gods" of the nations.

By repeated cycles of rebellion and injustice, God's covenant people pushed Him away, leaving themselves open to enemy oppression. While suffering affliction from enemies, they cried out to God for deliverance. And, as in the time of the judges, over and over God heard their cries and delivered them. But soon afterward, they rebelled again, often even worse than before.[179] "Again and again" their cruelty to one another and evil practices "pained the Holy One of Israel."[180]

God not only provided repeated warnings but also opportunities to turn along with ways of escape. But the covenant people pushed God away. Only when there was nothing more God could do to deliver His people, after centuries of repeated, sustained rebellion that included egregious evils like depraved fertility rites, child sacrifice to the demon "gods," and oppression of the poor and disinherited among them, God's special presence departed and, with it, His protection.

Israel fell to Assyrian conquest in 722 BC, and the ten tribes of the northern kingdom were dispersed.[181] Despite this and still more warnings through many prophets, the southern kingdom of Judah (consisting of the tribes of Judah and Benjamin) rebelled further until there was nothing more God could do for them "until there was no remedy."[182] God's special presence departed from the temple and from Jerusalem.[183] The empire of Babylon swept in, conquered Judah, and destroyed Solomon's temple (in 586 BC), sending many of the people of Judah into exile in foreign lands.[184]

Yet, God was not finished with His people. All but a remnant of God's covenant people had forsaken and rejected Him, but God had not forsaken them.

According to His great compassion and grace, God was with His people even in exile. Prior to the destruction of Jerusalem, King Nebuchadnezzar of Babylon had taken some captives to Babylon, including Daniel and his three friends Hananiah, Mishael, and Azariah (better known by their Babylonian names—Shadrach, Meshach, and Abednego).[185]

God was with them and blessed them. And they remained faithful to God even when it seemed it would cost their lives.

They refused to defile themselves by partaking of the king's food and wine, and God blessed them.[186] Later, faced with the decision to bow down to a great golden statue or be cast into a fiery furnace to die, Shadrach, Meshach, and Abednego refused to worship the Babylonian king's idol, even if it meant they would die.[187] They assured King Nebuchadnezzar that God *could* deliver them, but even if God did not, they would not serve Nebuchadnezzar's gods or worship the golden image.[188]

They were cast into the fiery furnace.

But then, another appeared in the furnace with them, whom Nebuchadnezzar described as "like a son of the gods" (who was actually the pre-incarnate Christ). God was with them and protected them, and the fire had no effect on them—not even their hair was singed.[189]

Later, under Medo-Persian rule, Daniel was faced with the decree that anyone who prayed to any god or man other than King Darius the Mede would be cast into the lions' den. Daniel prayed publicly anyway, just as he always did. He was cast into the lions' den overnight. But Daniel was unharmed, for God miraculously shut the lions' mouths.[190]

Through Daniel, God had revealed to King Nebuchadnezzar dreams and visions of the future. These foretold the fall and rise of empires in great detail—from Babylon to Rome and beyond—promising that eventually all oppressive empires would be destroyed. God would set up an everlasting kingdom, just as He promised David.[191]

In a prophecy given to Daniel (the seventy-week prophecy), God foretold the very year the Messiah would be anointed and begin His ministry and the very year He would be "cut off" and die (among many other things foretold in the prophecy).[192]

Further, God did not leave His covenant people in exile. Just as He foretold through the prophet Isaiah over one hundred years before, God raised up Cyrus, the Persian emperor who defeated Babylon and allowed the exiles to return to Judah and eventually restore and rebuild Jerusalem.[193]

Later, God delivered His people through Esther, a Jew who became Queen of Persia and risked her life to intercede before the king of Persia to save her people from destruction.[194]

Eventually, the Second Temple was built in Jerusalem.[195] But, it was nothing compared to Solomon's temple.

God's glory had dwelled in Solomon's temple but did not return to dwell in this Second Temple. And, for centuries, there was a drought of *covenantal* prophets—during a period sometimes called the intertestamental period.

The people remained under the rule of foreign empires, from Persian rule to that of the Greek and Roman Empires.

They waited for the promised Son of David—the Messiah—to come deliver them from the oppressive empires that ruled them. But it seemed like God's special presence would remain absent forever. It seemed like God's covenant promises to David of an everlasting kingdom ruled by the Son of David would be left unfulfilled.[196]

2

THE STORY OF GOD WITH US: PRESENCE COMING AND COMING AGAIN

Mary seemed to be an ordinary teenage girl. She was to marry a good man, Joseph the carpenter.

Then, everything changed.

An angel appeared and told her she would "give birth to a son" and "name Him Jesus."[1]

Pregnant? "How can this be, since I am a virgin?" Mary asked.

"The Holy Spirit will come upon you," the angel Gabriel answered, "and the power of the Most High will overshadow you; for that reason also the holy Child will be called the Son of God."[2]

"He will be great," Gabriel explained, "and will be called the Son of the Most High; and the Lord God will give Him the throne of His father David; and He will reign over the house of Jacob [Israel] forever, and His kingdom will have no end."[3]

Mary was chosen to bear the Messiah, the promised Son of David and the Son of God, who would fulfill the promise of Eve's Seed and many other promises.

Presence with Us Coming

Like everyone else, Mary's husband-to-be knew what causes *natural* pregnancies. It seemed like Mary had been unfaithful. But Joseph did not want to shame her, so he planned to break off the engagement quietly.

But then an angel appeared to Joseph in a dream, saying, "do not be afraid to take Mary as your wife; for the Child who has been conceived in her is of the Holy Spirit." And "you shall name Him Jesus, for He will save His people from their sins."[4]

Joseph listened and married Mary.

Though she was a virgin, Mary gave birth to a Son, fulfilling the ancient prophecy given hundreds of years before: "'BEHOLD, THE VIRGIN WILL CONCEIVE AND GIVE BIRTH TO A SON, AND THEY SHALL NAME HIM IMMANUEL,' which translated means, 'GOD WITH US.'"[5]

Just as foretold hundreds of years earlier, the promised Son was born in Bethlehem, the city of David.[6] He was not born in a palace, but Mary "laid Him in a manger, because there was no room for them in the inn."[7]

No one would know by looking at Him, but Mary's little baby was God in the flesh. The world's rulers should have lined up to worship Him. But they did not receive Him.

He was born with little human fanfare, but hosts of angels celebrated. They appeared to shepherds and announced that the Savior, the Messiah, had been born in the city of David.[8]

When Jesus's parents brought Him to the temple to be circumcised and dedicated, under the Holy Spirit's direction, a devout man named Simeon and a faithful prophet named Anna recognized Him as the Messiah and blessed Him.[9]

Also, wise men (magi) from far away in the East, who'd been looking for the promised Messiah based on study of ancient prophecies pointing to that very time, visited and worshiped the child Messiah.[10]

King Herod of Judea should have also worshiped Jesus. Instead, Herod sought to destroy Him by decreeing that all male children in Bethlehem two years old and under were to be killed.[11] Thus the empire did the will of the dragon, Satan, seeking to devour the Christ child.[12]

However, an angel warned Joseph to flee with Jesus to Egypt, "for Herod is going to search for the Child to kill Him." So he and Mary fled, returning when the angel told them Herod had died.[13]

This was part of a long line of events that seemed to jeopardize the birth and life of the Messiah.

The gospel promise given in Eden foretold the Seed of the woman would defeat the serpent. Thus, through childbirth, the world would be saved.[14]

The Messiah was to come through the covenant line of Israel, descended from Abraham, Isaac, Jacob, and David. But the promised sons in the covenant line themselves were frequently in jeopardy. Yet God preserved the covenant line, and the Messiah was born to Mary as promised.

Jesus's lineage manifests *many unexpected* twists and turns. Among Jesus's ancestors we find Tamar (who disguised herself as a prostitute to become pregnant because Judah would not keep his promise), the Canaanite woman Rahab of Jericho, the Moabite woman Ruth, and Bathsheba, a married woman whom David wickedly and rapaciously took for himself, having her husband Uriah killed.[15]

Talk about a circuitous and scandalous route to the Messiah's birth. No one concocting a story of the Messiah would fabricate this lineage.

The promised Son of David was born into poverty and scandal—of "questionable" birth in a poor family of an oppressed people ruled and oppressed by the brutal Roman empire.

By the time Jesus came, the covenant people were desperate for deliverance from centuries of rule by oppressive empires. But, the Messiah did not come the way most expected.

Many awaiting the Messiah expected a glorious warrior king to conquer their Roman oppressors. But Christ chose to come among the oppressed and disinherited. Should one wish to devise a hero's backstory to garner first-century followers, this was not it.

Unlike earthly, power-hungry kings, Christ left His throne as the ruler of the universe. He came not to be served, but to serve, showing how God's rule of unselfish love is the opposite of the self-serving rule of the devil.[16] With a wave of His little finger, Christ could have toppled all earthly empires, but He came as a humble servant to suffer and die even for His enemies, to demonstrate God's love and justice, reconciling the world to God.

> Christ came not to be served, but to serve, showing how God's rule of unselfish love is the opposite of the self-serving rule of the devil.

Jesus came as a seemingly ordinary man, but He was not *only* a man. He was "Immanuel"—"God with us." He was not only "born of a woman" as the Son of David, He was also the unique Son of God.[17]

What could be more amazing and exciting than this? God (the Son), the Creator of all, *became* human to save the cosmos.

The Life and Teachings of Jesus

Baptize Jesus? John was not worthy. Therefore, he protested, "I have the need to be baptized by You."[18] So said John the Baptist, the great prophet whose preaching prepared the way for the Messiah.

Jesus insisted. So John baptized Him and "heaven was opened, and the Holy Spirit descended upon Him in bodily form like a dove, and a voice came from heaven: 'You are My beloved Son, in You I am well pleased.'"[19]

John testified that Jesus was the "Son of God" and "Lamb of God," the One the sanctuary services and sacrifices prefigured, who would be sacrificed to make atonement for human sins, reconciling us to God.[20]

Before His baptism at the age of thirty, Jesus grew up in Nazareth, a town in Galilee.[21] At twelve years old, Jesus went with His family to Jerusalem for the Passover. When they left Jerusalem, Joseph and Mary thought Jesus was in the caravan they traveled with, but Jesus had stayed behind. After three days, they found Him in the temple, teaching the teachers of Israel, and "all who heard Him were amazed at His understanding and His answers."[22] In Jesus, God's special presence and glory finally returned to the temple, but most did not recognize Him.

After Jesus's baptism, "the Spirit brought Him out into the wilderness. And He was in the wilderness for forty days, being tempted by Satan."[23] But, "He ate nothing during those days."[24] After forty days, Satan tempted Jesus to prove that He was the Son of God, tempting Him to turn stones into bread, throw Himself down from the temple's pinnacle in confidence angels would save Him, and bow down and worship Satan. In this regard, Satan showed Jesus the world's kingdoms and declared, "I will give You all this domain and its glory, for it has been handed over to me, and I give it to whomever I want. Therefore if You worship before me, it shall all be Yours."[25]

Jesus rejected each temptation by quoting from Scripture, repeatedly saying "it is written."[26] The devil was defeated and left Jesus until an opportune time.

> *Jesus rejected each temptation by quoting from Scripture, repeatedly saying "it is written."*

Thereafter, Jesus repeatedly "cast out the demons," declaring "the kingdom of God has come" over and against the kingdom of Satan, whom Jesus repeatedly called "the ruler of this world."[27]

At every turn, Jesus's ministry undid the devil's work. Scripture identifies Satan as:

1. the deceiver of the whole world from the beginning,[28]
2. the slanderer and accuser of God and His people in the heavenly court,[29] and
3. the usurping dragon ruler of this world.[30]

In direct contrast, Jesus:

1. came "into the world, to testify to the truth,"[31]
2. demonstrated God's perfect righteousness and love, defeating Satan's slanderous allegations in the heavenly court,[32] and
3. will finally destroy the kingdom of Satan (who knows "he has only a short time" left) and "will reign forever and ever."[33]

Indeed, Jesus "appeared for this purpose, to destroy the works of the devil" and to "destroy the one who has the power of death, that is, the devil."[34]

After defeating Satan in the wilderness, Jesus called common fishermen, zealots, and even a tax collector to "Follow Me." Many men and women left everything and followed Him as His disciples. Among these, Jesus specially appointed twelve apostles.[35]

One of these was Peter, a fisherman. One day, after fishing all night and catching nothing, Jesus told Peter to sail into deep water and let down the nets. Peter obeyed, and the nets became so filled with fish that they began to break. They called another boat to help them haul in their catch but there were so many fish that both boats began to sink. Amazed, Peter "fell down at Jesus' knees," and he and others "left everything and followed Him."[36] Later, Jesus healed Peter's mother-in-law and many others in Capernaum, both curing illnesses and casting out demons.[37]

For three and a half years, Jesus ministered; teaching and healing many. At a wedding feast in Cana, He turned water into wine.[38] Then, He went throughout "all of Galilee, teaching in their synagogues and proclaiming the gospel of the kingdom, and healing every disease and every sickness among the people."[39]

One day, a royal official implored Jesus to go to his home and heal his extremely ill son. Then and there, Jesus declared, "Go; your son is alive." The man believed and went home, receiving news on the way that his son became better at the very hour Jesus said, "Your son is alive."[40]

Once on the seventh day of the week, the day God set apart as holy at creation (known as the Sabbath), Jesus was teaching in the synagogue. And, a demon-possessed man cried out, "What business do you have with us, Jesus of Nazareth? Have You come to destroy us? I know who You are: the Holy One of God!" Then Jesus commanded the demon, "Be quiet, and come out of him!" With convulsions and a loud cry, the demon departed, amazing the onlookers.[41]

Later, a leper fell on his knees before Jesus, saying, "If You are willing, You can make me clean." Most would not dream of touching a man with leprosy, but "moved with compassion," Jesus touched the man and declared, "'I am willing; be cleansed.' And immediately the leprosy left him, and he was cleansed."[42]

After this, four men brought a paralytic to Jesus, but such a crowd surrounded Jesus that they "removed the roof" and let the paralytic down on a pallet. "Seeing their faith," Jesus told the paralytic, "Son, your sins are forgiven" and "get up, pick up your pallet, and go home." The man did. And the crowd glorified God.[43]

Another time, a synagogue official named Jairus begged Jesus to come and heal his dying daughter. Jesus went with him. Along the way, a woman who'd suffered from a hemorrhage for twelve years and spent all she had trying to get well came amidst the crowd. She touched Jesus's cloak in faith, believing she would be healed. And, immediately, she was.[44]

Then, word arrived that Jairus's daughter had died. Hearing this, Jesus declared, "Do not be afraid, only believe."[45] When they arrived at Jairus's home, Jesus declared: "Little girl, I say to you, get up!" Immediately, she rose from the dead.[46]

On other occasions, Jesus raised more people from death to life, including His beloved friend Lazarus, whom Jesus called forth from the tomb four days after he died.[47]

Jesus not only healed the sick and lame, repeatedly cast out demons, and even raised the dead, but on numerous occasions, He miraculously provided food to thousands of hungry people, being "moved with compassion" for them. In these and many other ways, Jesus felt and showed compassion for people, seeing them as sheep without a shepherd, counteracting the devil's domain of darkness.[48]

These are but a few of the many miracles Jesus worked, demonstrating He was the promised Messiah "anointed" by the Spirit "to bring good news to the poor" and "proclaim release to captives, and recovery of sight to the blind, to set free those who are oppressed, to proclaim the favorable year of the Lord."[49]

Critics accused Jesus of blasphemy for healing on the Sabbath, forgiving sins (the right of God alone), "calling God His own Father, making Himself equal with God," and declaring things like, "before Abraham was born, I am."[50]

Many powerful people hated Him—seeing Him as a threat to their power. But children flocked to Him, and the poor, sick, and downtrodden hurried to Him wherever He was.

Jesus called all to repent, turn from their sins, and be saved. At the same time, He drew especially near to those whom the religious leaders shunned as wicked and untouchable—prostitutes, lepers, and many others.

Many leaders disparagingly labeled Jesus the friend of "tax collectors and sinners."[51] But, for Jesus this was a badge of honor. He proclaimed that He came to call sinners and save the sick.[52] Unlike those who seek people of high position, Jesus sought out the despised and weak—the disinherited. And, He—the King of the universe—was not ashamed to be counted among them.

He served the downtrodden and stood up against those who oppressed them. Thus, He drove the moneychangers from the temple, declaring they'd made God's house a "DEN OF ROBBERS" by using the very system God designed as a symbol of reconciling sinners to Himself as a way to cheat people. Just after driving out the moneychangers, "those who were blind and those who limped came to Him in the temple area, and He healed them."[53]

In all this, Jesus never committed any wrongdoing. He lived a perfect life without *any* sin.[54] He showed how humans should relate to God as Father, living in complete submission to God.

His ministry was filled not only with acts of love but also with the most profound teachings about God's love. People "were amazed at His teaching," for He taught "as *one* having authority, and not as the scribes."[55]

The grand central theme of Christ's teaching was love. This included His teachings on the kingdom of unselfish love that He brought, emphasizing the golden rule—"treat people the same way you want them to treat you"— and the two greatest commandments—love God and love your neighbor as yourself, which sum up the Ten Commandments and God's moral law of unselfish love as a whole.[56] Jesus continually called people to not neglect "the weightier provisions of the Law: justice and mercy and faithfulness," and by His life, death, and resurrection, He made a way to bring mercy to all people without compromising justice.[57]

> **The grand central theme of Christ's teaching was love.**

While rabbis customarily taught only men, Jesus welcomed and taught women too. For example, Jesus praised Mary of Bethany for choosing the greater part—sitting at His feet and learning the things of God.[58]

Jesus often taught in parables, drawing stories from everyday life. This made difficult topics easy to understand for the humble and poor who were willing to hear but struck the proud as hard sayings, for which some hated Him. For a taste of His many profound teachings, I invite you to pause here and read His Sermon on the Mount (Matt. 5–7) and some of His parables, such as that of the good Samaritan (Luke 10:30–37), the lost sheep, the lost coin, the prodigal son (Luke 15:3–32), and the sheep and the goats (Matt. 25:31–46).[59]

In one parable, Jesus cautioned that even if one rose from the dead, many would still not believe.[60] Later, when He rose from the dead, many refused to believe, just as He predicted.

Yet, some religious leaders themselves became believers.

A ruler and teacher named Nicodemus came to Jesus by night. Jesus taught Nicodemus, "you must be born again."[61] Jesus spoke not of literal birth, but spiritual birth. To enter God's kingdom, one must be *spiritually* born from above—leaving one's old life behind and being *"reborn"* by the Holy Spirit's power to new life in Christ, by faith.[62] In this context, John 3:16 declares, "For God so loved the world, that He gave His only Son, so that everyone who believes in Him will not perish, but have eternal life."

Another time, Jesus met a Samaritan woman at Jacob's well by divine appointment. At that time, there was great animosity between Jews and

Samaritans such that Jews had no dealings with Samaritans. But, Jesus surprised her by asking for a drink. When she replied by asking how He, a Jew, could ask her for a drink, Jesus told her that if she only knew who was asking, she would ask Him for *living* water, whoever drinks of which shall never thirst. Jesus also told her things about her life only a prophet could know. Then, after she spoke of the coming Messiah, Jesus told her plainly, "I am He, the One speaking to you."[63] She went and told her entire city about Jesus, and many came to Him through her ministry.[64]

Many other times, Jesus also revealed prophetic knowledge, making striking predictions of things to come, foretelling (among other things) that Judas would betray Him, Peter would deny Him, and He Himself would be put to death but would rise again on the third day.[65]

The Death of Jesus

The disciples could hardly believe it. They expected the Messiah to conquer Rome and deliver them from oppression.

How could He die at the hands of the very empire He was to overthrow? They were right that the Messiah would overthrow the scourge of oppressive earthly empires and bring liberation, but they were very wrong regarding the timing and the manner in which He would do so.

"The Son of Man must suffer many things and be rejected by the elders and chief priests and scribes, and be killed and be raised on the third day," Jesus foretold.[66] But, the disciples did not understand His words until much later.

Many wanted to make Jesus king, hoping He'd immediately overthrow Rome. When Jesus rode through Jerusalem on a donkey and colt, fulfilling prophecy, a crowd spread their coats and tree branches before Him shouting, "Hosanna to the Son of David; BLESSED IS THE ONE WHO COMES IN THE NAME OF THE LORD."[67]

Jesus was the Son of David—the Messiah—but Jesus did not come to establish an earthly kingdom.[68] Shortly after this triumphal entry, Jesus mourned over Jerusalem, displaying God's great love and desire to save the people, saying: "Jerusalem, Jerusalem, who kills the prophets and stones those who have been sent to her! How often I wanted to gather your children together, the way a hen gathers her chicks under her wings, and you were unwilling."[69]

When the chief priests and scribes heard the crowds shouting "Hosanna," they were indignant and sought to kill Jesus.[70] Judas, one of the twelve apostles, agreed to betray Jesus for money.[71]

Just before this, a woman of questionable reputation came to Jesus at the home of Simon, the leper. She broke a vial of very costly perfume, poured it on Jesus's head, and washed His feet with her hair. Some were indignant at what she did. But, Jesus defended her: "Why are you bothering the woman? For she has done a good deed for Me" and "did it to prepare Me for burial. Truly I say to you, wherever this gospel is preached in the whole world, what this woman has done will also be told in memory of her."[72]

What a contrast between the seemingly respectable Judas who sold Jesus out and the woman who lovingly anointed Jesus with costly perfume far beyond her means.

Soon after, Jesus and His disciples gathered in an upper room for Passover, a ritual meal that itself pointed to Jesus as the Lamb of God who would take away the world's sins.

Before they ate, Jesus washed the disciples' feet.[73] The King of kings washed His followers' feet like a servant. In direct contrast to Satan, who seeks to rise to God's place, Jesus willingly lowered Himself to save the world. Jesus even washed the feet of one He knew was betraying Him, Judas Iscariot.

"One of you will betray Me," Jesus announced while they were eating.

"Surely it is not I, Rabbi?" Judas replied.

"You have said it yourself," Jesus answered.[74]

Judas departed, but the other disciples did not know what he went to do.

Jesus took some bread, blessed it, and gave it to the disciples, saying, "Take it; this is My body." He gave them a cup and gave thanks and they drank. And Jesus said: "This is My blood of the covenant, which is being poured out for many."[75]

They sang a hymn together. Then, they went to the Mount of Olives.

Knowing His death was fast approaching, Jesus told His disciples that when He was struck down, they would *all* fall away, as prophesied long ago. Peter protested that others may fall away, but he wouldn't. Jesus replied, "this very night, before a rooster crows twice, you yourself will deny Me three times."[76]

They came to the garden of Gethsemane. Jesus was "deeply grieved, to the point of death."[77] A little way from the disciples, Jesus fell to the ground and prayed, "My Father, if it is possible, let this cup pass from Me; yet not as I will, but as You will."[78]

Soon after, Judas arrived, accompanied by a crowd with swords and clubs. Then, Judas betrayed Jesus with a kiss, signaling who they were to seize.

While they were seizing Jesus, Peter drew a sword and cut off the ear of Malchus, the high priest's servant. *But*, Jesus healed Malchus and told His followers not to defend Him, declaring that He could call legions of angels, but then Scripture would not be fulfilled.[79] Thus, He declared to those seizing Him, "this is your hour and the power of darkness!"[80]

Jesus gave Himself and laid down His life *willingly*. No one took it from Him.[81] No one could. Jesus *allowed* them to seize Him and later kill Him.

> **Jesus gave Himself and laid down His life willingly.**

As Jesus foretold, the disciples left Him and fled.[82]

Jesus was taken to be examined by Annas, the former high priest and father-in-law of Caiaphas the high priest. After questioning Jesus, Annas sent Him to Caiaphas, who oversaw an unlawful trial by night before the Council of scribes and elders.[83]

Therein, "the chief priests and the entire Council kept trying to obtain false testimony against Jesus, so that they might put Him to death." But "they did not find any" adequate testimony, "even though many false witnesses came forward" with accusations.

They told Jesus to answer such accusations, but "Jesus kept silent."

"I place You under oath by the living God," the high priest said, "to tell us whether You are the Christ, the Son of God."

"You have said it yourself," Jesus replied. "But I tell you, from now on you will see the Son of Man sitting at the right hand of power, and coming on the clouds of heaven."

At this, "the high priest tore his robes and said, 'He has blasphemed! What further need do we have of witnesses?'"

The Council members answered, "He deserves death!"

Then they spat in His face, beat Him with fists, slapped Him, and said, "Prophesy to us, You Christ; who is the one who hit You?"[84]

Meanwhile, three times Peter was accused of being with Jesus. And, three times Peter denied this, cursing and proclaiming that he did not know Jesus.

Then, Jesus "turned and looked at Peter." Remembering Jesus's prediction, Peter "went out and wept bitterly."[85]

Morning came. The Council decided to put Jesus to death.

They bound Jesus and sent Him to Pilate, the Roman governor of Judea, alleging Jesus should be killed for forbidding paying taxes to Caesar (a false charge) and claiming: "He Himself is Christ, a King."[86]

Pilate questioned Jesus but found no guilt in Him. Learning Jesus was a Galilean, Pilate sent Jesus to Herod Antipas, who ruled Galilee.

Herod questioned Jesus at length, but Jesus did not answer. Herod and his soldiers then mocked Jesus and sent Him back to Pilate.

Pilate declared to the chief priests and rulers of the people, "I have found no basis at all in the case of this man for the charges which you are bringing against Him" and "nor has Herod," so "I will punish Him and release Him."[87]

But the crowd repeatedly demanded Jesus's death, shouting, "crucify Him!" Eventually, Pilate consented and "handed Jesus over to their will."[88]

Pilate had Jesus beaten with a whip with metal pieces that caught on and tore off swaths of skin. Then, he handed Jesus over to be crucified.

The Roman cohort of soldiers stripped Jesus, put a scarlet robe on Him, and twisted a crown of thorns onto His head. Then, they mockingly knelt, saying, "Hail, King of the Jews!" They spat on Him and beat Him. Then, they put His own garments back on Him and took Him to crucify Him.[89]

A large crowd followed, including many women who were His followers, mourning over Him.[90]

They took Him to a place called Golgotha (i.e., Calvary).[91]

They nailed His arms and legs to a wooden cross, crucifying Him with a thief on His right and His left.

Even in His agony, Jesus prayed, "Father, forgive them; for they do not know what they are doing."

Roman soldiers cast lots to divide His garments among themselves, fulfilling another prophecy.[92] They mocked Him, offered Him sour wine, posted a sign above Him stating He was King of the Jews, and said, "If You are the King of the Jews, save Yourself!"[93]

Others, including rulers, also mocked Jesus, saying, "He saved others; let Him save Himself if this is the Christ of God, His Chosen One."[94]

One of the thieves beside Him also mocked Him, but the other thief rebuked him, saying, "we are receiving what we deserve for our crimes; but this man has done nothing wrong." Then, the other thief said, "Jesus, remember me when You come into Your kingdom!" And Jesus assured him, "you will be with Me in Paradise."[95]

Though it was mid-day (about the sixth hour, which we call noon), "darkness came over the entire land until the ninth hour, because the sun stopped shining."[96]

Then, Jesus cried out, "MY GOD, MY GOD, WHY HAVE YOU FORSAKEN ME?"[97]

Afterward, Jesus again cried out, "'Father, INTO YOUR HANDS I ENTRUST MY SPIRIT.' And having said this, He died."[98]

Then, "the veil of the temple was torn in two from top to bottom; and the earth shook and the rocks were split."[99]

Seeing this, a Roman centurion "began praising God, saying, 'This man was in fact innocent.'"[100] And he and other soldiers concluded, "Truly this was the Son of God!"[101]

Not wanting the bodies to remain on the crosses on Sabbath, which was approaching, the leaders "requested of Pilate that their legs be broken" so they would die more quickly.

But, they found Jesus was already dead and thus broke none of His bones, again fulfilling ancient prophecy.[102]

Jesus not only suffered the physical agony of crucifixion, but He suffered even more from carrying the colossal, crushing weight of the world's sins, which broke His heart.

To make sure Jesus was dead, a soldier thrust a spear into His side, fulfilling another prophecy, "and immediately blood and water came out."[103]

By His life and death, Jesus demonstrated God's perfect righteousness and unfathomable love, proving Satan's slanderous allegations against God's character to be utterly false.

According to the plan of the Father, Son, and Spirit to save the world, Jesus gave Himself as the once-for-all sacrifice, the one whom all the offerings of the sanctuary services and feasts prefigured—"the atoning sacrifice for our sins, and not for ours only but also for the sins of the whole world."[104]

There is no greater love than this.[105]

Joseph of Arimathea, a member of the Council who had become a disciple of Jesus, asked Pilate for Jesus's body. Receiving permission, Joseph took Jesus's body from the cross, wrapped it in linen, and "laid it in his own new tomb, which he had cut out in the rock; and he rolled a large stone against the entrance of the tomb and went away."[106]

And "the women who had come with Him from Galilee followed [including Mary Magdalene, Mary the mother of James and Joseph, and the mother of the sons of Zebedee], and they saw the tomb and how His body was laid." And they went to prepare spices and perfumes for His body, but "on the Sabbath they rested according to the commandment."[107]

The Resurrection of Jesus

When "the Sabbath was over," some of the women who faithfully followed Jesus—Mary Magdalene, Mary the mother of James, Joanna, Salome, and others—mournfully set out to the tomb to anoint Jesus's body.[108]

But the tomb was empty!

When "Mary Magdalene came early to the tomb, while it was still dark, and saw the stone already removed from the tomb," "she ran and came to Simon Peter" and John. She told them, "They have taken the Lord from the tomb, and we do not know where they have put Him."[109] Other women came also and found the stone rolled away and the tomb empty.[110]

But they were not alone. They met angels who looked like men in shining clothing.[111]

One "angel said to the women, 'Do not be afraid; for I know that you are looking for Jesus who has been crucified. He is not here, for He has risen, just as He said. Come, see the place where He was lying. And go quickly and tell His disciples that He has risen from the dead; and behold, He is going ahead of you to Galilee. There you will see Him; behold, I have told you.'"[112]

He has risen! What wonderful news! Soon they would see Him!

So "they left the tomb quickly with fear and great joy, and ran to report to His disciples."[113]

After the crucifixion, the chief priests and Pharisees had gone to Pilate to request that guards be stationed at the tomb because Jesus predicted He would rise after three days. After receiving permission, they secured the tomb with Roman guards and set a seal on the stone.[114]

But the tomb could not hold Him. The grave could not keep Him. Death itself could not triumph over Him.

"A severe earthquake had occurred, for an angel of the Lord descended from heaven and came and rolled away the stone, and sat upon it. And his appearance was like lightning, and his clothing as white as snow. The guards shook from fear of him and became like dead men."[115]

> The tomb could not hold Him. The grave could not keep Him. Death itself could not triumph over Him.

Even as the women Jesus appeared to went to tell the other disciples, some of those who'd guarded the tomb went "into the city and reported to the chief priests all that had happened. And when they had assembled with the elders and consulted together, they gave a large sum of money to the soldiers, and said, 'You are to say, 'His disciples came at night and stole Him while we were asleep.' 'And if this comes to the governor's ears, we will appease him and keep you out of trouble.' And they took the money and did as they had been instructed; and this story was widely spread."[116]

To disprove the resurrection account, the leaders need only have produced the body of Jesus. But they could not, because the tomb was empty. So, they made up a story instead, a very implausible one.

Do you know what would happen to a Roman soldier who fell asleep on the job? The penalty was death. How likely is it, then, that an entire group of Roman guards fell asleep on the job and the disciples rolled away the massive stone without disturbing even one of them? *Extremely* unlikely. The guards' cover story, however, itself confirms that Christ's tomb was indeed empty, despite having been heavily guarded.

The tomb was empty because Jesus rose from the dead.

The *first* disciples to discover the empty tomb were women. This is striking. Sadly, in that place and time, women were considered far less credible witnesses than men.[117] If one were trying to fabricate a compelling resurrection account in that place and time, one would not choose women to be the first witnesses. The story thus rings true.

At first, the apostles did not believe the women's report.[118] Peter and John ran to the tomb and saw for themselves that Jesus was not there; only His linen and face cloth, folded neatly by themselves.[119] They returned to Jerusalem, but Mary Magdalene had followed them to the tomb and remained behind.

She stood there, weeping. Then, in the tomb, "she saw two angels in white sitting, one at the head and one at the feet, where the body of Jesus had been lying.[120]

"Woman, why are you weeping?" they asked.

"Because they have taken away my Lord, and I do not know where they put Him," she responded.

Then, through tear-filled eyes, she saw a man standing there, but she thought it was the gardener.

"Woman, why are you weeping?" the man asked.

"Sir," she replied, "if you have carried Him away, tell me where you put Him, and I will take Him away."

Then, she heard His voice again, "Mary!"

It was Jesus, standing alive before her!

"Teacher!" she cried out, rushing to embrace Him.[121]

"Do not hold on to me," Jesus instructed, "because I have not yet ascended to the Father. But go to my brothers and say to them, 'I am ascending to my Father and your Father, to my God and your God.'"[122]

While Mary returned to the disciples, Jesus went to present Himself before the throne of God and before the heavenly council as the Lamb who was slain to defeat the enemy and death itself. There, Christ's sacrifice was accepted.[123]

Jesus appeared to the other women also: "And behold, Jesus met them and said, 'Rejoice!' And they came up and took hold of His feet, and worshiped Him. Then Jesus said to them, 'Do not be afraid; go, bring word to My brothers to leave for Galilee, and there they will see Me.'"[124] And they did.

Afterward, Jesus appeared to two followers on the road to Emmaus. At first, they didn't recognize Him. Before revealing Himself, Jesus taught them from Scripture that it was "necessary for the Christ to suffer these things and to come into His glory."[125] Specifically, "beginning with Moses and with all the Prophets, He explained to them the things written about Himself in all the Scriptures."[126] Only after such teaching, "their eyes were opened and they recognized Him; and He vanished from their sight."[127] And they quickly returned to Jerusalem to report to the disciples. That very evening, they found the eleven apostles gathered with other disciples who were reporting, "The Lord has really risen and has appeared to Simon" (Peter). Then, the two travelers told the disciples about meeting Jesus on the way to Emmaus.[128]

Now, "the doors were shut where the disciples were." Nevertheless, "Jesus came and stood in their midst, and said to them, 'Peace be to you.' And when He had said this, He showed them both His hands and His side."[129] And He invited them, "touch Me and see, because a spirit does not have flesh and bones as you plainly see that I have."[130]

"While they still could not believe it because of their joy and astonishment, He said to them, 'Have you anything here to eat?' They served Him a piece of broiled fish; and He took it and ate it in front of them."[131]

They not only saw Him, they were also invited to touch Him. And He even ate with them. This was no spirit. It was Jesus of Nazareth in the flesh, risen from the dead!

One of the apostles, Thomas, was not with them when Jesus came. Afterward, they told him, "We have seen the Lord!"

But Thomas replied, "Unless I see in His hands the imprint of the nails, and put my finger into the place of the nails, and put my hand into His side, I will not believe."

"Eight days later His disciples were again inside, and Thomas was with them. Jesus came, the doors having been shut, and stood in their midst and said, 'Peace be to you.' Then He said to Thomas, 'Place your finger here, and see My hands; and take your hand and put it into My side; and do not continue in disbelief, but be a believer.'"

"My Lord and my God!" Thomas cried out in reply.

And "many other signs Jesus also performed in the presence of the disciples."[132]

On another occasion, some of the disciples—Peter, Thomas, Nathanael, James, and John—went fishing on the Sea of Galilee. They fished all night but caught nothing.

Then, a man standing on the beach said, "Children, you do not have any fish to eat, do you?"

"No," they answered.

"Cast the net on the right-hand side of the boat," the man answered, "and you will find the fish."

So they did. And so many fish filled their net that they were not able to haul it in.[133]

It was Jesus!

They ate breakfast together.

Afterward, Jesus asked Peter, who was still grieved he'd denied Jesus three times, "do you love Me?"

"Yes, Lord; You know that I love You," Peter replied.

"Do you love Me?" Jesus asked again.

"Yes, Lord: You know that I love You," Peter replied again.

"Do you love Me?" Jesus asked a third time.

"Peter was hurt because He said to him the third time, 'Do you love Me?' And he said to Him, 'Lord, You know all things; You know that I love You.'"

Just as Peter had denied Jesus three times, Jesus here restored Peter three times. Then, He told Peter, "Follow Me!"[134]

Peter did follow Him for the rest of his life, until he was crucified upside down because he would not give up his faith in Jesus. Other disciples also faced great persecution and even death for their faith.[135]

One very strong line of evidence that Jesus truly rose from the dead is the first-hand testimony of the disciples, who were willing to die rather than give up their faith (more on this later). Against all odds, in the face of persecution by the Roman Empire, Jesus's disciples turned the world upside down.

> *Against all odds, in the face of persecution by the Roman Empire, Jesus's disciples turned the world upside down.*

There were not only a few such eyewitnesses to the risen Jesus. Many different people, in many different places and times, met the risen Jesus. Among these, Jesus appeared to Paul, a sworn enemy and persecutor of Christianity, who amazingly became a Christian after meeting the risen Jesus.

And, in what scholars recognize to be very early testimony (within just a few years of the resurrection), Paul reported that Jesus appeared to Peter, "then to the twelve. After that He appeared to more than five hundred brothers and sisters at one time, most of whom remain until now, but some have fallen asleep; then He appeared to James [the brother of Jesus], then to all the apostles; and last of all, as to one untimely born, He appeared to me also. For I am the least of the apostles, and not fit to be called an apostle, because I persecuted the church of God."[136]

Presence with Us Comforting and Empowering

Jesus rose from the dead and "presented Himself alive after His suffering, by many convincing proofs, appearing to them over a period of forty days and speaking of things regarding the kingdom of God."[137] But now, Jesus was to ascend to heaven. Would they, then, be without Him again? Would they be left alone?

Before the crucifixion, Jesus promised He would go away but would not leave them alone. He and the Father would send *another* Comforter, the Holy Spirit, to be *with* them wherever they would go. The Holy Spirit, Jesus promised, will "be with you forever," and "you know Him because He remains with you and will be in you." Further, Jesus promised, "I will not leave you as orphans; I am coming to you. After a little while, the world no longer is going to see Me, but you are going to see Me; because I live, you also will live."[138] Jesus would no longer be *physically* present with them in the flesh, but the Holy Spirit would be with them.

Jesus was to work as our high priest in the heavenly sanctuary, taking "His seat at the right hand of the throne of the Majesty in the heavens, a minister in the sanctuary and in the true tabernacle, which the Lord set up, not man."[139] Every person can "come to God through Him, since He always lives to make intercession for" us.[140]

Before His ascension, Jesus reminded them of what He said before His death, "that all the things that are written about Me in the Law of Moses and the Prophets and the Psalms must be fulfilled." Then, He explained, "it is written, that the Christ would suffer and rise from the dead on the third day, and that repentance for forgiveness of sins would be proclaimed in His name to all the nations, beginning from Jerusalem. You are witnesses of these things. And behold, I am sending the promise of My Father upon you; but you are to stay in the city until you are clothed with power from on high."[141]

Later, at Mount Olivet, Jesus delivered the Great Commission: "All authority in heaven and on earth has been given to Me. Go, therefore, and make disciples of all the nations, baptizing them in the name of the Father and the Son and the Holy Spirit, teaching them to follow all that I commanded you; and behold, I am with you always, to the end of the age."[142]

After this, Jesus "lifted up His hands and blessed them," and while "blessing them, He parted from them and was carried up into heaven."[143]

"He was lifted up while they were watching, and a cloud took Him up, out of their sight. And as they were gazing intently into the sky while He was going," two angels said, "why do you stand looking into the sky? This Jesus, who has been taken up from you into heaven, will come in the same way as you have watched Him go into heaven."[144]

Then, "after worshiping" Jesus, they "returned to Jerusalem with great joy, and were continually in the temple praising God."[145]

Before ascending, Jesus had commanded them to wait in Jerusalem "for what the Father had promised," for "you will be baptized with the Holy Spirit not many days from now." And "you will receive power when the Holy Spirit has come upon you; and you shall be My witnesses both in Jerusalem and in all Judea, and Samaria, and as far as the remotest part of the earth."[146]

The apostles gathered in Jerusalem in "the upstairs room," and "all these were continually devoting themselves with one mind to prayer, along with the women, and Mary the mother of Jesus, and with His brothers."[147]

Pentecost, the Spread of the Gospel, and Persecution

After rising from the dead, Jesus appeared to His followers numerous times "over a period of forty days," then He ascended to heaven.[148]

Ten days after Jesus ascended, on the day of Pentecost, it happened.

People from many nations were in Jerusalem for the feast of Pentecost (i.e., the Feast of Weeks). Pentecost was fifty days after the day of the wave sheaf offering—the day on which a sheaf of the first fruits of the harvest was given as an offering, waved by the priest before God.[149]

Fifty days before Pentecost, Jesus rose from the dead on the day of the wave-sheaf offering. He was the first fruit of the resurrection prefigured by the wave sheaf offering.[150] Fifty days later, the feast of Pentecost was also fulfilled in awesome fashion.

"When the day of Pentecost had come," the disciples "were all together in one place. And suddenly from heaven there came a sound like the rush of a violent wind, and it filled the entire house where they were sitting. Divided tongues, as of fire, appeared among them, and a tongue rested on each of them. All of them were filled with the Holy Spirit and began to speak in other languages, as the Spirit gave them ability."[151]

A crowd, including people "from every nation under heaven," came together "when this sound occurred." And they were amazed and puzzled because each one heard the disciples speak in their own language.[152]

Then, Peter preached the gospel, the good news of Jesus the Messiah, who gave Himself on the cross for all people and rose from the dead, conquering death itself so "EVERYONE WHO CALLS ON THE NAME OF THE LORD WILL BE SAVED."[153] The gospel pierced their hearts, and Peter called them to repent and "be baptized in the name of Jesus Christ for the forgiveness of your sins; and you will receive the gift of the Holy Spirit." Three thousand people were baptized that day, and they continually devoted themselves "to the apostles' teaching and to fellowship, to the breaking of bread and to prayer."[154]

"Awe came upon everyone because many wonders and signs were being done through the apostles. All who believed were together and had all things in common; they would sell their possessions and goods and distribute the proceeds to all, as any had need." And "day by day the Lord added to their number those who were being saved."[155]

The Holy Spirit had been at work from the very beginning of creation, but on Pentecost and beyond, the Holy Spirit came with a special kind of power unleashed by Christ's victory over the powers of darkness at the cross and in the resurrection.[156]

One day, Peter and John met a man lame from birth, asking for alms. "I have no silver or gold," Peter replied, "but what I have I give you; in the name of Jesus Christ of Nazareth, stand up and walk."[157] Then, Peter took the man by the hand and raised him up, "and immediately his feet and ankles were made strong. Jumping up, he stood and began to walk, and he entered the temple with them, walking and leaping and praising God."[158]

The people looking on were amazed. Peter again preached the gospel, proclaiming the resurrection and calling people to repent.[159] Greatly annoyed, the leaders arrested Peter and John. Nevertheless, many people who heard the word believed.[160]

After Peter and John had spent the night in jail, the leaders questioned them and "commanded them not to speak or teach at all in the name of Jesus."[161] When Peter and John refused, the Council further threatened them but let them go because the people around were praising God for the miraculous healing.[162]

Peter and John returned to their companions and reported what had happened. They all prayed to God, "grant" that we may "speak Your word with all confidence."[163] After they prayed, the place they gathered "was shaken, and they were all filled with the Holy Spirit and began to speak the word of God with boldness."[164]

The congregation of Jesus's followers held all property in common, and "there was not a needy person among them, for all who were owners of land or houses would sell them" and give the proceeds to "be distributed to each to the extent that any had need."[165]

The Holy Spirit worked more signs and wonders, and "increasingly believers in the Lord, large numbers of men and women, were being added to their number."[166]

Again, the leaders arrested "the apostles and put them in a public prison. But during the night an angel of the Lord opened the gates of the prison" and told them to preach the gospel to the people in the temple. And they did.[167]

The leaders again arrested them and brought them before the Council. The high priest said, "We gave you strict orders not to continue teaching in this name." "But Peter and the apostles answered, 'We must obey God rather than men.'" They testified that God raised Jesus from the dead and exalted Him saying, "we are witnesses of these things; and so is the Holy Spirit, whom God has given to those who obey Him."[168]

Enraged by this, the Council (i.e., the Sanhedrin) intended to kill them. But a teacher named Gamaliel cautioned them, "stay away from these men and leave them alone, for if the source of this plan or movement is men, it will be overthrown; but if the source is God, you will not be able to overthrow them; or else you may even be found fighting against God."[169] So, they flogged the apostles instead and again "ordered them not to speak in the name of Jesus, and then released them." The apostles went their way, "rejoicing that they had been considered worthy to suffer shame for His name. And every day, in the temple and from house to house, they did not stop teaching and preaching the good news of Jesus as the Christ."[170]

"The word of God kept spreading; and the number of the disciples continued to increase greatly in Jerusalem," and even "a great many of the priests were becoming obedient to the faith."[171]

The apostles called together "the whole community of the disciples," and they appointed seven deacons to take care of the growing congregation.[172] One of those deacons, named Stephen, performed "great wonders and signs among the people." But some accused Stephen of blasphemy and "stirred up the people, the elders, and the scribes," and they dragged him away to be tried before the Council, bringing false witnesses against him.[173] When questioned, Stephen called them to repent for persecuting the prophets and "always resisting the Holy Spirit."[174]

Upon hearing this, the Council was enraged. But Stephen was "full of the Holy Spirit" and announced, "I see the heavens opened and the Son of Man standing at the right hand of God." Still more enraged, they drove him out of the city and stoned him to death. But, as he died, he cried out, "Lord, do not hold this sin against them!"[175]

Saul of Tarsus had taken a leading part against Stephen, approving his killing. "And on that day a great persecution began against the church in Jerusalem, and they were all scattered throughout the regions of Judea and Samaria, except for the apostles." Indeed, "Saul began ravaging the church, entering house after house; and he would drag away men and women and put them in prison."[176]

Nevertheless, Christ's disciples continued to spread the good news of Christ's kingdom of unselfish love. Another of the deacons, Philip, preached the word and proclaimed Christ in Samaria, performing signs, casting out evil spirits, and healing the lame and paralyzed.[177]

And an angel told Philip to "go south to the road that descends from Jerusalem to Gaza." Philip went and met "an Ethiopian eunuch, a court official of Candace, queen of the Ethiopians," who'd come to Jerusalem to worship. He was sitting in his chariot, reading Isaiah. "Then the Spirit said to Philip, 'Go up and join this chariot.'" Philip did and "preached Jesus to him," explaining the words the man was reading from Isaiah, describing one "led like a sheep to slaughter," were about Jesus.

The man believed in Jesus and Philip baptized him. Then, the Spirit took Philip away and he "kept preaching the gospel to all the cities, until he came to Caesarea."[178]

Saul of Tarsus: A Most Unlikely Convert

Meanwhile, Saul of Tarsus continued to persecute Christians relentlessly. On his way to Damascus to arrest more, "suddenly a light from heaven flashed around him." Saul "fell to the ground and heard a voice saying to him, 'Saul, Saul, why are you persecuting Me?'"

"Who are You, Lord?" Saul answered.

"I am Jesus whom you are persecuting, but get up and enter the city, and it will be told to you what you must do."[179]

Saul got up, but found he could not see. So those traveling with him led him to Damascus. For three days, he neither ate nor drank and could see nothing.[180]

Jesus then appeared to a disciple in Damascus named Ananias, saying, "go to the street called Straight, and inquire at the house of Judas for a man from Tarsus named Saul, for he is praying, and he has seen in a vision a man named Ananias come in and lay his hands on him, so that he might regain his sight."[181]

Fearing Saul would arrest him, Ananias protested. "But the Lord said to him, 'Go, for he is a chosen instrument of Mine, to bear My name before the Gentiles and kings and the sons of Israel."[182] So Ananias went and laid hands on Saul, telling him, "the Lord Jesus, who appeared to you on the road by which you were coming, has sent me so that you may regain your sight and be filled with the Holy Spirit."[183]

Immediately, something like scales fell from Saul's eyes, and he could see. Saul was baptized. And "immediately he began to proclaim Jesus in the synagogues, saying, 'He is the Son of God.'"[184]

Amazing. The most avid persecutor of Christians himself became a Christian. He testified that he met the risen Christ and eventually died a martyr's death for his testimony.

> Amazing. The most avid persecutor of Christians himself became a Christian.

Even then, leaders in Damascus plotted to kill Saul for his testimony, watching the gates day and night. But some disciples helped Saul escape at night by lowering him in a large basket through an opening in the gate.[185]

Saul of Tarsus is better known as Paul, the great apostle who wrote many New Testament books. After these events, Paul went to Arabia and later returned to Damascus. Three years later, he returned to Jerusalem and met with a disciple named Barnabas, and with Peter and James, the brother of Jesus.[186]

In Jerusalem, some were also seeking to kill Paul, so the brethren sent him away to Tarsus.[187] Paul traveled to many places, and many Christians rejoiced, saying, "The man who once persecuted us is now preaching the faith which he once tried to destroy."[188]

Christianity Continues to Spread through the Mighty Works of the Holy Spirit

Meanwhile, the Holy Spirit performed many more miracles, and the church continued to increase.[189] In Lydda, a man named Aeneas was paralyzed and "bedridden for eight years." Peter met him and said, "'Aeneas, Jesus Christ heals you; get up and make your own bed.' Immediately he got up."[190]

In Joppa, "a disciple named Tabitha" (translated as Dorcas) was continually doing deeds of kindness and charity. But she became sick and died. Peter knelt down and prayed beside Tabitha's body. Then, he said, "Tabitha, arise." And she rose from the dead.[191]

In Caesarea, an angel told a Roman centurion named Cornelius to send men to Joppa to summon Peter.[192] The next day, while praying, Peter "saw the sky opened up" and a great sheet lowered to the ground with various animals on it. Then, a voice said, "Get up, Peter, kill and eat!" Now, according to the laws given to Moses, these particular creatures were not to be eaten because they were unclean. So, Peter protested, "I have never eaten anything unholy and unclean." Then, the voice said, "What God has cleansed, no longer consider unholy."[193] This vision was not about food but to show Peter it was wrong to think Gentiles were unclean.

Then, "the Spirit said to him, 'Behold, three men are looking for you,'" go with them, "for I have sent them Myself." He went with them to Caesarea, and many people assembled, for it was against custom for a Jew such as Peter "to associate with a foreigner or visit a foreigner." Against such human-made customs, Peter explained, "God has shown me that I am not to call any person unholy or unclean."[194]

Cornelius invited Peter to preach to the assembly. And Peter explained further, "I most certainly understand now that God is not one to show partiality, but in every nation the one who fears Him and does what is right is acceptable to Him."[195] Peter then testified of Christ's resurrection and declared that "all the prophets testify of Him, that through His name everyone who believes in Him receives forgiveness of sins."[196]

As Peter preached, "the Holy Spirit fell upon all those who were listening." The people "were amazed, because the gift of the Holy Spirit had also been poured out on the Gentiles."[197] And, Peter ordered them to be baptized in Jesus's name.[198]

Afterward, Peter went to Jerusalem. There, some took issue with Peter because he ate with Gentiles. To respond to their objections, Peter told them of his vision and the Spirit's instructions and that while he preached, "the Holy Spirit fell upon them just as He did upon us at the beginning."[199] When they heard all this, they "glorified God, saying, 'Well then, God has also granted to the Gentiles the repentance that leads to life.'"[200]

Meanwhile, the gospel was preached to Gentiles in other places, and many believed and turned to Jesus, including many in Antioch. Barnabas and Paul went and ministered to them there for an entire year.[201]

About that time, Herod Agrippa was persecuting Christians. He had the apostle James, the brother of John, "executed with a sword."[202] Then, Herod imprisoned Peter, "but prayer for him was being made to God intensely by the church."[203]

Peter was bound in chains, surrounded by soldiers. Suddenly an angel woke Peter and told him to get up. The chains fell off Peter's hands. And Peter followed the angel past the guards. When they came to the gate, it opened before them. They went out and the angel left. And when the disciples saw Peter, they were amazed.[204]

Paul's First Missionary Journey and the Jerusalem Council

After this, Paul went on many missionary journeys. First, the Holy Spirit sent Paul and Barnabas to proclaim God's word in Cyprus and many other places.[205] In Pisidian Antioch, Paul preached to both Jews and some God-fearing Gentiles in the synagogue on Sabbath. Many believed, but others persecuted them and drove them out.[206]

So, they went and preached in the synagogue in Iconium and many Jews and Gentiles believed.[207] Others rose up against them there also, however, and arranged to stone them. But Paul and Barnabas escaped and preached in other cities.[208]

In Lystra, Paul preached and met a man lame from birth and, seeing faith in his eyes, said, "'Stand upright on your feet!' And the man leaped up and began to walk."[209] This attracted a crowd. Some claimed Barnabas and Paul were gods, called them Zeus and Hermes, and arranged to offer sacrifices to them. But Barnabas and Paul corrected them and called them to worship the one true Creator God.

Then, some from other cities who'd persecuted Paul "won over the crowds," and "they stoned Paul and dragged him out of the city, thinking that he was dead."[210] But Paul survived and went with Barnabas to continue preaching, making many disciples in Derbe. They later returned to Lystra, Iconium, and (Pisidian) Antioch to continue the work there and in many other places. Finally, they returned to Antioch and reported the many great things God had done, highlighting God's bringing many Gentiles into the church.[211]

While many Gentiles became Christians, disputes arose regarding whether they needed to be circumcised like the Jews and keep all the laws of Moses—such as the ritual (ceremonial) laws.

So, the apostles and elders came together for a council in Jerusalem regarding this matter. Much debate ensued. Then, Peter stood up and reminded them that in his ministry God testified to the Gentiles and even gave them the Holy Spirit "and He made no distinction between us and them, cleansing their hearts by faith." He continued, saying, "why are you putting God to the test by placing upon the neck of the disciples a yoke which neither our forefathers nor we have been able to bear? But we believe that we are saved through the grace of the Lord Jesus, in the same way as they also are."[212]

Then, Paul and Barnabas related the many "signs and wonders that God had done through them among the Gentiles."[213] James, the brother of Jesus, who was presiding over the Council, declared that "the words of the Prophets" (in the Old Testament) agreed with what Peter preached about bringing Gentiles into the faith, quoting from Scripture the promise that God would come and restore the fallen tent of David "SO THAT

THE REST OF MANKIND MAY SEEK THE LORD, AND ALL THE GENTILES WHO ARE CALLED BY MY NAME."[214] "Therefore," James continued, "it is my judgment that we do not cause trouble for those from the Gentiles who are turning to God, but that we write to them that they abstain from things contaminated by idols, from acts of sexual immorality, from what has been strangled, and from blood."[215]

Yet, some difficulties continued in the relations between Jews and Gentiles. Later, at Antioch, Peter himself waffled under pressure by those who demanded that Gentiles be circumcised. Paul rebuked him for his hypocrisy, and Peter repented.[216]

Even apostles like Peter were fallible in their personal lives, which is one reason the testimony of those claiming to be prophets was to be tested by others, especially by the teaching of the apostles, who collectively stood as a cloud of first-generation witnesses.[217]

The teachings of the apostles themselves were to be tested by previously attested Scripture (e.g., the Old Testament).[218] Accordingly, those in the synagogue at Berea were commended for receiving the word preached by Paul and Silas "with great eagerness" but also "examining the Scriptures daily to see whether these things were so." And many of them believed, including a number of prominent Gentiles.[219]

> **The teachings of the apostles themselves were to be tested by previously attested Scripture.**

Although Peter was prominent among the apostles, he did not have a position of authority over the other apostles. As we saw, James, the brother of Jesus, presided over the Jerusalem Council.

The fact that James, the brother of Jesus, became a dedicated believer is itself amazing. Imagine if you had a brother who claimed to be the Messiah. You and I would never believe such a claim unless there was some amazing evidence . . . like resurrection.

At first, James and the other brothers of Jesus did not believe. But, after the resurrection, James came to believe and became a leader in the church in Jerusalem, eventually being brutally killed for his testimony.[220] According to early Christian testimony, James wrote the book of James while Jude, another brother of Jesus, wrote the book of Jude.

Paul's Second Missionary Journey

After the Jerusalem Council, Paul taught in Antioch for some time. Then, he went on his second missionary journey. He planned to take Barnabas, but Barnabas wanted to take John Mark, who had deserted them previously. Paul refused to take Mark, and they disagreed so sharply that they went to preach in separate places. Barnabas went with Mark, and Paul chose Silas and traveled about preaching and strengthening the churches.[221]

At Derbe, a young disciple named Timothy joined Paul and Silas. Guided by the Holy Spirit, they sailed to Philippi in Macedonia, found a place of prayer on the Sabbath, and preached to a group of women assembled outside the gate. One of the women, named Lydia, believed. She and her household were baptized, and the evangelists stayed at her house.[222]

Later, Paul cast a demon spirit out of an enslaved girl. Her masters were enraged because they profited much from using her as a fortune-teller. So "they seized Paul and Silas and dragged them into the marketplace before the authorities."[223]

Paul and Silas were severely beaten with rods and thrown into prison, but that did not stop them: "About midnight Paul and Silas were praying and singing hymns of praise to God, and the prisoners were listening to them; and suddenly there was a great earthquake, so that the foundations of the prison were shaken; and immediately all the doors were opened, and everyone's chains were unfastened."[224]

Finding the prison doors open, the jailer drew his sword to kill himself, but then he heard the voice of Paul cry out, "Do not harm yourself, for we are all here!" The jailer fell down before Paul and Silas, saying, "Sirs, what must I do to be saved?" And they told him, "Believe in the Lord Jesus, and you will be saved, you and your household." They preached further to him and his household and baptized them that very night. The next morning, the jailer received word to release Paul and Silas.[225]

They departed and preached the gospel wherever they went; in Thessalonica, Berea, Athens, and Corinth. In Thessalonica, Paul went to the synagogue and "for three Sabbaths reasoned with them from the Scriptures, explaining and giving evidence that the Christ had to suffer and rise from the dead."[226] Some were persuaded, including many Gentiles and leading women. But others formed a mob, tried to attack them, and persecuted believers.[227]

Paul and Silas departed to Berea and those in the synagogue there "received the word with great eagerness," and many prominent Gentile women and men believed.[228] From there, Paul went to Athens and spoke with Epicurean and Stoic philosophers, preaching Jesus and the resurrection on Mars Hill. Some sneered at the resurrection, but others joined Paul and believed.[229]

Then, Paul went to Corinth, where he met Priscilla and her husband, Aquila. Paul stayed with them and preached in the synagogue every Sabbath, trying to persuade Jews and Gentiles. Some rejected his message, but "Crispus, the leader of the synagogue, believed in the Lord together with his entire household; and many of the Corinthians" believed and were baptized.[230] Then, Jesus spoke to Paul in a vision by night, telling him not to be afraid and to continue to preach there. So Paul remained in Corinth for a year and six months, "teaching the word of God among them."[231]

Attempts by *some* Jews to persecute Paul arose there, so Paul departed with Priscilla and Aquila and went to Ephesus. There, Paul "entered the synagogue and reasoned with the Jews" and thereafter went to Caesarea and down to Antioch, completing his second missionary journey.[232]

Paul's Third Missionary Journey

Thereafter, Paul set out on his third missionary journey, beginning with the Galatian region and Phrygia.

Priscilla and Aquila remained behind in Ephesus. And, they took aside a man named Apollos, an eloquent man who was preaching the gospel mightily in Ephesus, and "explained the way of God more accurately to him."[233] Apollos went on to be a missionary, powerfully demonstrating from Scripture that Jesus was the Christ.[234]

Paul returned to Ephesus and remained there for some time, preaching God's word in the region. There, God performed many miracles through Paul—healing diseases and casting out evil spirits.[235] And many people abandoned the worship of false "gods" and other occult practices prominent in Ephesus.[236]

This, however, disrupted the business of many craftsmen in Ephesus who made shrines to the goddess Artemis. Enraged, they cried out,

"Great is Artemis of the Ephesians," and attacked some of Paul's traveling companions.[237]

After this uproar, Paul departed to Macedonia and spent three months in Greece. There, a plot formed against him, so he departed for Syria.[238] Along the way, Paul preached a lengthy message in Troas. A young man named Eutychus sat on the window sill listening, but fell asleep and fell from the third floor and was dead. Paul went and embraced him, and the boy lived again.[239]

Later, Paul set sail to go to Jerusalem. Along the way, many warned him not to go to Jerusalem because of the dangers. The prophet Agabus directly told Paul he would be bound there. But, Paul declared, "I am ready not only to be bound, but even to die in Jerusalem for the name of the Lord Jesus."[240]

From Jerusalem to Rome

Sure enough, while in Jerusalem, many sought to kill Paul. They dragged him out of the temple and severely beat him. Reports of the uproar reached a Roman commander, who ordered Paul to be bound in chains.[241]

Paul begged to be allowed to address the people.[242] Receiving permission, he told them of his education under Gamaliel, of his zeal and persecution of Christians, and finally, how he met the risen Jesus on the road to Damascus and became a Christian.[243] But, when he told them Jesus commissioned him to preach to the Gentiles, they stopped listening and cried out, "he should not be allowed to live!"[244]

The commander brought Paul into the barracks to examine him. He planned to scourge Paul until Paul informed him he was a Roman citizen. The next day, Paul was brought before the Council. As Paul spoke with them, a tumult arose, and the commander "was afraid that Paul would be torn to pieces by them," so he sent soldiers to remove him.[245]

The next night, "the Lord stood near" Paul "and said, 'Be courageous! For as you have testified to the truth about Me in Jerusalem, so you must testify in Rome also."[246]

Forty men planned an ambush to kill Paul the next time he would appear before the Council. But Paul's nephew heard of it, warned Paul, and the Roman commander was informed. At night, he sent Paul under guard by many soldiers to Caesarea, to Felix, the governor, with a letter explaining what happened and called Paul's accusers to bring charges before Felix.[247]

A few days later, Paul's accusers came and brought charges before Felix, claiming Paul stirred up dissension as a ringleader of Jesus's followers and tried to desecrate the temple.[248] Paul denied the charges while affirming his faith in Jesus and the resurrection, declaring, I believe "everything that is in accordance with the Law and is written in the Prophets."[249] Hearing this, Felix deferred judgment, hoping a bribe would be forthcoming, and ordered that Paul's friends could visit and minister to him.[250]

Two years passed. Felix was succeeded as governor by Porcius Festus. Then, Paul was brought before Festus for a hearing. Paul again denied the charges, stating, "I have not done anything wrong either against the Law of the Jews, or against the temple, or against Caesar."[251] Festus then asked Paul if he was willing to stand trial in Jerusalem. In response, Paul appealed to Caesar. Festus answered, "You have appealed to Caesar, to Caesar you shall go."[252]

But Paul was not immediately sent to Caesar in Rome. Several days later, King Herod Agrippa II and his sister Bernice visited Festus. Hearing of Paul's case, Agrippa asked to hear Paul himself. So, Paul was brought to speak before Agrippa in the auditorium, before commanders and the great men of Caesarea.[253]

Paul testified that he'd persecuted Christians but became one after meeting the risen Christ on the road to Damascus, who commissioned Paul to preach that many "may turn from darkness to light, and from the power of Satan to God."[254] Paul testified further, some "seized me in the temple and tried to murder me," for preaching so, but "I stand to this day testifying both to small and great, stating nothing but what the Prophets and Moses said was going to take place, as to whether the Christ was to suffer, and whether, as first from the resurrection of the dead, He would proclaim light both to the Jewish people and to the Gentiles."[255]

Hearing this, Agrippa said, "In a short time you are going to persuade me to make a Christian of myself."[256] Then, Agrippa and Festus agreed Paul had not done anything worthy of death or imprisonment and, had he not appealed to Caesar, might have been set free.[257]

Eventually, Paul was sent to Caesar in Rome, fulfilling what Jesus told him before.[258] Along the way, the ship carrying Paul and his companions under Roman guard (and many others) was caught in a storm and shipwrecked on the island of Malta. In the midst of the storm, an angel told Paul, "Do not be afraid, Paul; you must stand before Caesar; and behold, God has graciously granted you all those who are sailing with you."[259] Everyone on the boat—276 people—reached land safely, just as the angel foretold.[260]

The natives of Malta kindly received them. Then, a poisonous viper bit Paul. The islanders expected Paul to die from the poison, but Paul shook the viper off and was unharmed. So, they thought he was a god. Afterward, an islander was sick with recurrent fever and dysentery, but Paul prayed, laid hands on him, and healed him. Then, many others on the island came to Paul to be healed.[261]

After three months, they sailed on another ship to Rome. There, Paul stayed in rented quarters, with a soldier guarding him. People could come and visit him, and he could preach the message of Jesus there. And Paul testified to the Jews there, "trying to persuade them concerning Jesus, from both the Law of Moses and from the Prophets."[262] Some were persuaded, while others did not believe. Paul stayed in Rome for two years, writing various letters and "preaching the kingdom of God and teaching things about the Lord Jesus Christ with all openness, unhindered."[263]

Paul was eventually released from house arrest in Rome and traveled again to preach in various places. But, later, Paul was imprisoned again (in Rome).

Finally, Paul was killed for his witness to Jesus.[264]

Near the end of his life, Paul wrote in a letter to Timothy: "I have fought the good fight, I have finished the course, I have kept the faith; in the future there is reserved for me the crown of righteousness, which the Lord, the righteous Judge, will award to me on that day; and not only to me, but also to all who have loved His appearing."[265]

> **Though far from perfect, Paul's life was an amazing testimony of the power of the risen Jesus.**

Though far from perfect, Paul's life was an amazing testimony of the power of the risen Jesus. Not only did he convert from being a great persecutor of Christianity, but he also spent the rest of his life traveling and preaching, despite persecution and beatings, with numerous attempts on his life over the years.

According to early Christian sources, James, the brother of Jesus, Peter, and many other disciples also died for their faith in Him.[266] They also tried to kill John (the brother of James) by boiling him in oil, but he survived.[267] While imprisoned on the island of Patmos, John received and wrote down many visions in the book known as Revelation.

Presence with Us Coming Again

"I go to prepare a place for you," Jesus promised His disciples. "And if I go and prepare a place for you, I will come again and will take you to myself, so that where I am, there you may be also."[268]

And, just after Christ's ascension, an angel promised, "This Jesus, who has been taken up from you into heaven, will come in the same way as you have watched Him go into heaven."[269]

But *when* will He come? What is taking so long?

Nearly two thousand years have passed. Many today scoff at the very idea of Christ's Second Coming. Such scoffing itself, however, was foretold. Peter wrote, "in the last days mockers will come with their mocking." They will say, "Where is the promise of His coming? For ever since the fathers fell asleep, all things continue just as they were from the beginning of creation."[270]

> **Many today scoff at the very idea of Christ's Second Coming. Such scoffing itself, however, was foretold.**

Yet, Peter writes further, "The Lord is not slow about His promise, as some count slowness, but is patient toward you, not willing for any to perish, but for all to come to repentance."[271]

Just before Jesus ascended, His disciples asked Him when He would restore the kingdom to Israel. "It is not for you to know periods of time or appointed times which the Father has set by His own authority," Jesus replied.[272]

We are not told precisely when Jesus will return, but Scripture does foretell many things that will occur before Christ's Second Coming.[273] Many imposters will come and mislead many, Jesus foretold, claiming, "I am He!" And there will be many "wars and rumors of wars," Jesus foretold, "but that is not yet the end." Indeed, "nation will rise up against nation, and kingdom against kingdom; there will be earthquakes in various places" and "famines," but these "are only the beginning of birth pangs."[274]

Christ's followers will be persecuted, delivered to courts, flogged, and brought to stand before governors and kings *"as testimony to them."*[275] And, before the Second Coming, Jesus explained, "the gospel must first be preached to all the nations."[276]

When the end finally comes, Jesus foretold, "then they will see THE SON OF MAN COMING IN CLOUDS with great power and glory. And then He will send forth the angels, and will gather together His elect from the four winds, from the end of the earth to the end of heaven."[277]

In the meantime, however, prophecies also foretold that the dragon ruler (Satan) would have significant authority as the ruler of this world for a limited time. He would persecute Christ's followers for more than a thousand years. They would flee to find refuge and be preserved by God.[278] But, the dragon would continue to persecute Christ's followers, going off "to make war with the rest of her children," those who follow Christ, those "who keep the commandments of God and hold to the testimony of Jesus."[279]

Over the centuries, the prophecies revealed, this dragon ruler (Satan) gives great power, his throne, and great authority to oppressive earthly empires that persecute God's people. They enslave people, change God's times and laws, counterfeit Christ and the Holy Spirit, and attempt to force everyone to worship the dragon and earthly rulers instead of God, who alone is worthy of worship.[280]

Finally, however, Jesus will return, deliver the world from imperial oppression, and reclaim the world from the usurping rule of the devil.

Then, "many of those who sleep in the dust of the ground [the dead] will awake, these to everlasting life, but the others to disgrace and everlasting contempt."[281]

Death itself will be defeated "in a moment, in the twinkling of an eye, at the last trumpet; for the trumpet will sound, and the dead will be raised imperishable, and we will be changed."[282]

"Then will come about the saying that is written: 'DEATH HAS BEEN SWALLOWED UP in victory.'"[283]

Indeed, Paul explained, "if we believe that Jesus died and rose from the dead, so also God will bring with Him those who have fallen asleep through Jesus," and "we who are alive and remain until the coming of the Lord will not precede those who have fallen asleep. For the Lord Himself will descend from heaven with a shout, with the voice of the archangel and with the trumpet of God, and the dead in Christ will rise first. Then we who are alive, who remain, will be caught up together with them in the clouds to meet the Lord in the air, and so we will always be with the Lord. Therefore, comfort one another with these words."[284]

From beginning to end, the story of Scripture is the story of God *with us*—the story of God's special presence that was first established, then ruptured, then renewed by covenant, then with us in a new way with the first Advent of Christ (God with us in the flesh), then with us again in a new way with the work of the Holy Spirit as the Comforter, and finally will be restored to its original heights when Christ comes again.

> **From beginning to end, the story of Scripture is the story of God with us.**

In the end, the relentless mission of God to be with us will be accomplished forever. The special presence of God will be restored in fullness, and God will be *with us* again the way He intended from the beginning, forevermore. In the end, "the holy city, new Jerusalem" will come "down out of heaven from God, prepared as a bride adorned for her husband."[285] Then, it will be true in some special and unimaginable sense that "the tabernacle of God is among the people, and He will dwell among them, and they shall be His people, and God Himself will be among them, and He will wipe away every tear from their eyes; and there will no longer be any death; there will no longer be any mourning, or crying, or pain; the first things have passed away."[286]

This is only the beginning of the never-ending story of God *with us*.

3

IS THE STORY TRUE?
PRESENCE WITH US IN TRUTH

It could not be. He could not believe it. The other disciples reported to Thomas that Jesus had risen from the dead, saying, "We have seen the LORD!" But, Thomas replied, "Unless I see in His hands the imprint of the nails, and put my finger into the place of the nails, and put my hand into His side, I will not believe" (John 20:24–25).

Eight days later, Thomas and the other disciples were inside, and the doors were shut. Then, suddenly, Jesus came and stood in their midst and told Thomas, "Place your finger here, and see My hands; and take your hand and put it into My side; and do not continue in disbelief, but be a believer." Thomas responded by crying out, "My Lord and my God!" And Jesus replied, "Because you have seen Me, have you now believed? Blessed are they who did not see, and yet believed" (John 20:26–29).

A bit like Thomas, some ask today: Why should I believe? Is the story of Scripture true? I, for one, am thoroughly convinced this story *is* true. But how might one decide for himself or herself whether to believe?

As we will see, *everything* hinges on whether Jesus of Nazareth rose from the dead. As Paul wrote, "if Christ has not been raised, then our preaching is in vain" and our "faith also is in vain," and those who have hoped in Christ "are of all people most to be pitied" (1 Cor. 15:14, 19).

I, for one, believe the story and teachings of the Bible are true and provide the best framework for understanding the various dimensions of human existence as well as the biggest questions and issues of life. Before I share with you just why I believe this, however, let me begin by clearing the ground with respect to how the issue of faith itself might be approached.

Decisions of Faith

"If anyone is willing to do His will," Jesus said that one "will know about the teaching, whether it is of God, or I am speaking from Myself" (John 7:17). This raises a question for you and for me:

Are you willing? If you *could* believe, *would* you?

Every belief system requires some decisions of *faith*. I do not mean that every belief system requires *religious* faith or that each belief system requires *blind* faith, but every person must make some decisions (consciously or unconsciously) about whom or what they will believe, regarding what or whom they will trust or place confidence in relative to their beliefs.[1]

> *If you could believe, would you?*

For example, you believe the continent of Antarctica exists, right? But, most likely, you've never been there, so you have no first-hand experience. On what basis, then, do you believe Antarctica exists? Those of us who've never been to Antarctica believe it exists based on "faith" in the testimony of what we consider to be reliable sources.

A great many of your beliefs are grounded in this way, and rightly so. If you were to pause now to take inventory of just how many things you believe based on the testimony of others, without first-hand experience, you would very quickly lose count. Consciously or unconsciously, you regularly make decisions to believe based on the testimony of sources you consider to be reliable, without first-hand experience.

Yet, suppose you have been to Antarctica. At least you have a *memory* of visiting there. How would you know your memory of such a visit is reliable? Perhaps you simply dreamed that you visited Antarctica, or your mind could be playing tricks on you. Could you be *absolutely* certain you've been there? Would it not at least be possible you dreamed this or otherwise imagined this to be true? How could you know if your memory is reliable in this regard?

Here, again, some decision of faith is required. Not blind faith, but a decision about whether you should trust your memory in this regard. If you have a strong memory of having gone to Antarctica and no evidence defeating this memory, then you have good reason (that is, warrant) to believe you have indeed been there. Yet, this does involve trusting your memory, the kind of ordinary "faith" decision we repeatedly make every day, without thinking about it.

Suppose, instead, that you are actually in Antarctica right now. At least, you believe you're there. How would you know you were, in fact, in Antarctica? To answer this, you might appeal to your sight or your sense of touch. You might think, I can know I am in Antarctica because I can see it and touch it, etc. This kind of evidence based on sensory experience is known as empirical evidence. And, in our everyday life, we rely on our sensory experience all the time, typically without thinking about it.

But, how do you know your sensory experiences are reliable? How do you know, with certainty, that your senses are not deceiving you right now? Perhaps your senses are typically reliable, but you are on some powerful medication that causes hallucinations. Or, perhaps you are on a movie set made to look like Antarctica. Or, maybe you're dreaming. Of course, there are ways to rule out some of these possibilities, but there does not seem to be any way to entirely rule out the possibility that your sensory experience is wrong (about where you are located or about a great many other things).

You might attempt to *prove* your senses are not deceiving you by testing them, but it seems that any test you would attempt would already involve some reliance on your sensory experience.[2] Even asking someone else what they see and where you both are would itself rely on your sensory experience relative to their responses (e.g., *hearing* their response). And, if you're hallucinating or dreaming, the "person" you ask might not actually be there either!

Now, do not worry, I do indeed believe that my senses and cognitive faculties are *generally* reliable, but I cannot *prove beyond the shadow of a doubt* that they are. Any "evidence" I would posit to prove this (or anything else about the world) would itself require the use of my reason and/or senses.

How, then, can we believe anything with confidence? How can we truly *know* anything?

First, we should recognize that if knowing something requires proof beyond the possibility of *any* doubt, there would be very little (if anything) we could claim to know. Both our "big" beliefs and our "little" beliefs rest on decisions of faith at one juncture or another. Indeed, we regularly make decisions of "faith," often without thinking about it.

When I sit down in a chair, I don't pause to question whether it will support me. When I'm driving my car, I believe my brakes will work and continue to work. When I look out my window, I believe my eyesight is functioning in a generally reliable way, and, unless I have some reason to doubt it, I do not give much thought to the possibility that it is not.

Yet, all these beliefs rest on (conscious or unconscious) decisions to trust my senses. In this regard, most would agree that—absent compelling evidence to the contrary—we are justified in trusting our senses. But, doing so nevertheless involves "faith," minimally defined here as believing something that you cannot prove beyond any and all doubt. The question, then, is not whether you will have faith, but where will you place your faith?

> The question, then, is not whether you will have faith, but where will you place your faith?

Matters of the utmost importance hinge on decisions of faith. For example, I firmly believe that my wife loves me. But how could I know for sure, beyond the shadow of a doubt? I have a host of reasons to believe she does. But it is *possible* (although extremely unlikely) she is a great actor and is deceiving me. I nevertheless trust that she does indeed love me, and I have excellent reasons for doing so, rooted in the experiences of our relationship over many years. Yet, to believe she loves me still requires decisions of faith (as defined above). Indeed, love itself inherently involves trust and, thus, faith. I *could* doubt that she genuinely loves me, but I do not doubt it at all.

Just because I *can* doubt something does not mean I *should*. And the fact that something *can* be doubted does not count as evidence against it. One who decides they will only believe things that *cannot* be doubted and that do not require any decisions of faith will end up believing very little, if anything. In the process, such a one will miss out on a great deal of what makes the human experience most valuable and enjoyable. For one thing, such a one will not be in a position to believe anyone loves them, depriving oneself of the profound joys of genuine love relationships.

That some decisions of faith are required not only of religious beliefs, but also of secular ones is widely recognized by philosophers who study epistemology; the branch of philosophy that investigates the origin, nature, methods, and limits of human knowledge. Decisions of faith can be defeated and overturned, but all belief systems must start somewhere. Even empirical evidence requires commitment to the belief that my sensory experience (and cognitive function that interprets my experience) is generally reliable.[3]

Every belief system, then, religious or otherwise, rests on decisions to believe in something, whether that something is the closed universe of naturalism (the belief that everything arises from natural properties and causes, excluding supernatural explanations), a personal God who created the universe (theism), or anything in between.[4] Again, the question is not whether you will have "faith" but where will you place your faith?

"Natural" Beliefs?

If you've never thought about it, you've likely never made a *conscious* decision to trust your sensory experience (or cognitive faculties more broadly). But, upon reflection, the question remains as to whether and why you *should* trust them.

But you might say, it seems like I automatically trust my sensory experience (and cognitive faculties). I seem to trust them by default. It thus seems *natural* to me to trust my sensory experience and cognitive faculties unless I have some reason to do otherwise.

This seems right, as far as it goes. It is worth noting at this juncture, however, that if you ask some people why they believe in God, their answer might sound strikingly similar to the line of thought above. For many, it seems *natural* to believe in God. Many have believed in God as long as they can remember, and it's hard for them to imagine not believing in God. To them, it seems like the default belief is to believe in God—like it's *natural* to believe in God.

Here, while there are many interesting philosophical *arguments* for the existence of God (e.g., the moral, ontological, cosmological, teleological, historical, and others—see "Some Prominent Arguments for the Existence of God" below), world-class philosophers like Alvin Plantinga have offered rigorous philosophical arguments concluding that one can be *warranted* to believe in God even without (or prior to) such belief being evidentially based on other beliefs (that is, apart from basing belief in God on separate evidences or arguments).[5]

If theism is true, Plantinga contends, it stands to reason that God created human nature with faculties that are designed or aimed toward producing belief in God (cf. Rom. 1:19-21). If so, humans with properly functioning cognitive faculties have something like a sixth sense, so to speak, which John Calvin referred to as the sense of divinity (the *sensus divinitatis*), which might explain why the vast majority of people who've ever lived have believed in God or some gods.[6] In brief, Plantinga argues that belief in God is *properly basic*, meaning that (in the absence of a defeater) belief in God is the kind of belief one can be warranted in holding without first basing it on other evidence or arguments, that is, even if it is "not accepted on the evidential basis of other beliefs."[7]

Some Prominent Arguments for the Existence of God

There is not space here to adequately introduce the *many* arguments for the existence of God in circulation today. Here, I will simply list a few of the most prominent ones in simplified form without further comment.[8] Such arguments may not prove that God exists beyond the shadow of a doubt, but together form an impressive cumulative case worthy of consideration. However, as explained further below, I believe God exists not on the basis of any philosophical arguments but I believe the grand story of Scripture (including the many amazing prophecies contained therein) and the testimony of the Holy Spirit provide amazing evidence. Indeed, I am convinced that the Holy Spirit provides testimony to believers—an inner witness of God's presence and work in us and through us. I will discuss this and much more later in this chapter. Before doing so, it will be helpful for the reader to be aware of some arguments for the existence of God discussed most often today.

The cosmological argument maintains that God is the best explanation of the existence of the cosmos. God is the first cause—the uncaused cause of everything else that exists. The kalam version maintains, more specifically, that anything that begins to exist has a cause. The universe began to exist and therefore has a cause. The cause of the universe (the first cause of everything else) must transcend the universe, be uncaused, and have always existed. This *uncaused* cause is God.

The contingency argument (another kind of cosmological argument) maintains that God is the best explanation of contingent (non-necessary) things. In order for contingent things to exist, some necessary being must exist, and God is the necessary being—the explanation of why anything exists at all. This approach argues that every contingent thing has an explanation of its existence *in an external cause*. The universe is a contingent thing. The universe thus has an explanation of its existence *in an external cause*, and that explanation is God; the necessary being that explains the existence of contingent things.

The ontological argument claims that God is the greatest possible being and thus *must* exist. One version of this argument goes as follows. It is possible that a maximally great being exists. If it is *possible* that a maximally great being exists, however, then a maximally great being exists in *some* possible world. If a maximally great being exists in some possible world, then such a being must exist in every possible world (otherwise, that being would not be *maximally* great) and thus exists in the actual world. Therefore, a maximally great being (God) exists in the actual world.

The teleological argument maintains that God is the best explanation for the apparent design of the universe. This argument claims the universe is designed, and God is the designer of the universe. The fine-tuning version of this argument claims that the apparent fine-tuning of the universe is due to either physical necessity, chance, or design. But it is not due to physical necessity or chance and is, therefore, due to design. God is the designer.[9]

The moral argument maintains that God is the best explanation for (objective) moral values. Indeed, God is the basis of (objective) moral values. This argument claims that if God did not exist, objective moral values and duties would not exist. Yet, objective moral values and duties do exist. Therefore, God exists.

Even if one thinks philosophical arguments are not compelling, however, there are other reasons to believe in God apart from such philosophical arguments—including the beauty, relevance, goodness, and power of the story of Scripture itself, which I believe is the greatest story ever told.[10] A historical argument for the existence of God, the one I find most important, is based on the most crucial element of this story, the resurrection.

The historical resurrection argument maintains that God is the best explanation of the evidence that Jesus rose from the dead. There is abundant evidence that Jesus of Nazareth existed, claimed to be God (the Son), and rose from the dead in confirmation of His claims.[11] As Paul proclaimed, Jesus is the One whom God "appointed, having furnished proof to all people by raising Him from the dead" (Acts 17:31; cf. Rom. 1:4). Christ's resurrection provides amazing evidence of God's existence because it provides the best explanation of the evidence that Jesus of Nazareth rose from the dead (see further discussion later in this chapter).

Many have argued further, that life without God ultimately amounts to absurdity; without God there is no transcendent purpose, value, or meaning such that life without God is ultimately purposeless, valueless, and meaningless. This itself is not an argument for God's existence, but it is a widespread conclusion reached by many prominent *atheist* philosophers (e.g., Jean-Paul Sartre and Albert Camus).[12] If there is no God, death is the ultimate end for everyone. Eventually, *everything* will perish. There is, then, no transcendent goodness, no transcendent meaning, and no transcendent purpose. All things are permitted. All is meaningless. All is vanity, a chasing after the wind (see, e.g., Eccles. 2:11; 3:19–20).

Some have given up atheism because they found it wanting relative to the biggest questions of life. For example, former atheist Lee Strobel, who converted to Christianity after a two-year quest to disprove it, wrote: "To continue in atheism, I would need to believe that nothing produces everything, non-life produces life, randomness produces fine-tuning, chaos produces information, unconsciousness produces consciousness, and non-reason produces reason. I simply didn't have that much faith."[13]

If God exists, however, there is transcendent goodness, meaning, and purpose. In this regard, many have argued that God provides the best explanation of the ultimate purpose of life, the best explanation of the amazing effectiveness of mathematics and the scientific method (which presupposes the world is orderly and intelligible to human minds), and the best explanation of transcendent value and beauty, and love itself.[14] Alongside these (and a great many other) arguments, I believe the grand story of Scripture (including the many amazing prophecies contained therein), and the testimony of the Holy Spirit provide amazing evidence. Indeed, I believe the story of Scripture provides the best framework for making sense of the human experience—of existence, meaning, the purpose of life, and love itself. Further, I am convinced that the Holy Spirit provides testimony to believers—an inner witness of God's presence and work in us and through us.

While the testimony I have personally experienced is not available as evidence for someone else (outside of the external fruits in my life), it counts as evidence for me. One of the main reasons I am convinced that God exists is because of the testimony of the Holy Spirit and what I recognize as God's work in my life and the lives of others. The truth of the story of Scripture resounds in the stories of people's lives today, a contemporary cloud of witnesses (more on this below).

The "Default" Position?

The idea that it might be "natural" for humans to believe in God (that is, by divine design) seems consistent with the way Scripture approaches belief in God. Scripture does not make arguments for God's existence, but tells the story of God *with us*, sets forth God as the basis of everything else, and indicates humans ought to already know that God exists. Indeed, Paul writes against those "who suppress the truth in unrighteousness, because that which is known about God is evident within them; for God made it evident to them. For since the creation of the world His invisible attributes, that is, His eternal power and divine nature, have been clearly perceived, being understood by what has been made, so that they are without excuse. For even though they knew God, they did not honor Him as God or give thanks, but they became futile in their reasonings, and their senseless hearts were darkened" (Rom. 1:18–21; cf. Ps. 14:1; 19:1ff.). This passage indicates that God has made some things about Himself "evident to" humans so as to be "understood by what has been made."

If God created human nature with a disposition to recognize and believe in God (for the sake of love relationship), then belief in God would be "natural."

Why, then, does belief in God not seem "natural" or like the default position to many? Well, I cannot speak for all, but many (particularly in the West) have been conditioned by modernism to believe that one's beliefs must start from some *neutral* standpoint in order to be scientific. Then, some assume that a naturalistic standpoint is neutral.

But, naturalism is *not* neutral. Disbelief in God (or the supernatural more generally) is no more neutral than belief in God. While one might be agnostic about the existence of God, there is no strictly neutral starting point. Just as there can be no view from nowhere, every starting point has to start somewhere. The starting point itself could be defeated and abandoned later in one's thinking, but one cannot start without some starting point. To begin with, belief in God is at least as justified as starting with belief in naturalism or any other starting point.[15]

> **Disbelief in God is no more neutral than belief in God.**

In this regard, most people who've ever lived, including most people alive today, have believed in supernatural agents, and a great many have believed in one supreme God. This fact does not make belief in supernatural agents true, but it does suggest that "naturalistic" belief is not the *default* or *natural* position that humans tend to start from. Arguably, naturalism is a learned perspective, while belief in supernatural agents might not be. Indeed, some psychologists claim to have shown evidence that "children are naturally *tuned* to believe in gods of one sort or another."[16]

Here, one might pose a difficult question facing naturalism: why should naturalists believe their sensory experience and/or cognitive function is reliable in the first place? Plantinga argues that if (Darwinian) naturalism is true, there does not seem to be any good reason to think human faculties would correspond to truth (because adaptive *behavior* rather than true beliefs would be sufficient for natural selection). However, if theism is true and God created humans, one has good reason to trust such faculties (on the view that God created humans with such faculties aimed at truth). In brief, Plantinga argues that the naturalist has no sufficient overarching explanation for why our sensory experience and cognitive faculties are generally reliable or generally aimed at truth, but theists do.[17] In this regard, much scientific inquiry as we know it today arose and flourished on the basis of belief in a Creator God who designed the world to function in an orderly manner according to laws or law-like regularities and gave humans faculties (minds) such that the world is actually intelligible to us.

Whatever else we say here, we should be clear that scientific inquiry is very helpful and good when undertaken within the context of its intrinsic limits. Contrary to popular opinion, faith and science need not be perpetually at odds with one another. On the contrary, I believe they should be understood as close companions, and science should be highly valued.[18] Yet, as any good scientist will tell you, there are many questions the scientific method cannot answer because the method includes only things subject to empirical observation and is thus limited to observations regarding the physical realm. Any approach to knowledge as a whole that limits itself to what can be known *by the scientific method* alone (known as scientism) thereby cuts itself off from answering questions that transcend (physical) empirical observation, which include many questions humans consider to be the most important.[19]

For example, what is the meaning of life? What is love? Why are we here? Why is there anything at all? What is wrong with this world? What is good and virtuous and beautiful? What is my purpose? Who am I? How can I find true and lasting joy? Why do we even search for meaning? Why do we have a longing for a better world?[20]

These are metaphysical questions, which, by definition, transcend observation of the physical realm and are thus beyond strictly empirical observation.[21] Such *metaphysical* questions and issues, the most profound questions and experiences of life, transcend the limitations of empirical observation and investigation and thus transcend the limits of the scientific method. This is not a criticism of the scientific method, properly employed, but simply a recognition of its inherent limits when it comes to the big questions—the questions most significant to human existence and meaning.

There is far more to life than what we empirically observe. Where, then, might we turn relative to such questions? I, for one, believe the story and teachings of the Bible are true and provide the best framework for understanding both the empirical and metaphysical dimensions of human experience and, indeed, all of the biggest questions and issues of life.

Yet, you might ask, why should I or anyone else believe the Bible?

Why I Believe the Bible: A Christocentric Approach

There is much more to say about epistemology, but here I simply want you to recognize that *all* belief systems require some decisions of faith, religious or otherwise. The question once again, then, is not whether you will have faith, but where will you place your faith.

As we have seen, many of our beliefs are based on "faith" in what we consider to be reliable sources or testimony. When it comes to matters of history (historical events that are beyond our first-hand experience), we have to make decisions about what or whom we consider to be reliable sources. If you believe that people such as Alexander the Great and Cleopatra existed, you do so on the basis of historical testimony. Notably, as we will see, there is a great deal of historical (and other) testimony relative to the story of Scripture.

I am not in a position to tell you what to believe, and I will not try to do so. But, I am in a position to share with you some of the reasons why I believe the Bible is a reliable source.

Historical Revelation of the Personal God of the Bible

The God of the Bible is a personal God who cares about us and desires relationship *with us* (see chapter 7). If the personal God of the Bible exists, then, it is reasonable to expect Him to reveal Himself in some reliable way.[22] The Bible presents itself as exactly this kind of personal and reliable revelation of God.

The God of the Bible is a personal God who cares about us and desires relationship with us.

According to the Bible, Jesus of Nazareth claimed to provide in Himself the ultimate historical revelation of God (see John 14:9). While the claims of many religions are not rooted in history (indeed, many are *ahistorical*, appealing to transcendent, inaccessible realms), the Bible claims that God revealed Himself *historically*, in time and space, and did so supremely in Jesus, who claimed to be the Son of God. The entirety of Christian faith hinges on this claim.

If Jesus was (and is) who He claimed to be, then we have the best of good reasons to believe His testimony more broadly, including His testimony about the origin, nature, and authority of Scripture, which Jesus claimed "cannot be broken" (John 10:35, NKJV), and which He repeatedly quoted as having unique authority over human teachings and traditions (see, e.g., Matt. 15:3-9; cf. 5:17-18; Luke 24:25-27).

Who was Jesus, then? And how do we know?

In addition to biblical sources, numerous other ancient sources (including hostile sources) attest to Jesus's existence and to the fact that He was indeed crucified under the governance of Pontius Pilate.[23] The abundant extra-biblical evidence for the existence of Jesus of Nazareth includes references by non-Christians such as the Jewish historian Josephus (ca. 90-95, *Antiquities*, 18.3, 20.9), the Roman historian Tacitus (ca. 115, *Annals*, 15.44), the Roman historian (and contemporary of Tacitus) Suetonius (*Claudius*, 25), the Roman official Pliny the Younger writing to Emperor Trajan (ca. 112, *Letters*, 10:96-97), and others, including the central text of Rabbinic Judaism known as the Talmud (ca. 135, *Sanhedrin* 43a).[24] Indeed, the Talmud *inadvertently* attests that Jesus was a miracle worker by including the allegation that Jesus "practiced sorcery and enticed Israel to apostasy."[25]

Given the abundant evidence, the historical existence of Jesus of Nazareth and His death by crucifixion under the Roman governor Pilate is overwhelmingly affirmed by informed scholars. Some question, however, whether Jesus was in fact the Son of God, a question that hinges on whether Jesus *actually* rose from the dead, on which the truth of Christianity itself hinges. As Paul put it, if Jesus is not risen, the Christian faith is in vain (1 Cor. 15:14-19).

The Testimony of the Resurrection

Today, he might be classified as a terrorist. Paul relentlessly persecuted Christians for their faith, and he was thus greatly feared among Christians. Then, Paul himself *became* a Christian, thereby giving up everything and subjecting himself to persecution. What accounts for this amazing, highly unlikely turnaround?

Paul testified that the risen Christ met him on the way to Damascus (e.g., Acts 9:1-9), a meeting that completely changed his life. Indeed,

Paul attested that the risen Christ "appeared to Cephas [Peter], then to the twelve" and afterward "He appeared to more than five hundred brothers and sisters at one time, most of whom remain until now" and "then He appeared to James, then to all the apostles; and last of all . . . He appeared to me also" (1 Cor. 15:5–8).

Should we believe such testimony? There is far more historical evidence that Jesus rose from the dead than many people realize. In this regard, the vast majority of critical scholars (*including skeptics*) who specialize in New Testament and related fields affirm the following historical facts relative to the death of Jesus:[26]

- Jesus of Nazareth died by crucifixion.
- Very soon after Jesus's death, His followers had *real* experiences they thought were actual appearances of the risen Jesus.
- The lives of those followers were transformed as a result, even to the point of being willing to die specifically for their faith in the resurrection message.
- Jesus died, rose from the dead, and appeared to His followers was taught very early, soon after the crucifixion.
- James, the brother of Jesus, who at first did not believe, became a Christian due to his own experience that he thought was of the resurrected Christ.
- The Christian persecutor Paul (Saul of Tarsus) also became a believer after his own experience that he thought was an encounter with the risen Jesus.

Perhaps the world's leading expert on the resurrection of Jesus, Gary Habermas, calls these "minimal facts," each of which is "confirmed by several strong and independent arguments."[27] And, Habermas argues that, taken together, the best explanation of these minimal facts, *by far*, is that Jesus rose from the dead.

Even many skeptical, agnostic, and atheist scholars affirm these historical facts, Habermas explains, because "each one is virtually undeniable. Most of the half-dozen Minimal Facts typically used are confirmed by ten or more historical considerations each. That is simply an amazing foundation, especially for events that occurred in the First Century AD!"[28]

Beyond these facts, there is considerable evidence that the tomb in which Jesus's body was sealed was found empty on the first day of the week after the crucifixion.

The authorities did everything they could to discredit Jesus—they hated Him so much that they had Him crucified. But news spread that Jesus rose from the dead, and with such news, Christianity itself spread. To utterly discredit the resurrection accounts (and thus Christianity itself), all the authorities need have done was produce the dead body of Jesus.

They knew where He had been entombed; in the tomb belonging to Joseph of Arimathea, a member of the ruling Council (the Sanhedrin).[29] The authorities had made sure Roman guards were stationed there. And, if Jesus's body remained there, they had the power to open the tomb and reveal it.

But, they did not reveal the body of Jesus.

They could not because the tomb was indeed empty.[30]

According to the Gospels, women were the first to discover the empty tomb. This, many scholars point out, is strong evidence that the tomb was indeed empty. Sadly, at that time and place, women were viewed as far less credible witnesses in civil and criminal hearings than men. Anyone attempting to fabricate a credible resurrection story, then, would have been *extremely* unlikely to choose to list women as the first witnesses.

That the tomb was indeed empty is further attested by the reaction of the authorities themselves. They claimed Jesus's disciples had stolen His body—a claim that would be unnecessary if the tomb was not empty. Moreover, their claim that the disciples stole the body is implausible in the extreme. The tomb was heavily guarded because the authorities themselves had stationed Roman guards at the tomb precisely to prevent this possibility.[31]

Given that the penalty for a Roman soldier who fell asleep on duty was death, how likely would it be that an entire group of Roman guards would fall asleep on guard duty? It is *extremely* unlikely. And, how likely is it that the disciples could roll away the massively heavy stone that sealed the tomb from the entrance, and do so without waking up even one of the guards? Again, extremely unlikely.

The best explanation for the empty tomb is that Jesus truly rose from the dead. As the angel declared, according to Matthew 28:6, "He is not here, for He has risen, just as He said."

Notably, in this regard, Habermas explains that "contemporary critical scholars, whether skeptical or not, are virtually unanimous in rejecting" the hypothesis that the disciples stole the body. "If the disciples stole the body, they would not have been willing to die, in all probability, for a known lie or fraud."[32]

> *The best explanation for the empty tomb is that Jesus truly rose from the dead.*

Indeed, the very fact that many people claimed to have met the risen Christ and were *willing to die* for this testimony stands as strong evidence in favor of the historicity of the resurrection.

According to New Testament accounts, the risen Jesus appeared to Mary Magdalene, to a number of other women in a group, to Peter, to two other followers on the road to Emmaus, then to a gathering of many disciples during which Jesus ate with them and invited them to touch Him, then again about a week later to a group of disciples during which Jesus invited (doubting) Thomas to touch His wounds from the crucifixion, then later to a group of disciples by the Sea of Galilee, still later to a group of over five-hundred people, to James, to all the apostles, and to Paul on the road to Damascus, among other occasions.[33]

One might argue that those who claimed to have encountered the risen Jesus were lying. Yet, how likely is it that so many people could maintain such a lie in the face of severe persecution and on pain of death? People have died for false beliefs, but who dies for a belief they *know* to be false and without any earthly benefit to them or their family? What motivation would they have to die for what they knew to be a lie? They had everything to lose and virtually nothing to gain. They were harshly persecuted for their faith and, for many of them, the earthly "reward" for their testimony about Jesus Christ was a grisly death. For example, according to ancient tradition, Peter was crucified upside down for his testimony about Jesus, James (Jesus's brother) was stoned, and Paul was also martyred (likely beheaded) for his witness.[34] It does not seem plausible, then, to conclude that the disciples' testimony about Christ's resurrection was *intentionally* deceptive.

One might argue, instead, that those who claimed to encounter the risen Jesus were mistaken. Some have suggested such reported experiences might have been hallucinations. However, such accounts cannot be plausibly explained as the product of hallucinations because group hallucinations are extremely improbable. And one would have to posit *repeated* group hallucinations to account for the recurring appearances of Jesus to groups of followers over weeks (which included conversations, physical contact, and even dining with the risen Christ).[35] Additionally, hallucination hypotheses provide no help to account for the empty tomb.

For three and a half years, the apostles (and others) traveled with Jesus, ate with Him, observed His daily life, and had every opportunity to know first-hand the truth or falsehood of His claims. Yet, these and other disciples were willing to be violently killed rather than recant their faith in Jesus's resurrection because they were utterly convinced that Jesus was the Christ, the Son of God, and truly rose from the dead.

The best explanation of this is that Jesus really did rise from the dead, which accounts for the amazing origin and growth of Christianity, which is otherwise exceedingly unlikely given that its first proponents were faithful Jews, and Christianity took root under very unfavorable conditions and in the face of repeated persecutions in the Roman Empire.

The resurrection provides the best explanation *by far* for (*among other things*) the empty tomb, the prominence of women as witnesses, the various claims of post-mortem appearances by Jesus to individuals *and groups* in many different times and places (including to over five hundred people), the willingness of many to die specifically for their faith in the resurrection message, the amazing and otherwise highly unlikely origin and growth of Christianity, and highly unlikely conversions like those of Paul and James, the brother of Jesus.[36]

Defending Jesus's resurrection on purely historical grounds, Wolfhart Pannenberg said: "The evidence for Jesus' resurrection is so strong that nobody would question it except for two things: First, it is a very unusual event. And second, if you believe it happened, you have to change the way you live."[37] Indeed, as I see it, the most likely conclusion (by far) is that Jesus really did rise from the dead, just as He foretold. If so, Jesus truly was (and is) the Son of God, just as He claimed. Jesus "was declared the Son of God with power according to the Spirit of holiness by the resurrection from the dead" (Rom. 1:4) and God "furnished proof to all people by raising Him from the dead" (Acts 17:31).[38]

The Testimony of the Manuscript Evidence

Yet, one may protest: perhaps the stories about Jesus that have come down to us in the New Testament have been corrupted or tampered with. How do we know such stories are based on eyewitness testimony of first-generation witnesses and have been reliably transmitted?

First, recall that the above lines of evidence do not require that one first have confidence in the New Testament. Even merely treating the New Testament documents as sources on par with other ancient sources provides a mountain of evidence pointing toward the historicity of the resurrection.

Further, the New Testament sources claim to provide historically reliable and inspired eyewitness testimony of the life, death, and resurrection of Jesus. For example, Luke informs us he intended to write an accurate account, including the testimony of living eyewitnesses, so the reader might "know the exact truth" (Luke 1:1–4; cf. John 21:31). And, according to multiple early sources, each of the four Gospels was written by an apostle (Matthew, John) or a close associate of an apostle (Luke, an associate of Paul, and Mark, believed to have written Peter's account).[39]

As noted earlier, we can reasonably discount worries that the apostolic Gospels might be unreliable due to ignorance or deception.[40] The apostles, having spent daily life with Christ for three and a half years, certainly would have known what they were talking about, and they had nothing to gain by lying.[41] In fact, they lost everything in this world for their testimony. It is very unlikely that anyone who did not truly believe would have been willing to endure such harsh persecutions, including crucifixion and other forms of torture. The most plausible explanation of the apostolic witness to Christ, then, is that the apostles told the truth about Jesus.

But, how do we know their eyewitness testimony has been reliably transmitted over the centuries? This question might be answered by addressing three further questions:

- How close in time was the original account to the actual events?
- How close in time are the earliest manuscripts we possess to the original time of writing?
- How many manuscripts do we possess, and to what extent do they agree with one another?

The Date of Original Writing

We have good reason to believe that all four Gospels were written within thirty to sixty-five years of Christ's death and resurrection (in AD 31), within the lifetime of many eyewitnesses.[42]

Specifically, we have good reason to believe Luke was written before Acts because Acts continues Luke's account. Acts ends with Paul under house arrest in Rome, without reporting what happened to Paul. We know from extra-biblical sources that Paul was released but later executed in Rome (sometime between AD 62 and 67). Why doesn't Acts tell us what happened to Paul? Many scholars believe the best explanation is Acts was written before those events occurred, meaning Acts was written no later than AD 67, and Luke was thus written sometime before that.[43]

Further, Luke's Gospel shows evidence of using the Gospels of Matthew and Mark as sources, indicating Matthew and Mark were written even earlier.[44] These three Gospels (known as the Synoptic Gospels), then, were written within a few decades of Christ's resurrection. As Craig Blomberg puts it, the evidence "adds up to a strong case that all three [Synoptic] Gospels were composed within about thirty years of Christ's death," which is "well within the period of time when people could check up on the accuracy of the facts they contain."[45]

What about the Gospel of John? Critical scholars used to date John to the mid to late second century. But then, an early fragment of John (p[52]) was discovered, leading to the widely held conclusion that "any date between about 55 and 95 is possible," placing the writing of John within sixty-five years of Christ's death at the latest.[46]

All four Gospels, then, were written within the lifespan of first-generation apostles and other witnesses to Jesus's life, death, and resurrection. Thus, the claims therein could be verified or falsified by contemporaries, rendering it very unlikely that myth or legend could creep in by the time of their writing.[47]

Ancient biographies of other individuals were often written centuries later than the events they depict but are nevertheless generally relied upon by historians. In comparison, the Gospels are very early accounts indeed. And Paul was writing letters quite early, including testimony about Christ's death and resurrection in the form of early creeds that scholars trace to within just a few years of Christ's resurrection (e.g., 1 Cor. 15:3–5).[48]

The Age, Abundance, and Agreement of Ancient New Testament Manuscripts

But how do we know the documents were reliably transmitted?

The proximity of the earliest manuscripts we have to the date of the original writings is quite early, especially when compared to other ancient manuscripts. We have a number of second and third-century New Testament fragments, some that date from within a couple of generations of the originals or earlier. And we have the entire New Testament corpus in very important fourth-century codices.[49] Other ancient writings, by comparison, often have five hundred, eight hundred, or even one thousand years between the writing of the original and the earliest surviving copy.[50]

In all, we possess thousands of ancient New Testament manuscripts, far more than any other ancient work (which often exist in only a few ancient copies). Indeed, there are more ancient New Testament manuscripts than any other ten ancient works combined![51] Further, the New Testament books were so widely quoted by early Christians that nearly the entire New Testament (save a handful of verses) could be reconstructed from the writings of the second to fourth-century church fathers alone.[52]

Comparison of the many New Testament manuscripts shows an amazing extent of agreement between them. In fact, the New Testament "has not only survived in more manuscripts than any other book from antiquity, but it has survived in a much purer form than any other great book . . . a form that is over 99 percent pure."[53]

At this juncture, some point to the sheer number of variations among the ancient manuscripts. Indeed, there are some four hundred thousand textual variants, but most are very minor variants, and "the large number of variants is due to the large number of manuscripts."[54] As leading New

Testament textual scholar, Daniel Wallace writes, "the vast majority of textual alterations are accidental and trivial, and hence easy for textual critics to spot."[55] Further, according to New Testament textual scholar Bruce Metzger, "generally they're inconsequential variations" such as "differences in spelling" and other differences that do not change the meaning of the text.[56]

In all this, F. F. Bruce correctly states, "There is no body of ancient literature in the world which enjoys such a wealth of good textual attestation as the New Testament."[57] Indeed, he adds, "if the New Testament were a collection of secular writings, their authenticity would generally be regarded as beyond doubt."[58] If it is reasonable for me to believe other, less-attested accounts of ancient history are reliable, then it is reasonable to believe the New Testament, which is by far the most attested and accurately preserved work of antiquity, is reliable.

The Testimony of Jesus: Christ Confirms and Commissions the Biblical Canon

If, as argued above, the New Testament provides accurate eyewitness accounts of Jesus's life, death, and resurrection, then we have excellent reasons to believe that Jesus truly was (and is) the Son of God, as He claimed.[59]

We ought to pay very close attention, then, to Christ's own claims regarding the reliability and authority of the rest of Scripture. In numerous places, Jesus affirms the authority and reliability of the Old Testament (e.g., Matt. 5:17–18; 21:42; 22:29; 26:54, 56; Luke 24:44, 45; John 2:22; 5:39; 10:35; 17:12). And the rest of the New Testament likewise testifies of the authority and reliability of the Old Testament. As 2 Timothy 3:16 states, "All Scripture is inspired by God and beneficial for teaching, for rebuke, for correction, for training in righteousness" (cf. Acts 17:2; 18:28; Rom. 1:2; 4:3; 9:17; 10:11; 11:2; 1 Cor. 15:3, 4; Gal. 3:8; 2 Pet. 1:20–21, for more on this, see chapter 10).

We also have good reason to be confident that the Old Testament has been passed down to us with a high degree of accuracy. The Dead Sea Scrolls, discovered at Qumran in 1947 and onward, include Old Testament manuscripts dating from the third century BC to the first century AD (the time of Jesus), yielding strong evidence that the Old Testament has come down to us basically as it was at the time of Jesus.[60]

Furthermore, both the Old Testament and New Testament (the biblical canon) are confirmed by connection with Christ as divinely commissioned writings, revealed and inspired by the Holy Spirit. The Old Testament is confirmed by Christ's direct testimony and that of His apostles, and the New Testament is the inspired first-generation apostolic testimony about and commissioned by Christ, written by apostles or close associates of apostles (see also chapter 10).

The decision of faith Christ's testimony evokes, then, is quite straightforward. Either Christ is who He claimed to be (according to the New Testament), or He is not.[61] If Christ is indeed God incarnate, as He claimed (according to the New Testament), then the correct belief system is that which is accurately derived from the Scriptures that Christ Himself confirmed and commissioned—divinely revealed, inspired, and preserved by the operation of the Holy Spirit (see chapter 10).

One needn't first investigate every other religion in order to have warrant to accept the teachings of Scripture. Even as counterfeit money can be recognized as counterfeit by comparing it to money that is known to be genuine, if the conclusion that Christ is and was the Son of God is warranted, all other truth claims might be tested by comparison to Christ and His teachings, which attest to the reliability and authority of the entirety of the Bible.

> *You and I are confronted with a momentous choice. You must decide what you believe about who Jesus was. He was certainly no ordinary man.*

In this regard, you and I are confronted with a momentous choice. You must decide what you believe about who Jesus was. He was certainly no ordinary man.

The great historian Philip Schaff once wrote:

> Jesus of Nazareth, without money and arms, conquered more millions than Alexander the Great, Caesar, Mohammed, and Napoleon; without science and learning, he shed more light on things human and divine than all philosophers and scholars combined; without the eloquence of schools, he spoke such words of life as were never spoken before or since, and produced effects which lie beyond the reach of orator or poet; without writing

a single line, he set more pens in motion and furnished themes for more sermons, orations, discussions, learned volumes, works of art and songs of praise, than the whole army of great men of ancient and modern times. . . . There never was in this world a life so unpretending, modest, and lowly in its outward form and condition, and yet producing such extraordinary effects upon all ages, nations, and classes of men. The annals of history furnish no other example of such complete and astounding success, in spite of the absence of those material, social, literary, and artistic powers and influences which are indispensable to success for a mere man. Christ stands, in this respect also, solitary and alone among all the heroes of history, and presents to us an insolvable problem, unless we admit him to be more than man, even the eternal Son of God.[62]

Some have nevertheless tried to take a middle way, affirming that Jesus was a great man, a great moral teacher, but denying that He was, in fact, the Son of God. C. S. Lewis famously argued this is not a viable option if Jesus made the claims about Himself that are reported in the New Testament (see chapter 4). Lewis wrote:

I am trying here to prevent anyone saying the really foolish thing that people often say about Him: "I'm ready to accept Jesus as a great moral teacher, but I don't accept His claim to be God." That is the one thing we must not say. A man who was merely a man and said the sort of things Jesus said would not be a great moral teacher. He would either be a lunatic—on the level with the man who says he is a poached egg—or else he would be the Devil of Hell. You must make your choice. Either this man was, and is, the Son of God: or else a madman or something worse. You can shut Him up for a fool, you can spit at Him and kill Him as a demon; or you can fall at His feet and call Him Lord and God. But let us not come with any patronizing nonsense about His being a great human teacher. He has not left that open to us. He did not intend to.[63]

Later in this book, we'll see more about how Jesus Himself confirmed the Old Testament and commissioned the New Testament. Given this, if

Jesus was (and is) the Son of God, as the resurrection strongly confirms (cf. Acts 17:31; Rom. 1:4), then we have good reason to place confidence in the Old Testament and the New Testament that Christ Himself confirmed and commissioned. Put differently, if Jesus is who He said He was (as reported in the Gospels) and Jesus both confirms the Old Testament and commissions the New Testament, we have very good reasons to believe the Bible.

The Testimony of the Archaeological Evidence

An abundance of archaeological evidence further supports the Bible's reliability and historicity. Like other lines of evidence we've considered, archaeological evidence cannot *prove* the historicity of the Bible, nor should we expect it to. We have only a small fraction of the total possible archaeological evidence, and it would thus be unreasonable to expect it to confirm all the details of Scripture. Nevertheless, despite the relatively small fraction of the evidence that archaeologists have excavated and reported, biblical archaeology has provided an abundance of amazing confirmations of the Bible's historical reliability.[64]

For example, it was once believed that the Hittites referred to in biblical stories never existed until their capital and records were discovered at Boğazköy, Turkey. Further, some critical scholars used to claim that Sargon (II) of Assyria, mentioned in Isaiah 20:1, never existed. But Sargon's palace was later discovered in Khorsabad, Iraq.

Some also raised doubts about the historical existence of King David. Then, archaeologists found the Tel Dan Stele (ninth or eighth century BC), which includes an inscription testifying to the Davidic dynasty, confirmed further by other later finds. In this regard, Michael Hasel comments: "It is remarkable that in a matter of two years not one, but four separate references to David were identified by scholars in Egyptian, Aramean, and Moabite inscriptions testifying to the foundational influence of this early Israelite king."[65] Additionally, we have abundant archaeological evidence attesting to many kings of Israel and Judah, with many seals and other artifacts from the reigns of numerous kings, and references to Israel and its rulers in the records of other nations (e.g., the Merneptah Stele [ca. 1200 BC], the Moabite Stone [ca. 850 BC, i.e., the Mesha Stele], the Black Obelisk of Shalmaneser III [ca. 840 BC], the Taylor Prism [ca. 690 BC], and the Babylonian Chronicles [sixth century BC]).

Relative to Babylonian history, many critics claimed the author of Daniel was incorrect in recording Belshazzar as the ruler of Babylon when Babylon fell to Persia (in 539 BC). However, the discovery of the Cyrus Cylinder and Nabonidus Chronicle offered evidence that Belshazzar was co-regent with his father, Nabonidus, when Babylon fell. This would explain why Belshazzar made Daniel the "third ruler in the kingdom" after he provided the interpretation of the writing on the wall (Dan. 5:16). The third place would have been the highest place after the co-regents, Nabonidus and Belshazzar.

To take another striking example, some critics also previously questioned the historicity of Pontius Pilate, the Roman governor under whom Jesus was crucified. Then, in 1961, a first-century inscription was found at Caesarea Maritima with the words "Pontius Pilate Prefect of Judea" (known as the Pilate stone).[66]

There have been many other amazing archaeological finds that support the historicity of Scripture.[67] Indeed, the great archaeologist William F. Albright was at one time very skeptical about the historicity of biblical accounts, but through his work in archaeology came to the conclusion: "There can be no doubt that archaeology has confirmed the substantial historicity of the Old Testament tradition."[68] Of course, some critics interpret some archaeological data in a way that they claim contradicts Scripture.[69] However, as Norman Geisler puts it, "no archaeological find has ever refuted a biblical claim."[70]

The Testimony of Prophecy

The Bible also includes many amazing predictive prophecies. For example, Isaiah (writing ca. 740–700 BC) prophesied of Cyrus (the Persian ruler who conquered Babylon in 539 BC) by name over one hundred years before Cyrus was born! (Isa. 44:28–45:1)[71] Likewise, hundreds of years before King Josiah was born, a prophecy mentioned him by name and foretold a specific action of Josiah that later took place (1 Kings 13:1–2; see also 2 Kings 23:19–20).

Further, the prophecies of Daniel 2 and 7 (explained in chapter 16) outline the history of successive empires and other history from the time of Babylon (when the prophecies were given) all the way down to Christ's Second Coming! Indeed, these prophecies are so accurate and specific that some contend they could not have been written at the time of Daniel (sixth century BC). Presupposing that foretelling the future is impossible—because their conceptual framework does not allow for it—some claim these prophecies were written in the second century BC (the time of the Maccabees). However, the evidence strongly supports the view that the book of Daniel was written in the sixth century BC, as indicated in the book itself.[72]

Moreover, the most amazing prophecies of Daniel would not be explained by dating Daniel to the second century BC, since it predicts momentous events that occurred nearly two hundred years thereafter. Specifically, the seventy-week prophecy (Dan. 9:24–27) predicts, over five hundred years in advance, the precise year that Christ was anointed (being baptized and beginning His ministry in AD 27, Luke 3:1, 15) and the precise year He was "cut off" and brought an end to sacrifice and offering, fulfilling the ritual/ceremonial law by His own once-for-all effective sacrifice (AD 31, for more on this, see chapter 16).

The Old Testament includes *many* other amazing prophecies foretelling specific things about the Messiah, all of which Jesus fulfilled exactly. For example, hundreds of years before Jesus was born, Scripture prophesied the Messiah would: be born in Bethlehem (Mic. 5:2), be born of a virgin (Isa. 7:14), be from the tribe of Judah (Gen. 49:10) and a descendant of David (Isa. 11:1–10), bring good news and healing (Isa. 61:1–2), be betrayed by a close friend (Ps. 41:9), be numbered with wrongdoers/criminals (Isa. 53:12), be scourged but have no bones broken (Ps. 34:20; Isa. 53:5), and would be pierced for the transgressions of others (Isa. 53:5; cf. Ps. 22:16).[73] These prophecies (and many others) were each fulfilled in the life of Jesus of Nazareth. Taking just these few prophecies together, the probability that any one person would fulfill all these is infinitesimally small.

This is not even to mention the amazing correspondence between the rituals and festivals of the Old Testament sanctuary system and the atoning works of Christ in the New Testament and beyond (see chapter 16) and other amazing patterns of promise and fulfillment throughout Scripture (see, e.g., Acts 3:20–26).

Further, as we will see later, Jesus Himself made many predictions that were fulfilled exactly (e.g., of Judas's betrayal, Matt. 26:20–25, and

Peter's denial, Mark 14:27–30), including prophesying of His own death and resurrection after three days, and teaching His followers how the Scriptures themselves foretold "that the Christ would suffer and rise from the dead on the third day" (Luke 24:46; cf. 1 Cor. 15:4).[74] The best explanation of this and other evidence is that Jesus of Nazareth was (and is) the Son of God and the Scriptures that testify of Him and to which He attests (see Luke 24:44–48; John 5:38) are reliable and authoritative for faith and practice.

In this regard, Jesus Himself appealed to miracles and fulfilled prophecy as evidence of the truth (see, e.g., Luke 24:25–27; John 14:11). Christ's apostles likewise appealed to miracles, fulfilled prophecies, and the resurrection (itself a miracle and a fulfilled prophecy) as evidence of the truth of the Christian gospel (see, e.g., Peter's sermon in Acts 2:14–36; cf. 17:31).

The Testimony of the Holy Spirit

The testimony offered above does not *prove beyond any possible doubt* that the Bible is reliable, although it strongly supports its trustworthiness. If one assumes that God does not exist or that predictive prophecy is impossible, one might come up with some other *possible* explanations of the evidence surveyed earlier.

In the end, a decision of faith is still required, as is the case for any belief system. If I look at the above evidence from a standpoint of faith, or even simply express willingness to believe and ask God to give me faith (Mark 9:24; John 7:17), there are more than enough good reasons to believe. Yet, as will be discussed further later in this book, God is love, and love does not coerce or force the human will. Thus, God always leaves humans with the freedom and choice to believe or disbelieve the evidence that is available.

Accordingly, however impressive the "evidence" may be, there will remain those who doubt or refuse to believe altogether. In a parable, Jesus Himself predicted that some "will not be persuaded even if someone rises from the dead" (Luke 16:31).

The apostle Thomas himself found it difficult to believe that Jesus had risen from the dead. Yet, Jesus did not reject Thomas for his lack of faith. Instead, He graciously appeared to Thomas and let Thomas feel

His body and wounds, giving Thomas a personal experience confirming that He did indeed rise from the dead. After which, Thomas fell to the ground and proclaimed, "My Lord and my God!" (John 20:28). Because Thomas saw, he believed, but Jesus proclaimed, "Blessed are they who did not see, and yet believed" (John 20:29).

Jesus did not reject Thomas for initially doubting. And, He will not reject you or anyone else who has sincere questions either.[75] God can handle your questions and doubts and He commends and welcomes those who faithfully seek the truth.[76]

Beyond the testimony surveyed earlier, the most important testimony is the witness of the Holy Spirit, which authenticates the Bible as the word of God, the power of which is manifested in the changed lives of countless people across the ages.[77]

> God can handle your questions and doubts and He commends and welcomes those who faithfully seek the truth.

As a believer, by the work of the Holy Spirit, I can know God and know that Jesus is alive. By faith, I am united with Him. In this regard, Jesus told His apostles: "I will ask the Father, and He will give you another Helper, so that He may be with you forever; the Helper is the Spirit of truth, whom the world cannot receive, because it does not see Him or know Him; but you know Him because He remains with you and will be in you" and "you will know that I am in My Father, and you are in Me, and I in you" (John 14:16–17, 20; cf. 1 Cor. 2:10–16). John likewise taught, "All who obey his [God's] commandments abide in him, and he abides in them. And by this we know that he abides in us, by the Spirit that he has given us" (1 John 3:24, NRSVue; cf. 4:13; 5:6–10).

Those of us who've experienced the living God can witness to Him by manifesting His love in all that we say and do. Individually, demonstration of Scripture's origin and nature can be found in the personal experience of reading and studying Scripture itself with intentional openness to the guidance of the Holy Spirit.

What is your experience with the Bible? From my own experience, I can attest it is surely not just another book. I have often wondered in the past, are these things really true? And, the more I've studied, the more I've come to believe firmly. Careful study manifests the beauty and majesty of Scripture, written by more than forty different authors from all walks of life over a 1,600-year span, yet presenting a unified picture of God and corresponding belief system that meets the longings and needs of the human condition and experience.

Through the Bible, I have met the living God and seen the revealed testimony of His perfect love and justice. I am convinced the story of Scripture offers the best framework and answers to the biggest questions and issues of the human experience.[78] Through Scripture, I have met the risen Jesus, who was dead but is now alive. You ask me how I know He lives? I know that He lives within my heart. I have felt the inner testimony of the Holy Spirit strangely warm my heart (cf. Rom. 8:15–17; Gal. 4:6). And, by the illumination of the Holy Spirit, Scripture reveals to me my true self and need of a Savior as well as the promises of the future God has in store for me and all who believe in Christ.[79]

You need not take my word for it. You can also have such experiences. You can also meet the living God in Scripture and commune with Him in prayer. Pray to God with an open heart (or, if you find your heart is not open, just ask Him to open it). Dive into the Bible for yourself, drink deeply from its wells, and you will not be left thirsty (John 4:14), you will find rest for your soul (Matt. 11:29), and you will meet Christ, "the way, and the truth, and the life" (John 14:6)—your Creator and Sustainer. If you are willing to be saved, Christ will be your Savior forevermore—*God with us*.

> **Dive into the Bible for yourself, drink deeply from its wells, and you will not be left thirsty.**

As we saw earlier in this chapter, Jesus promised: "If anyone is willing to do His [God's] will," that person "will know about the teaching, whether it is of God, or I am speaking from Myself" (John 7:17). So, I ask again. Are you willing? If you could believe, would you? Do you find that you are stirred in your heart to believe even now? Perhaps you worry that you do not have enough faith. If so, do not worry, but simply pray like the man who brought his demon-afflicted son to Jesus to be healed and cried out to Jesus, "I do believe; help my unbelief!" (Mark 9:24). Jesus did not tell the man to come back when he had more faith. He cast the demon out and restored the man's son. If you pray likewise, God will hear you too.

Perhaps you haven't made your mind up yet. Perhaps you are troubled by issues like the problem of evil, or you wonder why God has not made Himself known even more clearly, both of which relate to matters of the cosmic conflict discussed in chapter 9 and beyond. Wherever you stand now, I invite you to keep reading and consider the story and teachings of Scripture for yourself, some of which are unpacked in the chapters to come. As you read, I hope you will get a glimpse of the beauty of Scripture and how its story and framework meet the deepest worries and fears and the greatest desires, hopes, and dreams common to the human condition—from the meaning and purpose of life and love to the final destiny of humankind.

Come and see. Whether or not you know Him, He already knows you. And He loves you more than you can imagine. He came to die to save you to be *with* Him forever and sent the Holy Spirit to testify of Him, and you might feel His inner witness pricking your conscious or warming your heart even now. And Jesus Himself calls to you, "Behold, I stand at the door and knock; if anyone hears My voice and opens the door, I will come in to him and will dine with him, and he with me" (Rev. 3:20).

For Further Reading

Adventist Perspectives:

Goldstein, Clifford. *Risen: Finding Hope in the Empty Tomb.* Nampa, ID: Pacific Press, 2020.

Hasel, Gerhard F. *Understanding the Living Word of God.* Adventist Heritage Library. Nampa, ID: Pacific Press, 2018 (reprint).

Hasel, Michael G. "History, the Bible, and Hermeneutics." In *Biblical Hermeneutics: An Adventist Approach.* Edited by Frank M. Hasel, 105–29. Biblical Research Institute Studies in Hermeneutics, vol. 3. Silver Spring, MD: Biblical Research Institute/Review and Herald Academic, 2020.

Pfandl, Gerhard. "Is the Bible Historically Reliable?" In *Interpreting Scripture: Bible Questions and Answers.* Edited by Gerhard Pfandl, 43–51. Silver Spring, MD: Biblical Research Institute, 2010.

Wahlen, Clinton. "Variants, Versions, and the Trustworthiness of Scripture." In *Biblical Hermeneutics: An Adventist Approach.* Edited by Frank M. Hasel, 63–103. Biblical Research Institute Studies in Hermeneutics, vol. 3. Silver Spring, MD: Biblical Research Institute/Review and Herald Academic, 2020.

Other Christian Perspectives:

Blomberg, Craig. *The Historical Reliability of the Gospels*, 2nd ed. Downers Grove, IL: IVP Academic, 2007.

Bruce, F. F. *The New Testament Documents: Are They Reliable?* 3rd ed. Grand Rapids, MI: Eerdmans, 1981.

Craig, William Lane. *Reasonable Faith: Christian Truth and Apologetics*. Wheaton, IL: Crossway, 2008.

Gould, Paul M. *Cultural Apologetics: Renewing the Christian Voice, Conscience, and Imagination in a Disenchanted World*. Grand Rapids, MI: Zondervan, 2019.

Habermas, Gary R. and Mike Licona, *The Case for the Resurrection of Jesus*. Grand Rapids, MI: Kregel Publications, 2004.

Kaiser, Walter C., Jr. *The Old Testament Documents: Are They Reliable & Relevant?* Downers Grove, IL: InterVarsity, 2001.

Lewis, C. S. *Mere Christianity*. New York: Macmillan, 1952.

Mason, Eric, ed. *Urban Apologetics: Restoring Black Dignity with the Gospel*. Grand Rapids, MI: Zondervan, 2021.

Meyer, Stephen C. *Return of the God Hypothesis: Three Scientific Discoveries that Reveal the Mind Behind the Universe*. New York: HarperOne, 2021.

Plantinga, Alvin. *Knowledge and Christian Belief*. Grand Rapids, MI: Eerdmans, 2015.

Sharp, Mary Jo. *Why I Still Believe: A Former Atheist's Reckoning with the Bad Reputation Christians Give a Good God*. Grand Rapids, MI: Zondervan, 2019.

Strobel, Lee. *The Case for Christ: A Journalist's Personal Investigation of the Evidence for Jesus*. Grand Rapids, MI: Zondervan, 1998.

Wallace, Daniel B. "The Reliability of the New Testament Manuscripts." In *Understanding Scripture: An Overview of the Bible's Origin, Reliability, and Meaning*, 111–20. Wheaton, IL: Crossway, 2012.

Wegner, Paul D. "The Reliability of the Old Testament Manuscripts." In *Understanding Scripture: An Overview of the Bible's Origin, Reliability, and Meaning*, 101–10. Wheaton, IL: Crossway, 2012.

Williams, Peter J. *Can We Trust the Gospels?* Wheaton, IL: Crossway, 2018.

PART TWO

GOD WITH US IN THREE PERSONS

4

CHRIST: GOD WITH US IN THE FLESH

"Who do men say that I, the Son of Man, am?" Jesus asked His disciples.

"Some say John the Baptist, some Elijah, and others Jeremiah or one of the prophets," they replied.

"But who do you say that I am?" Jesus asked (Matt. 16:13–15, NKJV).

Everything hinges on this question.

"You are the Christ, the Son of the living God," Peter answered (Matt. 16:16). He was right. This, Jesus told Peter, was revealed to him by "My Father who is in heaven" (Matt. 16:17).

Here and elsewhere, Jesus is identified as both the Son of Man and the Son of God. But what does that mean?

Jesus came into this world as a human son, born to Mary. Yet, Jesus was also the Son of God. When Jesus became human (in what is known as the incarnation), God became human.

You might be so familiar with this concept that it is no longer shocking to you. But it is shocking indeed. God becoming human is the most amazing event in the history of the cosmos. And it is deeply connected to the meaning and significance of your life and my life and the life of every person who has ever lived.

The very idea that God could and would become human is itself deeply mysterious. It is integral to the mystery of the gospel—"the mystery which had been hidden from the past ages and generations, but now has been revealed" (Col. 1:26). The gospel itself is the good news of the story of Jesus, the true King—the story of God *with us*.

> *God becoming human is the most amazing event in the history of the cosmos. And it is deeply connected to the meaning and significance of your life.*

The gospel is so simple that even a young child can understand it, yet so profound that it involves deep questions into which even angels long to look (cf. 1 Pet. 1:12).

This chapter focuses on some of the crucial questions about who Jesus is and why it matters:

- Who is Jesus? What is His story? Why did He become human, and what did He come to accomplish?
- What does Jesus reveal about who God is and who we are in relation to God?
- Is Christ truly God? Is Christ truly human? If so, how can this be? How could God *become* human?
- And, if Jesus was God, could He *truly* be human? To be truly human, must Jesus have been just like us?
- Why do the answers to these questions matter?

Relative to this last question, if Jesus is who He claimed to be—God in the flesh—then the answers to these and many other related questions profoundly impact *everything else*. For example, Jesus could reconcile humans to God and save the world only if Jesus was both truly God and truly human. The very destiny of creation, then, hinges on who Jesus was, what Jesus did, what Jesus is doing even now, and what Jesus will do in the future.

In the end, each of us must answer Jesus's question for ourselves, "who do you say that I am?" (Matt. 16:15, NKJV).

The Story of Immanuel: God with Us

If you passed Jesus on a dusty path in first-century Galilee, you might not have even noticed Him. He was a seemingly ordinary man, a craftsman from Nazareth.

But, He was far more. He was the promised One.

"We have found Him of whom Moses wrote in the Law, and the prophets also wrote: Jesus the son of Joseph, from Nazareth!" Philip excitedly told his friend, Nathanael.

"Can anything good be from Nazareth?" Nathanael asked.

"Come and see," Philip replied (John 1:45–46).

Nathanael did go. And he, along with Philip, became one of the original twelve apostles of Jesus.

I bid you also, dear reader, *come* and *see*.

Who is Jesus of Nazareth, and why does it matter? Jesus was and is the Son of God—God incarnate. He became human to save the world. On His works your life, my life, and the entire fabric of the universe depend.

Whether we recognize it or not, we need a hero. And Jesus is the hero we need—the only one who can save us and save the world. He is the ultimate hero of which every other hero is but a shadow—the Hero of heroes.

> *Whether we recognize it or not, we need a hero. And Jesus is the hero we need.*

Yet, Jesus is an unexpected kind of hero—one who lifts others up by willingly lowering Himself. He, the Son of God, gave up the splendor of heaven to become human—to be God *with us* in the flesh. In so doing, He revealed what God is like, finally giving Himself to be killed by the Empire for us on the cross—the ultimate demonstration of God's surpassing love (cf. John 15:13; Rom. 5:8).

But that was not the end of the story. If it were, we'd be hopeless. If Jesus is not risen, the Christian faith is in vain (cf. 1 Cor. 15:14–19). But Jesus did rise from the dead. His tomb is empty, and He appeared to many witnesses who testified of the risen Jesus and were willing to die for their testimony.

Because of Jesus, who is called *Immanuel* (which means "God with us," Matt. 1:23), we can be with God in the way God intended from the beginning.

Who Is Jesus, the Christ?

If Jesus rose from the dead just as He predicted He would, then we have the best of reasons to believe Jesus is who He said He was (see chapter 3). The apostles in the book of Acts and elsewhere repeatedly refer to the resurrection as evidence of who Jesus was, of which they were chosen witnesses (see Acts 10:40–42; cf. 2:32; 3:15; 4:10; 5:30; 13:30–37). Indeed, Acts 17:31 declares, God has "furnished proof to all people by raising Him from the dead."

But who did Jesus say He was? Jesus claimed to be both the Son of Man and the Son of God. In this regard, as we will see, Scripture testifies that Jesus was both truly human and truly divine. Only as both human and divine could Jesus fulfill the mission of the promised Messiah (the *Christ*, from the Greek translation of Messiah).

Before discussing the humanity and divinity of Jesus, however, we will first discuss the mission and works of Jesus, the promised Messiah (the Christ) who fulfilled the ancient prophecies of the hero to come. In doing so, we will see more clearly that only one who is both human and divine could accomplish these works and reconcile humans to God.

The Mission of Christ

Mary was a virgin, but the angel told her she was to bear a son. "He will be great and will be called the Son of the Most High; and the Lord God will give Him the throne of His father David; and He will reign over the house of Jacob forever, and His kingdom will have no end" (Luke 1:32–33).

These words revealed that her Son was to be the promised one, the Messiah, the son of David (see Matt. 9:27; 12:23; 21:9, 15; 22:14).

The coming of Jesus fulfilled a myriad of prophecies about the Messiah (see chapter 3), which in Hebrew means "anointed one." According to the ancient prophecies, the Messiah would be a son of Abraham and a son of David (meaning a descendant of both) and would fulfill the covenant promises made to Abraham and David, including the promise of an everlasting Davidic kingdom (see, e.g., 2 Sam. 7:13; cf. Jer. 23:5–6). This covenantal Son of David would also be the Son promised to Adam and Eve, the "Seed" of the woman whom God prophesied would crush the head of the serpent, later identified as Satan (see Gen. 3:15, NKJV; cf. Rom. 16:20; Rev. 12:9).

To understand the importance of the Messiah's coming as the promised son of David who would fulfill God's covenant promises, we need to remember the situation the people of Israel were in.

Israel, a nation blessed beyond measure, had been chosen by God as His covenant people in order to bless all nations (Gen. 12:3). God raised up Israel as His allotment—His inheritance whom He called "My son, My firstborn" (Exod. 4:22). Through Israel, God would reclaim the entire world from enemy rulership, the rulership given over to Satan by Adam and Eve at the Fall (cf. Gen. 1:28; John 12:31).

But, in the first century AD, the children of Abraham were suffering under oppression by the Roman Empire. For centuries, they had been ruled over by a succession of brutal empires—Babylon, Medo-Persia, Greece, and now Rome (just as prophesied in Dan. 7; see chapter 16). They desperately awaited the promised Messiah, whom they expected to deliver them from Rome just as God had delivered Israel from oppressive enemies countless times before, putting the "gods" of the nations to shame.

When the Messiah came, they thought, God would make His presence known, wrongs would be righted, and their oppressors would be overthrown. The sum of all their hopes and dreams was bound up with the Messiah's coming.

Imagine (if you can) that your family has been suffering severe hardship and oppression for ages, but an ancient contract stipulates that once a special promised son comes, you and your family will be freed from oppression, inherit a massive estate with enormous wealth, and enjoy vibrant health, prosperity, and bliss. What many in Israel were hoping and waiting for was a bit like that. The coming Messiah, they believed, would free them from centuries of Imperial oppression and usher in a kingdom of unimaginable prosperity.

When Jesus came but did not break the yoke of Rome, many were profoundly disappointed. The first coming of Jesus did not match their expectations of the Messiah, who was envisioned as the warrior king who would overthrow Rome. They looked for the conquering lion of Judah, but Jesus came as the lamb led to slaughter. Jesus came not as the conquering king ushering in a glorious earthly reign but as the crucified king who suffered what seemed like a shameful, cursed death.

Yet, as Jesus explained many times before His crucifixion and further explained after His resurrection, the ancient prophesies foretold that the Messiah must suffer, die, and rise on the third day (Luke 24:6–8, 25–27, 44–48). Jesus was indeed the promised Son. He would fulfill the covenant promises of old. But He would do so in two phases and by way of two comings—a first Advent and a second Advent.

Jesus, the Ultimate Prophet, Priest, and King

Jesus fulfills the prophecies of the coming of the greatest prophet, the highest high priest, and the King of kings.

The Mosaic covenant was given through a specially appointed and divinely attested prophet, Moses. And God promised to send another prophet like Moses (Deut. 18:15), a promise that ultimately referred to Jesus (Acts 3:22). As the Prophet of prophets, Jesus revealed God to humans, being Himself the ultimate revelation of God (cf. John 14:9).

In the Mosaic covenant, God also made a way to dwell *with* His people, despite their sinfulness. Without mediation, the presence of God's holiness would destroy sin and everything tainted by it. As the earthly place of such mediation, God established an earthly sanctuary, which was a copy of the sanctuary in heaven (Exod. 25:40; Heb. 8:5), "the true tabernacle, which the Lord set up, not man" (Heb. 8:2). To minister in the earthly sanctuary, God appointed a priesthood from the descendants of Levi.

Much earlier, specially appointed humans functioned as priests (in Eden and beyond). And a priest named Melchizedek appeared to Abraham (Gen. 14:18–20). In the fullness of time, Jesus came as the ultimate priest—identified as the second Adam (1 Cor. 15:45) and a priest after the order of Melchizedek (Heb. 7:13–17; cf. Ps. 110:4).

Even now, Jesus serves as our "high priest" in the heavenly sanctuary, "a minister in the sanctuary and in the true tabernacle, which the Lord set up, not man" (Heb. 8:1–2; cf. 9:11–12). Through His work as our high priest, we can "approach the throne of grace with confidence" (Heb. 4:15–16), for He "always lives to make intercession for" us (Heb. 7:25) as "the mediator of a new covenant" (Heb. 9:15).

In the Davidic covenant, God promised a Davidic kingdom that would never end. The line of *merely* human kings descending from David failed,— but God's promise did not fail. The coming Messiah, the Son of David, would not fail. He would fulfill the promises as the Davidic King whose reign would never end. This Davidic King would take up the failed and forfeited kingship of Adam, coming as the second Adam—the seed of the woman, who crushes the serpent's head (Gen. 3:15), fulfilling the human side of the covenant for humanity, thereby reclaiming the rulership of this planet that Adam lost and establishing an unending kingdom of perfect love and justice, peace and flourishing. The work of Jesus—the King of kings and Lord of lords—fulfills these promises.

The Coming King: The Two Advents of the Messiah Priest-King

Yet, if the ultimate King has come already, why is there not yet a kingdom of perfect love and justice? Because the Messiah's work was to take place in two stages.

First, the Messiah was to come as the Lamb slain for the world's sins, providing forgiveness to repentant sinners without compromising justice, demonstrating God's righteousness and love, and thereby defeating the devil's allegations (Rom. 3:25–26; 5:8). Second, the Messiah will return as the Lion of Judah, uprooting injustice and eradicating evil, ushering in the final age with no sin, suffering, or death (Rev. 21:3–4).

Christ's two Advents correspond to two stages wherein Christ defeats and eliminates Satan in the cosmic conflict. First, Christ's sacrifice on the cross makes atonement and legally defeats the devil's allegations in the heavenly court (see chapter 9). Second, Christ will execute final judgment against the domain of darkness and eradicate evil. These correspond to two stages of atonement, wherein all the enemy's allegations are first defeated in the heavenly court and, only thereafter, judgment is executed.

> **Christ's two Advents correspond to two stages wherein Christ defeats and eliminates Satan in the cosmic conflict.**

Many awaiting the Messiah in the first century, however, conflated the two Advents. They were correct that the Messiah would come as the conquering King (Isa. 9:6–7; Dan. 2:44). However, they failed to recognize that the Messiah would first come as the suffering servant (Isa. 53), the Lamb slain for the world's sins (Exod. 12:22–23; Isa. 53:7; 1 Cor. 5:7), whom the ancient prophecies foretold would be "cut off" in the first century (Dan. 9:26; see chapter 16).

Before the promised Son would crush the serpent's head, the serpent would first strike Him (Gen. 3:15; cf. Ps. 22:14–18; Isa. 50:6). Before the Messiah would destroy the devil's kingdom, He would first reclaim rulership of this world in a way the selfish rulers of this world would never imagine (1 Cor. 2:7–8)—coming as a humble servant and giving Himself over to torture and death in the ultimate display of unselfish love and righteousness (Rom. 5:8; 3:25–26; Phil. 2:6–8).

As the prophecy foretold:

> However, it was our sicknesses that He Himself bore, and our pains that He carried; yet we ourselves assumed that He had been afflicted, struck down by God, and humiliated. But He was pierced for our offenses, He was crushed for our wrongdoings; The punishment for our well-being was laid upon Him, and by

His wounds we are healed. All of us, like sheep, have gone astray, each of us has turned to his own way; but the Lord has caused the wrongdoing of us all to fall on Him. He was oppressed and afflicted, yet He did not open His mouth; like a lamb that is led to slaughter, and like a sheep that is silent before its shearers, so He did not open His mouth. By oppression and judgment He was taken away; and as for His generation, who considered that He was cut off from the land of the living for the wrongdoing of my people, to whom the blow was due? And His grave was assigned with wicked men, yet He was with a rich man in His death, because He had done no violence, nor was there any deceit in His mouth. But the Lord desired to crush Him, causing Him grief; if He renders Himself as a guilt offering, He will see His offspring, He will prolong His days, and the good pleasure of the Lord will prosper in His hand. As a result of the anguish of His soul, He will see it and be satisfied; by His knowledge the Righteous One, My Servant, will justify the many, for He will bear their wrongdoings. Therefore, I will allot Him a portion with the great, and He will divide the plunder with the strong, because He poured out His life unto death, and was counted with wrongdoers; yet He Himself bore the sin of many, and interceded for the wrongdoers (Isa. 53:4–12).

Between the two Advents, Christ ministers as our "high priest" in the heavenly "sanctuary," the "true tabernacle, which the Lord set up, not man" (Heb. 8:1–2; cf. 9:11–12).

Eventually, He will return and overthrow the earthly empires that oppressed His children and set up an everlasting kingdom of peace and justice (cf. Dan. 2:44). By two Advents rather than one, the ancient prophecy is fulfilled:

> For a Child will be born to us, a Son will be given to us; and the government will rest on His shoulders; and His name will be called Wonderful Counselor, Mighty God, Eternal Father, Prince of Peace. There will be no end to the increase of His government or of peace on the throne of David and over his kingdom, to establish it and to uphold it with justice and righteousness from then on and forevermore (Isa. 9:6–7).

The Works of Christ

A great storm on the sea was raging, and the boat they were in was "being covered by the waves; but Jesus Himself was asleep." His disciples woke Him, pleading, "Save us, Lord; we are perishing!" Jesus replied, "'Why are you afraid, you men of little faith?' Then He got up and rebuked the winds and the sea, and it became perfectly calm." Amazed, the disciples asked, "What kind of a man is this, that even the winds and the sea obey Him?" (Matt. 8:24–27).

What kind of man is this, indeed. Christ worked many other signs and wonders during His earthly ministry. Yet, even before Christ's first Advent, He was at work among humans.

The "angel of the Lord" who appeared to Moses in the burning bush was actually a manifestation of God's presence. We know this because "God called to him from the midst of the bush," telling Moses, "I am the God of your father," and "Moses hid his face, for he was afraid to look at God" (Exod. 3:4, 6).

Later, God told Moses, "I am going to send an angel before you." He commanded Moses to "obey his voice" for "My name is in him" (Exod. 23:20–21; cf. 14:19). The "name" of God, however, belongs to God alone (Isa. 42:8), so this also identifies this "angel" with God.

This same "angel" is referenced in Isaiah 63:8–9, which recounts that the Lord "became their Savior. In all their distress He was distressed, and the angel of His presence saved them; in His love and in His mercy He redeemed them, and He lifted them and carried them all the days of old." This corresponds to language Isaiah elsewhere uses of Christ's work as the Savior who was afflicted for humanity and redeemed humanity (see Isa. 53). The divine "angel of His presence," then, was none other than the pre-incarnate Christ, whom Paul identifies as the "spiritual rock which followed" Israel in the Exodus (1 Cor. 10:4).[1]

Why was He called an "angel," then? The word "angel" (the Hebrew term *malak*) simply means "messenger" or "one sent with a message." It may refer to celestial creatures sent by God, but it can also refer to human messengers (e.g., Hag. 1:13) and even to the divine messenger Himself.[2] This "angel of the Lord" was the special messenger who is Himself God (the Son) *and* was sent from God (the Father; cf. John 3:17).

This same "angel of the Lord" appeared to Hagar and was identified as "the Lord" and the "God who sees" (Gen. 16:13; cf. 21:17; 22:11–12; 31:11–13; 48:16). Later, Jacob wrestled with this "angel" in the form of a man who turned out to be God such that Jacob declared, "I have seen God face to face" (Gen. 32:30; cf. 32:38). Of this, Hosea 12:3–4 explains, Jacob "contended with God. Yes, he wrestled with the angel and prevailed."

This same divine "angel of the Lord" also appeared to Gideon (Judg. 6:11–23) and to Samson's parents, Manoah and his wife, such that Manoah said, "We will certainly die, for we have seen God" (Judg. 13:21–22; cf. 13:13–20; Zech. 3:1–5; Mal. 3:1).

The works of Christ did not begin with such visitations, however. Colossians 1:16–17 explains, "by Him [Christ] all things were created, both in the heavens and on earth, visible and invisible, whether thrones, or dominions, or rulers, or authorities—all things have been created through Him and for Him. He is before all things, and in Him all things hold together" (cf. John 1:1–3; Heb. 1:2, 10). And Christ "upholds all things by the word of His power" (Heb. 1:3).

This same Christ came as a baby, born to Mary; "when the fullness of the time came, God sent His Son, born of a woman" (Gal. 4:4). This same "Jesus Christ our Lord . . . was born of a descendant of David according to the flesh" and "was declared the Son of God with power according to the Spirit of holiness by the resurrection from the dead" as "promised beforehand through His prophets in the holy Scriptures" (Rom. 1:2–4). This same "Christ died for our sins according to the Scriptures" and "was buried" and "was raised on the third day according to the Scriptures" (1 Cor. 15:3–4).

"God anointed" this same Christ "with the Holy Spirit and with power" and "He went about doing good and healing all who were oppressed by the devil." They "put Him to death by hanging Him on a cross," but "God raised Him up on the third day." He appeared to many "witnesses," whom He had "chosen" as apostles and "ordered . . . to preach to the people, and to testify solemnly that this is the One who has been appointed by God as Judge of the living and the dead. All the prophets testify of Him, that through His name everyone who believes in Him receives forgiveness of sins" (Acts 10:38–43).

This same Christ lowered Himself to become human. "He humbled Himself by becoming obedient to the point of death: death on a cross," after which He was highly exalted so that "every knee will bow" and "every tongue will confess that Jesus Christ is Lord, to the glory of God the Father" (Phil. 2:6–11; cf. Eph. 1:20–23).

All this and more Christ did to make atonement, that is, to reconcile the world to God (2 Cor. 5:19).

Among other works:

- Christ was active in creating the universe and upholds the universe (Heb. 1:3).
- Christ came to make a way to restore the fullness of God's presence *with* us.
- Christ came to fulfill and confirm God's covenant promises (e.g., Gen. 3:15).
- Christ came to reveal and testify of the character of God (John 17:3).
- Christ came to demonstrate the righteousness and love of God (Rom. 3:25–26; 5:8).
- Christ came to bring justice and deliverance to the oppressed, to preach the gospel to the poor, and proclaim liberty to the captives (Luke 4:16–21; cf. Isa. 61:1–3; Matt. 11:4–5; Luke 7:22).
- Christ came as the Good Shepherd who laid down His life for His sheep (John 10:11) and also as the judge who restores justice in favor of the oppressed (Ezek. 34:11–31; John 5:22).
- Christ came to defeat the devil and liberate those oppressed by the devil (Acts 10:38; Heb. 2:14; 1 John 3:8).
- Christ cast out demons (Mark 9:20–27) and healed illnesses of many kinds (Matt. 4:23). He provided a way to finally defeat all illness and death itself.
- Christ came to establish the kingdom of God (Matt. 4:17), ruling with perfect love and justice.
- Yet, Christ also came as a humble servant—to serve rather than be served (Matt. 20:28).
- Christ came to save sinners through His death on the cross (1 Tim. 1:15).

- Christ came to forgive sinners while upholding justice (Rom. 3:25–26).
- Christ came to call humans to repentance, show the exceeding sinfulness of sin, and teach humans how to follow Him, providing an example of the way humans should relate to God (1 Pet. 2:21).
- Christ was resurrected as the first fruit of all who might be resurrected to eternal life in Him (1 Cor. 15:20).
- Christ became human so He could "become a merciful and faithful high priest" (Heb. 2:17) and later ascend to minister as our high priest in the heavenly sanctuary (Heb. 8:1–2; 9:11–12).
- Christ went to make a place for us to be with Him where He is (John 14:1–3) while also promising, "I am with you always, to the end of the age" (Matt. 28:20).
- Christ will return in the second Advent, re-establish justice, eradicate sin and evil forevermore, and finally restore all creation (see Rev. 19–22, especially 21:4–5).

In these and so many other ways, Christ is not only God *with* us, but He is in every way God *for* us.

Many of the works of Christ listed above relate to what are traditionally viewed as different models of atonement (reconciliation).

> *Christ is not only God with us, but He is in every way God for us.*

Yet, these are actually complementary facets of a much broader work of atonement that cannot be fully articulated by any single metaphor or model. Rather than viewing these facets as competing "models," it is better to think of them as essential pieces of a puzzle.

Christ's work of atonement is:

- substitutionary, meaning He died for us as our substitute (Isa. 53:6; Rom. 3:18; 5:8; Gal. 3:13; Eph. 5:2; Heb. 9:28; 1 Pet. 2:24; cf. Exod. 34:7; 2 Cor. 5:14).
- sacrificial, meaning Christ sacrificed His life as an offering for sinners (Rom. 3:25; 8:3–4; 1 Cor. 5:7; Heb. 9:22; cf. 9:12).
- one of ransom and redemption (Eph. 1:7; 1 Tim. 2:6; Titus 2:14; cf. Matt. 20:28; Mark 10:45; Rom. 3:24; Heb. 9:12, 15; 1 Pet. 1:18–19), meaning Christ deals with sinners' "debts" (metaphorically

referring to their sins), which they could never resolve by themselves.
- the work of expiation (i.e., removal of guilt), justification, and reconciliation, meaning Christ removes sinners' guilt, forgives sinners, and reconciles sinners to God (e.g., Rom. 3:24–25; 8:1–4).
- exemplary, meaning Christ set an example of what God is like *and* how humans should relate to God (John 14:9; 1 Pet. 2:21).
- victorious over the power of Satan and his dominion (Gen. 3:15; Heb. 2:14; 1 John 3:8; Rev. 12:7–9; 20:2, 10).

Each of these aspects of atonement (and more) are addressed further in chapter 13.[3]

In all, the work of Christ is aimed at restoring God's rule and reconciling creation to God, so God can again be God *with us* in the way He intended from the beginning. Yet, only one who is both human and divine could accomplish these works and reconcile humans to God. Only such a one could be "God with us" in the way Christ was and is with us.

The Son of the Promise: The Humanity of Christ

"And the Word became flesh, and dwelt among us" (John 1:14). In the incarnation, the Son of God became human. Jesus was the promised Son of Adam, Abraham, and David, but also the unique Son of God.

Only one who was both human and divine—the Son of Adam and the Son of God—could bridge the divide and reconcile fallen humanity to God, thus saving humanity. Only a human could be the promised covenantal Son and fulfill the covenant on behalf of humans, demonstrating that a human with an unbroken connection to God could be faithful to God's unselfish law of love (cf. Rom. 8:3–4). To be the suffering servant and take on and defeat human suffering and death, Jesus had to be genuinely human and suffer as a human.

Only one who is truly human could be the second Adam—the Son of Man who would succeed on behalf of humanity precisely where the first Adam failed, the promised seed of the woman who would crush the serpent's head (Gen. 3:15). Even as through "one man," Adam, "sin entered into the world, and death through sin," through "one Man,

Jesus Christ," sin would be undone and death defeated (Rom. 5:12–21; cf. 1 Cor. 15:45–49).

Only Jesus could accomplish this—"there is one God, and one mediator also between God and mankind, the man Christ Jesus" (1 Tim. 2:5).

We know Jesus was truly human because Scripture teaches that:

- Christ "became flesh, and dwelt among us" (John 1:14) and was "born in the likeness of men" (Phil. 2:7).
- Jesus experienced hunger and thirst (John 19:28; cf. 4) in the way that humans do.
- Jesus ate and drank (Mark 2:16), walked and talked, and otherwise lived as humans live.
- Jesus became physically tired, weary, and even slept (Matt. 8:24).
- Jesus prayed as a human to God (Matt. 6:9; John 17) and experienced temptations distinct to humans, being "tempted in all things just as we are" (Heb. 4:15; cf. Matt. 4:1–11)—yet without sin.
- Jesus identified with humanity and sympathized with our weaknesses in ways that only a human could.
- Jesus suffered *physical* pain and suffered in many other ways that are distinct to human experience.
- Jesus died on the cross as a mortal human.

Later, we will address the question, if Jesus was genuinely human and thus (among other things) mortal, how could He be God? For now, it is sufficient to recognize that Jesus was truly human, but not *merely* human. He was also divine (see the later discussion) and thus holds power over death itself (see John 11:25). Thus, He told His disciples, "I lay down my life in order to take it up again. No one takes it from me, but I lay it down of my own accord. I have power to lay it down, and I have power to take it up again" (John 10:17–18, NRSVue; cf. 11:25).[4]

In this and other ways, Jesus was not *just* like us. Unlike all other humans, Jesus existed before He was born (see, e.g., John 8:58). "When the fullness of the time came, God sent His Son, born of a woman, born under the Law, so that He might redeem those who were under the Law, that we might receive the adoption as sons and daughters" (Gal. 4:4–5).

Amazing. He became a son of Adam so we could be sons and daughters of God. Indeed, "though he existed in the form of God," Jesus lowered

Himself, "taking the form of a slave, assuming human likeness," and He "humbled himself and became obedient to the point of death—even death on a cross" (Phil. 2:6–8, NRSVue).

Jesus left His heavenly throne not to identify with the rulers of this world but with the weak and helpless. If Jesus wanted to come as a man of privilege and status, with the pedigree thought to befit an emperor, He could have come as a Roman. He could have taken the place of the Roman emperor.

But He did not. He chose not to. Instead, Jesus was born into a poor family, into a nation oppressed by the empire of Rome, of an ethnicity (Jewish) that was treated as inferior, from a town out of which some wondered whether anything good could come (John 1:46).

Instead of a plush, royal bed, He was laid in a manger (Luke 2:7). Instead of a palace, He possessed no place to lay His head (Matt. 8:20). Instead of a magnificent crown of jewels, He received a crown of thorns (John 19:2).

Instead of taking His rightful place on the throne, He willingly took His place with the disinherited—those in bondage and oppression.[5] He submitted Himself to abuse, cruelty, and a torturous death in order to heal the brokenhearted and set the captives free (cf. Isa. 61:1–2; Luke 4:16). And "though He was rich, yet for your sake He became poor, so that you through His poverty might become rich" (2 Cor. 8:9).

Jesus voluntarily identified Himself with the poor, the suffering, and the oppressed—those Scripture so often refers to as objects of God's special concern and compassion. Jesus thereby nullified the stigma of suffering and being oppressed, showing once and for all that it is not the case that those who prosper must therefore be divinely favored and those who suffer must deserve it.

In contrast to the devil, a mere creature who seeks to elevate himself and take the place and worship that belong to God alone in the ultimate demonstration of selfishness, Jesus was and is God yet willingly lowered Himself to become a creature to save creation in the ultimate demonstration of love. Christ "clothed His divinity with humanity, and for

> *Jesus was and is God yet willingly lowered Himself to become a creature to save creation in the ultimate demonstration of love.*

our sakes He became poor, that we through His poverty might be made rich" (cf. 2 Cor 8:9).[6]

He became human to save humans. He was, in truth, the "Son of Man" (e.g., Matt. 9:6; 12:32), a phrase that not only signals His humanity but also points to the ancient prophecy of the divine Messiah (Dan. 7:13–14).

The Man Who Was God: The Divinity of Christ

"Your father Abraham was overjoyed that he would see My day, and he saw it and rejoiced," Jesus told the leaders who had called Him demon-possessed.

"You are not yet fifty years old, and You have seen Abraham?" They replied.

Then, Jesus said it, declaring in no uncertain terms who He really was. "Truly, truly I say to you, before Abraham was born, I am" (John 8:56–58).

This stunning reply was not only a claim to pre-existence. By declaring "I am," Jesus identified Himself with the eternal God who declared "I AM" to Moses from the burning bush (Exod. 3:14; see also Isa. 43:10–13).[7]

Recognizing this amounted to a claim to be God, "they picked up stones to throw at Him, but Jesus hid Himself and left the temple grounds" (John 8:59).

This was not the only time they sought to kill Jesus for identifying Himself as God. When they accused Jesus of breaking the Sabbath after He healed a man, Jesus replied, "My Father is working until now, and I Myself am working" (John 5:17). Then, they sought to kill Him because He "was calling God His own Father, making Himself equal with God" (John 5:18). They rightly understood Jesus's claim to be the Son of God as a claim to be "equal with God."

Accordingly, Peter's answer to Jesus's question, "who do you yourselves say that I am," was a stronger claim beyond recognizing Jesus as the Messiah, the Son of David. Peter declared, "You are the Christ, the Son of the living God!" (Matt. 16:16). Likewise, John repeatedly refers to Jesus as the "only Son" of God (e.g., John 3:16). While mere humans can be God's children in a different sense, Jesus alone is the Son of God in the unique sense of being equal with God (John 5:18; cf. Phil. 2:6–8).

John further identifies Jesus as "the Word," teaching that "the Word was God" and, later, "the Word became flesh" (John 1:1, 14). So, Jesus is also the unique Son of God in that only He "was God" and then *became* a human son, born of a woman, but uniquely conceived of the Holy Spirit. Indeed, the angel Gabriel explained to Mary, *because* Jesus was conceived of the Holy Spirit, "for that reason also the holy Child will be called the Son of God" (Luke 1:35).

For this reason also, Christ was called Immanuel, which literally means "God with us" (Matt. 1:23; cf. Isa. 7:14). The Word who was God, "became flesh, and dwelt among us" (John 1:1, 14). Amazing.

Unlike all *merely* human sons, Christ had no beginning. "In the beginning was the Word, and the Word was with God, and the Word was God. He was in the beginning with God. All things came into being through Him, and apart from Him not even one thing came into being that has come into being" (John 1:1–3).[8]

This passage teaches many essential truths about Christ. First, it teaches "the Word was God" and, yet, "the Word was with God." It thus identifies Jesus as God while also distinguishing Jesus from at least one other person who is also rightly called God. This is a difficult concept to grasp, especially at first. We will further address how to understand this when we discuss the Trinity doctrine (in chapter 6). For now, I simply want you to notice that Jesus "was God," yet He was also "with God."

This passage also teaches that Christ is the Creator and *did not* Himself come into being. "All things came into being through Him, and apart from Him not even one thing came into being that has come into being" (John 1:3).[9] Christ is eternal—He "was God" and was "with God ... in the beginning" (John 1:1).

> **Christ is the Creator and did not Himself come into being.**

Many other texts also refer to Jesus as God. Long before Jesus was even born, Isaiah referred to the promised Messiah as "Mighty God" (Isa. 9:6). Later, when the risen Jesus appeared to him, Thomas proclaimed, "My Lord and my God!" (John 20:28; cf. Rom. 9:5; 2 Thess. 1:12; Titus 2:13; 2 Pet. 1:1). Further, in Hebrews 1:8, God the Father Himself says to the Son (Christ): "Your throne, God, is forever and ever."

Scripture also repeatedly teaches that Jesus possesses attributes that only God possesses (uniquely divine attributes), indicating that Jesus must be *truly* God in the fullest sense.

For instance, Scripture identifies Jesus as the proper object of worship. Indeed, the Father Himself commands, "Let all the angels of God worship Him [Christ]" (Heb. 1:6). And Jesus repeatedly accepts worship (John 9:38; cf. Matt. 2:11; 14:33; 28:9, 17; Luke 24:52; Heb. 1:6; Rev. 5:8–14). Yet, Scripture repeatedly teaches that God *alone* is to be worshiped (Exod. 34:14; cf. Matt. 4:10; Luke 4:8; Rev. 19:10). If Christ is not God, to worship Him would be blasphemous idolatry. Conversely, if Christ is the proper object of worship, He must be God. Being the proper object of worship is a uniquely divine attribute.

Likewise, Scripture identifies Christ as the Creator. Colossians 1:16–17 declares, "by Him [Christ] all things were created, both in the heavens and on earth, visible and invisible, whether thrones, or dominions, or rulers, or authorities—all things have been created through Him and for Him. He is before all things, and in Him all things hold together" (cf. John 1:3; Heb. 1:2, 10). Yet, being the Creator is a uniquely divine characteristic. God Himself declares in Isaiah 44:24: "I, the Lord, am the maker of all things, stretching out the heavens by Myself and spreading out the earth alone" (cf. 2 Kings 19:15; Neh. 9:6; Isa. 37:16). If Christ is the Creator, then, He must be God.

Scripture also identifies Christ as the Sustainer of all things, saying Christ "upholds all things by the word of His power" (Heb. 1:3; cf. Col. 1:17). In order to sustain "all things" by His power, however, Christ must be all-powerful. But *only* God is all-powerful and upholds all things. If Christ upholds all things, then He must be God.

Likewise, Scripture teaches that Christ has always existed—He is eternal. As we have seen, John 1:2–3 declares that Christ "was in the beginning with God" and did not Himself "come into being." Many other passages also teach that Christ is eternal (see, e.g., Col. 1:16–17; Rev. 22:13; cf. Isa. 9:6; Mic. 5:2; John 8:58; Gal. 4:4). Yet, being eternal is a divine attribute—only God is eternal and has life in Himself (cf. John 5:26; 1 Tim. 1:17); everything outside of God came into being and depends on God to exist. If Christ is eternal, upholds all things, and has life in Himself (John 5:26; 11:25), as Scripture teaches, He must be God.

Scripture also teaches that Christ is unchanging (immutable) in ways that Scripture elsewhere reserves for the eternal God.[10] Specifically, Christ is described as "the same yesterday and today, and forever"

(Heb. 13:8) and ever "the same" (Heb. 1:12). In fact, Hebrews 1:10–12 quotes statements that refer to the LORD (YHWH) as the everlasting, unchanging Creator in Psalm 102:25–27 and applies them to Christ.

Similarly, Scripture teaches that Jesus "knew all people" and "knew what was in everyone" (John 2:24–25, NRSVue; cf. Matt. 9:4; Rev. 2:23). And Jesus's disciples proclaimed to Christ: "Now we know that You know all things" (John 16:30; cf. 21:17). Yet, 1 Kings 8:39 teaches that God "alone knows every human heart" (NIV).

Further, Christ not only "upholds all things by the word of His power," but Christ "is the radiance of His [God's] glory and the exact representation of His [God's] nature" (Heb. 1:3). And, Jesus refers to "My glory which You [Father] have given Me" (John 17:24; cf. 17:5; Heb. 1:3) and declares, "all will honor the Son just as they honor the Father" (John 5:23). However, Scripture repeatedly teaches "there is no one like" God (1 Chron. 17:20, NRSVue), and God declares "I will not give My glory to another" (Isa. 42:8). Only one who is God, then, could be the "radiance" of God's "glory and the exact representation of His nature" (Heb. 1:3).[11]

Here, it is crucial to recognize that Scripture teaches there is no one who is "like" God (1 Chron. 17:20). One cannot be "God-like," or partially divine, then. That is, if being divine refers to being "like" God, the supreme being who alone is worthy of worship (Deut. 10:20; Luke 4:8), then one cannot be partially divine. One is either divine or not. There is no middle ground.

> **One is either divine or not. There is no middle ground.**

Hence, to be the "radiance" of God's "glory and the exact representation of His nature" (Heb. 1:3), Christ must Himself be God. If Christ possesses uniquely divine characteristics (e.g., equality with God, eternity, omnipotence, being the Creator and Sustainer of all who alone is worthy of worship), as Scripture teaches, then Christ must be God.

In this regard, Scripture explicitly declares the (full) divinity of Christ, saying, "in Him all the fullness of Deity dwells in bodily form" (Col. 2:9; cf. Phil. 2:6).[12] And, as we have seen, the pre-incarnate Christ repeatedly appeared in the Old Testament as the divine "Angel of the LORD."

Further, the teaching that Jesus is God is built into His name. The name Jesus, in Hebrew, literally means YHWH saves. Thus, the angel declared, "you shall name Him Jesus, for He will save His people from their sins" (Matt. 1:21). Yet, only God can save humans from sin (cf. Isa. 45:21–22). Hence, Jesus could only save people from their sins—and thus live up to His name—if He was not only human but also God.

Jesus Himself made many direct or indirect claims to divinity. Not only did Jesus call "God His own Father," thus "making Himself equal with God" (John 5:18; cf. Matt. 14:33), but He also spoke of "His angels" (Matt. 13:41) and "My kingdom" that is "not of this world" (John 18:36; cf. 8:23) and claimed to be "Lord even of the Sabbath" (Mark 2:27–28). Christ even claimed "authority" to "forgive sins" (Mark 2:10)—the ability of God alone (Mark 2:7; Luke 5:20–21) and claimed all judgment was given to Him and "all will honor the Son just as they honor the Father" (John 5:22–23; cf. Matt. 25:31–46; John 17:5). Further, Jesus claimed, "I and the Father are one" (John 10:30) and "The one who has seen Me has seen the Father" (John 14:9).

Additionally, not only did Jesus identify Himself as the great "I AM" (John 8:58; cf. Exod. 3:14), but Christ further declares, "I am the Alpha and the Omega, the first and the last, the beginning and the end" (Rev. 22:13; cf. Isa. 44:6).[13] Not only did Christ have no beginning, but "His kingdom will have no end" (Luke 1:33; cf. Isa. 9:7; Dan. 2:44; 7:14; Heb. 1:8; Rev. 11:15).

Jesus is both truly human and divine. But how can the same person be both divine and human? To this question, we now turn.

Son of Man and Son of God: The Two Natures of Christ

"What do you think about the Christ? Whose son is He?" Jesus asked some Pharisees.

"The son of David," they replied.

"Then how," Jesus asked, "does David in the Spirit call Him 'Lord,' saying, 'The Lord said to my Lord, 'Sit at My right hand, Until I put Your enemies under Your feet'? Therefore, if David calls Him 'Lord,' how is He his son?" (Matt. 22:42–45).

The answer is that the Messiah was not only the son of David but also the eternal Son of God.

Yet, how could Christ be both human *and* divine? In what follows, we will address this relative to three questions:

- How could Christ be the Son of God if He was truly divine?
- How could Christ be truly divine if He became human and thus "emptied Himself" (Phil. 2:7)?
- How could Christ be truly human if He was sinless?

Competing Theories in Christian Theology: The Divinity and Humanity of Christ

Before turning to these three questions, it is important to be aware of some approaches that Christians widely consider to be erroneous.

Some have claimed that Jesus was God but was not truly human. This view is known as docetism and claims that Jesus only seemed to be human, but this was an illusion.

On the other hand, some have claimed that Jesus was truly human but not truly divine. One form of this claim is known as adoptionism, which teaches that Jesus was an ordinary human whom God adopted to be His "Son." Adoptionism is one form of subordinationism. Subordinationism (relative to Christ) is the view that Christ is, by nature, less than God the Father.

Another form of subordinationism, known as Arianism, claims that Christ is not eternal and by nature less than the Father, being brought into existence at some time in the past by the Father such that "there was a time when he [the Son] was not."[14]

The false teaching of Arianism is named after Arius of Alexandria (ca. 250–336), whose views caused a stir in the fourth century. This view was overwhelmingly rejected and condemned at the Council of Nicea in AD 325, which set forth the Nicene Creed. A later, significantly expanded version of this creed (known as the Nicene-Constantinopolitan Creed) affirms Christ as "the only-begotten Son of God, begotten of the Father before all worlds" and "very God of very God, begotten, not made, being of one substance [*homoousios*] with the Father."[15]

While affirming that Jesus was and is truly God, the Nicene-Constantinopolitan view is typically understood as affirming the eternal generation of the Son—which is the view that the Son is *eternally* "begotten" or *eternally* generated by the Father such that the person of the Son originates from the Father—but there was never a time when the Son did not exist because this generation is understood as *eternal*. Many Christians affirm this, but many others reject eternal generation while upholding the divinity of Christ.[16] This is discussed further in chapter 6, including some reasons why Adventists typically question or reject this doctrine.

Some have falsely claimed that the teaching that Jesus is God was a late development, the result of a vote at the Council of Nicea (AD 325). However, not only does Scripture itself teach that Jesus is truly divine, but many other early Christian writings beyond the New Testament likewise attest (long before AD 325) that Jesus is God.

For example:

- Ignatius of Antioch referred to Christ as "God Himself being manifested in human form" (c. AD 108).[17]
- Justin Martyr stated, "the Father of the universe has a Son," who "is even God" (c. AD 155–157).[18]
- Irenaeus affirmed of Jesus, "He is God (for the name Emmanuel indicates this)" (c. AD 180).[19]
- Tertullian referred to "Christ our God"[20] (c. AD 200). And, he says further, we "believe that God really lived on earth" in "human form" (c. AD 207/8).[21]
- Origen wrote that "no one ought to be offended . . . that the Saviour is also God" (c. AD 220–230).[22]
- Cyprian of Carthage (c. AD 210–258) referred to "Jesus Christ, our Lord and God."[23]
- Lactantius affirmed, "we believe Him to be God" (AD 303–311).[24]

These and many other examples show that Christians believed Jesus is God long before the Council of Nicea (AD 325).

The Sonship of Christ: How Could Christ Be the Son of God if He Was Truly Divine?

To address how one who is truly divine could yet be the "Son of God," we need to address some issues relative to what Scripture means when it calls Jesus the *Son* of God.

Many have been confused by references to Christ as the "firstborn" (e.g., Col. 1:15) and "only begotten Son" of God (e.g., John 3:16, NKJV). Some believe such references support the traditional doctrine of the eternal generation of the Son, the view that the Son is *eternally* generated or "begotten" by the Father.[25] However, many others (including many Adventists) believe this view is not biblically warranted (more on this in chapter 6).

Others mistakenly believe such references mean that Christ is not eternal but came into existence. Consider Colossians 1:15, which calls Jesus "the image of the invisible God, the firstborn of all creation." The verses that follow indicate that Christ did not have a beginning to His existence. Rather, "all things have been created through Him and for Him. He is *before all things*" (Col. 1:16–17, emphasis mine). Likewise, John 1:3 teaches: "All things came into being through Him, and apart from Him not even one thing came into being that has come into being" (John 1:3). This entails that Christ Himself did not come into being.

What does the language of Christ as "firstborn" mean, then? In Scripture, the term "firstborn" often refers to one's special status, sometimes associated with one's birthright and later associated with covenant promises, particularly those about the Davidic Messiah. For example, God said of David, "I will also make him My firstborn, the highest of the kings of the earth" (Ps. 89:27). Of course, David was not literally "born" of God. Nor was David "firstborn" in any literal sense (even in his own family). But David was the chosen covenantal king, through whose lineage the Messiah (the King of kings) would come.

Accordingly, when used of Christ, "firstborn" is *covenantal* language that refers to Christ's special status as the promised Messiah—the promised covenantal "Son of David," the Davidic King who would usher in the everlasting kingdom (cf. Dan. 2) and fulfill the promises of the Davidic covenant.

Similar language of Christ's covenantal, Messianic role appears in Hebrews 1, which identifies Christ as fully divine, that is, as "the radiance of His [God's] glory and the exact representation of His [God's] nature" (1:3). Then, Hebrews 1:5–6 adds, "to which of the angels did God [the Father] ever say, 'You are my Son; today I have begotten you' [Ps. 2:7]? Or again, 'I will be his Father, and he will be my Son' [2 Sam. 7:14]? And again, when he brings the firstborn into the world, he says, 'Let all God's angels worship him'" (NRSVue, cf. Ps. 97:7).

Notice that angels already exist in Hebrews 1:5–6, but Scripture teaches that Christ existed "before all things" (Col. 1:16–17) and did not come into being (e.g., John 1:3; cf. Isa. 9:6; Mic. 5:2; John 8:58; Rev. 22:12). Hebrews 1 cannot, then, refer to Christ coming into being, but refers to the eternally pre-existent Christ entering the world in some special manner in the plan of redemption (cf. Acts 13:33; Rom. 1:4).

Accordingly, Hebrews 1:5–6 quotes from a royal coronation psalm (Ps. 2:6–7) and the Davidic covenant (2 Sam. 7:14), applying such language to Christ as the covenantal Son of David, the promised Davidic King (who is also the promised Priest of priests, *the* Royal Priest).[26] Here, the language "You are my Son; today I have begotten you" means something like: "Today I have installed you as My king, as My covenantal Son" (cf. Ps. 2:6–7). In Hebrews 1, to be "begotten" relates to being coronated or installed as king, and the language of "firstborn" likewise refers to Christ's Messianic status. And that chapter also identifies this *Messianic* Son as God: "But regarding the Son He [the Father] says, 'Your throne, God, is forever and ever'" (Heb. 1:8; quoting Ps. 45:6; cf. 110:1). Here, "God" (the Son) is anointed as the Messianic King by "God" (the Father).

This closely relates to references to Christ, sometimes translated as the "only begotten Son" (*monogenēs huios,* e.g., John 3:16, NKJV). Many New Testament scholars believe "*monogenēs*" is not derived from the Greek term for being conceived or born (*gennaō*) and conclude that *monogenēs* "means no more than 'only,' 'unique.'"[27] Yet, even if *monogenēs* is derived from *gennaō*, it might be used to refer to the incarnation since Jesus was actually born of a woman and "conceived [*gennaō*] ... of the Holy Spirit" (Matt. 1:20), though that was not the beginning of Christ's existence. Beyond this, *monogenēs* might be covenantal language similar to the language of Christ as *"firstborn"* and *"begotten"* in Hebrews 1. In numerous cases, *gennaō* is used figuratively, sometimes referring to the new "birth" of believers (John 3:3; 1 John 4:7; cf. Philem. 10).

The term *monogenēs* refers to Christ only in John's writings (John 1:14, 18; 3:16, 18; 1 John 4:9). It cannot mean Christ came into being, however, for that would contradict John's own words elsewhere (John 1:3). Notably, while other writers sometimes call believers "sons" (*huios*) of God (e.g., Gal. 3:26; Heb. 12:5–7), John calls believers children (*teknon*) of God (John 1:12; 1 John 3:1) but never "sons" (*huios*) of God.[28] In John's writings, only Jesus is called "Son" (*huios*) of God, and it makes sense that John would use the phrase *monogenēs huios* to emphasize Jesus's unique Sonship. The term *monogenēs* is closely associated with the Greek term for "beloved" (*agapētos*). And, it has been argued that *monogenēs* is itself a "hyperbole of affection" such that the best rendering of *monogenēs* in John 3:16 is "uniquely" or "only beloved."[29]

To this point, we have seen that many references to Christ's Sonship refer to Christ's status as the promised Messianic King, the covenantal Son of David, even as David himself was referred to as God's "begotten" (Ps. 2:7, NRSVue; cf. 2 Sam. 7:14) and God's "firstborn" (Ps. 89:27). These examples of covenantal Sonship do not depend on being literal offspring. Even among mere humans, one might be the "son" of one's "father" by adoption and one might refer to another as one's "begotten" child in a metaphorical sense that refers to one's "spiritual" son—as Paul refers to "my son Onesimus, whom I have begotten [*gennaō*] while in my chains" (Philem. 10, NKJV; cf. John 3:3).

In at least one sense, however, Jesus is the "Son of God" in the literal sense of being born of the virgin Mary. Because Jesus was conceived (*gennaō*, Matt. 1:20) in Mary of the Holy Spirit, the angel explained, "for that reason also the holy Child will be called the Son of God" (Luke 1:35). Christ, then, is not only the covenantal Son but also the Son of God in the unique sense of the incarnation (incarnational Sonship). He was a literal son, then, but a son unlike any others, Himself eternally pre-existent and by nature "equal with God" (John 5:18; cf. 1:1–3).

Here, it is crucial to recognize that one can be a "son" without being subordinate or inferior in nature, status, position, or function. Merely human sons are subordinate to their fathers and mothers when they are children because they are young children under their parents' protection and authority. However, even a merely human son might not be subordinate to his father. A son might become his father's supervisor in the workplace or his caretaker when his father is elderly or ill. David was the "son of Jesse." But, as king, David would not be subordinate to his father, Jesse. Further, in his last years, David shared his throne with his son Solomon as co-regent (1 Chron. 23:1). Sonship, then, does not always entail subordination.

In this regard, while Jesus is frequently called the "son of David," He was not subordinate to David. Rather, as Jesus Himself pointed out, David referred to the Messiah, the "son of David," as "Lord" (Matt. 22:41–46; cf. Ps. 110:1). Further, Christ's claim to be the "Son of God" amounted to a claim to be "equal with God" (John 5:18) such that "all will honor the Son just as they honor the Father" (John 5:23; cf. 2 Sam. 7:14; Ps. 2:6–7; Heb. 1:2–14). In order to save the world, the Son willingly lowered and submitted Himself to the Father and the Holy Spirit, according to the plan of redemption (see Phil. 2:5–8), even declaring "the Father is greater than I" (John 14:28). But being "equal with God" (John 5:18; cf. Col. 2:9), the Son is not subordinate *by nature*. Christ *became* temporarily subordinate in His role in the plan of redemption—a temporary and functional subordination (discussed further in chapter 6).

> In order to save the world, the Son willingly lowered and submitted Himself to the Father and the Holy Spirit, according to the plan of redemption.

Divinity Combined with Humanity

This brings us to the question: How could Christ be truly divine if He became human and thus "emptied Himself?" (Phil. 2:7). This has been a controversial question in the history of Christian thought.

Some early theologians thought of divinity in a way that seemed utterly incompatible with humanity. As Christian theologians sought to set forth a "respectable" form of Christianity that might avoid ridicule by the dominant Greco-Roman thought world of the age, some came to think of God's nature in terms deeply impacted by numerous streams of Greek philosophy. Later chapters will discuss this further. For now, it is sufficient to note that some claimed God could not experience the succession of time (before and after), could not change at all, and could not suffer or otherwise be affected by creatures.

Most of the controversies over Christ's nature, which caused significant strife and division in the first millennium of Christianity, were rooted in questions arising from this concept of God. For example, adopting the view that God could not change or suffer, Arius (ca. 256–336, the father of Arianism) argued that Christ could not be *fully* divine (in the full sense of equality with the Father) because Christ changed and suffered.

Yet, if God suffers *with us* as Scripture repeatedly depicts (which we will see in coming chapters), then the suffering of Christ presents no problem relative to Christ's divinity, as Arius and others mistakenly thought.

Competing Theories in Christian Theology: The Relationship between Christ's Divinity and Humanity

Throughout Christian history, there have been many controversial attempts to define the relationship between Christ's divinity and humanity.

Most Christians affirm that Christ is one person with two natures, having a truly divine nature and a truly human nature that are neither confused nor separated but both united and distinct in the singular person of Christ. This is often referred to as the hypostatic union, *part* of what is known as the Chalcedonian view, taught in the creed made during the Council of Chalcedon in AD 451, a creed affirmed by the Eastern Orthodox Church, Roman Catholic Church, and many Protestants, but rejected by the Oriental Orthodox Churches and others, and questioned by some relative to its affirmation of eternal generation.

The Chalcedonian view is typically set in contrast to other theories that most Christians have rejected.

On the one hand, Nestorianism separates the two natures of Christ into two persons, asserting that Christ consists of distinct human and divine *persons*.

On the other hand, Monophysitism teaches there are not two natures (divine and human) in Christ, but only one nature (*monos + physis*), humanity merged into a single divine nature.

This is similar to (and sometimes identified with) Miaphysitism, the view of the Oriental Orthodox Churches (such as the Coptic Orthodox Church and others) that the humanity and divinity of Jesus are united together, neither mingled nor confused nor altered, in one nature. Recently, a number of churches that affirm Chalcedonian and Miaphysite views, respectively, have issued statements concluding the difference between the two views is essentially a semantic difference.

Another view, rejected by most Christians, is known as Apollinarism (i.e., Apollinarianism), which maintains that Jesus had a normal human body but a divine mind or soul.

There are also related debates about whether Jesus has two wills—a human will and a divine will (dyothelitism) or one will (monothelitism)—and whether Christ's human nature was sinful or sinless.

An Adventist approach to understanding Christ as both truly divine and truly human is laid out below.[30]

Both Human *and* Divine?

Yet, how could Jesus possess both a human nature and a divine nature? Is divine nature compatible with human nature? If Christ has all the attributes of humanity, would that make Him less than God?

To be truly human, all that is needed is to possess every attribute that is *essential* to being human. Likewise, to be truly divine, one must possess all the *essential* attributes of divinity. As long as the essential attributes of humanity are compatible with divinity, then Christ could *become* human without ceasing to be God.

Yet, some claim human nature is incompatible with some divine attributes. For instance, mere humans are not all-knowing (omniscient), but God knows all things (1 John 3:20). Human presence is limited to bodily presence, but God is present everywhere (omnipresent, Ps. 139:7–10). How, then, could Jesus remain divine when He became human?

Some avoid this difficulty by claiming Christ "emptied Himself" (Phil. 2:7) in the sense of laying aside some or all of His divine attributes (often known as kenotic Christology, of which there are nuanced versions). However, most Christians reject versions of kenotic Christology that amount to Christ divesting Himself of divinity.

Instead, most Christian theologians believe Christ "emptied Himself" (Phil. 2:7) in a way that did not involve divesting Himself of divinity, consistent with Paul's writing elsewhere that "in Him [Christ] all the fullness of Deity dwells in bodily form" (Col. 2:9). Without ceasing to be divine, Christ took on human nature and emptied Himself in the sense of lowering Himself, "taking the form of a bond-servant (Phil. 2:6) and "becoming obedient to the point of death" (Phil. 2:8).[31]

Relative to omniscience and omnipresence, for example, one might maintain such attributes are not *essential* to divinity, such that Christ could lay them aside without ceasing to be divine. However, if one thinks such attributes are essential to divinity, this would be problematic.

Instead, many Christian theologians believe the incarnate Christ is omniscient and omnipresent with respect to His divine nature but limited in knowledge and presence with respect to His human nature. Omnipresence will be further discussed in chapter 8. Relative to divine omniscience, many believe that even during His earthly ministry, Christ possessed all knowledge (as divine) but voluntarily restricted Himself from accessing His divine knowledge about some things (according to some rules that He was not to use His divine powers for His own benefit). Christ might, then, "know all things" (John 16:30; cf. Matt. 9:4; John 2:24–25; 13:19; 21:17) in the sense of possessing all knowledge, but did not access some knowledge while on earth such that it was true He did not know the day or hour of His Second Coming (Mark 13:32). In this and other regards, some Christian theologians believe Christ's humanity imposed some "functional limitations" on His divine powers, without rendering Christ less than divine.[32]

More than one avenue is possible here without contradiction, and we might simply not be in a position to know just how Christ possesses a human nature and divine nature simultaneously. There are numerous mysteries in this regard, and when we think about Christ's nature, we are treading on holy ground and should be exceedingly careful. For our purposes, it is enough to see that there is more than one way in which Christ becoming human is compatible with Christ being divine.

Whether or not we know and fully understand just how Christ is both divine and human, Scripture teaches that Christ is truly divine *and* truly human. When Christ became human, He did not cease to be God. By taking on human nature in the incarnation without ceasing to be divine, Christ took on all essential human attributes without losing any essential divine attributes. While it would be impossible for humanity to elevate to the level of divinity, the greater (divinity) can condescend to the lesser (humanity). And Jesus did so for us.

> **Christ took on all essential human attributes without losing any essential divine attributes.**

Affected by Sin, but Not Infected by Sin

Yet, if God is not "tempted by evil" (James 1:13), how could Jesus be "tempted in all things just as we are" (Heb. 4:15)?[33] The key words here are "by evil." Evil is not desirable to God and thus would not (in and of itself) tempt Him. However, this is consistent with God (in Christ) condescending to become human and thus placing Himself in situations where He might be tempted not directly *by being attracted to evil itself* but tempted by desires that are not evil in themselves but would amount to sin given the circumstances.

Christ is the only human who never sinned, and in Him there was no sin (1 John 3:5). Yet, some claim, to be truly human, Christ must have taken on a human nature *corrupted* by sin, including an inclination to sin (often referred to by theologians today as a sinful nature).[34]

This issue has been controversial in the history of Adventist thought, particularly regarding whether Jesus inherited an inclination toward sin. The disagreement has sometimes been framed as between those who believe Jesus inherited a fallen, sinful nature like Adam after the Fall (postlapsarian) and those who believe Jesus inherited an unfallen nature like Adam before the Fall (prelapsarian).

However, framing the discussion this way can be misleading because many Adventist theologians who believe Jesus did *not* inherit an inclination toward sin nevertheless affirm Jesus was affected by the Fall and otherwise inherited a nature that was affected by sin and debilitated over the ages.

Adventist theologians on all sides affirm that Jesus *in some sense* inherited a "sinful" and "fallen" nature. The disagreement is over what kind of "sinful" and "fallen" nature Jesus inherited—specifically, whether it included an *inclination* or *propensity* toward sin.

Some have argued Jesus inherited the *same* fallen, sinful condition and inclinations toward sin that plague us (see chapter 12). If not, some argue, Jesus was not *fully* human like us and could not be our example.

The majority of Adventist theologians, conversely, believe Jesus did not inherit an inclination toward sin. On this view, Christ's human nature was neither just like Adam's before the Fall (prelapsarian) nor just like Adam's after the Fall (postlapsarian). Rather, Christ's human nature was like Adam's after the Fall with respect to inheriting things like physical weaknesses and infirmities common to humanity since the Fall, but different from Adam's nature after the Fall in that Jesus did not inherit the "taint" or "corruption" of sin manifested in inclinations or propensities toward sin. Proponents of this view argue that if Jesus took on a tainted and corrupted human nature with inclinations and propensities toward sin, Jesus Himself would have been *infected* by sin and under bondage to Satan such that Jesus could not save humanity from sin and bondage to Satan.[35]

Scripture does not include much information that directly addresses this point. However, no text or passage of Scripture explicitly teaches that Jesus had any inclination or propensity toward sin.

Yet, some who believe Jesus took on a human nature with inclinations toward sin argue that their view follows from the facts that Jesus became *fully* human and Jesus came to serve as an example for humanity in relation to God.

Both sides agree that Jesus became fully human and did so to provide an example for humans in relation to God (among other reasons). However, those who believe Jesus did not have any inclination toward sin maintain Jesus could be fully human and serve as our example without possessing any inclination toward sin (as discussed further below).

One might argue, however, that to redeem *corrupted* human nature, Jesus must have taken on *corrupted* human nature. In this regard, from ancient times, Christians have argued: "what is not assumed is not redeemed." However, this phrase is typically meant to affirm that, to be our Savior, Jesus must have been truly human such that through becoming human, Christ redeemed humanity.

If this principle is employed to mean *anything whatsoever* Christ did not assume was not redeemed, however, then one might arrive at the false conclusion that (for example) Jesus cannot redeem females because He was male or cannot redeem Gentiles because He was a Jew. To avoid such false conclusions, theologians typically conclude that to redeem humanity, Jesus needed to take on all *essential* human attributes (i.e., whatever attributes are necessary to being human; for more on human nature, see chapters 11 and 12).

If being truly human simply requires that one possess all essential human attributes, it follows that Jesus could be truly human without a *corrupted* human nature. To see this, consider the following. Before the Fall, were Eve and Adam truly human? Of course they were. But they did not have a corrupted human nature or an inclination toward sin before the Fall. Therefore, being truly human does not require having a corrupted human nature or an inclination toward sin.

Yet, if Jesus did not have an inclination toward sin, how could He be our example? Here, it is crucial to recognize that Jesus can be our example without being by nature just like us.

Jesus became *truly* human, but He is not *merely* human. Jesus is human *and* divine. Accordingly, during His earthly ministry (and beyond), Jesus possessed divine attributes and powers that *mere* humans do not possess. For example, Jesus could turn stones into bread as Satan tempted Him to do in the wilderness after Jesus had fasted for forty days (Matt. 4:3). While you and I have never been tempted to turn stones into bread because we cannot, Jesus was so tempted because He could have done so.

> *Jesus became* truly *human, but He is* not merely *human.* Jesus is human *and divine.*

Yet, there is nothing *intrinsically* immoral about turning stones into bread. So, for this temptation to make sense, it must have been somehow against the rules for Jesus to use His power for His own benefit in this struggle. Accordingly, Adventists believe Jesus never used His divine power *for His own benefit,* relying only on the power available to mere humans by faith and prayer. In this way, though Christ is far greater than us, He could serve as our example because He voluntarily limited Himself to using only power available to mere humans (relative to His own benefit).

I fondly recall teaching my son how to shoot a basketball when he was about five years old. While doing so, I did it myself as an example of how to do it. One might object that I was not a suitable example for him because I was taller and stronger than he was. I had the strength to shoot the ball high enough to reach the basket, but he did not.

Similarly, some contend it would be unfair if Jesus had no inclination to sin. How could He be our example if He did not possess the inclinations toward sin with which we wrestle?

Importantly, as the story of Jesus's temptations shows (Matt. 4), Jesus did wrestle with temptations. Indeed, "we do not have a high priest who cannot sympathize with our weaknesses, but One who has been tempted in all things just as we are, yet without sin" (Heb. 4:15; cf. 2:17–18; 7:26). Jesus was tempted, "yet without sin." Relative to temptations, then, Jesus was both like us and unlike us. On the one hand, He was "tempted in all things just as we are." On the other hand, He alone was "without sin."

Unlike us, Jesus had no evil desires, and He was not *naturally* attracted to sin (see John 14:30; 1 John 3:5; cf. James 1:13–15). Accordingly, Satan tempted Him by using desires that were not intrinsically sinful but sinful only in relation to the circumstances or rules involved (i.e., turning stones into bread). Nevertheless, the temptations Jesus faced were far greater and more severe than those faced by any mere human.[36] Jesus carried the weight of the world's sins all the way to the cross and was tempted to provide a way of escape for Himself, which He had the power to do at any moment. Indeed, Jesus had the power to do anything He wanted. Imagine how much greater temptations would be if you had unlimited power.

If there is anything unfair in this regard, it is in our favor. It is only because Christ was human *and* divine and was not Himself in need of a Savior that He could save us. On His own behalf, Christ only used power that is available to mere humans in relation to God. And, through His work, Christ provides the way for us to access such divine power so that, united with Christ, we can overcome sin.

Although my five-year-old son was not strong enough to make a basketball shot on his own like I could, I could still teach him and be his example. Further, precisely because I was bigger and stronger than he, I could help him. I could put him on my shoulders; from that height, he could shoot and make the basket.

This is part of the wonderful good news of the gospel. As we will see in chapter 13, we cannot overcome sin in our own strength, but we can by the power of God that is accessible through Christ by faith. And Christ Himself provided an example for us of how we can access this power by faith and prayer.

Unlike all other humans, however, Jesus did not need a Savior because Jesus was not *infected* with sin. While "all" mere humans "have sinned and fall short of the glory of God" (Rom. 3:23), Jesus alone "knew no sin" (2 Cor. 5:21) and "committed no sin" (1 Pet. 2:22; cf. Isa. 53:9). In contrast, mere humans are "conceived" in "sin" (Ps. 51:5), "go astray from the womb" and "err from their birth" (Ps. 58:3, NRSVue), and all mere humans are described as being "by nature children of wrath" (Eph. 2:3).

But, while still in Mary's womb, Jesus was described as "the holy Child" (Luke 1:35). This might be why Paul does not say Jesus came in sinful flesh, but rather writes that Jesus was sent "in the *likeness* of sinful flesh" (Rom. 8:3, emphasis mine; cf. Phil. 2:6–7).

Jesus was the only human who never sinned and the only human in whom there was *no sin at all*—"in Him there is no sin" whatsoever (1 John 3:5). Unlike all other humans, Jesus could truly declare, the devil "has nothing in Me" (John 14:30, NKJV).

Precisely because the devil had nothing in Him, Jesus could be our Savior. If Jesus was infected by sin, He would need a Savior. If Jesus's relationship with God was broken by His iniquity, He would need to be reconciled to God by some work of atonement that He would then not be suited to perform. But, praise God, even as the lamb that represented Christ in the sanctuary services was unblemished, Christ was unblemished, the spotless Lamb who takes away the world's sins (John 1:29).

Conclusion: Why Does It Matter?

"Who do you say that I am?" Jesus addressed this question to Peter (Matt. 16:15, NRSVue). But you and I and every other person must also answer this question for ourselves. On the answer to this question, *everything* hinges. The significance of your story is bound to *His* story by an unbreakable bond.

Have you ever pondered the true significance of who Jesus was and who Jesus is? If Jesus is who He claimed to be and truly rose from the dead, nothing could be more significant. If Jesus was and is the Son of God, this is the best of best news, for that means that you and I can inherit eternal life through Him.

This chapter introduced who Jesus is, His mission and works for us, and why it matters, highlighting that Jesus was and is God in the flesh—*God with us*. In Christ, God became human—the Son of God and the Son of Man. This is crucial because only one *truly* divine and *truly* human could rescue us from the evil of this world; only such a one could reconcile fallen humans to God and save the world so that God can be *with us* again in the special manner He intended from the beginning.

Jesus came as the promised Son, the Messiah who would fulfill the covenant promises made to Abraham and David, including the promise of an everlasting kingdom. He fulfilled the prophecies of the coming of the greatest prophet, the highest high priest, and the King of kings.

Yet, His mission and work of bringing His everlasting kingdom of peace takes place in two stages. First, the Messiah came and gave His life as the Lamb slain for the sins of the world and rose from the dead, conquering death so that anyone who believes in Him can have eternal life. That is, in order to defeat the devil and save the world, Christ not only lowered Himself to become human but willingly took on suffering and death by crucifixion *for us*. Second, Christ will return as the Lion of Judah, uprooting injustice and eradicating evil forevermore, ushering in an eternity with no sin, suffering, or death.

Your story and my story are bound up with these two stages—the *now* and the not yet—that which is and that which is to come. The situation you are in now is not all that there is. There is a future of eternal bliss beyond your wildest dreams that is available for you and for me in Christ. In Christ, you have a hero who will save you from fear, suffering, hardship, and death itself.

> *In Christ, you have a hero who will save you from fear, suffering, hardship, and death itself.*

So, who do *you* say that Jesus is? Do you believe in Him? Do you want to believe in Him? He calls to you even now. If you are willing, accept Him as your Savior and Lord. If you do, He will save you, and He "will never leave you nor forsake you" (Heb. 13:5, NKJV). Even now, you can simply invite Him into your heart, and He will accept your invitation. He promised: "Behold, I stand at the door and knock; if anyone hears My voice and opens the door, I will come in to him and will dine with him, and he with Me" (Rev. 3:20).

Christ not only calls you to follow Him and be saved, however. Christ also calls you to join Him in mission, to follow Christ, the Lamb. Anyone who wishes to follow Christ must follow Christ's teachings, as summed up in the two great love commands: wholeheartedly love God and love your neighbor as yourself (Matt. 22:37–38). In this regard, Jesus commanded, "love one another; just as I have loved you.... By this all people will know that you are My disciples: if you have love for one another" (John 13:34–35).

Following Christ in this way, however, is bound up with the work of the Holy Spirit, to which we turn in the next chapter. In the meantime, I invite you to pause and reflect on Mary's song of praise in Luke 1:46–55 and reflect on just how awesome God is and how amazing it is that, in Christ, God became human to save you and me—to be God *with us* forever.

Questions for Reflection

1. What struck you most about the works Christ does for us and in us? How is Christ's work relevant to your life now and in the future?
2. How important is the humanity of Jesus? What difference does it make whether or not Jesus was truly human and identified Himself with humanity, even the "least of these"?
3. Why is the divinity of Christ important to Christianity? How would you teach someone else about Christ's divinity from Scripture?
4. How could Christ be both truly human and truly divine? Did Christ remain truly divine when He became human? How is it important to your relationship with God that Christ was both?
5. How would you explain the sinlessness of Christ to someone else? In what way is Christ like us and unlike us in this respect? How might it help you to remember that Christ experienced temptations even more powerful than any that mere humans experience and that we can access divine power to overcome through Him?
6. Jesus asked Peter, "Who do you say that I am?" How do you answer this question of who Jesus is? What would you say to someone else seeking an answer to this question?
7. You can invite Jesus into your heart even now. Do you wish to do so? If so, you can simply pray to Jesus that He come into your heart. And, He will.

For Further Reading

Adventist Perspectives:
Adams, Roy. *The Nature of Christ: Help for a Church Divided Over Perfection.* Hagerstown, MD: Review and Herald, 1994.

Dederen, Raoul. "Christ: His Person and Work." In *Handbook of Seventh-day Adventist Theology*. Edited by Raoul Dederen. Hagerstown, MD: Review and Herald, 2000.

Donkor, Kwabena. *The Nature of Christ: The Soteriological Question*. Biblical Research Institute Release, no. 4. Silver Spring, MD: Biblical Research Institute, 2005.

Gallusz, Laszlo. *The Seven Prayers of Jesus*. London: InterVarsity, 2017.

Gulley, Norman R. *Systematic Theology: Creation, Christ, Salvation*. Berrien Springs, MI: Andrews University Press, 2012.

Heppenstall, Edward. *The Man Who Is God: A Study of the Person and Nature of Jesus, Son of God and Son of Man*. Washington, DC: Review and Herald, 1977.

Johnsson, William G. *Jesus of Nazareth: His Life, His Message, His Passion*. Berrien Springs, MI: Andrews University Press, 2018.

Rodrigues, Adriani Milli. *Toward a Priestly Christology: A Hermeneutical Study of Christ's Priesthood*. Lexington/Fortress Academic, 2018.

Talbott, Elizabeth Viera. *John: God Became Flesh*. Jesus 101, Book 2. Nampa, ID: Pacific Press, 2010.

Whidden, Woodrow W. *Ellen White on the Humanity of Christ*. Hagerstown, MD: Review and Herald, 1997.

White, Ellen G. *The Desire of Ages*. Mountain View, CA: Pacific Press, 1898.

See also the resources on the Biblical Research Institute website: https://adventistbiblicalresearch.org/materials/.

Other Christian Perspectives:

Bauckham, Richard. *Jesus: A Very Short Introduction*. New York: Oxford University Press, 2011.

Cole, Graham A. *The God Who Became Human: A Biblical Theology of Incarnation*. Downers Grove, IL: IVP Academic, 2013.

Erickson, Millard J. *The Word Became Flesh: A Contemporary Incarnational Christology*. Grand Rapids, MI: Baker, 2000.

Hurtado, Larry W. *One God, One Lord: Early Christian Devotion and Ancient Jewish Monotheism*, 3rd ed. London: T&T Clark, 2015.

MacLeod, Donald. *The Person of Christ*. Downers Grove, IL: InterVarsity, 1998.

Kärkkäinen, Veli-Matti. *Christology: A Global Introduction*. Grand Rapids, MI: Baker Academic, 2003.

Longenecker, Richard N. *Contours of Christology in the New Testament*. Grand Rapids, MI: Eerdmans, 2005.

Murpy, Francesca Aran, ed. *The Oxford Handbook of Christology*. New York: Oxford University Press, 2015.

Stott, John. *The Incomparable Christ*. Downers Grove, IL: InterVarsity, 2004.

Strauss, Mark L. *Four Portraits, One Jesus: A Survey of Jesus and the Gospels*, 2nd ed. Grand Rapids, MI: Zondervan, 2020.

Thurman, Howard. *Jesus and the Disinherited*. New York: Abingdon-Cokesbury, 1949.

Wright, N. T. *Simply Jesus: A New Vision of Who He Was, What He Did, and Why He Matters*. New York: HarperOne, 2018.

5

THE HOLY SPIRIT: GOD WITH US IN THE SPIRIT

"I tell you the truth," Jesus told His followers, "it is to your advantage that I am leaving; for if I do not leave, the Helper will not come to you; but if I go, I will send Him to you" (John 16:7). How could this be? How could anyone else's coming be so significant that it is to the disciples' advantage that Jesus "go away"?

Imagine being one of Jesus's disciples and hearing these words. How could it be better that the physical presence of Christ "go away" so that this other "Helper" would come? How could anyone make up for the physical absence of Christ—God with us in the flesh?

Jesus earlier identified this "Helper" as the Holy Spirit, telling His disciples: "I will ask the Father, and He will give you another Helper, so that He may be with you forever; the Helper is the Spirit of truth" (John 14:16–17). Notice the phrase, "that He may be with you forever." The disciples would not be left alone. The Holy Spirit would be *with* them forever.

But who is the Holy Spirit? This chapter addresses this and a host of other questions about the Holy Spirit's nature and works. We will see that the Holy Spirit is a divine person; thus, Christ's promise "that He may be with you forever" is a promise of God's permanent presence with Christ's followers via "another Helper" sent in Christ's place. As truly divine, the Holy Spirit could effectively take Christ's place as God with us *in the Spirit*. Thus, through the ministry of the Holy Spirit, the story of God's presence *with us* continues in a special way after Christ's ascension.

While many issues relative to the Holy Spirit warrant attention, this chapter focuses on the following questions:

- Who is the Holy Spirit?
- Is the Holy Spirit God?
- Is the Holy Spirit a person, and what does that mean?
- Is the Holy Spirit distinct from the Father and Son?
- Why does Scripture refer to the Holy Spirit as "the Spirit of the Father" and "the Spirit of Jesus"?
- What does the Holy Spirit do and why do these questions matter?

Regarding this last question, the Holy Spirit is far more prominent in Scripture than often recognized. Throughout the story of Scripture, God reveals Himself progressively, but always consistent with His past revelation. The Spirit is active throughout Scripture but is more clearly revealed when the fullness of time comes for the Spirit's more prominent role as "another Helper" sent in Christ's place, unleashed to witness of Christ and empower the church accordingly (cf. John 7:39).

In a myriad of ways, the Holy Spirit is central to Christian faith, and the Holy Spirit's works are essential to the lives of Christians *individually and collectively*. Indeed, the very possibility that humans might have eternal life hinges on the Holy Spirit's work. For, as Jesus Himself proclaimed, in order to enter the kingdom of heaven, one must be born again—that is, born of the Spirit (John 3:3–8).

The Holy Spirit is central to Christian faith, and the Holy Spirit's works are essential to the lives of Christians individually and collectively.

The Story of the Holy Spirit

Nicodemus came to Jesus under the cover of night. He was a respected ruler of the Jews, a member of the Sanhedrin—the council of elders that functioned (among other ways) as something like a Supreme Court of the Jews in Jerusalem.

"Truly," Jesus told Nicodemus, "unless someone is born again he cannot see the kingdom of God."

Born again? "How can a person be born when he is old? He cannot enter his mother's womb a second time and be born, can he?" Nicodemus replied.[1]

"Truly," Jesus continued, "unless someone is born of water and the Spirit, he cannot enter the kingdom of God. That which has been born of the flesh is flesh, and that which has been born of the Spirit is spirit. Do not be amazed that I said to you, 'You must be born again.' The wind blows where it wishes, and you hear the sound of it, but you do not know where it is coming from and where it is going; so is everyone who has been born of the Spirit" (John 3:3–8).

Born of the Spirit? Who is this Spirit? Here, Jesus employs a play on words. The word translated "Spirit" (*pneuma*) can also mean "wind" or "breath." Like the wind, the comings and goings of the Spirit are often mysterious.

This Spirit not only makes believers "born again" or "born from above," but Jesus the Son of God was "conceived" of this same "Holy Spirit" (Matt. 1:20). "The Holy Spirit will come upon you," the angel told the virgin Mary, "and the power of the Most High will overshadow you; for that reason also the holy Child will be called the Son of God" (Luke 1:35). Utterly amazing.

As the story of Jesus unfolds, so does the story of the Holy Spirit. When Jesus was baptized, "the Holy Spirit descended upon Him in bodily form like a dove" (Luke 3:21–22; cf. Matt. 3:16; Acts 10:38). Afterward, "Jesus, full of the Holy Spirit" was driven into the wilderness by the Holy Spirit to a prearranged confrontation wherein Jesus would be tempted by the devil (Mark 1:12; Luke 4:1–2).

Jesus was both the Son of God, conceived of the Spirit, and a man filled by the Spirit. While often not in the foreground of the story, a close reading of the Gospels shows the Spirit at work throughout Christ's ministry and demonstrates that the Spirit is a central player in the gospel story. The story and works of Christ are inextricably linked to the story and works of the Spirit.

So closely linked are the Son and the Spirit that when Jesus explained to His apostles He would be going away to the Father, He told them the Holy Spirit would be sent to be with them in His place.

"I will ask the Father," Jesus told them, "and He will give you another Helper, so that He may be with you forever; the Helper is the Spirit of truth, whom the world cannot receive, because it does not see Him or know Him; but you know Him because He remains with you and will be in you" (John 14:16–17). This is all about presence; the presence of God *with us*. While Jesus was physically going away, and though the Spirit was already present and active, the Spirit would come to "be with" Christ's followers in a *special* way "forever," to abide "with us" and "be in" us.

Further, Jesus told them, "it is to your advantage that I am leaving; for if I do not leave, the Helper will not come to you; but if I go, I will send Him to you" (John 16:7). But how could the Spirit's coming be so significant that it was to their advantage? This could be so because the Holy Spirit's presence with us is God's presence with us, unlocked and unleashed (cf. John 7:39) in a special way by the work of Christ for us on earth and in the heavenly sanctuary.

In the New Testament, the word translated "Helper" (*paraklētos*, sometimes translated "Comforter" or "Advocate") is used to refer only to the Holy Spirit (John 14:16, 26; 15:26; 16:7) and Jesus (1 John 2:1). Even as Jesus is our *paraklētos* "with the Father" (1 John 2:1), the Spirit is *another paraklētos*—another comforter and advocate *of the same kind*.[2] Both are sent by the Father according to the plan of redemption to perform the divine work of reconciliation.

Some, confused by the close link between the Spirit and Son, mistakenly suppose the Son and Spirit might be the *same* person. This is ruled out by (among other things) the way this passage and others refer to the Spirit and the Son as distinct from one another. The Spirit is not the *same* Helper as Jesus, but "*another* Helper" who "comes" from the Father after Jesus "goes away" to the Father. Further, Scripture depicts Christ as dependent on the Holy Spirit throughout His earthly ministry—driven into the wilderness by the Spirit and empowered by the Spirit throughout His ministry. Conversely, the Spirit Himself is later sent by the Son (John 15:26; 16:7).

Indeed, not only does Christ submit to the Father during His earthly ministry, but Christ also operates in submission to the Holy Spirit throughout His earthly ministry. Christ is incarnated via the Spirit (Matt. 1:18–20; Luke 1:35), filled and anointed by the Spirit (Luke 4:1, 18; cf. Matt. 12:28; Acts 10:38), and driven into the wilderness by the Spirit (Mark 1:12; cf. Matt. 4:1; Luke 4:1). And, according to Hebrews 9:14, Christ "through the eternal Spirit offered Himself without blemish to God."

Later, however, the Spirit is sent by both the Father and the Son (e.g., John 14:26; 15:26) and testifies about Jesus (John 15:26), thus operating in a distinct and apparently *functionally* submissive role relative to the

Father and Son (cf. John 16:13, see the further discussion in chapter 6).[3] Not only do the Son and Spirit play different (though always harmonious) roles in the plan of redemption, then, but their roles in relation to one another change over time. First, the Son is dependent on the Spirit. Later, the Spirit is sent by the Son.[4]

While distinct from the Son, the Spirit can effectively take the Son's place as "another *paraklētos*" with Christ's followers because the Spirit is *one with* the Son—not one in the sense of being the same person, but one in that the Spirit and Son and Father are one God (explained further in chapter 6).

Christ's promise that the Spirit would be sent to be with Christ's followers was fulfilled on the day of Pentecost. The risen Jesus had appeared to many people after the resurrection in the span of forty days (Acts 1:3). Then, Jesus ascended into heaven (Acts 1:9–11). Just before He ascended, however, Christ instructed His disciples "not to leave Jerusalem, but to wait for what the Father had promised" and "you heard of from Me" for "you will be baptized with the Holy Spirit not many days from now" (Acts 1:4–5). And Jesus further proclaimed, "you will receive power when the Holy Spirit has come upon you; and you shall be My witnesses both in Jerusalem and in all Judea, and Samaria, and as far as the remotest part of the earth" (Acts 1:8).

Ten days later, just as promised, the Holy Spirit came on the disciples with power on the day of Pentecost. This is one of many examples where crucial events of the story of redemption line up with feast days in the Hebrew calendar. For example, the Passover corresponds to Christ's crucifixion as the Lamb offered for us, the wave sheaf offering corresponds to Christ's resurrection as the first fruit, and Pentecost corresponds to the coming of the Holy Spirit in power.[5]

On the day of Pentecost, "suddenly a noise like a violent rushing wind came from heaven, and it filled the whole house where they were sitting. And tongues that looked like fire appeared to them, distributing themselves, and a tongue rested on each one of them. And they were all filled with the Holy Spirit and began to speak with different tongues, as the Spirit was giving them the ability to speak out" (Acts 2:1–4). A crowd gathered upon hearing the noise, and people from nations throughout the world gathered and were "amazed and astonished" for "each one of them was hearing them speak in his own language," the language to which they were born (Acts 2:6–8).

This was one of many great acts of the Holy Spirit recorded in the book of Acts. In large part, the story of the acts of the apostles therein is the story of the acts of the Holy Spirit. From the day the Spirit fell on Christ's followers at Pentecost forward, the Spirit worked miracles and inspired the apostles to testify and preach of the risen Christ.

The story of the Spirit is bound up with the Spirit's works, not only in the life of Christ and acts of the apostles, but going all the way back to before the creation of the world. The Holy Spirit is "the eternal Spirit" (Heb. 9:14). Before creation itself, the Holy Spirit already was and was already at work.

> *Before creation itself, the Holy Spirit already was and was already at work.*

The Mission and Works of the Holy Spirit

"In the beginning God created the heavens and the earth. And the earth was a formless and desolate emptiness, and darkness was over the surface of the deep, and the Spirit of God was hovering over the surface of the waters" (Gen. 1:1–2). The Holy Spirit's first act recorded in Scripture appears at the beginning of the Bible in the narrative of creation. Along with the Father and the Son, the Holy Spirit was also active in creation.

At Pentecost and beyond, the Spirit was sent by the Father and Son on a special mission in the plan of redemption, the role of another *paraklētos*. Because of what Jesus accomplished—defeating the devil via the cross, rising from the dead, and ascending to minister as our high priest in the heavenly sanctuary, the Holy Spirit came upon the followers of Christ with new power, as if the Spirit was in some sense unleashed via the victory of Christ (see chapter 9). In this regard, previously, "the Spirit was not yet given, because Jesus was not yet glorified" (John 7:39; cf. 16:7).

This was one fulfillment of the promise God gave long before through the prophet Joel, "I will pour out My Spirit on all mankind; and your sons and your daughters will prophesy, your old men will have dreams, your young men will see visions. And even on the male and female servants I will pour out My Spirit in those days" (Joel 2:28–29). And there will also be a latter rain of the Spirit before Christ's return (see Joel 2:23).

The Works of the Spirit throughout Creation

Yet, long before the Spirit came with power at Pentecost, the Spirit was active in this world, not only at creation but throughout the story of the Old Testament. For instance, the Spirit is mentioned before the flood, striving with humans (Gen. 6:3).[6] Later, the Holy Spirit was active in the Exodus; God "put His Holy Spirit in the midst of" the people of Israel and "the Spirit of the LORD gave them rest" (Isa. 63:11, 14; cf. Hag. 2:5). "But they rebelled and grieved His Holy Spirit" (Isa. 63:10).

Earlier, Joseph was referred to as "a man in whom is the Spirit of God" (Gen. 41:38, NKJV; cf. Dan. 5:11). Here and elsewhere, the Spirit is frequently referred to as filling special chosen individuals, especially chosen leaders and prophets.

For example, God filled chosen individuals with the Holy Spirit, so they received gifts of craftsmanship. Of the craftsman Bezalel, God declares: "I have filled him with the Spirit of God in wisdom, in understanding, in knowledge, and in all kinds of craftsmanship" (Exod. 31:3; cf. 35:30–35).

Further, the Spirit was upon Moses, and God placed the Spirit also upon seventy chosen elders. Indeed, God told Moses, "I will take of the Spirit that is upon you and will put the same upon them" (Num. 11:17, NKJV). "And when the Spirit rested upon them, they prophesied" (Num. 11:25), and Moses proclaimed, "If only all the LORD's people were prophets, that the LORD would put His Spirit upon them!" (Num. 11:29). Later, "the Spirit of God came upon" Balaam, and he prophesied a blessing on Israel (Num. 24:2). Still later, God instructed Moses to commission Joshua as the next leader of Israel, referring to Joshua as "a man in whom is the Spirit" (Num. 27:18). And, throughout the book of Judges, the Spirit repeatedly came upon chosen judges in power (see Judg. 3:10; 6:34; 11:29; 13:25; 14:6, 19; 15:14).

Likewise, the Spirit of God came upon kings. For example, "the Spirit of God rushed upon" King Saul "so that he prophesied" (1 Sam. 10:10; cf. 10:6; 11:6). Later, when Samuel anointed David as the future king, "the Spirit of the LORD rushed upon David from that day forward," but "the Spirit of the LORD left Saul," whom David eventually replaced (1 Sam. 16:13–14). And David wrote many *inspired* Psalms and declared: "The Spirit of the LORD spoke through me, and His word was on my tongue" (2 Sam. 23:2).

In many other cases, the Holy Spirit bestowed the gift of prophecy on humans. For example, Isaiah wrote: "The Spirit of the Lord GOD is upon me, because the LORD anointed me to bring good news to the humble; he has sent me to bind up the brokenhearted, to proclaim release to captives and freedom to prisoners" (Isa. 61:1–2).

Later, the prophet Ezekiel recounts, "the Spirit entered me" and "I heard Him speaking to me" (Ezek. 2:2). Further, Ezekiel recounts: "The hand of the LORD was upon me, and He brought me out by the Spirit of the LORD and set me down in the middle of the valley; and it was full of bones" (Ezek. 37:1). In what follows, Ezekiel sees a vision of dry bones, is asked whether such bones could live, and is commanded to prophesy to these bones God's words that God will "make breath enter" them that they "may come to life" (Ezek. 37:5).

Amazingly, in the vision the dry bones came together, sinews came upon them, flesh grew, and skin covered them. Finally, "the breath entered them, and they came to life and stood on their feet, an exceedingly great army" (Ezek. 37:7–10). These bones represented the house of Israel and God's promise to bring them back to life. Indeed, God declares, "I will put My Spirit within you and you will come to life" (Ezek. 37:14). Here and elsewhere, the Spirit is not only active relative to prophecy, but also relative to bringing life to that which is dead.

Earlier, God declared, "I will put My Spirit within you and bring it about that you walk in My statutes" (Ezek. 36:27).[7] In this and other examples, the Spirit of God dwells in some humans in a special way; active in the creative process of giving humans a "new heart," transforming their hearts of stone to a new heart of flesh, and thus raising them from *spiritual* death to *spiritual* life. Indeed, God declared, "I will give them one heart, and put a new spirit within them. And I will remove the heart of stone from their flesh and give them a heart of flesh, so that they may walk in My statutes, and keep My ordinances and do them. Then they will be My people, and I shall be their God" (Ezek. 11:19–20; cf. 18:31).[8]

Ezekiel and the other prophets of old spoke and wrote by inspiration of the Holy Spirit. Indeed, the law and the words of God were "sent by His Spirit through the former prophets" (Zech. 7:12). Accordingly, just before quoting a statement of God, Paul says, "The Holy Spirit rightly spoke through Isaiah the prophet to your fathers" (Acts 28:25; cf. Isa. 6).

Similarly, before introducing quotations from the Psalms (69:25 and 109:8), Peter declared, "the Scripture had to be fulfilled, which the Holy Spirit foretold by the mouth of David" (Acts 1:16; cf. 3:18, 21; 4:25; Rom. 1:2). Hebrews 3:7 likewise introduces a quotation of God's words by saying, "as the Holy Spirit says" (cf. Ps. 95:9-11).

In this regard, Peter teaches further, "no prophecy of Scripture becomes a matter of someone's own interpretation, for no prophecy was ever made by an act of human will, but men moved by the Holy Spirit spoke from God" (2 Pet. 1:20-21; cf. 2 Tim. 3:16). The Holy Spirit revealed and inspired the prophetic and apostolic testimony recorded in Scripture.

As Jesus told His apostles, "the Spirit of truth who comes from the Father, He will testify about Me, and you are testifying as well, because you have been with Me from the beginning" (John 15:26-27). Here and elsewhere, the New Testament highlights the crucial role of the Holy Spirit as testifying to the exaltation and coronation of the risen Jesus, an event in heaven revealed and attested on earth through the visible and observable outpouring of the Spirit at Pentecost, which unmistakably signals that Jesus is "both Lord and Christ" (see, e.g., Acts 2:33-36; 5:31-32; cf. John 15:26-27; Heb. 1:3-13; Rev. 4-5).[9]

Those chosen to be Christ's witnesses were inspired by the Holy Spirit to testify of the truth alongside the Spirit (John 15:26-27), even as Jesus came "to testify to the truth" (John 18:37), combatting the devil's lies at the center of the cosmic conflict (see chapter 9)—testifying of the exaltation of Jesus to the throne in heaven (see, e.g., Acts 5:31-32; cf. 7:55-56), which vindicated Christ in the heavenly court in a great reversal of the earthly judgments against Jesus that led to the cross, "prov[ing] the world wrong about sin and righteousness and judgment ... because the ruler of this world [the devil] has been condemned" (John 16:8, 11, NRSVue; cf. 12:31-32; for much more on this, see chapter 16).[10] To this end, Jesus gave "instructions through the Holy Spirit to the apostles whom he had chosen" and promised His chosen apostles, "you will receive power when the Holy Spirit has come upon you, and you will be my witnesses" even "to the ends of the earth" (Acts 1:2, 8, NRSVue).

Prophetic and apostolic testimony is *inspired* testimony in the literal sense that it is Spirit-filled testimony. In this regard, Peter teaches that the Old Testament prophets had the Holy Spirit within them; they were "seeking to know what person or time the Spirit of Christ within them was indicating as He predicted the sufferings of Christ and the glories to follow" (1 Pet. 1:11). Likewise, the Holy Spirit inspired the apostles to testify and they "preached the gospel" far and wide "by the Holy Spirit sent from heaven—things into which angels long to look" (1 Pet. 1:12).

God "revealed" His truth to chosen messengers (prophets and apostles) "through the Spirit" (1 Cor. 2:10). Indeed, the Holy Spirit acted to bring chosen prophets and apostles to understand the things of God (the process of revelation) and guided those chosen recipients of revelation as they shared God's messages in the spoken and written word (the process of inspiration). Thus, Paul identifies his own messages as "the word of God" (1 Thess. 2:13), and Peter proclaims that "men moved by the Holy Spirit spoke from God" (2 Pet. 1:21).

Apart from these special revealing and inspiring works of the Spirit, we would not have the special revelation of God contained in Scripture (on Scripture, see chapter 10). Paul explains, "the thoughts of God no one knows, except the Spirit of God" and "we have not received the spirit of the world, but the Spirit who is from God [the Holy Spirit], so that we may know the things freely given to us by God. We also speak these things, not in words taught by human wisdom, but in those taught by the Spirit, combining spiritual thoughts with spiritual words" (1 Cor. 2:11–13).

The Works of the Spirit for Us and in Us

Further, the Spirit also helps those who are not chosen prophets or apostles to understand divine revelation—a work of the Spirit called illumination (1 Cor. 2:14).[11] Without this work of the Spirit, we would not properly understand divine revelation, for "a natural person does not accept the things of the Spirit of God, for they are foolishness to him; and he cannot understand them, because they are spiritually discerned" (1 Cor. 2:14). To know God, then, we are dependent on the Holy Spirit in crucial ways! And this is why those seeking to understand the Scriptures should always seek the guidance of the Holy Spirit who inspired them.

> *To know God, then, we are dependent on the Holy Spirit in crucial ways!*

This same Holy Spirit further connects believers to God. The Spirit is the One "by whom" believers are "sealed for the day of redemption." Thus, Paul warns, "Do not grieve the Holy Spirit of God" (Eph. 4:30). As we have seen, this Spirit brings the spiritually dead back to spiritual life (Ezek. 36:26–27; 37:1–14). Believers are "born again" by the Spirit (John 3:7–8), a work known as regeneration. And the Spirit "dwells *in*" believers in a special way (known as indwelling, 1 Cor. 3:16; cf. Ezek. 11:19; 36:26–27; Rom. 8:9, 11; 1 Cor. 6:19; 2 Tim. 1:14).

Indeed, Jesus promised, "The one who believes in Me, as the Scripture said, 'From his innermost being will flow rivers of living water.' But this He said in reference to the Spirit, whom those who believed in Him were to receive; for the Spirit was not yet given, because Jesus was not yet glorified" (John 7:38–39). Later, at Pentecost and beyond, the Holy Spirit came with a special kind of power unleashed by Christ's victory over the powers of darkness at the cross and in the resurrection.

Accordingly, the apostles received a special baptism of the Holy Spirit at Pentecost as Jesus foretold, "John baptized with water, but you will be baptized with the Holy Spirit not many days from now" (Acts 1:5; cf. 2:4). And, of the wider body of believers, Paul writes, "by one Spirit we were all baptized into one body, whether Jews or Greeks, whether slaves or free, and we were all made to drink of one Spirit" (1 Cor. 12:13). The Spirit overcomes the ethnic and other boundaries that often divide people, uniting believers in the one body of Christ (a metaphor of the church). Indeed, baptized by the Spirit, believers are "built together into a dwelling of God in the Spirit" (Eph. 2:22). Baptism itself involves imagery that symbolizes spiritual death and rebirth—the old person enslaved by sin "dies" and is spiritually reborn in Christ, through the Spirit (see, e.g., Rom. 8:1–11). Without the Holy Spirit, we would be dead in our sins, cut off from God, but by the Holy Spirit, God abides *with us* and dwells in us (e.g., John 14:17).

Indeed, through the Spirit's regenerating work, we are adopted into God's very family as the (spiritual) children of God. As Paul explains, "all who are being led by the Spirit of God, these are sons and daughters of God," for "you have received a spirit of adoption as sons and daughters by which we cry out, 'Abba! Father!' The Spirit Himself testifies with our spirit that we are children of God, and if children, heirs also, heirs of God and fellow heirs with Christ, if indeed we suffer with Him so that we may also be glorified with Him" (Rom. 8:14–17). Indeed, Paul explains further: "Because you are sons, God has sent the Spirit of His Son into our hearts, crying out, 'Abba! Father!'" (Gal. 4:6).

Closely connected with this, the Spirit actively works to make believers holy—that is, to sanctify believers. The process of sanctification refers to the growth of believers in holiness and love, believers chosen "for salvation through sanctification by the Spirit and faith in the truth" (2 Thess. 2:13). Here, faith and obedience go together, for we are told that God has given "the Holy Spirit . . . to those who obey Him" (Acts 5:32).

Without the Holy Spirit's work, we would remain enslaved to sin and death, but the Holy Spirit liberates us from sin and evil for "where the Spirit of the Lord is, there is freedom" (2 Cor. 3:17). The Holy Spirit brings liberty to humans, who otherwise would be dead in their sins and captive to the enemy. In these and other depictions of the Holy Spirit's activity, we begin to get a picture of just how important the Holy Spirit's work is for our salvation.

Without the Holy Spirit's work, we would be hopeless. We are weak, but the Holy Spirit "helps our weakness; for we do not know what to pray for as we should, but the Spirit Himself intercedes for us with groanings too deep for words" (Rom. 8:26).

Without the Spirit's work, we would also be loveless and joyless. We only love in the first place because God first loves us (1 John 4:19), and by the Spirit's work humans are enabled to love. Indeed, "the fruit of the Spirit is love, joy, peace, patience, kindness, goodness, faithfulness, gentleness, self-control" (Gal. 5:22–23). Paul writes further: "If we live by the Spirit, let us also be guided by the Spirit," which involves living according to love (Gal. 5:25, NRSVue). Finally, Paul adds, "the one who sows to the Spirit will reap eternal life from the Spirit. Let's not become discouraged in doing good, for in due time we will reap, if we do not become weary," so "let's do good to all people" (Gal. 6:8–10). While humans (since the Fall) are naturally selfish, the work of the Holy Spirit spreads love in us, "the love of God has been poured out within our hearts through the Holy Spirit who was given to us" (Rom. 5:5). What could be better? What could be more important?

Without the Spirit's work, we would be destitute, but the Spirit gives special gifts to build up His people and advance God's mission. As seen earlier, the Spirit gave chosen people gifts in the Old Testament (see, e.g., Exod. 31:1–5; 35:30–36:1; Num. 11:25). In the New Testament church, further, "there are varieties of gifts, but the same Spirit" and "to each one is given the manifestation of the Spirit for the common good. For to one is given the word of wisdom through the Spirit, and to another the word of knowledge according to the same Spirit; to another faith by the same Spirit, and to another gifts of healing by the one Spirit, and to another the effecting of miracles, and to another prophecy, and to another the distinguishing of spirits, to another various kinds of tongues, and to another the interpretation of tongues. But one and the same Spirit works all these things, distributing to each one individually just as He wills" (1 Cor. 12:4, 7–11; see, e.g., Rom. 12:6–8; 1 Cor. 12:28–31; Eph. 4:11–13; 1 Pet. 4:10–11). These spiritual gifts are discussed further in chapter 17.

For now, it is crucial to note that the Spirit's work is not only important for the lives of individual believers but also corporately in the church, the fellowship of believers. The most crucial elements of the Christian life, individually and corporately, depend on the work of the Holy Spirit for us and in us, which is itself inseparably linked to the work of Christ for us and in us.

Among other works, then:

- The Holy Spirit was active at creation, moving over the waters (Gen. 1:2).
- The Holy Spirit is active in re-creation, bringing to life the dead (see Ezek. 37; cf. John 3:7–8).
- The Holy Spirit dwelled in the people's midst and gave rest to the people (Isa. 63:11, 14).
- The Holy Spirit was grieved by human rebellion (Isa. 63:10).[12]
- The Holy Spirit testifies of the truth (John 15:26) and teaches (Neh. 9:20 Luke 12:13; cf. John 14:26).
- The Holy Spirit glorifies the Son (John 16:14; cf. 15:26–27; Acts 2:33–36; 5:31–32).
- The Holy Spirit speaks through the prophets (Zech. 7:12), revealing God's messages and inspiring the prophets and the apostles

to speak and write the word of God (1 Cor. 2:11–14; 2 Tim. 3:16; 2 Pet. 1:21).
- The Holy Spirit convicts of sin (John 16:8), regenerates believers so they are "born again" (John 3:7–8), transforms hearts (Titus 3:5; cf. 2 Cor. 3:18), and sanctifies believers (2 Thess. 2:13).
- The Holy Spirit baptizes believers into one body (1 Cor. 12:13), transcending ethnic and other barriers, and in this and other ways, brings forth unity in the church.[13]
- The Holy Spirit dwells in (indwells) believers in a special way (e.g., John 7:38–39; 1 Cor. 3:16; 6:19–20; cf. Ezek. 11:19–20; 36:26).
- Through the work of the Holy Spirit, we can be adopted into God's family as children of God (Rom. 8:14–17).
- The Holy Spirit brings liberty to humans, who otherwise would be dead in our sins and captive to the enemy (see 2 Cor. 3:17).
- The Holy Spirit helps our weaknesses and intercedes for us (Rom. 8:26).
- The Holy Spirit brings the fruits of the Spirit into human lives (Gal. 5:22–25).
- The Holy Spirit pours the love of God out within our hearts (Rom. 5:5).
- The Holy Spirit gives spiritual gifts to whomever He wills in order to build up His people and advance His mission (1 Cor. 12:7–11)

The Divinity and Distinct Personhood of the Holy Spirit

The story and the works of the Holy Spirit reveal that the Holy Spirit is a person *distinct from* the Father and the Son, yet *united with* the Father and the Son. Indeed, close attention to the story and works of the Holy Spirit reveals that the Holy Spirit is a divine person; a person who *is* God, but is distinct from the Father and from the Son. Only a (fully) divine person could accomplish the works of the Holy Spirit.

The Holy Spirit is a person distinct from the Father and the Son, yet united with the Father and the Son.

We will return to the issue of the Holy Spirit's divinity later. First, we will focus on the biblical warrant for the conclusion that the Holy Spirit is a person who is distinct from the Father and the Son.

Competing Theories in Christian Theology: The Nature of the Holy Spirit

The most prominent controversies over the nature of the Holy Spirit have revolved around whether the Spirit is truly divine and whether the Spirit is a distinct person, both of which Christians generally affirm.

Regarding the former, some have claimed that the Holy Spirit is less than truly divine. One form of this view is known as the Pneumatomachian heresy (i.e., Macedonianism), a fourth-century view that claimed the Holy Spirit was created and, thus, by nature, subordinate to the Father and the Son. Others have thought the Holy Spirit was not created but emanated or otherwise proceeded from the Father and/or the Son at some point in the past such that the Holy Spirit is not eternal. Still others have thought the Holy Spirit is divine but eternally subordinate to the Father and the Son (see chapter 6). The Nicene-Constantinopolitan view, in contrast, holds that the Spirit eternally proceeds from the Father (and perhaps the Son) but is not by nature subordinate to the Father or the Son. This eternal procession view, which many believe does not have sufficient biblical warrant, is further discussed in chapter 6, including some reasons why Adventists typically do not affirm this doctrine.[14]

Regarding the personality of the Holy Spirit, some have claimed the Spirit is not a person at all, but merely a power or force. Others have claimed the Holy Spirit is a person, but not a *distinct* person, with some claiming the Holy Spirit is the person (or part of the person) of the Father and/or the Son (see the discussion of this further below).

An Adventist approach to these issues is offered below, affirming that the Holy Spirit is truly divine and a distinct person.[15]

The Personhood of the Holy Spirit

Jesus warned His followers that persecution would come. But He assured them they would not be alone. They will "bring you before the synagogues and the officials and the authorities," Jesus foretold, but "do not worry about how or what you are to speak in your defense, or what you are to say; for the Holy Spirit will teach you in that very hour what you ought to say" (Luke 12:11–12).

This not only highlights one of the ways God is *with us* in the Spirit, but this also exhibits one of the many *personal* characteristics attributed to the Holy Spirit that indicate the *personhood* of the Spirit (in this case, teaching).

Before proceeding, we need to clarify what it means and does *not* mean to be a "person." Regarding the latter, many have difficulty thinking of the Holy Spirit as a person because when they hear the word "person," they think of a *human* person with all the natural and physical limitations that go along with being a mere human. However, one can be a "person" without having the natural and physical limitations of *mere* humans. In the context of this discussion, a person is one who possesses *personal* attributes or capacities such as self-consciousness, reason, will, and love. Given that God possesses these capacities that only persons possess, God is personal. But God does not have the natural or physical limitations that humans have. As Jesus explained to the Samaritan woman at the well, God is not restricted to particular locations in the way that mere humans are because "God is spirit [*pneuma*]" (John 4:24).

To be a person, then, does not require that one is a *human* person or that one is physically limited in the way that humans are. Not only is God personal, but the celestial creatures Scripture identifies as angels are "persons," yet not *human* persons. This includes the fallen angels, which Scripture often calls demons or "unclean spirits." Such unclean spirits can enter into humans (indeed, many spirits can enter a single human), depart from humans, and also enter into animals (see, e.g., Mark 5:1–13; 9:17–29). Obviously, then, they are not limited in the natural and physical ways that mere humans are limited. Yet, though different from humans in numerous ways, angels (fallen or unfallen) are nonetheless "persons" (in the sense defined above). Accordingly, "persons" need not be physically constituted (cf. Luke 24:39) or limited in the same ways mere human persons are.

Even more so, the Holy Spirit is very different from human persons. But, according to Scripture, the Holy Spirit is a person. However, unlike all creaturely persons such as humans and angels, the Holy Spirit is uncreated and eternal and (as we shall see later) possesses other attributes that only God possesses. In countless ways, then, the Holy Spirit is different from creaturely persons because the Holy Spirit is a *divine* person (more on this later).

Just what does it mean, then, to be a person? Again, in the context of this discussion, a person is one who possesses *personal* attributes or capacities, defined as attributes or capacities that persons possess but mere powers or forces do not possess (such as self-consciousness, reason, will, and love). To be self-conscious is to be aware of oneself as an individual self, distinct from other selves (such that one thinks or refers to oneself as "I"). Whereas mere forces or powers do not possess the capacity for self-consciousness, persons do. Likewise, whereas a mere force does not have a faculty of reason or will or capacity to love, persons do.[16] If the Holy Spirit has *personal* attributes such as these, then the Holy Spirit is a person.

Given this understanding of personhood, we have already seen considerable evidence of the personhood of the Holy Spirit. Many of the actions and works of the Spirit depicted throughout Scripture are *personal* actions that involve distinctly *personal* attributes.

For example, the Holy Spirit:

- shares a name with the Father and Son (Matt. 28:19)
- teaches (Luke 12:12; cf. Neh. 9:20; John 14:26)
- testifies or bears witness (John 15:26; cf. Rom. 8:16)
- can be lied to and tested (Acts 5:3–4, 9)
- speaks (Acts 8:29; cf. Ezek. 2:2; Acts 10:19–20; 28:25; 1 Tim. 4:1; Heb. 3:7)
- admonishes (Neh. 9:30)
- leads and guides (Ps. 143:10; Acts 8:29)
- calls to ministry and sends out (Acts 13:2–4)
- forbids or allows and commands (Acts 8:29; 10:19–20; 16:6–7)
- intercedes (Rom. 8:26–27; cf. 15:16; Titus 3:5)
- reveals, searches, and knows the thoughts of God (1 Cor. 2:10–11)
- gives spiritual gifts to whom He *wills*—indicating the Holy Spirit has a will (1 Cor. 12:11; cf. Exod. 31:3; Acts 20:28; Rom. 8:27)
- can be "grieved" (Eph. 4:30; cf. Isa. 63:10; Mic. 2:7; Heb. 3:7–10; 10:29)[17]

These and other instances depict the Holy Spirit as performing actions only persons perform—*personal* actions that involve distinctly *personal* attributes. A mere force or power cannot know the thoughts of God (requiring reason), cannot will to give spiritual gifts to particular persons (requiring will), and cannot be grieved (requiring self-consciousness). Only a person could know, will, and be grieved—and, for that matter, teach, intercede, and testify.[18] The many kinds of distinctly personal actions attributed to the Holy Spirit throughout Scripture have long been recognized by Christians as conclusive evidence regarding the personhood of the Holy Spirit, going back to the early centuries of Christian thought.[19]

Scripture, then, depicts the Holy Spirit as possessing *personal* attributes, which means Scripture identifies the Holy Spirit as a person. This should affect the way we think of and relate to the Holy Spirit. As a person, the Holy Spirit personally works in our lives, willing and working good for us and in us, rather than a mere power that we might think we could *use* or *manipulate.*

The Distinctness of the Holy Spirit

"When the Helper comes," Jesus told His disciples, "whom I will send to you from the Father, namely, the Spirit of truth who comes from the Father, He will testify about Me" (John 15:26). This is one of many instances that identify the Spirit as distinct from both the Son and the Father. Here, the Spirit is sent by the Son and proceeds from the Father, and is thus distinct from both (see the entire discourse in John 14–16 in this regard).

Some, however, have claimed the Holy Spirit is the same person (or part thereof) as the Father or the Son, pointing to phrases like the "Spirit of God" (e.g., Rom. 8:9; Eph. 4:30), the "Spirit of your Father" (Matt. 10:20; cf. Mark 13:11), the "Spirit of Jesus" (e.g., Acts 16:7), and the "Spirit of Christ" (Rom. 8:9; 1 Pet. 1:11).

Such phrases, however, do not indicate that the Spirit is the same person as the Father or the Son. Interpreting such phrases that way would contradict the way the Father, Son, and Spirit are distinguished from one another in Scripture. In this regard, Romans 8:9–11 refers to the same Spirit as "the Spirit of God," "the Spirit of Christ," and "the Spirit of Him who raised Jesus from the dead." Yet, if the phrase "Spirit of Christ" here meant the Spirit is the same person as Christ and "Spirit of Him who raised Jesus from the dead" here meant the Spirit is the same person as the Father, then it would follow that Christ and the Father are the same person. But it is clear throughout Scripture that the Father and the Son are not the same person.

Why, then, is the Holy Spirit called, for example, the "Spirit of Christ" and the "Spirit of your Father"? In short, this is because the Father, Son, and Spirit are united together in special relationship (as one God, see chapter 6).

Consider the following language: My wife is the *spouse of* John, and I am the *spouse of* Brenda. Such language refers to a special kind of relationship and union my wife and I share. Similarly, phrases like "Spirit of Christ" and "Spirit of your Father" refer to the special relationship and union between the Spirit, Christ, and the Father. I do not mean to suggest that I am related to my wife in the way the Spirit is related to Christ and the Father. Certainly not! The union of the Spirit, Son, and Father is unique, far greater and different from any creaturely relationship (see chapter 6).

Even as the Father is the Father *of the* Son and the Son is the Son *of the* Father, the Holy Spirit is the Spirit *of the* Son and the Spirit *of the* Father. In other words, each of the persons is related to and belongs to the others in a special manner. Such language points to the special relationship (the union) of the Father, Son, and Spirit (as one God), which is consistent with the distinctness of the Father, Son, and Spirit. That is, overlapping references to Father, Son, and Spirit point to the unity of Father, Son, and Spirit—the one God, while references to the distinctness of the Father, Son, and Spirit emphasize they are distinct *persons*. This will be clarified further when we discuss the Trinity doctrine in the following chapter.

For now, it is evident from the way Scripture portrays the Holy Spirit as distinct from the Father and Son that the Spirit cannot be the same person as the Father or Son (or merely a part or aspect thereof). For example, the story of Christ's baptism portrays the Father, the Son, and the Holy Spirit as distinct agents who perform distinct actions at the baptism of Jesus. The Father speaks, the Spirit descends, and the Son is baptized (Luke 3:21–22).

Many other biblical instances also distinguish the Spirit from the Father and the Son. Jesus identified the Holy Spirit as "*another* Helper" distinct from Himself (John 14:16, emphasis mine), one who would "teach" the apostles further (John 14:26; cf. Luke 12:12) and testify about Christ (John 15:26; cf. 16:7–8, 13). The Holy Spirit, then, is not Christ, but *another* who would testify about Christ.[20]

Specifically, Jesus taught His followers, "the Holy Spirit whom the Father will send in My name, He will teach you all things, and remind you of all that I said to you" (John 14:26).[21] Here, the Holy Spirit is sent by the Father in the name of Jesus. Thus, the Spirit is not the Father or Jesus.

Then, one chapter later, Jesus added, "When the Helper comes, whom I will send to you from the Father, namely, the Spirit of truth who comes from the Father, He will testify about Me" (John 15:26). Here, the Holy Spirit is sent *by* the Son *from* the Father to testify *about* the Son. Thus, the Spirit cannot be the Son or the Father.[22] Accordingly, Jesus explained, when "the Spirit of truth, comes, He will guide you into all the truth; for He will not speak on His own, but whatever He hears, He will speak; and He will disclose to you what is to come" (John 16:13).

This distinction between persons is further apparent when Jesus says that one who "speaks a word against" Jesus can be "forgiven ... but whoever speaks against the Holy Spirit, it shall not be forgiven him, either in this age or in the age to come" (Matt. 12:32).

In these and other passages, Scripture explicitly identifies the Spirit as a person distinct from the Father and the Son. Yet, as shall be seen in the next section, the Spirit is (fully) divine.

The Divinity of the Holy Spirit

They lied. Ananias and Sapphira promised an offering to God, the proceeds from the sale of land they owned. But then, they decided to keep some of the proceeds, while pretending they gave all. Who would know?

Peter knew. "Ananias," Peter said, "why has Satan filled your heart to lie to the Holy Spirit and to keep back some of the proceeds of the land? While it remained unsold, did it not remain your own? And after it was sold, was it not under your control? Why is it that you have conceived this deed in your heart? You have not lied to men, but to God" (Acts 5:3–4).

Notice that in this story, Peter first says Ananias lied "to the Holy Spirit." But then, *in parallel* he tells Ananias, "You have not lied to men, but to God." Here, the parallelism indicates that lying to the Holy Spirit equals lying to God, which indicates the Holy Spirit is God. Thus, Scripture refers to the Holy Spirit as God.[23]

The conclusion that the Holy Spirit is God is also apparent from the works of the Holy Spirit. For example, only a (fully) divine person could effectively take the place of Jesus *with* the apostles after Christ's ascension (e.g., John 14:16).[24] Likewise, only one who is *divine* could pour the love of God into human hearts (Rom. 5:5) and only one who is *divine* could indwell humans such that humans in the church are a temple of God (1 Cor. 3:16–17; 6:19–20). And only a *divine* person could share a singular name with the Father and Son, the name in which Christ's followers are baptized (Matt. 28:19).

Here, it is crucial to remember that "there is none like" God (1 Chron. 17:20) and that there is no such thing as *partial* divinity. One is either God or not; one is either divine or not divine. If one is divine, then one is God, the supreme One who alone possesses uniquely divine attributes (see the discussion in the previous chapter).

And Scripture repeatedly teaches that the Holy Spirit possesses uniquely divine attributes (attributes that only God possesses). If this is so (as shall be articulated below), then Scripture teaches that the Holy Spirit is divine. Specifically, Scripture attributes to the Holy Spirit uniquely divine attributes such as eternity, omniscience, and omnipresence. Only God is eternal, but Scripture indicates the Holy Spirit is eternal by referring to the Spirit as "the eternal Spirit" (Heb. 9:14). Only God is all-knowing (omniscient), but Scripture teaches the Holy Spirit is all-knowing by declaring the Holy Spirit "knows" and "searches all things, even the depths of God" (1 Cor. 2:10–11). Only God can be present everywhere (omnipresent), but Scripture teaches the Holy Spirit would be present *"with"* Christ's followers "forever," with them wherever they would go (John 14:16; cf. Ps. 139:7), even as they dispersed to preach the gospel to the ends of the earth.

> **Scripture attributes to the Holy Spirit uniquely divine attributes such as eternity, omniscience, and omnipresence.**

Moreover, the New Testament quotes words attributed to God in the Old Testament and attributes them to the Holy Spirit. For instance, in Isaiah 6:8-10, the Lord declares a specific message to Isaiah to deliver to the people. But, in Acts 28:25, just before quoting this message, Paul says, "The Holy Spirit rightly spoke through Isaiah the prophet to your fathers" (Acts 28:25). The one who spoke to Isaiah and was identified as the Lord in Isaiah 6 is thus identified as the Holy Spirit in Acts 28:25. This complements Paul's words in 2 Corinthians 3:17 when he states, "the Lord is the Spirit."

Likewise, Hebrews 3:7 introduces a quotation spoken by the voice of God in Psalm 95:7-11 by saying, "as the Holy Spirit says." Not only does Hebrews 3 thereby identify the Holy Spirit as God, but careful attention to the quoted passage itself further illuminates the person and work of the Holy Spirit. The passage speaks of times the Israelites in the wilderness hardened their hearts against God. With respect to these, the Holy Spirit says, "YOUR FATHERS PUT ME TO THE TEST, AND SAW MY WORKS FOR FORTY YEARS. THEREFORE I WAS ANGRY WITH THIS GENERATION" (Heb. 3:9-10; cf. Exod. 16:7; Ps. 95:9-10).

Notice, here, that the Holy Spirit is not only identified as the one who spoke the words the Old Testament attributes to God but here uses personal terminology of self-consciousness—"your Fathers put *Me* to the test" and "saw *My* works" (cf. Ezek. 2:2-4). Here, then, is evidence of not only the divinity of the Holy Spirit, but also evidence of the distinct personhood of the Spirit.

In these passages and others, Scripture repeatedly teaches that the Holy Spirit is a divine person, distinct from the Father and the Son, while also being united with the Father and the Son.

Conclusion: Why Does It Matter?

You already know the Holy Spirit, even if you have not realized you do. If you have ever been convicted of sin, you have experienced the work of the Spirit. If you have ever felt the special presence of God, you have felt the work of the Spirit. If you have ever had the experience of having your mind illuminated, you have experienced the work of the Spirit. If you have love and kindness, you have known the Spirit's work in your life. The Spirit knows you better than you know yourself, and if you are in Christ by faith, the Spirit dwells in you, and you are a temple of God.

This is amazing news, rooted in the identity of the Holy Spirit. This chapter introduced the nature and works of the Holy Spirit, highlighting that the Holy Spirit is (fully) God. The Holy Spirit is not a mere force or power, but a person (possessing self-consciousness, reason, will, and love) who thus can (among other things) be grieved by evil, bear witness of Christ, intercede for us, pour God's love into our hearts, and will to give spiritual gifts to whomever He will.

Not only does Scripture identify the Holy Spirit as a "person," Scripture portrays the Father, the Son, and the Holy Spirit as *distinct* persons. Because the Holy Spirit is (fully) God and a person *distinct* from the Father and the Son, the Spirit can do the works He does for us, being sent by the Father and the Son to (among other things) testify about the Son, help our weaknesses and intercede for us, bring liberty to those enslaved by sin, pour the love of God in our hearts, and sanctify those who believe in Christ.

As we have seen, the Holy Spirit's works are essential to our lives, *individually and collectively*. Thus, David prayed, "Do not cast me away from Your presence, and do not take Your Holy Spirit from me" (Ps. 51:11). The very possibility that we might have eternal life hinges on the Spirit's work. As Christ proclaimed, in order to enter the kingdom of heaven, we must be born again—that is, born of the Spirit.

Do you wish to be filled with the Holy Spirit? If so, believe in Christ and invite God into your heart. If you accept Christ by faith, the Spirit will dwell in you. As Jesus proclaimed, "If anyone is thirsty, let him come to Me and drink. The one who believes in Me, as the Scripture said, 'From his innermost being will flow rivers of living water.' But this He said in reference to the Spirit, whom those who believed in Him were to receive" (John 7:37–39).

This understanding of who the Spirit is and the Spirit's work for us and in us is bound up with the biblical doctrine of the Trinity, to which we turn in the next chapter. Before turning to that chapter, however, I invite you to read John 14–16 and reflect on Christ's promise of the Spirit and how we can abide with God and in the love of God even now.

Questions for Reflection

1. What did you find most significant about the story and works of the Holy Spirit? How crucial is the Holy Spirit in people's lives today? Which works of the Holy Spirit are most relevant to your spiritual life?
2. How did the Holy Spirit work in the ministry of Jesus? How does the Holy Spirit work in the life of the church? How is this similar and different from the way the Spirit worked in the Old Testament?
3. Why is the divinity of the Holy Spirit important? What difference does it make to your life that the Holy Spirit is truly divine?
4. Why is it important to understand that the Holy Spirit is a distinct person? Why do you think this is so often misunderstood? How would you explain what it means for the Spirit to be a "person"?
5. Jesus promised that if one believes in Him, out of that person "will flow rivers of living water" (speaking of the Spirit, John 7:38–39). What does this mean to you personally?
6. You can ask of God to be filled with the Holy Spirit even now. Do you wish to be filled with the Holy Spirit? If so, simply believe in Jesus and pray to God with faith, asking God to fill you with the Holy Spirit. He will hear your prayer.
7. You can enter into the love relationship of the Trinity even now. Do you wish to do so? As Christ promised, you can abide with the Father, Son, and Spirit by faith. Simply ask God to give you His love—to evoke in your heart love for Him and love for others. He will do so, and you will be filled with God's love to share.

For Further Reading

Adventist Perspectives:

Canale, Fernando. "Doctrine of God." In *Handbook of Seventh-day Adventist Theology*. Edited by Raoul Dederen. Hagerstown, MD: Review and Herald, 2000.

Clouzet, Ron. *Adventism's Greatest Need: The Outpouring of the Holy Spirit*. Nampa, ID: Pacific Press, 2011.

Davidson, Jo Ann. "A Power or Person: The Nature of the Holy Spirit." *Journal of the Adventist Theological Society* 27, no. 1 (2016): 24–36.

Donkor, Kwabena. *God in 3 Persons—In Theology*. Biblical Research Institute Release, no. 9. Silver Spring, MD: Biblical Research Institute, 2015.

Froom, Le Roy E. *Coming of the Comforter: The Holy Spirit, the Secret of a Successful Christian Life*. Hagerstown, MD. Review and Herald, 1956.

Gulley, Norman R. *Systematic Theology: God as Trinity*. Berrien Springs, MI: Andrews University Press, 2011.

Hasel, Frank M. "The Holy Spirit: His Divinity and Personality." In *Biblical and Theological Studies on the Trinity*. Edited by Paul Petersen and Rob McIver. Cooranbong, NSW, Australia: Avondale Academic Press, 2014.

McVay, John K. "The Holy Spirit in the New Testament." *Journal of the Adventist Theological Society* 29, no. 1–2 (2018): 156–91.

Moskala, Jiří. "The Holy Spirit in the Hebrew Scriptures." *Journal of the Adventist Theological Society* 24, no. 2 (2013): 18–58.

Siqueira, Reinaldo and Alberto R. Timm, eds. *Pneumatology: The Person and the Work of the Holy Spirit*. Biblical Research Institute (forthcoming).

White, Ellen G. *The Acts of the Apostles*. Mountain View, CA: Pacific Press, 1911.

See also the resources on the Biblical Research Institute website: https://adventistbiblicalresearch.org/materials/.

Other Christian Perspectives:

Bruner, Frederick Dale. *A Theology of the Holy Spirit: The Pentecostal Experience and the New Testament Witness*, 2nd ed. Grand Rapids, MI: Eerdmans, 1987.

Cole, Graham A. *He Who Gives Life: The Doctrine of the Holy Spirit*. Wheaton, IL: Crossway, 2007.

Kärkkäinen, Veli-Matti. *The Holy Spirit: A Guide to Christian Theology*. Louisville, KY: Westminster John Knox, 2012.

Holmes, Christopher R. J. *The Holy Spirit*. New Studies in Dogmatics. Grand Rapids, MI: Zondervan, 2015.

Jones, Beth Felker. *God the Spirit: Introducing Pneumatology in Wesleyan and Ecumenical Perspective.* Eugene, OR: Cascade, 2014.

——— and Jeffrey W. Barbeau, eds. *Spirit of God: Christian Renewal in the Community of Faith.* Downers Grove, IL: IVP Academic, 2015.

Keener, Craig. *Gift and Giver: The Holy Spirit for Today.* Grand Rapids, MI: Baker Academic, 2020.

Pinnock, Clark. *Flame of Love: A Theology of the Holy Spirit.* Downers Grove, IL: IVP Academic, 1996.

Thiselton, Anthony C. *A Shorter Guide to the Holy Spirit.* Grand Rapids, MI: Eerdmans, 2016.

Yong, Amos. *Who is the Holy Spirit? A Walk with the Apostles.* Brewster, MA: Paraclete Press, 2011.

6

FATHER, SON, AND HOLY SPIRIT: THE TRINITY OF LOVE

"I have the need to be baptized by You, and yet You are coming to me?" John protested when Jesus came to be baptized.

"Allow it at this time," Jesus answered, "for in this way it is fitting for us to fulfill all righteousness" (Matt. 3:14–15).

So John baptized Jesus, and while Jesus "was praying, heaven was opened, and the Holy Spirit descended upon Him in bodily form like a dove, and a voice came from heaven: 'You are My beloved Son, in You I am well pleased'" (Luke 3:21–22; cf. Matt. 3:16–17; Mark 1:9–11). Here, Jesus (the Son), the Holy Spirit, and the Father are each active. The Son is baptized, the Spirit descends, and the Father speaks.

Scripture identifies the Son, the Spirit, and the Father as God. Yet, Scripture also teaches that there is only one God (Deut. 6:5; John 5:44; James 2:19). How can this be? How can the Son, Spirit, and Father be God if there is only one God? This is one of many questions often raised about the Trinity doctrine; the teaching that there is only one God *and* God is three persons—Father, Son, and Spirit.

Another prominent question is whether the Trinity doctrine is biblical. Many who claim it is not mean either that the word "Trinity" is not in the Bible or the nuances of some particular articulation of the Trinity doctrine are not taught by Scripture.

The word "Trinity" does not appear in Scripture, but this does not present a special problem for the Trinity doctrine because many other terms and phrases Christians affirm are not found in Scripture (e.g., incarnation, millennium, and theodicy). The crucial question is not whether a particular term is found in the Bible but whether the concept the term represents is *taught by* the Bible. If the concept of the Trinity is taught by Scripture, then the Trinity is biblical.

Yet, here it is crucial to recognize that there are various nuanced kinds of Trinity doctrines in Christian theology (more on this later), not all of which are taught by Scripture. So, which Trinity doctrine are we talking about? In this chapter, I will focus on what I call the *core* Trinity doctrine—the doctrine that there is only one God *and* God is three distinct, (fully) divine persons. And we will see that this core Trinity doctrine is taught by Scripture.

Beyond the core doctrine, however, a number of other questions arise, particularly regarding how to understand the relations between the Father, Son, and Spirit within the Trinity.

Before briefly addressing such questions, this chapter focuses on the core Trinity doctrine, particularly the two questions:

- Is the core Trinity doctrine biblically warranted?
- Is the core Trinity doctrine coherent?

First, however, we turn to an introduction of the story of the Trinity, which reveals that God is love within the Trinity—prior to and apart from creation—and that God is love in relation to creation.

The Story of the Father, Son, and Spirit— the Trinity of Love

He was in agony. His sweat was like drops of blood. Very soon, Jesus would go to the cross and die for the world's sins, but already the world's sins weighed on His shoulders. He was "deeply grieved," even "to the point of death" (Matt. 26:38). In His agony, He prayed, "Father, if You are willing, remove this cup from Me; yet not My will, but Yours be done" (Luke 22:42; cf. Matt. 26:36–42).

In obedience and submission to the Father's will, the Son willingly gave Himself to die on the cross for all humans. Indeed, Jesus declared, "For this reason the Father loves Me, because I lay down My life so that I may take it back. No one has taken it away from Me, but I lay it down on My own. I have authority to lay it down, and I have authority to take it back. This commandment I received from My Father" (John 10:17–18).

No one compelled Him. He was murdered under the authority of the Roman Empire, but this could take place only because Jesus gave Himself of His own will and in obedience to the Father's will. This was in accordance with the jointly willed plan of redemption, covenanted within the Trinity before creation (the covenant of redemption). This plan included the distinct roles the Father, Son, and Spirit would play in the story of redemption; each essential to saving the world from sin and evil and restoring God's intimate presence *with us*.

According to this plan, Christ "gave Himself for our sins so that He might rescue us from this present evil age, according to the will of our God and Father" (Gal. 1:4; cf. John 5:30; 6:38–40; 17:4–12). Indeed, the Son "loved" us and "gave Himself up for us" (Eph. 5:2; cf. Gal. 2:20), laying down His life for us of His own will, and according to the will of the Father (John 10:18).

That the Son would give Himself to save humanity, as the ultimate demonstration of God's love and righteousness, was central to the plan of redemption from *before* the foundation of the world (see Acts 2:23; 1 Pet. 1:20; Rev. 13:8). Scripture repeatedly calls this the "mystery" of the gospel, "God's wisdom in a mystery, the hidden wisdom which God predestined [that is, planned beforehand] before the ages to our glory" (1 Cor. 2:7; see also Rom. 16:25–25; Col. 1:26; 2 Tim. 1:9, Titus 1:2). This is "the plan of the mystery hidden for ages in God, who created all things," the "eternal purpose that he has carried out in Christ Jesus our Lord" (Eph. 3:9, 11, NRSVue; cf. Rom. 8:28–30; Eph. 1:4, 10–11; 2 Thess. 2:13; 2 Tim. 1:9; 1 Pet. 1:2).

Likewise, according to this plan, the Son was sent by the Father (John 5:36, 37; 6:44, 57; 8:16, 18; 10:36; 12:49; 1 John 4:14) and carried out His mission in obedience to the Father (e.g., John 14:31), acting only in accordance with the Father's will (e.g., John 5:30; 6:38; 8:28). Indeed, Jesus stated, "Truly, truly, I say to you, the Son can do nothing of Himself, unless it is something He sees the Father doing; for whatever the Father does, these things the Son also does in the same way" (John 5:19). Jesus acted voluntarily, of His own free will, yet always in accord with the Father's will.

> **Jesus acted voluntarily, of His own free will, yet always in accord with the Father's will.**

Christ shared glory and love relationship with the Father "before the world existed" (John 17:5, 24). Then, at the appointed time in the plan of redemption (Gal. 4:4), Christ willingly lowered and humbled Himself to become human and give Himself for humans (Phil. 2:5–8). Indeed, Christ's condescension was a voluntary lowering of Himself in the context of mutual (covenantal) love relationship. "For this reason the Father loves Me," Christ declared, "because I lay down My life so that I may take it back. No one has taken it away from Me, but I lay it down on My own. I have authority to lay it down, and I have authority to take it back" (John 10:17–18; Gal. 2:20; Eph. 5:2).

In the working out of this plan of redemption, not only does the Son lovingly obey the Father, but the Father also delegates to the Son within the context of love relationship, effectively "binding Himself to the results of Christ's salvific mission" (1 John 4:14; cf. 2 Cor. 5:19).[1] Indeed, Jesus states, the "Father loves the Son and has entrusted all things to His hand" (John 3:35; cf. 5:22–23; 13:3; 16:15). The Father Himself thereby "submits" to the Son relative to whatever He has "entrusted . . . to [the Son's] hand."

Eventually, the Son is re-elevated to His rightful throne—"the throne of God and of the Lamb" (Rev. 22:3), "highly exalted" with a "name which is above every name, so that at the name of Jesus EVERY KNEE WILL BOW, of those who are in heaven and on earth and under the earth, and that every tongue will confess that Jesus Christ is Lord, to the glory of God the Father" (Phil. 2:9–11; cf. Matt. 28:18; 1 Cor. 15:24–28; Eph. 1:20–23; Heb. 1:3–4).[2] Ultimately, as Christ Himself taught, "all will honor the Son just as they honor the Father" (John 5:23).

According to the plan of redemption, during His earthly ministry the Son operated in dependence and submission to the Holy Spirit. Christ was incarnated via the Spirit (Matt. 1:18–20; Luke 1:35), filled and anointed by the Spirit (Luke 4:1, 18; cf. Matt. 12:28; Acts 10:38), and driven into the wilderness by the Spirit (Mark 1:12; cf. Matt. 4:1; Luke 4:1). After defeating Satan's temptations in the wilderness, "Jesus returned to Galilee in the power of the Spirit" (Luke 4:14). Then, on the Sabbath, Jesus read from Isaiah 61:1–2 in the synagogue: "THE SPIRIT OF THE LORD IS UPON ME, BECAUSE HE ANOINTED ME TO BRING GOOD NEWS TO THE POOR. HE HAS SENT ME TO PROCLAIM RELEASE TO CAPTIVES, AND RECOVERY OF SIGHT TO THE BLIND, TO SET FREE THOSE WHO ARE OPPRESSED, TO PROCLAIM THE FAVORABLE YEAR OF THE LORD" (Luke 4:16–19). Then, Jesus declared, "Today this Scripture has been fulfilled in your hearing" (Luke 4:21), thus identifying Himself as the anointed one, the Messiah, "upon" whom was "the Spirit of the LORD."

After Christ's resurrection, however, the roles are somewhat reversed. Then, the Holy Spirit is sent by both the Father and the Son (e.g., John 14:26; 15:26) and operates in a *functionally* submissive role (cf. John 16:13) relative to the Father and Son.

Long before, the Father, Son, and Spirit were active in various ways throughout the Old Testament stories. Notably, the three appear in Isaiah 63, which refers to the great lovingkindness, goodness, and compassion of the Lord, who said of Israel, "Certainly they are My people, sons who will not deal falsely" (Isa. 63:8). This language of fatherhood is followed by the declaration, "He became their Savior. In all their distress He was distressed, and the angel of His presence saved them; in His love and in His mercy He redeemed them, and He lifted them and carried them all the days of old" (Isa. 63:8–9). Then, the passage recounts how the people "rebelled and grieved His Holy Spirit," the very "Spirit of the Lord" who "gave them rest" (Isa. 63:10, 14; cf. Eph. 4:30). These verses describe some of the redemptive works of:

- the Lord who speaks of Himself as the Father to Israel (His "sons"),
- the "angel of His presence," which we saw in the last chapter refers to the pre-incarnate Son, and
- "His Holy Spirit."

Not only here, but from the beginning to the end of the biblical story, the Father, Son, and Spirit work together to redeem creation and restore the intimate presence of God *with* us. The Father, Son, and Spirit were each active in the creation of the universe (see Gen. 1:1–2; John 1:1–3). And, from the time of creation onward, Scripture reveals the loving acts of the Father, Son, and Spirit *with us and for us*.

> *The Father, Son, and Spirit work together to redeem creation and restore the intimate presence of God with us.*

At every turn, the works of the Father, Son, and Spirit manifest that God is love. In love for us, the Son willingly gave Himself for us. And, in love for us, the Father, Son, and Spirit all willed this plan (cf. John 16:27). And, Paul writes, "the love of God has been poured out within our hearts through the Holy Spirit who was given to us" (Rom. 5:5).

In all, "God demonstrates His own love toward us, in that while we were still sinners, Christ died for us" (Rom. 5:8). While each play distinct roles in the plan of redemption, the loving work of redemption and reconciliation is the collaborative work of the Father, Son, and Spirit. God "reconciled us to Himself through Christ," and "God was in Christ reconciling the world to Himself" (2 Cor. 5:18–19). Altogether, the works of God—Father, Son, and Spirit—are aimed at restoring intimate love relationship between God and humans.

God not only loves creation, however. God is love. God was love. And God always will be love. Prior to and apart from creation, God *is* love. Before the world began, the persons of the Trinity were united in love relationship—the Trinity of love (see John 17:24). The Father loves the Son (John 3:35; 5:20; cf. Matt. 3:17), the Son loves the Father (John 14:31), and the Spirit shares in this love, glorifying the Son (John 16:14) and pouring the love of God out within our hearts (Rom. 5:5; cf. Rom. 15:30; Gal. 5:22).

The intimate love relationship that exists between the persons of the Trinity is one of indwelling, that is, abiding in one another. Jesus explains, "The words that I say to you I do not speak on My own, but the Father, as He remains in Me, does His works. Believe Me that I am in the Father and the Father is in Me" (John 14:10–11). And Jesus explains further to His followers, the Spirit "remains with you and will be in you" (John 14:17; cf. 14:20–21; 1 Cor. 3:16).

Amazingly, Christ's love for us mirrors the Father's love for Him. "Just as the Father has loved Me," Jesus explained, "I also have loved you; remain in My love" (John 15:9; cf. 15:4–7). Likewise, Jesus assured His followers, "the Father Himself loves you" (John 16:27). And Christ prayed to the Father that His followers "may be one, just as We are one; I in them and You in Me, that they may be perfected in unity, so that the world may know that You sent Me, and You loved them, just as You loved Me" (John 17:22–23). This Jesus prays not only for His first-generation disciples but "for those who believe in Me through their word, that they may all be one; just as You, Father, are in Me and I in You, that they also may be in Us" (John 17:20–21).

In response to God's love, then, humans can be united in love with God and with one another. Jesus promised, "I will ask the Father, and

He will give you another Helper, so that He may be with you forever; the Helper is the Spirit of truth" and "you know Him because He remains with you and will be in you" (John 14:16–17; cf. 1 John 2:27; 3:24). Further, Jesus explained, "The one who has My commandments and keeps them is the one who loves Me; and the one who loves Me will be loved by My Father, and I will love him and will reveal Myself to him" (John 14:21; cf. 16:27). Further, "If anyone loves Me, he will follow My word; and My Father will love him, and We will come to him and make Our dwelling with him" (John 14:23). Indeed, Jesus taught, "If you keep My commandments, you will remain in My love; just as I have kept My Father's commandments and remain in His love" (John 15:9–10; cf. 14:15; 15:14; 1 John 5:3).

As we will see later, God's commandments themselves express God's law of unselfish love (see chapter 14). In response to God's love, humans are to love God and love one another. Abiding in God's love, then, entails loving one another. "This is His commandment, that we believe in the name of His Son Jesus Christ, and love one another, just as He commanded us. The one who keeps His commandments remains in Him, and He in him. We know by this that He remains in us, by the Spirit whom He has given us" (1 John 3:23–24; cf. 4:13). Those who follow Christ by loving, then, are promised the Father, Son, and Spirit will abide with them and in them.

God is love (1 John 4:8, 16). It is no coincidence that Christ's followers are identified as those who love one another (John 13:34–35; 15:12, 17). As John writes: "Beloved, let's love one another; for love is from God, and everyone who loves has been born of God and knows God. The one who does not love does not know God, because God is love.... In this is love, not that we loved God, but that He loved us and sent His Son to be the propitiation for our sins. Beloved, if God so loved us, we also ought to love one another," and "if we love one another, God remains in us, and His love is perfected in us. By this we know that we remain in Him and He in us, because He has given to us of His Spirit. We have seen and testify that the Father has sent the Son to be the Savior of the world" (1 John 4:7–8, 10–14).

Prior and apart from the world, God is love within the Trinity. In relation to the world, God is love for us and with us. In all, "God is love, and the one who remains in love remains in God, and God remains in him" (1 John 4:16).

The Core Trinity Doctrine

The story of the Trinity is the story of love, unspeakably profound love manifest in the acts of the Father, Son, and Spirit to redeem and reconcile the world to God. The story of redemption is the story of the Trinity of love for us and with us.

As we will see later, this story only makes sense if the Father is God, the Son is God, and the Holy Spirit is God. That is, the story of redemption itself is bound up with the Trinity doctrine.

As noted earlier, the core Trinity doctrine teaches: There is only one God, and God is three distinct, fully divine persons.[3]

> *The core Trinity doctrine teaches: There is only one God, and God is three distinct, fully divine persons.*

This can be outlined in the following four tenets:

- There is only one God (the oneness of God).
- There is a *Trio* of Father, Son, and Holy Spirit (the threeness of God).
- The Father, Son, and Spirit are (fully) divine and therefore coequal and coeternal (the full divinity of the persons).
- The Father, Son, and Spirit are distinct persons. The Father is not the Son or Spirit, the Son is not the Father or Spirit, and the Spirit is not the Father or Son (the distinctness of the persons).

The core Trinity doctrine thus affirms God's oneness; God's threeness; the full divinity of Father, Son, and Spirit; and the distinct personhood of Father, Son, and Spirit.

The following four sections survey some of the biblical support for each of these four premises, which (taken together) amount to the core Trinity doctrine. If these four premises are biblically warranted, as I argue below that they are, then the core Trinity doctrine is biblically warranted.[4]

Competing Theories in Christian Theology: The Trinity

The core Trinity doctrine excludes a number of views that have historically been identified as heresies. The most prominent of these are:

- tritheism—the view that there are three gods (overemphasizing the threeness of God),
- modalism—the view that God is only one person who manifested Himself in three modes of appearance (overemphasizing the oneness of God), and
- subordinationism—the view that the Son and/or Spirit are, by nature (i.e., ontologically), less than or subordinate to the Father.

The Nicene-Constantinopolitan Trinity doctrine also excludes these but goes beyond the core Trinity doctrine to affirm some nuanced claims about relations within the Trinity. Specifically, the Nicene-Constantinopolitan doctrine is typically understood as affirming eternal relations of origin, the view that the Son is eternally generated or begotten by the Father (eternal generation) and the Spirit eternally proceeds from the Father and, perhaps, also from the Son (eternal procession).

When Christians refer to the Nicene doctrine, they often mean the creedal form that arose from the Council of Nicea (AD 325) and later significant expansions of that creed—traditionally attributed to the Council of Constantinople (AD 381), though "there is no certain account of the [Nicene-Constantinopolitan] creed itself until the Council of Chalcedon" (AD 451).[5]

The Council of Nicea roundly condemned Arianism, which claimed the Son was created by the Father at some point in time and thus is not of the same substance as the Father (*heteroousios* rather than *homoousios*). Whereas Arianism claimed "there was a time when he [the Son] was not," the Nicene-Constantinopolitan view affirms the Son originates from the Father as "begotten" but does so *eternally* such that there was never a time when the Son did not exist.[6]

Many who affirm the core Trinity doctrine, however, do not affirm the eternal relations of origin, believing the doctrines of eternal generation and eternal procession lack biblical warrant (discussed later in this chapter, including some reasons why Adventists typically do not affirm eternal relations of origin).

Scripture Teaches There Is Only One God

Scripture explicitly teaches there is only one God: "The LORD, He is God; there is no other besides Him" (Deut. 4:35; likewise, Deut. 4:39). Likewise,

Deuteronomy 6:4 adds, "The LORD is our God, the LORD is one!" (cf. Gen. 2:24).[7] 2 Samuel 7:22 further states: "You are great, Lord GOD; for there is no one like You, and there is no God except You" (cf. 1 Chron. 17:20).

Elsewhere, God Himself declares, "Before Me there was no God formed, and there will be none after Me" (Isa. 43:10; cf. 42:8). And "I am the LORD, and there is no one else; there is no God except Me" (Isa. 45:5; cf. 2 Kings 19:19; Ps. 83:18; 86:10; Isa. 37:20; 44:6-7).

Further, Scripture repeatedly emphasizes that God is unique and strictly forbids the worship of anyone other than the one true God (Exod. 34:14; cf. Deut. 4:39; 5:7-9; Matt. 4:10; Luke 4:8; Rev. 19:10). Jesus Himself affirmingly quoted Deuteronomy 6:4, "THE LORD IS OUR GOD, THE LORD IS ONE" (Mark 12:29; cf. 12:32) and referred to "the one and only God" (John 5:44).

James likewise explicitly affirms the oneness of God: "You believe that God is one. You do well; the demons also believe, and shudder" (James 2:19). Similarly, Paul writes, "there is no God but one" (1 Cor. 8:4; cf. 1 Tim. 1:17). In these and other texts, Scripture expressly teaches there is only one God.

Scripture Refers to a Trio of Father, Son, and Holy Spirit

"Go, therefore, and make disciples of all the nations," Jesus commanded, "baptizing them in the name of the Father and the Son and the Holy Spirit" (Matt. 28:19). Strangely, the word "name" here is singular, which many believe indicates the unity of Father, Son, and Holy Spirit.[8]

In this and other passages, Scripture repeatedly refers to the Trio of Father, Son, and Holy Spirit.[9] As we have seen, the Spirit (descending like a dove), Father (speaking from heaven), and the Son (being baptized) are depicted at Christ's baptism (Matt. 3:16-17). Further, John 14-16 includes many descriptions of the interrelationship of Father, Son, and Spirit. Conversely, something like a counterfeit "Trinity" (the Dragon, Sea Beast, and Earth Beast) that imitates and seeks to replace the Father, Son, and Spirit is highlighted in Revelation 12-13 (see chapter 18).[10]

Many Trinitarian references appear elsewhere. Indeed, there are at least seventy-five passages in the New Testament in which all three persons of the Trinity are mentioned within a range of one to five verses.[11] For example, 2 Corinthians 13:14 states: "The grace of the Lord Jesus Christ, and the love of God, and the fellowship of the Holy Spirit, be with you all." Ephesians 4:4–6 adds: "There is one body and one Spirit, just as you also were called in one hope of your calling; one Lord, one faith, one baptism, one God and Father of all." Likewise, 1 Corinthians 12:4–6 teaches, "there are varieties of gifts, but the same Spirit. And there are varieties of ministries, and the same Lord. There are varieties of effects, but the same God who works all things in all persons."[12]

The Old Testament also provides evidence regarding the Trinity. There are numerous indications of plurality in God, such as when God refers to "Us" and "Our" (e.g., Gen. 1:26; 3:22; 11:17; cf. Isa. 6:3). And, as we have seen (chapter 4), the pre-incarnate Christ makes numerous appearances as the divine "Angel of the LORD" (see Gen. 16:7–13; 21:17; 22:11–12; 31:11–13; 32:38 with Hosea 12:3–5; Exod. 3:2–4; 23:20–23; Judg. 13:13–22).[13]

Further, Isaiah 63 refers to the Father (who speaks of Israel as "My people, sons who will not deal falsely"), the Son (identified as "the angel of His presence" who "saved them" and "redeemed them"), and the Holy Spirit (who they "grieved" and who "gave them rest" (Isa. 63:8–10, 14; cf. 48:16).[14] Isaiah 63 thus refers to all three persons of the Trinity.

Scripture Teaches That the Father, the Son, and the Holy Spirit Are (Fully) Divine

As we have seen, no one is *like* God (1 Chron. 17:20), and there is thus no such thing as partial divinity. If being divine refers to being "like" God, the supreme Being who alone is worthy of worship (Luke 4:8) and who alone possesses the uniquely divine attributes, one cannot be *partially* divine. One is either divine or not.

Questions are not typically raised regarding the divinity of the Father, but some question the divinity of the Son and/or the Holy Spirit. Regarding the former, Scripture repeatedly affirms Christ's divinity.

As we saw in chapter 4, John 1:1–3 proclaims: "In the beginning was the Word, and the Word was with God, and the Word was God. He was in the beginning with God. All things came into being through Him, and apart from Him not even one thing came into being that has come into being." This passage declares that the Word, later identified as Christ, is "God." Further, this passage teaches that Christ is the eternally pre-existent Creator. Christ was "with God ... in the beginning" (cf. Mic. 5:2; Gal. 4:4) and did not Himself come into being since "apart from Him not even one thing came into being that has come into being" (cf. Col. 1:16–17; Rev. 22:13).[15]

Later in John, Thomas addressed Jesus as "My Lord and my God" (John 20:28). Further, though Scripture teaches that only God is to be worshiped (Exod. 34:14; cf. Matt. 4:10; Luke 4:8; Rev. 19:10), Jesus repeatedly accepts worship (John 9:38; cf. Matt. 2:11; 14:33; 28:9, 17; Luke 24:52; Heb. 1:6; Rev. 5:8–14) and the Father Himself commands angels to "worship" Christ (Heb. 1:6).

Elsewhere, Paul explicitly identifies Christ as God, calling Him "the image of the invisible God" and declaring, "by Him all things were created, both in the heavens and on earth, visible and invisible, whether thrones, or dominions, or rulers, or authorities—all things have been created through Him and for Him. He is before all things, and in Him all things hold together" (Col. 1:15–17).[16] Further, Paul teaches of Christ, "in Him all the fullness of Deity dwells in bodily form" (Col. 2:9; cf. Phil. 2:6; Col. 1:19–20).

Likewise, Scripture identifies Christ as "the radiance of His [God's] glory and the exact representation of His nature" and the One who "upholds all things by the word of His power" (Heb. 1:2–3). Yet, only One who is God could be the "radiance" of God's "glory and the exact representation of His nature" (see Isa. 42:8). Hebrews 1 later quotes the Father referring to Christ as God, saying: "But regarding the Son He [the Father] says, 'Your throne, God, is forever and ever, and the scepter of righteousness is the scepter of His kingdom. You have loved righteousness and hated lawlessness; therefore God, Your God, has anointed You with the oil of joy above Your companions'" (Heb. 1:8–9; quoting from Ps. 45:6–7; cf. 110:1).

Jesus Himself made many claims to divinity. He called "God His own Father," thus "making Himself equal with God" (John 5:18; cf. Matt. 14:33). He spoke of "His angels" (Matt. 13:41) and "My kingdom" (John 18:36) and claimed "authority" to "forgive sins" (Mark 2:10)—the ability of God alone (Mark 2:7; Luke 5:20–21). Further, Jesus claimed, "all will honor the Son just as they honor the Father" (John 5:22–23), "I and the Father are one" (John 10:30), and "the one who has seen Me has seen the Father" (John 14:9).

Perhaps most strikingly, when He said "before Abraham was born, I am," Jesus identified Himself as the great "I AM" (God Himself) who spoke to Moses from the burning bush (John 8:58; Exod. 3:14). Likewise, Christ declared, "I am the Alpha and the Omega, the first and the last, the beginning and the end" (Rev. 22:13; cf. Isa. 44:6).

Scripture also explicitly teaches the (full) divinity of the Holy Spirit (as we saw in chapter 5). In Acts 5:3, Peter said, "Ananias, why has Satan filled your heart to lie to the Holy Spirit?" Then, in parallel, Peter adds, "You have not lied to men, but to God" (Acts 5:4). The parallel indicates that the Holy Spirit is God.

Further, Scripture attributes to the Holy Spirit uniquely divine attributes, identifying the Spirit as "the eternal Spirit" (Heb. 9:14), indicating omniscience in saying that the Spirit "knows" and "searches all things, even the depths of God" (1 Cor. 2:10–11), and indicating omnipresence in that the Spirit could be with Christ's followers forever, wherever they would go (John 14:16; cf. Ps. 139:7), even as they dispersed across the globe to preach. And the Holy Spirit shares a name with the Father and Son, in which Christ's followers are to baptize (Matt. 28:19).

Moreover, the New Testament quotes words attributed to God in the Old Testament and attributes them to the Holy Spirit. Just prior to quoting God's words from Isaiah 6, Paul says, "The Holy Spirit rightly spoke through Isaiah the prophet to your fathers" (Acts 28:25). Likewise, Hebrews 3:7 introduces a quotation of divine speech from Psalm 95:7–11 by saying, "as the Holy Spirit says." And, notably, some of the words of God attributed to the Holy Spirit here are "YOUR FATHERS PUT *ME* TO THE TEST, AND SAW *MY* WORKS" (Heb. 3:9, emphasis mine; cf. Exod. 16:7).

All this and more explicitly teaches that the Son and the Spirit are (fully) divine.

Scripture Teaches That the Father, Son, and Spirit Are Distinct Persons

Most parties to the discussion readily recognize the Father is a person, and the Son is a person, but some question the personhood of the Holy

Spirit. Recall, here, that by "person" we do not mean a *human* person or one that is otherwise limited in physical, creaturely ways, but one who possesses *personal* attributes, defined as attributes that persons possess but mere powers or forces do not (such as self-consciousness, reason, will, and love, see chapter 5).

In this regard, as seen earlier, Scripture repeatedly attributes to the Holy Spirit characteristics and actions that only refer to persons.

For example, the Holy Spirit:

- shares a name with the Father and Son (Matt. 28:19)
- teaches (Luke 12:12; cf. Neh. 9:20; John 14:26)
- testifies or bears witness (John 15:26; cf. Rom. 8:16)
- can be lied to and tested (Acts 5:3–4, 9)
- speaks (Acts 8:29; cf. Ezek. 2:2; Acts 10:19–20; 28:25; 1 Tim. 4:1; Heb. 3:7)
- admonishes (Neh. 9:30)
- leads and guides (Ps. 143:10; Acts 8:29)
- calls to ministry and sends out (Acts 13:2–4)
- forbids or allows and commands (Acts 16:6–7; cf. 8:29; 10:19–20)
- intercedes (Rom. 8:26–27; cf. 15;16; Titus 3:5)
- reveals, searches, and knows the thoughts of God (1 Cor. 2:10–11)
- gives spiritual gifts to whom He *wills*—indicating the Holy Spirit has a will (1 Cor. 12:11; cf. Exod. 31:3; Acts 20:28; Rom. 8:27)
- can be "grieved" (Eph. 4:30; cf. Isa. 63:10; Mic. 2:7; Heb. 3:7–10; 10:29)

These and other instances depict the Holy Spirit as possessing distinctly *personal* attributes. Only a person can be grieved, will to give gifts to particular persons, know the thoughts of God, teach, testify, guide, call to ministry, forbid, command, and intercede.

Not only is the Holy Spirit identified as a "person," Scripture portrays the Father, the Son, and the Holy Spirit as *distinct* persons. The Father, Son, and Spirit act as distinct persons at Christ's baptism—the Father speaks, the Spirit descends as a dove, and the Son is baptized (Matt. 3:16–17). Further, the Father, Son, and Spirit relate to one another as distinct persons in what are known

> *Scripture portrays the Father, the Son, and the Holy Spirit as distinct persons.*

as I-Thou relations (where one references oneself as "I" and the other as "You"). For instance, Christ prays in Gethsemane, "My Father, if it is possible, let this cup pass from Me; yet not as I will, but as You will" (Matt. 26:39). Likewise, Jesus prays to the Father, "You loved Me before the foundation of the world" (John 17:24; cf. 3:35; 5:20).

Further, Jesus identifies the Holy Spirit as "another Helper," distinct from Himself (John 14:16), sent *by* the Father *in* Christ's name who will "teach" the apostles further (John 14:26; cf. Luke 12:12) and also sent *by* Christ *from* the Father to testify about Christ (John 15:26; cf. 16:7–8, 13).[17] The Holy Spirit, then, is neither Christ nor the Father (nor a part thereof) but another sent by Christ and the Father who would testify about Christ. Likewise, Jesus teaches that one who "speaks a word against" Him can be "forgiven . . . but whoever speaks against the Holy Spirit, it shall not be forgiven him, either in this age or in the age to come" (Matt. 12:32).

In these and other passages, Scripture explicitly teaches that the Holy Spirit is not the Son or the Father, the Son is not the Holy Spirit or the Father, and the Father is not the Son or the Holy Spirit.

The Core Trinity Doctrine Is Biblically Warranted

In the above passages and elsewhere, Scripture expressly affirms the four tenets of the core Trinity doctrine: (1) God's oneness; (2) God's threeness; (3) the full divinity of the Father, Son, and Spirit; and (4) the distinct personhood of the Father, Son, and Spirit. Taken together, these amount to the core Trinity doctrine: There is only one God, and God is three distinct, (fully) divine persons.[18]

Yet, some have claimed that neither the Son nor the Spirit could be (fully) divine because Jesus refers to the Father as "the only true God" (John 17:3), and Paul writes, "there is one God, the Father, from whom are all things and for whom we exist" (1 Cor. 8:6a, NRSVue; cf. Eph. 4:6).

However, in the very same verse, Paul goes on, "and one Lord, Jesus Christ, through whom are all things and through whom we exist" (1 Cor. 8:6b, NRSVue; cf. Eph. 4:5). If Paul's words "there is one God, the Father" entails that Jesus is not God, then Paul's further words "and one Lord, Jesus Christ" would indicate the Father is not Lord. But, many texts call the Father "Lord" (e.g., Matt. 11:25). Therefore, 1 Corinthians 8:6 cannot be consistently understood as meaning that Jesus is Lord to the exclusion of the Father. But, then, Paul's words in 1 Corinthians 8:6 likewise should not be taken to mean the Father is God to the exclusion of Jesus.

Further, to be consistent, the phrases "one God, the Father" and "the only true God" should *not* be understood as statements excluding the divinity of the Son or Spirit. That would contradict the biblical teachings seen earlier that explicitly affirm the full divinity of the Son and Spirit. Instead, such phrases emphatically affirm monotheism over and against false gods.[19] Monotheism, however, is consistent with the view that the one true God *is* three persons such that speaking of the Father as the "only true God" does not exclude the Son, who is "one" with the Father (John 10:30; cf. 14:9). Likewise, speaking of the Son as the "one Lord" would not exclude the Father from being "Lord" since the Father and Son "are one" (John 10:30).

Understanding the Trinity

This, however, raises some questions about how we should understand the Trinity. For example, how can three persons be one God? How should we understand the internal relations among the persons in the Trinity? To these and other questions we turn in the following sections.

Is the Core Trinity Doctrine Coherent?

First, we turn to the question: How can *three* persons be *one* God? To say God is one and God is three only amounts to contradiction if one claims God is one and three *in the same way.*

A three-leaf clover is one and three in different respects. A three-leaf clover is one and only one clover but has three leaves. This is no contradiction. Now, I am not suggesting the Trinity is one and three in the same way as a three-leaf clover. All analogies of the Trinity are deeply inadequate. I refer to the three-leaf clover not as an analogy of the Trinity but as a simple example showing that something can be one and three, in different respects, without any contradiction.

The God of the Bible is *one* in the sense of being one God and *three* in the sense of being three persons. As long as the three persons—Father, Son, and Spirit—are united in some way such that there is only *one* God, this is consistent with the biblical teaching that there is only one God.

But, just *how* are the Father, Son, and Spirit united? Scripture does not explicitly tell us. But, as we have seen, Scripture does teach that there is only one God and, yet, God is three distinct persons. This teaching entails that God somehow transcends creaturely limitations such that the three persons of the Trinity are united as one God. Even if the way in which this is so may be beyond our comprehension, affirming this does not entail any contradiction.

While we might not understand just *how* the three persons are united, we should not be surprised that the all-powerful Creator God transcends creaturely limitations and the creaturely categories and conceptions of being familiar to us. After all, even the best human thinkers still do not understand just how to make sense of how light sometimes appears to behave like a wave and other times like a particle (the so-called wave-particle duality of light). There is mystery, but no actual contradiction, in affirming God is *one* and *three* in different respects; specifically, *one* God and *three* persons.

Some additional confusion arises, in this regard, because people sometimes suppose the persons of the Trinity are "persons" in all the same ways mere humans are persons, with the same natural and *physical* limitations. Since three *human* persons are three separate (physically individuated) humans, some mistakenly assume three divine persons would amount to three "gods." Yet, God is not *physically* (or otherwise) limited in the way that mere creatures are. Jesus taught that "God is spirit" (John 4:24) and, while God does take on physical form, the all-powerful Creator of the physical universe is not Himself bound by physical or other limitations as creatures are (see chapter 8). God transcends physical and other creaturely limitations. Here, it is crucial to recall that by "person" in theology, we simply mean one with the capacity of self-consciousness, reason, will, and love.

God transcends physical and other creaturely limitations.

Yet, if the Father is God, the Son is God, and the Holy Spirit is God, how does that not amount to three "gods"? Here, there is a crucial difference between what is called the "is" of identity and the "is" of predication. The statement "Mark Twain is Samuel Clemens" is an example of the "is" of identity because Mark Twain was the pen name of Samuel Clemens. Mark Twain and Samuel Clemens were the same, identical person. The statement "Mark Twain is famous" is an example of the "is" of predication. Being famous is something true about Mark Twain, but being famous is not the same as being Mark Twain; "famous" is a true predication about Mark Twain.[20]

When Christians say the Father is God, the Son is God, and the Spirit is God, Christians mean this in the sense of the "is" of predication. It is a true predication about the Father that He is divine. Likewise, with respect to the Son and the Spirit. However, it is not true that (for example) the Father is God in the sense of the "is" of identity. The Father is God (in the sense of the "is" of predication), but God is more than the Father. A true statement about God using the "is" of identity would be: God is the Father, Son, and Spirit. As such, there are three persons who are God, but there are not three "gods." There is only one God, and God is three persons.

Competing Theories in Christian Theology: Relations within the Trinity

There are a number of competing theories about relations within the Trinity. Here, I will introduce three prominent areas about which some Trinitarians disagree.

First, while the widely affirmed Nicene-Constantinopolitan Trinity doctrine affirms eternal relations of origin within the Trinity (eternal generation of the Son and eternal procession of the Spirit), many other Christians (including many Adventists) do not affirm these doctrines, believing these doctrines are not taught by Scripture and might be incompatible with other teachings of Scripture.[21] For example, while proponents argue otherwise, some argue that the doctrine of eternal generation amounts to subordinationism.[22] Further, some Christian theologians believe the eternal relations of origin might require commitments regarding the divine nature that they believe conflict with biblical teachings (e.g., divine timelessness, see chapter 8).[23]

Second, Christian theologians hold differing views regarding the way in which God is three and one (i.e., the nature of triunity). The most prominent two views are commonly known as Latin theories (i.e., singularity theories) and social theories (with some nuanced forms preferring the label relational theories).[24] Social or relational theories claim the persons of the Trinity each possess a distinct faculty of self-consciousness, reason, and will. In direct contrast, Latin or singularity theories claim the "persons" of the Trinity do not each possess such faculties but share one unitary faculty of self-consciousness, reason, and will.[25]

The debate is a bit technical but boils down to whether the persons of the Trinity are distinct persons of the kind that can engage in I-Thou relations, that is, relations in which one is conscious of oneself as "I" and relates to another as "you." Believing Scripture repeatedly depicts this kind of relationship between the persons of the Trinity (e.g., in Christ's prayer in Gethsemane, Matt. 26:39, and the claims of love relationship between the persons, John 17:24), Adventists tend to affirm social or relational theories of the Trinity.[26]

Third, there is some disagreement about whether the Son and Spirit are *eternally* subordinate in relation to the Father.[27] Recently, a few Christian theologians have claimed that the Son and Spirit are eternally subordinate (a view known as eternal functional subordination or eternal relations of authority and submission). Most Christians, however, deny eternal subordination within the Trinity, with some affirming that the Son and Spirit are *temporarily* subordinate in a *functional* manner in order to carry out their respective roles in the plan of redemption (a view known as temporary functional subordination). This upholds that the Son and Spirit are not subordinate by nature, but only with respect to some functions taken on temporarily to carry out specific missions in the plan of redemption.

Not all Adventists agree, but many Adventists hold a view akin to temporary functional subordination (or what some might prefer to call voluntary submission), meaning the Son and Spirit voluntarily and temporarily lowered themselves to take on specific roles in the plan of redemption during which they submitted to one or more of the other persons of the Trinity. Once the mission for which they took on such roles is complete, however, the persons return to their state of functional equality that flows from the nature of the persons as co-equal. Hence, the subordination is both functional (for a particular mission) and temporary (lasting only until the mission is complete).[28]

We have already seen that sonship does not entail subordination (see chapter 4). Here, the fact that Christ takes on a submissive role, obeying the commands of the Father during his earthly life, does not entail that Christ is *always* in such a submissive role. Likewise, the fact that the Spirit takes on a submissive role in relation to the Father and the Son does not require that the Spirit is *always* in such a submissive role.

Notably, as seen earlier, Scripture depicts Christ as dependent on and submissive to the Spirit during his earthly ministry (e.g., Matt. 12:28; Mark 1:12; Luke 4:1), but the roles are somewhat reversed later. Specifically, after Christ ascends, the Son (along with the Father) sends the Spirit (e.g., John 14:26; 15:26), who then operates in a *functionally* submissive role (cf. John 16:13) relative to the Father and the Son. In these cases, the persons of the Trinity take on different, functionally submissive roles at various times in the history of redemption.

Further, though the Son shared glory with the Father before the world existed (John 17:5), at the appointed time (Gal. 4:4), the Son voluntarily lowers Himself and lovingly submits to and obeys the Father (see, e.g., John 5:19; 10:17–18; 14:28–31; Phil. 2:5–8) throughout His mission as the second Adam who came to restore what was lost and thus *"learned* obedience from the things which He suffered" (Heb. 5:8, emphasis mine). Conversely, there is a real sense in which the Father delegates to the Son and thereby "binds Himself" in a way that renders the Father dependent (and, at least in that sense, submissive) on the Son successfully carrying out His mission on behalf of the Trinity (1 John 4:14; cf. John 3:35; 5:22–23; 13:3; 16:15; 2 Cor. 5:19).[29]

Eventually, the Son is re-elevated to His rightful throne (Phil. 2:9–11; Rev. 22:3; cf. Matt. 28:18; 1 Cor. 15:24–28; Eph. 1:20–23; Heb. 1:3–4). His kingdom will have no end (Dan. 7:14, 27; Luke 1:33; 2 Pet. 1:11; cf. Heb. 1:8), but "all will honor the Son *just as* they honor the Father" (John 5:23, emphasis mine).[30]

Whatever else one concludes, it is crucial to deny any kind of subordinationism (any view that affirms one person of the Trinity is by nature less than another person of the Trinity) because Scripture teaches the persons of the Trinity are (fully) divine and thus co-equal.

Trinity of Love: Triunity as Eternal Relations of Love

God is love (1 John 4:8, 16). Yet, how could God be love prior to creation when there were no creatures for God to love? The answer is, within God, there was already love relationship between the persons of the Trinity before the foundation of the world (John 17:24). Accordingly, prior to the creation of the universe, the persons of the Trinity could be distinguished (at least) in that each person loved the other two persons as *other* than Himself (e.g., the Son eternally loves the Father and Spirit as persons other than Himself).[31]

Some believe this is itself evidence for the Trinity doctrine. In order for God to be love before God created creatures, the argument goes, there must have been love relationship in God and this requires both lover and beloved in the Godhead. Further, many note that love between *three* persons includes a dimension of love that is not present in love between only two persons. With a third person involved, the focus is not simply "I love you, and you love me," but includes a third person who my beloved loves and I also love (e.g., the love of parents for their child). With three persons, then, there is not only reciprocal love but also shared love—unselfish love shared with another beyond the reciprocal relationship.

Such eternal relations of love might not only distinguish the persons of the Trinity but such relations of love also highlight one possible way in which God is one. Specifically, the biblical concept of mutual indwelling (cf. John 10:30; 14:7–11) might be understood in terms of what theologians refer to as perichoresis. While there are various understandings of perichoresis, I use it here to refer to the idea that the three persons of the Trinity somehow indwell or coinhere in one another as *one* God. The Father, the Son, and the Spirit are eternally related in love relationship in a way that unites (or reflects the unity of) the persons as one God—the Father in the Son and the Spirit, the Son in the Father and the Spirit, and the Spirit in the Son and the Father—the Trinity of love.

Conclusion: Why Does It Matter?

At night, while all alone, she sometimes lay in bed wondering if anyone truly loved her, if anyone could truly love her. Maybe if people truly knew everything there was to know about her, they would not love her.

Maybe those who seem to love her now one day will stop. Even thinking about this made her feel more alone than she already felt.

Have you ever felt similarly? Have you ever longed for love deeper than any you've experienced—love of the kind that you can be sure will never, ever fail you?

The deepest longing of the human heart is to be loved and to love. You and I profoundly desire love and belonging. Many people spend their whole lives looking for love, looking for a place to belong where they are valued, secure, and safe. I am convinced there is only one place to find that love that truly satisfies the deepest longing of the human heart—what some have called the God-shaped hole inside our hearts. Only God can truly fulfill this deepest human desire.

God *is* love, and God already loves you more than you can imagine. You can rest secure in His love, knowing that He *is* love. Within God's very nature, God has always been and always will be love. Even apart from creation, God enjoys eternal love relationship within the Trinity—the love shared by Father, Son, and Spirit. And, amazingly, God invites you, me, and everyone else into love relationship with the one true God who is love.

Love itself is grounded in the Trinity of Father, Son, and Spirit. And the story of redemption itself only makes sense if the Father is God, the Son is God, and the Holy Spirit is God. Why is that?

First, the central point of the redemption story is that, in Christ, God became human to reconcile humans to God. Such reconciliation could only be accomplished by one who was both God and human, a central claim of the Trinity doctrine. If Christ is not God, the crucifixion was a merely human sacrifice, akin to pagan child sacrifice. But, if Christ is God and chose to give Himself for us (see John 10:18; Gal. 2:2), His sacrifice is a voluntary sacrifice of God (in Christ) giving *Himself* for us.

The sacrifice of a mere creature could not be an effective sacrifice to "demonstrate [God's] righteousness" or to demonstrate God's "love toward us" (Rom. 3:25–26; 5:8). But God (in Christ) sacrificed *Himself* for us. As Fleming Rutledge put it: God "has not required human sacrifice; he has himself become the human sacrifice."[32] Kathryn Tanner adds, "God is both the one sacrificing and the one sacrificed. The whole act is God's."[33] Christ willingly gave His life (John 10:18; cf. Gal. 2:20) according to the covenant of redemption, such that the story of redemption is the story of the Trinity of love.

Second, the Holy Spirit's identity is inseparable from the Trinity doctrine and the Spirit's crucial role in this plan of redemption. Only if the Holy Spirit is God could the Holy Spirit be "another Helper" or advocate (John 14:16) with us in Christ's place, sent by Father and Son to be God *with* us; that is God with Christ's followers wherever they would go (John 14:16–17; 15:26; cf. 7:38–39; 16:7–16). Further, the Spirit's works are crucial to the Christian faith. But the Holy Spirit could only connect us to God—interceding for us (Rom. 8:26–27) and otherwise carrying out divine works on our behalf—if the Holy Spirit is God. Here, again, the plan of redemption itself is bound up with the Trinity—the story of redemption is the story of the Trinity of love.

Understanding the Trinity is essential to understanding who God is and how we should relate to God. Only God is worthy of worship. If Christ is not God, it is blasphemy to worship Christ, and Christianity is utterly false. But Christ is God and the Father Himself commands creatures to worship Christ (Heb. 1:6).

In this and other ways, the Trinity doctrine is not an extraneous theological puzzle; it is central to *everything*. God is love. And, amazingly, we are invited to enter into love relationship *with* the one true God who is love—Father, Son, and Holy Spirit, the Trinity of love, whose love endures forever and never fails.

> **Understanding the Trinity is essential to understanding who God is and how we should relate to God.**

Do you want to be united in love with God? Although God already loves you more than you can imagine, He invites you into a deeper relationship with Him. Will you accept His invitation? Even now, Christ knocks at the door of your heart, desiring to draw you closer to Himself and fill you with the joy of the love of God and the peace that passes understanding that comes with it.

Have you ever felt like something is missing? Have you felt empty inside? Perhaps you have not realized that what you are longing for can only ultimately be filled by your Creator. Sure, other things may seem to dull the emptiness for a time, but the lasting joy you and I and every other human seek is found ultimately in the God who made you and gave Himself on the cross (in Christ) to save you and every other person. Accept God's love today, whether for the first time or as a renewal of your love relationship with God.

If you feel drawn to God even now, I invite you to pray. If you do not know how to pray, consider starting with the Lord's Prayer (Matt. 6:9–13). Then, ask the Father to fill your heart with God's presence, with the confidence that the Father does not need to be convinced to favor you, for (as Jesus assured His followers who loved Him) "the Father Himself loves you" (John 16:27; cf. 3:16). Pray, further, with the confidence that though you (and I) do not know how to pray as we should—we often do not know the right words—the Holy Spirit intercedes and "helps our weakness" in this and other regards (Rom. 8:26–27) and we can approach God's heavenly throne in confidence through Jesus Christ who "always lives to make intercession for" us (Heb. 7:25).

Finally, if you'd like to reflect on the steadfast, forever-enduring, never-failing love of God, I invite you to slowly and prayerfully read Psalm 136 and focus on the repeated refrain, "his steadfast love endures forever" (NRSVue).

Questions for Reflection

1. How would you answer a person who wonders if the Trinity is taught in the Bible? On the basis of Scripture, how would you respond?
2. What do you find most significant about the biblical material regarding the story of the Trinity?
3. What are some ways the Trinity doctrine has been misunderstood in the past and today?
4. What does it mean to be a "person" relative to the Trinity? Are the Father, Son, and Spirit distinct persons? If so, does it make sense to believe Father, Son, and Spirit are one (and only one) God?
5. Why does affirming both the oneness and threeness of the Trinity matter? How would you explain the practical implications of this?
6. What does it mean to you personally to consider Christ's call that those who believe in Him would be one and abide with one

another even as the Father, Son, and Spirit are one and abide with one another?
7. Why does the Trinity matter? What difference does it make to your life and the lives of those around you? Does understanding the Trinity shed important light on God's love?

For Further Reading

Adventist Perspectives:

Bediako, Daniel. *God in 3 Persons—In the Old Testament*. Biblical Research Institute Release, no. 10. Silver Spring, MD: Biblical Research Institute, 2015.

Canale, Fernando. "Doctrine of God." In *Handbook of Seventh-day Adventist Theology*. Edited by Raoul Dederen. Hagerstown, MD: Review and Herald, 2000.

Donkor, Kwabena. *God in 3 Persons—In Theology*. Biblical Research Institute Release, no. 9. Silver Spring, MD: Biblical Research Institute, 2015.

Donkor, Kwabena. *Eternal Subordination of Jesus?: A Theological Analysis and Review*. Biblical Research Institute Release, no. 23. Silver Spring, MD: Biblical Research Institute, 2022.

Gulley, Norman R. *Systematic Theology: God as Trinity*. Berrien Springs, MI: Andrews University Press, 2011.

Moon, Jerry. "The Adventist Trinity Debate, Part 1: Historical Overview," *Andrews University Seminary Studies* 41, no. 1 (Spring 2003): 113–29.

Moon, Jerry. "The Adventist Trinity Debate, Part 2: The Role of Ellen G. White," *Andrews University Seminary Studies* 41, no. 2 (Autumn 2003): 275–92.

Moskala, Jiří, and John Reeve, eds. *The Trinity*. Nampa, ID: Pacific Press (forthcoming).

Peckham, John C. *Divine Attributes: Knowing the Covenantal God of Scripture*. Grand Rapids, MI: Baker Academic, 2021.

Petersen, Paul. *God in 3 Persons—In the New Testament*. Biblical Research Institute Release, no. 11. Silver Spring, MD: Biblical Research Institute, 2015.

────── and Rob McIver, eds. *Biblical and Theological Studies on the Trinity.* Cooranbong, NSW, Australia: Avondale Academic Press, 2014.

Whidden II, Woodrow, John Reeve and Jerry Moon. *The Trinity: Understanding God's Love, His Plan of Salvation, and Christian Relationships.* Hagerstown, MD: Review and Herald, 2002.

See also the resources on the Biblical Research Institute website: https://adventistbiblicalresearch.org/materials/.

Other Christian Perspectives:

Copan, Paul. "Is the Trinity a Logical Blunder? God as Three and One." In *Contending with Christianity's Critics: Answering New Atheists & Other Objectors.* Edited by Paul Copan and William Lane Craig. Nashville, TN: B&H, 2009.

Emery, Gilles, and Matthew Levering, eds. *The Oxford Handbook of the Trinity.* Oxford: Oxford University Press, 2011.

Erickson, Millard J. *Who's Tampering with the Trinity? An Assessment of the Subordination Debate.* Grand Rapids, MI: Kregel Academic and Professional, 2009.

Hasker, William. *Metaphysics and the Tri-Personal God.* Oxford: Oxford University Press, 2013.

Kärkkäinen, Veli-Matti. *Christian Understandings of the Trinity: The Historical Trajectory.* Minneapolis, MN: Fortress, 2017.

McCall, Thomas H. *Which Trinity? Whose Monotheism? Philosophical and Systematic Theologians on the Metaphysics of Trinitarian Theology.* Grand Rapids, MI: Eerdmans, 2010

Phan, Peter C., ed. *The Cambridge Companion to the Trinity.* Cambridge: Cambridge University Press, 2011.

Sexton, Jason S., ed. *Two Views on the Doctrine of the Trinity.* Grand Rapids, MI: Zondervan, 2014.

PART THREE

GOD FOR US WHO LOVES, PROVIDES, AND REVEALS

7

THE ALMIGHTY CREATOR WHO SUFFERS WITH US: THE COVENANTAL GOD OF LOVE

The bush was on fire. Yet, it was not consumed. The bush kept burning without burning up. How could this be? Moses turned aside to see this amazing sight. Then, he heard the voice.

"Moses, Moses!"

"Here I am," Moses replied.

"Do not come near here," the voice answered; "remove your sandals from your feet, for the place on which you are standing is holy ground."

Finally, the speaker identified Himself. "I am the God of your father—the God of Abraham, the God of Isaac, and the God of Jacob."

Realizing he was in the presence of God, "Moses hid his face, for he was afraid to look at God" (Exod. 3:1–6).

Who is this God? What is God like?[1] Throughout the story of Scripture, this God of Abraham, Isaac, Jacob, and many others relates to creatures in striking ways—creating, speaking, hearing, willing, loving, promising, covenanting, suffering, grieving, relenting, responding to prayer, dwelling with humans, and otherwise engaging in a back-and-forth relationship with creatures.

These activities display some of the most significant attributes of God, discussed in this and the following chapter. Among other things, we will see that the God of the Bible is a covenantal God who freely engages in a back-and-forth relationship with creatures, makes promises to foster and grow love relationships, and always keeps His promises.

In this chapter, we will consider questions like:

- Is God all-powerful? If so, what does that mean?
- Is God reliable? Can God change?

- Does God care about me? Does God experience emotions?
- What does it mean to say God is love? What about God's wrath?
- The way we answer such questions affects our answers to other questions like:
- What kind of God do we worship?
- To what kind of God does it make sense to pray?

As we will see, the God of the Bible is supremely worthy of worship in light of His perfect goodness, love, wisdom, power, and personal presence. It makes sense to pray to this God because God hears us, cares about us, is deeply affected by what happens to us, has the power to save us, and precisely knows what is best for all concerned.

We will also see other amazing things about God, but along the way we must remember that God is far greater than we can imagine. Even "as the heavens are higher than the earth," so God's "ways" are "higher than" ours and God's "thoughts than" ours (Isa. 55:9). We should, then, approach these topics with great humility, remembering that when it comes to the things of God, there is always more to the story and "we see through a glass, darkly" (1 Cor. 13:12, KJV).

The Story of the God Who Creates, Loves, Covenants, Suffers, and Responds

Who was Moses to accomplish this great feat? How could he possibly free his people from centuries of bondage in Egypt? Nothing short of the miraculous could even begin to ease the oppression Israel suffered.

It seemed like a lost cause. Moses was chosen by the God of Abraham, Isaac, and Jacob—the Creator Himself. Through Moses, God promised to liberate Israel from slavery. But would the people believe? What if they were to ask who this God is?

Moses put this very question to God Himself.

"I AM WHO I AM," God replied. "This is what you shall say to the sons of Israel: 'I AM has sent me to you'" (Exod. 3:14).

At first, this answer seems mystifying, but it reveals more than first meets the eye. God has always existed and will always exist. Everything else exists only in dependence on God, the Creator of all, who alone exists *of Himself,* not depending on anyone or anything else to be who He is essentially (see further discussion below).

He is who He is. Indeed, the personal name of God—YHWH—is believed to be based on the Hebrew verb meaning "to be" so that it could be translated as "He is who He is." In English translations, this personal name YHWH is often translated as "Lord" (with all caps), a name many of the Jewish faith consider too holy to pronounce.

After identifying Himself as "I AM," God calls Himself "the Lord, the God of your fathers, the God of Abraham, the God of Isaac, and the God of Jacob" (Exod. 3:15). Here, the "I AM" who is self-existent and transcends all creation further identifies Himself by personal relationship to a particular covenant people. Amazing.

The almighty Creator of all is also the covenantal God of love, who freely enters into a back-and-forth covenant relationship with humans and always keeps His promises. He created all things, speaking many things into existence over the course of six days. But, on the sixth day, God intimately "formed the man of dust from the ground, and breathed into his nostrils the breath of life; and the man became a living person" (Gen. 2:7). Later that day, "the Lord God caused a deep sleep to fall upon the man" and "He took one of his ribs and closed up the flesh at that place. And the Lord God fashioned into a woman the rib which He had taken from the man" (Gen. 2:21–22).

Utterly astounding. "By the word of the Lord the heavens were made, and by the breath of His mouth all their lights" (Ps. 33:6), and "the world has been created by the word of God" (Heb. 11:3). Yet, the same God who created the worlds by His word condescended to personally and intimately create Adam and Eve.

This God is unlike anyone else! Mere humans who possess great power typically do everything they can to retain it, avoiding lowering themselves at all costs. Yet, the Creator of the universe, whom no one could compel, chooses to condescend to create humanity and enter into a genuine back-and-forth relationship, in which He even binds Himself by making promises to creatures who exist only by His power (Heb. 1:3).

This same God who is Creator of all is also the great Liberator. It is no coincidence that the two instances of the Sabbath commandment highlight God's great acts of creating (Exod. 20:11) and liberating His people from bondage in Egypt (Deut. 5:15; see chapter 15). Through miracle after miracle, demonstrating His unfathomable power, God delivered Israel from slavery. The Creator of all things, sovereign over the universe, concerns Himself with healing the broken-hearted and oppressed and, finally, setting the captives free (Isa. 61:1–2; Luke 4:16–19).

This God is the covenantal God who keeps His promises—the God of abundant compassion, grace, patience, lovingkindness, and justice. God saw the oppression of His people, heard their cries, and showed His great concern for them, liberating them "from the power of the Egyptians" in accordance with the covenant promises He made to Abraham (Exod. 3:7–17; cf. 2:24–25).

But, shortly after God liberated them, the people rebelled. While God met Moses on Mount Sinai, the people made a golden calf to worship as if it had delivered them from slavery. By this egregious evil, they forfeited any right to God's covenant promises and blessings.

God had every right to cut Israel off. But He did not. He sought out Moses to intercede for the people.[2] In response to Moses's intercession, God renewed the covenant, which apart from God's compassionate grace would have been utterly shattered.

Just after Israel's golden calf rebellion, God again appeared to Moses and proclaimed, "The LORD, the LORD God, compassionate and merciful, slow to anger, and abounding in faithfulness and truth; who keeps faithfulness for thousands, who forgives wrongdoing, violation of His Law, and sin; yet He will by no means leave the guilty unpunished" (Exod. 34:6–7). The God of the Bible is the God of love *and* justice.

In this story and beyond, God freely maintains relationships with creatures even after they rebel. Later, despite His people's countless rebellions and atrocities, God declared, "I will heal their apostasy, I will love them freely, because My anger has turned away from them" (Hosea 14:4). Indeed, it is only by God's freely granted mercy and grace, which exceeds all reasonable expectations, that humans continue to exist despite our evil.

Throughout the story of redemption, God freely engages in back-and-forth relationships with profoundly unworthy creatures and always keeps His promises. By doing so, God opened Himself up to enormous grief and pain, willingly suffering for us and *with* us. What wondrous love!

God made covenants with Adam and Eve and with Noah, which extended to every living creature. The nations, however, rejected God and His covenant promises. So, God made a covenant with Abraham and his chosen descendants, creating a covenant people chosen not only for their sake but to bless all nations (Gen. 12:1–3). Redemption itself, for all nations, would eventually come through a descendant of Abraham—Jesus.

God built on His covenant promises to Abraham, covenanting further with Israel at Sinai (the Mosaic covenant) and much later with David (the Davidic covenant), promising his throne would be established forever (2 Sam. 7:16). While David's merely human descendants failed and the earthly kingdom perished, the promise of the everlasting kingdom (and other covenant promises) is ultimately fulfilled in Jesus, the covenantal son of David.

Further, while God's people were often unfaithful, God was perfectly constant in faithfulness, bearing with them far beyond any obligations—indeed, beyond any reasonable expectations. Humans are unreliable, but God's character of love is unchanging—His "compassions do not fail" (Lam. 3:22) and His "steadfast love endures forever" (Ps. 136, NRSVue; cf. 1 Chron. 16:34; Jer. 31:3; 33:11; Rom. 8:35, 39). He is the exceedingly "compassionate God" who never fails His people and never forgets or breaks the covenants He makes (Deut. 4:31).

God takes pleasure in and passionately loves His people (Ps. 149:4; cf. Zeph. 3:17), metaphorically depicted as the passionate love of a long-suffering husband for his repeatedly adulterous wife (see Isa. 62:4; Jer. 2, 3; Ezek. 16, 23; Hosea 1–3; Zech. 8:2). Even as His people scorn Him, God is the unrequited lover who refuses to stop loving.

> **God is the unrequited lover who refuses to stop loving.**

Likewise, Scripture metaphorically depicts God's love as the tender love of a parent who adopts and affectionately cares for her child. Even "as a mother comforts her child," God promises, "so I will comfort you" (Isa. 66:13, NRSVue). And, "just as a father has compassion on his children, so the LORD has compassion on those who fear Him" (Ps. 103:13). Yet, the compassionate love of God is inestimably greater than any human parent. God Himself declares, "Can a woman forget her nursing child and have no compassion on the son of her womb? Even these may forget, but I will not forget you" (Isa. 49:15).

While His people are unfaithful, God calls them "my dear son," the "child in whom I delight," proclaiming, "I am deeply moved for him; I will surely have mercy on him" (Jer. 31:20, NRSVue; cf. Luke 15:20). Because God so loves humans, He is deeply grieved by human evil, which always harms God's children—even when self-inflicted. Accordingly, God laments, "I reared children and brought them up, but they have rebelled against me ... Woe, sinful nation, people laden with iniquity, offspring who do evil, children who act corruptly, who have forsaken the LORD, who have despised the Holy One of Israel ... Why do you continue to rebel?" (Isa. 1:2, 4–5, NRSVue; cf. Ps. 81:13; Jer. 3).

Nevertheless, God wanted to deliver His people from hardship, being repeatedly "moved to pity by their groaning" (Judg. 2:18). Deeply grieved over His rebellious people, God even declared, "My heart is turned over within Me, all My compassions are kindled" (Hosea 11:8).

Jesus displayed the same kind of compassion for people. "When he saw the crowds, he had compassion for them because they were harassed and helpless, like sheep without a shepherd" (Matt. 9:36, NRSVue). In this and many other instances, the sight of people in need or distress moved Jesus to compassion (Matt. 14:14; Mark 1:41; 6:34; Luke 7:13; cf. Mark 10:21).

The God of the Bible both delivers His people with power and suffers for and with His people. Indeed, "in all their distress He was distressed." Even though God "lifted" the people and "carried them all the days of old," God's covenant people repeatedly "rebelled and grieved His Holy Spirit" (Isa. 63:9–10; cf. Ps. 78:40–41).

The extent of God's passionate and compassionate love is displayed supremely in the sacrifice of Christ. No mere human sacrifice, God in the flesh suffered and gave *Himself* for us. Words cannot adequately describe such marvelous love.

God, the All-Powerful Creator

"In the beginning God created the heavens and the earth" (Gen. 1:1). From beginning to end, the story of Scripture emphasizes that God is the only Creator; God alone "created the heavens" and the earth (Isa. 45:18; cf. Gen. 1:1; Ps. 33:6; Col. 1:16; Heb. 11:3). God's act of creation is the starting point for everything that is, except God Himself who alone has no beginning. Therefore, it also provides the starting point for thinking about everything else.

God Created the Universe

God is the Creator of all. Apart from God, nothing would exist, and before God created, nothing existed other than God. Put in technical theological language, God created *ex nihilo* (from nothing). This follows from Scripture's teachings that God created all things, God is "before all things," and by God's will, all things exist (e.g., Col. 1:16–17; Rev. 4:11).

"Worthy are You, our Lord and our God, to receive glory and honor and power; for You created all things, and because of Your will they existed, and were created" (Rev. 4:11). God is worthy of worship because He is the Creator of "all things." God did not need to create anything but created the universe of His own free will.

Before anything else existed, the Father, Son, and Holy Spirit were united in love relationship (see John 17:24). But the Father, Son, and Spirit chose to create others on whom to bestow their love, and all three were active in creating (Gen. 1:2; Heb. 1:2).

Competing Theories in Christian Theology: Issues in Origins

The biblical teaching that God created all things stands in contrast to the theory of naturalistic evolution, the theory that the existence of the universe and life itself is the result of natural causes alone (without any supernatural action) and all that exists resulted from long ages of undirected evolutionary processes. According to this theory, all life forms result from long ages of descent with modification (by natural selection) from a universal common ancestor.

Christian theologians reject naturalistic evolution but hold various views regarding the nature and timing of God's creation. Advocates of theistic evolution (i.e., evolutionary creationism) believe God created through the natural processes of macroevolution. On this view, what exists today is the result of long ages of evolutionary processes, but God is the force behind these processes. Advocates of this view tend to believe the Genesis 1 creation week narrative is not a historical narrative but a poetic way of teaching that God (somehow) created the world.

Progressive creationism (sometimes spoken of as old earth creationism), instead, attempts to affirm the historicity of the Genesis creation narrative by suggesting that God created by a series of special acts of creation, separated by long periods of time, such that new kinds of organisms that appear in geological history were created by God over long ages. Some progressive creationists propose the *"days"* of creation week correspond to long ages between various special creative acts of God.

Other Christians believe the days of the Genesis creation week refer to seven literal days, treating Genesis 1 as a historical narrative that tells the story of God creating in six days and resting on the seventh.[3] Many who hold this view believe that other views fail to accord with the biblical data and face other problems such as long ages of suffering and death before sin. This view, often known as creationism, is endorsed by the Seventh-day Adventist Church.[4] Some who affirm this view, however, affirm young *earth* creationism, while others affirm young *life* creationism.[5]

Young earth creationists believe planet earth and life on earth were created thousands of years ago during the six-day creation week. To answer puzzles like the apparent age of the earth and distant starlight (how light could have reached earth by now from stars that are billions of light years away from earth), some young earth creationists posit the mature earth theory, which maintains the earth (and perhaps the *known* universe itself) was created in a mature state so that it appears to be much older than it is (analogous to the way creationists believe Adam and Eve were created as mature humans who, moments after they were created, would have appeared to be considerably older than they were).[6]

Young life creationists instead believe that during the six-day creation week, God *formed* planet earth and its ecosystems—creating all life on earth just as the narrative describes, but the raw material of our planet (and the known universe) was created by God at some point in the past, perhaps when the entire universe was created. On this view, the earth is old, but *life* on earth is young—the raw material of earth could be billions of years old, and the stars could likewise be very old, but the events of creation week took place during a literal six-day week just as Genesis narrates.[7]

Both of these versions of creationism affirm the historicity of the Genesis 1 narrative of the days of creation.

Creation: An Act of Love

Creation was an act of love. Though God needs nothing, God desired to share His love with creatures who could freely receive and freely give love. God desired to be *with us* for our good because God *is* love. Creation, then, is about more than merely *what* occurred but, just as importantly, *why* it occurred. God created humans for relationship. Creation is a relational event, not just the beginning of a creaturely being, but of being *in relationship with* God. It is the beginning of God *with us* in love.

> *Though God needs nothing, God desired to share His love with creatures who could freely receive and freely give love.*

Scripture does not specify precisely how long ago creation took place. Genesis describes God performing a series of creative acts over six days, then resting on the seventh day (Gen. 1–2:4). Yet, Scripture elsewhere reveals that some creatures in the universe existed before the Genesis creation week. When God "laid the foundation of the earth," the "morning stars sang together and all the sons of God shouted for joy" (Job 38:4, 7). The phrases "morning stars" and "sons of God" refer to celestial creatures such as angels, often called the heavenly host (see Col. 1:16). To sing *when* God "laid the foundation of the earth," such creatures must have been created *before* such events.

The events of creation week, then, were not the beginning of God's creation of the *universe*. Some unknown period of time passed between the creation of the universe and the events of the Genesis creation week relative to this world.

The creation of humans was the crowning act of creation week, in which God condescended to form Adam from the dust, personally breathing life into Adam's body (Gen. 2:7). What an amazing image! In creation, God knowingly committed Himself to relationship with creatures that would ultimately lead to taking on Himself the death of the cross to save the world from evil (Phil. 2:8). God need not have done so, but willingly did so, knowing full well the cost to Himself.

Everything God created was "very good" (Gen. 1:31; cf. 1 Tim. 4:4). But, through no fault of God's, creation was corrupted by the entrance of evil (see chapter 9). Evil was alien to this world. Evil came from elsewhere. Initially, moral harmony reigned in God's creation. The world was not as it is now. Creatures, however, made evil choices and thus fell from moral perfection. Adam and Eve's Fall in particular brought curses on this planet, changing our world in various adverse ways (Gen. 3:16–19). God intended that there be no human sickness, suffering, or death at all. So, it would have always been, were it not for human choice to depart from God's law of unselfish love, which unbroken would have ensured endless universal harmony and bliss.

God Is Self-Existent and All-Powerful and Sustains All

"I AM WHO I AM." These words God spoke to Moses from the burning bush (Exod. 3:14). Creation exists because of God's will (Rev. 4:11), but God alone has "life in Himself" (John 5:26; cf. 11:25). That is, only God is self-existent; only God exists *of Himself* as the great "I AM" who does not depend on anyone or anything else to be who He is essentially.[8]

Not only did God create all things, but God "upholds all things by the word of His power" (Heb. 1:3). God is the Sustainer of all. Everything else depends on God to exist, but God does not depend on anything to exist or to be who He essentially is (Acts 17:25). He is who He is.

There is, then, an absolute distinction between God and creation—the Creator-creature distinction. God is uncreated and transcends creation. Everything else depends on God. "For from Him, and through Him, and to Him are all things. To Him be the glory forever" (Rom. 11:36).[9] For this and many other reasons, the Creator God is worthy of worship.

Because God is who God is, those who trust in Him don't have to worry about tomorrow. Jesus explained, "do not be worried about your life, as to what you will eat or what you will drink; nor for your body, as to what you will put on. Is life not more than food, and the body more than clothing? Look at the birds of the sky, that they do not sow, nor reap, nor gather crops into barns, and yet your heavenly Father feeds them. Are you not much more important than they?" (Matt. 6:25–26).

God did not need to create. God needs nothing (Acts 17:25). Because of the eternal love within the Trinity, the statement "God is love" was true even before God created any world (1 John 4:8, 16; cf. John 17:24). Yet, God created out of unselfish love and generosity so as to share love *with* creatures. How marvelous! "See what great love the Father has lavished on us, that we should be called the children of God" (1 John 3:1, NIV). Amazingly, the self-existent God enters into back-and-forth love relationship with creatures who, in turn, also love one another. Creation is not only a manifestation of God's infinite power, then, but equally an expression of God's infinite love.

Yet, creation is nevertheless a manifestation of God's awesome power. God is *all-powerful* (that is, omnipotent). "I am the Alpha and the Omega," God states, "who is and who was and who is to come, the Almighty" (Rev. 1:8). Likewise, Revelation 19:6 proclaims: "Alleluia! For the Lord God Omnipotent reigns!" (NKJV; see also 2 Cor. 6:18; Rev. 4:8; 11:16–17; 15:3; 16:7, 14; 19:15; 21:22). "Nothing is too hard for" the "great and mighty God whose name is the LORD of hosts, great in counsel and mighty in deed," who "showed signs and wonders in the land of Egypt and to this day in Israel and among all humankind" (Jer. 32:17–20, NRSVue; cf. 32:27; Job 42:2; Ps. 147:5). Accordingly, Jesus teaches, "with God all things are possible" (Matt. 19:26; cf. Mark 10:27; 14:36; Luke 1:37).

To say God is omnipotent, however, is not to say God can do just anything. Scripture teaches there are some things God *cannot* do. For example, God "cannot deny Himself" (2 Tim. 2:13). As such, God cannot do anything that would contradict His own essential nature. Further, "God cannot be tempted by evil" (James 1:13), God "cannot lie" (Titus 1:2; cf. Num. 23:19), and God's promises are unbreakable because "it is impossible for God to lie" (Heb. 6:18). Accordingly, if God makes a promise or commitment, His future action is (*morally*) limited by that promise or commitment. As God Himself proclaims: "I will not violate My covenant, nor will I alter the utterance of My lips" (Ps. 89:34). While God is all-powerful, God also always keeps His promises.

This might explain why in some instances God's power to work miracles appears to be restricted. For example, Mark 6:5 reports that Jesus "could not do any miracle" in His hometown, "except that He laid His hands on a few sick people and healed them." This was "because of their unbelief" (Matt. 13:58; see also Mark 6:6). Yet, how could unbelief restrict the Almighty, who "upholds all things by the word of His power" (Heb. 1:3)? This could be so only if God committed Himself to acting in some way that is tied to human faith. Because God always keeps His promises, the exercise of divine power is restricted by whatever commitments God has made.

To take another example, a man brought his demon-afflicted son to Jesus and begged Jesus to cast the demon out, noting His disciples had not been able to do so. To this plea, Jesus replied, "All things are possible for the one who believes" (Mark 9:23; cf. Eph. 1:19). The man immediately cried out, "I do believe; help my unbelief" (Mark 9:24). And Jesus cast the demon out. Afterward, Jesus's disciples asked why they could not cast the demon out. "This kind cannot come out by anything except prayer," Jesus explained (Mark 9:29; cf. Matt. 17:20).

From these instances and others, we learn that divine action might *sometimes* be limited by the absence of faith and/or prayer. The way God works in the world (divine providence) is discussed further in chapter 9. For now, we have seen that God is all-powerful, yet there are *moral* restrictions on how God exercises His power in the world.

God is morally perfect and thus never does anything immoral or that contradicts His perfect goodness. Further, even God cannot perform contradictory actions such as making a square circle. This is not because God lacks any power but because it is intrinsically impossible to bring about a logical impossibility. This is explicit in Christ's prayer shortly before the crucifixion. Therein, Christ prays, "Abba! Father! All things are possible for You; remove this cup from Me; yet not what I will, but what You will" (Mark 14:36). Yet, Jesus also prays, "My Father, if it is possible, let this cup pass from Me; yet not as I will, but as You will" (Matt. 26:39).

> God is morally perfect and thus never does anything immoral or that contradicts His perfect goodness.

Praying "if it is possible" does not contradict affirming that "all things are possible for" God. The phrase "all things are possible for God" teaches that God possesses the power to do anything *that can be done*. Yet even the omnipotent God cannot bring about *contradictory* outcomes because (by definition) two contradictory outcomes cannot both occur. For example, God cannot both give all creatures free will and *not* give all creatures free will at the same time.[10] God cannot be both all-powerful *and* entirely powerless. More specifically, relative to Christ's prayer, God could not make it so that Jesus could avoid the cross and still save the world (on the atonement, see chapter 13).

In Christ's prayer, the phrase "if it is possible" does not mean "if it is possible" by itself, but "if it is possible" to avoid the cross while still accomplishing God's work of saving the world. As Hebrews 12:2 teaches, it was "for the joy set before Him" that Christ "endured the cross." What was the joy set before Him? The joy of saving His beloved creatures. Christ need not have died *for us* but did so voluntarily because it was the only way to save us (John 10:18; Eph. 5:2) and be *with us* for eternity. Christ is not only God *with us* (Immanuel) but God *for us*. What love!

In this way and others, the exercise of God's power is governed by God's perfect character of love. God always (freely) does what is loving for all concerned. If God "cannot lie" and "cannot deny Himself," as Scripture teaches, God's actions must accord with His essential nature and moral character of love. Scripture teaches then, that God is all-powerful but acts only in ways consistent with His essential nature and character of perfect goodness and love.

Recognizing that the all-powerful God loves us and wants to save us is exceedingly good news. The God of the Bible who wants to save us is mighty to save. God not only creates and sustains the world but God is the great liberator, healing the broken-hearted and setting the captives free.

> **God not only creates and sustains the world but God is the great liberator, healing the broken-hearted and setting the captives free.**

While much has gone wrong in this world, through no fault of God's, God has the power to make all things right in the end. And one day soon, He will. In the end, the same God powerful enough to speak the world into existence will make all things new, including "a new heaven and a new earth" (Rev. 21:1, 5; cf. Isa. 65:17; 66:22; 2 Pet. 3:13).

The Unchanging God Who Willingly Suffers with Us

"I knew this would happen. I just knew You would relent and not destroy them. That is why I refused to go to Nineveh in the first place!" Jonah was very angry and he made his complaints known to God (Jon. 4:1–2). Jonah thought God was being *too* merciful, *too* gracious, and *too* compassionate. "I knew that you are a gracious and merciful God, slow to anger, and abounding in steadfast love, and relenting from punishment" (Jon. 4:2, NRSVue). Imagine that! Imagine being angry with God for being so merciful, gracious, and compassionate!

This was an embarrassing display of self-righteousness, which was not righteous at all, for it lacked love. Yet, Jonah's misconceived complaint displays a precious truth about who God is—the God of mercy, grace, and compassion. God has revealed that He *is* love, not only in words but also in deeds. Indeed, Jonah's complaint draws on God's words to Moses in the aftermath of the golden calf rebellion (Exod. 34:6–7). The covenantal God of the Bible is the God of grace and compassion.

God's Changeless Character—Perfect Faithfulness, Holiness, and Goodness

God's grace and compassion toward Nineveh did not involve His going back on His word. Not at all. Throughout Scripture, God proclaims that He will act this very way, turning judgment away from those willing to turn from evil (e.g., Jer. 18:7–10). The opportunity to repent and be saved was implicit in the warning message God delivered through Jonah. That is why Jonah was sent and why Jonah did not want to go.

Indeed, "the Lord longs to be gracious" and "waits on high to have compassion" (Isa. 30:18). God is eager to relent from judgment precisely because His character of love is changeless.

"I, the Lord, do not change," God proclaims, "therefore you, the sons of Jacob, have not come to an end" (Mal. 3:6). Then, God adds, "Return to Me, and I will return to you" (Mal. 3:7).[11] Here, God both declares that He does not change *and* that if people will change in relation to Him, He will change in relation to them. There is some sense in which God is changeless, then, but God does change *relationally* in response to creatures.[12]

Some theologians cite Malachi 3:6 as support for the view that God cannot change *in any way* (strict immutability). Yet this verse actually teaches that God changes relationally, but His character does not change. God is always reliable, and precisely because of God's unwavering faithfulness, God's covenant people were preserved despite their repeated rebellions.

Likewise, James 1:17 teaches, "Every good thing given and every perfect gift is from above, coming down from the Father of lights, with whom there is no variation or shifting shadow." This verse also teaches that God's character is utterly constant, without "variation or shifting shadow." This is exceedingly good news. While humans are often unfaithful and otherwise change in arbitrary ways, God's character of perfect goodness is constant. Humans will let you down, but God never will. "The steadfast love of the LORD never ceases, his mercies never come to an end" (Lam. 3:22, NRSVue).

> **Humans will let you down, but God never will.**

The God of the Bible is eternally faithful and always keeps His promises. As Isaiah 25:1 proclaims, "LORD, You are my God; I will exalt You, I will give thanks to Your name; for You have worked wonders, plans formed long ago, with perfect faithfulness." Psalm 117:2 adds, "the faithfulness of the LORD endures forever. Praise the LORD!" (NRSVue).

God loves justice (Isa. 61:8). In God, "steadfast love and faithfulness will meet; righteousness and peace will kiss each other" (Ps. 85:10, NRSVue). As such, even "if we are faithless, He remains faithful, for He cannot deny Himself" (2 Tim. 2:13). This is why, as we have seen, God's promises are unbreakable (see also Num. 23:19; Titus 1:2; Heb. 6:17–18). The God of Scripture is the unwaveringly faithful covenant-maker and promise-keeper.

God's faithfulness is inseparable from His holiness. God is entirely "faithful, the Holy One of Israel" (Isa. 49:7), who "alone" is "holy" in and of Himself (Rev. 15:4). God is holy not only in terms of perfect goodness and faithfulness but also as the One who is essentially "set apart" from creation (the Creator-creature distinction).[13] As such, God alone is worthy of worship: "HOLY, HOLY, HOLY IS THE LORD GOD, THE ALMIGHTY, WHO WAS AND WHO IS AND WHO IS TO COME" (Rev. 4:8; cf. Isa. 6:3).

Wherever God is, it is holy. Thus, from the burning bush, God warned Moses, "Do not come near here; remove your sandals from your feet, for the place on which you are standing is holy ground" (Exod. 3:5). The sanctuary on earth was holy because of God's presence. Creatures may also be holy by proximity to God—the source of holiness, goodness, and love. Indeed, sinful humans can be made holy (sanctified) by relationship with God through Christ's atoning work (Heb. 10:10) and the mediation of the Holy Spirit (1 Thess. 2:13; 1 Pet. 1:2).

Because God is perfectly holy, our sins separate us from God—"your wrongdoings have caused a separation between you and your God, and your sins have hidden His face from you so that He does not hear" (Isa. 59:2). Indeed, "no evil can dwell with" God (Ps. 5:4). Without mediation, evil cannot be in God's presence because "God is a consuming fire" (Heb. 12:29). God's holy presence is to evil like fire to gasoline. But God makes a way to defeat evil, cleanse sinners, and reconcile us to Himself.

All the while, God remains perfectly holy and good. "His work is perfect, for all His ways are just; a God of faithfulness and without injustice, righteous and just is He" (Deut. 32:4). Indeed, "the LORD is good; his steadfast love endures forever and his faithfulness to all generations" (Ps. 100:5, NRSVue). "God is Light, and in Him there is no darkness at all" (1 John 1:5; cf. Hab. 1:13). These and other passages teach that God is morally changeless (i.e., morally immutable).

God is also changeless (immutable) with respect to His essential nature (e.g., with respect to His *unchanging* divine attributes such as being omnipotent). While creation is transient and ever-changing, God is always "the same," and His "years will not come to an end" (Ps. 102:27). His promises are sure. He "is the same yesterday and today, and forever" (Heb. 13:8).

Competing Theories in Christian Theology: Divine Immutability and Passibility

Christian theologians hold different theories of divine immutability. Some affirm strict immutability, the view that God does not change *at all*. If so, God cannot engage in back-and-forth relationship or experience relational change. Others affirm qualified immutability, the view that God does not change with respect to His character and essential nature but does change relationally in response to creatures.

Closely related to debates over divine immutability are debates over divine impassibility, which denies God has passions (whether of some or all kinds). Strict impassibilists maintain that God cannot be affected by anything outside of Himself and has no passions of any kind. God, then, cannot experience emotional change or suffering or be pleased or displeased by creatures but remains in a constant state of bliss, unmoved by the evil in the world. Qualified impassibilists instead affirm that God can be affected and experience emotions, but never "against his will by an outside force.'"[14] Some who hold this view maintain that God's emotions are determined by God alone.[15]

Others affirm divine passibility. Some affirm *essential* passibility, believing God is *essentially* passible in relation to the world (meaning the universe), meaning that by nature, God must be in relationship to some world and affected by that world from all eternity. In process theology, this means the universe is *eternally* part of God's being such that God necessarily feels the feelings of every creature.

Qualified passibility instead maintains God is not *essentially* related to the world but is voluntarily passible in relation to the world in a way that upholds the Creator-creature distinction.[16] God experiences changing emotions relative to the world because God freely chose to create (and thus bring the world into existence) and open Himself up to being affected by creation.[17] This is the view that is consistent with Seventh-day Adventist beliefs about God and God's relationship to creation.

God Engages in Back-and-Forth Relationship with Creatures

"If my people who are called by my name humble themselves, pray, seek my face, and turn from their wicked ways, then I will hear from heaven and will forgive their sin and heal their land" (2 Chron. 7:14, NRSVue). Here, God promises to hear and respond to His people's sincere prayers.

In this way and many others, while God's essential nature and character are changeless, God voluntarily engages in back-and-forth relationship with humans that involves *relational* changes on God's part (qualified immutability). Accordingly, God "was moved to pity by" the "groaning" of His covenant people "because of those who tormented and oppressed them" (Judg. 2:18). And, the LORD was moved and "responded to prayer for the land" (2 Sam. 24:25) and elsewhere responded to human pleas and prayers (e.g., Exod. 33:12–34:10; 2 Kings 20:5; Jon. 3:10).

However, God does not change or experience emotions in just the way humans do. Indeed, while describing deep emotions over His people, God declares, "I am God and not a man," thus "I will not come in wrath" (Hosea 11:9). Human emotions are imperfect and sometimes irrational, but God's emotions are never irrational, but always perfect and proportional to the state of affairs.

Whereas humans may lie and break promises, God never will. "God is not a man, that He would lie, nor a son of man, that He would change His mind" (Num. 23:19). God "will not lie nor change His mind; for He is not a man, that He would change His mind" (1 Sam. 15:29). God does not change in the way humans change.

Some have interpreted these verses to mean God does not change course or "relent" at all. But Scripture frequently depicts God relenting from judgment in response to human repentance (e.g., the case of Jonah), including twice in 1 Samuel 15 itself (15:11, 35). Indeed, God promised, "if" a "nation against which I have spoken turns from its evil, I will relent of the disaster that I planned to bring on it" (Jer. 18:8; cf. 18:10; 42:10). In accord with God's changeless character of merciful love, God is eager to relent if only His people will repent.

Throughout the story of Scripture, human actions affect God's actions. Indeed, when God heard the cry of His people, God "relented according to the greatness of His mercy" (Ps. 106:45; see also Gen. 18:23–32; Exod. 32:14; Ezek. 18:26–31; Jon. 4:2; Luke 13:34).

Yet, pleas and petitionary prayers do not convince God or move God to provide some blessing He did not already want to provide. Rather (as discussed further in chapter 9), petitionary prayer sometimes provides God the moral and legal grounds to bring about good for people that He already wanted to bring about. This is why, repeatedly in Scripture, God seeks out someone to intercede for His people (see Ezek. 22:30) to provide such moral and legal grounds. God eagerly desires to forgive and save, but He (morally) cannot do so in a way that breaks the commitments He has made (e.g., not to violate creaturely freedom, see chapter 9) or that is otherwise unjust.

God does change relationally in response to creatures, then, but only in ways that accord with God's unchanging character and essential nature. The incarnation itself is the most striking and significant divine change. Though Christ "already existed in the form of God," He "did not consider equality with God something to be grasped, but emptied Himself by taking the form of a bond-servant" and "humbled Himself by becoming obedient to the point of death: death on a cross" (Phil. 2:6–8). God the Son *became* human and suffered *for us* while remaining truly God—God *with us*.

> **God the Son became human and suffered for us while remaining truly God—God with us.**

God of Passion? Does God Have Emotions?

Has your heart ever been broken? In Scripture, God is repeatedly brokenhearted over His people, whom He loves more deeply than any love known to mere humans. Scripture repeatedly portrays God as a husband whose wife abandoned Him for others lovers, the victim of unrequited love, grieved by love lost.

In Hosea 11:8–9, God laments over the evil His people have done: "How can I give you up, Ephraim? How can I surrender you, Israel? How can I make you like Admah? How can I treat you like Zeboiim? My heart is turned over within Me, all My compassions are kindled. I will not carry out My fierce anger; I will not destroy Ephraim again. For I am God and not a man, the Holy One in your midst, and I will not come in wrath" (Hosea 11:8–9; cf. Isa. 30:15, 18–19; Jer. 3:1, 4, 8, 12).

Have you ever been so upset or grieved that it felt like your stomach was churning? This is the imagery of the depth of God's compassionate emotional response for His wayward people.[18]

Again, in Jeremiah 31:20, God expresses profound emotions for His people: "Is Ephraim My dear son? Is he a delightful child? Indeed, as often as I have spoken against him, I certainly still remember him; therefore My heart yearns for him; I will certainly have mercy on him" (Jer. 31:20; cf. Isa. 63:15). Elsewhere, "the LORD was moved to pity by" the "groaning" of His people (Judg. 2:18; cf. 10:16). In the Gospels, Jesus experienced these same kinds of emotions. For example, when seeing crowds of people in distress, like sheep without a shepherd, "He felt compassion for them" (Matt. 9:36).

The entire story of Scripture testifies of the "tender mercy of our God" (Luke 1:78). God loves His people even as "one whom his mother comforts" (Isa. 66:13) and even as "a father has compassion on his children" (Ps. 103:13). Further, God states: "Can a woman forget her nursing child and have no compassion on the son of her womb? Even these may forget, but I will not forget you" (Isa. 49:15). Notably, the Hebrew word translated compassion here (*raham*) is believed to be derived from the Hebrew word for womb (*rehem*). The compassion of God, then, might be described as a "womb-like mother love."[19]

While Scripture repeatedly depicts God experiencing changing emotions such as these, God does not experience changing emotions *in just the way* humans do. The language of Scripture is accommodative, meaning it teaches in a way that accommodates limited human understanding, and analogical, meaning there is both similarity and dissimilarity between what words mean when applied to humans and when applied to God.[20] Biblical language used of God conveys *true* teachings about God, but God is far greater than could be conveyed in human language. God is always greater and better than even our best conceptions of Him.

Scripture explicitly identifies *some* of the many differences between human and divine emotions. Human love often fades away, but God's love is everlasting (Ps. 100:5). Even the compassion of a mother for her young child may fail (Isa. 49:15), but God's "compassions do not fail" (Lam. 3:22). Human emotions are often irrational and sometimes evil, but God's emotions are never irrational and always perfectly good, displeased by evil while delighting in goodness (see Prov. 15:8). Humans often overreact and may be controlled by their anger, but God restrains His anger (Ps. 78:38) and *freely* bestows grace and compassion (Exod. 33:19; cf. Hosea 14:4; Rom. 9:15–16).

Many humans would do almost anything to avoid pain and suffering, but God voluntarily took on the suffering of the world to redeem the world and defeat suffering. God, then, is not *essentially* passible in relation to the world (i.e., the world is not *eternally* related to God), but God freely created and by His will *freely* brought the world into existence (Rev. 4:11) and, accordingly, *freely* opened Himself up to being affected by creation (*qualified* passibility).

What About God's Wrath?

Imagine watching your beloved child playing on a swing set. Suddenly, a man knocks your child off the swings and kicks her repeatedly. Would you be angry? If not, there is something wrong with you. If you love your child, such evil would anger you with *rightful* anger (i.e., righteous indignation).

Jesus Himself displayed righteous indignation against those who used the temple system to take advantage of widows, orphans, and the poor. "Jesus entered the temple area and drove out all those who were selling and buying on the temple grounds, and He overturned the tables of the money changers and the seats of those who were selling doves," declaring they were making God's house "a DEN OF ROBBERS" (Matt. 21:12–13; cf. Jer. 7:6, 9–11; Mark 11:15–18; Luke 19:45–48; John 2:14–15).[21] The very place that was to represent God's gracious forgiveness and cleansing of repentant sinners was being used to exploit and oppress the most vulnerable, exchanging people's money into the standard coinage for an additional fee, a hardship to the poor. It is no coincidence, then, that the language Jesus uses draws on Jeremiah 7, which emphasizes to "not oppress the stranger, the orphan, or the widow" (Jer. 7:6; cf. 7:11). Notably, Matthew 21 reports that just after Jesus thus cleansed the temple, the "blind and those who limped came to Him in the temple area, and He healed them" and "children... were shouting in the temple area, 'Hosanna to the Son of David'" (Matt. 21:14–15). Christ's righteous indignation against those who were making God's house "a den of robbers" was an expression of His love for the downtrodden and oppressed.

Indeed, the anger expressed by God in the Old and New Testaments is simply the righteous anger of love. Indignation against evil and compassion for the downtrodden is the proper reaction of righteous love.[22] While some mistakenly think God is perpetually angry in the Old Testament, attention to the timeline of Scripture shows long gaps between instances where God brought judgment, during which God did everything He could to restore and save His people. Thus, the prophets describe God as exceedingly longsuffering and merciful beyond any reasonable expectations. While people today (especially in the West) tend to ask why God brought judgment, the biblical authors repeatedly asked why God did not bring judgment more swiftly and more often to re-establish justice.

Because God loves deeply, God is deeply pained and angered by evil.[23] Some think a God of love should not become angry—that love and wrath are incompatible. Scripture paints a different picture, teaching that divine wrath is just the appropriate response of love against evil.

What kind of "love" would not be angered by the abhorrent suffering that humans inflict on one another? Should we not be angered by human trafficking, slavery, racism, misogyny, and oppressive evils of all kinds? Throughout Scripture, humans persistently perpetrated immense atrocities, including child sacrifice and many other depraved behaviors (cf. 2 Chron. 33:6). God is pained by every instance of evil because every instance hurts at least one of His children (even when self-inflicted) and separates people from Him (cf. Isa. 59:2). The mother of a child with terminal cancer rightly hates cancer. Much more so, God hates sin and evil, for it is the disease that ravages His creation and is behind all other diseases and ills.

Today, love is often thought of as merely a nice feeling. In Scripture, however, love and justice are inseparable.[24] Love without justice is crippled, and justice without love is cold and heartless. The God of the Bible loves justice (Ps. 37:28; Isa. 61:8). God is deeply moved out of concern for the oppressed and downtrodden and calls people also to be concerned about injustice in the world and make a difference where we can: "Seek justice, rebuke the oppressor, obtain justice for the orphan, plead for the widow's case" (Isa. 1:17; cf. 10:1–3; Mic. 6:8; Zech. 7:9–10; Matt. 23:23). The God of the Bible is thus the God of the oppressed—"a stronghold for the oppressed, a stronghold in times of trouble" (Ps. 9:9; cf. 103:6; 146:7). God not only "longs to be gracious" and "waits on high to have compassion," but "the LORD is a God of justice" (Isa. 30:18; cf. Exod. 34:6–7).

> **Love without justice is crippled, and justice without love is cold and heartless.**

While many in privileged situations find divine wrath distasteful, those who are or have been victims of cruel oppression and injustice (which still runs rampant in our sin-filled world) may see wrath from a different point of view. Throughout Scripture, the prophets cry out for God to bring judgment against oppressors and restore justice, to "defend the cause of the poor of the people, give deliverance to the needy, and crush the oppressor" (Ps. 72:4, NRSVue).

The prophets understood that looking the other way from evil and injustice simply multiplies the victims and oppression and is complicit in evil. In this regard, Miroslav Volf writes:

> I used to think that wrath was unworthy of God. Isn't God love? Shouldn't divine love be beyond wrath? God is love, and God loves every person and every creature. That's exactly why God is wrathful against some of them. My last resistance to the idea of God's wrath was a casualty of the war in former Yugoslavia, the region from which I come. According to some estimates, 200,000 people were killed and over 3,000,000 were displaced. My villages

and cities were destroyed, my people shelled day in and day out, some of them brutalized beyond imagination, and I could not imagine God not being angry. Or think of Rwanda in the last decade of the past century, where 800,000 people were hacked to death in one hundred days! How did God react to the carnage? By doting on the perpetrators in a grandparently fashion? By refusing to condemn the bloodbath but instead affirming the perpetrators basic goodness? Wasn't God fiercely angry with them? Though I used to complain about the indecency of the idea of God's wrath, I came to think that I would have to rebel against a God who wasn't wrathful at the sight of the world's evil. God isn't wrathful in spite of being love. God is wrathful because God is love.[25]

Accordingly, it is extremely significant that God is not only abundantly gracious, compassionate, and longsuffering but also "will by no means leave the guilty unpunished" (Exod. 34:6–7). Writing about the reaction to the case of Botham Jean, a black man murdered by a police officer in 2018 in his own apartment while he was minding his own business, Dorena Williamson highlights the mistake of emphasizing forgiveness and grace to the exclusion of justice. After the police officer was convicted of murder, Jean's brother publicly forgave and hugged the police officer—a moment of forgiveness and grace that quickly went viral. However, the response of Jean's mother did not go viral. On the juxtaposition of a brother's forgiveness going viral, while a mother's pain and cry for justice went largely overlooked, Williamson wrote: "When a black person extends radical forgiveness, we see the grace of the gospel. But when we ignore a black person's call for justice, we cheapen that grace. Both are acting like the God we serve; we need to listen to them both."[26]

God's response to evil keeps in mind the victims of evil, identifying the interests of the oppressed as His own. "One who oppresses the poor taunts his Maker, but one who is gracious to the needy honors Him" (Prov. 14:31; cf. James 2:5–8).

Divine anger, however, is never misplaced. It is always the appropriate, rational response to evil. God only becomes angry in response to evil, and even then, God *restrains* His anger, often postponing and mitigating the execution of divine judgment (Ps. 78:38). Whenever possible, divine judgment seeks restoration and reconciliation. God disciplines His people "as a [good and loving] man disciplines his son" (Deut. 8:5) in order "to do good" for them "in the end" (Deut. 8:16). "For whom the LORD loves He disciplines, just as a father disciplines the son in whom he delights" (Prov. 3:12; cf. Heb. 12:6). Here, it should be noted that human discipline is not always just or appropriate (even loving parents often fall short), but God's discipline always is.

At times, God's corrective discipline is the only way to save people from destroying themselves. If your best friend was unknowingly running toward a cliff and you had no way to stop them other than tackling them to keep them from falling and dying, would you do it? Of course.

> At times, God's corrective discipline is the only way to save people from destroying themselves.

Eventually, love requires action against persistent evil (the problem of evil is discussed in chapter 9). Yet, even when God brings judgment, God does not want to do so; God "does not afflict willingly" (Lam. 3:33). God brings judgment only as a last resort (cf. Isa. 30:18; Luke 13:34). Before doing so, God provides warning and makes a way of escape for those willing to turn from evil into the loving arms of God, having no pleasure in the death of anyone (Ezek. 33:11).

Not only does God make a way of escape, but He actually seeks after people as a shepherd seeks his lost sheep (Ezek. 34:11–12; cf. Luke 15:4–7). God does everything to save people without undermining the freedom necessary for love (more on that in chapter 9). Over and over, God sent His prophets to call people back to Him, but they despised the prophets' warnings and even killed some of them. God repeatedly called "because He had compassion on His people," but they continually "despised His words... until there was no remedy" (2 Chron. 36:15–16; cf. Judg. 10:13; 2 Kings 22:17; Heb. 8:9).

Divine wrath is God's loving reaction against persistent sin and evil (Deut. 9:7; 2 Chron. 36:16; Jer. 7:20–34; Hosea 12:14; Rom. 2:5; Col. 3:5–6). Yet, God's compassion far exceeds His anger. God's "anger is but for a moment," but "His favor is for a life time. Weeping may last for the night, but a shout of joy comes in the morning" (Ps. 30:5; cf. Exod. 34:6; Judg. 10:16; Isa. 30:18; 54:7–10; Luke 13:34).

The Covenantal Love of God

God becomes angry at evil because God loves passionately, but unlike human jealousy, God's *passionate* love (sometimes translated "jealousy") is perfect, always rational and appropriate—unfathomably holy, pure, and loving. Descriptions of divine "jealousy" in Scripture refer to God's rightful passion for exclusive relationship with His people without any of the faults akin to human *jealousy*. In the sense of only rightful, passionate love akin to such love for one's spouse, God is the *"jealous"* or *"passionate"* God (Deut. 4:24; cf. Exod. 20:5; 34:14; Deut. 5:9; 6:15; Josh. 24:19; Nah. 1:2) even as He is the compassionate God (Deut. 4:31; cf. Isa. 49:15). Indeed, God so loves the world that God Himself suffers when we suffer (cf. Isa. 63:9).

Christ's parable of the prodigal son highlights God's profound and amazing compassion for His children. In the parable, a son prematurely claimed his inheritance, left his father's home, and went off and squandered his inheritance. The son had effectively disowned his father but returned home to seek refuge, even if only as one of his father's servants. But, when the father saw his son returning, while "still a long way off," the father "felt compassion for him, and ran and embraced him and kissed him" (Luke 15:20). God's amazingly gracious and compassionate love for you and me and all His children is like this, but unimaginably greater.

The God of Scripture continually seeks back-and-forth covenant relationship with humans aimed at reciprocal love relationship. He is "the faithful God who keeps covenant and steadfast love with those who love him and keep his commandments, to a thousand generations" (Deut. 7:9, ESV; cf. Exod. 20:6; 1 Kings 8:23; Dan. 9:24).[27]

God's love is unfailing and everlasting (Ps. 103:15–17; 136; Lam. 3:22; Rom. 8:35–39), and God *freely* bestows love on everyone (John 3:16), even after rebellion (see Exod. 33:19; Neh. 9:31; Hosea 14:4). Yet, continuing to enjoy love relationship with God for eternity is contingent upon one's response to God's love (see Deut. 7:9–13; John 14:21–23; 16:27; Rom. 11:22; Jude 21; cf. Jer. 11:15; 14:10; 16:5; Hosea 9:15; John 1:12).[28] Accordingly, "the steadfast love of the LORD is from everlasting to everlasting on those who fear him" (Ps. 103:17, NRSVue; cf. Deut. 7:9–13; Matt. 18:27–33). We can never make God stop loving us, but we can finally reject that love *relationship* with God and, in so doing, cut ourselves off from the source of love and life itself, thus breaking God's heart.

God Himself is the source and ground of all love. We can only "love, because He first loved us" (1 John 4:19; cf. 4:7). Indeed, God proclaims to His people, "I have loved you with an everlasting love; therefore with lovingkindness I have drawn you" (Jer. 31:3, NKJV). God takes delight in humans (cf. Ps. 149:4; Zeph. 3:17), who are precious in His sight (Isa. 43:4; cf. Matt. 10:31). And, how we relate to God and others makes a difference to God. "The sacrifice of the wicked is an abomination to the LORD, but the prayer of the upright is His delight. The way of the wicked is an abomination to the LORD, but He loves the one who pursues righteousness" (Prov. 15:8–9; cf. Ps. 146:8; 2 Cor. 9:7; Heb. 13:16).

In all, God's love is *freely* given, passionate and compassionate, long-suffering, and covenantal. When God described His character of love to Moses in Exodus 34:6–7, He "proclaimed, 'The LORD, the LORD, a God merciful and gracious, slow to anger, and abounding in steadfast love and faithfulness, keeping steadfast love for the thousandth generation, forgiving iniquity and transgression and sin, yet by no means clearing the guilty, but visiting the iniquity of the parents upon the children and the children's children to the third and the fourth generation'" (NRSVue).[29]

Conclusion: Why Does It Matter?

If only someone knew how he felt. The pain inside seemed to be constant, always gnawing at him—day and night. He hid it well by day, not sure anyone else would understand or could understand. He was afraid to share his pain with other people, fearing they'd make fun of him, reject him, or worse, use his pain to hurt him more. If only there were someone who knew just the way he felt. If only there were someone who he could trust to confide in and find comfort.

Perhaps you've felt pain and suffering and wished for someone who knew your pain and would comfort you. Maybe you, like me, have longed for comfort beyond that which mere humans might provide when they show empathy and compassion for us, which often seems fleeting and a bit removed. I often long for the kind of empathy that is deeper than can be spoken in words. And I've found it in God.

God is the God of compassion. His compassions fail not, and He already knows just how you and I and everyone else feels. And, because He loves us so, He suffers *with* us. You are never alone in your suffering.

Whether you know it or not, God is *with* you and He desires to comfort and heal you.

God's compassion is central to His nature and character of love. We have seen in this chapter that God is the all-powerful (omnipotent) Creator of all, who alone is self-existent and sustains all things by His power. While God could remain in imperturbable bliss, enjoying eternal love within the Trinity without anyone else, God chose to create the universe *and* open Himself up to being affected by creatures. God thus willingly suffers with His creation while remaining all-powerful such that He can and will put an end to suffering once and for all. As such, God changes relationally *with us*, yet always remains the same God He always has been and always will be, remaining changeless (immutable) relative to His essential nature and character—always perfectly faithful, holy, good, and loving. God is love; and He freely and generously invites every person into a covenant love relationship with Him and voluntarily takes our sufferings and sorrows on His own shoulders, always willing to carry them for us and with us.

> Whether you know it or not, God is with you and He desires to comfort and heal you.

Is that not an amazing thought? Perhaps you feel drawn to a deeper relationship with the God of love and compassion even now. If so, simply ask Him to draw you into a deeper relationship with Him. And consider how you might reflect God's compassionate love to others. Given that God cares so much for you, how might you also be compassionate toward those around you? Here, also, if we ask God to show us and guide us, He will help us to not only be motivated to compassion for others but also lead us along the way to make a tangible difference in others' lives.

If you would like to reflect further on the Creator God, who nevertheless "humbles Himself to behold the things that are in the heavens and in the earth" (Ps. 113:6, NKJV), I invite you to prayerfully read and reflect on Psalm 113.

Questions for Reflection

1. What is the importance of understanding God as the Creator of all things? How should we relate to God as the Creator?

2. What comfort can we take in understanding that God exists of Himself and that His essential nature and character never change? What does this mean for how we can relate to Him?
3. Have you ever considered the depths of God's emotions as depicted in Scripture? Why is it so important to understand that God's emotions have none of the flaws of human emotions?
4. Is anger compatible with love? What would you say to someone who thinks the God of the Bible is an "angry" God? What is the importance of righteous indignation, and how does it relate to justice and love?
5. Do you think God's love is like human love? In what ways is it the same? In what ways is it different?
6. What does it mean to you to know that God loves you as you are and God wants a still closer relationship with you? What steps can you take to respond to God's invitation and enter into a deeper love relationship with Him?
7. You can enter into a deeper love relationship with God even now. Do you wish to do so? God has been seeking and calling you for your entire life like a good shepherd calls his sheep. Simply ask Him for a deeper relationship with Him. Tell Him: "I want to know you and your love more." Pray this in faith, and God will hear you.

For Further Reading

Adventist Perspectives:

Brand, Leonard and Arthur Chadwick. *Faith, Reason, & Earth History: A Paradigm of Earth and Biological Origins by Intelligent Design*, 3rd ed. Berrien Springs, MI: Andrews University Press, 2017.

Canale, Fernando. *Basic Elements of Christian Theology*. Berrien Springs, MI: Andrews University Lithotech, 2005.

———. "Doctrine of God." In *Handbook of Seventh-day Adventist Theology*. Edited by Raoul Dederen. Hagerstown, MD: Review and Herald, 2000.

Davidson, Jo Ann. *Glimpses of Our God*. Nampa, ID: Pacific Press, 2011.
Gibson, L. James, Ronny Nalin, and Humberto M. Rasi, eds. *Design and Catastrophe: 51 Scientists Explore Evidence in Nature*. Berrien Springs, MI: Andrews University Press, 2021.
Gulley, Norman R. *Systematic Theology: God as Trinity*. Berrien Springs, MI: Andrews University Press, 2011.
Klingbeil, Gerald A., ed. *The Genesis Creation Account and Its Reverberations in the Old Testament*. Berrien Springs, MI: Andrews University Press, 2015.
Peckham, John C. *Divine Attributes: Knowing the Covenantal God of Scripture*. Grand Rapids, MI: Baker Academic, 2021.
———. *The Doctrine of God: Introducing the Big Questions*. London: T&T Clark, 2019.
———. *Fervent Prayer: Cosmic Conflict and Petitionary Prayer*. Grand Rapids, MI: Baker Academic, forthcoming.
———. *The Love of God: A Canonical Model*. Downers Grove, IL: IVP Academic, 2015.
Shea, William H. "Creation." In *Handbook of Seventh-day Adventist Theology*. Edited by Raoul Dederen. Hagerstown, MD: Review and Herald, 2000.
See also the resources on the Biblical Research Institute website: https://adventistbiblicalresearch.org/materials/.

Other Christian Perspectives:
Cone, James. *God of the Oppressed*. New York: Seabury Press, 1975.
Fretheim, Terence E. *The Suffering of God: An Old Testament Perspective*. Philadelphia, PA: Fortress, 1984.
González, Justo L. *Mañana: Christian Theology from a Hispanic Perspective*. Nashville, TN: Abingdon, 1990.
Matz, Robert and A. Chadwick Thornhill, eds. *Divine Impassibility: Four Views*. Downers Grove, IL: IVP Academic, 2019.
Meyer, Stephen C. *Return of the God Hypothesis: Three Scientific Discoveries that Reveal the Mind Behind the Universe*. New York: HarperOne, 2021.
Mullins, R. T. *God and Emotion*. Cambridge: Cambridge University Press, 2020.

Perry, Jackie Hill. *Holier Than Thou: How God's Holiness Helps Us Trust Him*. Nashville, TN: B&H, 2021.

Rogers, Katherin A. *Perfect Being Theology*. Edinburgh: Edinburgh University Press, 2000.

Scrutton, Anastasia Philippa. *Thinking Through Feeling: God, Emotion, and Passibility*. London: Continuum, 2011.

8

THE ETERNAL, ALL-KNOWING GOD WHO DWELLS WITH US: THE EVER-PRESENT GOD OF LOVE

It was deeply frightening. There was thunder, flashes of lightning, and the sound of a trumpet. The mountain was smoking, and "when the people saw it all, they trembled and stood at a distance" (Exod. 20:18). They were so afraid that they pleaded with Moses not to let God speak to them.

At Mount Sinai, God manifested His presence before Israel in a thick cloud, and while the people remained at a distance, "Moses approached the thick darkness where God was" and received many covenant instructions and laws (Exod. 20:21). Afterward, Moses went up the mountain (with some others) "and they saw God" (Exod. 24:11). Then, Moses alone was called to meet with God on the mountain. The "glory of the Lord settled on Mount Sinai," looking "like a consuming fire on the mountain top" (Exod. 24:16–17).

On the mountain, God commanded Moses, Let the people "construct a sanctuary for Me, so that I may dwell among them" (Exod. 25:8). This sanctuary was to mediate God's presence so God could dwell in the midst of the people, despite their sinfulness. After the wilderness tabernacle was built, "the cloud covered the tent of meeting, and the glory of the Lord filled the tabernacle" (Exod. 40:34). Likewise, when Solomon's temple in Jerusalem was inaugurated centuries later, "the cloud filled the house of the Lord, so that the priests could not stand to minister because of the cloud, for the glory of the Lord filled the house of the Lord" (1 Kings 8:10–11). Then, Solomon proclaimed in amazement, "But will God indeed dwell on the earth? Behold, heaven and the highest heaven cannot contain You, how much less this house which I have built!" (1 Kings 8:27).

How can God dwell in the midst of mere humans? How could the Creator of all genuinely dwell *with* us? If God dwelled in the sanctuary, or in any particular place, God must be able to dwell in space and time. But how can this be?

These questions relate to contested issues about God's relationship to space and time, with implications for whether God can truly relate to humans and for God's knowledge—especially knowledge of the future. To introduce these issues, this chapter considers questions like:

- Is God present everywhere? Can God be genuinely *with us* in particular places?
- Does God have a past? Does God have a future? Can God be *with us* in time?
- Does God know everything, including the future?

Before addressing these questions, however, we will first consider how the stories of the Bible depict God's presence *with us.*

The Story of God's Presence with Us

All seemed lost. While Moses was on the mountain with God for forty days, the people fell into great evil. They made and worshiped a golden calf and engaged in morally depraved acts, even as Moses was receiving the Ten Commandments and instructions to build the sanctuary where God was to dwell among them.

When Moses "saw the calf and the people dancing," he was so angry that "he threw the tablets from his hands and shattered them to pieces at the foot of the mountain" (Exod. 32:19). The covenant God made with Israel seemed to be like those shards of the Ten Commandments, shattered in countless pieces.

Would the covenant continue? How could God dwell *with* them after such rebellion? If God would not go *with* them, what hope could they have?

If God would not go *with* the people, despite their sin, the sanctuary would not be built, and God's presence *with* them would be lost. This was an unimaginably awful prospect. Without God's special presence, they would be at the mercy of the wilderness and surrounding nations, with no hope of survival. If God would not go with them, all would be lost.

Moses pleaded with God to go *with* Israel. God replied, "My presence shall go with you, and I will give you rest" (Exod. 33:12–14). Yet, Moses persisted, asking God to confirm He would indeed go *with* the people in their very midst. God assured Moses He would do just what Moses asked (Exod. 33:15–17).

At the pinnacle of this dialogue, Moses requested, "Please, show me Your glory!" In response, God proclaimed, "I Myself will make all My goodness pass before you, and will proclaim the name of the LORD before you; and I will be gracious to whom I will be gracious, and will show compassion to whom I will show compassion" (Exod. 33:18–19).

However, God warned, "You cannot see My face, for mankind shall not see Me and live!" (Exod. 33:20). To protect Moses, God told him, "while My glory is passing by . . . I will put you in the cleft of the rock and cover you with My hand until I have passed by. Then I will take My hand away and you shall see My back, but My face shall not be seen" (Exod. 33:22–23).[1]

Moses could not see the *fullness* of divine presence, but he did experience God's *special* presence, veiled to protect him. Indeed, God spoke to Moses "face to face, just as a man speaks to his friend" (Exod. 33:11; cf. Deut. 34:10).[2] Even then, Moses could not see the *fullness* of God's presence. God's special presence was sometimes made visible to Moses (and others), but "no one has seen God" in His fullness (John 1:18). God "dwells in unapproachable light, whom no one has seen or can see" (1 Tim. 6:16; cf. Exod. 33:20).

God's presence is a dangerous thing indeed. Without God's special presence (explained further below), the people would surely perish in the wilderness. But, with God's special presence, they were also in danger of perishing due to God's holiness. God is a consuming fire and, absent mediation, any sin in God's presence would be destroyed (like fire to gasoline). If God were to go in the midst of sinful people without mediation, they would be destroyed (Exod. 33:5).

God could go *with* Israel in the way He intended only if God's special presence was mediated. The sanctuary was to fulfill this function (among others). God's promise that He would indeed go with them, even after their rebellion, assured the covenant would be renewed and the sanctuary built so God could dwell *with* them in their midst. Here and elsewhere, the story of the Bible is the story of God's presence, upon which *everything* depends.

Apart from God, nothing but God would exist. If God's presence were entirely absent, we would not exist. Further, if God would not go *with* Israel, God's covenant promises to save the world through them could not come to fruition. If the covenant was shattered and God's special presence was lost, all hope was lost.

> **The story of the Bible is the story of God's presence, upon which everything depends.**

But, God made a way. God did go *with* the people, demonstrating His abundant grace and compassion. After it was built, "the glory of the LORD filled the tabernacle," and God went *with* the people and before the people in a pillar of fire by night and a pillar of cloud by day (Exod. 40:34, 36–38; 13:21). And, God promised, "I will make My dwelling among you, and My soul will not reject you. I will also walk among you and be your God, and you shall be My people" (Lev. 26:11–12).

Centuries later, God's glory also filled Solomon's temple. While recognizing that "heaven and the highest heaven cannot contain [God], how much less this house which I have built," Solomon nevertheless proclaimed, "I have truly built You a lofty house, a place for Your dwelling forever" (1 Kings 8:27, 13).

God's special presence would have remained *with* Israel. But, in repeated cycles of rebellion, the people rejected God and pushed Him away (cf. Ps. 78:40–41). When they suffered affliction or oppression (often from the surrounding nations), they cried out to God for deliverance and restoration of His special blessings and protection. God heard and delivered them. But they rebelled again and again, often to a worse degree than before (see Ps. 78). The people thus removed themselves further and further from God—"again and again" they "pained the Holy One of Israel" (Ps. 78:41).

Eventually, after centuries filled with rebellion and apostasy—including evils like child sacrifice—there was nothing more God could do to deliver His people (cf. Isa. 5:1–7). Only after the people pushed God so far away that there was no remedy (2 Chron. 36:16) did God's special presence depart from the temple and from Jerusalem. "Then the cherubim lifted up their wings with the wheels beside them, and the glory of the God of Israel hovered over them. The glory of the LORD went up from the midst of the city and stood over the mountain which is east of the city" (Ezek. 11:22–23; see also Ezek. 9:9; 10:18–19). Then, Babylon conquered Judah and destroyed the temple (in 586 BC).

But that was not the end of the story of God's special presence with His covenant people. The people had forsaken and rejected God, but God was not finished with them. In His great mercy, God was with Daniel and others during their exile in Babylon. Just as He foretold, He raised up Cyrus, the Persian ruler who defeated Babylon and allowed the exiles to return and rebuild Jerusalem. Eventually, a second temple was built in Jerusalem. But it paled in comparison to Solomon's temple, and the glory of God did not fill it.

Yet, the glory of God did eventually visit this second temple in Jesus (cf. Hag. 2:9; Mal. 3:1). "When the fullness of the time came, God sent His Son, born of a woman, born under the Law" (Gal. 4:4).[3] "And the Word became flesh, and dwelt among us" (John 1:14). Jesus Himself was a "temple" of God's presence (John 2:19–21; cf. Matt. 12:6).

Yet, as they had previously persecuted and killed God's prophets, the leaders killed Jesus. Even as God's glory stopped on the mountain east of the city when it departed from Solomon's temple (Ezek. 11:23), centuries later, Jesus lamented over Jerusalem (Matt. 23:37–39) and soon afterward departed and ascended from the Mount of Olives east of Jerusalem (Acts 1:9–12). The second temple was also destroyed, this time by the Romans (AD 70). Today there is still no temple in Jerusalem, only some remains of the second temple.

But God made a way to remain God *with us*. When Jesus ascended, He entered the heavenly sanctuary as our high priest, "the greater and more perfect tabernacle, not made by hands, that is, not of this creation" (Heb. 9:11–12).[4] Christ and the Father sent the Holy Spirit "that He may be with you forever" and "He remains with you and will be in you" (John 14:16–17). Because "the Spirit of God dwells in" Christ's followers, they also "are a temple of God" (1 Cor. 3:16; cf. 6:19; Rom. 8:9).

The fullness of God's special presence with us was disrupted by the entrance of evil. Eventually, however, God will be with us again even as He was with Adam and Eve, "walking in the garden in the cool of the day" (Gen. 3:8). Jesus promised His followers, "I go to prepare a place for you" and "I will come again and receive you to Myself; that where I am, there you may be also" (John 14:2-3, NKJV). In the end, "the holy city, new Jerusalem," will come "down out of heaven from God, prepared as a bride adorned for her husband" (Rev. 21:2; cf. 2 Pet. 3:13; Rev 21:10).

From Genesis to Revelation, the story of Scripture is the story of God's desire to be specially present with us in the fullness of the intimate love relationship God intended from the beginning.[5] This personal presence of God in love relationship *with us* is the best possible good for all creation. The covenantal God of love wants to restore this presence with us so much that God became human to be "God with us" in the flesh.

Thus, all along the way, God Himself enters the story to be with us in space and time. "I will be with you and be your God," He promises (e.g., Lev. 26:12). And, this promise dovetails with Scripture's emphasis on sacred places such as the sanctuary and sacred times like the Sabbath. In the end, God will be with us in a way beyond imagining—greater than our greatest hopes and dreams. Then, it will be proclaimed, "the tabernacle of God is among the people, and He will dwell among them, and they shall be His people, and God Himself will be among them, and He will wipe away every tear from their eyes; and there will no longer be any death; there will no longer be any mourning, or crying, or pain; the first things have passed away" (Rev. 21:3-4; cf. 1 Cor. 2:9).

> All along the way, God Himself enters the story to be with us in space and time.

The Omnipresence and Special Presence of God

"Where can I go from Your Spirit? Or where can I flee from Your presence? If I ascend to heaven, You are there; If I make my bed in Sheol [the grave], behold, You are there. If I take up the wings of the dawn, if I dwell in the remotest part of the sea, even there Your hand will lead me, and Your right hand will take hold of me" (Ps. 139:7-10). Wherever the psalmist may go, God is there. God is present everywhere (omnipresent).

"'Am I a God who is near,' declares the LORD, 'and not a God far off? Can a person hide himself in hiding places so that I do not see him?' declares the LORD. 'Do I not fill the heavens and the earth?'" (Jer. 23:23-24; cf. Eph. 4:6). God is *both* near *and* far and somehow fills the heavens and the earth.

God's power extends to every location, for He "upholds all things by the word of His power" (Heb. 1:3). And nothing escapes God's sight, for "the eyes of the LORD are in every place, watching the evil and the good" (Prov. 15:3; cf. Job 34:21; Ps. 139:1–3; Ezek. 8:12; Amos 9:2–4).[6] No matter where something takes place, God is aware of it because God "knows all things" (1 John 3:20). Thus, *at least* in the sense of God's power and knowledge reaching everywhere, God is omnipresent.

Competing Theories in Christian Theology: Divine Presence

While Christian theologians typically agree God is omnipresent, there are various theories about the nature and manner of God's presence. Some believe God is omnipresent in the sense that His power and knowledge extend to every location, a view known as derivative omnipresence.[7] Some (but not all) who hold this view believe God *cannot* actually occupy space. Others claim God is somehow spatially present at every location, a view we might call nonderivative omnipresence.[8]

A minority of Christian theologians (e.g., some process theologians) believe the universe itself is *in* God and, thus, part of God's own being. This is a kind of panentheism, the view that everything that exists is *in* God.[9] This should not be confused with pantheism, the view that everything that exists *is* God such that God equals the universe. In contrast, Adventists affirm a strong view of the Creator-creature distinction such that creation is not to be identified with God (in part or in whole).

In contrast to panentheists and pantheists, most Christian theologians maintain God is utterly distinct from creation, cannot be contained in any spatial location, and is not by nature restricted to any physical or bodily form (*corpus*). Some believe God cannot have any physical body or take any physical form (*strict* incorporeality). Others instead (including Adventist theologians) maintain God is not bound to any physical form but can take on physical form (citing the incarnation as an instance of God doing so).[10] In what follows, I lay out an Adventist approach that affirms both divine omnipresence and *special* divine presence while recognizing that there is much that does not appear to be revealed in Scripture regarding the *precise manner* of divine presence.

God's Special Presence

"Go out and stand on the mountain before the Lord," God commanded Elijah. "And behold, the Lord was passing by! And a great and powerful wind was tearing out the mountains and breaking the rocks in pieces before the Lord; but the Lord was not in the wind. And after the wind there was an earthquake, but the Lord was not in the earthquake. And after the earthquake, a fire, but the Lord was not in the fire; and after the fire, a sound of a gentle blowing" (1 Kings 19:11–12).

While Scripture teaches God is omnipresent, in this and many other instances, Scripture also teaches that God is sometimes present in particular places in a special way. God was specially present with Adam and Eve in the garden, appeared in the form of a man to Abraham (Gen. 18:1–19:1) and Jacob (Gen. 32:24–30; Hosea 12:3–5), met with Moses at the burning bush and on many other occasions (Exod. 3:4–5; cf. 34:5–7), manifested Himself to the people of Israel (Exod. 24:9–11), "filled" the wilderness sanctuary and Solomon's temple (Exod. 40:34; 1 Kings 8:11), and met Elijah on the mountain in spectacular fashion (1 Kings 19:11–12). Such visible manifestations of divine presence are known as theophanies. The greatest theophany was the incarnation itself, when "the Word became flesh, and dwelt among us; and we saw His glory" (John 1:14).

In these and many other instances, God was *specially* present with people in particular times and places. In some *special* way, God's presence was concentrated in the Most Holy Place of the wilderness sanctuary and Solomon's temple. Yet, God's special presence may come and go, such as when God departed from Solomon's temple (Ezek. 11:22–23). And creatures may come before or flee from God's presence. Psalm 95:2 encourages people to "come before His presence with a song of thanksgiving." Conversely, "Cain left the presence of the Lord" (Gen. 4:16), "Jonah got up to flee to Tarshish from the presence of the Lord" (Jon. 1:3), and "Satan departed from the presence of the Lord" (Job 1:12; cf. 2:7).

At least at times, then, the special presence of God was conditional and could be forfeited (such as in the garden of Eden, and relative to the departure of God's glory from the temple). Thus, a prophet once told Asa, king of Judah, "the Lord is with you when you are with Him. And if you seek Him, He will let you find Him; but if you abandon Him, He will abandon you" (2 Chron. 15:2; see also Deut. 31:17–18; Acts 17:27; James 4:7–8).

And, elsewhere, God Himself states, "I dwell in a high and holy place, and also with the contrite and lowly of spirit" (Isa. 57:15; see also Rev. 3:20).

In the end, God will be with His people forevermore and a loud voice will proclaim, "Behold, the tabernacle of God is among the people, and He will dwell among them, and they shall be His people, and God Himself will be among them, and He will wipe away every tear from their eyes; and there will no longer be any death; there will no longer be any mourning, or crying, or pain; the first things have passed away" (Rev. 21:3–4).

I can hardly wait. When God's presence is finally restored in fullness, all the longings of the human heart will be met. There will be unending bliss because God is with us, and where God is, there is no pain or suffering, only holiness and goodness and unimaginable joy.

> When God's presence is finally restored in fullness, all the longings of the human heart will be met.

In the meantime, God is with His people wherever they go. Israel was promised, "the LORD is the one who is going ahead of you; He will be with you. He will not desert you or abandon you. Do not fear and do not be dismayed" (Deut. 31:8). Likewise, Joshua assured Israel: "Be strong and courageous! Do not be terrified nor dismayed, for the LORD your God is with you wherever you go" (Josh. 1:9; see also Isa. 43:2; Zech. 2:10–11).

Jesus similarly assured His followers, "where two or three have gathered together in My name, I am there in their midst" (Matt. 18:20). Likewise, Jesus promised His disciples in the Great Commission, "behold, I am with you always, to the end of the age" (Matt. 28:20). Even after He ascended, then, Jesus was somehow present *with* His disciples wherever they went. Somehow, via the Holy Spirit or otherwise, Jesus is still God *with us* even now.

Yet, we await the far greater special presence *with* Jesus in the Second Coming. Then, Christ's promise will be fulfilled, "I go to prepare a place for you" and "I will come again and receive you to Myself; that where I am, there you may be also" (John 14:2–3, NKJV).

God Is Near and Far—Immanent and Transcendent

God is somehow present everywhere, then, but not present everywhere in precisely the same way. God is sometimes specially present in particular places and times.

Yet, God cannot be contained. Solomon made this clear when he stated, "will God really dwell with mankind on the earth? Behold, heaven and the highest heaven cannot contain You; how much less this house which I have built!" (2 Chron. 6:18; cf. 1 Kings 8:27; Isa. 66:1; Acts 7:48).

Thus, when asked by the Samaritan woman at the well whether God should be worshiped at Mount Gerizim (where Samaritans worshiped at the time) or Jerusalem, Jesus replied, "a time is coming when you will worship the Father neither on this mountain nor in Jerusalem.... God is spirit, and those who worship Him must worship in spirit and truth" (John 4:21, 24). As Spirit, God is not restricted to particular places the way physical creatures are (cf. Luke 24:39).[11] Thus, God can be worshiped in many locations at the same time, present with us wherever we worship Him.

Though God is the all-powerful Creator who is not limited to any physical location or form, God has manifested Himself in physical form (cf. Exod. 24:10), especially in the incarnation (John 1:14).

God has drawn *near* to us, via the incarnation and otherwise, yet God is also *far* off, independent from the universe as the Creator and Sustainer of all (Gen. 1:1; Heb. 1:3). In these and other ways, God is transcendent, meaning God is above and beyond all creation. Yet, God is also immanent, meaning God is present with us and involved within creation.

The God of Scripture is both immanent and transcendent without contradiction. God is near to us and far off at the same time. As a children's story that I treasured growing up put it, the King "is as far away as you could ever suppose and yet he's as close as the tip of your nose."[12]

> **The God of Scripture is both immanent and transcendent without contradiction. God is near to us and far off at the same time.**

In all this, God is omnipresent and can be specially present. God is not incompatible with space. God can and does occupy and act within space, but God is not bound by space.

God with Us "in" Time

Even as God is not restricted by space in the way creatures are, God does not relate to time in the way mere creatures do. Yet, just as God can occupy space in ways unique and appropriate to God—being specially present in particular places—throughout Scripture, God acts and interacts in time, albeit in ways unique and appropriate to God.

Competing Theories in Christian Theology: Divine Eternity

Christian theologians agree God is eternal, meaning God had no beginning and will have no end. However, there are differing views of God's relation to time.

Many believe God is timeless, which (in the strict sense) means God cannot experience the passing of time. So understood, to be timeless (or atemporal) is to have no before or after—no succession of moments such that one has no past and no future. Among other things, this would mean God cannot do one thing and then another, nor perform any action that requires the passing of time. This is closely related to strict immutability and strict impassibility (discussed in chapter 7) because change takes time. Thus, a timeless God could not experience *any* change.

The idea of (strict) timelessness (alongside strict immutability and impassibility) is often traced to the influence of prominent streams of Greek philosophy, especially the pre-Christian philosophy of Plato (ca. 428/427–348/347 BC). For example, Augustine (AD 354–430), the most influential Christian theologian outside of Scripture, was heavily influenced by a later version of Plato's thought known as neoplatonism. Another highly influential theologian, Thomas Aquinas (AD 1225–1274), built on Augustine's theology while incorporating the philosophy of Aristotle (384–322 BC) that was becoming dominant at the time.

According to many historians, while the Protestant Reformation challenged numerous tenets of medieval Christianity, many leaders (e.g., Martin Luther, John Calvin) did not challenge the Augustinian concept of God.[13] Many identify this Augustinian conception as a form of (strict) classical theism, which views God as (among other things) strictly timeless, immutable, and impassible.

Other theologians believe God is not timeless but temporal (not to be confused with *temporary*). To say God is temporal means God experiences the passing of time—God has a past and a future. Many who affirm divine temporality, however, emphasize that God transcends creation and thus experiences "time" very differently from creatures (analogical temporality).[14]

Some who affirm divine temporality believe God *was* timeless but *became* temporal at the very moment He created the physical universe (and, with it, time itself). Others distinguish between time as we know it (called physical time or created time) and time in God's own life (metaphysical time or uncreated time), maintaining God has always been temporal in a way unique and appropriate to divinity, which cannot be measured (unmetricated).[15]

Others claim God is *both* timeless and temporal. However, doing so involves a contradiction *unless* one defines timeless to mean something other than strictly atemporal. If God experiences any passing of time (i.e., any temporality), then God cannot be strictly timeless (or *atemporal*).

An Adventist approach to these issues, affirming *analogical* temporality, is laid out below.

God Is Eternal and Temporal

"On that day it will be said to Jerusalem," the "Lord your God is in your midst, a victorious warrior. He will rejoice over you with joy, He will be quiet in His love, He will rejoice over you with shouts of joy" (Zeph. 3:16–17). This and other biblical passages depict God as having a future.

While Scripture does not say much specifically about the nature of time or of God's relation to it, Scripture does frequently depict God in distinctly temporal terms. For example, God's steadfast love is "from everlasting to everlasting" (Ps. 103:17), and God's "years will not come to an end" (Ps. 102:27; cf. Job 36:26). Further, God identifies Himself as "the Alpha and the Omega . . . who is and who was and who is to come, the Almighty" (Rev. 1:8).

Some believe texts like these (and others) might not definitively teach that God is temporal but simply use temporal language common to humans. However, beyond passages that refer to God and time specifically, many other texts depict God as performing actions and relating to creatures in temporal ways (i.e., ways that involve the passing of time).

For example, Scripture frequently depicts God performing one action and then *later* performing a different action, undergoing *changing* emotions, and otherwise *changing* relationally (see chapter 7). If God does such things (as Scripture depicts), then God cannot be timeless (in the strict sense discussed earlier). Since change requires the passing of time, if God were timeless, God could not change at all (strict immutability) and thus could not experience changing emotions (strict impassibility). If, however, God changes relationally (as Scripture teaches, see chapter 7), then God cannot be timeless.

While Scripture depicts God as temporal, however, Scripture also emphasizes that God is not temporal *in precisely the way humans are*. God is eternal, without beginning or end. God is the "Everlasting God, the Creator of the ends of the earth" (Isa. 40:28). God is "the eternal God" (Rom. 16:26), the "King eternal, immortal, invisible,"

> God is eternal, without beginning or end.

who deserves "honor and glory forever and ever" (1 Tim. 1:17). Thus, Psalm 90:2 proclaims: "Before the mountains were born or You gave birth to the earth and the world, even from everlasting to everlasting, You are God."

"Your years [God] are throughout all generations. In time of old You founded the earth, and the heavens are the work of Your hands. Even they will perish, but You endure; all of them will wear out like a garment; like clothing You will change them and they will pass away. But You are the same, and Your years will not come to an end" (Ps. 102:24–27). While things in creation are temporary, God is everlasting (cf. Ps. 103:15–17).

God acts and interacts temporally in this world, yet God is not contained by time, and God does not relate to time just as creatures do (cf. Job 10:4–5). As 2 Peter 3:8 proclaims, "with the Lord one day is like a thousand years, and a thousand years like one day" (cf. Ps. 90:4). Scripture depicts God as temporal in a way that is unique to God and appropriate to divinity (analogical temporality). God experiences temporal succession but relates to time differently than creatures do, transcending creation and time as we know it.

Even as the manner of divine presence is somewhat mysterious, God's relation to time remains mysterious. I do not claim to know exactly *how* God relates to time, but simply wish to affirm that God is capable of doing the things Scripture describes God as doing (e.g., engaging in back-and-forth relationship with creatures and changing relationally). If God were timeless, then God could not experience the passing of time.

God could not do one thing, then another. God could not experience emotional or other change. Yet, throughout Scripture, God performs *successive* actions, experiences changing emotions, and engages in back-and-forth covenantal relationships of love. Events such as creation and the cross are past even from God's perspective, and God Himself looks forward to the future when He will be reconciled with His people forevermore (see, e.g., Zeph. 3:17).

God Knows All Things: Divine Omniscience

If they could not tell the king what he wanted to know, they would be "torn limb from limb," and their homes would be "turned into a rubbish heap" (Dan. 2:5). A dream had greatly troubled Nebuchadnezzar, king of Babylon. He demanded that his wise men not only interpret the dream but first tell him what his dream was. They could not. No man could, they protested: "there is no one else who could declare it to the king except gods, whose dwelling place is not with mortal flesh" (Dan. 2:11).

So, the king decreed that all the wise men of Babylon be killed. This included Daniel, Hananiah, Mishael, and Azariah, exiles from Judah who had been trained as wise men. So, they prayed fervently.

God heard their prayers and revealed the dream and its meaning to Daniel, who reported what God revealed to the king while giving all the credit to the "God in heaven who reveals secrets" and "made known to King Nebuchadnezzar what will take place in the latter days" (Dan. 2:28). In response, Nebuchadnezzar declared, "Your God truly is a God of gods and a Lord of kings and a revealer of secrets, since you have been able to reveal this secret" (Dan. 2:47).

The dream foretold with amazing accuracy the succession of empires over many centuries, from Babylon to Rome and beyond. In many other prophecies in Daniel and beyond, God likewise foretold the future in astonishing detail (see, e.g., Dan. 7–12). Elsewhere, God contrasts His ability to predict the future with the inability of the "gods" of the nations to do so, citing this as conclusive evidence that He is the one true God (see, e.g., Isa. 41:22–23; 44:7–8, 21).

While creaturely knowledge is finite, God's "understanding is infinite" (Ps. 147:5); "there is no limit to His understanding" (Isa. 40:28, HCSB; cf. Job 37:16). Indeed, "there is no creature hidden from His sight, but all things are open and laid bare to" Him (Heb. 4:13). God is omniscient, which means God is all-knowing. God "knows all things" (1 John 3:20).

God's knowledge of all things includes intimate knowledge of every person. "LORD," the psalmist states, "You have searched me and known me. You know when I sit down and when I get up; You understand my thought from far away. You scrutinize my path and my lying down, and are acquainted with all my ways. Even before there is a word on my tongue, behold, LORD, You know it all. You have encircled me behind and in front, and placed Your hand upon me" (Ps. 139:1–5).

God's knowledge is both universal—including knowledge of all things that can be known—and particular, down to the number of hairs on your head (Ps. 44:21; 139:1–5; Matt. 6:8, 31; Luke 16:15; Acts 15:8; cf. Ps. 139:16; Isa. 46:9–10; Acts 2:23; 15:16–18; Rom. 8:28–30). As such, God is perfectly wise. God always knows what is best, so His plans and commands can be trusted.

Yet, does God know the future? Does God know what you and I will decide to do tomorrow, next week, and beyond? If so, do we have free will? If God knows the future, including the future decisions of creatures, how could we have free will?

> **God always knows what is best, so His plans and commands can be trusted.**

Competing Theories in Christian Theology: Divine Foreknowledge

God's knowledge of all future events, including knowledge of creatures' future decisions, is typically labeled exhaustive definite foreknowledge.

Many theologians believe God could have knowledge of *all* future events only if God causally determines creatures' future decisions; that is, if theistic determinism is true. Theistic determinism is the view that God causally determines everything that occurs, whether directly or indirectly *causing* everything to occur such that everything *must* occur precisely as it does.

If theistic determinism is true, creatures do not have freedom to will otherwise than God prefers. Theistic indeterminists, conversely, deny that God causally determines history, believing God grants creatures free will of the kind that is incompatible with determinism (libertarian free will).

With these definitions in mind, the main views about divine foreknowledge can be grouped into three categories:

- **Determinism and exhaustive foreknowledge:** Determinists maintain God knows the future exhaustively because He determines the future. God can predict all future events because all future events occur just as God has determined by Himself.
- **Indeterminism, but no exhaustive foreknowledge:** Process and open theists maintain God does not know the future exhaustively. They typically believe God can only know all creatures' future decisions if determinism is true, but they reject determinism.
- **Indeterminism and exhaustive foreknowledge:** Many other indeterminists believe God has exhaustive foreknowledge such that God knows creatures' future *free* decisions. Many such indeterminists believe God knows what creatures will decide in the future *and* creatures possess the ability to choose otherwise than God prefers (libertarian free will).

There are many theories regarding *how* God might possess exhaustive foreknowledge in a way compatible with the (libertarian) free will of creatures. For example, simple foreknowledge maintains God knows the future in some way that is not complex, with some proponents saying God somehow knows the future directly without thereby determining the future.[16] Instead, middle knowledge affirms God knows what any creature would freely do in any given circumstance. With such knowledge, God could know the future completely by adding His own decisions about what He will bring about in a way that respects creatures' free decisions.

Undoubtedly, there is mystery here, with different views held by intelligent and faithful Christians.[17] An Adventist approach to these issues is laid out below.

God Knows the Future

As I understand it, Scripture teaches both that God has exhaustive foreknowledge and that God consistently grants creatures the ability to will otherwise than God prefers. Creaturely free will is discussed in chapter 9. Here, we survey a small sample of what Scripture teaches about God's foreknowledge.[18]

"Your eyes have seen my formless substance," the psalmist says to God. "And in Your book were written all the days that were ordained for me, when as yet there was not one of them" (Ps. 139:16). This passage indicates that the psalmist's entire life, including his free decisions, was *foreknown* by God.

Elsewhere, God Himself proclaims: "I am God, and there is no other; I am God, and there is no one like Me, declaring the end from the beginning, and from ancient times things which have not been done" (Isa. 46:9–10; cf. Acts 15:16–18). The phrase "end from the beginning" seems to be a merism, a phrase that uses two contrasting words in order to refer to an entirety (like when one says, "young and old are welcome," meaning *all* are welcome). If so, this refers to God's knowledge not only of the end and the beginning but of everything in between—including the entirety of the future.

This understanding is consistent with Paul's teaching that God "works all things in accordance with the plan of His will" (Eph. 1:11, more on this later) and is supported by the context. Isaiah 46:9–10 appears in a section some call "the trial of the gods" (Isa. 41–48), wherein God highlights numerous ways the so-called "gods" the nations worship are deficient and thus false gods. One way God demonstrates this is by highlighting that those "gods" cannot tell the future, but He can.

"'Present your case,' the LORD says . . . 'Let them bring them forward and declare to us what is going to take place . . . announce to us what is coming; declare the things that are going to come afterward, so that we may know that you are gods" (Isa. 41:21–23). Later, God proclaims further, "I am the first and I am the last, and there is no God besides Me. Who is like Me? Let him proclaim and declare it" and "let them declare to them the things that are coming and the events that are going to take place" (Isa. 44:6–7). In these passages, God highlights foreknowledge as evidence of divinity (cf. John 13:19).

Then, God declares: "It is I who says of Cyrus, 'He is My shepherd, and he will carry out all My desire.' And He says of Jerusalem, 'she will be built,' and of the temple, 'Your foundation will be laid.' This is what the LORD says to Cyrus His anointed, whom I have taken by the right hand, to subdue nations before him and to undo the weapons belt on the waist of kings; to open doors before him so that gates will not be shut" (Isa. 44:28–45:1).[19] Cyrus was the Persian ruler who conquered Babylon in 539 BC and permitted the exiles to return and rebuild the temple in Jerusalem. Yet, this prophecy was recorded by Isaiah the prophet (writing ca. 740–700 BC) over one hundred years before Cyrus was born. Amazing! Likewise, hundreds of years before King Josiah was born, a prophecy mentioned him by name and foretold a specific action of Josiah that came to pass later on (1 Kings 13:1–2; see also 2 Kings 23:19–20).

Much later, Paul teaches about God's foreknowledge, saying, "we know that God causes all things to work together for good to those who love God, to those who are called according to His purpose. For those whom He foreknew, He also predestined to become conformed to the image of His Son, so that He would be the firstborn among many brothers and sisters; and these whom He predestined, He also called; and these whom He called, He also justified; and these whom He justified, He also glorified" (Rom. 8:28–30).

The Greek word translated "foreknew" in this passage (*proginōskō*) literally means to know beforehand and thus explicitly refers to foreknowledge. The Greek word translated "predestined" (*proorizō*) is a combination of two words and literally means "decide beforehand." One could decide something beforehand unilaterally (as determinists think God does), or one could decide something beforehand in a way that takes into account the free decisions of others. I believe Scripture teaches the latter (explained further in chapter 9) such that "predestined" (in Rom. 8:28–30 and elsewhere) refers to what God planned for the future after taking into account what God foreknows about creatures' free decisions. As I understand it, God providentially guides history to *restore* the good God has planned for us, while respecting the creaturely freedom that is essential to love relationship.

Elsewhere Paul writes, "we also have obtained an inheritance, having been predestined according to the purpose of Him who works all things in accordance with the plan of His will" (Eph. 1:11). Read in isolation, this text could be interpreted in a way consistent with determinism. However, this text is also consistent with the view that God *decides* or *plans* all things beforehand in a way that takes into account creatures' future free decisions (indeterminism with foreknowledge). How do we know whether to interpret this text as affirming determinism or indeterminism with foreknowledge? We should look to other biblical passages to see which interpretation makes sense of all relevant passages without twisting any of them. In the next chapter, I will discuss evidence that Scripture teaches indeterminism. Whatever one concludes about this, however, the teaching that God "works *all things* in accordance with the plan of His will" does not seem to be consistent with the view that God lacks exhaustive foreknowledge.

Many biblical stories also depict divine foreknowledge. For example, God gave Joseph dreams foretelling that his brothers would bow to him someday (Gen. 37:5–11, fulfilled in Gen. 42:6; 44:14). And Joseph interpreted the dreams of Pharaoh's cupbearer and baker, which correctly foretold just how Pharaoh would deal with them (Gen. 40:12–22; cf. Deut. 31:16–21).

Prophecies recorded in Daniel 2 and 7 foretold that Persia would arise to defeat and replace the Babylonian empire, that Greece would thereafter defeat and replace the Persian empire, and that Rome would thereafter arise and replace the Greek empire, along with many other things culminating with Christ's return. Daniel 9 records a prophecy given five hundred years before Jesus's birth, which foretold the precise year Christ would be baptized and begin His ministry and the precise year He would be crucified (one of many Messianic prophecies, see chapter 3). These amazing prophecies are discussed further in chapter 16.

Jesus Himself foretold that the twelve disciples would all abandon Him leading up to the crucifixion, saying: "'You will all fall away, because it is written: "I WILL STRIKE THE SHEPHERD, AND THE SHEEP WILL BE SCATTERED." But after I am raised, I will go ahead of you to Galilee.' But Peter said to Him, 'Even if they all fall away, yet I will not!' And Jesus said to him, 'Truly I say to you, that this very night, before a rooster crows twice, you yourself will deny Me three times'" (Mark 14:27–30). Just as Jesus foretold, after He was arrested, Peter denied he knew Jesus three times, then the rooster crowed.

Some who deny God has exhaustive foreknowledge argue Jesus might have predicted Peter's denial either by knowing Peter's character so well

He could predict Peter would deny Him or by selectively determining Peter's will. As I see it, the second hypothesis is unsatisfactory because it would mean God does not *consistently* grant free will and would mean that God sometimes causally determines that creatures do *evil* things (e.g., lying, denying Christ). The first hypothesis also seems unsatisfactory because Peter's character was not settled when He denied Christ, evidenced by the fact that Peter later repented and was restored. Moreover, this "settled character" hypothesis would not explain how Christ predicted the many details surrounding Peter's denials, such as the rooster crowing twice, and details regarding just when Peter would deny Jesus. Further, Jesus did not only predict that Peter would deny Him; He told the twelve disciples they would "all fall away" and identified this as fulfilling a centuries-old prophecy in Zechariah 13:7 (cf. Mark 14:27).

Likewise, Jesus foretold that Judas would betray Him and identified this also as a fulfillment of centuries-old prophecy (Ps. 41:9), saying, "I am not speaking about all of you. I know the ones whom I have chosen; but this is happening so that the Scripture may be fulfilled, 'HE WHO EATS MY BREAD HAS LIFTED UP HIS HEEL AGAINST ME'" (Mark 14:18–21; John 13:18). John reports, "Jesus knew from the beginning who they were who did not believe, and who it was who would betray Him" (John 6:64).[20] Right after predicting Judas's betrayal in John 13:18, Jesus explained, "From now on I am telling you before it happens, so that when it does happen, you may believe that I am He" (John 13:19). Similar to how God highlighted His ability to foretell future events as evidence He was the true God (e.g., as seen above in Isaiah), here Jesus pointed to His ability to predict the future as evidence "that I am He" (cf. John 8:58).

Jesus also repeatedly foretold His own death, including specific events that involved creatures' free decisions. For example, Jesus predicted: "Behold, we are going up to Jerusalem, and the Son of Man will be handed over to the chief priests and the scribes; and they will condemn Him to death and will hand Him over to the Gentiles. And they will mock Him and spit on Him, and flog Him and kill Him; and three days later He will rise from the dead" (Mark 10:33–34).

Indeed, the events surrounding Jesus's crucifixion are frequently described as occurring according to God's plan, indicating foreknowledge. For example, Acts 2:23 states, "this Man, delivered over by the predetermined plan and foreknowledge of God, you nailed to a cross by the hands of godless men and put Him to death" (cf. 1 Pet. 1:20). If one interprets this to mean God causally determined such evil events, it follows that God causally determines that creatures do evil, a conclusion that seems to contradict the biblical teaching that God's "work is perfect" and "all His ways are just" and "without injustice" (Deut. 32:4). The phrase "predetermined plan and foreknowledge," however, does not require the conclusion that God causally determined such events. This phrase is consistent with the view that God used His foreknowledge to plan beforehand what would occur in a way that incorporates creatures' free decisions. God's plan brings about the most preferable outcomes that are achievable, given the bad decisions of creatures (which are not up to God, see chapter 9).

In my view, these and other biblical passages teach God has exhaustive foreknowledge without teaching determinism.

God Asks Questions and Relents

Some believe other passages indicate God does not know the future exhaustively, such as when God asks Adam, "Have you eaten the fruit?" Or, when God asks Cain, "Where is your brother?"

However, God asks such questions not because He does not know the answers but for other reasons. Suppose I see my son with cookie crumbs on his face, with an open box of cookies on the counter, and ask him, "did you get into the cookies?" I already know the answer.

God sometimes asks people questions or tests them to bring them to a point that requires their response or manifests their decisions to themselves or others. For instance, after testing Abraham, God tells him, "now I know that you fear God" (Gen. 22:12). Yet, this cannot consistently be interpreted to mean God learned what was in Abraham's heart from this test. Even apart from foreknowledge, based on present knowledge alone God already knew Abraham feared God, for God "know[s] the human heart" (1 Kings 8:39, NRSVue; cf. Ps. 44:21; 139:1-5).

Further, some point to divine emotions as evidence God is sometimes surprised. However, emotional reactions do not require the element of surprise. One can feel genuine emotions in reaction to an event even if one knew that event would occur. This is true even of emotions that express frustration. Imagine a mother in a courtroom for a custody hearing concerning her young daughter. Imagine, further, that the child's father told the mother beforehand that during the hearing, he would falsely testify in court that she is an abusive mother. Even though she knew in advance, would she not still feel frustrated when he lies about her in court? Evidently, one can be deeply frustrated in reaction to events that one knew beforehand would occur.

Some also point to instances where some English translations say God "changed His mind" or repented (e.g., 1 Sam. 15:11, 35; Jon. 3:10), arguing that if God changed His mind, He must have encountered something He did not foreknow.[21] First, it is crucial to recognize that the Hebrew word, sometimes translated as "changed His mind" (*naham*) does not itself indicate or entail any change of mind. The term (*naham*) basically refers to sorrow or emotional pain, which may be "extended to describe the release of emotional tension" by God's relenting or "retracting a declared action" such as "punishment" or "blessing."[22] The term, then, indicates God's sorrow about something or that God compassionately changes His course of action in response to what has occurred (e.g., when God relented [*naham*] from destroying Nineveh in Jonah 3:10; cf. Jer. 18:7–10).

God changing His course in response to events does not indicate that God did not know such events beforehand. My son loves the beach. If I say to him, "if you clean your room, I will take you to the beach," I already know that he will clean his room. Nevertheless, his actual cleaning of his room changes my course of action from what it would have been if he did not clean his room to taking him to the beach.

What about God being sorry or even regretting something? To take one representative example, God said, "I regret [*naham*] that I have made Saul king" (1 Sam. 15:11). Some think this means God was surprised by Saul's disobedience. However, God could regret Saul's disobedience without being surprised by it. First, God had warned Israel what would occur if they had a king and told them He did not want them to have a king at that time (1 Sam. 8:6–22; cf. Deut. 17:14–20). Of course, then, God "regretted" making Saul king. God did not want them to have a king at that time in the first place.

Notably, one can regret and be sorrowful over something one has done even if one knew the results beforehand and would do the same thing again. For example, I regret that my family had to euthanize our beloved family cat years ago, but in light of the pain she was in and given that we had no preferable alternatives, I would do the same thing again.

Why, then, did God make Saul king? Israel rejected God as king, demanded a human king, and God let them have what they demanded (see 1 Sam. 8:7). Why Saul specifically? We are not told, but perhaps Saul was the most preferable option that the people would accept at the time.

Examples like these do not provide evidence that God lacks exhaustive foreknowledge, and I am not aware of any biblical passages that do.[23] Conversely, as seen earlier, many passages seem to teach God does know the future exhaustively.

How Can God Know the Future?

Yet, one might ask, if creatures have (libertarian) free will, *how* could God know the future? People often intuitively think that if God knows what I will decide to do tomorrow, I am not free to decide otherwise tomorrow. Based on this intuition, some claim God's having exhaustive foreknowledge is incompatible with God's consistently granting creatures (libertarian) free will.

The argument goes something like this:

God cannot be wrong.

So, if God knows what I will do tomorrow, then I *must* do whatever God knows I will do tomorrow.

However, this line of thinking actually involves a logical fallacy (called the fallacy of necessity). It need not be true that if God knows what I will do tomorrow, then I *must* do it. It *is true* that God must not be wrong. If God believes I will go for a walk tomorrow, He must not be wrong about that. But it does not follow from the fact that God must not be wrong that I *must* do whatever God believes I will do. If I have libertarian free will, I can choose *not* to take a walk tomorrow, and all that would follow from that is that God would not have believed that I would take a walk tomorrow.

The fact that God cannot be wrong about what I will decide does not cause or constrain my decision. If God's knowledge is *descriptive* rather than *prescriptive*, then events do not occur because God foreknows them, but God foreknows them because they will occur. As the Protestant

Reformer Jacobus (or James) Arminius (1560–1609) wrote: "For a thing does not come to pass because it has been foreknown or foretold; but it is foreknown and foretold because it is yet (*futura*) to come to pass."[24] God's foreknowledge, then, is not causative and does not restrict creaturely freedom. If so, God has foreknowledge of *whatever I freely* choose to do tomorrow. If I choose A tomorrow, God has foreknowledge of that. If I choose B tomorrow, God has foreknowledge of that instead.[25]

Yet, one may wonder, *how* does this work? *How* does God know the future? Scripture does not tell us *how* God knows the future. Yet, Scripture also tells us *that* God is eternal and omnipotent without telling us *how* God is eternal and omnipotent. Unless there is some contradiction involved, we do not need to know *how* something is the case in order to coherently affirm *that* it is the case.[26]

There are various theories of how divine foreknowledge *might* work (see the earlier discussion), but we do not have space to adequately consider them further here. Suffice it to say that God can do many things that are beyond creaturely understanding and imagination. The supposed problem, here, is not that God knows what everyone does at all times but that God knows what creatures will do *beforehand*. The supposed problem is a *timing* problem. However, if God can transcend the limitations that we experience relative to time and knowledge, why should I have difficulty believing God does so with respect to His knowledge of the future, even if I am not in a position to understand *how* He does so? Why should I expect to know *how* God knows the future? After all, Isaiah 40:28 tells us that God's "understanding is unsearchable" and Isaiah 55:8–9 teaches that God's thoughts and ways are far higher than our thoughts and ways. There are many things of God that are beyond our understanding.

Although there is considerable mystery here, I do not see any actual contradiction between believing that the Bible teaches that God knows the future completely and that God gives humans libertarian free will. And I believe the Bible teaches both, so I believe both.

Conclusion: Why Does It Matter?

She could not shake the feeling that God had rejected her. Surely God knew how evil she was, she thought. God must have known her sins and her selfishness from all eternity. She tried to hide it from others. Many thought she was a "good" person, but (when she let herself think about it) she saw her selfishness. But, she thought, if God knew she'd be like this, surely He had rejected her already. What kind of God would "waste" time with her, she wondered.

For some time, she had tried to make herself feel better by comparing herself to others. I am not as bad as that person over there, she thought. Compared to him, I am a "good" person. That has to count for something, right? But she could not shake the feeling. She knew in her heart her own inclination to selfishness and how very different that inclination is from the perfection of God.

More people than we realize worry that God might have already rejected them—that there is no hope for them. Perhaps you've thought like this or know someone who has. Well, let me assure you, God has not rejected you or them. God's invitation to live with Him forever is open—and remains open, for anyone who is willing to consider accepting that invitation. His compassionate seeking after us, to save us, goes far beyond any reasonable expectations.

> *God's invitation to live with Him forever is open for anyone who is willing to consider accepting that invitation.*

God longs to be with you more than you long to be with Him. God does not long for this because He needs you (or me). God needs nothing (cf. Acts 17:25). But, He longs for this because He loves you and me so very much, and He knows that the very best thing for us is to be with Him. Indeed, we were created for just this—to flourish in the special presence of God forever.

We've seen in this chapter that God is omnipresent; God is everywhere. Yet, God can also be specially present in particular places in addition to His general presence everywhere. We do not understand precisely how this works. Like many other things, we know and see only in part, for we see through a glass darkly (1 Cor. 13:12). But this should not surprise us. Because God is God and we are mere creatures, there will always be more for us to come to know about God. No creature could ever *fully* comprehend God.[27] We can know what God has revealed, but we should never make the mistake of forgetting that God is far greater than we can conceive.[28]

God is not only *with us* in space but also dwells *with us* in history—present with us in the past, present, and future while not being bound by time in the ways mere creatures are.

And God knows us more intimately than we know ourselves. He not only knows all our present experiences but He knows the past and the entire future—the end from the beginning. Because God knows this, we can be sure that He knows what He is doing, and He will bring about His promises.

God's knowledge, including foreknowledge, is exceedingly good news. If God knows the future, we can be sure that God has not taken unnecessary or reckless risks. We can be sure that God knows with certainty just which course of action is preferable for all concerned regarding every situation, and God knows with certainty that sin and evil will never rise again. If God knows the future, God foreknew you and me and every other person. And Christ chose to die for you and me specifically. Indeed, God chose to create *this* world, despite knowing the enormous cost to Himself, and can guarantee that He made the right decision in doing so.

In this regard, suppose a doctor is treating you for an infection that could become very serious if not treated. There is only one medicine available for the infection, but it has a potential side effect; it *might* cause terminal cancer, and it might not work to treat the infection effectively. If you take the medicine, the medicine might not work, and you could die because of it. But, if you do not take the medicine, your infection could itself become very serious, maybe even life-threatening. In this situation, would you rather have a physician who knows with certainty whether the medicine would effectively treat the infection and just what side effects, if any, it would have? Or, would you prefer the physician who only knows that the treatment *might* work and *might* have such side effects? The answer seems obvious.

Because God knows the future, we can be certain that He knows what is best, His loving commands are best for all concerned, and His promises are sure.

Even now, this God is with us, though not in the fullness of special presence He intended from the beginning and will bring about in the end. To assure and remind humans of His special presence, God gave His people the sanctuary as a place where He would specially dwell with them, and gave them the Sabbath as a kind of temple in time (see chapters 15 and 16). And He Himself (in Christ) became human—the ultimate example of God *with us*.

Whether you have an earthly father or mother, brother or sister, wife or husband, son or daughter, or no one on earth, you have a Father in heaven who is with you even now and desires to bring you into closer relationship with Himself, that you will one day dwell where Christ is and be with Him forever. As Jesus Himself promised: "In My Father's house are many mansions; if it were not so, I would have told you. I go to prepare a place for you. And if I go and prepare a place for you, I will come again and receive you to Myself; that where I am, there you may be also" (John 14:2–3, NKJV).

Whether you realize it or not, you belong to Him, and He is with you. But He longs to be more closely present with you still. Do you also long for this? If you do, respond to His drawing and calling of you even now. Invite His Spirit to dwell in you and give yourself wholeheartedly to Him. You can have a special encounter with the living God, who is with you right now.

> Whether you realize it or not, you belong to Him, and He is with you.

I invite you now to reflect further on the God who is with us in space and time. Read and reflect on Psalm 139, pondering the greatness of God; who is always with us and knows us better than we know ourselves and, despite our shortcomings, loves us and does everything He can to save us.

Questions for Reflection

1. What does it mean to you to know that God is present everywhere? What is the significance of the difference between God's omnipresence and special presence?
2. What practices can you begin or continue that might bring you into an experience of God's special presence?
3. Why does it matter whether God is strictly timeless or (analogically) temporal? How would you explain the significance of this to someone else?
4. Does it matter whether God can interact with creatures in space and time? What would it mean for the biblical stories if God has no past and no future?

5. How might knowing that God knows the future give you confidence that God knows what is best and can assure His promises will come to fruition in the end?
6. At the risk of getting ahead of ourselves, reflect on how God's ability to be present with us in space and time relates to core Adventist beliefs such as the sanctuary, the Sabbath, and the Second Coming (discussed in chapters 15, 16, and 19).
7. You can experience the special presence of God even now. Do you wish to experience God's presence? Simply ask for God's special presence in and with you. Pray in humility and faith, and God will be *with* you in a special way. "Draw near to God and He will draw near to you" (James 4:8).

For Further Reading

Adventist Perspectives:

Canale, Fernando. *Basic Elements of Christian Theology.* Berrien Springs, MI: Andrews University Lithotech, 2005.

———. "Doctrine of God" in *Handbook of Seventh-day Adventist Theology.* Edited by Raoul Dederen. Hagerstown, MD: Review and Herald, 2000.

Gulley, Norman R. *Systematic Theology: God as Trinity.* Berrien Springs, MI: Andrews University Press, 2011.

Hanna, Martin F. "Foreknowledge and the Freedom of Salvation." In *Salvation: Contours of Adventist Soteriology.* Edited by Martin F. Hanna, Darius W. Jankiewicz, and John W. Reeve, 33–60. Berrien Springs, MI: Andrews University Press, 2018.

Peckham, John C. *Divine Attributes: Knowing the Covenantal God of Scripture.* Grand Rapids, MI: Baker Academic, 2021.

———. *The Doctrine of God: Introducing the Big Questions.* London: T&T Clark, 2019.

———. *Theodicy of Love: Cosmic Conflict and the Problem of Evil.* Grand Rapids, MI: Baker Academic, 2018.

See also the resources on the Biblical Research Institute website: https://adventistbiblicalresearch.org/materials/.

Other Christian Perspectives:

Beilby, James K. and Paul R. Eddy, eds. *Divine Foreknowledge: Four Views*. Downers Grove, IL: InterVarsity, 2001.

Craig, William Lane. *The Only Wise God: The Compatibility of Divine Foreknowledge and Human Freedom*. Grand Rapids, MI: Baker, 1987.

Duvall, J. Scott, and J. Daniel Hays, *God's Relational Presence: The Cohesive Center of Biblical Theology*. Grand Rapids, MI: Baker Academic, 2019.

Lister, J. Ryan. *The Presence of God*. Wheaton, IL: Crossway, 2015.

Ganssle, Gregory, ed. *God and Time: Four Views*. Downers Grove, IL: InterVarsity, 2001.

Mullins, R. T. *The End of the Timeless God*. New York: Oxford University Press, 2016.

Nash, Ronald. *The Concept of God: An Exploration of Contemporary Difficulties with the Attributes of God*. Grand Rapids, MI: Zondervan, 1983.

Wolterstorff, Nicholas. *Inquiring About God: Selected Essays*, Vol. 1. Cambridge: Cambridge University Press, 2010.

Zagzegbski, Linda. *Omnisubjectivity: A Defense of a Divine Attribute*. Marquette: Marquette University Press, 2013.

9

THE GOD WHO PROVIDES ALL GOOD THINGS AND CONQUERS EVIL: DIVINE PROVIDENCE AND COSMIC CONFLICT

Why? It made no sense. He had followed God's call. John the Baptist had been a miracle child, chosen and called to prepare the way for the Messiah. He baptized Jesus, and Jesus even said of him, "among those born of women there is no one greater than John" (Luke 7:28). Yet, John languished in prison. Was Jesus truly the Messiah? If so, why was John left in prison to suffer and die?

Why do bad things happen to "good" people? Why is there evil in this world at all? In the end, John was beheaded. It seemed like evil triumphed. How could God let this happen? God's faithful servant was killed by wicked people who desired to silence him.

Job also suffered undeservedly. He questioned God's justice (Job 9:24) and even "cursed the day of his birth" (Job 3:1). He thought God was "cruel" to him (Job 30:21), but we will see later that such cruelty was inflicted by another. There was far more to the story that Job could not see.

Others throughout Scripture also questioned God's justice in the face of evil:

- "Where is the God of justice?" (Mal. 2:17)
- "Why do You stand far away, O Lord? Why do You hide Yourself in times of trouble?" (Ps. 10:1)
- "How long shall the wicked triumph?" (Ps. 94:3)
- "Why has the way of the wicked prospered?" (Jer. 12:1)
- "Why has the Lord our God done all these things to us?" (Jer. 5:19)
- "Why have these things happened to me?" (Jer. 13:22)

- Jesus, Himself the greatest victim of undeserved suffering, asked: "My God, My God, why have You forsaken Me?" (Mark 15:34; cf. Ps. 22)

If God is good, why is there so much evil? Why does evil seem to reign on our planet? These questions voice the problem of evil: If God is entirely good (omnibenevolent) and all-powerful (omnipotent), why does evil occur?

Alongside the problem of evil, this chapter addresses questions about God's providence—God's sustaining and guiding actions in history. Such questions include:

- Is God in control of history?
- Does God control everything that happens?
- Does God always get what He wants?

Along the way, we will see that God engages in back-and-forth relationship with creatures, always keeps His promises, and always wants and wills what is best for us. Yet, many things occur that God does not want to occur. Nevertheless, God can be trusted and will make things right in the end.

The Story of the Cosmic Conflict

He had not eaten for forty days. Jesus was in the wilderness and famished. There, the devil confronted Him. The arch-deceiver tempted Jesus, "If You are the Son of God, command that these stones become bread."

"It is written," Jesus replied, "Man shall not live on bread alone, but on every word that comes out of the mouth of God."

Taking Him to the pinnacle of the temple, Satan challenged Jesus, "If You are the Son of God, throw Yourself down."

"It is written," Jesus answered, "You shall not put the Lord your God to the test."

Then, "the devil took Him to a very high mountain and showed Him all the kingdoms of the world and their glory; and he said to Him, 'All these things I will give You, if You fall down and worship me.'"

"Go away, Satan!" Jesus responded. "For it is written, 'You shall worship the Lord your God, and serve Him only.' Then the devil left Him; and behold, angels came and began to serve Him" (Matt. 4:1–11).

According to Luke's account, Satan declared, "I will give You all this domain and its glory, for it has been handed over to me, and I give it to whomever I want. Therefore if You worship before me, it shall all be Yours" (Luke 4:6–7). Just imagine how tempting this was. If He would just bow down and worship, the devil claimed, Jesus could reclaim rulership of this world without the suffering and excruciating death before Him. No other has ever faced so great a temptation.

Here and elsewhere, central to the cosmic conflict between Christ and Satan is Satan's attempt to take God's place and receive the worship due to God alone.

The Serpent of Old

When God finished creating our world, "God saw all that He had made, and behold, it was very good" (Gen. 1:31). Evil had no part in God's good creation. Evil came from elsewhere.[1] How, then, did evil infect our planet?

Adam and Eve lived in perfect moral harmony with God and one another (Gen. 2:25), and they possessed moral freedom. The fruit of every tree of the garden was theirs to enjoy, except one tree God commanded them not to eat from (Gen. 2:16–17). They could obey God or disobey God, doing evil.[2]

One day, Eve went to that tree. There, she met a serpent who asked: "Has God really said, 'You shall not eat from any tree of the garden'?"[3] The serpent's question drew Eve into a dangerous, ultimately tragic, dialogue. In reply, Eve corrected the serpent's twisting of God's command, explaining that there was only one tree from which they could not eat, lest they die.

The serpent then directly contradicted God's words, asserting, "You certainly will not die! For God knows that on the day you eat from it your eyes will be opened, and you will become like God, knowing good and evil" (Gen. 3:1–5).

This was a direct attack on God and His character.[4] The serpent alleged that God is a liar who didn't really want what was best for Eve but was withholding something good (knowledge) from her to oppress her. Eve was thus confronted with a choice: believe what God had said or entertain the serpent's insidious slander of God's character.

Suppose everything you thought you knew about the person you love most in the world was challenged in a convincing, even spectacular, way. Suppose someone convinced you that your beloved was just using you, seeking to control and oppress you. If believed, such allegations would fracture your love relationship.

Likewise, the serpent's allegations attacked love relationship between God and humans. Either God or the serpent had lied. Who would Eve believe? Tragically, she chose to distrust God and eat the fruit. Adam also ate, with horrendous consequences.

This narrative spotlights a conflict over the truth about God's character. Central to the conflict is the choice of what or whom to believe. From Genesis to Revelation, the cosmic conflict revolves around whether creatures will choose to believe God or the serpent's lies about God.

Scripture later identifies this "serpent of old" as the devil himself, "who deceives the whole world," the "accuser of our brothers and sisters... who accuses them before our God day and night" (Rev. 12:9-10; cf. 20:2-3).[5] And Jesus Himself alluded to this Genesis story when He identified the devil as "a murderer from the beginning" and "a liar and the father of lies" (John 8:44).[6] Later, Paul identifies Satan as "the god of this world" who "has blinded the minds of the unbelieving" (2 Cor. 4:4; see also Acts 26:18).

> From Genesis to Revelation, the cosmic conflict revolves around whether creatures will choose to believe God or the serpent's lies about God.

Satan was once a perfect angel of light, but he fell, leading other "angels" who rebelled and "sinned" against God (2 Pet. 2:4; cf. Jude 6; Rev. 12:4). He and "his angels waged war" against God's kingdom (Rev. 12:7-9). Ezekiel 28 depicts the fall of this once-perfect angel who chose to rebel against God.[7]

While directed to the "king of Tyre," Ezekiel's message is directed beyond the human king to an angelic ruler—one who was a *covering* cherub (Ezek. 28:16; cf. Exod. 25:19). Specifically, the message addresses one who "had the seal of perfection, full of wisdom and perfect in beauty," who was present "in Eden, the garden of God," and was "the anointed cherub who covers" on "the holy mountain of God" (Ezek. 28:12-14). Twice, the text declares this angel was "perfect," the second time declaring, "You were blameless in your ways from the day you were created until unrighteousness was found in you" (Ezek. 28:15; cf. 28:12). Only one person fits this description of a formerly perfect angel who was present in Eden—"the serpent of old who is called the devil and Satan" (Rev. 12:9).

How did evil arise from this "perfect" creature?[8] This angel turned inward in pride, his "heart was haughty because of" his "beauty" and he "corrupted" his "wisdom" (Ezek. 28:17). Elsewhere, Isaiah describes Satan's attempt to exalt himself above God: "How you have fallen from heaven, you star of the morning, son of the dawn!" You "said in your heart, 'I will ascend to heaven; I will raise my throne above the stars of God" and "I will make myself like the Most High'" (Isa. 14:12–14).

Toward this end, Satan became "filled with violence" by the "abundance of [his] trade"

(Ezek. 28:16; cf. 18). The term translated "trade" (*rekullah*) derives from the Hebrew root (*rakil*), which refers to "slander" (cf. Lev. 19:16; Prov. 20:19).[9] Even as Satan slandered God's character and God's law in Eden by alleging God is a self-serving liar, Satan slandered God and sowed discord in heaven.

God commissioned Adam and Eve to rule this world (Gen. 1:28). But, through their fall, Satan became the temporary "ruler of this world" (John 12:31; 14:30; 16:11; cf. 2 Cor. 4:4), "handed over to" him through Adam and Eve's fall (cf. Luke 4:6). We thus live in enemy-ruled territory. Later, at Babel, the peoples of the world likewise rejected God's covenant promises and further gave themselves over to enemy rule (more on this later).

Despite repeated rebellions, God bestowed amazing grace. Shortly after Adam and Eve's fall, God proclaimed the good news that deliverance would come through Christ's conquest over Satan. Specifically, God told the serpent, "I will put enmity between you and the woman, and between your seed and her Seed; He shall bruise your head, and you shall bruise His heel" (Gen. 3:15, NKJV). The "Seed" of the woman here refers to Jesus, the Messiah. The serpent would bruise Christ's heel at the cross, but via the cross, Christ would crush the serpent's head (Gen. 3:15, often referred to as the *protoevangelium*, the "first gospel"). Here, the gospel is framed in the context of the cosmic conflict unfolded throughout Scripture. Christ came to "destroy the works of the devil" (1 John 3:8) and to "destroy the one who has the power of death, that is, the devil" (Heb. 2:14). By voluntarily suffering and dying for us, Christ defeated Satan and made certain the final eradication of evil, suffering, and death.

The Loving Providence of God: Divine Providence and Human Freedom

"I called, but no one answered; I spoke, but they did not listen. Instead, they did evil in My sight and chose that in which I did not delight" (Isa. 66:4). Here, God laments the evil humans have chosen, contrary to God's desires. According to this text (and many others like it), God does not always get what He wants because creatures often exercise their free will to choose otherwise than God prefers.

The very question of whether or not God always gets what He wants, discussed in more detail further below, is integrally related to broader questions about God's providence. Divine providence refers to God's sustenance and governance of the world, with special attention to God's action to bring about God's purposes in the world.

Competing Theories in Christian Theology: Divine Providence and Human Free Will

Divine providence and human free will are among the most heavily debated issues in Christian theology. Determinism teaches that every occurrence is caused by prior factors such that it must occur just as it does. Theistic determinism, more specifically, teaches that God causes everything to happen precisely as it does, whether directly or indirectly. In Christian theology, many trace determinism to Augustine (AD 354–430), and some contend that Christian theologians before Augustine rejected determinism.[10] In Protestant circles, theistic determinism is often associated with (and sometimes even labeled) Calvinism, but Calvinism (named after the French Protestant Reformer John Calvin, 1509–1564) as a system is complex, with many nuances among Calvinists.

Indeterminism, conversely, maintains that history is not entirely causally determined to occur just as it does. Theistic indeterminists maintain that God grants creatures free will of a kind that is incompatible with determinism, such that God does not causally determine creatures' decisions (libertarian free will). In Protestant circles, indeterminism is often labeled Arminianism, but here again, Arminianism (named after the Dutch Reformer Jacob Arminius, 1560–1609) as a system is complex, and some Protestants before Arminius affirmed indeterminism (e.g., Philip Melanchthon, 1497–1560).[11]

Libertarian free will is what most people intuitively think of when they hear the phrase "free will." Many determinists, however, maintain that humans possess *compatibilist* free will, meaning humans are free to do what they want, but what they want is itself entirely determined by prior factors outside their control. Adopting compatibilism, many determinist theologians believe humans are "free" to do what they want, but what humans want to do is itself causally determined by God.

These very different definitions of "free will" complicate the debate over whether Scripture teaches that humans have free will. Many biblical texts appear to affirm human free will (e.g., Deut. 30:19; Josh. 24:15). Yet, compatibilists often argue that such texts refer only to the freedom of humans to do what they want, consistent with the compatibilist view that what humans want to do is itself determined by God. This sometimes brings the discussion to an impasse.

Such an impasse might be overcome, however, by asking whether Scripture teaches that God always gets what He wants. If theistic determinism is true, all events occur as they do because God has causally determined history to take place just as it does. Yet, if God causally determines *all* history, nothing would occur that is otherwise than what God *actually* prefers. If things occur that God *actually* prefers not to occur, then theistic determinism is false.

To address what Scripture teaches relative to this debate, then, I will focus on texts relevant to the question: Does God always get what He wants?[12] That is, does everything occur as God *actually* prefers?

In what follows, I will lay out an Adventist approach to these issues, affirming the indeterministic view that God grants humans (and other creatures, such as angels) *libertarian* free will.

Does God Always Get What He Wants?

Throughout Scripture, creatures frequently choose otherwise than God prefers.[13] For instance, Isaiah proclaimed, God "longs to be gracious" to

His people and "waits on high to have compassion," but they were "not willing" (Isa. 30:18, 15).[14] Elsewhere, God lamented that His people "are not willing to listen to Me" (Ezek. 3:7; cf. Ps. 81:11–14; Isa. 65:12; 66:4; Jer. 19:5).

Likewise, Jesus sadly announced, "Jerusalem, Jerusalem, who kills the prophets and stones those who have been sent to her! How often I wanted to gather your children together, the way a hen gathers her chicks under her wings, and you were unwilling" (Matt. 23:37; cf. Luke 13:34; John 5:40).[15] Further, "the Pharisees and the lawyers rejected God's purpose for themselves" (Luke 7:30; cf. Mark 7:24).[16] God's will, then, can be rejected.

This is particularly highlighted relative to God's desire to save everyone. Scripture teaches that God "wants all people to be saved and to come to the knowledge of the truth" (1 Tim. 2:4), "not willing for any to perish, but for all to come to repentance" (2 Pet. 3:9). "'I take no pleasure in the death of anyone who dies,' declares the Lord GOD. 'Therefore, repent and live!'" (Ezek. 18:32; cf. 18:23; 33:11).[17] Tragically, however, some reject God's gift of salvation (see Dan. 12:2; John 3:18; 5:11–12, 28–29; 2 Thess. 1:7–10; 2:10–12; Rev. 20:12–15). God wants to save *everyone,* but some finally reject salvation. In these and many other instances, God does not get what He wants.

These and many other instances indicate that creatures possess freedom to will otherwise than God prefers. If so, creatures possess free will of the kind that is incompatible with determinism (free will of this kind is known as *libertarian* free will).

If God consistently grants this kind of free will such that creatures can do otherwise than God prefers, then God cannot determine that creatures always *freely* do good. Put differently, if God consistently grants creatures (libertarian) free will to act in the world, then it is not up to God whether a creature uses that free will to do good or evil.

As we have seen in part, the story of Scripture reveals that evil is the result of creatures misusing free will. Our fallen world includes many events that God does not want to occur. What, then, of divine providence?

God's Ideal and Remedial Wills

Throughout Scripture, people often will otherwise than God prefers. Yet, Scripture also teaches that God "works all things in accordance with the plan of His will" (Eph. 1:11). How can both be true? Do all events happen according to God's will, or do some events go against God's will?

Both can be true if we distinguish between God's ideal will and God's remedial will. God's ideal will is what God actually prefers, what would occur if everyone always did what God wants. If everything occurred according to God's *ideal* will, there would be no evil. Yet, God's ideal will is often unfulfilled because creatures often do otherwise than God prefers. God's remedial will, on the other hand, is what God wills *after* taking into account the free decisions of creatures, including creatures' bad decisions. It consists of God's will (and plan) to remedy the evils in the world brought about by creatures' bad decisions.

Imagine a cooking competition in which the chefs are required to use some set of ingredients but are free to also use any other ingredients to make the meal of their choosing. The final meal includes some ingredients the chef did not choose and others the chef did choose.

God's *remedial* will is somewhat like this. Because God consistently grants creatures free will, many "ingredients" of history result from creatures' decisions, including many bad ones. Yet, God also makes decisions and works to bring about the most preferable outcomes God can without breaking His commitment to creaturely freedom, a commitment that itself is for the sake of love (as we will see later).

It can be true that God's (ideal) will is sometimes unfulfilled (Luke 7:30) *and* that God "works all things in accordance with the plan of His will" (Eph. 1:11) if Ephesians 1:11 refers to God's *remedial* will, which includes creatures' free decisions (including those contrary to God's ideal will).[18] God indeed accomplishes all things according to His *remedial* will, but many things occur that God does not prefer because creatures often do otherwise than God *ideally* wills.

One of the many biblical examples of this is the case of Joseph being sold into slavery by his brothers. When Joseph meets his brothers many years later, after rising to a position of high authority in Egypt and thereby helping to save many lives (including those of his family) during the long famine, regarding their evil act of selling him into slavery Joseph declares: "As for you, you meant evil against me, but God meant it for good in order to bring about this present result, to keep many people alive" (Gen. 50:20). In this case, Joseph's brothers committed the evil of selling him into slavery *of their own free will*, working against God's *ideal will* (since it was evil), yet God nevertheless worked to bring about good in the end, to save many people, according to His remedial will.[19]

In all this, evil does not catch God by surprise. As we have seen, God foreknows creatures' free decisions, and thus God's providential plan (God's remedial will) includes the remedy for all evils. God does *not* cause all things. Many things occur that God does not want to occur. Yet, God always works to *remedy* all situations such that God "causes all things to work together for good to those who love God, to those who are called according to His purpose" (Rom. 8:28; cf. 8:18). God's remedial will culminates with the restoration of all things so that there is no evil or suffering forevermore, but only the perfect goodness and bliss that God always intended (see Rev. 21:3–4).

Love and Freedom

If you've ever participated in a group project, you know the outcome does not reflect only your input but is partially based on what you do and partially based on others' contributions. Likewise, because God grants creatures free will to bring about consequences in the world, history includes the results of countless decisions of creatures—including myriads of bad ones.

Yet, why does God grant creatures such freedom in the first place? Why not make everything happen according to His ideal will? The short answer is: God grants freedom for the sake of love. God is love, and genuine love relationship *requires* freedom.[20]

> God grants freedom for the sake of love. God is love, and genuine love relationship requires freedom.

Imagine you possessed the power to make someone else believe, will, and do whatever you wish. Could you, then, *make* them love you? No, you could not. Why? Because love requires freedom.[21] Love can only be *freely* given and *freely* received. Love relationship cannot be brought about by one party alone, no matter how powerful. Love relationship is, by nature, a cooperative outcome that involves more than one *free* party. God Himself loves freely and will not compel anyone else to act as He ideally desires because that would eradicate love.

This is why God *calls* creatures to love Him and one another (in the two greatest commands, see Matt. 22:37–40), but God does not *compel* creatures to love. If love did not require freedom, God would determine that everyone love perfectly all the time, just as He ideally wills and commands. But love *cannot* be compelled or otherwise determined, even by God.[22] The nature of love itself is not external to God as if there is some external principle to which God is beholden, but grounded in God's nature itself ("God is love," 1 John 4:8), and God "cannot deny Himself" (2 Tim. 2:13).

Genuine love relationship with creatures is possible only if God consistently grants creatures freedom to will otherwise than God ideally desires. But, to will otherwise than God ideally desires is to will evil. For creatures to possess the ability to love, then, requires that such creatures possess the freedom to reject love, which is the freedom to do evil. The very possibility of creaturely love relationship, then, requires the *possibility* of evil (but not its necessity). Were God to negate the *possibility* of evil, God would thereby also negate the very possibility for creatures to enjoy love relationship, contradicting His own character of love.

God is love (1 John 4:8, 16). As such, love is the highest value and best good in the universe (cf. 1 Cor. 13:13). Accordingly, God desires that creatures have the capacity to love and be loved. But such love requires free will, including the freedom to do evil. God consistently grants creatures such free will, then, because to do otherwise would exclude love.

Consequential Freedom Requires Laws

More specifically, creaturely love relationship requires freedom to act in ways that bring about intended outcomes in the world, which might be loving or not loving (i.e., good or evil). In order for creatures to have this kind of *consequential* freedom, creatures must possess the ability to act within limits that are relatively constant and within a context wherein (relatively) predictable effects follow from one's actions.[23] That is, there must be some way things typically work, some order in nature governed by laws that allow you to form intentions with the reasonable belief that what you do will bring about those intentions.[24] Your actions can have the consequences you intend only if your actions occur in an environment with (relatively) predictable laws or processes that govern the relationship of causes and effects.

Imagine trying to play a game without any rules or a video game that is not programmed with any regularity. When you press the "x" button, sometimes your character jumps, sometimes it crouches, and sometimes it does nothing at all. You never know what any button on the control pad will bring about on the screen because there is no regular pattern of what pressing "x" (or any other button) brings about. What you intend when you press "x" would be *inconsequential* because you would have no idea whether pressing this or that button would cause what you intend.

In a somewhat similar fashion, some "natural" order is required in our world in order for us to bring about intentionally loving or unloving outcomes. Without such order, our intentions would be inconsequential—there would be no impactful difference between loving (good) and unloving (evil) intentions. However, since genuine love relationship requires not only the freedom to *intend* loving actions but also to *perform* loving actions, genuine love relationship requires some law-governed natural order.

Not only is love the fulfillment of the law (Rom. 13:10), then, but the law itself is necessary for love. Accordingly, there is much evidence that God has ordered the created world to operate according to some consistent laws of nature, which God Himself *covenants* not to contravene because such order is crucial to the flourishing of love. Indeed, Scripture is filled with God making covenants, including covenants relative to nature operating in consistent, orderly ways (see Jer. 33:20–26; 31:35–37; cf. Gen. 8:20–22; 9:15–17).

Because God cannot deny Himself (2 Tim. 2:13) and always keeps His commitments and promises (Titus 1:2; Heb. 6:17–18), God's own action is *morally* limited according to whatever covenants He makes. Put differently, when God makes promises or gives laws, He thereby limits His future action to that which accords with His promises and laws yet without diminishing His sheer power (this is often called divine self-limitation).

> **Just as God does not break His promises, God does not break His own laws.**

Just as God does not break His promises, God does not break *His* own laws (see, e.g., Ps. 80:34; 111:7–8; 119:160). If God commits to consistently granting creatures consequential freedom (for the sake of love), along with the laws and forces of nature such consequential freedom requires, God will always act within the bounds of such commitments, both with regard to His laws relative to the workings of nature and His moral laws (on the latter, see chapter 14). This does not prevent God from working miracles but means the kinds of miracles God works always accord with God's promises and covenants (including *His* laws, with respect to the workings of nature and otherwise) because God never works contrary to His own commitments or His own laws.[25] God can nevertheless work mighty miracles (such as parting the Red Sea or raising people from the dead) because, as the Creator of nature who transcends and sustains nature by His *supernatural* power (see Heb. 1:3), God can work in *accordance* with *His* laws in *supernatural* ways that are far beyond the abilities (and limited understanding) of mere humans.[26]

We'll say more about the importance of divine law and its very good ends in a later chapter. Here it is important to recognize that, for the sake of goodness and love (grounded in God's very nature), God orders our world in a way that functions according to some consistent laws. And God Himself always works in accordance with such laws.

God is a God of order—a covenantal God who governs the world according to covenantal parameters consisting of divine promises and laws. God created the universe of His own free will (Rev. 4:11), and God sustains the universe by His power (Heb. 1:3). God sustains the world in accordance with His laws relative to the order and forces of nature, which He instituted in creation, and providentially governs the world in a way that makes room for the kind of freedom necessary for love.

The Problem of Evil and Theodicy

With this understanding of divine providence in place, we are now in a position to return to the problem of evil.[27]

Competing Theories in Christian Theology: The Problem of Evil

The question of theodicy is the question of how God's goodness can be reconciled with the evil in the world. Many theodicies attempt to resolve the logical problem of evil, which asserts that if an entirely good and all-powerful God exists, there would be no evil. Thinkers attempt to resolve this problem in various ways, including:

Denying or Modifying the Premises: Some deny that God is entirely good or that God is all-powerful such that God simply lacks the power to prevent evil. Denying these, however, is inconsistent with biblical teachings that God is entirely good (e.g., Deut. 32:4; 1 John 1:5) and omnipotent (e.g., Jer. 32:17–20; Rev. 1:8). Some, instead, deny that God has exhaustive knowledge of the future (exhaustive foreknowledge) and claim this helps relative to the problem of evil. However, denying that God possesses exhaustive foreknowledge (see chapter 8) provides no discernible advantage relative to the problem of evil. Even if God lacked foreknowledge, God's comprehensive *present* knowledge would be sufficient for God to anticipate any instance of evil at least a fraction of a second before it occurred. If God has some good reason(s) for not preventing an instance of evil that He anticipates (at least) just before it occurs, then the same good reason would apply relative to why God does not prevent an evil that He foreknows from before the creation of the world. God either has good and sufficient reasons for acting or refraining from acting relative to evil, or He does not. If God has such reasons, then those reasons are sufficient whether or not God possesses foreknowledge.[28]

Felix culpa (Latin for "happy fault"): Some claim it is actually better that evil occurs—God either permits or determines evils to bring greater good out of evil. For example, some claim God determines evil in order to bring about the greater good of manifesting His glory and wrath against evil (the divine glory defense). This, however, faces problems like affirming that God determines evil, evil is necessary for good, evil is an instrumental good, and evil somehow manifests God's glory (among other problems). Another example, the soul-making theodicy, claims evils are necessary for humans to grow into mature souls with freedom to love. This, however, rejects the biblical doctrine of the Fall, claiming God created the world by macroevolution so that mature humans would emerge through struggle. In general, *felix culpa* approaches are difficult to square with Paul's rejecting that we should "do evil that good may come" (Rom. 3:8).

Skeptical Theism: Some believe God has good reasons relative to evil, but we are not in a position to know what they are. This approach is not skeptical about God but skeptical that humans are in a position to know what God's reasons are relative to the evil in the world.

The Free Will Defense: Some claim evil is the result of the misuse of free will, which God has sufficiently good reasons to grant.

Cosmic Conflict: Some emphasize there is more to the story—a conflict between God's kingdom and a realm of demonic creatures who rebelled against God.

These last three avenues are discussed further below, with emphasis on the cosmic conflict perspective (i.e., the Great Controversy), which is integral to Adventist theology.[29]

God's Ways Are Not Our Ways

Job suffered deeply and undeservedly. He was faithful. He was not being punished for evil, as his "friends" claimed. He cried out to God for answers. Eventually, God answered Job but God did not answer many of Job's questions. Instead, God reminded Job there was much that Job did not know.

Job was embroiled in a cosmic conflict, horribly afflicted by Satan. Job's friends did well at first, sitting with him in silence for a week, but when they tried to explain his affliction as God's judgment, they only brought more suffering. Job knew they were wrong, but he did not understand what was happening to him.

Eventually, God "answered Job from the whirlwind and said, 'Who is this who darkens the divine plan by words without knowledge?'" (Job 38:1–2). One translation renders this: "Why do you talk so much when you know so little?" (CEV). "Where were you when I laid the foundation of the earth?" God goes on. "Tell Me, if you have understanding" (Job 38:4; cf. 11:7; 38:33). Humbled, Job responds, "I have declared that which I did not understand, things too wonderful for me, which I did not know" (42:3; cf. 40:3–5).

In His discourse with Job, God makes clear there are many things Job is not in a position to know. In some ways, this mirrors the approach known as skeptical theism, which affirms God has good reasons for acting (or refraining from acting) as He does, but given our limited capacities and knowledge, we are not in a position to know just what those reasons are.[30] Again, this approach is not skeptical about God but skeptical that humans are in a position or have the capacity to know what God's reasons are for acting (or refraining from acting) as He does.

Suppose you are camping. Your arm begins to itch. A very tiny bug called a "noseeum" (because they are very difficult to see) bit you. Does the fact you do not see the tiny bug mean there are no tiny bugs around? Of course not. The fact that you cannot see tiny bugs does not mean there are not tiny bugs around.[31] Similarly, even if one cannot see what God's reasons are, that does not mean God does not have good reasons.

"'My thoughts are not your thoughts, nor are your ways My ways,' declares the Lord. 'For as the heavens are higher than the earth, so are My ways higher than your ways and My thoughts than your thoughts'" (Isa. 55:8–9). As we consider the problem of evil, we should remember this. There are many things we are not in a position to know or understand.

Years ago, our eighteen-month-old son required a blood draw to determine whether he needed a potentially life-saving medical procedure. The nurse instructed my wife and me to hold Joel's little arms and legs while she stuck him with the needle to draw blood. I'll never forget the way Joel looked at me. He was too young to speak, but I could see the questions in his tear-filled eyes: "Why are you doing this to me, daddy? It hurts! Why aren't you keeping me from being hurt?"

Nothing I could have said to Joel at the time would have made him understand why I was doing what I was doing. It seemed like I was hurting him when I was actually trying to help him. Joel turned out to be fine, but I'll never forget that look in his eyes.

Even as Joel was in no position to understand why I held him down, we also are often not in a position to understand why God does not prevent evils that we might think He should prevent. Even as I had good, loving reasons for holding Joel down, God has good and loving reasons for what He does and refrains from doing, even if we are not in a position to know just what they are.

God has good and loving reasons for what He does and refrains from doing, even if we are not in a position to know just what they are.

As Paul writes, now we only "know in part" (1 Cor. 13:12). We are not in a position to see all the factors involved (cf. 1 Cor. 4:5), and we lack the ability (cognitive and otherwise) and the moral standing to "judge" God's actions. One might initially think that they could come up with a better way that God should have governed the world, but no one other than God is aware of all the factors involved. Given the number of factors and how even a small change in one way can have massive repercussions down the road, we are not capable of knowing how things would actually turn out if history took a different course. We should, then, remain humble with respect to such issues, recognizing how little we know, always remembering that "God is the holy and righteous One, the One before whom we ourselves will be judged, not someone subject to our judgment," and thus trusting in God's revelation as our rule and standard rather than our own fallible faculties (for more on God's revelation in Scripture, see the following chapter).[32]

Evil Is the Result of Misuse of Creaturely Free Will: The Free Will Defense

Beyond skeptical theism, the free will defense understands evil as the result of creatures' misuse of free will. God grants creatures free will such that He does not determine what creatures decide. What creatures *freely* do, then, is not up to God. Tragically, creatures have misused their free will to do evil, with horrendous effects.[33]

This free will defense is rooted in biblical teachings. As we have already seen, Scripture teaches God's ideal will is often unfulfilled (e.g., Ps. 81:11–14; Isa. 30:15–18; 66:4; Luke 7:30; 13:34). But why doesn't God use His power to determine that everyone always does what He wants?

If God determined creatures' decisions, they could not have free will of the kind necessary for love. Even God cannot *determine* that all beings *freely* do what God desires. As Katherin Rogers puts it: "God can no more make a controlled free being than He can make a round square."[34] This is not because God lacks any power, but because it is impossible to *determine* that someone *freely* do something (in the libertarian sense).

Creaturely love does not require the *actuality* of evil, but it does require the *possibility* of evil because love requires freedom. Whether *free* creatures do evil, then, is not up to God. And evil occurs because creatures choose otherwise than God prefers. God consistently grants free will, even when creatures do evil, because it is a necessary prerequisite of love.

Even many *atheist* philosophers recognize the free will defense resolves the *logical* problem of evil.[35] But, in its place, they raise the evidential problem of evil, which claims it is unlikely God exists given the *amount* of evil in our world. Couldn't God have prevented many evils without undermining free will? What about evils in nature that do not appear to be directly tied to the free will decisions of humans, such as "natural" disasters (e.g., hurricanes or viruses)?

Or, what about evils it seems God could prevent simply by providing a warning or special revelation? Suppose someone dies in a plane crash that was the result of a mechanical problem. It seems God could prevent that without undermining human freedom. In biblical stories, God repeatedly warned individuals of disasters (e.g., the famine in Egypt). Could God not do so again today?

These and other questions face the free will defense. What if, however, there is far more to the story than initially meets the eye?

An Enemy Has Done This: Cosmic Conflict Theodicy

A landowner "sowed good seed in his field," Jesus narrated, "but while his men were sleeping, his enemy came and sowed weeds among the wheat, and left" (Matt. 13:24–25). When the noxious weeds became evident, the landowner's servants asked, "Sir, did you not sow good seed in your field? How then does it have weeds?" (Matt. 13:27). This mirrors the question asked today: If God created the world entirely good, why is there evil?

The landowner's answer in Christ's parable is simple yet profound: "An enemy has done this!" (Matt. 13:28).

The servants then asked, "Do you want us, then, to go and gather them up?" (Matt. 13:28). This mirrors another question asked today: Why doesn't God eliminate evil immediately?

"No," the landowner replied, "while you are gathering up the weeds, you may uproot the wheat with them. Allow both to grow together until the harvest" (Matt. 13:29–30). Prematurely uprooting the weeds would also uproot the wheat. Likewise, prematurely uprooting evil would result in irreversible collateral damage to the good.[36]

Jesus explained later that, in this parable, He is the landowner, and the enemy who sowed the noxious weeds is the devil (Matt. 24:37–39). Christ's parable of the wheat and the weeds thus outlines the cosmic conflict between Christ and Satan. Evil is the result of Satan's action, not God's, allowed temporarily because doing otherwise would result in even greater tragedy. In Christ's words, the short answer to the problem of evil is: "An enemy has done this."

This cosmic conflict appears all throughout Scripture. In this often-invisible war between good and evil, God's kingdom is under assault by fallen angels who rebelled against God's government (see, e.g., Col. 1:16–17; 2 Pet. 2:4). The New Testament is filled with references to Satan and demons opposing God's kingdom.[37] Indeed, Jesus repeatedly "cast out the demons," declaring "the kingdom of God has come" over and against Satan's "kingdom" (Matt. 12:28, 26).[38]

Satan himself is "the ruler of the demons" (Matt. 9:34; 12:24–29), the dragon ruler who with "his angels waged" war against God in heaven, the "serpent of old ... who deceives the whole world" (Rev. 12:7–9) and gives power to kingdoms and rulers who oppress God's people throughout history (see Rev. 13), attempting to take God's place and receive the worship that belongs to God alone.

The "power of Satan" directly opposes God's kingdom (Acts 26:18), and "the whole world lies in the power of the evil one" (1 John 5:19; cf. Eph. 6:11–12; Col. 1:13–14). Indeed, Jesus Himself calls Satan the "ruler of this world" (John 12:31; 14:30; 16:11; cf. Luke 4:5–6; Eph. 2:2). The devil's strategy is continual deception; he not only "disguises himself as an angel of light" (2 Cor. 11:14), but Paul even calls him "the god of this world" who "has blinded the minds of the unbelieving" (2 Cor. 4:4).

In this regard, the "gods of the nations" central to Old Testament stories were actually demons in disguise, seeking to usurp worship (as Satan sought in the temptation) and destroy God's people.[39] In the Old Testament, God's people "made Him jealous with strange gods.... They sacrificed to demons, who were not God, to gods whom they have not known, new gods who came lately" (Deut. 32:16–17; cf. Ps. 106:37). Likewise, Paul explained, the Gentiles "sacrifice to demons and not to God" (1 Cor. 10:19–20; cf. Rev. 9:20; 2 Cor. 6:14–15).[40] All the instances of the "gods" of the nations and idolatry throughout Scripture, then, are instances of the cosmic conflict over rulership and worship. Satan seeks to overthrow God's kingdom by slander so he can usurp God's rule and receive worship that belongs only to God. It is no coincidence, then, that the devil attacks God's law, uses deceptive means to divert worship away from the one true God to himself, and continually seeks to enslave humans (more on all this later).

This cosmic conflict is central to the gospel story itself, the good news of the coming of the true King, Jesus Christ the righteous, who defeats Satan and reclaims the world from the temporary domain of the devil, liberating creation from bondage.[41] Indeed, "the Son of God appeared for this purpose, to destroy the works of the devil" (1 John 3:8) and "that through death He might destroy the one who has the power of death, that is, the devil, and free those who through fear of death were subject to slavery all their lives" (Heb. 2:14–15; cf. Gal. 1:4; Rev. 12:9–11).

But, since God is all-powerful, how could anyone oppose God in the first place? To this question and more, we now turn.

The Nature of the Conflict

Their lack of faith amazed Him. In His hometown, Nazareth, "they took offense at Him . . . and He could not do any miracle there except that He laid His hands on a few sick people and healed them" (Mark 6:3, 5).

How could this be? What could possibly restrict the One who "upholds all things by the word of His power" (Heb. 1:3) from doing more miracles? It could not be a matter of sheer power. God is all-powerful. Something else must have been going on.

According to Matthew 13:58, Jesus "did not do many miracles there because of their unbelief." Somehow, then, the people's unbelief affected Jesus's ability to work miracles. This suggests that Jesus was working within some specific parameters in the cosmic conflict, discussed later in this chapter.

For now, it is important to note that a conflict between God and creatures is only possible if God has committed Himself to working within some limitations such that His kingdom can be opposed. No one could oppose God in terms of sheer power. There could be no conflict between the all-powerful God and any creature if the conflict was a matter of sheer power or brute force. The conflict, then, must be of another kind.

What, then, is the nature of the conflict? Scripture depicts it as a conflict over Satan's slanderous allegations against God's character and government (including God's law of unselfish love, see chapter 14). It is a conflict over claims about what is true and who is good, *an epistemic conflict*. In this cosmic conflict, Satan wages a war of misinformation. Thus, in Genesis 3, the serpent claimed God was lying in order to withhold some good from Eve. This slanderous attack against God was a truth claim, requiring a decision regarding whom to believe.

> **In this cosmic conflict, Satan wages a war of misinformation.**

Accordingly, Jesus identifies Satan as "a murderer from the beginning" who "does not stand in the truth because there is no truth in him" for "he is a liar and the father of lies" (John 8:44; cf. 2 Cor. 11:3). From Genesis to Revelation, Satan's strategy is continual slander of God's character and government, deception aimed at overthrowing God's kingdom of truth and love. Satan thus "blinded the minds of the unbelieving" (2 Cor. 4:4; cf. Acts 5:3) and "deceives the whole world" (Rev. 12:9). In response, Jesus came "to testify to the truth" (John 18:37).

Truth matters far more than most realize.

Suppose someone told you that your beloved who promised to be faithful to you alone has repeatedly been romantically involved with others behind your back, with every intention to continue. Even if you merely thought this report *might* be true, the love relationship would be damaged. Unless shown to be false, such claims would damage trust. And, unless trust is restored, your love relationship would be irreparably damaged.

In a somewhat similar fashion, allegations against God's character and law threaten the harmony of the entire universe. If creatures believe God might be a tyrant, as Satan claims, the trust and love that undergirds the perfect harmony of heaven would be broken. God commits Himself to answering the allegations not for His own sake but out of love for the world, the restoration of which depends on God demonstrating that the enemy's allegations are false and reconciling the world to Himself in a way consistent with justice and love.

The devil's allegations, however, could not be proven false by force. How much power must a king exercise to prove to his subjects he is not unjust? What show of executive power could clear the name of a governor accused of corruption? No amount of power or force, however great, could defeat slanderous allegations against one's character. Indeed, exercising power to silence accusers would only make the allegations worse. A conflict over character, then, cannot be settled by sheer power but only by demonstration of character that falsifies the allegations.

Christ's work provides such demonstration, undoing and defeating Satan's work at every turn:

- While Satan is the deceiver of the world (Rev. 12:9; cf. John 8:44), Jesus came "into the world" in order "to testify to the truth" (John 18:37).
- While Satan is the slanderer and accuser of God and His people in the heavenly court (Rev. 12:10; cf. Job 1–2; Zech. 3:1–2; Jude 9; Rev. 13:6), Christ supremely demonstrates God's perfect righteousness and love via the cross (Rom. 3:25–26; 5:8), thereby defeating Satan's allegations in the heavenly court (Rev. 12:10–11).
- While Satan is the usurping ruler of this world (John 12:31; 14:30; 16:11; cf. Matt. 12:24–29; Luke 4:5–6; Acts 26:18; 2 Cor. 4:4; Rev. 12–13), Christ defeats Satan's kingdom and will finally destroy his domain and "reign forever and ever" (Rev. 11:15).

Jesus "appeared for this purpose, to destroy the works of the devil" (1 John 3:8; cf. Gen. 3:15) and to "destroy the one who has the power of death, that is, the devil" (Heb. 2:14).[42] Accordingly, Satan knows "that he has only a short time" (Rev. 12:12; cf. Rom. 16:20).

In the plan of redemption, God demonstrates His perfect righteousness and love. He does so not for Himself but because of His love for the world. "For God so loved the world, that He gave His only Son" (John 3:16). In so doing, "God demonstrates His own love toward us, in that while we were still sinners, Christ died for us" (Rom. 5:8).

Cosmic Courtroom Drama in the Heavenly Council

"Now there was a day when the sons of God came to present themselves before the Lord, and Satan also came among them" (Job 1:6). What is going on here? Who are these "sons of God," and why are they coming to "present themselves before the Lord"? And why is Satan there? This is a heavenly council scene, one of many in Scripture which depict celestial beings as having some ruling authority relative to events on earth.[43] This scene in Job peels back the curtain on a cosmic courtroom drama behind the scenes of earth's history.

"From where do you come?" God asked Satan before this heavenly court.

"From roaming about on the earth and walking around on it" (Job 1:7), Satan answered. This back-and-forth, repeated in Job 2:2, suggests Satan was present before the heavenly council as earth's ruler.

"Have you considered My servant Job?" God asked. "For there is no one like him on the earth, a blameless and upright man, fearing God and turning away from evil" (Job 1:8). This question and Satan's response open to view a pre-existing dispute between God and Satan.

Job did not "fear God for nothing," Satan claimed, but only because God had blessed and "made a fence around him." If met with calamity, Satan further alleged, Job would bitterly curse God (Job 1:9–11; cf. 2:5). Here, Satan acted as "the accuser of our brothers and sisters" who "accuses them before our God day and night" (Rev. 12:10; cf. Zech. 3:1–2).

Satan's allegations were not only against Job but also against God. By claiming Job's faithfulness was self-serving rather than genuine, Satan directly contradicted God's judgment that Job was "blameless," "upright," "fearing God and turning away from evil" (Job 1:8; cf. 2:3).[44] Further, Satan argued before the heavenly court that the "fence" around Job prevented him from proving that God's judgment of Job was false (cf. Rev. 12:10).

Before the heavenly court, God responded to Satan's charges by publicly agreeing to modify the limits on Satan's power, allowing Satan to put his allegations to the test, but still within limits—some modified *"rules of engagement"* that are the result of the court proceedings over which God presides. Yet, although Satan brought numerous horrible calamities against Job and his household, Job did not curse God, falsifying Satan's allegations (Job 1:20–22; 2:9–10).

Here, it is crucial to remember that this was *not* a private dialogue between God and Satan but *part of* open court proceedings before the heavenly court that involved charges Satan had brought against God's judgment and protection of Job.[45] God, the Creator and ruler over all, was not subject to the heavenly council. Still, in His infinite wisdom,

God responded to Satan's allegations in a way that took into account how members of the heavenly council (and others) viewed the case.[46] If Satan was not allowed to make his case, his allegations would have remained open, casting significant doubt on God's justice, with massive ramifications for all creation.[47]

The case of Job reveals numerous things about the cosmic conflict. First, bad things happen to "good" people (cf. Eccles. 7:15; 8:14; Jer. 5:28; 12:1; Luke 13:1–5), in contrast to the view of Job's "friends."[48] Second, Satan, not God, is the monster who afflicts Job (e.g., Job 2:7; 1:12). Third, Satan possesses the power to work evil in this world (as earth's ruler after the Fall), but only within limits set in the heavenly council that are known to both him and God, what Satan referred to as the "fence" that protected Job from Satan's designs.

Satan's restricted power as the temporary "ruler of this world" (John 12:31), then, functions within some "rules of engagement" that are known to both God and Satan (but not known to us).[49] Indeed, in order for there to be a conflict between God and a mere creature like the devil, there must be some consistent parameters—or rules of engagement—within which Satan was allowed to make his case against God. Since God always keeps His promises and commitments (Titus 1:2; Heb. 6:18), insofar as God agrees to such "rules," God's future action is *morally* limited by such rules.[50] As we will see in the next section, many evidences of such "rules of engagement" appear throughout Scripture.

Rules of Engagement in Scripture

"What business do You have with us, Son of God? Have You come here to torment us before the time?" Demons shouted these words at Jesus from within two "demon-possessed men" who "were so extremely violent that no one could pass by that way" (Matt. 8:28–29). Undeterred, Jesus cast the demons out, displaying His authority over all. Yet, the demons claimed that *final* judgment was not to be brought against them until a specified future time, indicating some "rules of engagement" at work.

On another occasion, a father pleaded with Jesus's disciples to cast a demon out of his son. But they couldn't. Later, this father asked Jesus to cast the demon out. And Jesus did. Afterward, Christ's disciples asked why they could not cast the demon out. "This kind cannot come out by anything except prayer," Jesus explained (Mark 9:29; cf. Matt. 17:20). Earlier, due to the lack of faith in Nazareth, Jesus "could not do any miracle there except that He laid His hands on a few sick people and healed them" (Mark 6:5). These instances show that some "rules" in the cosmic conflict are tied to prayer and faith (more on this later). Likewise, human behavior impacts what the devil can accomplish, opening or closing avenues for demonic influence. Thus, Paul warns Christians, "do not give the devil an opportunity" (Eph. 4:27) and James exhorts, "resist the devil, and he will flee from you" (James 4:7).

Later, Jesus told Peter, "Satan has demanded to sift you men like wheat" (Luke 22:31). The term translated as "demanded" suggests "the one making the request has a right to do so," indicating God and Satan "operate within certain constraints."[51] Something like this appears in Jude 9, when "Michael the archangel . . . disputed with the devil and argued about the body of Moses" and "did not dare pronounce against him an abusive judgment" (cf. Zech. 3:1–2).[52] Still later, Paul reports he wanted to visit the Thessalonians, but "Satan blocked our way" (1 Thess. 2:18, NRSVue; cf. Rev. 2:10).

These are not isolated instances. Relative to a message that "concerned" a "great conflict" (Dan. 10:1), Daniel fervently prayed for three weeks for understanding. God heard Daniel's words *"from the first day,"* but the "prince of the kingdom of Persia opposed" God's angel for "twenty-one days," until Michael "came to help" (Dan. 10:2, 12–13, NRSVue; cf. 10:20). The majority of scholars believe this "prince" of Persia is a celestial being, a heavenly ruler at work behind the human ruler (cf. Dan. 10:20–21).[53]

Daniel 10 thus depicts a cosmic conflict wherein an angel sent by God is delayed three weeks.[54] But how could the "prince" of Persia oppose God's angel for three weeks? God possessed the sheer power to respond to Daniel immediately. Yet, Scripture presents a real conflict between forces of goodness and darkness.[55] For such a conflict to transpire, God must not be exercising His full power; the enemy must be afforded some genuine freedom and power that is not arbitrarily removed, governed by some rules of engagement known to both parties (the details of which are not revealed to us). As noted earlier, for a mere creature such as the devil to oppose God, there must be some consistent parameters (or "rules") within which the enemy is allowed to operate. Insofar as God agrees to abide by such "rules," God's own action would be *morally* limited because God never breaks His word.

Notably, Jesus Himself repeatedly identified Satan as the "ruler of this world" (John 12:31; 14:30; 16:11). John explained, "the whole world lies in the power of the evil one" (1 John 5:19). For this to be true, Satan must have been granted some *significant* jurisdiction and power over this world to work out his government within some specified limits or "rules of engagement," which correspondingly limit God's action (morally). In this regard, Satan claimed rulership over this world "has been handed over to me, and I give it to whomever I want" (Luke 4:6; cf. John 19:11).

This rulership is manifest in the way the Old Testament demons masqueraded as "gods" of the nations (celestial rulers behind earthly rulers, see Deut. 32:16–17; cf. 1 Cor. 10:19–20). The New Testament even more explicitly reveals the cosmic war between the kingdom of light and the kingdom of darkness—the "power of Satan" (Acts 26:18; cf. 2 Cor. 4:4; Eph. 2:2; Col. 1:13) and demonic principalities and powers, "rulers and the authorities in the heavenly places" that war against goodness (Eph. 3:10; cf. Rom. 8:38; 1 Cor. 4:9; Col. 2:15; 1 Pet. 1:12).[56]

According to the New Testament, the demonic realm wields significant power in this world. Thus, Paul urges: "Put on the full armor of God, so that you will be able to stand firm against the schemes of the devil. For our struggle is not against flesh and blood, but against the rulers, against the powers, against the world forces of this darkness, against the spiritual forces of wickedness in the heavenly places" (Eph. 6:11–12; cf. Rom. 13:12; 2 Cor. 10:3–5; Eph. 4:27).

Yet, while demonic "rulers" have real power in our world, the cosmic conflict is *not* a conflict between equals. Not even close. Satan and his demonic horde are mere creatures (Col. 1:16). Their reign is limited and temporary. Indeed, Christ came to "destroy the one who has the power of death, that is, the devil" (Heb. 2:14) and "to destroy the works of the devil" (1 John 3:8). Christ "gave Himself for our sins so that He might rescue us from this present evil age" (Gal. 1:4; cf. Eph. 5:15). And, Paul testifies, through Christ God has "rescued us from the domain of darkness, and transferred us to the kingdom of His beloved Son" (Col.

1:13; cf. Dan. 2:44–45; Luke 4:6). He "disarmed the rulers and authorities" and "made a public display of them, having triumphed over them" (Col. 2:15; cf. 1 Cor. 2:6–8; 1 Pet. 3:22; 1 John 4:4).[57] And, in the end, God will utterly eradicate evil forevermore (see chapter 19).

The cosmic conflict is front and center in the apocalyptic imagery of Revelation. Therein, Satan is presented as "the great dragon" who opposes God and "deceives the whole world" (Rev. 12:9), having robust and widespread ruling authority on earth. The dragon (Satan) not only wars against God and God's people (e.g., Rev. 12:1–9) but is identified as the celestial ruler behind earthly empires that persecute God's people throughout the ages.

Specifically, the dragon "gave" a beast from the sea "his power and his throne, and great authority" (Rev. 13:2; cf. 13:5; 17:13–14), and "the whole earth" followed the beast and "worshiped the dragon because he gave his authority to the beast; and they worshiped the beast" (Rev. 13:3–4; cf. 13:6–8, 12). This sea beast blasphemes God, and "authority to act for forty-two months was given to him" to "make war with the saints and to overcome them, and authority was given to him over every tribe, people, language, and nation" (Rev. 13:5–7).

The characteristics of this sea beast ("like a leopard," with "feet" like a "bear," "the mouth of a lion" and ten horns, Rev. 13:1–2) correspond to the four beasts of Daniel 7 (see the discussion in chapter 16). This sea beast is thus a composite beast symbolizing the previous successive oppressive empires of Babylon, Persia, Greece, and Rome *and* the system that rises out of and follows Rome, which follows the way of the dragon.

Satan is thus depicted as the celestial ruler of this world who gives power and worldwide authority to the earthly empires and systems that set themselves up against God and God's people, directing worship to the dragon and themselves. Yet, there are clear indications of limits on Satan and his agencies as well. Satan "knows that his time is short" (Rev. 12:12, NRSVue). Scripture universally maintains that God finally triumphs and eradicates all evil, never to arise again. "He will wipe away every tear from their eyes; and there will no longer be any death; there will no longer be any mourning, or crying, or pain; the first things have passed away" (Rev. 21:4).

Understanding the Rules of Engagement

We have seen a number of instances of "rules of engagement" in the cosmic conflict. Importantly, as depicted in Job, such "rules" are the result of proceedings wherein God takes into account other minds in the heavenly court, setting rules that govern the limits within which Satan is permitted to make his case. As the result of proceedings that take into account how particular courses of action would be perceived by the creatures in the heavenly court and beyond, God does not set these rules of engagement unilaterally or arbitrarily. As such, they may be far from ideal. Yet, insofar as God agrees to such rules of engagement, God's action is (morally) limited to within the confines of such rules.[58]

Because God never lies (Titus 1:2) and never breaks His promises (Heb. 6:18), any commitment God makes is binding on God's future action. The rules of engagement might (morally) prevent God from doing what He otherwise wants to do, holding significant implications for whether it is within God's *moral* purview or jurisdiction to *immediately* reduce or eliminate evil in this world.

You and I might sometimes be tempted to think God should have prevented this or that evil occurrence. Yet, from our limited human perspective, we cannot see or adequately account for the rules of engagement and the multitude of other factors operating within the cosmic conflict. Perhaps some courses of action we think God should take are not available to Him within the parameters of the rules of engagement. Other actions we think God should take might contravene the extent of free will God has covenantally (and thus irrevocably) granted to creatures for the sake of love. Still others might result in a far worse outcome than the course God, in His perfect wisdom, chooses in light of all factors and *available* options. Put briefly, in any instance where God does not intervene to prevent some horrendous evil, to do so might have (1) been against the rules, (2) negated the kind of creaturely free will that is intrinsic to love relationship, and/or (3) resulted in far greater evil or less flourishing of love.

As seen earlier, numerous biblical passages link divine activity to faith and prayer (see Matt. 17:20; Mark 9:23–29; 11:22–24; cf. 2 Chron. 7:14). Prayer, then, might grant God jurisdiction to act in ways that otherwise would not be (morally) available to God within His commitments to human free will and the rules of engagement. Petitionary prayer might open up avenues for God to bring about goods He already wanted to bring about but was (morally) restricted by the rules of engagement from bringing about in the absence of prayer.[59]

At the same time, since there are many unseen factors, we should not think that when God does not bring about the outcome we want, it must be because we did not pray enough or have enough faith. Perhaps we prayed for the wrong outcome (cf. Rom. 8:26; 1 John 5:14–15) or with the wrong motives (James 4:2–3). Or, perhaps some things we pray for would nevertheless contravene God's commitments to free will or the rules of engagement more broadly, regardless of how much and how faithfully believers pray (cf. Matt. 26:39; Luke 22:32).

Yet, some might ask, why would God agree to such rules of engagement in the first place? For the good of all concerned, it is crucial that God defeat Satan's allegations, which would otherwise unravel the harmony and love of the universe. But perhaps there was no other way to defeat Satan's allegations and settle the conflict without even greater collateral damage to all concerned (cf. Matt. 13:29).

As noted earlier, just as a king cannot prove he is just by force and a governor cannot clear her name of corruption by executive power, Satan's slanderous allegations against God cannot be defeated by sheer power but require some fair and open demonstration to prove the allegations true or false (see 1 Cor. 4:9; cf. Matt. 13:29; 1 Cor. 6:2–3). A mere creature such as Satan, however, could not make a case against the omnipotent God unless permitted to operate within some *consistent* parameters—some rules of engagement which God commits not to contravene or override. Given that other minds in the heavenly council are involved, such rules might be far from ideal, but they might be the best available to God that *He knows* will settle the conflict in the minds of all creatures once and for all, with the least collateral damage to all concerned while guaranteeing a future eternity of perfect bliss and love relationship.[60]

More questions remain, of course, and there is much we do not know, which should caution us against premature judgments (cf. 1 Cor. 4:5). But we should note a significant

God always does what is preferable given the avenues available to Him.

biblical principle here: God always does what is preferable given the avenues available to Him (cf. Gen. 18:25; Deut. 32:4; 1 Sam. 3:18; Ps. 145:17; Dan. 4:37; Hab. 1:13; Rom. 3:25–26; Rev. 15:3). As such, whenever God does or refrains from doing something in a way that initially seems less than optimally good, it follows from this principle that it was not in God's purview to do something more preferable.[61]

In short, if left unresolved, Satan's allegations in the cosmic conflict would unravel the harmony and love in the *entire* universe. Such charges cannot be resolved by sheer force but require some kind of demonstration by both parties in the dispute, which in turn requires some parameters or "rules of engagement" for such demonstration by which both parties in the dispute abide.

We, mere creatures, are not in a position to judge precisely what parameters such a demonstration would require or even what would count as a sufficient demonstration. This demonstration is to answer the devil's allegations once and for all and inoculate the universe from evil ever arising again (Rev. 21:3–4; cf. Nah. 1:9), but only the One who is omniscient could perfectly calculate just what is sufficient to this end.

What More Could He Do?

Within this framework of understanding the cosmic conflict as a conflict of character rather than sheer power, love provides the morally sufficient reason for God's allowance of evil. That God has morally sufficient reasons in this regard does not amount to *justification* of the evils in our world themselves. Evil remains evil. God does not want or need evil to accomplish His entirely good purposes. The freedom required for love relationship only requires the *possibility* of evil, not the necessity of evil. Against God's ideal will, creatures chose to do evil. And, insofar as God irrevocably grants creatures free will (because it is intrinsic to love relationship), the avenues available to God to restore the universe to perfect harmony are limited by the free decisions of creatures (including those of angels and demons).

Yet, some might ask, should God have done more to prevent or stop evil? As the servants of the landowner in Christ's parable asked, why not uproot the weeds without delay (Matt. 13:28)? Why not eliminate the horrendous evils around us?

In this regard, timing matters a great deal. As Christ taught in His parable of the wheat and the weeds, prematurely uprooting evil would involve unthinkable collateral damage (Matt. 13:29–30). Accordingly, the harvest is delayed until "when the crop permits" (Mark 4:29). Before the devil's kingdom can be fully eradicated, Satan must first be legally defeated by way of demonstration and judgment in the heavenly court. Thus, the *execution* of judgment involving the final eradication of evil is delayed until the appointed time (Matt. 8:29; cf. Ps. 75:2; 1 Cor. 4:5; Heb. 10:12–13; Jude 9), after judgment is conducted in the heavenly court (Dan. 7:13–14; see also chapter 16). Thus, Christ's victory over evil takes place in two stages, the first consisting of Christ's legal defeat of Satan and his slanderous allegations in the heavenly court via the cross (e.g., Rev. 12:10–11; cf. John 12:31; Col. 2:15), the second to be accomplished through Christ's ministry in the heavenly sanctuary (see chapters 13 and 16), finally culminating with His return to set all captives free forevermore (see chapter 19).[62]

Yet, some might nevertheless persist in asking, could God have done more to prevent or stop evil? God answers a similar situation with His own question: "What more was there to do for my vineyard that I have not done in it?" (Isa. 5:4, NRSVue). This question arises in a passage that depicts God as a vineyard owner who makes every preparation for His vineyard, locating it on "a fertile hill," clearing its stones, planting the "choicest vine," and building a watchtower (Isa. 5:1–2). The vineyard should have yielded good grapes, but instead yielded rotten grapes (Isa. 5:2). Given this, God states: "Judge, please, between Me and My vineyard. What more could have been done to My vineyard that I have not done in it?" (Isa. 5:3–4, NKJV). What more could He do?

Jesus's parable in Matthew 21 picks up where Isaiah 5 ended, adding that the vineyard owner "leased it to vine-growers and went on a journey" (Matt. 21:33). Yet, when the owner twice sent his servants (the prophets) to collect the produce, the renters beat and killed his servants (Matt. 21:34–36). Finally, he sent his son (Jesus), saying, "They will respect my son" (Matt. 21:37). But the renters murdered his son (Matt. 21:38–39).

What more could He do? The Father loved us so much that He gave His beloved Son. The cosmic conflict could not be settled by sheer power but could only be settled by a public demonstration of God's character, set forth in Christ. Indeed, "God displayed [Christ] publicly as a propitiation in His blood through faith. This was to demonstrate His righteousness, because in God's merciful restraint, He let the sins previously committed go unpunished; for the demonstration, that is, of His righteousness at the present time, so that He would be just and the justifier of the one who has faith in Jesus" (Rom. 3:25–26). In this also, "God demonstrates His own love toward us, in that while we were still sinners, Christ died for us" (Rom. 5:8).

The cross demonstrates that God has done everything that could be done to remove evil without undermining the flourishing of love. If there was any preferable way, wouldn't He have chosen it? Whenever we suffer, God suffers *with us*, taking all the world's sufferings on His shoulders, including suffering for us by becoming the sacrifice (in Christ) for us. God, then, suffers most of all. Not only suffering for us via the cross but also suffering *with us* in all our sufferings.[63] What more could He do?

> **The cross demonstrates that God has done everything that could be done to remove evil without undermining the flourishing of love.**

In the end, God Himself will not only answer the problem of evil but will end all evil forever. In the meantime, however, looking to the cross provides us good reasons to trust that God has done everything He could do and has always done what is best for all concerned (given available avenues). Even though we may not see the reasons for God's action or apparent inaction in any given situation, that does not mean God has no such good reasons. There are many factors that we do not see. While we only see in part and know in part, we can look to the cross as the ultimate manifestation of God's love. The God who is willing to sacrifice Himself (in Christ) on the cross can be trusted, and we should remember that much that God is doing is unseen, at least for now.

Yet, the question remains, why does evil continue? As seen in the parable of the wheat and the weeds, prematurely eradicating evil would inflict massive collateral damage, uprooting the good with the evil (Matt. 13:28–29). God will finally put an end to evil, but it is allowed for a time. To do otherwise would eliminate freedom of the kind necessary for love.

If God destroyed evil prematurely, love itself would be severely damaged. The questions would not be answered. Creatures would not understand and would serve God out of fear rather than love.

When the cosmic conflict is finally ended, it will be clearly seen once and for all that God has only and always done what is good and loving. The enormity of evil will be clearly seen by all the universe—by angels and humans (1 Cor. 4:9; see chapter 16). All will see that God's laws and actions have only been loving and the inevitable result of departing from God's will is tragedy because God's law and ideal will is precisely what ensures a totally harmonious universe of unending love.

All God's creatures will understand that God is love—all of God's commands have always been, and always will be, out of love, for the ultimate happiness of all. Then, God's name will finally be vindicated (cf. Phil. 2:10) and the eternal, uninterrupted flourishing of love thereby secured. Only then will God make an utter end of evil and "wipe away every tear" and "there will no longer be any death; there will no longer be any mourning, or crying, or pain; the first things have passed away" (Rev. 21:4; see also chapter 19).

In the meantime, Paul assures us it will all be worth it; "the sufferings of this present time are not worthy to be compared with the glory that is to be revealed to us" (Rom. 8:18; cf. 2 Cor. 4:17). Paul does not mean to trivialize the immense suffering in our world but highlights how much greater the joy is that God has in store (see 1 Cor. 2:9). The very fact that God Himself came, taking on humanity, humbling Himself unto death, even the death of the cross (Phil. 2:8), demonstrates that He considered this world to be worth the cost to Himself. In giving Himself for us, God demonstrated His unfathomable love (Rom. 5:8) and "His righteousness" as "just and the justifier" (Rom. 3:25–26).

The solution to evil, the ultimate theodicy, will be fully understood in the world to come. In the meantime, however, the suffering God of the cross unequivocally demonstrates the depth of God's love and goodness. If there had been any other way to ensure that the universe would continue in unceasing love and uninterrupted goodness forevermore, He would have chosen it. God Himself has suffered most of all and knew in excruciating detail the suffering that He Himself would endure by creating this world, but He did so anyway because of His great love for us. Christ has done all He could do, even unto death. There is no greater love (John 3:16; 15:13). God is love (1 John 4:8, 16).

Conclusion: Why Does It Matter?

He felt like God was absent. Is God even there? If God truly was there, why did He seem to be hidden? Why, while he was experiencing so much suffering, did God appear to be silent? If a child in distress called out to her loving mother, that loving mother would respond, wouldn't she? Why, then, does God sometimes seem to not respond when we call out to Him in our distress? Why does God seem to be hidden, particularly in the midst of evil and suffering?

Have you ever felt like God is absent or silent? In those times and all others, God is indeed present. But why, then, does God sometimes seem to be hidden?

We have seen in this chapter that Scripture teaches there is an ongoing cosmic conflict, and understanding this is crucial to understanding the situation our world is in. Imagine viewing a work of art in a gallery. How you understand a work of art will differ greatly depending on whether you believe it is the work of one person or if you come to know it was the work of one person that was later vandalized by the artist's enemy. The way the world is now is a bit like this. God created this world, but it has been vandalized by the enemy, by the dragon, and by all who follow his ways. Much in this world does not seem to make sense because God's good design was vandalized by the enemy within an ongoing cosmic conflict.

Within this cosmic conflict, there are some parameters, or rules of engagement, that are the result of proceedings in the heavenly court presided over by God (wherein God takes into account other minds) and which God has committed to abide by, morally limiting His action to operating within such parameters to settle the conflict. As such, some courses of action God might otherwise take are not (morally) available to Him within the confines of the rules of engagement.

Relative to the problem of evil, then, when God does not intervene to prevent evil, it might be that for God to do so would have (1) been against the rules of engagement in the cosmic conflict, (2) negated the kind of creaturely free will that is intrinsic to love relationship, and/or (3) resulted in far greater evil or less flourishing of love.

This same line of thought is highly relevant to the problem of divine hiddenness, which runs parallel in many respects to the problem of evil. If God is (temporarily) operating within some (moral) constraints in the cosmic conflict, it might be against the rules for God to make Himself more visible or known in some contexts such that God might appear to be hidden or silent even though He is present and active in ways we might not see. This also holds implications for why *special* communications from God in history are so important (as we will see in the next chapter) and provides a framework in which it makes sense that God does not reveal Himself in the same ways to every person but works to provide *special* revelation to the world (such as that found in Scripture) through intermediaries such as prophets and apostles.

If you feel like God is hidden or silent, be assured that He is not absent. He is there with you. And He desires to be closer to you still, particularly in your distress and sufferings. God is near—suffering *with us*. Outside of select cases of special revelation (such as those recorded in the Bible), humans do not see the invisible God (cf. 1 Tim. 1:17) or audibly hear words from God, but Christ came as the ultimate revelation of God to humans, "the image of the invisible God" (Col. 1:15), so that whoever has seen Christ "has seen the Father" (John 14:9). You and I were not there to see and hear Jesus in person, but we can "see" and "hear" Him through the testimony recorded in Scripture, the nature of which is discussed further in the next chapter.

> *If you feel like God is hidden or silent, be assured that He is not absent. He is there with you.*

The question for you to answer, however, is do you want to know Him more? Do you want to experience the revelation of God? If you do, I invite you to pray and seek God in the revelation He has provided in the Bible. As I have sought to commune with God through prayer and studying Scripture, I have often felt the presence of God with me in a special way. Your experience might be different from mine, but if you seek God, He will let you find Him. As God promised His covenant people in Jeremiah 29:13, "you will seek Me and find Me when you search for Me with all your heart."

Even now, I invite you to reflect on Christ's teaching in this regard, found in Matthew 7:7–11. Then, consider the concern of God for justice by reading and reflecting on Psalm 82.

Questions for Reflection

1. Do you struggle with the problem of evil? Do you know anyone who does? How might the content of this chapter help?
2. What do you think is the most helpful response to the problem of evil? How can we remember that helping and consoling those in suffering is often needed more than attempts at explanation (consider the examples of Job's friends)? Further, what might we learn from God's response to Job about how little we know and our need to trust Him?
3. How is God's providence compatible with human free will? Why does this matter, relative to the problem of evil and more broadly?
4. What is the nature of the cosmic conflict? How would you describe this to someone who has never heard of it before?
5. How would you explain the rules of engagement in the cosmic conflict? How might understanding that there are some "rules" help us understand issues like providence, prayer, and apparent divine hiddenness?
6. Reflect on this question: What more could He do? Then, ask yourself: What more could I do? Specifically, what might I do to relieve suffering and contribute to justice in the world around me? As you ponder this, keep in mind the parameters of love (God's law of unselfish love, see chapter 14) in keeping with which God commands His followers to operate.
7. You can take your stand on the side of love in the cosmic conflict even now. Do you wish to do so? If so, I invite you to declare your faith in God and also take tangible steps to faithfully live in a way that spreads God's love and relieves suffering and injustice within your sphere of influence.

For Further Reading

Adventist Perspectives:

Adams, Roy. *Crossing Jordan: Joshua, Holy War, and God's Unfailing Promises* (Hagerstown, MD: Review and Herald, 2004).

Caesar, Lael. "The Issue of Suffering: Nine Christian Responses to Suffering." *Journal of the Adventist Theological Society* 10, no. 1–2 (1999): 73–89.

Davidson, Richard M. "Cosmic Metanarrative for the Coming Millennium," *Journal of the Adventist Theological Society* 11, no. 1–2 (2000).

Duah, Martha O. "A Study of Warfare Theodicy in the Writings of Ellen G. White and Gregory A. Boyd." PhD dissertation, Andrews University, 2012.

Gulley, Norman R. "Love at War: The Cosmic Controversy." In *Salvation: Contours of Adventist Soteriology.* Edited by Martin F. Hanna, Darius W. Jankiewicz, and John W. Reeve. Berrien Springs, MI: Andrews University Press, 2018.

Holbrook, Frank B. "The Great Controversy." In *Handbook of Seventh-day Adventist Theology.* Edited by Raoul Dederen. Hagerstown, MD: Review and Herald, 2000.

Peckham, John C. *Fervent Prayer: Cosmic Conflict and Petitionary Prayer.* Grand Rapids, MI: Baker Academic, forthcoming.

———. *Theodicy of Love: Cosmic Conflict and the Problem of Evil.* Grand Rapids, MI: Baker Academic, 2018.

Pfandl, Gerhard, ed. *The Great Controversy and the End of Evil.* Silver Spring, MD: Review and Herald/Biblical Research Institute, 2015.

Rice, Richard. *Suffering and the Search for Meaning.* Downers Grove, IL: IVP Academic, 2014.

White, Ellen G. *The Great Controversy.* Mountain View, CA: Pacific Press, 1911, 492–93.

See also the resources on the Biblical Research Institute website: https://adventistbiblicalresearch.org/materials/.

Other Christian Perspectives:

Acolatse, Esther. *Powers, Principalities, and the Spirit: Biblical Realism in Africa and the West.* Grand Rapids, MI: Eerdmans, 2018.

Beilby, James K. and Paul Rhodes Eddy, eds., *Understanding Spiritual Warfare: Four Views.* Grand Rapids, MI: Baker Academic, 2012.

Boyd, Gregory A. *Satan and the Problem of Evil: Constructing a Trinitarian Warfare Theodicy.* Downers Grove, IL: IVP Academic, 2001.

Cary, Phillip, William Lane Craig, William Hasker, Thomas Jay Oord, and Stephen Wykstra. *God and the Problem of Evil: Five Views.* Edited by Chard Meister and James K. Dew, Jr. Downers Grove, IL: IVP Academic, 2017.

Davis, Stephen T., ed. *Encountering Evil: Live Options in Theodicy.* Louisville, KY: Westminster John Knox Press, 2001.

Hart, David Bentley. *The Doors of the Sea: Where Was God in the Tsunami?* Grand Rapids, MI: Eerdmans, 2005.

Heiser, Michael S. *The Unseen Realm: Recovering the Supernatural Worldview of the Bible.* Bellingham, WA: Lexham Press, 2015.

Keener, Craig S. *Miracles Today: The Supernatural Work of God in the Modern World.* Grand Rapids, MI: Baker Academic, 2021.

Plantinga, Alvin. *God, Freedom, and Evil.* Grand Rapids, MI: Eerdmans, 1974.

10

THE TESTIMONY OF THE KING: DIVINE REVELATION AND SCRIPTURE AS COVENANT WITNESS DOCUMENT

The crushing grief weighed heavy on their hearts as they walked on the road to Emmaus. A couple of days earlier, Jesus was crucified. What now? He on whom all their hopes and dreams rested was gone. Was there any hope? Was their faith in Jesus misplaced?

Then, *He* came. But His identity was hidden. He walked with them and, "beginning with Moses and with all the Prophets, He explained to them the things written about Himself in all the Scriptures" (Luke 24:27). First, Jesus showed them what the Scriptures taught about the Messiah and His suffering, calling them to "believe in all that the prophets have spoken" (Luke 24:25; cf. Matt. 5:17–18; John 10:35). Only *after* teaching them from Scripture, "their eyes were opened and they recognized Him" (Luke 24:31).

Amazing. Before manifesting Himself to them as risen from the dead, He first taught them from Scripture. They thought He was gone, but He was actually walking *with* them. After the crucifixion, they nearly despaired of making sense of the prophecies of the Messiah, but the risen Messiah Himself taught them from Scripture.

To many today, God seems absent and hidden. But He is *with us*. Many question whether God can be known. But God can be known, for His Spirit is *with us* to teach us through the Scriptures He inspired. Yet, one might wonder: why God does not reveal Himself in the same ways *to every person*? Why does God provide *special* revelation through intermediaries such as prophets and apostles rather than directly revealing Himself to each person? The previous chapter provided the framework of the cosmic conflict in which this and other questions may be addressed.[1]

In light of this framework, this chapter addresses a number of questions about Scripture, including:
- Does God reveal Himself to humans? If so, how?
- What are revelation and inspiration? How do they work?
- If God wants us to know Him, why work through special messengers and writings? Why not make all people know Him directly?
- What is Scripture? Is the Bible trustworthy and true?

To even begin to address these questions, we must first see some of the story of how God revealed Himself to His people.

The Story of Special Revelation

They had much to learn, unlearn, and relearn. The people of Israel had been enslaved for generations in Egypt. God had foretold the centuries of enslavement and eventual liberation (Gen. 15:13–16), but God seemed absent and hidden.

Soon, God would reveal Himself in astonishing ways. Keeping His covenant promises to Abraham, God heard Israel's cries and raised up a special prophet, Moses, to lead Israel out of slavery.

By many miracles, God mightily broke the yoke of Egyptian bondage. Such miracles not only liberated Israel but *revealed* Israel's God as the one true God to the Egyptians and others throughout the ancient world. Indeed, the Canaanite woman Rahab who joined Israel and became an ancestor of Jesus Himself, came to know of the one true God through reports of God's mighty acts in the Exodus that reached her and the others in Jericho (see Josh. 2:8–11).

God's special revelation relative to the Exodus and beyond was to be preserved and passed down. God raised up and commissioned Moses to record His *covenantal* revelation—the special revelation of God's great acts for His covenant people and the teachings, promises, and laws God gave His covenant people for their good, and to bless all nations. This covenantal revelation was to be written and passed down as a rule or standard for future generations (Exod. 17:14; 24:4; 31:18; 34:27; Deut. 6:1–25; 10:5; 29:29; 31:9–12, 25–26).[2]

Special Revelation through Covenant People and Prophets

God had specially revealed Himself before. God personally spoke to Adam, Eve, Cain, and Noah. But, later, much *special* revelation was given to and through God's covenant people of Israel. Yet, why would God *specially* reveal Himself to a particular covenant people? Why not reveal Himself to everyone in the same way?

Recall that the Fall ruptured the divine-human relationship and made Satan the temporary and limited ruler of this world. Evil separated Adam and Eve (and thereafter all of humanity) from the intimate presence of God (cf. Isa. 59:2). Due to this separation, apart from where God *specially* revealed Himself, humans were left to "feel around for Him" in relative darkness, even "though He is not far from each one of us" (Acts 17:27).

After the Fall, humans descended in an evil, downward spiral. At Babel, the peoples of the world turned away from God's promises and light to relative darkness (Gen. 11). But God did not leave the world in utter darkness. He called Abraham and through him created a special covenant people with special covenant privileges (see chapter 14) for the sake of blessing all nations (Gen. 12:1–3; cf. Deut. 4:32–36), to whom and through whom He specially revealed Himself for the sake of all peoples. God worked in many ways to reveal Himself to this specially chosen covenant people, through whom God's special revelation would reach throughout the world.

From the time of the Abrahamic covenant onward, much of God's special revelation came through the covenant people of Israel. God personally spoke to Abraham, Hagar, Sarah, Isaac, Jacob, and Joseph. Later, God spoke further to Moses, Aaron, Miriam, the nation of Israel collectively, many judges, prophets, kings, apostles, and many others. Yet, God did not leave others in darkness. Beyond the exceptional special revelation given to and through Israel, non-Israelites such as Job and Balaam were also recipients of special revelation. Much special revelation, however, came through the special covenant people of Israel.

Many of those to whom God specially revealed Himself passed down their testimony of the events of revelation orally, but from Moses onward, God chose some prophets, whom He specially prepared and commissioned, to write down God's special, covenantal revelation that was to be preserved and passed down through the ages.

Moses was divinely commissioned to write down a record of God's great acts, teachings, laws, and promises that were to govern the special covenant relationship between God and His people over the ages. For example, at Sinai, Moses proclaimed "the words of the LORD" to the people and also "wrote down all the words of the LORD" (Exod. 24:3-4). The divinely revealed covenant teachings, laws, and promises were prescribed as the "rule" or standard of God's covenant relationship with His people, to be preserved and passed down to future generations (without alteration) and to hold continuing covenantal authority (Deut. 4:2ff.; cf. 6; 29:29; 31:10-13; Josh. 1:8; 23:6; 1 Kings 2:3; Neh. 8:8-18; 9:3).

God set up Moses as a *special* prophet, directly attesting of Moses's special role as *covenantal* prophet by many signs before Israel. Indeed, God proclaimed that, unlike with other prophets, He even spoke to Moses "mouth to mouth" (Num. 12:8). After Moses, God commissioned many other prophets who carried on the writing of covenantal revelation (e.g., Josh. 24:26; 1 Sam. 10:25; Isa. 30:8; Jer. 30:2; Hab. 2:2-3).

All prophets after Moses were to be tested by the books of Moses (known as the Torah or Pentateuch—the books of Genesis, Exodus, Leviticus, Numbers, and Deuteronomy). Already in the time of Joshua (Moses's successor as prophet and leader of Israel), Moses's writings were recognized as authoritative Scripture (see Josh. 1:7-8).[3] Thus, Joshua commanded the people, "Be very determined, then, to keep and do everything that is written in the Book of the Law of Moses, so that you will not turn aside from it to the right or to the left" (Josh. 23:6; cf. Deut. 17:18-19; 31:24-26; Josh. 1:7-9). Not only did the writings of Moses hold continuing normative authority throughout the ages (e.g., 1 Kings 2:3; 2 Kings 23:1-3; Ezra 3:2; Neh. 8-9), but later prophets also recognized as authoritative the writings of other earlier divinely commissioned prophets after Moses (Jer. 26:18; Dan. 9:2; et al.).

In this regard, the prophet Isaiah taught that divine revelation is a rule or standard by which teachings are to be judged: "To the Law and to the testimony! If they do not speak in accordance with this word, it is because they have no dawn" (Isa. 8:20; cf. 8:16). Accordingly, God's prophets continually called the people to be careful to hear and keep the word of the Lord, which was to function as their covenantal rule of faith and practice (Deut. 11:22; Josh. 22:5; Jer. 2:4; Ezek. 6:3; Hosea 4:1; Amos 3:1; cf. Neh. 9:30; Zech. 7:12).

Joshua himself proclaimed and wrote down covenantal revelation like Moses (Josh. 24:25-26). Indeed, the "book Joshua wrote received scriptural standing as the inspired word of God right away, just as the Book of the Law of Moses (the Pentateuch) had after Moses died (see 1:8 and 23:6)."[4] After Joshua, the book of Judges recounts the tragic history of Israel's repeated cycle of rebellion; forsaking God's covenant promises and commands, and committing many egregious evils, for "everyone did what was right in his own eyes" (Judg. 21:25). This rebellion against God's rule led to a period when, according to 1 Samuel 3:1, "word from the LORD was rare in those days; visions were infrequent."

But God raised up Samuel, the great prophet and judge who anointed the first kings of Israel, Saul and David. God called Samuel as a child, "revealed Himself to Samuel," and made sure "all Israel from Dan even to Beersheba knew that Samuel was confirmed as a prophet of the LORD" (1 Sam. 3:20–21). According to 1 Chronicles 29:29, "the acts of King David, from the first to the last, are written in the chronicles of Samuel the seer, in the chronicles of Nathan the prophet, and in the chronicles of Gad the seer," which many believe refer to the books of 1 Samuel and 2 Samuel. The prophet Samuel and others, then, proclaimed and recorded covenantal revelation that attested to (among other things) the Davidic covenant.

The rest of Old Testament Scripture attests to God's steadfast love, compassion, righteousness, and faithfulness to His covenant promises even amidst Israel's repeated and tragic unfaithfulness to the covenant. Under the kings that followed David, the covenant people repeatedly rebelled against God over many centuries. In His love and mercy, God repeatedly sent prophets who proclaimed and wrote down the "word of the Lord" to call the people back to Him. But, more often than not, God's prophets were not heeded (see, e.g., 2 Chron. 24:19). God "sent word to them again and again by His messengers, because He had compassion" on them, "but they continually mocked the messengers of God, despised His words, and scoffed at His prophets . . . until there was no remedy" (2 Chron. 36:15–16). Finally, Babylon conquered Jerusalem, ended the kingship, and sent most of the people of Judah into exile.

Yet, God did not forsake His people. During the exile in Babylon, God worked through the prophet Daniel (and other prophets) to reveal Himself, including to a foreign king. And Daniel wrote down prophecies of many empires to come and of the time of the end. Later, during Persian rule, God worked through Mordechai and Queen Esther to save God's covenant people from plots to destroy them. God also worked through Ezra and Nehemiah to return the people from Exile to the promised land, to restore and rebuild Jerusalem, and continued to send special revelation to His covenant people through chosen prophets. A remnant of the people returned from exile, but the kingship was not restored. They lived under the rule of foreign empires. The promised Son of David, the Messiah, had not come.

Special Revelation of the Messiah, Attested by Chosen Apostles

But then, the desire of all nations Himself came. The One in whom the promises would be fulfilled—the covenantal Son of David, the Messiah, the Son of Man, and the Son of God. He was the ultimate revelation of God on earth (see Heb. 1:1–2), "the true Light that, coming into the world, enlightens every person" (John 1:9; cf. 14:6). Among other things, Jesus came "to testify to the truth" (John 18:37).

> *The One in whom the promises would be fulfilled—the covenantal Son of David and the Son of God—was the ultimate revelation of God on earth.*

To prepare the way for Jesus, God "spoke long ago to the fathers in the prophets in many portions and in many ways," preceding the ultimate revelation of God on earth in Christ Himself (Heb. 1:1–2). To further prepare the way, in the first century AD the great prophet John the Baptist "came as a witness, to testify about the Light" (John 1:7). Later, Jesus commissioned apostles to testify of Him, to be His Spirit-filled and empowered "witnesses" of what Christ did and what He taught "as far as the remotest part of the earth" (Acts 1:8). Specifically, Christ commissioned them: "Go, therefore, and make disciples of all the nations, baptizing them in the name of the Father and the Son and the Holy Spirit, teaching them to follow all that I commanded you; and behold, I am with you always, to the end of the age" (Matt. 28:19–20).

To fulfill this commission to spread the gospel to the entire world, the testimony of the apostles was not only preached but also written down, copied, and spread abroad.[5] The New Testament consists of this testimony of the first-generation apostles commissioned by Christ, who were eyewitnesses to the resurrected Christ and were thereby appointed as His special witnesses (cf. Acts 1:2-4; 9:13-15; 10:41-42; 26:12-18).[6] These were Christ's "witnesses who had been chosen beforehand by God," including those "who ate and drank with Him after He arose from the dead" and whom Christ "ordered" to "preach to the people, and to testify solemnly that this is the One who has been appointed by God as Judge of the living and the dead. All the prophets testify of Him, that through His name everyone who believes in Him receives forgiveness of sins" (Acts 10:41-43; cf. Luke 1:1-3; John 15:26-27; 21:24; Acts 26:16; 2 Pet. 3:2; 1 John 1:1-5).[7]

Both the Old Testament and New Testament, then, testify of Christ (cf. John 5:39). Even as the Old Testament witnesses to God's great covenantal acts, teachings, and commands prior to Christ's coming and thus is a covenant witness document of the "old" covenant, the New Testament is a covenant witness document of God's great covenantal acts relative to the New Covenant—the coming of Christ, Christ's teachings, and the testimony of the apostles Christ commissioned as His special, Spirit-empowered, witnesses. And Jesus Himself confirmed the prophetic witness of the Old Testament (e.g., Luke 24:27, 44; cf. Matt. 5:17-18; John 5:39) and commissioned the apostolic witness of the New Testament (more on this later).[8]

As Jesus Himself explained, "the wisdom of God said, 'I will send them prophets and apostles'" (Luke 11:49). Likewise, Paul later explained, "God's household" has "been built on the foundation of the apostles and prophets, Christ Jesus Himself being the cornerstone" (Eph. 2:19-20; cf. 3:5). Still later, just before warning that mockers will come in the last days, Peter exhorted readers "to remember the words spoken beforehand by the holy prophets and the commandment of the Lord and Savior spoken by your apostles" (2 Pet. 3:2; cf. Jude 17).

In all, God revealed Himself in various ways and in diverse manners, including in many *special* ways such as through many specially chosen prophets and apostles and, ultimately, in the supreme revelation of God prior to the Second Coming, the incarnation, life, teachings, death, and resurrection of Christ (see Heb. 1:1-2). This special revelation of God is available to us today in writings passed down from God's divinely commissioned and inspired witnesses (chosen prophets, apostles, and their close associates), of which the Bible consists.

Revelation and Inspiration: The Word of God in Human Words

They were surrounded by enemy troops. It seemed hopeless. Yet, the prophet Elisha proclaimed: "Do not be afraid, for those who are with us are greater than those who are with them." Then, Elisha prayed for his attendant's eyes to be opened, and he saw that "the mountain was full of horses and chariots of fire all around Elisha" (2 Kings 6:16-17). An angelic army, otherwise unseen, was with them. In this case and others, there is much we would not see if God did not reveal it to us.

Yet, God has revealed Himself. If God did not, we could not know God. Knowledge of God depends on revelation. Simply defined, revelation is God's disclosure of, or about, Himself.

God revealed Himself because God wants humans to know Him and live. As Jesus proclaimed, "this is eternal life, that they may know You, the only true God, and Jesus Christ whom You have sent" (John 17:3). The significance of divine revelation, then, cannot be overstated.

God has revealed Himself through His works generally but also in special ways to chosen people in particular times and places. God's universal revelation through His works in all creation, available to all humans, is known as general revelation. God's special acts of revelation to chosen people in particular times and places is known as special revelation.

Through general revelation, some things about God have been made known to *all* people everywhere. Indeed, "The heavens declare the glory of God, and the sky above proclaims his handiwork. Day to day pours out speech, and night to night reveals knowledge. There is no speech, nor are there words, whose voice is not heard. Their voice goes out through all the earth, and their words to the end of the world" (Ps. 19:1-4, ESV). Likewise, Paul teaches, "what can be known about God is plain" even to the wicked who suppress the truth "because God has made it plain to them. Ever since the creation of the world God's eternal power and divine nature, invisible though they are, have been seen and understood through the things God has made. So they are without excuse, for though they knew God, they did not honor him as God or give thanks," but worshiped images of creatures rather than the Creator Himself (Rom. 1:18-23, NRSVue).

God, then, has provided general revelation of Himself to all peoples everywhere through nature itself. We should, then, diligently study what can be known through nature. While general revelation is valid and important, it is also significantly limited. Nature is marred by sin, history includes evils brought by rebellious creatures, the minds of humans are fallen, our reason is fallible (cf. Jer. 17:9), and many things about God cannot be known through general revelation alone.

Making inferences about God from nature is somewhat similar to making inferences about an artist based on her art. Some things about an artist can be known by pondering her art, but much about the artist is not revealed by her work. Moreover, this world is under enemy rule and filled with evils against God's designs and wishes. God's work has been marred by sin and evil, analogous to an artist's painting that has been vandalized by her enemy. Without explanation by the artist, we'd be left to draw inferences about the artist from the damaged painting alone, perhaps not even recognizing it is damaged. Similarly, without special revelation, we'd be left to draw inferences only from our severely damaged world.

In this and other ways, the content of special revelation is crucial to understanding God. Special revelation provides information that otherwise would not be known (see Eph. 3:3–5). The God of Scripture "reveals the profound and hidden things; He knows what is in the darkness, and the light dwells with Him" (Dan. 2:22; cf. 2:47).

Yet, why is there a need for *special* revelation at all? Why not reveal the contents of special revelation directly to *all* people? As we have seen, sin made some separation between God and humans (cf. Isa. 59:2). And, during the cosmic conflict, God operates within some rules of engagement such that even an angel sent with special revelation for Daniel could be delayed for three weeks (Dan. 10:12–13).

By human rebellion, the world gave itself over to enemy rule. In Eden, Adam and Eve fell. At Babel, the nations of the world rejected God and thus gave themselves over to the enemy's jurisdiction. But God reserved the right within the rules of engagement to raise up a special people through whom He could work to reclaim the world from enemy rule (somewhat akin to a "bridgehead" in the cosmic conflict). God thus raised up and chose Israel as His special covenant people (His "allotted share," Deut. 32:9, NRSVue)—not merely for their own sake, but to bless all nations through them. Israel was to function as a conduit of special revelation (among other blessings), which was to reach not only Israel but to spread throughout the world.

The special revelation given to Israel seems to be one of the special privileges of the covenant people, afforded according to the rules of engagement in the cosmic conflict (see chapter 9). If so, it makes sense that God would reveal Himself in the special and limited ways that He does throughout history. And it makes sense that Jesus would come to (among other things) "testify to the truth" (John 18:37) and commission chosen followers to also testify as special "witnesses" in the cosmic courtroom drama.

> *It makes sense that God would reveal Himself in the special and limited ways that He does throughout history.*

God Reveals Himself to Chosen Witnesses in Ways Humans Can Understand

"I will raise up for them a prophet from among their countrymen like you," God told Moses, "and I will put My words in his mouth, and he shall speak to them everything that I command him" (Deut. 18:18). Here and elsewhere, God promised to communicate *special* revelation through chosen prophets.

A prophet is God's *special* witness and messenger, one chosen and commissioned by God to receive and convey *special* messages. For example, God told Jeremiah, "before you were born I consecrated you; I have appointed you as a prophet to the nations" and "I have put My words in your mouth" (Jer. 1:5, 9). Likewise, God commissioned Ezekiel, "go to the house of Israel and speak with My words to them" and tell them, "This is what the Lord GOD says" (Ezek. 3:4, 11; cf. 3:17; Exod. 3; Deut. 18:15–19; 1 Sam. 3:20–21; Isa. 6; 22:14).

Later, Christ commissioned *special* witnesses known as apostles, chosen as first-hand eyewitnesses to the risen Christ (see Luke 24:48; Acts 1:2–8, 21–22; 3:15; 5:32; 9:13–15; 10:39–43; 26:12–18; cf. Eph. 2:20; 2 Pet. 3:2). These received special revelation. As Paul testifies, "the mystery [of Christ] was made known to me by revelation," a mystery that "was not made known to humankind" in previous generations "as it has now been revealed to his holy apostles and prophets by the Spirit" (Eph. 3:3–5, NRSVue; cf. Matt. 16:17; 1 John 1:5).

You might initially think special revelation is like a lightning bolt, as if God merely supernaturally implants knowledge in human minds. Scripture teaches, however, that God "spoke to our ancestors in many and various ways by the prophets" and "in these last days he has spoken to us by a Son" (Heb. 1:1–2, NRSVue).

At Sinai, God's people "heard the voice of God speaking from the midst of the fire" that they "might know that the LORD, He is God; there is no other besides him" (Deut. 4:33, 35). Earlier, God appeared and spoke to Moses from the burning bush (Exod. 3:2–4; cf. Num. 12:6–8). In these and many other instances, God manifested His presence visibly (in theophanies) and spoke directly to chosen humans (e.g., 1 Kings 19:11–12; Isa. 6; Ezek. 3). Many other instances introduce prophetic messages by phrases like "God said" or "the LORD spoke" (Gen. 1:3, 6, 9, 11, 14, 20, 24, 26; cf. Exod. 20:22; 25:1; 34:1, 6; Lev. 1:1; Num. 1:1; Deut. 32:48). These and other instances of revelation, such as visions (Luke 1:22; Acts 9:10; 10:3; 11:5; 2 Cor. 2:7) and dreams (Matt. 1:20; 2:12, 19, 22) and messages delivered by angels, come in *obviously* supernatural ways.

However, divine revelation also came in less obvious ways, including ways that seem "natural." At first glance, Jesus of Nazareth appeared to be an ordinary man. But He was, in fact, the supreme revelation of God. At least in some cases, then, special revelation might not *seem* so special; it might not seem to be miraculous or obviously supernatural.[9]

Indeed, God often used seemingly natural, ordinary means in the process of revelation. For example, Luke tells us he "investigated everything carefully from the beginning," considering what has been "handed down to us by those who from the beginning were eyewitnesses and servants of the word" (Luke 1:2–3). What Luke communicated, then, was revealed to him in part via researching the testimony of "eyewitnesses and servants of the word." Scripture, then, includes writings that make use of oral and written sources. Likewise, much found in the book of Lamentations or in wisdom literature such as Ecclesiastes is not *obviously* supernatural revelation (i.e., revelation that comes in an obviously supernatural manner) but nevertheless consists of the testimony of inspired prophets.[10] God sometimes communicates revelation by *seemingly* ordinary historical actions and sources.[11]

In each of the various patterns of revelation represented in Scripture, God reveals Himself historically—within the context of time and space such that revelation is historically constituted. That is, divine revelation comes through a historical process where God performs successive actions to progressively reveal more and more about Himself to humans He has chosen as recipients of *special* revelation.

Divine revelation is also given at a level that humans can understand. That is, divine revelation comes in ways that do not bypass the way human minds work but in ways that humans can cognitively grasp according to the way God created human minds to work.

> *Divine revelation comes in ways that do not bypass the way human minds work but in ways that humans can cognitively grasp.*

Revelation, then, is both *historical* and *cognitive*.[12] The God of the Bible can and does reveal Himself within the context of space and time in ways that normal human cognition can understand—in ways that relate to humans as temporal and thus historical beings, as well as *free* historical agents with the God-given (libertarian) freedom of thought and belief.

Competing Theories in Christian Theology: Divine Revelation

The view that God reveals Himself within the context of space and time in ways normal human cognition can understand is known as the historical-cognitive model of divine revelation.[13]

In contrast to this, many theologians adopt a kind of classical model, wherein divine revelation involves God timelessly infusing knowledge into prophets' minds, bypassing the normal historical and deliberative functioning of human minds so the prophet *passively* receives timeless data.[14] Some argue this *manner* of divine revelation would protect the content of revelation from error.

However, if divine revelation is *timelessly* infused, the contents of divine revelation could only be *timeless* data. If so, anything that *takes time* to communicate or understand could not be divinely revealed. This means historical events such as God appearing to Moses at the burning bush could not be part of divine revelation because such events transpire *over time*. Given this understanding, the only revelation such narratives could convey would be *timeless* ideas, conveyed symbolically or allegorically. According to this view, then, whether or not the historical events actually occurred may be irrelevant to what is revealed (symbolically) by biblical narratives, and most of what is contained in Scripture is *not* the product of divine revelation.

Some have questioned and finally rejected this classical model, however, wondering why God would bypass the function of human minds that He created and whether *timeless* ideas could even be received by human minds, which classical models viewed in terms of *timeless* human souls. Some modern understandings of the nature of knowledge (epistemology) concluded that human thought is unavoidably temporal and structures everything according to temporal categories.[15] Accordingly, many modernistic thinkers believed humans are incapable of receiving *timeless* information. Since many early modern thinkers inherited the classical presupposition that God is timeless and therefore divine revelation must be timeless, this amounted to the conclusion that God cannot reveal information about Himself to humans.

If there is any divine revelation, advocates of a modern model of revelation (i.e., the liberal model) thought, it could only consist of some kind of mysterious feeling of divine presence, devoid of the transmission of information (*a kind of non-cognitive encounter revelation*).[16] On this view, the Bible does not contain revealed information about God, but merely historically and culturally conditioned human opinions and mythologies of what God is like.

If God is not timeless, however, then even if humans are incapable of receiving timeless knowledge, such human inability would not prevent God from revealing knowledge about Himself to humans. In this regard, the historical-cognitive model (*affirmed by many Adventists*) contends that God can and does encounter humans in space and time *and* also reveals information about Himself historically in ways that do not bypass the ordinary functioning of the human mind, which God desires and expects humans to understand and preserve (cf. Deut. 29:29).[17]

Even as a healthy human love relationship involves both experiences of one another's presence and communication, the kind of relationship God desires and works to bring about by revealing Himself to humans involves the experience of divine presence, but it also involves knowledge of what God is like and how to relate to God. Such an understanding of divine revelation attempts to avoid the false dichotomies of reason versus experience, and theory versus practice. According to the historical-cognitive model, divine revelation is not the timeless transmission of reason to a timeless human soul (classical models) nor a timeless non-cognitive encounter (modern models). Rather, divine revelation is a historical activity whereby God reveals Himself to human agents in ways humans can understand cognitively.

Special Revelation

Special revelation may be defined as the process by which God brings specially chosen prophets to understand the contents of divine revelation that God wants them to understand. Closely related to this is inspiration, the process by which divine revelation is put into human words to share with others (discussed later in this chapter). The recipients of special revelation were not only chosen but also prepared by God to receive and communicate special revelation (more on this later). Yet, because God consistently grants humans the ability to *freely* think, believe, and choose, God does not simply implant or download information into a prophet's brain. Rather, God brings chosen prophets to sufficiently understand the contents of divine revelation through ways that do not undermine human free will and accord with the rules of engagement in the cosmic conflict (see chapter 9).

Sufficient understanding, however, does not require *total* understanding. For example, Daniel did not understand some things about the revelations given to him. Daniel "heard but did not understand" and was told, "these words will be kept secret and sealed up until the end time" (Dan. 12:8–9). The Spirit guides prophets and apostles to sufficient understanding (cf. John 16:13), but some things are not made known. As Deuteronomy 29:29 teaches, "The secret things belong to the LORD our God, but the revealed things belong to us and to our children forever, to observe all the words of this law" (NRSVue).

God reveals knowledge of Himself in *various* ways because truth is manifold and the audience God is trying to reach is manifold. Accordingly, no single pattern of divine activity by itself adequately accounts for all the kinds of material in the Bible. God uses a variety of patterns of revelation to reach various audiences, including dreams, visions, direct speech from God, messages delivered by angels, and theophanies. Yet, God also reveals Himself in less obviously supernatural ways, such as appear in the case of Luke, in wisdom literature like Ecclesiastes, and so on. In some cases, God provides the precise words of His message, such as when God Himself wrote the Ten Commandments on tablets of stone (Exod. 31:18). In most cases, however, prophets express the contents of divine revelation in their own words, under the supervision and guidance of the Holy Spirit (discussed further below).

> God reveals knowledge of Himself in various ways because truth is manifold and the audience God is trying to reach is manifold.

As 2 Timothy 3:16 puts it, "All Scripture is inspired by God [literally "God-breathed"] and beneficial for teaching, for rebuke, for correction, for training in righteousness." I will address the question of which writings count as "Scripture" later in this chapter (relative to the biblical canon). For now, it is important to note that to say Scripture is "God-breathed" does not mean that all that is written in Scripture is the product of divine activity alone. It is not. But it does teach that all "Scripture" is the product of some special divine activity such that it is correct to understand it as "inspired" or "God-breathed."

But, just what does it mean for some writing to be *inspired*? To this question, we now turn.

God Inspires Chosen Prophets and Apostles to Communicate Divine Revelation

While revelation is the cognitive process that makes special revelation known to chosen prophets and apostles, inspiration is the linguistic process wherein prophets and apostles express in human words the content of what God has revealed to them.[18] Just as the nature of revelation is historical—taking place over an extended period of time, so also is the nature of inspiration. And, like the process of revelation, the process of inspiration does not violate the freedom of thought God grants humans or otherwise override the mind of biblical authors.

In some cases, God Himself chooses and communicates the words, then prophets or apostles record the very words God gave them. In most cases, however, the prophets and apostles are commissioned to freely put the content of revelation into their own words.

Scripture includes the writing of many witnesses who provide their own particular perspective with various styles of writing. For example, each of the four Gospels (Matthew, Mark, Luke, and John) tells the story of Jesus in different ways, from different perspectives.

Yet, how can we be confident that what God intends to reveal makes it into the words biblical writers use? Might the writers hold mistaken presuppositions, misunderstand divine revelation, or miscommunicate it to others?

At least two categories of God's providential action ensure the trustworthiness of Scripture relative to the processes of revelation and inspiration. First, God works in the lives of chosen prophets and apostles to prepare them to receive special revelation. Second, the Holy Spirit supervises the process of putting divine revelation into words and, occasionally (when necessary), intervenes to correct human messengers.

For example, the prophet Nathan initially told David God was with him to build the temple, but that same night "the word of the LORD came to Nathan" and told him David was *not* to build the temple (2 Sam. 7:2–4, 12–13; cf. 1 Chron. 28:3). Long before this, God did not permit the prophet Balaam to curse Israel in His name (see Num. 22–24). When necessary, God intervened to correct His prophets from delivering a false message. By the time many false prophets arose among God's people later on, God had already provided an abundance of divine revelation by which false prophets could be recognized and rejected (cf. Isa. 8:20).

To prepare and equip His chosen messengers to receive revelation, God worked in various providential ways. All humans understand things from their particular perspective, impacted by their personal history, background, and social location.[19] The writers of Scripture lived in particular times, places, and cultures, with their thinking shaped *in part* by various cultural influences and personal experiences and impacted by their distinct personality, temperament, and other inherited characteristics.[20] Divinely chosen prophets and apostles, however, were providentially prepared for their tasks. Like all humans, their cultural background included numerous shared attitudes, values, beliefs, goals, and practices.[21] Yet, God worked to shape the history, culture, and beliefs of His covenant people Israel in many providential ways. Israel's culture was divinely impacted by ages of special revelations.

Before his Egyptian education as the adopted son of Pharaoh's daughter, Moses was prepared by the teaching of his God-fearing mother, Jochebed (Exod. 2:9–10; cf. Heb. 11:23). Later, God further prepared Moses during forty humbling years in the wilderness (cf. Acts 7:30), culminating with speaking to Moses from the burning bush and regularly speaking with and instructing Moses thereafter.

After Moses, the Torah was passed down and taught to subsequent generations as a rule of faith and practice. Sadly, the covenant people frequently strayed far from God, and many raised in the culture of Israel were not positioned to be faithful and trustworthy recipients and messengers of divine revelation. Yet, Israel's culture was nevertheless a Torah-impacted culture, from which God chose those He knew would be best suited for His purposes and worked in the lives of such chosen ones to specially prepare them for their calling, equipping them to receive and transmit divine revelation in a trustworthy manner.[22]

Moses's successor Joshua was prepared as a kind of apprentice to Moses. Later, Samuel was an answer to his mother Hannah's prayer, and she raised him to worship and love God and dedicated him to serve God at the temple (1 Sam. 1–2). And Jeremiah was chosen before birth. "Before I formed you in the womb," God told him, "I knew you. And before you were born I consecrated you; I have appointed you a prophet to the nations" (Jer. 1:5). We do not know as much about the lives of some other prophets, but the pattern of Scripture indicates that God worked in the lives of chosen prophets to prepare them to receive and *sufficiently* understand revelation. Whomever God calls to special tasks, He prepares and equips.

> **Whomever God calls to special tasks, He prepares and equips.**

Much later, Christ Himself prepared chosen apostles whom He taught and discipled as they followed Him day after day for years of His ministry. The apostle Paul was otherwise prepared, "educated under [the highly esteemed teacher] Gamaliel, strictly according to the Law of our fathers" (Acts 22:3) and later encountering the risen Christ and undergoing conversion that brought his understanding into accord with "the mind of Christ."

Yet, God did not unilaterally determine the contents of His chosen messenger's minds. This can be seen from the fact that the prophets and apostles *themselves* were not infallible and did not always immediately understand divine revelation. For example, the prophet Nathan was initially wrong about David building the temple (as seen earlier), and the apostle Peter received a vision to correct his view of Gentiles (see Acts 10) and also was rebuked by Paul (see Gal. 2:11ff.). The great prophet Daniel struggled to understand many things revealed to him (e.g., Dan. 12:8–9), and the prophets of old "made careful searches and inquiries" to try to understand what the Spirit revealed about the coming of Christ (1 Pet. 1:10–11). While in prison, even John the Baptist himself questioned whether Jesus was the Christ (Matt. 11:2–3). Further, the disciples of Jesus frequently misunderstood Christ's actions and teachings but eventually came to understand because the Holy Spirit came to "guide [them] into all the truth," as Christ had promised (John 16:13). God, then, did not immediately or unilaterally determine the contents of His chosen messengers' minds, but instead God providentially shaped the understanding of such chosen messengers in the course of their lives in a way congruent with their freedom of thought.

God not only prepared and equipped chosen prophets and apostles to receive revelation, but the Holy Spirit also inspired them, not typically choosing the words but supervising the process of human messengers putting revelation into their own words and intervening to correct them when necessary (as in the cases of Nathan, Balaam, Peter, and others).[23] Thus, "no prophecy of Scripture becomes a matter of someone's own interpretation, for no prophecy was ever made by an act of human will, but men moved by the Holy Spirit spoke from God" (2 Pet. 1:20–21). Here, inspiration is described as operating on the prophets themselves such that humans were "moved by the Holy Spirit" and thereby "spoke from God."[24]

Through the work of God to prepare, equip, and inspire the writers of Scripture, including the Holy Spirit's supervision and occasional intervention, *all* of Scripture is inspired (cf. 2 Tim. 3:16) and, as such, all Scripture is trustworthy. In this regard, 1 Samuel 3:19 declares of the prophet Samuel that God "let none of his words fail." If all Scripture is inspired this way, with God intervening when necessary to safeguard *the reliable communication of divine revelation*, it follows that Scripture is unfailingly trustworthy in all that it teaches. That is to say, Scripture is infallible or, as Jesus Himself put it, "the Scripture cannot be broken" (John 10:35, NKJV; cf. Matt. 5:17–18). Thus, Jesus called His followers to "believe in all that the prophets have spoken" (Luke 24:25; cf. Acts 24:14).

Competing Theories in Christian Theology: Inspiration

Some view the Bible not as God's word but as a collection of merely human writings, with some thinking of inspiration as merely a high gift like an artistic ability common to other human geniuses (the intuition theory of inspiration). Others believe the Holy Spirit influenced biblical authors, but only in the sense of heightening the experience all believers experience (the illumination theory of inspiration).[25]

Many others hold a high view of Scripture, believing the Bible is God's word and *all* of Scripture is inspired (plenary inspiration). Some in the past have thought God dictated each word of Scripture to human writers (the dictation theory of inspiration), but this is not a prominent view today. The more prominent view of many Evangelical and other Christians is the verbal plenary theory of inspiration, wherein *every word* is inspired by God in a way that allows for individual writing styles of human authors, and yet every word is (in some broader sense of divine providence, often thought of as deterministic) chosen by God.[26]

While believing *all* of Scripture is inspired, Adventists typically deny the theory of plenary *verbal* inspiration. Instead, Adventists affirm a view often labeled as thought inspiration, affirming that, while *some* words of Scripture are directly given by God (e.g., the Ten Commandments), God usually does not choose the words in Scripture.[27] Rather, inspiration operates primarily on the prophets themselves such that the concepts or *thoughts* expressed by the prophets in their own words are not merely their "own interpretation" but remain trustworthy as the product of inspiration (see 2 Pet. 1:20–21).[28] As such, inspiration works not only on the thoughts but also reaches the words the biblical writers use to express those thoughts such that Scripture is the word of God in human words (cf. Deut. 18:18; 2 Sam. 23:2; Jer. 1:9), though God usually does not choose the specific words of Scripture.[29] Thus Paul wrote we have "received . . . the Spirit who is from God, so that we may know the things freely given to us by God. We also speak these things, not in words taught by human wisdom, but in those taught by the Spirit, combining spiritual thoughts with spiritual words" (1 Cor. 2:13). Since the Adventist understanding of inspiration involves a synergy of divine and human elements in the writing of Scripture, it is closest to the category that many other Christians call the dynamic theory of inspiration.[30]

Treasure in Earthen Vessels

Scripture is the result of both divine and human activity, inspired by God but written by *imperfect* humans.[31] Here, it is crucial to distinguish between the *content* of revelation and the *mode* of revelation. The content of revelation includes the information or message God brings for the prophet to understand. The mode of revelation refers to the vehicle or medium by which the content of revelation is communicated.[32]

The *content* of revelation is divine, but the *mode* is human. Revelation communicated to and by humans is limited according to the inherent limitations of humans.[33] Even as the amount of water that can flow through a hose is limited by the hose's size, any message communicated to or by way of humans is necessarily limited by human nature. Just as humans cannot drink from a fire hose, humans cannot receive divine revelation in an unlimited fashion.

Because humans are imperfect creatures of limited capacity, messages that humans can receive and convey are necessarily limited to being expressed in ways that humans can understand, according to the limited modes of human languages. Whereas a divine mode of communication would be capable of total reach, any human mode of communication is capable of only partial reach. Whereas a divine mode would be absolutely accurate and precise, human modes are not capable of *absolute* accuracy and precision. Whereas a divine mode would be unlimited, human modes are necessarily limited. As such, if God is to communicate with humans, He must do so via limited modes.[34] As Paul writes, "we have this treasure in earthen containers" (2 Cor. 4:7).[35]

Yet, this does not mean such revelation is thereby faulty, untrue, or untrustworthy. I can teach my ten-year-old son about God in a way that remains true and trustworthy, even though what I teach and the way I teach it is limited by his capacity to understand. If I can do so, how much more could God communicate to humans in ways that remain true and trustworthy, even while the mode of communication is limited according to human capacities? Here, just as it would be a mistake to judge my vocabulary and theological understanding on the basis of a letter to my ten-year-old son, it would be a mistake to judge God on the basis of the limitations of human language that appear in Scripture.

Scripture is not only the result of divine action, which (by itself) is always perfect, but is also the result of human action, which is necessarily limited. Even in those cases where God spoke to humans, He did so in *human* language that humans could understand, which necessarily limits what could be transmitted through it.

> In those cases where God spoke to humans, He did so in human language that humans could understand.

Any product of humans will necessarily be limited in some way, at least in the sense of being incomplete. Even the best human products fall incalculably short of absolute perfection. Bethoven composed 822 brilliant works written over fifty-five years. But his greatest composition falls far short of the music of heaven. Serena Wiliams is among the greatest athletes in history. She has won 22 Grand Slam Tennis tournaments and three Olympic gold medals. Her success on the Tennis court is unmatched. But her talents do not match the talents of heaven. Even the greatest human achievements are finite and thus imperfect.

If you check the previous paragraph, you'll notice numerous mistakes (misspelled names and slightly incorrect numbers). Do such mistakes, however, change the meaning in any significant way? No. None of the mistakes concern anything integral to the subject matter communicated or make any material difference to the message communicated.

Minor mistakes or discrepancies by themselves, then, do not necessarily compromise the message. Even sentences that contain minor mistakes might nevertheless convey an intended message in a way that remains true. With regard to Scripture, the important question is not whether there are any apparent mistakes in the Bible as we now have it (there are, for example, minor copying errors) but whether any such apparent mistakes compromise the message Scripture communicates.[36]

As seen above, mistakes would only compromise the message if the mistakes materially affect the subject matter of the message. One way to quickly see whether an apparent mistake materially affects the subject matter of the message is to ask whether correcting the mistake would change the meaning of the message in some significant way. If not, the apparent mistake does not *materially* affect the message's subject matter. In this regard, I am not aware of any apparent mistakes in Scripture that materially compromise the subject matter of the message or entail that Scripture teaches falsehoods.[37]

One might initially think *any* apparent "mistakes" or apparent discrepancies in Scripture would compromise Scripture's trustworthiness. An *inspired* book should not contain apparent mistakes, some suppose. If determinism were true, it would be difficult to see why or how anything inspired by God could contain apparent mistakes. However, if God inspired Scripture in the ways outlined earlier, consistent with upholding (indeterministic) human freedom and working within some rules of engagement in the cosmic conflict, it is not surprising that Scripture *as we have it now* contains some things that appear to be minor mistakes. Yet, if God intervenes when necessary to protect the subject matter of His intended message, such apparent mistakes would not compromise the message God intends.[38] Further, it is important to remember that some things that initially appear to be mistakes might, on closer inspection, turn out not to be mistakes after all.[39]

Many advocates of biblical inerrancy recognize there are mistakes in the copies of Scripture we have but claim the original documents written by the original authors (the original autographs) contained no mistakes. Any errors in Scripture, some suppose, are copying errors. Even if so, however, determinist advocates of inerrancy face the difficulty of answering why God did not determine that there be no errors in the copies as well. Further, while the many ancient copies we have demonstrate that the biblical text has been passed down very accurately (see chapter 3), we have no original autographs. Thus, in some cases, we have no way to know from extant evidence whether an apparent mistake in the text(s) we have was in the original or is a copying mistake.

What matters most is whether the copies we actually have are truthful and trustworthy. That is, whether the biblical texts that have been passed down to us faithfully transmit the message of divine revelation.[40] I believe the testimony of many witnesses provides us with good reasons for believing Scripture is truthful and trustworthy in all that it teaches (infallible) and the manuscript evidence indicates the text of Scripture has come down to us very accurately (see chapter 3). In this regard, apparent mistakes that do not affect the subject matter of the message of Scripture should not undermine confidence in the truthfulness and trustworthiness of Scripture as a whole. And I do not know of any mistakes in Scripture that compromise the overarching trustworthiness of what Scripture teaches.[41]

Many problems people perceive relative to apparent mistakes in Scripture depend on the way people expect divinely inspired writings to look. Yet, if Scripture looked exactly the way *you* think it should, it would look very different from what many other people throughout the world (past and present) would expect or be in a position to understand. If, for example, the Bible was tailored to twenty-first century Americans, it would look very different. But then, how could it reach second-century Romans, eighth-century Indians, or many other peoples in various places and times? Further, writings tailored too specifically to a twenty-first century people will likely seem primitive to audiences of a later century (if time lasts).

Some criticize Scripture for not exhibiting the scientific precision seen in twenty-first century science textbooks. In this regard, it is crucial to recognize that Scripture often describes phenomena as they appear to the naked eye, without thereby making *scientific* claims about the nature of the cosmos.[42] Put technically, Scripture uses phenomenological language, such as speaking of the sun rising or setting. But we also use such phenomenological language of "sunrise" and "sunset" today even though we know the sun's appearing to "rise" and "set" is caused by the rotation of the earth.

If, however, Scripture was written with the precision of a twenty-first century science textbook, how could it have been understood by people prior to the scientific age? And would it not look very primitive to a twenty-second century audience (if time lasts)? Why, then, not produce it with *perfect* precision? If it were thus produced, no mere human would understand it! An absolutely "perfect" book could be understood only by God.

To effectively communicate to the vast and diverse audience God intended to address throughout the ages, Scripture must communicate in ways that can be understood in diverse times and places. And that is what it does. Scripture thus not only communicates at a level that can be understood by manifold audiences over time, but it is also expressed in a variety of forms and styles such that Scripture can speak to so many different kinds of people throughout the ages.[43] This should, at the same time, cause us to remember that the biblical passages we read were originally written in and to a particular time and place, which we should take into account in our process of interpretation (see the excursus on interpreting Scripture following this chapter).

> *To effectively communicate to the vast and diverse audience God intended to address throughout the ages, Scripture must communicate in ways that can be understood in diverse times and places.*

Word of God in Human Words

"You are experts at setting aside the commandment of God in order to keep your tradition," Jesus said in rebuke of some teachers. "Moses said, 'HONOR YOUR FATHER AND YOUR MOTHER,'" Jesus continued, "but you say, if one pledges their belongings as a gift to God, they are not to do anything for their parents, "thereby invalidating the word of God by your tradition" (Mark 7:9–13). Not only does Jesus here emphasize the uniquely normative authority of Scripture over human traditions, He also identifies Old Testament writings as "the word of God."[44]

Elsewhere, the contents of Scripture are repeatedly identified as the word of God. For example, God frequently tells prophets things like, "speak with My words" (Ezek. 3:4) and "I have put My words in your mouth" (Jer. 1:9; cf. Deut. 18:18).[45] Accordingly, many biblical texts are introduced by phrases like:

- "God said"
- "The Lord said"
- "Thus says the Lord"
- The "hand of the Lord came upon"
- The "word of the Lord came"[46]

Likewise, New Testament authors repeatedly identify the Old Testament as the word of God. For example, New Testament writers repeatedly use the phrase "it is written" to refer to Old Testament messages from God. Further, New Testament writers quote the Old Testament in a way that identifies it as the word of God (e.g., Heb. 1:5–13).[47]

As we've seen, Jesus Himself identified teachings from the Old Testament as "the word of God" (Matt. 15:6; Mark 7:13) and promoted a high view of Scripture, proclaiming things like "the Scripture cannot be broken" (John 10:35, NKJV; cf. Matt. 5:17–18) and "It is written: 'MAN SHALL NOT LIVE ON BREAD ALONE, BUT ON EVERY WORD THAT COMES OUT OF THE MOUTH OF GOD'" (Matt. 4:4; cf. Deut. 8:3). Likewise, in 2 Timothy 3:16, Paul teaches that "all Scripture is inspired by God [literally, "God-breathed]."[48] Just before this, Paul writes, "from childhood you have known the sacred writings which are able to give you the wisdom that leads to salvation through faith which is in Christ Jesus" (2 Tim. 3:15).

Elsewhere, Paul teaches that Israel was "entrusted with the actual words of God" (Rom. 3:2) and proclaims, while on trial for His faith, "I confess this to you, that in accordance with the Way, which they call a sect, I do serve the God of our fathers, believing everything that is in accordance with the Law and is written in the Prophets" (Acts 24:14). This and other references to the "Law" and the "Prophets" refer to the Old Testament Scriptures. In this regard, Jesus taught, "all the things that are written about Me in the Law of Moses and the Prophets and the Psalms must be fulfilled" (Luke 24:44). And, earlier in his ministry, Jesus explained: "Do not presume that I came to abolish the Law or the Prophets; I did not come to abolish, but to fulfill. For truly I say to you, until heaven and earth pass away, not the smallest letter or stroke of a letter shall pass from the Law, until all is accomplished!" (Matt. 5:17–18).

With respect to the New Testament, the gospel taught by the apostles is repeatedly described as the "word of God" (Acts 8:14; 11:1; 12:24; 13:46; 17:13;

18:11; 19:20; John 17:14; Eph. 1:13), recorded by eyewitnesses and contemporaries and faithfully passed down (i.e., Luke 1:1–3; cf. 24:48; John 20:31).

For example, Paul writes, we "thank God that when you received the word of God which you heard from us, you accepted it not as the word of mere men, but as what it really is, the word of God, which also is at work in you who believe" (1 Thess. 2:13). Here, Paul refers to the proclamation of the apostles and, insofar as the New Testament consists of apostolic proclamation in written form (as I believe it does, see the discussion below), then this claim applies not only to the spoken word of the apostles but also to the New Testament writings.

So, the authors of Scripture repeatedly identify their messages as the word of God. And, based on the testimony of many witnesses (see the discussion of reasons to believe the Bible in chapter 3), I am convinced this claim is true. Indeed, I believe that Scripture is the word of God in human words. The Bible was written by humans inspired by God such that Scripture may be identified as "God-breathed" (2 Tim. 3:16). Though communicated in language that humans can understand, in words often chosen by humans, prophets and apostles inspired by the Holy Spirit effectively communicated divine revelation in a way that is trustworthy in what it teaches, such that human words express the word of God.

What Is the Canon of Scripture?

Yet, this leads to a final question: How do we know the writings in the Bible are the writings God commissioned as Scripture? That is, how do we know we have the right books in the Bible?

These are questions about the biblical canon. The term canon refers to a "rule" or "standard," often used in reference to an authoritative collection of writings or works. The biblical canon refers to the uniquely authoritative books of the Bible that Christians view as the word of God.

In what follows, we will briefly address questions such as:

- What is the nature of the biblical canon?
- Who decided which books should be included in the biblical canon?
- How do we know which books should be included in the biblical canon today?

Competing Theories in Christian Theology: The Biblical Canon

There are two main approaches to the nature of the biblical canon: the community canon approach and the intrinsic canon approach.[49]

The community canon approach maintains the biblical canon is determined by some community (e.g., a church) and is authoritative by virtue of that community's authority.[50] The intrinsic canon approach instead maintains the biblical canon was determined by God Himself and is merely recognized by humans.[51] On this view, writings are intrinsically *canonical* by virtue of being divinely commissioned to be the rule or standard of faith and practice.[52] Such writings are intrinsically authoritative by virtue of God's action, whether or not humans recognize them to be so.[53]

Advocates of the community canon approach tend to believe there was no biblical canon until some authoritative community (e.g., a church council) voted a list of such books. Thus, they tend to look for canon lists and council votes to identify the canon. Conversely, advocates of the intrinsic canon approach believe canonical writings are intrinsically canonical as soon as they are written. To recognize which books are intrinsically canonical, they focus on traits that intrinsically canonical writings would have (such as being prophetic or apostolic testimony, being consistent with past revelation, and having self-authenticating features), discussed later in this chapter.

Given the intrinsic canon approach, the history of canon recognition is interesting and important, but the dating of canon recognition itself is not crucial. In this view, the post-apostolic community of Christians is not invested with authority to *determine* the canon. It does, however, play a crucial role in preserving both the writings themselves and a great deal of historical materials and testimony about those writings that counts as strong evidence today (as a *witness* does in a trial).[54]

Recognizing the books as canonical is important because writings will not function as the rule (that is, as functionally *canonical*) for a person or group unless recognized as holding canonical authority. However, *recognition* of the books is not what makes them canonical. Whether or not any person or group recognizes Him as such, Jesus is intrinsically *the* Messiah and Lord.

Similarly, those writings commissioned by God to be canonical are intrinsically canonical whether we recognize them or not.

Many prophets and apostles in Scripture were initially rejected by their community. Some were even killed for their testimony, as Jesus Himself was. Evidently, human communities often get it wrong, raising serious questions for community canon approaches. If their own contemporaneous communities initially rejected many prophets and apostles and many contemporaries rejected even Jesus Himself, how can we have confidence in human communities to *determine* which writings are canonical? The evidence of history indicates that human communities are inadequate to determine the canon.

For this and other reasons, Adventists tend to understand the biblical canon along the lines of an intrinsic canon approach. No community has the authority to determine which books are canonical. Rather, individuals and communities are themselves to be judged as true or false Christians *by* the canon of Scripture.

The Biblical Canon Is a Christocentric Covenant Witness Document

Given an intrinsic canon approach, the biblical canon consists of those writings God commissioned to be the uniquely normative rule of faith and practice.[55] God commissioned such canonical writings as an authentic, inspired witness of what He has done, what He wants humans to know about Him, and how to relate to Him—a testimony of love.

More specifically, the biblical canon is a *covenant* witness document containing the testimony of *covenantal* prophets and apostles—those specially chosen and inspired to testify of God's great *covenantal* acts and teachings.[56] Covenantal prophets and apostles recorded *covenantal* revelation—the special revelation given in the context of and as an inspired witness to the Old and New Covenants, including the amazing revelation of God's nature and work to save the human race, and much more. The biblical canon, then, consists of the inspired witness of *covenantal* prophets relative to the Old Covenant leading up to Christ (the

> *God commissioned such canonical writings as an authentic, inspired witness of what He has done, what He wants humans to know about Him, and how to relate to Him—a testimony of love.*

Old Testament) and the inspired witness of covenantal apostles to Christ and the New Covenant (the New Testament, cf. John 5:39; Heb. 1:1-2).[57]

The Old Testament is confirmed by Christ (evidenced by the way Christ and His apostles speak of and use the Old Testament), and the inspired testimony of the apostles contained in the New Testament is commissioned by Christ.[58] The biblical canon, then, consists of the *rule* publicly confirmed and commissioned by the *Ruler* Himself (see, e.g., Luke 24:44-49; Acts 1:8; 10:39-43; 22:14-15).

The New Testament, in particular, is the inspired testimony of the apostles to the incarnate and risen Christ; Himself the ultimate revelation of God, who promised the apostles that the Holy Spirit "will teach you all things, and remind you of all that I said to you" (John 14:26) and "guide you into all the truth" (John 16:13; cf. 8:31; Acts 1:8; Jude 3). These promises not only attest to the truth of the apostolic testimony; they also testify to the sufficiency of the truth revealed to the apostles.

The New Testament, then, consists of the unrepeatable, first-generation apostolic witness to the incarnate Christ (Himself the supreme and sufficient revelation of God) and Christ's teachings, manifested historically and publicly in a manner attested to by a cloud of witnesses (1 Cor. 15:3-15).[59] No further prophetic messages could be so attested prior to the Second Coming of the Ruler Himself. Once the Ruler (Christ) has come, any future claim to the prophetic gift must be tested by the rule confirmed and commissioned by the Ruler Himself, attested to by a cloud of specially chosen and inspired first-generation witnesses. The biblical canon, then, is closed historically, by the end of the first-generation apostolic witness to Christ and the New Covenant.[60]

Traits of Canonicity

Yet, how do we know which books should be recognized as canonical? In simplest terms, we look for evidence (internal and external) regarding divine commission.[61] Specifically, we look for particular traits that books commissioned by God *to be the rule of faith and practice* would thereby possess.[62]

Such traits can be distilled into three categories:
- Divinely Commissioned as (Covenantal) Prophetic and/or Apostolic Testimony

- Consistency with Past Revelation
- Self-Authenticating

The first trait is attested in both Scripture and the history of canon recognition. Scripture frequently highlights the foundational authority of the testimony of chosen prophets and apostles. For example, Peter instructs, "remember the words spoken beforehand by the holy prophets and the commandment of the Lord and Savior spoken by your apostles" (2 Pet. 3:2; cf. Luke 11:49). Paul further teaches that God's household is "built on the foundation of the apostles and prophets, Christ Jesus Himself being the cornerstone" (Eph. 2:20). In this regard, Jesus and His apostles consistently affirm the ruling authority of the Old Testament Scriptures of the prophets (e.g., Luke 24:25–27, 44; Acts 24:14). And the apostles are repeatedly identified as Christ's foundational "witnesses" (Luke 24:48; Acts 1:8, 22; 3:15; 5:32; 10:39–42; 26:16).

To recognize a book as canonical, then, we first look for evidence the book consists of (*covenantal*) prophetic and/or apostolic testimony. That is, was it written by a divinely commissioned (covenantal) prophet and/or first-generation apostle or first-generation close associate thereof who recorded such testimony? Christians believe the thirty-nine Old Testament books and twenty-seven New Testament books do consist of such divinely commissioned testimony.[63]

This leads to the second trait—consistency with past revelation. Since God does not contradict Himself (2 Tim. 2:13; cf. Titus 1:2–3; Heb. 6:17–18), any new divine revelation would not contradict previous divine revelation (Deut. 4:1–2; Matt. 5:17–18; Heb. 13:7–9). As Isaiah 8:20 teaches, "To the law and to the testimony! If they do not speak according to this word, it is because there is no light in them" (NKJV; cf. Luke 24:25; Acts 17:11; 24:14).

In Old Testament times, new messages were to be judged by the previous testimony of covenantal prophets. For example, Moses's writings were a *covenantal* rule by which later messages were tested (Deut. 13:1–5). Early Christians were to judge teachings by those delivered to them by the apostles (Gal. 1:8; cf. Titus 1:9; 1 John 4:1; 2 John 10), while the apostolic teachings themselves were tested for consistency with previous Scriptures (Acts 17:11; cf. 24:14).

The third trait is self-authentication. With respect to this trait, one looks for evidence in the writings themselves (e.g., fulfilled prophecies) that attest to them being revealed and inspired by the Holy Spirit (1 Cor. 2:10–14; cf. John 7:17; 10:27).

These three traits do not work in isolation, but any canonical book must not fail with respect to any of these three traits.

Recognizing Canonical Books

There is both internal and external evidence that supports recognizing the thirty-nine Old Testament books and twenty-seven New Testament books as canonical.[64]

Regarding the Old Testament, Jesus repeatedly identified the "Law and the Prophets" as authoritative Scripture (see Matt. 5:17; 7:12; 11:13; 22:40; Luke 16:16; cf. Matt. 11:13; Luke 16:29). Further, the way Christ and New Testament authors referenced Old Testament Scripture (e.g., Matt. 26:56; John 5:39; 1 Cor. 15:3) indicates they and their audiences knew which writings were "the Scriptures."

Specifically, Jesus taught, "all the things that are written about Me in the Law of Moses and the Prophets and the Psalms must be fulfilled" (Luke 24:44; cf. 24:27). The Hebrew Bible (*Tanakh*) is organized in three sections—the Law (*Torah*), Prophets (*Nevi'im*), and Writings (*Ketuvim*, of which Psalms is the first book), including the same books as the Protestant Old Testament canon, but in different groupings and with a different order (see chart below). Many believe that in Luke 24:44 Christ referred to these three sections, thus referring to the same Old Testament we have today.[65]

THE BOOKS OF THE HEBREW BIBLE		
THE TORAH ("LAW")	**THE NEVI'IM ("PROPHETS")**	**THE KETUVIM ("WRITINGS")**
Genesis Exodus Leviticus Numbers Deuteronomy	Joshua Judges Samuel (I & II) Kings (I & II) Isaiah Jeremiah Ezekiel Minor Prophets	Psalms Proverbs Job Song of Solomon Ruth Lamentations Ecclesiastes Esther Daniel Ezra-Nehemiah Chronicles (I & II)

Further, after noting God promised to send "prophets and apostles," some of whom would be persecuted and killed, Jesus proclaimed, "the blood of all the prophets, shed since the foundation of the world, may be charged against this generation, from the blood of Abel to the blood of Zechariah, who was killed between the altar and the house of God" (Luke 11:49–51). Abel was the first person in Scripture killed for his faith (Genesis 4), and the Zechariah referenced here was the last person killed for his faith in the last book of the Hebrew Bible (2 Chron. 24:20–21).

These instances, combined with other evidence, such as the extensive use of the Old Testament by Jesus and the apostles, suggests Jesus and the apostles affirmed the same Old Testament books contained in our biblical canon today.[66] This aligns with numerous lines of external evidence.[67]

Some External Evidence of Old Testament Recognition by About the Time of Jesus

- **The Prologue to *Sirach*** (ca. 130–110 BC) mentions the Law, Prophets, and "the others that followed them . . . the other books of our ancestors."[68]
- **2 Maccabees 3:12–14** (ca. 150–120 BC) mentions the "memoirs of Nehemiah" and says Nehemiah "founded a library and collected the books about the kings and prophets, and the writings of David, and letters of kings" and states Judas Maccabeus made a similar collection.
- ***b. Baba Batra* 14b–15a** (ca. 164 BC–AD 200) identifies by name all twenty-four books of the Tanakh (corresponding to the thirty-nine books of our Old Testament) and explicitly distinguishes between the Prophets and the Writings.
- **Josephus, *Against Apion* 1.8** (late first century AD) mentions a three-part corpus of "justly accredited" prophetic books and notes "no one has been so bold as either to add anything to them, to take anything from them, or to make any change in them" and "it is an instinct with every Jew, from the day of his birth, to regard them as the decrees of God, to abide by them, and, if need be, cheerfully to die for them."[69]

- **4 Ezra 14:45** (late first century AD) references a twenty-four-book collection.

The Old Testament Scriptures, then, are confirmed by Jesus Himself (e.g., Luke 24:27, 44) and identified as testimony of Christ (see John 1:45; 5:39; Acts 10:43; 1 Pet. 1:10–12). Further, Christ Himself commissioned the apostolic testimony of which the New Testament consists. Specifically, Christ chose apostles and commissioned them as His "witnesses" to the ends of the earth (e.g., Luke 24:48; Acts 1:8; 10:39–42; 26:16; cf. Matt. 28:19–20). The biblical canon, then, is a Christocentric canon—the Old Testament confirmed by Christ and the apostolic testimony contained in the New Testament commissioned by Christ (e.g., Luke 24:44, 48). The biblical canon is the rule confirmed and commissioned by the Ruler Himself.

The apostles not only affirm the Old Testament Scriptures but also identify New Testament writings as "Scripture." Specifically, Paul writes, "the Scripture says, 'YOU SHALL NOT MUZZLE THE OX WHILE IT IS THRESHING,' and 'The laborer is worthy of his wages'" (1 Tim. 5:18). The first quotation is from Deuteronomy 25:4, but the second corresponds to the very words in Luke 10:7, thus seeming to identify Luke as "Scripture."[70] Likewise, Peter calls Paul's letters "Scripture," referring to what Paul wrote "in all his letters," including "some things that are hard to understand, which the untaught and unstable distort, as they do also the rest of the Scriptures" (2 Pet. 3:16).

> **The biblical canon is the rule confirmed and commissioned by the Ruler Himself.**

The way the apostles referred to their own messages supports these conclusions. For instance, Paul writes, "we also constantly thank God that when you received the word of God which you heard from us, you accepted it not as the word of mere men, but as what it really is, the word of God, which also is at work in you who believe" (1 Thess. 2:13).

Some External Evidence of Early New Testament Recognition

Because there was no centralized church authority that decided which books would be canonical, canon recognition was a messy organic process. Statements by church councils regarding canonical books did not appear until the late fourth century and did not decide the canon but reported what Christians already held to be canonical.

Long before such councils, New Testament books were widely treated as "canonical." Athanasius's Festal Letter 39 (AD 367) is sometimes cited as the first extant list of all twenty-seven New Testament books. However, over a century earlier, Origen's *Homilies on Joshua* (ca. AD 250) seems to refer to all twenty-seven New Testament books.[71] Still earlier, Irenaeus (ca. AD 180) quoted extensively from the Old Testament and New Testament *as* Scripture (quoting every New Testament book except Philemon and 3 John) and referred to the authority of "Scripture" in ways that indicate his audience knew which books are "Scripture."[72] Further, Michael Kruger presents extensive evidence that "Christians began to view their books as Scripture much earlier than Irenaeus—perhaps even by the turn of the century."[73]

With regard to the New Testament, evidence suggests early Christians recognized whatever writings were believed to consist of first-generation *apostolic* testimony. For example, *The Shepherd of Hermas* was initially thought to be an inspired book but was not recognized as canonical because it was written "after [the apostles'] time."[74]

The Testimony of the Community and the Old Testament Apocrypha

While the community does not possess the authority to *determine* the canon, the testimony of Christians over the ages counts as strong supporting evidence (akin to a credible witness in a trial whose testimony does not *make* someone innocent or guilty but counts as significant evidence). Today, Christians nearly unanimously recognize the thirty-nine Old Testament books and twenty-seven New Testament books as *canonical*. Some Christians affirm more books (which Protestants call the Old Testament Apocrypha), but very few Christians accept fewer than the thirty-nine Old Testament books and twenty-seven New Testament books.[75]

The Old Testament Apocrypha consists of books written during what Protestants call the intertestamental period—from when the last of the thirty-nine Old Testament books was written in the fifth century BC to roughly the time of the apostles (with the books of the Old Testament Apocrypha typically dated from roughly the third century BC to the first century AD). Roman Catholics and Eastern Orthodox Christians (and others) affirm the Old Testament Apocrypha (which they call deuterocanonical), but Eastern Orthodox Christians accept more books than Roman Catholics.

Protestants, however, typically do not accept the Apocrypha as canonical. In brief, Protestants do not accept the Apocrypha as canonical because the books are not believed to possess the traits of canonicity (divinely commissioned as covenantal testimony, consistent with past revelation, and self-authenticating). More specifically, some of the prominent reasons often given for not affirming the Old Testament Apocrypha are:

- Jewish writings (from the Second Temple period) indicate there was a cessation of recognized normative (covenantal) prophecy in the intertestamental period.[76] Specifically, ancient documents (e.g., Josephus, *Against Apion* 1.7, 8; *b. Sotah* 48b; cf. 1 Macc. 9:27, 14:41) testify that such *authoritative* prophecy ceased after the time of Artaxerxes (fifth century BC).[77]
- Evidence suggests that first-century Jews did not view the books of the Old Testament Apocrypha as authoritative Scripture. Philo of Alexandria (ca. 20 BC–AD 50) did not quote the Old Testament Apocrypha *as authoritative Scripture* but copiously quotes from the thirty-nine Old Testament books as such. And, Josephus (AD 37–ca. 100) explicitly excluded the books known today as the Old Testament Apocrypha, writing: "It is true, our history has been written since Artaxerxes very particularly, but has not been esteemed of the like authority with the former by our forefathers, because there has not been an exact succession of prophets since that time" (Josephus, *Against Apion*, 1.8).
- Many Protestants argue that Jesus did not appear to treat any Old Testament Apocryphal books *as authoritative Scripture*, but He regularly referred to writings contained in the Hebrew Bible (Old Testament) *as authoritative Scripture.*[78] Jesus makes

references that appear to correspond to the contents and scope of the Hebrew Bible (see the earlier discussion of Luke 11:49–51; 24:44), which many take as evidence that Jesus affirmed the same Old Testament writings as those contained in the Hebrew Bible (corresponding to the thirty-nine books of the Old Testament).[79]
- Many Protestants contend that the Apocryphal books are not used in the New Testament *as authoritative Scripture* (e.g., no "it is written" or "the Scriptures say" referencing such works, in contrast to many such references to the books of the Hebrew Bible *as authoritative Scripture*, including nearly all of the thirty-nine books of the Old Testament).[80]
- Such works are excluded from the modern Hebrew Bible (Tanakh) and, according to Craig Blomberg, the "actual discussions of the contents of Scripture in ancient Judaism show no trace of an expanded canon that included the Apocrypha."[81] He writes further, "no *Jews* ever seriously supported the canonization of any of the Apocrypha."[82]
- Many early Christians did not consider the Apocrypha to be canonical (e.g., Melito of Sardis, the Bryennios List, Origen, Jerome, Athanasius). Accordingly, the apocryphal books were placed in a separate section of many Bibles because they were not deemed as of equal authority.
- Many believe the Old Testament Apocrypha includes false teachings (e.g., offering of money to atone for the sins of the dead, 2 Macc. 12:43–45).

While Protestants deny the Old Testament Apocrypha are canonical, however, they are widely viewed as helpful to read as (non-authoritative) background material, along with other extra-canonical literature from the Second Temple period.[83]

Other ancient writings pertinent to the discussion include the Old Testament Pseudepigrapha and the New Testament Pseudepigrapha/Apocrypha. The term Pseudepigrapha refers to pseudonymous writings; that is, writings that falsely claim to be written by a past figure. These works fail with respect to the traits of canonicity, not being written during the time period of the Old Testament covenantal prophets or the first-generation apostles, and sometimes including teachings inconsistent with past revelation. Nearly all Christians agree that these writings are not canonical.

While some Christians accept more books, however, the sixty-six books of the Bible (thirty-nine Old Testament books and twenty-seven New Testament books) are nearly unanimously affirmed among Christians.

Conclusion: Why Does It Matter?

She was in prison and her communication with the outside world was severely restricted. She often wondered what was happening in the lives of her beloved family, but she had access to no electronic communications. For a host of reasons, they could not visit her, though they would if they could. This caused her to treasure all the more the letters they frequently sent. It was not the same as being with them, but what the letters revealed nevertheless brought her great joy, helped her to cope with her imprisonment, and reminded her of how much she had to look forward to when her sentence would end and she would be free to be with her family once again.

It is not difficult to imagine how letters from loved ones would be so prized when other communication has been cut off. In some ways, the Bible provides special communication from God while we are in a context that is largely cut off from God's special presence—as we abide in "enemy territory" in the cosmic conflict. Understood this way, we should recognize the revelation given to us in Scripture as very precious, for through these special communications from God, we can know Him and know how to live and reflect the light of God's love in this dark world.

In this chapter, we have seen that Scripture is the product of divine revelation and inspiration, which operates in many ways and various patterns, such that Scripture is the word of God in human words. Along the way, we have taken up numerous questions about the nature of Scripture as inspired and as "canonical," but one crucial, practical question remains that each person must answer for himself or herself. Have you met God through Scripture?

If you want to meet God through Scripture, simply open your heart to Him, pray for the guidance and illumination of the Holy Spirit, and read carefully and slowly what God has given to us in the Bible. Do not worry if you do not understand everything immediately and, as you progress, follow the steps for the interpretation of Scripture that can be found in the excursus section that immediately follows this chapter.

As preparation for such reading, consider praying for what Paul prayed for the audience of his letter to the Ephesians, "that the God of our Lord Jesus Christ, the Father of glory, may give you a spirit of wisdom and of revelation in the knowledge of Him. I pray that the eyes of your heart may be enlightened, so that you will know what is the hope of His calling, what are the riches of the glory of His inheritance in the saints, and what is the boundless greatness of His power toward us who believe" (Eph. 1:17–19).

Before moving on, I invite you now to reflect on the great gift that God has given to humans by revealing Himself and His teachings in human words by reading Psalm 119, wherein the psalmist proclaims to God: "Your word is a lamp to my feet and a light to my path" (Ps. 119:105).

Questions for Reflection

1. How would you explain the meaning of revelation and inspiration to someone else? What is the difference between them?
2. What is the difference between general revelation and special revelation? In what ways is special revelation more reliable and adequate?
3. How much of Scripture is inspired? Why does this matter?
4. What does it mean to you to understand Scripture as the word of God in human words? Why is it so crucial to recognize Scripture is inspired by God but is conveyed through limited human language?
5. How do we know which books are those books God commissioned to be authoritative (that is, to be "canonical")? What are some traits of canonicity?
6. What is your experience in Scripture? How can you share that experience with someone else?
7. You can experience hearing God's voice through Scripture even now. Do you wish to do so? If so, pray to God, and ask for the

Holy Spirit to guide you and illuminate your mind. Then, open Scripture (perhaps beginning with one of the Gospels) and read carefully and prayerfully, listening for the voice of God.

For Further Reading

Adventist Perspectives:

Canale, Fernando L. *Back to Revelation-Inspiration: Searching for the Cognitive Foundation of Christian Theology in a Postmodern World*. Lanham, MD: University Press of America, 2001.

———. *The Cognitive Principle of Christian Theology: An Hermeneutical Study of the Revelation and Inspiration of the Bible*. Berrien Springs: Andrews University Lithotech, 2005.

Davidson, Richard M. "Biblical Interpretation." In *Handbook of Seventh-day Adventist Theology*. Edited by Raoul Dederen. Hagerstown, MD: Review and Herald, 2000.

———. "Interpreting Scripture: An Hermeneutical 'Decalogue,'" *Journal of the Adventist Theological Society* 4, no. 2 (1993): 95–114.

Gulley, Norman R. *Systematic Theology: Prolegomena*. Berrien Springs, MI: Andrews University Press, 2003.

Hanna, Martin. *The Cosmic Christ of Scripture: How to Read God's Three Books. Comparing Scripture Perspectives with the Writings of Ellen G. White*. Berrien Springs, MI: Cosmic Christ Connections, 2006.

Hasel, Frank M., ed. *Biblical Hermeneutics: An Adventist Approach*. Silver Spring, MD: Review & Herald Academic/Biblical Research Institute, 2021.

——— and Michael G. Hasel, *How to Interpret Scripture*. Nampa, ID: Pacific Press, 2020.

Peckham, John C. *Canonical Theology: The Biblical Canon, Sola Scriptura, and Theological Method*. Grand Rapids, MI: Eerdmans, 2016.

Pfandl, Gerhard, ed. *Interpreting Scripture: Bible Questions and Answers*. Silver Spring, MD: Biblical Research Institute, 2010.

Reid, George, ed. *Understanding Scripture: An Adventist Approach*, Vol. 1. Biblical Research Institute, 2005.

van Bemmelen, Peter M. "Revelation and Inspiration." In *Handbook of Seventh-day Adventist Theology*. Edited by Raoul Dederen. Hagerstown, MD: Review and Herald, 2000.

White, Ellen G., *Selected Messages*. Vol. 1. Washington, DC: Review and Herald, 1958, especially chapter 1.

See also the resources on the Biblical Research Institute website: https://adventistbiblicalresearch.org/materials/.

Other Christian Perspectives:

Anyabwile, Kristie. *Literarily: How Understanding Bible Genres Transforms Bible Study*. Chicago: Moody, 2022.

Castleman, Robbie F. *Interpreting the God-Breathed Word: How to Read and Study the Bible*. Grand Rapids, MI: Baker Academic, 2018.

Duvall, J. Scott and J. Daniel Hays. *Grasping God's Word: A Hand-On Approach to Reading, Interpreting, and Applying the Bible*. Grand Rapids, MI: Zondervan, 2020.

Erickson, Millard J. *Introducing Christian Doctrine*, 3rd Edition. Grand Rapids, MI: Baker Academic, 2015, chapters 3–7.

Fee, Gordon D. and Douglas Stuart. *How to Read the Bible for all Its Worth*, 4th ed. Grand Rapids, MI: Zondervan, 2014.

Osborne, Grant R. *The Hermeneutical Spiral: A Comprehensive Introduction to Biblical Interpretation*. Rev. and expanded, 2nd ed. Downers Grove, IL: InterVarsity Press, 2006.

Carson, D. A., ed. *The Enduring Authority of the Christian Scriptures*. Grand Rapids, MI: Eerdmans, 2016.

Gorman, Michael J., ed. *Scripture and Its Interpretation: A Global, Ecumenical Introduction to the Bible*. Grand Rapids, MI: Baker Academic, 2017.

Heyward, Orpheus J. *God's Word: The Inspiration and Authority of Scripture*. Renew, 2021.

Kruger, Michael J. *Canon Revisited*. Wheaton, IL: Crossway, 2012.

McCaulley, Esau. *Reading While Black: African American Biblical Interpretation as an Exercise in Hope*. Downers Grove, IL: IVP Academic, 2020.

Spellman, Ched. *One Holy Book: A Primer on How the Bible Came to Be and Why It Matters*. Codex Books, 2021.

EXCURSUS

THE EMMAUS APPROACH: HOW TO UNDERSTAND SCRIPTURE AND DO THEOLOGY

They did not recognize Him. Before revealing who He was, He first taught them from Scripture, "beginning with Moses and with all the Prophets, He explained to them the things written about Himself in all the Scriptures" (Luke 24:27). Astonishing. Instead of simply convincing them by manifesting Himself as risen from the dead, Jesus first directed them to Scripture.

Jesus thus appealed to Scripture as the authoritative basis of what was true about Himself, expositing the teachings of Old Testament Scripture as a whole, and calling them to "believe in all that the prophets have spoken!" (Luke 24:25; cf. Matt. 5:17–18; Luke 16:31; John 10:35). Accordingly, Paul later testified that he believed "everything that is in accordance with the Law and is written in the Prophets" (Acts 24:14; cf. 17:11); that is, everything in accordance with Old Testament Scripture.

As we have seen, Christ confirmed the Old Testament and commissioned the New Testament (e.g., Luke 24:44, 48). Following Christ's approach today, then, entails believing *all* that the Old Testament and New Testament Scriptures teach, believing and living by "every word that comes out of the mouth of God" (Matt. 4:4; cf. Deut. 8:3); that is, treating Scripture as a whole as *the* rule of faith and practice.

This excursus briefly introduces ten principles for interpreting Scripture in keeping with this "Emmaus approach."[1] Before diving into these principles, let me share with you that I used to think reading the Bible was boring. It contained so much information that was not interesting to me and did not seem relevant. Reading it could feel like a chore.

I no longer feel that way. What changed? In short, I began to read Scripture prayerfully and intentionally as a means to know God better and help others to come to know Him. Along the way, I learned to read Scripture more closely and deeply, informed by questions that arose from engaging others. In doing so, I began to see so much more in the text than ever before.

Whereas I once thought of Bible study as something I needed to do to check off a box, I have come to approach it in terms of building relationship with the living God. I would never want to approach relationship with my wife as if talking with her was something I needed to do to check a box. No, I want to spend time with her, talk with her, and get to know her more and more. In somewhat analogous fashion, I have come to approach the reading and studying of Scripture as an opportunity to spend time with and come to know the living God more and more.

Today, I see Scripture as a gold mine containing inexhaustible treasure. Many gems lie on the surface, but others require digging more deeply. Although Scripture's basic message is so simple even children can understand it, Peter taught that "some things" in Scripture "are hard to understand, which the untaught and unstable distort . . . to their own destruction" (2 Pet. 3:16). We cannot rely, then, on just a first glance reading of Scripture and should not make the mistake of assuming our initial interpretation is correct. Rather, one should study and "be diligent to present yourself approved to God as a worker who does not need to be ashamed, accurately handling the word of truth" (2 Tim. 2:15).

I have found the effort involved in "excavating" the treasures of Scripture, so to speak, to be more than worth it. It has filled not only my mind but my heart with love for God and abiding hope and purpose. By the ministry of the Holy Spirit, you can have this experience too. It will not come all at once. It is a journey. But, let me tell you, there is great joy in this journey.

We turn now to the ten principles for interpreting Scripture in keeping with the "Emmaus approach."

(1) The Bible "Alone" (*sola Scriptura*)

The first principle affirms the Bible as the supreme standard given by God as the uniquely normative rule of faith and practice, by which all doctrines and practices should be tested (see, e.g., 2 Tim. 3:16; 2 Pet. 1:20–21).[2]

This *sola Scriptura* principle distills the biblical teaching that the prophetic and apostolic testimony commissioned by God as the rule (contained in the canon of Scripture) is to be uniquely authoritative over all other factors. Whereas Jesus encouraged His followers to "believe in all that the prophets have spoken" (Luke 24:25), other theological factors such as our reason, experience, and traditions are fallible (see, e.g., Prov. 28:26; Jer. 17:9; Matt. 15:3–6; 1 Cor. 3:19–20).[3] Such factors, then, should be continually measured and tested against the *infallible* rule of Scripture (see, e.g., Luke 24:25; John 10:35; Acts 5:29; cf. 17:11–13; 24:14; Gal. 1:8; 1 John 4:1; 2 John 10). If Scripture is to rule, its interpretation cannot be ruled by anything else, whether one's private interpretation or community traditions.[4]

This principle, however, does *not* mean the Bible is the only writing we should read or the only source from which we should learn. Scripture itself teaches there is partial revelation of God in nature (general revelation, see Ps. 19:1–4; Rom. 1:18–23) and genuine prophecy outside of Scripture (see Acts 2:17; 1 Cor. 14:29). Thus, we can and should learn from things outside Scripture, seeking to understand the world around us by careful study of nature and scientific inquiry, but we should test *all* things by the standard of Scripture (keeping in mind our own interpretation of Scripture is fallible and sometimes needs to be corrected by Scripture).

There are two primary dangers in approaching *sola Scriptura*: isolationism and creedalism (or any form of making a community or community-determined standard finally normative).

Isolationism treats one's theological understanding as if it is the product of Scripture without the influence of any other factors.[5] But, in reality, no one reads Scripture in a way that is entirely free from influence by factors outside Scripture. We each read Scripture from our perspective, bringing a framework of prior understandings to our interpretation, whether we intend to or not (for example, we unavoidably bring to our reading some prior understanding of the very words we read, and we each read from some social location).[6] The influences of known presuppositions can be mitigated and corrected, but we cannot arrive at an interpretation that is free from *all* presuppositions. Accordingly, we should recognize we have presuppositions and continually seek to test what we bring to our reading of Scripture by the standard of Scripture itself. Otherwise, we risk confusing our fallible, private interpretation with the meaning of Scripture—unintentionally shifting authority from Scripture to ourselves.

Creedalism, on the other hand, treats creeds or confessional statements as the normative standard for interpreting Scripture, shifting *functional* authority from Scripture to whatever confessions, creeds, or statements a community adopts. If biblical interpretation is governed by a standard or set of presuppositions outside of Scripture, then Scripture's authority is functionally undercut, being superseded by that external standard. No one should develop their theological understanding in isolation from Christian community (see Heb. 10:23–25; cf. Acts 8:30–35). We should read Scripture within community and across various communities, which might help us see our own presuppositions and blind spots. But the conclusions we reach should always be measured and tested by Scripture itself.

God's Two Books: Scripture and Nature

"The heavens declare the glory of God, and the sky above proclaims his handiwork. Day to day pours out speech, and night to night reveals knowledge. There is no speech, nor are there words, whose voice is not heard. Their voice goes out through all the earth, and their words to the end of the world" (Ps. 19:1–4, ESV). Here and elsewhere, Scripture itself teaches that there is revelation of God in creation that is available to everyone, everywhere, at all times (general revelation).

Some refer to God's general revelation in nature and God's special revelation in Scripture as God's two books—the "book" of nature and the book of Scripture.[7] Some believe these two books are in conflict, and such a view contributes to the perceived conflict between science and theology that often undermines charitable and productive dialogue. However, rightly understood, these two books agree. The supposed conflict between them (sometimes more broadly thought of as a conflict between faith and science) is a matter of hermeneutics—differing interpretations of the data. As Adventists often understand it, where there is disagreement, or even apparent contradiction between them, it is because we have misunderstood one or both of the two books of nature and Scripture.[8]

There are many things revealed in Scripture and in nature and we should do our best to pursue truth to the best of our abilities. Believers in God should pursue the sciences with great rigor. Yet, even our best understanding of God and the world God created is a fallible understanding. This should evoke humility and the recognition that we do not have a perfect theology, and we do not have a perfect scientific understanding of the world. Both should be continually subjected to the data of revelation itself. Whereas God's two books always agree, our fallible interpretations of them may not. Where there is disagreement, or even apparent contradiction, I believe that is because we have misunderstood one or both of these books. Such issues should not cause us to abandon either faith or science but should drive us back to the sources, humbly proceeding in a way that continually distinguishes what is revealed from our fallible understandings of what is revealed.

(2) The Totality of Scripture (*tota Scriptura*)

This principle treats *all* of Scripture as the final rule of faith and practice (cf. 2 Tim. 3:16). One part of Scripture should not be emphasized while neglecting or downplaying other parts of Scripture. The *entire* biblical canon (*tota Scriptura*) should be allowed to actually function as *the* rule of faith and practice.

Many (false) arguments can be made from a few texts in isolation. The question is which understanding makes sense of *all* of the biblical data without injury to or twisting of any of it. In this regard, as seen in the temptation narrative, even the devil can quote Scripture (Matt. 4:6). But he twists it and takes it out of context, not rendering it in a way consistent with *all* of Scripture. Christ repeatedly responded to Satan's temptations and misuse of Scripture with other texts of Scripture that exposed Satan's misinterpretation, declaring (among other things): "It is written: 'man shall not live on bread alone, but on every word that comes out of the mouth of God'" (Matt. 4:4, quoting Deut. 8:3; see also Matt. 4:7, 10).

(3) The Analogy (or Harmony) of Scripture
(*analogia Scripturae*)

Closely related to the previous principle, the analogy of Scripture approaches Scripture as a unified and internally coherent corpus such that each passage should be understood in light of the entire biblical canon (see Isa. 8:20; Luke 24:27, 44–45). Scripture, then, should function as its own norm of interpretation.

Whenever we read something, we are also interpreting it. And we should be willing to recognize our interpretation is fallible. I believe Scripture is infallible, but my interpretation of it is not. If Scripture is truly to rule my faith and practice, I must be open to allowing Scripture to correct me, including my cherished interpretations. This is easier said than done and cannot be accomplished by interpretive procedures alone but requires a posture of humility and willing obedience to God that itself only comes from God (see principle #4 below).

Students of Scripture should always seek the wider teachings of Scripture to help understand any part of Scripture. Interpreters should continually go back and forth between considering what individual passages of Scripture teach and what the Bible as a whole has to say on given matters (in a hermeneutical spiral). Every interpretation of Scripture should be continually subjected back to the rule of Scripture itself, interpreting each individual part of Scripture in accordance with the rest of Scripture.

(4) Spiritual Discernment
(*spiritalis spiritaliter examinatur*)

This brings us to the crucial principle of spiritual discernment. Scripture teaches that spiritual things are spiritually discerned (1 Cor. 2:11–14). Accordingly, the Holy Spirit should be continually sought for guidance, illumination, and to foster in us the humility to be formed and corrected by Scripture's teachings. Scripture is the rule because it was given by the divine Ruler. As such, we should continually submit to the guidance of the Holy Spirit, who inspired Scripture.

In short, pray for the Holy Spirit's guidance. Then pray some more. Always begin your study of Scripture with prayer and continually approach Scripture with a prayerful and humble attitude.

The first four principles above lay out the basic approach to Scripture as the rule (the "canonical approach"). The last six principles offer specific guidelines for interpreting biblical passages. All these principles seek to draw meaning out of the text rather than reading into the text what is not there. The process of drawing meaning out of the text is known as exegesis.[9]

(5) Text and Translation

Because all translations involve interpretation, it is best to consider the text in its original languages. Today, it is more accessible than ever for anyone to learn some basic principles of Hebrew and Greek, the languages most of Scripture was originally written in.[10]

For those who never acquire skills in the original languages, however, there are hosts of resources available for the reader to be less reliant on the interpretations inherent in translations. By accessing a good, scholarly commentary, one can be alerted to instances where translations depart from one another (as well as historical information, to which we turn in our next principle).

Before consulting secondary sources such as good biblical commentaries, however, it is important to make sure you use a good translation. For study, the best kinds of translations are formal translations, which tend to be closer to a word-for-word translation, in contrast to those that aim for "sense-for-sense" translation, sometimes known as dynamic translations.[11] What kind of translation approach a version uses is typically stated in the introduction of the Bible.

Dynamic translations tend to be easier to read and more pleasing literarily, but formal translations stick closer to the original wording and thus are best for close study. Do not limit yourself to one translation for study but compare multiple versions and use secondary sources like commentaries to learn about what is behind the different translations.

(6) Historical Context/Questions of Introduction

Every biblical passage was written in some historical context—to particular people in particular times and places. To best understand Scripture, we should pay close attention to what we can know about the historical context.

When we study a passage, we should pay close attention to what the Bible reveals about its historical context and issues such as authorship, chronology, and the setting of the text. To further illuminate the historical background, one should consult good reference works such as Bible dictionaries, commentaries, and surveys of biblical history and archaeology. These secondary sources, however, should themselves be subjected to and tested by what Scripture itself teaches.

(7) Literary Context and Analysis

Close attention to the literary context and close analysis of the text are also crucial. First, consider what kind of literary composition the passage is (the literary genre). Is it prose (e.g., narratives, legal texts, and cultic material) or a form of poetry (characterized by various kinds of parallelism and, to a lesser degree, by meter and stanzas)?[12]

Second, analyze the text itself. Words mean what they are used to mean in sentences, paragraphs, and so on. Thus, one of the most important keys to understanding a text is to pay attention to the way writers have structured their material and to the literary context. Consider the verses that precede and follow the passage you are studying (immediate context), the wider context of the book (book context), and the wider context of the entirety of Scripture (the canonical context).

Of course, one cannot read all of Scripture every time one studies an individual passage. This is one reason it is important to read and reread Scripture as a whole over the course of time to become more and more familiar with Scripture as a whole. Ideally, we will read and study Scripture both broadly (reading all of it slowly over time) and deeply (delving into individual passages and Scripture more closely). We want to see both the forest as a whole and the individual trees, so to speak.

Ask questions like: What immediately precedes and follows the passage? How does the passage relate to the wider book? What other passages shed light on this text? How does this passage relate to the wider teachings of Scripture?

(8) Grammatical/Syntactical/Semantic Analysis

As noted earlier, the meaning of words is tied to the way they are used in sentences, paragraphs, and so on. Accordingly, to understand the meaning of texts, we must pay attention to the specific words of the texts and the way they are arranged in sentences (the syntax). What is emphasized by the ordering of the words? Is there meaning that becomes apparent by the way the words and concepts are constructed? Pay attention to the clues in the text as to when idioms and other figurative expressions are employed.

Examine the key words that appear in the text and (if possible) consider the range of meaning (semantic range) of the words in the original language. Here, it is helpful to survey the way the term is used throughout Scripture, keeping in mind that words do not always mean the same thing but have a range of meaning.[13] The context and usage of the term determine the meaning in individual passages, and you should be careful not to read the meaning of a word in one context into another context.

In all languages, words have shades of meaning across a range of meaning, which change with usage over time. Do not focus on a single, definitive meaning of the term but focus on understanding the range of meaning of the word as used in Scripture. Then, look to the usage in your passage to indicate what the word means based on the way it is used in the passage you are studying. Here, the use of good grammars, lexicons, concordances, and commentaries can be helpful, but the primary context of meaning should be the context of Scripture itself.

(9) Theological Context/Analysis

Next, consider what the text teaches about God and God's relationship with creatures. Identify specific issues raised or touched on by the passages under consideration and think about how they might reflect on who God is, how God relates to us, and the doctrines of the Christian faith.

Ask questions like: What picture of God does the text present? To what Christian doctrine or doctrines does the passage relate? How does the theological content of this passage relate to similar questions and issues elsewhere in the Bible? How does it relate to other doctrines? Here, employ the analogy of Scripture that was discussed earlier, allowing individual texts and the entirety of Scripture to mutually inform one another without any twisting, allowing the biblical text as a whole to shape and reshape your presuppositions and conclusions.

(10) Practical Application

Once time has been taken to let the text speak for itself, seeking to understand the meaning conveyed by the text in its own immediate and canonical context, consider the way the passage you are studying applies to your life and the lives of those around you. List the life issues touched on by the passage and ask how it might apply to life. What might the Holy Spirit be calling you to do? How might such an understanding of God and how He relates to creation affect your daily life? Is the text informing or instructing you to live a particular way, directly or indirectly? Pay attention to who the original audience was and any limitations of the application that might have been intended for a particular person or group in a particular time (such as civil laws given to Israel, see chapter 14). If the instruction or command was limited to a particular place and time, ask what principles might be gleaned from it that apply to our context today.

While the particular applications of God's good and always benevolent counsel might differ over time, the principles behind God's instructions are as unchanging as God's own immutable character of love. What does the passage mean to you in light of what you have studied? How is it relevant to the people around you? How can you apply it to your life in a way that is faithful to all of Scripture, carefully considered?

Presuppositions: Large, Small, and In-Between

Alongside these ten principles, it is crucial to recognize that we all unavoidably bring our presuppositions to our understanding of anything, including to our reading of Scripture.

Given this, we should carefully aim at recognizing more and more of the presuppositions we bring to the text and continually and progressively put our known presuppositions "on the table" (so to speak) to be judged according to what Scripture teaches in its own context (both its immediate context and in light of the totality of Scripture).

Whenever we attempt to interpret Scripture theologically, there are three levels of presuppositions that are operating (whether we are aware of them or not):

- presuppositions at the level of interpreting individual texts and passages (micro-level)

- presuppositions at the level of particular theological doctrines (meso-level)
- overarching presuppositions about the nature of God and the universe as a whole (macro-level)[14]

Each of these three levels always affects the others, even if one is not aware that one's presuppositions are operating this way.

For example, consider Genesis 1:1, "In the beginning God created the heavens and the earth." Ideally, the way you understand the words and phrases in the text will be attuned to the teachings of the rest of Scripture. Yet, whenever you read this text, you are already supplying some meaning to the words in the text. For example, one might ask, who is God? The text does not tell you much about who the God referenced here is. The concept of God you have in mind when you read this text might differ from the concept of God that is taught throughout Scripture. To allow Scripture to be the rule and judge at all three levels, you will need to ask (and continually keep asking) whether the concept you have in mind matches with that portrayed in the individual text of Scripture (and in Scripture as a whole). This can be done by applying the analogy of Scripture in an ongoing hermeneutical spiral.

If you stick just to this verse, you can see that the "God" referenced in this text was in the beginning and created the heavens and the earth. But then, a number of other questions arise. What does it mean to create? What are the heavens and the earth? What is the beginning referred to in this text? Here, again, the way you think about answering these questions will ideally be informed by the teachings of the rest of Scripture.

In all this, we should not only recognize that we all have presuppositions operating at these levels (no one is a blank slate), but we should attempt to become more aware of what our presuppositions are so they can be tested by Scripture.

One good way to become more aware of the presuppositions we bring to our reading of Scripture at all three levels is to read Scripture within community and across various communities (without giving priority to any community to provide the final meaning, for Scripture alone should hold such priority).

The Adventist church is blessed with great diversity, and we can learn from one another. Engagement with others from different backgrounds and cultures will broaden our horizons, may expose some blind spots we have, and help us to see things that are in the biblical text that we might not have seen before (or to see them in a new light). Of course, what we each bring from our various backgrounds should itself be continually tested by the Bible.

Conclusion

This all might seem complex and even daunting, but each of the principles outlined above can be employed in a simplified manner whenever you read the text, whether or not you have the time or resources to carry out all the steps in a manner you would if attempting an *academic* exegesis of the text.

In short, the principles can be simplified as follows:

- Approach Scripture as the unique rule of faith that God has commissioned to rule as a whole so that the parts of Scripture should be understood in light of the whole and vice versa, and all should be understood under the guidance and illumination of the Holy Spirit in a prayerful and humble attitude.
- Carefully read the passage in a good translation. Consider its immediate context and take into account the book context and canonical context (as practical in the time you have) and what you can know of the historical context, all the while being open to correction and reform of any presuppositions you might be bringing to the text (seeking to allow the text to speak for itself, understood in light of all of Scripture).

Whatever you do, please do not be intimidated by the principles laid out here. If you are unfamiliar with some of them, do not allow that to dissuade you from starting the journey of studying the Bible more deeply—one small step at a time. If you do not have the time or resources to attend to each principle now, just keep them in mind and hold your conclusions tentatively in light of what you have been able to consider and in light of the elements you know you have not been able to carefully consider. Hold more confidently to those things for which you have the most biblical warrant, after careful consideration, and hold more loosely those things that you have less biblical warrant for at the moment and regarding which more study is required.

Remember, the study of Scripture is not simply a destination but a journey. Your attempt should not be to master the text, but to allow Scripture to shape you and inspire you toward "taking every thought captive to the obedience of Christ" (2 Cor. 10:5).

The treasures to be found in Scripture are inexhaustible, so do not focus on an endpoint of understanding but on the joy of the journey of coming to know God better and still better, to bask in His love for you and grow in your love for Him and others.

PART FOUR

GOD FOR US WHO MAKES US, SAVES US, AND COVENANTS WITH US

11

GOD CREATES US IN GOD'S IMAGE: HUMAN NATURE, IDENTITY, AND VALUE

Leave everything he knew? His family? His life? The "gods" he'd been raised to worship? He would not just be leaving his home. It was as if he was leaving his *entire identity* behind.

But, he'd heard the one true God's voice: "Go from your country, and from your relatives and from your father's house, to the land which I will show you; and I will make you into a great nation, and I will bless you, and make your name great; and you shall be a blessing; and I will bless those who bless you, and the one who curses you I will curse. And in you all the families of the earth will be blessed" (Gen. 12:1–3).

What promises! So, "Abram went away as the LORD had spoken to him" (Gen. 12:4). Despite many missteps, he eventually became the father of many nations, including the covenant people of Israel, through whom God would reclaim and save the world. And God gave him a new name, Abraham, which means "father of many."

Bound up with Abraham's story, the story of Israel, and indeed the story of all peoples, are questions of human identity and value. Who am I? Where am I from? Where is home? In what does human value consist? Why am I here? This chapter takes up these questions, as well as the closely related issues of human equality, race, and sexuality.

The Human Story: Made in God's Image

She was devastated. What would become of her? Not only had her husband died, but her father-in-law and brother-in-law had died also. Only she, her sister-in-law, and her mother-in-law remained. Three widows in the land of Moab.

While Ruth and her sister-in-law Orpah were Moabites, their mother-in-law Naomi was an Israelite and decided to return to Israel. Naomi gave Ruth and Orpah leave to return to their extended families in Moab. Naomi kissed them goodbye, and they wept.

But Ruth and Orpah refused to leave Naomi. So, Naomi told them, "Return, my daughters. Why should you go with me? Do I still have sons in my womb, that they may be your husbands? Return, my daughters!" (Ruth 1:11–12). And they wept together again. Then, Orpah kissed Naomi goodbye, "but Ruth clung to" Naomi (Ruth 1:14). So, Naomi told Ruth, "your sister-in-law has gone back to her people and her gods; return after your sister-in-law" (Ruth 1:15).

Three times Naomi gave Ruth license to return to her people. Ruth would have to give up so much to leave her homeland of Moab. To be a widow in a strange land did not offer many good prospects. Returning to her extended family was far more promising. But she loved Naomi. Naomi had lost her husband and her two sons. Ruth would not leave her, despite the cost and bleak prospects.

"Do not plead with me to leave you or to turn back from following you," Ruth said, "for where you go, I will go, and where you sleep, I will sleep. Your people shall be my people, and your God, my God. Where you die, I will die, and there I will be buried. May the LORD do so to me, and worse, if anything but death separates me from you" (Ruth 1:16–17).

Wow. What amazingly loyal love.

Who, then, was Ruth? Before her husband died, some would have identified her as the wife of Mahlon, son of Elimelech. But was that *who* she was? After Mahlon's death, she was no longer the wife of Mahlon. Was she then less than before? Or was she *always more* than Mahlon's wife?

Who was Ruth before her husband died? Who was she after? To whom did she belong, and who belonged to her? Was she a Moabite? An Israelite? A worshiper of the gods of Moab or of the God of Israel? By choice, she became loyal to the God of Israel. But, even before she did, she was in the most broad and fundamental sense already a daughter of Eve and a daughter of the God of Abraham, Isaac, Jacob, and (eventually) Jesus.

Moabite by birth, Ruth joined Israel and married Boaz, himself the son of Rahab—the Canaanite woman from Jericho who'd joined Israel long before. Eventually, Ruth became the great-grandmother of King

David and an ancestor of Jesus Himself! That is one reason we know her story. But Ruth also represented vulnerable people—the poor, widows, and immigrants, whom God deeply cares for. Even if you and I had never heard of Ruth, God knew her and cared about her story. And He cares about your story, too, more than you could possibly imagine.

Many judge by outward appearance, but God looks at the heart. We often mistakenly identify people by their lineage and their perceived value in terms of external features and productivity. But, according to Scripture, human identity and value run much deeper. Most fundamentally, human identity and value are not rooted in lineage or externals but in relationship to the living God, the Creator of all.

> *Many judge by outward appearance, but God looks at the heart.*

Israelites often prided themselves on being children of Abraham, but like all others, they were descended from Eve, the mother of all. Eve had received the promise that one day her descendant—her Seed—would bring deliverance by crushing the head of the great enemy of humanity, the serpent (Gen. 3:15).

Deliverance was necessary because Eve and Adam had sinned. Because of their sin, the human race is fallen, infected with sin. Apart from Christ, humans are "by nature children of wrath" (Eph. 2:3, see chapter 12). But it was not always so and will not always be so.

Humans are God's special creation: "the Lord God formed the man of dust from the ground, and breathed into his nostrils the breath of life; and the man became a living person" (Gen. 2:7). Amazing. The almighty God personally formed man from dust and breathed life into his nostrils. Through the combination of the body God formed from dust and the breath of life God breathed into him, "man became a living person" (Gen. 2:7).

God also personally formed Eve: "the Lord God caused a deep sleep to fall upon the man, and he slept; then He took one of his ribs and closed up the flesh at that place. And the Lord God fashioned into a woman the rib which He had taken from the man, and brought her to the man" (Gen. 2:21-22).

And, even as the woman was "taken out of man" so that one became two, in marriage two become one—"a man shall leave his father and his mother, and be joined to his wife; and they shall become one flesh" (Gen. 2:23-24).

According to Genesis 1, God created *both* Adam and Eve in the image of God. Indeed, "God said, 'Let Us make mankind in Our image, according to Our likeness; and let them rule over the fish of the sea and over the birds of the sky and over the livestock and over all the earth, and over every crawling thing that crawls on the earth.' So God created man in His own image, in the image of God He created him; male and female He created them" (Gen. 1:26–27). Humans are unique among God's creatures, created in God's image and commissioned to rule the earth as God's own vice-regents.

As specially created by God, Adam is called "the son of God" (Luke 3:38). But Adam fell. Another son of God was needed to succeed where Adam failed. To redeem the first Adam and his progeny, a second Adam was needed. So, Jesus lowered Himself and became human, the Son of God born of a woman. "'The first man, Adam, became a living being'; the last Adam [Christ] became a life-giving spirit" (1 Cor. 15:45, NRSVue). Where Adam failed, Christ succeeded on behalf of all humanity so that "just as we have borne the image of the one of dust [Adam], we will also bear the image of the one of heaven [Christ]" (1 Cor. 15:49, NRSVue; cf. Rom. 5:12–21; 1 Cor. 15:22).

Christ, the unique Son of God, was also the truly human son of Mary. He revealed true humanity—*just* what humanity should be in relation to God—and redeemed humanity in Himself. Humanity itself must ultimately be understood, then, in relation to Jesus.

Human Identity and Value

Human identity and value are rooted in God (at least) twice over. God *created* humans in His image, and Christ *became* human to redeem humanity.

Human identity, value, and purpose stem first from the fact that humans were created in the very "image of God" (Gen. 1:26–27). Both humans and animals received "the breath of life" (Gen. 7:15; cf. 1:30). The story of Genesis 2 gives special prominence to the creation of man and woman, emphasizing God's special forming of Adam and Eve.

As all-powerful (Jer. 32:17; Rev. 19:16), God could have spoken humans into existence. But God chose to form Adam and Eve *intimately*. Imagine Almighty God personally shaping Adam from the dust, then breathing life into him. Amazing! God not only stoops to create but, in doing so, commits Himself to relationship *with us* that involves Christ taking humanity and dying *for us* (Phil. 2:8).

> God not only stoops to create but, in doing so, commits Himself to relationship *with us* that involves Christ taking humanity and dying *for us*.

Human uniqueness is further highlighted in that humans—male and female—were created in God's "own image," in "the image of God" (Gen. 1:27; cf. James 3:9). And "God blessed them" and commissioned them to "rule over" the other creatures of this planet (Gen. 1:28). Of all earth's creatures, only humans were made in God's image and tasked to rule as God's vice-regents.

Competing Theories in Christian Theology: The Image of God

Theologians offer multiple accounts of the image of God (*imago dei*), many of which fit into four categories: structural or ontological, functional, relational, and multifaceted.

The structural (or ontological) understanding views the image of God in terms of capacities (e.g., rational, moral, and others). On this view, the image of God corresponds to some capacity like reason, morality, or other attributes. A minority have thought the image of God involves some correspondence of physical form. Most often in classical Christian thought, however, the image is linked to human capacity for reason. Yet, this understanding faces criticism regarding what it means for humans who lack or have diminished capacities.

The functional understanding views the image of God in terms of human function as God's representatives, often understood in terms of priestly and royal functions, including dominion or rulership over this planet (see Gen. 1:26–28).[1] This "rulership" is often recognized to involve caretaking, a co-regency with significant stewardship implications.

The relational understanding views the image in terms of human relations to God, other humans, and (sometimes) creation more broadly. For some, this involves the ability to love, requiring moral freedom. In this regard, God's first recorded words to humanity are both command and prohibition (Gen. 2:16-17), indicating humans are morally responsible and judged according to God's law.[2]

The multifaceted understanding views the image of God as a combination of some or all of the above.[3] This seems to be the preferable approach to the image of God (held by many Adventists), avoiding reducing the image to one aspect.[4]

The Image of God

Whatever else one concludes regarding the image of God, Scripture expressly teaches that humans were *specially* created with a purpose designed by God, who profoundly loves us. Amazing. As Psalm 8 puts it: "When I consider your heavens, the work of your fingers, the moon and the stars, which you have set in place, what is mankind that you are mindful of them, human beings that you care for them? You have made them a little lower than the angels and crowned them with glory and honor. You made them rulers over the works of your hands; you put everything under their feet" (Ps. 8:3-6, NIV).

To be human in the fullest sense is to reflect the image of God—the God who in Christ became human to restore God's intimate presence with us. Christ Himself "is the image of the invisible God" (Col. 1:15) and "the radiance of His glory and the exact representation of His nature" (Heb. 1:3). Christ is also the exact representation of what humanity should be in relation to God and one another. To be human in a way that reflects God's image, then, is to be like Christ.

God's plan of redemption thus includes that humans "become conformed to the image of His Son, so that He would be the firstborn among many brothers and sisters" (Rom. 8:29; cf. 1 John 2:6; 4:17). We cannot rightly understand our humanity, then, apart from attention to Christ's humanity and our high calling to be redeemed as children of God in and through Jesus.

Jesus lived a life of perfect love. For us to reflect God's image, then, involves reflecting God's love to others, treating others in a Christlike manner, and thus rightly exercising our God-given freedom in accord with God's perfect law of love (see chapter 14).

In all this, the concept of the image of God "is fundamentally relational, or covenantal, and takes as its ground and focus the graciousness of God's own covenantal relations with humanity and the rest of creation."[5]

Rulers and Stewards

God gave humans a special duty of rulership relative to creation. As Psalm 8:5-8 puts it, God "crowned them [humans] with glory and honor. You made them rulers over the works of your hands; you put everything under their feet: all flocks and herds, and the animals of the wild, the birds in the sky, and the fish in the sea" (Ps. 8:5-8, NIV).

Indeed, "God said, 'Let Us make mankind in Our image, according to Our likeness; and let them rule over the fish of the sea and over the birds of the sky and over the livestock and over all the earth, and over every crawling thing that crawls on the earth.' So God created man in His own image, in the image of God He created him; male and female He created them. God blessed them; and God said to them, 'Be fruitful and multiply, and fill the earth, and subdue it; and rule over the fish of the sea and over the birds of the sky and over every living thing that moves on the earth'" (Gen. 1:26-28).

When Scripture declares humans are to "rule over" this world, however, it does not license a domineering or exploitative approach to creation. Human "rulership" must be understood in light of God's ordering in Genesis 2:15, which says Adam was put "in the Garden of Eden to cultivate it and tend it." The term *cultivate* (*avad*) often means to serve (the noun form refers to a servant). God's intention for humans to cultivate and tend the garden indicates humans were to be caretakers of creation, not exploiters of it.[6]

Whatever kind of "rule" humans were tasked with must be consistent with the way God rules—with love and justice as the Good Shepherd (see Ezek. 34:11-31). It cannot be the kind of "rule" God rebuked when He lamented: "Those who are sickly you have not strengthened, the diseased you have not healed, the broken you have not bound up, the scattered you have not brought back, nor have you searched for the lost; but with force and with violence you have dominated them" (Ezek. 34:4). God calls humans not to "rule" with domineering force and severity, but with love and justice.

Sadly, Adam and Eve forfeited their unique rulership status over this world when they succumbed to Satan's temptations, who thereby usurped temporary and limited rulership in this world and works through human rulers to oppress and foster injustice (see, e.g., Ps. 82;

Eph. 6:11–12). In contrast, humans are called to reflect God's benevolent rule in this world within our limited sphere of influence—both taking care of the natural world and relating to other humans with mercy, love, and justice, with concern for the oppressed and structural justice.

All of creation is God's creation such that any *good* human "rule" involves taking care of what belongs to God as good stewards. Every animal is His. As God Himself declares, "every animal of the forest is Mine, the cattle on a thousand hills. I know every bird of the mountains, and everything that moves in the field is Mine" (Ps. 50:10–11). Recognizing this should direct the way we treat God's creation and the resources God has given us.

Adventists believe that, as stewards of what God has entrusted to us (time, health, abilities, possessions, the earth, and its resources), we have a duty to properly use all the good things with which God has entrusted us.[7] When we "give" to support God's mission (e.g., tithe and offerings), then we are actually only returning to God a small portion of what He has freely given us (1 Chron. 29:14).[8] Conversely, when we exploit or damage creation, we are damaging *God's* creation.

If humans are to be caretakers rather than dominators, valuing fellow creatures as God's creation and treating them accordingly, then we ought to encourage practices aimed at taking better care of creation, doing what we can, and encouraging change that is better for the environment and all creatures.[9] We should practice and promote ways of life that cherish slowing down and resting, patterned after God Himself resting on the seventh day (Gen. 2:2–3). Our very lifestyle, both in terms of resting on the Sabbath and otherwise, might be aimed at rest not only from labor but also from mass consumerism and economic exploitation that drives much of the depletion of natural resources and greatly contributes to environmental and other harms.

God's profound concern for creation is apparent throughout Scripture. God Himself "formed" animals out of the ground (Gen. 2:19) and "protect[s] mankind and animals" (Ps. 36:6). And God responded to Jonah's anger at God's compassion for Nineveh by saying: "Should I not also have compassion on Nineveh, the great city in which there are more than 120,000 people, who do not know the difference between their right hand and their left, as well as many animals?" (Jon. 4:11). Did you catch that last part? God was concerned for the people *and* the animals, having compassion on both. Scripture teaches repeatedly that God cares for animals and a "righteous person has regard for the life of his animal" (Prov. 12:10; cf. Ps. 36:6; Jon. 4:11).[10] In short, God loves animals. So should we.

> **In short, God loves animals. So should we.**

Just after the verses on the image of God and human rule, God explains to the humans, "I have given you every plant yielding seed that is on the surface of all the earth, and every tree which has fruit yielding seed; it shall be food for you" (Gen. 1:29). Here, the original diet is identified as a plant-based diet, which required no animal death.

We do not have space to sufficiently elaborate on this here (on health laws, see chapter 14), but the original diet remains the ideal diet, not only in terms of being best for human health but also in terms of what is good for animals and the environment more broadly. We should be mindful of the fact that the way we eat has ethical implications for animals and the world around us. Concern for ethical eating and moving toward diets that are more earth-friendly and (as my colleague and friend Rahel Wells puts it) "cruelty-free" is very much in line with the ideals treasured in Adventism.[11] Just imagine the positive impact widespread vegetarianism, coupled with Sabbath-keeping, would have on the environment.[12]

Uniquely Valuable in the Sight of God

Humans, however, are of unique value to God. We should recognize all humans are deeply beloved of God and should treat each person accordingly. "Look at the birds of the sky," Jesus taught, "that they do not sow, nor reap, nor gather crops into barns, and yet your heavenly Father feeds them. Are you not much more important than they?" (Matt. 6:26). Indeed, not even one sparrow "will fall to the ground apart from your Father.... So do not fear; you are more valuable than a great number of sparrows" (Matt. 10:29, 31; cf. 12:12).

Unique human value and identity is grounded in *connection* with God, being created in the image of God, specially commissioned to rule creation in ways that reflect God's loving rule. However, the exceptional value and identity of humans is also manifest in the incarnation and work of Christ. God (in Christ) *became* human. This, by itself, displays God's special and gracious favor toward humanity, occasioned not by human merit but by human need and God's desire to be "with us," even after human rebellion fractured the intimate relationship God originally intended.

Christ suffered and gave His life, paying the ultimate price to redeem and rescue humanity. God loved and valued us so much that He gave *Himself* for us. Given the incalculable cost of redemption, it follows that humans are of infinite value in God's eyes. How much, then, should we value ourselves and others?

Today, many value humans only in terms of extrinsic values, such as what humans can do or produce.[13] Yet, contrary to what some have claimed, humans are not primarily sexual beings or economic beings. We are not machines, nor merely valuable as means of production. Humans are exponentially more valuable than any such things. Human value cannot be reduced to extrinsic values—economic or otherwise.

As God's special creation, in God's image and for whom Christ died, humans possess *intrinsic* value as God's creatures, apart from any functional and/or extrinsic value. As the psalmist puts it, "I am awesomely and wonderfully made" (Ps. 139:14). This is crucial to our understanding of ourselves and one another in the contemporary landscape inclined toward pragmatism and devaluation of human life. Prior to anything we do, God loves us, and we are His children. We may embrace that status and enjoy love relationship with God or ultimately reject it, but one needn't strive to create or prove self-worth in the eyes of the world. We are already invaluable to the One who is the source of all value. On this understanding, we should strive to take care of ourselves and one another.

> **We are already invaluable to the One who is the source of all value.**

Tragically, some Western thought has viewed humans as of little value. In this regard, Holocaust survivor Viktor E. Frankl wrote:

> If we present a man with a concept of man which is not true, we may well corrupt him. When we present man as an automaton of reflexes, as a mind-machine, as a bundle of instincts, as a pawn of drives and reactions, as a mere product of instinct, heredity and environment, we feed the nihilism to which modern man is,

in any case, prone. I became acquainted with the last stage of that corruption in my second concentration camp, Auschwitz. The gas chambers of Auschwitz were the ultimate consequence of the theory that man is nothing but the product of heredity and environment—or, as the Nazi liked to say, of "Blood and Soil." I am absolutely convinced that the gas chambers of Auschwitz, Treblinka, and Maidanek were ultimately prepared not in some Ministry or other in Berlin, but rather at the desks and in the lecture halls of nihilistic scientists and philosophers.[14]

Many humans today suffer from lack of understanding of the intrinsic worth of themselves and others. For many, life itself seems meaningless, full of pain, and without hope. Many are at least functional nihilists, living as if life is without transcendent value or meaning and thus amounts to absurdity. Accordingly, many humans live only for today, suppressing and sometimes drowning their fears and sorrows by various means of self-medication, focus on personal achievements, amusements, and/or unhealthy relationships where one locates one's own value in how much someone else appears to value them.

But the meaning and value of human life is not found in the way the world views and values things; meaning and value are secure in the God who gives us life, love, and hope. Jesus not only died for us, demonstrating just how beloved and valuable we are to God, but promised to come back for us, saying: "Do not let your heart be troubled; believe in God, believe also in Me. In My Father's house are many rooms; if that were not so, I would have told you, because I am going there to prepare a place for you. And if I go and prepare a place for you, I am coming again and will take you to Myself, so that where I am, there you also will be" (John 14:1–3). Those who believe in Jesus, then, have incomparable hope.

When all else seems meaningless, perhaps even hopeless, if Jesus is your Savior, you have nothing to fear for the future. Hope is yours—hope that surpasses all other hopes. Hardships and suffering will endure for a time, but a future draws near when there will be no more suffering forever (Rev. 21:4). Weeping may endure for a night, but joy comes in the morning (Ps. 30:5). In the meantime, God is *with* you always. In Him, you may have peace that passes understanding (Phil. 4:7), sustaining you through life's storms. Christ will never leave you (Heb. 13:5) and will instill in you a peace that passes all understanding, a deep calm and hopefulness that does not make you impervious to the storms of life but will sustain you through the storms.

God created humans to live *with* Him forever. Human identity and value, then, cannot be rooted in that which is transient and fading; it cannot be rooted in extrinsic values. We were made for a divine purpose. You and I are children of God, God's beloved, special creation imbued with inestimable and enduring value.

How then should we live? We should recognize our worth and the worth of all others in God's sight. All human lives are precious to God. We should reject views predicated on the survival of the fittest and instead employ an ethic of love. In the words of Paul: "Do nothing from selfishness or empty conceit, but with humility consider one another as more important than yourselves; do not merely look out for your own personal interests, but also for the interests of others. Have this attitude in yourselves which was also in Christ Jesus," who "emptied Himself" for us (Phil. 2:3–7).

> We should recognize our worth and the worth of all others in God's sight.

The Equal Value of All Humans

According to Scripture, *all* humans are of inestimable and enduring value and should be treated as such. The creation narrative demonstrates the basic equality of all humans. All humans are created in the image of God, and Christ died for *all* humans. This rules out *every* kind of ethnic prejudice and racism as entirely contrary to following Christ.

Scripture Condemns Racism

Racism and *genuine* Christianity are utterly incompatible. While many atrocities have been carried out in Christ's name, and many people falsely claim Christ's name to undergird their evil schemes, there is no place among genuine Christ-followers for any kind of racism. Christians should stand against all systems and structures that are racist or otherwise unjust.

As Paul taught, God "made from one man every nation of mankind to live on all the face of the earth" (Acts 17:26). The nations beyond Israel "also are His descendants"—all humans are children of God (Acts 17:28, 29) for whom Christ died, and those saved in the end include people "from every nation and all the tribes, peoples, and languages" (Rev. 7:9).[15] "For God so loved the world, that He gave His only Son, so that everyone who believes in Him will not perish, but have eternal life" (John 3:16). God not only calls us to love Him in return but commands us to love our neighbor as ourselves (Mark 12:30–31).

This is directly contrary to the great sin of racism, an egregious form of one of the two greatest sins the Bible condemns: the sins of idolatry and the sin of social injustice. These great sins correspond to a lack of love toward God and one another, breaking the two greatest commandments (Mark 12:30–31).

Tragically, racism and ethnocentrism have plagued humanity throughout history, from atrocities like the Holocaust to the displacement and slaughter of Native Americans and other indigenous peoples to the transatlantic slave trade and chattel slavery and the tragic legacy of racism in America and elsewhere.

Even apart from such atrocities, humans are prone to privilege those they consider to be their "tribe" (tribalism), mistreating others as less than or outsiders. "Otherizing" humans that are superficially unlike ourselves (relative to skin color, place of birth, or otherwise) fosters the oppression of foreigners and the mistreatment of immigrants and refugees.

Scripture teaches that all humans are made in God's image, children of God for whom Christ died, and should be treated as such. How could it be, then, that slaveholders in the American South appealed to Scripture to support their horrible system of slavery? They did so in ways that twisted Scripture beyond recognition.[16] The kind of chattel slavery practiced in America is entirely ruled out and condemned by Scripture.[17] For one thing, according to biblical law, it was a capital offense to kidnap a person and sell that person into slavery or keep that person in slavery (Exod. 21:16; cf. 20:15). Likewise, Paul directly condemns those who kidnap people for enslavement (*man-stealers/slave-traders*), thus condemning slave trading (1 Tim. 1:10).[18] This prohibits and condemns *the entire* transatlantic slave trade. And many other biblical principles condemn such evil practices.[19] There is no biblical sanction whatsoever for the reprehensible evil of chattel slavery perpetrated in America and elsewhere.[20] Quite the opposite, such is unequivocally condemned.

In this regard, an edited Bible for enslaved Africans was created, now known as the "Slave Bible." The compilers deliberately removed huge portions of Scripture, recognizing that so many biblical teachings would unravel their evil system of slavery and were thus deemed too dangerous to allow enslaved people to read (such as Scripture's repeated emphasis on God's ideals of justice, deliverance, and liberation of the oppressed). The very creation of this "Slave Bible" evidences that the Bible teaches anti-slavery principles promoting liberation, freedom, human equality, and justice.

It is no coincidence that the great British abolitionist William Wilberforce was a man of deep faith in Scripture. And many American abolitionists drew their inspiration from the Scriptures. Indeed, Esau McCaulley states that while earlier Christians made "strong theological cases against slavery" long before, "no society that preceded the eighteenth-century abolitionists contended that slavery itself was fundamentally immoral. The widespread move to abolish slavery is a Christian innovation."[21]

Early Adventists themselves were avid abolitionists (and otherwise protestors against racism) on the basis of the teachings of the Bible, appealing (for example) to Deuteronomy 23:15–16 to support people escaping from slavery.[22] It reads, "You shall not return to their owners slaves who have escaped to you from their owners. They shall reside with you, in your midst, in any place they choose in any one of your towns, wherever they please; you shall not oppress them" (NRSVue).

Here, it is crucial to recognize that the kind of "slavery" that was regulated by some laws of Israel in the Bible was nothing like the chattel slavery of the transatlantic slave trade and slavery in America and gives no sanction to such evil practices but was more akin to a kind of indentured servitude (typically the product of economic forces leading to servitude to repay a debt or subjugation in war).[23] It was also *far* from ideal, however, and biblical instructions regulating such practices (in the Old Testament and New Testament) were instructions regarding how to conduct oneself "within an existing social practice, without condoning that practice," analogous to laws regulating divorce (see below).[24]

Why, then, did God not give only *ideal* laws in the first place? In short, *some* laws given to Israel were less than ideal because they met and aimed to improve *real-life* situations that were *far* from ideal and could not simply be legislated away (to see this, one need only consider how often God's people rejected God's laws and did the opposite).

God repeatedly set forth *ideals* regarding the way humans should treat one another, which (if followed) would exclude *every* kind of injustice and oppression. Indeed, taken to their logical conclusions, the golden rule—"do to others as you would have them do to you, for this is the Law and the Prophets" (Matt. 7:12, NRSVue)—and the great commandment to "love your neighbor as yourself" (Lev. 19:18; Matt. 22:39; Luke 10:27) rules out slavery and other forms of oppression.[25] In this regard, James W. C. Pennington (c. 1807–1870), who himself escaped from slavery in western Maryland and became an active abolitionist, proclaimed: "My sentence is that slavery is condemned by the general tenor and scope of the New Testament. Its doctrines, its precepts, and all its warnings against the system. I am not bound to show that the New Testament authorizes me in such a chapter and verse to reject a slaveholder. It is sufficient for me to show what is acknowledged by my opponents, that it is murdering the poor, corrupting society, alienating the brethren, and sowing the seed of discord in the bosom of the whole church. . . . Let us always bear in mind of what slavery is and what the gospel is."[26]

The same could be said with respect to other overarching commands of the Old Testament, such as, "The stranger who resides with you shall be to you as the native among you, and you shall love him as yourself, for you were strangers in the land of Egypt" (Lev. 19:34) and "You shall also love the stranger, for you were strangers in the land of Egypt" (Deut. 10:19, NRSVue). Slavery, in any form, is utterly incompatible with the ideals of God's moral law of love, as are racism, oppression, and social injustice.

> **Slavery, in any form, is utterly incompatible with the ideals of God's moral law of love.**

It is no coincidence that the Old Testament prophets continually railed against injustice and oppression. For example, God declares: "Dispense true justice and practice kindness and compassion each to his brother; and do not oppress the widow or the orphan, the stranger or the poor; and do not devise evil in your hearts against one another" (Zech. 7:9–10; cf. Isa. 1:17; 10:1–3; 58:6; Mic. 6:8; Matt. 23:23; Luke 4:18 et al.).[27] And, in Luke, just after stating the great love commandment, Jesus responds to the question "who is my neighbor?" by telling the parable of the good Samaritan, which exemplifies ideals that directly counter racism and makes clear that love for one's neighbor is to include *all* peoples, particularly those in need or distress (Luke 10:29–37; cf. Matt. 25:31–46). Long before this, God's posture toward all the peoples of the earth was clear from (for example) His promises in the Abrahamic covenant that *all* peoples of the earth would be blessed through Abraham's descendants (Gen. 12:3) and His promises to gather and bless all nations through the work of the Messiah (see chapter 14).

Yet, knowing the hardness of human hearts, God also provided *remedial* laws to meet actual real-life situations and curtail human evils (cf. the distinction between God's ideal and remedial will be discussed further in chapter 14). While less than ideal, such remedial laws significantly and progressively improved human life, in contrast to typical laws of the age. For example, when asked about Old Testament laws regarding divorce, Jesus said: "Because of your hardness of heart Moses permitted you to divorce your wives; but from the beginning it has not been this way" (Matt. 19:8). As Esau McCaulley points out, Jesus here teaches that such "laws" included "allowances for human sin" rather than "the ideal for human interactions." Such "passages accept the world as broken and attempt to limit the damage that we do to one another . . . they seek to limit the damage arising from a broken world."[28]

God might have given *only* ideal laws that would look better in our day and age, but in the absence of any remedial laws (such as laws regulating divorce), the overall positive effect would have been less relative to actually improving people's lives at that time, particularly given that God's ideal laws themselves were frequently ignored (as were many of God's laws). For example, divorce is less than ideal, but imagine God commanded "do not *ever* divorce" and gave no commands to regulate divorce. People would divorce anyway, and there would be none of the protections for women that divorce laws in the Bible provided (more on this later).

In this regard and others, God sometimes gave laws that did not thereby sanction particular practices (such as laws relative to polygamy, divorce, conducting war, etc.) but would mitigate some of the most harmful results that would ensue without any regulation of such practices, which God knew would take place anyway (due to human evil). Such laws regulated bad systems and practices that already existed while setting in place trajectories that would eventually dismantle such systems.

If people kept God's *ideal* law of love perfectly (see chapter 14), there would never be a need for such *remedial* laws to curtail and deal with evils and *regulating systems until they could be dismantled*. But, if God only gave *ideal* laws, there would be no laws to regulate and mitigate the effects of the kinds of sins and practices that humans perpetrated in spite of knowing what God ideally desired and commanded (e.g., justice and mercy, Mic. 6:8).

Read canonically (i.e., employing the principles of *tota Scriptura* and the analogy of Scripture), biblical teachings regarding the way humans should love one another and treat one another are utterly inconsistent with slavery. And the trajectory of many other biblical statements also utterly undoes every form of slavery. Already in the Old Testament, the law of Moses commanded: "You shall not withhold the wages of poor and needy laborers, whether other Israelites or aliens who reside in your land in one of your towns. You shall pay them their wages daily before sunset, because they are poor and their livelihood depends on them" and "You shall not deprive a resident alien or an orphan of justice.... Remember that you were a slave in Egypt and the Lord your God redeemed you from there; therefore I command you to do this" (Deut. 24:14–15, 17–18, NRSVue).

And in the New Testament, for example, Paul's counsel to Philemon about the escaped slave Onesimus calls on Philemon to do "what is proper" and relinquish his claim on Onesimus, instead treating him as an equal brother in Christ. Specifically, Paul asks Philemon to receive Onesimus "no longer as a slave, but more than a slave, a beloved brother" and to "accept him as you would me," even offering that if Onesimus owes Philemon anything, "charge that to my account ... I will repay it" (Philem. 16–19).

Here and elsewhere, if followed, Paul's teachings would have turned slavery on its head. For example, Paul counseled slaves, "Were you called as a slave? Do not let it concern you. But if you are also able to become free, take advantage of that. For the one who was called in the Lord as a slave, is the Lord's freed person; likewise the one who was called as free, is Christ's slave" (1 Cor. 7:21–22).[29] Elsewhere, Paul proclaimed: "There is neither Jew nor Greek, there is neither slave nor free, there is neither male nor female; for you are all one in Christ Jesus" (Gal. 3:28).[30] In this regard, Ellen White commented of Paul: "It was not the apostle's work to overturn arbitrarily or suddenly the established order of society. To attempt this would be to prevent the success of the gospel. But he taught principles which struck at the very foundation of slavery and which, if carried into effect, would surely undermine the whole system."[31]

Here, it is crucial to emphasize that biblical teachings give no sanction to the kind of slavery practiced in America and beyond (again, Scripture condemns kidnapping/slave trading, Exod. 21:16; 1 Tim. 1:10). Such practices are evil (cf. Rev. 18:13). They are not only reprehensible crimes against humanity (made in the image of God) but crimes against God and against nature. And, we who call ourselves Christians must not turn a blind eye to the residual effects of these heinous crimes in our world—to the way the descendants of enslaved peoples still suffer in a myriad of ways, contributed to by ongoing racism and oppression of people groups in various forms throughout the world.

In short, genuine Christianity is utterly opposed to racism and xenophobia in any and all forms. If we are genuine Christians, we will stand against racism and injustice in ways consistent with the principles of God's kingdom of love and righteousness. One cannot follow Christ while hating one's brothers and sisters in feelings or in actions. As 1 John 4:20–21 states, "If someone says, 'I love God,' and yet he hates his brother or sister, he is a liar; for the one who does not love his brother and sister whom he has seen, cannot love God, whom he has not seen. And this commandment we have from Him, that the one who loves God must also love his brother and sister."

> *One cannot follow Christ while hating one's brothers and sisters in feelings or in actions.*

The Equal Value of Men and Women

"God created man in His own image, in the image of God He created him; male and female He created them" (Gen. 1:27; see also 5:1–2). Both *men and women* are created in the image of God and should be treated accordingly. Men are not better than women, and women are not better than men.

The narrative in Genesis 2 displays the equality (but not sameness) of men and women. After creating Adam, God declared, "It is not good for the man to be alone; I will make him a helper suitable for him" (Gen. 2:18). But God did not immediately do so.

First, animals were brought to Adam to be named, highlighting that Adam had no partner (Gen. 2:19-20). Then, God created Eve from the side of Adam (Gen. 2:21-23), not from Adam's head or foot as if she was to be above or below him, but from his side as his equal.[32] Notably, the term used to describe Eve as Adam's helper (*ezer*) in Genesis 2 does *not* indicate subservience but typically refers to one who provides help to another in need. Indeed, most Old Testament instances of *ezer* refer to God Himself. For example, the psalmist cries to God, "You are my help [*ezer*] and my savior" (Ps. 70:5; cf. Exod. 18:4; Deut. 33:29; Ps. 33:20; 146:5).

What, then, of Paul's statements that "women are to keep silent in the churches" (1 Cor. 14:34) and "I do not allow a woman to teach or to exercise authority over a man, but to remain quiet" (1 Tim. 2:12)? Like all other biblical texts, these should be understood in light of their own context and the rest of Scripture (*tota Scriptura*), particularly given that Paul often gives *contextual instructions*—instructions intended for a specific audience at a specific place and time that are not universal policies (e.g., having Timothy circumcised "because of the Jews," Acts 16:3, and giving instructions relative to slavery in the Roman empire).

Read in context, whatever Paul means when he states "women are to keep silent in the churches" (1 Cor. 14:34) cannot *consistently* be taken to mean that women are not to speak *at all* in church because that would contradict Paul's teachings earlier in this same letter about women praying and prophesying (1 Cor. 11:5; cf. Acts 21:9) as well as the teachings of the wider New Testament, such as God's promise, "I will pour out my Spirit upon all flesh, and your sons and your daughters shall prophesy . . . both men and women" (Acts 2:17-18, NRSVue).[33]

In the preceding verse, Paul emphasizes, "God is not a God of confusion, but of peace" (1 Cor. 14:33), and Paul afterward emphasizes "all things must be done properly and in an orderly way" (1 Cor. 14:40).

This suggests Paul is here addressing some particular issues that caused disorder and confusion in the church at Corinth at that time (a rather troubled church as can be seen from the rest of the letter, which struggled with sexual immorality in a city known for sexual promiscuity).[34]

Likewise, the context of 1 Timothy 2 is crucial. Paul was writing to Timothy at Ephesus, where Timothy remained in order to "instruct certain people not to teach strange doctrines, nor to pay attention to myths and endless genealogies" (1 Tim. 1:3-4). Ephesus was a major center of goddess worship, home to the great temple of Artemis (i.e., Diana, see Acts 19:23-41), the goddess who, according to mythology, "renounced all idea of marriage, supposedly because she was appalled at the birth pains her mother had suffered in bearing her, and remained the unattainable virgin goddess."[35] In this context, we know from the letter of 1 Timothy itself that Paul was countering some false teachers in Ephesus who espoused some particularly "strange doctrines" with attention to "myths and endless genealogies" (1 Tim. 1:3-4; cf. 4:1-7), including some "who forbid marriage" (1 Tim. 4:3) and thus also childbearing within marriage.[36]

Paul's instruction in 1 Timothy 2 is directly contrary to such "strange doctrines" (cf. Paul's *corrective* teachings in 1 Tim. 2:13-15). Notably, in this regard, the Greek word translated "exercise authority" (*authentein*) appears in the New Testament only in 1 Timothy 2:12, but evidence from other sources indicates the term was used to refer to *abuse* of authority and domineering over others.[37] If this is the meaning of *authentein* in this passage, then what Paul is prohibiting is an abuse of authority (domineering) by women, which some believe was a particular problem in Ephesus due to the prominent "goddess" cult there.[38]

However one understands precisely what Paul is arguing against here, read in context, Paul's words in 1 Timothy 2:12 cannot consistently be taken to mean women are not permitted to teach or have authority *at all* because such a claim would directly contradict the wider teachings of Scripture, including evidence from Paul's own ministry and teachings. For example, "when Priscilla and Aquila heard" Apollos teaching about God in Ephesus, "they took him aside and explained the way of God more accurately to him" (Acts 18:26). Here, Priscilla (a woman), along with her husband Aquila, taught Apollos (a man) the "way of God." Priscilla and her husband Aquila had traveled to Ephesus with Paul (Acts 18:18), and

Paul elsewhere identifies Priscilla and Aquila as "my fellow workers in Christ Jesus, who risked their own necks for my life, to whom not only do I give thanks, but also all the churches of the Gentiles" (Rom. 16:3-4; see also 2 Tim. 4:19).

In Romans 16, Paul sends greetings to numerous other prominent women, specifically commending "our sister Phoebe, a deacon [*diakonon*] of the church at Cenchreae" and "benefactor" of Paul (Rom. 16:1-2, NRSVue), and women named Mary, Tryphaena, Tryphosa, and Persis for their hard work (Rom. 16:6, 12; cf. 16:7).[39] Many other women were also teaching (Titus 2:3) and doing gospel work in the early New Testament church (e.g., Euodia and Syntyche in Phil. 4:2-3), with places of meeting often being the homes of prominent women who supported Christianity.

Decades earlier, the prophet Anna recognized the baby Jesus as the Messiah (Luke 2:36-38). The New Testament also mentions other female prophets (e.g., Acts 21:9; 1 Cor. 11:5). Further, Jesus intentionally met and taught the Samaritan woman at the well, who testified and brought many to believe in Christ (John 4:39). And, the *first* witnesses to the resurrection were women (see Matt. 28:5-10).

Indeed, on resurrection morning, an angel and Jesus Himself instructed the women to witness and testify to Christ's disciples of His resurrection. Specifically, the angel told Mary Magdalene and another Mary to "go quickly and tell His disciples that He has risen from the dead" (Matt. 28:7). Then, "Jesus met them" and told them, "Do not be afraid; go, bring word to My brothers to leave for Galilee, and there they will see Me" (Matt. 28:9-10). In this and other regards, many have noted how striking Jesus's interactions with women would have been in first-century Judea. Jesus consistently welcomed and elevated women and included women among His students, followers, and witnesses (see, e.g., Luke 10:38-42).

Numerous female heroes also appear in the Old Testament, including prophets. Scripture explicitly identifies Miriam (Exod. 15:20; cf. Mic. 6:4), Deborah (Judg. 4:3-6), Huldah (2 Kings 22:14-20), and others, as prophets. And, in Joel 2:28, God proclaims, "I will pour out My Spirit on all mankind; and your sons and your daughters will prophesy" (quoted in Acts 2:17). Deborah is also identified as a judge, a position of high authority and leadership in Israel (Judg. 4:4), and Scripture also speaks of a number of wise women (e.g., Judg. 5:28–30; 2 Sam. 14:2ff.; 20:16ff.).

Further, all humans since Adam have been born of women. As Paul writes, "as the woman originated from the man, so also the man has his birth through the woman; and all things originate from God" (1 Cor. 11:12). In this regard, in his discourse in 1 Timothy 2, Paul highlights that women are saved through childbirth (1 Tim. 2:15; cf. Gen. 3:15–16). Yet, not only women are saved through childbirth. Through childbirth, the world is saved—through the promised Seed of the woman, the Messiah (Gen. 3:15). It is no coincidence that Satan and his agents repeatedly work against childbirth throughout the story of Scripture (cf. Exod. 1:15–21; Matt. 2:16; Rev. 12:4).

Whatever else we say, the way we understand Scripture's teachings relative to men and women must be consistent with Paul's countercultural teaching that "There is neither Jew nor Greek, there is neither slave nor free, there is neither male nor female; for you are all one in Christ Jesus" (Gal. 3:28). Here, Paul is not denying or undermining the reality or significance of biological (and other) differences between the male and female sexes, but is affirming that all who are in Christ are one in Christ. All people, men and women, are made in God's image as equal before God.[40] If we call ourselves Christians, we should treat one another accordingly.

> *All people, men and women, are made in God's image as equal before God.*

Marriage and Sexuality

The special joining of a man and woman in marriage is a sacred, covenantal union instituted during creation. After describing God's forming woman from man, Genesis 2:24 explains, "For this reason a man shall leave his father and his mother, and be joined to his wife; and they shall become one flesh."[41]

The kind of unselfish love manifest in a *good* marriage (and other human relationships) is to reflect the perfect and unselfish love of God. As Paul explains: "Love is patient, love is kind, it is not jealous; love does not brag, it is not arrogant. It does not act disgracefully, it does not seek its own benefit; it is not provoked, does not keep an account of a wrong suffered, it does not rejoice in unrighteousness, but rejoices with the truth; it keeps every confidence, it believes all things, hopes all things, endures all things. Love never fails" (1 Cor. 13:4–8).

Some have thought, however, that husbands are supposed to *rule over* their wives. This, however, is contrary to God's original intention. As seen earlier, Eve's being formed from Adam's *side* indicates Eve was neither to rule over Adam nor to be ruled and trod under his foot, "but to stand by his side as an equal."[42] The statement in Genesis 3:16 that the woman's husband would "rule over" her describes one of the *curses* that was a result of the Fall, not the way God intended husbands and wives to relate to one another *ideally*.[43]

This curse was a description of what would ensue because of the Fall. The Fall fractured the ideal relationship between men and women, and tragically, throughout history men have oppressed and abused women. Such evils, however, are not in accord with God's ideals (cf. Col. 3:19). Today, we should stand against all oppression and abuse and aim at returning to the Eden ideal that preceded the Fall.

In this regard, Scripture does not only teach that wives should submit to their husbands but also teaches that *all* Christians should submit to one another in love. Indeed, *before* Paul states, "Wives, subject yourselves to your own husbands" (Eph. 5:22), Paul instructs Christians to "subject yourselves to one another in the fear of Christ" (Eph. 5:21).[44]

On the one hand, Paul teaches, "the husband is the head of the wife, as Christ also is the head of the church" and "as the church is subject to Christ, so also the wives ought to be to their husbands in everything" (Eph. 5:23–24). At the same time, Paul instructs, "Husbands, love your wives, just as Christ also loved the church and gave Himself up for her" (Eph. 5:25) and "husbands also ought to love their own wives as their own bodies. He who loves his own wife loves himself" and thereby "nourishes and cherishes" her (Eph. 5:28–29; cf. Col. 3:18–19). The key to successful marriage is a deep, unselfish love that is willing to give of oneself for the other.

Just as wives are called to submit to their husbands, husbands are called to love their wives *as Christ loved the church*. With what kind of love did Christ love the church? With self-sacrificial love—He laid down His very life for the church! This is the deepest kind of submission and the greatest manifestation of love. In Scripture, Christ-like leadership *is* sacrificial servant leadership—the opposite of domination.

Ephesians 5 is not about dominance, but about the beautiful, unselfish love relationship between a *good* husband and a *good* wife, in which *each* lovingly seeks the other's well-being and thus each submits himself or herself to serving the other's well-being (cf. Paul's reference to the *mutual* authority of husband and wife over one another's bodies in 1 Cor. 7:4).[45] In such a relationship of unselfish love, the well-being of the other is part and parcel of one's own happiness, the opposite of relationships in which men dominate women (or vice versa). Paul specifically admonishes husbands not only to "love your wives" but also to "never treat them harshly" (Col. 3:19, NRSVue).

> **Christ-like leadership is sacrificial servant leadership— the opposite of domination.**

All of this, as noted earlier, is couched in Paul's immediately prior instruction to "subject yourselves to one another in the fear of Christ" (Eph. 5:21). While our Bible translations add headings, in Paul's letter there was no break between verse 21 ("subject yourselves to one another") and verse 22 ("wives, subject yourselves to your own husbands"). The instructions to wives and husbands follow as ways in which the prior instruction to "subject yourselves to one another" is to be carried out.

Human relationships are to be relationships of unselfish love—to God and one another (Matt. 22:37–40). Humans are to reflect God's love to Him and others, including service toward God and fellow humans, loving one another even as Christ loves us (John 13:34). Here, contrary to popular myths, unselfish love should not be understood as incompatible with proper self-care and self-regard. Tragically, the myth that *agapē* love is incompatible with proper self-regard has significantly harmed women and others who've been told true love allows oneself to be abused and treated like a doormat, enabling spousal and other forms of abuse (see further below).[46] But Christ loved you so much that He died for you (Rom. 5:8), and you should treat yourself (and others) accordingly, but "do not throw your pearls before pigs" (Matt. 7:6; cf. 10:13–14).

The creation narrative sets forth the ideal for our relationship to God, to other humans, and to God's creation (cf. Gen. 1:26–28). Here we find that all humans should live in harmony as one family, and we find the more specific marriage ideal of union between one husband and one wife as what is to continue for life as "one flesh" (Gen. 2:24; Matt. 19:5).

In this regard, sex is a precious and sacred gift of God, and Scripture clearly specifies that sexual activity is to be reserved for the marriage relationship between one man and one woman.[47] Because it is so precious and sacred, the enemy continually seeks to pervert it.

According to Scripture, sexual activity outside of marriage between husband and wife is sinful. Scripture frequently condemns adultery (when a married person has sex with someone other than their spouse) and other kinds of sexual immorality (fornication/*porneia*).[48]

This includes homosexual sexual activity (see Rom. 1:24-27; cf. Lev. 18:22; 20:13) but is not limited to such activity.[49] For example, Paul writes, "Or do you now know that wrongdoers will not inherit the kingdom of God? Do not be deceived: Neither the sexually immoral nor idolaters nor adulterers nor men who have sex with men nor thieves nor the greedy nor drunkards nor slanderers nor swindlers will inherit the kingdom of God" (1 Cor. 6:9-10, NIV). Unfortunately, however, these verses are often quoted without also stressing the very important verse that follows: "And that is what some of you were. But you were washed, you were sanctified, you were justified in the name of the Lord Jesus Christ and by the Spirit of God" (1 Cor. 6:11, NIV).[50]

Notice Paul says to Christians at Corinth, "that is what some of you were." There is hope and redemption for *all* in Christ. All have sinned and fallen short of the glory of God (Rom. 3:10), but there is redemption for each of us in Christ (see chapter 13). Too many people have been abused and harmed by unloving attitudes and actions by those who call themselves Christians. If we follow Christ, however, we are to love others regardless of whether we agree with their lifestyle. We should love *each person* even as Christ has loved us, remembering that all have sinned and fallen short of God's glory, and it is only by God's grace that any of us can be called children of God. If we recognize our own sinfulness and God's amazing grace to us, how much more gracious and loving should we be to others?

> **There is hope and redemption for all in Christ.**

Nevertheless, sexual immorality of any kind is sinful and harmful. Being sinful, it harms the very ones who practice it. Pre-marital and extra-marital sex harms people.⁵¹ "Flee from sexual immorality," Paul instructs. "All other sins a person commits are outside the body, but whoever sins sexually, sins against their own body" (1 Cor. 6:18, NIV). To take just one example, as Nancy Pearcey explains relative to evidence of deep emotional harm resulting from so-called casual sex outside marriage, "the desire to attach to the other person when we have sex is not only an emotion but also part of our chemistry" such that "when we have intercourse, we create 'an involuntary chemical commitment.' The upshot is that even if you *think* you are having a no-strings-attached hookup, you are in reality creating a chemical bond—whether you mean to or not.... Sex involves our bodies down to the level of our biochemistry." Humans "do not, by nature, thrive on casual, meaningless sexual encounters," but "crave emotional intimacy and fidelity."⁵² In this regard, Pearcey recounts one young woman asking her counselor, "why do they tell you how to protect your body—from herpes and pregnancy—but they don't tell you what it does to your heart?"⁵³

The fact that one's natural inclinations or passions might incline one toward sex outside of marriage (between a man and a woman or otherwise) does not justify the action or render it harmless. While Joseph's natural passions might have inclined him toward accepting the demand of Potiphar's wife to engage in sexual activity with her, Joseph refused, saying, "How then could I do this great evil, and sin against God?" (Gen. 39:9). Of *all* kinds of sexual immorality, Paul writes, "this is the will of God, your sanctification; that is, that you abstain from sexual immorality; that each of you know how to possess his own vessel in sanctification and honor, not in lustful passion, like the Gentiles who do not know God" (1 Thess. 4:3–5).

In this regard, contrary to the way our culture often portrays matters, celibacy and singleness are *not* evils. Indeed, Paul commends celibacy as good (1 Cor. 7:1; cf. 7:8) and of his own singleness and celibacy says, "I wish that all men were even as I myself am. However, each has his own gift from God, one in this way, and another in that" (1 Cor. 7:7; cf. Matt. 19:12). Love relationship in marriage is a gift, but according to Paul singleness may also be a gift and sometimes involves a special calling.

With respect to those who are married, however, Paul sets forth the consistent biblical ideal that "the wife is not to leave her husband" and "the husband is not to divorce his wife" (1 Cor. 7:10–11; cf. Matt. 19:6). Yet, while Scripture consistently sets forth and emphasizes the ideal of marriage as a lifelong union, it also makes provision for handling situations that fall short of the ideal.

Deuteronomy 24 includes provision for a man to divorce his wife in the case of "indecency" (Deut. 24:1). And, while stressing the ideal, Jesus identifies this as a (remedial) provision made by God "because of your hardness of heart" (Matt. 19:8). Knowing humans would fall short of the ideal, God made provisions that would help to protect women and improve their situation.[54] Paul mentions other provisions for abandonment by an unbelieving spouse (1 Cor. 7:15), wherein the one abandoned is not culpable for the dissolution of the marriage. By extension, this provision includes victims of spousal abuse because one committing spousal abuse (or child abuse) has thereby abandoned their duty to faithfully keep the marriage covenant of unselfish love that loves and treats one's spouse as one would love their own bodies, nourishing and cherishing one's spouse rather than harming them (cf. Eph. 5:27–28).[55]

Christians should be very concerned and vigilant about standing against the abuse of women and children (and all others), relative to domestic violence and otherwise—such as all forms of sexual abuse. In this regard, rape is an example of intrinsic evil since it is an anti-love act. Love must be freely given and freely received, and thus, coercion is anti-love. Sexual relations are to be freely and consensually given and freely and consensually received as acts of love in the context of an exclusive relationship of covenant love known as marriage. Rape (and sexual abuse more broadly) utterly contradicts this, taking a gift of sacred love and making it a weapon of cruelty. Instead of freely given love in the context of marriage, it substitutes dominance and domination—it is thus the opposite of the way of the Lamb (Christ). It is of the dragon, who delights in evil and cruelty and hates love itself.

As seen earlier, Paul emphasizes that husbands are to "never treat" their wives "harshly" (Col. 3:19, NRSVue). Wives are *not* to submit to abuse, sexual or otherwise. A man who abuses his wife or children has broken the marriage covenant and forfeited marital rights. Such a relationship *might* be repaired *if* the wife is willing and it becomes safe to reconcile, but the wife is under no obligation to remain in an unsafe situation with her husband in such circumstances. Christians should be careful not to enable abuse by pressing for superficial reconciliation in such cases. The priority should be the safety of the abused and oppressed.[56]

Here, it is significant to notice that Scripture portrays God Himself as the victim of a broken marriage covenant. God was abandoned by His covenant people, and because of His people's apostasy and repeated spiritual adultery, God Himself is described as giving His people a "certificate of divorce" (Jer. 3:8).

Those who have been the victims of the pain that results from a broken marriage and other instances of lost love might take some solace in recognizing that God knows the sufferings of the broken-hearted, unrequited lover. And God will never leave you nor forsake you. God loves you (and every human) more than you could possibly imagine. You and I and every person are of unfathomable value to the Creator of all things. The One who created all things loves you and desires that you live with Him in paradise forever.

We are all broken, but the One who made us can restore us. Knowing God values us so much that Christ became human and died *for us*, how much more should we value *every* person around us, also made in the image of God and for whom Christ also died? Imagine if we treated each person according to the incalculable value they have in God's sight, protecting others from harm where we can and not being satisfied to leave some behind in oppression or squalor, but aiming our actions at individual and collective human flourishing. What if we followed Christ and truly loved others not only in word but also in costly action? We do not possess the power to utterly end evil here and now—only God can do that, and He will in the end—but we might bring a little slice of heaven to people in distress and need here and now (see Matt. 25).

> *We are all broken, but the One who made us can restore us.*

Conclusion: Why Does It Matter?

Even the memory of visiting that place haunted him. It had been many decades since the atrocities that had taken place there were ended. Yet, the place itself still felt like it was filled with evil.

The place he visited was Dachau, one of the most notorious concentration camps of Nazi Germany during World War II. By then, it was a museum, the mission of which was conveyed by a large sign with the words "never forget" printed in many different languages of the world. Nearby that sign, a sculpture of a group of emaciated and mangled bodies struck him and filled him with grief and sorrow. How could this have happened?

How can it be that people are treated like animals and exterminated as if they were worthless husks of matter merely because of their ethnicity or their sexual orientation or for being complicit with those deemed to be of the wrong ethnicity or sexual orientation?

These, and many other instances of atrocities by humans against other humans, should prompt us never to forget the true value of humans—all humans.

As we have seen in this chapter, all humans are made in the image of God and, as such, are of infinite value in the sight of God. Human life is thus precious, and each person should be treated with dignity and respect. There is no place for racism, ethnocentrism, sexism, or other prejudices against humans. We should never forget that Christ died for each and every human being and loves each one far more than you and I love ourselves (or anyone else).

God created humans in the image of God, with the capacity for covenantal relationship—the capacity to make morally significant decisions in relation to God and others. Thus, we are called to love and to do so with "ethical consciousness." As the theologian Dietrich Bonhoeffer, who lost his life standing against Hitler and his atrocities, once put it: "Your Yes to God demands your No to all injustice, to all evil, to all lies, to all oppression and violation of the weak and the poor, to all godlessness and mocking of the Holy."[57]

If you believe in the value of all humans and the importance of human rights, know that God cares far more. Accordingly, one primary way to love God in action is to tangibly show love to humans, all of whom God loves more than we can imagine. In this regard, Ellen White comments: "True religion never fosters ideas or develops character after the attributes of Satan. False religion teaches men to place a cheap estimate

> *One primary way to love God in action is to tangibly show love to humans, all of whom God loves more than we can imagine.*

upon human beings whom Christ has regarded of such value as to give His own life for them. False or mistaken Christianity is always careless of human needs, sufferings, and rights."[58]

If you would follow Christ, you must care about the needs, sufferings, and rights of fellow humans. Do you love your neighbor? What about your "enemies"? Do you recognize the infinite value of *every* human as one loved by God and one for whom Christ died? If so, I invite you to live accordingly. You may find it difficult to find love in your heart, even for those who might posture themselves as your enemies. Love for such ones cannot be generated by you by yourself, but if you ask God—the source of all love—He will work in and on your heart to make you more like Him so that instead of hatred, you can be a beacon of light and love to those around you.

Now, I invite you to read and reflect on Psalm 8, especially verse 4.

Questions for Reflection

1. What does the biblical story of humanity tell us about the identity and value of humans?
2. What does it mean to be created in the image of God? What implications does this biblical teaching have for the value of humans? What does it mean for your value in God's sight?
3. If humans were to be ruler-stewards of God's creation, how then should we treat the world around us? What implications does this have regarding care for the environment (creation care)?
4. What is the difference between seeing humans as extrinsically or intrinsically valuable? How does the fact that Christ became human to save us shed light on human worth? What does that mean for the way we should treat ourselves and others?
5. How would you help someone understand the biblical teachings on race and racism? In light of racism and other injustices in our world, what is the significance of the great love commandments in Scripture?
6. What is the biblical ideal for marriage and sexuality? Are men and women created equal? Does that mean men and women are the same? Why does this matter?

7. You can intentionally recognize the priceless value of humans even now and put that recognition into practice. Do you wish to do so? Ask God to help you see the value of all humans—including those who may present themselves as your enemy. And prayerfully make plans to be a beacon of God's light and love for humanity.

For Further Reading

Adventist Perspectives:

Bradford, Charles E. "Stewardship." In *Handbook of Seventh-day Adventist Theology*. Edited by Raoul Dederen. Hagerstown, MD: Review and Herald, 2000.

Cairus, Aecio C. "The Doctrine of Man." In *Handbook of Seventh-day Adventist Theology*. Edited by Raoul Dederen. Hagerstown, MD: Review and Herald, 2000.

Davidson, Jo Ann. "Women in Scripture: A Survey and Evaluation." In *Women in Ministry: Biblical and Historical Perspectives*. Edited by Nancy Vyhmeister, 157–86. Berrien Springs, MI: Andrews University Press, 1998.

Davidson, Richard M. *Flame of Yahweh: Sexuality in the Old Testament*. Grand Rapids, MI: Baker Academic, 2012.

Gane, Roy E., Nicholas P. Miller, and H. Peter Swanson, eds., *Homosexuality, Marriage, and the Church: Biblical, Counseling, and Religious Liberty Issues*. Berrien Springs, MI: Andrews University Press, 2012.

Gulley, Norman R. *Systematic Theology: Creation, Christ, Salvation*. Berrien Springs, MI: Andrews University Press, 2012.

McDugal, Sarah, Jennifer Jill Schwirzer, and Nicole Parker. *Safe Churches: Responding to Abuse in the Faith Community*. Abide Counseling Press, 2019.

Mueller, Ekkehardt and Elias Brasil de Souza, eds. *Marriage: Biblical and Theological Aspects*. Biblical Research Institute Studies in Biblical Ethics. Silver Spring, MD: Biblical Research Institute, 2015.

——— and Elias Brasil de Souza, eds. *Sexuality: Contemporary Issues from a Biblical Perspective*. Biblical Research Institute Studies in Biblical Ethics. Silver Spring, MD: Biblical Research Institute/Review and Herald, 2022.

Rock, Calvin B. "Marriage and Family." In *Handbook of Seventh-day Adventist Theology*. Edited by Raoul Dederen. Hagerstown, MD: Review and Herald, 2000.

———. *Protest and Progress: Black Seventh-day Adventist Leadership and the Push for Parity*. Berrien Springs, MI: Andrews University Press, 2018.

Schafer, A. Rahel. "'You, YHWH, Save Humans and Animals': God's Response to the Vocalized Needs of Non-human Animals as Portrayed in the Old Testament," PhD diss., Wheaton College, 2015.

Wahlen, Clinton, ed. *What Are Human Beings That You Are Mindful of Them?* Silver Spring, MD: Review & Herald, 2015.

Wells, A. Rahel. "Why Care for the Earth if It Is All Going to Burn? Eschatology and Ecology." In *Eschatology from an Adventist Perspective*. Edited by Elias Brasil de Souza, A. Rahel Wells, Laszlo Gallusz, and Denis Kaiser. Silver Spring, MD: Biblical Research Institute, 2021.

See also the Resources on the Biblical Research Institute website: https://adventistbiblicalresearch.org/materials

Other Christian Perspectives:

Cortez, Marc, *Theological Anthropology: A Guide for the Perplexed*. London: T&T Clark, 2010.

Eastman, Susan. *Paul the Person*. Grand Rapids, MI: Eerdmans, 2017.

Green, Joel B. *Body, Soul, and Human Life: The Nature of Humanity in the Bible*. Grand Rapids, MI: Baker Academic, 2008.

Jones, Beth Felker. *Faithful: A Theology of Sex*. Grand Rapids, MI: Zondervan, 2015.

Kilner, John F. *Dignity and Destiny: Humanity in the Image of God*. Grand Rapids, MI: Eerdmans, 2015.

McCaulley, Esau. *Reading While Black: African American Biblical Interpretation as an Exercise in Hope*. Downers Grove, IL: IVP Academic, 2020.

Moo, Douglas J. and Jonathan A. Moo, *Creation Care: A Biblical Theology of the Natural World*. Grand Rapids, MI: Zondervan, 2018.

Middleton, J. Richard, *The Liberating Image: The Imago Dei in Genesis 1.* Grand Rapids, MI: Brazos, 2005.

Pearcey, Nancy R. *Love Thy Body: Answering Hard Questions about Life and Sexuality.* Grand Rapids, MI: Baker, 2019.

Peterson, Ryan S. *The Imago Dei as Human Identity: A Theological Interpretation.* Winona Lake, IN: Eisenbrauns, 2016.

Richter, Sandra L. *Stewards of Eden: What Scripture Says About the Environment and Why It Matters.* Downers Grove, IL: IVP Academic, 2020.

Westfall, Cynthia Long. *Paul and Gender: Reclaiming the Apostle's Vision for Men and Women in Christ.* Grand Rapids, MI: Baker Academic, 2016.

12

LIFE AND DEATH: HUMAN FREEDOM, SINFULNESS, AND CONDITIONAL IMMORTALITY

"From any tree of the garden you may freely eat; but from the tree of the knowledge of good and evil you shall not eat, for on the day that you eat from it you will certainly die" (Gen. 2:16–17). God spoke these solemn words to Adam and Eve in the garden of Eden, indicating that God granted them moral freedom to will good or evil.

Embedded in God's command is the tragic prospect of human death. Humans could live forever, but they also could die. As a "branch cannot bear fruit of itself but must remain in the vine," humans cannot live—or do anything for that matter, apart from the Life-giver (John 15:4). Life depends on God and, if *utterly* cut off from God, the source of life, humans would die. In relationship to God, humans can live forever, but human immortality is *conditional*.

The way humans use their God-granted freedom, then, is a matter of life and death. As God later told His covenant people, "I have placed before you life and death, the blessing and the curse. So choose life in order that you may live, you and your descendants" (Deut. 30:19).

This chapter takes up some big questions about human nature, specifically relative to human freedom, sin, human constitution, and death. What is the extent of human free will? What is sin, and what are the consequences of sin regarding human nature? What happens when we die? Are humans strictly material beings or immaterial souls or something else? Do humans live forever?

The Human Story: Free to Love and Live Eternally

"Why are you angry? And why is your face gloomy?" God asked Cain these questions after his brother Abel's sacrifice was accepted, while Cain's was not. Cain was very angry indeed. God reminded Cain, however: "If you do well, will your face not be cheerful? And if you do not do well, sin is lurking at the door; and its desire is for you, but you must master it" (Gen. 4:6–7).

Like his parents (Adam and Eve) before him, Cain faced a choice. Would he "do well," following God's commands, or go his own way—the way of sin? Tragically, "Cain rose up against his brother Abel and killed him" (Gen. 4:8). He murdered his own brother, the first death recorded in Scripture. The tragic consequences of Adam and Eve's sins struck home. Sin quickly took root and only increased. By the time of Noah, "the wickedness of mankind was great on the earth," and "every intent of the thoughts of their hearts was only evil continually" (Gen. 6:5).

Adam and Eve originally lived in perfect moral harmony with God and one another (Gen. 2:25). Humans were created with the capacity to love and be loved. They were loved by God, an expression of His love. And they were to love God and one another in return.

Love, however, can only be *freely* given and *freely* received. Humans can reject God's love, but to reject God's love itself is evil. To love, then, requires the capacity of moral freedom—freedom to will good or evil (see chapter 9).

This moral freedom is apparent in God's instruction to Adam and Eve that they could eat from every tree in the garden except one (Gen. 2:16–17).[1] Tragically, both Eve and Adam decided to disobey God and eat the forbidden fruit.

Immediately, their eyes were opened to evil. They had been naked and unashamed (Gen. 2:25), but after eating the fruit, they tried to cover their guilt and became afraid of God, their loving Creator who desired only their good (Gen. 3:7–10).[2] Sin immediately brought relational strife. Adam blamed Eve and, indirectly, God who gave him Eve. Eve blamed the serpent (Gen. 3:12–13). Sin separates us from God, repelling love and fracturing relationships.

Through Adam and Eve's Fall, Satan became the temporary "ruler of this world" (John 12:31; 14:30; 16:11; cf. 2 Cor. 4:4). Evil, with its consequences of suffering and death, became part of the universal human experience.

And, because of Adam and Eve's sin, the human race is fallen, infected with sin. Apart from Christ, humans are "by nature children of wrath"

(Eph. 2:3). Each descendant of Adam and Eve inherit a bent toward sin (i.e., a sinful nature; cf. Rom. 5:19). "Through one man [Adam] sin entered into the world, and death through sin, and so death spread to all mankind, because all sinned" (Rom. 5:12; cf. 6:23).

Humanity fell in the garden (Gen. 3). Cain killed his brother Abel (Gen. 4). Humanity became so evil the thoughts of their hearts were "only evil continually" (Gen. 6:5). After the flood, humans rebelled and rejected God's promises at Babel (Gen. 11). Ever since, humans have inflicted horrendous evil upon one another, in rebellion against God. Human history is filled with strife—violence, exploitation, and oppression.

Yet, God did not leave humans without hope. God made a way to crush the serpent and save the world so that anyone willing can be saved and inherit eternal life (Gen. 3:15; John 3:16; see chapter 13). "Through one offense [that of Adam] the result was condemnation to all mankind." But, there is good news, for "through one act of righteousness [that of Christ, the second Adam] the result was justification of life to all mankind," specifically to "those who receive the abundance of grace and of the gift of righteousness" (Rom. 5:18, 17).

Human Freedom and Sinfulness

From creation onward (see Gen. 2:16–17), God granted humans moral freedom—free will of the kind necessary for genuine love relationship, which allows humans to freely receive and give love.

Since to reject or oppose God's love is itself evil, however, such freedom requires the ability to do evil—to do otherwise than God ideally desires (cf. Luke 7:30, see chapter 9). But none need have ever exercised their freedom to do evil. Tragically, however, creatures did, bringing separation from God and other disastrous consequences (Isa. 59:2).

From the beginning, human freedom was *limited freedom*, and could not be otherwise. Only One who is all-powerful could have *unlimited* freedom and even God has (morally) limited His own freedom insofar as He has committed Himself to grant creaturely freedom and otherwise made commitments (see chapter 9).

No creature, however, could be all-powerful. Thus, all creaturely freedom is necessarily limited according to our finite power and capacities. I cannot, for example, flap my arms and fly, however much I will to do so. Our exercise of freedom is further limited in relation to the way others use their freedom to affect the world around us. I may wish to enjoy peace and quiet at the beach, but if someone blasts music there, I cannot do so. My freedom is limited, then, both relative to my natural capacities and what others do around me.

The world is ordered in such a way that what I do not only affects me, but also the world around me. And, as seen in chapter 9, for us to even exercise freedom to act in the world, there must be some consistent parameters—an orderly way nature works according to regular "laws" so I can form intentions with reasonable expectations of bringing them about.[3] Creaturely freedom, then, always operates within parameters and constraints. Love itself requires some context of "laws" within which the freedom required for love can be exercised.

Our freedom would actually be much greater today if everyone acted not only within natural constraints but also *freely* acted within the bounds of *moral* laws, that is, laws given for the good of everyone. In this and other ways, God's law is good, and *for our good* in a myriad of ways we often fail to recognize (see more on this in chapter 14).

In the beginning, Adam and Eve possessed moral freedom that was unfettered by any inclination to do evil or by harmful actions of others. Their sin, however, ruptured the harmonious relationship between God and humans and between humans and one another (see Gen. 2:25; 3:7–13). Sin and its wages, death, became part of all human experience (Rom. 6:23; cf. 5:12). Ever since, humans have inflicted evil and suffering of all kinds on one another.

Because of sin, human freedom today is far more limited than God originally intended. First, the entrance of sin affected humans such that we *all* inherit a bent toward sin—an inborn inclination of selfishness (sinful nature) that inclines us toward sinning (discussed further below). And Satan became the temporary ruler of this world (John 12:31; 14:30; 16:11; cf. 2 Cor. 4:4), the arch-tempter and deceiver who seeks to fill human hearts with evil (Acts 5:3) and hold humans "captive . . . to do his will" (2 Tim. 2:26; cf. John 8:44; 1 Cor. 7:5; Eph. 4:26–27; 1 Thess. 3:5; 1 Pet. 5:7; 1 John 3:8). Second, humans often act in ways that harm others and otherwise restrict human and environmental flourishing. *Apart from Christ*, humans are in bondage to sin (e.g., John 8:34; Rom. 6:6,

17; 2 Pet. 3:19), both relative to our sinful natures and to the structures of sin and evil all around us, from which Christ came to set us free (cf. John 8:36; Rom. 6:7, 11, 18).

Indeed, Paul explains, "through one man [Adam] sin entered into the world, and death through sin, and so death spread to all mankind, because all sinned" (Rom. 5:12). And "death reigned from Adam until Moses, even over those who had not sinned in the likeness of the violation committed by Adam, who is a type of Him who was to come," that is, a type of Christ—the second Adam (Rom. 5:14). Indeed, "through one offense [that of Adam] the result was condemnation to all mankind" and "through the one man's disobedience [that of Adam] the many were made sinners" (Rom. 5:18-19). By Adam's sin, then, humans "were made sinners," and Adam's sin resulted in "condemnation to all."

Competing Theories in Christian Theology: The Nature of Sin

Many have identified the Christian doctrine of sin as Christianity's most self-evident teaching. You don't need anyone to tell you something is very wrong with humanity. The problem, Christianity teaches, is sin, from which humanity needs a Savior.[4] In this regard, many Christians agree with some form of the doctrine of total depravity, which teaches that because of the Fall, every aspect of human nature is corrupted (or depraved) such that one cannot save oneself but needs a Savior. Total depravity does not mean humans are as bad as they possibly could be, but that no aspect of humanity is untainted by sin. Nevertheless, Christians hold competing theories about the nature and extent of human sinfulness.

One primary issue is whether and to what extent humans inherit *sin*. The doctrine of sin (hamartiology) involves many nuances that defy neat categorization, but for simplicity we might identify three broad categories relative to the first sin in Eden, known as original sin.

The Pelagian view (named after Pelagius, ca. 354-418), almost universally rejected as heretical, claims the original sin in Eden did *not* taint human nature with a bent toward sin; humans do *not* inherit guilt from the original sin, and the human will is capable of choosing good or evil without special divine aid. The Semi-Pelagian view instead affirms that original sin tainted human nature with a propensity toward sinning, but the human will is nevertheless capable of choosing good or evil *without* special divine aid.

In direct contrast, the Augustinian view (named after Augustine, AD 354–430, who wrote in direct opposition to Pelagius) maintains that original sin tainted and depraved human nature, removing human freedom to choose good such that humans can choose good only by divine predestination. Further, humans inherit guilt from the original sin (known as original guilt).[5] Some, like Augustine, believe every later human was somehow present in the loins of Adam and thus culpable for his sin. Many others affirm original guilt but take various nuanced positions regarding how such guilt is inherited (e.g., the federal headship view maintains Adam's guilt is imputed (that is, attributed or credited) to all humans because Adam was the federal (or representative) head of the human race.

Many Christians, however, depart from Pelagian and Augustinian views, affirming (in contrast to Pelagianism) that original sin tainted and depraved human nature, rendering human sin inevitable and requiring *special divine aid* to turn from slavery to sin, while maintaining (in contrast to Augustinian views) that humans *can* choose to positively respond to God's invitation to be saved or reject God's invitation because God's grace enables fallen humans to accept God's gift of salvation (this is often labeled prevenient grace, grace that *precedes* human decision).[6] In contrast to semi-Pelagian views, this view (sometimes labeled the Semi-Augustinian view) emphasizes that humans can only reach out to God because God first reaches out to us (cf. 1 John 4:19), offering humans the choice to accept or reject divine deliverance from sin.

Some claim that nearly all Christian theologians prior to Augustine held something like this view, which continued in Eastern Christianity apart from the influence of the Pelagian controversy and has been adopted by many Protestant Christians, with Eastern Orthodox Christians and many Protestants affirming that original sin tainted and depraved human nature, but denying that humans inherit guilt from Adam (original guilt).[7] This view is closest to what many Adventists have historically affirmed.[8]

The Nature of Sin

"God made people upright, but they have sought out many schemes" (Eccles. 7:29). According to Scripture, while the first humans were created in God's image without any sin or sinful inclinations, the Fall corrupted human nature (see Rom. 5:19; Eph. 2:3; cf. Ps. 58:3), affecting the human will from then onward and opening the way for Satan to have more access to influence humans toward evil as the temporary ruler of this world.[9] The human will was initially inclined only toward goodness and love but is now *bent* toward sin and evil—we possess crooked wills, inclined toward selfishness rather than unselfish love. Infected by sin, our will itself is corrupt, tainted with selfishness.

To understand this, we must understand the nature of *sin* itself. As 1 John 3:4 describes it, "sin is lawlessness." Because God's law is the law of unselfish love (see chapter 14), inseparable from justice, breaking God's law or otherwise being *lawless* is contrary to love and love's counterpart, justice. Acts of sin, then, are instances of relational injustice that damage love relationship.

According to Scripture, however, while sin *includes* actions contrary to God's law, *sin is more* than particular acts of sin. Sin is like a disease involving an inner state of *lawlessness*, a corrupted nature bent toward sin (e.g., Eph. 2:3), which humans cannot resist without special divine aid.[10] Accordingly, the problem of sin requires a new heart, replacing our "heart of stone" with "a heart of flesh" (Ezek. 11:19).

> Acts of sin, then, are instances of relational injustice that damage love relationship.

It is no coincidence that "all have sinned and fall short of the glory of God" (Rom. 3:23). Indeed, "There is no righteous person, not even one; there is no one who understands, there is no one who seeks out God; they have all turned aside, together they have become corrupt; there is no one who does good, there is not even one" (Rom. 3:10–12, quoting Ps. 14:1–3). In this regard, John emphasizes, "If we say that we have no sin, we are deceiving ourselves and the truth is not in us" and "If we say that we have not sinned, we make Him a liar and His word is not in us" (1 John 1:8, 10; cf. 2:1–2).

With only one exception (Jesus, 1 John 3:5), *every human* (with the capacity to make moral choices) who has ever lived has sinned. Again, this is no coincidence but a result of the Fall (see Rom. 5:19). Indeed, "the intent of man's heart is evil from his youth" (Gen. 8:21; cf. 6:5). Humans "go astray from the womb; they err from their birth" (Ps. 58:3, NRSVue). Indeed, David wrote, "I was brought forth in iniquity, and in sin my mother conceived me" (Ps. 51:5, NKJV). As the context elaborates, this refers to David's sinfulness *from birth*. Likewise, Paul explains, "we too all previously lived in the lusts of our flesh, indulging the desires of the flesh and of the mind, and were by nature children of wrath, just as the rest" (Eph. 2:3).

By Adam's sin, "many were made sinners" (Rom. 5:19) and all "go astray" and "err from their birth" (Ps. 58:3). Thus, "there is no person who does not sin" (1 Kings 8:46; cf. Rom. 3:9–12). Indeed, "there is not a just man on earth who does good and does not sin" (Eccles. 7:20, NKJV; cf. Ps. 14:1–3; 143:2; Matt. 19:17), but we are "all under sin" (Rom. 3:9; cf. 3:10, 23).

Jeremiah 17:9 further describes the diseased moral condition of humanity, saying, "The heart is deceitful above all things, and desperately wicked; Who can know it?" (NKJV, cf. 13:23). Even our seemingly good deeds are tainted: "For all of us have become like one who is unclean, and all our righteous deeds are like a filthy garment" (Isa. 64:6). This is because even our desires are selfish and sinful.

We are, by nature, attracted to sin, but we should hate it. Everything sinful is harmful. Sin is killing us and all we love. As James 1:14 explains, "each one is tempted when he is carried away and enticed by his own lust. Then when lust has conceived, it gives birth to sin; and sin, when it has run its course, brings forth death."

Paul describes his experience of the depraved human nature this way:

> For I do not understand what I am doing; for I am not practicing what I want to do, but I do the very thing I hate. However, if I do the very thing I do not want to do, I agree with the Law, that the Law is good. But now, no longer am I the one doing it, but sin that dwells in me. For I know that good does not dwell in me, that is, in my flesh; for the willing is present in me, but the doing of the good is not. For the good that I want, I do not do, but I practice the very evil that I do not want. But if I do the very thing I do not want, I am no longer the one doing it, but sin that dwells in me. I find then the principle that evil is present in me, the one

who wants to do good. For I joyfully agree with the law of God in the inner person, but I see a different law in the parts of my body waging war against the law of my mind, and making me a prisoner of the law of sin, the law which is in my body's parts. Wretched man that I am! Who will set me free from the body of this death? (Rom. 7:15-24).

Who will set us free, indeed? Some think they can be righteous before God by willing themselves to be good, but the sin problem is far deeper than external actions. As Paul put it, "sin" itself "dwells in" us (Rom. 7:17). You cannot save yourself. Only God can save you. Thus, Paul continues, "Thanks be to God through Jesus Christ our Lord. . . . there is now no condemnation at all for those who are in Christ Jesus. For the law of the Spirit of life in Christ Jesus has set you free from the law of sin and of death" (Rom. 7:25-8:2). Apart from God's work in us, however, we are *not even able* to turn from sin, "the mind set on the flesh is hostile toward God; for it does not subject itself to the law of God, for it is not even able to do so" (Rom. 8:7; cf. Jer. 13:23).

> You cannot save yourself. Only God can save you.

In Scripture, "sin" sometimes describes lawless actions, but *"sin"* also often describes the depraved nature and *bent* state of humanity. Specifically, Scripture depicts sin as:

- bad deeds (e.g., Rom. 1:18-3:20)
- depravity of heart (e.g., Gen. 6:5; 8:21; Ps. 51:5; 58:3; Jer. 17:9; Eph. 2:3; cf. Jer. 11:8; 16:12; Matt. 7:18-23; James 1:14-15; 4:1-2)
- an enslaving power (e.g., John 8:34; Rom. 6:6, 17; 7:17, 20; 2 Pet. 2:19)

Regarding this last point, Ivan Blazen explains:

> The Bible describes sinful actions as the product of living under the rule of an alien, evil, and enslaving power such as is described in Romans 5-8. Always occurring in the singular except in Romans 7:5, sin is pictured as king or lord (Rom. 5:12-14, 21) to whom humans yield themselves in obedient service (Rom. 6:6, 12, 13). Like a harsh tyrant or wicked taskmaster, sin holds people in slavery (verses 6, 16-18, 20; 7:14) and pays them wages

> (Rom. 6:23). Like a demon it can dwell in a person (Rom. 7:17, 20), deceive that person (verse 11), as the serpent deceived Eve (Gen. 3:13), and even effect death in the person (Rom. 6:16, 23; 7:11, 14). Its suppression of mankind can be produced by the imposition of its own law (Rom. 7:23; 8:2) or, by subversively working its destructive purposes through God's law (Rom. 7:8, 11, 13; cf. 1 Cor. 15:56). It can lie dormant or suddenly spring to life, stirring the sinful passions to action (Rom. 7:5–9). Sin as a power stands opposed to God (Rom. 6:23) and, like a criminal, is condemned by God (Rom. 8:3). To speak of sin as a power expresses the paradox that sin is something we do, and yet which precedes and determines our doing. In sinning it is we who sin, yet not we ourselves (Rom. 7:17, 20).[11]

Not only are individual humans corrupt, but there is also corporate evil and injustice rooted in oppressive structures around us (e.g., tribalism and systemic racism, systems contributing to warmongering and other violence, human trafficking, the violation of human rights, and oppression of the poor and various economic injustices rooted in human greed and the "love of money," which "is a root of all sorts of evil"; 1 Tim. 6:10). At the root of such structural evils is sin. Yet, such structural evils are not only the result of *human* depravity. As we've seen (chapter 9), demonic "principalities and powers" work behind the scenes. The devil is the temporary "ruler of this world" in the cosmic conflict.[12] Accordingly, God's work to save the world involves more than individual salvation; it involves liberating the world from systemic evil and the power of darkness. The world is affected by sin such that "the whole creation groans and suffers," but will one day "be set free from its slavery to corruption into the freedom of the glory of the children of God" (Rom. 8:21–22).

At the root of injustice, systemic and otherwise, is the selfishness of sin. Justice for all, however, can only be the product of *unselfish* love. Many people today call for justice while seeking to leave aside discussion of sin, but to do so is to treat the symptoms without treating the disease behind them. The disease of sin, however, can only be cured by the Creator, who alone can replace our "heart of stone" with "a heart of flesh" (Ezek. 11:19). Only God can bring full liberation from systemic evil, which is rooted in sin—the problem that only God can fully resolve. The ultimate defeat and eradication of *all* kinds of evil will only come about through Christ's work of salvation, in which Christ first deals with the sin problem at the root of all evils, defeating the devil's allegations through giving Himself as the all-sufficient atoning sacrifice for sins (in His first Advent) and only later, after and on the basis of defeating the devil's allegations and resolving the sin problem, finally destroys the devil and his works and brings justice in all its fullness (after His second Advent). Nevertheless, without losing focus on our primary mission of helping people find salvation and eternal life in Christ and prepare for Christ's soon return, we should work against the powers of darkness in our sphere of influence here and now (always working in love), while remembering only God can ultimately save us from sin and its horrible effects—individually and collectively.[13]

God will save everyone who is willing to be saved. *Not one person* will be lost because of their sinful nature. God has made provision for everyone such that the only reason anyone will be lost is because they reject God's grace, offered freely to everyone (see chapter 13). As John 3:16–18 explains: "For God so loved the world, that He gave His only Son, so that everyone who believes in Him will not perish, but have eternal life. For God did not send the Son into the world to judge the world, but so that the world might be saved through Him. The one who believes in Him is not judged; the one who does not believe has been judged already, because he has not believed in the name of the only Son of God."

Perhaps you wonder whether you are beyond saving. If you are at all concerned about being saved, you are not beyond saving. The only unpardonable sin is to finally reject and cut yourself off from the work of the Holy Spirit (cf. Mark 3:28–29).[14] If you have even the smallest desire to be with God, you have not done so, for you would have no such desire were it not for the Holy Spirit's work on your heart (cf. Rom. 2:4). But do not wait. Call on the name of the Lord and He will save you (Rom. 10:13; see chapter 13).

> **If you are at all concerned about being saved, you are not beyond saving.**

Human Mortality, Constitution, and Destiny

Life is a gift. When young, it is easy to think you are immortal. It is easy to forget that humans eventually die.

Death, however, is the opposite of what God intended for us (cf. Ezek. 33:11; 2 Pet. 3:9). Life is from God, and Christ came and gave His life so we could have eternal life (see John 10:10), demonstrating that every human life is of incalculable value to God.

But there can be no life apart from God, the only source of life who sustains all things (Heb. 1:3). Nothing can exist apart from God. Thus, human existence entirely depends on connection with God. God *with us* is essential to life.

Is human life, then, eternal? Humans can live forever in connection with God—"everyone who believes in [Christ] will not perish, but have eternal life" (John 3:16). Yet, what about those who reject life with God? Do they live forever? Are humans immortal?

The Conditional Immortality of Humans

"For God so loved the world, that He gave His only Son, so that everyone who believes in Him will not perish, but have eternal life" (John 3:16). Here and elsewhere, Scripture teaches that human eternal life is *conditional*. Thus, Jesus proclaimed of His followers, "I give them eternal life, and they will never perish" (John 10:27–28). All creaturely life depends on God. Creatures live only by divine sustenance. Human life is a gift that can be lost.

In the very first book of the Bible, the serpent tempted Eve with the lie, "You certainly will not die!" (Gen. 3:4). Had Adam and Eve not sinned, they could have taken "from the tree of life, and eat, and live forever" (Gen. 3:22). But, because of their rebellion, God sent them from the garden and stationed an angel and a flaming sword "to guard the way to the tree of life" (Gen. 3:23–24).

The last book of Scripture likewise refers to the tree of life. To everyone "who overcomes," Jesus promises, "I will grant to eat from the tree of life, which is in the Paradise of God" (Rev. 2:7). Further, Revelation 22:14 proclaims: "Blessed are those who wash their robes, so that they will have the right to the tree of life, and may enter the city by the gates."[15]

Such references to the tree of life indicate that humans do not innately possess eternal life but are innately mortal—dependent on divine sustenance, which is conditional. Indeed, Jesus calls Himself "the living bread that came down out of heaven," teaching that "if anyone eats from this bread, he will live forever" (John 6:51; cf. 14:6; 15:1–6). Here and elsewhere, from beginning to end, Scripture teaches that humans are *conditionally* immortal.

Paul thus speaks of "those who by perseverance in doing good seek glory, honor, and immortality," to whom "He will give eternal life" (Rom. 2:7). Later, Paul identifies the "outcome" of salvation as "eternal life," adding, "the wages of sin is death, but the gracious gift of God is eternal life in Christ Jesus our Lord" (Rom. 6:22–23). Notice the contrast between "death" and the "gift" of "eternal life."

Eternal life is God's gift, freely available to anyone willing to live *with* God in a world of perfect, unselfish love. Further, Jesus proclaimed, those who (by Christ's work) "are considered worthy to attain to that age and the resurrection from the dead . . . cannot even die anymore, for they are like angels, and are sons of God, being sons of the resurrection" (Luke 20:35–36). In the end, only the saved "put on immortality." As Paul writes of the redeemed, "the trumpet will sound, and the dead will be raised imperishable, and we will be changed. For this perishable must put on the imperishable, and this mortal must put on immortality" (1 Cor. 15:52–53).

Humans, then, are only *conditionally* immortal. Only God is immortal in the sense of *unconditional* immortality, for God "alone possesses immortality" (1 Tim. 6:16). But this means humans do not possess an unconditionally immortal soul, a soul that *cannot* die. Indeed, Jesus Himself warned, God "is able to destroy both soul and body" (Matt. 10:28). Further, Jesus warned, "whoever wants to save his life will lose it; but whoever loses his life for My sake will find it. For what good will it do a person if he gains the whole world, but forfeits his soul? Or what will a person give in exchange for his soul?" (Matt. 16:25–26). We will talk more about the meaning of the term "soul" in Scripture a bit later, but here we see that human life can be lost.

Thus, Jesus urged, "Enter through the narrow gate; for the gate is wide and the way is broad that leads to destruction, and there are many who enter through it. For the gate is narrow and the way is constricted that leads to life, and there are few who find it" (Matt. 7:13–14). Thus, Christ elsewhere contrasts the redeemed who will "come out" from the tomb "to a resurrection of life" with the unsaved who will come forth "to a resurrection of judgment" (John 5:29). Those who reject God's gift of eternal life finally perish (cf. Ps. 37:20; 145:20; Mal. 4:1)—they cease to live and never live again.[16]

Elsewhere, Jesus taught the unredeemed wicked "will go away into eternal punishment, but the righteous into eternal life" (Matt. 25:46). Since Jesus contrasts it with eternal life, "eternal punishment" cannot refer to eternal conscious torment.[17] Rather, this "eternal punishment" is the second death, resulting in the destruction of the unrepentant wicked that *forever* ends their life (see chapter 19).[18] Here, eternal punishment is the opposite of eternal life; it is *cessation of life that lasts forever*.

Paul likewise refers to this when he teaches the unredeemed wicked "will pay the penalty of eternal destruction, away from the presence of the Lord and from the glory of His power" (2 Thess. 1:9). This does not refer to a process of destruction that goes on forever, but the result of destruction that is final and thus "eternal." Since human existence depends on God, a human utterly separated from God's presence ceases to live (and thus perishes). Those who *finally* reject life *with* God thereby finally cut themselves off from eternal life, being entirely destroyed forever.

That the destruction of the wicked refers to the final destruction of the *whole* human is apparent when Jesus teaches, "do not be afraid of those who kill the body but are unable to kill the soul; but rather fear Him who is able to destroy both soul and body in hell [*gehenna*]" (Matt. 10:28; cf. 13:40–42; 2 Pet. 2:6).[19]

The biblical data regarding what "hell" is will be discussed further in chapter 19, alongside final events. There, we will see that none of the words in Scripture translated as "hell" (e.g., *hadēs* and *gehenna*) refer to a place of endlessly burning fire or teach eternal conscious torment. Rather, as we will see in chapter 19, Scripture consistently teaches that those saved by Christ inherit eternal life, but those who are lost perish forever, dying the second death, which extinguishes life and from which there is no return. The wicked will not endure endless suffering, but in accordance with the loving mercy of God, they will finally perish forever.

> *The wicked will not endure endless suffering, but in accordance with the loving mercy of God, they will finally perish forever.*

Only those whose names are written in the book of life will live forever. But eventually, there will be no more death (Rev. 21:4); death itself will be destroyed. As Paul writes, "the last enemy that will be destroyed is death" (1 Cor. 15:26, NKJV). And, according to Revelation 20:14, in the end, Death and *Hades* (a term sometimes mistakenly translated as hell, but actually referring to the grave in Scripture, see chapter 19) are themselves "thrown into the lake of fire" to be destroyed. For "our Savior Christ Jesus" has "abolished death and brought life and immortality to light through the gospel" (2 Tim. 1:10). Jesus conquered death for all of us (cf. Heb. 2:14; Rev. 1:18).

Competing Theories in Christian Theology: The State of the Dead and Human Constitution

Many Christians believe *every* human lives forever. Some believe all humans will finally be saved. This is known as universalism, of which there are various forms. Others believe only some will be saved, and the unsaved will suffer eternal conscious misery or torment—the eternal conscious punishment view.

Others maintain, however, that only humans saved by Christ live forever while the unsaved perish and ultimately cease to exist forever—the conditional immortality view (i.e., conditionalism or annihilationism). This is the view Adventists affirm.[20]

The views above are closely related to and yet distinct from theories regarding the state humans are in between their death and resurrection, known as the intermediate state (which Adventists typically call the state of the dead). Adventists (and others) believe that when humans die, they are unconscious and remain so until being resurrected—the unconscious state of the dead view, akin to what some Christians call "soul sleep" (though Adventists do not believe humans have a conscious, separable soul).

Many Christians, however, believe humans remain conscious after death (the conscious state of the dead view), with varying views regarding what happens to humans after death. Some believe that upon death, humans (in a disembodied state typically spoken of as one's "soul" and/or "spirit") immediately go either to heaven or hell (believed to be a place of eternal conscious punishment). Others believe there is a middle place that is neither heaven nor hell, known as Purgatory, where some disembodied humans go after death to be purged of their sins/sinfulness and prepared to live in God's presence.

Distinct from these views, some believe there is a place of the dead (sometimes identified with Sheol and/or Hades) where the dead reside in a shade-like conscious existence until resurrection, with the saved and lost in different compartments.

The above views are closely related to, yet also distinct from, competing theories of human constitution, regarding which there are *many* nuanced views.[21] A basic definition of some prominent categories follows:

Substance Dualism affirms a dichotomy of body and soul/spirit (or mind). For example, both Platonic Dualism and Cartesian Dualism affirm that humans possess an immaterial soul (or mind) and a material body, which are entirely different kinds of substances (raising questions of whether and how they might interact).[22] Distinct from dualism is the trichotomist view, which believes humans consist of *three* distinct parts—body, soul, *and* spirit.

The common view that humans possess a soul that is distinct and separable from the body (sometimes called radical dualism)[23] is often traced to the influence of the Greek philosopher Plato, particularly the view that the material world is a shadow world—a lesser realm of things always changing and passing away, while ultimate reality is an immaterial world of ideas or forms (to which the soul properly belongs)—timelessly eternal, immaterial, and utterly unchanging (Plato's two-world theory).

Plato wrote of humans possessing pre-existent souls, which fell into bodily existence by failing to focus sufficiently on immaterial reality. The early Christian theologian Origen (ca. AD 184–ca. 253) adopted this view, but most Christians have rejected this pre-existence theory of the soul.[24] Many affirm traducianism, the view that human souls are passed down from parents to children, stemming ultimately from Adam's soul. Alternatively, some affirm the creationism theory of the soul, believing God creates a new soul out of nothing (*ex nihilo*) for each human at conception.

Distinct from these is a view known as emergent dualism, which views the soul as an "emergent" substance dependent on the body from which it emerges.[25] This is a kind of holistic dualism, which refers to kinds of dualism that affirm substance dualism but hold that "the human person, though composed of discrete elements, is nonetheless to be identified with the whole, which then constitutes a functional unity."[26]

Hylomorphism, a theory developed by the Greek philosopher Aristotle, holds that physical objects, including humans, are a combination of matter (the physical "stuff") and form (that which "unifies matter into a single object"). According to Aristotle, humans are a hylomorphic union of body (matter) and soul (form).

Building on Aristotle, the medieval theologian Thomas Aquinas affirmed a kind of hylomorphism that is sometimes identified as a kind of dualism but distinct from *Cartesian* dualism because it emphasizes the *unity* of the human being. Accordingly, some reject the label of dualism for this view to avoid confusion in this regard. Specifically, Thomas Aquinas believed bodily nature is essential to humans, but the soul is immaterial and immortal and thus survives the death of the body (according with many forms of dualism, at least in this respect).

Yet, *some* advocates of hylomorphism deny that a human soul can exist apart from a body. Thus, one *might* affirm a kind of hylomorphism that identifies humans as having "form" and "matter" in *some* sense, such that humans are more than merely physical or material without affirming that humans have a separable, conscious soul.

Physicalism (or Materialism) maintains that humans are fundamentally physical (or material) beings (a kind of monism or "one substance" view). Some affirm non-reductive physicalism, wherein human constitution is fundamentally physical, but human nature is not reducible to or fully explained by the laws, properties, and concepts of the physical sciences.[27] Non-reductive physicalism is sometimes identified as a form of emergentism (in contrast to emergent dualism, introduced above). Emergentism includes the view that human properties like consciousness emerge from other properties humans possess while being different from them.

Idealism, another kind of monism, maintains that everything consists of ideas (or mind, *nous*). There is no mind-body or mind-matter problem because everything we call "matter" is actually merely idea(s) we perceive as material. Humans (and everything else) consist only of immaterial idea(s).

Neutral monism, however, rejects the dichotomy of mind and matter, believing humans consist of one substance that is neither fundamentally mental nor physical but *inclusive* of both "mind" and "matter," so to speak.

Physicalism (or materialism), idealism, neutral monism, and *some forms of* dualism (e.g., holistic dualism) and hylomorphism are distinct kinds of wholism. Relative to human constitution, wholism refers to views that emphasize the unity of the human being such that humans are either wholly material or wholly immaterial or consist of an inseparable union of material and immaterial components or properties without which one would not be human.

Adventists typically affirm some kind of wholism, emphasizing the unity of human nature and denying both that humans have an immortal soul and that humans have a separable, conscious soul—that is, a soul that may exist consciously apart from the body.

The State of the Dead and Human Constitution

"Lord, if You had been here, my brother would not have died" (John 11:32). These words Mary of Bethany spoke through tears to Jesus after her brother Lazarus's death. Jesus was "deeply moved," and "Jesus wept" (John 11:33, 35).

"Remove the stone" from this tomb, Jesus said. Then, Martha (another sister of Lazarus) protested, "Lord, by this time there will be a stench, for he has been dead four days."

"Did I not say to you that if you believe, you will see the glory of God?" Jesus replied.

They removed the stone and, after praying to the Father, Jesus "cried out with a loud voice, 'Lazarus, come out!'" (John 11:38–43).

Then, Lazarus, "the man who had died," came out of the tomb alive (John 11:44).

Simply astounding. Jesus is Lord even over death.

This is a comforting thought indeed, especially in the midst of great suffering and death all around us. In times of exceptional hardship, such as in the midst of a pandemic or war, we might simply hope for that hardship to be over—for the suffering and death associated with it to cease and life to return to "normal." But, even after a particular time of significant trial and hardship is over, people will continue to suffer and die of various causes. And, we will endure other maladies and hardships.

Yet, there is hope beyond whatever might plague you as you read now. In Jesus, Christians have the hope of the resurrection and the final defeat of suffering and death forevermore. In the end, God "will wipe away every tear from their eyes; and there will no longer be any death; there will no longer be any mourning, or crying, or pain; the first things have passed away" (Rev. 21:4).

But what is death? What happens to humans when we die? These questions not only deal with the state of the dead but also with questions about human constitution. In this regard, while many believe humans have (or are) immortal souls, no text in Scripture affirms the immortality of the soul. On the contrary, as seen earlier, Scripture teaches that God "alone possesses immortality" (1 Tim. 6:16), humans are mortal, and eternal life is a gift *conditional* upon accepting salvation. In these and other ways, Scripture consistently teaches that humans are only *conditionally* immortal. The saved live forever *with* God, but the lost perish forever.

> *Scripture teaches that God "alone possesses immortality," humans are mortal, and eternal life is a gift conditional upon accepting salvation.*

Regarding the state of the dead, biblical scholars widely recognize that Scripture consistently depicts human death as an unconscious sleep. Daniel 12:2 states, "those who sleep in the dust of the ground will awake," some "to everlasting life, but the others to disgrace and everlasting contempt." Likewise, Paul writes of the dead awaiting the resurrection as "those who are asleep" (1 Thess. 4:13; see also 4:14–15) and those who "sleep" (1 Cor. 15:51–52; see also 1 Cor. 15:6, 18, 20; 2 Pet. 3:4). According to these texts, from the time humans die until resurrection they are in a state referred to as "sleep."

When Stephen died from stoning, the text says, "he fell asleep" (Acts 7:60). And Jesus Himself referred to death as "sleep." When He received news of Lazarus's death, Jesus said, "Our friend Lazarus has fallen asleep; but I am going so that I may awaken him from sleep." While the disciples initially thought Jesus "was speaking about actual sleep," the text tells us that Jesus "had spoken of his death" and Jesus "said to them plainly, 'Lazarus died'" (John 11:11–14; see also Matt. 9:24; Mark 5:39; Luke 8:52). Then, after Lazarus was dead for four days, Jesus resurrected him (John 11:44).

Significantly, in this regard, Peter preached that King David (who died roughly one thousand years earlier) was not in heaven but remained in the grave awaiting resurrection (Acts 2:29, 34). Peter emphasized this to show that David prophesied of Christ's resurrection when David wrote, "My flesh also will live in hope; for You will not abandon my soul to Hades [that is, the grave; see below], nor will You allow Your holy one to undergo decay" (Acts 2:26–27, quoting Ps. 16:10). David must have been writing about the resurrection of the Davidic Messiah (Christ), Peter explained, because David himself "both died and was buried, and his tomb is with us to this day" and "it was not David who ascended into heaven" (Acts 2:29, 34).

Specifically, Peter declared, "because he [David] was a prophet and knew that GOD HAD SWORN TO HIM WITH AN OATH TO SEAT ONE OF HIS DESCENDANTS ON HIS THRONE, he looked ahead and spoke of the resurrection of the Christ, that HE WAS NEITHER ABANDONED TO HADES, nor did His flesh SUFFER DECAY. It is this Jesus whom God raised up, a fact to which we are all witnesses," but "it was not David who ascended into heaven" (Acts 2:30–32, 34).

If the saved dead go to heaven when they die, Peter's exposition would not make sense. But, Peter emphasizes, given that we know David "died and was buried, and his tomb is with us to this day" and "it was not David who ascended into heaven" (Acts 2:29, 34), those verses from David's Psalm are rightly understood as a prophecy of the Messiah, the covenantal Son of David. Later, Paul likewise preached of this prophecy, "YOU WILL NOT ALLOW YOUR HOLY ONE TO UNDERGO DECAY" (Acts 13:35, quoting Ps. 16:10), emphasizing that David "fell asleep, and was buried among his fathers and underwent decay; but He [Christ] whom God raised did not undergo decay" (Acts 13:36–37).

Notably, throughout Scripture, the term *hadēs* (*sheol* in Hebrew in Psalm 16) refers to the grave—the place of the dead wherein (as we will see below) no one is conscious.

Indeed, the death Scripture describes as "sleep" is an unconscious state. According to Ecclesiastes 9, "the living know that they will die; but the dead do not know anything, nor do they have a reward any longer, for their memory is forgotten. Indeed their love, their hate, and their zeal have already perished, and they will no longer have a share in all that is done under the sun" and "there is no activity, planning, knowledge, or wisdom in Sheol where you are going" (Eccl 9:5–6, 10). Psalm 6:5 adds, "there is no mention of You [God] in death; in Sheol [the grave], who will praise You?" Psalm 115:17 likewise teaches, "the dead do not praise the LORD, nor do any who go down into silence" (cf. Ps. 146:3–4).

Yet, if humans are conscious in death, as many suppose, how could it be that in death there is no mention or praise of God? If a righteous worshiper of God were conscious in death, surely that person would pray to God and praise God and otherwise "mention" God and give God "thanks." There is no mention of God in death because, as Ecclesiastes 9:5, 10 reveals, "the dead do not know anything" and "there is no activity, planning, knowledge, or wisdom in Sheol [i.e., the grave]."

According to these passages, the dead know nothing and have no reward. This is incompatible with the view that when humans die, their soul or spirit departs and exists consciously in heaven or "hell" or a middle place. Rather, these passages teach that human death is an unconscious state. When humans die, no conscious entity survives. Death is the cessation of human life as a whole.

What, then, about the "soul" or "spirit," concepts regarding which there is so much discussion? Here, there is much confusion because of popular (mis)conceptions of what terms like "soul" and "spirit" mean in Scripture.

First, as seen earlier, there is no human "soul" or "spirit" that survives the final destruction of the wicked (the result of the second death, see chapter 19). Jesus makes this clear when He warns, "do not be afraid of those who kill the body but are unable to kill the soul; but rather fear Him who is able to destroy both soul and body in hell" (Matt. 10:28).

Second, Scripture portrays human living beings as the product of a material body and the breath of life from God. As Genesis 2:7 explains, "God formed the man of dust from the ground, and breathed into his nostrils the breath of life; and the man became a living person [*nephesh hayyah*]." It is the *combination* of the material body and the breath of life that amounts to the human living being or, as the King James Version puts it, the human "living soul [*nephesh hayyah*]."

Third, Scripture portrays death as the *reversal* of this combination of the material body and breath (or spirit) of life. Specifically, Ecclesiastes 12:7 describes death by saying, "then the dust will return to the earth as it was, and the spirit [*ruah*] will return to God who gave it." Likewise, Psalm 104:29 states: "You [God] take away their breath [*ruah*], they perish and return to their dust" (cf. 104:30). And Psalm 146:4 teaches, "His spirit [*ruah*] departs, he returns to the earth; On that very day his plans [or "thoughts"] perish." Notice, here, that the "spirit" (*ruah*) that "departs" is *not* conscious for "on that very day his plans [or "thoughts"] perish." When the breath/spirit departs, the human is dead (Eccles. 12:7), with no conscious existence remaining (Eccles. 9:5–10).

In this regard, many biblical references to the human "spirit" (*ruah* in the Old Testament and *pneuma* in the New Testament) refer to that which gives life or animates humans. For instance, James 2:26 states, "the body without the spirit [*pneuma*] is dead."

Here, it is crucial to recognize that the Hebrew and Greek terms translated as "soul" and "spirit" are used in Scripture with a range of meanings in different contexts.[28] For instance, the terms sometimes translated as "soul" often refer to the entirety of the person or the life of the person that might be lost. For example, God states, "Behold, all souls [*nephesh*] are Mine; the soul [*nephesh*] of the father as well as the soul [*nephesh*] of the son is Mine. The soul [*nephesh*] who sins will die" (Ezek. 18:4). Here, notice, that the "soul" (*nephesh*) can die. Likewise, Jesus warns, "whoever wants to save his life [*psychē*] will lose it; but whoever loses his life [*psychē*] for My sake will find it. For what good will it do a person if he gains the whole world, but forfeits his soul [*psychē*]? Or what will a person give in exchange for his soul [*psychē*]?" (Matt. 16:25–26).

Here, the New Testament term often translated as "soul" (*psychē*) refers to one's life, which can *finally* be lost.

The term sometimes translated as *"soul"* in the Old Testament (*nephesh*) sometimes refers in Scripture to the entire person, the life or self of a person, or the seat of human desires, appetite, emotions, and passions. The corresponding term, often translated *"soul"* in the New Testament (*psychē*), also sometimes refers to the whole person or one's life or one's self, but other times refers to some aspect of humans such as the seat of human spirituality, morality, thinking, and emotions (cognitive/affective/spiritual/moral aspects).[29] Notably, however, animals also have "the breath of life" (Gen. 7:15, 22) and become "living creatures [*nephesh hayyah*]" (Gen. 1:20; cf. 1:24; 2:19) and are spoken of as "creatures" who "had life [*psychē*]" (Rev. 8:9; cf. 16:3). The terms by themselves, then, do not refer to unique aspects of human nature.[30]

Further, the term often translated as spirit throughout the Old Testament (*ruah*), when used of humans, often refers to the breath or life principle that animates human beings but also has other nuanced meanings (including often referring to the Spirit of God).[31] Likewise, when used of humans, the term most often translated as spirit throughout the New Testament (*pneuma*) often refers to the human life force but may also refer to aspects of humanity and frequently refers to the Holy Spirit.[32]

The biblical terms translated soul and spirit, then, sometimes refer to the entire human, but at other times refer to aspects of a human or to the life and vitality of a human. In this regard, "although the Bible views the nature of man as a unity, it does not precisely define the relationship among body, soul, and spirit."[33] Sometimes, the terms for soul and spirit are used interchangeably, such as when Mary proclaims, "My soul [*psychē*] exalts the Lord, and my spirit [*pneuma*] has rejoiced in God my Savior" (Luke 1:46–47). Most often, human beings are described in terms of body and soul (Matt. 10:28) or body and spirit (1 Cor. 7:34; cf. James 2:26), but other instances speak of humanity in terms of body, soul, *and* spirit (1 Thess. 5:23; Heb. 4:12) and even with wording like "heart," "soul," "mind," and "strength" (Mark 12:30). But, in Scripture, the terms translated "soul" (*nephesh* and *psychē*) or "spirit" (*ruah* and *pneuma*) never depict an *immortal* human soul or an entity that exists consciously apart from the human body after death.[34]

Here, some might raise questions about Revelation 6:9–10, "I saw underneath the altar the souls [*psychē*] of those who had been killed because of the word of God . . . and they cried out with a loud voice, saying, 'How long, O Lord, holy and true, will You refrain from judging and avenging our blood on those who live on the earth?'" (cf. Rev. 20:4). However, this should not be taken as a literal description; it is apocalyptic imagery that figuratively expresses the injustice of the martyrdom of faithful persons, to be rectified in the coming judgment.[35] Something akin to this figurative language appears in Genesis 4:10 when God says to Cain after he killed his brother, "the voice of your brother's blood is crying out to Me from the ground."[36]

What, however, about the story of the witch of Endor? After the prophet Samuel's death, King Saul inquired of God for counsel, but God did not answer. So, in direct disobedience against God's many clear commands to have nothing to do with spiritualism and occult practices like necromancy (e.g., Deut. 18:10–15; Isa. 47:13–14), Saul went to consult a witch and asked her to conjure Samuel up from the grave. When Saul asked what the woman saw, she said, "I see a divine being [*elohim*] coming up from the earth" (1 Sam. 28:13). This is crucial. We have already seen that the term *elohim*, which usually refers to God, in a few cases refers to celestial creatures such as fallen "demons" who are evil spirits (e.g., Deut. 32:17). In light of all the biblical evidence, Adventists believe Saul did not communicate with Samuel, but with an evil spirit impersonating Samuel.[37]

This highlights one reason why understanding the state of the dead matters today. Before Christ's return, the enemy will seek to deceive the world through spiritualism—sending "unclean spirits" that "are spirits of demons, performing signs" to deceive and gather the world against the truth of God (Rev. 16:13). It is crucial, then, that we understand the dangers of spiritualism and are not susceptible to being tricked into thinking one of our dead loved ones is communicating with us today, leaving us susceptible to the doctrines of demons. Again, Scripture commands us to have nothing to do with occult practices, such as attempting to communicate with the dead; the devil can use such practices to deceive people.

In all this, Adventists believe that humans do not possess an immortal soul but are only conditionally immortal (for God "alone possesses immortality," 1 Tim. 6:16). And humans do not possess a soul or spirit that exists consciously apart from the body (a conscious, separable soul).

That is, Adventists believe the biblical data teaches a kind of wholism, emphasizing the unity of human nature and denying both that humans have an immortal soul and that humans have a soul that exists consciously apart from the body. Instead, Adventists believe that when humans die, they are unconscious until resurrection. And only those who are saved by God will inherit eternal life, while those who are not will experience the second death and perish forever.

In keeping with this wholistic understanding of human nature, Adventists place considerable emphasis on healthy living, believing that it is our duty to care for the body that God has given us and, in doing so, extend the positive impact we might have on the world (cf. 1 Cor. 6:19–20; see also chapter 14).

The Future Hope for Humanity: The Embodied Destiny of Humans

Death is an enemy—the last enemy to be destroyed (1 Cor. 15:26). The fact that death is a sleep (an unconscious state) is good news, for it means saved persons who die are not aware of the struggles and suffering of loved ones here on earth. They are not consciously waiting for ages to reunite with loved ones. Since "the dead do not know anything" (Eccles. 9:5) and their "plans [thoughts] perish" when they die (Ps. 146:4), the dead do not experience the time passing from their death to resurrection. Instead, they rest in perfect, unconscious peace (spared from awareness of this world's ongoing evils), and the very next thing they know, they will see Jesus in the resurrection. As far as their experience is concerned, it is *as if* they are raised to eternal life with Christ and loved ones immediately after death.[38]

> Death is an enemy—the last enemy to be destroyed.

As Paul writes, "we who are alive and remain until the coming of the Lord will not precede those who have fallen asleep. For the Lord Himself will descend from heaven with a shout, with the voice of the archangel and with the trumpet of God, and the dead in Christ will rise first. Then we who are alive, who remain, will be caught up together with them in the clouds to meet the Lord in the air, and so we will always be with the Lord" (1 Thess. 4:15-17). Notice, when Christ returns "the dead in Christ will rise first." They are not risen yet. When Christ returns, those who remain alive waiting *and* those "dead in Christ" will be "caught up together" and be with God forevermore. Hallelujah!

What about the thief on the cross, then, whom Jesus told, "Truly I say to you today you will be with Me in Paradise". (Luke 23:43)? I intentionally omitted the comma included in the translation here because there was no comma in the Greek text. In isolation, the verse could be read as "Truly I say to you, today you will be with Me in Paradise." Or, it could be read as: "Truly I say to you today, you will be with Me in Paradise." Read the second way, Jesus is not saying they would be together in paradise that very day but is using the word "today" to emphasize the surety of His promise—something like saying, "I am telling you right now."

Which reading is correct? The reading consistent with the immediate and wider context of Scripture. As seen earlier, Scripture repeatedly teaches that the state of human death is a state of unconsciousness (referred to as "sleep"). That is, from death until resurrection, humans are not conscious. Moreover, when Jesus met Mary after He rose from the dead, He said, "Do not cling to Me, for I have not yet ascended to My Father" (John 20:17, NKJV). Jesus Himself was not in heaven personally on the day of His crucifixion. He could not, then, have personally been there with the thief on the cross that day. So, the second reading is the one that best fits the context and is consistent with Scripture's wider teaching.

Some might wonder, here, about Paul's statements about "having the desire to depart and be with Christ" rather than "remain on in the flesh" (Phil. 1:23-24) and "prefer[ring] rather to be absent from the body and to be at home with the Lord" (2 Cor. 5:8). Do these texts indicate Paul hoped to *immediately* be with Christ in a disembodied state when he died?

First, the context is key. In 2 Corinthians 5, Paul contrasts the body he possessed then (which he calls the "earthly tent") with the resurrection body the redeemed will receive (which he calls "our dwelling from heaven"). Specifically, he writes, "in this tent [one's present body] we groan, longing to be clothed with our dwelling from heaven [one's resurrection body], since in fact after putting it on, we will not be found naked. For indeed, we who are in this tent groan, being burdened, because we do not want to be unclothed but to be clothed, so that what is mortal will be swallowed up by life" (2 Cor. 5:2-4; cf. Rom. 7:24).

Here, Paul talks of being clothed when "what is mortal will be swallowed up by life," indicating that being "clothed with our dwelling from heaven" refers to a heavenly body, what Paul called the "spiritual body" in his first letter to the Corinthians (1 Cor. 15:44). There, Paul contrasts the "natural body" of humans prior to death with the "spiritual body" of resurrected humans. Specifically, Paul there writes of "the resurrection of the dead," teaching, "It is sown a perishable body, it is raised an imperishable body; it is sown in dishonor, it is raised in glory; it is sown in weakness, it is raised in power; it is sown a natural body, it is raised a spiritual body. If there is a natural body, there is also a spiritual body.... For this perishable must put on the imperishable, and this mortal must put on immortality" (1 Cor. 15:42-44, 53).

In this context, Paul states, "while we are at home in the body [his present body] we are absent from the Lord" (2 Cor. 5:6), and we "prefer rather to be absent from the body and to be at home with the Lord" (2 Cor. 5:8). Read in context, Paul is not speaking of a disembodied state after death (he already stated he does "not want to be unclothed," 2 Cor. 5:4), but is metaphorically speaking of his longing to put off the *clothing* of his mortal body and be *clothed* instead with his "spiritual" resurrection body (cf. Rom. 7:24).

Notably, Paul's teaching affirms that bodily existence is good, but our current bodily state has been corrupted. Bodily human existence was part of God's good creation in the beginning. As such, we should neither deny bodily needs nor think of material existence as something less than good that is to be escaped. The pain and suffering of our present bodily existence, from which we rightly long to escape, is a result of the Fall rather than an intrinsic part of bodily existence. In the end, humans will again enjoy bodily existence in "spiritual" bodies, but without suffering or death (see Rev. 21:4).

Second, elsewhere Paul repeatedly speaks figuratively of being "absent in body but present in spirit" (1 Cor. 5:3; Col. 2:5) *with* those to whom he writes. But such statements do not indicate Paul was literally absent from his body and present with them in some disembodied ("spirit") state. These are figurative expressions similar to saying to a loved one with whom I cannot be physically present, "I'm with you in spirit."

Third, given Scripture's teaching that human death is an unconscious state until resurrection, once Paul died the next experience he would have would be to awaken in Christ's presence. As such, Paul's expressed "desire to depart and be with Christ" (Phil. 1:23) and "be absent from the body and to be at home with the Lord" (2 Cor. 5:8) is consistent with understanding human death as an unconscious state. As far as Paul's experience is concerned, if he were to die, it would be *as if* Paul were with Christ in the very next moment.

Thus, consistent with Paul's own teaching that those who are dead "have fallen asleep" and "the dead in Christ will rise" when Christ returns (1 Thess. 4:14–16; cf. John 5:28–29; Acts 2:29, 34), Paul looks forward to receiving his reward on resurrection day, emphasizing the blessed hope of the resurrection at Christ's return, when the dead who "have fallen asleep through Jesus" (1 Thess. 4:14) will be raised to life (cf. Job 19:25–26; 2 Tim. 4:7–8; Rev. 22:12). As he proclaims: "Behold, I am telling you a mystery; we will not all sleep, but we will all be changed, in a moment, in the twinkling of an eye, at the last trumpet; for the trumpet will sound, and the dead will be raised imperishable, and we will be changed. For this perishable must put on the imperishable, and this mortal must put on immortality. But when this perishable puts on the imperishable, and this mortal puts on immortality, then will come about the saying that is written: 'DEATH HAS BEEN SWALLOWED UP in victory. WHERE, O DEATH, IS YOUR VICTORY? WHERE, O DEATH, IS YOUR STING?'" (1 Cor. 15:50–55). Amen and Amen.[39]

Conclusion: Why Does It Matter?

The thought of death terrified him. So, he did everything he could to try not to think of it often. He stayed busy with work or entertainment. But the more he tried to fill his life with distractions, the more miserable he became.

Unless Jesus returns before then, one day you will die. I am sorry to be the bearer of bad news. But it is true, for it is appointed "for people to die once, and after this comes judgment" (Heb. 9:27).

Even now, you and I are in the process of dying. We do everything we can to hide from this reality. Many humans live their lives as if they will never end. And much of the world around us is designed so that we will not take the time to ponder the harsh reality of this life in this world—so we will not reflect on the transience and relative meaninglessness of *this* life in and of itself.

Some have thought that because death is inevitable, we might as well live life to the fullest now. *Carpe diem!* Seize the day! Others proclaim, "eat, drink, and be merry, for tomorrow we die." This way leads only to misery and emptiness and what many have described as the meaninglessness and absurdity of life without God.

It is true that we should live life to the fullest now with the recognition that we are mortal and one day will die (unless Christ returns first). But what it means to live life to the fullest is rather different from what society depicts.

The only life that satisfies the deepest longings of the human heart is life with God, for humans have been created and designed by God for relationship with God. Just as hunger is satisfied only by food, nothing else can satisfy our deep longing for meaning, value, and love that is found ultimately in relationship with God—the source of these and all other good things.

> **The only life that satisfies the deepest longings of the human heart is life with God, for humans have been created and designed by God for relationship with God.**

If this is all there is, life would seem to be without meaning. But there is more. There is hope beyond what we can imagine. Eternal life with God is better than anything we could wish for (1 Cor. 2:9).

The sinfulness of human nature has blinded many to these and other truths. But we have seen in this chapter that Scripture teaches that humans are not immortal but depend on connection with God in order to live. Because of sin, all humans are subject to death and (apart from God's work in and for us) enslaved to sin. But death is not God's will for us. Life is a precious gift. What are you doing with yours?

There is only one full and effective solution to the corruption and mortality that plagues all humans, taken up in the next chapter, but to receive its benefits, we must recognize the problem. We are sinners, and we need a Savior outside of ourselves. You cannot save yourself from sin. Just as a leopard cannot change its spots, you cannot rid yourself of your sinful nature. And you cannot live apart from God. Life is only possible in relationship with God. Those who live seemingly apart from Him are nevertheless sustained by God's grace, even if they do not know it. But finally, each person must choose whether they will live with God in accordance with unselfish love or whether they will choose to cut themselves off from God (and thus from life itself).

Do you want to live? Do you want to be free from sin and evil and death? We are so accustomed to evil that sometimes it does not seem so bad to us. After being in a dark room for a long time, our eyes become accustomed to darkness, so much so that sudden light hurts our eyes. Even so, some of us have grown so accustomed to sin and darkness that we do not recognize our deep desire and longing for the light and love that flows from Christ.

But simply ask yourself, do you want to live? Do you want to be loved and to love forever? If so, God loves you already, and He will transform and save you; He will rescue you *"from the domain of darkness"* and transfer you to Christ's kingdom of light and love (Col. 1:13).

Perhaps you think you are beyond hope. You are not. God calls to you even now: "'As I live!' declares the Lord GOD, 'I take no pleasure at all in the death of the wicked, but rather that the wicked turn from his way and live. Turn back, turn back from your evil ways! Why then should you die?" (Ezek. 33:11).

If you hear His voice, do not harden your heart. Open your heart to Him, and He will come in and heal you and save you, so that you can live in light and love *with Him* forever.

Even now, I invite you to read and reflect on Psalm 51 and consider praying the words of David as your own prayer of repentance from sin. If you do, God will hear you. God will forgive. And God will make you a new creation, as described in the next chapter.

Questions for Reflection

1. Are humans free? Are there senses in which humans are free, but not entirely free? Why does it matter?
2. How do you make decisions about what you will do and how you will live?

3. Are humans born sinners? If so, what does that mean? Is it unfair that humans inherit a "sinful" nature?
4. Why does it matter how humans are constituted? Does this hold implications for human value?
5. Do all humans live forever? What happens after we die? What are some practical implications of beliefs in this regard? What about practices that some engage in attempting to communicate with the dead?
6. Have you ever contemplated your own death? How does realizing that eventually (unless Christ returns first) you and everyone you know will die put life in perspective? What really matters, given this understanding?
7. You can have eternal life even now. Though you are by nature mortal, God can give you eternal life. Do you want to live with Him forever? If so, ask Him now to save you to be with Him forever. Invite Him to do whatever it takes to cleanse you from sin and save you. He will do it. He wants to deliver you from sin and death even more than you want to be delivered. He promised He will hear you, and He always keeps His promises.

For Further Reading

Adventist Perspectives:

Adams, Roy. "The Nature of Sin: Understanding Its Character and Complexity." In *Salvation: Contours of Adventist Soteriology*. Edited by Martin F. Hanna, Darius W. Jankiewicz, and John W. Reeve. Berrien Springs, MI: Andrews University Press, 2018.

Bacchiocchi, Samuele. *Immortality or Resurrection? A Biblical Study on Human Nature and Destiny*. Berrien Springs, MI: Biblical Perspectives, 1998.

Cairus, Aecio C. "The Doctrine of Man." In *Handbook of Seventh-day Adventist Theology*. Edited by Raoul Dederen. Hagerstown, MD: Review and Herald, 2000.

Fowler, John. "Sin." In *Handbook of Seventh-day Adventist Theology*. Edited by Raoul Dederen. Hagerstown, MD: Review and Herald, 2000.

Froom, Le Roy Edwin. *The Conditionalist Faith of Our Fathers*. 2 vols. Washington, DC: Review and Herald, 1965–1966.

Gulley, Norman R. *Systematic Theology: The Church and Last Things*. Berrien Springs, MI: Andrews University Press, 2016.

Hanna, Martin. "What Shall We Say About Sin? A Study of *Hamartia* in Paul's Letter to the Romans." In *God's Character and the Last Generation*. Edited by Jiří Moskala and John C. Peckham. Nampa, ID: Pacific Press, 2018.

Jankiewicz, Darius. "Sin and Human Nature: Historical Background," in *Salvation: Contours of Adventist Soteriology*, ed. Martin F. Hanna, Darius W. Jankiewicz, and John W. Reeve. Berrien Springs, MI: Andrews University Press, 2018.

Knight, George R. "The Sinful Nature and Spiritual Ability." In *Salvation: Contours of Adventist Soteriology*. Edited by Martin F. Hanna, Darius W. Jankiewicz, and John W. Reeve. Berrien Springs, MI: Andrews University Press, 2018.

Moskala, Jiří and John Reeve, eds. *God and Death* (Berrien Springs, MI: Andrews University Press, forthcoming).

Wahlen, Clinton, ed. *What Are Human Beings That You Are Mindful of Them?* Silver Spring, MD: Review & Herald, 2015.

See also the resources on the Biblical Research Institute website: https://adventistbiblicalresearch.org/materials/.

Other Christian Perspectives:

Cullmann, Oscar. *Immortality of the Soul or Resurrection of the Dead: The Witness of the New Testament*. London: Epworth Press, 1958.

Fudge, Edward. *The Fire That Consumes: A Biblical and Historical Study of the Doctrine of Final Punishment*, 3rd ed. Cambridge: Lutterworth, 2012.

Green, Joel B. *Body, Soul, and Human Life: The Nature of Humanity in the Bible*. Grand Rapids, MI: Baker Academic, 2008.

—— and Stuart L. Palmer, eds., *In Search of the Soul: Four Views on the Mind-Body Problem*. Downers Grove, IL: InterVarsity, 2005.

McCall, Thomas H. *Against God and Nature: The Doctrine of Sin*. Wheaton, IL: Crossway, 2019.

Murphy, Nancey. *Bodies and Souls, or Spirited Bodies?* Cambridge: Cambridge University Press, 2006.

——— and Warren S. Brown. *Did My Neurons Make Me Do It? Philosophical and Neurobiological Perspectives on Moral Responsibility and Free Will.* Oxford: Clarendon, 2007.

Sprinkle, Preston, ed. *Four Views on Hell*, 2nd ed. Grand Rapids, MI: Zondervan, 2016.

13

GOD SAVES US: THE PROCESS OF SALVATION

"What must I do to inherit eternal life?" the man asked Jesus.

"You know the commandments," Jesus replied, then listed many of them.

"All these things I have kept since my youth," the man answered, perhaps hoping this revered teacher and miracle worker would commend him.

"One thing you still lack," Jesus replied. "Sell all that you possess and distribute the money to the poor, and you will have treasure in heaven; and come, follow Me."

When the man heard this, "he became very sad, for he was extremely wealthy. And Jesus looked at him and said, 'How hard it is for those who are wealthy to enter the kingdom of God! For it is easier for a camel to go through the eye of a needle, than for a rich person to enter the kingdom of God!'"

This astonished the audience, accustomed to thinking of riches as a sign of God's favor. "And so who can be saved?" they asked.

Jesus replied, "The things that are impossible with people are possible with God" (Luke 18:18–27).

Christ's replies indicate that salvation is costly *and* that salvation by human effort is impossible. The man might have thought his good works would save him. But only God's work can save humans.

Yet, God's work to save is costly. At the cross, God in Christ paid the highest price, giving His life to save humans even while humans murdered Him. However, while more costly than we can fathom, salvation is offered to us *freely* (cf. Rom. 6:23).

> *No amount of good works will procure salvation for you. Only Christ can.*

You cannot buy salvation, and you cannot earn it. No amount of good works will procure salvation for you. Only

Christ can. But, to receive the gift of salvation, an exchange is required. One must give oneself to Christ unreservedly—all one is and all one has. When Christ told the man to sell all his possessions and give the proceeds to the poor, He did not mean doing so would *earn* the man salvation. But He was teaching the man (and any who hear His message) that to follow Jesus, one's love and loyalty must be redirected from oneself to God's kingdom of unselfish love. Only by being willing to give what *filled* his heart, what he prized most, could the man be *filled* instead with God's unselfish love.

Sadly, the riches the man held onto were worthless in comparison to what Christ offered Him. Imagine clinging to filthy rags when offered the most magnificent and costly robe, which also granted admission to the King's banquet table (cf. Matt. 22:11–12). Invited to follow Jesus, the man instead held onto a little treasure in this world, which would pass away, thereby refusing to grasp the gift of eternal life and love, treasure of a kind that surpasses anything you could imagine and will never pass away (see 1 Cor. 2:9).

This chapter addresses crucial questions about salvation, such as: How can I be saved? How are we saved? Who can be saved? What does it look like to be saved?

The Story of Liberation by Way of the Cross

"Remember me when You come into Your kingdom!" the man said to Jesus (Luke 23:42). He was hanging on a cross next to Jesus in the midst of a most cruel and agonizing torture devised by the Roman imperial war machine—so extremely painful that from it the term "excruciating" is derived.

He had seen Jesus mocked and reviled by rulers and soldiers, who sneeringly jeered, "He saved others; let Him save Himself if this is the Christ of God, His Chosen One" and "If You are the King of the Jews, save Yourself!" (Luke 23:35–37).

But somehow, he recognizes that the man being crucified next to him at that very moment could save him. To this criminal's request of faith, Jesus replied, "Truly I say to you today you will be with Me in Paradise" (Luke 23:43).[1]

Little did that criminal know, the innocent One hanging next to him had worked to save the world from the moment sin entered it. Indeed, even before, Christ covenanted the plan of redemption with the Father and Spirit.

The Promised One

Throughout the history of Israel, this very One visited humans as the "angel of the Lord" (see chapter 4). Of this very One, Isaiah prophesied: "In all their distress He was distressed, and the angel of His presence saved them; in His love and in His mercy He redeemed them, and He lifted them and carried them all the days of old" (Isa. 63:9).

Indeed, more than seven hundred years prior to Christ's crucifixion, Isaiah prophesied:

> He was despised and abandoned by men,
> A man of great pain and familiar with sickness;
> And like one from whom people hide their faces,
> He was despised, and we had no regard for Him.
> However, it was our sicknesses that He Himself bore,
> And our pains that He carried;
> Yet we ourselves assumed that He had been afflicted,
> Struck down by God, and humiliated.
> But He was pierced for our offenses,
> He was crushed for our wrongdoings;
> The punishment for our well-being was laid upon Him,
> And by His wounds we are healed.
> All of us, like sheep, have gone astray,
> Each of us has turned to his own way;
> But the Lord has caused the wrongdoing of us all
> To fall on Him.
> He was oppressed and afflicted,
> Yet He did not open His mouth;
> Like a lamb that is led to slaughter,
> And like a sheep that is silent before its shearers,
> So He did not open His mouth.
> By oppression and judgment He was taken away;
> And as for His generation, who considered
> That He was cut off from the land of the living
> For the wrongdoing of my people, to whom the blow was due?

> And His grave was assigned with wicked men,
> Yet He was with a rich man in His death,
> Because He had done no violence,
> Nor was there any deceit in His mouth. (Isa. 53:3–7)

He "renders Himself as a guilt offering, He will see His offspring" and "will justify the many, for He will bear their wrongdoings.... Because He poured out His life unto death, and was counted with wrongdoers; yet He Himself bore the sin of many, and interceded for the wrongdoers" (Isa. 53:10–12).

In the midst of near despair after the Fall in Eden, God prophesied of this same One—the woman's Seed who would crush the serpent's head (Gen. 3:15). Here and elsewhere, the gospel itself is framed within the context of the cosmic conflict (cf. Heb. 2:14; 1 John 3:8). Via the cross, Christ would fulfill this promise, defeating Satan and making certain the liberation from the devil's domain of darkness and the final eradication of evil, suffering, and death.

Early in His ministry, Jesus announced that He was the anointed One (the Messiah) promised in Isaiah 61:1–2, the One "anointed" to "bring good news to the poor" and "proclaim release to captives, and recovery of sight to the blind, to set free those who are oppressed, to proclaim the favorable year of the LORD" (Luke 4:18–21).

Jesus did all this and more, even raising people like Lazarus from the dead. Yet, the people healed eventually died. Lazarus died again. Demons continued to oppress people individually, and demonic rulers continued to work through earthly rulers to oppress and enslave people.

Jesus came to bring more than such temporary healing and respite. He came to establish a kingdom of unselfish love unlike all human kingdoms, which would eventually eradicate the kingdom of darkness and the oppressive earthly kingdoms beholden to it (cf. Ps. 82), liberating people from demonic oppression of all kinds. Indeed, Jesus came not only to save individual persons but also to liberate this world and rid the cosmos of evil and injustice.

The "favorable year of the LORD" mentioned in the passage above referred to the year of Jubilee, which was to occur every fifty years, at the end of seven cycles of seven years wherein the seventh year was the *sabbatical* year in which (among other things) enslaved Israelites were to be released. The year of Jubilee was an even greater year of liberation, in which not only were slaves freed, but lands were to revert to their original owners, preventing landowning from being centralized in the hands of a wealthy few.

As the Messiah, Jesus would bring the ultimate fulfillment of the year of Jubilee, with full liberation and redemption and the eventual destruction of all oppressive systems. Even as the original Passover (see Exod. 12) was instituted when God liberated Israel from Egyptian slavery via the Exodus, Christ came as our Passover lamb (1 Cor. 5:7) to liberate the cosmos from sin and evil.

By His work—at the cross and beyond—Christ not only provides personal salvation but defeats the devil and his domain. Christ's kingdom brings perpetual truth, justice, and love, providing not only spiritual freedom but breaking every chain of bondage—bringing freedom from demonic principalities and powers and the earthly systems of oppression they foster.

To eradicate evil and set up a kingdom of unselfish love, however, God must first defeat the kingdom of darkness in a way that itself upholds all the principles of love and justice. Evil and injustice cannot be defeated by more evil and injustice. To eliminate evil and injustice, God Himself must act justly—according to His own law of unselfish love. The exact opposite of earthly rulers who grasp for power, Christ possessed the power to dominate everyone and everything but instead sacrificed Himself to save His murderers. God thus conquers evil, injustice, and oppression with their opposite—pure unselfish love that brings liberation and justice.

> To eliminate evil and injustice, God Himself must act justly—according to His own law of unselfish love.

This would be accomplished in two stages, the first consisting of Christ's legal defeat of Satan and his slanderous allegations in the heavenly court via the cross, and the second to be accomplished through Christ's ministry in the heavenly sanctuary (see chapter 16), finally culminating with His return to set all captives free forevermore.

The Cross

They came with swords and clubs and arrested Him at Gethsemane (Mark 14:43–46). Knowing what was to come, Jesus had been "deeply grieved, to the point of death" and prayed, "Abba! Father! All things are possible for You; remove this cup from Me; yet not what I will, but what You will" (Mark 14:34, 36). Thus, Jesus voluntarily gave Himself. No one took life from Him—He laid His life down on His own initiative (John 10:18) according to the plan of redemption covenanted within the divine Trinity before the foundation of the world.

They took Him by night to be tried by the Council. They brought false testimony against Him, charged Him with blasphemy for claiming to be the Son of God, and "condemned Him as deserving of death." Some spit on Him, blindfolded Him, and beat Him, saying, "Prophesy!" (Mark 14:64–65).

In the morning, they sent Him to Pilate, the Roman prefect of Judea. "Pilate questioned Him: 'So You are the King of the Jews?'" Jesus answered, "It is as you say" (Mark 15:1–2). Pilate then asked Jesus to answer the charges against Him, but Jesus did not answer them, "so Pilate was amazed" (Mark 15:3–5).

Being "aware that the chief priests had handed Him over because of envy," Pilate found no fault in Jesus. But the crowd shouted at Pilate, "Crucify Him!"

"Why, what evil has He done?" Pilate asked.

But they shouted all the more, "Crucify Him!" (Mark 15:10, 13–14).

So, "intent on satisfying the crowd," Pilate had "Jesus flogged" and "handed Him over to be crucified" (Mark 15:15).

Though innocent, Jesus was condemned to a torturous and agonizing death.

The soldiers took Him and "dressed Him in purple" to mock Him. They put a twisted "crown of thorns" on His head and mocked, "'Hail, King of the Jews!' And they repeatedly beat His head with a reed and spit on Him, and kneeling, they bowed down before Him." Finally, "they led Him out to crucify Him" (Mark 15:16–20).

Then, they crucified Him.

Crucifixion was a notoriously agonizing method of execution meant to deter any who would think to challenge Roman supremacy. But it was not the physical agony of the crucifixion that brought Jesus the most suffering, but the weight of the world's sins on His shoulders that crushed Him (see Isa. 53:4–5).

Even before they seized Him, Jesus was "deeply grieved, to the point of death" (Matt. 26:38) and in so much "agony" that "His sweat became like drops of blood, falling down upon the ground" (Luke 22:44).

As we have seen, sin and the (full) presence of God are incompatible—sin separates from God (Isa. 59:2). What Jesus, Himself human *and* divine, experienced by taking the world's sins on His shoulders is beyond description.

While Jesus was on the cross, "darkness fell over the whole land" from "the sixth hour ... until the ninth hour" and, finally, "Jesus cried out with a loud voice ... 'MY GOD, MY GOD, WHY HAVE YOU FORSAKEN ME?'" (Mark 15:33–34).

Even in the midst of unfathomable anguish, Jesus prayed for the very ones who tortured and killed Him. "Father, forgive them; for they do not know what they are doing" (Luke 23:34).

Though He possessed the power to deliver Himself from the cross at any time, Christ freely paid the infinite price so that we may be saved freely, without cost. He "gave Himself as a ransom for all" (1 Tim. 2:6). He willingly took on Himself what we deserve so that we may receive what He deserves. Though He "committed no sin ... He Himself brought our sins in His body up on the cross, so that we might die to sin and live for righteousness; by His wounds you were healed" (1 Pet. 2:22, 24; cf. Isa. 53:4–5; 2 Cor. 5:21).

Thus, Christ provided the ultimate demonstration of God's righteousness and love, both the just and the justifier of those who believe (Rom. 3:25–26; 5:8). Christ "suffered for sins once for all time, the just for the unjust, so that He might bring us to God, having been put to death in the flesh, but made alive in the spirit" (1 Pet. 3:18).

"Jesus let out a loud cry, and died. And the veil of the temple was torn in two from top to bottom. And when the centurion ... saw that He died in this way, he said, 'Truly this man was the Son of God!'" (Mark 15:33, 37–39).

The story of redemption is the story of God's love. God (the Son) became a man, suffered torture and human death, and thereby provided the ultimate demonstration of righteousness and love (Rom. 3:25–26; 5:8; cf. John 15:13), defeating the devil's charges in order to save the world.

And His death was not the end.

He rose to life as the "firstborn from the dead" (Col. 1:18), that we may also be resurrected.

He died *by* sin so we might die *to* sin (cf. Rom. 6:11) and live forever *with* Him in whom there is no sin, but only perfect, unselfish love.

Through Him, the unique Son of God, we might be adopted as children of God, with an inheritance beyond imagining (Rom. 8:15, 23; Eph. 1:5).

Yet, the reconciliation of God and humans is not complete. Christ's work of atonement continues. Even now, Christ intercedes and ministers for us in the heavenly sanctuary (Heb. 8:1–6; 9:11–12) to provide both forgiveness and cleansing (1 John 1:9).

One day, He will return as He promised (John 14:1–3) to take all who love Him to live *with* Him forever in eternal bliss.

How Does God Save?

Sin did not catch God by surprise. God's plan of salvation, the mystery of the gospel (Eph. 3:9), was in place before the world began (1 Cor. 2:7; cf. Rom. 16:25–26; Rev. 13:8). Christ would manifest God's unfathomable love and thus triumph over evil by taking on humanity, giving Himself and submitting to death on the cross as an innocent victim of evil, offering Himself as a substitute for sinners so that all who believe in Him might not perish but have everlasting life (see John 3:16; 10:15–18; 15:13; Phil. 2:7; 1 John 2:1).

To foreshadow this plan of redemption, God instituted a symbolic system of sacrifices, which prefigured the remedy to sin and evil—the perfect life and death of the Son of God, "the Lamb of God who takes away the sin of the world!" (John 1:29).[2]

After they sinned, Adam and Eve unsuccessfully tried to cover their guilt and shame with fig leaves. But God Himself covered their guilt—He made "garments of skin ... and clothed them," requiring the first animal sacrifice (Gen. 3:21). This sacrifice, like all others in the sacrificial system, pointed to Christ's sacrifice.

No animal death could provide the remedy (that is, atone) for sin, no skin could cover the enormity of iniquity, and no ritual or human action of any kind could heal the rift created by evil. Only God could. Christ Himself provided the once-for-all atonement (Heb. 9:12; 10:10; 1 Pet. 3:18).

What Is Atonement and Why Did Christ Die for Us?

Atonement is God's remedy for evil, which ruptured the God-world relationship.[3] Atonement is God's way of repairing that relationship, *reconciling* the world to Himself. God can do this, however, *only* in ways consistent with His perfect justice and love—for God "cannot deny Himself" (2 Tim. 2:13).

God desires to save sinners (2 Pet. 3:9), but the wages of sin is death (Rom. 3:23). How, then, can God save sinners without being unjust?

God justifies sinners while Himself remaining just by substituting Himself in our place so the consequences of sin fall on Him (see Rom. 3:23–26; 1 Tim. 2:6; 1 Pet. 1:18–19; 2:24; 3:18).[4] He is thus the "just and the justifier" (Rom. 3:26), defeating evil and injustice without Himself succumbing to evil or injustice, thereby defeating Satan's allegations in the cosmic conflict, redeeming and eventually liberating the cosmos (see Rev. 12:10–11; cf. Heb. 2:14; 1 John 3:8).

Here, though, numerous questions arise: Why was Christ's death needed for atonement? What did Christ thereby accomplish? Is atonement by substitution (substitutionary atonement) immoral or merely a legal fiction?

The cosmic conflict sheds significant light on these questions, ultimately manifesting there was no other way for God to save sinners without Himself being unjust and thus unloving because love and justice are intertwined and inseparable (see Ps. 33:5; 89:14; cf. Isa. 61:8; Jer. 9:24).

Why Was Christ's Death Needed for Atonement?

Sin requires a remedy. But why couldn't God reconcile sinners to Himself without Christ's death? Why couldn't God simply forgive sin without such sacrifice? Did God require blood to be satiated?[5]

No. Death is the opposite of what God desires (cf. Ezek. 18:32). It is not that God is unwilling to forgive without atonement. It is that God (morally) *cannot* forgive sin without atonement because doing so would itself be unjust, and God cannot deny Himself (2 Tim. 2:13).

The Father, Son, and Spirit *all* desire to save sinners. But, since God "cannot deny Himself" (2 Tim. 2:13) and "cannot lie" (Titus 1:2) and His promises are unbreakable (Heb. 6:18), God could not simply cancel or break His perfect law of unselfish love.[6] To overlook sin or change His law to accommodate it would mean God's moral law was arbitrary and unjust in the first place, as Satan alleged, and would amount to God Himself being unjust and unloving (either by prescribing *immoral* law in the first place or by transgressing the very law of love itself, on which the harmony of creation depends).[7]

Only by the law of unselfish love could a universe filled with free beings exist in perfect harmony without conflict of interest (self vs. other), in stark contrast to our world plagued by billions driven by incessant selfishness.[8] The flourishing of all beings in the universe depends on creatures unwaveringly living by the law of unselfish love—not out of fear or by force, but love, evoked by God's revelation of His unsurpassable love.

On the one hand, if humans could save themselves through lawkeeping, there would be no need for Christ's work (including His death) to save us—to accomplish for us what we could not accomplish for ourselves. Yet, on the other hand, if God could change or break the law of love, Christ need not have fulfilled the law and died for us, carrying for us "the wages of sin," which "is death" (Rom. 6:23). Sin inevitably leads to death because, absent a remedy for sin, it inevitably cuts one off from the perfectly holy God, the source of life, with whom evil cannot dwell (Ps. 5:4). In this regard, even as God does not break His promises (Heb. 6:18), God does not break His own laws (cf. Ps. 89:34). God is love and God's moral law is a perfect transcript of His character of love, not an external norm to which He must submit, nor an arbitrary norm, but one internal to His nature of love.[9]

In this regard, we've already seen it is impossible for creatures to live (totally) apart from God. Since sin necessarily separates from God (cf. Isa. 59:2), without a remedy for sin, sinners would inevitably perish.

Sin, then, inevitably leads to death. Yet, to justify repentant sinners *and* uphold the law of love, God (in Christ) took sin's consequences on Himself, ensuring that evil will finally be vanquished. God thus demonstrates to all that He is entirely just and loving and only desires what is best for us. Had there been any other way, would not Christ have chosen it instead of excruciating suffering and death? Christ Himself prayed in Gethsemane, "if it is possible, let this cup [of suffering and death] pass from Me; yet not as I will, but as You will" (Matt. 26:39).

It is not that God Himself needs to be satisfied or convinced to forgive. God is and was willing to forgive but can only do so in ways that uphold justice and love. So, God did what only He could do, "sending His own Son in the likeness of sinful flesh and as an offering for sin, He condemned sin in the flesh, so that the requirement of the Law might be fulfilled in us" (Rom. 8:3-4). In all this, "God was in Christ reconciling the world to Himself" (2 Cor. 5:19). That which God did not desire in itself, Christ's death, was God's will in this instance only because it was the only way to achieve His greater desire to save us while upholding His love and justice, the foundation of His kingdom (Ps. 89:14) and essential to who God is (Exod. 34:6-7).

> *Christ's death was God's will because it was the only way to achieve His greater desire to save us while upholding His love and justice.*

Competing Theories in Christian Theology: Models of Atonement

There are numerous views regarding just how Christ's work brought about atonement or reconciliation between God and creation, known as theories or models of atonement.

The main models are often categorized as objective or subjective. Objective models of the atonement emphasize what Christ's death accomplishes for humans apart from human response to Christ's work. Subjective models of the atonement emphasize the way Christ's death inspires humans to respond, often focusing on Christ as the example for humans to follow (exemplarist theories).[10]

Among models often classified as objective theories, the Christus Victor model emphasizes that through His death, Christ defeats Satan and the kingdom of darkness.[11] Because it was prevalent in the early centuries of Christianity, this model is sometimes called the classic theory of the atonement. Some early Christians depicted this as if Christ "tricked" the devil into accepting His death as a ransom, with the devil not realizing Christ would rise from the dead. This questionable version is often called the ransom theory of the atonement, but the Christus Victor approach does not require it.

The satisfaction theory, set forth by Anselm (1033/34-1109), identifies sin as an offense that dishonors God that can only be cleared by Christ's death, rendered to *satisfy* divine justice by balancing out injustice (providing a surplus of honor that can pay for the human deficit, such as in a feudal system).

In contrast to Anselm, Peter Abelard (1079-1142) is often identified as the father of the moral influence theory of the atonement. This theory stresses that Christ's death was the supreme revelation of God's love that serves to morally influence humans to follow Christ's example. This is typically categorized as a subjective theory, but some scholars note that Abelard's view included objective aspects and is not reducible to seeing Christ's death as *merely* an example.[12] Some who affirm a moral influence theory, however, deny Christ's death was needed as a *substitution* for sinners.

The penal substitution theory of the atonement emphasizes that Christ took upon Himself the penalty or punishment for sin that humans deserve as our substitute. It is typically traced to the Protestant Reformers, though some argue it was present far earlier in Christian thought.

The governmental theory of the atonement, typically traced to Hugo Grotius (1584-1645), characterizes Christ as a penal *example* whereby the justice of God's law and the moral government is upheld while sinners are pardoned.

Many classify the theories above as either subjective or objective, but many such theories involve both subjective and objective aspects. To take one more example, Irenaeus's (AD 130-202) recapitulation theory emphasized that Christ recapitulated history in His life, death, and resurrection—succeeding where the first Adam and humanity failed *and* that humanity is now to imitate Christ. For Irenaeus, Christ's life is accepted in place of all the sins of humanity, but Christ is also our teacher and example.

These models are often pitted against one another. But the problem with some theories of atonement is often not what they affirm but what they deny. Some will say Christ is your substitute, not your example (or vice versa), but this is a false dichotomy, pitting aspects of atonement affirmed in Scripture against one another.

What Does Christ Accomplish by His Work of Atonement?

No one aspect of the atonement is sufficient to capture the majesty, grandeur, and magnitude of salvation through Christ. Scripture presents the atonement as multi-faceted: Christ's work of atonement provides (among other things) the all-sufficient and perfect sacrifice, the effective mediator, our substitution, a ransom and redeemer, expiation (that is, removal of guilt) resulting in justification and reconciliation, victory over the power of evil, and an example of how humans should live in love relationship to God as well as a demonstration of God's righteousness and the depth and vastness of His love for us.

> *No one aspect of the atonement is sufficient to capture the majesty, grandeur, and magnitude of salvation through Christ.*

Let's take a closer look at some of these facets.

A Demonstration *and* Example of Unselfish Love

Christ died for us because God loves us, demonstrating His amazing love for us. As John 3:16 explains, "For God so loved the world, that He gave His only Son, so that everyone who believes in Him will not perish, but have eternal life." And Romans 5:8 proclaims, "God demonstrates His own love toward us, in that while we were still sinners, Christ died for us."

This demonstration provides the supreme example of unselfish love and inspires and awakens love in humans. In His life and death, Christ set an example of what God is like *and* provided the perfect example of humanity in relation to God. In giving Himself for us, He showed how humans should act in relation to God and others—the way of the Lamb, which is the way of unselfish love. As 1 Peter 2:21 teaches, Christ "suffered for you, leaving you an example, so that you would follow in His steps." The way of the Lamb calls us to love one another, for Christ loved us and gave Himself for us (Eph. 5:2; cf. Gal. 2:20).

A Substitutionary Atonement

Christ died for us, in our place, as our substitute. Scripture repeatedly teaches that Christ died for us (e.g., Isa. 53:6; Gal. 3:13; Eph. 5:2; Heb. 9:28; 1 Pet. 2:24; cf. 2 Cor. 5:14, 21). Specifically, Christ "suffered for sins once for all time, *the just for the unjust*, so that He might bring us to God" (1 Pet. 3:18, emphasis mine; cf. Rom. 4:25; 1 Cor. 5:7; 1 Tim. 2:6; 1 John 4:10).[13] Notice, Christ's sacrifice for our sins somehow makes it possible for Christ to bring us to God—to reverse the separation caused by sin.

Further, Peter writes, "Christ also suffered for you" and "He Himself brought our sins in His body up on the cross, so that we might die to sin and live for righteousness; by His wounds you were healed" (1 Pet. 2:21, 24). This last part quotes Isaiah 53:5, which in full reads: "he was wounded for our transgressions, crushed for our iniquities; upon him was the punishment that made us whole, and by his bruises we are healed" (NRSVue).[14]

This substitutionary aspect of atonement is intertwined with the demonstration of God's justice *and* love. Christ gave Himself for us "to demonstrate His [God's] righteousness" or justice so that He would *be just* even as He *justified* sinners—that is, "so that He would be just and the justifier of the one who has faith in Jesus" (Rom. 3:25-26). In parallel, Paul teaches, "God demonstrates His own love toward us, in that while we were still sinners, Christ died for us" (Rom. 5:8). In atonement, as elsewhere in Scripture, love and justice go together.

Christ's death was not *merely* a demonstration, however. It would make no sense for me to throw myself in front of a speeding car as a demonstration of love for my son. But, if my son were about to be struck by that speeding car, it would make sense to throw myself in front of the car and knock him out of the way to save him. In analogous fashion, Christ's death for our sins demonstrated God's love because Christ gave Himself to save us from sin, which inevitably brings death.

Faced with the choice of leaving us to "the wages of sin," which "is death" (Rom. 6:23) or taking those wages upon Himself, Christ chose to die for us, manifesting the greatest love (John 15:13). God could not simply acquit guilty sinners, for that would conflict with justice (Exod. 34:7). To save sinners, while remaining perfectly loving and just, God (in Christ) willingly took upon Himself the consequences of sin in our place (cf. 2 Cor. 5:21). This was the only way God could pardon humans without breaking the law of love that flows from God's nature and character of perfect love and justice, which would be impossible because God cannot deny Himself (2 Tim. 2:13).

A Sacrificial Atonement

Accordingly, Christ's substitutionary death was a sacrificial death, "a sacrifice of atonement by his blood, effective through faith" (Rom. 3:25,

NRSVue). Christ "is the atoning sacrifice for our sins, and not for ours only but also for the sins of the whole world" (1 John 2:2, NRSVue).

Just as the Passover lamb was the substitutionary offering for the firstborn Hebrews prior to the Exodus, Christ's death provided a vicarious offering for sinners (1 Cor. 5:7; Heb. 9:22; cf. Exod. 12; Heb. 9:12). Thus, Christ is our "Passover" lamb who "has been sacrificed" for us (1 Cor. 5:7); "the Lamb of God who takes away the sin of the world!" (John 1:29; cf. 1 Pet. 1:19; Rev. 5; 13:8).

Christ's sacrifice for our sins satisfies the just requirements of God's perfect law of unselfish love. Christ came "as an offering for sin," and thus God "condemned sin in the flesh, so that the requirement of the Law might be fulfilled in us" (Rom. 8:3–4).

This, however, was utterly *unlike* pagan sacrifices, which were given to manipulate gods to be benevolent toward offerers. First, Christ's sacrifice was not to appease the Father, so He would love and forgive us. Rather, Christ died for us because God *already* loved us (John 3:16; Rom. 5:8). Second, God did not sacrifice someone else for us. Rather, God (in Christ) voluntarily *gave Himself* to die for us so that we could be saved (see John 10:18; 2 Cor. 5:19). As Fleming Rutledge puts it: God "has not required human sacrifice; he has himself become the human sacrifice."[15] Kathryn Tanner adds, "God is both the one sacrificing and the one sacrificed. The whole act is God's."[16] What amazing love!

Atonement as Ransom, Redemption, and Reconciliation

Scripture also depicts Christ's sacrifice in terms of ransom and redemption. Christ "gave Himself as a ransom for all" (1 Tim. 2:6; cf. Matt. 20:28; Mark 10:45). And Christ "gave Himself for us to redeem us from every lawless deed" (Titus 2:14). Accordingly, "in Him we have redemption through His blood, the forgiveness of our wrongdoings, according to the riches of His grace" (Eph. 1:7; cf. Rom. 3:24; Heb. 9:12, 15; 1 Pet. 1:18–19).

In simplest terms, to provide redemption for someone (in the literal sense) is to make a payment on their behalf. This imagery arises from the Hebrew background of ransom payments to free people from bondage and/or cover debts they could not pay (Exod. 21:7–11; Ruth 1–4; Job 6:23).

This facet of the atonement relates to three significant questions: Is substitution immoral? Who is the recipient of redemption/ransom? Is justification brought about by atonement merely a legal fiction?

Regarding the first question, while in criminal cases substitution might be considered unjust, in civil cases one can *voluntarily* pay the fine of another. The judge can pay the traffic offender's fine if she chooses. Even in merely human legal systems, then, *voluntary* payment of one's penalties by another is not deemed unjust.[17] Further, in American law, a corporation can be criminally liable for crimes its employees commit and might pay restitution (among other legal consequences) and, in severe cases, even be dissolved (known as the "corporate death penalty"). Further, an entity that acquires a corporation takes on that corporation's liabilities.

In a somewhat analogous fashion, God can justly take on our liabilities or pay the wages of sin for all who are united with Christ by faith (analogous to the way one might assume and pay off the debts of another without any illegality or injustice). The wages of sin are not thereby removed, nor is the law thwarted or nullified, but God takes the "wages" upon Himself.

In doing so, God does not trivialize the heinousness of sin and the pain and suffering it causes victims. God is willing to forgive sin, but He will not pretend sin (which always harms people) is no big deal or not so bad after all or otherwise break the law of love. To do so would be neither just nor loving. No, sin must be dealt with. It cannot simply be swept under the rug because every sin affects relationships, and we know what happens when unresolved issues are allowed to fester continually in our relationships.

So, God Himself pays the price.

Who, then, is the recipient of the ransom/redemption transaction?

Scripture identifies Satan as "the accuser of our brothers and sisters" who continually points out that without penalty, the law would be breached, which would vindicate his charges against God and require his own acquittal (Rev. 12:10; cf. Zech. 3). Satan is the one who brings the accusations that must be answered in the heavenly court, but Satan does *not* receive any payment. God makes restitution relative to His law of unselfish love (cf. Rom. 8:3–4), Himself suffering the loss by way of the cross so we might lose nothing in the transaction while no one can rightly claim the law has not been fulfilled.

In the process of atonement, Christ removes the guilt from sinners by taking it upon Himself and dealing with it once and for all (Rom. 3:24–25; 1 John 2:2). This is called expiation, the removal of guilt, which results in what is technically called propitiation, the removal of wrath, rendering those in Christ justified and no longer under condemnation (Rom. 8:1). God's righteous wrath, itself a product of His love and justice, is always directed only at sin/guilt. Where there is no sin or guilt, there is no wrath. In much the same way any sane person should be angry at child abuse, God is always appropriately angry at sin since sin always harms God's children.

Expiation, however, is *not* appeasement of a bloodthirsty god but consists of God Himself taking on the cost of sin. God shoulders the world's guilt and the horrendous consequences of evil, thus removing the enormous weight of guilt from all who accept Him as their substitute so He may, in turn, bestow upon us the eternal weight of glory (cf. 2 Cor. 4:17).

In this way, those who accept Christ are justified—that is, declared to be just as a consequence of the removal of their guilt (see Rom. 3:26), removing that which separated them from God and thus reconciling them to God (Rom. 5:10–11; 2 Cor. 5:18–20; Eph. 2:11–16; Col. 1:19–22).

Is justification, then, a legal fiction? How can God declare us just if we are sinners? If God simply acquits the guilty, Satan's accusation that God is unjust would be valid.

But justification is not legal fiction. God does not clear the guilty (Exod. 34:7). This is why He took the penalty on Himself—to remove guilt from those who accept Him. Further, God's declaration of the believer's righteousness is not fictional as if God *pretends* that sinful and unjust people are actually sinless and just, but akin to a promissory note because God assures that His declaration regarding the righteousness of believers will become true in reality such that all who trust in Christ will be perfectly sinless and just in the end (at glorification, see below). God will finish in believers what He has begun (Phil. 1:6), *making* them righteous.

God's reconciling work—atonement—thus includes *both* the phase of forgiveness (justification) *and* cleansing (sanctification; cf. 1 John 1:9).

Though theologically distinct, justification and sanctification are inseparable.[18] Those in Christ by faith are covered by Christ's righteousness and thus accounted (reckoned) as righteous (Rom. 4:3–9; Gal. 3:6) while at the same time being made righteous over time by the process of God's work in them.

Christus Victor: Is God Truly Just in Saving Sinners?

Christ's work of atonement defeats the devil and liberates us from his kingdom of darkness. Indeed, the "Son of God appeared for this purpose, to destroy the works of the devil" (1 John 3:8). And Jesus died for us "so that through death He might destroy the one who has the power of death, that is, the devil, and free those who through fear of death were subject to slavery all their lives" (Heb. 2:14–15; cf. Gen. 3:15).

> **Christ's work of atonement defeats the devil and liberates us from his kingdom of darkness.**

The atonement thus encompasses more than the redemption of humans. Indeed, "the whole creation groans and suffers the pains of childbirth together until now" (Rom. 8:22), and through Christ, God will "reconcile all things to Himself, whether things on earth or things in heaven, having made peace through the blood of His cross" (Col. 1:20). Evil needs to be expunged and reconciliation accomplished not only at the level of individual humans but also corporately, systemically, and structurally. Christ came to (among other things) bring justice to the oppressed and downtrodden, heal the broken-hearted, set captives free (Luke 4:18), and deliver creation itself from bondage (see Rom. 8:19–23).[19] God's work of salvation includes finally replacing the earthly kingdoms of injustice and oppression with a kingdom of perfect, unselfish love.

The facets of atonement discussed in previous sections make a great deal of sense within a cosmic conflict context, which helps us understand why God (morally) could not simply overlook evil, but saving sinners required atonement. The very way God saves sinners (see also, chapter 16) triumphs over Satan's slanderous lies against God's character and government and his accusations against God's people in the heavenly court, claiming God cannot justly save such sinners (see Zech. 3:1–5; Jude 9; Rev. 12:10; cf. Job 1–2).

In the midst of this cosmic courtroom drama, Christ "came into the world, to testify to the truth" (John 18:37, NRSVue; cf. Rev. 3:14), exposing the lies of the enemy, the "father of lies," the arch-slanderer who "deceives the whole world" (John 8:44–45; Rev. 12:9). Indeed, Revelation 12:10–11 explicitly links Christ's sacrificial death with the defeat of Satan and his accusations before the heavenly court, saying: "Now the salvation, and the power, and the kingdom of our God and the authority of His Christ have come, for the accuser of our brothers and sisters has been thrown down, the one who accuses them before our God day and night. And they overcame him because of the blood of the Lamb and because of the word of their testimony" (Rev. 12:10–11).

Supremely demonstrating God's perfect righteousness (Rom. 3:4, 25–26) and love (Rom. 5:8), Christ's death on the cross legally defeated the devil's allegations against God's character and government (Rev. 12:10–11), bringing judgment to cast out the usurping "ruler of this world" (John 12:31; 14:30; 16:11) and disarming the powers of darkness (cf. Col. 2:15).[20]

The phase of atonement completed at the cross was the prerequisite for Christ's atoning ministry in the heavenly sanctuary after Christ's resurrection (Heb. 8:1–6; 9:11–12), mirrored by the Holy Spirit's coming in power to testify on earth (cf. John 7:39), and for the eventual eradication of the devil and death and evil itself that is still to come (see Rev. 21). Even after Christ's death on the cross, sessions in the heavenly court continue (see Rev. 4–5), with judgment in the heavenly court to take place prior to Christ's Second Coming (Dan. 7:9–10; Rev. 14:7, i.e., pre-Advent judgment, see much more on this in chapter 16).

In this regard, God's saving of sinners raises crucial questions like: Is God truly just in saving humans whose sins merit death? Is God just with regard to who is saved and who is not? Has God truly done all He could do to save the lost and done so with perfect justice for all concerned?

God answers these questions and others via the cross *and* Christ's ministry in the heavenly sanctuary, in the context of a preliminary judgment in the heavenly court prior to Christ's coming (the pre-Advent judgment, Dan. 7:9–10; Rev. 14:7), which precedes the final judgment after Christ's coming (the post-Advent judgment), described in Revelation 20:4–5 (cf. John 5:28–29; 1 Cor. 6:3; see chapter 16).

In His plan of redemption, God has made provision to save everyone, "not willing for any to perish, but for all to come to repentance" (2 Pet. 3:9; cf. John 3:16; 1 Tim. 2:4–6; Titus 2:11). Yet, because some reject Christ's provision, including even some who *claim* to accept Christ as Lord (see Matt. 7:21–23), not all will be saved. Yet, all will come into judgment (2 Cor. 5:10; cf. Matt. 12:36–37; Acts 17:31; Rom. 2:16; Heb. 10:27–11:2; Rev. 14:7; 20:12; 22:12).[21]

Before Christ's return, those who have truly accepted Christ as their Savior and Lord will be vindicated by heavenly court judgment (Dan. 7:9–10; 8:14, see chapter 16). Accordingly, when Christ comes again, all cases will have been decided such that Christ can justly "reward each according to his works" (Matt. 16:27, NKJV; cf. Rev. 20:12; 22:12).[22]

Since God is omniscient, God has no need of any investigation or judgment proceedings to reveal to Him who can justly be saved (2 Tim. 2:19). The pre-advent judgment, then, does not supply information to God but clearly manifests to others in the heavenly court and beyond that God is perfectly just (cf. 1 Cor. 4:9; see further discussion in chapter 16). God *justly* saves all sinners who can be saved, all who have true faith in Christ, which is manifested in love (see Matt. 25:31–46; cf. 22:11–12).

> **God justly saves all sinners who can be saved, all who have true faith in Christ, which is manifested in love.**

Christ gave everything for us, giving Himself to die as an innocent victim, thus laying to rest once and for all any claim that God is selfish or that His law is arbitrary or unjust. As such, God has done everything He could do to save every person and defeat evil without in any way compromising His justice (cf. Isa. 5; Matt. 21). Those who are not saved are lost due to their own decision to reject God's love—sadly, yet justly, condemned by their own refusal to have faith in Christ (cf. John 3:18).

In all this, just as God prophesied in Genesis 3:15, Christ's work of atonement triumphs over the devil and his domain, completely debunking the Satanic allegations that began the cosmic conflict and brought evil into the universe. The plan of redemption thus not only *justly* provides salvation for sinners but, while doing so, also accomplishes the vindication of God's character, not for God's sake, but for the good of the entire universe, reconciling all things to God (Col. 1:19).

How Can I Be Saved?
The Process of Being Redeemed

I was four years old. My sister was seven. While playing hide and seek in some cupboards, we found some old cans of paint. We opened some, and before we knew it, we were covered in blue paint, and it was all over the cupboards and the floor. We knew we were in big trouble.

Have you ever been covered in paint? It's not easy to get off. We could not possibly clean up the mess we'd made. So, we headed downstairs to tell our mother, tracking paint all the way.

Of course, my mother was not happy with what we'd done, but she loved us despite our mess. She did not tell us to clean ourselves up. She knew that even our attempts to clean up the mess would only make it worse. She painstakingly cleaned us and the mess we'd made. She bore the consequences of our mess and cleaned up what we could not.

God Makes Provision to Save Each Person

Just as my sister and I were covered in paint, all humans are covered in sin (Rom. 3:23), incapable of cleaning up our mess and in need of a Savior. But God so loved the world that He gave His uniquely beloved Son, who gave His own life to make a way to forgive and cleanse us (John 3:16; 1 John 1:9).

God is willing to forgive (Deut. 29:29; Ps. 103:3; Jer. 5:1; Amos 7:2) and wants to save every person. Accordingly, Jesus came to seek and save the lost (Luke 19:10) and has made provision for every sinner by His death and ongoing mediation so that anyone who accepts Him will be saved (John 3:16; 1 John 2:2).

God "wants all people to be saved and to come to the knowledge of the truth" and "gave Himself as a ransom for all" (1 Tim. 2:4, 6; 4:10; cf. John 3:16; 12:32; Titus 2:11). And God "is patient toward" us, "not willing for any to perish, but for all to come to repentance" (2 Pet. 3:9; cf. Ezek. 18:23, 32; 33:11; Matt. 12:14). Accordingly, Jesus Himself "is the atoning sacrifice for our sins, and not for ours only but also for the sins of the whole world" (1 John 2:2, NRSVue). God's offer of salvation, then, is universal. Yet, while God does everything He can (consistent with love and justice) to save every person, some refuse to be saved and finally reject salvation (see, e.g., Dan. 12:2; John 3:18; 5:11-12, 28-29; 2 Thess. 1:7-10; 2:10-12; Rev. 20:12-15).

What about those who have never heard the gospel, however? Can they be saved?

Many Christians believe only those who've heard of Christ and *consciously* believed in Him can be saved. However, Scripture teaches that some light from God reaches every person. Christ is "the true light, which enlightens everyone" (John 1:9, NRSVue), and He promised, "I, when I am lifted up from the earth, will draw all people to myself" (John 12:32, NRSVue; cf. 1:16; 3:16–17; Rom. 1:20; 2:15).

Further, God promised Abraham, "in you all the families of the earth will be blessed" (Gen. 12:3) and, as Peter learned, "God is not one to show partiality, but in every nation the one who fears Him and does what is right is acceptable to Him" (Acts 10:34–35; cf. Isa. 25:6–8; John 10:16; Acts 15:13–18; Rom. 1:5; 2:6–16; 3:9, 29).

In this regard, there is evidence in Scripture that (in some sense) Christ "enlightens everyone" (John 1:9, NRSVue) and draws all people to Himself (John 12:32) and that God holds each person accountable for their response to the light available to them (however small; cf. Rom. 1:19–21; 2:6–16; James 4:17), but not for light unavailable to them, for God "overlooked the times of ignorance" (Acts 17:30; cf. Luke 12:47–48; John 9:40–41; Acts 14:16–17; 17:31; Rom. 3:25).[23] Adventists believe that God does not condemn anyone due to circumstances beyond their control, but each one is given some opportunity so that no one is condemned due to *unwillful* ignorance (cf. John 3:16–21; 1 Tim. 4:10).[24] Not all are saved, however, because some (tragically) reject the light given them. And, all who are saved are saved through the work of Christ, for "there is salvation in no one else; for there is no other name under heaven that has been given among mankind by which we must be saved" (Acts 4:12).

Throughout Scripture, God consistently provides both warnings prior to judgment and a way of escape (e.g., preaching through Noah prior to the flood, warning Lot and his family in Sodom, warning Nineveh through Jonah, the warnings in the Three Angels' Messages prior to Christ's Second Coming, and many others). As the righteous judge, God always does what is right and is supremely fair to each one (e.g., Gen. 18:25; Ps. 19:9; Jer. 12:1; Acts 10:34–35; Rev. 15:3; 16:7), seeking to save everyone and giving a fair opportunity to all.

Nevertheless, Jesus is the only Savior—"there is salvation in no one else; for there is no other name under heaven that has been given among mankind by which we must be saved" (Acts 4:12; see also Luke 2:11; John 4:42; Acts 5:31; Eph. 5:23; Phil. 3:20; 2 Pet. 1:1; 1 John 4:14). Indeed, Jesus proclaimed, "I am the way, and the truth, and the life; no one comes to the Father except through Me" (John 14:6). Only through Christ's atoning work can one be saved. But God has made provision for all to be saved through Christ's "atoning sacrifice... for the sins of the whole world" (1 John 2:2, NRSVue).

God's Gracious Work Precedes Human Response: Prevenient Grace

If God did not draw us first, we would be hopeless. But Christ promised to "draw all people to myself" (John 12:32, NRSVue). As a good shepherd seeks after every wayward lost sheep, God seeks after each person (Matt. 18:12–14; Luke 15:3–7; cf. Ezek. 34:11–12, 16; John 10:11, 16). Even as a lost sheep would be unable to find its way back, if God did not come to us first, we would be hopelessly lost.

God's action of seeking and drawing us to Himself is sometimes called *prevenient* grace—grace bestowed previously to any action toward God on our part, which makes it possible for humans to respond to God's call. As Adventists understand it, this consists of God's seeking, drawing, and acting on human hearts in the course of history (not timelessly, see chapter 8). God takes the initiative, which we are unable to take.

As 1 John 4:19 declares, "We love, because He first loved us." Likewise, God proclaims, "I have loved you with an everlasting love; therefore with lovingkindness I have drawn you" (Jer. 31:3; cf. 1:5).

Because of human sinful nature, without divine prompting no one would turn to God in faith or repentance (see Rom. 2:4).[25] No one can come to Christ unless the Father draws that person (John 6:44), but Christ, the "true light," which "enlightens everyone" (John 1:9), draws all people to Himself (John 12:32).

> *No one can come to Christ unless the Father draws that person, but Christ, the "true light," which "enlightens everyone," draws all people to Himself.*

Salvation by Faith: Trust, Allegiance, and Repentance

What must *I* do, then, to be saved? Although the emphasis must always remain on what God has done and is doing for us, to be saved, one must respond to God's work in us. As Paul puts it, "work out your own salvation with fear and trembling; for it is God who is at work in you, both to desire and to work for His good pleasure" (Phil. 2:12-13).

Whoever *believes in* Christ will be saved. "Believe in the Lord Jesus, and you will be saved" (Acts 16:31; cf. John 3:16; Rom. 5:6-11; 10:9; 1 Cor. 1:23-24). "For God so loved the world, that He gave His only Son, so that everyone who believes in Him will not perish, but have eternal life" (John 3:16).

To believe in Christ is more than simply believing that Christ is *the* Savior—even the demons believe that much (James 2:19). Such faith *in* Jesus means to accept Christ as one's Savior *and* Lord.[26] This involves not merely cognitive belief but *trust in* and *allegiance to* Him, surrendering your life to Him (Ezek. 11:19; 16:26; John 15:5; Gal. 2:20; James 4:7-8).

Such faith requires repentance—genuine sorrow for sin and willingness to turn from sin through God's power (Acts 2:37-38; 3:19; 2 Cor. 7:10). Alongside true repentance will be the desire to bring about restitution for wrongs we have done.

Though we have a choice whether to cooperate with God, repentance is also a work of God in us, only possible because "the kindness of God leads you to repentance" (Rom. 2:4). In this regard, God proclaims: "I take no pleasure at all in the death of the wicked, but rather that the wicked turn from his way and live. Turn back, turn back from your evil ways! Why then should you die, house of Israel?" (Ezek. 33:11; cf. 2 Chron. 7:14; Mark 1:14,15; Luke 3:3; Acts 2:37, 38; 3:19).

Justified by Faith

Those who repent and exercise faith in response to God's prior gracious calling and drawing are justified by faith. That is, God forgives their sins, covering them by Christ's atonement. Put simply, to be *justified* means to be forgiven by God and, in virtue of being forgiven, counted as righteous. Justification, then, is God's declaration

> *Put simply, to be* justified *means to be forgiven by God and, in virtue of being forgiven, counted as righteous.*

of a sinner's righteousness (i.e., forgiveness, pardon), accompanied by the removal of guilt (expiation) by His work of atonement.

Although Paul is careful to emphasize that justification does not nullify the Law (Rom. 3:31), justification does not come by works of the Law. Humans are "justified by faith apart from works of the Law" (Rom. 3:28). Justification cannot be earned but is the product of God's "gracious gift . . . resulting in justification" (Rom. 5:16).

Yet, justification is not a once-for-all action. We are called to confess our sins and seek forgiveness day after day (cf. 1 John 1:9). Even as marriage is not sustained simply by saying one's wedding vows but requires day-by-day commitment, one's saving relationship with God does not consist of a one-time confession of faith but an ongoing connection with God.

Just as a plant's branches cannot bear fruit apart from the vine, we are hopeless if we do not remain connected to Christ. As Jesus taught, "I am the vine, you are the branches; the one who remains in Me, and I in him bears much fruit, for apart from Me you can do nothing" (John 15:5).

One can abandon faith in Christ and thus lose salvation. Paul explains, you "are saved" by the gospel, "if you hold firmly to the word which I preached to you, unless you believed in vain" (1 Cor. 15:2).[27] Paul himself could have fallen away and thus wrote, "I strictly discipline my body and make it my slave, so that, after I have preached to others, I myself will not be disqualified" (1 Cor. 9:27). Accordingly, Jesus taught, "the one who endures to the end will be saved" (Mark 13:13, NRSVue).

Competing Theories in Christian Theology: Justification and Sanctification

Here, it should be noted that the Roman Catholic concept of justification is different from the way most Protestants understand justification.

In Roman Catholicism, justification includes God's declaring one righteous *and* making one righteous. According to the typical Protestant understanding, conversely, justification refers to God's declaration of righteousness, while sanctification refers to the process whereby God makes one righteous. Distinct from these, the Eastern Orthodox conception of rightness with God involves theosis, a kind of union with God that is sometimes referred to as deification or divinization (or apotheosis, which literally means "making divine").[28]

As many Protestants understand it, a justified person is declared righteous solely on the grounds of Christ's *imputed* righteousness—righteousness that is legally *declared* or *ascribed* to the sinner. At the same time, the one justified is in the process of being sanctified—actually *becoming* righteous by faith, referred to as *imparted* righteousness).[29] Adventism affirms this understanding, with emphasis on the importance of growth in holiness (sanctification).[30]

There have been some disagreements among Adventists regarding sanctification, particularly whether one can reach a state of "perfection" prior to Christ's Second Coming and, if so, of what kind. Some have claimed the last generation of believers must be sinlessly "perfect" prior to Christ's Second Coming in order to provide the grounds for the vindication of God's character. Some thus believe it is possible for humans to become *completely* sinless prior to the transformation of the redeemed by Christ at the Second Coming (1 Cor. 15:52–55). This view is often labeled Last Generation Theology, a controversial view strongly denied by most Adventist theologians.[31]

The view that humans can become completely sinless is a form of perfectionism. Perfectionism tends to place the emphasis on human works and suggests one might reach a stopping point prior to glorification when one is perfectly "sanctified" and thus no longer in need of Christ's imputed righteousness.

Most Adventist theologians reject *perfectionism*, maintaining that believers may be "perfect" in Christ—justified by faith and continually becoming more like Christ by faith, but not *completely* sinless prior to the transformation of the redeemed from corruptible to incorruptible at Christ's Second Coming (1 Cor. 15:52–55), known as glorification. On this view, Christians may achieve character "perfection," but this kind of "perfection" is not the same as the absolutist conception of "perfection" in Greek thought.[32]

Rejecting perfectionism, however, does not entail licentiousness or downplaying the Christian duty of holy living. Christians should be holy, exemplifying love in action, "in holy conduct and godliness" (2 Pet. 3:11; cf. Eph. 1:4; 5:27; 1 Pet. 1:15–16). Believers motivated by love will not only be concerned with abstaining from sins but also about making a positive impact by actively loving and serving others, not focusing only on sins of *commission* but also sins of *omission* (see the parable of the Good Samaritan in Luke 10:25–37 and Christ's teaching regarding the sheep and the goats in Matt. 25:34–46).

Genuine holiness, both overcoming sinful thoughts and actions and exemplifying unselfish love in action toward others, can only be accomplished by God's work in us that we embrace by faith. This is because *genuine* obedience itself flows from a disposition of love. Yet, selfish by nature due to our fallenness, we are incapable of generating a genuine disposition of unselfish love in and of ourselves.[33]

In this regard, "love" should never be set in opposition to God's law or law-keeping: "love is the fulfillment of the law" (Rom. 13:10). And the greatest commandments are love for God and love for one's neighbor, on which the entire Law depends (Matt. 22:37–40; Mark 12:29–31; cf. Lev. 19:34; Deut. 6:5). Attempts at law-keeping without love, however, are worse than clanging cymbals (cf. Rom. 13:1). One cannot genuinely *keep* the law without love because the law is a transcript of God's character of love and any action truly in keeping with God's law of unselfish love must be motivated by unselfish love.

In this regard, Adventists reject both legalism and antinomianism. Legalism maintains that one can be saved by keeping God's law. Adventists believe keeping God's law cannot save anyone—one can only be saved by Christ through faith. Yet, those who place their faith in Christ will follow Christ as Savior *and* Lord, meaning they will seek to follow God's law, the law of love that is best for creaturely flourishing. This is directly in contrast to antinomianism, which claims Christians do not have a duty to follow God's moral law.

Sanctified by Faith

In addition to God forgiving sinners (justification), God's work of salvation also involves the process of sanctification—the process of being made holy, that is, becoming righteous. Sanctification is the process by which believers become more and more like Christ, growing in love and holiness toward more fully reflecting Christ's character.

Whereas justification is a declaration of God made in a moment, sanctification is the work of a lifetime. Yet, both are *by faith* (not meritorious works; Acts 26:18) and depend upon the primary and prior (prevenient) action of God. You cannot earn salvation—you cannot work your way to justification and sanctification; only Christ in you by faith can accomplish this. In both respects, "the one who is righteous will live by faith" (Rom. 1:17, NRSVue; cf. Gal. 3:11). True faith, however, is manifest in works of unselfish love (see James 2).

Just as faith in God and love for God go together, justification and sanctification go together. As John explains, "If we confess our sins, He is faithful and righteous, so that He will forgive us our sins and cleanse us from all unrighteousness" (1 John 1:9). Justification corresponds to forgiveness, and sanctification corresponds to cleansing. Justification and sanctification are thus distinct from one another but inseparable.

> *True faith, however, is manifest in works of unselfish love.*

To be saved by faith involves accepting Christ as *both* one's Savior *and* Lord—both belief in Christ as my substitute who died for me and atoned for my sins and allegiance to Christ as my King whom (motivated by gratitude and love) I wish to serve as faithfully as possible, by the power of the Holy Spirit. One is not saved by any such works, nor does one accrue merit, but in the end, there is a judgment according to works (e.g., Matt. 7:2; 12:36-37; 16:27; Rom. 2:5-8; 14:12; 2 Cor. 5:10; 1 Pet. 1:17; Rev. 2:23; 20:12; 22:12), which manifests where one's allegiance truly resides—with God and therefore unselfish love for others or with the enemy and therefore selfishness and self-serving.[34]

The one who is justified is not only forgiven and thus acquitted of any guilt (Rom. 5:16), accounted righteous (Rom. 4:1-5, 22-24), but is also in the process of being sanctified by faith and receives the divine promise of a future reality of righteousness when "we will be like Him" (1 John 3:2).[35]

Sanctification is an ongoing process of being made holy—past, present, and future. Thus, it is appropriate for believers to say, "we *have been* sanctified (Heb. 10:10), we are *being* sanctified (Heb. 10:14), and we *will be* sanctified" (1 John 3:2-3; emphasis mine). In different senses, sanctification (being made holy) is accomplished in the believer's past (Acts 20:32; Eph. 5:25, 26; Heb. 10:10, 29), is an ongoing process in the present (Rom. 6; Heb. 10:14), and *points to* a final result that the believer experiences in the future (Phil. 3:12-14; 1 John 3:2-3) known as glorification (discussed below). Thus, even "now we are children of God," but "when He appears, we will be like Him" (1 John 3:2).

Perfect in Christ: Awaiting Glorification

In the meantime, those in Christ by faith are counted as "perfect" in Christ. Indeed, Hebrews 10:14 declares, "by one offering He has perfected for all time those who are sanctified."

The meaning of perfection, however, is often misunderstood. In this regard, there are two perilous extremes: (1) believing I must achieve absolute moral perfection before I die (or before Christ comes) in order to be saved, and (2) believing I cannot be morally perfect, so why even try?

The first extreme is utterly false. Was the thief on the cross, who Jesus promised would be in paradise with Him (Luke 23:43), already morally perfect? Far from it! Yet, he was saved. So, it cannot be true that in order to be saved, one must have achieved moral perfection in this life.

Not long before his death, Paul himself testified he had not "already become perfect" (Phil. 3:12). And Scripture teaches that we will not attain perfection in the sense of being incorruptible until Christ's Second Coming (glorification): "We shall not all sleep, but we shall all be changed—in a moment, in the twinkling of an eye, at the last trumpet. For the trumpet will sound, and the dead will be raised incorruptible, and we shall be changed. For this corruptible must put on incorruption, and this mortal must put on immortality" (1 Cor. 15:51–53, NKJV; cf. 1 John 3:2).

Yet doesn't God command us to be "perfect"? Indeed, He does. Jesus Himself commanded: "Therefore you shall be perfect, as your heavenly Father is perfect" (Matt. 5:48). How can it be, then, that we will not be "incorruptible" until the Second Coming—until glorification?

Much of the difficulty here stems from a mistaken understanding of the kind of perfection in view. Terms like "blameless" and "perfect" have ranges of meaning and in Scripture often do not refer to *absolute* perfection or blamelessness.[36] For example, Genesis 6:9 states, "Noah was a righteous man, blameless in his generation." Yet, Noah was not *absolutely* morally perfect or blameless. Likewise, Job 1:1 declares that Job "was blameless." But Job also was not *absolutely* morally perfect. Even apart from individual descriptions of their moral failings, we know that neither of these—and no one else, save Jesus alone—was entirely morally perfect or blameless because Scripture teaches "there is no righteous person, not even one" and "all have sinned and fall short of the glory of God" (Rom. 3:10, 23).

In Scripture, "perfection" can refer to maturity or being "complete" at any given stage of the process of salvation.[37] Thus, one can be "perfect" in the sense of maturity or completeness at a particular stage of growth while not yet attaining *absolute* moral perfection. Thus, Paul can both say he has *not* "already become perfect" (Phil. 3:12) while just three verses later referring to himself and others as those who are "perfect" (Phil. 3:15, KJV; cf. Heb. 10:14). In a very important sense, everyone who has genuine faith in Christ is already perfect *in Christ*—that is accounted as morally perfect before God through Christ's mediation for us. Yet, we are not yet absolutely morally perfect—that is, morally perfect in every respect.

Notably, the context of Christ's command to be perfect illuminates what kind of perfection is in view in Matthew 5:48. In the verses leading up to verse 48, Jesus contrasts those who love only those who love them with God's love that extends to *all* (Matt. 5:43–47). Whereas human love is incomplete and thus imperfect, God's love is complete (for all) and thus perfect. In context, Christ commands His followers to be perfect in love.[38] This understanding is supported by the fact that in his parallel account of Christ's discourse in Matthew 5, instead of the command "you shall be perfect" (Matt. 5:48), Luke reports Christ's teaching in these words, "Be merciful, just as your Father is merciful" (Luke 6:36). To be merciful is to extend love for others, including the undeserving, and to thus be complete or perfect in love. To be perfect in the sense Christ commands in Matthew 5:48 is to love completely—to love everyone, even as God loves everyone.

This is not in contrast to growing in holiness. Holiness and love go together. We are to be perfect in love, even as God is, and holy, even as God is (cf. Matt. 5:58; 1 Pet. 1:15–17). Yet, as seen earlier, love itself is the fulfillment of the law and the greatest commands are to love God and one another (Matt. 22:37–40; Rom. 13:10). The command to love completely entails the command to holiness and doing justice that extends even to those we might think of as our enemies (Matt. 5:44; Luke 6:35; cf. Mic. 6:8).

Yet, why can't we be absolutely morally perfect prior to glorification? Why can we not be entirely free from our fallen nature right now? The same question can be asked relative to why we struggle with death prior to the Second Coming. God has the sheer power to stop death, even as He has the power to make us absolutely morally perfect. It is not a question of God's power, then, but *timing* in the history of redemption, within the rules of engagement and timeline of the cosmic conflict.[39]

The tension of already being perfect in Christ yet awaiting the fullness of perfection at glorification corresponds to the tension between Christ having established the kingdom of God already, defeating Satan at the cross, and the final establishment of His eternal kingdom that we still await, when the domain of darkness and death and evil itself will be eradicated and the fullness of God's presence *with us* will be re-established forevermore (see Rev. 21:3–4).[40] In the meantime, however, even as we await glorification on resurrection day, Paul exhorts us to "consider yourselves to be dead to sin, but alive to God in Christ Jesus" (Rom. 6:11).

Here, though, one might mistakenly arrive at the other extreme: I cannot be absolutely (morally) perfect now, so why even try?

Here, consider again Paul's words in Philippians 3: "Not that I have already grasped it all or have already become perfect, but I press on if I may also take hold of that for which I was even taken hold of by Christ Jesus. Brothers and sisters, I do not regard myself as having taken hold of it yet; but one thing I do: forgetting what lies behind and reaching forward to what lies ahead, I press on toward the goal for the prize of the upward call of God in Christ Jesus. Therefore, all who are mature [or "perfect"], let's have this attitude; and if in anything you have a different attitude, God will reveal that to you as well; however, let's keep living by that same standard to which we have attained" (Phil. 3:12–16).

Notice the metaphor of running a race Paul uses. He has not attained perfection, but he presses on, not looking back, but looking forward. You cannot win a sprint while looking backward (unless you are Usain Bolt in his prime!), and thus Paul counsels not to focus on the fact of not yet attaining but instead to press on with eyes on the prize.

Yet, one might protest, if I cannot be morally perfect here and now, why even try? Imagine you are playing basketball: will you make all your shots? No. Inevitably, you will miss some shots—even professionals inevitably miss. However, do you *have to* miss any particular shot? No, you could make the next one. And you could make the next shot after that. The fact that you will inevitably sometimes miss does not in any way make it impossible for you to make your next shot and certainly does not remove the reason for trying. Not trying to make any shots because you cannot make all of them would be absurd.

Similarly, even though we may fail at times, that is no reason to turn away from God's commands to be holy and loving like God—as much as possible. Nothing necessitates that I will fail at any particular time. While Paul is very clear that we have a sinful nature that remains until glorification (1 Cor. 15:51–53; cf. Rom. 7), he equally emphasizes that this provides no excuse for continuing in sin. For example, he writes in Romans 6:1–4: "What shall we say then? Are we to continue in sin so that grace may increase? Far from it! How shall we who died to sin still live in it? Or do you not know that all of us who have been baptized into Christ Jesus have been baptized into His death? Therefore we have been buried with Him through baptism into death, so that, just as Christ was raised from the dead through the glory of the Father, so we too may walk in newness of life."

You will be tempted to continue in the way of sin, but "God is faithful" and "will not allow you to be tempted [or tested] beyond what you are able, but with the temptation will provide the way of escape also, so that you will be able to endure it" (1 Cor. 10:13). Peter could not walk on water. But somehow, he did! How did Peter walk on water? By the power of Christ alone. And he continued walking on water only as long as he kept his eyes on Christ.[41] As soon as Peter looked away, he sank (Matt. 14:28–31). Likewise, we can overcome by clinging to Christ by His divine power.

> **We can overcome by clinging to Christ by His divine power.**

Instead of concluding that (1) I must attain absolute moral perfection in this life to be saved or (2) I cannot be absolutely morally perfect now, so why even try, I conclude that (3) Christ has justified me by faith. He has thus set me apart and is sanctifying me by faith and will transform me from corruptible to incorruptible when He returns. Although I am not absolutely morally perfect yet, I am counted as *perfect in Christ* (justification), I am being perfected in Christ (sanctification), and I will be perfected in Christ (glorification).[42]

In all this, it is only by the mediation of Christ that we, otherwise hopelessly condemned according to our sins, can be saved. It is only in virtue of Christ's righteousness that we can stand in the presence of the holy God in the day of judgment (more on this in chapter 16).

"Jesus imparts all the powers, all the grace, all the penitence all the inclination, all the pardon of sins, in presenting His righteousness for man to grasp by living faith which is also the gift of God. If you would gather together everything that is good and holy and lovely in man and then present the subject to the angels of God as acting part in the salvation of the human soul or in merit, the proposition would be rejected as treason."[43]

Conclusion: Why Does It Matter?

Nothing seemed to satisfy her. What she wanted most always seemed just out of reach. She had imagined that if only she were successful and prosperous, she would feel content. But she had achieved success in her career and acquired greater wealth than she'd ever dreamt of having. Yet, she felt empty inside, nonetheless.

No matter how much success you achieve in this life, no matter how much wealth or possessions you accumulate, you will not find the deepest and truest joy that can be found unless you find it in relationship to God—the source of all joy. He has made a way, at great cost to Himself, for all who are willing to find the deepest and most profound joy and live eternally in bliss with Him and others in His kingdom of unselfish love.

What, then, must you do to find this deepest and most profound joy? What must you do to inherit eternal life? In brief, the process of salvation may be summed up as follows:

- Universal Provision: Christ provides universal provision for the salvation of all, including you and me.
- Prevenient Grace: God reaches out to humans first and draws us to Himself.
- Repentance: The Holy Spirit convicts us of sin, and the kindness of God leads us to repentance.
- Faith: God moves us to place saving faith in Christ, surrendering to Him in total allegiance.
- Justification: God justifies us (declares us forgiven of our sins).

- Sanctification: God sanctifies us (makes us holy, righteous, and loving over time).
- Glorification: God will finally glorify us (make us perfect, change us from corruptible to incorruptible).

This process may be framed simply in terms of faith, love, and hope. As a sinner, I can only be saved by faith in Christ (justification) and, through His work in my life, grow in love toward God and fellow humans (sanctification) while expectantly hoping and waiting for the day when I will be like Him (glorification).[44] As Paul puts it: "But now faith, hope, and love remain, these three; but the greatest of these is love" (1 Cor. 13:13).

Even now, you can respond to God's call to give Him your heart: "if you confess with your mouth Jesus as Lord, and believe in your heart that God raised Him from the dead, you will be saved" (Rom. 10:9). You will face trials along the way. Jesus foretold: "In this world you will have trouble. But take heart! I have overcome the world" (John 16:33, NIV; cf. Rom. 8:18).

One final crucial question remains: What does it look like to be saved?

In a word: love—love for God and others.

Micah 6:8 succinctly explains what is expected of those who would follow God: "He has told you, mortal one, what is good; and what does the LORD require of you but to do justice, to love kindness, and to walk humbly with your God?"

Tying salvation and doing justice together, Isaiah further explains: "Wash yourselves, make yourselves clean; remove the evil of your deeds from My sight. Stop doing evil, learn to do good; seek justice, rebuke the oppressor, obtain justice for the orphan, plead for the widow's case. 'Come now, and let us debate your case,' says the LORD, 'Though your sins are as scarlet, they shall become as white as snow; though they are red like crimson, they shall be like wool'" (Isa. 1:16–18).

Here, I invite you to consider pausing and reading the calls for justice that are the perpetual emphasis of the prophets throughout the Old Testament and which also resonate in the New Testament (see, e.g., James 2). While you may have encountered people who call themselves Christians who are not concerned about the oppressed and downtrodden, the Christianity taught in Scripture is deeply concerned about those whom Jesus refers to as "the least of these" (see

Matt. 25:31–46). To reflect such concern, in word and deed, is to reflect the heart of God.

Questions for Reflection

1. Have you felt the need of a Savior? What does it mean to be saved?
2. What does Christ's work of atonement accomplish? How is it that humans are saved by Christ's work? What does this tell us about God's character?
3. How can you be saved? What is the process of salvation?
4. What is the difference between justification, sanctification, and glorification? How can understanding this distinction keep us from extremes on both sides (e.g., perfectionism)?
5. What kind of perfection does Scripture call humans to? Why does this matter?
6. Are you saved? What would you say to someone who asks how one can know they are saved? Where does the assurance of salvation lie?
7. You can be saved even now. God freely offers you and all humans the gift of salvation. Are you willing to be saved? If so, pray to God even now, asking for forgiveness of sins and declaring that you accept Him as your Lord and Savior. He will save you forever if you put your trust in Him and keep putting your trust in Him day by day. For "He who began a good work in you will perfect it until the day of Christ Jesus" (Phil. 1:6).

For Further Reading

Adventist Perspectives:

Blazen, Ivan. "Salvation." In *Handbook of Seventh-day Adventist Theology*. Edited by Raoul Dederen. Hagerstown, MD: Review and Herald, 2001.

Gulley, Norman R. *Systematic Theology: Creation, Christ, Salvation*. Berrien Springs, MI: Andrews University Press, 2012.

Hanna, Martin F., Darius W. Jankiewicz, and John W. Reeve, eds. *Salvation: Contours of Adventist Soteriology*. Berrien Springs, MI: Andrews University Press, 2018.

Knight, George R. *Sin and Salvation: God's Work for Us and in Us.* Hagerstown, MD: Review and Herald, 2009.

LaRondelle, Hans. *Christ Our Salvation: What God Does for Us and in Us.* Mountain View, CA: Pacific Press, 1980.

Moskala, Jiří and John C. Peckham, eds. *God's Character and the Last Generation.* Nampa, ID: Pacific Press, 2018.

Ott, Helmut. *Perfect in Christ: The Mediation of Christ in the Writings of Ellen G. White.* Hagerstown, MD: Review and Herald, 2010.

Rodríguez, Ángel Manuel. *Living Without an Intercessor in the Writings of Ellen G. White.* Biblical Research Institute Release, no. 17. Silver Spring, MD: Biblical Research Institute, 2020.

Whidden, Woodrow W. *The Judgment and Assurance: The Dynamics of Personal Salvation.* Hagerstown, MD: Review and Herald, 2012.

———. *Ellen White on Salvation: A Chronological Study.* Hagerstown, MD: Review and Herald, 1995.

White, Ellen G., *Steps to Christ.* Historical Introduction and Notes by Denis Fortin. Berrien Springs, MI: Andrews University Press, 2017.

See also the resources on the Biblical Research Institute website: https://adventistbiblicalresearch.org/materials/.

Other Christian Perspectives:

Bates, Matthew W. *Salvation By Allegiance Alone: Rethinking Faith, Works, and the Gospel of Jesus the King.* Grand Rapids, MI: Baker Academic, 2017.

Gospel Allegiance: What Faith in Jesus Misses for Salvation in Christ. Grand Rapids, MI: Brazos, 2019.

Beilby, James and Paul R. Eddy, eds. *The Nature of the Atonement: Four Views.* Downers Grove, IL: IVP Academic, 2006.

Craig, William Lane. *Atonement and the Death of Christ: An Exegetical, Historical, and Philosophical Exploration.* Waco, TX: Baylor University Press, 2020.

MacKinnon, Donald. "Subjective and Objective Conceptions of Atonement." In *Prospect for Theology: Essays in Honour of H. H. Farmer.* Edited by F. G. Healey, 167–82. Welwyn: James Nisbet & Co, 1996.

McNall, Joshua M. *The Mosaic of Atonement: An Integrated Approach to Christ's Work.* Grand Rapids, MI: Zondervan, 2019.

Morris, Leon. *The Atonement: Its Meaning and Significance.* Downers Grove, IL: InterVarsity, 1983.

Rutledge, Fleming. *The Crucifixion: Understanding the Death of Christ.* Grand Rapids, MI: Eerdmans, 2015.

Stott, John R. W. *The Cross of Christ.* Downers Grove, IL: InterVarsity Press, 1986.

14

GOD COVENANTS WITH US: UNDERSTANDING COVENANT AND LAW

Unfaithful. She abandoned her husband for other lovers. Yet, God commanded Hosea to love this woman though she was "committing adultery," even "as the Lord loves the sons of Israel, though they turn to other gods" (Hosea 3:1; cf. 2:2, 14).

In this striking object lesson, and in many other instances, Scripture portrays God as a grieving husband whose wife has abandoned him for other lovers—the heartbroken victim of unrequited love (cf. Hosea 11:8). Though God's people were repeatedly unfaithful, God continued to love them.

Throughout Scripture, the metaphor of marriage depicts God's covenant relationship with His people. A covenant is a binding agreement between two or more parties, typically including promises and privileges as well as conditions and responsibilities.[1]

The marriage between my wife and me is a kind of covenant. When we were married, we exchanged vows (promises) and took on responsibilities toward one another, entering into a covenant of love. In analogous fashion, the covenants God makes with humans throughout Scripture are covenants of love, initiated by and flowing from God's perfect, unselfish love (cf. Deut. 4:37–38; 7:7–13; 10:15; 1 John 4:19). As such, the covenants are often depicted by family imagery of love relationship such as marriage and the parent-child relationship.

God's choice of Israel as His covenant people, intended to ultimately bless all peoples, was *because* of His love (see Gen. 12:3; Deut. 4:37). As we will see, God's covenants—with Israel and otherwise—include both divine promises and human obligations. Through Israel, God planned to redeem, reclaim, and reconcile the world to Himself. The story of redemption itself, which is largely the story of God's covenants, can be framed as stages of the restoration of God's presence *with us*.

> *The story of redemption itself, which is largely the story of God's covenants, can be framed as stages of the restoration of God's presence with us.*

God was present with Adam and Eve in Eden in very special ways. But the covenant relationship between God and humans was ruptured by the Fall. Though God graciously continued to be present with us, sin separated humans from the full presence God intended.

Subsequently, God initiated covenants with Noah, Abraham, Moses, and David, finally establishing the New Covenant with Christ's own blood. These covenants were invariably preceded by great acts of divine deliverance. And, through it all, God showed Himself to be perfectly faithful, always keeping His promises.

This chapter addresses crucial questions about the nature of God's covenants and God's law of unselfish love, including: How do covenants between God and humans operate, and what does it mean for how we should relate to God today? Do God's laws given in the context of these covenants still apply to us today?

Answering these questions involves a number of other questions, such as whether God's covenants with humans are:

- continuous or discontinuous?
- particular or universal?
- promissory or obligatory?
- conditional or unconditional?

The Story of Covenant

"If it is possible, let this cup pass from me," Jesus prayed shortly before His crucifixion.

Jesus could have avoided the cross, but it was not possible for Him to *both* avoid the cross *and* save the world. To save the fallen world required a remedy for sin and a way to forgive sinners without compromising God's love and justice, upholding the law of unselfish love such that God is both just and the justifier of those who believe (Rom. 3:25–26), defeating the devil's allegations against God's character and government.

The story of God's plan of redemption, the way God saves the world while upholding love and justice, is bound up with the story of the covenants God makes with humans—with Adam and Eve, Noah, Abraham, Moses, David, and beyond into the New Covenant. And, embedded in this story of God's covenants is the story of God's law of unselfish love given for the flourishing of all creation.

The Eden Covenant

God's relationship with Adam and Eve included elements common to God's covenants with humans throughout Scripture, including: God's gracious initiation of relationship, divine law to govern the relationship, and blessings that flowed from the relationship, conditional upon the relationship's continuance.

By graciously creating Adam and Eve, God initiated relationship with humans. And divine law appears in God's commandment to the first humans: "From any tree of the garden you may freely eat; but from the tree of the knowledge of good and evil you shall not eat, for on the day that you eat from it you will certainly die" (Gen. 2:16–17). Adam and Eve, then, were given moral freedom—they could trust God and obey His commands, or distrust and disobey.

Why there was a tree of knowledge of good and evil in Eden in the first place has puzzled many. Here, one must remember the cosmic conflict began earlier in heaven with the devil's allegations against God's character and government (see chapter 9). Later, in Eden, the devil was allowed an opportunity to tempt Adam and Eve relative to this one tree in the garden, apparently as part of the rules of engagement in the cosmic conflict (decided in the heavenly council). If Satan could get the humans to fall, he would become the ruler of this world in their place.

In the guise of a serpent, the devil misrepresented and twisted God's command to make God seem arbitrary and unfair. "Has God really said, 'You shall not eat from any tree of the garden'?" (Gen. 3:1). Of course, God had said almost the opposite—they could eat from *every* tree except one.

Only one who is all-powerful could have *unlimited* freedom. For creatures, then, unlimited freedom is inherently impossible. For *creatures* to be free to make choices in the first place requires some parameters or laws within which such choices can be made. Nevertheless, the devil grasped for absolutely unlimited freedom, seeking absolute autonomy and desiring to be a law unto himself and others in God's place. He thus insinuated that even one dietary restriction was too much.

After thus misrepresenting God's command, the serpent claimed God lied when He told them they'd die if they ate the fruit, and he further insinuated that God did so to oppress them—to keep them from becoming like God (Gen. 3:1-5).

The serpent's allegations amounted to a referendum on God's commands—that is, on God's law, thus also amounting to a referendum on God's character of love (more on this later). God's commands are oppressive and should be rejected, the serpent alleged, as part of his quest to overthrow God's government and law.

The opposite was true on all counts, and throughout the rest of the story of God's covenants, God demonstrates the perfect love and justice of His character and law, which in the end will be shown beyond any reasonable doubt.

The Law in Eden

The core principles of God's moral law of unselfish love were already in place in Eden—apparent in the institutions of marriage, work, and the Sabbath.

During creation week, God rested on the seventh day and "blessed the seventh day and sanctified it" (i.e., set it apart for holy use, Gen. 2:3). The Sabbath stands as (among other things) a memorial that God is the only Creator and thus the only true God, alone worthy of worship (see chapter 15). Given this, Roy Gane explains, the institution of the Sabbath during creation week not only establishes the fourth commandment regarding the Sabbath (Exod. 20:8-11) but also rules out having other gods, idolatry, and misusing the Lord's name (corresponding to the first three of the Ten Commandments).[2]

On the sixth day, God instituted marriage between Adam and Eve (Gen. 2:24). As Gane further explains, this marriage leads to procreation, which relates to the commandment that parents are to be honored (the fifth commandment) and involves respect for human life that rules out both murder (the sixth commandment) and bearing false witness (the ninth commandment). And the sacredness of marriage itself rules out adultery (the seventh commandment) and coveting someone else's spouse (the tenth commandment).

Finally, God gave Adam and Eve the tasks of cultivating and keeping the garden (Gen. 2:15), thus instituting work. In this regard, Gane explains that work and respect for the fruits of one's work rules out stealing (the eighth commandment), bearing false witness to gain benefits due someone else (the ninth commandment), and coveting such benefits (the tenth commandment).[3]

Blessings, Curses, Grace, and the Promise

Had Adam and Eve trusted God, they would have forever enjoyed the unparalleled blessings of never-ending life *with* God. Their distrust and disobedience, however, ruptured relationship with God, forfeiting the blessings of unbroken relationship with God. These blessings were replaced by curses that followed as consequences of sin, corrupting nature itself, which had been perfectly ordered to yield creation's flourishing (Gen. 3:14–17; cf. Rom. 8:20–22).

Yet, God continued to bestow grace and many blessings on Adam and Eve, including life itself. And God promised that one day the woman's Seed would crush the serpent's head (Gen. 3:15), bringing deliverance. Christ came in fulfillment of this promise, "to destroy the works of the devil" (1 John 3:8; cf. Heb. 2:14). Christ, the second Adam, succeeded where the first Adam failed (Rom. 5; 1 Cor. 15), enabling Him to reverse the curses of sin and conquer death itself.

God's relationship with Adam and Eve thus included both divine commands (obligations) and divine promises, predicated on God's gracious provisions. And, as we will see, the basic divine institutions of Sabbath, marriage, and work (and laws implied in them) extended to all the descendants of Adam and Eve. While some divine blessings were conditional, humans bring very little to the relationship, with God supplying the very life, power, and freedom with which humans can freely love and obey the Creator (or not). And, whereas the curses brought by sin were universal in this world, so is the provision for redemption and the blessings of eternal life *with* God brought by Christ's work of atonement, according to the promise.

The Noahic Covenant

By the time of Noah, "the wickedness of mankind was great on the earth" and "every intent of the thoughts of their hearts was only evil continually" (Gen. 6:5). But, "Noah found favor in the eyes of the LORD. . . . Noah was a righteous man, blameless in his generation. Noah walked with God" (Gen. 6:8–9). And, God promised Noah, "I will establish My covenant with you; and you shall enter the ark—you, your sons, your wife, and your sons' wives with you" (Gen. 6:18).

Left unchecked, the ubiquitous wickedness and violence on the earth would have eventually led to the total self-destruction of humanity (cf. Gen. 6:11–13). Accordingly, some see God's bringing of judgment in the flood as not only bringing judgment against such wickedness but also saving humanity from itself by giving humanity a kind of new start with Noah and his descendants rather than leaving humanity to destroy itself eventually. In this regard, Scripture continually teaches that God is the entirely righteous judge who has the right to bring judgment to end evil but does so only as a last resort while providing ways of escape for those willing to take them (in this case, the ark).

God graciously delivered Noah and his family and would have delivered others had they heeded God's warnings. With such deliverance, however, came commands and obligations. For instance, Noah was to build the ark and prepare for the flood *precisely* as God instructed. After the flood, vegetation was scarce, and God allowed humans to eat animals. But, God commanded, "you shall not eat flesh with its life, that is, its blood" (Gen. 9:4).

Alongside such commands, God promised: "I Myself am establishing My covenant with you, and with your descendants after you; and with every living creature that is with you: the birds, the livestock, and every animal of the earth. . . . I establish My covenant with you; and all flesh shall never again be eliminated by the waters of a flood, nor shall there again be a flood to destroy the earth." God identified the rainbow as "the sign of the covenant which I am making between Me and you and every living creature that is with you, for all future generations. . . . between Me and all flesh that is on the earth" (Gen. 9:9–12, 17; cf. 8:20–22).

This covenant was universal—including all humans and animals. And, because of God's promise that no flood will destroy the earth again, this is often labeled an *unconditional* covenant. However, while this promise is not attached to conditions, we have seen this covenant also included obligations and commands.

The Abrahamic Covenant

After the flood, the peoples of the earth rebelled with the tower of Babel, effectively rejecting God's covenant promises to Noah and giving themselves over to other gods (see chapter 9). God then called Abraham out of the nations to create a new nation to be His allotted covenant people (see Deut. 32:8–9). The Abrahamic covenant thus shifted toward particularity. Yet, Israel's election was not merely for their own sake but to bless *all* peoples (Gen. 12:3) and (eventually) reclaim all peoples as part of God's covenant people.

"Go from your country," God told Abraham, "To the land which I will show you; and I will make you into a great nation, and I will bless you, and make your name great; and you shall be a blessing.... And in you all the families of the earth will be blessed" (Gen. 12:1–3; see also 17:1–11). Here, God promises posterity, land, continued relationship with God, and blessing to *all* peoples.

This covenant follows the pattern of royal grant covenants in the ancient Near East, wherein a royal figure *granted* land and/or other blessings to a faithful servant and his descendants.[4] Some have thought of grant covenants as strictly promissory and unconditional, but such covenants may include conditions, as the Abrahamic covenant does.

For instance, when introducing the Abrahamic covenant, God proclaimed: "I am God Almighty; walk before Me, and be blameless. I will make My covenant between Me and you, and I will multiply you exceedingly" (Gen. 17:1–2). After proclaiming numerous promises and identifying this as "an everlasting covenant" between God and Abraham and his descendants "throughout their generations," God added, "you shall keep My covenant, you and your descendants after you throughout their generations" and commanded circumcision of Abraham and his male descendants as "the sign of the covenant between Me and you" (Gen. 17:7, 9–11). This sign was also a condition since any "uncircumcised male" was to be "cut off from his people" because "he has broken My covenant" (Gen. 17:14).

Later, God said of Abraham, "I have chosen him, so that he may command his children and his household after him to keep the way of the LORD by doing righteousness and justice, so that the LORD may bring upon Abraham what He has spoken about him" (Genesis 18:19). Here, the phrase "so that" indicates that some of God's intended blessings were conditional upon covenant faithfulness by Abraham's descendants.

Likewise, some promises were partially conditional on Abraham's covenant faithfulness. For example, God told Abraham's son Isaac: "I will multiply your descendants as the stars of heaven, and will give your descendants all these lands; and by your descendants all the nations of the earth shall be blessed, because Abraham obeyed Me and fulfilled his duty to Me, and kept My commandments, My statutes, and My laws" (Gen. 26:4–5; likewise, see 22:16–18; cf. Gal. 3:6; Heb. 11:17–19).

While this covenant includes blessings and obligations (e.g., circumcision) particular to Israel, it also includes universal blessings. Indeed, the overarching promises of the Abrahamic covenant relative to relationship with God are not limited to the particular nation of Israel, but "those who are of faith" (including Gentiles) are children "of Abraham" and "blessed with Abraham" (Gal. 3:6, 9; cf. 3:28–29).[5]

The Mosaic Covenant

The Mosaic covenant was built on the Abrahamic covenant.

While Israel was enslaved in Egypt, "God heard their groaning; and God remembered His covenant with Abraham, Isaac, and Jacob" (Exod. 2:24). This does not imply God had forgotten, but biblical references to God "remembering" signal that God is about to act relative to past promises (akin to how one "remembers" marriage vows by acting in accordance with those vows).

Likewise, God explained to Moses, "I appeared to Abraham, Isaac, and Jacob" and "established My covenant with them, to give them the land of Canaan" and "I have heard the groaning of the sons of Israel, because the Egyptians are holding them in bondage, and I have remembered My covenant" (Exod. 6:2–5; cf. 3:6, 15–16; 4:5; Deut. 29:9–15).

Further, God promised Israel, I will "rescue you from [Egyptian] bondage" and "take you as My people, and I will be your God" and "bring you to the land which I swore to give to Abraham, Isaac, and Jacob"

(Exod. 6:6–8; cf. Gen. 15:16; Deut. 9:5). In these and other instances, Scripture identifies the Exodus as God's action in keeping with His promises in the Abrahamic covenant.

Later, just before articulating the Ten Commandments, God declared: "I am the LORD your God, who brought you out of the land of Egypt, out of the house of slavery" (Exod. 20:2; cf. 19:4). While the Ten Commandments were "written by the finger of God" on stone tablets in the Mosaic covenant (Exod. 31:18; Deut. 9:10), the core of these already appeared in the context of the Eden covenant (as seen earlier). Beyond the Ten Commandments, the Mosaic covenant also included many other laws of various types (discussed later in this chapter), including laws establishing and regulating the Levitical priesthood and sanctuary services.

Many scholars believe the Mosaic covenant follows the pattern of ancient suzerain-vassal treaties—covenants between chiefs or lords (suzerains) and servants (vassals), including:

- introduction of parties
- historical prologue
- stipulations (the parameters of the covenant, including commands)
- document clause—including instructions for preservation and reading
- witnesses to the treaty
- blessings and curses

Such treaty-type covenants included a number of obligations prescribed for the servants on which continued covenant blessings depended. Some emphasized the servants' obligations in treaty-type covenants in contrast to the rulers' promises in grant-type covenants but, in Scripture, both kinds of covenants include divine promises and commands (or obligations).[6]

As noted earlier, the Mosaic (treaty-type) covenant itself is built onto the Abrahamic (grant-type) covenant. The Mosaic covenant continues many aspects of the Abrahamic covenant, while including elements distinct to the Mosaic covenant, some of which applied only to the ancient nation of Israel while others apply to God's people throughout the remaining covenants; including the New Covenant (more on this below). For instance, while many Mosaic laws were particular to the ancient nation of Israel and thus temporary (at least in their specifics), the Ten Commandments were universal and thus continue beyond the nation of Israel (discussed later in this chapter).

While including many promises, the Mosaic covenant is repeatedly framed in strongly conditional terms. For example, God declared, "if you will indeed obey My voice and keep My covenant, then you shall be My own possession among all the peoples, for all the earth is Mine; and you shall be to Me a kingdom of priests and a holy nation" (Exod. 19:5–6; cf. 24:3–8; Lev. 26; Deut. 7:9–26).

Elsewhere, God declared, "I will confirm My covenant with you," and "make My dwelling among you," and "I will also walk among you and be your God, and you shall be My people. I am the Lord your God, who brought you out of the land of Egypt so that you would not be their slaves, and I broke your yoke and made you walk erect. But if you do not obey Me and do not carry out all these commandments" and "break My covenant," then "I will set My face against you" (Lev. 26:9–17; cf. Deut. 29:24–25).

Yet, even then, if the rebellious people "confess their wrongdoing and the wrongdoing of their forefathers . . . then I will remember My covenant with Jacob" and "Isaac" and "Abraham." Indeed, "in spite of this, when they are in the land of their enemies, I will not reject them. . . . But I will remember for them the covenant with their ancestors" (Lev. 26:40–45).

Throughout the Mosaic covenant, God called people to a covenant relationship of love, grounded in God's prior love for them (see Deut. 7:7–8; cf. 4:37–38; 10:15–19). In this context, God declared, "it shall come about, because you listen to these judgments and keep and do them, that the Lord your God will keep His covenant with you and His faithfulness which He swore to your forefathers. And He will love you, bless you, and make you numerous. . . . in the land which He swore to your forefathers to give you" (Deut. 7:12–13).

Alongside calling the people to such loyal covenant love, however, God promised that He would transform the hearts of the willing, saying, "the Lord your God will circumcise your heart and the hearts of your descendants, to love the Lord your God with all your heart and all your soul, so that you may live" (Deut. 30:6).

While the people often failed to reflect God's love, God never failed. God repeatedly showed extravagant grace and compassion, from the golden calf rebellion and beyond, God showed Himself to be: "The LORD, the LORD God, compassionate and merciful, slow to anger, and abounding in faithfulness and truth; who keeps faithfulness for thousands, who forgives wrongdoing, violation of His Law, and sin" and at the same time one who "will by no means leave the guilty unpunished" (Exod. 34:6–7).

> While the people often failed to reflect God's love, God never failed.

The Davidic Covenant

Centuries later, against God's warnings and expressed wishes (1 Sam. 8:6–22; see also Deut. 17:14–20), the people wickedly demanded a king (1 Sam. 12:17) and thus "rejected [God] from being King over them" (1 Sam. 8:7; cf. 10:19; 12:12–13). In response to Israel's demands, Saul was chosen as Israel's first *human* king (1 Sam. 10:24; cf. 12:13).

Nevertheless, had Saul been faithful, God "would now have established [Saul's] kingdom over Israel forever" (1 Sam. 13:13). But, by repeated disobedience Saul eventually forfeited his kingdom (see 1 Sam. 13:8–14; 15:3, 9–11, 23).

To replace Saul, God chose David, "a man after His own heart" (1 Sam. 13:14). And God made a covenant with David and his posterity that built on both the Abrahamic and Mosaic covenants. While the Mosaic covenant established the Levite priesthood and sanctuary services, the Davidic covenant established David's kingship, promising to "establish the throne of his kingdom forever" and adopted David as His covenantal son, declaring, "I will be a father to him and he will be a son to Me" (2 Sam. 7:13–14).

Like the Abrahamic covenant, this is a royal grant covenant, with the promise of everlasting kingship and covenantal sonship passed down to David's descendants. Indeed, God told David, after you die, "I will raise up your descendant after you" and "establish his kingdom. He shall build a house for My name, and I will establish the throne of his kingdom forever. I will be a father to him and he will be a son to Me." And, "Your house and your kingdom shall endure before Me forever; your throne shall be established forever" (2 Sam. 7:12–16).

Further, God states, "I have made a covenant with My chosen; I have sworn to My servant David, I will establish your descendants forever and build up your throne to all generations" (Ps. 89:3–4). And, "I will also make him My firstborn, The highest of the kings of the earth.... I will not violate My covenant, nor will I alter the utterance of My lips. Once I have sworn by My holiness; I will not lie to David. His descendants shall endure forever, and his throne as the sun before Me" will "be established forever" (Ps. 89:27, 34–37).

The line of Davidic kings, however, was broken at the time of the Babylonian conquest and exile of Judah (sixth century BC). What, then, of these promises of an everlasting Davidic kingdom (cf. Ps. 89:38, 49)?

The Mosaic covenant had emphasized that covenant privileges and blessings could be forfeited by sustained unfaithfulness to the covenant (as seen earlier). This conditionality was re-emphasized in the Davidic covenant. While the overarching promise of granting an everlasting kingdom to David was unconditional, God repeatedly warned that the continued enjoyment of the blessings of the Davidic covenant by subsequent generations was conditional on covenant faithfulness.

Thus, David instructed Solomon: "Do your duty to the LORD your God, to walk in His ways, to keep His statutes, His commandments, His ordinances, and His testimonies, according to what is written in the Law of Moses, so that you may succeed in all that you do and wherever you turn, so that the LORD may fulfill His promise which He spoke regarding me, saying, 'If your sons are careful about their way, to walk before Me in truth with all their heart and all their soul, you shall not be deprived of a man to occupy the throne of Israel'" (1 Kings 2:1–4; cf. 3:6–7). Likewise, God told Solomon, "if you walk before Me as your father David walked, in integrity of heart and honesty, acting in accordance with everything that I have commanded you, and if you keep My statutes and My ordinances, then I will establish the throne of your kingdom over Israel forever, just as I promised to your father David, saying, 'You shall not be deprived of a man on the throne of Israel.' But if you or your sons indeed turn away from following Me, and do not keep My commandments and My statutes which I have placed before you, but you go and serve other gods and worship them, then I will cut

Israel off from the land which I have given them, and the house which I have consecrated for My name, I will expel from My sight" (1 Kings 9:4–7; see also Ps. 132:11–12).

Tragically, in a downward spiral of rebellion, most of David's successors abandoned God and His laws and committed egregious evils (even child sacrifice). God bore long with His covenant people but, despite repeated warnings through many prophets, they pushed God away "until there was no remedy" (2 Chron. 36:16), until there was nothing more God could do for them (see Isa. 5:1–7). After hundreds of years, mostly filled with apostasy, Babylon came and conquered Judah.

The line of merely human Davidic kings thus failed miserably. How, then, could God's promise of an everlasting Davidic kingdom be fulfilled?

The New Covenant

The Davidic covenant is fulfilled in the New Covenant through the Messiah—the Son of David and Son of God—whose kingdom will endure forever. Indeed, all the covenants surveyed earlier point to and are fulfilled in the New Covenant, confirmed by Christ's blood, which itself extended the Abrahamic covenant. Thus, at the Last Supper, Jesus explained, "This cup, which is poured out for you, is the new covenant in My blood" (Luke 22:20; cf. Matt. 26:28; Mark 14:24; 1 Cor. 11:25). Hebrews 13:20 identifies this as "the blood of the eternal covenant."

While extending beyond all preceding covenants, the New Covenant is not an *entirely* new thing but the fulfillment of overarching promises and other elements of the Old Covenant(s).[7] It is both old *and* new, part and parcel of the everlasting covenant, fulfilled ultimately through Christ. As Zechariah (John the Baptist's father) prophesied, God "raised up a horn of salvation for us in the house of His servant David" in order "to remember His holy covenant, the oath which He swore to our father Abraham" (Luke 1:69, 72–73).

What, then, is *new* about the New Covenant? And, what is *old* about the New Covenant?[8]

What Is New about the New Covenant?

In short, what is new about the New Covenant is the work of Christ as our perfect king, our perfect substitutionary sacrifice and high priest in the heavenly sanctuary. Christ's death took "place for the redemption of the violations that were committed under the first covenant," such that He is "the mediator of a new covenant" (Heb. 9:15). Christ gave Himself as the perfect, "once for all" sacrifice for us (Heb. 10:10) and now ministers as our "high priest of the good things having come" in the "greater and more perfect tabernacle, not made by hands, that is, not of this creation" (Heb. 9:11), the heavenly sanctuary, of which the earthly sanctuary, temples, and sacrifices were only figures (or types)—copies and shadows that could not actually deal with sin, but pointed to Christ's work (see Heb. 8:1–6; 9:11–15).

What is new about the New Covenant is the work of Christ as our perfect king, our perfect substitutionary sacrifice and high priest in the heavenly sanctuary.

The New Covenant is a "better covenant" (Heb. 8:6) because of Christ's atoning work, which was pointed to, but not yet actual, in the Old Covenant(s). Specifically, through Christ, the New Covenant includes a better priesthood (Heb. 7:22–28; 8:6), a better sacrifice (Heb. 9:12–14, 23), a better temple—the real heavenly sanctuary (Heb. 9:11), and "better promises" guaranteed by Christ Himself (Heb. 8:6).

The first covenant was faulty, but not due to any imperfection or fault on God's part—the fault lay in the creaturely parties involved; the sinful priests, imperfect sacrifices, and human-made sanctuary, and the sinfulness of the people who repeatedly broke the covenant (see Heb. 8:7–8; cf. Jer. 31:32). Thus, "finding fault with the people," God declared, "I will bring about a new covenant" (Heb. 8:7–8; cf. Jer. 31:31ff.). Humans and earthly systems failed such that Christ was needed to make atonement and fulfill the human part of the covenant that sinful humans could not fulfill on their own. In short, the Old Covenant(s) was incomplete without the New Covenant works of Christ as our sacrifice and high priest in the heavenly sanctuary.

To effectively deal with the problem of sin required better sacrifices, a better priesthood, and a greater temple promised in the better promises of the New Covenant. Whereas "it is impossible for the blood of bulls and goats to take away sins" (Heb. 10:4), Jesus is "the Lamb of God who takes away the sin of the world" (John 1:29). Whereas the blood of goats and calves needed to be offered over and over again, and still could not take away sins (Heb. 10:1, 4), Christ offered Himself as the "once for all" sacrifice, the "one sacrifice for sins for all time" (Heb. 10:10, 12; cf. 9:11–12, 26). The Old Covenant could not actually deal with sin but included only copies and shadows of that which could—the ministry of Christ promised in the New Covenant (see Heb. 10:1–4; 8:5).

Humans utterly broke the Old Covenant (cf. Heb. 8:7–9), which would leave humans hopelessly cut off from God without divine mediation to make atonement for sin. Thus, there was need of a human who would not fail but would perfectly keep the covenant. This God provided in Christ. In the New Covenant, Christ perfectly fulfilled the human part of the covenant and made the full atonement no mere human or earthly system could provide—He Himself is the *perfect* sacrifice and *perfect* priest who ministers in the "greater and more perfect" sanctuary in heaven, the guarantor of the better "promise of the eternal inheritance" (Heb. 9:11, 15), the free gift of salvation through Christ.

Since sin amounts to relational injustice that breaks love relationship, unavoidably separating humans from God, sin could not be dealt with by merely earthly rituals and animal sacrifices performed by sinful humans in a human-made sanctuary on behalf of humans who kept on sinning. The work of Christ is alone effective to deal with sin, providing atonement that makes *righteous* forgiveness possible on God's side and demonstrates God's righteousness and love, while also fulfilling the covenant on behalf of humans (as the second Adam) by His perfect life of obedience, even unto death.

In the New Covenant, Christ Himself (the God-man—Son of God and covenantal Son of David) fulfills both the divine and human sides of the covenant relationship, thus reconciling humans to God. In Christ, the New Covenant has both a perfect atonement made by God on our behalf, and a perfect human party who perfectly fulfills the Law—Jesus Christ the righteous; who stands as our substitute, making all who are willing heirs to the (overarching) promises of the eternal covenant. This stands in direct contrast to any attempts to fulfill the covenant obligations without Christ as our substitute and intercessor, which is utterly impossible. Anyone who tries to fulfill the covenant requirements by himself or herself (without surrendering to Christ) inevitably fails. Likewise, the Old Covenant(s) without the New Covenant would inevitably fail (i.e., *without Christ* providing the better sacrifice and priesthood in the more perfect heavenly sanctuary).

"For what the Law could not do, weak as it was through the flesh [of sinful humans], God did: sending His own Son in the likeness of sinful flesh and as an offering for sin, He condemned sin in the flesh, so that the requirement of the Law might be fulfilled in us" (Rom. 8:3–4; cf. Heb. 10:1ff.). Notice, Christ's work in the New Covenant does not annul the law but fulfills "the requirement of the Law" (more on this later). As Christ Himself taught, "Do not presume that I came to abolish the Law or the Prophets; I did not come to abolish, but to fulfill. For truly I say to you, until heaven and earth pass away, not the smallest letter or stroke of a letter shall pass from the Law, until all is accomplished!" (Matt. 5:17–18).

Among the "better promises" of the New Covenant is God's promise: "I WILL PUT MY LAWS INTO THEIR MINDS, AND WRITE THEM ON THEIR HEARTS" (Heb. 8:10; quoting from Jer. 31:33). In contrast to the mistaken view that one could be saved by one's works of keeping the law, salvation comes through Christ's works of atonement that fulfill the law for us, so any who accept Him as Savior and Lord are heirs to the promise.

In this regard, Paul presents the story of the two sons of Abraham (Ishmael and Isaac) as an allegory of the two covenants, contrasting the son born through Hagar—the product of Abraham's attempt to fulfill God's promise for himself (representing the old/first covenant)—with the son born to Sarah "through the promise," representing the New Covenant (Gal. 4:22–24). Thus, Paul contrasts Abraham's failed attempt to help God fulfill His promise of the covenantal son through Hagar (human works attempting to fulfill the covenant) with God's miracle of providing the promised son through Sarah, who was barren and past normal child-bearing age (God's work to fulfill the covenant). Abraham's failed attempt corresponds to every human attempt to fulfill the first covenant by *our works*, without the all-sufficient works of Christ that are provided *for us* in the New Covenant, according to God's promise.[9] Paul further identifies the first covenant as "Mount Sinai" and the earthly Jerusalem (the locations of the wilderness tabernacle and earthly temples of the Old Covenant) in contrast to the New Covenant, which Paul identifies as "the Jerusalem above" (the location of the heavenly sanctuary of the New Covenant, Gal. 4:24–25). The rituals and works of the earthly sanctuary system could not resolve the sin problem, but Christ's work in the heavenly sanctuary can and does (see chapter 16). Indeed, it "was necessary" that the heavenly sanctuary "be cleansed ... with better sacrifices" (Heb. 9:23), a work Christ accomplishes by His ministry in the heavenly sanctuary (see chapter 16). Hallelujah!

The needed atonement, cleansing of the heavenly sanctuary, and transformation of human hearts promised in the New Covenant—inscribing God's laws on our hearts (Jer. 31:33)—could be accomplished *only* through the ministry of Christ (the promised Son) and the Holy Spirit; itself "unlocked" by Christ's victorious death on the cross (see chapter 9, cf. John 7:39), which was necessary for the New Covenant to be put "in force" (Heb. 9:16–17; cf. Matt. 26:28). None of this could be provided by earthly rituals or human works of the Old Covenant, but could only be provided by the New Covenant works of Christ (the promised Son) on the cross and in the heavenly sanctuary.

This is the promise of the work God will eventually complete on behalf of all who believe in Christ. "He who has begun a good work in you will complete it until the day of Jesus Christ" (Phil. 1:6, NKJV). In the meantime, though we are faulty, Christ stands as the promised Son who is the faultless and unblemished sacrifice *in our stead*, the perfect unblemished "Lamb of God who takes away the sin of the world" (John 1:29; cf. Gen. 22; Matt. 26:28) and is "able to save to the uttermost those who come to God through Him, since He always lives to make intercession for them" (Heb. 7:25; cf. 1 John 1:9).

What Is Old *about the New Covenant?*

The very promises of the New Covenant themselves appear in the Old Testament (e.g., the Davidic covenant, see Jer. 31). The New Covenant itself is the fulfillment of the overarching promises of the Old Covenant(s), including God's promises that the woman's Seed would crush the serpent's head (Gen. 3:15), that all nations would be blessed through Abraham's seed (Gen. 22:18; cf. 12:3), and the seed of David (ultimately fulfilled in the covenantal Son of David) would rule over an everlasting kingdom (Ps. 89:4, 36–37; cf. 2 Sam. 7:13, 16).

The New Testament makes clear that the overarching promises of the Abrahamic covenant are not limited to biological descendants of Abraham or a particular nation but transcend national boundaries, including all those who "belong to Christ." Indeed, Paul writes: "There is neither Jew nor Greek, there is neither slave nor free, there is neither male nor female; for you are all one in Christ Jesus. And if you belong to Christ, then you are Abraham's descendants, heirs according to promise" (Gal. 3:28-29; cf. 3:6-9). Thus, there can be no *nationalistic* Christianity. Christ's kingdom is not of this world, not beholden to human kingdoms and their caste systems, but utterly transcends national and other boundaries that separate people (cf. Gal. 3:26-29, see more on this in chapter 17).

In a transnational way, the New Covenant fulfills God's promises to Abraham of a great posterity (all who belong to Christ), land (the new earth), blessing to all peoples (through Christ's work of atonement), and continued fellowship with God *with us* forever (cf. Gen. 12:1-3). Indeed, Paul writes, "it is those who are of faith who are sons of Abraham. The Scripture, foreseeing that God would justify the Gentiles by faith, preached the gospel beforehand to Abraham, saying, 'ALL THE NATIONS WILL BE BLESSED IN YOU.' So then, those who are of faith are blessed with Abraham, the believer" (Gal. 3:7-9).

In the Old Covenant, one became heir to the covenant blessings and promises and obligations by being a member of the Israelite nation (either by birth or by otherwise joining oneself to the nation). In the New Covenant, however, one becomes heir by faith in Christ (which, as we have seen, involves trust and allegiance to the promised covenantal Son).

Notably, however, even in the Old Covenant, people were not saved by simply being a member of the covenant community (even if some might have thought they were). Salvation was neither limited to the nation of Israel (e.g., Rahab, Ruth, and prophesied remnants of other nations), nor was every Israelite automatically saved.

One can only be saved through the work of Christ, prefigured by the sanctuary system of sacrifices and rituals laid out in the Mosaic covenant. In the New Covenant, those elements that were bound up with the nation of Israel (particular civil laws for governing society) and which pointed to Christ as their ultimate fulfillment (the system of ritual and ceremonial types, see Heb. 10:9) pass away, being replaced by the better sacrifices, priesthood, temple,

> *One can only be saved through the work of Christ, prefigured by the sanctuary system of sacrifices and rituals laid out in the Mosaic covenant.*

and promises of the New Covenant. The principles behind the civil and ceremonial laws remain, but the particular civil and ceremonial laws and obligations do not (see the later discussion in this chapter). In these respects, and others, by the "new covenant," God has "made the first old" and "ready to vanish away" (Heb. 8:13, KJV). However, the New Covenant does not do away with God's *moral* law but rather makes God's moral law of unselfish love internal to humans (Jer. 31:33; cf. Deut. 30, more on this later). If the New Covenant was to annul God's moral law (specified in the Old Testament and beyond), Christ need not have died to uphold justice with respect to it.[10] Again, Christ did not come to "abolish the Law or the Prophets" "but to fulfill" them (Matt. 5:17).

The particular Old Testament covenants are not entirely done away with, then, but are fulfilled. Those elements limited to the nation of Israel, or which were merely types of Christ's work, are the "shadow of the good things to come" (Heb. 10:1) that passed away with the New Covenant instituted by Christ. Yet, there is continuity between the New Covenant and the Old Covenant(s) at the level of the *transnational* promises of God and God's unchanging moral law of unselfish love that was already established in Eden.[11]

This raises a number of other questions and issues with regard to God's law, in particular, which we will turn to below.

Competing Theories in Christian Theology: Covenant Issues

The three most prominent approaches to covenant issues are known as covenant theology, dispensationalism, and New Covenant theology.

Covenant theology (prominent among Reformed thinkers) views the story of redemption in terms of two or three covenants. First, the covenant of redemption refers to a pre-creation covenant within the Trinity, including the plan of redemption (although some omit this). Second, the covenant of works refers to God's covenant with Adam (seen as the federal head or representative of the human race), in which perfect obedience would result in eternal life and disobedience would result in death. Third, the covenant of grace refers to God's covenant of salvation by grace through Christ's mediation. This covenant includes numerous "administrations" in the Old Testament and New Testament, differing in the so-called times of "law" (prior to Christ's coming) and "gospel" (from Christ's coming onward).

Covenant theology maintains that every person who is saved is saved by grace through faith. Covenant theology also views the Christian church as "spiritual Israel" (a kind of spiritual replacement of the nation of Israel), and holds that biblical civil laws (laws for governing Israelite society) and ceremonial laws (ritual, sacrificial laws) have been done away with, but the moral law (i.e., the Ten Commandments) remains.

Dispensationalism organizes biblical history into numerous "dispensations" (or administrations; distinct ways God ordered the divine-human relationship), emphasizes literal interpretation of Scripture, and teaches that Israel and the church are utterly distinct peoples of God such that divine promises and commands to one do not apply to the other.

Dispensationalists believe there are identifiable ages wherein God dealt with people differently, according to different "dispensations."[12] Dispensationalists differ regarding how many "dispensations" are identifiable. Classical dispensationalism identifies seven dispensations; the Age of:

- Innocence (Creation—Fall, Gen. 1:1–3:7),
- Conscience (Aftermath of Fall—Flood, Gen. 3:8–8:22),
- Human Government (Aftermath of Flood—Babel, Gen. 9:1–11:32),
- Promise (Abraham—Just Prior to Ten Commandments, Gen. 12:1–Exod. 19:25),
- Law (Ten Commandments—Pentecost, Exod. 20:1–Acts 2:4),
- Grace (Pentecost—Millennium, Acts 2:4–Rev. 20:3, i.e., Church Age), and
- (Millennial) Kingdom (Millennium, Rev. 20:4–6).

In each dispensation, people are saved by grace, but the content of faith differs. The church does not replace Israel but is always distinct and operates under an utterly distinct dispensation with different promises and commands. Promises and commands given prior to the Age of Grace (the Church Age) do *not* apply to the Church. Old Testament laws (and others given prior to the Church Age) only apply to Israel.

Most dispensationalists believe the Church Age began at Pentecost (Acts 2), but some (known as ultradispensationalists) believe the Church Age began later (e.g., Acts 9, Acts 13, or even as late as Acts 28). This holds significant implications regarding what promises and commands (laws) apply to the church.

The Church Age ends with Christ's return prior to the millennium (the "thousand years" referenced in Revelation 20). Many dispensationalists believe Christ will take believers to heaven and will leave others behind prior to the tribulation on earth prophesied in Revelation (a pretribulation view of the rapture, sometimes called the "secret rapture").

Given their belief that promises and commands made to Israel do not apply to the church, and their emphasis on literal interpretation of prophecy, dispensationalists believe all the (unconditional) promises given to Israel must be fulfilled to the *nation* of Israel.[13] Any such Old Testament promises yet to be fulfilled, they believe, will be fulfilled in a literal manner to the literal nation of Israel during a literal one thousand year kingdom on earth, ruled by Christ.

New Covenant theology teaches the Old Covenant (particularly the Mosaic covenant) has been abolished, superseded, and replaced by the New Covenant.[14] In this view, people are saved by grace through faith, but the Old Covenant was a "covenant of works" that was not sufficient for spiritual redemption. According to New Covenant theology, the church replaces and supersedes Israel as God's people. All promises prefigured (or typified) in the Old Covenant are somehow (often figuratively) realized in the church. Old Testament law has been canceled (a view known as antinomianism)—having been nailed to the cross and replaced by the "law of Christ," limited to what is specified in the New Testament.

Of these three, Adventist theology is closest to covenant theology; agreeing that civil and ceremonial laws are fulfilled, but the moral law remains in place for Christians. However, Adventist theology differs regarding (among other things) the seventh-day Sabbath, the nature of election/predestination, and the nuanced relationship between Israel and the church as one of both difference and "continuity."[15] For an abbreviated comparison of these four views, see the following chart.

OVERVIEW OF FOUR APPROACHES TO COVENANT ISSUES

	COVENANT THEOLOGY	DISPENSATIONALISM	NEW COVENANT THEOLOGY	ADVENTIST THEOLOGY
Overview	Two or three covenants: (redemption), works, grace	Various distinguishable economies in the outworking of God's purpose	Old (Mosaic) Covenant replaced by New Covenant	Many particular covenants, with considerable continuity among them, sometimes spoken of as one overarching covenant, the overarching promises of which are fulfilled in Christ's New Covenant works
Salvation	Saved by grace through faith (election) in OT and NT	Different dispensations of salvation	By grace through faith (election)	Saved by grace through faith in the OT and NT, as depicted in the sanctuary
Law	Civil and ceremonial laws have been done away with; moral laws remain in effect	Grace replaces law in the age of the church; law remains for Israel	Old Covenant law has been done away with—nailed to the cross	Civil and ceremonial laws no longer in effect (but principles remain); moral laws and "health" laws remain in effect
Israel/ Church	The church is "spiritual Israel"	Absolute distinction between Israel and the church—literal application of texts	The church has replaced Israel	Nuanced understanding of the relationship between Israel and the church as one of both difference and continuity
Eschatology	Typically postmillennialist or amillennialist	Dispensational premillennialist (secret rapture— pre-, mid-, or post-tribulation)	Various; often similar to Covenant Theology	Historicist and premillennialist (very different from dispensationalist premillennialism)

Understanding and Applying God's Law of Unselfish Love

"You shall love the LORD your God with all your heart, and with all your soul, and with all your mind," Jesus proclaimed. "This is the greatest and foremost commandment. The second is like it, 'You shall love your neighbor as yourself.' Upon these two commandments hang the whole Law and the Prophets" (Matt. 22:37–40).

God's law is the law of unselfish love. Even as God's covenants are grounded in love, aimed at healthy divine-human relationship and human flourishing, divine laws are all about love relationships—the vertical relationship of humans with God and horizontal relationships among humans (and other creatures).

> **God's law is the law of unselfish love.**

God's moral law is a transcript of God's character of perfect, unselfish love.[16] Indeed, as we will see, the Ten Commandments themselves are exemplifications of this law of unselfish love. The first four commandments exemplify love for God, and the last six (and part of the fourth) exemplify love for others.

God's moral law is simply God's instruction regarding *how* to love Him and one another—"love is the fulfillment of the Law" (Rom. 13:10).

Categories of Biblical Law

To understand which biblical laws apply today, it is crucial to recognize different kinds of laws according to their functions. Regarding any particular law, we might ask: Is this a *moral* command, a civil or ceremonial law, or something else?

Moral commands deal with things that are *fundamentally* good or evil. Moral laws, then, are descriptive of what is good and are opposed to what is evil in all times and places. Moral laws are thus universal and eternal rather than particular and temporary.[17]

Civil laws are temporary laws that apply to a particular civilization. The civil laws of the Old Testament governed Israelite society as a theocracy (with God as ruler) but do not apply to societies in other times and places.

Ceremonial laws are ritual or cultic laws that prescribed the sacrifices, rituals, and services that prefigured the plan of redemption fulfilled in

Christ and His work. These laws are temporary—to be kept until they are fulfilled by Christ's work, of which they are merely copies and shadows (cf. Col. 2:16-17; Heb. 8:5; 10:1-10)—though of continual educational value thereafter.

While many Christians recognize these categories of laws, Scripture itself does not *explicitly* identify these categories, and these categories can be employed in ways that oversimplify the complexity of biblical laws. Nevertheless, I believe the various *functions* (moral, civil, or ceremonial) of different laws are apparent in Scripture such that these categories are useful, when carefully handled.[18] Here, however, it is crucial to recognize that many biblical verses include more than one category of law (e.g., a verse might consist of a *moral* command followed by a *civil* penalty for breaking that command).

Additionally, Adventists typically identify biblical instructions that promote physical health (e.g., dietary benefits) as health laws.[19] Because the fundamental nature of humans and the principles of physical health remain (relatively) constant in this life, Adventists believe these health laws remain in effect as ways we should be good stewards of our God-given bodies.[20]

Overall, it might be preferable to affirm that the *principles* behind all biblical laws remain even after the particulars of some laws (e.g., civil, ceremonial) pass away. In this regard, Roy Gane suggests: "A biblical law should be kept to the extent that its principle can be applied unless the New Testament removes the reason for its application."[21]

Ceremonial Laws

The ceremonial laws of the Old Testament included sacrifices and rituals to be carried out by Levite priests at the sanctuary/temple—some daily, some weekly, some monthly, and some on particular feast days. These were "a copy and shadow of the heavenly things" (Heb. 8:5), "a shadow of the good things to come" (Heb. 10:1; cf. Col. 2:16-17), which prefigured Christ's works of atonement at the cross and in the heavenly sanctuary.[22]

Because of Christ's work of atonement pertaining to the heavenly sanctuary, the ritual or ceremonial laws that prefigured His works no longer need to be performed on earth. With the New Covenant, Christ "takes away the first in order to establish the second" (Heb. 10:9)—that is, Christ takes away the "shadow of the good things to come" (Heb. 10:1) prescribed in the ceremonial law, and establishes the New Covenant with its better sacrifices, priesthood, and temple (cf. Acts 15:5–7, 10, 28–29; Eph. 2:14–15; Heb. 8–10).

When Christ died on the cross, "the veil of the temple was torn in two from top to bottom; and the earth shook and the rocks were split" (Matt. 27:51; cf. Mark 15:38; Luke 23:45). This dramatically signaled the end of the ceremonial system that prefigured Christ's works of atonement.[23]

The ceremonial laws are no longer in force because their temporary function is fulfilled in Christ's work. And today, the ceremonial laws cannot be kept as written because we no longer have an earthly temple, a Levite priesthood, or animal sacrifices (see, e.g., Heb. 10:9–14). All these are replaced by Christ's work as our perfect once-for-all sacrifice and high priest ministering for us in the heavenly sanctuary (see Heb. 9:11–15, 23–28).

Civil Laws

Old Testament civil laws are no longer in force because they were prescribed to govern Israelite society as a theocracy—ruled by God as God's unique covenant people. Civil laws and penalties were not given for all times and places and thus do not remain in force today, when God's covenant people consist of all who "belong to Christ" (cf. Gal. 3:29), whose "kingdom is not of this world" (John 18:36).

The civil penalties, in particular (such as death penalties for various infractions), seem very harsh today. Here, it is crucial to remember the context in which the civil laws and penalties were given. Israel had just come out of centuries of slavery in Egypt. They had never governed themselves. They were without a homeland, traveling through a hostile wilderness in the midst of nations that sought to destroy them. At every turn, their collective lives were in peril. If strife and civil war erupted, the people would destroy themselves in the wilderness.

Both naturally and in terms of cosmic forces in the cosmic conflict, Israel's continued existence depended on the special protection and sustenance of God (who miraculously fed them and protected them from poisonous snakes and hostile nations ruled by demons, cf. Heb. 8:14–17). Without God's special preservation, they would have *all* perished in the wilderness. Yet, God's special preservation itself hinged on the people remaining in special covenant relationship with Him. Given the rules of engagement in the cosmic conflict (see chapter 9), if the people rejected God and gave themselves over to other "gods," they would thereby cut themselves off from the special covenant privileges as God's allotted portion (cf. Deut. 32:8–9).

In this regard, it is easy to forget that even a slight deviation from God's commands is a very serious matter. Were it not for God's amazing grace, even one sin would cut us off from the life giver Himself, resulting in death. Many people take God's grace for granted, not recognizing that we only continue to live because God graciously makes a way to preserve us despite our sin.

Given that all the Israelites' lives were at risk, it makes sense that penalties for violations of the law would be strict, functioning as deterrents that might save the people from destruction. An airplane passenger who decides to disobey a flight attendant's commands faces serious legal penalties. However, the same person can disobey a flight attendant's commands at (for example) a ballgame without legal penalty. Why? Because, in an airplane, even slight deviations from flight crew instructions can put all passengers' lives at risk.

In the wilderness, even slight deviations from God's instructions put the lives of all Israelites at risk. Everyone was in the same boat (or plane), so to speak. Such penalties were not to be applied in all circumstances—they were neither ideal nor universal instructions. They were not to remain in force forever (Jesus Himself later stood against the crowd assembled to stone a woman caught in adultery according to the civil law; see John 8). They were given for a particular people in a particularly dangerous context, as guidelines and deterrents to ultimately keep them safe from destruction.[24]

As discussed (in part) in chapter 11, some laws given to Israel were far from ideal because God was dealing with sinful humans mired in a cosmic conflict. Sinful practices ingrained in ancient Near Eastern culture could not simply be legislated away. So, God gave *ideal* laws—articulating the ideals of unselfish love, but God also articulated *remedial* laws that would mitigate and curtail some of the harm of practices God knew people would engage in contrary to and despite His ideal commands (see the discussion of remedial laws regarding slavery and divorce in chapter 11). While far from ideal, such remedial laws were significant improvements over ancient Near Eastern customs and laws of the time. If followed, the remedial laws would greatly improve people's lives and guard against more heinous practices of the day. And, if God's ideal laws of unselfish love were perfectly followed, there would be no occasion for such remedial laws in the first place.

To take just one example for now, many critics of Scripture quote Deuteronomy 22:28-29, "If a man finds a girl who is a virgin, who is not betrothed, and he seizes her and has sexual relations with her, and they are discovered, then the man who had sexual relations with her shall give the girl's father fifty shekels of silver, and she shall become his wife, because he has violated her; he is not allowed to divorce her all his days."

Critics often construe this law as if it commands that a woman who is raped must marry her rapist. But is that what this remedial law commands? The word translated "seizes" (*taphas*) here is different from the word used to describe rape earlier in the chapter, and likely refers not to rape but to seduction. There is good reason to understand Deuteronomy 22:28 as a law dealing with *consensual* extra-marital sex between a man and woman who are neither married nor engaged to anyone.[25]

What supports this conclusion? This law appears in a series of three cases that all involve a man having sex with a virgin woman outside of marriage; the differences between them being whether the woman was engaged, and whether she was raped.

In the first case (Deut. 22:23-24), the woman is engaged, but no rape is involved (indicated by the phrase, "she did not cry out for help... in the city," Deut. 22:24). Thus, both the man and woman are to be penalized for their infraction (on the severity of the penalties, see the earlier discussion of the perilous context of civil laws).

In the second case, the woman is engaged to be married, and she is the victim of rape, "the man seizes her and rapes her [*hazaq + shakav*]," and she "cried out, but there was no one to save her" (Deut. 22:25, 27). In this case, the rapist is to be put to death, but "you are not to do anything to the girl" because she "cried out, but there was no one to save her" (Deut. 22:26-27). This stands *in direct contrast* to other ancient laws, such as middle Assyrian laws that included "honor killings" of the *victims* of rape and "revenge rapes," which consisted of the wife or daughter of the rapist being raped in revenge.[26]

In the third case (Deuteronomy 22:28), the woman is *not* engaged and is *not* the victim of rape. The phrase translated as (the man) "seizes her" (*taphas* + *shakav*) uses a different word than the terminology for rape in the previous case, and here likely refers to seduction. That both the man and woman are to blame seems to be indicated by the words "they are discovered." If so, this law does not command women to marry their rapists. Rather, it commands the man who engaged in consensual extra-marital sex to marry the woman and *never* divorce her (cf. Exod. 22:16–17), protecting her from being left in a destitute state (unmarried women had few options to support themselves in ancient Near Eastern cultures).[27]

Here and elsewhere throughout the story of Scripture, God is often performing triage; giving ideal moral laws (such as the Ten Commandments) that would have prevented the kinds of problems dealt with in remedial laws but which were often ignored, while also giving *remedial* laws that were far from ideal in order to deal with far from ideal real-life situations that could not simply be legislated away, while moving people to a trajectory toward the ideal.

Health Laws

As noted earlier, many Adventists categorize biblical laws that promote physical health as health laws, believed to remain in effect because the fundamental nature of human physical health remains (relatively) constant in this life.

While not directly identified in Scripture as *health* laws, in retrospect, some laws greatly improved sanitation and hygiene, mitigated the spread of disease (e.g., Lev. 13:45–46), and prescribed dietary restrictions that (we now know) yield considerable health benefits.

Scripture teaches that our bodies are to be temples of God (see 1 Cor. 6:19–20; cf. 3:16–17). Accordingly, Adventists believe humans have a solemn and sacred duty to take care of our health as much as possible, as good stewards of our bodies (and lives as a whole), which are gifts of God. Far from being bad news or burdensome commands, laws that would improve health are good news, helping humans to flourish and enjoy more abundant life.

Regarding dietary laws, Adventists typically believe the laws given to Israel regarding clean and unclean foods remain in effect today (see Lev. 11; Deut. 14).[28] Such laws command dietary practices that we now know improve health.

Further, the distinction between clean and unclean animals appears in the flood story long before the Mosaic law was given. Only two of each unclean animal were preserved in Noah's ark—just enough to reproduce—while seven pairs of the clean animals were brought (Gen. 7:2-3; cf. 8:20). Given that only some clean animals were designated as proper sacrifices, provision for seven pairs of *all* clean animals would not be needed only for sacrificial purposes. Such provision would make sense, however, in light of the permission given humans to eat animals (after the flood devastated much of the edible vegetation, Gen. 9:3-4). The prohibition of eating unclean animals is thus implicit; since eating one of only one pair would render the animal extinct.

The distinction between clean and unclean animals, then, preceded the nation of Israel and cannot thus be limited to Israel. Further, God referenced this distinction when instructing Israel not to follow the "detestable" customs of the nations (Lev. 20:23-26).

What about New Testament passages that some believe annul such food laws? Upon inspection, such passages do not annul the food laws but address defilement by association—that is, traditional restrictions regarding not eating or touching anything that had touched something unclean.

For example, Jesus declared, "whatever goes into the person from outside cannot defile him, because it does not go into his heart, but into his stomach, and is eliminated" (Mark 7:18-19). Then, many translations add, "Thereby He declared all foods clean" (Mark 7:19). Translated literally, however, this last phrase simply reads, "cleansing all foods" or "purging all foods." The idea that Christ "declared" all foods clean is added by translators. But, translated literally, the text teaches that the process of digestion cleanses the food in the ways relevant to the context. Specifically, what one eats "does not go into his heart, but into his stomach, and is eliminated, thus cleansing all foods." By considering the wider context of Mark 7, one can see that Christ is not addressing the distinction between clean and unclean foods.[29] Rather, Jesus is responding to the Pharisees' criticism of Christ's disciples for "eating their bread with unholy hands, that is, unwashed" hands—meaning without first ritually washing their hands according to "the traditions of the elders" (Mark 7:2–3).[30] Here, Jesus challenges the extra-biblical traditions regarding ritual cleansing that were part of the false view of defilement by association that was customary then.[31]

Elsewhere, Peter was shocked by a vision where he saw unclean animals, and a voice told him to "kill and eat." Peter protested, "I have never eaten anything unholy and unclean." The voice responded, "What God has cleansed, no longer consider unholy" (Acts 10:12–15). The context indicates this vision was not about clean and unclean foods but about Peter's negative view of Gentiles and defilement by association. Contrary to the human-made, extra-biblical law that Jews were not "to associate with or visit a foreigner," Peter explained, "God has shown me that I am not to call any person unholy or unclean" (Acts 10:28). Rather than overturning food laws, the vision was to teach Peter not to discriminate against people based on their ethnicity, and to recognize that "God is not one to show partiality, but in every nation the one who fears Him and does what is right is acceptable to Him" (Acts 10:34–35; cf. 10:45).

While God allowed humans to eat animals after the flood (without consuming blood, due to the sacredness of life, Gen. 9:4), the ideal diet from the beginning was a vegetarian diet. Such a diet is not only better for human health but also better regarding the treatment of animals and the environment as a whole. The mass production of meat is a major contributor to environmental harm and resource depletion, expending a staggering number of resources, including a huge amount of food that could relieve human hunger throughout the world.[32] Widespread practices of "ethical eating" would help to mitigate some of this harm.

Seventh-day Adventist teaching does not mandate vegetarianism, but many Adventists are vegetarian or vegan in an attempt to get closer to the ideal diet as stewards of one's own health and the environment. Historically, the Adventist faith has stressed a holistic approach to human health (the health message).[33] This includes limiting consumption of unhealthy food and other unhealthy substances, and refraining entirely from other harmful substances (such as alcohol, tobacco, and illicit drugs), alongside positive health practices such as regular exercise and proper rest. Some best health practices emphasized by Seventh-day Adventists are summarized in the acronym NEWSTART, which stands for: Nutrition, Exercise, Water, Sunshine, Temperance, [Fresh] Air, Rest, and Trust in God.[34]

Such practices also benefit mental health, which is extremely important. Viewing humans as wholistic beings, the Seventh-day Adventist faith is concerned with human health as a whole: physical, mental, and spiritual. Notably, many studies show that, on average, Adventists are healthier and live longer than the general population.[35] Part of the Adventist mission is to help people come to ways of healthy living that result in more abundant life now.[36]

All of creation is *God's* creation, and concern for health (our own, that of animals, and creation as a whole) is one way of living in accordance with God's own love and care for creation.

Moral Laws

God's moral law is the law of unselfish love, a reflection of God's own righteousness and character of perfect love (Luke 6:36; cf. Lev. 19:2; Ps. 19:7–8; 119:142, 172). This law is not arbitrary (as if one could make evil good or good evil) but flows immutably from God's essential nature for "God is love" (1 John 4:8, 16).[37]

> *God's moral law is the law of unselfish love, a reflection of God's own righteousness and character of perfect love.*

The most prominent group of moral laws are the Ten Commandments in Exodus 20:3–17:

1. "You shall have no other gods before Me."
2. "You shall not make for yourself an idol, or any likeness of what is in heaven above or on the earth beneath, or in the water under the earth. You shall not worship them nor serve them; for I, the LORD your God, am a jealous God, inflicting the punishment of the fathers on the children, on the third and the fourth generations of those who hate Me, but showing favor to thousands, to those who love Me and keep My commandments."
3. "You shall not take the name of the LORD your God in vain, for the LORD will not leave him unpunished who takes His name in vain."

4. "Remember the Sabbath day, to keep it holy. For six days you shall labor and do all your work, but the seventh day is a Sabbath of the Lord your God; on it you shall not do any work, you, or your son, or your daughter, your male slave or your female slave, or your cattle, or your resident who stays with you. For in six days the Lord made the heavens and the earth, the sea and everything that is in them, and He rested on the seventh day; for that reason the Lord blessed the Sabbath day and made it holy."
5. "Honor your father and your mother, so that your days may be prolonged on the land which the Lord your God gives you."
6. "You shall not murder" [or "kill," depending on which translation is to be preferred].
7. "You shall not commit adultery."
8. "You shall not steal."
9. "You shall not give false testimony against your neighbor."
10. "You shall not covet your neighbor's house; you shall not covet your neighbor's wife, or his male slave, or his female slave, or his ox, or his donkey, or anything that belongs to your neighbor."

While most of these commandments follow the "you shall not..." pattern, the fourth and fifth commandments are stated as positive commands. These serve as a hinge between the first four commandments, which focus on relationship to God, and the last six (and part of the fourth), which focus on human relationships with one another.

These ten laws themselves are exemplifications of the greatest commandments, which Jesus identified as wholeheartedly loving God and loving one's neighbor as oneself (Matt. 22:37–39). Notably, Jesus quoted both of these commandments from the Old Testament (Deut. 6:5; Lev. 19:18) and said, "Upon these two commandments hang the whole Law and the Prophets" (Matt. 22:40).

At the root of the moral law, then, is love.[38] The Ten Commandments themselves exemplify how to love God and one another. God's moral law is the law of unselfish love and, accordingly, "love is the

> **At the root of the moral law, then, is love.**

fulfillment of the Law" (Rom. 13:10). When God and creatures uphold this law, we uphold love.

The two greatest commands of love correspond to what the Old Testament prophets identify as the greatest sins—idolatry (corresponding to lack of love for God) and social injustice (corresponding to lack of love for our neighbors). The God of Scripture loves justice (Ps. 33:5; Isa. 61:8) and detests injustice, continually commanding humans to foster justice according to God's law of unselfish love. For example, God commands: "Learn to do good; seek justice, rebuke the oppressor, obtain justice for the orphan, plead for the widow's case" (Isa. 1:17; cf. Mic. 6:8). Likewise, God declares: "Dispense true justice and practice kindness and compassion each to his brother; and do not oppress the widow or the orphan, the stranger or the poor; and do not devise evil in your hearts against one another" (Zech. 7:9-10). A myriad of other texts emphasize justice and love; highlighting the works of mercy and love for the poor and oppressed that accompany true faith, without which faith is dead (see James 2).[39]

There are many moral laws in Scripture beyond the Ten Commandments, but all such laws are laws of unselfish love. Accordingly, Jesus emphasized the ideals of love and justice as far weightier than lesser matters, saying, "woe to you Pharisees! For you pay tithes of mint, rue, and every kind of garden herb, and yet you ignore justice and the love of God; but these are the things you should have done without neglecting the others" (Luke 11:42). In the parallel in Matthew 23:23-24, Jesus says, you "have neglected the weightier provisions of the Law: justice and mercy and faithfulness; but these are the things you should have done without neglecting the others. You blind guides, who strain out a gnat and swallow a camel!"

Applied today, these teachings call Christians to stand against evil in whatever form, with special concern for the way sin and evil harms people; all of whom God loves, and for whom Christ died. In this regard, Ellen White comments: "Every false religion teaches its adherents to be careless of human needs, sufferings, and rights."[40] The Christianity of Scripture, however, consistently teaches us to be deeply concerned about human needs, sufferings, and rights. As the enemy of humans and all God's beloved creatures, it is no coincidence that the devil opposes

God's law of unselfish love, attempting to change God's "times and laws" through his beastly agents (Dan. 7:25, see chapter 18).

The Moral Law Is Good and Continues for Our Good

If you've flown on an airplane, you should be thankful for air traffic controllers. They direct planes regarding when and where to take off and land, and what flight patterns to use. Although pilots have every intention of avoiding collisions, without air traffic control, countless collisions would occur. Even when everyone has *only* good intentions, some rules and guidelines are needed for everyone's good.

Even in a perfect world, we will need God's law of unselfish love to avoid unintentional conflicts of interest. If (at least) billions of free creatures do whatever they want without any regard for overarching laws, conflicts would occur even if everyone intended only good.

Contrary to the serpent's insinuations in Eden and beyond, as mere creatures, we cannot be a law unto ourselves because we do not know what is best in all circumstances—we cannot even fathom all the factors involved. Only one who knows everything—the end from the beginning—could lovingly direct the "traffic" of creaturely interests such that there would be no conflict, ensuring perfect peace, harmony, and the greatest flourishing of all. God's moral law—the law of unselfish love—is necessary for the harmony of the universe.

> God's moral law—the law of unselfish love—is necessary for the harmony of the universe.

Why does Paul, then, sometimes speak negatively of "the Law"? In brief, Paul is *often* referring to laws, or interpretations of laws, insofar as they were used to separate Jews from Gentiles (e.g., circumcision). Through His New Covenant ministry, Christ broke down the walls of separation between Jews and Gentiles. Thus, Paul writes, Christ "Himself is our peace, who made both groups [Jews and Gentiles] into one and broke down the barrier of the dividing wall, by abolishing in His flesh the hostility, which is the Law composed of commandments expressed in ordinances, so that in Himself He might make the two one new person, in this way establishing peace" (Eph. 2:14–15).[41]

Some interpret these verses (and others) as nullifying God's moral law (i.e., the Ten Commandments) but such an interpretation does not fit since the moral law *itself* did not separate Jews from Gentiles but applied to all people.[42] Further, such an interpretation contradicts Paul's teachings elsewhere. For example, Paul wrote: "Do we then nullify the Law through faith? Far from it! On the contrary, we establish the Law" (Rom. 3:31) and "the Law is holy, and the commandment is holy and righteous and good" (Rom. 7:12; cf. Ps. 19:7; 111:7–9).

Paul did not reject God's law, but the *misuse* of divine laws relative to continuing to separate Jews from Gentiles, or thinking one can save oneself by law-keeping (legalism)—whether by rituals (relative to the ceremonial law) or by good works (relative to the moral law; cf. Rom. 3:28; Gal. 3:11).

The law is not a means of salvation: "For by grace you have been saved through faith; and this is not of yourselves, it is the gift of God; not a result of works, so that no one may boast" (Eph. 2:8–9).[43] Accordingly, Paul teaches "the Law" is like a tutor to lead us to Christ—who alone can save us and through whom *anyone* can be "Abraham's descendants, heirs according to promise" (see Gal. 3:24–29). We are not "under the Law" as a means of salvation but "under grace." Yet, this does not give us license to continue to sin and break God's moral law (Rom. 6:14–15; cf. 1 John 3:4). The problem is not God's law itself, then, but its misuse. Indeed, "the Law is good, if one uses it lawfully" (1 Tim. 1:8).

When Paul says, "Christ is the end of the Law for righteousness to everyone who believes" (Rom. 10:4), Paul does not mean Christ puts an end to God's moral law (which would amount to Paul contradicting himself and the rest of Scripture, see Rom. 3:31), but uses the word "end" (*telos*) in the sense of goal.[44] Indeed, why would Christ put an end to the law He died to uphold? If the *moral* law could just be abolished, why die for our sins?[45]

In this regard, Christ Himself taught: "Do not presume that I came to abolish the Law or the Prophets; I did not come to abolish, but to fulfill. For truly I say to you, until heaven and earth pass away, not the smallest letter or stroke of a letter shall pass from the Law, until all is accomplished! Therefore, whoever nullifies one of the least of these commandments, and teaches others to do the same, shall be called least in the kingdom of heaven; but whoever keeps and teaches them, he shall be called great in the kingdom of heaven" (Matt. 5:17–19).[46]

Christ's work did not cancel the moral law but "canceled the certificate of debt consisting of decrees against us, which was hostile to us; and He has taken it out of the way, having nailed it to the cross" (Col. 2:13–14). This "certificate of debt consisting of decrees against us" might refer to our indebtedness relative to the Law, covered by Christ's sacrifice, or it might be understood as a reference to the ceremonial laws fulfilled by Christ. But, given Paul's teachings and those of the rest of Scripture, this cannot consistently be understood as referring to the cancellation of God's *moral* law. In this regard, a *lawless* "god" would not be good news for the abused and oppressed.[47] But, the one true God does not simply cancel the law of love and sweep evils like abuse, oppression, and injustice under the rug. God deals with sin in ways that uphold the law (see chapter 13) *because* God is love.[48]

As such, "all [God's] precepts are trustworthy. They are upheld forever and ever" (Ps. 111:7–8). Accordingly, Christ taught, "If you love Me, you will keep My commandments" (John 14:15; cf. 1 John 2:3–4; 3:4). And, in the end, "the saints" are those "who keep the commandments of God and their faith in Jesus" (Rev. 14:12; cf. 12:17).

Although the Law cannot save, it is not invalidated by redemption. Paul writes, "Are we to continue in sin so that grace may increase? Far from it! How shall we who died to sin still live in it?" (Rom. 6:1–2). Further, "Is the Law sin? Far from it! On the contrary, I would not have come to know sin except through the Law; for I would not have known about coveting if the Law had not said, 'You shall not covet'" (Rom. 7:7).

The Law itself is not the problem; the problem is our sin and inclination to sin, which rebels against God's law. Thus, Paul writes, "sin, taking an opportunity through the commandment, deceived me, and through it, killed me. So then, the Law is holy, and the commandment is holy and righteous and good" (Rom. 7:11–12). Does this mean, Paul asks, "that which is good become a cause of death for me? Far from it! Rather it was sin, in order that it might be shown to be sin by bringing about my death through that which is good [the Law], so that through the commandment sin would become utterly sinful" (Rom. 7:13).

While "the Law is spiritual," Paul goes on, "I am fleshly, sold into bondage to sin" and find "the principle [literally "law," *nomos*] that evil is present in me" (Rom. 7:14, 21). "For I joyfully agree with the law of

God in the inner person, but I see a different law in the parts of my body waging war against the law of my mind, and making me a prisoner of the law of sin, the law which is in my body's parts" (Rom. 7:22–23).

The law of God is against us because of our sin *and* our sinful nature—the "law of sin" in us. God's law exposes and condemns our sins and sinfulness. In this sense, "the power of sin is the law" (1 Cor. 15:56). Unless a Savior makes atonement for our sins, we cannot be righteous before God's law (cf. Gal. 3:11–14).

Further, God's law is contrary to our sinful inclinations. Even as telling a child not to touch a hot stove often prompts them to do so, because of our sinful nature, we are prone to rebel against God's laws. We thus need a heart transplant, which only God can provide and promises to provide in the New Covenant, saying, "'this is the covenant which I will make with the house of Israel after those days,' declares the Lord: 'I will put My law within them and write it on their heart; and I will be their God, and they shall be My people'" (Jer. 31:33; quoted in Heb. 8:10; cf. Ps. 40:8).

Good though it is, the law given by Moses cannot defeat the law of sin in us—our sinful nature. Only Christ's work of atonement in the New Covenant accomplishes that. Yet, Paul assures those who are in Christ by faith, "the law of the Spirit of life in Christ Jesus has set you free from the law of sin and of death. For what the Law could not do, weak as it was through the flesh, God did: sending His own Son in the likeness of sinful flesh and as an offering for sin, He condemned sin in the flesh, so that the requirement of the Law might be fulfilled in us" (Rom. 8:2–4).

While there are many things the law cannot do (such as make righteous or save), the "Law" itself is "holy and righteous and good" (Rom. 7:12), and God intends our good through it. Among its many positive functions, God's law:

- reveals God's character of perfect love.
- teaches us what is good and just.
- guides us in the best ways of abundant life—the Lamb's ways of love and justice.
- shows our sin, like a mirror (Rom. 3:2; 7:7; James 1:22–25).
- shows our need of a Savior and functions as a schoolmaster to lead us to Christ (Gal. 3:22–24).[49]

While God's laws might sometimes seem strict, particularly when considered out of context, God's law is (among other things) intended to serve as guardrails to keep us from destroying ourselves—from falling off the side of a cliff, as it were. The law serves to protect us from cutting ourselves off from the only source of life, light, and joy—the living God who is Himself love.

God is *the* single source of life and light and love and joy. There is no life, light, love, or joy apart from Him. Anything you might identify as a source of these things actually depends on God. To finally reject God's law of love is to reject God, who Himself is love, and thus cut oneself off from love and life altogether.

> The law serves to protect us from cutting ourselves off from the only source of life, light, and joy—the living God who is Himself love.

We may now enjoy relationship with the perfectly holy and loving God, despite our sinfulness, only because God has graciously made a way to reconcile us to Him—a bit like a tunnel under a mountain that will eventually collapse. God holds this "tunnel" open to rescue as many as possible. But many mistakenly think the "tunnel" we live in now is the way things "naturally" are, not recognizing it is only God's grace that gives us this path back to Him, with His law of love to guide us. When God warns us against sin, He warns us out of profound concern and love for us to spare us from harm, given that sin is always harmful. He does not want to condemn you but to save you from all harm and give you unending, abiding joy.

The authors of Scripture treasured God's law as a precious gift. While ancient Near Eastern "gods" were immoral, fickle, arbitrary, and petty such that people never knew just what might please them, the God of Scripture is just the opposite. Imagine living in constant fear that the "gods" would not be happy with you, whatever you might think, say, or do! In contrast, the prophets throughout Scripture frequently praise God for His law because it clearly displays what God desires and expects, revealing God's constancy, perfect love, and justice. A dichotomy between law and grace would have puzzled ancient Israelites, who saw God's giving of His law itself as a great display of God's gracious favor, providing assurance, peace, and hope.[50]

Thus, the psalmist wrote, "How I love Your Law! It is my meditation all the day. . . . How sweet are Your words to my taste! Yes, sweeter than honey to my mouth! From Your precepts I get understanding" and "Your word is a lamp to my feet and a light to my path" (Ps. 119:97, 103-105).

Many think of God's law as abstract "dos and don'ts," but God's law of love expresses the principles of abundant life—the avenue to true contentment and *genuine* happiness. God's moral laws are not abstract principles but commands and instructions for the harmonious flourishing of all creation.

Imagine driving a car in busy city traffic. Now, imagine there are no traffic laws, stoplights, stop signs, traffic directions, nor lines on the road. Similar to the chaos, death, and destruction that would ensue if everyone drove cars on busy streets without any traffic laws or guidelines, apart from God's law, creation could not flourish. God's law of unselfish love is for everyone's good.

If God's law keeps you from what is currently your heart's desire, that is only because your heart and its desires are diseased (cf. Jer. 17:9). God's law of love never keeps you from what you would desire if you knew what God knows with only loving intentions. As David Asscherick put it, "You do not really want what the law forbids. Even if you think you do, you don't want what Jesus doesn't want for you."[51]

God knows you better than you know yourself, loves you far more than you love yourself (or anyone else), knows just what is best for you and all others, wants only what is best for you and others, and possesses the power to finally bring about everyone's best good. God's law is good and can be trusted because God is love.

> **God's law is good and can be trusted because God is love.**

Conclusion: Why Does It Matter?

It was the happiest day of her life. Her wedding day was everything she'd imagined it would be. She'd dreamed of it since she was a child. He, she thought, was everything she had longed for. She believed they would be happy together forever.

As they exchanged vows, she had meant every word—"to have and to hold, in sickness and in health, till death do us part."

Those words were bitter in her memory now. He had recited them, just as she had; words that were to commit them to a covenant of marriage that was never to be broken. But he—her beloved husband—had broken the marriage covenant. After months of secrecy, she discovered he was intimately involved with another woman. She was devastated.

Maybe you are familiar with this kind of betrayal. If you are, I am sorry for the pain someone's lack of loyal love has caused. If you are not, you can easily imagine how you might feel in this woman's place.

The love commitment of marriage matters deeply to us, as it should. We have been created and designed for exclusivity in romantic relationships to matter at the core of our being. We have been created for committed, loving relationship with God and others (whether in marriage or other relationships such as other family relationships and/or loyal friendships). The commitment of covenant love matters even more to God.

As we've seen briefly, Scripture depicts God as the unrequited lover, the husband scorned by an unfaithful wife. He not only lowers Himself to establish and enter into covenant relationship with mere creatures voluntarily, He also does everything He can to maintain covenant love relationship *with us*, despite the fact that we have been unfaithful.

Among other things, God provides instructions for how we can enjoy covenant love in a way that is best for all concerned, found in God's law of unselfish love. This law provides a roadmap to the most abundant life, about which we will see more in the following chapter, relative to the great gift of the Sabbath. In this and other regards, God's law of unselfish love does not consist of abstract commands, but every part of it is that which is necessary for the flourishing of love relationship. Not one part of God's law is arbitrary or petty—it is all motivated by the perfect unselfish love of God for the best good of all. God's law is not given to keep us from any good thing but to protect us from that which would harm us.

Do you desire covenant love relationship with God and others? Anyone who wishes to enter or continue in such relationship must be willing to live according to the eternal principles of unselfish love. You need not, indeed you *cannot*, do so by yourself. If you ask God, He will perform in you (over time) the work of writing His law of unselfish love on your heart.

In this regard, I invite you to read and reflect on Jeremiah 31, focusing on how it describes God's everlasting love for humans that draws people even before they love in return (see v. 3) and the way God works in the New Covenant to put His law of unselfish love in human hearts, promising "I will be their God, and they shall be My people" (Jer. 31:33).

Questions for Reflection

1. Is there one covenant between God and humans in Scripture or many? In what sense(s) are there many, and in what other sense(s) is there one overarching covenant?
2. What is the difference between the Old and New Covenant(s)? In what ways is Christ Himself at the center of this distinction?
3. Does the New Covenant do away with the laws of the Old Testament? Why is this important relative to our understanding of biblical law?
4. What are the different kinds of laws in the Old Testament? How does this help us know how to relate to biblical laws today?
5. Can one be saved by keeping the law? How can one avoid legalism?
6. What might you say to someone who thinks of God's laws as burdensome? How could you help them see they are for our good?
7. You can be in special covenantal relationship with God even now. Do you want to enter into such relationship? If so, invite God to write His law on your heart, to fill you with His unselfish love, and to help you reflect that love to others.

For Further Reading

Adventist Perspectives:

Doukhan, Jacques. *Israel and the Church: Two Voices for the Same God.* Peabody, MA: Hendrickson, 2002.

Frey, Mathilde. "Sabbath Theology in the Book of Revelation." In *Toward a Theology of the Remnant: An Adventist Ecclesiological Perspective.* Edited by Ángel Manuel Rodríguez. Studies in Adventist Ecclesiology 1. Silver Spring, MD: Biblical Research Institute, 2009.

Gane, Roy E. *Old Testament Law for Christians.* Grand Rapids, MI: Baker Academic, 2017.

———. "The Role of God's Moral Law, Including Sabbath, in the 'New Covenant.'" Accessed November 3, 2021. https://adventistbiblicalresearch.org/materials/the-role-of-gods-moral-law-including-sabbath-in-the-new-covenant.

Hasel, Gerhard F., *Covenant in Blood.* Mountain View, CA: Pacific Press, 1982.

——— and Michael G. Hasel, *The Promise: God's Everlasting Covenant.* Nampa, ID: Pacific Press, 2021.

LaRondelle, Hans K. *Our Creator Redeemer: An Introduction to Biblical Covenant Theology.* Berrien Springs, MI: Andrews University Press, 2005.

———. *The Israel of God in Prophecy: Principles of Prophetic Interpretation.* Berrien Springs, MI: Andrews University Press, 1983.

McCarty, Skip. *In Granite or Ingrained? What the Old and New Covenants Reveal About the Gospel, the Law, and the Sabbath.* Berrien Springs, MI: Andrews University Press, 2007.

Peckham, John C. *The Concept of Divine Love in the Context of the God-World Relationship.* New York: Peter Lang, 2014.

Reid, George W. "Health and Healing." In *Handbook of Seventh-day Adventist Theology.* Edited by Raoul Dederen. Hagerstown, MD: Review and Herald, 2000.

Veloso, Mario. "The Law of God." In *Handbook of Seventh-day Adventist Theology.* Edited by Raoul Dederen. Hagerstown, MD: Review and Herald, 2000.

See also the resources on the Biblical Research Institute website: https://adventistbiblicalresearch.org/materials/.

Other Christian Perspectives:

Bahnsen, Greg L., Walter C. Kaiser, Jr., Douglas J. Moo, Wayne G. Strickland, and Willem A. VanGemeren. *Five Views on Law and Gospel.* Grand Rapids, MI: Zondervan, 2010.

Genry, Peter and Stephen Wellum. *Kingdom Through Covenant: A Biblical-Theological Understanding of the Covenants.* Wheaton, IL: Crossway, 2012.

Hahn, Scott W. *Kinship by Covenant: A Canonical Approach to the Fulfillment of God's Saving Promises.* New Haven, CT: Yale University Press, 2009.

Imes, Carmen Joy. *Bearing God's Name: Why Sinai Still Matters*. Downers Grove, IL: IVP Academic, 2019.

Kaiser, Jr. Walter. *The Promise-Plan of God: A Biblical Theology of the Old and New Testaments*. Grand Rapids, MI: Zondervan, 2009.

———. *Toward Old Testament Ethics*. Grand Rapids, MI: Zondervan, 1983.

McKnight, Scott and B. J. Oropeza, eds. *Perspectives on Paul: Five Views*. Grand Rapids, MI: Baker Academic, 2020.

Tamez, Elsa. *The Scandalous Message of James: Faith Without Works is Dead*. New York: Crossroad, 2002.

Thiessen, Matthew. *Jesus and the Forces of Death: The Gospels' Portrayal of Ritual Impurity within First-Century Judaism*. Grand Rapids, MI: Baker Academic, 2020.

Walton, John H. *Covenant: God's Purpose, God's Plan*. Grand Rapids, MI: Zondervan, 1994.

Wright, Christopher J. H. *Old Testament Ethics for the People of God*. Downers Grove, IL: IVP Academic, 2013.

15

THE GIFT OF THE SABBATH: TEMPLE IN TIME AND DAY OF REST, GRACE, AND DELIVERANCE

They accused Jesus of breaking the Sabbath law. While passing through grain fields on the Sabbath, Christ's disciples became hungry and picked some heads of grain to eat as they went. "Now when the Pharisees saw this, they said to Him, 'Look, Your disciples are doing what is not lawful to do on a Sabbath!'" (Matt. 12:2; cf. Luke 6:2).

Jesus responded not by denying the Sabbath law but by appealing to Scripture to show the accusers misunderstood and misapplied it. Jesus recounted that while traveling, David and his companions ate consecrated bread in the temple, which normally was unlawful for anyone but the priests to eat. And, He asked, "have you not read in the Law that on the Sabbath the priests in the temple violate the Sabbath, and yet are innocent? But I say to you that something greater than the temple is here" (Matt. 12:3–6).

To refute their accusations of breaking the law, Jesus appealed to the Law in Scripture itself, referencing His own place relative to it as "greater than the temple." Jesus did not condone *breaking* the Sabbath law. Rather, He explained that the disciples had not broken it by picking a few heads of grain while traveling with Jesus, who was the ultimate Davidic king and high priest. He further chastised the accusers, saying they had "condemned the innocent" and would not have if they had understood God's words, "'I desire compassion, rather than sacrifice'" (Matt. 12:7, quoting Hosea 6:6).

Further, He proclaimed: "The Sabbath was made for man, and not man for the Sabbath. So the Son of Man is Lord, even of the Sabbath" (Mark 2:27–28; cf. Matt. 12:8).[1] By these few words, Jesus identified

Himself (the Son of Man) as *the Creator*, the very One who created humankind and also instituted the Sabbath at creation (Gen. 2:1–3)—the Lawgiver Himself.

Afterward, Jesus went into the synagogue and encountered a man with a withered hand. Then, the accusers asked Him, "Is it lawful to heal on the Sabbath?"

"What man is there among you," Jesus replied, "who has a sheep, and if it falls into a pit on the Sabbath, will he not take hold of it and lift it out? How much more valuable then is a person than a sheep! So then, it is lawful to do good on the Sabbath" (Matt. 12:9–12).

After "looking around at them with anger, grieved at their hardness of heart," Jesus told the man, "Stretch out your hand." And the man's hand was restored (Mark 3:5; cf. Matt. 12:13).

It is *lawful* to do good on the Sabbath. God's law *is* the law of unselfish love—a blessing rather than a curse. The Sabbath itself is a gift from God for the well-being of humans and all creation in relationship *with* our loving Creator.

Jesus was not guilty of breaking the Sabbath law. He, the Creator and Lawgiver Himself, upheld the law of unselfish love as it was intended—as a blessing for the flourishing of creation (cf. Matt. 5:17–18). The "Lord of the Sabbath" Himself kept the Sabbath in a way that was a blessing to others.

Hypocritically, Christ's accusers denounced Jesus for healing—doing good on the Sabbath—while on the same Sabbath they themselves "conspired against Him, as to how they might destroy Him" (Matt. 12:14; cf. Mark 3:6).

Some had made Sabbath-keeping itself a curse, a yoke of oppression, turning the blessing God intended on its head. For some, the focus was on precisely what one should not do on the Sabbath, which distracted from the overarching meaning of the Sabbath, detracted from joyful fellowship with the Creator, and distracted from caring for the poor and oppressed (see Isa. 58, discussed later).

It is no coincidence that before Matthew recounts these stories about the Sabbath, He quotes these words of Jesus: "Come to Me, all who are weary and burdened, and I will give you rest. Take My yoke upon you and learn from Me, for I am gentle and humble in heart, and YOU WILL

FIND REST FOR YOUR SOULS. For My yoke is comfortable, and My burden is light" (Matt. 11:28–30).

Are you weary or troubled or distressed? In Jesus, you will find rest and refreshment. As the Lord of the Sabbath, He has given you and all creation a day set apart for rest *with* Him. An amazing gift!

In the Sabbath, God invites us to *stop* working, slow down, and find rest and peace in Him. The enemy has sought to turn this great blessing into a curse, to turn *resting from* work into its opposite—a work itself.

Many believe this gift—the Sabbath—has been done away with for Christians. But was the Sabbath set apart for Jews only? Should Christians still celebrate Sabbath? What is the meaning and value of the Sabbath today? This chapter addresses these and other questions.

In the Sabbath, God invites us to stop working, slow down, and find rest and peace in Him.

Competing Theories in Christian Theology: The Sabbath

Christians hold competing views of the Sabbath. Many believe the Sabbath commandment does not apply to Christians today.

Dispensationalism maintains the Sabbath commandment was for Israel and thus applies only to Israel, not Christians (the church).

New Covenant Theology believes the New Covenant made the Old Covenant obsolete, abolishing Old Testament laws except those the New Testament explicitly affirms. They believe the Sabbath is not affirmed in the New Testament.

Covenant Theology maintains instead that the moral law remains, including the Ten Commandments, but Christians are under no obligation to keep the seventh-day Sabbath. *Some* believe the particular day is not essential, so Christians can keep the Sabbath commandment by observing one day of the week. Many of these observe Sunday, known as first-day Sabbatarians.

Adventists and other seventh-day Sabbatarians conversely believe the Sabbath commandment remains in place relative to the seventh-day Sabbath specifically (more on this below).[2]

Why do many Christians worship on Sunday instead of Sabbath? Many do so based on belief in church authority and tradition. Peter Geiermann, in *The Convert's Catechism of Catholic Doctrine,* claims

"Saturday is the Sabbath day," but "we observe Sunday instead of Saturday... because the Catholic Church transferred the solemnity from Saturday to Sunday."[3]

The history of the shift from Sabbath to Sunday worship, however, is more complex and somewhat obscure (and cannot be adequately recounted here). In brief, the shift from Sabbath to Sunday observance took place over the course of many centuries, with evidence of Sunday worship in some places in the early second century but also evidence that Sunday did not begin to replace Sabbath *as a day of rest* until the fourth century.[4]

The Roman emperor Constantine issued a Sunday law in AD 321: "On the venerable Day of the Sun let the magistrates and people residing in cities rest, and let all workshops be closed."[5] Later, the Council of Laodicea (a regional synod of approximately thirty clerics held in AD 363–364) also issued a Sunday law, saying, "Christians shall not Judaize and be idle on Saturday but shall work on that day; but the Lord's day [by which they meant Sunday] they shall especially honor, and as being Christians, shall, if possible, do no work on that day."[6]

Nevertheless, Sabbath observance was still widespread throughout Christianity into the fifth century and beyond. Indeed, fifth-century church historian Socrates Scholasticus wrote: "For although almost all churches throughout the world celebrate the sacred mysteries on the sabbath of every week, yet the Christians of Alexandria and at Rome, on account of some ancient tradition, have ceased to do this."[7] Another fifth-century church historian Sozomen added, "The people of Constantinople, and almost everywhere, assemble together on the Sabbath, as well as on the first day of the week, which custom is never observed at Rome or at Alexandria.[8] Centuries later, the Sabbath was one of the issues involved in the split between the Western (Roman Catholic) and Eastern (Orthodox) Church in AD 1054.[9]

Today, many Christians cite Christ's resurrection on the first day as the precedent for Sunday worship, but there is no biblical support for the change.[10]

The Story of Sabbath: Day of Rest, Grace, and Deliverance

"By the seventh day God completed His work which He had done, and He rested on the seventh day from all His work which He had done. Then

God blessed the seventh day and sanctified it, because on it He rested from all His work which God had created and made" (Gen. 2:2-3). The Creator, who needs no rest, rested on the seventh day of creation week, setting apart the seventh day as *holy*.

Instituted at Creation

God Himself thus instituted the Sabbath in the beginning—a day set apart to rest and celebrate creation with the Creator Himself. The fourth commandment delivered at Sinai thus grounds the Sabbath in creation and begins with the word *remember* (Exod. 20:8-11). The Sabbath thus functions as (among other things) a memorial of creation—set apart as "holy to the Lord" and "a sign between Me [God] and the sons of Israel forever; for in six days the Lord made heaven and earth, but on the seventh day He ceased from labor, and was refreshed" (Exod. 31:15, 17).

Although a sign of God's covenant people, the Sabbath is not a day set apart *only* for the nation of Israel. Being set apart ("sanctified") by God at creation, the Sabbath long precedes the nation of Israel.

As further evidence of the ancient origin of the Sabbath, some point to the fact that in many languages throughout the world, the word for the seventh day of the week means "Sabbath" (see chart below).

"SABBATH" AS THE NAME OF THE SEVENTH DAY IN VARIOUS LANGUAGES	
Croatian	Subota
Esperanto	Ŝabato
(modern) Greek	Sabbato
Hungarian	Szombat
Italian	Sabato
Polish	Sobota
Portuguese	Sábado
Russian	Subbota
Slovenian	Sobota
Spanish	Sábado

The Sabbath Was in Place among Israel before Sinai

After being liberated from slavery in Egypt, Israel remained in danger. Without divine providence, they would perish in the wilderness. But

God did provide. Among other things, God provided bread from heaven known as manna, "a fine flake-like thing, fine as the frost on the ground," which was "like coriander seed, white, and its taste was like wafers with honey" (Exod. 16:14, 31).

Regarding the manna, God told Moses, "I will rain bread from heaven for you; and the people shall go out and gather a day's portion every day, so that I may test them, whether or not they will walk in My instruction. On the sixth day, when they prepare what they bring in, it will be twice as much as they gather daily" (Exod. 16:4–5).

The people were told not to keep manna overnight, but to gather only one day's portion each day except the sixth day, when they were to gather a double portion because they were not to gather the manna on the seventh day because it "is a Sabbath observance, a holy Sabbath to the LORD" (Exod. 16:23). When some tried to keep manna overnight other than on the sixth day, it "bred worms and stank" (Exod. 16:20). But, when they kept another day's portion overnight from the sixth day, "it did not stink nor was there a maggot in it" (Exod. 16:24).

And Moses told them, "Eat it today, for today is a Sabbath to the LORD; today you will not find it in the field. Six days you shall gather it, but on the seventh day, the Sabbath, there will be none" (Exod. 16:25–26). Later, Moses added, "the LORD has given you the Sabbath; for that reason He gives you bread for two days on the sixth day. . . . So the people rested on the seventh day" (Exod. 16:29, 30).

This was *before* the Ten Commandments were delivered in Exodus 20, showing again that the Sabbath was already established. Even before the Law was delivered at Sinai, the people already knew about God's law and were expected to keep the Sabbath.

The Sabbath Commandment at Sinai as a Memorial of Creation

"Remember the Sabbath day, to keep it holy. For six days you shall labor and do all your work, but the seventh day is a Sabbath of the LORD your God; on it you shall not do any work, you, or your son, or your daughter, your male slave or your female slave, or your cattle, or your resident who stays with you. For in six days the LORD made the heavens and the earth, the sea and everything that is in them, and He rested on the seventh day; for that reason the LORD blessed the Sabbath day and made it holy" (Exod. 20:8–11).

The commandment here frames the Sabbath as a memorial of creation (cf. Exod. 31:13–17). It not only points back to God resting on the seventh day of creation week, blessing the Sabbath and making it holy, but begins with the word *"remember."*

Imagine a teacher telling her students about a research paper for the first time, saying, *"Remember* the thirty-page research paper due next week." Invariably, her class would respond: "What research paper? You never told us about any research paper!" It would make little sense to use the word *"remember"* to refer to something that is being put in place for the first time. The very call to *"remember"* indicates the Sabbath was already in place, instituted at creation for humans to practice from then onward.[11]

The commandment here also identifies the seventh day as God's Sabbath—the "Sabbath of the LORD your God," blessed and made holy by Him (Exod. 20:9). On God's Sabbath, humans are not asked to do anything. Instead, humans are told to *refrain* from working and to rest instead, following God's example of resting on the seventh day during creation week. It is a day to remember God as our Creator and rest *from* our work *in His* creative work (cf. John 5:17). The God-given rest on the Sabbath extends even to the land.

Although often misrepresented or twisted from a blessing to a curse, the command itself simply instructs creatures to *rest* from work on the Sabbath. Imagine that your employer commanded you to take an extra day off every week, with no loss to you. Would you complain? Quite the opposite, right? The Sabbath is not an onerous command but a great gift. Stop working, God commands, and rest in My work for you as your Creator. This great gift is for all, extending to servants and foreigners and even animals (Exod. 20:10).

> The Sabbath is not an onerous command but a great gift. Stop working, God commands, and rest in My work for you as your Creator.

A Memorial of Liberation from Slavery and Oppression

Decades later, just before the next generation of Israelites were about to cross over into the promised land of Canaan, Moses reiterated the Ten Commandments. In his restatement of the fourth commandment,

Moses framed the Sabbath as a memorial of liberation from slavery:

> Keep the Sabbath day to treat it as holy, as the Lord your God commanded you. For six days you shall labor and do all your work, but the seventh day is a Sabbath of the Lord your God; you shall not do any work that day, you or your son or your daughter, or your male slave or your female slave, or your ox, your donkey, or any of your cattle, or your resident who stays with you, so that your male slave and your female slave may rest as well as you. And you shall remember that you were a slave in the land of Egypt, and the Lord your God brought you out of there by a mighty hand and an outstretched arm; therefore the Lord your God commanded you to celebrate the Sabbath day (Deut. 5:12–15).

The Sabbath commandment is firmly situated in the center of the Ten Commandments. As seen previously, the first four commandments are ways of keeping the greatest command—to love God wholeheartedly—and the last six commandments are ways of keeping the other great command, to love one's neighbors. The Sabbath commandment, then, is a bit like a hinge between the vertical (toward God) and horizontal (toward others) emphases of the Ten Commandments.

Indeed, the fourth commandment actually exemplifies *both* great love commands, emphasizing not only the vertical dimension of faithful love for God but also the horizontal dimension of love toward others, which requires *justice* for others. The commandment not only calls the hearer or reader to rest but also to make sure their children, anyone who works for them, anyone who might be visiting, and even their animals are allowed to rest. It explicitly calls people to rest not only for their own sake but also "so that your male slave and your female slave may rest as well as you" (Deut. 5:14). Remembering the Sabbath is an act of love toward God but also an act of love toward others, allowing others to rest, especially the oppressed.

The commandment further emphasizes, "you shall remember that you were a slave in the land of Egypt, and the Lord your God brought you out of there by a mighty hand and an outstretched arm; therefore the Lord your God commanded you to celebrate the Sabbath day." Here, the Sabbath is identified as a memorial of God's liberation and deliverance of His people from slavery. Beyond celebrating creation, then, the Sabbath is also a day that celebrates liberation from oppression and injustice. The Sabbath commandment also brings justice and equality in that the Sabbath is a day of rest for *everyone* and is, in a sense, a great equalizer, treating all people equally. This makes perfect sense because celebrating God's creation goes hand-in-hand with caring for God's creation, including practical love toward others.

The Universal *and* Particular Nature of the Sabbath

Yet, some may ask, wasn't the Sabbath just for Jews?

We've already seen the Sabbath could not be for Jews only. It was instituted before Abraham, at Creation itself (Gen. 2:2–3; cf. Exod. 20:11) and is thus universal. Even in Israel, the Sabbath was not only for literal descendants of Abraham but also for sojourners and even their animals (Exod. 20:10; Deut. 5:14).

Beyond this, God later promises a blessing for foreigners who keep the Sabbath. Specifically, God promises: "Also the foreigners who join themselves to the Lord, to attend to His service and to love the name of the Lord, to be His servants, every one who keeps the Sabbath so as not to profane it, and holds firmly to My covenant; even those I will bring to My holy mountain, and make them joyful in My house of prayer. Their burnt offerings and their sacrifices will be acceptable on My altar; for My house will be called a house of prayer for all the peoples" (Isa. 56:6–7). Further, God speaks of a future wherein "from Sabbath to Sabbath, all mankind will come to bow down before Me" (Isa. 66:23).

Then, in the New Testament, we find Gentiles attending weekly Sabbath meetings during which Paul preached to them (Acts 13:42–44; 18:4).

But some may protest, why does the particular day of the week matter? Why not just keep any day of the week for God?

Imagine I told my wife, "Your birthday is inconvenient for me. Let's just celebrate your birthday on mine." Or, suppose I said to her: "I have trouble remembering our anniversary, but I have no trouble remembering my anniversary with an ex-girlfriend. Let's celebrate our anniversary on that day instead." Before you assume I'm an insensitive fool, except for the purpose of this illustration, I'd never even dream of saying this!

Obviously, *particular* days of remembrance and celebration matter. We care deeply about days that are significant to us, particularly those concerning our most intimate relationships.

God sets aside one day every week to be *with* us in a special way, a day for us to rest and foster relationships of love. The particular day God established should matter to us because our relationship with God, our loving Creator and Savior, matters.

Even as my anniversary with my wife is a day we remember our marriage covenant and celebrate our love for one another, the Sabbath is a day we should remember that God is the covenantal God who is our Creator and our Liberator. As Jo Ann Davidson puts it, "the Sabbath is one of the great proofs that God is love—for lovers like to set apart specific times to be together."[12]

> God sets aside one day every week to be with us in a special way, a day for us to rest and foster relationships of love.

The Sabbath is universal and particular—instituted at creation for all as a particular day to commune with God, a gift to remember and celebrate what God has done and is doing for us—to rest in His work rather than focusing on ours. Being instituted before the Fall, the Sabbath has universal significance for the flourishing of humanity.

The Custom of Jesus

On the sixth day, which we call Friday, Jesus was crucified. They broke the legs of the criminals beside Jesus to speed their deaths "since it was the day of preparation, to prevent the bodies from remaining on the cross on the Sabbath" (John 19:31). Jesus died on the sixth day, before the Sabbath, and did not rise again until the first day. During the Sabbath, Jesus rested in the tomb.

And His followers kept the Sabbath on crucifixion weekend. Just after describing Jesus's body being placed in the tomb belonging to Joseph of Arimathea, Luke reports further that it was the "preparation day, and a Sabbath was about to begin. Now the women who had come with Him from Galilee followed, and they saw the tomb and how His body was laid. And then they returned and prepared spices and perfumes. And on the Sabbath they rested according to the commandment. But on the first day of the week, at early dawn, they came to the tomb bringing the spices which they had prepared" (Luke 23:54-24:1).

It is quite striking that Luke tells us, "they rested according to the commandment," without any other commentary. If, as some Christians believe, the resurrection transferred solemnity from the Sabbath to Sunday, this would have been a good place for Luke (writing decades later) to tell readers of this change. But Luke tells us this with no hint of any change. And there is no evidence in Scripture of any change or abrogation of the Sabbath commandment.

On the contrary, the consistent witness of Scripture is that both Jesus and His followers kept the Sabbath. For example, Luke tells us of Christ's Sabbath observance, "as was His custom, He entered the synagogue on the Sabbath" (Luke 4:16).

The "custom" of Jesus was to observe the Sabbath, as evidenced in many other texts that report Christ's Sabbath observance. For instance, Mark tells us: "They went into Capernaum; and immediately on the Sabbath Jesus entered the synagogue and began to teach" (Mark 1:21; cf. Luke 4:31; 13:10). Again, "when the Sabbath came, He began to teach in the synagogue" (Mark 6:2).

If Christ's resurrection were to transfer solemnity from Sabbath to Sunday, one would think Christ would have mentioned this. He had repeated opportunities to do so when His accusers challenged Him regarding healing on the Sabbath. And Jesus forecasted other momentous changes to religious practice. For example, Jesus made clear the earthly temple would pass away: prophesying that the Second Temple would be destroyed (Matt. 24:2; Mark 13:2), proclaiming that "something greater than the temple is here" (Himself, Matt. 12:6; cf. John 2:19), and telling the Samaritan woman at the well, "a time is coming when you will worship the Father neither on this mountain nor in Jerusalem" (John 4:21; cf. 4:24). And Jesus implicitly identified Himself as the true sacrifice (cf. Matt. 26:26-28; Luke 22:18-20) and true priest (cf. Matt. 12:5-6; Mark 2:23-28) in place of the earthly ceremonial system.[13]

But Jesus did not forecast a coming day when the Sabbath would be annulled. And, while the "veil of the temple was torn in two from top to bottom" when Christ died (Matt. 27:51), signaling the end of the ceremonial system of rituals and sacrifices, and Christ instituted the Lord's

Supper as a memorial of the New Covenant in His blood saying "do this in remembrance of Me" (Luke 22:19), nothing in the Gospels (or the rest of the New Testament) indicates any change relative to the Sabbath commandment. On the contrary, amidst His discourse on momentous events to come, including the destruction of the temple (Matt. 24:2), the way Jesus speaks indicates that the Sabbath will still be in place much later, warning His followers they will need to flee to the mountains when persecution comes and saying "pray that when you flee, it will not be in the winter, or on a Sabbath" (Matt. 24:20).

Far from indicating any change relative to the Sabbath, Christ repeatedly corrected misunderstandings and misapplications of it that were not in keeping with God's everlasting law of unselfish love, teaching "it is lawful to do good on the Sabbath" and pointing out the hypocrisy of those who would save their sheep from a pit on the Sabbath but not lift a finger to help a fellow human in distress (Matt. 12:12; cf. Luke 14:3–5). In this regard, Jesus also proclaimed Himself the Lord of the Sabbath. Specifically, emphasizing the Sabbath is a *gift* for humanity, Jesus proclaimed: "The Sabbath was made for man, and not man for the Sabbath. So the Son of Man is Lord, even of the Sabbath" (Mark 2:27–28).

The Custom of the Apostles

Likewise, observing the Sabbath was the custom of the apostles, which continued after Christ's resurrection.

For example, Paul and Barnabas attended synagogue on Sabbath. Paul preached to the people, including Gentiles, and "the people repeatedly begged to have these things spoken to them the next Sabbath" (Acts 13:14, 42–43). And, "the next Sabbath nearly all the city assembled to hear the word of the Lord" (Acts 13:44).

Later, Paul and Silas (and others) met with a group in the countryside on Sabbath in Philippi. Specifically, "on the Sabbath day we went outside the gate to a riverside, where we were thinking that there was a place of prayer; and we sat down and began speaking to the women who had assembled" (Acts 16:12–13).[14]

Indeed, like Jesus, it was Paul's *custom* to observe Sabbath. Thus, "according to Paul's custom, he visited them, and for three Sabbaths reasoned with them from the Scriptures" (Acts 17:2). Thus, Paul "was reasoning in the synagogue every Sabbath and trying to persuade Jews and Greeks" (Acts 18:4).

In these and other ways, the New Testament does not abolish the Sabbath but affirms it.

The Sabbath and the Three Angels' Messages

The book of Revelation includes material that points to the Sabbath being an important issue prior to Christ's Second Coming. There, in what is known as the Three Angels' Messages, John "saw another angel flying in midheaven with an eternal gospel to preach to those who live on the earth, and to every nation, tribe, language, and people; and he said with a loud voice, 'Fear God and give Him glory, because the hour of His judgment has come; worship Him who made the heaven and the earth, and sea and springs of waters'" (Rev. 14:6–7).

As Jon Paulien has demonstrated, this first angel's message directly alludes to the fourth commandment.[15] Specifically, the language "worship Him who made the heaven and the earth and the sea" draws on the language of the fourth commandment, "For in six days the LORD made the heavens and the earth, the sea and everything that is in them, and He rested on the seventh day; for that reason the LORD blessed the Sabbath day and made it holy" (Exod. 20:11).

While the Sabbath is not mentioned directly, this allusion demonstrably points to the Sabbath commandment (which we have seen is, among other things, a memorial of creation). Then, at the end of the Three Angels' Messages, the third angel warns of a beast—an antichrist power that attempts to usurp the worship due God alone, the same one who in Daniel attempts to change *times* and *laws* (Dan. 7:25; see chapter 18). Specifically, the third angel warns against worshiping this beast and his image and receiving his mark (Rev. 14:9–11) and then proclaims: "Here is the perseverance of the saints who keep the commandments of God and their faith in Jesus" (Rev. 14:12).

Thus, the Three Angels' Messages point to the Sabbath commandment in the midst of a warning that the hour of judgment has come and to worship only the Creator and then emphasizes that the "saints ... keep the commandments of God."[16]

The Sabbath Gift Remains for Christians

Scripture thus repeatedly affirms God's gift of the Sabbath as:

- instituted at creation and set apart as holy (Gen. 2:1-3)
- in place before Sinai as evidenced in the story of manna (Exod. 16:13-35)
- commanded in the Ten Commandments as a memorial of creation (Exod. 20:8-11; cf. 31:13-17)
- commanded in the Ten Commandments as a memorial of liberation from slavery and oppression (Deut. 5:12-15)
- the custom of Jesus, who affirmed the Sabbath (Luke 4:16; cf. Matt. 12:12; 24:20; Mark 1:21; 2:27-28; 6:2; Luke 4:31; 13:10; John 19:31)
- the custom of the Apostles, who also affirmed the Sabbath (Acts 13:14, 42-44; 16:12-13; 17:1-2; 18:4; cf. Luke 23:54-24:1)
- embedded in the Three Angels' Message (Rev. 14:6-12; cf. Exod. 20:11; Dan. 7:25).

Some, however, refer to a few texts as purported evidence that the Sabbath is no longer in place for Christians (e.g., Acts 20:7; Rom. 14:5; 1 Cor. 16:2; Col. 2:16-17; Rev. 1:10). None of these passages, however, teach that the Sabbath is abolished (for Christians or others) or transfer solemnity from Sabbath to Sunday.

Specifically, some appeal to Revelation 1:10, wherein John says, "I was in the Spirit on the Lord's day," and claim this refers to Sunday. However, there is no evidence that "the Lord's day" referenced here was the first day of the week. As we have seen, Christ identifies Himself as the "Lord of the Sabbath" (Matt. 12:8; Luke 6:5; cf. Mark 2:28), and many Adventists believe "the Lord's day" here refers to a Sabbath day.

Further, some contend that Acts 20:7 and 1 Corinthians 16:2 indicate Sunday observance among early Christians. In the latter, Paul states: "On the first day of every week, each of you is to put aside and save as he may prosper, so that no collections need to be made when I come" (1 Cor. 16:2). But this text says nothing about observing Sunday or worshiping together on Sunday; it is merely an instruction to individuals ("each of you") to set aside money on the first day of every week to be ready when Paul comes, so "no collections" are made when he comes.

In the former text, Luke tells us: "On the first day of the week, when we were gathered together to break bread, Paul began talking to them, intending to leave the next day, and he prolonged his message until midnight" (Acts 20:7). Some interpret this as evidence of a worship gathering on Sunday.

Yet, the evidence suggests this was actually a meeting on the Sabbath that continued into what we call Saturday night, which at that time would have been called the first day of the week. (In Scripture, days begin at sundown. Thus the Sabbath begins on what we call Friday night at sunset; see Gen. 1:5; Lev. 23:32.) Notice, they were gathered to eat together, and Paul was speaking to them and "prolonged his message until midnight." This indicates the meal was an evening meal. But an evening meal on the first day of the week after sundown would be on what we call Saturday night. So, it is likely that this was a continuance of a Sabbath meeting late into what we call Saturday night.

Moreover, even if Christians sometimes gathered together to worship on Sunday, that would not be evidence of either the abolishing of seventh-day Sabbath observance or of the solemnity of Sunday as a regular day of worship. Adventists meet on days other than the Sabbath (e.g., prayer meetings on weeknights or chapel services on select weekdays), but doing so does not abolish or replace the Sabbath. Eight texts in the New Testament mention the first day of the week, but not one of them instructs us to worship on Sunday in honor of the resurrection.

Some also quote Romans 14:5, "One person values one day over another, another values every day the same. Each person must be fully convinced in his own mind." However, there is nothing in this text or the context that suggests this is about the seventh-day Sabbath. The context references disputes over "opinions" (Rom. 14:1), including whether to eat or refrain from eating, with Paul concluding: "The one who observes the day, observes it for the Lord ... and the one who does not eat, it is for the Lord that he does not eat, and he gives thanks to God" (Rom. 14:6; cf. 14:1–3). Paul's counsel might pertain to disputes over observing ceremonial feast days or designated days of fasting or whether Christians must refrain from meat sacrificed to idols, which Paul addressed in 1 Corinthians 8. The *Andrews Study Bible* comments, "day" here "cannot refer to the seventh-day Sabbath, as Paul's own practice and writing regularly attest. It is probably a reference to the various Jewish feast days such as Passover and the Day of Atonement, and the days of fasting that preceded them."[17]

Finally, many Christians quote Colossians 2:16–17: "Therefore, no one is to act as your judge in regard to food and drink, or in respect to a festival or a new moon, or a Sabbath day—things which are only a shadow of what is to come; but the substance belongs to Christ."

What Paul addresses here is somehow connected to regulations observed in Colossae in recognition of "elementary spirits" (see Col. 2:20). Further, it is crucial to recognize that the language of Colossians 2:16 parallels the way the Old Testament speaks of the ceremonial law relative to the feast days. For example, Ezekiel 45:17 states of ceremonial feast days (i.e., festivals), "it shall be the prince's part to provide the burnt offerings, the grain offerings, and the drink offerings, at the feasts, on the new moons, and on the Sabbaths, at all the appointed feasts of the house of Israel" (cf. Hosea 2:11). The sequence in Colossians 2:16 is the same—food (corresponding to burnt and grain offerings), drink (corresponding to drink offerings), festival (corresponding to feasts), new moon, and sabbath day, indicating the same ceremonial law relative to feast days is referenced in Colossians 2:16.

Notably, distinct from the *weekly* seventh-day Sabbath, the Old Testament also refers to seven *annual* ceremonial "sabbaths"—that is, festival days in the Israelite calendar that occurred annually according to the ceremonial law (e.g., the Day of Atonement; Lev. 23:27–32). In this regard, some scholars believe the reference to "sabbaths" in Colossians 2:16 is simply referring to those seven annual ceremonial sabbaths (feast days), *not* to the seventh-day Sabbath.[18] Other scholars believe Colossians 2:16 references the weekly Sabbath, but not with respect to Sabbath rest according to the commandment, but instead relative to the weekly sacrifices and rituals that the ceremonial law prescribed to be performed on the weekly Sabbaths.[19]

Either way, the Sabbath command itself is not what is referenced here, but the ceremonial laws (e.g., rituals and sacrifices) pertaining to festivals, new moons, and sabbaths. That these verses do not refer to observing the seventh-day Sabbath can be seen from the fact that Colossians 2:17 identifies the things at issue as "things which are only a shadow of what is to come; but the substance belongs to Christ." We have already seen that the sacrifices and rituals of the ceremonial law are elsewhere identified as "a copy and shadow of the heavenly things" (Heb. 8:5) and "a shadow of the good things to come" (Heb. 10:1; cf. Col. 2:16–17), which prefigured Christ's works of atonement at the cross and in the heavenly sanctuary.

However, the weekly Sabbath is not "only a shadow of what is to come."[20] On the contrary, the Sabbath is a memorial of God's past work, a memorial of God's great work of creation (among other things). Whereas things set up to prefigure a greater reality to come (e.g., types in the ceremonial law) are no longer necessary once that greater reality comes, memorials of great things worth remembering remain as continual reminders. As Gane puts it: "God instituted the seventh day Sabbath for human beings before the Fall into sin (Gen. 2:2–3). Therefore it cannot be one of the temporary types/symbols that God set up after the Fall in order to lead human beings to salvation from sin. In other words, the Sabbath cannot be a temporary type because it pre-existed the need for temporary types."[21]

Notably, in this regard, the Presbyterian commentator Albert Barnes wrote:

> There is no evidence from this passage that he [Paul] would teach that there was no obligation to observe *any* holy time, for there is not the slightest reason to believe that he meant to teach that one of the ten commandments had ceased to be binding on mankind.... he had his eye on the great number of days which were observed by the Hebrews as festivals, as a part of their ceremonial and typical law, and not to the *moral* law, or the ten commandments. No part of the moral law—no one of the ten commandments could be spoken of as "a *shadow* of good things to come." These commandments are, from the nature of moral law, of perpetual and universal obligation.[22]

Beyond this, Roy Gane argues, "if Paul had touched the original function of the Sabbath itself, there surely would have been an uproar of biblical proportions, calling for a council like the one in Jerusalem that dealt with the controversy over circumcision (Acts 15)."[23] There was no such uproar because the gift of Sabbath rest remained.

Sabbath Theology: The Sabbath as a Gift of Rest, Grace, Liberation, and Deliverance

"Martha, Martha, you are worried and distracted by many things." Jesus spoke these words to Martha, who had welcomed Jesus to her home. While her sister Mary was "seated at the Lord's feet, and was listening to His word," Martha "was distracted with all her preparations." Finally, Martha came to Jesus and said, "Lord, do You not care that my sister has left me to do the serving by myself? Then tell her to help me." To this, Jesus replied, "Martha, Martha, you are worried and distracted by many things; but only one thing is necessary; for Mary has chosen the good part, which shall not be taken away from her" (Luke 10:38-42). Martha was working so hard that she was missing the blessing that awaited her *with* Jesus.

Today, it is very easy to be distracted by work or other things such that we neglect the far better things God has in store for us, including dedicated time to rest *with* Him.

This reminds me of a story of a woman who was very busy and in a great hurry. On her way to a meeting, she hurriedly got on a bus with her four-month-old son. On the way, she was constantly on business calls on her phone while anxiously awaiting her stop. When her stop came, she hurried off the bus and went on her way.

> *Today, it is very easy to be distracted by work or other things such that we neglect the far better things God has in store for us, including dedicated time to rest with Him.*

Before long, she realized she'd made a horrible mistake. She had forgotten her baby on the bus! She was so busy and distracted that she had *forgotten* her own son. Eventually, she was reunited with her baby boy, safe and sound. But her "busyness" might have cost her what she held most dear.

In our world, many people are constantly in motion—always going somewhere fast. There's a lot going on in our lives. Through devices like smartphones, we are constantly connected—never more than a fingertip away from work and other concerns of life. Burnout is all too common.

Day of Rest: A Temple in Time

Humans simply cannot thrive without proper rest. If we constantly work seven days a week, our bodies and our mental health suffer, and we eventually break down and burn out. Our spiritual health likewise requires rest and time to *slow down*. This is especially important in an age where we are more and more lonely, anxious, busy, and distracted—with so much vying for our time and attention.[24]

Healthy relationships with my wife and son require quality time where we give one another our undivided attention. Likewise, healthy relationship with God requires time apart from the distractions of everyday life, dedicated to spending quality time with the One who is most dear of all. *Time matters not just to us but to God Himself.* Even as my young son and I long to spend quality time together, the Creator God desires quality time with us. With the gift of the Sabbath, God invites us to come apart and rest, to experience the Sabbath as a gift of God's special presence—a temple in time to commune *with* God. As Sigve Tonstad puts it: "By the act of hallowing the seventh day God drives the stake of divine presence into the soil of human time."[25]

What Martha needed, we also need. To refrain from the *busyness* of life, sit at Jesus's feet, and rest in Him. Thus, Jesus invites you and me: "Come to Me, all who are weary and burdened, and I will give you rest. Take My yoke upon you and learn from Me, for I am gentle and humble in heart, and YOU WILL FIND REST FOR YOUR SOULS. For My yoke is comfortable, and My burden is light" (Matt. 11:28–30).[26] The very One who is the Lord of the Sabbath, the Creator, invites you to rest with Him. He gives us the Sabbath as a shelter in which to rest.

As I write this, it is Friday afternoon. I am tired, and I am very much looking forward to the opportunity to rest soon. But, given current commitments, I would not feel free to do so were it not for the Sabbath. This week (like many others), the deadlines feel like they are pressing around me and I would feel compelled to work through the seventh day were it not for God's gift of the Sabbath, which frees me from the sense of duty to keep working. My Creator *commands* me to rest. What a lovely, life-giving command, for which I am extremely grateful! I can rest guilt-free without feeling remorse about all of the things I "should" be doing with the time.

But the Sabbath is far more than a day of rest so that we can recover to return to our labors. As Abraham Heschel put it, "the Sabbath as a day of rest, as a day of abstaining from toil, is not for the purpose of recovering one's lost strength and becoming fit for forthcoming labor. The Sabbath is a day for the sake of life. . . . The Sabbath is not for the sake of the weekdays; the weekdays are for the sake of the Sabbath. It is not an interlude, but the climax of living."[27]

The older I get, the more I long for peace and rest. In a world of hustle and bustle, the Sabbath offers us a slice of life as God intended, not filled with meaning-making or money-making or other temporary pursuits, but rest *in Him* and relationship *with Him*. The Sabbath affords us the opportunity to stop working and producing and recognize that we are worth far more than our work and far more than what we produce, and so is every other person. We are of infinite value to the one who invites us to rest in and with Him.

> We are of infinite value to the one who invites us to rest in and with Him.

In this and other ways, the Sabbath is a gift from God—a day of rest that is a gift of rest. Notice, what the Sabbath commandment asks of us is not to do something but to *refrain from doing*—to slow down and stop working. God commands you simply to *rest* with Him. He is working to sustain you and everything else, so you do not have to (see John 5:17). What a gift!

At the same time, this is not a *passive* rest but involves an invitation to worship God, praising Him for what He has done and continues to do for us and in us.[28] God has set the Sabbath apart as a day for relationship, somewhat similar to the way humans in love set dates and celebrate those dates with quality time together. Amazing!

The Sabbath is to be a day of rest *and* relationship. A day to remember the creation purpose of love relationship with God and with others. A day to take time to remember who we are in Christ, how we came to be—created and redeemed as God's children—and what the future holds for us with eternal life in a fully restored (re-created) world with no strife or suffering or evil, but only everlasting peace and joy. A day to bask in the love of the One who made us and is worthy of all love and worship and a day to remember how we should reflect love toward one another.

Day of Grace and Sign of Sanctification

As a gift of rest, the Sabbath is also a gift of grace—a sign between God and His people that God Himself sanctifies us as *His* work of grace, in which we can rest with confidence.

God graciously created us and He graciously sustains us even after the Fall. The Sabbath stands as a testament to the Creator's work for us and in us, apart from which we could do nothing and, indeed, could not even exist. As Jacques Doukhan explains, "Because God meets humans on their own turf, His divine rest becomes their rest; it is shared *with* humans." Further, "humans did not need nor deserve to rest, since they did not work during creation week; God worked for them, while they were still absent. As such, this rest is pure grace, an undeserved gift from God to humans, indeed it is God's rest they are invited to enter (Matt. 11:28; Heb. 3:18; Heb. 4:1–11)."[29]

The Sabbath stands as a sign that God is the one who saves us. It is God who makes us whole and holy, not we ourselves. As God said to the prophet Ezekiel, "I gave them My Sabbaths to be a sign between Me and them, so that they might know that I am the LORD who sanctifies them" (Ezek. 20:12; cf. Exod. 31:13–17; Ezek. 20:20). The Sabbath is thus a sign between God and His people, a testament of God's creative and restorative power, in which all who belong to Christ can rest knowing that Christ will complete His good work in us and in the entire cosmos. The Sabbath "is the sign of the power of Christ."[30]

As Jacques Doukhan explains: "In obeying the fourth commandment, the believer does not negate the value of grace. On the contrary, the awareness of grace is implied. Through obedience to God's law, the believer expresses faith in God's grace."[31]

Keeping the Sabbath as intended by God, then, is the opposite of works-based religion. Again, the Sabbath commandment calls us to *refrain* from working and rest in the grace of our Creator, Sustainer, and Savior. The Sabbath is a sign of God's gracious love and care for us and for all of creation. As Jennifer Jill Schwirzer puts it, "The Sabbath is an outward practice of the inward principle of resting in unearned love and righteousness. If we treat Sabbath-keeping as if it earns something, we deny the principle that enlivens the practice, turning this temple in time into a religious trinket."[32]

While the enemy has sought to transform this day of rest into a day of burdens, God intended the Sabbath to be a day of delight *with* Him, wherein we can rest in His perfect love and grace, trusting in what God has already done and is doing *for us*.

This is a particular blessing in our anxiety-ridden, achievement-obsessed, burnout cultures, in which many of us are always trying to make something of ourselves. The Sabbath, as a gift of rest, offers us a temple in time to celebrate God's work for us instead of focusing on our works—to commune *with* Him, enjoying what He has made instead of relentlessly chasing after what we hope to make of ourselves or for ourselves. As Abraham Heschel puts it, "The meaning of the Sabbath is to celebrate time rather than space. Six days a week we live under the tyranny of things of space; on the Sabbath we try to become attuned to holiness in time. It is a day on which we are called upon to share in what is eternal in time, to turn from the results of creation to the mystery of creation; from the world of creation to the creation of the world."[33]

The Sabbath subverts all perspectives that locate value in productivity and achievement. The Sabbath stands as resistance against viewing ourselves and others as merely means of production, only valuable for what we can do, produce, or achieve. God does not see you that way. God sees you as a beloved child on whom He freely bestows grace and love, in which you can safely and peacefully rest, put aside the cares of this world, and *Sabbath* in Him.

Alongside this, the Sabbath stands as a subversive rebuke to both works-based righteousness on the one hand and consumption culture on the other, calling humans to come apart and cease from our "busyness" and business in ways that would reap inestimable benefits to nature were humans to Sabbath regularly. Recall that concern for creation is embedded in the Sabbath commandment itself, including the fact that God also intended to bless animals with rest through the Sabbath. Just imagine the benefits in terms of creation care if humans the world over rested on the Sabbath. The Sabbath that stands as (among other things) a memorial of creation would then also be an exceedingly great benefit to creation.

Day of Liberation and Justice

As a day of rest and grace, the Sabbath is also a day of liberation, justice, and resistance to oppression.[34] As seen earlier, the Sabbath commandment emphasizes that *all* workers are to be allowed to rest on the Sabbath, whatever their economic status or class. And the restatement of the Ten Commandments in Deuteronomy 5 identifies the Sabbath as a memorial of God's deliverance and liberation from slavery: "you shall remember that you were a slave in the land of Egypt, and the LORD your God brought you out of there by a mighty hand and an outstretched arm; therefore the LORD your God commanded you to celebrate the Sabbath day" (Deut. 5:15).

It is no coincidence that Isaiah 58 speaks of the Sabbath in the context of highlighting God's concern for justice and calling God's followers to do justice. In the midst of a running discourse on justice and overturning oppression, God states:

> If, because of the Sabbath, you restrain your foot from doing as you wish on My holy day, and call the Sabbath a pleasure, and the holy day of the LORD honorable, and honor it, desisting from your own ways, from seeking your own pleasure and speaking your own word, then you will take delight in the LORD, and I will make you ride on the heights of the earth; and I will feed you with the heritage of Jacob your father, for the mouth of the LORD has spoken. (Isa. 58:13–14)

These verses are sometimes mistakenly understood to mean that we should have no pleasure on the Sabbath. But these verses say no such thing. Rather, the Sabbath is to be "a pleasure." The Sabbath was never intended to be a burden, even though some have made it so. God wants us to delight in the Sabbath.

But what kind of delight? In these verses, God calls people to turn from their *own private* pleasure (or business) to the delight of God, similar to the way I might turn from my own private delight to spend time with my wife—for the greater delight we might share in doing something together.

What kind of delight, then, is God's delight? That is, what delights God? The context in Isaiah 58 holds the answer:

> Cry loudly, do not hold back; raise your voice like a trumpet, and declare to My people their wrongdoing, and to the house of Jacob their sins. Yet they seek Me day by day and delight to know My ways, as a nation that has done righteousness and has not forsaken the ordinance of their God. They ask Me for just decisions, they delight in the nearness of God. "Why have we fasted and You do not see? Why have we humbled ourselves and You do not notice?"

Behold, on the day of your fast you find your desire, and oppress all your workers. Behold, you fast for contention and strife, and to strike with a wicked fist. You do not fast like you have done today to make your voice heard on high! Is it a fast like this that I choose, a day for a person to humble himself? Is it for bowing one's head like a reed and for spreading out sackcloth and ashes as a bed? Will you call this a fast, even an acceptable day to the Lord? Is this not the fast that I choose: to release the bonds of wickedness, to undo the ropes of the yoke, and to let the oppressed go free, and break every yoke? Is it not to break your bread with the hungry and bring the homeless poor into the house; when you see the naked, to cover him; and not to hide yourself from your own flesh? Then your light will break out like the dawn, and your recovery will spring up quickly; and your righteousness will go before you; the glory of the Lord will be your rear guard. Then you will call, and the Lord will answer; you will cry for help, and He will say, "Here I am." If you remove the yoke from your midst, the pointing of the finger and speaking wickedness, and if you offer yourself to the hungry and satisfy the need of the afflicted, then your light will rise in darkness, and your gloom will become like midday. And the Lord will continually guide you, and satisfy your desire in scorched places, and give strength to your bones; and you will be like a watered garden, and like a spring of water whose waters do not fail. Those from among you will rebuild the ancient ruins; you will raise up the age-old foundations; and you will be called the repairer of the breach, the restorer of the streets in which to dwell (Isa. 58:1–12).

Among other things, God delights in loosening the bonds of injustice, doing good, feeding the hungry, and housing the homeless—the very kinds of things Jesus was criticized for doing *on the Sabbath* (see Matt. 12; John 5). Indeed, on the Sabbath, when Jesus read in the synagogue from Isaiah 61:1–2, He proclaimed His work as the Messiah "to bring good news to the poor" and "proclaim release to captives, and recovery of sight to the blind, to set free those who are oppressed, to proclaim the favorable year of the Lord" (Luke 4:18–19). Some had made Sabbath a yoke of oppression and otherwise oppressed others, but Jesus came to remove the yoke of oppression and replace it with peace and rest in Him (Matt. 11:28–30).

If we are to follow Christ's example and turn from our own "pleasure" to that which pleases God, relative to the Sabbath and otherwise, we must turn "to release the bonds of wickedness, to undo the ropes of the yoke, and to let the oppressed go free, and break every yoke" and to share our "bread with the hungry" and "bring the homeless poor into" our house, to clothe the naked and not hide ourselves from our brothers and sisters and their needs (Isa. 58:6–8). In these and other ways, God calls His people to turn from our own private delights (or business) to bestow love, relieve suffering and oppression, and bring justice to others.

Over and over again throughout Scripture, God calls His people to seek justice and relieve oppression. To take just a few examples:

- Isaiah 1:17 proclaims: "Learn to do good; seek justice, rebuke the oppressor, obtain justice for the orphan, plead for the widow's case."
- Isaiah 10:1–2 adds, "Woe to those who enact unjust statutes and to those who constantly record harmful decisions, so as to deprive the needy of justice and rob the poor among My people of their rights, so that widows may be their spoil and that they may plunder the orphans."
- Likewise, Micah 6:8 explains, "He has told you, mortal one, what is good; and what does the LORD require of you but to do justice, to love kindness, and to walk humbly with your God?"
- And Jesus Himself cries out, "Woe to you, scribes and Pharisees, hypocrites! For you tithe mint and dill and cumin, and have neglected the weightier provisions of the Law: justice and mercy and faithfulness; but these are the things you should have done without neglecting the others. You blind guides, who strain out a gnat and swallow a camel!" (Matt. 23:23–24).

Scripture reveals that God is concerned not only about sins of commission (doing wrong things) but also sins of omission (neglecting to do good). Many of those who reject or misapply God's law put the emphasis in the wrong place, not recognizing that God's law is the law of unselfish love. As such, God's law cannot be kept simply by refraining from doing explicitly wrong things—the only one who keeps the law is the one who loves. "If someone says, 'I love God,' and yet he hates his brother or sister, he is a liar; for the one who does not love his brother and sister whom he has seen, cannot love God, whom he has not seen" (1 John 4:20).

There are people today who are saved who do not keep the Sabbath, and there are people who keep the Sabbath who are not saved. We are not saved by keeping the Sabbath, but (*observed in the spirit of love*) the Sabbath *is* a sign of allegiance. However, you cannot be a genuine follower of Christ if you do not care about the poor and the oppressed. Those who follow Christ are those who follow the Lamb wherever He goes, and this involves active love toward others (see Matt. 25:31-46).

> **We are not saved by keeping the Sabbath, but (observed in the spirit of love) the Sabbath is a sign of allegiance.**

The Sabbath is not only a day for us to rest in what God has done and is doing for us, but the Sabbath also calls us to provide rest to others by dismantling oppressive systems and improving the situation of others. While resting from work on the Sabbath, we might signal resistance against economic exploitation and all other forms of oppression. Notably, in a chapter on the Sabbath, Ellen White wrote: "Every false religion teaches its adherents to be careless of human needs, sufferings, and rights."[35] The Sabbath stands against idolatry—the great sin that corresponds to breaking the greatest commandment, to love God, but the Sabbath also stands against social injustice (the great sin that corresponds to breaking the second great commandment, to love our neighbors as ourselves).

In this way and others (see chapter 18), the Sabbath stands as a sign of true allegiance to the true King and His ways of unselfish love and justice. The Lamb's kingdom of unselfish love and justice stands utterly opposed to the empires of this world—the oppressive, enslaving regimes of the dragon. Those who follow the way of the Lamb rather than the way of the dragon produce the fruits of love—showing concern about injustice and oppression and doing what they can to overturn it in keeping with the principles of love, opposing evil without doing evil.

Sabbath-keepers, then, are to be chain-breakers who relieve oppression and injustice wherever possible, feeding the hungry, caring for the ill or impoverished, and aiming our lifestyles toward the ideal for our fellow humans and for all creation, treating each weekly Sabbath as a foretaste of the ultimate day of Jubilee, when all creation will be forever set free. Doing so itself is a way of worshiping our Creator. As Proverbs 14:31 puts it, "Those who oppress the poor insult their Maker, but those who are kind to the needy honor him" (NRSVue).

Day of Deliverance

In all these ways and many others, the Sabbath is a day of deliverance provided by the God who is *with us* and wants to be even more closely *with us* still.

Sabbath is a great gift; it is good for us, it is good for others, it is good for animals and the environment, and it provides temporal space for us to connect with God and our loved ones in deeper ways.

I once came across the statement: "Childhood ends when you understand that sleep is a gift not a punishment." In analogous fashion, Sabbath is a gift, not a laborious requirement. As Kessia Reyne Bennett once put it, the Sabbath is not "a fence to jump over" but "a shelter in which to rest."[36]

Conclusion: Why Does It Matter?

His father was always busy. Not because he wanted to be busy—he worked many hours to provide for the family as best he could. He would have loved to spend more time with his children. He was a good father, but he could not always be present.

The son longed to spend more time with his dad, quality time with dedicated attention where the work and worries and cares of this life were put to the side, and they could be together.

For this family and many others, the Sabbath was and is a great gift. The Sabbath is a day God sets aside for relationship, a day God calls His followers to set aside for shared attention with God, to commune *with* Him.

Such sacred time is extremely important today. We live in an age when people are increasingly lonely, busy, anxious, and distracted. So many things compete for our attention. We have technology that we were told would connect us to others (and sometimes it does in helpful ways), but it often distances us from intimate personal relationships rather than drawing us into them.

Many people today thus desperately long for significant, personal presence with closeness and wherein persons pay attention to one another (shared attention).[37] Even when people are together in person, such significant presence is absent when people are together in the same place, but one or more is not "present" in the sense that their attention is on their smartphone. Significant, personal presence of the kind we long for involves intentional attention to one another. Among other things, the Sabbath provides sacred time for this kind of relationship with God and with others. What a gift!

Even as a son longs for quality time with his loving father, the Creator of all desires quality time with you and with me. He invites us to come away from our burdens and rest in and with Him. Christ calls: "Come to Me, all who are weary and burdened, and I will give you rest" (Matt. 11:28).[38]

Are you weary? Do you desire rest? You can find the greatest peace and rest in relationship with God. God seeks you, draws you, calls you, and freely offers to draw you even closer to Himself into relationship that will fulfill that which your heart most longs for.

> *Do you desire rest? You can find the greatest peace and rest in relationship with God.*

I invite you now to read and reflect on Isaiah 58 in full, recognizing that the rest God desires to give to you and me is to be accompanied with rest and deliverance for all of His people from suffering and oppression of every kind.

God offers you and me sacred time with Him in the great gift of the Sabbath. In the next chapter, we turn to the sanctuary in relation to God's work to be *with* His people in space, in their very midst.

Questions for Reflection

1. What stands out to you about the story of the Sabbath? How does it change your perspective to see it as an integral part of the story of God's love for His people?

2. Why is it significant that the Sabbath was in place as a memorial of creation before there was any nation of Israel?
3. How does understanding the Sabbath as also a memorial of liberation shed light on the gift and meaning of the Sabbath? How does this relate to the teachings of Isaiah 58? How should it motivate us to help others today?
4. Does it matter which day we set aside to worship God? Why do special days you share with someone matter to you?
5. Do you find any personal significance in understanding the Sabbath as a gift of rest, the opposite of work, but a call to stop working and rest in God's grace and God's work of liberation and deliverance for all peoples?
6. What can you do to make the Sabbath a delight and a blessing, not only for you but also for others around you?
7. You can enjoy the Sabbath rest as a gift of God this very next Sabbath. Do you want to enter into this special rest with God? If so, prayerfully prepare to make this next coming Sabbath a special day to commune with God and to reflect His light and love to others. If you give yourself to Him, He will carry your burdens and give you rest, as Christ promised (Matt. 11:28–30).

For Further Reading

Adventist Perspectives:

Andreasen, Neils-Erik. *Rest and Redemption*. Berrien Springs, MI: Andrews University Press, 1978.

———. *The Old Testament Sabbath: A Tradition-Historical Investigation*. Missoula, MT: Society of Biblical Literature, 1972.

Andrews, J. N. *History of the Sabbath and First Day of the Week*. Battle Creek, MI: Steam Press, 1873.

Bacchiocchi, Samuele. *From Sabbath to Sunday*. Rome: Pontifical Gregorian University Press, 1977.

Bediako, Daniel and Ekkehardt Mueller, eds. *The Sabbath in the Old Testament and the Intertestamental Period: Implications for

Christians in the Twenty-First Century. Silver Spring, MD: Biblical Research Institute, 2021.

——— and Ekkehardt Mueller, eds. *The Sabbath in the New Testament*. Silver Spring, MD: Biblical Research Institute, 2023.

Davidson, Jo Ann. *Rediscovering the Glory of the Sabbath*. Nampa, ID: Pacific Press, 2021.

Davidson, Richard M. *A Love Song for the Sabbath: How to Experience the Joy that God Intended When He Gave Us the Sabbath*. Hagerstown, MD: Review and Herald, 1988.

du Preez, Ron. *Judging the Sabbath: Discovering What Can't Be Found in Colossians 2:16*. Berrien Springs, MI: Andrews University Press, 2008.

Strand, Kenneth. "The Sabbath." In *Handbook of Seventh-day Adventist Theology*. Edited by Raoul Dederen. Hagerstown, MD: Review and Herald, 2000.

———, ed. *The Sabbath in Scripture and History*. Washington, DC: Review and Herald, 1982.

Tonstad, Sigve. *The Lost Meaning of the Seventh Day*. Berrien Springs, MI: Andrews University Press, 2009.

See also the resources on the Biblical Research Institute website: https://adventistbiblicalresearch.org/materials/.

Other Perspectives:

Baab, Lynne M. *Sabbath Keeping: Finding Freedom in the Rhythm of Rest*. Downers Grove, IL: IVP, 2005.

Barack, Nathan A. *A History of the Sabbath*. New York: Jonathan David Press, 1965.

Brueggemann, Walter. *Sabbath as Resistance: Saying No to the Culture of Now*. Louisville, KY: Westminster John Knox, 2014.

Donato, Christopher John, ed. *Perspectives on the Sabbath: Four Views*. Nashville: B&H Academic, 2011.

Eskenazi, Tamara Cohn, Daniel J. Harrington, and William H. Shea, eds. *The Sabbath in Jewish and Christian Traditions*. New York: Crossroad, 1991.

Heschel, Abraham Joshua. *The Sabbath*. New York: Farrar, Straus and Giroux, 1951.

Myers, Ched. *The Biblical Vision of Sabbath Economics*. Washington, DC: Church of the Saviour, 2001.

Swoboda, A. J. *Subversive Sabbath: The Surprising Power of Rest in a Nonstop World*. Grand Rapids, MI: Brazos, 2018.

PART FIVE

GOD WITH US AGAIN, FOREVER

16

GOD MAKES A WAY TO DWELL WITH US: THE SANCTUARY

Banished from their home. They'd lost nearly everything. Sin separated them from the close fellowship with God they had enjoyed. And they could no longer eat from the tree of life. They would die and, in the meantime, witness decay and death all around them.

Almost immediately after they fell, they tried to cover their shame and guilt—"they sewed fig leaves together and made themselves waist coverings" (Gen. 3:7). And, when God came walking in the midst of the garden, they were afraid and hid themselves (Gen. 3:8–10).

They could not repair what they'd broken or restore what was lost. Their makeshift fig-leaf coverings were not even adequate to cover their nakedness, let alone cover their shame and guilt. Yet, God Himself "made garments of skin for Adam and his wife, and clothed them" (Gen. 3:21). This, however, required the first animal sacrifice. Imagine how they must have felt, seeing another die to cover them.

That first sacrifice, like others in the sacrificial system that followed, was a figure (or type) pointing to the true sacrifice—"the Lamb of God who takes away the sin of the world!" (John 1:29). Indeed, the entire sanctuary system was a type of the mediating work of Christ to defeat sin and death and save the world.

This chapter turns to consider the sanctuary, which paints an amazing and beautiful picture of the story of redemption and much more. Among other questions, this chapter will address questions like:

What is the sanctuary? What should we learn from it? What does the sanctuary system represent? Why does it matter?

It is no coincidence that a significant percentage of Scripture is about the sanctuary, which is far more than a place or a mere doctrine, as we will see.[1]

> *It is no coincidence that a significant percentage of Scripture is about the sanctuary, which is far more than a place or a mere doctrine.*

The Story of Mediation and the Place of the Sanctuary

Overtaken with grief and nearing despair, John wept. In a vision of the heavenly court, he saw a scroll "written on the inside and on the back, sealed with seven seals" at the "right hand of the one seated on the throne." And a mighty angel shouted, "Who is worthy to open the scroll and break its seals?" But, "no one in heaven or on earth or under the earth was able to open the scroll or to look into it." So, John "began to weep bitterly because no one was found worthy to open the scroll or to look into it" (Rev. 5:1–4, NRSVue).[2]

Why was John so upset? Far more is going on here than initially meets the eye.

A sealed document in the ancient world was typically a legal document. "Only the owner could break the seals and disclose the contents."[3] The owner was usually a king or his official.

In the Old Testament, when a king took the throne, he received the royal crown and the scroll of the covenant (the book of Deuteronomy, see 2 Kings 11:12; cf. Deut. 17:18–20; 1 Sam. 10:25). Thus, the "Covenant Scroll became a symbol of installation upon the throne."[4]

In this scene, the scroll is at the right hand of the Father on the throne, "waiting for a worthy candidate to come and take it, and, subsequently, to sit in that place on the throne at the right hand" of the Father.[5] "The ability to take and open the scroll would represent the right to rule."[6]

Nothing less is at stake here than whether anyone will be found worthy to rule. If no one is found, who could deliver this world from the enemy's demonic rule?

No one was found worthy. So, John wept.

But then, John was told, "Do not weep. See, the Lion of the tribe of Judah, the Root of David, has conquered, so that he can open the scrolls and its seven seals" (Rev. 5:5, NRSVue; cf. 12:10–11).

John looked and "saw between the throne and the four living creatures and among the elders a Lamb standing as if it had been slaughtered" (Rev. 5:6, NRSVue). This Lamb took the scroll, and "myriads of myriads and thousands of thousands" of angels sang songs of praise and worship, proclaiming: "Worthy is the Lamb that was slaughtered to receive power and wealth and wisdom and might and honor and glory and blessing!" (Rev. 5:11–12, NRSVue).

Jesus—the Lamb who was slain—was found worthy to open the scroll, to rule and fulfill God's covenant promises as the covenantal son of David. John's bitter tears turned to joy.

In another time and place, bitter tears also turned to joy. Mary Magdalene went to Jesus's tomb, but the stone was rolled away, and Jesus's body was gone. At first, this only added to her grief. But then, Jesus called her name, "Mary!" And, she cried out to Him, "Rabboni!"

Jesus said to her, "Stop clinging to Me, for I have not yet ascended to the Father; but go to My brothers and say to them, 'I am ascending to My Father and your Father, and My God and your God'" (John 20:17).

Afterward, Jesus ascended to the Father and presented Himself before the throne and before the heavenly council as the Lamb who was slain and thereby conquered the enemy—legally defeating Satan via the cross (Rev. 5; 12:10–11; cf. John 16:8, 11). In a great reversal of the earthly judgments against Jesus that led to the cross, Christ was vindicated in the heavenly court and thereafter exalted back to His rightful place on the throne "at the right hand of God" (Rom. 8:34; Eph. 1:20; Col. 3:1; Heb. 10:12; 1 Pet. 3:22), now as the covenantal Son of David, fulfilling the ancient prophecies (Ps. 110:1; cf. Matt. 22:41–45; 26:62–65; Acts 2:33–36).

The risen Christ also took up His work as our high priest in the heavenly sanctuary, the long-promised king *and* "priest forever according to the order of Melchizedek" (Ps. 110:4; see also Ps. 110:1; Heb. 7:13–17). Therefore, "we have such a high priest, who has taken His seat at the right hand of the throne of the Majesty in the heavens, a minister in the sanctuary and in the true tabernacle, which the Lord set up, not man" (Heb. 8:1–2; cf. Rom. 8:34; Heb. 9:11).

> *Who is worthy? Only the Lamb who was slain. Only the long-promised priest-king can save the world.*

Who is worthy? Only the Lamb who was slain. Only the long-promised priest-king can save the world.

When the risen Christ ascended to His Father in the heavenly court, as "the Lamb that was slaughtered" (Rev. 5:12), Christ was found worthy to rule (having defeated the devil via the cross, Rev. 12:10–11) and *inaugurated* the heavenly sanctuary, being installed as the cosmic royal priest. That is, Christ opened "a new and living way which He inaugurated for us through the veil, that is, through His flesh," so we can now "have confidence to enter the [most] holy place by the blood of Jesus" (Heb. 10:19–20; cf. Dan. 9:24).

The first phase of Christ's work of atonement was completed at the cross. Christ's once-for-all sacrifice on the cross (Heb. 9:12; 10:10) was sufficient provision for full atonement for the sins of the whole world (1 John 2:2). Yet, we have not yet been fully reconciled to God. Christ's atoning sacrifice must be accepted and applied individually. For this and other reasons, Christ's work continues in the heavenly sanctuary.

Here, again, is the motif of "already, but not yet" that we've seen in the cosmic conflict. Christ announced His work brought judgment that involved casting out the devil, declaring: "Now judgment is upon this world; now the ruler of this world will be cast out" (John 12:31; cf. 16:11). Christ legally defeated Satan at the cross (Rev. 12:10–11), but Satan's rule has not yet been completely uprooted, though the devil "knows that his time is short!" (Rev. 12:12, NRSVue). The two phases of Christ's defeat of Satan correspond to the two phases of Christ's work of atonement—as our sacrifice at the cross and our high priest in the heavenly sanctuary.

As we have seen, Christ's work of atonement is necessary because sin separates from God (Isa. 59:2), the source of Life, such that "the wages of sin is death" (Rom. 6:23). Adam and Eve's sin condemned this world to degradation and death and rule by the devil. If not for the promise that the woman's Seed would one day crush the serpent and save the world (Gen. 3:15), all hope would have been lost. To crush the serpent's head, though, the Seed was first Himself crushed on the cross. He thus demonstrated God's righteousness and love, defeating the enemy's allegations and making a way to reconcile sinners to God while remaining righteous—to justify sinners while remaining just (Rom. 3:25–26).

As Hebrews 2:14 explains it, "since the children share in flesh and blood, He Himself [Christ] likewise also partook of the same, so that through death He might destroy the one who has the power of death, that is, the devil" (Heb. 2:14). Thus, Paul proclaimed: "The God of peace will soon crush Satan under your feet" (Rom. 16:20).

Even as God clothed Adam and Eve with animal skins from the first animal sacrifice (Gen. 3:21), which prefigured Christ's sacrifice, Christ covers our sins with His robe of righteousness resulting from giving Himself as our sacrificial lamb (see 1 Pet. 1:18–19), a self-sacrificial act in which Christ voluntarily lowered Himself and demonstrated God's perfect character of unselfish love, in direct contrast to the devil's allegations and his egomaniacal quest to elevate himself and rule in Christ's place.

From the story of Cain and Abel, we see that a system of animal sacrifices was already in place (Gen. 4:4). A few chapters later, animal sacrifice appears again in the story of Noah (Gen. 8:2). Later, numerous sacrifices are embedded in the story of Abraham. And (as a test) God told Abraham to sacrifice his son Isaac, but then Himself provided a ram as a sacrifice in Isaac's place (Gen. 22), prefiguring Christ's sacrifice in our place.

In the Exodus, while delivering Israel from slavery, God instituted the Passover, wherein each Israelite home was to sacrifice a lamb and put its blood on the lintel and doorposts so the destroying angel of the tenth plague would *pass over* the homes covered by the blood. This also prefigured Christ's work, such that Paul identifies Christ as "our Passover" who "has been sacrificed" (1 Cor. 5:7).

Then, God instituted the ceremonial laws of the Mosaic covenant, a ritual system of sacrifices and festivals that all prefigured Christ's work for us (more on this later). God instituted an elect priesthood and commanded, "make me a sanctuary so that I may dwell among them" (Exod. 25:8, NRSVue). This earthly sanctuary was a model (or "type," a special kind of symbolic representation) of the heavenly sanctuary, to be made "by the pattern" that "was shown to" Moses "on the mountain" (Exod. 25:40), "a copy and shadow of the heavenly things," of the "true tabernacle" in heaven, "which the Lord set up, not man" (Heb. 8:5, 2; cf. Ps. 102:19).

Notice the *express* purpose of this sanctuary was so that God could dwell *with* and among His people. For the perfectly holy God to dwell among sinful people, mediation is required. The sanctuary and its services prefigured (as "types") the mediating work that the God-man Christ performs to reconcile humans to God.

When inaugurated, the special presence of God filled the wilderness sanctuary (Exod. 40:34) and, later, the temple built in Jerusalem known as Solomon's temple (1 Kings 8:10-11). When the Babylonian empire conquered Judah, Solomon's temple was destroyed (586 BC). After the Babylonian exile, the Second Temple was built (515 BC), but God's special presence did not fill it.

Later, however, God's special presence visited the Second Temple in Jesus Himself—God incarnate, the true sacrifice and high priest of whom the earthly sacrifices and priests were types.

By His death as the once-for-all sacrifice on the cross (see Heb. 9:12; 10:10), Christ brought the earthly sanctuary system with all its ritual sacrifices and festivals to an end as prophesied (see Dan. 9:27), signaled when "the veil of the temple" was miraculously "torn in two from top to bottom" (Matt. 27:51; see chapter 14). Later, the Roman empire destroyed the Second Temple, and no earthly temple has replaced it.

The true temple in heaven, however, remains (see Heb. 8:2-5; 9:11-12). Thus, in a vision of heaven, John saw furniture that corresponds to the earthly sanctuary—the lampstand (Rev. 4:5), the golden altar of incense (Rev. 8:3), and the ark of the covenant (Rev. 11:19). Indeed, Revelation 11:19 states: "And the temple of God which is in heaven was opened; and the ark of His covenant appeared in His temple, and there were flashes of lightning and sounds and peals of thunder, and an earthquake, and a great hailstorm."

Even as the earthly temples were attacked by earthly empires empowered by the dragon Satan (cf. Dan. 7:3-7; Rev. 13:2; see chapter 18), this heavenly sanctuary has been under attack of a different kind. According to the prophecies of Daniel and Revelation, another imperial regime empowered by the dragon (a distinctly religious power) wages spiritual war against this heavenly sanctuary, attempting to take Christ's place and instituting a false system of salvation and worship (cf. Dan. 7:7-12, 19-27; 8:9-14; Rev. 13:1-14:12; more on this later and in chapter 18).

Notably, before he fell, Satan himself was a covering cherub in the heavenly sanctuary—"the anointed cherub who covers . . . on the holy mountain of God" (Ezek. 28:14; cf. Exod. 25:19-20; 37:7-9).[7] As seen previously, though created perfect, he corrupted himself (Ezek. 28:14-19; see chapter 9). The place where sin and evil first arose (the heavenly sanctuary, referred to in Ezekiel 28:14 as "the holy mountain of God"), then, is the place the solution to sin and evil is ultimately worked out.

Even now, Christ is our high priest and "a minister in the sanctuary and in the true tabernacle, which the Lord set up, not man" (Heb. 8:2). Indeed, "when Christ appeared as a high priest of the good things having come, He entered through the greater and more perfect tabernacle, not made by hands, that is, not of this creation; and not through the blood of goats and calves, but through His own blood, He entered the holy place [better translated as "sanctuary," *ta hagia*] once for all time, having obtained eternal redemption" (Heb. 9:11-12; cf. 6:19-20).

Whereas "the copies of the things in the heavens" (the earthly sanctuary elements) were "cleansed" by the blood of calves and goats (the sacrifices of the earthly system), Christ cleanses "the heavenly things [the heavenly sanctuary] themselves with better sacrifices than these. For Christ did not enter a holy place [or "sanctuary"] made by hands, a mere copy of the true one, but into heaven itself, now to appear in the presence of God for us" (Heb. 9:23-24).

While the Old Covenant included chosen priests and ritual animal sacrifices and services in an earthly sanctuary/temple, the New Covenant includes the once-for-all sacrifice of Christ, who ministers as the true high priest in the heavenly sanctuary. Christ's ministry encompasses both the first and second phases of the earthly priestly ministry—the daily sacrifices and the yearly Day of Atonement (discussed below). Christ Himself is the true (antitypical) sacrifice and the true (antitypical) high priest prefigured by the earthly sacrifices and services. He takes sin on Himself and into the heavenly sanctuary in the first phase and cleanses the heavenly sanctuary in the second phase. The next section will help you understand these phrases.

The Sanctuary Doctrine: The Basic Elements

In brief, the sanctuary doctrine includes the teaching that the elements of the earthly sanctuary system of the Old Covenant were types of Christ's works of atonement in the New Covenant, involving the heavenly sanctuary.[8] Christ offered Himself as the once-for-all sacrifice (Heb. 10:10) and now ministers as our true "high priest" in the heavenly sanctuary—the "true tabernacle, which the Lord set up, not man" (Heb. 8:1-2; cf. 8:3-5; 9:11-12).[9]

As types of Christ's work of atonement, the rituals and ceremonies of the earthly sanctuary system correspond to Christ's sacrifice for us on the cross *and* ministry for us in the heavenly sanctuary, by which God saves sinners while demonstrating God's righteousness and love, defeating the devil's allegations and ultimately bringing reconciliation and restoration to the entire cosmos.

After He legally defeated the devil at the cross (Rev. 12:10-11) and rose from the dead, Christ ascended to heaven, inaugurated the heavenly sanctuary (Rev. 5), and began a special intercessory ministry, prefigured in the *daily* rituals of the sanctuary.[10] Later, Christ entered into the second phase of His atoning work, prefigured by the *yearly* rituals of the Day of Atonement (discussed further below).

This second phase of Christ's atoning work includes a judgment in the heavenly court that takes place prior to Christ's Second Coming (the pre-advent judgment depicted in Dan. 7:9-10 and elsewhere). Among other things, this pre-advent judgment deals with the sins of the world in a way that demonstrates God's perfect righteousness and love and thereby "cleanses" the heavenly sanctuary, prefigured by the cleansing of the earthly sanctuary on the Day of Atonement.

This pre-advent judgment plays a crucial role in vindicating God's character in the cosmic conflict, condemning evil and injustice without sweeping it under the rug while revealing to celestial creatures (both fallen and unfallen) that God has done everything He could to save everyone willing to be saved and that God saves the redeemed in a way that is perfectly just—in accord with His immutable character and law of unselfish love, utterly defeating Satan's allegations in the cosmic conflict.

The Basic Purpose of the Sanctuary

The sanctuary is all about divine presence, making a way for God to be *with us* in a special, intimate fashion. As many scholars have recognized, Genesis depicts Eden as an earthly sanctuary for God's dwelling, a copy of the original heavenly Eden sanctuary.[11] In Eden, God was intimately present to Adam and Eve, but their sin brought separation, fracturing their relationships with God and one another.

> *The sanctuary is all about divine presence, making a way for God to be with us in a special, intimate fashion.*

Later, God commanded Moses, "Have them construct a sanctuary for Me, so that I may dwell among them" (Exod. 25:8). Notice the express purpose of the earthly sanctuary was so that God could dwell *with* His people. Somehow the sanctuary system made a way for God to dwell among His people.

Yet, many wonder, why would sanctuary rituals and ceremonies matter in the first place? Here, it is crucial to recognize that some ceremonies are not merely for show but accomplish important things. Consider, in this regard, an adoption ceremony. In the United States, legal processes are embedded in the adoption ceremony that are essential to making the adoption legal. The declaration by the judge and other court proceedings actually change the status of the child to a legal son or daughter of his or her adoptive parents, with momentous life-changing results for the parties concerned.

Likewise, Scripture presents Christ's ministry in the heavenly sanctuary as a reality through which the world is saved, and we are reconciled to God. *What could be more important?* And the earthly sanctuary rituals and services pointed beyond themselves to Christ's mediating work to save and reconcile people to Himself. The perfectly holy God can dwell in the midst of a sinful people only through mediation.

Competing Theories in Christian Theology: Typology

Many parts of Scripture portray in advance—or prefigure—the work of Christ. These are examples of "types." While the word "type" is sometimes broadly used of natural analogies, as Adventists understand it, a biblical type is a historical reality (person, event, or institution) that God designed to prefigure a greater reality to come, known as the antitype. And typology is the study of such types.[12]

Richard Davidson identifies six basic "typological" passages (Rom. 5:14; 1 Cor. 10:6, 11; Heb. 8:5; 9:24; 1 Pet. 3:21). Each uses the words "type" (*typos*) or "antitype" (*antitypos*) as technical terms relative to the author's interpretation of the Old Testament.[13] For example, Hebrews 8:5 explicitly teaches sanctuary typology, explaining that the priests in the earthly sanctuary/temple served "a copy and shadow of the heavenly things" and noting "Moses was warned by God when he was about to erect the tabernacle" to "make all things by the pattern [*typos*] which was shown to you on the mountain" (cf. Exod. 25:40).

The earthly sanctuary was a type of the heavenly sanctuary, and the earthly sanctuary services were types of Christ's atoning works—His sacrifice on the cross and ministry in the heavenly sanctuary. Thus, Hebrews teaches that the earthly sanctuary "made by [human] hands" was "a mere copy of the true one"—the heavenly sanctuary (Heb. 9:24). Indeed, as our "high priest," Christ "entered through the greater and more perfect tabernacle, not made by hands, that is, not of this creation; and not through the blood of goats and calves, but through His own blood, He entered the holy place once for all time, having obtained eternal redemption" (Heb. 9:11–12).

Davidson further identifies five distinguishing characteristics of typology. A type (1) is rooted in history; (2) points forward or predictively prefigures; (3) prefigures, but not explicitly, not verbally; (4) involves a heightened correspondence; and (5) is divinely ordained to function as a prefiguration of the antitype.[14] These five characteristics set typology in contrast to *allegorizing*. A literary allegory is a symbolic story or poem that figuratively conveys abstract or spiritual meaning through representative elements. Scripture includes some allegories (e.g., Christ's parables), and careful interpreters should recognize when the context indicates the presence of allegory and interpret such accordingly. However, allegorizing (in the sense meant here) refers to ways of reading that interpret texts allegorically, even when the presence of allegory is not indicated by the text or its context. For example, many who affirm strict classical theism (see chapter 8) employ allegorizing as a way of interpreting Scripture to make it fit with the strictly timeless, immutable, and impassible conception of God their system affirms.

For many Adventists and other biblical interpreters, however, allegorizing is problematic because it often reads into literature symbolic meanings not intended by the author(s) or discernible in the text itself and which run counter to or ignore the historical sense of the text, *potentially* allowing *any* fanciful symbolic interpretation or arbitrary assignment of meaning the reader imagines. Scripture thus might be treated like a "wax nose," which can be twisted and pointed any direction one wishes, potentially undermining the meaning and authority of Scripture. Historically, *allegorizing* readings have reinterpreted biblical depictions of God (e.g., God's emotional reactions reinterpreted based on the presupposition that God is timeless and impassible and thus cannot actually have emotional reactions, see chapter 7) to fit with the timeless conception of God in strict classical theism, downplaying the historical or literal sense of the text in favor of the so-called spiritual (timeless) sense of the text.

While insisting that typology should operate with consistent principles of interpretation and interpretive controls (grounded in Scripture itself), Davidson further distinguishes his understanding of typology from what he calls "post-critical" approaches. Such post-critical approaches maintain that historicity is not essential, viewing types as merely *retrospective* analogies or loose correspondences to similar modes of divine activity with little or no predictive elements. Instead, the Adventist approach to typology (as explained by Davidson) views types as predictive, divinely designed prefigurations rooted in historical realities.

Sanctuary Layout and Services

The earthly sanctuary functioned as a conduit of God's presence, connecting heaven and earth—something like a portal to heavenly realities.[15] The earthly sanctuary/temples served as a meeting place, a center of divine revelation, a center of worship, and a type of the heavenly sanctuary (Exod. 25:9).

The earthly sanctuary and temples had the following layout:

LAYOUT OF THE EARTHLY SANCTUARY

A – Holy Place | B – Most Holy Place

1. Bronze Altar | 2. Laver | 3. Table | 4. Lampstand | 5. Gold Altar | 6. Ark of the Covenant

The wilderness sanctuary was surrounded by a courtyard, entered from the east. Moving east to west, one would pass the altar of burnt offering and the laver (a large basin filled with water) before coming to the entrance of the sanctuary itself—a veil through which one would enter into the compartment known as the Holy Place. Inside the Holy Place were the table of shewbread, the seven-branched lampstand/menorah, and the altar of incense. At the western end of the Holy Place, there was another veil, the entrance to the Most Holy Place, a cube that contained the ark of the covenant and where God's special presence (Shekinah glory) dwelled.[16]

The furniture in the courtyard and the sanctuary prefigured various aspects of Christ's ministry and the heavenly sanctuary.[17] For example, the altar of burnt offering and the *daily* sacrifices offered thereon prefigured Christ's once-for-all and all-sufficient sacrifice for us on the cross (cf. Heb. 10:11–12; 13:10–12). The laver and the ceremonial washings performed there prefigured (among other things) the cleansing aspects of Christ's work (cf. Eph. 5:25–27).

The lampstand prefigured (among other things) Christ as the Light of the world (cf. John 1:9; 8:12). The table of shewbread (i.e., the bread of the presence) primarily prefigured Christ, "the bread of life" (cf. John 6:47–51). The altar of incense (the smoke and aroma of which would waft into the Most Holy Place) prefigured the intercession of Christ (cf. Heb. 7:25), offering the merits of His righteousness to cover our unrighteousness.[18]

Finally, in the Most Holy Place, the ark of the covenant corresponded to God's throne in heaven, with God "enthroned above [or upon or between] the cherubim" (e.g., Ps. 80:1; 99:1; Isa. 37:16), with Christ Himself identified in Romans 3:25 with language that literally means the cover of the ark of the covenant—"the mercy seat" (CSB) or place of forgiveness/atonement.

From east to west, one moved toward God's special presence, which filled the Most Holy Place. In this regard, some have seen the layout as prefiguring the way humans can move toward God's presence via the steps of salvation, being justified by faith through Christ's sacrifice (corresponding to the altar of burnt offering), being cleansed by faith and growing in holiness through Christ's intercession *and sustenance* (corresponding to the laver, shewbread, lampstand, and altar of incense), and through Christ "approach the throne of grace with confidence" (Heb. 4:16).

Daily and Yearly Sacrifices and Services

The sanctuary services were carried out by Levite priests, who functioned as God's representatives before the people and the people's representative before God—mediators between God and humans who made intercession for human sin (Exod. 28:9–12; Lev. 10:11; Deut. 33:10). This mediating ministry included two crucial phases: the daily sacrifices and the yearly Day of Atonement, prefiguring Christ's sacrifice on the cross and priestly ministry for us in the heavenly sanctuary.

The daily sanctuary services included a number of things that were done continually or regularly (*tamid*),[19] including the:

- continual/regular wearing of the breastplate by the high priest over his heart, containing twelve stones with the names of the twelve tribes, "as a memorial before the LORD continually" (Exod. 28:29)
- continual/regular burnt offering, a one-year-old male lamb offered every morning and evening (Num. 28:3–8), kept burning continually on the altar (Lev. 6:9–13). These were types of Christ's sacrifice, highlighting our *constant* dependence on His atoning sacrifice, which *continually* covers the sins of those who are in Christ by faith[20]
- continual/regular offering of the bread of the presence, placed "before the LORD" in the Holy Place every Sabbath as offering to God (Exod. 25:30; Lev. 24:8; 2 Chron. 2:4). This also highlighted humanity's constant dependence on God for physical and spiritual food—Christ Himself being the "bread of life" (John 6:35)
- continual/regular light of the lampstand, continually supplied with olive oil to make the "lamp burn continually" (Exod. 27:20; cf. Lev. 24:2). This pointed to Christ as the Light of the world that continually shines in the darkness (cf. John 1:4–5, 9; 8:12)
- continual/regular burning of the incense, morning and evening incense was burnt on the altar of incense, for "perpetual incense before the LORD" (Exod. 30:7–8). This incense represented Christ's merits and continual intercession for us (Heb. 7:25).[21]

In addition to the burnt offerings, many other offerings (peace offerings, sin offerings, guilt/trespass offerings, and meal/grain offerings) represented the sacrifice of Christ in unique ways (see chart below).

		TYPES OF SACRIFICES			
REF.	OFFERING	BLOOD ON ALTAR TO	MEAT TO	UNIQUE ASPECT	CHRIST'S SACRIFICE
Lev. 1	burnt	sides	the Lord	all meat consumed	Christ's life consumed
Lev. 2	grain	(no blood)	(no flesh)	no death	Christ provides eternal life
Lev. 3:1–17; 7:11–36	peace (well-being)	sides	*priest + offerer	offerer ate	spiritually "partaking" of Christ
Lev. 4:1–35; 6:24–30	sin (purification)	horns	*priest	elevation of blood	Christ as ransom for life
Lev. 5:1–19; 7:1–7	guilt (reparation)	sides	*priest	prior payment of reparation	Christ pays debt of sin

*except when the offerer was a priest (e.g., Lev. 4:3–12).
Adapted with permission from *Andrews Study Bible: Light. Depth. Truth.*, NKJV (Berrien Springs, MI: Andrews University Press, 2010), 128. © by Andrews University Press.

Together, these various offerings represented the multi-faceted accomplishments of Christ's sacrifice for us.[22]

Through the daily services of animal sacrifices, the people's sins were symbolically brought into the sanctuary (representing God Himself taking responsibility for dealing with the sin) such that the sanctuary required cleansing.

Two types of sins committed throughout the year needed to be dealt with, both:

- intentionally defiant ("high-handed") sins (Num. 15:30–31) for which there was no prescribed ritual or sacrifice) and
- a category of sins sometimes called "unintentional" (*shegagah*) sins (see Lev. 4:2), but which also included intentional sins (see,

e.g., Lev. 6:1–7) that were not done rebelliously or defiantly (i.e., high-handedly).[23]

There were numerous animal sacrifices for this second category of sins. These were to be without blemish or defect (representing Christ's *perfect* offering).

When individuals brought animal sacrifices for themselves, they were to lay their hand on the animal's head "that it may be accepted for him to make atonement on his behalf" (Lev. 1:4; cf. 3:2, 8; 4:29) and then slay it. Even as they caused the innocent animal's death, their sin would eventually cause the death of the innocent Son of God.

When sin (purification) offerings were made for the high priest or the whole community throughout the year, blood from the animal sacrifice was brought into the Holy Place and sprinkled seven times before the inner veil and daubed on the horns of the altar of incense (Lev. 4:6–7, 17–18). The sin, symbolically carried by the blood, thus moved into the sanctuary toward the (symbolic) throne of God in the Most Holy Place (symbolizing God taking responsibility for dealing with these sins on Himself).

On the yearly Day of Atonement, however, the movement of the blood was reversed. Whereas the daily services symbolized sins coming into the sanctuary throughout the year, the Day of Atonement services symbolized sins being removed from the sanctuary—cleansing the sanctuary from the effects of sin.[24]

No one was to enter the Most Holy Place except the high priest, who entered only once a year on the Day of Atonement (except when the sanctuary was first inaugurated, see Exod. 40:1–16). It was a very holy and solemn day of judgment and cleansing, preceded by ten days during which trumpets were blown to call the people to prepare, humble themselves, repent, and call on God for forgiveness and cleansing.

On the Day of Atonement, the sprinkling of blood began in the Most Holy Place, with blood first sprinkled on the cover of the ark of the covenant, then sprinkled seven times in front of the ark's cover, then (moving eastward into the Holy Place) daubed on the horns of the altar of incense and sprinkled seven times in front of the inner veil, then (moving out of the sanctuary) daubed on the horns of the altar of burnt offering and finally sprinkled seven times on the altar of burnt offering (Lev. 16).

RITUAL CLEANSING OF THE SANCTUARY ON THE DAY OF ATONEMENT

Sins and impurities enter daily

Sins and impurities exit yearly

This chart draws on the work of Roy Gane.

This ritual cleansing of the sanctuary on the Day of Atonement (symbolically) removed the sins and impurities that had been (symbolically) brought into the sanctuary throughout the year (see Lev. 16:16). And, as a result of the cleansing of the sanctuary, the people were cleansed (Lev. 16:30; cf. 16:16–17; Heb. 10:22)—sins were *finally* wiped away.[25]

These two phases of atonement (daily and yearly) correspond to the following:

- Christ's atoning sacrifice as our sacrificial Lamb, applied by Christ as our high priest in the heavenly sanctuary for forgiveness of our sins (cf. Heb. 9:14–15), and
- Christ's high priestly work of cleansing the heavenly sanctuary (cf. Heb. 9:23–24) during the antitypical Day of Atonement.

The wonderful promise of 1 John 1:9 mirrors these two phases: "If we confess our sins, He is faithful and righteous, so that He will forgive us our sins [first phase] and cleanse us from all unrighteousness [second phase]."

There were two special sin offerings on the Day of Atonement, a bull for the priests (Lev. 16:11ff.) and a goat for the rest of the people (Lev. 16:15ff.). These were supplemented by two burnt offerings, a ram for the priests and a ram for the people (Lev. 16:3, 5, 11, 15).

The goat offered as sin offering for the people was the goat "for the LORD" (Lev. 16:8), its blood sprinkled on the cover of the ark of the covenant, then seven times in front of the ark, then sprinkled and daubed in other places moving eastward out of the sanctuary (as depicted earlier, Lev. 16:15–19), thus ritually cleansing the sanctuary.

After being removed from the sanctuary by this ritual cleansing, however, the sins still had to be banished from the camp. This was represented by a ritual with a second goat. This goat was *not* a sacrifice to the LORD and *not* a goat for the LORD, but was identified as the goat "for Azazel" (Lev. 16:8, NRSVue, often translated "scapegoat").[26] This goat "for Azazel" was (symbolically) loaded with the sins that had been ritually removed from the sanctuary. Then, this goat was sent away from the sanctuary and the camp "into the wilderness to Azazel" (Lev. 16:10, 20–22, NRSVue).

Azazel is not explicitly identified in Leviticus, but the next chapter refers to "the goat demons" that people made sacrifices to (Lev. 17:7), and there is considerable evidence that Azazel is a demonic enemy of God, fitting the profile of the devil himself.[27]

Accordingly, Adventists typically believe this goat for Azazel represents the devil, (symbolically) loaded with the refuse of sins that he himself instigated and for which he thus finally bears his own culpability. The devil does not in any way function as a substitute or sacrifice for us but bears his own culpability for the horrendous evil he instigated.[28] This ritual, then, represents the devil and evil itself being banished *from the universe* forever. When evil is finally eradicated, God's special presence with us will be fully restored, with no more suffering or death and no more sin or evil to separate us from the fullness of God's special presence.

> *When evil is finally eradicated, God's special presence with us will be fully restored, with no more suffering or death and no more sin or evil to separate us from the fullness of God's special presence.*

Atonement Processes: The Cross and Christ's Two-Phase Ministry in the Heavenly Sanctuary

Scripture repeatedly identifies Christ as the true (antitypical) once-for-all sacrifice (Heb. 10:10), "the Lamb of God who takes away the sin of the world" (John 1:29), "our Passover [paschal lamb]" who "has been sacrificed" (1 Cor. 5:7), and "the Lamb who has been slaughtered" (Rev. 13:8). Accordingly, believers are redeemed "with precious blood, as of a lamb unblemished and spotless, the blood of Christ" (1 Pet. 1:18–19; cf. Heb. 9:15, 26).

And Scripture also repeatedly identifies Christ as our true (antitypical) high priest who ministers for us in the heavenly sanctuary, "the true tabernacle, which the Lord set up, not man" (Heb. 8:1–2; 9:11–14). Even now, Christ ministers in the heavenly sanctuary "to save forever those who come to God through Him, since He always lives to make intercession for them" (Heb. 7:25).

The earthly sanctuary services of the Old Covenant, "only a shadow of the good things to come" (Heb. 10:1), could not resolve the sin problem, for "it is impossible for the blood of bulls and goats to take away sins" (Heb. 10:4). But Christ's (New Covenant) atoning sacrifice and priestly ministry in the heavenly sanctuary does take away sin so that we can be "sanctified through the offering of the body of Jesus Christ once for all time. Every priest stands daily ministering and offering time after time the same sacrifices, which can never take away sins; but He, having offered one sacrifice for sins for all time, SAT DOWN AT THE RIGHT HAND OF GOD" (Heb. 10:10–12; cf. 7:26–27; 10:13–14).

Indeed, "it was necessary" that the heavenly sanctuary "be cleansed ... with better sacrifices" (Heb. 9:23) through the ministry of a better, sinless priesthood. And Christ Himself provides the perfect sacrificial offering (of Himself on the cross) and ministers for us as the one true high priest in the true heavenly sanctuary (see, e.g., Heb. 8:1–5; 9:11–15).

After legally defeating Satan by His sacrifice on the cross (Rev. 12:10–11), Christ was exalted back to His rightful place on the throne, and Christ inaugurated the heavenly sanctuary (cf. Rev. 5) and took up His work as our high priest therein (Heb. 8:1–5; 9:11–15), the promised "priest forever according to the order of Melchizedek" (Ps. 110:4; see also Heb. 7:13–17). Christ's high priestly work in the heavenly sanctuary precedes His Second Coming.

The Pre-Advent Judgment

Daniel looked, and "thrones were set up, and the Ancient of Days took His seat; His garment was white as snow, and the hair of His head like pure wool. His throne was ablaze with flames, its wheels were a burning fire. A river of fire was flowing and coming out from before Him; thousands upon thousands were serving Him, and myriads upon myriads were standing before Him; the court convened, and the books were opened" (Dan. 7:9-10; cf. 7:22, 26-27).

This scene depicts a judgment in heaven that precedes Christ's Second Coming (cf. Rev. 14:7)—the Second Coming is depicted as taking place afterward (Dan. 7:13-14). This pre-advent judgment in the heavenly court/council renders verdicts regarding the salvation of those who belong to Christ by faith—rendering "judgment . . . in favor of the saints" (Dan. 7:22; cf. Rev. 12:10-11), while correspondingly condemning Satan and the oppressive imperial systems Satan works through on earth against God's sanctuary and God's people (represented by beasts and the counterfeit system of the little horn in particular; Dan. 7:11-12; cf. 7:25-27).[29]

This judgment "in favor of the saints" (Dan. 7:22) directly counters the devil's allegations in the heavenly court against God's people—the allegations of "the accuser of our brothers and sisters . . . who accuses them before our God day and night" (Rev. 12:10), thus vindicating God's people and also vindicating the justice of God in saving His people through Christ's atoning work.

As Adventists typically understand it, this pre-advent judgment corresponds to the cleansing of the sanctuary on the yearly Day of Atonement (the second phase of the atonement). By offering forgiveness of sins, God took responsibility for justly dealing with sin (symbolically represented by sins coming into the sanctuary via the daily sanctuary services). But, through Christ's works of atonement, God justly deals with sins such that He is both "just and the justifier of the one who has faith in Jesus" (Rom. 3:26). Christ's high priestly ministry in the heavenly sanctuary relative to the pre-advent judgment cleanses God's sanctuary and God's people, *justly* dealing with sin, thereby clearing God's name and refuting Satan's allegations while correspondingly condemning evil and injustice, leading to the final eradication of evil forevermore.

The Nature of Judgment

Scripture consistently teaches that "we will all stand before the judgment seat of God" (Rom. 14:10). Indeed, "we must all appear before the judgment seat of Christ, so that each one may receive compensation for his deeds done through the body, in accordance with what he has done, whether good or bad" (2 Cor. 5:10; cf. Rev. 20:12). God "has set a day on which He will judge the world in righteousness" (Acts 17:31; cf. Heb. 10:30; James 2:11–12; 1 Pet. 1:17) and God's "righteous judgment will be revealed" and God "will repay according to each one's deeds" (Rom. 2:5–6, NRSVue; see also Ps. 62:12; Prov. 24:12; Rom. 2:16). Accordingly, Ecclesiastes 12:13–14 teaches, "fear God and keep His commandments," for "God will bring every act to judgment, everything which is hidden, whether it is good or evil."

Jesus Himself likewise taught, "on the day of judgment you will have to give an account for every careless word you utter, for by your words you will be justified, and by your words you will be condemned" (Matt. 12:36–37, NRSVue). Further, Jesus proclaimed, "the Son of Man is going to come in the glory of His Father with His angels, and WILL THEN REPAY EVERY PERSON ACCORDING TO HIS DEEDS" (Matt. 16:27). In Revelation 22:12, Jesus likewise declares, "Behold, I am coming quickly, and My reward is with Me, to give to every one according to his work" (NKJV).

Adventists distinguish between the judgment in the heavenly court prior to Christ's Second Coming (the pre-advent judgment, Rev. 14:7; cf. Dan. 7:9–10) and the execution of judgment against the unrepentant wicked later on (e.g., Rev. 14:14–16; 20:12). Specifically, in Revelation 14:7, the first angel's message proclaims: "Fear God and give Him glory, because the hour of His judgment has come" (Rev. 14:7; cf. Eccles. 12:13–14). But only later is judgment *executed* (Rev. 14:14–16; 20:12; see chapter 19). Just as in regular earthly courts, verdicts precede the execution of sentences, Adventists believe the pre-advent judgment renders the verdicts that precede the final execution of judgment, doing so by way of a transparent process in the heavenly court whereby Satan's accusations (against the redeemed and against God) are defeated.

Most people fear judgment, viewing it only in negative terms, but in Scripture judgment is always a good thing for those faithful to God. In Scripture, judges bring deliverance for the oppressed and downtrodden, and thus God's people often cry out for God to bring judgment, which will amount to their deliverance.

Imagine someone has illegally claimed your home and taken your children. Would you want a perfectly just judge known for delivering victims of oppression to intervene and bring justice? Of course!

Unless you have given your allegiance to the devil, this is very much like the situation in which you stand now. The devil has effectively stolen and corrupted our home, claiming this world belongs to him and raining suffering on you and every person you love. Don't you want justice and deliverance to come? If so, you also thereby long for God's judgment to come.

Yet, perhaps you are afraid that God's judgment will be *against* you. After all, you've done evil. Unless someone delivers you from the wages of sin, you also will be condemned to eternal death. But there is good news of great joy: "the wages of sin is death, but the gracious gift of God is eternal life in Christ Jesus our Lord" (Rom. 6:23).

While no mere human could stand in the judgment alone, for "all have sinned" (Rom. 3:23), if you accept Christ, He will be your substitute and defender in the heavenly court. As John writes, "if anyone does sin, we have an advocate with the Father, Jesus Christ the righteous, and he is the atoning sacrifice for our sins, and not for ours only but also for the sins of the whole world" (1 John 2:1–2, NRSVue). Just imagine that! Christ will defend you by His own righteousness in the heavenly court. Christ defends us not against the Father—"the Father Himself loves you" (John 16:27) and wants to save everyone and is perfectly united with Christ and the Holy Spirit in the plan of salvation. Rather, Christ defends us against the accusations of the enemy, Satan, the accuser of our brethren who accuses God's people day and night (Rev. 12:10). And, since all judgment is given to Christ (John 5:22), if Christ is your Savior *and* Lord you cannot lose in the judgment. You can only lose if you reject Christ and choose to represent yourself in the judgment (cf. John 3:18).

> Christ will defend you by His own righteousness in the heavenly court.

As we have seen (see chapter 13), those who are in Christ by faith are justified and thus counted as righteous (cf. Rom. 8:1). God's work of love in them (Rom. 5:5; Gal. 5:6) will demonstrate that they have been justified in that their love will be manifest in their works (see Matt. 25:31–46).

If you claim to love me but do not lift a finger to help my child when he is drowning, then you manifestly do not *actually* love me. Similarly, "If someone says, 'I love God,' and yet he hates his brother or sister, he is a liar" (1 John 4:20). Many claim to be Christians but are not actually followers of Christ. Remember, many have claimed to be Christians while actually following the dragon (e.g., many involved in the transatlantic slave trade, various wars of conquest, advocating "Christian" nationalism, colonialism, economic oppression of the poor, sexual exploitation and other forms of sexual immorality, and other great evils have claimed to be Christians). The judgment exposes what is truly in one's heart, what and whom you love, and where your allegiance lies—whether you truly follow the Lamb or the dragon.

We will, then, be judged *according to* works (Eccles. 12:14; cf. Dan. 7:10; Matt. 25:31–46; Rom. 2:5–6; 2 Cor. 5:10; 1 Pet. 1:17; Rev. 20:12) because our works manifest what is truly in our heart—whether we truly love God and thus manifest "the obedience of faith" (Rom. 1:5). Yet, works cannot save us—they are not meritorious, but "only evidence of the faith through which we are saved (Eph. 2:8–9; James 2:26)."[30]

Through Christ's mediation in the heavenly sanctuary, you can be pleasing to God (e.g., 1 Pet. 2:5–6; cf. Heb. 11:6) and accounted perfect *in Christ*. Christ's mediation for every person who believes in Him provides forgiveness and cleansing (see 1 John 1:9–10) and makes up for the deficiencies of all who are "in Christ" by faith (Rom. 8:1).[31] That is, our "righteous deeds" are "like a filthy garment" (Isa. 64:6), but Christ makes up for our deficiencies by providing the all-sufficient sacrifice for us. Christ covers, as it were, our sinfulness with His own perfection—like the perfectly clean, vibrant, and majestic robe of a king being placed over the filthy, soiled rags of a pauper (see Isa. 61:10; Rev. 19:7–8; cf. Matt. 22:11–12).

Christians are called to pursue "the holiness without which no one will see the Lord" (Heb. 12:14) and "cleanse ourselves from all defilement of flesh and spirit, perfecting holiness in the fear of God" (2 Cor. 7:1). But we can have no confidence in our own ability to cleanse ourselves by ourselves. One can, however, be "confident . . . that He who began a good work among you will complete it by the day of Christ Jesus" (Phil. 1:6). Only Christ can forgive us and cleanse us, and He will effectively do so for everyone who places their faith in Him. As long as we continue to accept His transforming power *by faith*, we have complete assurance that our sins are forgiven (Rom. 8:1–17; Col. 1:21–23) and thus "have confidence to enter the holy place by the blood of Jesus, by a new and living way which He inaugurated for us" (Heb. 10:19–20).[32]

Why a Pre-Advent Judgment?

Adventists sometimes refer to the pre-advent judgment as the investigative judgment—descriptive of the heavenly court proceedings that render verdicts prior to Christ's Second Coming regarding who is saved.

Yet, given that God already "knows all things" (1 John 3:20), why would there be any "investigative" judgment? Put simply, the pre-advent judgment proceedings are not for God's information but for the sake of creatures looking on.

As we have seen (especially in chapter 9), there is an ongoing cosmic conflict involving the heavenly council/court—a cosmic courtroom drama such that events on earth are "a spectacle to the world [*cosmos*], both to angels and to mankind" (1 Cor. 4:9). God does not govern unilaterally. Instead, God shares governance (while remaining sovereign) and operates transparently relative to the heavenly council (i.e., heavenly court) and beyond. Judgment proceedings in heaven, and the heavenly council/court itself, serve a broader function that includes an open demonstration of the justice of God's government before celestial creatures, countering the cosmic allegations against God's character (see chapter 9).

The only way love can flourish is if everyone trusts and loves God unreservedly. But this is only possible if no doubt about God or His character remains. So, God opens up His judgment records to the scrutiny of the celestial creatures in the heavenly court (*and beyond*) and also, after the Second Coming, to redeemed humans who will "judge the world" and even "judge angels" (1 Cor. 6:2–3) in a post-advent judgment during the millennium (see chapter 19). The way God deals with sin and evil in the cosmic conflict demonstrates once and for all that God is perfectly righteous and loving—judgment proceedings in heaven open God's ways for all to see and know that God *is love* and can be trusted unreservedly.

> *The way God deals with sin and evil in the cosmic conflict demonstrates once and for all that God is perfectly righteous and loving.*

Specifically, the pre-advent judgment:

- displays that God did everything He could to save everyone He could, demonstrating God's justice *and* love,
- manifests that the redeemed have, in fact, been justified by true faith in Christ as their Savior and Lord,
- vindicates those who accept Christ *and, by extension,*
- vindicates God's justice and government as He both saves us and fulfills the law such that He is both "just and the justifier of the one who has faith in Jesus" (Rom. 3:26).
- condemns unrepentant oppressors (e.g., Dan. 7:26–27) in favor of justice for victims, including casting down and eventually destroying the oppressive earthly empires through which the dragon (Satan) works (more on this later).

God's approach to the final judgments matches the way He operates throughout Scripture. Specifically, throughout Scripture, God repeatedly initiates some kind of a (formal or informal) lawsuit or "investigative judgment" before pronouncing a verdict.[33]

For example, after the Fall, God questioned Adam and Eve: "Where are you?" "Have you eaten from the tree from which I commanded you not to eat?" "What is this that you have done?" (Gen. 3:9, 11, 13). Later, God questioned Cain after he murdered his brother Abel, saying: "Where is Abel your brother?" "What have you done? The voice of your brother's blood is crying out to Me from the ground" (Gen. 4:9–10). Elsewhere, before the heavenly council, God asked Satan questions like: "From where do you come?" "Have you considered My servant Job?" (Job 1:7–8).

In these and many other instances, God did not ask such questions to acquire information. He already knew the answers. Such questions were asked in the context of judgment, somewhat similar to the way a lawyer asks questions of a witness or defendant when she already knows the answers, doing so in order to get testimony on record before the court.

As Richard Davidson explains, these and a multitude of other "mini-lawsuits constitute a microcosm of the macrocosmic final 'assize,' the apocalyptic cosmic divine lawsuit described in such passages as Daniel 7 and throughout the book of Revelation."[34] Such covenant lawsuits, Davidson explains further, manifest a significant pattern: "Before God executes judgment (either positively or negatively) toward an individual or a people, He first conducts legal proceedings, not for Him to know the facts, but to reveal in open court, as it were, that He is just and fair in all of His dealings."[35] God's very process of judgment itself provides evidence of God's perfect fairness, thoroughly refuting the devil's accusations for the good of all in the universe.

The sanctuary services as a whole represent (among other things) the way God deals with sin for the entire cosmos, making atonement and providing forgiveness for the repentant without sweeping sin under the rug or failing to bring justice on behalf of victims and the oppressed. In the end, all evil is exposed and laid bare for all the universe to see and God deals with it at the greatest cost to Himself for the sake of all, never playing favorites but always working so that all of creation can be healed and restored in a way that accords with His perfect love and justice. Finally, only those who refuse redemption and healing bear the results of their sin and evil on their own shoulders by their own intractable choice to cling to evil and reject love (see chapter 19).

Sanctuary Prophecies

He couldn't sleep. The dream greatly troubled him. He demanded that his wise men not only provide its meaning but also tell him what the dream contained. His wise men protested that only the gods could do this. Furious, King Nebuchadnezzar of Babylon decreed that the wise men be killed because they could not reveal what he asked.

What troubled Nebuchadnezzar so? In his dream, he saw a great statue with a head of gold, chest and arms of silver, a mid-section of bronze, legs of iron, and feet partly of iron and clay. Then, he saw that "a stone was cut out without hands, and it struck the statue on its feet of iron and clay and crushed them" and crushed the entire statue. Then, "the stone that struck the statue became a great mountain and filled the entire earth" (Dan. 2:31–35).[36]

Through the prophet Daniel, God revealed the content of the dream and its interpretation to Nebuchadnezzar. The head of gold represented Babylon, and the other parts represented other empires that would arise one after the other, followed by a divided kingdom (the feet of iron and clay) after which "the God of heaven will set up a kingdom which will never be destroyed" (Dan. 2:36–44).

Years later, Daniel received another vision that built on this prophecy. He saw "four great beasts" that came "up from the sea." The first "was like a lion but had the wings of an eagle." The second resembled a bear "raised up on one side." The third was "like a leopard," with "four wings of a bird" and "four heads." And the fourth beast was "dreadful and terrible, and extremely strong; and it had large iron teeth. It devoured and crushed, and trampled down the remainder with its feet; and it was different from all the beasts that were before it, and it had ten horns" (Dan. 7:3–7).

These four beasts correspond to the same four successive empires represented by four metals of the statue in Daniel 2. The winged lion represented Babylon, which fell to the Persian ruler Cyrus in 539 BC. The bear represented the Medo-Persian Empire, raised up on one side to signify that the Persians were stronger than the Medes. The Medo-Persian empire was overtaken by Greece (331 BC), represented by the leopard with four heads and wings. Alexander the Great rapidly conquered huge amounts of territory (the speed signified by the leopard's wings) but then died, leaving the Greek empire to be divided and ruled by four of Alexander's generals (represented by the four heads). The Roman Empire followed (168 BC), represented by the fourth beast with iron teeth (representing Rome's crushing military strength) and ten horns, which represented the parts the Roman Empire eventually divided into (corresponding to the ten toes of the Daniel 2 statue; see illustration on the next page).

These amazing prophecies foretold the succession of massive empires over many centuries as well as the deterioration and division of Rome.

The prophecy of Daniel 7 further reveals that during the time of the ten horns, "another horn, a little one, came up among them, and three of the previous horns were plucked out before it; and behold, this horn possessed eyes like human eyes, and a mouth uttering great boasts" (Dan. 7:8).

Just after this, Daniel sees a judgment in the heavenly court (the pre-advent judgment; Dan. 7:9–10), followed by the execution of judgment against the beasts (Dan. 7:11–12) and Christ's Second Coming, establishing His "everlasting dominion" including "all the peoples, nations and populations of all languages" (Dan. 7:13–14).

THE PROPHETIC DREAMS OF DANIEL 2 AND 7

- BABYLON
- MEDO-PERSIA
- GREECE
- IMPERIAL ROME
- CHRISTIANIZED ROME /END OF TIME

Later, the little horn is identified as one who "will speak against the Most High and wear down the saints of the Highest One, and he will intend to make alterations in times and in law; and they will be handed over to him for a time, times, and half a time. But the court will convene for judgment, and his dominion will be taken away, annihilated and destroyed forever" (Dan. 7:25–26). This little horn, then, speaks against God, oppresses God's people, and attempts to change God's times and laws.

This little horn appears again in Daniel 8, which expands on Daniel 7. In a vision, Daniel saw "a ram which had two horns" with one horn "longer than the other" (Dan. 8:3), representing Medo-Persia (Dan. 8:20). Then, Daniel saw a goat with a large horn (representing Greece and its first king Alexander, Dan. 8:21) that "rushed at" and utterly defeated the ram (Dan. 8:5–7). Then, the goat's large horn was broken (representing Alexander's death), with four horns arising in its place "toward the four winds of heaven" (Dan. 8:8), representing the four parts of the kingdom divided among Alexander's four generals (Dan. 8:22).

The vision then turns to the little horn, "which grew exceedingly great toward the south, toward the east, and toward the Glorious Land. And it grew up to the host of heaven; and it cast down some of the host and some of the stars to the ground, and trampled them. He even exalted himself as high as the Prince of the host; and by him the daily sacrifices [*tamid*] were taken away, and the place of His sanctuary was cast down. Because of transgression, an army was given over to the horn to oppose the daily sacrifices [*tamid*]; and he cast truth down to the ground. He did all this and prospered" (Dan. 8:9–12, NKJV).[37] This description identifies this little horn with the one in Daniel 7, which arose from the fourth beast (Rome), uprooting three of that beast's ten horns (Dan. 7:24).

The prophetic descriptions of this little horn manifest that it is not merely a political power that oppresses God's people (e.g., Dan. 7:21) but also a religious power, opposing God and His sanctuary—speaking against God and attempting to change times and laws (Dan. 7:25), attempting to take the place of Christ (the "Prince of the host"), remove His regular sanctuary services (*tamid*), "cast down . . . the place of His sanctuary," and "cast truth down to the ground" (Dan. 8:10–12, NKJV; cf. 8:25; see chapter 18).

After this, Daniel heard a "holy one" ask, "'How long will the vision be, concerning the daily sacrifices [*tamid*] and the transgression of desolation, the giving of both the sanctuary and the host to be trampled underfoot?' And he said to me, 'For two thousand three hundred days; then the sanctuary shall be cleansed'" (Dan. 8:13–14, NKJV).

Two thousand three hundred days! Daniel greatly worried over what this could mean (Dan. 8:27). Would Daniel's people have to endure exile for far longer than the seventy years prophesied by Jeremiah (Jer. 25:11–12; 29:10)?

A number of years later, Daniel 9 picks up with Daniel studying Jeremiah's seventy-year prophecy (Dan. 9:2), then offering a stirring intercessory prayer for his people's forgiveness and deliverance, pleading with God to "let Your face shine on Your desolate sanctuary" (Dan. 9:17; see 9:3–19).

While Daniel was praying, the angel "Gabriel, whom [Daniel] had seen in the vision [of Daniel 8] previously, came to" give him "understanding of the vision" of Daniel 8 (Dan. 9:21–23). Specifically, Gabriel told Daniel:

> Seventy weeks are determined for your people and for your holy city, to finish the transgression, to make an end of sins, to make reconciliation for iniquity, to bring in everlasting righteousness, to seal up vision and prophecy, and to anoint the Most Holy. Know therefore and understand, that from the going forth of the command to restore and build Jerusalem until Messiah the Prince, there shall be seven weeks and sixty-two weeks; the street shall be built again, and the wall, even in troublesome times. And after the sixty-two weeks Messiah shall be cut off, but not for Himself; and the people of the prince who is to come shall destroy the city and the sanctuary. The end of it shall be with a flood, and till the end of the war desolations are determined. Then he shall confirm a covenant with many for one week; but in the middle of the week He shall bring an end to sacrifice and offering. And on the wing of abominations shall be one who makes desolate, even until the consummation, which is determined, is poured out on the desolate. (Dan. 9:24–27, NKJV)

This prophecy, known as the seventy-week prophecy, foretells a period of sixty-nine weeks from "the going forth of the command to restore and build Jerusalem until Messiah the Prince."

Jerusalem was restored and rebuilt approximately five hundred *years* before Jesus—the Messiah. This sixty-nine weeks, then, cannot refer to regular weeks of days (483 days) but makes sense if understood as "prophetic" weeks of years (483 years), with each prophetic "day" corresponding to a literal "year."

Were there 483 years from "the going forth [or, going into effect] of the command to restore and build Jerusalem until Messiah the Prince"? Let's check.

Luke identifies the year of Jesus's baptism, which effectively anointed Jesus as Messiah and began His public ministry, as "the fifteenth year of the reign of Tiberius Caesar" (Luke 3:1, 21), corresponding to AD 27. Counting back 483 years (remember there was no year 0) brings us to the year 457 BC. In that year, the decree of the Persian ruler Artaxerxes to restore and rebuild Jerusalem went into effect (Ezra 7:13–26).[38]

So, there was a period of 483 years from this decree until Jesus the Messiah began His public ministry, just as the prophecy foretold.

This prophecy further foretold that after those sixty-nine weeks, "the Messiah will be cut off" and "he will confirm a covenant with the many for one week, but in the middle of the week he will put a stop to sacrifice and grain offering" (Dan. 9:26–27).

Understood as weeks of years, the middle of the "week" would be three and a half years into the seventieth week of years. We know from the Gospels that Jesus's public ministry lasted three and a half years, ending with His crucifixion in AD 31 when He was "cut off" and His once-for-all sacrifice put an end to the earthly sanctuary system of rituals and sacrifices (cf. Matt. 27:51).[39]

Over five hundred years in advance, then, this seventy-week prophecy foretold the very years Christ began His ministry and was crucified. Amazing!

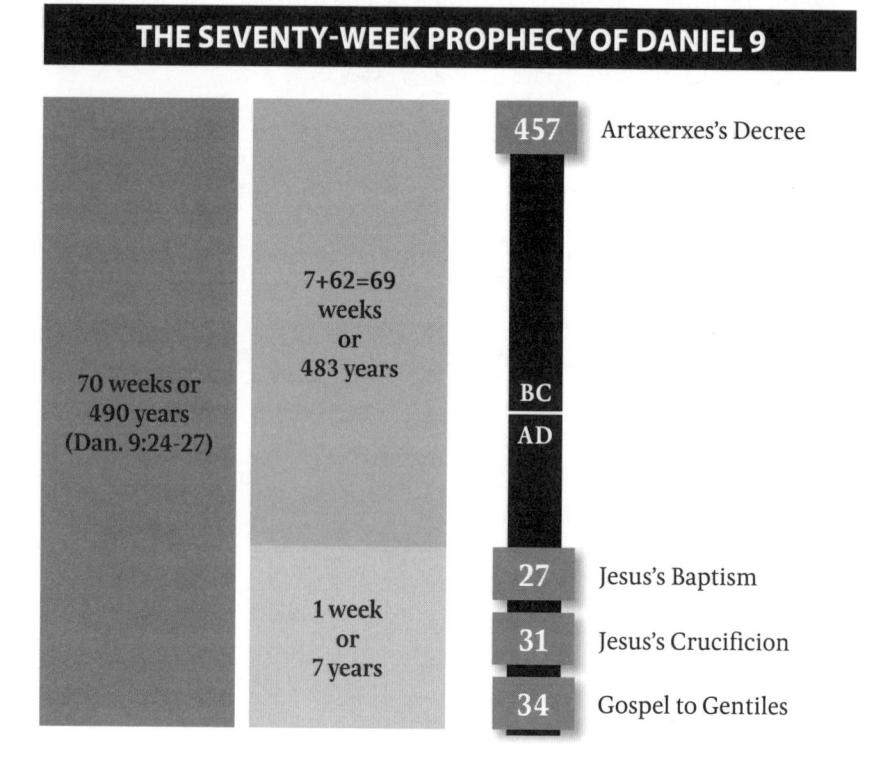

THE SEVENTY-WEEK PROPHECY OF DANIEL 9

- 70 weeks or 490 years (Dan. 9:24-27)
- 7+62=69 weeks or 483 years
- 1 week or 7 years
- 457 BC — Artaxerxes's Decree
- 27 AD — Jesus's Baptism
- 31 — Jesus's Crucificion
- 34 — Gospel to Gentiles

Adapted with permission from *Andrews Study Bible: Light. Depth. Truth.*, NKJV (Berrien Springs, MI: Andrews University Press, 2010), 1127. © by Andrews University Press.

The prophecies in Daniel are so strikingly accurate that skeptics have argued they must have been written by later authors after the events the prophecies predict. One popular hypothesis claims the book of Daniel was written centuries later, during the Maccabean period (ca. 165 BC). However, dating the book to the Maccabean period would still not explain how the seventy-week prophecy predicted the precise years Jesus would begin His public ministry and be crucified. Further, there is a great deal of evidence indicating the book of Daniel was written in the sixth century BC, as the book itself portrays.[40]

The end of the seventieth week brings us to AD 34, the year Stephen was stoned and Paul was converted, so the gospel went with power to the Gentiles. Later, as prophesied, a Roman leader (Titus) came and "destroy[ed] the city and the sanctuary" (Dan. 9:26) in AD 70.

Elsewhere in Scripture, years are also symbolically referred to as "days" (e.g., Ezek. 4:4–6; cf. Num. 14:34).[41] And the concept of weeks of years itself appears elsewhere. Specifically, after every seven weeks of years ("sabbaths of years"), there was to be a year of Jubilee in Israel (Lev. 25:8–10), which brought forgiveness of debts and deliverance to the poor and oppressed.

Notably, the seventy-week prophecy itself appears to be a large-scale Jubilee prophecy. Even as the regular year of Jubilee followed *seven weeks of years* in Israel (forty-nine years), Daniel 9 foretold *seventy weeks of years* (490 years) relative to the Messiah who would bring the "favorable year of the LORD" prophesied in Isaiah 61:1–2 with "good news to the humble," "bind[ing] up the brokenhearted," "proclaim[ing] release to captives and freedom to prisoners," and "comfort[ing] all who mourn."[42] Jesus announced this was fulfilled when He read Isaiah's prophecy in the synagogue (Luke 4:16–21).

The exile had ended when Cyrus allowed the Jews to return to Jerusalem and rebuild the temple, but the people still felt like exiles since they were oppressed and ruled over—effectively enslaved—in their own land. They awaited the Messiah's coming to deliver them from Roman oppression. While Jeremiah's prophecy foretold the exile would end after a period of *seventy* years (Jer. 29:10), Daniel's prophecy associated the Messiah's coming with a period of seventy times seven. Many Jews understood this and expected the Messiah's coming relative to this 490-year period.[43] The Messiah did come as the seventy-week prophecy foretold, but the deliverance He brought was different and far greater from what they were looking for (see chapter 4). He came to "make atonement for guilt," thus forgiving the ultimate debts, and "to bring in everlasting righteousness" (Dan. 9:24).

Christ's work "to bring in everlasting righteousness," however, was not complete at the cross. When He ascended to heaven after His resurrection, Christ inaugurated the heavenly sanctuary, fulfilling the prophecy relative to "anoint[ing] the Most Holy Place" (Dan. 9:24), and thereafter began His high priestly ministry in the heavenly sanctuary.

Christ's ministry in the heavenly sanctuary relates to another mysterious time prophecy—the 2,300-day prophecy of Daniel 8:14—the one that had deeply worried Daniel.

After describing the little horn's assaults against God, His people, and His sanctuary (Dan. 8:11–12), Daniel heard a "holy one" ask, "How long will the vision be, concerning the daily sacrifices [*tamid*] and the transgression of desolation, the giving of both the sanctuary and the host to be trampled underfoot?" The answer to this question was: "For two thousand three hundred days; then the sanctuary shall be cleansed" (Dan. 8:13–14, NKJV).

What *sanctuary* shall be cleansed? Recall that Christ's once-for-all sacrifice put an end to the earthly sanctuary system of rituals and sacrifices (cf. Matt. 27:51), and the Romans destroyed the Second Temple in AD 70. The little horn follows Rome and thus the sanctuary that the little horn assaults and replaces with its own system cannot be the earthly temple in Jerusalem (which was never rebuilt) but refers to the heavenly sanctuary where Christ ministers as the one true high priest (Heb. 8:1–4).[44]

Notably, the parallel sequence of Daniel 7 and 8 suggests the cleansing of the sanctuary referred to in Daniel 8:14 corresponds to the pre-advent depicted in Daniel 7:9–10 (see chart on the next page).

But when does this "cleansing" take place?

We've already seen Gabriel's instruction in Daniel 9 was to help Daniel understand the vision of Daniel 8, so the two are related in some significant way. For this and other reasons, Adventists typically believe the seventy-week prophecy of Daniel 9 provides the key regarding

THE PROPHECIES OF DANIEL 7 AND 8	
DANIEL 7	**DANIEL 8**
Babylon (Lion)	-
Medo-Persia (Bear)	Medo-Persia (Ram)
Greece (Leopard)	Greece (Goat)
Christianized Rome (Terrible Beast)	-
Little Horn	Little Horn
Judgment	Cleansing of the Sanctuary
Second Coming	-

the timing of the 2,300-day prophecy. Specifically, both time prophecies begin at the same time, with the seventy prophetic weeks (490 years) being the first part of the 2,300 prophetic days (understood as 2,300 years).

If so, the 2,300 prophetic days would also begin with Artaxerxes's decree in 457 BC and thus end in AD 1844 (remember, there was no year 0). Accordingly, Adventists believe the cleansing of the sanctuary prophesied in Daniel 8:14 began in 1844[45] (see chart on the next page).

As Adventists typically understand it, then, the seventy-week prophecy foretold the timing when Christ would begin the first phase of atonement, giving Himself as our sacrificial Lamb and rising again to inaugurate the heavenly sanctuary and minister there as our mediating high priest (corresponding to the "daily" sanctuary services). And the 2,300-day prophecy foretold the timing when Christ would begin the second phase of atonement—the pre-advent judgment and cleansing of the heavenly sanctuary (corresponding to the Day of Atonement).

Sanctuary Theology Matters

The sanctuary is *far more* than a doctrine.[46] Among other things, Scripture depicts the heavenly sanctuary as a real place (cf. Exod. 25:8–9; Heb. 6:19–20; 8:1–5; 9:11–12), and the earthly sanctuary services prefigure the two phases of Christ's atoning work in the heavenly sanctuary.

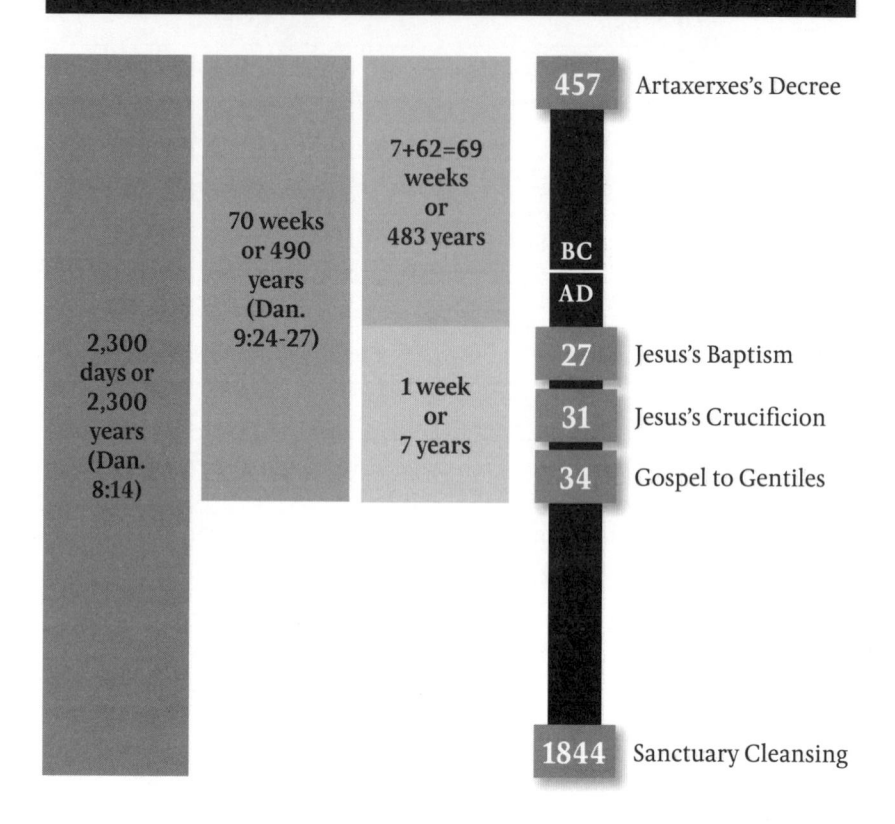

THE 2,300-DAY PROPHECY AND THE SEVENTY-WEEK PROPHECY

2,300 days or 2,300 years (Dan. 8:14)	70 weeks or 490 years (Dan. 9:24-27)	7+62=69 weeks or 483 years	457	Artaxerxes's Decree
			BC / AD	
		1 week or 7 years	27	Jesus's Baptism
			31	Jesus's Crucifixion
			34	Gospel to Gentiles
			1844	Sanctuary Cleansing

Timelines not to scale. Adapted with permission from *Andrews Study Bible: Light. Depth. Truth.*, NKJV (Berrien Springs, MI: Andrews University Press, 2010), 1127. © by Andrews University Press.

    The heavenly sanctuary, however, is *not* a copy of the earthly sanctuary/temples. It is the other way around. The earthly sanctuary/temples were each merely "a copy and shadow of the heavenly things," the true sanctuary in heaven, which is far greater (Heb. 8:5). We must be careful here not to conceptually reduce heavenly realities to earthly things— heavenly things are far greater and more glorious than we can imagine (cf. 1 Cor. 2:9). We have very little understanding of what heavenly *space and time* is like, and we should thus be careful not to project the limitations we experience on earth onto the reality of heaven and its processes.

We know, for example, that God is not limited to inhabiting any particular space but is omnipresent (see chapter 8). When Adventists affirm that God dwells in the sanctuary, we do not mean that God is limited to the sanctuary. As Solomon put it, "will God indeed dwell on the earth? Behold, heaven and the highest heaven cannot contain You, how much less this house which I have built!" (1 Kings 8:27; cf. 2 Chron. 2:6). No amount of space can contain God, who is not reducible to the plane of creaturely reality. God condescends to be specially present with us, but God is always greater than and transcends the bounds of creation.

> God condescends to be specially present with us, but God is always greater than and transcends the bounds of creation.

As Adventists understand it, the earthly sanctuary was (among other things) a typological ritual system that prefigured the heavenly sanctuary (Heb. 9:24). The heavenly sanctuary is a real place (though greater than any creaturely reality we know). Not only is it integral to the process of reconciliation between God and fallen creatures in the context of cosmic conflict, but even apart from its functions in dealing with the problem of sin it is God's heavenly "habitation" or "dwelling" and the place of His "throne" (Deut. 26:15; Ps. 11:4; 68:5), the command center of the universe where God convenes the heavenly council (cf. 1 Kings 22:19; Job 1:6).[47] Among many other instances, the heavenly sanctuary is prominent in the book of Revelation, which is structured around seven introductory sanctuary scenes (moving from imagery of the daily sacrifices/services to that of the Day of Atonement). These scenes flow from Christ's death and resurrection (Rev. 1:5, 17, 18; cf. 5:6, 9, 12) to the inauguration of Christ's ministry in the heavenly sanctuary made possible by His death and resurrection (Rev. 4–5), to Christ's intercessory ministry following His inauguration (Rev. 8:3–4), and on to the work of end-time judgment in the heavenly sanctuary (Rev. 11:18–19; 15:5–8; 19:1–10), followed by the tabernacle of God being with humans on earth (Rev. 21:1–22:5). This overall structure of Revelation follows "the sweep of salvation history as set forth in the festival typology of Leviticus 23" (with moments of salvation history corresponding to various festivals; see chart below).[48]

Christ's two-phase ministry in the heavenly sanctuary involves various activities—some in the past, some in the present, and some yet

SEVEN INTRODUCTORY SCENES IN REVELATION

PASSAGE	FOCUS	FESTIVAL	LOCATION
1:9–20	Earth-focus on Christ's earthly work (with Holy Place imagery)	Passover	Earth
4:1—5:14	Inauguration of heavenly sanctuary (mix of sanctuary imagery but Holy Place focus)	Pentecost	Heaven
8:2–6	Intercession in heavenly sanctuary (Holy Place)	Trumpets	Heaven
11:19	Judgment in heavenly sanctuary (Most Holy Place)	Day of Atonement (Investigative Judgment)	Heaven
15:5–8	Cessation of heavenly sanctuary ministry	Day of Atonement (Executive Judgment)	Heaven
19:1–10	Doxology in heaven (absence of explicit sanctuary imagery)	Day of Atonement (Review Judgment)	Heaven
21:1—22:5	Back to earth—tabernacle of God with men	Tabernacles	Earth

future. This requires that God is specially present (but not *contained*) in the heavenly sanctuary and there is some kind of temporal succession in God's life (contrary to claims that God is *strictly* timeless) such that words like "here" or "there" and "now" and "then" properly apply to God (though in ways unique to God).

Understanding the sanctuary holds many implications for one's theological understanding as a whole—that is, one's theological system. Below, we consider just a few important theological implications that show, in part, how integral the sanctuary is to Adventist theology.[49]

Competing Theories in Christian Theology: The Heavenly Sanctuary

The very idea of a *real* heavenly sanctuary is contested. For example, heavily influenced by streams of Greek philosophy, the traditional *Greco-Roman* system of strict classical theism (see chapter 8) claims God is *strictly* timeless (incompatible with temporal succession) and spaceless (incompatible with occupying space). If so, God cannot inhabit a spatio-temporal location, including (but not limited to) a heavenly sanctuary, and God cannot perform a sequential (and thus temporal) process relative to atonement (or otherwise). Given such a system, there could not be a *real* spatial and temporal, heavenly sanctuary and the sanctuary doctrine of two phases of atonement is impossible.

For example, *some* approaches claim God unilaterally and unconditionally determines who is saved and lost such that a heavenly judgment taking account of free human decisions makes no sense. Likewise, the conception *some* hold of human "souls" receiving their reward (of heaven or otherwise) immediately after death conflicts with the sanctuary doctrine regarding a pre-advent judgment "in favor of the saints" (Dan. 7:9–10, 22), who receive their reward later after Christ's Second Coming (see chapter 19).

Further, *some* approaches claim the church is the conduit of salvation such that humans can be reconciled to God only through the agency of human clergy. In some systems, this reconciliation takes place via earthly rituals and human mediators rather than the high priestly ministry of Christ in the heavenly sanctuary, substituting an earthly priesthood and system of sacraments in place of Christ's ministry as our one true high priest, whom Scripture identifies as the "one mediator between God and humankind" (1 Tim. 2:5, NRSVue), through whom humans may boldly draw near to the "throne of grace" (Heb. 4:16). Other systems obscure the sanctuary system and Christ's ongoing work as our high priest in the heavenly sanctuary by viewing the earthly (Old Testament) sanctuary system as *purely* symbolic and thus obsolete after Christ's death on the cross.

The Adventist approach to the heavenly sanctuary (laid out in this chapter) stands in direct contrast to the above theories.[50]

The Sanctuary and the God-World Relationship

In many ways, the sanctuary itself manifests the nature of the God-world relationship. The God revealed in and by the sanctuary is the God of love who is deeply involved in and affected by every facet of our lives and who takes our free decisions seriously. By creating this world, God voluntarily bestowed love upon us and opened Himself up to being profoundly affected by creatures, including the best interests of all creatures in His own interests (cf. Eph. 5:25–30) such that He is at times deeply grieved (Gen. 6:6; Ps. 78:40; Isa. 63:10; Jer. 31:20; Hosea 11:8–9; Matt. 23:37) but in the end will delight with profound joy over His redeemed children (Zeph. 3:17; cf. Ps. 147:10–11; Isa. 62:4; Col. 3:20; Heb. 13:21).

> *The God revealed in and by the sanctuary is the God of love who is deeply involved in and affected by every facet of our lives and who takes our free decisions seriously.*

The history of God's love for us is manifest in the story of redemption—the story of God's unceasing work to reconcile humans to Himself, displayed in the sanctuary system. Apart from God's work of mediation for us, any relationship between the perfectly holy God and sinful humans would be impossible. But God made a way to save us at great cost to Himself through the sacrifice and mediation of Christ.

As we have seen, the priestly and sacrificial system of the sanctuary prefigured Christ's work of reconciling sinners to God. Christ gave Himself as "an offering and a sacrifice to God as a fragrant aroma" (Eph. 5:2; cf. Ezek. 20:39–42; 2 Cor. 2:14–15), and through Him alone mediation is truly accomplished. Christ's mediation atones for the sins of those who are "in Christ" by faith (Rom. 8:1; cf. 15–17; Eph. 1:6). Thus, "through Christ," who is "choice and precious in the sight of God," humans may "offer spiritual sacrifices that are acceptable to God through Jesus Christ" as a "chosen people, a royal priesthood" (1 Pet. 2:4–5, 9) and be "pleasing in His sight" (Heb. 13:21; cf. Rom. 12:1–2; Heb. 15–16; 12:28; 1 John 3:21–22).

The Sanctuary and Cosmic Conflict

The cosmic conflict began in the heavenly sanctuary with the fall of a covering cherub who was created "blameless" but chose to slander

God's character such that iniquity was found in this cherub, who corrupted himself (Ezek. 28:12-19; cf. Exod. 25:19-20; Isa. 14:12-14). The conflict spread to earth in Eden, itself a type of the heavenly sanctuary.

The conflict stems from slanderous allegations against God's character raised by the devil, the "accuser of our brothers and sisters" who "accuses them before our God day and night" (Rev. 12:10; cf. Zech. 3:1-9; Jude 9). By accusing those God counts as His people, the devil thereby accuses God Himself, particularly with respect to God's law and God's judgment in favor of His people. Satan's allegations can be defeated only if God redeems sinners in a way that is perfectly just—in a way that upholds God's unchanging law of unselfish love. In the sanctuary system (via both phases of atonement), God defeats the devil's allegations, vindicates Himself in the heavenly council/court, and vindicates all those who belong to Christ by faith, who overcome through "the blood of the Lamb" (Rev. 12:10-11). Thus, God makes a way to dwell *with* His people (cf. Exod. 25:8-9), providing reconciling atonement in a way that is perfectly just and loving.

The Sanctuary, Sin, and Salvation

In the cosmic conflict, the horrendous nature of sin is unmasked, and the problem of sin ultimately resolved. But only God can resolve the problem of sin while saving sinners. Salvation cannot come from below, by human effort, but only from above by God's work for us (exemplified in the sanctuary system). God Himself provides the atoning sacrifice for us in Christ (cf. Gen. 22:8, 13-14), who gives Himself for us (e.g., Titus 2:14). We cannot cleanse our sin or change our hearts, but we can be cleansed by the blood of the Lamb and empowered by the Holy Spirit, who dwells in all who are in Christ by faith. We cannot defeat the enemy ourselves, but Christ will defeat the enemy's accusations for us and "through death ... destroy the one who has the power of death, that is, the devil" (Heb. 2:14; cf. Gen. 3:15; 1 John 3:8; Rev. 12:7-9).

The two-phase atonement of the sanctuary system continually manifests God's awesome holiness, justice, and love, calling for humans to humble themselves accordingly (e.g., the self-searching and divine cleansing aspects of the Day of Atonement; cf. Lev. 16:29–31; Dan. 8:14; 2 Tim. 2:21; 1 John 1:9). The ritual transference of responsibility for sin from humans into the sanctuary manifests the responsibility God takes on Himself in dealing with the sin problem (for which God was never culpable). And, Christ's Day of Atonement ministry cleanses the heavenly sanctuary, thereby vindicating God's own spotless character and vindicating those who trust in Him, finally making them spotless. As such, God is both the "just and the justifier" of those who believe in Christ (Rom. 3:26), who "is also able to save forever those who come to God through Him, since He always lives to make intercession for" us (Heb. 7:25).

The Sanctuary and Christology

The sanctuary system presupposes that Christ is both divine and human such that He alone—as the God-man—can mediate the relationship between God and humans (1 Tim. 2:5). Christ fulfills both the divine and human sides of the covenant relationship, thus reconciling humans to God. In Christ, the New Covenant includes both a perfect atonement made by God on our behalf and a perfect human party who fulfills the Law and stands as our substitute, taking sin and death on Himself in order to defeat them and "destroy the works of the devil" (1 John 3:8; cf. Gen. 3:15; Heb. 2:14–15). "God was in Christ reconciling the world to Himself" and "He made Him who knew no sin to be sin in our behalf, so that we might become the righteousness of God in Him" (2 Cor. 5:19, 21).

Christ is the true unblemished (absolutely sinless), perfect Lamb (prefigured by the various offerings; cf. 1 John 3:5) and the true Prophet, Priest, and King. Christ's priesthood is not merely symbolic or already completed, but Christ "holds His priesthood permanently" (Heb. 7:24) as our always-ministering, ever-interceding High Priest (cf. Rom. 8:34; Heb. 4:15–16; 7:25) such that Jesus "has become the guarantee of a better covenant" (Heb. 7:22).

Only through Christ's mediation can humans have peace with God (Rom. 5:1) and offer "spiritual sacrifices that are acceptable to God through Jesus Christ" (1 Pet. 2:5). Through the unique Son, we can become sons and daughters of God (Gal. 3:26; cf. Rom. 8:15–17; Heb. 2:9–17; 1 John 3:1–2). Through the truly elect One, we can be elect (Eph. 1:4–6;

cf. Luke 9:35). Through the uniquely beloved One, we are beloved (Eph. 1:6; 5:1; cf. Matt. 3:17; Col. 3:12; 1 Thess. 1:4; 2 Thess. 2:13). Through Christ, we can confidently approach God's throne of grace, which is in the Most Holy Place of the heavenly sanctuary (Heb. 4:16).

Christ also brought to earth the fullness of the Godhead bodily (Col. 2:9), the divine presence as God incarnate and the fullest revelation of God to humans—*God with us* (Immanuel). In the incarnation, "the Word" who both "was God" and was "with God" in "the beginning" and through whom "all things came into being" (John 1:1–3) also "became flesh, and dwelt [or "tabernacled"] among us" (John 1:14). He was the true Shekinah glory, greater than the earthly temple (Matt. 12:6). And He "will come again," that where He is, we might also be (John 14:3, NKJV).

The Sanctuary and the Nature of Humanity

The sanctuary system further presupposes that humans are morally responsible, culpable for our sinfulness, and possessing free will (thanks to God's prior action; Deut. 30:6; Jer. 31:3; 1 John 4:19) to accept God's love and be reconciled by Christ's atoning work (Deut. 6:5; Matt. 22:37; cf. Josh. 24:15; Ezek. 33:11; 1 John 4:8–16).

With regard to human constitution, the biblical teaching of conditional immortality (Gen. 2:7; Ps. 146:4; Eccles. 9:5; 12:7; Dan. 12:2; John 11:11–13; 1 Thess. 4:16–17; see chapter 11) complements the sanctuary teaching of a pre-advent judgment on the basis of which humans receive their reward (cf. Dan. 7:9–14; Matt. 12:36–37; 16:27; 2 Cor. 5:10; Heb. 10:27–39; Rev. 11:18; 22:12).

With regard to human value, the lengths that God has gone to save us and manifest His love for us, despite the unfathomable cost to Himself, demonstrates the inestimable value of *all* humans to God (cf. Matt. 10:31; 12:12; Luke 12:7, 24; John 15:13; Gal. 2:20; Eph. 5:2).

Finally, the sanctuary system points toward the destiny that God intends for us; we were created to be *with* God forever, and the God of the universe wants to dwell in our midst (cf. Ps. 23:6; John 14:3). Amazing.

The Sanctuary and Ecclesiology

The sanctuary system also sheds light on the doctrine of the church (ecclesiology, discussed in the next two chapters).

Christ is the only mediator between God and humans (1 Tim. 2:5) and the once-for-all sacrifice (Heb. 10:10; 1 Pet. 3:18; cf. Rom. 6:10; Heb. 7:27; 9:12). Thus, no earthly priesthood is needed any longer to mediate between God and humans and no additional sacrifices (or sacraments) are required in order to be in right relationship with God. Rather, "If we confess our sins, He is faithful and righteous, so that He will forgive us our sins and cleanse us from all unrighteousness" (1 John 1:9).

The church, then, is not a mediating conduit of salvation. Instead, Christ's church is to consist of a priesthood of all believers (1 Pet. 2:5-9; cf. Exod. 19:5-6; Heb. 13:15-16) who, as the collective body of Christ, are to be conduits of the *message* of what the true high priest has done and is doing (e.g., the everlasting gospel, Rev. 14:6-12).

The sanctuary, as the place of atonement (i.e., reconciliation), enables the unity of the church, possible only through union with Christ. This is not an artificial unity imposed by an institution, but true unity *in Christ* as "parts of His body" (Eph. 5:30), without removing our diversity as "many" who "are one body in Christ, and individually parts of one another" (Rom. 12:5). Those who are in Christ are the friends of the bridegroom (cf. Isa. 5:1-7; John 3:29), whose duty it is to proclaim and manifest Christ's love.

The Sanctuary, Judgment, Law, Hell, and Last Things

While many fear judgment, the judgment is exceedingly good news for those who are in Christ. We may have full assurance in Christ, rather than in ourselves, for all judgment has been given to Him (John 5:22; cf. 2 Tim. 4:1). If we trust in Christ, the judge Himself is also our Advocate who defends us in court, defeating all the enemy's accusations—vindicating Himself and His people (cf. Rom. 3:4-6, 21-26). Indeed,

> *While many fear judgment, the judgment is exceedingly good news for those who are in Christ.*

"we have an Advocate with the Father, Jesus Christ the righteous; and He Himself is the propitiation for our sins; and not for ours only, but also for the sins of the whole world" (1 John 2:1-2).

Notably, in the very next verse, John writes, "By this we know that we have come to know Him, if we keep His commandments" (1 John 2:3). God's commandments are themselves a reflection of His character of love (Matt. 22:37-40; cf. Rom. 13:8; Gal. 5:14; James 2:8). In the earthly sanctuary, the Ten Commandments were placed in the ark of the covenant (Deut. 31:24-26; 1 Kings 8:9; Heb. 9:4; cf. Exod. 2:16; Rev. 11:19), showing the relationship between God's law and the sanctuary. Indeed, "righteousness and justice are the foundation of [God's] throne" (Ps. 89:14), and Christ's ministry manifests that "mercy and truth have met together; righteousness and peace have kissed" (Ps. 85:10, NKJV).[51]

At the heart of God's law of unselfish love, as exemplified in the Ten Commandments, stands the Sabbath commandment. The Sabbath calls us to remember who God is as the Creator, what He has graciously done and is doing for us as the Liberator in whom we can rest, and how we should therefore treat others (Exod. 20:8-11; Deut. 5:12-15; cf. Rev. 14:7)

The Sabbath is rightly described as a *temple* in time and a sign of those who are in loving relationship with God (cf. Exod. 31:13; Ezek. 20:12). The Sabbath is thus integral to the Three Angels' Messages as the memorial to the Creator and judge who will judge with just judgment and create again a new heaven and a new earth (Rev. 14:7; 21:4).

Before Christ's return, those who have truly accepted Christ as Savior *and* Lord will be vindicated by heavenly judgment (Dan. 7:9-10; 8:14). When Christ comes in glory, all cases will have been decided and He will "reward each according to his works" (Matt. 16:27, NKJV; cf. Rev. 20:12; 22:12). Through Christ the righteous judge, Satan—the "accuser of our brothers and sisters" in the heavenly court—and those who follow him are cast down and defeated (Rev. 12:10). God is vindicated as He both saves us and fulfills the law of unselfish love, "demonstrat[ing] His righteousness" such that He is both "just and the justifier of the one who has faith in Jesus" (Rom. 3:25-26; cf. 5:8).

Through the judgment, all creatures will see that all God's ways are perfectly good, loving, and just (cf. Rev. 15:3-4). We are not to judge anyone "before the time," but when Christ comes, He will "bring to light the things hidden in the darkness and disclose the motives of human hearts" (1 Cor. 4:5). Then, the redeemed will "judge the world"; indeed, "we shall judge angels" (1 Cor. 6:2-3). Thereby, we will confirm that God's justice and mercy have indeed kissed (cf. Ps. 85:10), that God, in His infinite love and immeasurable compassion, has *justly* saved all those He could save—everyone willing to be saved, while God has rightly (yet unwillingly) condemned those who reject love and life itself (Lam. 3:33), who are condemned by their own unbelief (Rom. 2:5; cf. John 3:18). This astonishing demonstration of God's justice (Rom. 3:26) and love (Rom. 5:8) evokes love in response (1 John 4:19), contributing to *cosmic* reconciliation (cf. Rom. 5:10; 2 Cor. 5:18–21; Col. 1:21).

In the end, the judgments will manifest that God did everything He could (cf. 2 Chron. 36:16; Isa. 5:3–4)—nothing more could be done to save those who finally, intractably reject God's love. As such, the most loving thing God can do is put the unrepentant wicked out of their misery. As we will see also in chapter 19, there is no place of eternal conscious torment. Rather, God forever eradicates evil from the universe and, finally, "God will wipe away every tear from their eyes; there shall be no more death, nor sorrow, nor crying. There shall be no more pain, for the former things have passed away" (Rev. 21:4, NKJV). Reconciliation (atonement) will then finally be complete, and the universe will be restored.

The Cosmic Conflict and God's Reputation Revisited

The judgments finally manifest, once and for all, the perfect love and justice of God. The devil, not God, is culpable for the entrance of evil in the universe.

Satan sowed the seeds of evil all over and then turned around and blamed God for it (Matt. 13:24–30), manifesting himself as the "father of lies" (John 8:44) and the slanderer par excellence (cf. Gen. 3:1–5; Ezek. 28:16; Rev. 12:10). In this context, God desires to manifest His character because, if human beings think God is a tyrant who is responsible for evil, how could they love Him? If God does not vindicate His name (reputation), how will creatures know the truth about Him and come to love Him? For this reason, God is profoundly concerned with His reputation and character before the world (e.g., Gen. 18:24–25; Exod. 32:12–13; Num. 14:15–16; Deut. 9:28; Josh. 7:7–9; Ps. 23:3; 25:11; 31:3; 79:9; 106:8; 109:21; 143:11; Isa. 5:1–5; 48:9–11; 66:5; Jer. 12:1–4; 14:7; Ezek. 18:25; 20:9, 14, 22, 44; Dan. 9:19; Rom. 3:3–5). God's name is thus defended for the sake of love. Scripture, accordingly, depicts a crucial link between God's demonstration of His righteousness and love and His justification of sinners (see especially Rom. 3:25–26; 5:8).

The two phases of the atonement in the sanctuary system highlight this link. Via the daily (*tamid*) sanctuary sacrifices and rituals, the people's sin was transferred into the sanctuary. God thus took responsibility to deal with His people's sins (cf. 2 Sam. 14:9). In the second Day of Atonement phase, the sanctuary is cleansed and all sins are removed from the sanctuary as God completes the vindication of Himself and His saints, manifesting that He is "able to save to the uttermost those who come to God through" Christ (Heb. 7:25, NKJV) without in any way compromising His justice. God deals with sin righteously and fairly, shouldering it and taking responsibility though He is not at all culpable for it (cf. 2 Cor. 5:21; 1 John 3:5).

The sanctuary system thus manifests a theology of God's character as integral to His glory. Rather than history being about the manifestation of God's sovereignty and power, God's character of perfect, unselfish love is manifest in the way God deals with evil. God's power is shown not in dominating others but in taking upon Himself weakness to save others. God manifests His glory not by force but by revealing His character (cf. Exod. 33:19; 34:6–7; Ps. 78:2; Rom 3:26; 5:8), defeating the enemy's lies by shining the light of truth, of which Christ came to testify (John 18:37).

In the end, through the pre-advent and post-advent judgments, all the universe will conclusively see that God is fair. And every knee shall bow and every tongue confess that Jesus is Lord (Rom. 14:11; Phil. 2:10–11) and God is just, and the redeemed will proclaim: "Great and marvelous are Your works, Lord God, the Almighty; righteous and true are Your ways, King of the nations!" (Rev. 15:3; cf. Ps. 98:2; Rev. 16:5).

In the end, the solution to the problem of evil is found in the very place evil arose—in the sanctuary. In the end, justice will come and unselfish love will reign forever. In this regard, the psalmist Asaph was deeply troubled by the evil and injustice in the world. While Asaph served God with a pure heart and was nevertheless "stricken all day long," the wicked prospered, oppressing others and blaspheming God. When he sought to "understand this, it was troublesome" to him. That is, Asaph states: "Until I entered the sanctuary of God; then I perceived their end" (Ps. 73:14, 16–17).

> *In the end, the solution to the problem of evil is found in the very place evil arose—in the sanctuary.*

The cosmic conflict began in the sanctuary (in heaven) and spread to the earth in Eden (a type of the sanctuary). The solution was prefigured in the earthly sanctuary/temples and services, specifically prefiguring Christ's sacrifice on the cross and high priestly ministry in the heavenly sanctuary for us. Finally, when we look into the sanctuary, we see the love and justice of God. By looking in the sanctuary, with Asaph, we can trust God, make Him our refuge, and "tell of all [His] works" (Ps. 73:17, 22, 28).

Conclusion: Why Does It Matter?

Today was the day. Judgment day. The verdict would be in soon, and *everything* depended on it. Would the verdict be good or bad? He could not know for sure. So he waited, and he waited, and he waited some more.

Finally, the verdict was in. Guilty on all charges, with the perpetrator ordered to pay full restitution. He and his family were overjoyed. Justice was finally coming. They would get back what was lost. Deliverance had come.

If you are like most people, you think of judgment in negative terms. Most people do not want to be judged. If I tell you, judgment is coming, or soon I will be judging you, you're likely to react with displeasure.

As we've briefly seen, however, in Scripture, judgment is a good thing. It brings justice for the victims of evil and deliverance to the oppressed and downtrodden. So, instead of trying to avoid judgment, the faithful in Scripture long and cry out for God to bring judgment because they know that God is the just judge who will bring justice, deliverance, and a future filled with hope and assurance of goodness.

In the end, God will bring justice, and He does so through the proceedings of the sanctuary. As we have seen, God Himself makes atonement for us to reconcile us to Himself, so that all who are willing to be saved and cleansed by Him can live with Him forever in blissful love and joy for eternity.

This is exceedingly good news. The question for you and for me, though, is whose side are we on? Will we take the side of the oppressor, or will we be found with the victims, the downtrodden, and the oppressed? Do we long for justice?

The oppressive systems and those who give allegiance to them will finally be judged, while all who repent of evil in favor of embracing the love freely offered by God to all will be forgiven and cleansed. Then, the cry shall go forth to God: "Righteous and true are Your ways, King of the nations!" And "Your righteous acts have been revealed" (Rev. 15:3–4).

Even now, you have a decision regarding where your allegiance will lie. Will you embrace love and justice by faith? Will you follow the way of the Lamb (Jesus) or the way of the dragon (Satan)? Whose side will you be on? The side of love and justice or the side of evil, oppression, and injustice?

On the one hand, if we are honest with ourselves, without mediation we would be found on the side of the evildoers. Even if we have not actively and intentionally defied God or oppressed others, we have all sinned and fallen short of the glory of God. Our sin is worthy of death.

But atonement has been made for us. The spotless and sinless Lamb gave Himself for us and even now ministers for us in the heavenly sanctuary. Hallelujah!

The one to whom all judgment has been given is also your advocate, *if* you place your faith in Him—that is, if you surrender to Him as *your* Savior *and* Lord. Without Him you cannot win. But, with Him, you cannot lose.

He works even now not only for your personal deliverance but to restore justice and right all wrongs in the universe, to bring peace and an everlasting kingdom of unselfish love throughout all creation. Call on Him and He will save you. Jesus is enough. As Ellen G. White once put it: "You will come up from the grave without anything, but if you have Jesus, you will have everything. He is all that you will require to stand the test of the day of God, and is not this enough for you?"[52]

Now, I invite you to read and reflect on Psalm 73 and ponder the justice and deliverance that God brings through the sanctuary.

Questions for Reflection

1. How would you explain the nature of the sanctuary to someone? Is the sanctuary a doctrine or more than a doctrine? Why does it matter?
2. What does the basic purpose of the earthly sanctuary being built—so God could dwell with His people—tell us about God's love and care for humans? What does this imply for the sanctuary system as a whole?

3. What do you find most striking about the prophecies discussed in this chapter? Do they give you confidence in Scripture and in the God of Scripture?
4. Is judgment something to be worried about or afraid of? How does understanding God's work for us and in us relative to the judgment help us to recognize that judgment brings deliverance to those in need and is thus a very good thing?
5. How does understanding the cosmic conflict and the heavenly council motif (discussed in chapter 9) shed light on the background of the heavenly pre-advent judgment?
6. How does the sanctuary relate to and shed light on other doctrines such as the doctrine of Christ, salvation, humanity, the church, and so on?
7. You can have Christ as your Advocate even now. Do you wish for Christ to make full atonement for you and reconcile you to God? If so, simply ask Him to do so. Surrender yourself to Him as your Savior *and* Lord.

For Further Reading

Adventist Perspectives:

Adams, Roy. *The Sanctuary Doctrine: Understanding the Heart of Adventist Theology.* Hagerstown, MD: Review and Herald, 1993.

Cortez, Félix H. *In These Last Days: The Message of Hebrews.* Nampa, ID: Pacific Press, 2022.

———. *Within the Veil: The Ascension of the Son in the Letter to the Hebrews.* Dallas: Fontes, 2020.

Davidson, Richard M. *A Song for the Sanctuary: Experiencing God's Presence in Shadow and Reality.* Silver Spring, MD: Biblical Research Institute/Review and Herald Academic, 2022.

de Souza, Elias Brasil. *The Heavenly Sanctuary/Temple Motif in the Hebrew Bible,* Adventist Theological Society Dissertation Series, Vol. 7. Berrien Springs, MI: ATS Publications, 2005.

Doukhan, Jacques B. *Secrets of Daniel: The Wisdom and Dreams of a Jewish Prince in Exile.* Hagerstown, MD: Review and Herald, 2000.

Gane, Roy. *Altar Call*. Berrien Springs, MI: Diadem, 1999.

———. *Leviticus, Numbers*. The NIV Application Commentary. Grand Rapids, MI: Zondervan Academic, 2011.

———. *Who's Afraid of the Judgment?: The Good News About Christ's Work in the Heavenly Sanctuary*. Nampa, ID: Pacific, 2006.

Heppenstall, Edward. *Our High Priest: Jesus Christ in the Heavenly Sanctuary*. Washington, DC: Review and Herald, 1972.

Holbrook, Frank B. ed., *Doctrine of the Sanctuary: A Historical Survey (1845–1863)*, Daniel and Revelation Committee Series 5. Silver Spring, MD: Biblical Research Institute, 1989.

Moskala, Jiří. "The Gospel According to God's Judgment: Judgment as Salvation," *Journal of the Adventist Theological Society* 22, no. 1 (2011): 28–49.

Pröbstle, Martin. *Where God and I Meet: The Sanctuary*. Hagerstown, MD: Review and Herald, 2013.

Rodríguez, Ángel Manuel, "The Sanctuary." In *Handbook of Seventh-day Adventist Theology*. Edited by Raoul Dederen. Hagerstown, MD: Review and Herald, 2000.

Timm, Alberto R. *The Sanctuary and the Three Angels' Messages 1844–1863: Integrating Factors in the Development of Seventh-day Adventist Doctrines*. Berrien Springs, MI: Adventist Theological Society Publications, 1995.

Wallenkampf, Arnold V. and W. Richard Lesher, eds., *The Sanctuary and the Atonement: Biblical, Historical, and Theological Studies*. Washington, DC: Review and Herald, 1981.

See also the resources on the Biblical Research Institute website: https://adventistbiblicalresearch.org/materials/.

Other Perspectives:

Beale, G. K. *The Temple and the Church's Mission: A Biblical Theology of the Dwelling Place of God*. Downers Grove, IL: IVP Academic, 2004.

Dowley, Tim. *The Kregel Pictorial Guide to the Tabernacle*. Grand Rapids, MI: Kregel, 2002.

Edersheim, Alfred. *The Temple: Its Ministry and Services*. Peabody, MA: Hendrickson, 1994.

Levy, David M. *The Tabernacle, Shadows of the Messiah: Its Sacrifices, Services, and Priesthood.* Grand Rapids, MI: Kregel, 2003.

Milgrom, Jacob. *Leviticus 1–16.* Anchor Bible Commentary. New Haven, CT: Yale University Press, 1998.

Moffit, David M. *Atonement and the Logic of Resurrection in the Epistle to the Hebrews.* Leiden: Brill, 2011.

Morales, L. Michael. *The Tabernacle Pre-Figured: Cosmic Mountain Ideology in Genesis and Exodus.* Leuven: Peeters, 2012.

———. *Who Shall Ascend the Mountain of the Lord? A Biblical Theology of the Book of Leviticus.* Downers Grove, IL: IVP Academic, 2015.

Perrin, Nicholas. *Jesus the Temple.* Grand Rapids, MI: Baker, 2010.

———. *Jesus the Priest.* Grand Rapids, MI: Baker, 2019.

17

GOD WITH US IN THE CHURCH: THE FELLOWSHIP OF THE LAMB

After the flood, the people resolved to build "a tower whose top will reach into heaven" and make a "name" for themselves to avoid being "scattered abroad over the face of all the earth" (Gen. 11:4). This was in direct contrast to God's command to Noah and his descendants: "Be fruitful and multiply, and fill the earth" (Gen. 9:1; cf. 9:7).

So, God "scattered" the people "over the face of all the earth" by confusing their language (Gen. 11:7–8). The place was "named Babel, because there the Lord confused the language of all the earth; and from there the Lord scattered them abroad over the face of all the earth" (Gen. 11:9).

By rejecting the commands God gave Noah in the covenant He made after the flood, the people effectively rejected the covenant rule of God, leaving God without a covenant people. The people dispersed but followed after other "gods."

Yet, God did not remain without a covenant people. God called Abraham out of his country and through him created Israel, the people of God through whom He would redeem and reclaim the whole world, calling all peoples everywhere to become part of God's people *in Christ*.

This chapter seeks to understand the people of God the New Testament identifies as God's household, the church, addressing questions like:

- Who are the people of God today? What is the church?
- Are all churches genuine, or is there a *true* church?
- How is the church to operate relative to governance?
- Who is the head of the church?
- What is the extent of the church's authority in religious and other matters?

In what follows, I introduce an Adventist perspective on these difficult questions.

The Story of the Church—God's Household

They had met the risen Christ. He appeared to them many times over forty days. Then, He ascended to heaven. But, just before He did, Christ left His followers with instructions.

Specifically, "He commanded them not to leave Jerusalem, but to wait" and told them, "you will be baptized with the Holy Spirit not many days from now" and "you will receive power when the Holy Spirit has come upon you; and you shall be My witnesses both in Jerusalem and in all Judea, and Samaria, and as far as the remotest part of the earth" (Acts 1:3–8).

Then, as they looked on, "He was lifted up," and "a cloud took Him up, out of their sight" (Acts 1:9).

So, they waited.

On the day of Pentecost, they were all together. Then, "suddenly a noise like a violent rushing wind came from heaven, and it filled the whole house where they were sitting. And tongues that looked like fire appeared to them, distributing themselves, and a tongue rested on each one of them. And they were all filled with the Holy Spirit and began to speak with different tongues, as the Spirit was giving them the ability to speak out" (Acts 2:1–4).

For the great festival of Pentecost, Jerusalem was filled with worshipers "from every nation under heaven." And a great crowd of people gathered due to the noise, and "they were bewildered, because each one of them was hearing them speak in his own language. They were amazed and astonished, saying, 'Why, are not all these who are speaking Galileans? And how is it that we each hear them in our own language to which we were born?'" (Acts 2:5–8).

Then, Peter preached the gospel to them and appealed to them to repent and "be baptized in the name of Jesus Christ for the forgiveness of your sins; and you will receive the gift of the Holy Spirit. For the promise is for you and your children and for all who are far away, as many as the Lord our God will call to Himself" (Acts 2:37–39). And about three thousand were baptized that day!

Afterward, they "were continually devoting themselves to the apostles' teaching," and "many wonders and signs were taking place through the apostles. And all the believers were together and had all things in common; and they would sell their property and possessions and share them with all, to the extent that anyone had need" (Acts 2:42–45).

These events stood at the beginnings of the Christian church. The rest of the book of Acts tells the story of the acts of the apostles that spread the gospel, establishing churches throughout the world (see chapter 2).

The Holy Spirit's work at Pentecost was (among other things) a reversal of what occurred at Babel. There, language had been confused, separating the people. Now, God gave the apostles the gift of tongues—the ability to speak such that peoples from all over the world could understand in their native language and hear the call to become followers of Christ.[1] This new thing could only be done on the basis of Christ's victory via the cross.[2]

> The Holy Spirit's work at Pentecost was a reversal of what occurred at Babel.

By the works of the Holy Spirit, God worked to reclaim the world from enemy rule, calling all people to *freely* unite under the New Covenant rule of Christ, which does not distinguish between Jew and Gentile because in the New Covenant such walls of separation are removed (see Eph. 2:11–22; cf. Gal. 3:28).

As Peter explained, "the promise is" indeed "for all who are far away," whoever responds to God's universal invitation (Acts 2:39). Indeed, Paul explained further, *all* who are in Christ by faith are "one in Christ Jesus" and "Abraham's descendants, heirs according to the promise"—that is, children of Abraham relative to God's overarching promises, fulfilled in the New Covenant (see Gal. 3:26–29).

In the New Covenant, the people of God include all those who are in Christ by faith. The New Covenant, however, does not amount to a rejection of (ethnic) Israel and her descendants.[3] Throughout the story of Scripture, God repeatedly preserved for Himself a remnant of His people, as He repeatedly promised He would. And the New Covenant includes those of (ethnic) Israel who are in Christ by faith.

Instead of rejecting (ethnic) Israel, the New Covenant brings a shift from one kind of kingdom to another and, consequently, from one kind of identity as God's people to another.[4]

The *earthly* Davidic kingship failed—the line of kings was extinguished, and the nation of Israel was subjected to foreign rule. But the New Covenant King is unlike the former Davidic kings, and the kingdom He came to establish is unlike worldly kingdoms. Christ's is a kingdom that will never end, a kingdom of unselfish love that invites *all* peoples to covenant relationship with God—relationship of loving allegiance that never attempts to force allegiance.

All, then, can be part of God's special New Covenant people. Thus, Christ's Great Commission calls to "make disciples of all the nations" (Matt. 28:19). And, in the end, those saved by Christ will encompass "a great multitude which no one could count, from every nation and all the tribes, peoples, and languages" (Rev. 7:9). Indeed, by His blood the Lamb (Christ) ransomed people "from every tribe, language, people, and nation" and makes "them into a kingdom and priests to our God" who "will reign upon the earth" (Rev. 5:9–10). This New Covenant gathering from all nations was foretold in the Old Testament: "All nations whom You have made will come and worship before You, Lord" (Ps. 86:9).

Accordingly, God's end-time call is as inclusive as possible. In Revelation 14:6, John sees an angel "flying in midheaven with an eternal gospel to preach to those who live on the earth, and to every nation, tribe, language, and people." God calls *all* people to Himself, inviting all to join themselves to Christ by faith and follow the way of the Lamb (see chapter 18), serving as a kingdom of priests (Rev. 5:9–10) filled with the Holy Spirit and testifying with the Spirit of the cosmic royal priest, Jesus (see, e.g., Acts 5:30–32).

In Christ, God's people are not limited to a particular geo-political nation; all can be elect children of God through the Elect Son of God. As we will see, Christ—the one true high priest—establishes a kingdom of priests from *all* nations, tribes, tongues, and peoples (1 Pet. 2:5, 9–10; Rev. 5:9–10; cf. Exod. 19:6), over which Christ alone is the head—the cosmic royal high priest. This kingdom of priests is the body of Christ-followers who are "God's household, having been built on the foundation of the apostles and prophets, Christ Jesus Himself being the cornerstone" (Eph. 2:19–20).

The Doctrine of the Church: An Introduction

God called Abraham, Isaac, and Jacob in the Old Testament, entered into special covenant relationship with them and their descendants, and claimed them as His allotted covenant people—His special portion (Deut. 32:9).

In the New Covenant, God also calls a people, but not relative to a particular ancestry or national identity. Instead, God calls *all* people to special covenant relationship with the living God *in Christ*, fulfilling the overarching promises of the Old Testament.

In the Old Testament, God had already provided means for those outside (ethnic) Israel to be part of God's covenant people by joining themselves to the nation of Israel. In the New Covenant, however, all peoples can be part of God's household, the church, by joining themselves to Christ.

> **God calls all people to special covenant relationship with the living God in Christ, fulfilling the overarching promises of the Old Testament.**

What, then, is the church? The church consists of all who are united to Christ (by faith in Christ) and thus follow the way of the Lamb (allegiance to Christ), commissioned as a "royal priesthood" (1 Pet. 2:9). As Paul teaches, "you are all sons and daughters of God through faith in Christ Jesus." Thus, "there is neither Jew nor Greek, there is neither slave nor free, there is neither male nor female; for you are all one in Christ Jesus. And if you belong to Christ, then you are Abraham's descendants, heirs according to promise" (Gal. 3:26–29).

The term "church" may refer to all those who are united to Christ by faith—the universal church (cf. Matt. 16:18), or it may refer to a particular group of such people in a particular location. Thus, the New Testament speaks of the "churches of God in Christ" (1 Thess. 2:14; 2 Thess. 2:1) and "churches of Christ" (Rom. 16:16; Gal. 1:22).[5]

While the church's identity is grounded in union with Christ, Scripture speaks of the church in various ways. The church may refer to (among other things):

- a community of believers in a particular building, such as a house (e.g., 1 Cor. 16:19).
- a community of believers in a particular location, such as a city (e.g., the church at Corinth, 1 Cor. 1:2).
- a group of congregations in a broader geographical area (e.g., 1 Cor. 16:19; Gal. 1:2).

- the whole body of believers throughout the world (e.g., Eph. 1:22–23).

The church, then, is not a building. And the church is more than a particular church fellowship or institution. Christians who gather together for worship (1 Cor. 11:18; 14:19), prayer, and instruction (Acts 11:26; 12:5; 1 Cor. 14:4–5) are called the church, but the church is more than such gatherings. "The church is the community of believers who confess Jesus Christ as Lord and Saviour."[6]

Competing Theories in Christian Theology: The Nature of the Church

The nature and identity of the Christian church are variously understood. Here, I will focus on two overarching theories that stand in contrast to one another relative to what is the "true church."

Some believe the true church is the church whose leaders descend from the first-generation apostles in an unbroken line of historical succession. This is typically understood as a succession of bishops, each consecrated/ordained by other bishops going back to the first-generation apostles (known as apostolic succession).

On this basis, the Roman Catholic Church identifies itself as the one true church, claiming Peter was the first bishop of Rome—the first pope appointed as universal leader of the church, and all other *true* popes descended from Peter in an unbroken line of apostolic succession.

Many church historians, however, conclude apostolic succession itself is a later idea and there was no such unbroken line of popes (e.g., the bishop of Rome did not garner supremacy until centuries after Peter).[7] Further, on numerous occasions, more than one person simultaneously claimed to be pope and exercised pontifical functions.[8] And there have been many scandals regarding the buying and selling of church offices (simony), including allegations of some buying the office of pope and regarding the deeply corrupt behavior of some popes and other church leaders (e.g., the history of the Borgias).

Yet, even if an unbroken line could be established historically, such would not guarantee truth or faithfulness to the message and mission of Christ and the apostles any more than lines of successive kings in Israel and Judah kept Israel and Judah faithful to the one true God.[9]

Further, other churches also claim to be the one true church by apostolic succession, such as the Eastern Orthodox Church, the Oriental Orthodox communion, the Assyrian Church of the East, and the Ancient Church of the East. Many others also claim apostolic succession (e.g., Hussites, Anglicans, Moravians, and Scandinavian Lutherans), and a myriad of churches *could* claim their leaders were ordained by other ordained leaders going back to ordination by the first-generation apostles.

Many Christians deny the importance of apostolic succession, however, believing instead that the true church consists of the followers of the genuine apostolic teachings and message. This is understood to be in keeping with Paul's depiction of the church as "God's household" that is "built on the foundation of the apostles and prophets, Christ Jesus Himself being the cornerstone" (Eph. 2:19–20).

As Adventists and many other Protestants understand it, the followers of the apostolic teachings and message are those who follow the New Testament (consisting of the testimony of the first-generation apostles) and the Old Testament, which Jesus and His apostles affirmed. Adventists are among those known as restorationists, those Christian bodies who believe Christian faith and practice should be reformed and restored to be as close as possible to the teachings and practices affirmed by Scripture.[10]

As Adventists understand it, the true church consists of those who follow the teachings of Scripture as a whole, not necessarily limited to any single denomination. Yet, God has given specific groups at specific times special messages to proclaim. And Adventists believe the Three Angels' Message (see chapter 18) is a special end-time message which it is the mission of the Adventist Church to proclaim.[11]

The Universal Church

If the church is the community of those who belong to Christ, accepting Christ as Lord *and* Savior, then no particular denomination or church fellowship can rightly lay claim to *exclusively* being *the* only Christians such that there are not genuine Christians in other denominations.

There are true Christians in many different Christian denominations. Throughout history, God has worked in a diversity of peoples and movements. Accordingly, Jesus Himself taught, "I have other sheep that are not of this fold; I must bring them also" (John 10:16).[12]

Fellowship in a specific church is important. Scripture teaches, "let's consider how to encourage one another in love and good deeds, not abandoning our own meeting together, as is the habit of some people, but encouraging one another; and all the more as you see the day [of Christ's return] drawing near" (Heb. 10:24–25). However, being part of a specific church does not (by itself) make one a true Christian. Merely being in a church does not make one a Christian any more than being in a garage makes one a car.

In this regard, Seventh-day Adventists believe that "the universal church is composed of all who truly believe in Christ," consisting of everyone who belongs to Christ by faith throughout the whole world.[13] As such, the universal church is one in Christ and is not limited to one denomination, but "the Lord knows those who are His" (2 Tim. 2:19). Because someone may profess faith in Christ and hold membership in a particular church denomination or fellowship without actually having faith in Christ, we might not know whether someone is a true Christian simply by outward appearances. And, we are cautioned, "do not go on passing judgment before the time, but wait until the Lord comes, who will both bring to light the things hidden in the darkness and disclose the motives of human hearts" (1 Cor. 4:5).

Yet, Christians are warned to "be on the alert" for "savage wolves" that would come in among the church (Acts 20:29–31). Indeed, Christ Himself warned: "Beware of the false prophets, who come to you in sheep's clothing, but inwardly are ravenous wolves. You will know them by their fruits" (Matt. 7:15–16; cf. 1 John 4:1). In the end times, there will be those who in some sense look like a lamb, but speak like a dragon (see Rev. 13:11)—those who in some ways appear to be following Christ, but are actually in the service of the dragon ruler of this world, the devil (see chapter 18).

Conversely, Revelation identifies those faithful to Christ in the end times as those "who keep the commandments of God and their faith in Jesus" (Rev. 14:12). And, according to Christ's parable of the sheep and the goats, the difference between those who truly follow Christ (the sheep) and those who do not (the goats) is that those who follow Christ are those who care for the poor, oppressed, and incarcerated—in short, those who love their neighbor as themselves, which is to love Christ indirectly. As Jesus said, "to the extent that you did it for one of the least of these brothers or sisters of Mine, you did it for Me" (Matt. 25:40).

The Church as the Household of God, Bride of Christ, and Body of Christ

Scripture uses many metaphors to describe the church, including the household of God/Christ, the bride of Christ, and the body of Christ. Each of these are metaphors of intimate relationship, metaphors of belonging to Christ in profound ways. Let us briefly consider each of these in turn.[14]

The Household of God: Spiritual House for a Holy Priesthood

The metaphor of the church as God's household frequently appears in the New Testament. To be part of God's household is to belong to God's family through Christ, which comes with both privileges and responsibilities (see 1 Pet. 4:17). The church is to be a fellowship of love—Christ's followers are known by their love for one another (John 13:35).

Believers are adopted in Christ and, thus, heirs to the inheritance Christ won on behalf of all who are in Him by faith (e.g., Rom. 8:15–17). Those who belong to Christ are thereby "children of God" in a special sense.[15] As John writes, "See how great a love the Father has given us, that we would be called children of God" (1 John 3:1).

> *The church is to be a fellowship of love—Christ's followers are known by their love for one another.*

Thus, Paul wrote to believers in Ephesus, "you are no longer strangers and foreigners, but you are fellow citizens with the saints, and are of God's household, having been built on the foundation of the apostles and prophets, Christ Jesus Himself being the cornerstone, in whom the whole building, being fitted together, is growing into a holy temple in the Lord, in whom you also are being built together into a dwelling of God in the Spirit" (Eph. 2:19–22).

Here, the metaphor of "God's household" is connected with the metaphor of God's temple—the place of God's special presence. Likewise, Paul elsewhere speaks of believers as "God's building," the "foundation" of which "is Jesus Christ" (1 Cor. 3:9, 11). Elsewhere, believers themselves are referred to as "the temple of God" in which "the Spirit of God dwells" (1 Cor. 3:16; cf. 6:19; 2 Cor. 6:16). And Peter writes to believers, "you also, as living stones, are being built up as a spiritual house for a holy priesthood, to offer spiritual sacrifices that are acceptable to God through Jesus Christ," the "precious cornerstone" (1 Pet. 2:5–6).

The Bride of Christ

Closely related to the household metaphor is another family metaphor, the church as Christ's bride. In Scripture, God repeatedly depicts Himself as the husband of His covenant people (e.g., Isa. 62:5).[16] In the New Testament, the metaphor of bride refers to the church—those who belong to Christ by faith and fidelity.

For example, Paul writes: "Husbands, love your wives, just as Christ also loved the church and gave Himself up for her, so that He might sanctify her, having cleansed her by the washing of water with the word, that He might present to Himself the church in all her glory, having no spot or wrinkle or any such thing; but that she would be holy and blameless. So husbands also ought to love their own wives as their own bodies. He who loves his own wife loves himself; for no one ever hated his own flesh, but nourishes and cherishes it, just as Christ also does the church, because we are parts of His body. FOR THIS REASON A MAN SHALL LEAVE HIS FATHER AND HIS MOTHER AND BE JOINED TO HIS WIFE, AND THE TWO SHALL BECOME ONE FLESH. This mystery is great; but I am speaking with reference to Christ and the church" (Eph. 5:25–32; cf. 2 Cor. 11:2). Notice the intimacy of love portrayed here between Christ and His church.

In the end, Christ will be reunited with His people in what Revelation calls "the marriage of the Lamb." Then, it will be said, "the marriage of the Lamb has come, and His bride has prepared herself" (Rev. 19:7; cf. Matt. 22). Thus, John was instructed to write, "Blessed are those who are invited to the wedding feast of the Lamb" (Rev. 19:9; cf. 21:1–2).

The Body of Christ

The bride metaphor is itself closely connected with the metaphor of the church as the body of Christ. When Paul speaks of a man and woman becoming "one flesh" in marriage, he includes the metaphor of the body of Christ, emphasizing that Christ nourishes, cherishes, and loves "the church, because we are parts of His body" (Eph. 5:29–31).

Elsewhere, Paul adds, "we, who are many, are one body in Christ, and individually parts of one another" (Rom. 12:4–5). Further, "just as the body is one and yet has many parts, and all the parts of the body, though they are many, are one body, so also is Christ. For by one Spirit we were all baptized into one body, whether Jews or Greeks, whether slaves or free, and we were all made to drink of one Spirit. For the body is not one part, but many" and "you are Christ's body, and individually parts of it" (1 Cor. 12:12–14, 27).

Of this church body, Christ is repeatedly identified as the one and only head (see Eph. 1:22; 5:25; Col. 2:20; discussed below).

Functions and Ordinances of the Church

God tasks the church with numerous functions for the sake of mission, including:

- Proclaiming the gospel (Mission) and the message of Christ's second Advent
- Making disciples of all nations
- Worship and exhortation
- Christian fellowship
- Instruction in the Scriptures
- Caring for the needy and suffering
- The ordinances

The mission of the church is discussed further in chapter 18. Here, we will focus on the two ordinances of baptism and the Lord's supper, both of which are rooted in Christ's teachings and commands and model union with God.

Competing Theories in Christian Theology: Sacramentalism

Christians take *many* differing views regarding rituals like baptism, the Lord's Supper, and others. Many affirm various forms of sacramentalism, while others reject sacramentalism.

Sacramentalism maintains that certain rituals (called sacraments) confer grace and have efficacy relative to salvation. In Roman Catholicism, a sacrament is a holy or sacred object and/or rite thought to be a channel of divine grace (understood as spiritual power or energy).[17] Roman Catholics affirm seven sacraments: baptism, confirmation, eucharist, penance, anointing of the sick, marriage, and holy orders. Protestant Reformers such as Martin Luther, however, limited sacraments to only those commanded by Jesus: baptism and the Lord's Supper (Eucharist).[18] Some think of marriage along similar lines.

Some Protestants reject sacramentalism, adopting an alternative that views Christian rituals like baptism and the Lord's Supper (and sometimes marriage) as church ordinances, which do not themselves transmit divine power or grace but are *merely* outward symbols of the inner work of the Holy Spirit.

Disagreements about the nature of Christ's presence relative to the bread and wine (or juice) in the Lord's Supper (Eucharist) have been a significant source of division among Christians.

Many affirm some kind of "Real Presence" of Christ in the Lord's Supper (Eucharist). Roman Catholics believe that when the priest consecrates the bread and wine of the Eucharist, they *actually become* Christ's body and blood. Their external appearance remains the same, but their substance changes into Christ's broken body and blood (known as transubstantiation).[19] This sacrament is thus called the holy sacrifice of the Mass, through which they believe forgiveness of sin may be obtained.

The Eastern Orthodox Church affirms the Eucharist as one of the sacraments (referred to as "mysteries") and affirms both the Real Presence of Christ and the sacrificial nature of the Eucharist but does not attempt an explanation of how the change occurs.

Protestants, however, *typically* reject both the view that the bread and wine *become* Christ's body and blood and the view that the Lord's Supper is a sacrifice of Christ, which many believe contradicts Scripture's teaching regarding the once-for-all sufficiency of Christ's sacrifice on the cross (e.g., Heb. 10:10). Many Protestants, however, affirm some kind of real presence of Christ in the Eucharist.

Lutherans believe there is a sacramental union of the bread and wine with Christ's body and blood such that Christ is really present "in, with, and under" the bread and wine, yet distinct from them (with no change in substance). This view is sometimes referred to as consubstantiation, but some maintain this is a misnomer.[20]

Reformed and Presbyterian Christians maintain, instead, that Christ is not physically (corporeally) present *in* the bread and wine, but Christ is spiritually present. By receiving the bread and wine by faith, one can receive Christ through the Holy Spirit's power, which works through the sacrament. This view is sometimes called receptionism.

Some Christians, however, believe the Lord's Supper (i.e., Communion) is a commemoration of the Last Supper wherein the bread and wine (or juice) are symbolic of Jesus's body and blood that was broken for us on the cross, but Christ is not specially present (physically or spiritually) in or through these emblems specifically (though Christ is present as He always is "where two or three have gathered together in [His] name" (Matt. 18:20). This view is sometimes known as memorialism (often associated with the Swiss reformer Ulrich Zwingli). Adventists affirm a view that is similar to this.

Christians also hold differing views regarding the nature and manner of baptism. Many affirm baptismal regeneration, the view that regeneration (being "born again") occurs when one is baptized, with many viewing baptism as a sacrament. Others (including Adventists) deny this, maintaining that baptism is an outward sign of an inward commitment (a covenant between God and the person being baptized), distinct from regeneration.

Roman Catholics, Eastern Orthodox Christians, and many Protestants practice infant baptism (i.e., paedobaptism).[21] Other Protestants reject infant baptism, practicing only believer's baptism (i.e., credobaptism). Here, baptism is reserved for those who earnestly profess faith, requiring that those baptized are mature enough to understand and personally believe prior to baptism. During the Protestant Reformation, the Anabaptists (literally, re-baptizers) faced persecution for their insistence that baptism should be reserved for believers.

Christians also perform baptism in different ways. Those who practice infant baptism may do so by sprinkling water on the infant's head (aspersion), pouring water on the infant's head (affusion), or (less usually) by immersing the infant in water (immersion). Some perform believer's baptism by pouring (affusion), and others (including Adventists) practice believer's baptism by immersion, with many arguing immersion baptism is taught by Scripture.

Closely related to sacramentalism is sacerdotalism, the view that human priests are mediators between God and humans and, thus, conduits of divine grace. This stands in direct contrast to the way many Protestants (including Adventists) understand the priesthood of all believers, which claims there is no longer any mediator between God and humans save Christ alone, the "one mediator between God and humankind" (1 Tim. 2:5, NRSVue), such that through Christ all believers may approach the throne of grace (Heb. 4:16) as "a holy priesthood" (1 Pet. 2:5) via the ministry of the one true high priest, Jesus.

Baptism

An angel appeared to him and said, "Get ready and go south to the road that descends from Jerusalem to Gaza." Philip obeyed and met an Ethiopian eunuch, a court official of Candace, queen of the Ethiopians. This man was a believer in the God of Israel who "had come to Jerusalem to worship." Philip found him "reading Isaiah the prophet," and "the Spirit said to Philip, 'Go up and join this chariot.'"

Philip went and asked him, "Do you understand what you are reading?" The man replied, "Well, how could I, unless someone guides me?" The man then asked whether Isaiah was speaking of himself or another when he prophesied of one "like a lamb that is led to slaughter" (Isa. 53:7–8). Then, "beginning from this Scripture he [Philip] preached Jesus to him."

The man believed Philip's teachings; Philip invited him to be baptized, and "they both went down into the water," and Philip "baptized him." And "When they came up out of the water, the Spirit of the Lord snatched Philip away," and the man "no longer saw him, but went on his way rejoicing" (Acts 8:26–39). Amazing.

This was one example of fulfilling Christ's Great Commission to "go" and "make disciples of all the nations, baptizing them in the name of the Father and the Son and the Holy Spirit, teaching them to follow all that I commanded you" (Matt. 28:19-20). Here, Jesus linked baptism with making disciples and teaching them to observe His commandments. Baptism, then, is for disciples who commit to following Christ's commands.

At the outset of His ministry, Jesus Himself was baptized by John the Baptist. To prepare for the Messiah's coming, John continually called people to repent of their sins and be baptized. But Jesus was sinless. He was not baptized for sins of His own, but "He appeared in order to take away sins; and in Him there is no sin" (1 John 3:5). He thus provided an example for humans, and His baptism symbolized the death He would voluntarily undergo for our sins (Phil. 2:8; 1 John 2:2; cf. 2 Cor. 5:21).

For believers also, baptism symbolizes death and resurrection to new life, following Christ's example. As Paul writes, "all of us who have been baptized into Christ Jesus have been baptized into His death." Thus, "we have been buried with Him through baptism into death, so that, just as Christ was raised from the dead through the glory of the Father, so we too may walk in newness of life" (Rom. 6:3-4; cf. Gal. 2:20). Paul goes on to explain, "our old self was crucified with Him, in order that our body of sin might be done away with, so that we would no longer be slaves to sin; for the one who has died is freed from sin" (Rom. 6:6-7). So, "consider yourselves to be dead to sin, but alive to God in Christ Jesus" (Rom. 6:11).

Elsewhere, Paul connects this symbolism of baptism as figurative death to a figurative (spiritual) kind of circumcision. He writes, "in Him [Christ] you were also circumcised with a circumcision performed without hands, in the removal of the body of the flesh by the circumcision of Christ, having been buried with Him in baptism, in which you were also raised with Him through faith in the working of God, who raised Him from the dead. And when you were dead in your wrongdoings and the uncircumcision of your flesh, He made you alive together with Him, having forgiven us all our wrongdoings" (Col. 2:11-13).

Adventists thus understand baptism as a symbol of (figuratively) partaking in Christ's death, burial, and resurrection and also a symbol of belonging to God's New Covenant people *instead of circumcision*

(Col. 2:11–12).[22] As Adventists understand it, baptism does not provide forgiveness or cleansing but is a public display symbolic of the forgiveness and cleansing one receives when one confesses one's sins (cf. Matt. 3:6; 1 John 1:9) and repents in faith, accepting Christ and receiving the Holy Spirit.

> *Adventists understand baptism as a symbol of figuratively partaking in Christ's death, burial, and resurrection and also a symbol of belonging to God's New Covenant people.*

Given such meaning, Adventists believe baptism is reserved for believers who understand what Christ offers and commands and commit themselves to following Christ as Savior *and* Lord—following in Christ's footsteps in terms of being "dead to sin" and "alive to God" (Rom. 6:3–11). Because baptism itself does not regenerate or save, it can be reserved for when one is in a position to understand and commit to Christ's teachings and commands without posing any danger to one's salvation.

Adventists practice baptism by immersion, believing such practice is taught by Scripture and viewing the "burial" by water as symbolic of death to one's old life of sin and the rising out of the water as symbolic of spiritual resurrection to new life in Christ.

Regarding the biblical teaching, John 3:23 informs us John "was baptizing in Aenon, near Salim, because there was an abundance of water there." Yet, "an abundance of water" would not be needed if such baptism was by pouring or sprinkling. Further, we've already seen that the Ethiopian court official was baptized by immersion (Acts 8:38–39). And Jesus Himself was baptized by immersion: "After He was baptized, Jesus came up immediately from the water" (Matt. 3:16; cf. Mark 1:9–10). It seems to be no coincidence that the Greek term *baptizō* means "to dip in or under."

Baptism is not an extraneous detail of the Christian life, but an important public declaration of one's commitment to Christ and Christian fellowship administered to the one being baptized as a sign of entry into Christ's body (the church). Accordingly, Paul emphasizes there is "one baptism" even as there is "one body" (Eph. 4:4–5). Baptism is a most joyous occasion, a symbol of union with Christ, forgiveness of sins, and receiving the Holy Spirit.

The Lord's Supper

Shortly before His crucifixion, Christ shared a final Passover with His apostles. "I have eagerly desired to eat this Passover with you before I suffer," He said, for "I shall not eat it again until it is fulfilled in the kingdom of God" (Luke 22:15–16).

Jesus then took a cup, gave thanks, and told His apostles, "Take this and share it among yourselves." Afterward, Jesus took some bread, gave thanks, "broke it and gave it to them, saying, 'This is My body, which is being given for you; do this in remembrance of Me.' " Then, "in the same way He took the cup after they had eaten, saying, 'This cup, which is poured out for you, is the new covenant in My blood' " (Luke 22:17–20; cf. Matt. 26:26–28).

This first Lord's Supper—the Last Supper—was a Passover meal. The Lord's Supper (Communion) is thus rooted in the meaning of Passover, the feast that commemorated how the people of Israel sacrificed a lamb and put its blood on their lintel and doorposts so that the destroying angel *passed over* their households, sparing their firstborns (see Exod. 12:3–8, 15, 19–20). Via the cross, Christ became our Passover Lamb—"Christ our Passover . . . has been sacrificed" (1 Cor. 5:7).

With His death, Christ put an end to the ceremonial sacrifices and festivals—including Passover. In its place, Christ instituted the Lord's Supper, commanding His followers to "do this in remembrance of Me" (Luke 22:19; 1 Cor. 11:24). It was to be a "memorial of His great sacrifice," which also looks to the future, "until He comes" (1 Cor. 11:26).[23]

When Jesus said, "This is My body, which is being given for you" (Luke 22:19), His actual physical body was not yet broken, for He had not yet gone to the cross. The phrase "this is my body," Adventists believe, was figurative speech such that the elements of the Lord's Supper represent or symbolize Christ's body and blood, broken for us on the cross, the once-for-all sacrifice that does not need to be repeated (Heb. 9:12; 10:10).

Adventists thus practice communion as a symbolic ordinance and do not believe that Christ is specially present (e.g., corporeally present) *in* the elements. The service memorializes what Christ did for us, serving as a proclamation of "the Lord's death until He comes" (1 Cor. 11:26; cf. 10:16–17), but also reminds Christians to *spiritually* feast upon Christ through prayer and Bible study (cf. John 6:48–63).[24]

Adventists use unleavened bread and unfermented grape juice in the service, symbolic of Christ as the uncorrupted and unblemished sacrificial lamb. And Adventists practice open communion, allowing members and non-members to partake. Rather than attempting to determine who is worthily or unworthily taking communion, Adventists believe each person should make their own decision whether to participate relative to the disposition of one's heart. This, Adventists base on Paul's instruction: "Whoever, therefore, eats the bread or drinks the cup of the Lord in an unworthy manner will be answerable for the body and blood of the Lord. Examine yourselves, and only then eat of the bread and drink of the cup. For all who eat and drink without discerning the body eat and drink judgment against themselves" (1 Cor. 11:27–29, NRSVue).

Adventists also practice the ordinance of footwashing in preparation for partaking of the Lord's Supper, following Christ's example and words (John 13:14–15). Before eating the Last Supper, Jesus "poured water into the basin, and began washing the disciples' feet" (John 13:4–5). Amazing. Jesus humbled Himself to wash His disciples' feet, a total reversal of expectations and custom.

This was so shocking that Peter protested he'd never let Jesus wash his feet. But Jesus replied, "If I do not wash you, you have no place with Me" (John 13:8). So Peter said, "Lord, then wash not only my feet, but also my hands and my head!" (John 13:9). However, Jesus replied, "He who has bathed needs only to wash his feet; otherwise he is completely clean" (John 13:10).

After washing their feet, Jesus said, "if I, the Lord and the Teacher, washed your feet, you also ought to wash one another's feet. For I gave you an example, so that you also would do just as I did for you" (John 13:14–15). Adventists practice this ordinance of humility as a memorial of Christ's humility, understanding it also as a symbol of cleansing and a process that facilitates forgiveness and fellowship among Christians, with willingness to humbly serve one another, following Christ's example as one who came not to be served, but to serve (Matt. 20:28). Those who follow Christ are called to follow Christ's example not merely relative to this ordinance, but by serving people around us in practical ways—lifting up the poor and the oppressed as we are able.

The Unique Headship of Christ, Authority, and Governance of the Church

Who is the greatest? They frequently argued about this among themselves. Some of the disciples even went to Jesus privately to request seats of honor in His kingdom (Mark 10:37; cf. Matt. 20:20–23).

But they had it all wrong. They thought of greatness as position and power. But, Jesus explained, "the rulers of the gentiles lord it over them, and their great ones are tyrants over them. It will not be so among you, but whoever wishes to be great among you must be your servant, and whoever wishes to be first among you must be your slave, just as the Son of Man came not to be served but to serve and to give his life a ransom for many" (Matt. 20:25–28, NRSVue).

Do you want to be great? Be a servant. To lead, you must serve and give yourself, as Jesus did. Christ left the highest place to humble Himself even to the point of death (Phil. 2:5–8). Anyone who wishes to be a leader in the body of Christ must follow Christ's example of servant leadership.

In this regard, Christ instructed, "you are not to be called rabbi, for you have one teacher, and you are all brothers and sisters. And call no one your father on earth, for you have one Father, the one in heaven. Nor are you to be called instructors, for you have one instructor, the Messiah. The greatest among you will be your servant" (Matt. 23:8–11, NRSVue).

> *Anyone who wishes to be a leader in the body of Christ must follow Christ's example of servant leadership.*

What does this mean, then, for leadership and authority in the church?

Competing Theories in Christian Theology: Church Governance

The most prominent divisions in Christian history were largely motivated by disagreements over the nature of church government and authority.

Long before the Protestant Reformation, there was a Great Schism between East and West in 1054, splitting into the Eastern Orthodox Church and Roman Catholicism. One prominent factor in this divide was the Western Church's insistence on the primacy of the Bishop of

Rome (the Pope). The Orthodox and Catholic Churches both hold a high view of tradition and church authority and identify the church as normative interpreter of Scripture and tradition, but the Orthodox Church rejects the primacy of any one bishop.

In the sixteenth century came the Protestant Reformation, which protested and split from the Roman Catholic Church regarding (among other things) the following:

- primacy of the pope and his claim to be the vicar of Christ,
- infallibility of the Roman Catholic Church,
- replacement of Christ's high priestly ministry with a system of earthly priests (sacerdotalism) contrary to the priesthood of all believers,
- system of meritorious works, and
- system of penance and indulgences.[25]

As many Protestants (and others) understand it, these and other abuses of authority in medieval Christendom paved the way for many in the Enlightenment period (ca. 1650–1800) and beyond to reject Christianity altogether.[26]

Alongside these issues, there was disagreement over the authority of Scripture relative to tradition and the church. The Protestant Reformation affirmed Scripture as the uniquely normative rule of faith and practice (*sola Scriptura*), the supreme standard on earth by which all doctrines and practices are to be normed or ruled, which is not itself to be normed or ruled.[27] Roman Catholicism, conversely, claimed there is one sacred deposit of apostolic testimony, consisting of Scripture and the Tradition of the church (Scripture + Tradition), possessed by the Roman Catholic Church such that the church alone is the normative interpreter of Scripture and Tradition (specifically the Magisterium—the pope and the bishops).[28] The Magisterium thus functions as the supreme and final authority on earth.[29]

The Roman Catholic and Eastern Orthodox Churches are examples of the episcopal system of church government (as well as Coptics, Anglicans, many Lutherans, and others). Episcopal systems focus on the authority of a bishop or bishops as chief authorities (the head or heads of the church), with authority purported to derive from broken apostolic succession. The label derives from the Greek term *episkopos* (meaning "overseer"), which tradition came to identify with the office of bishop.

In Roman Catholicism, the Bishop of Rome (the Pope) claims primacy over all other bishops, claiming to be Peter's successor and that Jesus appointed Peter as the head of the church. Protestants argue there is no basis for this claim in Scripture (in Matthew 16:18–19 or elsewhere) and typically maintain that Christ *alone* is the foundation and head of the church (1 Cor. 3:11; Eph. 2:20–22; 1 Pet. 2:4–8). Many trace the development of such episcopal government to gradual increases in authority claimed by clergy over numerous generations, long after the first apostles passed away.[30]

The other two most prominent forms of church government are the presbyterian and congregational forms.

The Presbyterian form focuses on leadership by elders. Its name is derived from the Greek term *presbyteros*, typically translated "elder" in Scripture, an office many Protestants believe is the same in Scripture as that of *episkopos* (e.g., Acts 20:17, 28; Titus 1:5–7), understood as "overseer" (not bishop). This approach typically views authority as residing originally at the level of the local church elder. Ministers and pastors (or reverends) are elders of the local church with a specialized role. Leaders beyond the local level may be elected to serve and govern over the regional body or bodies of churches, but their authority is typically considered delegated authority rooted in the local level. Whereas episcopal systems centralize chief authority in bishops, presbyterian systems are somewhat decentralized by comparison.

Congregational forms are the most decentralized of these three, vesting authority in local congregations, independent (or relatively independent) from the authority and control of other religious bodies. Local churches often associate themselves with other local churches in a district, convention, or other association. In many congregational churches, primary leadership is vested in the senior or lead pastor, sometimes thought of as the principal elder. Other congregational churches are led by an elected council or leadership board holding final (or near-final) authority.

Seventh-day Adventists often classify their system as a representative form of church government. It has much in common with presbyterian systems (e.g., pastors as elders with special functions) and sometimes operates in ways that tend in an episcopal direction (particularly when authority is more centralized in church leaders).

The Adventist Church has five levels of church organization (four, if divisions are counted as part of the General Conference level):

- the local church, made up of individual members
- the local conference, made up of a number of local schools and churches within a region
- the Union Conference, made up of local conferences
- the Division, made up of unions in a particular geographical area
- the General Conference, made up of all unions in all parts of the world, organized into divisions that hold administrative responsibility for particular geographical areas

SEVENTH-DAY ADVENTIST CHURCH ORGANIZATIONAL STRUCTURE

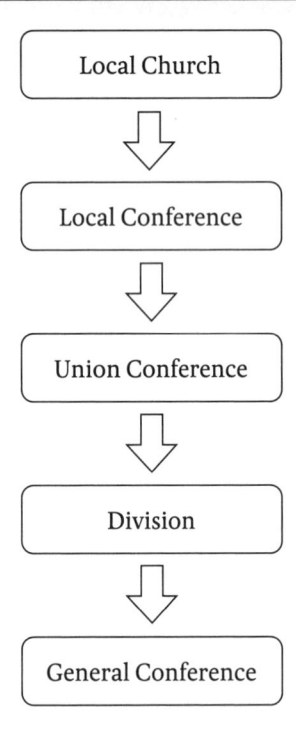

Local Church
⇩
Local Conference
⇩
Union Conference
⇩
Division
⇩
General Conference

At the local church level, the church in business session (duly called meetings consisting of *all* local church members who attend) has the final say. Regular operations run through a church board elected by the local church in business session, often chaired by a pastor (who does not vote except by secret ballot or to make or break ties), which makes recommendations to the church in business session regarding larger decisions.[31] The pastor, then, does not hold executive authority in the local church except that delegated to him or her by the local church.

For the world church, the church in business session is the General Conference in business session, which consists of delegates sent from various fields to represent their respective groups (as well as ex-officio and other appointed delegates).

The Unique Headship of Christ

Christ alone is *the* Head of the church—the unique Head.[32] "He is the head over every ruler and authority" (Col. 2:10). No one else can be the Head of the church, for the church is *His* body. After His resurrection, Christ was seated at the Father's "right hand" in "the heavenly places, far above all rule and authority and power and dominion, and every name that is named, not only in this age but also in the one to come. And He put all things in subjection under His feet, and made Him head over all things to the church, which is His body, the fullness of Him who fills all in all" (Eph. 1:20-23; cf. 5:23).

> Christ alone is the Head of the church—the unique Head.

Christ is the ultimate servant leader, the Creator who became human not to be served but to serve and give His life for us (Matt. 20:28). He rules with perfect justice and unselfish love, which no mere human can equal. All doctrines and practices are to be normed and ruled by the unique rule that Christ Himself confirmed and commissioned, the canon of Scripture (see chapter 10).

The Priesthood of All Believers

Christ is also the ultimate high priest. Through Him, all believers can approach God's throne of grace (Heb. 4:16). Salvation does not come by decisions or operations of the church but through the "one mediator between God and humankind, Christ Jesus" (1 Tim. 2:5, NRSVue; cf. Acts 4:12).

In the New Covenant, then, there is no need for human priests to mediate between God and humans. Instead, there is a priesthood of all believers to proclaim and witness regarding the all-sufficient work of Christ and vindication of God's character. As Peter explains to believers, you "are being built up as a spiritual house for a holy priesthood, to offer spiritual sacrifices that are acceptable to God through Jesus Christ" (1 Pet. 2:4–5). And, "you are A CHOSEN PEOPLE, A royal PRIESTHOOD, A HOLY NATION, A PEOPLE FOR GOD'S OWN POSSESSION, so that you may proclaim the excellencies of Him who has called you out of darkness into His marvelous light; for you once were NOT A PEOPLE, but now you are THE PEOPLE OF GOD; you had NOT RECEIVED MERCY, but now you have RECEIVED MERCY" (1 Pet. 2:9–10).

How marvelous!

If you are in Christ by faith, you belong to this "spiritual house" that is to be "a royal priesthood." In the Old Covenant, there was an elect priesthood to which only a few could belong, but the New Covenant ushers in the priesthood of *all* believers (1 Pet. 2:4–5; cf. Gal. 3:27–29). This is consistent with God's intentions all along, for God initially called Israel to be a "kingdom of priests" (Exod. 19:6), but they asked for someone to mediate for them because they were afraid. The New Covenant renews this divine intention. By Christ's "blood," He ransomed "people ... from every tribe, language, people, and nation" and "made them into a kingdom and priests to our God, and they will reign upon the earth" (Rev. 5:9–10).

This view of the priesthood of all believers stands in direct contrast to the view known as sacerdotalism, wherein human priests are viewed as mediators between God and humans and thus conduits of divine grace. Instead, Scripture teaches the priesthood of *all* believers while emphasizing that there is "one mediator between God and humankind, Christ Jesus" (1 Tim. 2:5, NRSVue).

The Gifts of the Spirit

All who belong to Christ are to be "a royal priesthood" (1 Pet. 2:9), with each serving according to the spiritual gifts the Holy Spirit bestows on "each one individually just as He wills" (1 Cor. 12:11) for the upbuilding and edification of the church.

As Paul explains, "there are varieties of gifts, but the same Spirit. And there are varieties of ministries, and the same Lord. There are varieties of effects, but the same God who works all things in all persons. But to each one is given the manifestation of the Spirit for the common good" (1 Cor. 12:4–7).

If you belong to Christ, this includes you. You are chosen, called, and gifted by the Holy Spirit. Your life has a greater purpose beyond the mundane things of life. You are called to ministry.

Scripture includes many lists of spiritual gifts, none of which are exhaustive.

> *Your life has a greater purpose beyond the mundane things of life. You are called to ministry.*

For example, Paul explains, "to one is given the word of wisdom through the Spirit, and to another the word of knowledge according to the same Spirit; to another faith by the same Spirit, and to another gifts of healing by the one Spirit, and to another the effecting of miracles, and to another prophecy, and to another the distinguishing of spirits, to another various kinds of tongues, and to another the interpretation of tongues. But one and the same Spirit works all these things, distributing to each one individually just as He wills" (1 Cor. 12:8–11).

And Paul goes on, "God has appointed in the church, first apostles, second prophets, third teachers, then miracles, then gifts of healings, helps, administrations, and various kinds of tongues" (1 Cor. 12:28). Elsewhere, Paul writes, "He gave some as apostles, some as prophets, some as evangelists, some as pastors and teachers, for the equipping of the saints for the work of ministry, for the building up of the body of Christ; until we all attain to the unity of the faith, and of the knowledge of the Son of God, to a mature man, to the measure of the stature which belongs to the fullness of Christ" (Eph. 4:11–13). Spiritual gifts, then, are given not for individuals to flaunt or claim as if such gifts were their unique possession but for the upbuilding and good of the church collectively.[33]

Here and elsewhere, Scripture speaks of specific appointed functions or offices in the church for the common good. The first-generation apostles were a special group, chosen as witnesses by Christ Himself (e.g., Acts 1:8; 10:38–41). Alongside the offices in the passages above, Scripture elsewhere speaks of overseers (*episkopos*), elders (*presbyteros*), and deacons (*diakonos*). With many Protestants, Adventists understand the biblical language of "overseers" and "elders" as referring to the same church function/office (as in, e.g., Acts 20:17, 28; Titus 1:5–7), one of servant leadership.

All the members of the body and their spiritual gifts are crucial to the church and her ministry. Indeed, "as in one body we have many members and not all the members have the same function, so we, who are many, are one body in Christ, and individually we are members one of another. We have gifts that differ according to the grace given to us: prophecy, in proportion to faith; ministry, in ministering; the teacher, in teaching; the encourager, in encouragement; the giver, in sincerity; the leader, in diligence; the compassionate, in cheerfulness. Let love be genuine; hate what is evil; hold fast to what is good; love one another with mutual affection; outdo one another in showing honor" (Rom. 12:4–10, NRSVue).

Among the best ways to discover one's spiritual gifts is to get involved in the ministries of the local church. Take part in service, pray for the guidance of the Holy Spirit, and see how God opens doors to use the gifts the Spirit has given for the common good. As Peter exhorts, "As each one has received a special gift, employ it in serving one another as good stewards of the multifaceted grace of God" (1 Pet. 4:10).[34]

Being a follower of Christ involves commitment to a life of service inside and outside the church—living missionally, with one's life aimed at fulfilling God's mission to call people into God's love. This mission is far bigger than any one person. But, if you believe in Christ, you are called to be part of this huge thing God is doing. If you desire to follow Christ, do not be satisfied to just "sit" by in the church pew or at home. Instead, follow Christ's commission and "go" (see Matt. 28:19–20).

The Gift of Prophecy and the Unique Authority of Scripture in the Church

It is no coincidence that in the lists of spiritual gifts, the offices of apostles and prophets are given priority. "God's household," the church, was "built on the foundation of the apostles and prophets, Christ Jesus Himself being the cornerstone" (Eph. 2:19–20).

Today, priority belongs to the testimony of those divinely commissioned *covenantal* prophets and apostles contained in the canon of Scripture—the uniquely authoritative rule of faith and practice because it was commissioned as such by the Ruler Himself (see chapter 10).

In addition to the *covenantal* prophets and apostles whose testimony is contained in Scripture, the Bible mentions numerous other prophets who did not write any of the books in Scripture (e.g., Enoch, Huldah, John the Baptist). Further, the New Testament speaks of the gift of prophecy and recognizes prophets in the church beyond the Old Testament prophets and New Testament apostles (e.g., 1 Cor. 14). Indeed, Scripture indicates that prophetic messages would be given long after New Testament times (see, e.g., Rev. 11:3; 6; 12:17; 19:10; cf. Joel 2:28–30; Acts 2:17–20).

How, then, should we understand the gift of prophecy today? Adventists believe Scripture teaches that the prophetic gift functions at various times and places even after New Testament times, but prophets outside Scripture are never to supersede, or add to, the biblical canon.

On the one hand, Scripture teaches: "Do not quench the Spirit, do not utterly reject prophecies" (1 Thess. 5:19–20; cf. 1 Cor. 14:1). Yet, Jesus strongly warned that many false prophets would arise in the last days and mislead many people (Matt. 24:11, 24; cf. 7:15). Accordingly, Paul instructed, "test everything; hold fast to what is good" (1 Thess. 5:21, NRSVue), and John added, "test the spirits to see whether they are from God" (1 John 4:1).

In this regard, Adventists believe any true prophet from God will pass the following four biblical tests of prophets.

- A true prophet recognizes Jesus Christ: "every spirit that does not confess Jesus is not from God," but is "of the antichrist" (1 John 4:2–3).
- The teachings of a true prophet agree with Scripture; if they do not teach according to the word of the prophets and apostles, there is no light in them (Isa. 8:20; James 1:17).
- A true prophet does not make false predictions (Deut. 18:21–22; cf. Jer. 28:9), though it is important to recognize that some prophecies are conditional prophecies and not to confuse a conditional prophecy with a false prediction.
- A true prophet is known by his or her fruits. As Jesus said while warning against false prophets, "every good tree bears good

fruit, but the bad tree bears bad fruit.... So then, you will know them by their fruits" (Matt. 7:15–20; cf. 2 Pet. 1:21).

The Prophetic Gift of Ellen G. White

"Other than the Bible, what is the best book on the life of Jesus?" I asked my parents one morning. I was ten years old, and we were on our way to some used book sales. I'd announced I would look for a book on David, proclaiming him the Bible's greatest hero.

"Jesus is the greatest hero," my father quickly corrected.

"Of course, dad," I replied. "Okay, then, I want to find the best book on Jesus's life other than the Bible."

Without hesitation, my dad replied, "that would be *The Desire of Ages* by Ellen White."

I was reminded that this book was part of a five-book series spanning the history of redemption—The *Conflict of the Ages* series, which I'd often admired on my parents' bookshelf.

"I'll make a deal with you," my father said. "If you read *The Desire of Ages*—the entire book—we'll get you your own set of the series."

I took the deal, and I read *The Desire of Ages* for the first time. Even though my little ten-year-old brain did not understand everything I read, I loved it. Looking back now, I see how reading that book, and then many others by Ellen White, instilled in me a deep love for God and profound awe at God's character of love. From then onward, I've treasured Ellen White's writings. I'm so thankful that I read many of her books myself long before I encountered people misusing her writings and taking them out of context. Otherwise, I might have mistakenly judged the writings of Ellen White on the basis of the way they are sometimes misused.

The Ellen White I encountered through her writings was quite different from the caricatures of her I've encountered since then, including some by well-meaning admirers of her work. I encourage you also to read her writings for yourself, starting with her masterpiece, *The Desire of Ages*. Or, for something shorter, consider reading her lovely book on salvation titled *Steps to Christ*.[35]

But, you might be wondering, just who is Ellen White?

Ellen Gould (Harmon) White (1827–1915) received her first prophetic vision in December of 1844 while still a teenager. For approximately seventy years thereafter, she preached and wrote voluminously of God's love, the nearness of Christ's Second Coming, and God's judgment hour message (Rev. 14:6–12).

She received many prophetic visions and dreams, ranging from a few minutes to four hours. These were sometimes accompanied by supernatural phenomena. Once, while in vision, she held up an eighteen-and-a-half-pound Bible in her outstretched arm for more than twenty minutes. And eyewitnesses, including medical doctors, reported that while in vision, she did not breathe.[36]

Though with little formal education beyond the third grade, she wrote approximately eighty books, two hundred tracts and pamphlets, 4,600 periodical articles, and another sixty thousand pages of manuscript materials. She wrote on a wide variety of subjects, including biblical theology, social justice, health, nutrition, education, psychology, interpersonal relationships, agriculture, and more. Her writings have been translated more than any woman in history; she is the most translated American author in history. *Smithsonian* magazine recently named her one of the one hundred most significant Americans of all time.[37] With Joseph Bates and her husband, James White, she was one of the founders of the Seventh-day Adventist Church.[38]

Adventists believe that the life and writings of Ellen White attest that she was a true prophet of God, exemplifying "the spirit of prophecy" (cf. Rev. 19:10). Accordingly, Adventists believe Ellen White's "writings speak with prophetic authority and provide comfort, guidance, instruction, and correction in the [Adventist] church."[39] At the same time, Adventists maintain that "the Bible is the standard by which all teaching and experience must be tested."[40] As her husband, James White put it, "the Bible is a perfect and complete revelation. It is our only rule of faith and practice."[41] Accordingly, Adventists do not base doctrines on Ellen White's writings but on the Bible alone, keeping with the *sola Scriptura* principle (see chapter 10 and the excursus that follows).

The Prophetic Gift and *Sola Scriptura*

Yet, this raises significant questions: Does recognition of prophetic writings outside of Scripture undermine the *sola Scriptura* principle?

How does the authority of Scripture relate to the authority of other prophetic messages, such as those of Ellen White?[42]

As we have seen, the *sola Scriptura* principle does not mean all knowledge (or even all divine revelation) is found in Scripture alone. Scripture itself attests to general revelation and extra-biblical prophecy. In a nutshell, the *sola Scriptura* principle simply affirms that Scripture is the uniquely normative rule of faith and practice (under the rule of God alone), the standard by which all other materials are to be tested and judged. Recognizing the prophetic gift and prophetic messages outside of Scripture is perfectly consistent with this principle as long as such extra-biblical prophetic messages are tested and ruled by Scripture.

In this regard, Paul explains that messages of prophets were to be tested according to the principle "the spirits of prophets are subject to prophets" (1 Cor. 14:32; cf. 11:4–5; 14:29–33; 1 Thess. 5:19–22; 1 John 4:1–2).

Further, Paul instructs that messages that claimed to be prophetic were to be subject to the authority of the apostles (1 Cor. 14:37–38). Such messages, then, were not of the same functional authority as the testimony of the first-generation apostles but were themselves subject to the testimony of the apostles. This is evidence of what Jon Paulien calls the "unique authority of the apostle[s]" due to their "special commission of leadership and the unique relationship in time to the first-century Christ event."[43]

Specifically, Paul writes: "Anyone who claims to be a prophet or spiritual must acknowledge that what I am writing to you is a command of the Lord. Anyone who does not recognize this is not to be recognized" (1 Cor. 14:37–38, NRSVue; cf. Luke 10:16; Rev. 1:3). Paulien infers from this that "any noncanonical prophet in the New Testament era was subject to the authority of the New Testament, which was written by the apostles."[44] From this, it follows that any noncanonical prophet is to be subject to the authority of the New Testament and the Old Testament that preceded it, by which the New Testament itself was tested (Acts 17:11–13), and to which the New Testament attests. That is, any noncanonical prophet is to be subject to the authority of the biblical canon confirmed and commissioned by Christ, the Ruler Himself (see chapter 10).

Yet, one might ask, since noncanonical prophetic messages are from God, aren't they just as divinely revealed and inspired as canonical writings and possess divinely granted authority? Indeed they are, and they do. Why, then, is there a difference between the biblical canon's authority and that of noncanonical prophetic messages?

Here, some mistakenly assume that the authority of any genuine prophet must be equivalent to the authority of any other. Scripture, however, records that God Himself sometimes distinguishes between the functional authority of some prophets. God did so when Moses was challenged by Aaron and Miriam (Num. 12:1–8), both recipients of the prophetic gift. And Paul highlights such a distinction, teaching of the apostles' authority over those prophesying in 1 Corinthians 14:37.

This makes sense if we understand that prophets are authoritative in virtue of, and to the extent that, *God* vests authority in them. Consider the relative functional authority of a judge and a minister. In some countries (such as the United States), both can perform weddings by the authority vested in them by the state, but the state grants judges additional functional authority that ministers do not possess.

In a somewhat similar fashion, the relative authority of prophetic messages corresponds to the relative *functional* authority granted by God (that is, whatever authority God grants for some function). As such, if the canon of Scripture is correctly recognized as the writings God commissioned to be the uniquely normative rule of faith and practice, it follows that the canon of Scripture holds divinely commissioned *functional* authority by which noncanonical prophetic messages (and all other material) are to be tested and ruled.

Why would God make such a distinction? It seems He did so in order to establish a unique rule or standard by which all other messages could be judged. In this regard, the difference between the authority of *canonical* prophets and apostles and *noncanonical* prophets is that the former hold uniquely normative ruling authority by virtue of the divine commission of their messages to function as the rule of faith and practice (as covenantal witnesses). In Paulien's words, while "[t]here are no degrees of inspiration," the apostles were "used as the standard to judge between those who exercised the true gift of prophecy and those who did not." As such, the apostles "functioned as an epistemological standard, and the New Testament would likewise do so after they were gone."[45]

In this regard, there is a significant historical—and thus functional—difference between canonical prophets/apostles and any later prophet. After Jesus came as the supreme revelation of God, any prophet thereafter has to be tested by the *covenantal* revelation the Ruler (Jesus) publicly confirmed and commissioned to function as *the rule of faith and practice* until He returns (the Old Testament and New Testament). Jesus publicly confirmed the Old Testament and commissioned the New Testament, with a cloud of appointed first-generation witnesses to the unrepeatable Christ event. No later prophetic revelation could meet this standard. All later claims to prophetic revelation must then be judged and ruled by this standard until the Ruler Himself returns.

Put differently, any prophet after Christ can only be properly recognized insofar as they recognize Christ (1 John 4:2). The one who properly recognizes Christ ought also to recognize the ruling authority of the Scriptures, the inspired writings of the covenantal prophets that Christ Himself recognized (the Old Testament Scriptures; cf. Luke 24:44-45) and of the apostles Christ commissioned as His uniquely authoritative historical witnesses (see Luke 10:16; 24:44-49; Acts 1:8, 22; 2:32; 3:15; 5:29-32; 10:39-43; 13:31; 22:14-15; 26:16; 1 Cor. 15:15). These apostles delivered not simply the "word of mere men," but truly "the word of God" (1 Thess. 2:13), resulting in the New Testament. Any prophetic message after Christ, then, is to be tested by and subject to the covenantal revelation Christ Himself attested and commissioned as the uniquely normative "ruling" authority—the canon of Scripture.

> **Any prophet after Christ can only be properly recognized insofar as they recognize Christ.**

This is precisely the way Ellen White understood her own prophetic writings in relation to Scripture. She repeatedly and consistently emphasized that Scripture is to be our only rule of faith and practice—the unequaled standard by which positions are to be judged. For example, she called people to "return to the great Protestant principle—the Bible, and the Bible only, as the rule of faith and duty."[46] Elsewhere she wrote, "God will have a people upon the earth to maintain the Bible, and the Bible only, as the standard of all doctrines and basis of all reforms."[47] Further, she repeatedly emphasized that Scripture is to be "the only rule of faith and doctrine."[48]

In keeping with this principle, she also consistently and repeatedly emphasized that noncanonical prophetic messages, including her own writings, are subject to the unequaled authority of the biblical canon—identifying her writings as a "lesser light to lead men and women to the greater light [the Bible]."[49]

She wrote, "Our position and faith is in the Bible.... And never do we want any soul to bring in the Testimonies [by which she meant her own writings] ahead of the Bible."[50] Elsewhere, she insisted her writings are not "an addition to the word of God," as some "make it appear."[51] She emphasized, in this regard, "the Spirit was not given—nor can it ever be bestowed—to supersede the Bible; for the Scriptures explicitly state that the Word of God is the standard by which *all* teaching and experience must be tested."[52] Simply put, Ellen White's consistent teaching was: "The Lord desires you to study your Bibles. He has not given any additional light to take the place of His Word."[53]

Accordingly, she instructed:

> In public labor do not make prominent, and quote that which Sister White has written, as authority to sustain your positions.... Bring your evidences, clear and plain, from the Word of God. A "Thus saith the Lord" is the strongest testimony you can possibly present to the people. Let none be educated to look to Sister White, but to the mighty God, who gives instruction to Sister White.[54]

White thus consistently insisted her writings were not to be used as the basis of doctrine or as a final and normative interpreter of Scripture—instead proclaiming, "we want Bible evidence for every point we advance."[55] In this regard, she called readers to judge her own prophetic writings *by* the Scriptures, urging that her own writings should be rejected if they conflict with Scripture: "If the Testimonies speak not according to this word of God, reject them."[56]

This principle can only be followed, however, if White's writings are not employed as a normative interpreter of Scripture. White's writings may serve as an aid in understanding the Bible, but they are not to be employed as a normative interpreter of the Bible. To employ White's writings that way would contradict the *sola Scriptura* principle as well as White's own counsels regarding her writings. In this regard, Frank Hasel explains that White did not advocate herself "as the authoritative source for the interpretation of Scripture. Rather, she time and again affirms the great Protestant principle: 'The Bible is its own expositor.' . . . She did not assume the role of being the authoritative interpreter of Scripture but encouraged others to be diligent students of Scripture themselves."[57]

Put simply, if Scripture is to be the *only* rule of faith and practice, Ellen White's own writings cannot also be a rule of faith and practice. Those who deeply respect and appreciate White's prophetic gift (as I do) should reserve normative "ruling" authority for the canon of Scripture, as she herself did and instructed others to do. To do otherwise would not only undermine the principle of *sola Scriptura* but also implicitly deny her authority as a prophet.

Accordingly, Adventists believe that Ellen White's writings are an important example of the gift of prophecy that should not be neglected. Still, her writings are themselves subject to the unequaled, ruling authority of Scripture.[58]

Conclusion: Why Does It Matter?

Lonely. She was surrounded by people—in real life and through social media. Yet, she felt deeply alone.

She longed for community, *real* community. Social media was fun and helped her to connect to people all over the world, but she was left wanting far more. She wanted to be in a community of fellowship and love, but she felt like she had no such community. Though all her "friends" were at the tip of her fingers through her smartphone, she felt very alone.

Have you felt like this? Do you long for community, *real* community?

A simple solution, one might think, would be to join a group in person to share life's sorrows and joys in some way. But social media and the media in general offer many reasons to distrust other people. More and more, people seem to wear their cruelty on their sleeves, unashamedly spouting hatred. So, it sometimes seems safer to keep to oneself, despite the loneliness such relative isolation brings in its wake.

We have seen in this chapter many things about the nature of God's church as God's household, the bride and body of Christ, of which Christ alone is the head. To this body, Christ invites you and me to be united.

In this regard, Hebrews 10:24–25 calls us to "consider how to encourage one another in love and good deeds, not abandoning our own meeting together, as is the habit of some people, but encouraging one another; and all the more as you see the day [of Christ's return] drawing near."

We should never confuse Christ with those who claim to follow Him. People (including people in the church) will let you down, but Christ never will. But do not let the shortcomings of people keep you from the gift of fellowship in Christ's body. Do not underestimate the significance of the support of a community pulling and growing in the same direction, a safe haven. The church is to be a place of refuge. Admittedly, local churches are not always places of refuge. Those of us committed to church fellowship, seeking communion with Christ's children, despite all our faults, should be committed to improving our church contexts, so they are safe places for all to come and be secure.

All who belong to Christ are to be part of the "royal priesthood" of *all* believers, with each one gifted individually by the Spirit for ministry. Some have unique gifts, like the rare gift of prophecy, but each of us is gifted to minister in some manner.

If you belong to Christ, you are called to serve Him according to your gifts. Whether you are called to be a professional minister or not, you are called to minister. To minister simply means to serve. All of God's people are called to be servants who build up the faith and well-being of the community as the body of Christ is filled with the Holy Spirit.

Who, then, can serve? Anyone and everyone who belongs to Christ, and is therefore equipped by the Holy Spirit, who gives gifts to *whomever* He wills (1 Cor. 12:11).

If you are not already, I invite you to become involved (or more involved) in a local church. Approach it not only as a place to worship God with others but as a place to serve others (and in doing so, serve God).

> *Approach a church not only as a place to worship God with others but as a place to serve others (and in doing so, serve God).*

In this regard, I invite you to read and reflect on 1 Corinthians 12–13, focusing especially on the importance of the members of the body to one another and the spiritual gifts God gives to edify this body—His church and the ultimate value of love above all.

Questions for Reflection

1. What is the nature of the church? What does the church mean to you?
2. Is the church a building or an organization? Or should it be understood as a group of people? How does the way we understand this affect our own relationship to the church?
3. What is the true church? Is there one true church or many true churches? What do you think Christ meant when He said, "I have other sheep, which are not of this fold" (John 10:16)?
4. What is the significance of baptism? Why and how might one get baptized, and what does it mean?
5. Who is the head of the church? Why does this matter in practice today? How does this relate to the priesthood of all believers?
6. Have you ever identified your spiritual gifts? What gifts do you have? How have you used them, or how might you use them in the church?
7. What is the relationship between the gift of prophecy and the church? How do Adventists understand the prophetic gift of Ellen White in relationship to the authority of Scripture?
8. You can be a part of God's body—the church—even now. Do you wish to belong to the fellowship of the Lamb? If so, prayerfully speak with your teacher or the leaders in your local church. If you have not already, ask them what preparations are needed to prepare for baptism. And ask how you can be involved.

For Further Reading

Adventist Perspectives:

Bradford, Charles E. *The King Is in Residence: A Beloved Leader Shares His Vision for the Church.* Nampa, ID: Pacific Press, 2018.

Bruinsma, Reinder. *The Body of Christ: A Biblical Understanding of the Church.* Hagerstown, MD: Review and Herald Publishing Association, 2009.

Dederen, Raoul. "The Church." In *Handbook of Seventh-day Adventist Theology.* Edited by Raoul Dederen. Hagerstown, MD: Review and Herald, 2000.

Fortin, Denis. *One in Christ: Biblical Concepts for a Doctrine of Church Unity*. Nampa, ID: Pacific Press, 2018.

Gulley, Norman R. *Systematic Theology: The Church and the Last Things*. Berrien Springs, MI: Andrews University Press, 2016.

Kiesler, Herbert. "The Ordinances: Baptism, Foot Washing, and Lord's Supper." In *Handbook of Seventh-day Adventist Theology*. Edited by Raoul Dederen. Hagerstown, MD: Review and Herald, 2000.

Knight, George R. *Meeting Ellen White: A Fresh Look at Her Life, Writings, and Major Themes*. Hagerstown, MD: Review and Herald, 1996.

———. *A Search for Identity: The Development of Seventh-day Adventist Beliefs*. Hagerstown, MD: Review and Herald, 2000.

Peckham, John C. "The Prophetic Gift and *Sola Scriptura*." In *Biblical Hermeneutics: An Adventist Approach*. Edited by Frank M. Hasel, 377–404. Silver Spring, MD: Review & Herald Academic/Biblical Research Institute, 2021.

Rice, George E. "Spiritual Gifts." In *Handbook of Seventh-day Adventist Theology*. Edited by Raoul Dederen. Hagerstown, MD: Review and Herald, 2000.

Rodríguez, Ángel Manuel, ed. *Message, Mission, and Unity of the Church*. Studies in Adventist Ecclesiology 2. Silver Spring, MD: Biblical Research Institute, 2013.

———, ed. *Toward a Theology of the Remnant: An Adventist Ecclesiological Perspective*. Studies in Adventist Ecclesiology 1. Silver Spring, MD: Biblical Research Institute, 2009.

———, ed. *Worship, Ministry, and the Authority of the Church*. Studies in Adventist Ecclesiology 3. Silver Spring, MD: Biblical Research Institute, 2016.

White, Ellen G. *The Acts of the Apostles*. Mountain View, CA: Pacific Press, 1911.

———. *The Desire of Ages*. Mountain View, CA: Pacific Press, 1898.

———. *The Great Controversy*. Mountain View, CA: Pacific Press, 1911.

Other Christian Perspectives:

Allison, Gregg R. *Sojourners and Strangers: The Doctrine of the Church*. Wheaton, IL: Crossway, 2012.

Avis, Paul, ed. *The Oxford Handbook of Ecclesiology*. Oxford: Oxford University Press, 2018.

Bantu, Vince L. *A Multitude of All Peoples: Engaging Ancient Christianity's Global Identity*. Downers Grove, IL: IVP Academic, 2020.

Bray, Gerald. *The Church: A Theological and Historical Account*. Grand Rapids, MI: Baker Academic, 2016.

Peterson, Cheryl M. *Who Is the Church? An Ecclesiology for the Twenty-First Century*. Minneapolis: Fortress Press, 2013.

McGrath, Alister. *Reformation Thought: An Introduction*, 4th ed. Malden, MA: Wiley-Blackwell, 2012.

Jennings, Willie James. *Acts: A Theological Commentary on the Bible*. Louisville: Westminster John Knox Press, 2017.

von Campenhausen, Hans. *Ecclesiastical Authority and Spiritual Power in the Church of the First Three Centuries*. Peabody, MA: Hendrickson, 1997.

Williams, Jarvis J. *Redemptive Kingdom Diversity: A Biblical Theology of the People of God*. Grand Rapids, MI: Baker Academic, 2021.

18

THE MISSION OF THE CHURCH: THE WAY OF THE LAMB VS. THE WAY OF THE DRAGON

"The thief comes only to steal and kill and destroy," Jesus warned, but "I came so that they would have life, and have it abundantly" (John 10:10). This Jesus told His followers while warning them about those who pretend to be shepherds but are actually thieves and robbers, following in the footsteps of the arch-thief, the devil.

True shepherds enter their sheepfolds by the door, Jesus explained. Thus, those who climb in over the fence thereby show themselves to be robbers. Then, Jesus proclaimed, "I am the door; if anyone enters through Me, he will be saved, and will go in and out and find pasture" (John 10:9). Anyone who does not enter through Christ or teaches others to enter some other way—advocating another means of salvation (cf. Acts 4:12)—is a robber.

"I am the good shepherd," Jesus further explained, who does not flee when the wolf comes, but "lays down His life for the sheep." "I am the good shepherd," Jesus continued, "and I know My own, and My own know Me" (John 10:11–14). Yet, Jesus emphasized, "I have other sheep that are not of this fold; I must bring them also, and they will listen to My voice; and they will become one flock, with one shepherd" (John 10:16).

There are true followers of Christ in various movements, but there are also many false teachers. Thus, Christ warned of wolves in sheep's clothing, those who claim Christ's name but work against His kingdom of unselfish love—who follow the way of the dragon rather than the way of the Lamb. "Beware of the false prophets, who come to you in sheep's clothing, but inwardly are ravenous wolves. You will know them by their fruits" (Matt. 7:15–16; cf. 24:24; Acts 20:29–31; 1 John 4:1).

This chapter addresses a number of remaining questions about the church, including:

- What is the unity of the church?
- What is the mission of the church?
- What is the role of the church in the cosmic conflict?
- What is the remnant, and what is her mission?
- How might we distinguish between the way of the dragon and the way of the Lamb?

The Unity and Mission of the Church

"There is one body and one Spirit, just as you also were called in one hope of your calling; one Lord, one faith, one baptism, one God and Father of all who is over all and through all and in all" (Eph. 4:4–6). This one body is the body of Christ, which consists of *all* those who belong to Christ. "There is neither Jew nor Greek, there is neither slave nor free, there is neither male nor female; for you are all one in Christ Jesus. And if you belong to Christ, then you are Abraham's descendants, heirs according to promise" (Gal. 3:28–29).

No organization, then, can claim to *comprehensively* be the body of Christ. Some think of church unity in terms of organizational structure or clergy leadership, but in Scripture, the unity of Christians as the body of Christ is not found in externals, but *in* Christ, *by* the Holy Spirit. As Paul puts it, "just as the body is one and yet has many parts, and all the parts of the body, though they are many, are one body, so also is Christ. For by one Spirit we were all baptized into one body, whether Jews or Greeks, whether slaves or free, and we were all made to drink of one Spirit" (1 Cor. 12:12–13).

Yet, not all those who claim Christ's name actually follow Christ, whatever their church membership status, and some institutions claim the name "Christian" but operate in ways that are anything but Christian. There is one church, but that church is not identified as or limited to a single denomination or fellowship, it consists of *everyone* who belongs to Christ all over the world—from every tribe, tongue, nation, and people. The universal church is one *in Christ* and is not limited to one denomination, but the "Lord knows those who are His" (2 Tim. 2:19; cf. John 10:14).[1]

The members of Christ's body need one another. One is not less than another, just as a hand is not less than a foot, nor an eye less than an ear, or vice versa. "If the whole body were an eye, where would the hearing be? If the whole body were hearing, where would the sense of smell be? But now God has arranged the parts, each one of them in the body, just as He desired. If they were all one part, where would the body be? But now there are many parts, but one body. And the eye cannot say to the hand, 'I have no need of you'; or again, the head to the feet, 'I have no need of you.' On the contrary, it is much truer that the parts of the body which seem to be weaker are necessary; and those parts of the body which we consider less honorable, on these we bestow greater honor, and our less presentable parts become much more presentable, whereas our more presentable parts have no need of it." God intends "that the parts may have the same care for one another. And if one part of the body suffers, all the parts suffer with it; if a part is honored, all the parts rejoice with it. Now you are Christ's body, and individually parts of it" (1 Cor. 12:17-27; cf. Rom. 12:4-5).

The unity of the church, then, is our unity in Christ as His body. All who belong to Christ are unified in Christ. This unity does not require uniformity and crosses the boundaries that often separate humans, including *everyone* who belongs to Christ by faith. When the church arose in the midst of the Roman Empire, this was very striking indeed because communities that transcended ethnic boundaries were typically unheard of in those days.[2]

> **All who belong to Christ are unified in Christ.**

As Christ's body, the mission of the church is to serve as Christ's hands and feet, making disciples of all nations. Followers of Christ are called to spread God's love in both word and in deed, carrying out the Great Commission given by Jesus: "Go, therefore, and make disciples of all the nations, baptizing them in the name of the Father and the Son and the Holy Spirit, teaching them to follow all that I commanded you; and behold, I am with you always, to the end of the age" (Matt. 28:19-20).

Additionally, Adventists seek to carry out a worldwide special mission of preparing the world for Christ's soon return, proclaiming the everlasting gospel of the Three Angels' Messages found in Revelation 14:6-12:

And I saw another angel flying in midheaven with an eternal gospel to preach to those who live on the earth, and to every nation, tribe, language, and people; and he said with a loud voice, "Fear God and give Him glory, because the hour of His judgment has come; worship Him who made the heaven and the earth, and sea and springs of waters."

And another angel, a second one, followed, saying, "Fallen, fallen is Babylon the great, she who has made all the nations drink of the wine of the passion of her sexual immorality." Then another angel, a third one, followed them, saying with a loud voice, "If anyone worships the beast and his image, and receives a mark on his forehead or on his hand, he also will drink of the wine of the wrath of God, which is mixed in full strength in the cup of His anger; and he will be tormented with fire and brimstone in the presence of the holy angels and in the presence of the Lamb. And the smoke of their torment ascends forever and ever; they have no rest day and night, those who worship the beast and his image, and whoever receives the mark of his name." Here is the perseverance of the saints who keep the commandments of God and their faith in Jesus.

To better understand these messages, we need to consider the context—the dramatic visions of cosmic conflict depicted in Revelation 12–14, which stand at the heart of Revelation. These portray the cosmic conflict relative to (among other things) the enemy's oppression and persecution of God's people in his attempt to take Christ's place and usurp worship.

Competing Theories in Christian Theology: The Mission of the Church

Christian history manifests various approaches to the mission of the church. Here, I briefly focus on two opposing trajectories.

The first views the mission of the church as a quest to establish God's kingdom *on earth*, by force if necessary; mission as imperialist conquest. Following this approach, many atrocities have been committed in the name of Christ.

In the early centuries of Christianity, the Roman Empire persecuted and killed many for their faith. In AD 312, however, the Roman emperor Constantine announced he had converted to Christianity. Constantine proceeded to use the cross as a war banner, advancing a militant, imperial form of Christianity, very different from the way of Christ. And Constantine set forth an edict promoting severe persecution against those deemed heretics by church leaders.[3]

Later, in AD 380, the reigning Roman emperors issued the Edict of Thessalonica, making the Catholicism of Nicene Christians the state religion of the Roman Empire, decreeing further persecution against those deemed heretics, with executions of Christians deemed heretics in the years that followed.[4]

Making a case for just war theory, the extremely influential theologian Augustine (AD 354–430) approved of war to preserve the unity of the church. He taught that error has no rights and justified torture and other "great violence" against those deemed heretics, teaching that those condemned by the church should be punished by the empire.[5] Some have thus thought of Augustine as a forerunner of the Inquisition, the office set up in the Roman Catholic Church centuries later to root out and punish heresy.

Many medieval theologians over the next thousand years and beyond agreed that those deemed heretics should be persecuted, with some even sanctioning the death penalty. In the mid-fifth century, Pope Leo I (c. 400–461) justified the earlier imperial execution of Priscillian, the bishop of Ávila who was deemed a heretic after other bishops brought allegations against him and he was executed by the state in AD 385, writing that "this rigourous treatment [execution by the sword of Priscillian and five of his companions] was for long a help to the church's law of gentleness which, although it relies upon the priestly judgment, and shuns blood-stained vengeances, yet is assisted by the stern decrees of Christian princes at times when men, who dread bodily punishment, have recourse to merely spiritual correction."[6]

Centuries later, the exceedingly influential Roman Catholic theologian Thomas Aquinas (1225–1274) advocated the death penalty for obstinate heretics, to be excommunicated by the church and turned over to the state to be killed, *some being burned alive*.[7] The death penalty for those deemed heretics had been formalized in the Canon Law of the Roman Catholic Church during the Lateran Councils of 1179 and 1215). In 1229, Pope Gregory IX declared it the duty of every Catholic to persecute heretics. And Emperor Frederick II (1194-1250) made the execution of heretics part of the civil and criminal code of the Holy Roman Empire.

Much persecution ensued. For example, the Waldensians were excommunicated as heretics in 1184 and severely persecuted for centuries. Many Waldensians and others were burned at the stake or worse. Movements to reform the church, based on the teachings of people like John Wycliffe (1328-1384) in England and Jan Hus (1370-1415) in Bohemia, were condemned as heretical, with Hus and many others burned at the stake.[8]

Sadly, Christian history is riddled with such persecution as well as imperialist oppression and war; including religious wars among Christians with the power of the state often wielded to enforce particular forms of Christianity. The Roman Catholic Church waged many religious wars; against Muslims (and Jews) in the Crusades in the late eleventh century and beyond, and against Protestants who departed from the Roman Catholic Church in the sixteenth century and beyond.

Further, in 1452 Pope Nicholas V issued the papal bull (decree) *Dum Diversas*, which authorized the king of Portugal to conquer and force any "Saracens [Muslims] and pagans and any other unbelievers" into perpetual slavery. Adding to this, in 1455, Pope Nicholas V issued another papal bull, *Romanus Pontifex*, which granted Portugal dominion over lands in Africa, extending the permission to conquer and force indigenous peoples into slavery.[9]

These were major parts of the Doctrine of Discovery, found in a series of papal bulls from the twelfth century onward that claimed territorial sovereignty for Roman Catholic monarchs over lands they claimed to "discover." This undergirded the global slave trade of the fifteenth and sixteenth centuries and the Age of Imperialism, effectively granting Roman Catholic European nations dominion over allegedly "discovered" lands, licensing exploitative colonialism and the enslavement of peoples in Africa, the New World, and elsewhere.[10]

Many Christians stood against the slave trade and led movements that resulted in abolishing slavery (e.g., William Wilberforce). Adventists and many others were staunch abolitionists, but others who claimed to be Christians—many Catholics and Protestants alike—promoted and participated in the great evil of slavery.

Further, while some Protestants refused to engage in warfare, many other Protestants engaged in religious wars against Catholicism and also persecuted other Protestants. For example, Anabaptists were persecuted by Catholics, Lutherans, and Calvinists. Tragically, even as early Christians were victims of persecution by the empire of Rome (the fourth beast of Daniel 7), later "Christians" followed in Rome's beastly footsteps, persecuting and attempting to force others to follow their religion, often on pain of death.

In stark contrast to this trajectory of conquest, persecution, and oppression, the second trajectory views the mission of the church as *peacefully* making disciples for God's kingdom of unselfish love, which is not of this (present) world (John 18:36)—mission as peaceful disciple-making, inviting rather than trying to force others, for neither love nor allegiance nor genuine worship can be coerced.[11] On this view, consistent with Adventism and many other forms of Christianity (e.g., the Anabaptist tradition), Christianity is not to be advanced by force of arms but is to follow the way of the Lamb—the Prince of Peace, seeking the ideals of nonviolence (turning swords into plowshares, Isa. 2:4) and justice (Isa. 1:17). Adventism itself has not been without its flaws and failures in these and other regards, but Adventists and other Christians who follow this second trajectory strongly advocate for religious freedom and the separation of church and state, viewing attempts to force people to worship or to worship in particular ways as directly opposed to the way of Christ.

The Serpent vs. the Woman: The Church in the Wilderness

She fell prey to the serpent's deception. She believed his lies that slandered God's character, portraying God's commands as motivated by selfishness and desire to oppress rather than their true motivation of unselfish love and justice. This confrontation between the serpent and the woman resulted in the woman (Eve) being driven from her safe and secure Eden home into a relative wilderness that would now be filled with danger, hardship, and death.

But there was hope. God foretold a future confrontation between the serpent and the Seed of the woman: "I will put enmity between you and the woman, and between your seed and her Seed; He shall bruise your head, and you shall bruise His heel" (Gen. 3:15, NKJV).

Fast forward to Revelation, which depicts another confrontation between the serpent and a woman:

> A great sign appeared in heaven: a woman clothed with the sun, and the moon under her feet, and on her head a crown of twelve stars; and she was pregnant and she cried out, being in labor and in pain to give birth. Then another sign appeared in heaven: and behold, a great red dragon having seven heads and ten horns, and on his heads were seven crowns. And his tail swept away a third of the stars of heaven and hurled them to the earth. And the dragon stood before the woman who was about to give birth, so that when she gave birth he might devour her Child. And she gave birth to a Son, a male, who is going to rule all the nations with a rod of iron; and her Child was caught up to God and to His throne. Then the woman fled into the wilderness where she had a place prepared by God, so that there she would be nourished for 1,260 days (Rev. 12:1–6).[12]

Who is this dragon? This same chapter later identifies him as "the serpent of old who is called the devil and Satan, who deceives the whole world," who made "war in heaven" against "Michael and his angels" and "was thrown down" with "his angels" (Rev. 12:7–9). The phrase "serpent of old" refers to the serpent who tempted Eve in the garden. In Revelation 12:1–6, this serpent persecutes another woman.

Who, then, is this woman? This scene is apocalyptic imagery, which is highly symbolic. And the book of Revelation frequently draws on imagery from the rest of the Bible. Elsewhere, Scripture frequently depicts God's covenant people as a woman (e.g., Jer. 6:2) and Christ's church as the bride of Christ (see, e.g., 2 Cor. 11:2; Eph. 5). Such imagery is consistent with the frequent figurative portrayal of God's people as His wife (e.g., Isa. 54:5-6). The pattern throughout Scripture thus indicates that the woman in Revelation 12 represents the people of God throughout the ages. This conclusion is supported by the mention of twelve stars on her crown. Scripture often associates the number twelve with God's elect people (e.g., the twelve tribes of Israel and twelve apostles of Christ).

> *The pattern throughout Scripture indicates that the woman in Revelation 12 represents the people of God throughout the ages.*

This "woman" gave birth to a child whom the dragon sought to devour. The child refers to Jesus, whom Herod sought to kill as a baby (Matt. 2:16) and who was "to rule all the nations with a rod of iron" and "was caught up to God and to His throne" (Rev. 12:5). The woman cannot be equated with Jesus's mother Mary specifically, however, for (as we will see below) the woman's further activities span far longer than the lifespan of any mere human. As Adventists understand it, the woman represents the people of God leading up to the birth of Christ (the nation of Israel through whom Christ was born as the covenantal Son of David) *and* the people of God after Christ's ascension (the universal church of all who belong to Christ over the ages).

Sometime after her child was "caught up to God" (the ascension of Christ, Rev. 12:5), the woman fled from the dragon into the wilderness to be nourished there for 1,260 days (Rev. 12:6).[13] One thousand two hundred sixty literal days would only be three and a half years. But, like the prophecies we've seen in Daniel, these are not literal days but prophetic days—part of symbolic, apocalyptic imagery of Revelation.[14]

This same time period, referred to as "a time, times, and half a time," appears later in the same chapter, which says the dragon "persecuted the woman," but "two wings of the great eagle were given to the woman, so that she could fly into the wilderness to her place, where she was nourished for a time, times, and half a time, away from the presence of the serpent" (Rev. 12:13-14). This same time period also appears in Daniel, during which the little horn would persecute God's people (Dan. 7:25; 12:7; cf. Rev. 13:5). Specifically, Daniel 7:25 prophesied that the little horn "will speak against the Most High and wear down the saints of the Highest One, and he will intend to make alterations in times and in law; and they will be handed over to him for a time, times, and half a time."

This same time period appears numerous other times in Revelation, referred to as forty-two months (Rev. 11:2; 13:5), 1,260 days (Rev. 11:3; 12:6), and "a time, times, and half a time" (Rev. 12:14). Numerically, these all add up to the *same* time period. Forty-two months, calculated with thirty days in a month (according to the lunar calendar), amounts to 1,260 days (42 x 30 = 1,260). Likewise, understanding "time" to refer to a year (as Nebuchadnezzar was described as becoming like a beast for "seven times," or years, Dan. 4:16, NKJV), a time, times (two times), and half a time amount to three and a half *prophetic* years. Counting 360 days in the (lunar) year, three and a half years amounts to 1,260 prophetic days.

In keeping with the historicist interpretation of prophecy affirmed by the Protestant Reformers and many others (explained in chapter 19), Adventists understand these 1,260 prophetic "days" as 1,260 literal years, typically understanding the time period as referring to the persecution of the church in the wilderness by the state-sponsored imperialist church from medieval times through the Enlightenment.[15]

During this time, the woman fled into a wilderness where she received help against the persecution of the dragon (Rev. 12:14–16). "And the dragon was enraged with the woman, and he went to make war with the rest of her offspring, who keep the commandments of God and have the testimony of Jesus Christ" (Rev. 12:17, NKJV).

Notice the dragon makes war with "the rest of her offspring" or "the remnant of her seed" (KJV), reminiscent of the language of Genesis 3:15 regarding the conflict between the serpent's "seed" and that of the woman. This second act of the serpent versus the woman and her seed thus comes full circle, with Revelation 12 effectively picking up where Genesis 3:15 left off.

This "remnant of her seed" refers to the descendants of the woman who remain faithful—the faithful remnant of God's people. Just as the devil persecuted God's people (Israel) throughout the Old Testament (e.g., through the influence of demons masquerading as the ruler "gods" of the nations, see chapter 9), this prophecy reveals that, from Christ's ascension onward, the devil persecutes the New Testament people of God—the church, finally going off to persecute the faithful "remnant of her seed," those who "keep the commandments of God, and have the testimony of Jesus Christ" (Rev. 12:17, KJV).

Before Christ's return, then, there is a remnant of the universal church, with two identifying marks, they: keep the commandments of God and have the testimony of Jesus. As Ranko Stefanovic puts it: "The text (Rev. 12:17) indicates that at the end of time, as the whole world renders their allegiance and loyalty to Satan and his allies (Rev. 13:4, 8), God will have a people who will be unreservedly faithful and obedient to him in keeping his commandments and holding to the testimony of Jesus given through the gift of prophecy (cf. Rev. 19:10)."[16]

The story of the dragon's war against the woman and her seed continues in Revelation 13.

The Way of the Dragon: Empires and Imperialist "Christianity" (Rev. 13)

He'd built a glorious and exceedingly powerful empire that he wanted to believe would never pass away. The dream of the statue of gold, silver, bronze, iron, and iron mixed with clay had greatly troubled him, but the interpretation might have troubled him even more. According to the dream, Nebuchadnezzar's empire of Babylon was represented by the statue's head of gold, but it would be replaced by a succession of empires that would finally end with the establishment of a kingdom that is not of this world—the kingdom of the Prince of Peace that will never end (Dan. 2).

Years later, King Nebuchadnezzar defiantly built a statue of pure gold from top to bottom, as if his kingdom would never end—despite the prophecy. He commanded that everyone bow down to it and worship, with the death penalty for anyone who refused.

Three young Hebrew men refused. Nebuchadnezzar was enraged. When they were brought to him, he said, "Is it true, Shadrach, Meshach, and Abednego, that you do not serve my gods, nor worship the golden statue that I have set up? Now if you are ready... to fall down and worship the statue that I have made, very well. But if you do not worship, you will immediately be thrown into the midst of a furnace of blazing fire; and what god is there who can rescue you from my hands?" (Dan. 3:13–15).

Despite Nebuchadnezzar's threats, the three Hebrews stood firm to God's commandments to worship only the one true God (e.g., Exod. 20:3–5). They replied, "If it be so, our God whom we serve is able to rescue us from the furnace of blazing fire; and He will rescue us from your hand, O king. But even if He does not, let it be known to you, O king, that we are not going to serve your gods nor worship the golden statue that you have set up" (Dan. 3:17–18).

What faithfulness! Whether God delivers us or not, we will not serve your gods or worship your golden image.

They were tied and thrown into the fiery furnace.

But miraculously, they were unharmed, "the fire had no effect on the bodies of these men, nor was the hair of their heads singed, nor were their trousers damaged, nor had even the smell of fire touched them" (Dan. 3:27).

Although only three men were thrown in, Nebuchadnezzar saw "four men untied and walking about in the middle of the fire unharmed" and declared, "the appearance of the fourth is like a son of the gods!" (Dan. 3:25). This fourth person was the pre-incarnate Christ, who was with them and preserved them in the midst of the fire.

This imagery of forced worship by an imperial power, directly contrary to God's commandments, appears again in Revelation 13, mirroring the story of Daniel 3 and intentionally building on prophetic imagery throughout Daniel. Just as the prophecies of Daniel build on one another (Daniel 7 builds on Daniel 2, Daniel 8 builds on Daniel 7, and so on), many prophecies of Revelation build on and explicitly parallel the prophecies of Daniel.

Specifically, in Revelation 13, John sees a vision of a beast from the sea which receives authority from the dragon, makes war with God's people, and receives worship from "every tribe, people, language, and nation" and a second beast from the earth who "makes the earth and those who live on it worship the first beast" (Rev. 13:7–8, 12).

Like the dragon, the sea beast had ten horns and seven heads. But, instead of having seven crowns on his *heads* as the dragon did, this beast had ten crowns on his *horns*, signaling that this prophetic vision would highlight the time of the horns. Further, this sea beast "was like a leopard, and his feet were like those of a bear, and his mouth like the mouth of a lion. And the dragon gave him his power and his throne, and great authority" (Rev. 13:2).

Where have we heard about a leopard, bear, lion, and beast before? In the vision of Daniel 7. There, the four successive empires of Babylon,

Medo-Persia, Greece, and Rome—all of whom oppressed the people of Israel—are represented by four beasts: a lion, bear, four-headed leopard, and dreadful, terrifying, and extremely strong beast with ten horns. If you're counting, that is seven heads and ten horns in all, just like the sea beast of Revelation 13. This sea beast has the characteristics of all four beasts of Daniel 7, put together into one composite beast.[17]

That is no coincidence. The sea beast of Revelation 13 is a composite of the oppressive powers prophesied of in Daniel 2, Daniel 7, and beyond. As we've seen, Daniel 7 identified beastly empires that oppressed God's people throughout the ages. Revelation 13 mirrors this in this composite sea beast, highlighting that the successive oppressive empires introduced in Daniel 7 were agents of the dragon all along. In the forms of various empires, this sea beast persecuted God's people (Israel) throughout the Old Testament and continues to persecute the New Testament people of God after Christ's ascension, wielding power and great authority given him by the dragon (Rev. 13:2).[18]

During the time of the nation of Israel, this sea beast took the form of successive empires that persecuted and oppressed God's people of Israel over the centuries. Sometime after Christ's ascension, this sea beast takes the form of the little horn that arose from the fourth beast of Rome in Daniel 7, who oppresses God's people, attempts to change God's times and laws, take Christ's place, and assault God's sanctuary in Daniel 7 and 8 (e.g., 7:21–22, 25; 8:11–14, 23–25). The essence of these powers in Daniel 7 and 8 and Revelation 13 is theological and religious apostasy which requires and guides the use of force (persecution) and is operative even when the use of force is not present.

Recognizing that this sea beast is a composite of the successive oppressive powers represented in Daniel 7, we can see that the ten horns of this sea beast correspond to the ten horns of the fourth beast of Daniel 7, the empire of Rome. As we've seen (in chapter 16), the ten horns on the head of this beast represented "kingdoms" that arose in the aftermath of the Roman empire—the time of the divided Roman empire and beyond (like the ten toes of the Daniel 2 statue; see illustration on page 557). The time of the horns, highlighted by the crowns on the horns in Revelation 13, can thus be identified as the aftermath of the Roman empire and beyond.

This matches the depiction of the woman identified as a harlot (imagery of a counterfeit people of God engaged in spiritual adultery) who rides on a beast with seven heads in Revelation 17–18.

Along with the dragon, this sea beast usurps the worship due to the one true God alone. Specifically, in the vision, John "saw one of his heads as if it had been fatally wounded, and his fatal wound was healed. And the whole earth was amazed and followed after the beast; they worshiped the dragon because he gave his authority to the beast; and they worshiped the beast, saying, 'Who is like the beast, and who is able to wage war with him?' A mouth was given to him speaking arrogant words and blasphemies, and authority to act for forty-two months was given to him. And he opened his mouth in blasphemies against God, to blaspheme His name and His tabernacle, that is, those who dwell in heaven. It was also given to him to make war with the saints and to overcome them, and authority was given to him over every tribe, people, language, and nation. All who live on the earth will worship him, everyone whose name has not been written since the foundation of the world in the book of life of the Lamb who has been slaughtered" (Rev. 13:3–8).

First, notice that this sea beast sets forth a counterfeit resurrection, receives worship alongside the dragon who gave him authority, and continues its work for forty-two months (amounting to three and a half *prophetic* years). All this (and more) counterfeits Christ, who actually rose from the dead, receives worship alongside the Father and received authority during His earthly ministry from the Father, and whose earthly ministry (from baptism to ascension) lasted three and a half years.[19]

This sea beast, then, is a counterfeit Christ and puts itself in Christ's place. It is thus anti-Christ ("*anti*" in the Greek New Testament typically means "instead of"). This anti-Christ seeks to take Christ's place and (as we will see) pretends to follow the way of the Lamb, while actually following the way of the dragon. Among other things, this sea beast seeks to receive the worship due to God alone and attempts to force by violence those who resist.

This beast is given authority to blaspheme God and His temple and make war with God's people for forty-two months. This time period is one of many characteristics revealing that, in the time of the horns (the aftermath of the Roman Empire) and beyond, this sea beast corresponds to the little horn of Daniel 7 and Daniel 8. Recall that in the prophecy of Daniel 7, from the head of the fourth beast (Rome), the little horn arose, which is depicted in these prophecies as an (imperialist) religious power (e.g., blaspheming God, boasting, and seeking to receive worship).

This little horn is given authority and wages war against God's people for the same time period that the sea beast is given authority and oppresses God's people ("a time, times, and half a time," which we saw earlier is the same time period as forty-two months (Dan. 7:25-26; Rev. 13:5; see chart below). Just like the sea beast in the time of the horns, this little horn "was waging war with the saints and overpowering them" (Dan. 7:21; cf. Rev. 13:7).

THE SEA BEAST OF REVELATION 13 AND THE LITTLE HORN OF DANIEL 7
*all quotations are from the NKJV

The sea beast of Revelation 13 had a "mouth speaking great things and blasphemies" (Rev. 13:5).	The little horn of Daniel 7 also had a "mouth speaking pompous words" (Dan. 7:8).
Satan's powers persecute God's people for 1,260 days, or "a time and times and half a time," or 42 months (Rev. 12:6, 14; 13:5).	"The saints" were "given into" the "hand" of the little horn for "a time and times and half a time" (Dan. 7:25).
"It was granted to" the sea beast "to make war with the saints and to overcome them" (Rev. 13:7).	The little horn was "making war against the saints, and prevailing against them" (Dan. 7:21).

This same little horn was predicted to "speak out against the Most High and wear down the saints of the Highest One, and he will intend to make alterations in times and in law; and they will be given into his hand for a time, times, and half a time" (Dan. 7:25). *Here, again, we see that God's law is at issue.* In Daniel 8, this same little horn is said to have "even exalted himself as high as the Prince of the host" (i.e., Christ) such that "the place of His sanctuary was cast down" and "he cast truth down to the ground. He did all this and prospered" (Dan. 8:11-12, NKJV). Likewise, "He will even oppose the Prince of princes" (Dan. 8:25).

All this describes an (imperialist) religious *and political* power that performs the same blasphemous and oppressive actions and wages war against God's people for the same time period as the sea beast of Revelation 13.

The little horn of Daniel and the sea beast of Revelation 13 (during the time of the horns and beyond) thus represent the same imperial religious power, which (among other things) puts itself in Christ's place and sets forth a counterfeit theological system, usurps the worship that belongs to God alone, blasphemes God and His temple, and seeks to change God's times and laws.

Who, then, does this sea beast represent? Adventists have consistently identified both the little horn of Daniel and Revelation's sea beast (during the time of the little horn's authority and beyond) as representative of the "medieval and post-medieval ecclesiastical authoritarian rule"[20] of the Roman Catholic Church and theological system. For our purposes here, I will speak of this power and those complicit with it (including those represented by the earth beast) by using the label "imperialist Christianity," which refers not merely to the use of force by such powers, but to the even more crucial underlying system of theological and religious apostasy that motivates the use of force and is present even when such powers do not use force to impose their religious system.

Put broadly, imperialist Christianity refers to systems that self-identify as "Christian" or that promote Christian ideals but advance a system of theological and religious apostasy and work to advance their ends by exercising power with the goal of dominance over others. Imperialist Christianity includes those churches that advance a counterfeit theological agenda and, when afforded the opportunity, are willing to force others to worship as they do and otherwise serve their goals relative to increasing wealth and power and blasphemously do so in Christ's name. In these respects, then, imperialist *Christianity* is a misnomer, for relative to such acts, it is actually *anti*-Christ, pretending to follow Christ but actually working according to the way of the dragon (e.g., forcing allegiance) that is directly opposite to the way of the Lamb.[21]

A primary exemplar of imperialist "Christianity" is medieval Christendom, which set forth a system of theological and religious apostasy wherein Christianity was viewed and promoted by violence as the heir of the Roman Empire (i.e., the so-called Holy Roman Empire) and styled itself as a distinctly Greco-Roman form of Christianity.

However, while specific oppressive powers (such as medieval and post-medieval Christendom) can be identified as greater or lesser iterations of imperialist Christianity, imperialist Christianity, as a general descriptor, is not limited to a single church or church organization alone. Tragically, the spirit of imperialist Christianity has manifested itself in many different organizations and in many different forms—even those organizations that officially oppose the spirit of imperialist Christianity are susceptible to sometimes acting in beastly ways in accordance with it. The dragon works and will work through whatever channels are available to him. From ancient times until today, he has been especially interested in corrupting "Christian" institutions to serve his anti-Christ ends.

> *The dragon works and will work through whatever channels are available to him.*

For example, in the antebellum South of the United States (and beyond), imperialist Christianity was at work in slaveholders who identified as Christians and even claimed that Christianity supported their reprehensible evils. These and many others throughout the world had the audacity to claim (and thus profane) the name of Christ even as they bought and sold and oppressed and abused human beings made in the image of God, thus blaspheming the name of Christ, egregiously sinning against God and human nature. In this regard, Frederick Douglass (who had experienced the evils of being enslaved for many years) wrote, "between the Christianity of this land, and the Christianity of Christ, I recognize the widest possible difference—so wide, that to receive the one as good, pure, and holy, is of necessity to reject the other as bad, corrupt, and wicked. . . . I love the pure, peaceable, and impartial Christianity of Christ: I therefore hate the corrupt, slaveholding, women-whipping, cradle-plundering, partial and hypocritical Christianity of this land [of America]. Indeed, I can see no reason, but the most deceitful one, for calling the religion of this land Christianity."[22]

In these and other egregious evils, such as many wars of conquest (often under religious pretexts) and widespread colonialism the world over, imperialist Christianity received support from powerful nations of the earth, many of which themselves justified their actions and place in the world in the name of Christ.

In this regard, a second beast appears in Revelation 13, a beast John saw "coming up out of the earth," which "had two horns like a lamb, and he spoke as a dragon." This earth beast "exercises all the authority of the first beast [from the sea] in his presence. And he makes the earth and those who live on it worship the first beast, whose fatal wound was healed. He performs great signs, so that he even makes fire come down out of the sky to the earth in the presence of people" and thereby "deceives those who live on the earth" by the signs he performs. And the earth beast tells "those who live on the earth to make an image to the beast who had the wound of the sword and has come to life. And it was given to him to give breath to the image of the beast, so that the image of the beast would even speak and cause all who do not worship the image of the beast to be killed. And he causes all, the small and the great, the rich and the poor, and the free and the slaves, to be given a mark on their right hands or on their foreheads, and he decrees that no one will be able to buy or to sell, except the one who has the mark, either the name of the beast or the number of his name" (Rev. 13:11–17).

Just as the sea beast was a counterfeit of Christ (an anti-Christ), this earth beast is a counterfeit Holy Spirit. As the Holy Spirit descended on the apostles at Pentecost and performed many other miracles to spread the gospel, the earth beast brings fire from heaven and performs other signs, but in order to deceive. And, as the Holy Spirit (among other things) testifies of and glorifies Christ, the earth beast directs worship to the sea beast. Unlike the Holy Spirit, however, the earth beast *forces* people to worship the sea beast, on pain of death. Like Nebuchadnezzar set up the image and forced people to worship it in Daniel 3, the earth beast sets up an image to the sea beast and forces people to worship it. Like the sea beast, then, this earth beast pretends to follow the way of the Lamb but actually follows the way of the dragon. Having "two horns like a lamb" but speaking "as a dragon" (Rev. 13:11), the earth beast is a little dragon in sheep's clothing.

Who is this two-horned earth beast? Adventists typically believe that none fits the profile like the United States of America. People fled to America for freedom, religious and otherwise. Yet, even before America formed itself into an independent nation, civil liberty was compromised by the great sins of violence against Native Americans and slavery.[23]

And, while America has a better track record regarding religious liberty than many nations, America has sometimes engaged in imperialistic actions in the name of Christ. As Adventists understand the prophecies of Revelation 13–14, such behavior will only worsen before Christ's return. Yet, early in Adventist history, the earth beast was viewed as *already* speaking like a dragon because "it professed to uphold religious and civil liberty (the two horns [of the earth beast]), but in reality denied those privileges to religious and racial minorities."[24] In this regard, Kevin M. Burton explains, "the second Advent movement," focused on the Three Angels' Messages relative to the Sabbath and the Second Coming, was accompanied by "the abolitionist call for the immediate and total destruction of slavery and demand for equal rights for the oppressed."[25]

Still today, the self-proclaimed American ideals of liberty and justice for all remain unmet for many people in America. Alongside this, a great danger facing America and elsewhere is that of "Christian" nationalism, which directly opposes the separation of church and state (conflating the advancement of the state with the advance of Christianity) that is crucial to religious liberty and is thus a major emphasis of Adventism.[26] This is the opposite of true Christianity, the way of the Lamb who never seeks to force allegiance or worship, for the genuine allegiance and worship that matters to the Lamb is only that of love, which *cannot* be forced. The dragon who temporarily rules this world (cf. John 12:31), conversely, works through human agencies and systems to foster oppression, injustice, and false worship wherever he can.

Christian nationalism falls prey to the blasphemy of Christian empire and ignores the biblical teaching that we are sojourners here awaiting the perfect kingdom of love and justice that only God can establish such that no earthly nation could ever be the final goal of genuinely Christian identity and existence. As Christ explicitly declared, "My kingdom is not of this world" (John 18:36). Christ's kingdom cannot be advanced by the sword, and any attempt to do so is not of Christ. The cross may have been emblazoned on the shields of the armies of Christendom, but they did not follow the way of Christ when they wielded the sword to dominate, destroy, oppress, and force the allegiance of others, committing atrocities in Christ's name.

The Christ of the Bible is thus not the *false*, militant "Christ" of empire. Whereas empire (and imperialism) grasps for power and wealth, Jesus gave up everything (Phil. 2)—He cast aside the ultimate place in riches and power and position to lower Himself for us. And He calls Christians to do likewise: "If any wish to come after me, let them deny themselves and take up their cross and follow me" (Matt. 16:24, NRSVue). Imperialist Christianity is not genuinely Christian because (in this and other ways) it is not Christ-like. In Christ's kingdom of unselfish love, there is no room for oppression and injustice.[27]

> **Whereas empire (and imperialism) grasps for power and wealth, Jesus gave up everything.**

As we have seen, many evils of colonialism and the transatlantic slave trade perpetrated throughout the world were undergirded by the ecclesiastical decrees of the Doctrine of Discovery (see the earlier discussion). In this, the sea beast and earth beast united, advancing false claims of supremacy for one group of people over others, attempting to baptize such a serpentine claim under the guise of divine right.

It should be no surprise, then, that Revelation 18 condemns imperialist Christianity (referred to as "Babylon" and depicted as a woman, a counterfeit people of God, sitting on a scarlet beast with seven heads and ten horns) and its associates in terms of (among other things) trading cargo that includes "slaves, and human lives" (Rev. 18:13). Such horrendous evils are part of a broader system focused on garnishing wealth without regard for human life and justice and the things of God such that "the merchants of the earth have become rich from the excessive wealth of her luxury" (Rev. 18:3). At her downfall, however, "the merchants of the earth weep and mourn over her, because no one buys their cargo any more" (Rev. 18:11).

This woman on the beast, which Adventists believe represents an example of imperialist Christianity, is not only guilty of the great evils of religious apostasy but also sins of economic injustice and severe oppression of humans. She is thus guilty of committing and perpetuating the two greatest sins decried repeatedly by the prophets—idolatry and social injustice, which amount to breaking the two greatest commands—unselfish love for God and unselfish love for our neighbor as ourselves.

By (among other things) thinking to change God's times and laws (e.g., the Sabbath commandment, see chapter 15), putting itself in Christ's place and counterfeiting Christ's priestly ministry in the heavenly sanctuary (see chapters 16 and 17), and usurping the worship that belongs to God alone, imperialist Christianity and her associates enshrine a system of idolatry (the theological and spiritual adultery of the harlot) that is directly contrary to the greatest commandment to love God and to the first four of the Ten Commandments that correspond to it. By oppressing people in Christ's name, forcing worship and allegiance, and even fostering the enslavement of people, imperialist Christianity directly breaks the second great command—love for neighbor—which corresponds to those of the Ten Commandments that focus on interpersonal relationships (commandments 5–10 and part of 4).

As the Old Testament people of God fell into repeated and systemic idolatry (spiritual adultery) and social injustice contrary to the way of the Lamb, many individuals and institutions who have called themselves "Christian" have likewise fallen and followed the way of the dragon.

Love is the opposite of the way of the dragon. The way of the dragon is the way of selfishness and the desire to oppress. The very evil schemes the devil seeks to advance he has projected onto God in his slanderous claims against God's character at the center of the cosmic conflict. Selfish grasping for power and oppression of others is the *modus operandi* of the devil, the utter opposite of the God of Scripture, who is unselfish love, manifested in the fact that the Son lowered and humbled Himself even to the point of death, as the Lamb to be sacrificed for us.

In short, the way of the dragon is the way of selfishness that forces itself upon and oppresses others. In contrast, the way of the Lamb is the way of unselfish love and justice,

> In contrast to the way of the dragon, the way of the Lamb is the way of unselfish love and justice.

with the Lamb and all who follow Him never seeking to force allegiance but to draw people into love relationship, which *cannot* be forced.

The Way of the Lamb: The Remnant and the Three Angels' Messages (Rev. 14)

The enemy's design, from beginning to end, is to take God's place, to usurp God's rule and the worship that belongs to God alone. Worship itself is a question of allegiance at the heart of the entire cosmic conflict.

The allegiance God desires is only the allegiance of love. In contrast, the allegiance the dragon demands and attempts to enforce through beastly agents is a forced allegiance, seeking to crush anyone who resists his power.

Despite the dragon's relentless attempts to force all peoples to worship and serve him, however, faithful remnants of God's people persist in the Old Testament and New Testament, consisting of those who remain faithful to God and His law of unselfish love even in the face of hardship and persecution. The remnant in the last days described in Revelation 12:17 consists of those "who keep the commandments of God and hold to the testimony of Jesus."

In this regard, just after the vision of the two-horned earth beast, John "looked, and behold, the Lamb was standing on Mount Zion, and with Him 144,000 who had His name and the name of His Father written on their foreheads." These are the "ones who follow the Lamb wherever He goes. These have been purchased from mankind as first fruits to God and to the Lamb. And no lie was found in their mouths; they are blameless" (Rev. 14:1–5).

The Three Angels' Messages immediately follow these verses (Rev. 14:6–12). Therein, the faithful remnant of God's people is again described as those "who keep the commandments of God and their faith in Jesus" (Rev. 14:12).[28] This remnant proclaims the approach of Christ's second Advent, a message integral to the culmination of the cosmic conflict, and is faithful in spite of persecution and the threat of death for refusing to abandon God's commandments and worship the beast and his image, refusing to sacrifice love on the altar of power.

Whereas the faithful remnant have the names of the Father and the Lamb written on their foreheads (Rev. 14:1), the two-horned earth beast causes all who worship the beast and his image to receive "a mark on his forehead or on his hand" (Rev. 14:9; see also 13:16). Here, again, the two-horned beast counterfeits the Holy Spirit who seals those faithful to God on their foreheads (Eph. 4:30; Rev. 7:3; cf. 2 Cor. 1:22; Eph. 1:13). Whereas the two-horned earth beast (the counterfeit of the Holy Spirit) marks those who give allegiance to and worship the sea beast and dragon (following the unjust, oppressive ways of human empire), the true Holy Spirit seals those who belong to Christ, which in the end consist of those who resist the counterfeit trinity of the dragon and his beasts, instead giving their allegiance and worship to the one true God.[29]

At the time when the beasts enforce worship (cf. Rev. 13:15–17), the difference between those who receive the mark of the beast and those who receive the seal of God has to do with faithfulness that includes keeping God's commandments (the law of unselfish love) as followers of Christ (Rev. 14:12; cf. 12:17). At that time, then, all people will have to decide whether they will give allegiance to and worship the beast (and the dragon) or reserve allegiance for the one true God alone and worship only Him, according to His commandments.

Will they side with those who would seek to force allegiance and force worship, oppressing and killing all who stand in the way of their self-seeking dominance, or will they side with those who follow the Lamb who never forces allegiance or worship but operates according to the principles of unselfish love and perfect justice, keeping God's commandments regardless of the consequences? In short, will they follow the way of the dragon or the way of the Lamb?

Here, it is crucial to recognize that the mark of the beast is only given and received at the time of the end, relative to the decisions people make as to whose side they are on. Is their allegiance to the God who is Himself perfect unselfish love, or do they worship and give allegiance to a beastly misrepresentation and counterfeit of the one true God? While church membership and fellowship are important in many other ways, the issue here is not church membership. Adventists believe that there are true Christians in many different denominations (see, e.g., John 10:16). And, before the end, there will be those from various denominations (including Adventism) who fall away from following Christ and also others who come to follow the Lamb and reject the way of the dragon that manifests itself in imperialist Christianity and beyond. Everyone alive in those last days will have opportunity to respond to God's call to come out of Babylon and thus reject the way of the dragon; God's call to "Come out of her, my people, so that you will not participate in her sins and receive any of her plagues" (Rev. 18:4). Just before the return of Christ, then, there will be two classes: those who follow the Lamb wherever He goes (Rev. 14:4) and keep God's commandments (His law of unselfish love) and those who follow the way of the dragon.

Just as in the story of the fiery furnace in Daniel 3, here, allegiance and worship are front and center. Just as God's people have faced persecution in past ages, in the end, beastly powers will try to enforce a false system of worship shortly before Christ's return, a system set in place of and over and against God's law of unselfish love (Rev. 13–14).

The centrality of the issue of worship, which itself strikes at the heart of whether we love God, is highlighted in the first of Three Angels' Messages: "Fear God and give glory to Him, for the hour of His judgment has come; and worship Him who made heaven and earth, the sea and springs of water" (Rev. 14:7, NKJV).

Notice that this message references creation, directly alluding to the language of the Sabbath commandment of Exodus 20:11, "in six days the LORD made the heavens and the earth, the sea and everything that is in them, and He rested on the seventh day" (cf. Ps. 146:6).[30] The end-time issue of worship is thus explicitly tied to the recognition of God as the Creator, which is itself embedded in the fourth commandment—to rest and allow others to rest on the Sabbath as a memorial of creation (Exod. 20:11) and liberation (Deut. 5), which imperialist Christianity (Babylon and her minions) opposes.[31] True worship of the one true God includes freely given obedience motivated by love, manifested in the remnant "who keep the commandments of God and the faith of Jesus" (Rev. 14:12, NKJV).

> *True worship of the one true God includes freely given obedience motivated by love.*

Here and elsewhere, the book of Revelation contrasts the true worship of God with the system of false worship the dragon sets up as a counterfeit, administered by the sea beast and eventually enforced by the two-horned earth beast. As part of this grand end-time counterfeit, false christs and false prophets will arise, deceiving many (Matt. 24:24–27).

The counterfeits will be extremely convincing. Perhaps, a false christ will offer miracles, the healing of a severely ill loved one perhaps, and many will desperately want to believe him as the voices around will likely ask: "What are you going to believe, some ancient book or that which you see with your own eyes?" The only safety against such strong delusions will be found in a personal love relationship with God that clings to the way of the Lamb, adhering to His Scripture as the rule of faith and practice, despite supernatural manifestations around us (2 Thess. 2:1–15). In this regard, those who follow the Lamb should be wary of groundless conspiracy theories, testing everything by Scripture. While the world marvels, follows the beast, and worships the dragon (Rev. 13:3–4), the remnant who love Christ will "follow the Lamb wherever He goes" and "keep the commandments of God and the faith of Jesus" (Rev. 14:4, 12, NKJV).

Those who follow the Lamb will be those who follow the way of the Lamb, the way of unselfish love of which God's law of love is a transcript, rather than the way of the dragon—the way of selfish power and dominance that is antithetical to unselfish love. This way places confidence in God's promises and ability to utterly defeat and end evil, focusing on spreading the good news of the gospel of Jesus Christ encapsulated in the Three Angels' Messages, which directs our attention to God, who alone can ultimately resolve the many evils this world faces.

Conclusion: Why Does It Matter?

Power. He longed for power. He wanted to be great. He wanted control. He wanted others to serve him and his interests. He did not realize it, but he worshiped power. He sought power with all his heart because he thought it would give him control, but his desire for power was actually controlling him, motivating every step he took on a path of selfishness.

He did not think of it much. But nearly everything he did was to advance his own interests, to achieve his goals of power and prestige. Helping people, visiting people in prison, feeding and clothing the poor, standing for justice, and seeking to build better lives for fellow humans—these were all fine things, he thought. But he did not have time for such things. He was too busy building his own kingdom. Maybe someday he could donate time and money to such causes. But, first, he had to look out for number one. If he didn't, who would? It is a dog-eat-dog world, after all, as they say.

Was he a Christian? He thought so. If asked, he would profess his faith in Jesus, who he thought of as the conquering Messiah. He was drawn to the thought of the glory and splendor of Christ's eternal kingdom and the thought of being near to God's throne—so close to power, strongly attracted him. Of course, he worshiped such power; who would not, he thought?

But that was just the problem. He valued and worshiped the power, not realizing that the glory of God's kingdom is not one of sheer power but of love—the power of love that is an altogether different kind of power than that manifested in earthly empires. The "glory" of empire, which seeks to dominate others. But the "glory" of domination and oppression is no glory at all.

It is no coincidence that when Moses asks God, "show me your glory," God showed Moses His goodness. The glory of God is bound up with His goodness—His character of love, such that rather than a theology of glory that worships power, I am convinced the Bible teaches a theology of God's glory that highlights God's character of unselfish love.

God's kingdom is a kingdom of unselfish love; the opposite of coercion and domination. While God possesses all power, He freely gives power to others, even lowering Himself to the place of humans to suffer and die for us. There is no greater love than this and no greater power than this power of self-control and self-sacrifice—power of another kind, the unstoppable, unending, and non-coercive power of *unselfish* love.

Whose kingdom do you seek? Do you seek power, prestige, or other goods for yourself only? Or, do you long for and seek the kingdom of unselfish love? Maybe you do not know at the moment. But ask yourself this, which kingdom would you rather live in? For my part, I'd rather live in the kingdom of unselfish love, and I wish to live even now as one who belongs to that kingdom.

In James 2:5–6, James strongly decries injustice in society, specifically decrying the dishonoring and oppression of the poor. Then, he calls attention to the law of love for one's neighbor, saying if you fulfill this law, then "you are doing well" (James 2:8).

How are you doing in this regard? How are we doing collectively? What more can we do, and what more should we be doing in our individual lives and in our community? The concern James shows for the poor here is not isolated in Scripture but is a major theme. Indeed, the Old Testament law included many provisions for the poor, including injunctions against driving people into hopeless poverty by imposing unbearable interest rates and debt (see Exod. 22:25–27), and commands to leave some of the corners of one's field unharvested so that the needy and foreigner could freely glean from what was left over (Lev. 23:22). How might we live today in a way that follows such principles?

Again, those who follow the Lamb will be those who follow the way of the Lamb, the way of unselfish love of which God's law of love is a transcript, rather than the way of the dragon—the way of selfish power and dominance that is antithetical to unselfish love. Will you follow the Lamb or the dragon? If you would follow the Lamb, I invite you now to dedicate (or rededicate) your life to Jesus—to knowing Him personally and to spreading His gospel so that as many as possible might receive the good news and hear the Three Angels' Messages before the soon return of Christ.

Further, I invite you to pause now and read and reflect on James 2:5–6 and Matthew 24:31–46, focusing especially on the difference between the sheep and the goats, on what it looks like to *truly* follow the Lamb not only in word but also in deeds of love.

Questions for Reflection

1. What should unity in the church look like? Does unity require uniformity?
2. How does the history of persecution by Christians throughout the ages serve as a warning to us today? How can we avoid the mistakes of the past and differentiate following Christ from so much of the evil that has been done in the name of Christ?
3. What is the significance of the woman in Revelation 12? What does it mean to be a "remnant" in this context?
4. What is the relationship between the fourth commandment (the Sabbath commandment) and the Three Angels' Messages (compare Exod. 20:11 and Rev. 14:7)? Why does this matter? How do the enemy's attempts to change laws and usurp worship belonging to God alone connect to the big issues of the cosmic conflict?
5. What are the crucial differences between the way of the Lamb and the way of the dragon? In what ways can we make sure we are following the Lamb and standing against the dragon?

6. What are the Three Angels' Messages, and how are they relevant today? Why are the issues of allegiance and worship so important?
7. You can follow the way of the Lamb even now. Do you wish to denounce the way of the dragon and embody the way of the Lamb? If so, give yourself wholeheartedly, with all your allegiance, to the Lamb. Prayerfully ask God to help you to imitate Christ and His ways of peace and love and prayerfully make plans to choose the way of love, in word and in deed, spreading God's love and helping others to encounter the good news of Jesus.

For Further Reading

Adventist Perspectives:

Campbell, Michael W. and Nikolaus Satelmajer, eds. *Here We Stand: Luther, the Reformation, and Seventh-day Adventism*. Nampa, ID: Pacific Press, 2017.

Damsteegt, P. Gerard. *Foundations of the Seventh-day Adventist Message and Mission*. Berrien Springs, MI: Andrews University Press, 1977.

Dederen, Raoul. "The Church." In *Handbook of Seventh-day Adventist Theology*. Edited by Raoul Dederen. Hagerstown, MD: Review and Herald, 2000.

Doss, Gorden. *Introduction to Adventist Mission*. Silver Spring, MD: Institute of World Mission, 2018.

Doukhan, Jacques. *Secrets of Revelation: The Apocalypse through Hebrew Eyes*. Hagerstown, MD: Review and Herald, 2002.

Goldstein, Clifford. *The Remnant: Biblical Reality or Wishful Thinking?* Nampa, ID: Pacific Press, 1994.

Gulley, Norman R. *Systematic Theology: The Church and Last Things*. Berrien Springs, MI: Andrews University Press, 2016.

Hasel, Gerard F. *The Remnant: The History and Theology of the Remnant from Genesis to Isaiah*. Berrien Springs, MI: Andrews University Press, 1980.

Kiš, Miroslav M. "Christian Lifestyle and Behavior." In *Handbook of Seventh-day Adventist Theology*. Edited by Raoul Dederen. Hagerstown, MD: Review and Herald, 2000.

LaRondelle, Hans K. *The Israel of God in Prophecy: Principles of Prophetic Interpretation*. Berrien Springs, MI: Andrews University Press, 1983.

———. "The Remnant and the Three Angels' Messages." In *Handbook of Seventh-day Adventist Theology*. Edited by Raoul Dederen. Hagerstown, MD: Review and Herald, 2000.

London, Samuel G., Jr. *Seventh-day Adventists and the Civil Rights Movement*. University Press of Mississippi, 2009.

Miller, Nicholas. *500 Years of Protest and Liberty: From Martin Luther to Modern Civil Rights*. Nampa, ID: Pacific Press, 2017.

Morgan, Douglas. *Adventism and the American Republic: The Public Involvement of a Major Apocalyptic Movement*. Knoxville, TN: University of Tennessee Press, 2001.

Muñoz-Larrondo, Rubén. *A Postcolonial Reading of the Acts of the Apostles*, Studies in Biblical Literature, vol. 147. New York: Peter Lang Publishing, 2012.

Peckham, John C. "Love and Justice," *Lake Union Herald* (January 2019): 18–21.

Rock, Calvin B. *Protest and Progress: Black Seventh-day Adventist Leadership and the Push for Parity*. Berrien Springs, MI: Andrews University Press, 2018.

Rodríguez, Ángel Manuel, ed. *Toward a Theology of the Remnant: An Adventist Ecclesiological Perspective*. Studies in Adventist Ecclesiology 1. Silver Spring, MD: Biblical Research Institute, 2009.

Skinner, Jerome. "Social Justice in the Minor Prophets." Six web articles. *The Compass Magazine*. https://web.archive.org/web/20211207063818/https://thecompassmagazine.com/tag/jerome-skinner-social-justice-minor-prophets.

Stefanovic, Ranko. *Revelation of Jesus Christ: Commentary on the Book of Revelation*, 2nd ed. Berrien Springs, MI: Andrews University Press, 2009.

White, Ellen G. *The Great Controversy*. Mountain View, CA: Pacific Press, 1911.

See also the resources on the Biblical Research Institute website: https://adventistbiblicalresearch.org/materials/.

Other Christian Perspectives:

Carter, Warren. *Jesus and the Empire of God: Reading the Gospels in the Roman Empire.* Eugene, OR: Cascade, 2021.

Charles, Mark, and Soong-Chan Rah. *Unsettling Truths: The Ongoing, Dehumanizing Legacy of the Doctrine of Discovery.* Downers Grove, IL: IVP Academic, 2019.

Hoang, Bethany Hanke and Kristen Deede Johnson. *The Justice Calling: Where Passion Meets Perseverance.* Grand Rapids, MI: Brazos, 2017.

Jennings, Willie James. *Acts: A Theological Commentary on the Bible.* Louisville, KY: Westminster John Knox Press, 2017.

Westfall, Cynthia Long and Bryan R. Dyer, eds. *The Bible and Social Justice.* Eugene, OR: Pickwick, 2016.

19

THE END OF THE BEGINNING: LAST THINGS

"Let not your heart be troubled; you believe in God, believe also in Me. In My Father's house are many mansions; if it were not so, I would have told you. I go to prepare a place for you. And if I go and prepare a place for you, I will come again and receive you to Myself; that where I am, there you may be also" (John 14:1–3, NKJV).

Everything depends on Christ's promised return. We need a hero, for without one this world is hopeless. The oppression of the dragon and his beasts will not be broken by human hands (see, e.g., Dan. 8:25) but can only be overcome by the return of the King—the covenantal son of David, who is Jesus Christ the righteous.

But, the promise of Christ's second Advent raises a host of questions, discussed in the field known as eschatology, the study of last things (from the Greek term *eschatos*, which means "last"). Scripture overflows with expectancy of the return of the King and the end of corruption, suffering, and evil forevermore.

In the end, all who are in Christ will be redeemed, and "the creation itself also will be set free from its slavery to corruption into the freedom of the glory of the children of God" (Rom. 8:21). In the meantime, creation "groans and suffers" and "we ourselves, having the first fruits of the Spirit, even we ourselves groan within ourselves, waiting eagerly for our adoption as sons and daughters, the redemption of our body. For in hope we have been saved, but . . . we hope for what we do not see" and "through perseverance we wait eagerly for it" (Rom. 8:22–25).

Repeatedly, Scripture speaks of the nearness of the end. For example, Peter writes, "The end of all things is near; therefore, be of sound judgment and sober spirit for the purpose of prayer" (1 Pet. 4:7). James 5:8

adds, "be patient; strengthen your hearts, for the coming of the Lord is near" (cf. Rom. 13:12; 1 John 2:18).

Yet, if Christ's return was "near" two thousand years ago, what is taking so long? And what will Christ's return be like? What is the final destiny of the saved and of the lost? This chapter takes up these and other questions.

Advent Again: The Story of the Return of the King

They met Him. They saw Him. They even ate with Him and touched Him after He rose from the dead. To many chosen apostles, Christ "presented Himself alive after His suffering, by many convincing proofs, appearing to them over a period of forty days and speaking of things regarding the kingdom of God" (Acts 1:3).

Many hoped Christ would restore the kingdom to Israel then (Acts 1:7). But, Jesus explained, "It is not for you to know periods of time or appointed times which the Father has set by His own authority; but you will receive power when the Holy Spirit has come upon you; and you shall be My witnesses both in Jerusalem and in all Judea, and Samaria, and as far as the remotest part of the earth" (Acts 1:7–8).

Then, they saw Him ascend into heaven. "He was lifted up while they were watching, and a cloud took Him up, out of their sight" (Acts 1:9). Then, two angels said, "Men of Galilee, why do you stand looking into the sky? This Jesus, who has been taken up from you into heaven, will come in the same way as you have watched Him go into heaven" (Acts 1:11).

Roughly *two thousand* years later, we still await His return.

Despite the apparent delay, we can be confident that Christ will return because God always keeps His promises, and Christ promised, "I will come again" (John 14:3, NKJV).

Throughout Scripture, the fulfillment of God's great promises were preceded by a lengthy period of waiting.[1] Christ's first coming was promised in Eden (Gen. 3:15) and prophesied many times thereafter, but it did not take place for ages.[2] Noah warned of the flood *long* before it took place and, after entering the ark, waited another seven days (cf. Gen. 7:4) until the rain came. Abraham and Sarah waited until they were one hundred and ninety years old, respectively, for the promised son, Isaac (Gen. 21:1–7), and did not live to see the fulfillment of the promise that their descendants would be numerous "as the stars of the heavens and as the sand, which is on the seashore" (Gen. 22:17). Later, as God foretold, Abraham's descendants were enslaved in Egypt for hundreds of years, *delaying* passage into the Promised Land for centuries, until after the time of probation granted the Canaanites came to an end (Gen. 15:13–16; cf. Exod. 2:23).[3]

Later, biblical authors repeatedly questioned God regarding when promised deliverance would come, "How long, Lord?" (e.g., Ps. 74:10; 89:46; cf. 42:9). When Habakkuk cried out to God: "How long, LORD, have I called for help, and You do not hear?" (Hab. 1:2), God answered: "Write down the vision and inscribe it clearly on tablets.... For the vision is yet for the appointed time; it hurries toward the goal and it will not fail. Though it delays, wait for it; for it will certainly come, it will not delay long" (Hab. 2:2–3).

In Ezekiel's day, the people in Babylonian captivity declared, "The days are long, and every vision fails." But, God responded, "The days are approaching as well as the fulfillment of every vision.... For I the LORD will speak whatever word I speak, and it will be performed. It will no longer be delayed" (Ezek. 12:22–25; cf. 12:28). Daniel was told there would be long time periods of waiting before the prophecies he received would be fulfilled and was instructed, "as for you, go your way to the end; then you will rest and rise for your allotted portion at the end of the age" (Dan. 12:13; cf. 12:4).

Likewise, Scripture repeatedly indicates there would be an (apparent) delay before Christ's Second Coming. For example, Christ tells a parable of ten women awaiting the coming of the bridegroom. "As the bridegroom was delayed, all of them became drowsy and slept. But at midnight there was a shout, 'Look! Here is the bridegroom! Come out to meet him.'" Five of them had wisely brought flasks of oil to keep their lamps burning and were there waiting, but five had foolishly taken "no oil with them" and were off buying more oil when the bridegroom came, leaving them shut out of the wedding banquet (Matt. 25:1–10, NRSVue). Christ follows this parable of His Second Coming by warning: "Keep awake, therefore, for you know neither the day nor the hour" (Matt. 25:13, NRSVue).

Elsewhere, Paul warns people not to be deceived by claims that "the day of the Lord has come... for it will not come unless the apostasy comes first, and the man of lawlessness is revealed, the son of destruction, who opposes and exalts himself above every so-called god or object of worship, so that he takes his seat in the temple of God, displaying himself as being God" (2 Thess. 2:2–4). This "man of lawlessness" is identified as "the one whose coming is in accord with the activity of Satan, with all power and false signs and wonders, and with all the deception of wickedness" (2 Thess. 2:9–10). Understood in the context of the works of the dragon and his beastly agents against God and His law of unselfish love, this refers to a long history of the enemy wielding power before Christ's return.

Accordingly, Scripture directly foretold that many in the last days would scoff at the (apparent) "delay" of Christ's second Advent. Indeed, Peter writes, "in the last days mockers will come with their mocking, following after their own lusts, and saying, 'Where is the promise of His coming? For ever since the fathers fell asleep, all things continue just as they were from the beginning of creation'" (2 Pet. 3:3–4). Yet, Peter assures, "with the Lord one day is like a thousand years, and a thousand years like one day. The Lord is not slow about His promise, as some count slowness, but is patient toward you, not willing for any to perish, but for all to come to repentance. But the day of the Lord will come like a thief, in which the heavens will pass away with a roar and the elements will be destroyed with intense heat, and the earth and its works will be discovered" and "according to His promise we are looking for new heavens and a new earth, in which righteousness dwells" (2 Pet. 3:8–10, 13).

The prophecies themselves foretold lengthy time periods before Christ's return, such as the 1,260 years and 2,300 years foretold in Daniel. The latter prophecy alone indicates Christ's return would not take place for around two thousand years after Christ's first coming, during which the enemy would persecute God's people and oppose God's law of unselfish love.

Today, Adventists believe these time prophecies have been fulfilled such that we are living close to the final events of history foretold in prophecy. However, no mere creature knows the day nor the hour of Christ's return (Matt. 24:36). And, believers are not to set times but are instructed to prepare and "be ready, for the Son of Man is coming at an hour you do not expect" (Matt. 24:44, NRSVue; see also 25:13; 1 Thess. 5:2–6).

In this regard, Christ warned, "many will come in My name, saying,

'I am the Christ,' and they will mislead many people. And you will be hearing of wars and rumors of wars. See that you are not alarmed, for those things must take place, but that is not yet the end. For nation will rise against nation, and kingdom against kingdom, and there will be famines and earthquakes in various places. But all these things are merely the beginning of birth pains" (Matt. 24:5–8).

Christ's followers will be persecuted, many will be killed, and they "will be hated by all nations because of My name" (Matt. 24:9). Many will fall away, and "many false prophets will rise up and mislead many people. And because lawlessness is increased, most people's love will become cold. But the one who endures to the end is the one who will be saved" (Matt. 24:11–13).

Before the end finally comes, Christ foretold, "this gospel of the kingdom shall be preached in the whole world as a testimony to all the nations, and then the end will come" (Matt. 24:14). The warning of judgment and the everlasting gospel will be proclaimed to the world—the Three Angels' Messages (Rev. 14:6–12). Finally, each person will be called to make a decision for or against Christ (Rev. 22:11), to follow the way of the Lamb or the way of the dragon.

> **Each person will be called to make a decision for or against Christ, to follow the way of the Lamb or the way of the dragon.**

The Second Coming

One morning, my then seven-year-old son told me: "I wish we could be in heaven now. When Jesus said, 'I am coming quickly,' this is not what I expected!"

Christ is coming back. The King will return. We do not know when, but we can be sure He will return because Christ always keeps His promises (John 14:1–3). Yet, what will the manner of His coming be?

Competing Theories in Christian Theology: The Second Advent

Christians hold differing views regarding the nature and timing of Christ's coming.

Some say Christ has already returned in some spiritual or mystical way, and eschatological passages in Scripture refer to the impact of

Christ's first coming and ministry, not to any future Second Coming (realized eschatology).

Others believe *all* promises about Christ's kingdom are predicted to be fulfilled in the future after Christ's resurrection (futuristic eschatology). One form of this (consistent eschatology) interprets Christ's references to the imminence of the coming kingdom as claims that it would come in the very near future after Christ's resurrection, but this (of course) did not happen.

Instead of this, many believe the kingdom is not yet here in fullness, but God's last-day kingdom began with Christ's first coming such that Christ's earthly life, death, and resurrection *inaugurated* God's last-day kingdom on earth (inaugurated eschatology). Some aspects of the kingdom are *already* in place, while others are *not yet* (the "already/not yet" motif).

Many Christians recognize that, in some significant senses, Christ's first Advent established Christ's kingdom. Yet, there are also many significant respects in which Christ's kingdom has not yet been established in full. From an Adventist perspective, this complements what we have seen regarding the two stages wherein Christ first legally defeated the allegations of the devil at the cross and will finally eradicate the devil's kingdom and destroy the devil and his minions.

Christians also hold various views regarding the manner of Christ's return. While some claim it already occurred spiritually or mystically, many affirm it will be a literal, physical return. Some of these, however, maintain Christ will come in secret and take the redeemed away, leaving the rest behind for another phase of history (the secret rapture view of dispensationalist eschatology). Many others (including Adventists), however, affirm that Christ's Second Coming will be literal and physical as well as visible and audible—not secret, but witnessed worldwide.

Behind specific interpretations of eschatology stand competing interpretive approaches to apocalyptic prophecies, the four most prominent of which are historicism, preterism, futurism, and idealism.[4]

Historicism maintains that apocalyptic prophecies are fulfilled in the course of history, from Bible times to the end.[5] While not as prominent today, this approach was very prominent in the early centuries of Christianity and the Reformation.[6] Historicism believes the prophecies of Daniel and Revelation are fulfilled during the time period that extends from the time when the prophecies were given (or shortly thereafter) to the final establishment of Christ's kingdom. From our perspective, then, some prophecies (or parts thereof) were fulfilled during the time of the respective prophets and beyond, while others refer to what is still future.

Preterism maintains that some (partial preterism) or all (full preterism) apocalyptic prophecies refer to events and concerns contemporary to the prophet who delivered them or relatively soon afterward. From our perspective, such prophesied events/concerns are in the past. The preterist approach was developed during the Counter-Reformation to counter the historicist interpretation of many Protestant Reformers by a Spanish Jesuit theologian named Luis de Alcázar (1554–1613), who argued the prophecies of Revelation (with the exception of the last three chapters) were fulfilled during the first six centuries of Christian history.[7]

Futurism maintains that apocalyptic prophecies refer not primarily to the times in which they were written but to future events (often those just prior to the Second Coming). The futurist approach is often associated with the Spanish Jesuit theologian named Francisco Ribera (1537–1591), who believed the introductory chapters of Revelation referred to ancient Rome, while the rest of the book refers to a literal three-and-a-half-year period in the last days.

Idealism, instead, interprets apocalyptic prophecies as symbolic such that they do not refer to literal, historical events but to themes. This is sometimes called the spiritual approach or allegorical approach.

Historically, Adventist theology has followed the historicist approach, believing this approach flows from the way apocalyptic prophecies such as those in Daniel and Revelation are introduced and interpreted in Scripture itself. For example, as Adventists typically understand it, historicism matches the interpretations given to Daniel by divine revelation. For instance, according to the interpretation given to Daniel (see Dan. 2:36–45), the parts of the statue in Nebuchadnezzar's dream referred to four kingdoms in history—the first being Nebuchadnezzar's kingdom of Babylon, then three kingdoms that followed one after the other, a divided kingdom, and finally God's eternal kingdom. The prophecy conveyed in the dream, then, begins with the time it was given and continues on to the final events of history. Building on Daniel 2, the vision of Daniel 7 follows the same pattern, with four beasts corresponding to the four parts of the statue, beginning from the time the prophecy was given (the first beast corresponding to Babylon) and extending to the end times.

The Manner of Christ's Return

"Behold, He is coming with the clouds, and every eye will see Him, even those who pierced Him; and all the tribes of the earth will mourn over Him. So it is to be. Amen" (Rev. 1:7). This and other biblical passages indicate that Christ's second Advent will be far from secret—*every* eye will see Him.

In this regard, Jesus warned, "false christs and false prophets will arise and will provide great signs and wonders, so as to mislead, if possible, even the elect. Behold, I have told you in advance. So if they say to you, 'Behold, He is in the wilderness,' do not go out; or, 'Behold, He is in the inner rooms,' do not believe them. For just as the lightning comes from the east and flashes as far as the west, so will the coming of the Son of Man be" (Matt. 24:24–27; cf. Luke 17:23–24; 2 Cor. 11:4).

Not only will Christ's coming be visible to *"every eye,"* but it will also be audible. "For the Lord Himself will descend from heaven with a shout, with the voice of the archangel and with the trumpet of God, and the dead in Christ will rise first. Then we who are alive, who remain, will be caught up together with them in the clouds to meet the Lord in the air, and so we will always be with the Lord" (1 Thess. 4:16–17).

These and other instances depict Christ's return as literal, physical, audible, and visible.[8] Thus, after Christ's ascension, two angels told Christ's followers, "This Jesus, who has been taken up from you into heaven, will come in the same way as you have watched Him go into heaven" (Acts 1:11). Just as Jesus ascended literally, physically, and visibly to heaven, so He will return.

These teachings stand in contrast to the idea of a "secret" rapture. Some have thought biblical passages describing Christ coming "like a thief" support the secret rapture view. However, such passages do not depict the manner of Christ's coming as "secret," but instead highlight that many will be *surprised* by the timing of Christ's coming such that it is crucial to be ready (see Matt. 24:43–44; cf. 25:13; 1 Thess. 2:2–6; Rev. 3:3; 16:15). The coming is "like a thief" in that it sneaks up and surprises many, but it is not secret or undetected when it actually occurs. For example, "the day of the Lord is coming just like a thief in the night. While they are saying, 'Peace and safety!' then sudden destruction will come upon them like labor pains upon a pregnant woman.... But you, brothers and sisters, are not in darkness, so that the day would overtake you like a thief" (1 Thess. 5:2–4). Likewise, 2 Peter 3:10 teaches, "the day of the Lord will come like a thief, in which the heavens will pass away with a roar and the elements will be destroyed with intense heat."

This is no *secret* coming.

Some advocates of the secret rapture view point to Christ's teaching that "on that night [of Christ's return] there will be two in one bed; one will be taken and the other will be left. There will be two women grinding at the same place; one will be taken and the other will be left" (Luke 17:34–35). Read in context, however, these texts do not teach that Christ will *secretly* come and take some while others will be left behind *to go on living*. Just a few verses prior, Jesus explained this end will come "just as it happened in the days of Noah" and "in the days of Lot" (Luke 17:26, 28). In both cases (the flood and the destruction of Sodom and Gomorrah), those who were not rescued but "left behind" perished in the destruction. Likewise, at the Second Coming, those who are not "caught up ... in the clouds" with Christ (1 Thess. 4:17) will die. Some will be taken and others left, but the coming is not secret and the ones left behind do not go on living—they are "destroy[ed] with the brightness of His coming" (2 Thess. 2:8, NKJV; cf. 1:7–8; Rev. 6:15–17).

> This is no secret coming.

Far from being a secret coming, when Christ returns, "the sign of the Son of Man will appear in the sky, and then all the tribes of the earth will mourn, and they will see the SON OF MAN COMING ON THE CLOUDS OF THE SKY with power and great glory. And He will send forth His angels with A

GREAT TRUMPET BLAST, and THEY WILL GATHER TOGETHER His elect from the four winds, from one end of the sky to the other" (Matt. 24:30–31).

However, things on earth will get worse before they get better. Before Christ's return, the dragon and his beasts will attempt to enforce a false system of worship, set against God's law of unselfish love (Rev. 13:14). As seen previously, the centrality of worship is highlighted in the first angel's message: "Fear God and give glory to Him, for the hour of His judgment has come; and worship Him who made heaven and earth, the sea and springs of water" (Rev. 14:7, NKJV). This directly alludes to the language of the Sabbath commandment of Exodus 20:11, "in six days the LORD made the heavens and the earth, the sea and everything that is in them, and He rested on the seventh day" (cf. Ps. 146:6).[9] The end-time test of worship is thus linked to recognizing God as Creator, with the remnant identified as those who "keep the commandments of God and the faith of Jesus" (Rev. 14:12, NKJV).

This remnant will be severely persecuted for refusing to participate in the counterfeit (antichrist) worship (Rev. 13, see chapter 18). Yet, these will finally receive the seal of God, whereas those who choose to worship the beast and accept his false system will receive the mark of the beast (Rev. 7:1–10; 13:15–18; 14:8–12).

This final test over worship will thus bring each person on earth to a point of final decision for or against God, thus ending the current period of probation such that everyone alive just prior to Christ's coming will have made their final choice, and it will be said: "He who is unjust, let him be unjust still; he who is filthy, let him be filthy still; he who is righteous, let him be righteous still; he who is holy, let him be holy still" (Rev. 22:11, NKJV).

Before Christ's return, the entire world will be plunged into a "time of trouble" such as the world has never seen (Dan. 12:1, NKJV), including the seven last plagues, judgment on the earth, and strife which God's angels have long held back (Rev. 16).

Although God's people will go through this "great tribulation," God does not forsake His people—they will "come out of the great tribulation" (Rev. 7:14). Those saved by the Lamb will be "a great multitude which no one could count, from every nation and all the tribes, peoples, and languages, standing before the throne and before the Lamb, clothed in white robes, and palm branches were in their hands" (Rev. 7:9).

In the end, the Lamb wins, and all who are united to the Lamb share in His victory. Thus, Jesus proclaimed, "These things I have spoken to you so that in Me you may have peace. In the world you have tribulation, but take courage; I have overcome the world" (John 16:33).

Finally, the King will come and bring deliverance, finally breaking the yoke of oppression, injustice, and evil of all kinds once and for all. Christ, the true King, will appear in the clouds, and His coming will be more wonderful than can be imagined.

While those who finally reject Christ will perish at the brightness of His coming (2 Thess. 2:8–10; cf. Mal. 4:1; Rev. 6:15–17), those who have accepted Christ will be caught up into the air, along with the righteous dead who will be resurrected from their sleep at Christ's coming and join Christ in the air. Indeed, "the Lord Himself will descend from heaven with a shout, with the voice of an archangel, and with the trumpet of God. And the dead in Christ will rise first. Then we who are alive and remain shall be caught up together with them in the clouds to meet the Lord in the air. And thus we shall always be with the Lord" (1 Thess. 4:16–17, NKJV).

At Christ's coming, those who have been justified and sanctified will finally be glorified, transformed in an instant to perfection (translation), never again to fall prey to sin, sickness, or death. "We shall not all sleep, but we shall all be changed—in a moment, in the twinkling of an eye, at the last trumpet. For the trumpet will sound, and the dead will be raised incorruptible, and we shall be changed. For this corruptible must put on incorruption, and this mortal must put on immortality. So when this corruptible has put on incorruption, and this mortal has put on immortality, then shall be brought to pass the saying that is written: 'Death is swallowed up in victory.' 'O Death, where is your sting? O Hades, where is your victory?'" (1 Cor. 15:51–55, NKJV).

Then our struggle with sin and evil will be over; "when He is revealed, we shall be like Him, for we shall see Him as He is" (1 John 3:2, NKJV). Humans who have accepted God's free offer of salvation will not only be fully restored to God's ideal of moral and physical perfection, but will also enjoy perpetual growth, including learning more of God, His creation, and the science of salvation, "things into which angels long to look" (1 Pet. 1:12).

Final Events Before the Millennium

- False prophets and false christs will arise, deceiving many.
- Christ will come with the blast of a trumpet and shout of the Archangel, accompanied by angels.
- Every eye will see Christ's Second Coming; it will not be secret.
- The redeemed dead will be resurrected to eternal life.
- The redeemed living will be taken to heaven (translated) without ever seeing death.
- The unrepentant wicked will be destroyed by the brightness of Christ's coming and the earth rendered desolate.
- The unrighteous dead remain dead until after the millennium.

The Millennium and the End of Evil

"Where are you?" "Have you eaten from the tree from which I commanded you not to eat?" (Gen. 3:9, 11). God posed these and other questions to Adam and Eve after they ate the forbidden fruit in Eden.

Yet, why did God ask such questions to which He already knew the answers? Throughout Scripture, God frequently asks questions in the context of (formal or informal) judgment proceedings (e.g., Job 1:7–8), analogous to questions attorneys ask in trials to get information on the record. God's way of fair, moral governance involves open judgment proceedings by which God brings the truth into the light of day for all intelligent creatures to see (cf. Luke 12:2–3).

Thus, as seen in chapter 16, the pre-advent judgment takes place before Christ's return (see, e.g., Dan. 7:9–10). This judgment condemns unrepentant agents of oppression (*individuals and empires*) while vindicating those who accept Christ, forever declaring them clean and showing God did all He could to *justly* save everyone, refuting the devil's accusations in the heavenly court and casting down and eventually destroying the little horn power. This judgment thus manifests God's perfect righteousness such that God Himself is vindicated as both "just and the justifier" (Rom. 3:25–26)—saving those who are in Christ by faith while also fulfilling His perfect law of unselfish love and justice.

After Christ's Second Coming, however, there is another judgment— the post-advent judgment, which Revelation 20 describes as taking place during a period of one thousand years known as the millennium. The saved will live and reign with Christ for a thousand years, and "judgment" will be "given to them" (Rev. 20:4).[10]

Competing Theories in Christian Theology: The Millennium

Christians hold various theories regarding the millennium. Here, I introduce four of the most prominent views.

Amillennialism understands the thousand years mentioned in Revelation 20 as symbolic rather than a literal period of time. Some hold that the symbolic millennium has already begun, referring to the church age, after which Christ will return.

Postmillennialism agrees that Christ's return will take place after the millennium (the second Advent is *postmillennial*) but believes the kingdom of God is established on earth during the millennium such that, prior to Christ's return, Christianity flourishes throughout the world (often conceived as a millennial rule of Christ's kingdom).

In contrast, premillennialists believe Christ will literally and physically return prior to the millennium, understood as a literal thousand-year period. There are significant differences, however, between *dispensationalist* premillennialism and *historic* premillenialism.

Dispensationalist premillennialism makes an utter distinction between Israel and the church, believing saved Christians will be secretly raptured prior to the millennium, during which God's promises to the nation of Israel are literally fulfilled in a millennial kingdom of Israel established by Christ on earth. Most believe Christians are raptured before the period of tribulation prophesied in Revelation (pre-tribulationists), but some believe the rapture takes place during (mid-tribulationists) or after the tribulation (post-tribulationists).

Historic premillennialism, on the other hand, differs from the dispensationalist approach and thus does not see the millennium with reference to a literal nation of Israel. Those who hold this view typically believe Christ returns after the tribulation, ushering in a millennial kingdom of peace. This view is called historic because it appears to have been affirmed by many early church fathers.[11] Many who hold this view believe the millennium is on earth.

Adventists hold a premillennialist view that also differs from the dispensationalist approach by (among other ways) not viewing the millennium as referring to a literal nation of Israel. However, as Adventists understand it, Christ's Second Coming renders the earth desolate, then the redeemed dwell for one thousand years in heaven, during which the post-Advent judgment takes place, and after which the redeemed inhabit the new earth. This view is explained further below.[12]

Millennium in Heaven

> Then I saw thrones, and they sat on them, and judgment was given to them. And I saw the souls of those who had been beheaded because of their testimony of Jesus and because of the word of God, and those who had not worshiped the beast or his image, and had not received the mark on their foreheads and on their hands; and they came to life and reigned with Christ for a thousand years. The rest of the dead did not come to life until the thousand years were completed. This is the first resurrection. Blessed and holy is the one who has a part in the first resurrection; over these the second death has no power, but they will be priests of God and of Christ, and will reign with Him for a thousand years. (Rev. 20:4-6)

According to these verses, the dead who belong to Christ "came to life and reigned with Christ for a thousand years," while the "rest of the dead did not come to life until" after the millennium. As we have seen earlier in this book, Scripture teaches that the first death is a "sleep" (Dan. 12:2; John 11:1-44; 1 Cor. 15:51-52), during which the dead are unconscious until they are resurrected (Ps. 146:3-4; Eccles. 9:5). And, here in Revelation, we see that the righteous are resurrected in the first resurrection, and the wicked are resurrected in the later second resurrection after the millennium (John 5:28-29; Rev. 20:4-6).

As Adventists understand it, Scripture teaches that the "first resurrection" (Rev. 20:5) takes place when Christ returns: "the Lord Himself will descend from heaven with a shout" and "the dead in Christ will rise first" (1 Thess. 4:16-17). Then, the saved who were already alive at Christ's coming "will be caught up together with them in the clouds to meet the Lord in the air" (1 Thess. 4:17) and be taken to heaven to dwell there for one thousand years.

During the millennium, Adventists believe, no humans are alive on the earth. The lost who are alive just prior to Christ's return will be "destroy[ed] with the brightness of His coming" (2 Thess. 2:8, NKJV; cf. 1:7-8; 2 Pet. 3:10; Rev. 6:15-17). And the lost dead do "not come to life until" after the thousand years (Rev. 20:5)—remaining in an unconscious state during the millennium.

During this "thousand years," Revelation 20 teaches, the devil is "bound," thrown "into the abyss" so he could "not deceive the nations any longer, until the thousand years were completed" (Rev. 20:2-3). Adventists understand this "abyss" in which the devil is "bound . . . for a thousand years" as referring to the earth in a desolate formless state matching its state at the outset of creation ("without form, and void," Gen. 1:2, NKJV; cf. 2 Pet. 3:10), without any humans on it to tempt and no nations to deceive "until the thousand years were completed," after which the devil is "released for a short time" (Rev. 20:3, 7).

During this millennium, the redeemed in heaven review the records of history and evaluate the verdicts of God's just judgment, seeing that all God has done is perfectly just and loving (Rev. 20:1-4). Paul refers to this post-advent judgment when he states, "do you not know that the saints will judge the world? . . . Do you not know that we will judge angels?" (1 Cor. 6:2-3; cf. 4:5).

While no one has authority to *bring* God into judgment, God Himself calls for us to judge between Him and His vineyard—to forever answer all questions about His justice and love (e.g., Isa. 5:3; Rom. 3:3-5). The universe can continue in perpetual harmony and bliss only if all creatures trust God unreservedly, which can only take place if all questions about God's character and the way He deals with injustice are answered once-and-for-all. Not for His own sake, then, but for the sake of the flourishing of the entire universe in perfect love and justice, God vindicates His own character before the universe by opening up His government to the review of all intelligent creatures (in the pre-advent and post-advent judgments). Thereby, *all* will see that all God's ways are "righteous and true" (Rev. 15:3)—God has done everything that could be done for the good of all, in accordance with His perfect goodness and love, and that

His law is perfect and just, answering once-and-for-all the question, "what more could He do?" (see Isa. 5:3–4).

Additionally, these thousand years will be a time of healing from the trauma that has been experienced, to make sense of what has occurred (cognitively), and to heal from the pain and suffering (emotional healing). There will be time to expose and process the evils and injustices of this world, ushering in the final age of perfect justice and love forevermore. This might be why the "leaves of the tree" of life are described as "for the healing of the nations" (Rev. 22:2).

After the "thousand years" are "completed," the lost "come to life" (the second resurrection, Rev. 20:5; cf. John 5:28–29; Rev. 20:13). Then, "Satan will be released from his prison, and will come out to deceive the nations," rallying the lost to attack the holy city that came down from heaven (Rev. 20:7–9; 21:2).

The dragon's final attempted assault on God and His people in the holy city manifests the intractable finality of the wickedness of the lost, who refuse to live in accordance with God's law of unselfish love. In their attempt to attack the holy city, they undeniably show their true colors as unrepentant and thus irredeemable followers of the way of the dragon, which selfishly grasps for power and dominance through violence.

"And they came up on the broad plain of the earth and surrounded the camp of the saints and the beloved city, and fire came down from heaven and devoured them" (Rev. 20:9). Why would God resurrect the lost if they are thereafter to die the second death? Scripture does not tell us. But it might have something to do with the fact that this final episode both manifests once and for all the irreversible choice the lost have made against love and in favor of unrelenting evil and brings the cosmic conflict to a final end wherein even those who finally reject life with God nevertheless ultimately recognize that all God's ways are just and thus finally see God's utter goodness and just judgment.

Had there been any question whether anyone lost might have turned around, if only given more opportunity, this forever lays it to rest.[13] Those who finally reject God's love would never be happy in God's kingdom of unselfish love and, if allowed to enter there, would only bring misery to all others while themselves remaining miserable. Accordingly, God does the most loving thing He could do for them and the entire universe. God puts the lost out of their misery so they will no longer suffer, and no one else will suffer anymore at their hands (discussed below).

Before the lost perish relative to the second death, however, "at the name of Jesus EVERY KNEE WILL BOW, of those who are in heaven and on earth and under the earth, and that every tongue will confess that Jesus Christ is Lord, to the glory of God the Father" (Phil. 2:10-11). As Adventists understand it, before the lost perish, every single person will recognize that God is just—even those who finally reject life with God because they love darkness and hate the light finally see God's utter goodness. And the redeemed will sing "the song of Moses" and "the song of the Lamb, saying, 'Great and marvelous are Your works, Lord God, the Almighty; Righteous and true are Your ways, King of the nations!'" (Rev. 15:3-4; cf. Deut. 32:4; Rev. 19:1-2).

In all this, the full manifestation of God's character in the cosmic conflict is not for our world alone; our world is itself a spectacle or theater to the cosmos (1 Cor. 4:9). In the final judgments, all questions about God's justice and love are forever answered. Finally, *every* knee will bow and *every* tongue will confess the Lordship of Christ and the justice and character of God (Phil. 2:10-11; cf. Is 45:23; Rom. 14:11; Rev. 5:13; 15:3; 19:1-6).

Events During the Millennium
- The saved dwell with God in heaven.
- The lost remain dead.
- Satan is "bound" on the earth.
- The earth is desolate.
- The post-advent judgment takes place.

The End of Hell: Love Destroys Evil

God "will wipe away every tear from their eyes; and there will no longer be any death; there will no longer be any mourning, or crying, or pain; the first things have passed away" (Rev. 21:4).

In the end, there will be no more death or crying or pain anywhere in the universe. Given this divine promise, there could not be a place of suffering that goes on forever (often called "hell").

Competing Theories in Christian Theology: Competing Views of "Hell"

Christians disagree about the reality and nature of what many call hell. The three most prominent views are eternal conscious punishment, conditionalism, and universalism.[14]

The eternal conscious punishment view maintains that the lost suffer everlasting conscious torment, with the place of such torment often identified as "hell."

Universalism, conversely, maintains that all humans will finally be saved.

In contrast to both, conditionalism (i.e., conditional immortality or annihilationism) maintains that saved humans live forever with

THREE VIEWS ON "HELL"

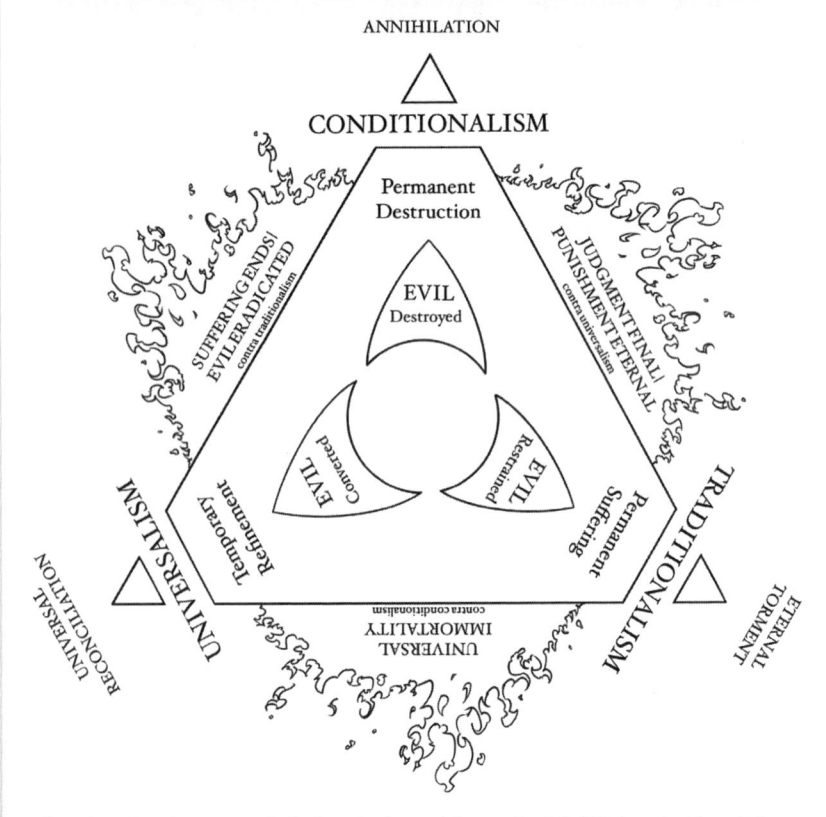

[Diagram: A triangle labeled with the three views — ANNIHILATION/CONDITIONALISM at the top, UNIVERSALISM/UNIVERSAL RECONCILIATION at the bottom-left, and TRADITIONALISM/ETERNAL TORMENT at the bottom-right. Inner sections show "Permanent Destruction / EVIL Destroyed" (top), "Temporary Refinement / EVIL Converted" (bottom-left), and "Permanent Suffering / EVIL Restrained" (bottom-right). Side labels: "SUFFERING ENDS / EVIL ERADICATED (contra traditionalism)," "JUDGMENT FINAL / PUNISHMENT ETERNAL (contra universalism)," and "UNIVERSAL IMMORTALITY (contra conditionalism)."]

This chart has been simplified and adapted from the "Hell Triangle Chart" from rethinkinghell.com/helltriangle (used by permission).

God, but the lost finally perish and cease to exist forever. Here, "annihilate" simply means to cause something to come to nothing (*nihil*). This is the view Adventists hold.

Christians also hold differing views regarding the intermediate state, which Adventists often refer to as the state of the dead.

As we have seen (in chapter 12), Adventists hold the unconscious state of the dead view, somewhat akin to what many other Christians call "soul sleep" (though Adventists do not believe humans have a conscious, separable soul).[15]

Many Christians instead believe humans remain conscious after death (the conscious state of the dead view). Some believe that after death, people immediately go either to heaven or hell (understood as a place of everlasting suffering) in a disembodied state. Others believe that after death one might go to a middle place called purgatory, where one is purged of sinfulness and made ready for heaven. Distinct from these, others believe that after death people go to a place of the dead (which some identify as Sheol and/or Hades) where they remain conscious in a shade-like kind of conscious existence until the resurrection at Christ's return, with the saved and lost in different compartments, with no opportunity of changing from lost to saved (or vice versa).

The Nature of "Hell"

For some, the doctrine of a place called "hell" where the wicked endure endless torture is linked to the belief of the immortality of the soul, which stems from Greek (Platonic) philosophy.[16] On this view, all humans live forever and thus the wicked endure perpetual punishment. However, Scripture proclaims that God "alone possesses immortality" (1 Tim. 6:16) and there is not a single mention of the immortality of the soul in Scripture.[17] Rather, as seen in chapter 12, creaturely immortality is conditional upon relationship with God (John 3:16; 6:51; cf. 2 Thess. 2:9–10). With God, there is life. Without God, there is no life. God alone is the immortal One who bestows (conditional) immortality on those who remain connected to Him in love relationship.[18]

With God, there is life. Without God, there is no life.

What, then, is the nature of "hell" spoken of in Scripture? The two words most often translated "hell" in the New Testament are *gehenna* and *hadēs*. But neither of these terms refer to a place of endlessly burning fire or everlasting torment.

Gehenna refers literally to the valley of Hinnom, which was a valley in the southern part of Jerusalem where, in times of apostasy, false "gods" of the nations (Canaanite Baals) were worshiped, and child sacrifices were offered to Molech (see 2 Chron. 28:2, 3; 33:6; cf. Jer. 32:35).[19] As such, the valley had been a place of rebellion against God, but Jeremiah proclaimed it would become a place of divine judgment and would be called "the Valley of the Slaughter" (Jer. 7:30–34; 19:1–9; cf. Isa. 30:33) and "Isaiah, though not specifically mentioning the valley, uses the concepts associated with it to refer to God's universal last-day judgment against the wicked" (see Isa. 66:16, 24).[20] Christ uses this term (*gehenna*) metaphorically of the final lake of fire (Matt. 5:22, 29–30; 10:28; 18:9; Mark 9:43–47; Luke 12:5).[21]

Hadēs, on the other hand, does not refer to the Greek mythological concept of a subterranean place of torture but refers to the grave (abode of the dead), corresponding to the Hebrew term *sheol* (grave).[22] According to Revelation 20:14, *hadēs* itself will be *destroyed* in the lake of fire, along with death. Thus, *hadēs* cannot itself be an eternally burning place.

Satan himself will be destroyed in the lake of fire (cf. Ezek. 28:19). Indeed, "the devil who deceived them was thrown into the lake of fire and brimstone, where the beast and the false prophet are also; and they will be tormented day and night forever and ever" (Rev. 20:10; cf. Matt. 25:41; Jude 7).

Yet, what about the phrase "forever and ever" in this and other passages?

The Greek term translated "forever" (*aiōn*) in this passage has a range of meaning. It may refer to "life span" but may also refer to:

- "a long time, duration of time, where both a specifically limited period of time as well as an unlimited period can be meant" (Luke 1:33, 55; John 6:51),
- an age, particular unit of history (Matt. 12:32; 13:39), or
- the world itself (Matt. 13:22; 24:3; Mark 4:19).[23]

In brief, the term *aiōn* sometimes refers to that which is eternal in the sense of quantity of time (everlasting in *some* sense) but may instead have a qualitative meaning, referring not to an everlasting period of time but an eon or age. The meaning of *aiōn* depends upon the nature of that to which it refers and the way it is used in context.[24]

With regard to the final execution of judgment, Adventists believe such language does not refer to fire that burns its object forever but to fire that completely and permanently destroys the wicked. It destroys "forever" in the sense of permanent destruction (or annihilation), destroying even death and hades (Rev. 20:14). This sense of "eternal" relative to permanent consequences is the meaning of *aiōnios* (the adjectival form of *aiōn*) in Jude 7, which refers to "Sodom and Gomorrah and the cities around them ... undergoing the punishment of eternal [*aiōnios*] fire. Since Sodom and Gomorrah are not still burning today, the phrase "eternal fire" cannot refer to fire that continues burning these cities forever. In context, this "fire" is "eternal" with respect to the consequences it brings about, eternal in the sense of bringing about *permanent* destruction.[25]

Similar imagery appears in Revelation 14:10–11, which says those who worship the beast "will be tormented with fire and brimstone in the presence of the holy angels and in the presence of the Lamb. And the smoke of their torment ascends forever and ever."[26]

Elsewhere in Scripture, this same imagery of smoke ascending "forever and ever" is metaphorical language that refers to permanent desolation. For example, Isaiah 34:9–10 states, Edom's "streams will be turned into pitch, and its loose earth into brimstone, and its land will become burning pitch. It will not be extinguished [or "quenched"] night or day; its smoke will go up forever [*olam*]. From generation to generation it will be desolate; none will pass through it forever and ever." While this passage speaks of smoke that "will go up forever," Edom is not still burning; no smoke is currently going up from Edom. Isaiah uses poetic language to refer to a *final and permanent* destruction of Edom, rendering it forever desolate (echoing the "smoke" Abraham saw that "ascended like the smoke of a furnace" when Sodom and Gomorrah were destroyed by "brimstone and fire ... from the LORD out of heaven," Gen. 19:28, 24; cf. Jude 7).

Revelation 14:10–11 and 20:10 picks up and uses this same poetic imagery (as does Rev. 19:3; cf. 18:9, 18). Just as the language in Isaiah 34 should not be taken to mean there is literally smoke rising from Edom for an everlasting duration, the highly symbolic *apocalyptic* language of Revelation should not be interpreted as if it refers to literal fire and smoke that burns and ascends for an everlasting duration. Such passages do not teach eternal conscious punishment but are best understood as poetic imagery about the final, permanent *destruction* that Scripture repeatedly teaches about elsewhere (see below), such that those destroyed will be no more *forever*.

Notice further that Isaiah 34:10 speaks of fire that "will not be extinguished [or quenched] night or day." Here and elsewhere in Scripture, imagery of fire that is not extinguished or quenched (i.e., "unquenchable fire") does not refer to fire that burns for an everlasting duration but to fire that cannot be put out (quenched or extinguished) and thus certainly accomplishes destruction (e.g., Jer. 7:20; 17:27; Ezek. 20:47–48; cf. 2 Kings 22:17).[27] Fire consumes (e.g., Heb. 10:27).

For example, Matthew 3:12 says of the final judgment, "He will gather His wheat into the barn, but He will burn up the chaff with unquenchable fire" (cf. Luke 3:17). That this fire is unquenchable does not indicate the fire burns the chaff forever. The chaff burns up. An unquenchable fire is not one that burns for an everlasting period of time but one that cannot be put out and thus *burns up* whatever it burns. This verse thus supports the conditional immortality view. Accordingly, Jesus taught that whereas the wheat (representing the sons of the kingdom) will be gathered up into His barn, the weeds (representing the sons of the evil one) will be bound "in bundles to burn them" and explained, further, that "just as the weeds are gathered up and burned with fire, so shall it be at the end of the age" (Matt. 13:30, 40).

Similar imagery of "unquenchable fire" appears in Isaiah 66:24, which states, "Then they will go out and look at the corpses of the people who have rebelled against Me. For their worm will not die and their fire will not be extinguished [or "quenched"]; and they will be an abhorrence to all mankind."

We've already seen that fire that is not extinguished (or "quenched") refers to fire that cannot be put out (not fire that burns forever). Further, notice that nothing in this passage speaks of humans continuing to live or suffer forever. The passage refers not to living humans but to corpses ("dead bodies") alongside imagery of worms (which feed on corpses) and fire (which consumes). Here, it is not humans who "will not die" but the worms that "will not die."

This phrase "will not die" appears numerous times in the Old Testament. There, it does not mean "will *never* die" but refers to something that will not die at a particular time or in particular circumstances (e.g., Gen. 42:20; Exod. 30:20; Jer. 38:24). In Isaiah 66:24, such language indicates the worm will not die before fully consuming the bodies. Such imagery is not about immortal worms but is imagery of worms that "will not die" *until* they consume the corpses they are feeding on.

In Isaiah 66:24, then, the two metaphors refer to the final and permanent consumption of the unrepentant wicked: (1) worms that will not die until after the corpses are consumed and (2) fire that will not be quenched but will consume the corpses.

Jesus Himself draws on this imagery when describing the final destruction of the unrepentant wicked. Specifically, Jesus warns, "it is better for you to enter life maimed, than, having your two hands, to go into hell, into the unquenchable fire" (Mark 9:43; cf. 5:30). And "it is better for you to enter the kingdom of God with one eye, than, having two eyes, to be thrown into hell, where THEIR WORM DOES NOT DIE, AND THE FIRE IS NOT EXTINGUISHED" (or "quenched," Mark 9:47–48).

In these instances, the word translated "hell" is *gehenna*, which we've already seen literally refers to the valley of Hinnom, which Jeremiah indicated would be the place of God's judgment (Jer. 7:32; 19:6). Christ often used the term *gehenna* metaphorically to refer to the lake of fire (Matt. 5:22, 29–30; 10:28; 18:9; Mark 9:43–47; Luke 12:5). As elsewhere, such imagery refers to the fire of divine judgment that cannot be put out (and is thus "unquenchable"), but burns up whatever it is burning and thus permanently destroys it.

What about other texts, however, that refer to "eternal fire" and "eternal punishment"? For example, Jesus said, "if your hand or your foot is causing you to sin, cut it off and throw it away from you; it is better for you to enter life maimed or without a foot, than to have two hands or two feet and be thrown into the eternal fire" (Matt. 18:8; cf. 5:30; 25:41; Mark 9:43). Does the phrase "eternal fire" refer to fire that burns humans forever or does it refer to fire that is eternal in another sense?

Some think "eternal fire" here might be a metaphorical reference to God Himself, whom Scripture elsewhere identifies as "a consuming fire" (Heb. 12:29). On this understanding, in the end, everyone comes into the unmediated presence of God, which consumes evil (and those who cling to it) like a consuming fire, but the redeemed who cling to Christ (by faith) are purified by the "fire" of God's presence. If correct, this understanding might make sense of Jesus's statement that "everyone will be salted by fire" (Mark 9:49).

Instead (or alongside this), the phrase "eternal fire" might refer to fire that is eternal in the sense that its effects are permanent (i.e., eternal), as the phrase is used in Jude 7 when it refers to "Sodom and Gomorrah and the cities around them" being "exhibited as an example in undergoing the punishment of eternal [*aiōnios*] fire." As noted earlier, since Sodom and Gomorrah are not burning today, "eternal fire" in Jude 7 cannot refer to fire that *continues burning* those cities forever. Rather, "eternal" here refers to punishment by fire that is "eternal" in the sense of being permanent.

Supporting this understanding, 2 Peter 2:6 states that God "condemned the cities of Sodom and Gomorrah to destruction by reducing them to ashes, having made them an example of what is coming for the ungodly." The "eternal fire" that destroyed Sodom and Gomorrah, then, was fire that consumed them until they were reduced "to ashes." The *effect* of that fire was eternal in the sense of being permanent, but the fire did not burn the cities forever; it *destroyed* them by reducing them to ashes.

Notably, both Jude 7 and 2 Peter 2:6 teach that the fire that destroyed Sodom and Gomorrah was "an example" of what will happen to the wicked in the end. This provides context for understanding Jesus's warning about being "thrown into the eternal fire" (Matt. 18:8) and other references to "eternal fire" (Matt. 25:41). Here and elsewhere, the "eternal fire" is not fire that burns something forever, but fire that finally consumes whatever it is burning, reducing it to ashes. Relative to the final judgment, such fire is "eternal" not in the sense that it burns something forever but in the sense that its effects are eternal; it brings about *permanent* (eternal) destruction.

This understanding is consistent with Jesus's teaching that the lost "will go away into eternal punishment, but the righteous into eternal life" (Matt. 25:46; cf. Mark 3:29; Heb. 6:2; 9:12). In isolation, "eternal punishment" could refer to eternal conscious punishment or to punishment that has eternal consequences (i.e., permanent punishment). But, here, Jesus contrasts "eternal punishment" with "eternal life." Given this contrast, "eternal punishment" must refer to something other than "eternal life." If only the redeemed inherit eternal life (a conclusion supported by abundant biblical data, as we saw in chapter 12), then the lost cannot *live* forever and thus cannot undergo eternal conscious punishment. In this verse, eternal punishment is the opposite of eternal life—it is death that lasts forever in the sense of being *permanent* (corresponding to the second death that lost humans experience).

> **Eternal punishment is the opposite of eternal life—it is death that lasts forever in the sense of being permanent.**

This same contrast is at work in Daniel 12:2, which teaches, "those who sleep in the dust of the earth shall awake, some to everlasting life and some to shame and everlasting contempt" (NRSVue). Since it is contrasted with "everlasting life," the result of "everlasting contempt" must not involve "everlasting life." The lost, then, go to "shame and everlasting contempt," not in the sense that they live forever, but the shame and contempt they brought on themselves is "eternal" in the sense of being permanent.

This corresponds to the meaning of Hebrews 6:2 when it refers to "the resurrection of the dead and eternal judgment." This does not refer to a process of judgment that goes on forever, but judgment that is permanent (cf. Mark 3:29). This sense of "eternal" relative to permanent consequences is likewise at work in Hebrews 9:12, which says that Christ has "obtained eternal redemption." This does not refer to a *process* of redemption that goes on forever but to redemption that is eternal in the sense of being permanent. The saved are permanently redeemed.

This sense of *permanent* consequences is what 2 Thessalonians 1:9 also refers to when it says the unredeemed wicked "will suffer the punishment of eternal destruction, separated from the presence of the Lord and from the glory of his might" (NRSVue). Creatures cannot live entirely apart from God. Thus, to be utterly separated from God's presence is to cease to exist (perish). Those who finally reject love relationship with God thus finally reject and cut themselves off from receiving God's gracious gift of eternal life and are thus *permanently* destroyed.

This is consistent with many other biblical passages that teach the unrepentant wicked will perish or be destroyed. For example, Psalm 37:20 declares, "the wicked will perish; and the enemies of the LORD will be like the glory of the pastures, they vanish—like smoke they vanish away." Likewise, Malachi 4:1 proclaims: "See, the day is coming, burning like an oven, when all the arrogant and all evildoers will be stubble; the day that comes shall burn them up, says the LORD of hosts, so that it will leave them neither root nor branch" (NRSVue, cf. 4:3; Isa. 47:14; Obad. 16; Matt. 3:10–12; 13:30, 40).

Further, Jesus Himself warns: "Do not fear those who kill the body but cannot kill the soul; rather, fear the one who can destroy both soul and body in hell" (*gehenna*, Matt. 10:28, NRSVue; cf. 7:13–14; 13:40–42; 2 Pet. 2:6). This teaching that "both soul and body" are destroyed in *gehenna* indicates that the final judgment is the end of life for the unrepentant wicked; they experience "the second death," resulting in the permanent privation of life such that they cease to be forever.[28]

Many other texts also depict the wicked as finally perishing (e.g., Rom. 2:12; 2 Thess. 2:10; cf. Heb. 10:27). Indeed, Scripture consistently teaches that the redeemed live forever, but those who reject the gift of life with God will perish and cease to be forever. "For the wages of sin is death, but the gracious gift of God is eternal life in Christ Jesus our Lord" (Rom. 6:23). Thus, God cries out, "I take no pleasure in the death of anyone who dies" so "repent and live!" (Ezek. 18:32; cf. 2 Thess. 2:9–10). And perhaps the most famous passage in Scripture proclaims that whoever believes in the Son "will not perish, but have eternal life" (John 3:16; cf. 10:28).

Eventually, suffering and death will be no more. God Himself "will wipe away every tear from their eyes; there shall be no more death, nor sorrow, nor crying. There shall be no more pain, for the former things have passed away" (Rev. 21:4, NKJV). Yet, if sorrow and crying and pain are no more, there could not be a place of perpetual torment and suffering in the universe.

Love Puts an End to Suffering and Evil

In the classic Disney story *Old Yeller*, a beloved family dog named Old Yeller is put to death. Why? Old Yeller had contracted rabies. Because no adequate treatment was available, the most loving and merciful thing the family could do was put him down, and they very reluctantly did so.

They loved Old Yeller, but the most loving thing they could do was to put Old Yeller out of his misery. In a somewhat analogous fashion, the most loving thing God can do for those who finally and intractably refuse His love is to put them out of their misery for the best good of all concerned.

Love cannot allow the disease of evil to continue forever. God's holy love will ultimately destroy all *evil* once and for all in an executive judgment, including anyone who clings to evil. This is the most loving thing God could do. If God preserved the lives of the lost, they would only endure in misery and continually spread misery. Imagine endless existence in an evil-filled world without the mediating effects of God's providence. It would be unimaginably worse than our present world (as bad as it is). Endless existence in such a world would be exponentially worse than torture. God's action in eradicating evil is a manifestation of His mercy and love toward the lost (mercifully ending their misery) and the rest of the universe, not allowing injustice and pain and suffering to go on forever (cf. Isa. 28:21; Lam. 3:32–33).

> **Love cannot allow the disease of evil to continue forever.**

Some think that a God of love should grant eternal life to all. However, the only reason God does not save all is because some finally refuse to be saved—they reject love itself.[29] God wants to save everyone and would if He could, but will not force anyone to live with Him forever. God has "no pleasure in the death of anyone who dies" (Ezek. 18:32; cf. 33:11) and does not want anyone to perish but wants to save everyone (e.g., 1 Tim. 2:4–6; 2 Pet. 3:9). Thus, God will save everyone who is willing to be saved. "For God so loved the world, that He gave His only Son, so that everyone who believes in Him will not perish, but have eternal life" (John 3:16). Yet, love requires freedom (see chapter 9), and God will not force anyone to be saved.[30] Thus, God would save everyone if He could, but if saving a person involves making that person a recipient and reflector of unselfish love (and love requires freedom), God cannot do this without the *free*, voluntary response of the persons He saves.

The lost "perish" only "because they did not accept the love of the truth so as to be saved" (2 Thess. 2:10). Those who are destroyed have finally rejected God's love, and there is nothing more that God can do for them except give them over to their own decisions (Isa. 5:4–6). The only reason God does not grant eternal life to everyone, then, is because some finally refuse life (by refusing God and His love).

Here, some mistakenly think God gives an arbitrary ultimatum like "love me or die." But, this fails to understand that creatures *cannot* exist apart from relationship to God, the source and sustainer of all life (cf. Heb. 1:3). God does not give any arbitrary ultimatum. It just is the case, and could not be otherwise, that a creature cannot exist entirely apart from God the Creator and Sustainer of all (Heb. 1:3)—the only One who has life in Himself and upon whom all other life depends.

What some people want—or think they want—is for God to give them eternal life apart from Him. But life apart from God is impossible and, if it were possible, would be devoid of all goodness and thus absolutely miserable. Thinking one can continue to enjoy life separated from God for eternity is a bit like thinking an electric light bulb could go on shining while being cut off from electricity and any other source of power. Apart from God, there can be no life.[31] Life with God is inseparable from love. If one finally rejects God and His love, then one rejects life itself. There is no other alternative because *there is no life apart from God*. To reject God is like cutting off the branch you are sitting on, but far worse.

So, those who finally reject God and His love (thus rejecting life itself) will experience the second death; utterly cut off from God (the source of life), they will cease to live forever. They permanently sever their relationship with God and thus permanently lose their life.

In this and in every other way, God is love. God does not subject humans to endless torture. Indeed, could a loving God really enjoy all eternity if He were conscious of such endless suffering? Would we? God is just in all His ways and will not endlessly torture people for sins they committed during a relatively short life span. For those who finally reject life with God, God does the most loving thing He could for them and for all concerned. In His mercy and love, God will eradicate evil forevermore, including its consequences of suffering and death.

There is, then, no eternally burning hell. The lake of fire that finally destroys the wicked will be here on earth, purging the earth of all evil prior to God's re-creation of the new earth. Finally, the devil and his minions and "Death and Hades" themselves are "thrown into the lake of fire. This is the second death, the lake of fire. And if anyone's name was not found written in the book of life, he was thrown into the lake of fire" (Rev. 20:10, 14–15).

As seen previously, without mediation, evil cannot be in God's presence because "God is a consuming fire" (Heb. 12:29; cf. Isa. 33:14) and "no evil can dwell with" God (Ps. 5:4). God's holy presence is to evil as fire is to gasoline. So, absent mediation, the fire of God's holiness finally consumes all evil. God will not let evil continue forever but lovingly brings evil to an end forever.

Evil will not merely be quarantined in some "corner" of the universe reserved for everlasting torture, as some believe. No, evil and pain shall be no more. Even the last enemy, death itself, will perish (1 Cor. 15:26; Rev. 21:4).

The New Earth: The Ultimate Promised Land

"Behold, the tabernacle of God is among the people, and He will dwell among them, and they shall be His people, and God Himself will be among them, and He will wipe away every tear from their eyes; and there will no longer be any death; there will no longer be any mourning, or crying, or pain; the first things have passed away" (Rev. 21:3–4).[32]

These words describe the future of this world in the new earth. Of all the words of Scripture I love so dearly, these are my favorite. No more death. No more mourning. No more crying. No more pain. God Himself will be *with us*, uninterrupted and forever. Can you even imagine?

> *No more death.*
> *No more mourning.*
> *No more crying.*
> *No more pain. God Himself will be with us, uninterrupted and forever.*

Just prior to the proclamation of these words, John saw "a new heaven and a new earth; for the first heaven and the first earth passed away, and there is no longer any sea." And John "saw the holy city, new Jerusalem, coming down out of heaven from God, prepared as a bride adorned for her husband" (Rev. 21:1–2). And, "He who sits on the throne said, 'Behold, I am making all things new.' And He said, 'Write, for these words are faithful and true'" (Rev. 21:5).

After evil is finally eradicated, God will effect a full restoration of this world, remaking it according to His original ideal, creating a "new heaven and a new earth; for the first heaven and the first earth passed away" (Rev. 21:1). And, in the new earth, believers will live *with God* forevermore (Rev. 21:3).[33]

Events After the Millennium

- The Holy City descends.
- The wicked dead are resurrected.
- Satan and his followers attack the city.
- The wicked are destroyed by fire.
- The earth is cleansed and renewed.

No injustice or oppression will be there. *The freedom of love will reign.* No illness or maladies and no pain, suffering, or death will be there (Rev. 21:4). The last enemy, death, is once and for all defeated (1 Cor. 15:26): "death is swallowed up in victory. O death, where is your victory? O death, where is your sting?" (1 Cor. 15:54–55, NKJV). The former things have passed away, and God declares, "Behold, I am making all things new" (Rev. 21:4–5).

The redeemed will be reunited with their family and loved ones who died in the Lord (cf. Rev. 14:13), *never* to part again. All who are in Christ will be reunited in the ultimate family with God Himself as the head. There will be no more orphans—none will be lonely or uncared for; all will have been adopted into God's perfect family through Christ.

Then, nature will be fully restored; "the creation itself also will be set free from its slavery to corruption into the freedom of the glory of the children of God" (Rom. 8:21). "And the wolf will dwell with the lamb, and the leopard will lie down with the young goat, and the calf and the young lion and the fattened steer will be together; and a little boy will lead them" (Isa. 11:6).

The world to come—the ultimate promised land—will be infinitely better than we can imagine. "Eye has not seen, nor ear heard, nor have entered into the heart of man the things which God has prepared for those who love Him" (1 Cor. 2:9, NKJV).[34] Even now, we await the soon return of our Lord and Savior Jesus Christ, which will set off a chain of events, culminating in the total eradication of evil and the re-creation of a new earth as the home of the redeemed where only goodness will dwell (2 Pet. 3:13)—and God Himself will dwell *with us* forever (Rev. 21:4).

Then, our greatest hopes will finally be fulfilled in the full glorification of those who belong to Christ, redeemed by the blood of the Lamb. Then, faith is fulfilled. Love is fully restored according to God's perfect law of unselfish love, to be enjoyed with all of the endless and unsurpassable bliss of love relationship with God and all other creatures. The cosmic conflict is finally ended. Sin will never rise again (Rev. 21:3–4; cf. Nah. 1:9). No one will ever again rebel; nothing will ever again mar God's perfect creation because the question of God's character, the problem of sin and evil, will have been dealt with once and for all.

We can be sure that sin and evil will never arise again because of the inspired promise (among others) that "there will no longer be any mourning, or crying, or pain; the first things have passed away" (Rev. 21:4). In the end, God will have answered and defeated all the devil's slanderous allegations *once and for all*, permanently inoculating the universe from evil ever arising again (Rev. 21:3–4; cf. Nah. 1:9).

The promise that "the sufferings of this present time are not worthy to be compared with the glory that is to be revealed" will be fulfilled (Rom. 8:18; cf. 2 Cor. 4:17). All will forever recognize that God is always and only good and just, the one who is love, His character and law of love vindicated beyond the shadow of a doubt. "The great controversy is ended. Sin and sinners are no more. The entire universe is clean. One pulse of harmony and gladness beats through the vast creation. From Him who created all, flow life and light and gladness, throughout the realms of illimitable space. From the minutest atom to the greatest world, all things, animate and inanimate, in their unshadowed beauty and perfect joy, declare that God is love."[35]

Conclusion: Why Does It Matter?

She had been waiting for what seemed like an eternity. Stay where you are, he'd told her. I will come back for you. Just stay put, and I will come for you. Trust me.

But he had been gone so long. She was hungry and tired and getting colder and colder by the minute. She did not know how much longer she could survive, out in the wilderness, if he did not return soon. Was he really coming back, as he'd promised? It was hard not to wonder.

If she struck out on her own to find deliverance and finally reach safety, however, she'd surely be caught by those who sought to exterminate her and her people. She was in a warzone, and her only hope for deliverance was him. Only if he came back as he promised would she have any hope of deliverance. Only if he came and saved her could she safely cross beyond enemy lines and finally be safe.

Most of us have not experienced anything like such clear and present physical danger. And, yet, whether cognizant of it or not, we have all been in even more grave danger, dwelling in enemy territory, temporarily ruled by the enemy who seeks to destroy us, "the devil," who "prowls around like a roaring lion, seeking someone to devour" (1 Pet. 5:8). For this reason, Peter instructs Christians in this same chapter to "be on the alert" and "resist" the devil and be "firm in your faith" for after "you have suffered for a little while, the God of all grace, who called you to His eternal glory in Christ, will Himself perfect, confirm, strengthen, and establish you" (1 Pet. 5:7–11). Thus, Peter tells us to cast all our anxiety on God, "for He cares for you" (1 Pet. 5:6, NKJV).

While the enemy seeks to devour us like a roaring lion, there is a far greater Lion who has promised to deliver all who place faith in Him, all who would follow the Lamb wherever He goes, following His instructions even when He seems hidden or absent—even when one might wonder if He will ever come back.

Jesus is coming again. No matter how dark things look, light is coming. "Weeping may endure for a night, but joy comes in the morning" (Ps. 30:5, NKJV).

Jesus is coming again. He will make all wrongs right. In the end, death will be no more. Suffering will be no more. No more illnesses like cancer and other diseases. No more pain. No more loneliness. No more sorrow. No more anxiety. Indeed, "according to His promise

> *Jesus is coming again. He will make all wrongs right.*

we are looking for new heavens and a new earth, in which righteousness dwells" (2 Pet. 3:13). God has things in store for us beyond what we can imagine, things beyond imagining for us to explore and enjoy forever. "Eye has not seen, nor ear heard, nor have entered into the heart of man the things which God has prepared for those who love Him" (1 Cor. 2:9, NKJV).

In the meantime, though, let us not be so heavenly-minded that we are of no earthly good. Now is the time to not only commit ourselves to the way of the Lamb as we await His return but to spread His love to others in word and in deed.

As we seek to do so, I invite you to reflect on the hope that lies before us by reading and reflecting on Revelation 21, focusing on what God has in store for those who love Him.

One day soon, it will be said: "Behold, the tabernacle of God is among the people, and He will dwell among them, and they shall be His people, and God Himself will be among them, and He will wipe away every tear from their eyes; and there will no longer be any death; there will no longer be any mourning, or crying, or pain; the first things have passed away" (Rev. 21:3–4).[36] Hallelujah!

Questions for Reflection

1. Reflect on Christ's promise that He went to prepare a place for His people and will come again. What does this promise mean to you?
2. If Christ's return was "near" two thousand years ago, what is taking so long? Why is there such an (apparent) delay? How does Scripture shed light on this? What would you say to someone who says we cannot expect Christ to return, given how long it has taken?
3. What will Christ's return be like? Why does it matter that we understand what Scripture teaches about Christ's return?
4. Some people think of preparing for the end as preparing for all kinds of earthly events. How might thinking of this preparation as preparing to meet Jesus and live in love relationship with Him and others forever change our focus?
5. What do you think the significance of the millennium is? How does this post-advent judgment shed light on God's character of love and justice?

6. What is the final destiny of the saved and the lost? Why doesn't God save everyone in the end? Do you think God would if He "could"? How should understanding this affect our lives today?
7. What do you look forward to most in the New Earth?
8. You can live forever on the New Earth. Do you wish to live with God forever, in perpetual bliss and joy? If so, make a commitment right now. Now is the time to not only commit ourselves to the way of the Lamb as we await His return but to spread His love to others in word and in deed.

For Further Reading

Adventist Perspectives:

Davidson, Jo Ann. "The Second Coming of Christ: Is There a 'Delay'?" In *God's Character and the Last Generation*. Edited by Jiří Moskala and John C. Peckham. Nampa, ID: Pacific Press, 2018.

de Souza, Elias Brasil, A. Rahel Wells, Laszlo Gallusz, and Denis Kaiser, eds. *Eschatology from an Adventist Perspective*. Silver Spring, MD: Biblical Research Institute, 2021.

Doukhan, Jacques B. *Secrets of Daniel: Wisdom and Dreams of a Jewish Prince in Exile*. Hagerstown, MD: Review and Herald, 2000.

———. *Secrets of Revelation: The Apocalypse through Hebrew Eyes*. Hagerstown, MD: Review and Herald, 2002.

Froom, Le Roy Edwin. *The Conditionalist Faith of Our Fathers*. 2 vols. Washington, DC: Review and Herald, 1965–1966.

———. *The Prophetic Faith of Our Fathers*. 4 vols. Washington, DC: Review and Herald, 1950–1954.

Gulley, Norman R. *Systematic Theology: The Church and Last Things*. Berrien Springs, MI: Andrews University Press, 2016.

Holbrook, Frank B., ed. *Symposium on Revelation—Book I*, Daniel and Revelation Committee Series 6. Silver Spring, MD: Biblical Research Institute, 1992.

———, ed. *Symposium on Revelation—Book II*, Daniel and Revelation Committee Series 7. Silver Spring, MD: Biblical Research Institute, 1992.

Johnsson, William G. "Biblical Apocalyptic." In *Handbook of Seventh-day Adventist Theology*. Edited by Raoul Dederen. Hagerstown, MD: Review and Herald, 2000.

LaRondelle, Hans K. *The Israel of God in Prophecy: Principles of Prophetic Interpretation*. Berrien Springs, MI: Andrews University Press, 1983.

Lehmann, Richard P. "The Second Coming of Jesus." In *Handbook of Seventh-day Adventist Theology*. Edited by Raoul Dederen. Hagerstown, MD: Review and Herald, 2000.

Moskala, Jiří, and John Reeve, eds. *God and Death*. Berrien Springs, MI: Andrews University Press (forthcoming).

Nam, Daegeuk. "The New Earth and the Eternal Kingdom." In *Handbook of Seventh-day Adventist Theology*. Edited by Raoul Dederen. Hagerstown, MD: Review and Herald, 2000.

Peckham, John C. "Conditionalism: A Systematic Case." In *What Is Hell?* Edited by Paul Copan and Christopher M. Date. Downers Grove, IL: IVP Academic (forthcoming).

Rodríguez, Ángel Manuel, ed. *Toward a Theology of the Remnant: An Adventist Ecclesiological Perspective*. Studies in Adventist Ecclesiology 1. Silver Spring, MD: Biblical Research Institute, 2009.

Stefanovic, Ranko. *Revelation of Jesus Christ: Commentary on the Book of Revelation*, 2nd ed. Berrien Springs, MI: Andrews University Press, 2009.

Webster, Eric Claude. "The Millennium." In *Handbook of Seventh-day Adventist Theology*. Edited by Raoul Dederen. Hagerstown, MD: Review and Herald, 2000.

White, Ellen G. *The Great Controversy*. Mountain View, CA: Pacific Press, 1911.

See also the resources on the Biblical Research Institute website: https://adventistbiblicalresearch.org/materials/.

Other Christian Perspectives:

Blomberg, Craig and Sung Wook Chung, eds., *A Case for Historic Premillennialism: An Alternative to "Left Behind" Eschatology*. Grand Rapids, MI: Baker Academic, 2009.

Copan, Paul and Christopher M. Date, eds. *What Is Hell?* Downers Grove, IL: IVP Academic, forthcoming.

Date, Christopher M., Gregory G. Stump, and Joshua W. Anderson, eds. *Rethinking Hell: Readings in Evangelical Conditionalism.* Eugene, OR: Cascade, 2014.

────── and Ron Highfield, eds. *A Consuming Passion: Essays on Hell and Immortality in Honor of Edward Fudge.* Eugene, OR: Pickwick, 2015.

Edwards, David L. and John R. W. Stott, *Evangelical Essentials: A Liberal-Evangelical Dialogue.* Downers Grove, IL: InterVarsity Press, 1989.

Fudge, Edward. *The Fire that Consumes: A Biblical and Historical Study of the Doctrine of Final Punishment*, 3rd ed. Cambridge: Lutterworth, 2012.

Middleton, J. Richard. *A New Heaven and a New Earth: Reclaiming Biblical Eschatology.* Grand Rapids, MI: Baker Academic, 2014.

Mühling, Markus, ed. *T&T Clark Handbook of Christian Eschatology.* London: T&T Clark, 2015.

Sprinkle, Preston, ed. *Four Views on Hell*, 2nd ed. Grand Rapids, MI: Zondervan, 2016.

Walls, Jerry L., ed. *The Oxford Handbook of Eschatology.* Oxford: Oxford University Press, 2010.

Wittmer, Michael. *Four Views on Heaven.* Grand Rapids, MI: Zondervan, 2022.

EPILOGUE

ASK, SEEK, KNOCK

We've covered quite a bit of ground in this book. Yet, many questions remain and warrant further treatment. Undoubtedly, you have more questions that come to mind even now, and I encourage you to keep seeking answers, aiming at finding truth (wherever it leads) and the beauty and goodness by which genuine truth is always ultimately accompanied.

In short, I encourage you to ask, seek, and knock, as Jesus Himself invited people to do. As Christ put it: "Ask, and it will be given to you; search, and you will find; knock, and the door will be opened for you. For everyone who asks receives, and everyone who searches finds, and for everyone who knocks, the door will be opened" (Matt. 7:7–8, NRSVue).

As you seek God, remember that He is already seeking you. Christ Himself stands at the door and knocks (Rev. 3:20) and, long before, God promised, "you will seek Me and find Me when you search for Me with all your heart" (Jer. 29:13).

This is not the end, but only the beginning of our quest to know God more—a quest that will continue forever. Do you, even now, have difficult questions in mind—perhaps even doubts? If so, let me encourage you that God can handle your questions and your doubts. Indeed, the God of the Bible encourages questions that are asked in good faith. So, keep asking, seeking, and knocking. Keep searching for the God who created all things, loves you more than you can imagine, and desires to be *with* you forever.

"He who testifies to these things says, 'Yes, I am coming quickly.' Amen. Come, Lord Jesus. The grace of the Lord Jesus be with all. Amen" (Rev. 22:20–21).

APPENDIX

SEVENTH-DAY ADVENTIST FUNDAMENTAL BELIEFS

The latest (2020) edition of these fundamental beliefs can be found here: https://www.adventist.org/wp-content/uploads/2020/06/ADV-28Beliefs2020.pdf

Seventh-day Adventists accept the Bible as their only creed and hold certain fundamental beliefs to be the teaching of the Holy Scriptures. These beliefs, as set forth here, constitute the church's understanding and expression of the teaching of Scripture. Revision of these statements may be expected at a General Conference Session when the church is led by the Holy Spirit to a fuller understanding of Bible truth or finds better language in which to express the teachings of God's Holy Word.

1 The Holy Scriptures

The Holy Scriptures, Old and New Testaments, are the written Word of God, given by divine inspiration. The inspired authors spoke and wrote as they were moved by the Holy Spirit. In this Word, God has committed to humanity the knowledge necessary for salvation. The Holy Scriptures are the supreme, authoritative, and the infallible revelation of His will. They are the standard of character, the test of experience, the definitive revealer of doctrines, and the trustworthy record of God's acts in history. (Ps. 119:105; Prov. 30:5, 6; Isa. 8:20; John 17:17; 1 Thess. 2:13; 2 Tim. 3:16, 17; Heb. 4:12; 2 Peter 1:20, 21.)

2 The Trinity

There is one God: Father, Son, and Holy Spirit, a unity of three coeternal Persons. God is immortal, all-powerful, all-knowing, above all, and ever present. He is infinite and beyond human comprehension, yet known through His self-revelation. God, who is love, is forever worthy of worship, adoration, and service by the whole creation. (Gen. 1:26; Deut. 6:4; Isa. 6:8; Matt. 28:19; John 3:16; 2 Cor. 1:21, 22; 13:14; Eph. 4:4-6; 1 Peter 1:2.)

3 The Father

God the eternal Father is the Creator, Source, Sustainer, and Sovereign of all creation. He is just and holy, merciful and gracious, slow to anger, and abounding in steadfast love and faithfulness. The qualities and powers exhibited in the Son and the Holy Spirit are also those of the Father. (Gen. 1:1; Deut. 4:35; Ps. 110:1, 4; John 3:16; 14:9; 1 Cor. 15:28; 1 Tim. 1:17; 1 John 4:8; Rev. 4:11.)

4 The Son

God the eternal Son became incarnate in Jesus Christ. Through Him all things were created, the character of God is revealed, the salvation of humanity is accomplished, and the world is judged. Forever truly God, He became also truly human, Jesus the Christ. He was conceived of the Holy Spirit and born of the virgin Mary. He lived and experienced temptation as a human being, but perfectly exemplified the righteousness and love of God. By His miracles He manifested God's power and was attested as God's promised Messiah. He suffered and died voluntarily on the cross for our sins and in our place, was raised from the dead, and ascended to heaven to minister in the heavenly sanctuary in our behalf. He will come again in glory for the final deliverance of His people and the restoration of all things. (Isa. 53:4-6; Dan. 9:25-27; Luke 1:35; John 1:1-3, 14; 5:22; 10:30; 14:1-3, 9, 13; Rom. 6:23; 1 Cor. 15:3, 4; 2 Cor. 3:18; 5:17-19; Phil. 2:5-11; Col. 1:15-19; Heb. 2:9-18; 8:1, 2.)

5 The Holy Spirit

God the eternal Spirit was active with the Father and the Son in Creation, incarnation, and redemption. He is as much a person as are the Father and the Son. He inspired the writers of Scripture. He filled Christ's life with power. He draws and convicts human beings; and those who respond He renews and transforms into the image of God. Sent by the Father and the Son to be always with His children, He extends spiritual gifts to the church, empowers it to bear witness to Christ, and in harmony with the Scriptures leads it into all truth. (Gen. 1:1, 2; 2 Sam. 23:2;

Ps. 51:11; Isa. 61:1; Luke 1:35; 4:18; John 14:16-18, 26; 15:26; 16:7-13; Acts 1:8; 5:3; 10:38; Rom. 5:5; 1 Cor. 12:7-11; 2 Cor. 3:18; 2 Peter 1:21.)

6 Creation

God has revealed in Scripture the authentic and historical account of His creative activity. He created the universe, and in a recent six-day creation the Lord made "the heavens and the earth, the sea, and all that is in them" and rested on the seventh day. Thus He established the Sabbath as a perpetual memorial of the work He performed and completed during six literal days that together with the Sabbath constituted the same unit of time that we call a week today. The first man and woman were made in the image of God as the crowning work of Creation, given dominion over the world, and charged with responsibility to care for it. When the world was finished it was "very good," declaring the glory of God. (Gen. 1-2; 5; 11; Exod. 20:8-11; Ps. 19:1-6; 33:6, 9; 104; Isa. 45:12, 18; Acts 17:24; Col. 1:16; Heb. 1:2; 11:3; Rev. 10:6; 14:7.)

7 The Nature of Humanity

Man and woman were made in the image of God with individuality, the power and freedom to think and to do. Though created free beings, each is an indivisible unity of body, mind, and spirit, dependent upon God for life and breath and all else. When our first parents disobeyed God, they denied their dependence upon Him and fell from their high position. The image of God in them was marred and they became subject to death. Their descendants share this fallen nature and its consequences. They are born with weaknesses and tendencies to evil. But God in Christ reconciled the world to Himself and by His Spirit restores in penitent mortals the image of their Maker. Created for the glory of God, they are called to love Him and one another, and to care for their environment. (Gen. 1:26-28; 2:7, 15; 3; Ps. 8:4-8; 51:5, 10; 58:3; Jer. 17:9; Acts 17:24-28; Rom. 5:12-17; 2 Cor. 5:19, 20; Eph. 2:3; 1 Thess. 5:23; 1 John 3:4; 4:7, 8, 11, 20.)

8 The Great Controversy

All humanity is now involved in a great controversy between Christ and Satan regarding the character of God, His law, and His sovereignty over the universe. This conflict originated in heaven when a created being, endowed with freedom of choice, in self-exaltation became Satan, God's adversary, and led into rebellion a portion of the angels. He introduced the spirit of rebellion into this world when he led Adam and Eve into sin. This human sin resulted in the distortion of the image of God in humanity, the disordering of the created world, and its eventual devastation at the time of the global flood, as presented in the historical account of Genesis 1-11. Observed by the whole creation, this world became the arena of the universal conflict, out of which the God of love will ultimately be vindicated. To assist His people in this controversy, Christ sends the Holy Spirit and the loyal angels to guide, protect, and sustain them in the way of salvation. (Gen. 3; 6-8; Job 1:6-12; Isa. 14:12-14; Ezek. 28:12-18; Rom. 1:19-32; 3:4; 5:12-21; 8:19-22; 1 Cor. 4:9; Heb. 1:14; 1 Peter 5:8; 2 Peter 3:6; Rev. 12:4-9.)

9 The Life, Death, and Resurrection of Christ

In Christ's life of perfect obedience to God's will, His suffering, death, and resurrection, God provided the only means of atonement for human sin, so that those who by faith accept this atonement may have eternal life, and the whole creation may better understand the infinite and holy love of the Creator. This perfect atonement vindicates the righteousness of God's law and the graciousness of His character; for it both condemns our sin and provides for our forgiveness. The death of Christ is substitutionary and expiatory, reconciling and transforming. The bodily resurrection of Christ proclaims God's triumph over the forces of evil, and for those who accept the atonement assures their final victory over sin and death. It declares the Lordship of Jesus Christ, before whom every knee in heaven and on earth will bow. (Gen. 3:15; Ps. 22:1; Isa. 53; John 3:16; 14:30; Rom. 1:4; 3:25; 4:25; 8:3, 4; 1 Cor. 15:3, 4, 20-22; 2 Cor. 5:14, 15, 19-21; Phil. 2:6-11; Col. 2:15; 1 Peter 2:21, 22; 1 John 2:2; 4:10.)

10 The Experience of Salvation

In infinite love and mercy God made Christ, who knew no sin, to be sin for us, so that in Him we might be made the righteousness of God. Led by the Holy Spirit we sense our need, acknowledge our sinfulness, repent of our transgressions, and exercise faith in Jesus as Saviour and

Lord, Substitute and Example. This saving faith comes through the divine power of the Word and is the gift of God's grace. Through Christ we are justified, adopted as God's sons and daughters, and delivered from the lordship of sin. Through the Spirit we are born again and sanctified; the Spirit renews our minds, writes God's law of love in our hearts, and we are given the power to live a holy life. Abiding in Him we become partakers of the divine nature and have the assurance of salvation now and in the judgment. (Gen. 3:15; Isa. 45:22; 53; Jer. 31:31-34; Ezek. 33:11; 36:25-27; Hab. 2:4; Mark 9:23, 24; John 3:3-8, 16; 16:8; Rom. 3:21-26; 8:1-4, 14-17; 5:6-10; 10:17; 12:2; 2 Cor. 5:17-21; Gal. 1:4; 3:13, 14, 26; 4:4-7; Eph. 2:4-10; Col. 1:13, 14; Titus 3:3-7; Heb. 8:7-12; 1 Peter 1:23; 2:21, 22; 2 Peter 1:3, 4; Rev. 13:8.)

11 Growing in Christ

By His death on the cross Jesus triumphed over the forces of evil. He who subjugated the demonic spirits during His earthly ministry has broken their power and made certain their ultimate doom. Jesus' victory gives us victory over the evil forces that still seek to control us, as we walk with Him in peace, joy, and assurance of His love. Now the Holy Spirit dwells within us and empowers us. Continually committed to Jesus as our Saviour and Lord, we are set free from the burden of our past deeds. No longer do we live in the darkness, fear of evil powers, ignorance, and meaninglessness of our former way of life. In this new freedom in Jesus, we are called to grow into the likeness of His character, communing with Him daily in prayer, feeding on His Word, meditating on it and on His providence, singing His praises, gathering together for worship, and participating in the mission of the Church. We are also called to follow Christ's example by compassionately ministering to the physical, mental, social, emotional, and spiritual needs of humanity. As we give ourselves in loving service to those around us and in witnessing to His salvation, His constant presence with us through the Spirit transforms every moment and every task into a spiritual experience. (1 Chron. 29:11; Ps. 1:1, 2; 23:4; 77:11, 12; Matt. 20:25-28; 25:31-46; Luke 10:17-20; John 20:21; Rom. 8:38, 39; 2 Cor. 3:17, 18; Gal. 5:22-25; Eph. 5:19, 20; 6:12-18; Phil. 3:7-14; Col. 1:13, 14; 2:6, 14, 15; 1 Thess. 5:16-18, 23; Heb. 10:25; James 1:27; 2 Peter 2:9; 3:18; 1 John 4:4.)

12 The Church

The church is the community of believers who confess Jesus Christ as Lord and Saviour. In continuity with the people of God in Old Testament times, we are called out from the world; and we join together for worship, for fellowship, for instruction in the Word, for the celebration of the Lord's Supper, for service to humanity, and for the worldwide proclamation of the gospel. The church derives its authority from Christ, who is the incarnate Word revealed in the Scriptures. The church is God's family; adopted by Him as children, its members live on the basis of the new covenant. The church is the body of Christ, a community of faith of which Christ Himself is the Head. The church is the bride for whom Christ died that He might sanctify and cleanse her. At His return in triumph, He will present her to Himself a glorious church, the faithful of all the ages, the purchase of His blood, not having spot or wrinkle, but holy and without blemish. (Gen. 12:1–3; Exod. 19:3–7; Matt. 16:13–20; 18:18; 28:19, 20; Acts 2:38–42; 7:38; 1 Cor. 1:2; Eph. 1:22, 23; 2:19–22; 3:8–11; 5:23–27; Col. 1:17, 18; 1 Peter 2:9.)

13 The Remnant and Its Mission

The universal church is composed of all who truly believe in Christ, but in the last days, a time of widespread apostasy, a remnant has been called out to keep the commandments of God and the faith of Jesus. This remnant announces the arrival of the judgment hour, proclaims salvation through Christ, and heralds the approach of His second advent. This proclamation is symbolized by the three angels of Revelation 14; it coincides with the work of judgment in heaven and results in a work of repentance and reform on earth. Every believer is called to have a personal part in this worldwide witness. (Dan. 7:9–14; Isa. 1:9; 11:11; Jer. 23:3; Mic. 2:12; 2 Cor. 5:10; 1 Peter 1:16–19; 4:17; 2 Peter 3:10–14; Jude 3, 14; Rev. 12:17; 14:6–12; 18:1–4.)

14 Unity in the Body of Christ

The church is one body with many members, called from every nation, kindred, tongue, and people. In Christ we are a new creation; distinctions of race, culture, learning, and nationality, and differences between high and low, rich and poor, male and female, must not be divisive among us. We are all equal in Christ, who by one Spirit has bonded us into one fellowship with Him and with one another; we are to serve and be served without partiality or reservation. Through the revelation of Jesus Christ in the Scriptures we share the same faith and hope, and reach out in one witness to all. This unity has its source in the oneness of the triune God, who has adopted us as His children. (Ps. 133:1; Matt. 28:19, 20; John 17:20-23; Acts 17:26, 27; Rom. 12:4, 5; 1 Cor. 12:12-14; 2 Cor. 5:16, 17; Gal. 3:27-29; Eph. 2:13-16; 4:3-6, 11-16; Col. 3:10-15.)

15 Baptism

By baptism we confess our faith in the death and resurrection of Jesus Christ, and testify of our death to sin and of our purpose to walk in newness of life. Thus we acknowledge Christ as Lord and Saviour, become His people, and are received as members by His church. Baptism is a symbol of our union with Christ, the forgiveness of our sins, and our reception of the Holy Spirit. It is by immersion in water and is contingent on an affirmation of faith in Jesus and evidence of repentance of sin. It follows instruction in the Holy Scriptures and acceptance of their teachings. (Matt. 28:19, 20; Acts 2:38; 16:30-33; 22:16; Rom. 6:1-6; Gal. 3:27; Col. 2:12, 13.)

16 The Lord's Supper

The Lord's Supper is a participation in the emblems of the body and blood of Jesus as an expression of faith in Him, our Lord and Saviour. In this experience of communion Christ is present to meet and strengthen His people. As we partake, we joyfully proclaim the Lord's death until He comes again. Preparation for the Supper includes self-examination, repentance, and confession. The Master ordained the service of foot-washing to signify renewed cleansing, to express a willingness to serve one another in Christlike humility, and to unite our hearts in love. The communion service is open to all believing Christians. (Matt. 26:17-30; John 6:48-63; 13:1-17; 1 Cor. 10:16, 17; 11:23-30; Rev. 3:20.)

17 Spiritual Gifts and Ministries

God bestows upon all members of His church in every age spiritual gifts that each member is to employ in loving ministry for the common good of the church and of humanity. Given by the agency of the Holy Spirit, who apportions to each member as He wills, the gifts provide all abilities and ministries needed by the church to fulfill its divinely ordained functions. According to the Scriptures, these gifts include such ministries as faith, healing, prophecy, proclamation, teaching, administration, reconciliation, compassion, and self-sacrificing service and charity for the help and encouragement of people. Some members are called of God and endowed by the Spirit for functions recognized by the church in pastoral, evangelistic, and teaching ministries particularly needed to equip the members for service, to build up the church to spiritual maturity, and to foster unity of the faith and knowledge of God. When members employ these spiritual gifts as faithful stewards of God's varied grace, the church is protected from the destructive influence of false doctrine, grows with a growth that is from God, and is built up in faith and love. (Acts 6:1-7; Rom. 12:4-8; 1 Cor. 12:7-11, 27, 28; Eph. 4:8, 11-16; 1 Tim. 3:1-13; 1 Peter 4:10, 11.)

18 The Gift of Prophecy

The Scriptures testify that one of the gifts of the Holy Spirit is prophecy. This gift is an identifying mark of the remnant church and we believe it was manifested in the ministry of Ellen G. White. Her writings speak with prophetic authority and provide comfort, guidance, instruction, and correction to the church. They also make clear that the Bible is the standard by which all teaching and experience must be tested. (Num. 12:6; 2 Chron. 20:20; Amos 3:7; Joel 2:28, 29; Acts 2:14-21; 2 Tim. 3:16, 17; Heb. 1:1-3; Rev. 12:17; 19:10; 22:8, 9.)

19 The Law of God

The great principles of God's law are embodied in the Ten Commandments and exemplified in the life of Christ. They express God's love, will, and purposes concerning human conduct and relationships and are binding upon all people in every age. These precepts are the basis of God's covenant with His people and the standard in God's judgment. Through the agency of the Holy Spirit they point out sin and awaken a sense of need for a Saviour. Salvation is all of grace and not of works, and its fruit is obedience to the Commandments.

This obedience develops Christian character and results in a sense of well-being. It is evidence of our love for the Lord and our concern for our fellow human beings. The obedience of faith demonstrates the power of Christ to transform lives, and therefore strengthens Christian witness. (Exod. 20:1-17; Deut. 28:1-14; Ps. 19:7-14; 40:7, 8; Matt. 5:17-20; 22:36-40; John 14:15; 15:7-10; Rom. 8:3, 4; Eph. 2:8-10; Heb. 8:8-10; 1 John 2:3; 5:3; Rev. 12:17; 14:12.)

20 The Sabbath

The gracious Creator, after the six days of Creation, rested on the seventh day and instituted the Sabbath for all people as a memorial of Creation. The fourth commandment of God's unchangeable law requires the observance of this seventh-day Sabbath as the day of rest, worship, and ministry in harmony with the teaching and practice of Jesus, the Lord of the Sabbath. The Sabbath is a day of delightful communion with God and one another. It is a symbol of our redemption in Christ, a sign of our sanctification, a token of our allegiance, and a foretaste of our eternal future in God's kingdom. The Sabbath is God's perpetual sign of His eternal covenant between Him and His people. Joyful observance of this holy time from evening to evening, sunset to sunset, is a celebration of God's creative and redemptive acts. (Gen. 2:1-3; Exod. 20:8-11; 31:13-17; Lev. 23:32; Deut. 5:12-15; Isa. 56:5, 6; 58:13, 14; Ezek. 20:12, 20; Matt. 12:1-12; Mark 1:32; Luke 4:16; Heb. 4:1-11.)

21 Stewardship

We are God's stewards, entrusted by Him with time and opportunities, abilities and possessions, and the blessings of the earth and its resources. We are responsible to Him for their proper use. We acknowledge God's ownership by faithful service to Him and our fellow human beings, and by returning tithe and giving offerings for the proclamation of His gospel and the support and growth of His church. Stewardship is a privilege given to us by God for nurture in love and the victory over selfishness and covetousness. Stewards rejoice in the blessings that come to others as a result of their faithfulness. (Gen. 1:26-28; 2:15; 1 Chron. 29:14; Haggai 1:3-11; Mal. 3:8-12; Matt. 23:23; Rom. 15:26, 27; 1 Cor. 9:9-14; 2 Cor. 8:1-15; 9:7.)

22 Christian Behavior

We are called to be a godly people who think, feel, and act in harmony with biblical principles in all aspects of personal and social life. For the Spirit to recreate in us the character of our Lord we involve ourselves only in those things that will produce Christlike purity, health, and joy in our lives. This means that our amusement and entertainment should meet the highest standards of Christian taste and beauty. While recognizing cultural differences, our dress is to be simple, modest, and neat, befitting those whose true beauty does not consist of outward adornment but in the imperishable ornament of a gentle and quiet spirit. It also means that because our bodies are the temples of the Holy Spirit, we are to care for them intelligently. Along with adequate exercise and rest, we are to adopt the most healthful diet possible and abstain from the unclean foods identified in the Scriptures. Since alcoholic beverages, tobacco, and the irresponsible use of drugs and narcotics are harmful to our bodies, we are to abstain from them as well. Instead, we are to engage in whatever brings our thoughts and bodies into the discipline of Christ, who desires our wholesomeness, joy, and goodness. (Gen. 7:2; Exod. 20:15; Lev. 11:1–47; Ps. 106:3; Rom. 12:1, 2; 1 Cor. 6:19, 20; 10:31; 2 Cor. 6:14–7:1; 10:5; Eph. 5:1–21; Phil. 2:4; 4:8; 1 Tim. 2:9, 10; Titus 2:11, 12; 1 Peter 3:1–4; 1 John 2:6; 3 John 2.)

23 Marriage and the Family

Marriage was divinely established in Eden and affirmed by Jesus to be a lifelong union between a man and a woman in loving companionship. For the Christian a marriage commitment is to God as well as to the spouse, and should be entered into only between a man and a woman who share a common faith. Mutual love, honor, respect, and responsibility are the fabric of this relationship, which is to reflect the love, sanctity, closeness, and permanence of the relationship between Christ and His church. Regarding divorce, Jesus taught that the person who divorces a spouse, except for fornication, and marries another, commits adultery. Although some family relationships may fall short of the ideal, a man and a woman who fully commit themselves to each other in Christ through marriage may achieve loving unity through the guidance of the Spirit and the nurture of the church. God blesses the family and intends that its members shall assist each other toward complete maturity. Increasing family closeness is one of the earmarks of the final gospel message. Parents are to bring up their children to love and obey the Lord. By their example and their words they are to teach them that Christ is a loving, tender, and caring guide who wants them to become members of His body, the family of God which embraces both single and married persons. (Gen. 2:18-25; Exod. 20:12; Deut. 6:5-9; Prov. 22:6; Mal. 4:5, 6; Matt. 5:31, 32; 19:3-9, 12; Mark 10:11, 12; John 2:1-11; 1 Cor. 7:7, 10, 11; 2 Cor. 6:14; Eph. 5:21-33; 6:1-4.)

24 Christ's Ministry in the Heavenly Sanctuary

There is a sanctuary in heaven, the true tabernacle that the Lord set up and not humans. In it Christ ministers on our behalf, making available to believers the benefits of His atoning sacrifice offered once for all on the cross. At His ascension, He was inaugurated as our great High Priest and, began His intercessory ministry, which was typified by the work of the high priest in the holy place of the earthly sanctuary. In 1844, at the end of the prophetic period of 2,300 days, He entered the second and last phase of His atoning ministry, which was typified by the work of the high priest in the most holy place of the earthly sanctuary. It is a work of investigative judgment which is part of the ultimate disposition of all sin, typified by the cleansing of the ancient Hebrew sanctuary on the Day of Atonement. In that typical service the sanctuary was cleansed with the blood of animal sacrifices, but the heavenly things are purified with the perfect sacrifice of the blood of Jesus. The investigative judgment reveals to heavenly intelligences who among the dead are asleep in Christ and therefore, in Him, are deemed worthy to have part in the first resurrection. It also makes manifest who among the living are abiding in Christ, keeping the commandments of God and the faith of Jesus, and in Him, therefore, are ready for translation into His everlasting kingdom. This judgment vindicates the justice of God in saving those who believe in Jesus. It declares that those who have remained loyal to God shall receive the kingdom. The completion of this ministry of Christ will mark the close of human probation before the Second Advent. (Lev. 16; Num. 14:34; Ezek. 4:6; Dan. 7:9-27; 8:13, 14;

9:24-27; Heb. 1:3; 2:16, 17; 4:14-16; 8:1-5; 9:11-28; 10:19-22; Rev. 8:3-5; 11:19; 14:6, 7; 20:12; 14:12; 22:11, 12.)

25 The Second Coming of Christ

The second coming of Christ is the blessed hope of the church, the grand climax of the gospel. The Saviour's coming will be literal, personal, visible, and worldwide. When He returns, the righteous dead will be resurrected, and together with the righteous living will be glorified and taken to heaven, but the unrighteous will die. The almost complete fulfillment of most lines of prophecy, together with the present condition of the world, indicates that Christ's coming is near. The time of that event has not been revealed, and we are therefore exhorted to be ready at all times. (Matt. 24; Mark 13; Luke 21; John 14:1-3; Acts 1:9-11; 1 Cor. 15:51-54; 1 Thess. 4:13-18; 5:1-6; 2 Thess. 1:7-10; 2:8; 2 Tim. 3:1-5; Titus 2:13; Heb. 9:28; Rev. 1:7; 14:14-20; 19:11-21.)

26 Death and Resurrection

The wages of sin is death. But God, who alone is immortal, will grant eternal life to His redeemed. Until that day death is an unconscious state for all people. When Christ, who is our life, appears, the resurrected righteous and the living righteous will be glorified and caught up to meet their Lord. The second resurrection, the resurrection of the unrighteous, will take place a thousand years later. (Job 19:25-27; Ps. 146:3, 4; Eccl. 9:5, 6, 10; Dan. 12:2, 13; Isa. 25:8; John 5:28, 29; 11:11-14; Rom. 6:23; 16; 1 Cor. 15:51-54; Col. 3:4; 1 Thess. 4:13-17; 1 Tim. 6:15; Rev. 20:1-10.)

27 The Millennium and the End of Sin

The millennium is the thousand-year reign of Christ with His saints in heaven between the first and second resurrections. During this time the wicked dead will be judged; the earth will be utterly desolate, without living human inhabitants, but occupied by Satan and his angels. At its close Christ with His saints and the Holy City will descend from heaven to earth. The unrighteous dead will then be resurrected, and with Satan and his angels will surround the city; but fire from God will consume them and cleanse the earth. The universe will thus be freed of sin and sinners forever. (Jer. 4:23-26; Ezek. 28:18, 19; Mal. 4:1; 1 Cor. 6:2, 3; Rev. 20; 21:1-5.)

28 The New Earth

On the new earth, in which righteousness dwells, God will provide an eternal home for the redeemed and a perfect environment for everlasting life, love, joy, and learning in His presence. For here God Himself will dwell with His people, and suffering and death will have passed away. The great controversy will be ended, and sin will be no more. All things, animate and inanimate, will declare that God is love; and He shall reign forever. Amen. (Isa. 35; 65:17-25; Matt. 5:5; 2 Peter 3:13; Rev. 11:15; 21:1-7; 22:1-5.)

ENDNOTES

PREFACE
1. What follows is drawn from an article previously published in *Ministry* magazine (John C. Peckham, "Questioning God?" *Ministry* 88/6 [June 2016]: 6-9), reprinted here from *Ministry*® International Journal for Pastors, www.MinistryMagazine.org. Used by permission.
2. Martin Luther King Jr., *Strength to Love* (Philadelphia, PA: Fortress, 2010), 2.

INTRODUCTION
1. For example, see J. Scott Duvall and J. Daniel Hays, *God's Relational Presence: The Cohesive Center of Biblical Theology* (Grand Rapids, MI: Baker Academic, 2019).
2. Justo L. González, *A History of Christian Thought: In One Volume* (Nashville, TN: Abingdon, 2014).
3. George R. Knight, *A Search for Identity: The Development of Seventh-day Adventist Beliefs* (Hagerstown, MD: Review and Herald, 2000).

CHAPTER I • THE STORY OF GOD WITH US: PRESENCE RUPTURED AND RENEWED
1. The story retold in this chapter and the one that follows is only an outline of the inexhaustibly rich story of the Bible. Nothing can replace that story. This is but a pale reflection of some elements of that marvelous story. The story can only be fully appreciated by reading it from the Bible itself and I strongly encourage that each one reading this book make a plan to do just that over time. The reading of the Bible itself, in a spirit of prayer, cannot be replaced. So, while I hope this and the chapters that follow will be helpful to you, I bid you, dear reader, to take up the Bible itself and read it for yourself and never stop reading it and prayerfully reflecting on it for the rest of your life.
2. Matthew 27:54.
3. See John 17:24.
4. See chapter 5.
5. See Acts 17:25.
6. See Revelation 4:11.
7. See Acts 17:25; Romans 11:36; Hebrews 1:3; Revelation 4:11.
8. See 1 John 4:8, 16.
9. See Genesis 1:1-25.
10. E.g., Psalm 36:6; Proverbs 12:10; Jonah 4:11.
11. See Genesis 1-3; Exodus 20:1-17; Jeremiah 31:35-37; 33:2-26; Matthew 22:37-40.
12. Genesis 2:7.
13. Genesis 2:21-24.
14. Genesis 1:26, NRSVue.
15. Genesis 1:31.
16. Genesis 2:2-3.
17. God's special presence will be explained further in chapter 8. For now, the reader need only understand it as God being present with His people in some special way or ways.
18. See Genesis 3; Romans 8:20.
19. Genesis 3:4.
20. See Genesis 2:16-17.
21. Genesis 3:5.
22. Genesis 3:6.
23. See Romans 8:21-22.
24. See Deuteronomy 32:4.
25. Genesis 2:16-17.
26. See, e.g., Psalm 145; James 1:17.
27. See Malachi 3:6; James 1:17; 1 John 4:8.
28. See Psalm 5:4; Isaiah 59:2.
29. See Revelation 12:7-9.
30. See Genesis 1:26; Psalm 8:4-6; Luke 4:6; John 12:31; Revelation 12-13 (discussed further in chapter 9).
31. John 8:44; 12:31; 14:30; 16:11.
32. 1 John 3:8; cf. Romans 3:25-26; 5:8; Revelation 12:10-11.
33. Genesis 3:4-5.
34. Genesis 1:31.
35. See Genesis 1:31; 3:4-5.
36. See Ezekiel 28:12-19; cf. Isaiah 14:12-14; Revelation 12:7-9. See the further discussion in chapter 9.
37. See Revelation 12:9-10; cf. Job 1-2. See chapter 9.

38. Genesis 3:8, 10.
39. Genesis 3:12–13.
40. See Genesis 2:16–17; 3:16–19.
41. For a further discussion of the Fall of Adam and Eve and its results, see chapter 12.
42. Genesis 3:15.
43. Genesis 4:1–8.
44. Genesis 6:5.
45. Genesis 6:6.
46. Genesis 6:11–12, NRSVue.
47. Genesis 6:8–9.
48. Genesis 6:13ff.
49. See Genesis 8:20–9:17.
50. See Genesis 11:1–9.
51. See Deuteronomy 32:8–9, 17. See also John C. Peckham, *Theodicy of Love: Cosmic Conflict and the Problem of Evil* (Grand Rapids, MI: Baker Academic, 2018), 69–70.
52. Genesis 12:1–3.
53. See Deuteronomy 32:8–9.
54. See, e.g., 1 John 4:8, 16.
55. See chapter 9. See also, Peckham, *Theodicy of Love*, 42–45.
56. See chapter 9.
57. See Genesis 1:26–28; Psalm 8:6; Luke 4:6; John 12:31; 14:30; 16:11; cf. Revelation 12–13.
58. See Genesis 11:1–9; cf. Deuteronomy 32:8–9, 17. See Peckham, *Theodicy of Love*, 69–70.
59. See Genesis 12–15.
60. See Genesis 12:1–3; Deuteronomy 32:9.
61. Genesis 17:5.
62. See Genesis 16:1–2.
63. Genesis 21:8–14.
64. Genesis 16:5–10.
65. Genesis 21:15–20; cf. 16:11–12.
66. Genesis 17:19.
67. Genesis 17:17; 18:12–15.
68. Genesis 21:1–3.
69. See Genesis 17:19; cf. 21:5–7.
70. Genesis 12:10–20; 20:1–18.
71. Genesis 22:1–14.
72. For more on this and other aspects of "covenant jeopardy," see John H. Walton, *Covenant: God's Purpose, God's Plan* (Grand Rapids, MI: Zondervan, 1994).
73. Genesis 25:21.
74. Genesis 25:23.
75. Genesis 25:29–34.
76. Genesis 27:1–28:5.
77. Genesis 28:12.
78. Genesis 28:13–15.
79. Genesis 37.
80. See Genesis 41–45; Exodus 1:8–14; 2:23–25.
81. Exodus 1:15–21.
82. Exodus 1:22.
83. Exodus 2:1–6.
84. Exodus 2:7.
85. Exodus 2:8–10.
86. Exodus 2:11–22.
87. Exodus 3:1–5.
88. Exodus 3:7–10.
89. Genesis 15:13–16, NRSVue.
90. Exodus 4:22–23.
91. Exodus 7:10–12:36.
92. Exodus 13:21.
93. Exodus 14:5–7.
94. Exodus 14:21.
95. Exodus 14:8–31.
96. See, e.g., Exodus 12:12.
97. Exodus 12:38; cf. 12:48–49.
98. Joshua 2:9–11.
99. Matthew 1:5.

100. Genesis 41:45, 50. And, Moses's wife Zipporah was a Midianite (Exod. 2:21; cf. Num. 12:1).
101. See, e.g., Exodus 12:48–49.
102. See Exodus 19–24.
103. Leviticus 26:11–12.
104. Exodus 24:9–11; 31:18.
105. Matthew 22:37–38.
106. See chapter 14.
107. See, e.g., Numbers 12:6–8.
108. Exodus 25:8.
109. John 1:29; cf. Hebrews 10:10. See chapter 16.
110. See Leviticus 16; cf. Hebrews 8:1–2.
111. See chapter 16.
112. See Exodus 32:1–8.
113. Exodus 32:6.
114. Exodus 32:19–20.
115. Exodus 33:14.
116. Exodus 33:18.
117. Exodus 33:19.
118. Exodus 33:20–34:6.
119. Exodus 3:14.
120. Exodus 34:6–7, NRSVue.
121. Exodus 32:26; 34:1ff.
122. Exodus 40:34–38.
123. Psalm 78:41; cf. Nehemiah 9; Psalm 78.
124. See Hosea 11:8–9; Jeremiah 31:20.
125. Numbers 13:28.
126. Numbers 13:31.
127. Numbers 14:6–10.
128. Numbers 14:20.
129. Numbers 14:22–24.
130. Numbers 14:34–35; cf. Exodus 13:17–18.
131. Deuteronomy 32:51–52; 34:5–6; cf. Numbers 20:10–11; Matthew 17:3; Jude 9.
132. See Joshua 1.
133. This cycle is seen throughout Judges (see Judges 2:8ff.) and onward in the history of the kings of Israel and Judah. For one recounting, see Nehemiah 9.
134. Judges 2:18.
135. Judges 2:19.
136. Judges 4:4.
137. Judges 4–5.
138. Judges 6–8.
139. See, e.g., Judges 17:1–6.
140. See Judges 19–21.
141. Judges 21:25.
142. 1 Samuel 2:22.
143. 1 Samuel 4:22.
144. 1 Samuel 5:1–7:1–2.
145. 1 Samuel 3:1.
146. 1 Samuel 1:11.
147. 1 Samuel 1:20, 27.
148. 1 Samuel 1:24–28.
149. 1 Samuel 3:1–18.
150. 1 Samuel 3:19–21.
151. E.g., 1 Samuel 7:3–4, 13–14.
152. 1 Samuel 8:1–3.
153. 1 Samuel 8:19–20.
154. See 1 Samuel 8:6–22; cf. Deuteronomy 17:14–20.
155. 1 Samuel 8:7.
156. 1 Samuel 10:21–24; 12:13.
157. 1 Samuel 13:13–14.
158. 1 Samuel 13:14.
159. Ruth 4:17.
160. Ruth 1–4.
161. Matthew 1:5–6.
162. 2 Samuel 7:13–14.

163. 1 Kings 2:1-4.
164. 1 Kings 9:4-7.
165. See, e.g., 1 Kings 10.
166. 1 Kings 3:5-28.
167. 1 Kings 8:10-11.
168. See 1 Kings 11.
169. See 1 Kings 12ff.; cf. 11:11-13.
170. 1 Kings 18:17-40.
171. See e.g., 2 Chronicles 24:19; cf. Psalm 81:11-14.
172. See Jonah 1-4.
173. Psalm 106:37-38; cf. Deuteronomy 32:17.
174. Psalm 81:11-14.
175. See, e.g., Isaiah 30:15-18.
176. Isaiah 66:4.
177. See e.g., Psalm 78:40; cf. Hosea 11:8.
178. Isaiah 1:16-17. See also Isaiah 10:1-3; Micah 6:8; Zechariah 7:9-10.
179. See Psalm 78.
180. Psalm 78:40-41.
181. See 2 Kings 17.
182. 2 Chronicles 36:16; cf. Isaiah 5:1-5.
183. See Ezekiel 11:22-23; cf. On God's *special* presence, see chapter 8.
184. 2 Chronicles 36:17-21.
185. Daniel 1.
186. See Daniel 1:8-21.
187. See Daniel 3.
188. Daniel 3:16-17.
189. Daniel 3:24-27.
190. See Daniel 6.
191. See Daniel 2 and 7.
192. Daniel 9:24-27. See also chapter 16.
193. 2 Chronicles 36:22-23; cf. Isaiah 44:28-45:1.
194. See Esther 1-10.
195. See Ezra 4-5.
196. See, e.g., Psalm 89.

CHAPTER 2 • THE STORY OF GOD WITH US: PRESENCE COMING AND COMING AGAIN
1. Luke 1:31.
2. Luke 1:34-35.
3. Luke 1:32-33.
4. Matthew 1:20-21.
5. Matthew 1:22-23; cf. Isaiah 7:14.
6. Luke 2:4-7; cf. Micah 5:2.
7. Luke 2:7.
8. Luke 2:8-14.
9. Luke 2:25-38.
10. Matthew 2:11.
11. Matthew 2:16-18; cf. Jeremiah 31:15; Revelation 12:4.
12. See Revelation 12:4-5.
13. Matthew 2:13-15, 19-21.
14. Genesis 3:15.
15. Matthew 1:3-6. See Genesis 38; Joshua 2:1-21; 6:23-25; Ruth 1-4; 2 Samuel 11.
16. See Matthew 20:28; cf. Philippians 2:5-8.
17. Galatians 4:4.
18. Matthew 2:14.
19. Luke 3:21-22.
20. John 1:34-36. See also chapter 16.
21. Matthew 2:23.
22. Luke 2:47.
23. Mark 1:12-13.
24. Luke 4:2.
25. Luke 4:6-7.
26. See Matthew 4:1-11; Luke 4:1-13.
27. See Matthew 12:27-29; John 12:31.
28. See Matthew 4:3; John 8:44; Revelation 12:9; cf. Acts 5:2; 2 Corinthians 11:3; 1 John 3:8; Revelation 2:10.

29. See Revelation 12:10; cf. Job 1–2; Zechariah 3:1–2; Jude 9; Revelation 13:6.
30. See John 12:31; 14:30; 16:11; cf. Matthew 12:24–29; Luke 4:5–6; Acts 26:18; 2 Corinthians 4:4; Ephesians 2:2; 1 John 5:19; Revelation 12–13.
31. John 18:37, NRSVue.
32. See Romans 3:25–26; 5:8; Revelation 12:10–11.
33. Revelation 12:12; 11:15; cf. Romans 16:20.
34. 1 John 3:8; Hebrews 2:14.
35. See Mark 2:14–15; 3:13–19; John 1:35–51; cf. Matthew 4:18–22; Mark 1:16–20; Luke 5:1–11.
36. Luke 5:1–11.
37. Matthew 8:14–17; Mark 1:30–34; Luke 4:38–41.
38. John 2:1–11.
39. Matthew 4:23; cf. Mark 1:38–39.
40. John 4:46–54.
41. Mark 1:21–27; cf. Luke 4:31–37.
42. Mark 1:40–42; cf. Matthew 8:1–4; Luke 5:12–16.
43. Mark 2:1–12; cf. Matthew 9:1–8; Luke 5:17–26.
44. Mark 5:25–34.
45. Mark 5:36.
46. Mark 5:41–42.
47. John 11:1–44.
48. See Mark 6:34–44; cf. Matthew 9:36; 14:14; Mark 1:41; 10:21; Luke 7:14.
49. Luke 4:16–19; cf. Isaiah 61:1–2.
50. John 5:16–18; 8:58, cf. Matthew 9:2–3; Mark 2:5–8; Luke 5:20–21;.
51. Mark 2:16; cf. Luke 7:34–35.
52. Matthew 9:11–13.
53. Matthew 21:12–14.
54. See, e.g., 2 Corinthians 5:21; 1 Peter 2:22; 1 John 3:5.
55. Mark 1:22.
56. See Matthew 7:12; 22:37–40.
57. Matthew 23:23; cf. Luke 11:42.
58. Luke 10:42.
59. For much more on Christ's teachings, see William G. Johnsson, *Jesus of Nazareth: His Life, His Message, His Passion* (Berrien Springs, MI: Andrews University Press, 2018), chapters 149–257.
60. Luke 16:31.
61. John 3:8.
62. John 3:3–8.
63. See John 4:26.
64. See John 4:5–42.
65. See Matthew 14:30; 16:21; John 13:18–19.
66. Luke 9:22.
67. Matthew 21:9.
68. John 18:36.
69. Matthew 23:37.
70. Matthew 21:15; Mark 11:18.
71. Matthew 26:14–16.
72. Matthew 26:6–13.
73. See John 13:1–17.
74. Matthew 26:20–25; John 13:25–27.
75. Mark 14:22–25.
76. Mark 14:27–30.
77. Mark 14:33–34.
78. Matthew 26:39.
79. Matthew 26:51–54; Luke 22:50–51; John 18:10–11.
80. Luke 22:53, NRSVue.
81. John 10:18.
82. Matthew 26:56.
83. John 18:12–13, 19–24.
84. Matthew 26:59–68.
85. Luke 22:60–62; cf. Matthew 26:69–75.
86. Matthew 27:1–2; Luke 23:1–2.
87. Luke 23:14–16.
88. Luke 23:21–25.
89. Matthew 27:26–31.
90. Luke 23:27.

91. Mark 15:22.
92. Luke 23:34; cf. Psalm 22:18.
93. Matthew 27:33–37; Luke 23:36–38.
94. Luke 23:35.
95. Luke 23:41–43.
96. Luke 23:44–45.
97. Matthew 27:45–46.
98. Luke 23:46.
99. Matthew 27:51; Luke 23:44–45.
100. Luke 23:47.
101. Matthew 27:54.
102. John 19:31–37; cf. Psalm 34:20.
103. John 19:34–35.
104. 1 John 2:2, NRSVue.
105. John 15:13.
106. Matthew 27:57–60; cf. Luke 23:50–53; John 19:38–42.
107. Luke 23:54–56; cf. Matthew 27:55–56.
108. See Mark 16:1; Luke 24:1–10.
109. John 20:1–2.
110. Luke 24:1–3.
111. Luke 24:4–5.
112. Matthew 28:5–7. See also Luke 24:4–8.
113. Matthew 28:8.
114. Matthew 27:62–66.
115. Matthew 28:2–4.
116. Matthew 28:11–15.
117. See, e.g., Josephus, *Antiquities*, 4.219.
118. Luke 23:9–11.
119. John 20:3–7.
120. John 20:11–12.
121. John 20:13–16.
122. John 20:17, NRSVue.
123. On the significance of this and the later inauguration of the heavenly sanctuary, see chapter 16.
124. Matthew 28:8–10.
125. Luke 24:26.
126. Luke 24:27.
127. Luke 24:31.
128. Luke 24:33–35.
129. John 20:19–20.
130. Luke 24:39.
131. Luke 24:41–43.
132. John 20:24–30.
133. John 21:1–6.
134. John 21:15–19.
135. On the martyrdom of many of the disciples see the ancient record in Eusebius, *The Church History*, II:IX; II:XXIII; II:XXV. For more on this, see Sean McDowell, *On the Fate of the Apostles: Examining the Martyrdom Accounts of the Closest Followers of Jesus* (New York: Routledge, 2015).
136. 1 Corinthians 15:3–9.
137. Acts 1:1–3.
138. John 14:16–19.
139. Hebrews 8:1–2.
140. Hebrews 7:25.
141. Luke 24:44–49.
142. Matthew 28:18–20.
143. Luke 24:50–51.
144. Acts 1:9–11.
145. Luke 24:52–53.
146. Acts 1:4–8.
147. Acts 1:13–14.
148. Acts 1:3, 9.
149. See Leviticus 23:9–16.
150. See Revelation 1:5.
151. Acts 2:1–4, NRSVue.
152. Acts 2:5–12.

153. Acts 2:21.
154. Acts 2:38–42.
155. Acts 2:43–47, NRSVue.
156. E.g., John 7:39.
157. Acts 3:6, NRSVue.
158. Acts 3:7–8, NRSVue.
159. Acts 3:11–26.
160. Acts 4:1ff.
161. Acts 4:18.
162. Acts 4:19–22.
163. Acts 4:29.
164. Acts 4:31.
165. Acts 4:32–35.
166. Acts 5:14.
167. Acts 5:17–21.
168. Acts 5:27–32.
169. Acts 5:38–39.
170. Acts 5:40–42.
171. Acts 6:7.
172. Acts 6:1–6, NRSVue.
173. Acts 6:8–12.
174. Acts 7:51.
175. Acts 7:54–60.
176. Acts 8:1–3.
177. Acts 8:4–8.
178. Acts 8:26–40.
179. Acts 9:1–6.
180. Acts 9:9.
181. Acts 9:11–12.
182. Acts 9:15.
183. Acts 9:17.
184. Acts 9:20.
185. Acts 9:23–25.
186. See Galatians 1:17–19.
187. Acts 9:30.
188. See Galatians 1:21–24.
189. Acts 9:31.
190. Acts 9:32–34.
191. Acts 9:36–42.
192. Acts 10:1–8.
193. Acts 10:9–16.
194. Acts 10:19–28.
195. Acts 10:34–35.
196. Acts 10:43.
197. Acts 10:44–45.
198. Acts 10:48.
199. Acts 11:15.
200. Acts 11:18.
201. Acts 11:19–30.
202. Acts 12:2.
203. Acts 12:5.
204. Acts 12:7–16.
205. Acts 13:4.
206. Acts 13:14–52.
207. Acts 14:1.
208. Acts 14:5–7.
209. Acts 14:8–10.
210. Acts 14:19.
211. Acts 14:20–27.
212. Acts 15:8–11.
213. Acts 15:12.
214. Acts 15:15–17; cf. Amos 9:11–12.
215. Acts 15:19–20.
216. Galatians 2:11–14.

217. See 1 Corinthians 14:29, 37–38.
218. See, e.g., Acts 17:10–11; Galatians 1:8; cf. Isaiah 8:20.
219. Acts 17:10–12.
220. See Acts 1:14; cf. Galatians 1:19. Josephus refers to the stoning of James, the brother of Jesus, in *Antiquities* 20.9.1. See also McDowell, *Fate of the Apostles*.
221. Acts 15:36–41.
222. Acts 16:6–15.
223. Acts 16:16–19.
224. Acts 16:25–26.
225. Acts 16:27–40.
226. Acts 17:2–3.
227. Acts 17:12–14.
228. Acts 17:11.
229. Acts 17:32–34.
230. Acts 18:1–8.
231. Acts 18:9–11.
232. Acts 18:19. See also 18:12–22.
233. Acts 18:26.
234. Acts 18:27–28.
235. Acts 19:11–12.
236. Acts 19:17–19; cf. 19:26.
237. Acts 19:28–29.
238. Acts 20:2–3.
239. Acts 20:7–12.
240. Acts 21:11–13.
241. Acts 21:27–36.
242. Acts 21:37–40.
243. Acts 22:1ff.
244. Acts 22:22.
245. Acts 23:10. See also 22:24–23:10.
246. Acts 23:11.
247. Acts 23:12–31.
248. Acts 24:1–9.
249. Acts 24:14.
250. Acts 24:22–26.
251. Acts 25:8.
252. Acts 25:9–12.
253. Acts 25:13–27.
254. Acts 26:18.
255. Acts 26:21–23.
256. Acts 26:28.
257. Acts 26:31–32.
258. See Acts 27.
259. Acts 27:24.
260. Acts 27:44.
261. Acts 28:1–9.
262. Acts 28:23.
263. Acts 28:31.
264. See, e.g., Eusebius, *The Church History*, II:XXV. See also, McDowell, *Fate of the Apostles*.
265. 2 Timothy 4:7–8.
266. See, e.g., Eusebius, *The Church History*, II:XXIII; II:XXV. And, the first-century Jewish historian Josephus himself reports the death of James the brother of Jesus by stoning. Josephus, *Antiquities* 20.9.1. See also McDowell, *Fate of the Apostles*.
267. On this tradition regarding John, see Tertullian (ca. AD 200) in *The Prescription Against Heretics*, 36. See also Ellen G. White, *Acts of the Apostles*, (Mountain View, CA: Pacific Press, 1911), 570.
268. John 14:2–3, NRSVue.
269. Acts 1:11.
270. 2 Peter 3:3–4.
271. 2 Peter 3:9.
272. Acts 1:6–7.
273. See Mark 13:32.
274. Mark 13:6–8.
275. Mark 13:9.
276. Mark 13:10; see also Mathew 24:14.

277. Mark 13:26-27.
278. See Revelation 12:1-17. See the further discussion in chapter 18.
279. Revelation 12:17.
280. See Revelation 13; cf. Daniel 7-8. See the further discussion in chapter 18.
281. Daniel 12:2. See also Revelation 20-22.
282. 1 Corinthians 15:52.
283. 1 Corinthians 15:54; cf. Isaiah 25:8.
284. 1 Thessalonians 4:14-17.
285. Revelation 21:2; cf. 21:10; 2 Peter 3:13.
286. Revelation 21:3-4.

CHAPTER 3 • IS THE STORY TRUE? PRESENCE WITH US IN TRUTH
1. Here, I use "faith" in the minimal sense of trust or confidence in something or someone.
2. As Thomas Reid put it: "If a man's honesty were called into question, it would be ridiculous to refer to the man's own word, whether he be honest or not. The same absurdity there is in attempting to prove, by any kind of reasoning, probable or demonstrative, that our reason is not fallacious, since the very point in question is, whether reasoning may be trusted." Thomas Reid, *Essays on the Intellectual Powers of Man* (Edinburgh: For John Bell, 1785), 592. See also Nicholas Wolterstorff, *Thomas Reid and the Story of Epistemology* (Cambridge: Cambridge University Press, 2004).
3. Here, it is worth noting that much that science studies is unseen and relates to things we do not understand such as so-called "dark matter" and "dark energy." In this regard, Michael Guillen writes, "When I was an atheist... my worldview rested on the core axiom that seeing is believing. When I learned that 95% of the cosmos is invisible, consisting of 'dark matter' and 'dark energy,' names for things we don't understand, that core assumption became untenable. As a scientist, I had to believe in a universe I mostly could not see. My core axiom became 'believing is seeing.' Because what we hold to be true dictates how we understand everything—ourselves, others and our mostly invisible universe, including its origin. Faith precedes knowledge, not the other way around." Michael Guillen, "Why Atheists Need Faith," The Wall Street Journal, accessed September 23, 2021, https://www.wsj.com/articles/atheists-need-faith-christianity-science-reason-physics-math-astronomy-11632426886?.
4. See Steven B. Cowan and James S. Spiegel, *The Love of Wisdom: A Christian Introduction to Philosophy* (Nashville, TN: B&H Academic, 2009), 47-100.
5. See Alvin Plantinga, *Knowledge and Christian Belief* (Grand Rapids, MI: Eerdmans, 2015).
6. As Plantinga defines it, "The *sensus divinitatis* is a belief-producing faculty (or power, or mechanism) that under the right conditions produces belief that isn't evidentially based on other beliefs." Plantinga, *Warranted Christian Belief* (Oxford: Oxford University Press, 2000), 179. See also John Calvin, *Institutes of the Christian Religion*, Book 1, Chapter 3.
7. See Plantinga, *Knowledge and Christian Belief*, 14. Roughly defined, a "basic belief" is one that is "not accepted on the evidential basis of other beliefs." Plantinga, *Knowledge and Christian Belief*, 14. For Alvin Plantinga, a *properly* basic belief is one that is warranted, which means it is "produced by cognitive faculties functioning properly in a congenial epistemic environment according to a design plan successfully aimed at truth." Plantinga, *Warranted Christian Belief*, 178. This approach is known as proper functionalism, a form of reliabilism.
8. For an introduction to some of these arguments, which I have drawn from in my summary of some of them, see J. P. Moreland and William Lane Craig, *Philosophical Foundations for a Christian Worldview* (Downers Grove, IL: InterVarsity Press, 2003), 463-500. See also Jerry L. Walls and Trent Dougherty, eds., *Two Dozen (or So) Arguments for God* (Oxford: Oxford University Press, 2018).
9. Stephen Meyer makes a strong case from the scientific data that undergirds both cosmological and teleological arguments. Specifically, Meyer argues that that scientific data supports three conclusions that strongly point to the existence of God: (1) the universe had a beginning, (2) the universe has been finely tuned for the possibility of life, and (3) there have been huge bursts of information into our biosphere. See Stephen Meyer, *Return of the God Hypothesis: Three Scientific Discoveries that Reveal the Mind Behind the Universe* (New York: HarperOne, 2021).
10. On the beauty of the Christian story, see Gregory E. Ganssle, *Our Deepest Desires: How the Christian Story Fulfills Human Aspirations* (Downers Grove, IL: InterVarsity Press, 2017), 73-102. See also, Jo Ann Davidson, *Toward a Theology of Beauty: A Biblical Perspective* (Lanham, MD: University Press of America, 2008).
11. See, e.g., Craig L. Blomberg, *The Historical Reliability of the Gospels*, 2nd edition (Downers Grove, IL: IVP Academic, 2007); Gary R. Habermas, *The Historical Jesus: Ancient Evidence for the Life of Christ* (Joplin, MO: College Press, 1996); Gary R. Habermas and Mike Licona, *The Case for the Resurrection of Jesus* (Grand Rapids, MI: Kregel Publications, 2004); Mike Licona, *The Resurrection of Jesus: A New Historiographical Approach* (Downers Grove, IL: IVP Academic, 2010). See also, Clifford Goldstein, *Risen: Finding Hope in the Empty Tomb* (Nampa, ID: Pacific Press, 2020).
12. See, for example, Albert Camus's novel, *The Stranger*, wherein the protagonist of the story (Meursault) concludes the universe is purely physical and life is ultimately meaningless. For him, "nothing had the least importance"; "the deaths of others, or a mother's love" made no difference to him.

He concluded it does not matter what one does or how one decides to live since eventually all will die. There is no God and no greater meaning to human life, but only "the benign indifference of the universe." Albert Camus, *The Stranger*, trans. Stuart Gilbert (New York: Vintage, 1958), 152, 154. See also Jean-Paul Sartre, *Being and Nothingness*, trans. Hazel E. Barnes (New York: Philosophical Library, 1956).

13. Lee Strobel, Twitter (@LeeStrobel, December 24, 2017). For his account of his quest, see Lee Strobel, *The Case for Christ: A Journalist's Personal Investigation of the Evidence for Jesus* (Grand Rapids, MI: Zondervan, 1998).

14. For arguments along these lines (and many others), see Walls and Dougherty, *Two Dozen (or So) Arguments for God*. Regarding the reliance of the development of the scientific method itself on theism, Jeffrey Koperski explains, the thinking of modern philosophers who rejected "Aristotelian metaphysics" in favor of what developed into modern science "was intrinsically theistic: There were laws for the whole of nature because there was a divine lawgiver." Jeffrey Koperski, "How the Laws of Nature were Naturalised," *Science and Christian Belief* 33/2 (2021): 63. In this regard, Craig Keener notes: "Modern science originally developed in contexts that affirmed that a superintelligent God created the universe and that it therefore should make sense." Craig Keener, "Miracles Don't Violate the Laws of Nature," *Christianity Today*, accessed May 13, 2022, https://www.christianitytoday.com/ct/2022/february-web-only/miracles-philosophy-skepticism-laws-nature.html.

15. This highlights one failure of the project of modernism and modernist epistemology that demands some neutral and indubitable foundation for beliefs. This was the quest of, for example, René Descartes (1596–1650), the rationalist philosopher often referred to as the father of modern philosophy. But, nearly all philosophers now recognize that this modernist (Cartesian) quest has failed, for there is no neutral standpoint and few, if any, things that *cannot* be doubted (especially relative to grounding a system of beliefs). Recognizing the failure of modernism, in this respect, frees one to recognize that *all* systems of belief require decisions of faith such that the starting point of the atheist-naturalist is no more neutral or indubitable than that of the theist.

16. Justin L. Barrett, "Out of the Mouths of Babes," *The Guardian*, accessed November 25, 2008, https://www.theguardian.com/commentisfree/belief/2008/nov/25/religion-children-god-belief#:.

17. See, in this regard, Alvin Plantinga, *Where the Conflict Really Lies: Science, Religion, and Naturalism* (New York: Oxford University Press, 2011), 307–50.

18. Indeed, I am convinced that the data of Scripture and the data of nature do not contradict one another. See the discussion of the relationship between them on page 334.

19. With respect to scientism: "When science is credited as the one and only way we have to describe reality, or to state truth, such restrictive epistemology might graduate into scientism. According to this view, the only rationality is scientific rationality. Poetry, literature, music, fine art, religion, or ethics could not be considered sources of knowledge, according to this view, because they are not generated by scientific methods. Such fealty to the deliverances of science, especially at the expense of other ways of knowing, can become ideological, and scientism is the preferred description of such a view. While enthusiasm for science has been a part of its ethos since the Enlightenment, scientism goes beyond enthusiasm in its insistence that whatever falls outside the scope of science is not knowledge." "Science and Ideology," *Internet Encyclopedia of Philosophy*, accessed October 20, 2021, https://iep.utm.edu/sci-ideo/#H6.

20. The approach known as logical positivism (i.e., logical empiricism) also cuts itself off from addressing metaphysical questions because it limits knowledge to that which can be verified by empirical observation or logical proof beyond any possible doubt (known as the verification principle).

21. In other words, the scientific method is limited to physics rather than metaphysics. However, as Ronald Nash explains, "worldviews should fit" not only our knowledge of the external world but they also should "fit what we know about ourselves" such as: "I am a being who thinks, hopes, experiences pleasure and pain, believes, desires. I am also a being who is often conscious of right and wrong and who feels guilty and sinful for having failed to do what was right. I am a being who remembers the past, is conscious of the present, and anticipates the future. I can think about things that do not exist. I can plan and then execute my plans. I am able to act intentionally; instead of merely responding to stimuli, I can will to do something and then actually do it. I am a person who loves other human beings. I can empathize with others and share their sorrow and joy. I know that someday I will die" but believe there will be an afterlife and "I seem often to be overcome by moods and emotions that suggest that the ultimate satisfaction I seek is unattainable in this life." Ronald Nash, *Worldviews in Conflict: Choosing Christianity in a World of Ideas* (Grand Rapids, MI: Zondervan, 1992), 59.

22. By "personal" God I mean one with self-consciousness, rationality, will, and love; not merely a force or a transcendent, disinterested deity.

23. For an introduction to the historical evidence regarding Jesus of Nazareth, see Habermas, *The Historical Jesus*, 187–242. See also, Blomberg, *The Historical Reliability of the Gospels*; Craig S. Keener, *The Historical Jesus of the Gospels* (Grand Rapids, MI: Eerdmans, 2012); Edwin Yamauchi, "Jesus Outside the New Testament: What is the Evidence?", in *Jesus Under Fire*, ed. by Michael J. Wilkins and J. P. Moreland (Grand Rapids, MI: Zondervan, 1995), 207–30; Gerd Theissen and Annette Merz, *The Historical Jesus: A Comprehensive Guide* (Minneapolis, MN: Fortress, 1998); F. F. Bruce, *Jesus and Christian Origins Outside the*

New Testament (London: Hodder and Stoughton, 1974); cf. Strobel, *The Case for Christ*, 19–130. Regarding some oft-repeated, but thoroughly debunked and spurious, claims that the biblical story of Jesus was copied from pagan mythology, see Mary Jo Sharp, "Does the Story of Jesus Mimic Pagan Mystery Stories?" in *Come Let Us Reason: New Essays in Christian Apologetics*, eds., William Lane Craig and Paul Copan (Nashville, TN: B&H Academic, 2012). See also, Ronald H. Nash, *The Gospel and the Greeks: Did the New Testament Borrow from Pagan Thought?* 2nd ed. (Phillipsburg, NJ: P & R Publishing, 2003); J. Ed Komoszewski, M. James Sawyer, and Daniel B. Wallace, *Reinventing Jesus: How Contemporary Skeptics Miss the Real Jesus and Mislead Popular Culture* (Grand Rapids, MI: Kregel Publications, 2006), 219–58.

24. Most scholars believe there have been some interpolations in the writings of Josephus in *Antiquities* Book 18 (known as the *Testimonium Flavianum*) relative to some statements about Jesus therein (such as calling Jesus the "Messiah"), but the vast majority of scholars also believe that there are genuine references to Jesus of Nazareth in Josephus's writings that are not interpolations (*Antiquities* 20.9 is typically not disputed and most scholars believe the core of Book 18 is authentic, including reference to Jesus's crucifixion under Pilate). For more on the evidence from Josephus and the *Testimonium Flavianum* in particular, see Thiessen and Merz, *The Historical Jesus*, 64–73.

25. *Baraitha Bab. Sanhedrin* 43a.

26. See Gary Habermas, "Minimal Facts on the Resurrection that Even Skeptics Accept," accessed October 20, 2021, https://ses.edu/minimal-facts-on-the-resurrection-that-even-skeptics-accept. See also Habermas and Licona, *The Case for the Resurrection*.

27. Habermas, "Minimal Facts." See also, Goldstein, *Risen*.

28. Habermas, "Minimal Facts."

29. Luke 23:50. Many scholars argue this detail also rings true because it would be unlikely Jesus's followers would make up a story about a member of the Sanhedrin taking Jesus's body and putting it in his tomb.

30. For a discussion of the multiple lines of evidence that the tomb way empty, see William Lane Craig, "The Resurrection of Jesus," in *Reasonable Faith: Christian Truth and Apologetics*, 3rd ed. (Wheaton, IL: Crossway, 2008), 303–404. Further, for an impressive maximal case for the resurrection, see Timothy McGrew and Lydia McGrew, "The Argument from Miracles: A Cumulative Case for the Resurrection of Jesus of Nazareth," in *The Blackwell Companion to Natural Theology*, ed. by William Lane Craig and J. P. Moreland (Malden, MA: Blackwell, 2009), 593–662.

31. See Matthew 27:63–28:15.

32. Habermas, *The Historical Jesus*, 226–7.

33. See Matthew 28:9–10, 16–20; Luke 24:13–31, 34, 36–51; John 20:11–17, 19–23, 26–29; 21:1–23; Acts 1:3–9; 9:3–6; 1 Corinthians 5:5; 15:1–8. Further, Stephen saw Jesus just before he was killed for his faith (Acts 7:55–56), and Jesus appeared to John on the island of Patmos (Rev. 1:12–20).

34. On the martyrdom of many of the disciples e.g., Eusebius, *The Church History*, II:IX; II:XXIII; II:XXV. Notably, the first-century Jewish historian Josephus himself reports the death of James the brother of Jesus by stoning. Josephus, *Antiquities* 20.9.1. See also Sean McDowell, *On the Fate of the Apostles: Examining the Martyrdom Accounts of the Closest Followers of Jesus* (New York: Routledge, 2015).

35. See Strobel, *The Case for Christ*, 225–43. Even less likely is the hypothesis that they were deceived by a massive conspiracy. What would have motivated such a conspiracy and who would have had the means to pull it off?

36. See Craig, "The Resurrection of Jesus" in *Reasonable Faith*, 333–404.

37. Wolfhart Pannenberg, in a conversation with Ron Sider, *Prism Magazine*, March/April, 1997, quoted in Erwin W. Lutzer, *Seven Reasons Why You Can Trust the Bible* (Chicago: Moody, 2015).

38. See Strobel, *The Case for Christ*, 191–260. See also N. T. Wright, *The Resurrection of the Son of God* (London: SPCK, 2003); Licona, *The Resurrection of Jesus*; Habermas and Licona, *The Case for the Resurrection of Jesus*; Craig A. Evans, N. T. Wright, and Troy A. Miller, *Jesus, the Final Days: What Really Happened* (Louisville, KY: Westminster John Knox Press, 2009); Habermas, *The Historical Jesus*.

39. See D. A. Carson and Douglas J. Moo, *An Introduction to the New Testament*, 2nd ed. (Grand Rapids, MI: Zondervan, 2005).

40. See Peter J. Williams, *Can We Trust the Gospels?* (Wheaton, IL: Crossway, 2018), 51–86. See also Richard Bauckham, *Jesus and the Eyewitnesses: The Gospels as Eyewitness Testimony*, 2nd ed. (Grand Rapids, MI: Eerdmans, 2017); Blomberg, *The Historical Reliability of the Gospels*.

41. Paul was not one of the original twelve, but was a true apostle by virtue of the risen Christ's special calling on the road to Damascus.

42. See Carson, Moo, and Morris, *An Introduction to the New Testament*. Some remain skeptical regarding the date or the writing of the Gospels and other New Testament books, but much evidence identifies the New Testament records as genuine apostolic testimony. For a recent case for very early dating of New Testament books, see Jonathan Bernier, *Rethinking the Dates of the New Testament: The Evidence for Early Composition* (Grand Rapids, MI: Baker Academic, 2022).

43. See Craig L. Blomberg, "Where Do We Start Studying Jesus?" in Michael J. Wilkins and J. P. Moreland, eds., *Jesus Under Fire: Modern Scholarship Reinvents the Historical Jesus* (Grand Rapids, MI: Zondervan, 1995), 29. Such dating would also explain the lack of mention of the destruction of

Jerusalem (AD 70) and of the death of James the brother of Jesus (ca. AD 62). Indeed, no event later than AD 62 is mentioned in Acts. On this and other reasons for this view, see Carson, Moo, and Morris, *An Introduction to the New Testament*, 116–17. Some date Luke ca. 75–80 based on their belief that predictive prophecy is impossible, but the book contains a "prediction" of the destruction of Jerusalem in AD 70. However, "the evidence for an early date seems more convincing than that for a later time, and while it comes short of complete proof, it should be accepted." Carson, Moo, and Morris, *An Introduction to the New Testament*, 117.

44. Although there are alternate theories (as is always the case with regard to historical investigation), it is "prevailing scholarly opinion that Luke used the canonical Mark as one of his key sources" and the best evidence places the writing of Mark in the late 50s, though some date it as early as the 40s and others as late as the 80s. Carson, Moo, and Morris, *An Introduction to the New Testament*, 98. With regard to Matthew alone, there is an upper limit on how late the book could have been written since Ignatius (who died, ca. 108) quotes from it. Moreover, the book itself suggests the temple was still standing when it was written (Matt. 5:23–24; 12:5–7; 17:24–27; 23:16–22), which would place an upper limit of AD 70. However, some critical scholars date the book from AD 80–100, generally due to the presupposition that predictive prophecy (particularly regarding the destruction of Jerusalem in AD 70) is impossible. Carson, Moo, and Morris, *An Introduction to the New Testament*, 152–56.

45. Blomberg, "Where Do We Start Studying Jesus?," 29.

46. For the Gospel of John, "dates in the second century are now pretty well ruled out by manuscript discoveries" including but not limited to p52. Carson, Moo, and Morris, *An Introduction to the New Testament*, 166.

47. As Craig Blomberg states, "Rabbis became famous for having the entire Old Testament committed to memory. So it would have been well within the capability of Jesus' disciples to have committed much more to memory than appears in all four Gospels put together—and to have passed it along accurately." Interviewed in Strobel, *The Case for Christ*, 43.

48. See, e.g., Anthony C. Thiselton, *The First Epistle to the Corinthians: A Commentary on the Greek Text* (Grand Rapids, MI: Eerdmans, 2000), 1206.

49. See Daniel B. Wallace, "The Reliability of the New Testament Manuscripts," in *Understanding Scripture: an Overview of the Bible's Origin, Reliability, and Meaning*, ed. Wayne A. Grudem, C. John Collins, and Thomas R. Schreiner (Wheaton, IL: Crossway, 2012), 113; Strobel, *The Case for Christ*, 55–72.

50. "By comparison, the average classical author has no copies for more than half a millennium." Wallace, "The Reliability of the New Testament Manuscripts," 113. For example, of the *Annals of Imperial Rome* written by Tacitus (ca. AD 116), the first six books exist today in only one manuscript, copied about AD 850. Books 11–16 are in another manuscript from the eleventh century. Books 7–10 are lost. Likewise, of Josephus's *The Jewish War* (late first century), we have nine Greek manuscripts from the tenth to twelfth centuries, one Latin translation from the fourth century, and Russian materials from the eleventh or twelfth century. And, the earliest copy of Caesar's Gallic Wars (50 BC) is from AD 900. See Strobel, *The Case for Christ*, 60–61.

51. We currently possess more than 5,800 ancient Greek manuscripts of the New Testament and more than 24,000 ancient manuscripts if one includes ancient translations. On the other hand, "the copies of the average ancient Greek or Latin author's writings number fewer than *twenty* manuscripts! Thus, the New Testament has well over one thousand times as many manuscripts as the works of the average classical author." Wallace, "The Reliability of the New Testament Manuscripts," 113.

52. For a full tabulation see Norman L. Geisler and William E. Nix, *A General Introduction to the Bible: Revised and Expanded* (Chicago: Moody Press, 1986), 419–33.

53. Norman L. Geisler and William E. Nix, *From God to Us: How We Got our Bible* (Chicago: Moody Publishers, 2012), 248.

54. Wallace, "The Reliability of the New Testament Manuscripts," 114. For more on the issue of textual variants, see Paul D. Wegner. *A Student's Guide to Textual Criticism of the Bible: Its History, Methods and Results* (Downers Grove, IL: InterVarsity), 2006—especially the discussion of transmissional errors that occur in the Bible, pages 44–57. See also, Clinton Wahlen, "Variants, Versions, and the Trustworthiness of Scripture" in *Biblical Hermeneutics: An Adventist Approach*, ed. Frank M. Hasel. Biblical Research Institute Studies in Hermeneutics, vol. 3 (Silver Spring, MD: Biblical Research Institute/Review and Herald Academic, 2020), 63–103.

55. Wallace, "The Reliability of the New Testament Manuscripts," 114.

56. Bruce Metzger, interviewed in Strobel, *The Case for Christ*, 64. Daniel Wallace has classified the four hundred thousand variants into four categories: (1) spelling and nonsense errors (at least 75%), (2) minor changes, including synonyms and alterations, that do not affect translation (since Greek is an inflected language one can say the same thing with many different constructions), (3) meaningful but not viable differences, and (4) meaningful and viable differences (less than 1% of variants). Wallace, "The Reliability of the New Testament Manuscripts," 114–18. Regarding the two classes of meaningful differences: First, meaningful but not viable differences refers to a variant that would affect the meaning of translation but where the variant is not viable because we see the variant pop up only in later manuscripts and there is not much chance that one late scribe got it right and all others were wrong (e.g., 1 John, 1 Thess. 2:9—"gospel

of Christ" in late medieval manuscript instead of "gospel of God" in all early manuscripts). That leaves only meaningful and viable differences, which are less than 1% and nearly all of which are minor variants.

57. F. F. Bruce, *The Books and the Parchments*, 3rd and rev. ed. (Westwood, NJ: Revell, 1963), 178.

58. F. F. Bruce, *The New Testament Documents: Are They Reliable*, 3rd ed. (Grand Rapids, MI: Eerdmans, 1981), 10. Daniel Wallace adds, "If one is skeptical about what the original New Testament text said, that skepticism needs to be multiplied many times over when it comes to the writings of all other ancient Greek and Latin authors." Wallace, "The Reliability of the New Testament Manuscripts," 113.

59. Some have argued against the reliability of the Gospels due to differences among Synoptic Gospel accounts (Matthew, Mark, and Luke) and the Gospel of John. However, in contrast to this view (which relies heavily on some questionable presuppositions), there are good reasons to believe in the reliability of the Gospel accounts as eyewitness accounts. In this regard, see Blomberg, *Historical Reliability of the Gospels*, 152-240. For a much briefer, introductory discussion, see Williams, *Can We Trust the Gospels?* 123-28. For an extended treatment of the abundant evidence that points to the Gospels as eyewitness accounts, see Bauckham, *Jesus and the Eyewitnesses*.

60. See Walter C. Kaiser, *The Old Testament Documents: Are They Reliable & Relevant?* (Downers Grove, IL: InterVarsity Press, 2001), 40-52. See also, Paul D. Wegner, "The Reliability of the Old Testament Manuscripts," in *Understanding Scripture*, eds. Wayne A. Grudem, C. John Collins, and Thomas R. Schreiner (Wheaton, IL: Crossway, 2012), 101-10.

61. In response to those critical scholars who claim Jesus did not actually make claims to be the Messiah or to be God in the flesh, William Lane Craig makes a strong case that even apart from belief in the reliability of the New Testament, there are very good reasons to believe Jesus did in fact claim to be the Messiah and the divine Son of God. Otherwise, Craig argues, it is extremely difficult to explain how such claims about Jesus arose so very early, particularly given the Jewish background in which Christianity arose. See, Craig, "The Self-Understanding of Jesus" in *Reasonable Faith*, 287-332.

62. Philip Schaff, *The Person of Christ* (New York: Charles Scribner's Sons, 1881), 29-30.

63. C. S. Lewis, *Mere Christianity* (New York: Macmillan, 1952), 55-56.

64. For an introduction, see Alfred J. Hoerth and John McRay, *Bible Archaeology: An Exploration of the History and Culture of Early Civilizations* (Grand Rapids, MI: Baker, 2006). See also, Randall Price with H. Wayne House, *Zondervan Handbook of Biblical Archaeology* (Grand Rapids, MI: Zondervan, 2017).

65. Michael G. Hasel, "History, the Bible, and Hermeneutics," in *Biblical Hermeneutics: An Adventist Approach*, ed. Frank M. Hasel. Biblical Research Institute Studies in Hermeneutics, vol. 3 (Silver Spring, MD: Biblical Research Institute/Review and Herald Academic, 2020), 121. Specifically in addition to the Tel Dan inscription in Aramaic discovered in 1993-1994, "the phrase 'house of David' was subsequently identified in 1994 by André Lemaire in line 31 on the Moabite Inscription found in Dibon, in Jordan" and "Kenneth Kitchen suggests that 'the heights of David' is a toponym listed among the Negev sites mentioned in the Shishak reliefs at the Temple of Amun at Karnak." Hasel, "History, the Bible, and Hermeneutics," 121. Further, Hasel explains, "new surveys and excavations at Khirbet Qeiyafa, Socoh, Khirbet el-Rai, Tel Burna, Khirbet Summeily and Lachish (2007-2020) have shown increasing evidence for major settlement and growth of the early kingdom of Judah" consistent with the biblical data regarding the reign of King David. Hasel, "History, the Bible, and Hermeneutics," 121-122.

66. See Jerry Vardaman, "A New Inscription Which Mentions Pilate as 'Prefect.'" *Journal of Biblical Literature* 81 (1962): 70-71

67. See Price, *Zondervan Handbook of Biblical Archaeology*.

68. William F. Albright, *Archaeology and the Religion of Israel* (Baltimore, MD: Johns Hopkins UP, 1956), 176.

69. For example, there is an ongoing debate regarding how to interpret the archaeological data about Jericho. For an introductory account, see Kaiser, *The Old Testament Documents*, 109-18. In this regard, it is important to keep in mind that the absence of evidence is not evidence of absence. That is, the fact that one does not have evidence of a particular occurrence does not count as evidence against the occurrence. For more on this, see Hasel, "History, the Bible, and Hermeneutics," 116-22.

70. Geisler and Nix, *A General Introduction to the Bible*, 557.

71. Numerous critics claim part of Isaiah must have been written after Cyrus because they believe such predictive prophecy is impossible. However, there is considerable evidence that the 8th century prophet Isaiah was the author of the entire book that bears his name, as is attested in the New Testament (John 12:38-41). See Gregory A. King, "Did Isaiah Write the Book of Isaiah?" in *Interpreting Scripture: Bible Questions and Answers*, ed. Gerhard Pfandl (Silver Spring, MD: Biblical Research Institute, 2010), 59-64.

72. See Jiří Moskala, "Did the Prophet Daniel Write the Book of Daniel?" in *Interpreting Scripture: Bible Questions and Answers*, ed. Gerhard Pfandl (Silver Spring, MD: Biblical Research Institute, 2010), 65-71. See also Gerhard Pfandl, *Daniel God's Beloved Prophet: His Life and His Prophecies* (Silver Spring, MD: Biblical Research Institute/Review and Herald Academic, 2021).

73. On Matthew's quotation of Isaiah 7:14 relative to the virgin birth see Richard Davidson, "Inner-Biblical Hermeneutics: The Use of Scripture by Bible Writers," in *Biblical Hermeneutics: An Adventist Approach*, ed. Frank M. Hasel (Silver Spring, MD: Biblical Research Institute/Review and Herald Academic, 2020), 259-62.

74. Notably, at Jesus's trial, hostile witnesses unintentionally confirmed that Jesus had predicted His death and resurrection after three days when they testified: "We heard Him say, 'I will destroy this temple that was made by hands, and in three days I will build another, made without hands'" (Mark 14:58; cf. Matt. 26:61). Further, during the crucifixion, some jeered at Jesus, "Ha! You who are going to destroy the temple and rebuild it in three days, save Yourself by coming down from the cross!" (Mark 15:29-30; cf. Matt. 27:38-40). John tells us Jesus had actually declared earlier in His ministry: "Destroy this temple, and in three days I will raise it up" and "He was speaking about the temple of His body. So when He was raised from the dead, His disciples remembered that He said this; and they believed the Scripture and the word which Jesus had spoken" (John 2:19-22).

75. Ellen G. White comments: "How shall I know the right way? If the Bible is indeed the Word of God, how can I be freed from these doubts and perplexities?" In answer, she wrote: "God never asks us to believe, without giving sufficient evidence upon which to base our faith. His existence, His character, the truthfulness of His word, are all established by testimony that appeals to our reason; and this testimony is abundant. Yet God has never removed the possibility of doubt. Our faith must rest upon evidence, not demonstration. Those who wish to doubt will have opportunity; while those who really desire to know the truth, will find plenty of evidence on which to rest their faith." Ellen G. White, *Steps to Christ* (Mountain View, CA: Pacific Press, 1892), 105. I encourage you to read the entire chapter therein, titled: "What to Do with Doubt." On Ellen White and her work, see chapter 17.

76. See the preface. Approaches of *blind* faith are referred to as fideism whereas approaches that require evidence prior to belief are forms of evidentialism. Instead of these, the approach advocated here recognizes that decisions of faith are required of *any* system of belief, religious or otherwise, while also recognizing that God gave humans the faculty of reason and considerable evidence. Here, the witness of the Holy Spirit plays a crucial role that may help us avoid both fideism and evidentialism or forms of rationalism.

77. For more on the testimony of the Holy Spirit, see John Calvin, *Institutes of the Christian Religion*, Book 1, Chapter 7.

78. Consider the testimony of William Miller, who wrote of wrestling with his own questions: "I saw that the Bible did bring to view just such a Savior as I needed; and I was perplexed to find how an uninspired book should develop principles so perfectly adapted to the wants of a fallen world. I was constrained to admit that the Scriptures must be a revelation from God; they became my delight, and in Jesus I found a friend." William Miller, *Apology and Defence* (Boston: J. V. Himes, 1845), 4.

79. Ellen G. White testified: "Do you ask why I believe in Jesus? Because He is to me a divine Saviour. Why do I believe the Bible? Because I have found it to be the voice of God to my soul. We may have the witness in ourselves that the Bible is true, that Christ is the Son of God. We know that we are not following cunningly devised fables." White, *Steps to Christ*, 112.

CHAPTER 4 • CHRIST: GOD WITH US IN THE FLESH

1. According to J. Alec Motyer (and many others), the "angel of the Lord" is "an Old Testament anticipation of Jesus." J. Alec Motyer, *The Prophecy of Isaiah* (Downers Grove, IL: InterVarsity, 1993), 387. John N. Oswalt adds: "The angel is the Lord himself as visibly present (see Exod. 20:21-23; 33:2, 14-15; Num. 20:16; Josh. 5:13-15; Judg. 13:6, 21-22). Delitzsch makes a good case for this being an expression of the second person of the Trinity." John N. Oswalt, *The Book of Isaiah, Chapters 40-66* (Grand Rapids, MI: Eerdmans, 1998), 607.

2. See *BDB*, 521; *HALOT*, 585-86.

3. See also, Seventh-day Adventist Fundamental Belief #9 in the Appendix.

4. Scripture does not reveal precisely how the cross affected Christ's divine nature, but we know Christ's death on the cross did not cause divinity to die in the sense of going out of existence since Jesus Himself taught that He possessed and retained the power take up His life again (John 10:17-18; cf. 11:25). In this regard, Ellen White comments: "Christ came forth from the grave to life that was in Himself. Humanity died; divinity did not die. In His divinity, Christ possessed the power to break the bonds of death. He declared that He has life in Himself to quicken whom he will." Ellen G. White, *Selected Messages*, vol. 1 (Washington, DC: Review and Herald, 1958), 301.

5. See Howard Thurman, *Jesus and the Disinherited* (New York: Abingdon-Cokesbury, 1949), 17-18.

6. Ellen G. White, "The Need of Love," *Review and Herald* (August 28, 1888), par. 1.

7. Regarding John 8:58, Leon Morris comments: "'I am' must here have the fullest significance it can bear. It is in the style of deity (see on vv. 24 and 28), 'a reference to his eternal being.'" Leon Morris, *The Gospel According to John* (Grand Rapids, MI: Eerdmans, 1995), 419.

8. Leon Morris comments on the phrase "the Word was God," saying: "Nothing higher could be said: all that may be said about God may fitly be said about the Word." Morris, *The Gospel According to John*, 68. D. A. Carson explains, further, the lack of the article in John 1:1 does not indicate the Word is a lesser "god" for "if John had included the article," he "would have been so identifying the Word with God" that "it would be nonsense to say . . . that the Word was *with* God." Carson, *The Gospel According to John* (Grand Rapids, MI: Eerdmans, 1991), 117 (emphasis original).

9. On John 1:3, Ellen G. White comments, "If Christ made all things, He existed before all things. The words spoken in regard to this are so decisive that no one need be left in doubt. Christ was God

essentially, and in the highest sense. He was with God from all eternity. God over all, blessed forevermore. The Lord Jesus Christ, the divine Son of God, existed from eternity, a distinct person, yet one with the Father." White, *Selected Messages* 1:247.

10. The "immutability" attributed to God in Scripture, however, should not be confused with the strict kind of immutability that rules out genuine back-and-forth relationship between God and creation. For more on this, see chapter 7.

11. On Hebrews 1:3, Paul Ellingsworth explains, the phrases "exact representation of His nature" and "radiance of His glory" together describe "the essential unity and exact resemblance between God and his Son." Ellingsworth, *The Epistle to the Hebrews* (Grand Rapids, MI: Eerdmans, 1993), 99.

12. Regarding Colossians 2:9, F. F. Bruce comments, in Christ "(truly man as he was) the plenitude of deity was embodied." F. F. Bruce, *The Epistles to the Colossians, to Philemon, and to the Ephesians* (Grand Rapids, MI: Eerdmans, 1984), 100.

13. Of Revelation 22:13, G. K. Beale writes: "The Apocalypse has already called God 'the Alpha and the Omega' (1:8; 21:6) and 'the Beginning and the End' (21:6), and Christ has been called 'the First and the Last' (1:17; 2:8). Now all these titles, which are used in the OT of God, are combined and applied to Christ to highlight his deity." G. K. Beale, *The Book of Revelation* (Grand Rapids, MI: Eerdmans, 1999), 1138.

14. See Philip Schaff, *The Creeds of Christendom*, vol. 1 (New York: Harper & Brothers, 1978), 29.

15. Quoted from the Anglican *Book of Common Prayer*, in Schaff, *The Creeds of Christendom*, 2:58–59.

16. In this regard, Ellen G. White maintained: "In Christ is life, original, unborrowed, underived." White, *The Desire of Ages* (Mountain View, CA: Pacific Press, 1898), 530. Adventists typically do not affirm the doctrine of eternal generation. For more on this, see Kwabena Donkor, *Eternal Subordination of Jesus?: A Theological Analysis and Review*. Biblical Research Institute Release, no. 23 (Silver Spring, MD: Biblical Research Institute, 2022), 34–36.

17. Ignatius of Antioch, *The Epistle of Ignatius to the Ephesians*, 19.3 (ANF 1:57).

18. Justin Martyr, *The First Apology of Justin*, 63 (ANF 1:184).

19. Irenaeus, *Against Heresies* 3.21.4 (ANF 1:452).

20. Tertullian, *Of Patience*, 13 (ANF 3:715).

21. Tertullian, *Against Marcion* 2.16 (ANF 3:309).

22. Origen, *On First Principles*, 1.2.10 (ANF 4:250). Around this time, a mosaic found in an ancient church at Megiddo also refers to "the God Jesus Christ" (ca. 230).

23. Cyprian of Carthage, *The Epistles of Cyprian*, 62.1 (ANF 5:359).

24. Lactantius, *Divine Institutes*, 5.3 (ANF 7:139). For much more on early Christian understandings of Christ's divinity, see Richard Bauckham, *Jesus and the God of Israel: God Crucified and Other Studies on the New Testament's Christology of Divine Identity* (Grand Rapids, MI: Eerdmans, 2008); Larry W. Hurtado, *One God, One Lord: Early Christian Devotion and Ancient Jewish Monotheism*, 3rd ed. (London: T&T Clark, 2015).

25. See, e.g., Fred Sanders and Scott R. Swain, eds., *Retrieving Eternal Generation* (Grand Rapids, MI: Zondervan, 2017), 29–146.

26. See Ellingsworth, *Hebrews*, 111. See also the reference to the "Branch" from David (Isa. 11:1, 10; Jer. 23:5; Zech. 3:8; 6:12) who will reign forever (Jer. 23:5–6; 33:14–18; Mic. 5:2), an eternal king who shall stand in the strength of *YHWH* and in the majesty of the name of *YHWH* His God (Mic. 5:4).

27. Morris, *The Gospel According to John*, 93. Murray J. Harris concludes, "As far as the evidence of the NT is concerned, it may be safely said that μονογενής is concerned with familial relations, not manner of birth. Neither the virgin birth of Jesus nor the 'eternal generation' of the Son is in John's mind when he uses the adjective μονογενής." Murray J. Harris, *Jesus as God: The New Testament Use of Theos in Reference to Jesus* (Eugene, OR: Wipf & Stock, 2008), 86–87.

28. Here and elsewhere, I usually gloss the singular form of Greek and Hebrew terms so readers can more easily recognize them when repeated, transliterated in accordance with the SBL general-purpose style.

29. R. L. Roberts, "The Rendering 'Only Begotten' in John 3:16," *Restoration Quarterly* 16 (1973): 15. See also Harris, *Jesus as God*, 85–86.

30. The Seventh-day Adventist fundamental belief regarding the Son states: "God the eternal Son became incarnate in Jesus Christ. Through Him all things were created, the character of God is revealed, the salvation of humanity is accomplished, and the world is judged. Forever truly God, He became also truly human, Jesus the Christ. He was conceived of the Holy Spirit and born of the virgin Mary. He lived and experienced temptation as a human being, but perfectly exemplified the righteousness and love of God. By His miracles He manifested God's power and was attested as God's promised Messiah. He suffered and died voluntarily on the cross for our sins and in our place, was raised from the dead, and ascended to heaven to minister in the heavenly sanctuary on our behalf. He will come again in glory for the final deliverance of His people and the restoration of all things. (Isa. 53:4–6; Dan. 9:25–27; Luke 1:35; John 1:1–3, 14; 5:22; 10:30; 14:1–3, 9, 13; Rom. 6:23; 1 Cor. 15:3, 4; 2 Cor. 3:18; 5:17–19; Phil. 2:5–11; Col. 1:15–19; Heb. 2:9–18; 8:1, 2)." Seventh-day Adventist Fundamental Belief #4.

31. Ellen G. White comments, "Christ had not exchanged his divinity for humanity; but he had clothed his divinity with humanity" (*Review and Herald*, Oct 29, 1895). Further, she writes, Christ "veiled

his divinity with the garb of humanity, but he did not part with his divinity" (*Review and Herald*, June 15, 1905). She also states, "although Christ's divine glory was for a time veiled and eclipsed by His assuming humanity, yet He did not cease to be God when He became man. The human did not take the place of the divine, nor the divine of the human. This is the mystery of godliness. The two expressions 'human' and 'divine' were, in Christ, closely and inseparably one, and yet they had a distinct individuality." Ellen G. White, "Christ Glorified," *Signs of the Times* (May 10, 1899), par. 11.

32. For one model, in this regard, see Andrew Loke, "On the Coherence of the Incarnation: The Divine Preconscious Model." *Neue Zeitschrift für Systematische Theologie und Religionsphilosophie* 51/1 (2009): 50–63.

33. Importantly, to say Christ was "tempted in all things as we are" does not claim Christ experienced every single temptation humans do, but is better understood as Christ undergoing the kinds of temptations common to humanity. In the temptation, for example, the three temptations are representative of the kinds of temptations all humans face. See Sakae Kubo, *Calculated Goodness* (Nashville, TN: Southern Publishing Association, 1974), chapter 1.

34. Some confusion in Adventist circles arises here because Ellen White used phrases like "fallen nature" and "sinful nature" quite differently than theologians tend to use them today. She affirmed that Christ "took upon Him our sinful nature." Ellen G. White, "The Word of God," *Advent Review and Sabbath Herald*, August 22, 1907. Yet, when she affirmed that Christ took a "sinful nature," she did not thereby affirm that Christ took on a nature corrupted by sin that included an inclination or propensity to sin. Rather, she taught, "we must not think that the liability of Christ to yield to Satan's temptations degraded His humanity and He possessed the same sinful, corrupt propensities as man. . . . Christ took our nature, fallen but not corrupted." Manuscript 57, 1890; Ellen G. White, *Manuscript Releases*, vol. 16 (Silver Spring, MD: Ellen G. White Estate, 1990), 182. She taught that Christ took on our human infirmities and weaknesses and thus could be tempted as we are. Yet, she clarified that Christ "is a brother in our infirmities, but not in possessing like passions. As the sinless one, His nature recoiled from evil." Ellen G. White, *Testimonies for the Church*, vol. 2 (Mountain View, CA: Pacific Press, 1868), 201. Indeed, Jesus took on "humanity, perfectly identical with our nature, except the taint of sin" and "His finite nature was pure and spotless." Manuscript 57, 1890; Ellen G. White, *Manuscript Releases*, 16:182. In this regard, she warned: "Be careful, exceedingly careful as to how you dwell upon the human nature of Christ. Do not set Him before the people as a man with the propensities of sin. He is the second Adam. The first Adam was created a pure, sinless being, without a taint of sin upon him; he was in the image of God. He could fall, and he did fall through transgressing. Because of sin, his posterity was born with inherent propensities of disobedience. But Jesus Christ was the only begotten Son of God. He took upon Himself human nature, and was tempted in all points as human nature is tempted. He could have sinned; He could have fallen, but not for one moment was there in Him an evil propensity." Letter 8, 1895; Ellen G. White, *Manuscript Releases*, vol. 13 (Silver Spring, MD: Ellen G. White Estate, 1990), 18. Further, she wrote: "Never, in any way, leave the slightest impression upon human minds that a taint of, or inclination to corruption rested upon Christ, or that He in any way yielded to corruption." Letter 8, 1895;

Ellen G. White, *Manuscript Releases*, 13:18. Indeed, Christ's "nature was more exalted, and pure, and holy than that of the sinful race for whom He suffered." Ellen G. White, *Review and Herald*, September 11, 1888, par. 10. For much more on this, see Tim Poirier, "Sources Clarify Ellen White's Christology," *Ministry*, December 1989, 7–9. See also Darius Jankiewicz, "Jesus Christ: Savior and Example," in *God's Character and the Last Generation*, eds. Jiří Moskala and John C. Peckham (Nampa, ID: Pacific Press, 2018); Woodrow W. Whidden, *Ellen White on the Humanity of Christ* (Hagerstown, MD: Review and Herald, 1997), 46–50; Eric C. Webster, *Crosscurrents in Adventist Christology* (Berrien Springs, MI: Andrews University Press, 1984), 115–33.

35. Ellen G. White comments, "Christ did not possess the same sinful, corrupt, fallen disloyalty we possess, for then He could not be a perfect offering." *Review and Herald*, April 25, 1893.

36. Ellen White comments, "Never will man be tried with temptations as powerful as those which assailed Christ." Ellen G. White, *Testimonies for the Church*, vol. 4 (Mountain View, CA: Pacific Press, 1876), 45. Indeed, she wrote: "The temptations that Christ withstood were as much stronger than ours as his nobility and majesty are greater than ours," *Atlantic Union Gleaner*, August 26, 1903, par. 5.

CHAPTER 5 • THE HOLY SPIRIT: GOD WITH US IN THE SPIRIT

1   The Greek term in the phrase translated "born again" is ambiguous. When Jesus uses the phrase, it could mean "born from above," but Nicodemus understands it as "born again," which he questions.

2.   Indeed, as many commentators have pointed out, when Jesus calls the Spirit "another Helper" or "another Comforter" (*paraklētos*) He does so in a way that indicates the Spirit is another like Himself. If this were not so, it would not have been to their advantage that Jesus go away (John 16:7). D. A. Carson comments, the words "'another Paraclete' [John 14:16] in the context of Jesus' departure implies that the disciples already have one, the one who is departing." Carson, *The Gospel According to John* (Grand Rapids, MI: Eerdmans, 1991), 500. George R. Beasley-Murray adds: "The implication of [John 14] v 16 is that Jesus has performed the role of a Paraclete during his earthly ministry, and after his departure he will ask the

Father to send another Paraclete to perform a like ministry for his disciples." George R. Beasley-Murray, *John* (Dallas: Word, 2002), 256.

3. See the discussion in Fernando Canale, "Doctrine of God," in *Handbook of Seventh-day Adventist Theology*, ed. Raoul Dederen (Hagerstown, MD: Review and Herald, 2000), 132–34.

4. Graham Cole sees "a story of successive subordinations. In the state of humiliation the Messiah is directed by the Spirit. In the state of glory, the vindicated Messiah directs the Spirit." Graham Cole, *He Who Gives Life: The Doctrine of the Holy Spirit* (Wheaton, IL: Crossway, 2007), 207. See also Norman Gulley, *Systematic Theology: God as Trinity* (Berrien Springs, MI: Andrews University Press, 2011), 147–48.

5. Canale notes, further, "it is possible to see Pentecost and the covenant at Sinai as types of the historical coming of the Holy Spirit. The historical coming of the Holy Spirit at Pentecost, then, would be the antitype of the Sinaitic covenant understood as the good gift of God to His people." Canale, "Doctrine of God," 131.

6. Some scholars think references like these in Genesis (e.g., 1:1–2; 6:3) and elsewhere might not be to the Holy Spirit, with some holding the critical view that Old Testament prophets would not have known about the Holy Spirit. But, taken canonically, I am convinced these are references to the Holy Spirit and if the same Spirit inspired the Old Testament (as the apostles declare), there is no reason to assume what the writers of Scripture knew or did not know in this regard.

7. For more on this and many other passages, see Jiří Moskala, "The Holy Spirit in the Hebrew Scriptures," *Journal of the Adventist Theological Society* 24/2 (2013): 18–58.

8. Some believe that the "spirit" mentioned in Ezekiel 11:19 refers merely to a power, but I believe the "spirit" referenced here is the "Spirit of God" referenced throughout Ezekiel (as in Ezek. 36:27) in personal terms, who (among other personal acts) lifts up Ezekiel and "speaks" to Ezekiel (Ezek. 11:1–2, 5; cf. 2:2). Nevertheless, the case made in this section does not hinge on the meaning of "spirit" in Ezekiel 11:19.

9. For more on this crucial role of the Holy Spirit, see John K. McVay, "The Holy Spirit in the New Testament," *Journal of the Adventist Theological Society* 29/1–2 (2018): 156–91. As McVay explains: "At the heart of the Christian message as it extends from Jerusalem to the ends of the earth (1:8) is the exaltation-coronation of Jesus. And it is the Holy Spirit who everywhere bears witness to that great event." McVay, "Holy Spirit," 165.

10. As Raymond E. Brown comments: "The very fact that Jesus stands justified before the Father means that Satan has been condemned and has lost his power over the world." Brown, *The Gospel According to John XIII–XXI* (Garden City, NY: Doubleday, 1970), 713. For more on this, see chapter 9.

11 On the interpretation of Scripture, see the excursus after chapter 10.

12. According to John Oswalt, "Most commentators recognize that the understanding of the Holy Spirit here [in Isaiah 63:10] and in v. 11 is close to the fully developed NT concept of the third person of the Trinity. Here he is clearly a person who is capable of being hurt by human behavior, and in v. 11 he is the empowering and enabling presence in the human spirit." Oswalt, *The Book of Isaiah, Chapters 40–66* (Grand Rapids, MI: Eerdmans, 1998), 607.

13. For more on this, see Frank M. Hasel, "The Doctrine of the Holy Spirit," in *Pneumatology: The Person and the Work of the Spirit*, ed. Reinaldo W. Siqueira and Alberto R. Timm (Silver Spring, MD: Biblical Research Institute, forthcoming).

14. Some have attempted to ground this view in texts like John 15:26, which speaks of "the Spirit of truth who proceeds from the Father." However, as D. A. Carson notes, "it is almost certain that the words 'who goes out from the Father', set in synonymous parallelism with 'whom I will send to you from the Father', refer not to some ontological 'procession' but to the mission of the Spirit." Carson, *John*, 529. As far as I can see, there is not sufficient biblical warrant to affirm the eternal procession view. See Canale, "Doctrine of God," 132; John C. Peckham, *Divine Attributes: Knowing the Covenantal God of Scripture* (Grand Rapids, MI: Baker Academic, 2021), 209–48. Additionally, there is a longstanding debate among Eastern and Western branches of Christianity over whether the correct form of the creed affirms that the Holy Spirit proceeds from the Father alone or from the Father and the Son. Centuries after the Councils of Nicea and Constantinople, "and the Son" (*filioque* in Latin) was added into the Nicene-Constantinopolitan creed in the West and became a major cause of the division between the Roman Catholic Church and Eastern Orthodox Church that took place in 1054.

15. The Seventh-day Adventist fundamental belief regarding the Holy Spirit states: "God the eternal Spirit was active with the Father and the Son in Creation, incarnation, and redemption. He is as much a person as are the Father and the Son. He inspired the writers of Scripture. He filled Christ's life with power. He draws and convicts human beings; and those who respond He renews and transforms into the image of God. Sent by the Father and the Son to be always with His children, He extends spiritual gifts to the church, empowers it to bear witness to Christ, and in harmony with the Scriptures leads it into all truth. (Gen. 1:1, 2; 2 Sam. 23:2; Ps. 51:11; Isa. 61:1; Luke 1:35; 4:18; John 14:16–18, 26; 15:26; 16:7–13; Acts 1:8; 5:3; 10:38; Rom. 5:5; 1 Cor. 12:7–11; 2 Cor. 3:18; 2 Pet. 1:21.)." Seventh-day Adventist Fundamental Belief #5.

16. Of course, these capacities might be damaged in a human person, but such are still part of human nature when properly functioning.

17. Regarding the Spirit being grieved in Ephesians 4:30, Andrew T. Lincoln comments: "Not only does the language of saddening or disappointing the Spirit by one's wayward actions provide a powerful

personal metaphor, but the identity of the one offended is also underlined forcefully. The one who is grieved is the holy Spirit of God—that Spirit who is characterized by holiness and who is God himself at work in believers." Andrew T. Lincoln, *Ephesians* (Dallas: Word, 1990), 306-7.

18. On the personhood of the Holy Spirit, Ellen White comments: "The Holy Spirit is a person, for He beareth witness with our spirits that we are the children of God.... The Holy Spirit has a personality, else He could not bear witness to our spirits and with our spirits that we are the children of God. He must also be a divine person else He could not search out the secrets which lie hidden in the mind of God." Manuscript 20, 1906; Ellen G. White, *Letters and Manuscripts*, vol. 21 (egwwritings.org). Further, she writes: "We need to realize that the Holy Spirit, who is as much a person as God [the Father] is a person, is walking through these grounds." Manuscript 66, 1899, par. 11; Ellen G. White, *Letters and Manuscripts*, vol. 14 (egwwritings.org).

19. Many Christians, from early times, believed biblical instances describing the *personal* works of the Holy Spirit provided a compelling argument for affirming the personhood of the Holy Spirit. See, e.g., Basil, *On the Holy Spirit*, 16.

20. In this regard, Ellen White not only affirms the personhood of the Holy Spirit (as seen in note 18), but she explicitly affirms that the Spirit is a *distinct* person. She writes: "The Holy Spirit is the Comforter, in Christ's name. He personifies Christ, yet is a distinct personality." Manuscript 93, 1892, par. 8; Ellen G. White, *Letters and Manuscripts*, vol. 8 (egwwritings.org).

21. Noting the "Trinitarian implications of v 26," George Beasley-Murray observes that the Spirit's "role as representative of Jesus and his task of recalling and interpreting the revelation brought by Jesus make very clear the [distinct] personal nature of the Spirit." Beasley-Murray, *John*, 261.

22. W. F. Albright and C. S. Mann comment that the "emphasis on the Paraclete [Holy Spirit]" is "common in John," being "clearly represented as being neither Father nor Son." W. F. Albright and C. S. Mann, *Matthew* (New Haven, CT: Yale University Press, 2008), 362.

23. Regarding Acts 5:3-4, Ben Witherington III comments, "the Spirit here is treated as a person, one who can be lied to, not merely a power" and "the Spirit is equated with God, as a comparison of vv. 3 and 4 shows". Witherington, *The Acts of the Apostles: A Socio-Rhetorical Commentary* (Grand Rapids, MI: Eerdmans, 1998), 216n80. As such, Ananias "is guilty of lying not merely to human beings but to God in the person of the Spirit." Witherington, *Acts*, 216.

24. In this regard, Ellen White comments: "The Comforter that Christ promised to send after He ascended to heaven, is the Spirit in all the fullness of the Godhead." Ellen G. White, *Evangelism* (Washington, DC: Review and Herald, 1946), 615. Elsewhere, she refers to "the Holy Spirit" as "the third person of the Godhead." White, *Evangelism*, 617. And, she also comments further of a time when the heavenly host "fall down and worship the Father and the Son and the Holy Spirit." Manuscript 139, 1906, par. 32; Ellen G. White, *Letters and Manuscripts*, vol. 21 (egwwritings.org).

CHAPTER 6 • FATHER, SON, AND HOLY SPIRIT: THE TRINITY OF LOVE

1. Fernando Canale, "Doctrine of God," in *Handbook of Seventh-day Adventist Theology*, ed. Raoul Dederen (Hagerstown, MD: Review and Herald, 2000), 128.

2. This re-elevation takes place in stages, corresponding to stages in the cosmic conflict (Satan is defeated at the cross, but not yet destroyed). See chapter 9 and John C. Peckham, *Theodicy of Love: Cosmic Conflict and the Problem of Evil* (Grand Rapids, MI: Baker Academic, 2018), 119-37.

3. This section draws on the four-point case I have laid out elsewhere in other forms. See, e.g., John C. Peckham, *Divine Attributes: Knowing the Covenantal God of Scripture* (Grand Rapids, MI: Baker Academic, 2021), 210-28.

4. The Seventh-day Adventist fundamental belief regarding the Trinity states: "There is one God: Father, Son, and Holy Spirit, a unity of three coeternal Persons. God is immortal, all-powerful, all-knowing, above all, and ever present. He is infinite and beyond human comprehension, yet known through His self-revelation. God, who is love, is forever worthy of worship, adoration, and service by the whole creation. (Gen. 1:26; Deut. 6:4; Isa. 6:8; Matt. 28:19; John 3:16 2 Cor. 1:21, 22; 13:14; Eph. 4:4-6; 1 Pet. 1:2)." Seventh-day Adventist Fundamental Belief #2.

5. Lewis Ayres, *Nicaea and Its Legacy: An Approach to Fourth-Century Trinitarian Theology* (Oxford: Oxford University Press, 2006), 253.

6. See Philip Schaff, *The Creeds of Christendom* (New York: Harper & Brothers, 1978), 1:29.

7. As many scholars have noted, the Hebrew term translated "one" (*ehad*) here does not require a strict, numerical unity (cf. the use of the term in Gen. 2:24) and thus does not require a unitarian understanding of God.

8. Craig Blomberg writes: "The singular 'name' followed by the threefold reference to 'Father, Son, and Holy Spirit' suggests both unity and plurality in the Godhead. Here is the clearest Trinitarian 'formula' anywhere in the Gospels." *Matthew* (Nashville, TN: B&H, 2001), 432. Leon Morris comments, similarly: "We should notice that the word name is singular; Jesus does not say that his followers should baptize in the 'names' of Father, Son, and Holy Spirit, but in the 'name' of these three. It points to the fact that they are in some sense one." *The Gospel According to Matthew* (Grand Rapids, MI: Eerdmans, 1992), 748. He notes, further: "That the early followers of Jesus thought of God as triune seems clear from the passages

that speak of the three together (e.g., Rom. 8:11; 1 Cor. 12:4–6; 2 Cor. 13:14; Gal. 4:6; Eph. 4:4–6; 2 Thess. 2:13, etc.). That God is a Trinity is a scriptural idea." Morris, *The Gospel*, 748. While some have questioned the authenticity of this text (claiming it is a later development), the passage is well-attested in early and later biblical manuscripts such that there is no ground for this view. There is good reason to believe the later formulations in Acts are abbreviations of the longer, original form in Matthew 28:19. As Blomberg puts it: as "the clearest Trinitarian 'formula' anywhere in the gospels," this text "is therefore often accused of being a very late development and not at all something Jesus himself could have imagined. But this view misjudges both the speed of the development of New Testament theology (cf. Jesus as God already in Acts 3:14–15—unless by circular reasoning this passage is also dismissed as late because of its high Christology), as well as how technical a formula this is. Acts 2:38 demonstrates that other baptismal formulae were also used in the earliest stages of Christianity. Jesus has already spoken of God as his Father (Matt. 11:27; 24:36), of himself as the Son (11:27; 16:27; 24:36), and of blasphemy against God's work in himself as against the Spirit (12:28)." Blomberg, *Matthew*, 432.

9. In this regard, Ellen White comments, "There are three living persons of the heavenly trio; in the name of these three great powers—the Father, the Son, and the Holy Spirit—those who receive Christ by living faith are baptized, and these powers will co-operate with the obedient subjects of heaven in their efforts to live the new life in Christ." Ellen G. White, *Evangelism* (Washington, DC: Review and Herald, 1946), 615.

10. For example, G. K. Beale comments, "the dragon, the sea beast, and the land beast form a competing trinity with the Father, the Son, and the Holy Spirit." *The Book of Revelation* (Grand Rapids, MI: Eerdmans, 1999), 729.

11. According to Roderick Durst, the New Testament contains "seventy-five triadic order passages." Roderick Durst, *Reordering the Trinity: Six Movements of God in the New Testament* (Grand Rapids, MI: Kregel, 2015), 68. Michael Horton adds: "The confession 'one God in three persons' arises naturally out of the triadic formulas in the New Testament in the context of baptism (Mt 28:19 and par.) and liturgical blessings and benedictions (Mt 28:19; Jn 1:18; 5:23; Ro 5:5–8; 1Co 6:11; 8:6, 12:4–6; 2Co 13:13–14; Eph 4:4–6; 2Th 2:13; 1Ti 2:5, 1Pe 1:2)." Michael Horton, *The Christian Faith: A Systematic Theology for Pilgrims on the Way* (Grand Rapids, MI: Zondervan, 2011), 274–75.

12. Gordon D. Fee comments, "one must note the clear Trinitarian implications in this set of sentences, the earliest of such texts in the NT." Gordon D. Fee, *The First Epistle to the Corinthians* (Grand Rapids, MI: Eerdmans, 1987), 588.

13. It is crucial to recognize that the Hebrew term translated angel (*malak*) has the basic meaning of "messenger" and does not necessarily refer to an angelic being. Throughout Scripture, the term *malak* can refer to a human messenger or a celestial messenger or even a divine messenger (as is the case in these passages).

14. On "the angel of His presence" as a reference to the pre-incarnate Christ, see chapter 4. On the Holy Spirit in this passage, see chapter 6.

15. John 1:1-3 rules out not only Arianism, but semi-Arianism, for if Christ did not come into being, He could not have been begotten at any point in time.

16. On the reference to Christ as "firstborn" in Colossians 1:15, 18, see chapter 4.

17. Ellen White explicitly affirms, in this regard, that the Holy Spirit is a *distinct* person. She writes: "The Holy Spirit is the Comforter, in Christ's name. He personifies Christ, yet is a distinct personality." Manuscript 93, 1892, par. 8; Ellen G. White, *Letters and Manuscripts*, vol. 8 (egwwritings.org).

18. Ellen G. White comments: "The Father is all the fullness of the Godhead bodily, and is invisible to mortal sight. The Son is all the fullness of the Godhead manifested. The Word of God declares Him to be 'the express image of His person.' 'God so loved the world that He gave His only-begotten Son. . . .' Here is shown the personality of the Father. The Comforter that Christ promised to send after He ascended to heaven, is the Spirit in all the fullness of the Godhead, making manifest the power of divine grace to all who receive and believe in Christ as a personal Saviour. There are three living persons of the heavenly trio; in the name of these three great powers—the Father, the Son, and the Holy Spirit—those who receive Christ by living faith are baptized, and these powers will co-operate with the obedient subjects of heaven in their efforts to live the new life of Christ." White, *Evangelism*, 614–15.

19. Gordon Fee comments regarding 1 Corinthians 8:6, "the formulae 'one God' and 'one Lord' stand in specific contrast to the 'many gods' and 'many lords' of the pagans" (1 Cor. 8:5). Fee, *1 Corinthians*, 374.

20. See Paul Copan, "Is the Trinity a Logical Blunder? God as Three and One" in *Contending with Christianity's Critics: Answering New Atheists & Other Objectors*, ed. Paul Copan and William Lane Craig (Nashville, TN: B&H, 2009), 212.

21. Adventists typically do not affirm the doctrine of eternal generation. For more on this, see Kwabena Donkor, *Eternal Subordination of Jesus?: A Theological Analysis and Review*. Biblical Research Institute Release, no. 23. Silver Spring, MD: Biblical Research Institute, 2022), 34–36.

22. For instance, J. P. Moreland and William Lane Craig claim that "although creedally affirmed, the doctrine of the generation of the Son (and the procession of the Spirit) is a relic of Logos Christology which finds virtually no warrant in the biblical text and introduces a subordinationism into the Godhead which anyone who affirms the full deity of Christ ought to find very troubling." J. P. Moreland and William

Lane Craig, *Philosophical Foundations for a Christian Worldview* (Downers Grove, IL: IVP Academic, 2003), 594; cf. Millard Erickson, *Who's Tampering with the Trinity* (Grand Rapids, MI: Kregel, 2009), 184.

23. According to Stephen Holmes, Gregory of Nazianzus affirmed that "The Father begets the Son and spirates the Spirit, impassibly, timelessly and incorporeally." Stephen Holmes, *The Quest for the Trinity* (Downers Grove, IL: IVP Academic, 2012), 112. See Gregory, *Orations*, 29.2. Augustine similarly writes, the Father "begot him [the Son] timelessly in such a way that the life which the Father gave the Son by begetting him is co-eternal with the life of the Father who gave it." Augustine, *The Trinity* 15.47, trans. Edmund Hill (Brooklyn: New City, 1991), 432. William Hasker, however, is one example of a theologian who attempts to affirm the eternal processions while also affirming divine temporality. See William Hasker, *Metaphysics and the Tri-Personal God* (Oxford: Oxford University Press, 2013), 214–25.

24. There are other theories, such as the lesser-known relative identity theory (i.e., Constitution Trinitarianism) of Jeffrey Brower and Michael Rea based on a medieval strategy, which suggests "the divine persons may be conceived on analogy with form-matter compounds (such as the difference between lumps and statues)" and argue for "numerical [and essential] sameness without identity" of the persons; "one God, but three persons who are genuinely distinct rather than identical." Thomas H. McCall, "Relational Trinity: Creedal Perspective," in *Two Views on the Doctrine of the Trinity*, ed. Jason S. Sexton (Grand Rapids, MI: Zondervan, 2014), 113–37.

25. Holmes argues any view of the Trinity as three centers of consciousness (e.g., social Trinity views) is "a simple departure from . . . the unified witness of the entire theological tradition." Holmes, *Quest for the Trinity*, 195. However, Tom McCall has argued that some theologians traditionally categorized as exemplars of so-called Latin Trinitarianism (e.g., Augustine, Richard of St. Victor) make claims that seem to affirm elements of social Trinitarianism. Augustine himself "views the divine persons as distinct agents with will and consciousness." Tom McCall, "Social Trinitarianism and Tritheism Again: A Response to Brian Leftow," *Philosophia Christi* 5/2 (2003): 410.

26. For more, see Peckham, *Divine Attributes*, 209–48.

27. For much more on this, see Donkor, *Eternal Subordination of Jesus*, 34–36.

28. For much more on this, see Norman Gulley, *Systematic Theology: God as Trinity* (Berrien Springs, MI: Andrews University Press, 2011), 142–56.

29. See Canale, "Doctrine of God," 128.

30. Some believe 1 Corinthians 15:28 teaches that the Son continues to be subjected to the Father for eternity: "When all things are subjected to Him, then the Son Himself will also be subjected to the One who subjected all things to Him, so that God may be all in all" (cf. Eph. 1:23). In my view, this verse is best understood as referring to the end of the Son's functional covenant role (and rule) as the second Adam, whose work ultimately defeats sin and the devil, thereby reclaiming the rulership the first Adam forfeited after which Christ resumes the place of glory He shared with the Father before the world began (John 17:5). Otherwise, this verse (and 15:24) would seem to contradict the many biblical passages that teach Christ's rule never ends (e.g., Daniel 7:14, 27; Luke 1:33; 2 Pet. 1:11). To be consistent with such biblical passages, the statements that Christ "must reign until He has put all His enemies under His feet" and thereafter "hands over the kingdom to our God and Father" (1 Cor. 15:24–25) cannot mean the Son actually ceases to rule. Indeed, the Father Himself elsewhere says to the Son: "Your throne, God, is forever and ever" (Heb. 1:8; cf. Isa. 9:7; Rev. 11:15). As I understand it, then, the Son rules as the second Adam until He fulfills His covenantal function (as the Messianic Son of David and of Adam) of defeating the devil's kingdom in the cosmic conflict, but thereafter resumes His place on His throne—"the throne of God and of the Lamb" (Rev. 22:3) and "He will reign forever and ever" (Rev. 11:15; cf. Isa. 9:6–7). This is the interpretation given in the *Andrews Study Bible* and shared by many theologians. As John Calvin puts it, Christ will not "resign the kingdom, but will transfer it in a manner from his humanity to his glorious divinity." Calvin, *Commentary on the Epistles of Paul the Apostle to the Corinthians*, trans. John Pringle (Edinburgh: Calvin Translation Society, 1849), 2:32–33. See also, Gulley, *Systematic Theology: God as Trinity*, 152–55.

31. In Romans 15:30, Paul speaks of the "love of the Spirit." Likewise, in Colossians 1:8, Paul refers to "love in the Spirit." Further, the "love of God is shed abroad in our hearts by the Holy Ghost" (Rom. 5:5, KJV), and love is itself a fruit of the Spirit (Gal. 5:22). Moreover, the "fellowship of the Holy Spirit" is placed in parallel with "the grace of the Lord Jesus Christ" and "the love of God" in a Trinitarian formula (2 Cor. 13:14; cf. Phil. 2:1), and it is further implied that the Spirit loves humans since the Spirit manifests love toward humans in action (not leastwise in Rom. 8:26). Likewise, the Spirit comes as the "comforter," thus replacing Christ on earth (John 14:16). As such, it is implied that the Spirit should likewise be seen as a partner in such love relationships, both intra-Trinitarian and divine-human. For more on the Trinity as a Trinity of love, see Peckham, *Divine Attributes*, 228–45. See also, Gulley, *Systematic Theology: God as Trinity*; Woodrow Whidden II, John Reeve and Jerry Moon, *The Trinity: Understanding God's Love, His Plan of Salvation, and Christian Relationships* (Hagerstown, MD: Review and Herald, 2002).

32. Fleming Rutledge, *And God Spoke to Abraham: Preaching from the Old Testament* (Grand Rapids, MI: Eerdmans, 2011), 302.

33. Kathryn Tanner, *Christ the Key* (New York: Cambridge University Press, 2010), 268.

CHAPTER 7 • THE ALMIGHTY CREATOR WHO SUFFERS WITH US: THE COVENANTAL GOD OF LOVE

1. This question involves how we approach Scripture and do theology, discussed in chapter 10.
2. Many read Exodus 32:10 (and onward) and think that God actually wanted to destroy Israel. But, had God actually wanted to destroy Israel, He need not have told Moses "leave Me alone" (Exod. 32:10). Had God chosen to destroy Israel, Moses could not have done anything to stop God from destroying Israel. God's statement to Moses had the opposite effect, opening the way for intercession and deliverance without compromising God's perfect goodness and law of love. A close reading of the narrative of Exodus 32 and onward indicates that God spoke to Moses as He did in order to elicit intercession that provides moral grounds for God to forgive His covenant people and renew the covenant (cf. Ezek. 22:30). For more on this narrative, see John C. Peckham, "Show Me Your Glory: A Narrative Theology of Exodus 33:12-34:10," in *Meeting with God on the Mountains: Essays in Honor of Richard M. Davidson*, ed. Jiri Moskala (Berrien Springs, MI: Andrews University, 2016), 583-603.
3. Many Adventists argue that the genre and language used in Genesis 1 is language of historical prose and demonstrates that the author intended to describe literal (rather than figurative) days. Further, many argue, the following four elements together demonstrate that a text refers to six literal twenty-four-hour periods: (1) the word "day" (*yom*), (2) the verb "to be" (*hayah*, here in the past tense, "was"), (3) evening and morning, and (4) the day is given a number. All four of these elements appear in the refrain, "so the evening and the morning were the _____ day." See Randall W. Younker, *God's Creation: Exploring the Genesis Story* (Nampa, ID: Pacific Press, 1999), 28-49. As Gerhard Hasel puts it: "The Hebrew language—its grammar, syntax, and linguistic structures, as well as its semantic usage—allows only for the literal meaning of 'day' for the creation 'days' of Genesis 1." Gerhard F. Hasel, "The 'Days' of Creation in Genesis 1: Literal 'Days' or Figurative 'Periods/Epochs' of Time?" in *Creation, Catastrophe, and Calvary: Why a Global Flood Is Vital to the Doctrine of Atonement*, ed. John Templeton Baldwin (Hagerstown, MD: Review and Herald, 2000), 40-68.

Many Adventists believe the data indicates the entire unit of Genesis 1-11 is historical prose and this is evident from a number of indicators, including the unity of the narrative, the vav-consecutive verbal form (a feature of Hebrew usually used in historical narrative), the repeated formula *"these are the generations of,"* and the general similarity of the style with later historical narratives in Genesis and elsewhere. Genesis 1-11 also manifests poetic qualities that supplement the basic prose genre without undercutting the demonstrable intent to communicate history. The historicity of Genesis 1-3 is further implied by the fact that the creation narrative is fundamental to prominent teachings throughout Scripture. Indeed, a great deal of biblical theology is directly dependent on the creation and fall narratives of Genesis 1-3. For example, Jesus Himself referred to the Genesis narrative of creation in ways that indicated He took it as a historical account (see, e.g., Matt. 19:4-6; Mark 10:6-9 wherein Jesus quotes from Gen. 1:27 and Gen. 2:24. See also, Mark 2:27-28; 13:19). In this regard, Ekkehardt Mueller argues: "By quoting from Genesis 1 and 2 Jesus affirms the creation account and the mode of creation as described there. He understands Genesis 1 and 2 literally and takes the two chapters at face value. Two human beings, male and female, were directly created by God and subsequently became one flesh in marriage, which he instituted." Mueller, "Creation in the New Testament," *Journal of the Adventist Theological Society* 15/1 (2004): 56.

4. For an introduction to creationism by Adventist scientists, see Leonard Brand and Arthur Chadwick, *Faith, Reason, & Earth History: A Paradigm of Earth and Biological Origins by Intelligent Design*, 3rd ed. (Berrien Springs, MI: Andrews University Press, 2017). The official Seventh-day Adventist belief on creation reads as follows: "God has revealed in Scripture the authentic and historical account of His creative activity. He created the universe, and in a recent six-day creation the Lord made 'the heavens and the earth, the sea, and all that is in them' and rested on the seventh day. Thus He established the Sabbath as a perpetual memorial of the work He performed and completed during six literal days that together with the Sabbath constituted the same unit of time that we call a week today. The first man and woman were made in the image of God as the crowning work of Creation, given dominion over the world, and charged with responsibility to care for it. When the world was finished it was 'very good,' declaring the glory of God (Gen. 1-2; 5; 11; Exod. 20:8-11; Ps. 19:1-6; 33:6, 9; 104; Isa. 45:12, 18; Acts 17:24; Col. 1:16; Heb. 1:2; 11:3; Rev. 10:6; 14:7)." Seventh-day Adventist Fundamental Belief #6. See the Appendix.
5. On young earth creationism and young life creationism, see Ariel Roth, *Origins: Linking Science and Scripture* (Hagerstown, MD: Review and Herald, 1998), 340-51. Distinct from these is the intelligent design movement, which challenges Darwinian theories of origins, claiming that an abundance of evidence is not accounted for by undirected processes of evolution, but points toward intelligent design (design by an intelligent agent or agents). The intelligent design movement is not restricted to Christians and takes no overarching stance on the biblical story of creation. See Stephen Meyer, *Return of the God Hypothesis: Three Scientific Discoveries that Reveal the Mind Behind the Universe* (New York: HarperOne, 2021).
6. For an example of a case for the "mature earth" theory, see Kurt P. Wise, *Faith, Form, and Time: What the Bible Teaches and Science Confirms about Creation and the Age of the Universe* (Nashville, TN: B&H, 2002).
7. In the young life creationism view, mention of the stars on the fourth day is understood as a parenthetical statement affirming that God created the stars also, without asserting they were created

on that day. See Younker, *God's Creation*, 30–36. Some also posit that the sun and the moon appeared on day four and the author presents a phenomenological reading, that is, from the author's perspective of their appearance (not that they came into existence then). See William H. Shea, "Creation," in *Handbook of Seventh-day Adventist Theology*, ed. Raoul Dederen (Hagerstown, MD: Review and Herald, 2000), 420. This is sometimes called the passive gap theory, distinguishing it from the active gap theory (prominent among some dispensationalists and others), which posits Satan was active in changing creation over the long ages between the initial creation of the universe and the recent six-day creation week.

8. The technical term for the divine attribute of self-existence is aseity, from the Latin *a se*, which means "of itself."

9. According to Douglas J. Moo, Romans 11:35–36 teaches God is "the source (*ek*), sustainer (*dia*), and goal (*eis*) of all things." Moo, *The Epistle to the Romans* (Grand Rapids, MI: Eerdmans, 1996), 743.

10. As C. S. Lewis puts it, God's "Omnipotence means power to do all that is intrinsically possible, not to do the intrinsically impossible. You may attribute miracles to him, but not nonsense. This is no limit to his power. If you choose to say 'God can give a creature free will and at the same time withhold free will from it,' you have not succeeded in saying *anything* about God: meaningless combinations of words do not suddenly acquire meaning simply because we prefix to them the two other words 'God can'. . . . It is no more possible for God than for the weakest of his creatures to carry out both of two mutually exclusive alternatives; not because his power meets an obstacle, but because nonsense remains nonsense even when we talk it about God." Lewis, *The Problem of Pain* (New York: HarperOne, 2001), 18.

11. Pieter Verhoef comments regarding Malachi 3:7, this phrasing "denotes a consequence: 'in order that I may turn to you,' or 'then I will turn to you. The transgressions of the people were the cause of God's turning away from them, the reason why he was no longer pleased with them (1:8, 10; 2:13)." Verhoef, *The Books of Haggai and Malachi* (Grand Rapids, MI: Eerdmans, 1987), 302.

12. See John C. Peckham, *Divine Attributes: Knowing the Covenantal God of Scripture* (Grand Rapids, MI: Baker Academic, 2021), 39–71.

13. The Bible uses the Hebrew term *qadosh* ("holy") of God to signify that God is "separate, apart, and so *sacred, holy*." "קָדוֹשׁ" BDB, 872. The term also refers to created objects that may be set apart or consecrated (and thus sacred or holy) in connection to God.

14. Daniel Castelo, *Apathetic God: Exploring the Contemporary Relevance of Divine Impassibility*. Paternoster Theological Monographs (Colorado Springs, CO: Paternoster, 2009), 16.

15. E.g., Rob Lister, *God Is Impassible and Impassioned: Toward a Theology of Divine Emotion* (Wheaton, IL: Crossway, 2013).

16. Here, a technical note may be helpful: whatever is *essential* to someone or something is thereby something without which that person or thing could not exist. As such, to say the world is *essential* to God or *essentially* related to God is to say that God cannot exist apart from being in relation to some world (which would require that the world is eternal). Because the world is not eternal, but came into existence as a result of God freely creating it (e.g., Rev. 4:11), the world cannot be essential to God or essentially related to God. Hence, God cannot be *essentially* passible in relation to the world because God existed without the world and could only be passible *in relation to the world* from the time the world began to exist onward.

17. On qualified passibility, see John C. Peckham, "Qualified Passibility," in *Divine Impassibility: Four Views*, eds. Robert Matz and A. Chadwick Thornhill (Downers Grove, IL: IVP Academic, 2019), 87–128.

18. Used of both God and humans, this kind of language is idiomatic and does not refer to literal body parts, but uses such language to refer to strong emotional reaction. Thus, in Lamentations 1:20, similar idiomatic usage appears when a human says: "My heart is overturned within me." For more on this, see Peckham, *Divine Attributes*, 58–60. See also, John C. Peckham, *The Love of God: A Canonical Model* (Downers Grove, IL: IVP Academic, 2015), 147–189.

19. See Phyllis Trible, *God and the Rhetoric of Sexuality* (Philadelphia, PA: Fortress, 1978), 31–59. See also H. J. Stoebe, "רחם" *TLOT*, 3:1226; *HALOT*, 1217–18; Mike Butterworth, "רחם" *NIDOTTE*, 3:1093.

20. For more on the accommodative and analogical nature of biblical language about God, see Peckham, *Divine Attributes*, 33–37.

21. Gerald Borchert comments, "anger and judgment can in fact be the obverse side of the coin of love." *John 1–11* (Nashville, TN: B&H, 2001), 164.

22. See John C. Peckham, "The Wrath of the God of Love," in *God and Death*, eds. Jiri Moskala and John Reeve (forthcoming). As Thomas McCall puts it: "God's righteous wrath is always portrayed in Scripture as God's antagonism toward sin. . . . It is the contingent [yet natural] expression of the holy love that is shared between Father, Son, and Holy Spirit." McCall, *Against God and Nature: The Doctrine of Sin* (Wheaton, IL: Crossway, 2019), 334. See also Frank M. Hasel, "The Wrath of God," *Ministry* 64/11 (1992): 10–12.

23. As Gordon Wenham puts it, God exhibits "the anger of someone who loves deeply." *Genesis 1–15* (Dallas: Word, 1987), 146.

24. D. C. K. Watson writes "Unless God detests sin and evil with great loathing, He cannot be a God of Love," since true love requires justice. Watson, *My God is Real* (London: Falcon, 1970), 39.

25. Miroslav Volf, *Free of Charge: Giving and Forgiving in a Culture Stripped of Grace* (Grand Rapids, MI: Zondervan, 2006), 138–39.

26. Dorena Williamson, "Botham Jean's Brother's Offer of Forgiveness Went Viral. His Mother's Calls for Justice Should Too," Christianity Today (website), accessed October 7, 2019, https://www.christianitytoday.com/ct/2019/october-web-only/botham-jean-forgiveness-amber-guyger.html.

27. The word translated "lovingkindness" (*hesed*) exemplifies the covenantal aspect of divine love (and much more). The word *hesed* expects relational responsiveness toward the goal of, or within, reciprocal relationship (often formal covenant relationship). On one hand, *hesed* is "characterized by permanence and reliability." Hans-Jürgen Zobel, "חֶסֶד," *TDOT*, 1:57. On the other hand, "Numerous texts witness to at least the hypothetical possibility of losing God's חֶסֶד or of having it taken away." David A. Baer and Robert P. Gordon, "חֶסֶד" *NIDOTTE*, 2:215. See Genesis 24:27; 2 Chronicles 6:42; Psalm 36:10 [11]; 77:8; 88:11; 106:45. God's *hesed* is extremely steadfast, reliable, and enduring. Yet, Katharine D. Sakenfeld explains, "God's *hesed* is conditional, dependent upon the good repair of the covenant relationship that it is up to Israel to maintain" (cf. Deut. 7:9, 12; 2 Sam. 22:26; 1 Kings 8:23; 2 Chron. 6:14; Pss. 25:10; 32:10). Sakenfeld, "Love in the OT," *B*, 4:379. See also John C. Peckham, *The Concept of Divine Love in the Context of the God-World Relationship* (New York: Peter Lang, 2014), 300–319.

28. See Peckham, *Love of God*, 191–247.

29. See Seventh-day Adventist Fundamental Belief #3 in the Appendix.

CHAPTER 8 • THE ETERNAL, ALL-KNOWING GOD WHO DWELLS WITH US: THE EVER-PRESENT GOD OF LOVE

1. Nahum Sarna suggests the term translated "back" here "means the traces of His presence, the afterglow of His supernatural effulgence." Nahum Sarna, *Exodus* (Philadelphia, PA: Jerusalem Publication Society, 1991), 215.

2. This does not contradict the statement elsewhere that Moses could not *"see"* God's *"face"* (Exod. 33:20), but is an idiom of intimate communication. The Hebrew words translated *"face to face"* form an idiom that means "something like 'person to person.'" See Peter C. Craigie, *Deuteronomy* (Grand Rapids, MI: Eerdmans, 1976), 148 (emphasis original). A. S. van der Woude adds, the phrase "face to face" (*panim el-panim*) "depicts the immediate and personal relationship between God and his chosen." *TLOT*, 2:1005. See also J. Scott Duvall and J. Daniel Hays, *God's Relational Presence: The Cohesive Center of Biblical Theology*. (Grand Rapids, MI: Baker Academic, 2019).

3. Duvall and Hays comment in this regard, "the restoration of God's presence is promised throughout the OT prophets and is fulfilled in the Gospels when Jesus, Immanuel (God with us), appears." *God's Relational Presence*, 1; cf. Ezekiel 43:1–12; Haggai 2:9.

4. David Moffit comments, "the author [of Hebrews] speaks in Heb. 9–10 about Jesus entering the tabernacle in heaven, the very tabernacle that Moses saw [cf. Exod. 25:8–9, 40; Heb. 8:5], and moving through its sancta into the place where God dwells. This concrete depiction of a heavenly structure where God dwells and where the angels serve as priests (Heb. 1) indicates the author's belief in a heavenly tabernacle upon which the earthly tabernacle/temple is modeled." David Moffit, *Atonement and the Logic of Resurrection in the Epistle to the Hebrews* (Leiden: Brill, 2011), 221n.7. Moffit comments further, the "language in [Hebrews] 9:11–12 encourages a spatial and temporal conception of Jesus entering and moving through a structure that actually exists in heaven," coinciding "with the author's claim that Jesus serves as a high priest in heaven." Moffit, *Atonement*, 225.

5. As J. Ryan Lister explains, the story of Scripture focuses on the "restoration of God's presence" in terms of God's relational nearness" that was "once lost in the fall." J. Ryan Lister, *The Presence of God* (Wheaton, IL: Crossway, 2015), 24. J. Scott Duvall and J. Daniel Hays add that "God's relational presence" is "the most comprehensive, pervasive, and unifying theme" of Scripture. J. Scott Duvall and J. Daniel Hays, *God's Relational Presence*, 329.

6. Proverbs 15:3 does not refer to physical eyes that are in every location, but uses figurative language to emphasize that nothing escapes God's "sight." Bruce K. Waltke comments, this "signifies [God's] presence in a situation and his evaluation of it." *The Book of Proverbs: 1–15* (Grand Rapids, MI: Eerdmans, 2004), 614.

7. Regarding the distinction between derivative and non-derivative presence, I draw on the work of Ross Inman, "Omnipresence and the Location of the Immaterial," in *Oxford Studies in Philosophy of Religion*, vol. 8, ed. Jonathan Kvanvig (Oxford: Oxford University Press, 2018).

8. Some believe God is "wholly present at every point in the universe." J. P. Moreland and William Lane Craig, *Philosophical Foundations for a Christian Worldview* (Downers Grove, IL: IVP Academic, 2003), 515.

9. Representative of process panentheism, Charles Hartshorne writes: "In an undiluted sense [God] has all the world for body." Charles Hartshorne, *Man's Vision of God and the Logic of Theism* (Hamden, CT: Archon, 1964), 200.

10. Richard Swinburne has argued that "God is essentially bodiless" such that "although he may sometimes have a body, he is not dependent on his body in any way." Swinburne, *The Christian God* (New York: Clarendon, 1994), 127.

11. In Luke 24, the risen Jesus assures His disciples He is not a spirit because "a spirit [*pneuma*] does not have flesh and bones." Then, Jesus eats "a piece of broiled fish . . . in front of them" (Luke 24:39, 42–43; cf. Isa. 31:3).

12. Jeff Wood and E. J. Irish, *Secrets of the Kingdom*. Chapel Records, 1983, vinyl.

13. According to the historian Richard A. Muller, "the Reformation altered comparatively few of the major loci of theology: the doctrines of justification, the sacraments, and the church received the greatest emphasis, while the doctrines of God, the trinity, creation, providence, predestination, and the last things were taken over [from the medieval and patristics] by the magisterial Reformation virtually without alteration." Richard A. Muller, *The Unaccommodated Calvin: Studies in the Foundation of a Theological Tradition* (New York: Oxford University Press, 2000), 39.

14. Regarding analogical temporality, see John C. Peckham, "Divine Passibility, Analogical Temporality, and Theo-Ontology," in *Scripture and Philosophy: Essays Honoring the Work and Vision of Fernando Luis Canale* (Berrien Springs, MI: Adventist Theological Society Publications, 2016), 32–53. See also, Fernando Canale, *Basic Elements of Christian Theology* (Berrien Springs, MI: Andrews University Lithotech, 2005), 71; cf. Thomas F. Torrance, *The Christian Doctrine of God: One Being Three Persons* (London: T&T Clark, 2016), 220, 241.

15. The unmetricated view is thought to avoid the potential problem of an infinite regress of time in God's life (or a non-traversable eternity in God's life). On this and other views, see John C. Peckham, *The Doctrine of God: Introducing the Big Questions* (London: T&T Clark, 2019), 69–107.

16. For an example of simple foreknowledge (advocated by David Hunt) and other views (e.g., middle knowledge advocated by William Lane Craig), see James K. Beilby and Paul R. Eddy, eds., *Divine Foreknowledge: Four Views*, (Downers Grove, IL: InterVarsity, 2001).

17. For more on various views of divine knowledge, see Peckham, *Doctrine of God*, 111–40.

18. For more regarding the biblical teaching of divine foreknowledge, see John C. Peckham, *Divine Attributes: Knowing the Covenantal God of Scripture* (Grand Rapids, MI: Baker Academic, 2021), 111–40.

19. Many interpret the last phrase of Isaiah 45:1 as predicting not only Cyrus's defeat of Babylon, but as accurately describing the way he did it. Further, according to John Oswalt, the "Cyrus predictions" (Isa. 41:2, 25; 44:28–45:1; 46:11) provide "evidence that God can and does tell the future" as part of God's argument "against the idols" centered on the fact "that they cannot declare the future." John Oswalt, *The Book of Isaiah, Chapters 40–66* (Grand Rapids, MI: Eerdmans, 1998), 196.

20. David Hunt notes that in Matthew 26 "we find Jesus predicting, in quick succession, that he will be betrayed on the feast of the Passover (v. 2) by a disciple (v. 21) 'who has dipped his hand into the bowl with me' (v. 23); that it is Judas in particular who will betray him (v. 25); that his other disciples will desert him (v. 31); and that Peter will deny him three times before morning (v. 34)—none of which looks like it could be foreknown with certainty in the absence of some supernatural insight into the future." David Hunt, "The Simple-Foreknowledge View," in *Divine Foreknowledge: Four Views*, eds. James K. Beilby and Paul R. Eddy. Downers Grove, IL: InterVarsity, 2001), 68.

21. See John C. Peckham, "Does God Change His Mind?" *Perspective Digest*, 14/1 (2009): 20–33. See also Robert B. Chisholm, Jr., "Does God 'Change His Mind'?" BSac 152/608 (2007): 387–99.

22. H. Van Dyke Parunak, "A Semantic Survey of *Nhm*," *Biblica* 56 (1975): 532.

23. For a discussion of other relevant passages, see Peckham, *Divine Attributes*, 111–40.

24. James Arminius, *The Writings of James Arminius*, trans. James Nichols (Grand Rapids, MI: Baker, 1977), 2:70 (Disputation 28.14).

25. For more on this, see Peckham, *Divine Attributes*, 111–40. See also, William Lane Craig, *The Only Wise God: The Compatibility of Divine Foreknowledge and Human Freedom* (Grand Rapids, MI: Baker, 1987).

26. Craig comments: "The Christian may quite correctly say, 'I do not in fact know how God foreknows future free decisions. But why *should* I know how God has such foreknowledge? Who are human beings that they should know how God foreknows the future? Unless there is some reason to think that such foreknowledge is impossible, it is perfectly rational to believe in it.'" Craig, *The Only Wise God*, 119 (emphasis original).

27. Ellen White comments, "It is impossible for finite minds fully to comprehend the character or the works of the Infinite One. To the keenest intellect, the most highly educated mind, that holy Being must ever remain clothed in mystery. 'Canst thou by searching find out God? canst thou find out the Almighty unto perfection? It is as high as heaven; what canst thou do? deeper than hell; what canst thou know?' Job 11:7, 8." Ellen G. White, *Steps to Christ*, (Mountain View, CA: Pacific Press, 1892), 105.

28. Ellen White comments, "The revelation of Himself that God has given in His word is for our study. This we may seek to understand. But beyond this we are not to penetrate. The highest intellect may tax itself until it is wearied out in conjectures regarding the nature of God, but the effort will be fruitless. This problem has not been given us to solve. No human mind can comprehend God. None are to indulge in speculation regarding His nature. Here silence is eloquence. The Omniscient One is above discussion." Ellen G. White, *The Ministry of Healing* (Mountain View, CA: Pacific Press, 1905), 429.

CHAPTER 9 • THE GOD WHO PROVIDES ALL GOOD THINGS AND CONQUERS EVIL: DIVINE PROVIDENCE AND COSMIC CONFLICT

1. Randall Younker explains that Genesis 2 foreshadows the entrance of evil into this world by its statements regarding four things that were not yet in the world, all of which were not present until

after the Fall. See Randall Younker, "Genesis 2: A Second Creation Account?" in *Creation, Catastrophe, and Calvary: Why a Global Flood Is Vital to the Doctrine of Atonement*, ed. John Templeton Baldwin (Hagerstown, MD: Review and Herald, 2000), 69–78.

2. Donald E. Gowan notes, the very "setting of a limit shows that" Eve "does indeed have a choice and thus establishes" her "freedom." *From Eden to Babel: A Commentary on the Book of Genesis 1–11*, ITC (Grand Rapids, MI: Eerdmans, 1988), 42.

3. Here, "the serpent discreetly avoids any reference to God's generous permission but magnifies God's prohibition, which is the reversal" of Gen. 2:16–17. Victor P. Hamilton, *The Book of Genesis, Chapters 1–17* (Grand Rapids, MI: Eerdmans, 1990), 172. "He grossly exaggerates God's prohibition, claiming that God did not allow them access to any of the orchard trees," presenting God as "spiteful, mean, obsessively jealous, and self-protective." Hamilton, *Genesis 1–17*, 188.

4. Hamilton characterizes this as "a direct frontal attack." There is a "mixture here of misquotation, denial, and slander fed to the woman by the snake." *Genesis 1–17*, 189. Nahum M. Sarna adds that the "serpent emphatically contradicts the very words of God used in 2:17" and "proceeds to ascribe self-serving motives to God." *Genesis: The Traditional Hebrew Text with New JPS Translation*, The JPS Torah Commentary (Philadelphia: Jewish Publication Society, 1989), 25. Kenneth A. Mathews, further, contends that the "motivation for God's command is impugned by the serpent. In the wisdom tradition the adversary argues the same case in Job (1:9–11; 2:4–5). God is not good and gracious; he is selfish and deceptive, preventing the man and woman from achieving the same position as 'Elohim' (v. 5)." *Genesis 1–11:26*, vol. 1a, The New American Commentary (New International Version): An Exegetical and Theological Exposition of Scripture, vol. 1a (Nashville, B&H, 1995), 236.

5. Tremper Longman III explains, the "serpent, as later Scripture (Rev. 12:9) makes clear, was not an ordinary animal, but rather an" appearance "of the evil one, Satan himself." Longman, *Daniel* (Grand Rapids, MI: Zondervan, 1999), 256.

6. Gerald L. Borchert contends that Jesus's "reference [in John 8:44] is obviously to the garden of Eden text where the deceit of the serpent/devil led to the 'death' of Adam and Eve (Gen 3:1–4; cf. Wis 2:24; Rom 5:12)." *John 1–11* (Nashville, TN: B&H, 2001), 305.

7. Both Ezekiel 28 and Isaiah 14 contain oracles addressed to human kings. However, the language in both passages points beyond a mere human audience to Satan himself as the intended addressee (cf. Gen. 3:15). Ezekiel 28:12 speaks of a "lamentation for the king of Tyre," a subtle shift from the "prince of Tyre" as the addressee earlier in the chapter (28:2). See José M. Bertoluci, "The Son of the Morning and the Guardian Cherub in the Context of the Controversy between Good and Evil" (ThD diss., Andrews University, 1985).

8. "How" is distinct from "why." *Why* any perfect being would originate sin will always remain a mystery because no rational explanation or excuse exists; Satan's sin was utterly nonsensical and unjustifiable. Ellen White comments, in this regard: "It is impossible to explain the origin of sin so as to give a reason for its existence. Yet enough may be understood concerning both the origin and the final disposition of sin to make fully manifest the justice and benevolence of God in all His dealings with evil. Nothing is more plainly taught in Scripture than that God was in no wise responsible for the entrance of sin; that there was no arbitrary withdrawal of divine grace, no deficiency in the divine government, that gave occasion for the uprising of rebellion. Sin is an intruder, for whose presence no reason can be given. It is mysterious, unaccountable; to excuse it is to defend it." Ellen G. White, *The Great Controversy* (Mountain View, CA: Pacific Press, 1911), 492–93.

9. See Richard M. Davidson, "And There Was Gossip in Heaven," *Adventist Review* (January 2013): 22–24. See also Richard M. Davidson, "Cosmic Metanarrative for the Coming Millennium," *Journal of the Adventist Theological Society* 11, no. 1–2 (2000): 108.

10. Richard Swinburne claims, "all Christian theologians of the first four centuries believed in human free will in the libertarian sense, as did all subsequent Eastern Orthodox theologians, and most Western Catholic theologians from Duns Scotus (in the fourteenth century) onwards." Swinburne, *Providence and the Problem of Evil* (Oxford: Clarendon Press, 1998), 35.

11. On the development of Melanchthon's nuanced views on free will, see Gregory Graybill, *Evangelical Free Will: Phillipp Melanchthon's Doctrinal Journey on the Origins of Faith* (Oxford: Oxford University Press, 2010).

12. In this context, that which God wants (or desires) is defined as that which He would bring about were He to unilaterally and causally determine the outcome. See John C. Peckham, *Theodicy of Love: Cosmic Conflict and the Problem of Evil* (Grand Rapids, MI: Baker Academic), 27–53.

13. See Peckham, *Theodicy of Love*, 27–53.

14. John N. Oswalt comments: "The Holy One had extended his arms to them with a gentle word of strength (28:12), but they refused." Oswalt, *Isaiah 1–39* (Grand Rapids, MI: Eerdmans, 1986), 554.

15. Craig Blomberg comments, "God never imposes His love by overriding human will." Blomberg, *Matthew* (Nashville, TN: B&H, 2001), 350. Whereas some limit Christ's statement in Matthew 23:37 to His humanity, His cry matches the depiction of God's will elsewhere (e.g., Ezek. 33:11).

16. Joseph Fitzmyer comments, "the Pharisees and lawyers thwarted God's design on their behalf." *Luke I–IX*, AB 28 (Garden City, NY: Doubleday, 1981), 670. H. J. Ritz adds that this assumes "that the *boulē*

of God can be hindered." H. J. Ritz "Βουλη," in *Exegetical Dictionary of the New Testament*, ed. Horst Robert Balz and Gerhard Schneider (Grand Rapids, MI: Eerdmans, 1990), 224.

17. Some argue that the terms *anyone* and *all* in passages such as 1 Timothy 2:4 may be referring to all kinds of people rather than each individual or that such terms may simply be referring to the specific addressees of the letter." See the discussion in Richard J. Bauckham, *2 Peter, Jude* (Dallas: Word, 2002), 313; Douglas J. Moo, *2 Peter and Jude* (Grand Rapids, MI: Zondervan, 1996), 188. However, Ezekiel 18:32 does not leave room for this kind of interpretation. As Peter H. Davids puts it, God wants "'everyone'/'all' to come to repentance.... God's will may not be done, but it will not be for lack of trying on his part." *The Letters of 2 Peter and Jude* (Grand Rapids, MI: Eerdmans, 2006), 281.

18. On Romans 9–11, see John C. Peckham, *Divine Attributes: Knowing the Covenantal God of Scripture* (Grand Rapids, MI: Baker Academic, 2021), 141–74.

19. For more on the case of Joseph and other examples of how God's ideal and remedial wills relate, see Peckham, *Divine Attributes*, 167–70.

20. For more on this, see Peckham, *Theodicy of Love*, 27–54. See also John C. Peckham, *The Love of God: A Canonical Model* (Downers Grove, IL: IVP Academic, 2015), 112–14, 226–28, 257–63; John C. Peckham, *The Concept of Divine Love in the Context of the God-World Relationship* (New York: Peter Lang, 2014), 204–34, 372–98, 500–2, 577–82.

21. Ellen G. White comments, "The exercise of force is contrary to the principles of God's government; He desires only the service of love; and love cannot be commanded; it cannot be won by force or authority. Only by love is love awakened." White, The *Desire of Ages* (Mountain View, CA: Pacific Press, 1898), 22. Elsewhere, she comments further: "The law of love being the foundation of the government of God, the happiness of all intelligent beings depends upon their perfect accord with its great principles of righteousness. God desires from all His creatures the service of love—service that springs from an appreciation of His character. He takes no pleasure in a forced obedience; and to all He grants freedom of will, that they may render Him voluntary service." White, *Patriarchs and Prophets*, 34. Further, she writes, "to deprive man of the freedom of choice would be to rob him of his prerogative as an intelligent being, and make him a mere automaton. It is not God's purpose to coerce the will. Man was created a free moral agent." Ellen G. White, *Patriarchs and Prophets* (Washington, DC: Review and Herald, 1890), 331.

22. As Richard Rice puts it, God can do "anything logically possible *that does not require creaturely cooperation.*" Rice, *Suffering and the Search for Meaning* (Downers Grove, IL: IVP Academic, 2014), 52 (emphasis original).

23. See Peckham, *Theodicy of Love*, 41–45.

24. As Michael Murray puts it, "free and effective choice" requires some "nomic regularity," that is, a "natural order" that "operate[s] by regular and well-ordered laws of nature," within which creatures may "form intentions" and have "reason to believe ... certain bodily movements" will likely actualize those intentions. Murray, *Nature Red in Tooth and Claw: Theism and the Problem of Animal Suffering* (New York: Oxford University Press, 2008), 7, 139–40. Alvin Plantinga adds, "intelligent free action would not be possible in a world without regularity and predictability ... *such* action would be possible in a world in which God often intervened, provided he did so in a regular and predictable way." Plantinga, *Where the Conflict Really Lies: Science, Religion, and Naturalism* (New York: Oxford University Press, 2011), 103.

25. Ellen G. White affirms that God does not break His own laws, but this does not prevent God from acting in history and working miracles. Specifically, she writes: "God does not annul His laws. He does not work contrary to them. The work of sin He does not undo. But He transforms. Through His grace the curse works out blessings." White, *Education* (Mountain View, CA: Pacific Press, 1903), 148. Again, she writes: "God does not annul His laws or work contrary to them, but He is continually using them as His instruments. Nature testifies of an intelligence, a presence, an active energy, that works in and through her laws." White, *Patriarchs and Prophets*, 114; cf. White, *Testimonies for the Church*, vol. 8 (Mountain View, CA: Pacific Press, 1904), 259. Contrary to those who believe God cannot work miracles because of the "laws of nature," White contends: "As commonly used, the term 'laws of nature' comprises what men have been able to discover with regard to the laws that govern the physical world; but how limited is their knowledge, and how vast the field in which the Creator can work in harmony with His own laws and yet wholly beyond the comprehension of finite beings!" White, *Patriarchs and Prophets*, 114. Likewise, she elsewhere comments that we should not think God is "bound by the laws of nature to be nature's servant" or that "nature is a self-sustaining agency apart from the Deity, having its own inherent power with which to work." And, yet, she declares: "The Lord does not work through His laws to supersede the laws of nature. He does His work through the laws and properties of His instruments." White, *Testimonies for the Church*, vol. 16 (Mountain View, CA: Pacific Press, 1901), 186.

26. As Craig Keener puts it: "Human beings regularly act within nature; they do not, for example, 'violate' the law of gravity by catching a falling pencil or lifting an eraser. Nor does a surgeon violate natural law when she restores someone's sight. Why should a putative creator be any less able to act within nature than those he created?" In this regard, special divine action *beyond* the so-called laws of nature does not entail a *violation* of laws of nature. In this regard, Keener explains further: "Today philosophers of science tend to define laws of nature in primarily descriptive ways. That is, these 'laws' describe what happens rather than causing it. If scientists find some things that do not fit the pattern, they may rethink

the law, but they do not ordinarily say that something violated the law. Moreover, laws of nature describe nature at particular levels and under particular conditions; they function differently in settings such as superconductivity or black holes. Why should special divine action not create a different set of conditions than those to which we are accustomed?" Craig Keener, "Miracles Don't Violate the Laws of Nature," *Christianity Today* (website), accessed May 13, 2022, https://www.christianitytoday.com/ct/2022/february-web-only/miracles-philosophy-skepticism-laws-nature.html.

27. Ellen G. White frames the problem of evil this way: "To many minds the origin of sin and the reason for its existence are a source of great perplexity. They see the work of evil, with its terrible results of woe and desolation, and they question how all this can exist under the sovereignty of One who is infinite in wisdom, in power, and in love. Here is a mystery of which they find no explanation. And in their uncertainty and doubt they are blinded to truths plainly revealed in God's word and essential to salvation." White, *The Great Controversy*, 492.

28. For more on this, see Peckham, *Theodicy of Love*, 142–45, 161–62.

29. See Seventh-day Adventist Fundamental Belief #8 in the Appendix.

30. "If God is good and powerful as the theist believes, then he will indeed have a good reason for permitting evil; but why suppose the theist must be in a position to figure out what it is?" Alvin Plantinga, "Reply to the Basingers on Divine Omnipotence." *Process Studies* 11/1 (1981): 28.

31. This draws on Stephen Wykstra's work. See Wykstra, "Rowe's Noseeum Arguments from Evil," in *The Evidential Argument from Evil*, ed. Daniel Howard-Snyder (Bloomington, IN: Indiana University Press, 1996), 126–50.

32. As William Hasker put it, it is "wholly inappropriate" to think as if God is "sitting nervously in the dock hoping that we, his attorneys, will be able to get him off from the charges." Rather, "God is the holy and righteous One, the One before whom we ourselves will be judged, not someone subject to our judgment." As such, "God does not need a theodicy, but we do—at least, some of us do." Hasker, *The Triumph of God Over Evil* (Downers Grove, IL: IVP Academic, 2008), 120.

33. This approach has a long history in Christian thought. Paul Gavrilyuk identifies it with "the common core of patristic theodicy," writing: "Relatively early among patristic theologians, a broad agreement emerged that the free will of some rational creatures accounted for the actualization of evil. The Creator could not be held responsible for the free evil choices that rational creatures made, since God did not causally determine these choices." Rather, the "misuse of angelic and human free will is the cause of evil." Gavrilyuk, "An Overview of Patristic Theodicies," in *Suffering and Evil in Early Christian Thought*, ed. Nonna Verna Harrison and David G. Hunter (Grand Rapids, MI: Baker Academic, 2016), 6, 4. For Alvin Plantinga's widely lauded recent version of this approach, see Plantinga, *God, Freedom, and Evil* (Grand Rapids, MI: Eerdmans, 1977).

34. Katherin Rogers, *Perfect Being Theology* (Edinburgh: Edinburgh University Press, 2000), 101.

35. For example, the atheist philosopher William Rowe wrote: "The logical problem of evil has been severely diminished, if not entirely resolved" as a "result of Plantinga's work." Rowe, "Introduction to Part II: The Logical Problem of Evil," in *God and the Problem of Evil* (Malden, MA: Blackwell, 2001), 76.

36. Ellen G. White comments: "Had he [Satan] been immediately blotted from existence, they would have served God from fear rather than from love. The influence of the deceiver would not have been fully destroyed, nor would the spirit of rebellion have been utterly eradicated. Evil must be permitted to come to maturity. For the good of the entire universe through ceaseless ages Satan must more fully develop his principles, that his charges against the divine government might be seen in their true light by all created beings, that the justice and mercy of God and the immutability of His law might forever be placed beyond all question." White, *The Great Controversy*, 498.

37. For example, see Matthew 4:1–10; 8:28–33; 9:33; 10:1, 8; 17:18; Mark 1:13; 3:15, 22–23; 5:13–15; 7:25–30; 9:17–30; Luke 4:33–36; 8:2, 27–33; 9:38–42; 10:18–19; 11:14; 13:16; John 8:44; cf. Acts 5:3; 26:18; Hebrews 2:14; 1 John 3:8. Brian Han Gregg comments, "the conflict between God and Satan is clearly a central feature of Jesus' teaching and ministry." Gregg, *What Does the Bible Say About Suffering?* (Downers Grove, IL: IVP Academic, 2016), 66.

38. David George Reese comments, God's "kingdom was confronting more than a loose confederation of hostile forces. It faced an opposing kingdom of evil spirits." Reese, "Demons: New Testament," *ABD* 2:141.

39. In this regard, John Goldingay writes that behind the idols were "so-called deities [that] do indeed exist, but they do not count as God, and they are subject to God's judgment," yet these "supernatural centers of power" can "deliberately oppose Yhwh's purpose." Goldingay, *Old Testament Theology, Volume 2: Israel's Faith* (Downers Grove, IL: IVP Academic, 2006), 43. In this regard, God "executed judgment on" Egypt's "gods" (Num. 33:4; cf. Exod. 12:12; 18:10–11). Many other instances refer to the "gods" of the nations (cf. Exod. 12:12; 15:11; 23:32; Deut. 4:19–20; 6:14; 32:8, 17; Josh. 24:15; Judg. 6:10; 10:6; 11:24; 1 Sam. 5:7; 6:5; 1 Kings 11:5, 33; 18:24; 20:23, 28; 2 Kings 17:29–31; 18:33–35; 19:12–13; 1 Chron. 5:25; 2 Chron. 25:14–15, 20; 28:23; 32:13–17; Ezra 1:2–3; Isa. 36:18–20; 37:12; Jer. 5:19, 30–31; 34:12–13; 46:25; 50:2; 51:44; Zeph. 2:11). Scripture explicitly highlights, however, that YHWH is utterly superior (1 Chron. 16:25–26; 2 Chron. 2:5–6), there is "no one like" YHWH "among the gods" (2 Chron. 6:14; Ps. 86:8; cf. 77:13; 95:3; 96:4–5; 97:9; 135:5). See also Daniel I. Block, *The Gods of the Nations*, 2nd ed. (Grand Rapids, MI: Baker Academic, 2000).

40. Reese explains that this refers to "pagan gods," the "spiritual reality behind the apparent nothingness of idols." "Demons," 2:140, 142. Gordon D. Fee adds, Israel "had rejected God their Rock for beings who were no gods, indeed who were demons" (Deut. 32:17). Fee, *The First Epistle to the Corinthians* (Grand Rapids, MI: Eerdmans, 1987), 472; Clinton E. Arnold, *Powers of Darkness: Principalities & Powers in Paul's Letters* (Downers Grove, IL: IVP Academic, 1992), 95; Stephen F. Noll, *Angels of Light, Powers of Darkness: Thinking Biblically about Angels, Satan, and Principalities* (Downers Grove, IL: InterVarsity, 1998), 81. See also the discussion in Sung Ik Kim, "Proclamation in Cross-Cultural Context: Missiological Implications of the Book of Daniel" (PhD diss., Andrews University, 2005), 82–83.

41. As C. S. Lewis put it: "One of the things that surprised me when I first read the New Testament seriously was that it talked so much about a Dark Power in the universe—a mighty evil spirit who was held to be the Power behind death and disease, and sin.... Christianity thinks this Dark Power was created by God, and was good when he was created, and went wrong.... this universe is at war ... [and] it is a civil war, a rebellion, and that we are living in a part of the universe occupied by the rebel. Enemy-occupied territory—that is what this world is." Lewis, *Mere Christianity* (New York: HarperOne, 2001), 45.

42. Ellen G. White comments: "The earth was dark through misapprehension of God. That the gloomy shadows might be lightened, that the world might be brought back to God, Satan's deceptive power was to be broken. This could not be done by force. The exercise of force is contrary to the principles of God's government; He desires only the service of love; and love cannot be commanded; it cannot be won by force or authority. Only by love is love awakened. To know God is to love Him; His character must be manifested in contrast to the character of Satan. This work only one Being in all the universe could do. Only He who knew the height and depth of the love of God could make it known." White, *Desire of Ages*, 22. See also Lael Caesar, "Religious Faiths and the Problem of Evil: A Biblical Perspective," https://christintheclassroom.org/vol_37b/37b-cc_059-100.pdf.

43. Many biblical texts depict a heavenly council of celestial beings, often describing them as possessing ruling authority relative to events on earth. See 1 Kings 22:19–23; 2 Chronicles 18:18–22; Job 1:6–12; 2:1–7; Psalm 29:1–2; 82; 89:5–8; Isaiah 6; Daniel 7:9–14; Zechariah 3:1–7; cf. Isaiah 24:21–23; 1 Corinthians 4:9; Revelation 4–5. "Several passages in the OT" appear "to assume that God governs the world through a council of the heavenly host." But, "in the OT the complete dependence of these sons of God on God himself and their total submission to him is not questioned. In this way Israel altered the ancient Near Eastern understanding of the divine council to conform to its monotheistic belief." John E. Hartley, *The Book of Job* (Grand Rapids, MI: Eerdmans, 1988), 71n6; cf. Michael S. Heiser, "Divine Council," in *The Lexham Bible Dictionary*, ed. John D. Barry et al. (Bellingham, WA: Lexham Press, 2016); E. T. Mullen, Jr., "Divine Assembly," in *ABD*, 2:214.

44. Lindsay Wilson notes that the court scenes have "implications for the character of Job but also for God's integrity. If God is treating Job as righteous when he is not, then God is not acting fairly. Much is at stake," for this "is a questioning not just of Job's motives but also of God's rule. The accuser is saying to God that Job does not deserve all his blessings, and thus God is not ruling the world with justice." Wilson, *Job* (Grand Rapids, MI: Eerdmans, 2015), 32, 34. Similarly, Frances Andersen astutely notes, "God's character and Job's are both slighted." *Job* (Nottingham: Inter-Varsity, 1976), 89.

45. John E. Hartley notes that "the main function of this assembly here is to provide an open forum in which Yahweh permits the testing of Job. That is, the plan to test Job was not hatched in a secret meeting between Yahweh and the Satan. Rather it was decided openly before the heavenly assembly. In this setting Yahweh's motivation, based on his complete confidence in Job, was fully known and thus it was above question." Hartley, *The Book of Job*, 72; cf. Wilson, *Job*, 34.

46. Carol Newsom comments: "The words that the *satan* utters in v. 11 are no wager but a challenge to a test." Carol Newsom, "The Book of Job," in *The New Interpreter's Bible*, ed. Leander E. Keck, vol. 4 (Nashville, Abingdon, 1994), 349. See also Frances I. Andersen, *Job* (Nottingham: Inter-Varsity, 1976), 89.

47. Frances Andersen argues that God has "good reason" for dealing with Satan's allegations before the heavenly council as He does, "namely to disprove the Satan's slander" of God's character." Andersen, *Job*, 95. So also, Wilson, *Job*, 32.

48. In the end, Job is vindicated on this point by God and Job's "friends" are shown to have been wrong. Yet, the text gives no indication that Job receives any understanding of the wider, cosmic significance of this test case—an amazing testament of Job's faith indeed. Elsewhere in Scripture, the theology of retribution of Job's friends is falsified. See, for example, Ecclesiastes 3:16–17; 8:12, 14; 9:2; Matthew 5:45; Luke 13:1–5; John 9:1–3. See also Lael Caesar, "Job As Paradigm for the Eschaton," *Journal of the Adventist Theological Society* 11/1–2 (2000): 148–62.

49. Any hint of cosmic dualism is utterly rejected by the biblical data (cf. Col. 1:16–17).

50. The cosmic conflict is apparent elsewhere in Job (even beyond the scenes in Job 1–2). For example, in Job, God repeatedly refers to a sea beast named Leviathan, saying: "Can you drag out Leviathan with a fishhook, and press down his tongue with a rope?" (Job 41:1). "Will he [Leviathan] make a covenant with you? Will you take him as a servant forever?" (Job 41:4). "No one is so reckless that he dares to stir him [Leviathan]; who then is he who opposes Me?" (Job 41:10). If Leviathan, here, is rightly understood as reference to a supernatural character (or, more specifically, a metaphorical depiction of Satan himself, as many Adventist scholars believe), these statements of God in Job not only reference the cosmic conflict,

but make it clear that God remains sovereign even in the midst of this conflict. Notably, in this regard, a multi-headed dragon (identified as representing Satan, the serpent of old) appears in Revelation 12, reminiscent of the multi-headed sea serpent Leviathan who is an enemy of God in the Old Testament (see Ps. 74:13-14; LXX 73:13-14; 104:26; LXX 103:26; cf. Job 26:13; 41:1; Ps. 148:7; Isa. 27:1).

51. Gregg, *What Does the Bible Say About Suffering?* 64.

52. Adventists believe that "Michael," which means in Hebrew "(the one) who is like God," is another name for Christ. Michael, then, is not an angelic being, but the ruler of the angels. The "arch" in archangel derives from the Greek term for chief or ruler, so "archangel" is taken to mean ruler of the angels (notice that Christ often refers to "His angels," Matt. 13:41; 24:31; cf. Rev. 12:7). This understanding complements the instances of the divine "angel of the Lord" (Gen. 16:7-13; 22:11; Ex 3:2-4; 14:19; 23:20-23; Judg. 13:13-22; Hosea 12:3-5), the "angel of His [YHWH's] presence" (Isa. 63:9), who is no mere angel, but is Himself God (see chapter 4).

53. Tremper Longman rejects the view of Calvin and others that the prince of Persia in Daniel 10 is "the human prince Cambyses," claiming that "these verses give us a hint at the cosmic battle that parallels the earthly struggles of God's people. The 'prince of the Persian kingdom' is a supernatural being who fights on behalf of that human kingdom. The Old Testament knows of such spiritual entities and events in other books besides Daniel, perhaps most notably in Deuteronomy 32:8-9" (cf. Deut. 4:19; Isa. 24:21-23). Tremper Longman III, *Daniel*, 250. John Goldingay also sees this and verses 20-21 as references to the "heavenly correspondents of these earthly powers [Persia and Greece]. *Daniel*, 292; cf. Stephen R. Miller, *Daniel* (Nashville: B&H, 1994), 285. Daniel L. Smith-Christopher comments that Daniel 10:13 "refers once again to the notion, apparently widespread in some circles of Jewish apocalyptic writing, that the various nations have spiritual counterparts, as Israel has the angel Michael (see Deut. 29:26; 32:8-9; see also Ecclus 17:17; Jub 15:31-32). The sources of this notion have been debated by scholars, many of whom see its roots in the idea of a heavenly council of celestial beings.... Whatever the source of the idea, its function within Daniel is of particular interest—a heavenly version of the conflicts on earth between the foreign nations and the Jewish people." Smith-Christopher, "The Book of Daniel," in NIB, 7:137. See also Louis F. Hartman and Alexander Di Lella, *Daniel*, AB (New Haven: Yale University Press, 2008), 282; Kim, "Proclamation in Cross-Cultural Context," 146-49.

54. As Longman puts it, "though the divine realm heard and began responding immediately to Daniel's prayers three weeks earlier, there was a delay because of a conflict, an obstacle in the form of the 'prince of the Persian kingdom' (v. 13)." *Daniel*, 249. Miller adds, "Gabriel had been on his way from heaven with a message for Daniel but had been prevented by the prince of Persia." *Daniel*, 284.

55. Gleason L. Archer comments, "The powers of evil apparently have the capacity to bring about hindrances and delays, even of the delivery of the answers to believers whose requests God is minded to answer. God's response was immediate, so far as his intention was concerned. But 'the prince of the Persian kingdom' (v. 13)—apparently the satanic agent assigned to the sponsorship and control of the Persian realm—put up a determined opposition to the actual delivery of the divine answer." "Daniel," in *Daniel and the Minor Prophets*, F. E. Gaebelein, ed., The Expositor's Bible Commentary 7 (Grand Rapids, MI: Zondervan, 1986), 124.

56. See also Arnold, *Powers of Darkness*.

57. Here, the "cross is seen as the point of decisive defeat" of the evil powers. Arnold, "Principalities and Powers," *ABD* 5:467. However, "[a]lthough defeated by the cross-resurrection event, the powers are still active (Eph. 6:12; Gal. 4:9)" but "will finally be destroyed at the consummation (1 Cor. 15:24)." Arnold, "Principalities and Powers," *ABD* 5:467. In this regard, Seventh-day Adventist Fundamental Belief #11 ("Growing in Christ") states, in part: "By His death on the cross Jesus triumphed over the forces of evil. He who subjugated the demonic spirits during His earthly ministry has broken their power and made certain their ultimate doom. Jesus' victory gives us victory over the evil forces that still seek to control us, as we walk with Him in peace, joy, and assurance of His love. Now the Holy Spirit dwells within us and empowers us. Continually committed to Jesus as our Saviour and Lord, we are set free from the burden of our past deeds. No longer do we live in the darkness, fear of evil powers, ignorance, and meaninglessness of our former way of life." See the Appendix.

58. Here, it should be recognized that no such rules are imposed upon God. No one has the power, authority, or jurisdiction to oppose things on God, the almighty Creator. Yet, because God does not determine the thoughts of creatures, relative to the rules of engagement and otherwise, God works in ways that take into account the way courses of action will be perceived by creatures, in the heavenly council and beyond, toward demonstrating once and for all that He is wholly good, just, and loving, a demonstration that is for the good of the entire universe (since, otherwise, the perfect harmony of the universe would be continually upset).

59. For a technical discussion of petitionary prayer, see John C. Peckham, "The Influence Aim Problem of Petitionary Prayer: A Cosmic Conflict Approach." *Journal of Analytic Theology* 8 (2020): 412-32.

60. Here, it is not as if God needed to be constrained, for God only and always does what is good and right and always keeps His promises. Rather, the rules of engagement themselves manifest God's fair and gracious character, providing the parameters needed for there to be an open demonstration in which all can see the devil is free to operate within some pre-arranged limits so that all could see Satan's claims that

God is unfair are false, parameters which also constrain the devil to operate within limits rather than wreaking all havoc on this world he otherwise would.

61. Some have raised questions about particular actions of God recorded in Scripture, with one prominent example raised by critics being the conquest of Canaan. For more on this issue, in light of the wider scope of the cosmic conflict, see Peckham, *Theodicy of Love*, 157–59; cf. Barna Magyarosi, *Holy War and Cosmic Conflict in the Old Testament* (Berrien Springs, MI: ATS Publications, 2010), esp. 112–24; Paul Copan and Matthew Flannagan, *Did God Really Command Genocide?* (Grand Rapids, MI: Baker, 2014); Roy Adams, *Crossing Jordan: Joshua, Holy War, and God's Unfailing Promises* (Hagerstown, MD: Review and Herald, 2004).

62. For much more on this two-stage victory of Christ, see Peckham, *Theodicy of Love*, 119–137.

63. In this regard, Ellen G. White comments: "Our world is a vast lazar house, a scene of misery that we dare not allow even our thoughts to dwell upon. Did we realize it as it is, the burden would be too terrible. Yet God feels it all. In order to destroy sin and its results He gave His best Beloved" and through His plan of redemption will finally "bring this scene of misery to an end." White, *Education*, 264.

CHAPTER 10 • THE TESTIMONY OF THE KING: DIVINE REVELATION AND SCRIPTURE AS COVENANT WITNESS DOCUMENT

1. This is a primary reason why the doctrine of Scripture appears after discussion of the cosmic conflict in this book.

2. For more on this, see John C. Peckham, *Canonical Theology: The Biblical Canon, Sola Scriptura, and Theological Method* (Grand Rapids, MI: Eerdmans, 2016).

3. Of Joshua 1:8, the *Andrews Study Bible* comments: "God's revelation to Moses was regarded as authoritative Scripture already in the time of Joshua, and it became the foundation of the OT canon." *Andrews Study Bible: Light. Depth. Truth.*, NKJV (Berrien Springs, MI: Andrews University Press, 2010), 265.

4. *Andrews Study Bible*, NKJV, 292.

5. The writing down of apostolic testimony (by apostles themselves or close contemporary associates thereof) was a way to permanently record the unique and unrepeatable apostolic witness beyond the limits of their personal presence (cf. Rev. 1:11), and for future generations. As Michael Kruger puts it, "written accounts were simply a way to make oral/eyewitness testimony permanently accessible." Michael J. Kruger, *The Question of Canon: Challenging the Status Quo in the New Testament Debate* (Downers Grove, IL: IVP Academic, 2013), 72. Further, Kruger writes, "the mission of the apostles" made "the resulting collection of authoritative books—a virtual inevitability." Kruger, *Question of Canon*, 76.

6. Here and elsewhere the apostolic testimony is often framed as a special "witness" (*martys*). See Luke 24:48–49; Acts 1:8, 21–22; 2:32; 3:15; 5:32; 10:39–41; 13:31; 22:15; 23:11; 26:16; 1 Peter 5:1; cf. Luke 1:2; John 15:26–27; 19:35; 20:30; 21:24; Acts 4:20; 1 Corinthians 15:15; Hebrews 12:1; 2 Peter 1:16; 1 John 1:1–4. Regarding this, Kruger comments: "Given the authoritative role of the apostles in early Christianity, and the manner in which they were commissioned to speak for Christ, an apostolic writing would bear the highest possible authority. Indeed, it would bear Christ's authority." Kruger, *Question of Canon*, 153.

7. "Paul, Peter, and John use expressions that clearly exhibit their consciousness of being moved, like the prophets of old, by the Holy Spirit (Eph. 3:4, 5; 1 Pet. 1:12; Rev. 1:10, 11). They are conscious of speaking and writing with divine authority." Peter M. van Bemmelen, "Revelation and Inspiration," in *Handbook of Seventh-day Adventist Theology*, ed. Raoul Dederen (Hagerstown, MD: Review and Herald, 2000), 37.

8. See Peckham, *Canonical Theology*.

9. On the many different patterns of revelation, see the work of Fernando L. Canale, *The Cognitive Principle of Christian Theology: An Hermeneutical Study of the Revelation and Inspiration of the Bible* (Berrien Springs: Andrews University Lithotech, 2005).

10. In this regard, it is important to pay attention to the distinct genres in Scripture (e.g., historical narrative, law, poetry, wisdom literature, apocalyptic, etc.). For more on this, see Kristie Anyabwile, *Literarily: How Understanding Bible Genres Transforms Bible Study* (Chicago: Moody, 2022).

11. However, the sources that are used by authors are not always inspired. Scripture teaches that God can use sources (human witnesses or even written documents passed down) as a *means* of revelation. At the same time, that does not mean every source is used by God for revelation or that such sources must themselves be revealed or inspired.

12. For much more on the historical and cognitive nature of divine revelation in Scripture, see Canale, *The Cognitive Principle of Christian Theology*. Fernando L. Canale, *Back to Revelation-Inspiration: Searching for the Cognitive Foundation of Christian Theology in a Postmodern World* (Lanham, MD: University Press of America, 2001). As cognitive, divine revelation in Scripture includes much propositional content, though it is not only propositional.

13. On the historical-cognitive model of revelation, see the pioneering work of Fernando Canale, *Back to Revelation-Inspiration*; Canale, *The Cognitive Principle of Christian Theology*.

14. For further explanation of the classical model, see Canale, *Back to Revelation-Inspiration*, 75–95.

15. The Enlightenment philosopher Immanuel Kant (1724–1804) was responsible for what some have referred to as a Copernican revolution in epistemology, the area of philosophy that deals with the nature of knowledge. For more on this, see Diogenes Allen and Eric O. Springsted, *Philosophy for Understanding Theology*, 2nd ed. (Louisville, KY: Westminster John Knox, 2007), 209–30.

16. Canale sometimes refers to this model as the modern model and other times labels it the liberal model. See Canale, *Back to Revelation-Inspiration;* Canale, *The Cognitive Principle of Christian Theology.*

17. Revelation, however, should never be conceived of in a way that reduces it to mere information. Divine revelation conveys far more than merely propositional knowledge, but it does include propositional knowledge, which is crucial. Revelation is not less than information about God, but it is far more than information.

18. As Peter M. van Bemmelen explains, "while the word 'inspiration' is not a precise translation of any Greek word used in the Bible to describe the process by which Scripture comes to the human mind, it may be appropriately used to represent a process in which the Holy Spirit works on selected human beings, to move them to proclaim messages received from God. Some spoke the word; some wrote it. The written form constitutes the God-breathed Scriptures (2 Tim. 3:16). 'Inspiration' refers to the Holy Spirit's work on these messengers or prophets, whether they spoke or wrote. Because these people were 'inspired' or 'moved by the Holy Spirit' (2 Pet. 1:21), their utterances and writings may be considered inspired as well (2 Tim. 3:16)." van Bemmelen, "Revelation and Inspiration," 34.

19. See Boubakar Sanou and John C. Peckham, "Canonical Theology, Social Location, and the Search for Biblical Orthodoxy," in *Scripture and Theology,* ed. Tomas Bokedal et al. (de Gruyter, forthcoming). See also Kwabena Donkor, "Presuppositions in Hermeneutics," in *Biblical Hermeneutics: An Adventist Approach,* ed. Frank M. Hasel. Biblical Research Institute Studies in Hermeneutics, vol. 3 (Silver Spring, MD: Biblical Research Institute/Review and Herald Academic, 2020), 7–30; Frank M. Hasel, "Presuppositions in the Interpretation of Scripture," in *Understanding Scripture: An Adventist Approach,* ed. George W. Reid. Biblical Research Institute Studies, vol. 1 (Silver Spring, MD: Biblical Research Institute, 2005), 27–46.

20. Ellen White comments: "They [writers] do not represent things in just the same style. Each has an experience of his own, and this diversity broadens and deepens the knowledge that is brought out to meet the necessities of varied minds. The thoughts expressed have not a set uniformity, as if cast in an iron mold, making the very hearing monotonous. In such uniformity there would be a loss of grace and distinctive beauty." Ellen G. White, *Selected Messages* (Washington, DC: Review and Herald, 1958), 1:22.

21. See Canale, *The Cognitive Principle of Christian Theology,* 338–41.

22. Ellen G. White comments, "God . . . by His Holy Spirit, qualified men and enabled them to do His work (to communicate His truth to the world). He guided the mind in the selection of what to speak and what to write. The treasure was entrusted to earthen vessels, yet it is, none the less, from heaven." White, *Selected Messages,* 1:26. Further, she writes: "Through the inspiration of His spirit the Lord gave His apostles truth, to be expressed according to the development of their minds by the Holy Spirit. But the mind is not cramped as if forced into a certain mold." White, *Selected Messages,* 1:22.

23. Ellen G. White comments that Scripture was "written by inspired men," yet "the writers of the Bible were God's penmen, not His pen." White, *Selected Messages,* 1:21.

24. Ellen G. White comments: "It is not the words of the Bible that are inspired, but the men that were inspired. Inspiration acts not on the man's words or his expressions but on the man himself, who, under the influence of the Holy Ghost, is imbued with thoughts. But the words receive the impress of the individual mind. The divine mind is diffused. The divine mind and will is combined with the human mind and will; thus the utterances of the man are the word of God." White, *Selected Messages,* 1:21. As she describes her experience, God was at work not only in the process of revelation but also relative to her process of writing. For example, she wrote: "I am just as dependent upon the Spirit of the Lord in relating or writing a vision, as in having the vision, yet the words I employ in describing what I have seen are my own, unless they be those spoken to me by an angel, which I always enclose in marks of quotation." White, *Selected Messages,* 1:37. On Ellen White's prophetic gift, see chapter 17.

25. On these and other theories, see Millard J. Erickson, *Introducing Christian Doctrine,* 3rd edition (Grand Rapids, MI: Baker Academic, 2015), 59–67.

26. See Erickson, *Introducing Christian Doctrine,* 52–53.

27. The official Seventh-day Adventist belief on Scripture reads as follows: "The Holy Scriptures, Old and New Testaments, are the written Word of God, given by divine inspiration. The inspired authors spoke and wrote as they were moved by the Holy Spirit. In this Word, God has committed to humanity the knowledge necessary for salvation. The Holy Scriptures are the supreme, authoritative, and the infallible revelation of His will. They are the standard of character, the test of experience, the definitive revealer of doctrines, and the trustworthy record of God's acts in history. (Ps. 119:105; Prov. 30:5, 6; Isa. 8:20; John 17:17; 1 Thess. 2:13; 2 Tim. 3:16, 17; Heb. 4:12; 2 Pet. 1:20, 21.)" Seventh-day Adventist Fundamental Belief #1. See the Appendix.

28. "God inspired men—not words [cf. 2 Pet. 1:21]. . . . In some instances writers were commanded to express the exact words of God, but in most cases God instructed them to describe to the best of their ability what they saw or heard. In these latter cases, the writers used their own language, patterns, and style. . . . Genuine inspiration does not obliterate the prophet's individuality, reason, integrity, or personality." For example, "Moses informed Aaron of God's messages, and, in turn, Aaron communicated them in his own vocabulary and style to Pharaoh. Likewise, Bible writers conveyed divine commands, thoughts, and ideas in their own style of language" such that "the vocabulary of the different books of the Bible varied and reflects the education and culture of the writers." *Seventh-day Adventists Believe:*

An Exposition of the Fundamental Beliefs of the Seventh-day Adventist Church, 2nd ed. (Boise, ID: Pacific Press, 2005), 14. "The Bible, then, is divine truth expressed in human language." *Seventh-day Adventists Believe*, 15. In this regard, as noted earlier, Ellen G. White comments: "It is not the words of the Bible that are inspired, but the men that were inspired. Inspiration acts not on the man's words or his expressions but on the man himself, who, under the influence of the Holy Ghost, is imbued with thoughts. But the words receive the impress of the individual mind. The divine mind is diffused. The divine mind and will is combined with the human mind and will; thus the utterances of the man are the word of God." White, *Selected Messages*, 1:21.

29. For more on this, see Fernando L. Canale, "Revelation and Inspiration," in *Understanding Scripture: An Adventist Approach*, ed. George W. Reid. Biblical Research Institute Studies, vol. 1 (Silver Spring, MD: Biblical Research Institute, 2005), 47–74. Therein, Canale critiques some understandings of "thought inspiration," particularly those that "assume a dichotomy between thoughts and words" such that revelation and inspiration "operates in the truth behind the words, but falls short of affecting the words." Canale, "Revelation and Inspiration," 56. That understanding of "thought inspiration" lends itself to the problematic "conclusion that large portions of Scripture present fallible human ideas." Canale, "Revelation and Inspiration," 58. Instead, Canale explains, although "as Adventists we do not believe that the words of Scripture were inspired, i.e., they were neither dictated nor do they represent the divine language per se, the process of R-I [revelation-inspiration] nevertheless reaches the words of the prophets." Canale, "Revelation and Inspiration," 59. In other words, Canale writes (commenting on the quote in the above note from *Selected Messages* 1:21), "White clearly says that divine inspiration . . . works not on the words (as the verbal theory affirms) but in the formation of the writer's thought. Nevertheless, inspiration reaches the words of the prophets, which 'are the words of God.'" Canale, "Revelation and Inspiration," 58–59 (the last part quoting White, *Selected Messages* 1:21). Likewise, rejecting the view that "only the thoughts behind the words [are] inspired," Peter van Bemmelen concludes, "thoughts as well as words are involved in this process" of revelation and inspiration." van Bemmelen, "Revelation and Inspiration," 39–40. As he puts it: "The Holy Spirit moved upon people to speak or write; yet what they spoke or wrote was the inspired word of God." van Bemmelen, "Revelation and Inspiration," 39.

30. As Erickson defines it: "The dynamic theory emphasizes the combination of divine and human elements in the process of inspiration and of the writing of the Bible. The Spirit of God worked by directing the writer to the thoughts or concepts he should have and allowing the writer's own distinctive personality to come into play in the choice of words and expressions. Thus, the writer gave expression to the divinely directed thoughts in a way that was uniquely characteristic of that person." This, Erickson differentiates from the "verbal theory," which "insists that the Holy Spirit's influence extends beyond the direction of thoughts to the selection of words used to convey the message. The work of the Holy Spirit is so intense that each word is the exact word God wants used at that point to express the message. Ordinarily, however, great care is taken to insist that this is not dictation." Erickson, *Introducing Christian Doctrine*, 53.

31. "The human shape of Scripture is unmistakable. Human authors—using human language, quoting human sources, operating in specific human contexts, describing human emotions—are subject to all the weaknesses and failures of humanity. Prophets and apostles were not free from sin. They doubted, they were afraid, at times they succumbed to temptation (Exod. 4:10–14; Num. 20:10–12; 2 Sam. 11:1–27; 1 Kings 19:1–3; Luke 22:54–62). Neither were they free from pride and prejudice, as is quite evident from Jonah and the Gospel narratives (Matt. 20:20–28)." van Bemmelen, "Revelation and Inspiration," 35.

32. See Canale, *The Cognitive Principle of Christian Theology*, 266–67.

33. Ellen G. White comments: "The Bible is written by inspired men, but it is not God's mode of thought and expression. It is that of humanity. God, as a writer, is not represented. Men will often say such an expression is not like God. But God has not put Himself in words, in logic, in rhetoric, on trial in the Bible. The writers of the Bible were God's penmen, not His pen." White, *Selected Messages*, 1:21.

34. See Canale, *The Cognitive Principle of Christian Theology*, 266–67.

35. Ellen G. White comments: "The Bible, perfect as it is in its simplicity, does not answer to the great ideas of God; for infinite ideas cannot be perfectly embodied in finite vehicles." White, *Selected Messages*, 1:22. Elsewhere, she explains further: "The Bible is not given to us in grand superhuman language. Jesus, in order to reach man where he is, took humanity. The Bible must be given in the language of men. Everything that is human is imperfect. Different meanings are expressed by the same word; there is not one word for each distinct idea. The Bible was given for practical purposes." White, *Selected Messages*, 1:20. Further, she explains: "The Lord speaks to human beings in imperfect speech, in order that the degenerate senses, the dull, earthly perception, of earthly beings may comprehend His words. Thus is shown God's condescension. He meets fallen human beings where they are. The Bible, perfect as it is in its simplicity, does not answer to the great ideas of God; for infinite ideas cannot be perfectly embodied in finite vehicles of thought. Instead of the expressions of the Bible being exaggerated, as many people suppose, the strong expressions break down before the magnificence of the thought, though the penman selected the most expressive language through which to convey the truths of higher education. Sinful beings can only bear to look upon a shadow of the brightness of heaven's glory." White, *Selected Messages*, 1:22.

36. In this regard, Frank Hasel writes, "there are a number of differences or discrepancies in the extant Hebrew and Greek texts upon which our Bible translations are based. For example, the Old Testament contains a number of numerical discrepancies in referring to the same events or things in the books of Samuel, Kings, and Chronicles. In 2 Samuel 8:4, David is said to have taken 700 horsemen from Hadadezer while in 1 Chronicles 18:3, 4 the figure is given as 7,000. According to 1 Kings 4:26, Solomon had 40,000 stalls for horses, but, in 2 Chronicles 9:25, he had only 4,000 stalls. In Matthew 27:54, the centurion says, 'Truly, this was the Son of God.' In Luke 23:47, however, the centurion is quoted as saying, 'Truly, this man was righteous.' In the book of Acts, Stephen told the Jews that Abraham bought the cave of Machpelah for a sum of money from the sons of Hamor in Shechem (Acts 7:16). According to the book of Genesis, however, Abraham bought the cave from Ephron the Hittite (Gen. 23:8), and it was Jacob who bought his plot of land from the sons of Hamor in Shechem (Gen. 33:19). Some of these discrepancies may have perfectly good explanations; others may be due to copyists' mistakes or human frailties. Ellen White wrote: 'Some look to us gravely and say, 'Don't you think there might have been some mistake in the copyist or in the translators?' This is all probable.... All the mistakes will not cause trouble to one soul, or cause any feet to stumble, that would not manufacture difficulties from the plainest revealed truth' (1SM 16). Do such minor discrepancies destroy our confidence in the Bible? No, unless we insist on a verbal inspiration of Scripture, which claims that 'all the words and all the verbal relationships are inspired by God.' As Seventh-day Adventists we do not hold this view. 'It is not the words of the Bible that are inspired, but the men that were inspired. Inspiration acts not on the man's words or his expressions but on the man himself, who, under the influence of the Holy Ghost, is imbued with thoughts' (1SM 21). Ellen White also stated that God 'by His Holy Spirit, qualified men and enabled them to do His work. He guided the mind in the selection of what to speak and what to write' (1SM 26; GC v–vi; cf. also 1SM 36, 37; 3SM 51, 52). Nevertheless, we cannot exclude the possibility of discrepancies or a lack of precision in minor details in the text—details that could be left out without changing the overall reliability of the historical records or the veracity of the theological message." Frank M. Hasel, "Are there Mistakes in the Bible?" in *Interpreting Scripture: Bible Questions and Answers*, ed. Gerhard Pfandl, vol. 2, Biblical Research Institute Studies (Silver Spring, MD: Biblical Research Institute, 2010), 35–36.

37. In this regard, Frank Hasel writes: "Are there mistakes in the Bible? If by mistake we mean that Scripture teaches error or is fallible and historically unreliable, the answer is 'No!' The Bible is God's infallible revelation of His truth and will. Many so-called 'problems' in the Bible often are not with the biblical text but rather with the interpreter. Furthermore, particularly since the rise of biblical criticism, the historical reliability of the Bible has often been confirmed by new discoveries in archaeology and other sciences. The suggestion that the Bible contains mistakes can easily be misunderstood to mean that God makes mistakes or that He has placed them there, but this is not the case. The discrepancies and imperfections in Scripture are due to human frailties. Without question, we do find challenging statements and even discrepancies in the Bible. But none of these discrepancies negatively affects the teaching or the historical reliability of Scripture. We can have full confidence that the Bible we have today is God's truth making every willing man and woman wise unto salvation." Hasel, "Are there Mistakes in the Bible?" 40–41.

38. Regarding the possibility of mistakes in Scripture as we have it now, Ellen G. White wrote: "Some look to us gravely and say, 'Don't you think there might have been some mistake in the copyist or in the translators?' This is all probable, and the mind that is so narrow that it will hesitate and stumble over this possibility or probability would be just as ready to stumble over the mysteries of the Inspired Word, because their feeble minds cannot see through the purposes of God. Yes, they would just as easily stumble over plain facts that the common mind will accept, and discern the Divine, and to which God's utterance is plain and beautiful, full of marrow and fatness. All the mistakes will not cause trouble to one soul, or cause any feet to stumble, that would not manufacture difficulties from the plainest revealed truth." White, *Selected Messages*, 1:16.

39. Thus, in some cases we should suspend judgment on seeming discrepancies while we await further information. For example, for some time many critical scholars believed there was no way to reconcile the chronologies of the kings of Israel and Judah in Kings and Chronicles. But, then, the Adventist scholar Edwin R. Thiele published his dissertation work, *The Mysterious Numbers of the Hebrew Kings*, 1st ed. (New York: Macmillan, 1951). Thiele's work has been published in many later revised editions and is still relied on today by many scholars.

40. Ellen G. White believed: "The Bible, and the Bible alone, is to be our creed, the sole bond of union; all who bow to this Holy Word will be in harmony. Our own views and ideas must not control our efforts. Man is fallible, but God's Word is infallible." White, *Selected Messages*, 1:416.

41. Regarding how to approach apparent mistakes in Scripture, see Frank M. Hasel, "Are There Mistakes in the Bible? *Ministry* 85/1 (2013): 20–23. See also, Richard M. Davidson, "Biblical Interpretation," in *Handbook of Seventh-Day Adventist Theology*, ed. Raoul Dederen (Hagerstown, MD: Review and Herald, 2000), 72–75. For some examples of how apparent mistakes are approached by other Christians, with numerous examples of instances that might appear to be errors at first, but turn out on closer inspection to not be errors, see Walter C. Kaiser, Jr., Peter H. Davids, F. F. Bruce, and Manfred T. Brauch, *Hard Sayings of the Bible* (Downers Grove, IL: IVP Academic, 2010 (reprint edition); Gleason F. Archer, Jr., *New*

International Encyclopedia of Bible Difficulties, 2nd ed. (Grand Rapids, MI: Zondervan, 2001); cf. Noel Weeks, *The Sufficiency of Scripture* (Edinburgh: The Banner of Truth Trust, 1988). For much more on the trustworthiness and enduring authority of Scripture, see D. A. Carson, ed., *The Enduring Authority of the Christian Scriptures* (Grand Rapids, MI: Eerdmans, 2016). For examples of Adventist approaches to difficult passages, see Gerhard F. Pfandl, ed. *Interpreting Scripture: Bible Questions and Answers.* Biblical Research Institute Studies 2 (Silver Spring, MD: Biblical Research Institute, 2010).

42. For more on this and other issues of biblical interpretation, see "Methods of Bible Study," in *Biblical Hermeneutics: An Adventist Approach*, ed. Frank M. Hasel. Biblical Research Institute Studies in Hermeneutics, vol. 3 (Silver Spring, MD: Biblical Research Institute/Review and Herald Academic, 2020), 463–73.

43. As Ellen G. White put it: "The creator of all ideas may impress different minds with the same thought but each may express it in a different way yet without contradiction." White, *Selected Messages*, 1:22. "Yet this variety (scarcely two leaves that are just alike) adds to the perfection of the tree as a whole." White, *Selected Messages*, 1:21. "As presented through different individuals the truth is brought out in its varied aspects." White, *Selected Messages*, 1:25.

44. Ellen G. White comments: "Never attempt to search the Scriptures unless you are ready to listen, unless you are ready to be a learner... Never let mortal man sit in judgment upon the Word of God or pass sentence as to how much of this is inspired and how much is not inspired, and that this is more inspired than some other portions." White, *Sermons and Talks* (Silver Spring, MD: Ellen G. White Estate, 1990), 1:66.

45. "There is sufficient evidence in the books of Moses and the prophets to show that God called them to speak and to write the words He had entrusted to them (Exod. 17:14; Deut. 31:19, 24; 1 Sam. 3:19, 21; 23:2; Jer. 36:2; Hab. 2:2)." van Bemmelen, "Revelation and Inspiration," 36.

46. Old Testament writers frequently use phrases that explicitly denote their divine origin/commission of Scripture as prophetic. These include "by the hand of" (Ezek. 1:3; 3:22; 37:1; 40:1), "the Word of the Lord" or something similar (e.g., Jer. 1:11, 13; Hosea 1:1; Joel 1:1; Jon. 1:1; Micah 1:1), "declares [or says] the Lord" (e.g., Gen. 22:16; Exod. 4:22; 5:1;7:17; 1 Sam. 10:18), and "thus says Yahweh" (e.g., Isa. 7:7; Amos 1:3; Obad. 1:1; Hag. 1:7; Zech. 12:1). According to Gerhard F. Hasel, these phrases are "the OT's way of saying that it is God-derived and 'God-breathed.'" Gerhard F. Hasel, "Divine Inspiration and the Canon of the Bible," *Journal of the Adventist Theological Society* 5/1 (1994): 78.

47. "Numerous times in the NT 'it is written' is equivalent to 'God says.' For example, in Hebrews 1:5–13, seven Old Testament citations are said to have been spoken by God, but the Old Testament passages cited do not always specifically ascribe the statement to God (see Ps. 45:6, 7; 102:25-27; 104:4). Again, Romans 9:17 and Galatians 3:8 (citing Exod. 9:16 and Gen. 22:18, respectively) reveal a close identification between Scripture and the Word of God: the NT passages introduce the citations with 'Scripture says,' while the Old Testament passages have God as the speaker. The Old Testament Scriptures as a whole are viewed as the 'oracles of God' (Rom. 3:2)." Davidson, "Biblical Interpretation," 63.

48. "The application of 2 Timothy 3:16, that all Scripture is God-breathed, should be made not only to the books of the OT but to those of the NT as well. That their writings were already recognized as inspired Scripture by Christian authors of the second century A.D. provides additional justification for such an application." van Bemmelen, "Revelation and Inspiration," 37.

49. On the nature of the biblical canon, see Peckham, *Canonical Theology*, 2–7, 16–72.

50. See James A. Sanders, "The Issue of Closure in the Canonical Process," in *The Canon Debate*, ed. Lee Martin McDonald and James A. Sanders (Peabody, MA: Hendrickson, 2002), 252.

51. Canonical "Scripture is something given by God" such "that only he can determine what it is. The role of the church, therefore, is essentially receptive, to recognize what he has given." Charles E. Hill, "The New Testament Canon: *Deconstructio ad Absurdum?*" *JETS* 52/1 (March 2009), 119. See also, Hasel, "Divine Inspiration and the Canon of the Bible," 69–70. As Anthony Thiselton explains, "the church did not 'make' the canon, but through its life and identity recognized the formative impact of divine revelation through the call of the 'prophets and apostles as a whole.'" Anthony Thiselton, "Canon, Community, and Theological Construction," in *Canon and Biblical Interpretation*, ed. Craig G. Bartholomew et al. (Grand Rapids, MI: Zondervan, 2006), 13. For Milton Fisher, "what is really meant by canonization—[is] recognition of the divinely authenticated word." Milton Fisher, "The Canon of the New Testament," in *The Origin of the Bible*, ed. Philip Wesley Comfort (Wheaton: Tyndale, 1992), 77; cf. Brevard S. Childs, *Biblical Theology in Crisis* (Philadelphia, PA: Westminster, 1970), 105; F. F. Bruce, *The Books and the Parchments* (Glasgow: Harper Collins, 1991), 86–104; Kruger, *Question of Canon*, 39.

52. As Gerhard Hasel put it, the "canon developed at the very point when the biblical books were written under inspiration" Hasel, "Divine Inspiration and the Canon of the Bible," 73. Bruce M. Metzger likewise stated: "The canon is complete when the books which by principle belong to it have been written" Bruce M. Metzger, *The Canon of the New Testament: Its Origin, Development, and Significance* (Oxford: Clarendon, 1987), 287.

53. Put simply, the difference between the two views of canon centers on where the authority to determine the canon lies. In the intrinsic canon approach, the canon is a collection of *authoritative books*. In the community canon approach the canon is an *authoritative collection* of books.

54. In this regard, Michael Kruger explains: "The role of the church [in canon recognition] is like a thermometer, not a thermostat. Both instruments provide information about the temperature in

the room—but one determines it and one reflects it." Michael J. Kruger, *Canon Revisited* (Wheaton, IL: Crossway, 2012), 106.

55. For more on these and other claims regarding the sixty-six-book canon of Scripture, see Peckham, *Canonical Theology*, 16–72.

56. To say the canon of Scripture is a covenant witness document is to say that the Old Testament canonical writings might be seen as depositing the written text of the covenantal relationship between God and His people and the New Testament might be seen as containing the Christ-commissioned canonical documentation of the New Covenant. See also Andreas J. Köstenberger and Michael J. Kruger, *The Heresy of Orthodoxy* (Wheaton, IL: Crossway, 2010), 109–15; Peckham, *Canonical Theology*, 22–28; cf. Kevin Vanhoozer's view of the "canon" as "a divinely initiated covenant document" in *The Drama of Doctrine: A Canonical-Linguistic Approach to Christian Theology* (Louisville, KY: Westminster John Knox, 2005), 134.

57. In other words: "Covenantal prophets and apostles include those recipients of revelation and inspiration commissioned by God to witness to and communicate God's covenantal revelation that pointed to Christ (the Old Testament) and God's covenantal revelation that testified to the Christ event—the incarnation, ministry, death, and resurrection of Christ (the New Testament). Covenantal prophets and apostles are intrinsically canonical (that is, they possess unique *ruling* authority) because they have been commissioned by God (the Ruler) to receive and transmit the divinely revealed and inspired rule of faith and practice." John C. Peckham, "The Prophetic Gift and Sola Scriptura," in *Biblical Hermeneutics: An Adventist Approach*, ed. Frank M. Hasel (Silver Spring, MD: Review & Herald Academic/Biblical Research Institute, 2021), 385–86.

58. On the New Testament attestation of the Old Testament, see, e.g., Luke 24:27, 44–45; 2 Timothy 3:16; 2 Peter 1:20–21; cf. John 1:45; 5:39; Acts 10:43; 1 Peter 1:20–12. Further, Matthew writes, "all this has taken place so that the Scriptures of the prophets will be fulfilled" (Matt. 26:56; cf. 1:22; 2:15–17, 23; Luke 1:70; 24:27, 44–45; Acts 1:16; 3:18). Likewise, Paul speaks of God establishing believers both "according to my gospel and the preaching of Jesus Christ" and "through the Scriptures of the prophets, in accordance with the commandment of the eternal God" (Rom. 16:25–26; cf. 1:2; 3:2; 15:4). Accordingly, Paul contends that he serves "the God of our fathers, believing everything that is in accordance with the Law and is written in the Prophets" (Acts 24:14; cf. John 1:45; Acts 23:5; 2 Cor. 4:2). Elsewhere, Paul "for three Sabbaths reasoned with them from the Scriptures" and "demonstrate[ed] by the Scriptures that Jesus was the Christ" (Acts 17:2; 18:28; cf. 1 Cor. 15:3). This and other New Testament evidence suggests the "canonical" authority of some recognized corpus of Old Testament Scripture.

59. Importantly, Jesus Himself commissioned the apostles to record, proclaim, witness to, and disseminate His acts, teachings, and commands, and make disciples of all nations (cf. Matt. 28:19–20; Acts 1:8). Jesus "appointed twelve" to "be with Him" and to "send them out to preach, and to have authority" (Mark 3:14–15). When sending them, Christ declared they would bear "testimony" to "governors and kings" and "to the Gentiles," but said, "it is not you who are speaking, but it is the Spirit of your Father who is speaking in you" such that those who do not "receive you nor listen to your words" will face judgment (Matt. 10:18, 20, 14–15; cf. John 14:26). In John 20:21, Jesus declared to the apostles, "just as the Father has sent Me, I also send you" (cf. John 17:8, 18). Further, Jesus told them, "The one who listens to you listens to Me, and the one who rejects you rejects Me," suggesting their commission as Christ's authoritative ambassadors (Luke 10:16).

60. In this regard, relative to the last book of the New Testament (Revelation) it is notable that John, the last of the twelve apostles, was "explicitly commissioned to 'write in a book what' he sees 'and send *it* to the seven churches' (Rev. 1:11) and depicts the content of his writing as the 'Revelation of Jesus Christ, which God gave Him to show to His bond-servants' (Rev. 1:1) wherein he 'testified to the word of God and to the testimony of Jesus Christ' (Rev. 1:2). Revelation thus testifies of itself as direct revelation from God and further evinces its 'canonical' authority by concluding with an inscriptional curse against anyone who 'adds' to or 'takes away from' the 'words of the book of this prophecy' (Rev. 22:18–19; cf. Deut. 4:2)." Peckham, *Canonical Theology*, 30. For more on divine commission relative to the New Testament, see Peckham, *Canonical Theology*, 28–31.

61. Here and elsewhere, I use "'divine commission' as an umbrella term for the various divine activities in the production of the canonical writings," including the processes of revelation and inspiration explained earlier in this chapter. Peckham, *Canonical Theology*, 20.

62. On traits of canonicity and recognizing the books of Scripture as "canonical," see Peckham, *Canonical Theology*, 16–47.

63. This trait of prophetic/apostolic authorship is consistent with recognizing some writings as written by scribes or amanuenses under the direction of prophets/apostles as well as with later editing and scribal activity by inspired individuals under the direction of the Holy Spirit.

64. It is beyond the scope of this brief introduction to present this evidence in any detail. For more, see Peckham, *Canonical Theology*, 16–72; Kruger, *Canon Revisited*.

65. For a discussion of this, see Kruger, *Question of Canon*, 49; cf. Roger T. Beckwith, *The Old Testament Canon of the New Testament Church* (Grand Rapids, MI: Eerdmans, 1986), 110–80; Stephen B. Chapman, "The Old Testament Canon and Its Authority for the Christian Church," *Ex Auditu* 19 (2003): 125–48.

66. "According to the Synoptic Gospels, Jesus quotes or alludes to twenty-three of the thirty-nine books of the Hebrew Bible." He "alludes to or quotes all five books of Moses, the three major prophets (Isaiah, Jeremiah, and Ezekiel), eight of the twelve minor prophets, and five of the Writings." Craig Evans, "The Scriptures of Jesus and His Earliest Followers," in *The Canon Debate* ed. Lee Martin McDonald and James A. Sanders (Peabody, MA: Hendrickson, 2002), 185; cf. R. T. France, *Jesus and the Old Testament* (Grand Rapids, MI: Baker, 1982), 259–63. While the presence or absence of a quote or allusion may not itself indicate how a source was viewed (numerous sources are alluded to without connoting authority of inspiration thereof, cf. Acts 17:28; Titus 1:12), it is notable that each section of the Hebrew Bible is well-represented by quotes and allusions throughout the New Testament (frequently quoted as authoritative Scripture). On Roger Nicole's count of "specific quotations and direct allusions," "278 different Old Testament verses are cited in the New Testament: 94 from the Pentateuch, 99 from the Prophets, and 85 from the Writings. Out of the 22 books in the Hebrew reckoning of the Canon only six (Judges-Ruth, Song of Solomon, Ecclesiastes, Esther, Ezra-Nehemiah, Chronicles) are not explicitly referred to" while there are "passages reminiscent of all Old Testament books without exception." Roger Nicole, "New Testament Use of the Old Testament," in Revelation and the Bible, ed. Carl F. H. Henry (Grand Rapids, MI: Baker, 1958), 138; cf. 135–51.

67. Thus, Childs believes: "From the evidence of the New Testament it seems clear that Jesus and the early Christians identified with the scriptures of Pharisaic Judaism." Childs, *Biblical Theology*, 26; cf. Peter Balla, "Evidence for an Early Christian Canon (Second and Third Century)," in *The Canon Debate*, 372–85; Beckwith, *The Old Testament Canon*, 165–66; F. F. Bruce, *The Canon of Scripture* (Downers Grove, IL: InterVarsity Press, 1988), 255; Robert I. Vasholz, *The Old Testament Canon in the Old Testament Church: The Internal Rationale for Old Testament Canonicity* (Lewiston: The Edwin Mellen Press, 1990). Consider, for instance, the way that Christ referred to and used Old Testament Scripture as authoritative (e.g., Matt. 4:4–10; 5:17–19; 11:13–14; 12:3–6, 39–42; 15:4–6; 19:4–9; 21:42–44; 22:29–32, 37–40, 43–45; 24:9–21; 26:31–32, 54–56; Mark 1:44; 7:6; 10:3; 12:26; Luke 8:21; 11:28; 16:16–17; 24:27, 44–45; John 2:22; 5:39; 10:34–35; 17:12, 17). See also the way the rest of the New Testament testifies to Old Testament writings as authoritative Scripture (e.g., Acts 17:2; 18:28; Rom. 1:2; 4:3; 9:17; 10:11; 11:2; 1 Cor. 15:3, 4; Gal. 3:8; 2 Tim. 3:16; 2 Pet. 1:20–21).

68. The prologue was written by Ben Sira's grandson, but many have pointed to evidence that Ben Sira himself held a similar Old Testament collection. See the discussion in Stephen Dempster, "Canons on the Right and Canons on the Left: Finding a Resolution in the Canon Debate," *JETS* 52 (2009): 59–61. "Clearly, there was a biblical text that Ben Sira had before him that was similar to what was later viewed as canonical in Judaism." Dempster, "Canons," 59.

69. Additionally, without naming each book, Josephus speaks of a three-part corpus as five books of Moses, thirteen of the Prophets (from death of Moses to time of Artaxerxes), and four containing "hymns to God and precepts for the conduct of human life." Josephus, *Against Apion*, 1.8 (LCL 186:179 [Josephus, *The Life. Against Apion*, trans. H. St. J. Thackeray. Loeb Classical Library 186. Cambridge, MA: Harvard University Press, 1926]).

70. Whether this is a quote from Luke's Gospel is a matter of much dispute. In this regard, Köstenberger and Kruger see Luke 10:7 as the "clear and obvious source for this citation." Köstenberger and Kruger, *Heresy*, 130.

71. See Metzger, *The Canon*, 139–40; Kruger, *Canon Revisited*, 284. Therein, Origen mentions all twenty-seven New Testament books without mentioning any others or making any distinctions among them. See also Metzger's survey of Origen's writings (Metzger, *The Canon*, 135–141), in which he concludes that Origen accepted the four Gospels, "fourteen Epistles of Paul, as well as Acts, 1 Peter, 1 John, Jude, and Revelation, but expressed reservation concerning James, 2 Peter, and 2 and 3 John." Metzger, *The Canon*, 141.

72. According to James Daniel Hernando, Irenaeus quoted from every New Testament book except Philemon and 3 John (in *Against Heresies* and *Fragments*) and his "writings contain quotations or verbal allusions to 77.9% (201 of 258) of the chapters in the canonical New Testament." Hernando thus concludes that "functionally Irenaeus is operating with a New Testament canon of Scripture." James Daniel Hernando, "Irenaeus and the Apostolic Fathers: An Inquiry into the Development of the New Testament Canon." (PhD diss., Drew University, 1990), 84. See also, John Behr, "The Word of God in the Second Century," *Pro Ecclesia* 9/1 (2000): 95.

73. Kruger, *Question of Canon*, 203.

74. The Muratorian Fragment claims that *Shepherd* was written "very recently, in our times" during the time of Pius, bishop of Rome (ca. AD 140–154). It thus "cannot be read publicly to the people in church either among the prophets, whose number is complete, or among the apostles, for it is after their time." Lines 74, 78–80, in Metzger, *The Canon*, 307. The Muratorian Fragment itself is perhaps the earliest extant *list* of New Testament books. We know little about the author of this fragment (which many scholars date ca. AD 180), but it appears to identify twenty-three of the New Testament books as Scripture (the four Gospels, Acts, thirteen Pauline epistles, Jude, 1 and 2 John, likely 3 John, and Revelation). In this regard and others, the messiness of the process of canon recognition shows that early Christians took recognition of Scripture seriously. The evidence regarding canon reception suggests that the Gospels were functioning as "canonical" very early, accepted as having ruling authority insofar as they were believed to record the

actions and teachings of Christ the Ruler Himself. Evidence also suggests that some collection of Paul's letters was also recognized quite early (cf. 2 Pet. 3:15–16) —recognized insofar as they were believed to be written by Paul and thus consisting of Christ-commissioned apostolic testimony. As John Barton put it, "astonishingly early, the great central core of the present New Testament was already being treated as the main authoritative source for Christians" with "little" suggestion of "any serious controversies about the Synoptics, John, or the major Pauline epistles." John Barton, *Holy Writings, Sacred Text: The Canon in Early Christianity* (Louisville, KY: WJK, 1997), 18. With respect to the other New Testament books known as the general epistles, there was dispute over a few of them in some places, seemingly because such writings were recognized if they were believed to consist of genuine first-generation apostolic testimony (written by a first-generation apostle or close associate within the purview of apostolic supervision), but churches in various parts of the world were not always immediately in a position to know whether some such writings were, in fact, first-generation apostolic testimony. In this regard, see also Peckham, *Canonical Theology*, 63–68; Kruger, *Canon Revisited*, 36–38.

75. In this regard, many discussions of the biblical canon speak of the church's recognition and usage of the canonical books as one of the criteria of canonicity. From an intrinsic canon perspective, however, community recognition and usage is not a *criterion* of canonicity (because no post-apostolic community possesses the authority to *determine* the canon). However, such widespread recognition and usage of the canonical books—including nearly unanimous consent regarding the thirty-nine books included in the Hebrew Bible (Old Testament) and the twenty-seven books included in the New Testament (what some call, the common canonical core)—does count as *significant evidence* in favor of the biblical canon (akin to a witness in a trial, as noted previously). In this regard, it is particularly notable that the New Testament books were so widely quoted that nearly the entire New Testament could be reconstructed from the writings of second- to fourth-century church fathers. See Norman L. Geisler and William E. Nix, *A General Introduction to the Bible: Revised and Expanded* (Chicago: Moody Press, 1986), 419–33.

76. In his monograph on the issue, L. Stephen Cook concludes: "Second Temple Jews did, on the whole, tend to believe that prophecy had ceased in the Persian period." L. Stephen Cook, *On the Question of the "Cessation of Prophecy" in Ancient Judaism* (Tübingen: Mohr Siebeck, 2011), 192. See also Cook, *On the Question*, 47–177.

77. First Maccabees 9:27 refers to a time of "great distress in Israel, such as had not been since the time that prophets ceased to appear among them" (cf. 1 Macc. 4:46; 14:41). More significantly, writing in the first century, Josephus referenced a three-part corpus of "[o]ur books, those which are justly accredited" as of "the prophets" who wrote through "inspiration" being "but two and twenty" and specified that the authoritative writings were "until Artaxerxes," saying: "From Artaxerxes to our own time the complete history has been written, but has not been deemed worthy of equal credit with the earlier records, because of the failure of the exact succession of the prophets." Josephus, *Against Apion* 1.7, 8 (LCL 186:179, 181). Though Josephus referred to twenty-two books, many scholars believe these are the same as the twenty-four books of the Hebrew Bible today, but numbered as twenty-two (perhaps combining Judges with Ruth and Jeremiah with Lamentations, counting these as two books rather than four) to correspond to the twenty-two letters of the Hebrew alphabet and would thus correspond to the same thirty-nine books in the Old Testament; cf. Beckwith, *The Old Testament Canon*, 235–73. Many have interpreted Josephus's statements to mean that he believed (like many others in first-century Judaism) that prophecy of the covenantal kind recognized as authoritative Scripture had ceased, such that "canonical" books were limited to those written by the mid-fifth-century BC. As Cook explains, Josephus does note some prophetic phenomena in later ages and does not exclude the possibility that true prophets could reappear, but he "does not seem to believe that true προφῆται (prophets) and προφητεία (prophecy) continued beyond the Persian period." Cook, *On the Question*, 136; cf. Cook, *On the Question*, 131–32. Cook views Josephus as "assuming some beliefs—probably common among Jews of his day—about the relationship of the ancient prophets to the collection of Jewish Scriptures, and about a fundamental change in the prophetic tradition around the time of Artaxerxes." Cook, *On the Question*, 133.

78. Craig A. Evans writes: "According to the Synoptic Gospels, Jesus quotes or alludes to twenty-three of the thirty-nine books of the Hebrew Bible." He "alludes to or quotes all five books of Moses, the three major prophets (Isaiah, Jeremiah, and Ezekiel), eight of the twelve minor prophets, and five of the Writings." Evans, "The Scriptures of Jesus and His Earliest Followers," cf. R. T. France, *Jesus and the Old Testament*, 259–63. Here, it is crucial to understand that the presence or absence of a quote or allusion from a source does not *by itself* indicate how a source was viewed by the one quoting it. In this regard, numerous sources are alluded to without connoting that such sources were viewed as holding the authority of Scripture (e.g., Acts 17:28; Titus 1:12; cf. Luke 16:19–31). Nevertheless, it is notable that each section of the Hebrew Bible is very well-represented by quotes and allusions throughout the New Testament. And, more significantly, such Old Testament books are frequently *quoted as authoritative Scripture*.

79. Michael Kruger concludes, in this regard: "Although it is disputed by some scholars, there are good reasons to think the threefold canonical structure of the Old Testament [the Law, Prophets, and Writings] would have been established by the time of Jesus." *Question of Canon*, 49. See also Beckwith, *The Old Testament Canon of the New Testament Church*, 110–80; Stephen B. Chapman, "The Old Testament Canon and Its Authority for the Christian Church," 125–48.

80. As noted earlier, according to Roger Nicole, "278 different Old Testament verses are cited in the New Testament: 94 from the Pentateuch, 99 from the Prophets, and 85 from the Writings. Out of the 22 books in the Hebrew reckoning of the Canon only six (Judges-Ruth, Song of Solomon, Ecclesiastes, Esther, Ezra-Nehemiah, Chronicles) are not explicitly referred to" while there are "passages reminiscent of all Old Testament books without exception." Roger Nicole, "New Testament Use of the Old Testament," 138; cf. 135–51. In this regard, Craig Blomberg finds it "particularly telling" that the New Testament "explicitly quotes from a broad-section of Old Testament documents but never quotes from the Apocrypha" as authoritative Scripture. Jude quotes once from a pseudepigraphic work, *1 Enoch*, but not in a fashion that necessarily implies that he understood the work to be part of the Hebrew canon [see Jude 14]. Paul at times quotes Greek poets and philosophers as well (e.g., Acts 17:28; Titus 1:12), without implying that he thought they were inspired or had authored Scripture. If one expands the database from quotations to allusions, one may speculate about numerous possible references to both apocryphal and pseudepigraphic texts in the New Testament. But good preachers have always alluded to well-known or important literature outside the Bible. One has to look for language that unambiguously shows that a given author is treating a book as canonical before declaring that quotations or allusions to it imply this kind of uniquely authoritative status." Blomberg, *Can We Still Believe the Bible?*, 49–50. For a list of numerous possible references to the Old Testament Apocrypha in the New Testament, see McDonald, *The Biblical Canon*, 452–64. Here again, it is important to recognize that a mere quotation or allusion to a source does not by itself thereby indicate that it was viewed as authoritative.

81. As Blomberg notes, "the earliest complete or nearly complete New Testament manuscripts still in existence (from the fourth and fifth centuries) have the LXX attached to them" and include the Apocrypha. Some suggest this is evidence that "Hellenistic or Diaspora Judaism thus must have had an expanded canon." Yet, the "actual discussions of the contents of Scripture in ancient Judaism show no trace of an expanded canon that included the Apocrypha." Blomberg, *Can We Still Believe*, 49.

82. Blomberg, *Can We Still Believe*, 51 (emphasis original). See also, Bruce, *The Canon of Scripture*, 44–50. In this regard, recall that the Talmud (in *b. Baba Batra* 14b–15a, ca. 164 BC–AD 200) identifies by name all twenty-four books of the Tanakh (corresponding to the thirty-nine books of our Old Testament) and explicitly distinguishes between the Prophets and the Writings.

83. For an excellent introduction to these writings, see David A. deSilva, *Introducing the Apocrypha: Message, Context, and Significance* (Grand Rapids, MI: Baker Academic, 2018).

EXCURSUS • THE EMMAUS APPROACH: HOW TO UNDERSTAND SCRIPTURE AND DO THEOLOGY

1. These ten principles are drawn from Richard M. Davidson, "Interpreting Scripture: An Hermeneutical 'Decalogue,'" *Journal of the Adventist Theological Society* 4/2 (1993): 95–114.

2. For more on *sola Scriptura*, see John C. Peckham, "Understanding *Sola Scriptura*: A Working Approach for the Church," in *Here We Stand: Luther, the Reformation, and Seventh-day Adventism*, eds. Michael W. Campbell and Nikolaus Satelmajer (Nampa, ID: Pacific Press, 2017): 57–64. See also John C. Peckham, *Canonical Theology: The Biblical Canon, Sola Scriptura, and Theological Method* (Grand Rapids, MI: Eerdmans, 2016), 140–65.

3. Recognizing Scripture as uniquely normative does not exclude the use of one's reason, but does call for one to recognize Scripture as a higher authority. Ellen G. White wrote: "God desires man to exercise his reasoning powers; and the study of the Bible will strengthen and elevate the mind as no other study can.... When we come to the Bible, reason must acknowledge an authority superior to itself, and heart and intellect must bow to the great I AM." White, *Steps to Christ*, 109. For more on the role of reason, see Frank M. Hasel, "Theology and the Role of Reason," *Journal of the Adventist Theological Society* 4/2 (1993) 172–98.

4. Ellen G. White believed: "The Bible, and the Bible alone, is to be our creed, the sole bond of union." White, *Selected Messages*, 1:416. Further, she wrote, "God will have a people upon the earth to maintain the Bible and the Bible only, as the standard of all doctrines and the basis of all reforms. The opinions of learned men, the deductions of science, the creeds or decisions of ecclesiastical councils, as numerous and discordant as are the churches which they represent, the voice of the majority—not one nor all of these should be regarded as evidence for or against any point of religious faith. Before accepting doctrine or precept, we should demand a plain Thus saith the Lord in its support." White, *The Great Controversy* (Mountain View, CA: Pacific Press, 1911), 595.

5. This corresponds, roughly, to what Alister McGrath labeled "tradition 0." Alister McGrath, *Reformation Thought: An Introduction*, 3rd ed. (Malden, MA: Blackwell, 2001), 154.

6. See Boubakar Sanou and John C. Peckham, "Canonical Theology, Social Location, and the Search for Biblical Orthodoxy," in *Scripture and Theology*, eds. Tomas Bokedal, et al. (de Gruyter, forthcoming). See also Kwabena Donkor, "Presuppositions in Hermeneutics," in *Biblical Hermeneutics: An Adventist Approach*, ed. Frank M. Hasel. Biblical Research Institute Studies in Hermeneutics, vol. 3 (Silver Spring, MD: Biblical Research Institute/Review and Herald Academic, 2020); Frank M. Hasel, "Presuppositions in the Interpretation of Scripture," in *Understanding Scripture: An Adventist Approach*, ed. George W. Reid. Biblical Research Institute Studies, vol. 1 (Silver Spring, MD: Biblical Research Institute, 2005).

7. See further, Leonard Brand, "Faith, Science, and the Bible," in *Biblical Hermeneutics: An Adventist Approach*, ed. Frank M. Hasel. Biblical Research Institute Studies in Hermeneutics, vol. 3 (Silver Spring, MD: Biblical Research Institute/Review and Herald Academic, 2020), 179–209.

8. See further, Frank M. Hasel, "Living with Confidence Despite Some Open Questions: Upholding the Biblical Truth of Creation Amidst Theological Pluralism," *Journal of the Adventist Theological Society* 14/1 (2003): 229–54.
9. For further explanation of these steps, see Davidson, "Interpreting Scripture," 95–114. See also, Ekkehardt Mueller, "Principles of Biblical Interpretation," in *Biblical Hermeneutics: An Adventist Approach*, ed. Frank M. Hasel. Biblical Research Institute Studies in Hermeneutics, vol. 3 (Silver Spring, MD: Biblical Research Institute/Review and Herald Academic, 2020), 211–34; "Methods of Bible Study," in *Biblical Hermeneutics: An Adventist Approach*, ed. Frank M. Hasel. Biblical Research Institute Studies in Hermeneutics, vol. 3 (Silver Spring, MD: Biblical Research Institute/Review and Herald Academic, 2020), 463–73.
10. One free resource can be found at: beta.stepbible.org.
11. See also Clinton Wahlen, "Variants, Versions, and the Trustworthiness of Scripture" in *Biblical Hermeneutics: An Adventist Approach*, ed. Frank M. Hasel. Biblical Research Institute Studies in Hermeneutics, vol. 3 (Silver Spring, MD: Biblical Research Institute/Review and Herald Academic, 2020), 63–103.
12. For more on this, see Kristie Anyabwile, *Literarily: How Understanding Bible Genres Transforms Bible Study* (Chicago: Moody, 2022)..
13. For example, the most prominent Greek term for love (the *agape* root) in Scripture typically has a positive connotation in reference to virtuous love, but it can also refer to misdirected love (2 Tim. 4:10; see, e.g., the use of the term in the Greek translation of the Old Testament in 2 Sam. 13:1, 4, 15 to refer to rapacious lust). For much more on this, see Peckham, *The Love of God*, 70–77.
14. See Fernando L. Canale, *Back to Revelation-Inspiration: Searching for the Cognitive Foundation of Christian Theology in a Postmodern World* (Lanham, MD: University Press of America, 2001), 148–49. See also, the discussion in John C. Peckham, *Divine Attributes: Knowing the Covenantal God of Scripture* (Grand Rapids, MI: Baker Academic, 2021), 31–33; Donkor, "Presuppositions in Hermenautics," 7–30.

CHAPTER 11 • GOD CREATES US IN GOD'S IMAGE: HUMAN NATURE, IDENTITY, AND VALUE
1. See J. Richard Middleton, *The Liberating Image: The Imago Dei in Genesis 1* (Grand Rapids, MI: Brazos, 2005).
2. Ellen G. White comments: "Every human being, created in the image of God, is endowed with a power akin to that of the Creator—individuality, power to think and to do." White, *Education* (Mountain View, CA: Pacific Press, 1903), 18.
3. See Marc Cortez, *Theological Anthropology: A Guide for the Perplexed* (London: T&T Clark, 2010), 18–20. See also Middleton, *Liberating Image*; Ryan S. Peterson, *The Imago Dei as Human Identity: A Theological Interpretation* (Winona Lake, IN: Eisenbrauns, 2016); and John F. Kilner, *Dignity and Destiny: Humanity in the Image of God* (Grand Rapids, MI: Eerdmans, 2015).
4. In this regard, Seventh-day Adventist Belief #7 on "The Nature of Humanity" states: "Man and woman were made in the image of God with individuality, the power and freedom to think and to do. Though created free beings, each is an indivisible unity of body, mind, and spirit, dependent upon God for life and breath and all else. When our first parents disobeyed God, they denied their dependence upon Him and fell from their high position. The image of God in them was marred and they became subject to death. Their descendants share this fallen nature and its consequences. They are born with weaknesses and tendencies to evil. But God in Christ reconciled the world to Himself and by His Spirit restores in penitent mortals the image of their Maker. Created for the glory of God, they are called to love Him and one another, and to care for their environment. (Gen. 1:26–28; 2:7, 15; 3; Ps. 8:4–8; 51:5, 10; 58:3; Jer. 17:9; Acts 17:24–28; Rom. 5:12–17; 2 Cor. 5:19, 20; Eph. 2:3; 1 Thess. 5:23; 1 John 3:4; 4:7, 8, 11, 20)." Seventh-day Adventist Fundamental Belief #7. See the Appendix.
5. Joel B. Green, *Body, Soul, and Human Life: The Nature of Humanity in the Bible* (Grand Rapids, MI: Baker Academic, 2008), 63.
6. On Genesis 2:15, Victor P. Hamilton comments, "*avad* is 'the normal Hebrew verb meaning 'to serve.' So again the note is sounded that man is placed in the garden as servant. He is there not to be served but to serve. The second verb—*keep* or 'tend' (Heb. *shamar*)—carries a slightly different nuance. The basic meaning of this root is 'to exercise great care over,' to the point, if necessary, of guarding." Hamilton, *The Book of Genesis, Chapters 1–17* (Grand Rapids, MI: Eerdmans, 1990), 171.
7. See Seventh-day Adventist Fundamental Belief #21 ("Stewardship") in the Appendix.
8. In response to the abundant blessings of God, Adventists believe God calls us to return tithe (ten percent of our income, see Hag. 1:3–11; Mal. 3:8–12; 1 Cor. 9:9–14) and give offerings to support the ministry and mission of the church.
9. See, in this regard, Sandra L. Richter, *Stewards of Eden: What Scripture Says About the Environment and Why It Matters* (Downers Grove, IL: IVP Academic, 2020); Douglas J. Moo and Jonathan A. Moo, *Creation Care: A Biblical Theology of the Natural World* (Grand Rapids, MI: Zondervan, 2018).
10. See A. Rahel Schafer, "'You, YHWH, Save Humans and Animals': God's Response to the Vocalized Needs of Non-human Animals as Portrayed in the Old Testament," (Ph.D. diss., Wheaton College, 2015).

11. See Schafer, "You, YHWH, Save Humans and Animals." See also, A. Rahel Wells, "Why Care for the Earth if It Is All Going to Burn? Eschatology and Ecology," in *Eschatology from an Adventist Perspective*, ed. Elias Brasil de Souza, A. Rahel Wells, Laszlo Gallusz, and Denis Kaiser (Silver Spring, MD: Biblical Research Institute, 2021).

12. The mass production of meat is responsible for an enormous amount of greenhouse gases and such practices also deplete resources in many other ways. E.g., Damian Carrington, "Avoiding meat and dairy is 'single biggest way' to reduce your impact on earth," The Guardian, accessed December 13, 2021, https://www.theguardian.com/environment/2018/may/31/avoiding-meat-and-dairy-is-single-biggest-way-to-reduce-your-impact-on-earth. See also, https://ourworldindata.org/meat-production.

13. The tragic view that some have of humans, which places value in terms of extrinsic values like capacities, can be seen in the words of the ethicist Peter Singer, who maintains: "If we compare a severely defective human infant with a nonhuman animal, a dog or a pig, for example, we will often find the nonhuman to have superior capacities" with regard to anything that can "plausibly be considered morally significant.... Only the fact that the infant is a member of the species Homo sapiens leads it to be treated differently from the dog or pig. Species membership alone, however, is not morally relevant.... Humans who bestow superior value on the lives of all human beings, solely because they are members of our own species, are judging along lines strikingly similar to those used by white racists who bestow superior value on the lives of other whites, merely because they are members of their own race." This "sanctity-of-life view" is "impossible to restore in full" because "the philosophical foundations of this view have been knocked asunder. We can no longer base our ethics on the idea that human beings are a special form of creation, made in the image of God." Peter Singer (Princeton University Bioethicist), "Sanctity of Life or Quality of Life?" *Pediatrics*, July 1983, 128–29.

14. Viktor E. Frankl, *The Doctor and the Soul: From Psychotherapy to Logotherapy* (New York: Vintage Books, 1986), xxvii.

15. Ellen G. White comments, "Christ tears away the wall of partition, the self-love, the dividing prejudice of nationality, and teaches a love for all the human family. He lifts men from the narrow circle that their selfishness prescribes; He abolishes all territorial lines and artificial distinctions of society. He makes no difference between neighbors and strangers, friends and enemies. He teaches us to look upon every needy soul as our neighbor and the world as our field." White, *Thoughts from the Mount of Blessings* (Mountain View, CA: Pacific Press, 1896), 41.

16. For a sample of the twisted interpretations of Scripture put forward by advocates of slavery in America, see Darius Jankiewicz, "Hermeneutics of Slavery: A 'Bible-Alone' Faith and the Problem of Human Enslavement," *Journal of Adventist Mission Studies* 12/1 (2016): 47–73. Then, see Esau McCaulley's treatment of these issues in McCaulley, *Reading While Black: African American Biblical Interpretation as an Exercise in Hope* (Downers Grove, IL: IVP Academic, 2020). For example, he reports that his mother "had always told me that the racists were the poor interpreters and that we were reading correctly when we saw in biblical texts describing the worth of all people an affirmation of Black dignity." He then laments that the debate over biblical texts dealing with slavery has all-too-often "been crafted and carried on without any regard for the Black testimony." McCaulley, *Reading While Black*, 9. See, for example, the position of James Pennington quoted in this chapter of *God with Us*.

17. On the heinous cruelties of antebellum slavery in America, see Frederick Douglass, *Narrative of the Life of Frederick Douglass: An American Slave*, ed., Benjamin Quarles (Cambridge, MA: Belknap Press, 1960).

18. In 1 Timothy 1:10 Paul thus "forbids, as does the OT, slave-trading, which thus amounts to forbidding the entire transatlantic slave trade." George W. Knight, *The Pastoral Epistles: A Commentary on the Greek Text* (Grand Rapids, MI: Eerdmans, 1992), 86.

19. On the issue of slavery in the Bible, see Esau McCaulley, *Reading While Black*, 137–163; Lisa M. Bowens, *African American Readings of Paul: Reception, Resistance, and Transformation* (Grand Rapids, MI: Eerdmans, 2020); cf. Paul Copan, *Is God A Moral Monster? Making Sense of the Old Testament God* (Grand Rapids, MI: Baker, 2011), 124–157.

20. Unequivocally condemning slavery in America, Ellen White wrote: "The people of this nation have exalted themselves to heaven, and have looked down upon monarchical governments, and triumphed in their boasted liberty, while the institution of slavery, that was a thousand times worse than the tyranny exercised by monarchial governments, was suffered to exist and was cherished. In this land of light a system is cherished which allows one portion of the human family to enslave another portion, degrading millions of human beings to the level of the brute creation. The equal of this sin is not to be found in heathen lands." Ellen G. White, *Testimonies for the Church*, vol. 1 (Mountain View, CA: Pacific Press, 1855), 258–259.

21. McCaulley, *Reading While Black*, 142.

22. See, in this regard, Kevin M. Burton, "The Seventh-day Adventist Pioneers and Their Protest against Systemic Racism," June 18, 2020, accessed October 31, 2021, https://www.nadministerial.com/stories/2020/6/18/the-seventh-day-adventist-pioneers-and-their-protest-against-systemic-racism. In this regard, Trevor O'Reggio writes, "by pointing out slavery as a fulfillment of America in prophecy, they were simply repudiating any notion of America being some type of the kingdom of God." O'Reggio, "Slavery,

Prophecy, and the American Nation as Seen by the Adventist Pioneers, 1854-1865," *Journal of the Adventist Theological Society* 17/2 (2006): 158.

23. For more on the issue of slavery and the Bible, see Clinton Wahlen and Wagner Kuhn, "Culture, Hermeneutics, and Scripture: Discerning What Is Universal," in *Biblical Hermeneutics: An Adventist Approach*, ed. Frank M. Hasel, Biblical Research Institute Studies in Hermeneutics, vol. 3 (Silver Spring, MD: Biblical Research Institute/Review and Herald Academic, 2020), 165-69.

24. Knight, *Pastoral Epistles*, 86.

25. This is not even to mention the prohibition of stealing in the Ten Commandments (Exod. 20:15), which would include prohibition against the stealing of humans or their livelihood. Likewise, Scripture teaches the principle that "the laborer deserves to be paid" (Luke 10:7; 1 Tim. 5:18, NRSVue).

26. James W. C. Pennington, *A Two Years' Absence, or, A Farewell Sermon, Preached in the Fifth Congregational Church, Nov. 2, 1845* (Hartford, CT: H. T. Wells, 1845), 27, quoted in McCaulley, *Reading While Black*, 163.

27. On God's great concern for *biblical* social justice, see John C. Peckham, "Love and Justice," *Lake Union Herald* (January 2019): 18-21.

28. McCaulley, *Reading While Black*, 141.

29. Some have interpreted the second part of 1 Corinthians 7:21 as exhorting slaves to remain in slavery even if they have an opportunity to become free and make use of that situation to witness. But, there are many reasons to understand this as Paul encouraging individuals to become free if they can. See the extensive case summarized by Gordon Fee, concluding that the "freedom" interpretation "seems by far the better one." Fee, *The First Epistle to the Corinthians* (Grand Rapids, MI: Eerdmans, 1987), 317-18.

30. Elsewhere, Paul gave counsel regarding how to navigate the realities of slavery in Roman society of the day in a way that nevertheless witnessed of Christ (e.g., 1 Tim. 6:1-3), but these should not be understood as sanctioning the practice of slavery—they were contextual instructions for the sake of the gospel. In this regard, Esau McCaulley comments: "I think that we should see 1 Timothy 6:1-3 in much the same way that we see the slave laws of the Old Testament. Paul is trying to make pastoral sense of a difficult situation. We are not limited to his solution, but we can be inspired by his example. Paul, despite claims to the contrary, sought to limit the damage done by slavery and rethought the whole institution in light of the cross and resurrection." McCaulley, *Reading While Black*, 161-62.

31. Ellen G. White, *Acts of the Apostles* (Mountain View, CA: Pacific Press, 1911), 459.

32. Ellen G. White comments, "God Himself gave Adam a companion . . . who could be one with him in love and sympathy. Eve was created from a rib taken from the side of Adam, signifying that she was not to control him as the head, nor to be trampled under his feet as an inferior, but to stand by his side as an equal, to be loved and protected by him. A part of man, bone of his bone, and flesh of his flesh, she was his second self, showing the close union and the affectionate attachment that should exist in this relation." White, *Patriarchs and Prophets* (Washington, DC: Review and Herald, 1890), 46.

33. On this, the *Andrews Study Bible* comments: "Note that earlier Paul does assume that women will pray and prophesy in public worship (11:5, 13). These verses perhaps address a problem that arose when women prophets tried to judge, test, and silence the prophetic utterances of their husbands and other men during public worship (see 14:29-30)." *Andrews Study Bible: Light. Depth. Truth.*, NKJV (Berrien Springs, MI: Andrews University Press, 2010), 1510.

34. The *Seventh-day Adventist Bible Commentary* interprets the instruction in 1 Corinthians 14:34 as pertaining to avoiding "bring[ing] reproach upon the church" relative to customs of the time. Specifically, the commentary notes the "place and service of women in Bible history (see Judges 4:4; 2 Kings 22:14; Luke 2:36, 37; Acts 21:9)" and that "Paul himself commended the women who labored with him in the gospel (Phil. 4:3)" and goes on to say: "There is no doubt that women played a definite part in the life of the church." Why this instruction for women to "keep silent in the churches," then? The answer the *Seventh-day Adventist Bible Commentary* gives is that this is "because both Greek and Jewish custom dictated that women should be kept in the background in public affairs. Violation of this custom would be looked upon as disgraceful and would bring reproach upon the church." Francis D. Nichol, ed., *The Seventh-day Adventist Bible Commentary*, vol. 6 (Washington, DC: Review and Herald Publishing Association, 1980), 793.

35. Walter A. Elwell, ed., "Diana," *Baker Encyclopedia of the Bible* (Grand Rapids, MI: Baker, 1988), 622.

36. In this regard, Philip H. Towner comments: "It should certainly be noted that one element of the false teaching was a prohibition of marriage." In this regard, he goes on: "It can hardly be accidental that Paul encourages the domestic path of bearing children (v. 15) while the false teachers prohibited marriage (4:3; i.e. sexual relations)." Philip H. Towner, *The Letters to Timothy and Titus*, The New International Commentary on the New Testament (Grand Rapids, MI: Eerdmans, 2006), 213, 219.

37. See Linda Belleville, "Lexical Fallacies in Rendering αὐθεντεῖν in 1 Timothy 2:12: BDAG in Light of Greek Literary and Nonliterary Usage," *Bulletin for Biblical Research* 29/3 (2019): 317-41.

38. Further, Craig Keener comments regarding 1 Timothy 2:11-12: "The proper way for any novice to learn was submissively and 'quietly' (a closely related Greek term appears in 2:2 for all believers). Women were less likely to be literate than men, were trained in philosophy far less often than men, were trained in rhetoric almost never, and in Judaism were far less likely to be educated in the law. Given the bias against

instructing women in the law, it is Paul's advocacy of their learning the law, not his recognition that they started as novices and so had to learn quietly, that was radical and countercultural." He goes on: "Given women's lack of training in the Scriptures (see comment on 2:11), the heresy spreading in the Ephesian churches through ignorant teachers (1:4–7), and the false teachers' exploitation of these women's lack of knowledge to spread their errors (5:13; 2 Tim. 3:6), Paul's prohibition here makes good sense. His short-range solution is that these women should not teach; his long-range solution is 'let them learn' (2:11). The situation might be different after the women had been instructed (2:11; cf. Rom. 16:1–4, 7; Phil. 4:2–3)." Craig S. Keener, *The IVP Bible Background Commentary: New Testament* (Downers Grove, IL: InterVarsity, 1993), 1 Timothy 2:11–12.

39. Whether the person referred to in Romans 16:7 as "outstanding among the apostles" was a woman (Junia) or a man (Junias) is a matter of some dispute, which is beyond the scope of this introductory volume. As Esther Yue L. Ng explains, among "many biblical scholars, there is a growing consensus that the 'Junia' mentioned in Romans 16:7 alongside Andronicus is the name of a woman" who was "a female apostle in her own right." "Was Junia(s) in Rom. 16:7 a Female Apostle? And So What?" *Journal of the Evangelical Theological Society* 63/3 (2020): 517. For one example of this position, see Richard Bauckham, *Gospel Women: Studies of the Named Women in the Gospels* (Grand Rapids, MI: Eerdmans, 2002), 165–85. On the other hand, Esther Yue L. Ng herself argues against this view in her article "Was Junia(s) in Rom. 16:7 a Female Apostle?"

40. As Seventh-day Adventist Fundamental Belief #14, on "Unity in the Body of Christ," reads (in part): "In Christ we are a new creation; distinctions of race, culture, learning, and nationality, and differences between high and low, rich and poor, male and female, must not be divisive among us. We are all equal in Christ, who by one Spirit has bonded us into one fellowship with Him and with one another; we are to serve and be served without partiality or reservation." For the full statement, see the Appendix.

41. See also Ekkehardt Mueller and Elias Brasil de Souza, eds. *Marriage: Biblical and Theological Aspects*, Biblical Research Institute Studies in Biblical Ethics (Silver Spring, MD: Biblical Research Institute, 2015). The official Seventh-day Adventist belief on "Marriage and the Family" states: "Marriage was divinely established in Eden and affirmed by Jesus to be a lifelong union between a man and a woman in loving companionship. For the Christian a marriage commitment is to God as well as to the spouse, and should be entered into only between a man and a woman who share a common faith. Mutual love, honor, respect, and responsibility are the fabric of this relationship, which is to reflect the love, sanctity, closeness, and permanence of the relationship between Christ and His church. Regarding divorce, Jesus taught that the person who divorces a spouse, except for fornication, and marries another, commits adultery. Although some family relationships may fall short of the ideal, a man and a woman who fully commit themselves to each other in Christ through marriage may achieve loving unity through the guidance of the Spirit and the nurture of the church. God blesses the family and intends that its members shall assist each other toward complete maturity. Increasing family closeness is one of the earmarks of the final gospel message. Parents are to bring up their children to love and obey the Lord. By their example and their words they are to teach them that Christ is a loving, tender, and caring guide who wants them to become members of His body, the family of God which embraces both single and married persons. (Gen. 2:18–25; Exod. 20:12; Deut. 6:5–9; Prov. 22:6; Mal. 4:5, 6; Matt. 5:31, 32; 19:3–9, 12; Mark 10:11, 12; John 2:1–11; 1 Cor. 7:7, 10, 11; 2 Cor. 6:14; Eph. 5:21-33; 6:1–4.)" Seventh-day Adventist Fundamental Belief #23. See the Appendix.

42. Again, Ellen G. White comments, "Eve was created from a rib taken from the side of Adam, signifying that she was not to control him as the head, nor to be trampled under his feet as an inferior, but to stand by his side as an equal, to be loved and protected by him." *Patriarchs and Prophets*, 46.

43. See the discussion of Genesis 3:16 in Nichol, ed., *The Seventh-day Adventist Bible Commentary*, 234. In this regard, Ellen G. White comments: "Eve was told of the sorrow and pain that must henceforth be her portion. And the Lord said, 'Thy desire shall be to thy husband, and he shall rule over thee.' In the creation God had made her the equal of Adam. Had they remained obedient to God—in harmony with His great law of love—they would ever have been in harmony with each other; but sin had brought discord, and now their union could be maintained and harmony preserved only by submission on the part of the one or the other. Eve had been the first in transgression; and she had fallen into temptation by separating from her companion, contrary to the divine direction. It was by her solicitation that Adam sinned, and she was now placed in subjection to her husband. Had the principles enjoined in the law of God been cherished by the fallen race, this sentence, though growing out of the results of sin, would have proved a blessing to them; but man's abuse of the supremacy thus given him has too often rendered the lot of woman very bitter and made her life a burden." White, *Patriarchs and Prophets*, 58.

44. On Ephesians 5:22, see Leo Ranzolin, Jr., "Are Wives to Submit to Their Husbands?" in *Interpreting Scripture: Bible Questions and Answers*, ed. Gerhard Pfandl, vol. 2, Biblical Research Institute Studies (Silver Spring, MD: Biblical Research Institute, 2010), 385–89. Ranzolin concludes, "marriage can be seen as an institution wherein the husband and wife, striving to follow Christ's model of sacrificial love, mutually and lovingly submit to one another (Eph. 5:21). Such a marriage displays a 'one flesh' unity, demonstrating the kind of unity that is at the heart of God's purposes to re-unify all of humankind and the cosmos (1:10)." Ranzolin, "Are Wives to Submit," 389.

45. Ellen G. White comments: "Neither the husband nor the wife should attempt to exercise over the other an arbitrary control. Do not try to compel each other to yield to your wishes. You cannot do this and

retain each other's love. Be kind, patient, and forbearing, considerate, and courteous. By the grace of God you can succeed in making each other happy, as in your marriage vow you promised to do." White, *The Adventist Home* (Hagerstown, MD: Review and Herald, 1952), 118. Further, she wrote: "In the married life men and women sometimes act like undisciplined, perverse children. The husband wants his way, and the wife wants her way, and neither is willing to yield. Such a condition of things can bring only the greatest unhappiness. Both husband and wife should be willing to yield his or her way or opinion. There is no possibility of happiness while they both persist in doing as they please." *The Adventist Home*, 118.

46. On the biblical meaning of love itself, with respect to self-sacrificial love specifically, see John C. Peckham, *The Love of God: A Canonical Model* (Downers Grove, IL: IVP Academic, 2015), 117–45.

47. On the issue of polygamy, see Ronald du Preez, *Polygamy in the Bible* (Berrien Springs, MI: Adventist Theological Society Publications, 1993). See also Ron du Preez, "Polygamy, Scripture, and the Institution of Marriage," in *Sexuality: Contemporary Issues from a Biblical Perspective*, ed. Ekkehardt Mueller and Elias Brasil de Souza, Biblical Research Institute Studies in Biblical Ethics (Silver Spring, MD: Biblical Research Institute/Review and Herald, 2022), 147–82.

48. On human sexuality, see Richard M. Davidson, *Flame of Yahweh: Sexuality in the Old Testament* (Grand Rapids, MI: Baker Academic, 2012). See also Ekkehardt Mueller and Elias Brasil de Souza, eds. *Sexuality: Contemporary Issues from a Biblical Perspective*, Biblical Research Institute Studies in Biblical Ethics (Silver Spring, MD: Biblical Research Institute/Review and Herald, 2022).

49. "Jesus' pronouncements against *porneia* (Matt. 5:32; 15:19; 19:9; Mark 7:21), when viewed against the OT background, include same-sex intercourse as well as other heterosexual practices (Matt. 10:15; 11:23–24; Mark 6:11; Luke 10:12; 17:29). The nature of *porneia* (without qualifiers) as used by Jesus and the various NT writers has been the subject of considerable debate, but the OT provides the key to its identification. Especially significant is its usage (again without qualifiers) in Acts 15:28–29, where, as we saw, intertextual allusions to Leviticus 17 and 18 are unmistakable." "An Understanding of the Biblical View on Homosexual Practice and Pastoral Care: Seventh-day Adventist Theological Seminary Position Paper," 2017, accessed October 31, 2021, https://www.andrews.edu/sem/about/statements/seminary-statement-on-homosexuality-edited-8-17-jm-final.pdf. See also: https://www.adventist.org/articles/homosexuality/. See also Roy E. Gane, Nicholas P. Miller, and H. Peter Swanson, eds., *Homosexuality, Marriage, and the Church: Biblical, Counseling, and Religious Liberty Issues* (Berrien Springs, MI: Andrews University Press, 2012). On *porneia*, specifically, see also Ekkehardt Mueller, *"Porneia:* Sexual Immorality," in *Sexuality: Contemporary Issues from a Biblical Perspective*, ed. Ekkehardt Mueller and Elias Brasil de Souza, Biblical Research Institute Studies in Biblical Ethics (Silver Spring, MD: Biblical Research Institute/Review and Herald, 2022), 17–32.

50. "While homosexuality is a distortion of the Edenic ideal, 'there is no condemnation' for homosexually oriented persons as long as they 'are in Christ Jesus' (Rom. 8:1) and do not harbor or act upon their orientation and propensities. The same principle applies to those who struggle with heterosexual immorality (see Matt. 5:27–28; Rom. 6:1–23; 8:1–4; Col. 3:1–10; James 1:14–15). Even as some individuals may experience a miraculous deliverance from sinful heterosexual and homosexual urges, others may have to wrestle with such tendencies all their lives (see Gal. 5:16–25). One is not culpable for these involuntary tendencies, but for acting upon them either in imagination or actual practice." "An Understanding of the Biblical View on Homosexual Practice and Pastoral Care: Seventh-day Adventist Theological Seminary Position Paper" (2017). See also Ekkehardt Mueller, "Homosexuality and Scripture," in *Sexuality: Contemporary Issues from a Biblical Perspective*, ed. Ekkehardt Mueller and Elias Brasil de Souza, Biblical Research Institute Studies in Biblical Ethics (Silver Spring, MD: Biblical Research Institute/Review and Herald, 2022), 415–34.

51. See Richard M. Davidson and Ekkehardt Mueller, "Does Sexual Intercourse Constitute Marriage? The Issue of Premarital Sex," in *Sexuality: Contemporary Issues from a Biblical Perspective*, ed. Ekkehardt Mueller and Elias Brasil de Souza, Biblical Research Institute Studies in Biblical Ethics (Silver Spring, MD: Biblical Research Institute/Review and Herald, 2022), 33–72; Johannes Kovar, "Uncommitted Relationships: Cohabitation from a Biblical and Historical Perspective," in *Sexuality: Contemporary Issues from a Biblical Perspective*, ed. Ekkehardt Mueller and Elias Brasil de Souza, Biblical Research Institute Studies in Biblical Ethics (Silver Spring, MD: Biblical Research Institute/Review and Herald, 2022), 73–102.

52. Nancy R. Pearcey, *Love Thy Body: Answering Hard Questions about Life and Sexuality* (Grand Rapids, MI: Baker, 2019), 127–28.

53. Quoted in Pearcey, *Love Thy Body*, 123.

54. Specifically, according to the *Seventh-day Adventist Bible Commentary*, "The purpose of the law here announced [in Deut. 24:1–4] was to better the lot of Hebrew women. This law, far from establishing a low moral standard, or approving of one, represented a far higher standard than the cruel customs of the time recognized. The law guaranteed a divorced woman certain rights, and actually protected her from being considered as an adulteress and an outcast." In ancient times, "The cast-off, unattached woman's lot was a deplorable one. The bill of divorce alleviated her unfortunate lot. This law simply recognized the prevailing situation and sought to improve it. This was a law of permission, not one of command. These precise restrictions were designed to eliminate the easy divorce procedure the Hebrews had apparently learned in their association with heathen peoples. It was against the concept of the wife as property that Christ spoke so emphatically (Matt. 5:27–32; 19:3–9)," which "had brought great misery and injustice." Nichol, ed., *The Seventh-day Adventist Bible Commentary*, 1037–38.

55. In this regard, *Seventh-day Adventists Believe* notes: "While the divine ideal for marriage is that of a loving and permanent union that continues until the death of one partner, at times a legal separation becomes necessary because of offenses such as physical abuse to spouse or child." *Seventh-day Adventists Believe: An Exposition of the Fundamental Beliefs of the Seventh-day Adventist Church,* 2nd ed. (Boise, ID: Pacific Press, 2005), 338.

56. Regarding how to respond to abuse of various kinds, see Sarah McDugal, Jennifer Jill Schwirzer, and Nicole Parker, *Safe Churches: Responding to Abuse in the Faith Community* (Abide Counseling Press, 2019).

57. Dietrich Bonhoeffer, *The Collected Sermons of Dietrich Bonhoeffer,* vol. 1., trans. Douglas W. Stott, et al. (Minneapolis: Fortress, 2012), 203.

58. Letter 81, 1894, par. 7; Ellen G. White, *Letters and Manuscripts,* vol. 9 (egwwritings.org).

CHAPTER 12 • LIFE AND DEATH: HUMAN FREEDOM, SINFULNESS, AND CONDITIONAL IMMORTALITY

1. Donald E. Gowan notes, the very "setting of a limit shows that" Eve "does indeed have a choice and thus establishes" her "freedom." *From Eden to Babel: A Commentary on the Book of Genesis 1–11* (Grand Rapids, MI: Eerdmans, 1988), 42.

2. Ellen G. White comments: "The sin of Adam and Eve caused a fearful separation between God and man. And here Christ steps in between fallen man and God, and says to man, You may yet come to the Father; there is a plan devised through which God can be reconciled to man, and man to God; and through a mediator you can approach God." White, "Christian Recreation," *Review and Herald* (May 31, 1870): 185–86.

3. As Alvin Plantinga puts it, "intelligent free action would not be possible in a world without regularity and predictability ... such action would be possible in a world in which God often intervened, provided he did so in a regular and predictable way." Plantinga, *Where the Conflict Really Lies: Science, Religion, and Naturalism* (New York: Oxford University Press, 2011), 103.

4. "Common to all the Fathers was the conviction that mankind needed a Saviour who was Jesus Christ, the incarnate *Logos* of God. It was this belief, rather than any specific understanding of human sin, which set them apart from their contemporaries." Gerald Bray, "Original Sin in Patristic Thought," *Churchman* 108, no. 1 (1994), 37.

5. See Bray, "Original Sin in Patristic Thought."

6. On prevenient grace, see George R. Knight, "The Grace that Comes Before Saving Grace," in *Salvation: Contours of Adventist Soteriology,* ed. Martin F. Hanna, Darius W. Jankiewicz, and John W. Reeve (Berrien Springs, MI: Andrews University Press, 2018).

7. See Bray, "Original Sin in Patristic Thought," 46–47.

8. On this, see Roy Adams, "The Nature of Sin: Understanding Its Character and Complexity," in *Salvation: Contours of Adventist Soteriology,* ed. Martin F. Hanna, Darius W. Jankiewicz, and John W. Reeve (Berrien Springs, MI: Andrews University Press, 2018); Darius Jankiewicz, "Sin and Human Nature: Historical Background," in *Salvation: Contours of Adventist Soteriology,* ed. Martin F. Hanna, Darius W. Jankiewicz, and John W. Reeve (Berrien Springs, MI: Andrews University Press, 2018). See also Gerhard Pfandl, "Some Thoughts on Original Sin," accessed November 1, 2021, https://adventistbiblicalresearch.org/materials/some-thoughts-on-original-sin/.

9. Ellen G. White comments: "The true object of education is to restore the image of God in the soul. In the beginning, God created man in his own likeness. He endowed him with noble qualities. His mind was well-balanced, and all the powers of his being were harmonious. But the fall and its effects have perverted these gifts. Sin has marred and well-nigh obliterated the image of God in man. It was to restore this that the plan of salvation was devised, and a life of probation was granted to man. To bring him back to the perfection in which he was first created, is the great object of life,—the object that underlies every other. It is the work of parents and teachers, in the education of the youth, to co-operate with the divine purpose; and in so doing they are 'laborers together with God.' " White, *Christian Education* (Battle Creek, MI: International Tract Society, 1894), 63.

10. On human depravity, Ellen G. White comments: "They [Adam and Eve] were told that their nature had become depraved by sin; they had lessened their strength to resist evil, and had opened the way for Satan to gain more ready access to them. In their innocence they had yielded to temptation; and now, in a state of conscious guilt, they would have less power to maintain their integrity." Ellen G. White, *Patriarchs and Prophets* (Washington, DC: Review and Herald, 1890), 61. Further, she writes: "There is in his [human] nature a bent to evil, a force which, unaided, he cannot resist." Ellen G. White, *Education* (Mountain View, CA: Pacific Press, 1905), 29.

11. Ivan Blazen, "Salvation," in *Handbook of Seventh-Day Adventist Theology,* ed. Raoul Dederen (Hagerstown, MD: Review and Herald, 2001), 275.

12. One might ask, in this regard, is the fact that we inherit a sinful nature unfair? Perhaps. But, the unfairness is not God's. It is unfairness that is part and parcel of sin itself—part and parcel of the temporary rule of the devil in the cosmic conflict. The situation humanity faces is the result of the devil's rebellion and our complicity with it.

13. In this regard, Seventh-day Adventist Belief #11 ("Growing in Christ") states, in part, "in Jesus, we are called to grow into the likeness of His character, communing with Him daily in prayer, feeding

on His Word, meditating on it and on His providence, singing His praises, gathering together for worship, and participating in the mission of the Church. We are also called to follow Christ's example by compassionately ministering to the physical, mental, social, emotional, and spiritual needs of humanity. As we give ourselves in loving service to those around us and in witnessing to His salvation, His constant presence with us through the Spirit transforms every moment and every task into a spiritual experience." See the Appendix.

14. In this regard, Ellen G. White comments: "It is through the medium of His Spirit that God works upon the human heart; and when men willfully reject the Spirit and declare it to be from Satan, they cut off the channel by which God can communicate with them. By denying the evidence which God has been pleased to give them, they shut out the light which had been shining in their hearts, and as the result they are left in darkness." White, *Testimonies for the Church*, vol. 5 (Mountain View, CA: Pacific Press, 1882), 634.

15. Instead of referring to those who "wash their robes," some manuscripts read: "Blessed are they that do his commandments, that they may have right to the tree of life, and may enter in through the gates into the city" (Rev. 22:14, KJV). Either way, this text refers to *conditional* immortality.

16. On these and other texts that teach regarding the final destruction of the wicked, see Edward Fudge, *The Fire That Consumes: A Biblical and Historical Study of the Doctrine of Final Punishment*, 3rd ed. (Cambridge: Lutterworth, 2012). See also Paul Copan and Christopher M. Date, eds. *What Is Hell?* (Downers Grove, IL: IVP Academic, forthcoming); Jiří Moskala and John Reeve, eds. *God and Death* (Berrien Springs, MI: Andrews University Press, forthcoming).

17. See, in this regard, Tom Shepherd, "Do the Wicked Burn Forever in Hell?" in *Interpreting Scripture: Bible Questions and Answers*, ed. Gerhard Pfandl (Silver Spring, MD: Biblical Research Institute, 2010), 293–95. See also Fudge, *The Fire that Consumes*, 39.

18. As Edward Fudge explains it, the "eternal punishment" referenced in Matthew 25:46 is "'eternal' in its results. The New Testament speaks in the same way of eternal salvation (Heb. 5:9), eternal judgment (Heb. 6:2), eternal redemption (Heb. 9:12), eternal punishment (Mt 25:46) and eternal destruction (2 Thess. 1:9). In each case, the outcome is everlasting, not the process." Edward Fudge and Robert A. Peterson, *Two Views of Hell: A Biblical and Theological Dialogue* (Downers Grove, IL: InterVarsity, 2000), 51.

19. In this case, I depart from the SBL general-purpose style to transliterate this as *gehenna* (rather than *geenna*) because this term is so often found in various literature by this spelling and I want to make sure the reader recognizes this as the same term that they encounter elsewhere that corresponds to the Valley of Hinnom.

20. While eternal conscious punishment and, to a lesser extent universalism, are represented as views held by early church fathers, conditionalism is also a view that was held by some early church fathers and many others down through the ages of the Christian tradition. In this regard, see Copan and Date, eds. *What Is Hell?* See also, Le Roy Edwin Froom, *The Conditionalist Faith of Our Fathers*, 2 vols. (Washington, DC: Review and Herald, 1965–1966).

21. For a discussion of some prominent views, see Joel B. Green and Stuart L. Palmer, eds., *In Search of the Soul: Four Views on the Mind-Body Problem* (Downers Grove, IL: InterVarsity, 2005).

22. Substance dualism must be distinguished from property dualism, the view that "mental phenomena are non-physical properties of physical phenomena, but not properties of non-physical substances. Property dualists are not committed to the existence of non-physical substances, but are committed to the irreducibility of mental phenomena to physical phenomena," of which consciousness is often adduced as an example. "Dualism and Mind," *Internet Encyclopedia of Philosophy*, accessed December 13, 2021, https://iep.utm.edu/dualism/#H6.

23. Joel Green refers to the view "that the soul (or mind) is separable from the body, having no necessary relation to the body, with the human person identified with the soul" as "radical dualism." On this view, "the soul acts apart from bodily processes, and the body is nothing more than a temporary and disposable holding tank for the soul." Green, "Body, Soul, Mind, and Brain: Critical Issues," 13. This is distinct from "holistic dualism," which "in its various renditions qualifies as a form of substance dualism, but it posits that the human person, though composed of discrete elements, is nonetheless to be identified with the whole, which then constitutes a functional unity." Green, "Body, Soul, Mind, and Brain," 13.

24. On the influence of Platonic and other lines of Greek philosophy on ideas like the pre-existence of the soul and the immortality of the soul, see Jaroslav Pelikan, *The Christian Tradition: A History of the Development of Doctrine*, vol. 1 (Chicago: University of Chicago Press, 1971), 47–52. Pelikan concludes: "Two Christian doctrines are perhaps the most reliable indications of the continuing hold of Greek philosophy on Christian theology: the doctrine of the immortality of the soul and the doctrine of the absoluteness of God." Pelikan, *The Christian Tradition*, 51.

25. On emergent dualism, see William Hasker, "On Behalf of Emergent Dualism," in *In Search of the Soul*.

26. Green, "Body, Soul, Mind, and Brain," 13.

27. E.g., Nancey Murphy, "Nonreductive Physicalism," in *In Search of the Soul*. For an alternative monist view, see "Kevin Corcoran, "The Constitution View of Persons," in *In Search of the Soul*.

28. As Joel Green puts it: "We must face the reality that neither the Old nor the New Testament writers developed a specialized or technical, denotative vocabulary for theoretical discussion of the

human person. And if this is so, then contemporary interpreters ought to exercise care when reading the biblical materials in light of specialized language that has developed subsequently." Green, *Body, Soul, and Human Life: The Nature of Humanity in the Bible* (Grand Rapids, MI: Baker Academic, 2008), 60.

29. For some examples of *psychē* relative to explicitly *mortal* life, see Matthew 2:20; Acts 15:26; 27:10; Romans 11:3; Philippians 2:30; Revelation 12:11.

30. In this regard, as Joel Green puts it, "Genesis 1-2 does not locate the singularity of humanity in the human possession of a 'soul,' but rather in the human capacity to relate to Yahweh as covenant partner, and to join in companionship within the human family and in relation to the whole cosmos in ways that reflect the covenant love of God." Green, *Body, Soul, and Human Life*, 65.

31. "Whereas the Hebrew word *nephesh*, translated *soul*, denotes individuality or personality, the Old Testament Hebrew word *ruach*, translated *spirit*, refers to the energizing spark of life essential to individual existence. It stands for the divine energy, or life principle, that animates human beings." *Seventh-day Adventists Believe: An Exposition of the Fundamental Beliefs of the Seventh-day Adventist Church*, 2nd ed. (Boise, ID: Pacific Press, 2005), 95. Yet, "Never in the Old Testament, with respect to man, does *ruach* denote an intelligent entity capable of sentient existence apart from the body." *Seventh-day Adventists Believe*, 96.

32. "As with *ruach*, there is nothing inherent in the word *pneuma* denoting an entity in man capable of conscious existence apart from the body, nor does New Testament usage with respect to man in any way imply such a concept." *Seventh-day Adventists Believe*, 96.

33. *Seventh-day Adventists Believe*, 96.

34. "Biblical evidence indicates that sometimes *nephesh* and *psuche* refer to the whole person and at other times to a particular aspect of man such as the affections, emotions, appetites, and feelings. This usage, however, in no way shows that man is a being made up of two separate and distinct parts. The body and the soul exist together; together they form an indivisible union. The soul has no conscious existence apart from the body. There is no text indicating that the soul survives the body as a conscious entity." *Seventh-day Adventists Believe*, 95.

35. Some might appeal to the parable of the rich man and Lazarus (Luke 16), but Adventists believe that because it is a parable it should not be taken as making a claim about what happens to people when they die. In this regard, Tom Shepherd outlines numerous reasons why this parable should not be taken to mean the dead are conscious after death and/or receive their final reward prior to the Second Coming:

"1. Elsewhere in the Gospels Jesus refers to death as a sleep from which He awakens people (Matt. 9:24; Mark 5:39; John 11:11, 12; see also Acts 7:60; 13:36; 1 Cor. 11:30; 15:6, 18, 20, 51; 1 Thess. 4:13-15 and 2 Pet. 3:4). This teaching of death as a sleep appears not only in the other Gospels and the writings of Peter and Paul but also in Luke 8:52.

2. According to the parable the rich man after he died had 'eyes' and a 'tongue,' that is, very real bodily parts. He asked that Lazarus 'dip the tip of his finger in water.' This corporeal state is contrary to the concept of immortal souls leaving the body at death.

3. If this is a literal account of the afterlife, then heaven and hell are near enough for a conversation to be held between the inhabitants of heaven and hell. Not a very desirable situation for either party.

4. To use this parable to prove that people receive their rewards at death would mean that Christ contradicted Himself when He said in another place that the righteous and the wicked receive their reward at the Second Coming (Matt. 16:27; 25:31-46; Luke 11:31, 32).

5. The Old Testament writers are very emphatic in stating that the dead, righteous and wicked alike, lie silent and unconscious in the grave until the resurrection day. See Job 14:12; Ps. 115:17; Eccles. 9:5, 6, 10." Tom Shepherd, "Does the Parable of the Rich Man and Lazarus Teach the Immortality of the Soul?" in *Interpreting Scripture: Bible Questions and Answers*, ed. Gerhard Pfandl, vol. 2, Biblical Research Institute Studies (Silver Spring, MD: Biblical Research Institute, 2010), 311.

36. Some might also wonder about the reference to "the spirits now in prison" in 1 Peter 3:19 and some of Paul's statements. Paul's statements will be taken up in the next section alongside the discussion of the resurrection body. Regarding 1 Peter 3:18-20, Adventists typically interpret verse 19 as referring to Christ preaching (through the preaching of Noah) to the humans alive at Noah's time (taking "spirits," *pneuma*, to refer to living human beings as in 1 Cor. 16:18 and akin to the way the eight persons saved in the ark are referred to by the term *psychē* in 3:20). See Francis D. Nichol, ed. *The Seventh-day Adventist Bible Commentary*, vol. 7 (Washington, DC: Review and Herald, 1980), 575-76. Alternatively, verse 19 might be interpreted as referring to the risen Christ proclaiming victory over evil demonic spirits who were at work at the time of Noah, which might complement Colossians 2:15.

37. Grenville J. R. Kent, "Did the Medium at Endor Really Bring Forth Samuel?" in *Interpreting Scripture: Bible Questions and Answers*, ed. Gerhard Pfandl, vol. 2, Biblical Research Institute Studies (Silver Spring, MD: Biblical Research Institute, 2010), 196-99. See also Grenville J. R. Kent, *Say It Again Sam: A Literary and Filmic Study of Narrative Repetition in 1 Samuel 28* (Eugene, OR: Pickwick, 2011).

38. Adventists believe only a few humans are with God in heaven prior to the resurrection, such as Enoch, Moses, Elijah, and (perhaps) those raised when Jesus was raised (Matt. 27:52-53).

39. On the first death and the second death, see chapter 19.

CHAPTER 13 • GOD SAVES US: THE PROCESS OF SALVATION

1. Here, again, I have intentionally left the comma out of this sentence as it is not in the Greek original and its placement affects the meaning. See the earlier discussion in chapter 12.

2. The study of things in Scripture that prefigure other things (known as types) is known as typology. Typology is "the study of persons, events, or institutions in salvation history [types] that God specifically designed to predictively prefigure their antitypical eschatological fulfillment in Christ and the gospel realities brought about by Christ." Richard M. Davidson, "Biblical Interpretation," in *Handbook of Seventh-Day Adventist Theology*, ed. Raoul Dederen (Hagerstown, MD: Review and Herald, 2000), 83.

3. The English word "atonement" is a concatenation of the words "at" and "one" to literally convey reconciliation (at-one-ment) in an attempt to adequately translate the rich Hebrew term *kipper*. When atonement is complete, humans will once again be "at one" with God. See Niels-Erik A. Andreasen, "Atonement/Expiation in the Old Testament" in W. E. Mills, ed., *Mercer Dictionary of the Bible* (Macon, GA: Mercer University Press, 1990), 30.

4. "Upon Christ as our substitute and surety was laid the iniquity of us all. He was counted a transgressor, that He might redeem us from the condemnation of the law. The guilt of every descendant of Adam was pressing upon His heart. The wrath of God against sin, the terrible manifestation of His displeasure because of iniquity, filled the soul of His Son with consternation." Ellen G. White, *The Desire of Ages* (Mountain View, CA: Pacific Press, 1898), 753.

5. Some aspects of the atonement are not immediately clear via our human attempts at understanding. Accordingly, that God's plan of redemption was a "mystery" that required revelation (Rom. 16:25; Eph. 6:19) and remains something into which even angels long to look (1 Pet. 1:12) should engender humility in us as we see through a mirror dimly (1 Cor. 13:12).

6. As Ellen G. White puts it, "Had it been possible for the law to be changed or abrogated, then Christ need not have died.... It was because the law was changeless, because man could be saved only through obedience to its precepts, that Jesus was lifted up on the cross." White, *Desire of Ages*, 762.

7. Ellen G. White comments, "the law of God is as sacred as God Himself. It is a revelation of His will, a transcript of His character, the expression of divine love and wisdom. The harmony of creation depends upon the perfect conformity of all beings, of everything, animate and inanimate, to the law of the Creator." White, *Patriarchs and Prophets*, 52.

8. Many have asked why God made the rules as they are and the best answer is that they are themselves the best rules that could have been—in agreement with God's character of love and producing the best possible consequences in a world of free beings. Only God knows the end from the beginning and only He can foresee the only way that all beings can live in harmony for eternity. Thus, God prescribes His perfect and unchanging law, which will lead to everyone's best happiness provided that all trust God unreservedly. Surrender to faith in God's goodness, love, and wisdom is necessary because only God can see the inevitable outcomes of the extremely complex results of billions of choices, while none of us can know the end from the beginning. Thus, some of God's laws may not be understood by us in the short run but we must trust that God has our best interest in mind. For an excellent treatment of the relationship between God's character of goodness, ethical grounding, and God's moral commands, see David Baggett and Jerry L. Walls, *Good God: The Theistic Foundations of Morality* (New York: Oxford University Press, 2011).

9. Thus, "the law of God is as sacred as God Himself. It is a revelation of His will, a transcript of His character, the expression of divine love and wisdom. The harmony of creation depends upon the perfect conformity of all beings, of everything, animate and inanimate, to the law of the Creator." White, *Patriarchs and Prophets*, 52.

10. See Donald MacKinnon, "Subjective and Objective Conceptions of Atonement," in *Prospect for Theology: Essays in Honour of H. H. Farmer*, ed. F. G. Healey (Welwyn: James Nisbet & Co, 1996), 167–82.

11. See Gregory A. Boyd, "Christus Victor View," in *The Nature of the Atonement: Four Views*, eds. James Beilby and Paul R. Eddy (Downers Grove, IL: IVP Academic, 2006). See also Gustaf Aulén, *Christus Victor: An Historical Study of the Three Main Types of the Idea of Atonement* (London: SPCK, 1931).

12. The moral influence theory is generally attributed to Peter Abelard (1079–1142) in his *Epitome of Christian Theology*, though he himself did not exclude other aspects of the atonement and thus did not advocate a simple moral influence perspective.

13. Ellen G. White comments, "Righteousness is obedience to the law. The law demands righteousness, and this the sinner owes to the law; but he is incapable of rendering it. The only way in which he can attain to righteousness is through faith. By faith he can bring to God the merits of Christ, and the Lord places the obedience of His Son to the sinner's account. Christ's righteousness is accepted in place of man's failure, and God receives, pardons, justifies, the repentant, believing soul, treats him as though he were righteous, and loves him as He loves His Son." White, *Selected Messages*, vol. 1 (Washington, DC: Review and Herald, 1958), 367.

14. Ellen G. White comments, "Christ was to die as man's substitute. Man was a criminal under the sentence of death for transgression of the law of God, as a traitor, a rebel; hence a substitute for man must die as a malefactor, because He stood in the place of the traitors, with all their treasured sins upon His divine soul. It was not enough that Jesus should die in order to fully meet the demands of the broken law, but He died a shameful death." White, *Review and Herald*, July 5, 1887, par. 8.

15. Fleming Rutledge, *And God Spoke to Abraham: Preaching from the Old Testament* (Grand Rapids, MI: Eerdmans, 2011), 302.

16. Kathryn Tanner, *Christ the Key* (New York: Cambridge University Press, 2010), 268.

17. Some reject the language of penal substitution because of an aversion to the language of "penalty." However, there is a crucial distinction between a penalty that is inflicted upon (or charged from) someone involuntarily and someone voluntarily taking a penalty upon themselves just as one would pay the fine of another or post bail to remove someone from prison. Thus, Christ is "the one who, seeing the helpless condition of the fallen race, came to redeem men and women by living a life of obedience to God's law and by paying the penalty of disobedience." Ellen G. White, *Acts of the Apostles* (Mountain View, CA: Pacific Press, 1911), 207.

18. "The righteousness by which we are justified is imputed; the righteousness by which we are sanctified is imparted. The first is our title to heaven, the second is our fitness for heaven." Ellen G. White, (June 4, 1895). Both of these are received by surrender to Christ: "both our title to heaven and our fitness for it are found in the righteousness of Christ. The Lord can do nothing toward the recovery of man until, convinced of his own weakness, and stripped of all self-sufficiency, he yields himself to the control of God." White, *Desire of Ages*, 300.

19. As James Cone put it, "Fellowship with God is now possible, because Christ through his death and resurrection has liberated us from the principalities and powers and the rulers of this present world." Cone, *God of the Oppressed* (New York: Seabury Press, 1975), 209.

20. This concept of Christus Victor makes even more sense when understood in light of the cosmic conflict. Language of a cosmic lawsuit or trial appears throughout Scripture. In the New Testament, Paul speaks of his own ministry as an exhibit in cosmic legal proceedings: "For I think, God has exhibited us, the apostles, last of all as men condemned to death, because we have become a spectacle to the world, both to angels and to mankind" (1 Cor. 4:9). In this regard, Gordon Fee comments, there is "a cosmic dimension to the spectacle: He is on display before the whole universe, as it were." *The First Epistle to the Corinthians* (Grand Rapids, MI: Eerdmans, 1987), 175.

21. The statement that the righteous will "not come into judgment" (John 5:24) is better rendered will "not come into condemnation." The Greek term (*krisis*) may refer to the negative decision of judgment (condemnation) rather than to judgment generally. That this term refers to condemnation here and does not exclude any judgment of believers is apparent by reference to other passages that teach that "we must all appear before the judgment seat of Christ" (2 Cor. 5:10; cf. Rom. 8:1).

22. Scripture emphasizes God's evaluation of His people, who are counted as "worthy" and "precious," "beloved," "pleasing," "acceptable" in His sight, not through their own merits but by being joined to Christ (Rom. 8:1, 15–17; 23:1–2; Eph. 1:4–6; 5:2; Col. 1:10; 2 Thess. 1:5, 11; Heb. 13:21; 1 Pet. 2:4–10). On this, see John C. Peckham, *The Love of God: A Canonical Model* (Downers Grove, IL: IVP Academic, 2015).

23. Notably, "J. Herbert Kane, in a careful and judicious discussion of the problem, argues that not all persons will be judged by God on the same basis. Romans 2 makes it clear that each one will be judged according to the light he or she had. No person will be judged on the basis of light that was unavailable. 'Every man possesses some form of light and he will be judged by that light and by no other.' Those without access to the gospel of Jesus Christ nevertheless have some light available to them. The unevangelized has the 'light of creation, providence, and conscience and will be judged by that light. If he is finally condemned it will not be because he refused to believe the gospel, but because he failed to live up to the little light he had.'" Harold A. Netland, *Dissonant Voices: Religious Pluralism and the Question of Truth* (Vancouver: Regent College Publishing, 1991), 269. See also J. Herbert Kane, *Understanding Christian Missions*, 4th ed. (Grand Rapids, MI: Baker, 1986), 135–137.

24. Ellen G. White comments, in this regard: "We shall not be held accountable for the light that has not reached our perception, but for that which we have resisted and refused. A man could not apprehend the truth which had never been presented to him, and therefore could not be condemned for light he had never had." White, *Last Day Events* (Boise, ID: Pacific Press, 1992), 218. See also Ángel Manuel Rodríguez, "World Religions and Salvation: An Adventist View," in *Message, Mission, and Unity of the Church*, ed. Ángel Manuel Rodríguez, Studies in Adventist Ecclesiology 2 (Silver Spring, MD: Biblical Research Institute, 2013).

25. "It is impossible for us, of ourselves, to escape from the pit of sin in which we are sunken. Our hearts are evil, and we cannot change them.... Education, culture, the exercise of the will, human effort, all have their proper sphere, but here they are powerless. They may produce an outward correctness of behavior, but they cannot change the heart; they cannot purify the springs of life. There must be a power working from within, a new life from above, before men can be changed from sin to holiness. That power is Christ. His grace alone can quicken the lifeless faculties of the soul, and attract it to God, to holiness." Ellen G. White, *Steps to Christ* (Mountain View, CA: Pacific Press, 1892), 18.

26. "Our righteousness is found in obedience to God's law *through the merits of Jesus Christ*.... Exceeding great is our salvation, for ample provision has been made through the righteousness of Christ, that we may be pure, entire, wanting nothing.... Man cannot possibly meet the demands of the law of God in human strength alone. His offerings, his works, will all be tainted with sin. A remedy has been provided in the Saviour, who can give to man the virtue of his merit, and make him co-laborer in the great work of

salvation. Christ is righteousness, sanctification, and redemption to those who believe in him, and who follow in his steps." Ellen G. White, *Review and Herald* (Feb. 4, 1890).

27. Adventists thus do not affirm "once saved always saved" (see Matt. 10:22; 24:13; Mark 13:13; 1 Cor. 9:27; 15:2; Heb. 6:4–6; 2 Pet. 2:19–22; Rev. 3:5).

28. The "Finnish school" of Luther interpretation, in dialogue with Russian Orthodox theology, claims that Luther's view was closer to the orthodox understanding of *theosis,* i.e., "deification," and that for Luther justifying righteousness was not solely an alien righteousness: "in line with Catholic theology, justification means both declaring righteous and making righteous." Veli-Matti Kärkkäinen, "Deification View," in *Justification: Five Views,* ed. James K. Beilby and Paul Rhodes Eddy (Downers Grove, IL: IVP Academic, 2011), 222. For a critique of this view, from the perspective of the traditional interpretation of Luther, see Michael S. Horton's "Traditional Reformed Response" to Kärkkäinen's chapter, in *Justification: Five Views,* 244–49.

29. R. C. Sproul explains: "Luther's famous dictum *simul justus et peccator* goes to the heart of the issue regarding forensic justification. The Latin phrase means 'at the same time just and sinner.' This simultaneous condition refers to the situation wherein the sinner is counted just forensically by virtue of the imputation of Christ, while he remains in and of himself, yet a sinner. Luther did not mean that the sinner who is still a sinner is an unchanged person. The sinner who has saving faith is a regenerate person. He is indwelt by the Holy Spirit. But he is still unjust in himself. Nor does it mean that the sinner is not in a real process of sanctification by which he is becoming just. Those who possess saving faith necessarily, inevitably, and immediately begin to manifest the fruits of faith, which are works of obedience. However, the *grounds* of that person's justification remain solely and exclusively the imputed righteousness of Christ. It is by His righteousness and His righteousness alone that the sinner is declared to be just." R. C. Sproul, "The Forensic Nature of Justification," in *Justification by Faith Alone: Affirming the Doctrine by Which the Church and the Individual Stands or Falls,* revised and updated edition, ed. John Kistler (Morgan, PA: Soli Deo Gloria Publications, 2003), 33–34.

30. On the view known as universal legal justification, which most Adventists reject, see Ángel Manuel Rodríguez, "Some Problems with Legal Universal Justification," accessed November 3, 2021, https://adventistbiblicalresearch.org/materials/some-problems-with-legal-universal-justification/.

31. For more on the view known as last generation theology, see Jiří Moskala and John C. Peckham, eds. *God's Character and the Last Generation* (Nampa, ID: Pacific Press, 2018).

32. E.g., Denis Fortin, "Sanctification and Perfection Are the Work of a Lifetime," in *God's Character and the Last Generation,* eds. Jiří Moskala and John C. Peckham (Nampa, ID: Pacific Press, 2018). See also Edward J. Heppenstall, "How Perfect Is 'Perfect' or Is Christian Perfection Possible?" accessed November 3, 2021, https://adventistbiblicalresearch.org/materials/how-perfect-is-perfect-or-is-christian-perfection-possible/; Hans K. LaRondelle, *Perfection and Perfectionism: A Dogmatic-Ethical Study of Biblical Perfection and Phenomenal Perfectionism* (Berrien Springs, MI: Andrews University Press, 1971). Helmut Ott, *Perfect in Christ: The Mediation of Christ in the Writings of Ellen G. White* (Hagerstown, MD: Review and Herald, 2010); Ángel Manuel Rodríguez, *Living Without an Intercessor in the Writings of Ellen G. White,* Biblical Research Institute Release, no. 17 (Silver Spring, MD: Biblical Research Institute, 2020).

33. "We love, because He first loved us" (1 John 4:19). That is, "only by love is love awakened." Ellen G. White, *The Desire of Ages,* 22. For much more on Ellen White's theology of salvation, see Woodrow W. Whidden, *Ellen White on Salvation: A Chronological Study* (Hagerstown, MD: Review and Herald, 1995).

34. "We do not earn salvation by our obedience; for salvation is the free gift of God, to be received by faith. But obedience is the fruit of faith." Ellen G. White, *Steps to Christ,* 61.

35. However, just like justification, sanctification is in no way the result of meritorious works but it is also the result of faith, meaning placing one's full trust in God and making Him both the Savior and Lord of one's life. As Ellen White puts it: "Every soul may say: 'By His perfect obedience He has satisfied the claims of the law, and my only hope is found in looking to Him as my substitute and surety, who obeyed the law perfectly for me. By faith in His merits I am free from the condemnation of the law. He clothes me with His righteousness, which answers all the demands of the law. I am complete in Him who brings in everlasting righteousness. He presents me to God in the spotless garment of which no thread was woven by any human agent. All is of Christ, and all the glory, honor, and majesty are to be given to the Lamb of God, which taketh away the sins of the world.'" Ellen G. White, *Selected Messages,* 1:396.

36. See LaRondelle, *Perfection and Perfectionism,* 51–245.

37. *BDAG,* 995, 996; *NIDNTT,* 2:59, 60–61, 62, 65 (see, e.g., 1 Cor. 14:20; Eph. 4:13; Col. 1:28; James 1:4). As Edward Heppenstall put it, rather than absolutely sinless perfection, biblical perfection relative to humans is a "spiritual maturity and stability that is possible in this life." Edward Heppenstall, "Let Us Go on to Perfection," in *Perfection: The Impossible Possibility,* ed. Herbert Douglass (Nashville, TN: Southern Publishing Association, 1975), 67. See also Heppenstall, "How Perfect Is 'Perfect' or Is Christian Perfection Possible?" in LaRondelle, *Perfection and Perfectionism,* 171–82.

38. In this regard, John Wesley wrote: "What is Christian Perfection? The loving God with all our heart, mind, soul, and strength. This implies that no wrong temper, none contrary to love, remains in the soul; and that all the thoughts, words, and actions are governed by pure love." John Wesley, "A Plain Account of Christian Perfection," in *The Works of John Wesley,* vol. 11 (Albany, OR: Ages, 1997), 461.

39. For reasons that it seems to me are built into the rules of engagement in the cosmic conflict (see chapter 9), God does not exercise His power to totally remove our sinful nature before Christ's return. It seems to be built into the cosmic conflict that the enemy can antagonize us (in limited fashion) until the end of his usurping reign. Just as God's presence is temporarily and partially impeded by sin during the soon-to-end rule of the devil, the exercise of God's power is limited according to the commitments He has made in the cosmic conflict relative to the temporary and limited domain of the devil.

40. Ellen G. White comments: "As we have clearer views of Christ's spotless and infinite purity, we shall feel as did Daniel, when he beheld the glory of the Lord, and said, 'My comeliness was turned in me into corruption.' We cannot say, 'I am sinless,' till this vile body is changed and fashioned like unto His glorious body. But if we constantly seek to follow Jesus, the blessed hope is ours of standing before the throne of God without spot or wrinkle, or any such thing, complete in Christ, robed in His righteousness and perfection." White, *Signs of the Times* (March 23, 1888). Elsewhere, she writes further: "Sanctification is not the work of a moment, an hour, or a day. It is a continual growth in grace. We know not one day how strong will be our conflict the next. Satan lives, and is active, and every day we need to earnestly cry to God for help and strength to resist him. As long as Satan reigns we shall have self to subdue, besetments to overcome, and there is no stopping place. There is no point to which we can come and say we have fully attained." "Ellen G. White Comments," *The Seventh-day Adventist Bible Commentary*, ed. Francis Nichol, vol. 7 (Washington, DC: Review and Hearld, 1980), 947.

41. Ellen G. White comments: "Christ is our pattern, the perfect and holy example that has been given us to follow. We can never equal the pattern; but we may imitate and resemble it according to our ability. When we fall, all helpless, suffering in consequence of our realization of the sinfulness of sin; when we humble ourselves before God, afflicting our souls by true repentance and contrition; when we offer our fervent prayers to God in the name of Christ, we shall as surely be received by the Father, as we sincerely make a complete surrender of our all to God. We should realize in our inmost soul that all our efforts in and of ourselves will be utterly worthless; for it is only in the name and strength of the Conqueror that we shall be overcomers." White, *Review and Herald*, February 5, 1895, par. 7.

42. I am indebted to my friend and colleague Martin Hanna for emphasizing this framework.

43. Ellen G. White, *Faith and Works* (Nashville, TN: Southern Publishing Association, 1979), 24. See also Seventh-day Adventist Fundamental Belief #10 ("The Experience of Salvation") in the Appendix.

44. Again, I am indebted to my colleague, Martin Hanna, for highlighting this framework in personal discussions.

CHAPTER 14 • GOD COVENANTS WITH US: UNDERSTANDING COVENANT AND LAW

1. According to Gary N. Knoppers, a covenant is a "formal agreement involving two or more parties," "inevitably bilateral," and thus "affects those parties." Gary N. Knoppers, "Ancient Near Eastern Royal Grants and the Davidic Covenant: A Parallel?" *Journal of the American Oriental Society* 116, no. 4 (1996): 696.

2. Roy E. Gane, "The Role of God's Moral Law, Including Sabbath, in the 'New Covenant,'" (2004), 13, accessed November 3, 2021, https://adventistbiblicalresearch.org/materials/the-role-of-gods-moral-law-including-sabbath-in-the-new-covenant/.

3. Gane, "The Role of God's Moral Law, 13.

4. See Moshe Weinfeld, "The Covenant of Grant in the Old Testament and in the Ancient Near East," *Journal of the American Oriental Society* 90, no. 2 (1970): 184–203.

5. On the relation between the Abrahamic covenant, Mosaic covenant, and the "New" Covenant, Ellen G. White comments: "And the Lord declared to him, 'I will establish My covenant between Me and thee and thy seed after thee in their generations, for an everlasting covenant, to be a God unto thee and to thy seed after thee.' Genesis 17:7. Though this covenant was made with Adam and renewed to Abraham, it could not be ratified until the death of Christ. It had existed by the promise of God since the first intimation of redemption had been given; it had been accepted by faith; yet when ratified by Christ, it is called a new covenant. The law of God was the basis of this covenant, which was simply an arrangement for bringing men again into harmony with the divine will, placing them where they could obey God's law. Another compact—called in Scripture the 'old' covenant—was formed between God and Israel at Sinai, and was then ratified by the blood of a sacrifice. The Abrahamic covenant was ratified by the blood of Christ, and it is called the 'second,' or 'new,' covenant, because the blood by which it was sealed was shed after the blood of the first covenant. That the new covenant was valid in the days of Abraham is evident from the fact that it was then confirmed both by the promise and by the oath of God—the 'two immutable things, in which it was impossible for God to lie.' Hebrews 6:18. But if the Abrahamic covenant contained the promise of redemption, why was another covenant formed at Sinai? In their bondage the people had to a great extent lost the knowledge of God and of the principles of the Abrahamic covenant." White, *Patriarchs and Prophets* (Washington, DC: Review and Herald, 1890), 370–71.

6. For more on this, see John C. Peckham, *The Concept of Divine Love in the Context of the God-World Relationship* (New York: Peter Lang, 2014).

7. See Gerhard Hasel and Michael Hasel, *The Promise: God's Everlasting Covenant* (Nampa, ID: Pacific Press, 2021).

8. For more on these questions and related issues, see Skip McCarty, *In Granite or Ingrained? What the Old and New Covenants Reveal About the Gospel, the Law, and the Sabbath* (Berrien Springs, MI:

Andrews University Press, 2007).

9. Skip McCarty refers to this as the Old Covenant mindset or experience. See McCarty, *In Granite or Ingrained*, 81–82.

10. In this regard, Ellen G. White comments: "It was because the law was changeless, because man could be saved only through obedience to its precepts, that Jesus was lifted up on the cross." White, *The Desire of Ages* (Mountain View, CA: Pacific Press, 1898), 762.

11. For more on the biblical theology of the "covenants," see Hans K. LaRondelle, *Our Creator Redeemer: An Introduction to Biblical Covenant Theology* (Berrien Springs, MI: Andrews University Press, 2005).

12. See Paul P. Enns, *The Moody Handbook of Theology* (Chicago, IL: Moody Press, 1997), 520.

13. As Enns explains the dispensationalist view: "The unconditional covenants of the Old Testament were given to Israel: the Abrahamic Covenant (Gen. 12:1–3) promised Israel a land, a posterity, and blessing; the Palestinian Covenant (Deut. 30:1–10) promised Israel would return to the land; the Davidic Covenant (2 Sam. 7:12–16) promised Israel that Messiah would come from Judah and have a throne and a kingdom, ruling over Israel; the New Covenant (Jer. 31:31–34) promised Israel the spiritual means whereby the nation would enter into blessing and receive forgiveness." Enns, *Moody Handbook of Theology*, 523.

14. On the "New Covenant theology" perspective, see William D. Barrick, "New Covenant Theology and the Old Testament Covenants," *The Masters Seminary Journal* 18, no. 1 (Fall 2007): 165–80.

15. In this regard, Seventh-day Adventist Fundamental Belief #12 states, in part: "The church is the community of believers who confess Jesus Christ as Lord and Saviour. In continuity with the people of God in Old Testament times, we are called out from the world." For the full statement, see the Appendix. For some nuanced Adventist perspectives on the relationship of Israel and the church (with some differences between them), see Raoul Dederen, "Church," in *Handbook of Seventh-day Adventist Theology*, ed. Raoul Dederen (Hagerstown, MD: Review and Herald, 2000), 543–45; Jacques Doukhan, *Israel and the Church: Two Voices for the Same God* (Peabody, MA: Hendrickson, 2002). On Israel in prophecy, with particularly helpful insights on why Adventists do not adopt dispensationalism, see Hans K. LaRondelle, *The Israel of God in Prophecy: Principles of Prophetic Interpretation* (Berrien Springs, MI: Andrews University Press, 1983).

16. Ellen G. White comments: "What an exalted idea of the law of God does this give us! To say that it is perfect may convey various ideas to different persons, for many would be apt to measure the law by their own standard of perfection; but when we learn that it is "the righteousness of God," we know that it must be infinite in its breadth. The law is a transcript of God's character, a photograph of character which is infinite in its perfection. It is his nature represented in words, for the benefit of his creatures, so that they may know what is required of them if they would be partakers of the divine nature." White, *Signs of the Times*, January 28, 1886, 55.

17. The great Protestant Reformer John Wesley declared: "The ritual or ceremonial law, delivered by Moses to the children of Israel, containing all the injunctions and ordinances which related to the old sacrifices and service of the Temple, our Lord indeed did come to destroy, to dissolve, and utterly abolish.... But the moral law, contained in the Ten Commandments, and enforced by the Prophets, he did not take away. It was not the design of his coming to revoke any part of this. This is a law which never can be broken, which 'stands fast as the faithful witness in heaven.' The moral stands on an entirely different foundation from the ceremonial or ritual law, which was only designed for a temporary restraint upon a disobedient and stiff-necked people; whereas this was from the beginning of the world, being 'written not on tables on stone,' but on the hearts of all the children of men, when they came out of the hands of the Creator. And, however the letters once wrote by the finger of God are now in a great measure defaced by sin, yet can they not wholly be blotted out, while we have any consciousness of good and evil. Every part of this law must remain in force upon all mankind, and in all ages; as not depending either on time or place, or any other circumstances liable to change, but on the nature of God, and the nature of man, and their unchangeable relation to each other." John Wesley, "Sermon 25: Upon Our Lord's Sermon on the Mount, Discourse 5" in *The Works of John Wesley*, vol. 5 (Albany, OR: Ages, 1997), 380–81.

18. However, Walter Kaiser makes a case that in the Pentateuch there are some indications (by terminology and concepts) of these differences between types of laws. See Walter Kaiser, *Toward Old Testament Ethics* (Grand Rapids, MI: Zondervan, 1983), 44–48. See also, Gane, "The Role of God's Moral Law." However, see also the caveats and nuances regarding such categories in Roy E. Gane, *Old Testament Law for Christians* (Grand Rapids, MI: Baker Academic, 2017), 174–78.

19. See Jiří Moskala, *The Laws of Clean and Unclean Animals of Leviticus 11: Their Nature, Theology, and Rationale* (An Intertextual Study), Adventist Theological Society Dissertation Series, vol. 4 (Berrien Springs, MI: Adventist Theological Society Publications, 2000); Gerhard F. Hasel. "The Distinction Between Clean and Unclean Animals in Lev. 11: Is It Still Relevant?" *Journal of the Adventist Theological Society* 2, no. 2 (1991): 91–125.

20. Ellen G. White comments: "We cannot be too often reminded that health does not depend on chance. It is a result of obedience to law. This is recognized by the contestants in athletic games and trials of strength. These men make the most careful preparation. They submit to thorough training and strict discipline. Every physical habit is carefully regulated. They know that neglect, excess, or carelessness,

which weakens or cripples any organ or function of the body, would ensure defeat.... We are waging a warfare upon which hang eternal results. We have unseen enemies to meet. Evil angels are striving for the dominion of every human being. Whatever injures the health, not only lessens physical vigor, but tends to weaken the mental and moral powers. Indulgence in any unhealthful practice makes it more difficult for one to discriminate between right and wrong, and hence more difficult to resist evil. It increases the danger of failure and defeat." White, *The Ministry of Healing*, 128.

21. Gane, "The Role of God's Moral Law," 19. Gane goes on: "Thus moral and health principles are timeless, ceremonial laws that served a prophetic function in pointing forward to Christ's saving activity are superseded by his ministry, and Christians should preserve principles encapsulated in civil laws even though the ancient Israelite judicial system has ended and culturally dependent specifics may no longer apply." See also Gane's progressive moral wisdom approach outlined in Gane, *Old Testament Law*, 202–3.

22. Additionally, there was the law of circumcision, which the New Testament explicitly teaches is no longer binding for Christians (see, e.g., Acts 15). Circumcision does not continue in the New Covenant because Christ's work ushers in a New Covenant world order in which God claims the whole world as His allotted portion so a particular sign for a particular covenant nation (Israel) is no longer in place. Indeed, through Christ, "there is no distinction between Greek and Jew, circumcised and uncircumcised" (Col. 3:11). The Sabbath was also a sign of God's special people, but it preceded the Mosaic covenant and always transcended the nation of Israel, being rooted in creation. It is thus universal and extends beyond the Mosaic covenant (see more on this in chapter 15).

23. Ellen G. White comments: "Christ was standing at the point of transition between two economies and their two great festivals. He, the spotless Lamb of God, was about to present Himself as a sin offering, that He would thus bring to an end the system of types and ceremonies that for four thousand years had pointed to His death. As He ate the Passover with His disciples, He instituted in its place the service that was to be the memorial of His great sacrifice. The national festival of the Jews was to pass away forever. The service which Christ established was to be observed by His followers in all lands and through all ages." White, *Desire of Ages*, 652.

24. For much more on the civil laws in the Old Testament and related issues, see Clinton Wahlen and Wagner Kuhn, "Culture, Hermeneutics, and Scripture: Discerning What is Universal," in *Biblical Hermeneutics: An Adventist Approach*, ed. Frank M. Hasel, Biblical Research Institute Studies in Hermeneutics, vol. 3 (Silver Spring, MD: Biblical Research Institute/Review and Herald Academic, 2020), 131–77.

25. On this, see Sandra L. Richter, "Rape in Israel's World . . . and Ours: A Study of Deuteronomy 22:23–29," *Journal of the Evangelical Theological Society* 64, no. 1 (2021): 59–76. The description I give of the different cases in Deuteronomy 22 also draws on Richter's work. See also, Richard Davidson, *Flame of Yahweh: Sexuality in the Old Testament* (Grand Rapids, MI: Baker Academic, 2012), 355–56, 359–61.

26. See Richter, "Rape in Israel's World . . . and Ours," 69–72.

27. For much more on this, see Richter, "Rape in Israel's World . . . and Ours."

28. See Moskala, *The Laws of Clean and Unclean Animals of Leviticus 11;* Gerhard F. Hasel. "The Distinction Between Clean and Unclean Animals in Lev. 11."

29. See Hasel, "The Distinction Between Clean and Unclean Animals," 113–14. Hasel concludes in this regard: "The debate in Mark is against the 'tradition of men,' the Rabbinic purity laws, that prescribed how hands had to be washed before eating so that one would not ritually defile oneself in eating." Hasel, "The Distinction Between Clean and Unclean Animals", 114. See also, Eike Mueller's extensive case that "Jesus, in Mark 7:1-23, is actually addressing a specific Second Temple period tradition (*halakah*) rather than the clean/unclean distinction of animals in Lev. 11." As such, "Rather than abrogating the law, Jesus in this study is seen citing the law as authoritative (Mark 7:10-13) and building on the law of the Hebrew Bible for his own teaching (Mark 7:20–23, cf. Lev. 17–20). . . . In Mark 7:1-23 Jesus does not elevate ethics above ritual, or vice versa, he instead argues that human tradition cannot displace divine ethics. As this concept is broadened to the Gentile mission (Mark 7:24–30; Acts 10), grace through Jesus in the form of healing and salvation does not warrant the rejection of the law." See Eike Mueller, "Cleansing the Common: Narrative-Intertextual Study of Mark 7:1–23" (Andrews University ThD diss., 2015), 250–51.

30. As Matthew Thiessen explains at the culmination of his monograph relative to ritual impurity in first-century Judaism: "The very introduction of the story [here in Mark 7] makes it clear that the controversy revolves around 'the traditions of the elders' (7:3). The question relates, then, to legal questions that these Pharisees and scribes believed Jesus's disciples should be observing. Mark's story stresses, though, that this handwashing tradition was *not* a commandment of God, and therefore Jesus's disciples do not need to observe it." Thiessen, *Jesus and the Forces of Death: The Gospels' Portrayal of Ritual Impurity Within First-Century Judaism* (Grand Rapids, MI: Baker Academic, 2020), 190 (emphasis original). He goes on: "any reading of this story that depicts Jesus as rejecting God's commandments to Israel to avoid eating unclean animals results in a Jesus who is irrational at best, and deeply hypocritical at worst." Thiessen, *Jesus and the Forces of Death*, 194.

31. Some have also appealed to Romans 14 in this regard. But, Romans 14 says nothing about clean or unclean foods. Paul's counsel likely pertains to disputes over observing ceremonial feast days or designated days of fasting or whether Christians must refrain from meat sacrificed to idols. Some thought such meat should never be eaten whereas Paul himself held a more nuanced view (see 1 Cor. 8–9).

32. E.g., Damian Carrington, "Avoiding Meat and Dairy Is 'Single Biggest Way' to Reduce Your Impact on Earth," The Guardian, accessed December 13, 2021, https://www.theguardian.com/environment/2018/may/31/avoiding-meat-and-dairy-is-single-biggest-way-to-reduce-your-impact-on-earth. See also, Hannah Ritchie, Pablo Rosado, and Max Roser, "Meat and Dairy Production," Our World in Data, accessed February 12, 2023, https://ourworldindata.org/meat-production.

33. See Seventh-day Adventist Fundamental Belief #22 ("Christian Behavior") in the Appendix.

34. See https://www.newstart.com.

35. E.g., Mary Kekatos, "Seventh-Day Adventists Live Longer and Have 30% Lower Cancer Risks Compared to Other Americans Thanks to the Religion's Strict Diet and Lifestyle Practices, Study Finds," DailyMail.com, accessed November 3, 2021, https://www.dailymail.co.uk/health/article-7731947/Seventh-Day-Adventists-longer-life-expectancy-lower-cancer-risk-study-finds.html.

36. See White, *The Ministry of Healing*.

37. While particular moral laws in time and space might result partially from things (contingently) willed by God that could be otherwise (e.g., the *particular timing* of the Sabbath being contingent on the timing of creation), the core principles of such moral laws are not arbitrary (else they would not be moral laws).

38. Ellen G. White comments, "the law of God is as sacred as God Himself. It is a revelation of His will, a transcript of His character, the expression of divine love and wisdom. The harmony of creation depends upon the perfect conformity of all beings, of everything, animate and inanimate, to the law of the Creator." White, *Patriarchs and Prophets*, 52. See also Seventh-day Adventist Fundamental Belief #19 ("The Law of God") in the Appendix.

39. In this regard, see Elsa Tamez, *The Scandalous Message of James: Faith Without Works is Dead* (New York: Crossroad, 2002).

40. White, *Desire of Ages*, 287.

41. Concerning Ephesians 2:15, which speaks of Christ "abolishing in His flesh the hostility, which is the Law composed of commandments expressed in ordinances," the *Andrews Study Bible* notes: "This does not mean that the Ten Commandments (Exod. 20:1–17; Deut. 5:6–21) are abolished, as Paul clearly demonstrates their continuing significance. He quotes the commandment about honoring one's parents (Eph. 6:1–3) and alludes to others as well (adultery, 4:17–24; 5:3–5, 21–33; bearing false witness, 4:25; stealing, 4:28). It does mean that the whole system of OT law, insofar as it was used to separate Jews from Gentiles, has come to an end." *Andrews Study Bible: Light. Depth. Truth.*, NKJV (Berrien Springs, MI: Andrews University Press, 2010), 1545–46. Further, *The Seventh-day Adventist Bible Commentary* notes: "This is generally thought of as referring to the ceremonial law. It is true that the ceremonial law came to an end at the cross, but it should be remembered that the ceremonial system as God gave it did not create the enmity Paul here describes. It was the interpretation" many "placed upon it, the additions they made to it, and the exclusive and hostile attitudes they adopted as a result, that were the basis of hostility.... The ceremonial law which pointed to Christ naturally came to an end when Christ fulfilled its types. Jewish civil law had already largely passed away with the passing of the nation's sovereignty. But the moral precepts, which are a transcript of the character of God, are as eternal as God Himself and can never be abrogated. In all his teaching concerning the end of the Jewish legal system, Paul made emphatically clear that the moral law was not abrogated (see on Rom. 3:31). When speaking of the end of circumcision Paul was careful to add, 'but the keeping of the commandments of God [is everything]' (see on 1 Cor. 7:19)." Francis D. Nichol, ed., *The Seventh-day Adventist Bible Commentary*, vol. 6 (Washington, DC: Review and Herald, 1980), 1009–10.

42. In contrast to antinomianism, which falsely teaches God's law has been abrogated, the fruits of grace are obedience to God's law of unselfish love (cf. Rom. 13:8–10; James 2).

43. Ellen G. White comments: "Our righteousness is found in obedience to God's law through the merits of Jesus Christ.... Exceeding great is our salvation, for ample provision has been made through the righteousness of Christ, that we may be pure, entire, wanting nothing.... Man cannot possibly meet the demands of the law of God in human strength alone. His offerings, his works, will all be tainted with sin. A remedy has been provided in the Saviour, who can give to man the virtue of his merit, and make him co-laborer in the great work of salvation. Christ is righteousness, sanctification, and redemption to those who believe in him, and who follow in his steps." White, "The Relation of Christ to the Law Is Not Understood," *Review and Herald*, February 4, 1890.

44. On Romans 9:4, see Roberto Badenas, *Christ the End of the Law: Romans 10.4 in Pauline Perspective*, Journal for the Study of the New Testament Supplement Series, vol. 10 (Sheffield: JSOT Press, 1985).

45. In this regard, Mario Veloso states: "A superficial way to eliminate sin would have been to invalidate the moral law. In this case Christ's sacrifice on the cross would not have been needed. But the reality of the Crucifixion proves that God did not abolish the moral law." Veloso, "The Law of God," in *Handbook of Seventh-day Adventist Theology*, ed. Raoul Dederen (Hagerstown, MD: Review and Herald, 2000), 463.

46. Here, Jesus is speaking not strictly of the Ten Commandments or moral law, but speaks broadly of all the law and the prophets—including all the parameters of the Old Covenant(s). Christ did not come to abolish these, but to fulfill *all* the law and the prophets as Himself the promised one of the covenants. This (along with what we saw earlier regarding the New Covenant as fulfillment of the Old Covenant) rules out the view that the New Covenant cancels or abolishes the Old Covenant(s).

47. Ellen G. White comments: "God does not annul His laws. He does not work contrary to them. The work of sin He does not undo. But He transforms. Through His grace the curse works out blessing." White, *Education* (Mountain View, CA: Pacific Press, 1903), 148.

48. "What wonderful promises are made to us in the Word of God. "For God so loved the world, that he gave his only begotten Son, that whosoever believeth in him should not perish, but have everlasting life." [John 3:16.] That is what the Lord gave Jesus for. The law of God had been transgressed. It could not be changed to meet man in his fallen condition. Jesus Christ, the maker of the law, came to our world in the image of God, and died that we might have eternal life. The law is a transcript of God's character. No more could the law of God be abolished, nor one precept of it altered, than you could tear away the throne of the infinite God. Christ who stood at the head could rescue men from the power of the enemy. He was the foundation of the whole Jewish economy. Type met antitype in Christ when He came to our world. Type met antitype on the cross of Calvary." Manuscript 9, 1893; Ellen G. White, *Letters and Manuscripts*, vol, 8 (egwwritings.org).

49. Compare the so-called "three uses of the law," recognized by many Christians, which appear in (among other places) the Formula of Concord (Article VI), to maintain outward discipline (and thus "curb" sin), provide people with knowledge of their sins (akin to a "mirror"), and provide a rule to regulate the whole lives of the regenerate (serving as a "guide").

50. See Andrew E. Hill and John H. Walton, *A Survey of the Old Testament*, 3rd ed. (Grand Rapids, MI: Zondervan, 2009), 204–15.

51. David Asscherick posted on Twitter (@dasscherick, January 13, 2021).

CHAPTER 15 • THE GIFT OF THE SABBATH: TEMPLE IN TIME AND DAY OF REST, GRACE, AND DELIVERANCE

1. For more on Jesus's view of the law, see Eike Mueller, "Cleansing the Common: Narrative-Intertextual Study of Mark 7:1–23" (ThD diss., Andrews University, 2015). Specifically, Mueller makes a case that: "Rather than abrogating the law, Jesus . . . is seen citing the law as authoritative (Mark 7:10–13) and building in the law of the Hebrew Bible for his own teaching (Mark 7:20–23; cf. Lev. 17–20)." In all, "grace through Jesus in the form of healing and salvation does not warrant rejection of the law." Mueller, "Cleansing," 250, 251.

2. See also Seventh-day Adventist Fundamental Belief #20 ("The Sabbath") in the Appendix.

3. Peter Geiermann, *The Convert's Catechism of Catholic Doctrine* (St. Louis: Herder, 1957), 50. In this regard, the sixteenth-century Protestant Reformer Philip Melanchthon wrote in the Augsburg Confession of Faith (1530): "Besides, they [Roman Catholics] cite the change from the Sabbath to the Lord's Day—contrary to the Decalogue, it appears. No case is made more of than this change of the Sabbath. Great, they say, is the power of the church, for it dispensed from one of the Ten Commandments!" *The Augsburg Confession of Faith*, Article 28.30, translated by Theodore G. Tappert (Philadelphia, PA: Fortress Press, 1959), 86.

4. See Kenneth A. Strand, "The Sabbath," in *Handbook of Seventh-day Adventist Theology*, ed. Raoul Dederen (Hagerstown, MD: Review and Herald, 2000), 517–29. See also, Kenneth Strand, ed. *The Sabbath in Scripture and History* (Washington, DC: Review and Herald, 1982).

5. See Philip Schaff, *History of the Christian Church*, vol. 3 (New York: Charles Scribner's Sons, 1910), 105.

6. Charles Joseph Hefele, *A History of the Christian Councils*, vol. 2, trans. and ed. by H. N. Oxenham (Edinburgh: T. and T. Clark, 1896), 316, quoted in Don F. Neufeld and Julia Neuffer, eds., *Seventh-day Adventist Bible Student's Source Book*, Commentary Reference Series (Washington, DC: Review and Herald, 1962), 879.

7. Socrates Scholasticus, *The Ecclesiastical History*, 5.22 (*NPNF2* 2:132).

8. Hermias Sozomen, *The Ecclesiastical History*, 7.19 (*NPNF1* 2:390). Relative to the quotations from both Socrates Scholasticus and Hermias Sozomon, William H. Shea points out that it is interesting that "the two earliest clear statements in the literature of the early Church relating to the Sabbath/Sunday controversy" are from Rome (in the writings of Justin Martyr) and Alexandria (The Epistle of Barnabas), respectively. See William H. Shea, "The Sabbath in the Epistle of Barnabas," *Andrews University Seminary Studies* 4, no. 2 (1966): 175.

9. See R. L. Odom, "The Sabbath in the Great Schism of A.D. 1054," *Andrews University Seminary Studies* 1, no. 1 (1963): 74–80.

10. In this regard, James Cardinal Gibbons, then Archbishop of Baltimore, wrote: "But you may read the Bible from Genesis to Revelation, and you will not find a single line authorizing the sanctification of Sunday. The Scriptures enforce the religious observance of Saturday, a day which we never sanctify." Gibbons, *The Faith of Our Fathers*, 83rd ed. (Baltimore, MD: John Murphy Company Publishers, 1917), 97.

11. Other Christians have also recognized this. For example, Dwight L. Moody wrote: "The sabbath was binding in Eden, and it has been in force ever since. This fourth commandment begins with the word 'remember,' showing that the sabbath already existed when God wrote this law on the tables of stone at Sinai. How can men claim that this one commandment has been done away with when they will admit that the other nine are still binding?" Moody, *Weighed and Wanting: Addresses on the Ten Commandments* (Chicago: The Bible Institute Colportage Association, 1898), 47. Further, Moody wrote, "I honestly believe

that this commandment is just as binding today as it ever was. I have talked with men who have said that it has been abrogated, but they have never been able to point to any place in the Bible where God repealed it." Moody, *Weighed and Wanting*, 46.

12. Jo Ann Davidson, *Rediscovering the Glory of the Sabbath* (Nampa, ID: Pacific Press, 2021), 126.

13. See Nicholas Perrin, "Jesus as Priest in the Gospels," *The Southern Baptist Journal of Theology* 22, no. 2 (2018): 81–99.

14. Here, again (relative to Acts 16:12-13), you would expect Luke (the Gentile) to tell us if the Sabbath was no longer in place. Instead, he both narrates that the women kept the Sabbath and then tells of preaching to them on the Sabbath.

15. See Jon Paulien, "Revisiting the Sabbath in the Book of Revelation," *Journal of the Adventist Theological Society* 9 (1998): 179–86. See also the additional biblical arguments in this regard in Johannes Kovar, "The Remnant and God's Commandments: Revelation 12:17," in *Toward a Theology of the Remnant: An Adventist Ecclesiological Perspective*, ed. Ángel Manuel Rodríguez, Studies in Adventist Ecclesiology 1 (Silver Spring, MD: Biblical Research Institute, 2009), 113–26.

16. Ellen G. White comments: "But Christians of past generations observed the Sunday, supposing that in so doing they were keeping the Bible Sabbath; and there are now true Christians in every church, not excepting the Roman Catholic communion, who honestly believe that Sunday is the Sabbath of divine appointment. God accepts their sincerity of purpose and their integrity before Him. But when Sunday observance shall be enforced by law, and the world shall be enlightened concerning the obligation of the true Sabbath, then whoever shall transgress the command of God, to obey a precept which has no higher authority than that of Rome, will thereby honor popery above God. . . . And it is not until the issue is thus plainly set before the people, and they are brought to choose between the commandments of God and the commandments of men, that those who continue in transgression will receive 'the mark of the beast.' " White, *The Great Controversy* (Mountain View, CA: Pacific Press, 1911), 449.

17. *Andrews Study Bible: Light. Depth. Truth.*, NKJV (Berrien Springs, MI: Andrews University Press, 2010), 1485.

18. See, e.g., Ron du Preez, *Judging the Sabbath: Discovering What Can't Be Found in Colossians 2:16* (Berrien Springs, MI: Andrews University Press, 2008).

19. See, e.g., Roy E. Gane, "The Role of God's Moral Law, Including Sabbath, in the 'New Covenant' " (2004), 20–21, accessed November 3, 2021, https://adventistbiblicalresearch.org/materials/the-role-of-gods-moral-law-including-sabbath-in-the-new-covenant/.

20. In this regard, some appeal to Hebrews 4. As Roy Gane explains: "It is true that in this passage Sabbath rest is used to characterize a life of peace resulting from faith in God. Sabbath as a microcosm of such a life is simply an extension of the significance that Sabbath has carried since Creation. But this does not mean that the seventh day Sabbath is a temporary, *historical/horizontal* kind of type like the Israelite sacrificial system. A historical/horizontal type consists of something that prefigures something in the future, which constitutes its antitype. When the antitype commences, the type becomes obsolete. Thus, for example, the levitical priesthood was superseded by the greater Melchizedek priesthood of Jesus Christ (Heb. 7-10). Another example is the ritual of Passover, which Christ fulfilled and therefore superseded when he died on the cross (see John 19:14). The type and antitype do not function at the same time. But in Hebrews 4, God's 'rest' has not suddenly become available for Christians; it was available all along and was not fully appropriated in Old Testament times only because of unbelief. Because the life of rest was available in Old Testament times, at the same time when the weekly Sabbath was in operation for the Israelites, the weekly Sabbath cannot be a historical type of the life of rest. Rather, it is an eternal memorial of Creation." Gane, "The Role of God's Moral Law," 14–15.

21. Gane, "The Role of God's Moral Law," 14.

22. Albert Barnes, *Notes on the New Testament: Ephesians, Philippians, and Colossians.* Barnes' Notes on the Old and New Testaments (Grand Rapids, MI: Baker, 1982), 267.

23. Gane, "The Role of God's Moral Law," 20.

24. See, in this regard, Frank M. Hasel's chapter "The Virtue of Rest" in Hasel, *Living for God: Reclaiming the Joy of Christian Virtue* (Nampa, ID: Pacific Press, 2020), 97–108, esp. 104–6.

25. Sigve Tonstad, *The Lost Meaning of the Seventh Day* (Berrien Springs, MI: Andrews University Press, 2009), 21.

26. The Sabbath is a day of rest in which we can enjoy personal presence and intimate relationship, for which many people today are starving. See A. J. Swoboda, *Subversive Sabbath: The Surprising Power of Rest in a Nonstop World* (Grand Rapids, MI: Brazos, 2018), esp. 65–82; cf. Tonstad, *The Lost Meaning of the Seventh Day*, esp. 118–23.

27. Abraham Heschel, *The Sabbath* (New York: Farrar, Strauss, and Giroux, 2005), 14.

28. See Frank M. Hasel, *Living for God*, 102.

29. Jacques B. Doukhan, *Genesis* (Nampa, ID: Pacific Press/Review and Herald, 2016), 69.

30. White, *The Desire of Ages* (Mountain View, CA: Pacific Press, 1898), 283.

31. Jacques Doukhan, "Loving the Sabbath as a Christian: A Seventh-Day Adventist Perspective," *The Sabbath in Jewish and Christian Traditions*, ed. Tamara Cohn Eskenazi, Daniel J. Harrington, and William H. Shea (New York: Crossroad, 1991), 155.

32. Jennifer Jill Schwirzer, Twitter (@JenniferJillS, July 10, 2021).
33. Heschel, *The Sabbath*, 10.
34. See Walter Brueggemann, *Sabbath as Resistance: Saying No to the Culture of Now* (Louisville, KY: Westminster John Knox, 2014).
35. White, *Desire of Ages*, 287. Further, she writes: "The necessities of life must be attended to, the sick must be cared for, the wants of the needy must be supplied. He will not be held guiltless who neglects to relieve suffering on the Sabbath. God's holy rest day was made for man, and acts of mercy are in perfect harmony with its intent. God does not desire His creatures to suffer an hour's pain that may be relieved upon the Sabbath or any other day." White, *Desire of Ages*, 207.
36. Kessia Reyne Bennett, Twitter (@kreyne, June 11, 2021).
37. See Eleonore Stump, *Wandering in the Darkness: Narrative and the Problem of Suffering* (Oxford: Oxford University Press, 2010), 116–18.
38. I do not mean to suggest or imply that Matthew 10:28 is about Sabbath rest specifically, but this verse signals God's concern for and provision for human rest.

CHAPTER 16 • GOD MAKES A WAY TO DWELL WITH US: THE SANCTUARY
1. Much of this chapter draws on the excellent work of Richard M. Davidson in his book, *A Song for the Sanctuary: Experiencing God's Presence in Shadow and Reality* (Silver Spring, MD: Biblical Research Institute/Review and Herald Academic, 2022).
2. Ranko Stefanovic comments: "At least two documents written on both sides are mentioned in the Old Testament: 'the two tablets of the testimony' which Moses brought down from the mountain (Exod. 32:15), and the scroll that Ezekiel saw spread before him which 'had writing on the front and on the back' (2:9–10)." Stefanovic, *Revelation of Jesus Christ: Commentary on the Book of Revelation*, 2nd ed. (Berrien Springs, MI: Andrews University Press, 2009), 201.
3. Stefanovic, *Revelation*, 201.
4. Stefanovic, *Revelation*, 205.
5. Stefanovic, *Revelation*, 205.
6. Stefanovic, *Revelation*, 205.
7. As Davidson comments on Ezekiel 28:14: "Think about it: if we are gazing at a heavenly scene that portrays an 'anointed covering cherub,' where are we looking? Informed by the parallels with the earthly sanctuary—where there were golden cherubim with wings that covered the ark of the covenant in the Most Holy Place (Exod. 37:9)—we may deduce that we are viewing nothing less than the very Holy of Holies of the heavenly sanctuary! So, not only does Ezekiel 28 reveal to us the origin of Satan who was once a beautiful unfallen angel, but it reveals the existence of the heavenly sanctuary before sin!" Davidson, *Song for the Sanctuary*, 21.
8. This heavenly sanctuary is referenced many times in the Old and New Testaments. Relative to the Old Testament, Elias Brasil de Souza identifies forty-three passages that contain the heavenly sanctuary/temple motif. Elias Brasil de Souza, *The Heavenly Sanctuary/Temple Motif in the Hebrew Bible*, Adventist Theological Society Dissertation Series, vol. 7 (Berrien Springs, MI: ATS Publications, 2005). Relative to the New Testament, Leonardo Nunes identifies at least thirty-five passages that deal with the heavenly sanctuary/temple motif. Leonardo G. Nunes, "Function and Nature of the Heavenly Sanctuary/Temple and Its Earthly Counterparts in the New Testament Gospels, Acts, and Epistles: A Motif Study of Major Passages" (ThD diss., Andrews University, 2020).
9. Notably, David M. Moffit, New Testament scholar at the University of St. Andrews, comments, "the author [of Hebrews] speaks in Heb. 9–10 about Jesus entering the tabernacle in heaven, the very tabernacle that Moses saw [cf. Exod. 25:8–9, 40; Heb. 8:5], and moving through its sancta into the place where God dwells. This concrete depiction of a heavenly structure where God dwells and where the angels serve as priests (Heb. 1) indicates the author's belief in a heavenly tabernacle upon which the earthly tabernacle/temple is modeled." Moffit, *Atonement and the Logic of Resurrection in the Epistle to the Hebrews* (Leiden: Brill, 2011), 221n.7; cf. Richard M. Davidson, *Typology in Scripture: A Study of Hermeneutical Typos Structures* (Berrien Springs, MI: Andrews University Press, 1981), 336–388. Moffit further comments, the "language in [Hebrews] 9:11–12 encourages a spatial and temporal conception of Jesus entering and moving through a structure that actually exists in heaven," coinciding "with the author's claim that Jesus serves as a high priest in heaven." Moffit, *Atonement*, 225.
10. In this regard, there is a close connection between the heavenly sanctuary and the book of Revelation. For example, Jacques Doukhan identifies a sevenfold structure of the book of Revelation around seven references to the heavenly sanctuary and to Israel's calendar of festivals. See Jacques B. Doukhan, *Secrets of Revelation: The Apocalypse through Hebrew Eyes* (Hagerstown, MD: Review and Herald, 2002), 13–14. See also the chart "Seven Introductory Scenes in Revelation" later in this chapter.
11. See the discussion in Davidson, *Song for the Sanctuary*, 103–30. See also Richard M. Davidson, "Sanctuary 101," *Adventist World*, published February 27, 2022, https://www.adventistworld.org/sanctuary-101/.
12. According to Richard Davidson, "typology is the study of persons, events, or institutions that God has designed to prefigure (point forward to) their eschatological (end-time) fulfillment in Christ or

the gospel realities brought about by Christ." Davidson, *Song for the Sanctuary*, 162. See also Davidson, *Typology in Scripture*.

13. Davidson, *Song for the Sanctuary*, 159.
14. Davidson, *Song for the Sanctuary*, 164–66.
15. Here, it is important to recall that Scripture depicts the heavenly "world" (or realm) and earthly "world" (or realm) as integrally connected. There is a crucial relationship between heaven and earth that is highlighted throughout Scripture—events on earth affect events in heaven and vice versa. Scripture frequently depicts a dual picture, with God depicted as dwelling in the heavenly sanctuary, while also dwelling with special presence in the earthly sanctuaries and temples of Israel (see 1 Kings 8:27; Ps. 78:69; 79:1; Isa. 66:1, 6). While God is omnipresent such that even "heaven and the highest heaven cannot contain" Him (1 Kings 8:27), God nevertheless dwelled in localized temples on earth, which were replicas (shadow types) of the heavenly original. In this regard, the earthly sanctuaries and temples seemed to function as a special hinge-point, almost like a portal in some respects, between heaven and earth. See, in this regard, Kim Papaioannou and Ioannis Giantzaklidis, eds. *Earthly Shadows, Heavenly Realities: Temple/Sanctuary Cosmology in Ancient Near Eastern, Biblical, and Early Jewish Literature* (Berrien Springs, MI: Andrews University Press, 2017).
16. The Shekinah (a rabbinic term) glory was the visible manifestation of God's presence (cf. Ps. 90:1).
17. For much more on each of these aspects, see Davidson, *Song for the Sanctuary*, 195–216, on which this section draws.
18. Ellen G. White comments: "The incense, ascending with the prayers of Israel, represents the merits and intercession of Christ, His perfect righteousness, which through faith is imputed to His people, and which can alone make the worship of sinful beings acceptable to God. Before the veil of the most holy place was an altar of perpetual intercession, before the holy, an altar of continual atonement. By blood and by incense God was to be approached—symbols pointing to the great Mediator, through whom sinners may approach Jehovah, and through whom alone mercy and salvation can be granted to the repentant, believing soul." White, *Patriarchs and Prophets* (Washington, DC: Review and Herald, 1890), 353.
19. The Hebrew term *tamid* can mean either "regular" or "continual," depending on the context.
20. Ellen G. White comments: "Christ as high priest within the veil so immortalized Calvary that though He liveth unto God, He dies continually to sin. . . . Christ Jesus is represented as continually standing at the altar, momentarily offering up the sacrifice for the sins of the world. . . . All incense from earthly tabernacles must be moist with the cleansing drops of the blood of Christ." White, Manuscript 50, 1900.
21. Davidson, *Song for the Sanctuary*, 279–81.
22. For much more on these offerings, see Roy Gane, *Altar Call* (Berrien Springs, MI: Diadem, 1999), 64–104; Davidson, *Song for the Sanctuary*, 223–44.
23. As Roy Gane comments: "In Leviticus 4 the sins remedied by purification offerings are limited to those committed 'inadvertently.' In 5:1–13, however, confession plus the graduated purification offering expands the scope of expiation beyond inadvertence, which is not mentioned here, to sins committed through omission or neglect, including failure to supply required testimony (v. 1) and forgetting to perform a duty to the Lord, whether ritual purification (vv. 2–3) or fulfilling an oath (v. 4)." And, "reparation offerings also remedy some deliberate sins (6:1–7; Num. 5:5–8). Nevertheless, each of these cases of non-inadvertent sin remedied by a purification or reparation offering involves some kind of mitigating factor that places it with inadvertent wrongs in the category of nondefiant offenses rather than with flagrant, defiant violations, for which no animal sacrifice can expiate (Num. 15:30–31)." Gane, *Leviticus, Numbers* (Grand Rapids, MI: Zondervan Academic, 2011), 123. Richard Davidson comments on this: "Even though some scholars see this term [*shegagah*] limited to sins involving some kind of ignorance (either of the act or of the sin), several lines of evidence lead to the conclusion that the Hebrew word *shegagah* includes intentional as well as unintentional sins, and these 'inadvertent' sins include the whole range of sins that are non-brazen, i.e., not done rebelliously, 'with a high hand.'" Davidson, *Song for the Sanctuary*, 288. Among a list of many reasons for this conclusion, Davidson comments further: "The noun *shegagah* is derived from the verb *shagag/shagah* ('to wander, go astray'), which is used in Scripture for both unintentional and intentional 'going astray' (Job 12:16; Ps. 119:67; Prov. 5:20). This verb is parallel to the New Testament term for 'sin,' (*hamartanō*), which means 'to miss the mark' (whether unintentionally or intentionally." Davidson, *Song for the Sanctuary*, 289. Further, "The noun *shegagah* elsewhere in Scripture refers to occasions that encompass both unintentional and intentional (but non-brazen) 'going astray' (Num. 35:11; Eccles. 5:6; 10:5)." Davidson, *Song for the Sanctuary*, 289. Moreover, "In discussing the case of the ruler or the common Israelite in the text of Leviticus 4:22–23 and 4:27–28," the text "shows two different kinds of *shegagah* sins being described, separated by the word 'or' (Heb. 'ō). Each set of verses 'consists of two clauses that introduce two alternative manners of sinning. The first alternative is to sin intentionally. . . and the second is to sin unintentionally.'" Davidson, *Song for the Sanctuary*, 289. And, "Numbers 15:22–31 presents two overarching classes of sin: Numbers 15:22–29 describes the *shagah/bishgagah* (intentional and unintentional 'inadvertent' non-rebellious) sins, and this is contrasted in 15:30–31 with the sin *beyad ramah* ('with a high hand')—that is, 'high-handed,' presumptuous, rebellious, brazen sin. The former class can be atoned for and forgiven (through the sin offering), while the latter class has no means of atonement in the sanctuary services. He is 'completely cut off; his guilt shall be upon him' (Num. 15:30)." Davidson, *Song for the Sanctuary*, 290; cf. Lev. 4:2; Isa. 53:7.

24. See the further discussion in Gane, *Altar Call*, 203–9.

25. See further, Gane, *Altar Call*, 204.

26. As Gane puts it, "The goat for Azazel was not offered as a sacrifice at all. It is true that Leviticus 16:5 refers to Azazel's goat as a 'sin ritual' along with the Lord's goat. The Hebrew word here for 'sin ritual' is elsewhere translated as 'sin offering.' But in the case of the scapegoat, the ritual was not an offering/sacrifice because the goat was not given *to* God as an offering. Rather, according to verse 10, it was sent *away* from God and His sanctuary 'into the wilderness to Azazel.'" Gane, *Altar Call*, 248.

27. There is considerable evidence indicating that "Azazel" in the Day of Atonement ritual (Lev. 16:8–10) refers to a demon enemy of God. See Roy Gane, *Cult and Character: Purification Offerings, Day of Atonement, and Theodicy* (Winona Lake, IN: Eisenbrauns, 2005), 247–51. Gane elsewhere states, further, just as the "Lord's goat belonged to the Lord and was offered to the Lord, but it also *represented* the Lord," the "goat that belonged to Azazel and was sent to him *must also represent* Azazel." Gane, *Altar Call*, 250. "Although Azazel is a shadowy figure in Leviticus, his overall profile is clear and there is only one being in the universe who fits it: Satan," who is "God's great enemy (Matt. 4:1–11; Luke 10:17–18; Rev. 12:7–17)." Gane, *Altar Call*, 250.

28. As Gane explains: "Azazel's goat, carrying the sins of the Israelites, represents Satan bearing responsibility with regard to human sins that is *his own responsibility*. . . . Satan does not carry a molecule of my own responsibility. Christ bore that at the cross. Satan is not my substitute in *any* sense whatsoever. Only Christ is my substitute." Gane, *Altar Call*, 254.

29. See, in this regard, the brief but informative article by Gerhard Pfandl, "The Pre-Advent Judgment: Fact or Fiction? (Part 2)," *Ministry*, accessed November 4, 2021, https://www.ministrymagazine.org/archive/2004/02/the-pre-advent-judgment-fact-or-fiction.html.

30. Gane, *Altar Call*, 337.

31. As Ellen G. White puts it: "Jesus loves His children, even if they err. . . . He keeps His eye upon them, and when they do their best, calling upon God for His help, be assured the service will be accepted, although imperfect. Jesus is perfect. Christ's righteousness is imputed unto them, and He will say, Take away the filthy garments from him, and clothe him with change of raiment. Jesus makes up for our unavoidable deficiencies." White, Letter 17a, 1891, par. 21; Ellen G. White, *Letters and Manuscripts*, vol. 7 (egwwritings.org).

32. See further, Davidson, *Song for the Sanctuary*, 743–62.

33. On the many covenant lawsuits in Scripture, see Richard M. Davidson, "The Divine Covenant Lawsuit Motif in Canonical Perspective," *Journal of the Adventist Theological Society* 21, no. 1–2 (2010). For more on the pre-advent judgment, see William H. Shea, *Selected Studies on Prophetic Interpretation*, Daniel and Revelation Committee Series, vol. 1 (Silver Spring, MD: Biblical Research Institute, 1992), 1–29.

34. Davidson, "Divine Covenant Lawsuit," 83. This concept of a cosmic courtroom drama, particularly Daniel 7's heavenly council judgment scene, relates to the heavenly council/court scenes of Revelation. David E. Aune identifies seven "heavenly court" or "heavenly throne-room scenes" in Revelation (4:1–5:14; 7:9–17; 8:1–4; 11:15–18; 14:1–5; 15:2–8; 19:1–10). The longest of these is in Revelation 4–5 and, according to Aune, focuses on "God enthroned in his heavenly court surrounded by a variety of angelic beings or lesser deities (angels, archangels, seraphim, cherubim) who function as courtiers. All such descriptions of God enthroned in the midst of his heavenly court are based on the ancient conception of the divine council or assembly." Aune, *Revelation 1–5:14*, Word Biblical Commentary (Dallas: Word, 1997), 277.

35. Davidson, "Divine Covenant Lawsuit," 83. Likewise, Richard Bauckham notes that, in Revelation, the "world is a kind of court-room in which the issue of who is the true God is being decided. In this judicial contest Jesus and his followers bear witness to the truth." Bauckham, *The Theology of the Book of Revelation* (Cambridge: Cambridge University Press, 1993), 73. Specifically, "Jesus' and his followers' witness to the true God and his righteousness" is what "exposes" the enemy's program of deceit and slander. Bauckham, *The Theology of the Book of Revelation*, 72–73. This is situated within the broader context of "the cosmic conflict between good and evil." Bauckham, *The Theology of the Book of Revelation*, 15.

36. For much more on these and other amazing prophecies in the book of Daniel, see Jacques B. Doukhan, *Secrets of Daniel: The Wisdom and Dreams of a Jewish Prince in Exile* (Hagerstown, MD: Review and Herald, 2000).

37. On Daniel 8, the *Andrews Study Bible* Notes comments: "The word 'sacrifices' is often supplied by translators but is not in the original text (see also 'sacrifice,' 'offering,' or 'burnt offering' in other translations). In the context of the earthly sanctuary/temple, the Hebrew term for 'regularity' [*tāmîd*] (sometimes referred to as the 'continual' or 'daily'), applied to a variety or system of regular rituals (lamps, burnt offerings, incense, placing bread) that were performed daily (Exod. 27:20; 29:38; 30:7–8) or weekly (Lev. 24:8). It designated the daily service of the priest in the court and inside the Holy Place of the tabernacle. It is used here to refer to the mediation of the Prince of the hosts in the heavenly sanctuary (see Heb. 7:25). The horizontal phase of the little horn represented by the Roman Empire extended beyond the destruction of the Jerusalem temple in A.D. 70. The religious phase of the little horn interfered with the daily ministration of Christ for us in the heavenly temple (see Rev. 13:6)." *Andrews Study Bible: Light. Depth. Truth.*, NKJV (Berrien Springs, MI: Andrews University Press, 2010), 1125–26. Martin Pröbstle comments, further: "In the Torah *tamîd* designates the regularity (with intervals) or continuity (without interruption) of activities, events, or states of affairs and, as such, describes the regular activities of the

daily service at the sanctuary.... In addition to *the* regular sanctuary service, the *tamid* also refers to the true worship by the people of God." Indeed, "in Daniel 11:31 and Daniel 12:11 the *tamid* is replaced by false worship ('abomination of desolation'), indicating that it is the true worship [cf. Dan. 6:16, 20]. In short, the *tamid* in Daniel 8 designates (a) the continual service of the 'Prince of the host' as high priest, and (b) the continual worship directed toward the 'Prince of the host' by believers. Daniel 8:11, 12 then describes how the horn interferes with the worship of the divine 'Prince of the host,' the true high priest. The horn acts as another 'prince of the host' and commands its own counterfeit 'host,' which the horn sets up against the *tamid* (verse 12)." Pröbstle, *Where God and I Meet: The Sanctuary* (Hagerstown, MD: Review and Herald, 2013), 106.

38. There were other decrees before and after this one, but this one best matches the wording of the prophecy of Daniel 9. See, in this regard, Gane, *Altar Call*, 289–90. See also Brempong Owusu-Antwi, *The Chronology of Daniel 9:24–27* (Berrien Springs, MI: Adventist Theological Society Publications, 1995).

39. For some arguments in support of dating Jesus's crucifixion to AD 31, see Grace Amadon, "Ancient Jewish Calendation," *Journal of Biblical Literature* 61 (1942): 227–280; Grace Amadon, "The Crucifixion Calendar," *Journal of Biblical Literature* 63 (1944): 177–90, cited in Michael Hasel, "History, the Bible, and Hermeneutics," in *Biblical Hermeneutics: An Adventist Approach*, ed. Frank M. Hasel, Biblical Research Institute Studies in Hermeneutics, vol. 3 (Silver Spring, MD: Biblical Research Institute/Review and Herald Academic, 2020), 125.

40. See Jiří Moskala, "Did the Prophet Daniel Write the Book of Daniel?" in *Interpreting Scripture: Bible Questions and Answers*, ed. Gerhard Pfandl (Silver Spring, MD: Biblical Research Institute, 2010), 65–71.

41. See also Shea's chapters on the year-day principle in *Selected Studies on Prophetic Interpretation*, 67–110.

42. As Gane explains: "For the Israelites, a week could be a week of years" and after "seven Sabbaths/weeks of years, the Jubilee year of freedom was to come for Israelites who had fallen into debt slavery or who had lost their land (Lev. 25:8–10).... The parallel is unmistakable. The 'seventy weeks' are a large-scale Jubilee period: seventy weeks of *years*, that is, 490 years," after which freedom from domination by foreign empires would come. "The fact that the 'seventy weeks' represent a period leading up to a Jubilee is reinforced by Daniel 9:25, which refers to a period of 'seven weeks' " of years at the beginning of the seventy weeks. Gane, *Altar Call*, 290–91. Notably, Jesus was likely alluding to this seventy weeks (and God's centuries of forbearance with His people) when He declared that one should extend forgiveness "up to seventy times seven" (Matt. 18:22).

43. See David J. Hamstra, "The Seventy-Weeks Prophecy of Daniel 9:24–27 and First-Century AD Jewish Messianic Expectation," *Andrews University Seminary Student Journal* 4, no. 1–2 (2020):19–30. Further, N. T. Wright comments: Daniel 9 "announces precisely that idea of an *extended exile*: the 'seventy years' that Jeremiah said Israel would stay in exile have been stretched out to seventy times seven, almost half a millennium of waiting until the One God would restore his people at last, by finally dealing with the 'sins' that had caused the exile in the first place. The scheme of 'seventy sevens' resonated with the scriptural promises of the jubilee—this would be the time when the ultimate debts would be forgiven. Devout Jews in the first century labored to work out when the 490 years would be up, often linking their interpretations of Daniel to the relevant passages in Deuteronomy. This was the long hope of Israel, the forward-looking narrative cherished by many who, like Saul of Tarsus, were soaked in the scriptures and eager for the long-delayed deliverance. And many of them believed that *the time was drawing near*. They knew enough chronology to do a rough calculation" and recognized that "the time was near." N. T. Wright, *Paul: A Biography* (New York: HarperOne, 2018), 19–20.

44. Notably, the first beast of Daniel 7 (the empire of Babylon) destroyed the first temple, the last beast of Daniel 7 (the empire of Rome) destroyed the second temple, and the little horn of Daniel (corresponding to the later iteration of the composite beast of Revelation 13) assaults the heavenly temple.

45. For an excellent and concise explanation of the prophecies of Daniel 8 and 9 relative to the sanctuary (to which I am indebted and draw on in this chapter), see Gane, *Altar Call*, 280–97.

46. For elaboration of the ideas in this "Sanctuary Theology Matters" section, see John C. Peckham, "Toward a Systematic Theology of the Sanctuary," in Davidson, *Song for the Sanctuary*, 679–712.

47. See also Davidson, "Sanctuary 101."

48. Davidson, *Song for the Sanctuary*, 650. See also Davidson, *Song for the Sanctuary*, 650–55.

49. It is no coincidence that the Adventist pioneers saw the sanctuary as the integrating factor of Adventist doctrines. See, in this regard, Alberto R. Timm, *The Sanctuary and the Three Angels' Messages 1844–1863: Integrating Factors in the Development of Seventh-day Adventist Doctrines* (Berrien Springs, MI: Adventist Theological Society Pubications, 1995). In this regard, Ellen White wrote, "the subject of the sanctuary was the key which unlocked the mystery of the disappointment of 1844. It opened to view a complete system of truth, connected and harmonious, showing that God's hand had directed the great advent movement and revealing present duty as it is brought to light the position and work of His people." Ellen G. White, *The Great Controversy* (Mountain View, CA: Pacific Press, 1888), 423.

50. See also Seventh-day Adventist Fundamental Belief #24 ("Christ's Ministry in the Heavenly Sanctuary") in the Appendix.

51. God's love is just love and His justice is loving. The love of God is inseparable from justice and vice versa in the biblical text. See John C. Peckham, *The Love of God: A Canonical Model* (Downers Grove, IL: IVP Academic, 2015), e.g., 82–83, 159–60.

52. Ellen G. White, *Evangelism* (Washington, DC: Review and Herald, 1946), 243.

CHAPTER 17 • GOD WITH US IN THE CHURCH: THE FELLOWSHIP OF THE LAMB

1. Adventists typically understand the gift of tongues (1 Cor. 14) as a gift that provides the ability to communicate in foreign languages through the power of the Spirit (Acts 2:4–6; cf. Mark 16:17) rather than in terms of speaking in unintelligible utterances. For more on the complexities and nuances of this issue, however, see Ángel Manuel Rodríguez, "The Gift of Tongues in 1 Corinthians 14," accessed October 1, 2021, https://adventistbiblicalresearch.org/materials/the-gift-of-tongues-in-1-corinthians-14/. See also Gerhard F. Hasel, *Speaking in Tongues: Biblical Speaking in Tongues and Contemporary Glossolalia* (Berrien Springs, MI: Adventist Theological Society Publications, 1994).

2. See also Denis Fortin, "The Holy Spirit and the Church," in *Message, Mission, and Unity of the Church*, ed. Ángel Manuel Rodríguez, Studies in Adventist Ecclesiology 2 (Silver Spring, MD: Biblical Research Institute, 2013).

3. To be clear, even in the Old Covenant(s) belonging to the people of God was not strictly based on ethnicity, but it was tied to identifying as part of God's elect people of Israel.

4. On God's people in the Old Testament, see Gerhard Pfandl, "The People of God in the Old Testament," in *Message, Mission, and Unity of the Church*.

5. The official Seventh-day Adventist Belief on "The Church" begins: "The church is the community of believers who confess Jesus Christ as Lord and Saviour." Seventh-day Adventist Fundamental Belief #12. See Appendix.

6. https://www.adventist.org/the-church/.

7. E.g., Hans von Campenhausen, *Ecclesiastical Authority and Spiritual Power in the Church of the First Three Centuries* (Peabody, MA: Hendrickson, 1997).

8. There have been more than thirty antipopes in the history of the Roman Catholic Church. See H. G. J. Beck, "Antipope," *New Catholic Encyclopedia* (New York: McGraw-Hill Book Company, 1967), 1:632–33.

9. See Frank M. Hasel, "The Apostolicity of the Church" in *Worship, Ministry, and the Authority of the Church*, ed. Ángel Manuel Rodríguez, Studies in Adventist Ecclesiology 3 (Silver Spring, MD: Biblical Research Institute, 2016), 217–20.

10. See further, Alberto Timm, "Seventh-day Adventist Ecclesiology, 1844–2012: A Brief Historical Overview," in *Message, Mission, and Unity of the Church*.

11. See Ángel Manuel Rodríguez, ed. *Toward a Theology of the Remnant: An Adventist Ecclesiological Perspective*, Studies in Adventist Ecclesiology 1 (Silver Spring, MD: Biblical Research Institute, 2009).

12. Here, Jesus refers to the fold of His church into which He will bring other sheep (other true followers of Christ) who do not yet belong to this fold. This relates to the concept of the remnant, discussed in the following chapter. For more, in this regard, see Frank M. Hasel, "The Remnant in Contemporary Adventist Theology," in *Toward a Theology of the Remnant*, 159–80.

13. Seventh-day Adventist Fundamental Belief #13. See Appendix. See also Ekkehardt Mueller, "The Universality of the Church in the New Testament," in *Message, Mission, and Unity of the Church*.

14. For more on biblical metaphors of the church, see John McVay, "Biblical Metaphors for the Church: Building Blocks for Ecclesiology," in *Message, Mission, and Unity of the Church*.

15. See also John C. Peckham, *The Concept of Divine Love in the Context of the God-World Relationship* (New York: Peter Lang, 2014), 452–53.

16. For much more on this marriage metaphor and other kinship metaphors, see Peckham, *Concept of Divine Love*, 290–300, 451–56.

17. The name "sacraments" combines the Latin word for "holy" (*sacer*) and the Greek word *mysterion*, here used to refer to a rite. Augustine defined a sacrament as "the visible form of an invisible grace." Augustine, quoted in J. C. Lambert, "Sacraments," in *The International Standard Bible Encyclopaedia*, ed. James Orr et al. (Chicago: The Howard-Severance Company, 1915), 2636.

18. See Mickey L. Mattox, "Sacraments in the Lutheran Reformation," in *The Oxford Handbook of Sacramental Theology*, ed., Hans Boersma and Matthew Levering (Oxford: Oxford University Press, 2015).

19. The Council of Trent (1551) declared, "by the consecration of the bread and wine there takes place a change of the whole substance of the bread into the substance of the body of Christ our Lord and of the whole substance of the wine into the substance of his blood," called "transubstantiation." *Catechism of the Catholic Church*, 2nd ed. (Washington, DC: United States Catholic Conference, 2000), 347.

20. On this Lutheran view and other views, see Alister E. McGrath, *Historical Theology* (Malden, MA: Blackwell, 1998), 195–200.

21. For those who hold the view that baptism is a sacrament that infuses grace and is thus effective for salvation, infant baptism *may* be thought of as needed to put the infant in a saved state.

22. See Seventh-day Adventist Belief #15 "Baptism" in the Appendix.

23. Ellen G. White comments: "Christ was standing at the point of transition between two economies

and their two great festivals. He, the spotless Lamb of God, was about to present Himself as a sin offering, that He would thus bring to an end the system of types and ceremonies that for four thousand years had pointed to His death. As He ate the Passover with His disciples, He instituted in its place the service that was to be the memorial of His great sacrifice. The national festival of the Jews was to pass away forever. The service which Christ established was to be observed by His followers in all lands and through all ages." White, *Desire of Ages* (Mountain View, CA: Pacific Press, 1898), 652.

24. See further, Seventh-day Adventist Belief #16 "The Lord's Supper" in the Appendix.

25. On the theology of the Protestant Reformation, see Alister McGrath, *Reformation Thought: An Introduction*, 4th ed. (Malden, MA: Wiley-Blackwell, 2012). See also Darius Jankiewicz, "The Sixteenth Century Protestant Reformation and Adventist Ecclesiology," in *Message, Mission, and Unity of the Church*. See also Ellen G. White, *The Great Controversy* (Mountain View, CA: Pacific Press, 1911).

26. For a helpful introduction to the Enlightenment, with special focus on its impact and relationship to religion, see James M. Byrne, *Religion and the Enlightenment: From Descartes to Kant* (Louisville, KY: Westminster John Knox Press, 1996).

27. For example, the Belgic Confession (1561) affirmed "the sufficiency of the Holy Scriptures to be the only rule of faith," saying: "We believe that these Holy Scriptures fully contain the will of God, and that whatsoever man ought to believe unto salvation, is sufficiently taught therein.... Neither may we compare any writings of men, though ever so holy, with those divine Scriptures; nor ought we to compare custom, or the great multitude, or antiquity, or succession of times or persons, or councils, decrees, or statutes, with the truth of God, for the truth is above all.... Therefore we reject with all our hearts whatsoever doth not agree with this infallible rule, which the Apostles have taught us, saying, *Try the spirits whether they are of God;* likewise, *If there come any unto you, and bring not this doctrine, receive him not into your house.*" The Belgic Confession, Article VII in Philip Schaff, ed., *The Creeds of Christendom*, vol. 3 (New York: Harper & Brothers, 1882), 389. Likewise, the Formula of Concord (1576) teaches, "the only rule and norm, according to which all dogmas and all doctors ought to be esteemed and judged, is no other whatever than the prophetic and apostolic writings of both the Old and of the New Testament." All "other writings, whether of the fathers or the moderns, with whatever name they come, are in nowise to be equaled to the Holy Scriptures, but are all to be esteemed inferior to them." The Formula of Concord, Epitome of the Articles I in *Creeds of Christendom*, 3:93–94. Thus, "Holy Scripture alone is acknowledged as the [only] judge, norm, and rule, according to which, as by the [only] touchstone, all doctrines are to be examined and judged." The Formula of Concord, Epitome of the Articles III in *The Creeds* 3:96. Note the formula's crucial distinction between "Scripture alone" as the "rule" and the Apostles, Nicene, and Athanasian Creeds. Whereas doctrine should conform to the latter, such creeds "do not possess the authority of a judge—for this dignity belongs to Holy Scripture alone; but merely give testimony to our religion," particularly how the "Scriptures have been understood and explained in the Church of God." Epitome III in *The Creeds* 3:97. Similarly, the Westminster Confession of Faith (1647) affirms that the "infallible rule of interpretation of Scripture is the Scripture itself." WCF 1.9 in *The Creeds* 3:605. Accordingly: "The Supreme Judge, by which all controversies of religion are to be determined, and all decrees of councils, opinions of ancient writers, doctrines of men, and private spirits, are to be examined, and in whose sentence we are to rest, can be no other but the Holy Spirit speaking in the Scripture." WCF 1.10 in *The Creeds* 3:605–606. Further, "The whole counsel of God, concerning all things necessary for his own glory, man's salvation, faith, and life, is either expressly set down in Scripture, or by good and necessary consequence may be deduced from Scripture: unto which nothing at any time is to be added, whether by new revelations of the Spirit, or traditions of men." WCF 1.6 in *The Creeds* 3:603.

28. Roman Catholicism teaches that the "apostles entrusted the 'Sacred deposit' of the faith (*depositum fidei*), contained in Sacred Scripture and Tradition, to the whole of the Church." *Catechism of the Catholic Church,* 27. And, "Both Scripture and Tradition must be accepted and honored with equal sentiments of devotion and reverence." *Catechism*, 26, quoting from *Dei Verbum*, 9. However, the Roman Catholic Church explicitly identifies the Magisterium (the pope and the bishops) as the normative interpreter of Scripture and Tradition: "the task of authentically interpreting the word of God, whether written or handed on, has been entrusted exclusively to the living teaching office of the Church [the Magisterium], whose authority is exercised in the name of Jesus Christ." *Dei Verbum* 10; cf. *Lumen Gentium*, 25.

29. Eventually, the Roman Catholic Church posited "doctrine of implicit tradition," which means that "the tradition of the church is to be found at its richest in its most developed form—the present teaching of the church," such that "Pope Pius IX could say that he himself was the tradition." Anthony N. S. Lane, "Scripture, Tradition and Church: An Historical Survey," *Vox Evangelica* 9 (1975): 47. On this view, which Heiko Oberman labeled Tradition III, "not only Scripture, but now also Scripture and tradition taken together are materially insufficient to support by simple explication" some "authoritative definitions" of the church such as the mariological dogmas of 1854 (the Immaculate Conception) and 1950 (the Assumption), leaving the "Teaching office of the Church" as a "norm" that "takes on the function of the source." Heiko A. Oberman, *The Dawn of the Reformation: Essays in Late Medieval and Early Reformation Thought* (Edinburgh: T&T Clark, 1986), 294–95.

30. E.g., von Campenhausen, *Ecclesiastical Authority*.

31. For more on this and other aspects of church government and practice, see the Seventh-day Adventist Church Manual: https://www.adventist.org/resources/church-manual/.

32. The official Seventh-day Adventist Belief on "The Church" reads, in part: "The church is the body of Christ, a community of faith of which Christ Himself is the Head. The church is the bride for whom Christ died that He might sanctify and cleanse her." Seventh-day Adventist Fundamental Belief #12. See Appendix.

33. See also Seventh-day Adventist Belief #17 ("Spiritual Gifts and Ministries") in the Appendix.

34. For much more, see Rodríguez, ed. *Worship, Ministry, and the Authority of the Church*.

35. Ellen G. White, *Steps to Christ*, Historical Introduction and Notes by Denis Fortin (Berrien Springs, MI: Andrews University Press, 2017).

36. For some eyewitness accounts about Ellen White in vision, see https://whiteestate.org/legacy/issues-eyewitns-html/.

37. See https://www.adventistreview.org/church-news/ellen-g.-white-named-among-100-most-significant-americans.

38. For much more on Ellen G. White's life and ministry, see George R. Knight, *Meeting Ellen White: A Fresh Look at Her Life, Writings, and Major Themes* (Hagerstown, MD: Review and Herald, 2013).

39. Seventh-day Adventist Fundamental Belief #18. See Appendix.

40. Seventh-day Adventist Fundamental Belief #18. See Appendix.

41. James White, *A Word to the Little Flock* (Gorham, ME: 1847), 13.

42. For much more on these issues, see John C. Peckham, "The Prophetic Gift and Sola Scriptura," in *Biblical Hermeneutics: An Adventist Approach*, ed. Frank M. Hasel (Silver Spring, MD: Review & Herald Academic/Biblical Research Institute, 2021), 377–404, from which this section draws.

43. Jon Paulien, "The Gift of Prophecy in Scripture," in *Understanding Ellen White*, ed. Merlin Burt (Nampa, ID: Pacific Press, 2015), 16–17.

44. Paulien, "Gift of Prophecy," 19.

45. Paulien, "Gift of Prophecy," 22–23.

46. Ellen G. White, *The Great Controversy*, 204.

47. White, *The Great Controversy*, 595.

48. Ellen G. White, "The Value of Bible Study," *Review and Herald*, July 17, 1888.

49. Ellen G. White, *Evangelism* (Washington, DC: Review and Herald, 1946), 257. As Tim Poirier understands it, this "greater light-lesser light" analogy communicates that "just as the moon derives its light from the sun and reflects only what that source emits, so her messages are seen as deriving their authority from scripture, serving only to mirror the principles presented therein." Tim Poirier, "Contemporary Prophecy and Scripture: The Relationship of Ellen G. White's Writings to the Bible in the Seventh-day Adventist Church, 1845–1915," research paper, Wesley Theological Seminary, March 1986, quoted in Merlin Burt, "Ellen G. White and *Sola Scriptura*, 7," paper presented at the Seventh-day Adventist Church and Presbyterian Church USA Conversation, Louisville, KY (August 23, 2007), 7, accessed January 2, 2018, https://adventistbiblicalresearch.org/sites/default/files/pdf/Burt%2C%20Ellen%20White%20%26%20Sola%20Scriptura.pdf.

50. White, *Evangelism*, 256.

51. Ellen G. White, *Testimonies for the Church*, vol. 4 (Mountain View, CA: Pacific Press, 1876), 246.

52. White, *The Great Controversy*, vii. Again, she explains, "God has, in that Word, promised to give visions in the 'last days,'" but this is "not for a new rule of faith, but for the comfort of His people, and to correct those who err from Bible truth." White, *Early Writings* (Washington, DC: Review and Herald, 1882), 78.

53. White, *Selected Messages*, vol. 3 (Washington, DC: Review and Herald, 1958), 29.

54. White, *Selected Messages*, 3:29–30. Indeed, she wrote: "If you had made God's word your study, with a desire to reach the Bible standard and attain to Christian perfection, you would not have needed the Testimonies. . . . The written testimonies are not to give new light, but to impress vividly upon the heart the truths of inspiration already revealed." White, *Testimonies for the Church*, 2:605.

55. Ellen G. White, *The Ellen G. White 1888 Materials* (Washington, DC: Ellen G. White Estate, 1987), 36. Just prior to this, in the same letter to Butler and Smith, she wrote, "If we have any point that is not fully, clearly defined, and [that] can bear the test of criticism, don't be afraid or too proud to yield it" (White, *1888 Materials*, 35. Later in the same letter, she writes, "Let none feel that we know all the truth the Bible proclaims," White, *1888 Materials*, 36. In this regard, Merlin Burt comments, "Ellen White's writings were not the source of any Seventh-day Adventist doctrine." Burt, "Ellen G. White and *Sola Scriptura*," 9. Likewise, Alberto R. Timm writes, "all Seventh-day Adventist doctrines were derived from and grounded on the Scriptures." Timm, "The Authority of Ellen White's Writings," in *Understanding Ellen White*, 60.

56. White, *Testimonies for the Church*, 5:691.

57. Frank M. Hasel, "Ellen G. White's Use of Scripture," in *The Gift of Prophecy in Scripture and History*, ed. Alberto R. Timm and Dwain N. Esmond (Silver Spring, MD: Review and Herald, 2015), 304, 306. As Merlin Burt puts it, in this regard "neither early Adventists nor Ellen White herself saw her prophetic experience as incompatible with" the "principle" of *sola Scriptura*. "Rather they saw her visions as a *fulfillment of biblical predictions* and *subject to biblical authority*." Burt, "Ellen G. White and *Sola Scriptura*," 11.

ENDNOTES

58. The official Seventh-day Adventist Belief regarding "The Gift of Prophecy" reads as follows: "The Scriptures testify that one of the gifts of the Holy Spirit is prophecy. This gift is an identifying mark of the remnant church and we believe it was manifested in the ministry of Ellen G. White. Her writings speak with prophetic authority and provide comfort, guidance, instruction, and correction to the church. They also make clear that the Bible is the standard by which all teaching and experience must be tested. (Num. 12:6; 2 Chron. 20:20; Amos 3:7; Joel 2:28, 29; Acts 2:14–21; 2 Tim. 3:16, 17; Heb. 1:1–3; Rev. 12:17; 19:10; 22:8, 9)," Seventh-day Adventist Fundamental Belief #18. See Appendix.

CHAPTER 18 • THE MISSION OF THE CHURCH: THE WAY OF THE LAMB VS. THE WAY OF THE DRAGON

1. See further, Ekkehardt Mueller, "The Universality of the Church in the New Testament," in *Message, Mission, and Unity of the Church*, ed. Ángel Manuel Rodríguez, Studies in Adventist Ecclesiology 2 (Silver Spring, MD: Biblical Research Institute, 2013); cf. Seventh-day Adventist Fundamental Belief #13 in Appendix.

2. See N. T. Wright, *Paul and the Faithfulness of God*, Book 1 (Minneapolis, MN: Fortress, 2013), 383. In this regard, N. T. Wright comments, "what was central to Paul's worldview was the fact of a new community, a community which transcended the boundaries of class, ethnic origin, location and (not least) gender, by all of which the pagan world in general, and the imperial world in particular, set so much store." Wright, *Paul and the Faithfulness of God*, 383.

3. Constantine had set forth the Edict of Milan (AD 313), which had granted Christianity license in the empire and "confirmed to each individual of the Roman world the privilege of choosing and professing his own religion. But this inestimable privilege was soon violated" and "the emperor imbibed the maxims of persecution; and the sects which dissented from the Catholic church were afflicted and oppressed by the triumph of Christianity. Constantine easily believed that the heretics, who presumed to dispute *his* opinions or to oppose *his* commands, were guilty of the most absurd and criminal obstinacy" and he issued "an edict which announced their total destruction." Edward Gibbon, *The History of the Decline and Fall of the Roman Empire*, vol. 2 (New York: Harper & Brothers, 1880), 477; cf. Eusebius, *The Life of the Blessed Emperor Constantine* 3.63–66 (*NPNF2* 1:538–40).

4. For more on apostasy in early Christianity, see John W. Reeve, "Understanding Apostasy in the Christian Church," in *Message, Mission, and Unity of the Church*, ed. Ángel Manuel Rodríguez, Biblical Research Institute Studies in Adventist Ecclesiology, vol. 2 (Silver Spring, MD: Biblical Research Institute, 2013), 155–89. See further, Jean Carlos Zukowski, *The Role and Status of the Catholic Church in the Church-State Relationship within the Roman Empire from A.D. 306 to 814*. Adventist Theological Society Dissertation Series (Berrien Springs, MI: Adventist Theological Society Publication, 2013).

5. At first, Augustine was strongly against the use of violence to resolve disputes over doctrine, but "Augustine eventually reversed his position and decided to endorse coercion," agreeing with practices already in place and defending the church's appeal to and welcoming of imperial force against those deemed heretics. Perez Zagorin, *How the Idea of Religious Toleration Came to the West* (Princeton, NJ: Princeton University Press, 2013), 27. Indeed, "Augustine insisted that the emperors and political authorities had the God-given right to crush the sacrilege and schism of the Donatists, since they were as obligated to repress false and evil religion as to prevent the crime of pagan idolatry." Zagorin, *How the Idea of Religious Toleration Came to the West*, 28. Augustine wrote against those who "think that no one can be justified in using violence" and against the position that "the true Church must necessarily be the one which suffers persecution, not the one inflicting it." Augustine, *A Treatise Concerning the Correction of the Donatists* 2.10 (*NPNF1* 4:636). Further, Augustine wrote: "If, therefore, we wish either to declare or to recognize the truth, there is a persecution of unrighteousness, which the impious inflict upon the Church of Christ; and there is a righteous persecution, which the Church of Christ inflicts upon the impious." Augustine, *A Treatise Concerning the Correction of the Donatists* 2.11 (*NPNF1* 4:637). Of those who were "corrected" through "terror," Augustine wrote: "Who is mad enough to deny that it was right that assistance should have been given through the imperial decrees [concerning violence to coerce heretics], that they might be delivered from so great an evil" as the heresy they were under. Augustine, *A Treatise Concerning the Correction of the Donatists* 3.13 (*NPNF1* 4:638). While he argued it is better "that men should be led to worship God by teaching," he contended those who do not yield to such should be "compelled by fear or pain, so that they might afterwards be influenced by teaching." Augustine, *A Treatise Concerning the Correction of the Donatists* 6.21 (*NPNF1* 4:641). Thus, he argued, "many must . . . be recalled to their Lord by the stripes of temporal scourging, like evil slaves, and in some degree like good-for-nothing fugitives." Augustine, *A Treatise Concerning the Correction of the Donatists* 6.21 (*NPNF1* 4:641). "Why, therefore, should not the Church use force in compelling her lost sons to return?" Augustine, *A Treatise Concerning the Correction of the Donatists* 6.23 (*NPNF1* 4:642). On the development of just war theory in church history that was significantly influenced by Augustine, see Zoltán Szallós-Farkas, "Military Service and Just War: An Historical Overview," in *Adventists and Military Service: Biblical, Historical, and Ethical Perspectives*, eds. Frank M. Hasel, Barna Magyarosi, and Stefan Höschele (Madrid: Safeliz, 2019), 87–116.

6. Leo the Great, *Letters* 15.1 (*NPNF2* 12:20).

7. Thomas Aquinas wrote: "As for heretics their sin deserves banishment, not only from the Church by excommunication, but also from this world by death. To corrupt the faith, whereby the soul lives, is

much graver than to counterfeit money, which supports temporal life. Since forgers and other malefactors are summarily condemned to death by the civil authorities, with much more reason may heretics as soon as they are convicted of heresy be not only excommunicated, but also justly be put to death." Thomas Aquinas, *Summa Theologiae*, IIa IIae, q. 11, art. 3 (Gilby 32:89).

8. For more on the Waldenses and other Christians persecuted for their faith, see White, *The Great Controversy*, 61ff. See also John Foxe, *Foxe's Book of Martyrs* (Springdale, PA: Whitaker House), 1981.

9. Mark Charles and Soong-Chan Rah, *Unsettling Truths: The Ongoing, Dehumanizing Legacy of the Doctrine of Discovery* (Downers Grove, IL: IVP Academic, 2019), 15–19.

10. On this and much more, see Charles and Rah, *Unsettling Truths*.

11. For much more regarding the emphasis on peace and reconciliation and conscientious objection to violence in the long history of the Seventh-day Adventist Church, see Frank M. Hasel, Barna Magyarosi and Stefan Höschele, eds., *Adventists and Military Service*.

12. For much more on this and the other prophecies of Revelation, see Ranko Stefanovic, *Revelation of Jesus Christ: Commentary on the Book of Revelation*, 2nd ed. (Berrien Springs, MI: Andrews University Press, 2009). See also Jacques Doukhan, *Secrets of Revelation: The Apocalypse through Hebrew Eyes* (Hagerstown, MD: Review and Herald, 2002).

13. "This period of 1260 days is referred to seven times in the books of Daniel and Revelation. As 1260 days it appears in Rev. 11:3; 12:6; as 42 months in Rev. 11:2; 13:5; and as 3 1/2 times in Dan. 7:25; 12:7; Rev. 12:14. For the calculation of this period see on Dan. 7:25. Adventists generally date this period as from A.D. 538 to A.D. 1798. During this period God's hand was over the church, preserving it from extinction." Francis D. Nichol, ed., *The Seventh-day Adventist Bible Commentary*, vol. 7 (Review and Herald Publishing Association, 1980), 809. See also Heinz Schaidinger, *Historical Confirmation of Prophetic Periods*. Biblical Research Institute Release, no. 7. (Silver Spring, MD: Biblical Research Institute, 2010).

14. See the section on the year-day principle in Gerhard Pfandl, "How Do Seventh-day Adventists Interpret Daniel and Revelation?" in *Interpreting Scripture: Bible Questions and Answers*, ed. Gerhard Pfandl (Silver Spring, MD: Biblical Research Institute, 2010), 81–83.

15. For much more, see Stefanovic, *Revelation*.

16. Stefanovic, *Revelation*, 404. See also Gerhard Pfandl, "Identifying Marks of the End-Time Remnant in the Book of Revelation," in *Toward a Theology of the Remnant: An Adventist Ecclesiological Perspective*, ed. Ángel Manuel Rodríguez, Studies in Adventist Ecclesiology 1 (Silver Spring, MD: Biblical Research Institute, 2009). See also Frank M. Hasel, "The Remnant in Contemporary Adventist Theology."

17. Stefanovic, *Revelation*, 410; G. K. Beale, *The Book of Revelation* (Grand Rapids, MI: Eerdmans, 1999), 683.

18. As Stefanovic puts it: "In Revelation, the beast stands as the symbol of the political power through which Satan works actively throughout the earth's history, in general, and in the last days, in particular (Rev. 11:7; 13:1–18; 14:9–11; 15:2; 16:2, 10, 13; 17:3–17; 19:19–20; 20:4, 10)." Stefanovic, *Revelation*, 410. See also Beale, *Revelation*, 683, 686.

19. Further, Stefanovic notes: "The rhetorical question: 'Who is like the beast?' is a parody of 'Who is like God?' in the Old Testament (Exod. 15:11; Ps. 35:10; Mic. 7:18). It is especially significant that Christ, while waging war with the dragon in heaven, is referred to as Michael (Rev. 12:7), which in Hebrew means 'Who is like God?' Here is another indication that in preparation for the final battle this beast imitates Christ." See Stefanovic, *Revelation*, 414.

20. Stefanovic, *Revelation*, 411.

21. "But what are the principles which each of these teach their political followers? The dragon and his political party, in whatever nation they may appear, (as all three of these political principles must pervade the whole earth) will support tyranny, slavery, and aggrandizement of the few at the expense of many. The beast and his political party will be known only by their hypocrisy, bigotry, and superstition. Their principal object will be to operate on the hopes and fears of men, and so gain an ascendancy over the minds of the individuals who may be so unfortunate as to be found in their ranks. The false prophet will fill his party with notions of infidelity, lust, and conquest." William Miller, *Evidence from Scripture and History of the Second Coming of Christ, About the Year 1843* (Boston: J. V. Himes, 1842), 226.

22. Frederick Douglass, *Narrative of the Life of Frederick Douglass: An American Slave*, ed., Benjamin Quarles (Cambridge, MA: Belknap Press, 1960), 185.

23. Ellen G. White wrote: "The Lord God of Israel has looked upon the vast number of human beings who were held in slavery in the United States of America. The United States has been a refuge for the oppressed. It has been spoken of as the bulwark of religious liberty. God has done more for this country than for any other country upon which the sun shines. It has been marvelously preserved from war and bloodshed. God saw the foul blot of slavery upon this land, he marked the sufferings that were endured by the colored people. He moved upon the hearts of men to work in behalf of those who were so cruelly oppressed. The Southern States became one terrible battle-field. The graves of American sons who had enlisted to deliver the oppressed race are thick in its soil. Many fell in death, giving their lives to proclaim liberty to the captives, and the opening of the prison to them that were bound. God spoke concerning the captivity of the colored people as verily as he did concerning the Hebrew captives, and said: 'I have surely seen the affliction of my people, ... and have heard their cry by reason of their taskmasters; for I

know their sorrows; and I am come down to deliver them.' The Lord wrought in freeing the Southern slaves." White, *Review and Herald*, December 17, 1895. Further, one of the founders of the Seventh-day Adventist Church, James White, once wrote: "It is the Anglo-Saxon race which boasts of being the great apostle of the principles of righteousness and just government, and yet poisons millions of the Chinese annually, enforcing the infliction with armed fleets; takes America from the Indians, and the Scinde from its lawful possessors, by robbery and murder; kills races of men to get territory to which it has no claim; makes treaties to plunder those who enter into them, breaks them to gain lands, blows the helpless to atoms because they dare to remonstrate and seek self-preservation by force of arms. The Anglo-Saxon race professes to be the messenger of peace, yet carries a sword ever warm with blood, and often with the blood of its own immediate kindred. The Anglo-Saxon race gives itself out as the missionary of Heaven, and the evangelizer of mankind; yet it is earth's most successful propagandist of atheism, infidelity, and resistance to lawful authority; the educator of nations in rebellion and supreme selfishness." With respect to America specifically, he goes on: "God can do without this nation of ours, if he sees fit just as well as with it." James White, *Advent Review and Sabbath Herald*, February 16, 1864, 90–91.

24. Kevin M. Burton, "The Seventh-day Adventist Pioneers and Their Protest against Systemic Racism" (June 18, 2020), accessed October 31, 2021, https://web.archive.org/web/20200626083551/https://www.nadministerial.com/stories/2020/6/18/the-seventh-day-adventist-pioneers-and-their-protest-against-systemic-racism. As James White put it: The United States "has two horns like a lamb. Its outward appearance and profession is the most pure, peaceful, and harmless, possible. It professes to guarantee to every man liberty and the pursuit of happiness in temporal things, and freedom in matters of religion; yet about four millions of human beings are held by the Southern States of this nation in the most abject and cruel bondage and servitude, and the theological bodies of the land have adopted a creed-power, which is as inexorable and tyrannical as is possible to bring to bear upon the consciences of men. Verily with all its lamblike appearance and profession, it has the heart and voice of a dragon; for out of the abundance of the heart the mouth speaketh." James White, *Advent Review and Sabbath Herald*, November 11, 1862, 188. Uriah Smith likewise wrote of the "beast with two horns like a lamb" who "spake as a dragon. This we believe means the United States. This government is lamb-like in appearance, but dragon-like in action. In profession it is the land of liberty; but in action it is the land of slavery and oppression." Smith, *Advent Review and Sabbath Herald*, June 10, 1858. Likewise, J. N. Loughborough wrote: "Where is a government to be found more lamb-like in its appearance than this our own nation, with its Republican and Protestant rulers?" Yet, "that very national executive body, who have before them this Declaration of Independence, and profess to be carrying out its principles, can pass laws by which 3,500,000 slaves can be held in bondage." Loughborough, *The Two-Horned Beast* (Rochester, NY, 1854), 12; cf. Ellen G. White, *Testimonies for the Church*, vol. 1 (Mountain View, CA: Pacific Press, 1855) 259, 358, 360.

25. Burton, "The Seventh-day Adventist Pioneers and Their Protest against Systemic Racism."

26. See Nicholas Miller, *500 Years of Protest and Liberty: From Martin Luther to Modern Civil Rights* (Nampa, ID: Pacific Press, 2017).

27. As Willie James Jennings puts it: "The imperial project of the Roman Empire also dies in the body of the disciple who has joined her or his body to the risen savior, Jesus. The Spirit is crumbling imperial design from within by destroying the divide between those enslaved and their masters. The hierarchies nurtured so carefully by the Roman Empire are being undone by the Spirit." Willie James Jennings, *Acts: A Theological Commentary on the Bible* (Louisville, KY: Westminster John Knox Press, 2017), 9.

28. For much more on the remnant, see Gerhard F. Hasel, *The Remnant: The History and Theology of the Remnant from Genesis to Isaiah* (Berrien Springs, MI: Andrews University Press, 1980). See also Gerhard F. Hasel, "Remnant," in *The International Standard Bible Encyclopedia*, 2nd ed. (Grand Rapids, MI: Eerdmans, 1988).

29. As my friend and colleague Ante Jerončić puts it, "we spurn bids to view historical developments and current societal arrangements through the eyes of the victors and their ideologies of 'exception' by which they justify the necessity of exploitation, oppression, and destruction of human life. Instead, apocalyptic identity presents a form of counter-memory; an orientation attentive to the underside of history and the muted voices of victims, the multitude of slain souls under the altar (verse 9). It refuses to sentimentalize their deaths, to abandon them to the logic of historical necessity and ideologies of collateral damage, and thus protests an 'unalterable bias toward inhumanity and destruction in the drift of the world.' Such a *solidarity consciousness* frames the apocalyptic lifestyle." Jerončić, "Inhabiting the Kingdom: On Apocalyptic Identity and Last Generation Lifestyle," in *God's Character and the Last Generation*, eds. Jiří Moskala and John C. Peckham (Nampa, ID: Pacific Press, 2018); cf. George Steiner, *The Death of Tragedy* (New Haven, CT: Yale University Press, 1996), 291.

30. The parallel of God making heaven, earth, and sea is only interrupted by Revelation 14's mention of the "springs of water," which very likely alludes to the first major judgment, the flood, in which the "fountains [or springs] of the deep" were broken up, water flooded from below and not just above (Gen. 7:11). See Jon Paulien, "Revisiting the Sabbath in the Book of Revelation," *Journal of the Adventist Theological Society* 9, no. 1 (1998): 179–86.

31. Notably, the first angel's message of Revelation 14:7 centering on faithful worship of the Creator went out even as the evolutionary theory denied the biblical account of creation. In mid-October 1844,

bookseller Robert Chambers anonymously published the widely influential bestseller *Vestiges of the Natural History of Creation*, which offered a completely naturalistic account of the origin of the universe and life and had a large impact on public thought. Further, in the summer of 1844, Charles Darwin had written his *1844 Sketches* and was arranging for his manuscript on origins to be published. See Art Chadwick and Ingo Sorke, "What on Earth Happened in 1844?" *Adventist Review* (October 17, 2013), 17–19.

CHAPTER 19 • THE END OF THE BEGINNING: LAST THINGS

1. See Jo Ann Davidson, "The Second Coming of Christ: Is There a 'Delay'?" in *God's Character and the Last Generation*, eds. Jiří Moskala and John C. Peckham (Nampa, ID: Pacific Press, 2018).

2. Ellen G. White comments: "The Saviour's coming was foretold in Eden. When Adam and Eve first heard the promise, they looked for its speedy fulfillment. They joyfully welcomed their firstborn son, hoping that he might be the Deliverer. But the fulfillment of the promise tarried." White, *The Desire of Ages* (Mountain View, CA: Pacific Press, 1898), 31.

3. "Through the symbols of the great darkness and the smoking furnace, God had revealed to Abraham the bondage of Israel in Egypt, and had declared that the time of their sojourning should be four hundred years. 'Afterward,' He said, 'shall they come out with great substance.' Gen. 15:14. Against that word, all the power of Pharaoh's proud empire battled in vain. On 'the selfsame day' appointed in the divine promise, 'it came to pass, that all the hosts of the Lord went out from the land of Egypt.' Ex. 12:41." Ellen G. White, *Desire of Ages*, 32.

4. Historicism relative to prophecy is not to be confused with another, unrelated view called historicism, which theorizes that social and cultural phenomena are determined by history.

5. "The earlier premillennialists in general, as well as the Millerites in particular, were *historicists;* that is, they held that the fulfillments of Bible prophecy, including those of Revelation, were to be seen in the course of history, from Bible times to the end. This was actually the view of the infant church; thus the early Christians were historicists even though, standing at the very beginning of Christian history, they necessarily looked to the future for most of the fulfillments." Don F. Neufeld, ed. *Seventh-day Adventist Encyclopedia* (Hagerstown, MD: Review and Herald Publishing Association, 1995). See also Gerhard Pfandl, "How Do Seventh-day Adventists Interpret Daniel and Revelation?" in *Interpreting Scripture: Bible Questions and Answers*, ed. Gerhard Pfandl (Silver Spring, MD: Biblical Research Institute, 2010); Gerhard Pfandl, "Understanding Biblical Apocalyptic," in *Biblical Hermeneutics: An Adventist Approach*, ed. Frank M. Hasel, Biblical Research Institute Studies in Hermeneutics, vol. 3 (Silver Spring, MD: Biblical Research Institute/Review and Herald Academic, 2020), 265–90.

6. "The historicist approach to prophetic interpretation was used by the early Church Fathers up to the fifth century A.D. Le Roy E. Froom has shown that a significant shift in prophetic interpretation occurred when Augustine defined the kingdom of God as the Christian church and spiritualized the millennium, making it a symbol of the Christian Era (*The Prophetic Faith of Our Fathers*, vol. 1, 473–91). His views prevailed during the Middle Ages, until the period of the Protestant reform. The Reformers restored historicism as the method to be used in the interpretation of Daniel and Revelation, and identified the papacy as a manifestation of the antichrist predicted in those books." Neufeld, ed., *Seventh-day Adventist Encyclopedia*.

7. "The Counter-Reformation developed a new system of prophetic interpretation that came to be known as preterism. This method was developed by a Spanish Jesuit named Luis de Alcazar (died 1613). According to him, the prophecies of Revelation were fulfilled during the first six centuries of the Christian Era. He identified Nero with the antichrist (*ibid.*, vol. 2, pp. 506–508). Preterism was later adopted by many Protestants and has become today the prevailing method of prophetic interpretation among religious scholars in general. According to them, Daniel deals with events that took place during the time of the Maccabbeans, and Revelation deals with the situation of the church during the time of John." Neufeld, ed., *Seventh-day Adventist Encyclopedia*.

8. See Seventh-day Adventist Fundamental Belief #25 ("The Second Coming of Christ") in the Appendix.

9. See Jon Paulien, "Revisiting the Sabbath in the Book of Revelation," *Journal of the Adventist Theological Society* 9, no. 1 (1998): 179–86.

10. For much more on this, see Eric Claude Webster, "The Millennium," in *Handbook of Seventh-day Adventist Theology*, ed. Raoul Dederen (Hagerstown, MD: Review and Herald, 2000).

11. For a recent case in favor of historic premillennialism, see Craig Blomberg and Sung Wook Chung, eds., *A Case for Historic Premillennialism: An Alternative to "Left Behind" Eschatology* (Grand Rapids, MI: Baker Academic, 2009).

12. See also Seventh-day Adventist Fundamental Belief #27 ("The Millennium and the End of Sin") in the Appendix.

13. I am not suggesting they receive a second chance at this juncture but, rather, that no second chance would matter as they have already made their final decision and grieved the Holy Spirit. "No second probation will ever be provided. If the unspeakable gift of God does not lead man to repentance, there is nothing that ever will move his heart." Ellen G. White, *The Signs of the Times* (December 20, 1889).

14. For more on these views, particularly the debate between eternal conscious punishment and conditionalism, see Paul Copan and Christopher M. Date, eds. *What Is Hell?* (Downers Grove, IL: IVP Academic, forthcoming).

15. See Seventh-day Adventist Fundamental Belief #26 ("Death and Resurrection") in the Appendix.

16. The Platonic tradition, with the view of an eternally pre-existing and immortal soul, heavily influenced many lines of Christian thought by way of Neoplatonism. See, e.g., Augustine, *The City of God* 21.3.2 (*NPNF1* 2:453-54). For a brief discussion, see Jaroslav Pelikan, *The Christian Tradition: A History of the Development of Doctrine*, vol. 1 (Chicago: University of Chicago Press, 1971), 47-51; Aecio E. Cairus, "The Doctrine of Man," in *Handbook of Seventh-day Adventist Theology*, ed. Raoul Dederen (Hagerstown, MD: Review and Herald, 2000), 223-25. Advocates of eternal conscious punishment typically depart from the Platonic idea that humans souls are pre-existent and *necessarily* immortal, but believe that God *confers* immortality on all humans. Nevertheless, Richard Swinburne contends, "belief in the natural immortality of the soul" influenced the church Fathers such that annihilation of the lost "would in their view require an [extraordinary] action of God" such that "extinction of the wicked was therefore seldom entertained as a possibility open to God." Swinburne, "The Future of the Totally Corrupt," in *Rethinking Hell: Readings in Evangelical Conditionalism*, ed. Christopher M. Date, Gregory G. Stump, and Joshua W. Anderson (Cambridge: Lutterworth, 2014), 240.

17. Notice that the redeemed receive immortality only at the resurrection (1 Cor. 15:50-54), conditioned upon their faith in Christ; "I am the living bread ... if anyone eats of this bread, he will live forever" (John 6:51). See Cairus, "The Doctrine of Man," 212-13; cf. Samuele Bacchiocchi, *Immortality or Resurrection? A Biblical Study on Human Nature and Destiny* (Berrien Springs, MI: Biblical Perspectives, 2006).

18. On the case for conditionalism, see Edward Fudge, *The Fire that Consumes: A Biblical and Historical Study of the Doctrine of Final Punishment,* 3rd ed. (Eugene, OR: Cascade, 2011). See also Stott's brief summary of his tentative case for conditionalism in David L. Edwards and John R. W. Stott, *Evangelical Essentials: A Liberal-Evangelical Dialogue* (Downers Grove, IL: InterVarsity Press, 1989), 312-20; Copan and Date, eds. *What Is Hell?* See also John G. Stackhouse, Jr.'s arguments in favor of conditionalism in *Four Views on Hell*, ed. Preston Sprinkle (Grand Rapids, MI: Zondervan, 2016). Further, see the essays by John W. Wenham, E. Earle Ellis, Anthony Thiselton, Richard Swinburne, and others who reject everlasting torment in *Rethinking Hell*.

19. Some secondary sources claim the valley of Hinnom was a kind of trash dump, "a place where the rubbish from the city was constantly being burned," Johannes P. Louw and Eugene A. Nida, eds., *Greek-English Lexicon of the New Testament Based on Semantic Domains* (New York: United Bible Societies, 1988), 5. But this claim appears to rest on later tradition (sometimes traced to a Rabbi around the turn of the thirteenth century). According to Moisés Silva, "Jewish apocalyptic" from before the time of Jesus "refers to 'a valley, deep and burning with fire' (*1 En.* 54.1; cf. 56.3 et al.), apparently assuming that the Valley of (Ben) Hinnom would become, after the final judgment, the hell of fire (this idea may have been influenced by the fact that the valley evidently was used for burning refuse and the bodies of criminals). Hence the name γέεννα came to be applied to the eschat. place of punishment in general and so attracted the corresponding ideas about Hades." Moisés Silva, "γέεννα," in *New International Dictionary of New Testament Theology and Exegesis* (Grand Rapids, MI: Zondervan, 2014), 548.

20. Ángel Manuel Rodríguez, "Crime and Punishment: What Is the 'Hell Fire' Mentioned in Matthew 5:22?" *Adventist World,* published November 28, 2020, https://www.adventistworld.org/crime-and-punishment/.

21. See *"gehenna," BDAG,* 190-91.

22. *Hades* "is not an eternal but only a temporary place or state." See H. Bietenhard, "*hadēs*," *NIDNTT,* 2:207. On the meaning of *sheol*, see Eriks Galenieks, "The Nature, Function, and Purpose of the Term *Sheol* in the Torah, Prophets, and Writings" (PhD Dissertation, Andrews University, 2005).

23. See J. Guhrt, "*aiōn*," *NIDNTT,* 3:827, 829, 830. See also *BDAG* 32-33. See also Fudge, *The Fire that Consumes*; Le Roy Edwin Froom, *The Conditionalist Faith of Our Fathers: the Conflict of the Ages Over the Nature and Destiny of Man*, 2 vols. (Washington, DC: Review and Herald, 1965). Likewise, the Old Testament equivalent, *olam*, often translated "forever" such as in Isaiah 34:10, does not necessarily mean eternal or refer to an everlasting duration but most often refers "to a future limited duration, i.e., to conditions that will exist continuously throughout a limited period of time, often a single life span." Anthony Tomasino, "'*ôlām*,' *NIDOTTE*, ed. Willem A. VanGemeren, 5 vols. (Grand Rapids, MI: Zondervan, 1997), 3:347. Like the equivalent New Testament *aiōn* (the noun form of the root of which *aiōnios* is the adjective), the meaning of *olam* depends on the referent. For example, Jonah was in the fish "forever" (*olam*), referring to three days (Jon. 2:6; cf. Exod. 19:9; Deut. 15:17; 1 Sam. 1:22).

24. S. Quezada Case explains, the Greek term *aiōn* "can be translated as 'age' (Matt. 12:32; 13:39), 'world' (Matt. 13:22; 24:3, KJV), 'forever' (Luke 1:33, 55; John 6:51), or 'never' (John 10:28; 11:26). It is the equivalent of the Hebrew word '*ôlām* which is generally translated as 'forever' (e.g., Exod. 19:9; 2 Sam. 7:29). However, neither the Hebrew ('*ôlām*) nor the Greek term (*aiōn*) carry in themselves the sense of endless or everlasting. Their meaning depends on the nature of the subject or entity to which they are applied. If God, who is immortal, or the righteous who receive immortality are the subject, the meaning

of *'ōlām* and *aiōn* is eternal without end (Gen. 21:33; Matt. 25:46). If anyone or anything that does not possess immortality is the subject, *'ōlām* and *aiōn* refer to a limited time period that can be long or short, i.e., as long as the nature of the subject allows." See S. Quezada Case, "What Does 'The Smoke of Their Torment Ascends Forever and Ever' Mean?" in *Interpreting Scripture: Bible Questions and Answers*, ed. Gerhard Pfandl (Silver Spring, MD: Biblical Research Institute, 2010), 444–45.

25. Tom Shepherd comments: "It is not the chaff or tares that endures forever. Since they are combustible they are consumed. But the fire is eternal in its effects. (cf. Mark 9:42–50 with the reference to the worm that does not die and the fire that is not quenched). It is instructive to note in this regard that Jesus does not call the wicked eternal, but rather the fire. The wicked are consumed by the eternal fire (just like the chaff or the tares), and the effect is eternal punishment, not *eternal punishing*." Tom Shepherd, "Do the Wicked Burn Forever in Hell?" in *Interpreting Scripture*, 294.

26. See Case, "What Does 'The Smoke of Their Torment Ascends Forever and Ever' Mean?" in *Interpreting Scripture*, 444–46. See also Ralph G. Bowles, "Does Revelation 14:11 Teach Eternal Torment? Examining a Proof-text on Hell," *Evangelical Quarterly* 73, no. 1 (2001): 21–36. After noting that "the theory of eternal torment stands on a very narrow exegetical base," resting heavily on two texts "from the most symbolic of biblical books," Revelation (specifically, Rev. 14:11; 20:10), Bowles proceeds to show that Revelation 14:11 does not, in fact, teach or support eternal conscious punishment. Bowles, "Does Revelation 14:11 Teach Eternal Torment?" 33. Neither does Revelation 20:10 (see the discussion in the main text). If this is right, as I believe it is, the theory of eternal torment is exegetically baseless.

27. As Edward Fudge explains: "Throughout Scripture unquenchable fire signifies fire that cannot be extinguished or resisted and that therefore consumes until nothing is left (Is 34:10–11; Ezek. 20:47–48; Amos 5:6; Mt 3:12)." Edward Fudge and Robert A. Peterson, *Two Views of Hell: A Biblical and Theological Dialogue* (Downers Grove, IL: InterVarsity, 2000), 29. Fudge explains further: "Because God's fire is irresistible and cannot be quenched, it keeps burning and consuming until nothing is left. Anything that is put into unquenchable fire is finally burned up." Fudge and Peterson, *Two Views of Hell*, 38.

28. Regarding Matthew 10:28, Edward Fudge comments: "The words *kill* and *destroy* are parallel and interchangeable in this passage" such that the destruction at issue here refers to the cessation of life. Fudge and Peterson, *Two Views of Hell*, 43.

29. As T. F. Torrance puts it: "It is upon the Yes of God's eternal love for us that our salvation rests, but that Yes is also the judgment of those who perish." Torrance, *The Christian Doctrine of God: One Being Three Persons* (New York: T & T Clark, 2001), 246.

30. As William Lane Craig puts it, "it is logically impossible to make someone freely do something." "The Coherence of Theism: Introduction," in *Philosophy of Religion: A Reader and Guide*, ed. William Lane Craig (New Brunswick, NJ: Rutgers University Press, 2002), 211. See also Alvin Plantinga, *God, Freedom, and Evil* (Grand Rapids, MI: Eerdmans, 1977). As Vincent Brümmer put it, "the fact that God allows us as persons to retain the ability to turn away from him, excludes any form of universalism which holds that God's love *must* triumph in the end and cause all to love him." *The Model of Love: A Study in Philosophical Theology* (Cambridge: Cambridge University Press, 1993), 179. David Fergusson adds: "Only a theology that recognizes the freedom finally to rebel against God can avoid the determinism of either double predestination or universalism." "Will the Love of God Finally Triumph?" in *Nothing Greater, Nothing Better: Theological Essays on the Love of God*, ed. Kevin J. Vanhoozer (Grand Rapids, MI: Eerdmans, 2001), 196.

31. As Claus Westermann states: "To say no to God—and this is what freedom allows—is ultimately to say no to life; for life comes from God." *A Continental Commentary: Genesis 1–11* (Minneapolis, MN: Fortress, 1994), 222.

32. For much more on this, see Daegeuk Nam, "The New Earth and the Eternal Kingdom," in *Handbook of Seventh-day Adventist Theology*, ed. Raoul Dederen (Hagerstown, MD: Review and Herald, 2000).

33. See also Seventh-day Adventist Fundamental Belief #28 ("The New Earth") in the Appendix.

34. Regarding 1 Corinthians 2:9, *The Seventh-day Adventist Bible Commentary* states: "In its primary application the statement deals with all that is provided through the gospel for the welfare and happiness of God's people while here on earth. This relates to forgiveness of sins, justification and sanctification, the joy and peace that the grace of God imparts to the believer, and his ultimate deliverance from this evil world. By extension the statement also comprehends the inexpressible wonder and beauty and joy of God's kingdom of glory, the eternal home of the saved." Francis D. Nichol, ed., *The Seventh-Day Adventist Bible Commentary*, vol. 6 (Washington, DC: Review and Herald Publishing Association, 1980), 671.

35. Ellen G. White, *The Great Controversy* (Mountain View, CA: Pacific Press, 1911), 678.

36. For much more on this, see Nam, "The New Earth and the Eternal Kingdom."